ABOUT THE EDITORS

Anne Commire developed and edited Gale's *Something About the Author* series (volumes 1–64) and *Yesterday's Authors of Books for Children* (2 volumes) and helped develop and edit *Authors and Artists for Young Adults* (volumes 1–6). As a playwright, she has written *Shay*, first produced in New York City at Playwrights' Horizons; *Put Them All Together* (cited in *Best Plays of 1978–79)*, first produced at the McCarter Theatre in Princeton; "Melody Sisters," first produced at the L.A. Public Theatre; and *Starting Monday* (nominated for the Outer-Critics' Circle John Gassner Award), first produced at the Yale Repertory Theatre. All four plays were initially presented at the Eugene O'Neill Playwright's Conference. Commire directed and co-wrote "The NOW Show" at the Dorothy Chandler Pavilion; she also co-wrote, with actress Mariette Hartley, *Breaking the Silence,* and is the recipient of a New York State CAPS grant and a Rockefeller grant in playwrighting.

Deborah Klezmer is a freelance author and editor who has been a frequent contributor to Gale's *Something About the Author* series and *Authors and Artists for Young Adults*. A graduate of New York University's Dramatic Writing Program, she is the author of the plays *Man-of-War* and *Underneath the Apple Tree* and has studied at Circle in the Square and Playwrights' Horizons.

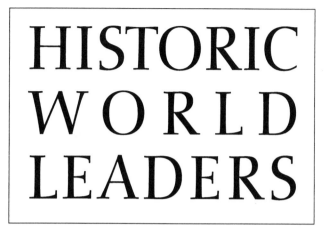

HISTORIC
WORLD
LEADERS

HISTORIC WORLD LEADERS

2

EUROPE
A-K

Anne Commire, Editor

Deborah Klezmer, Associate Editor

Gale Research Inc.

DETROIT • WASHINGTON DC • LONDON

Anne Commire, *Editor*
Deborah Klezmer, *Associate Editor*

Gale Research Inc. Staff

Lawrence W. Baker, *Senior Developmental Editor*
Peg Bessette, Jane Hoehner, Leslie Joseph, Allison McNeill, Rebecca Nelson, *Contributing Editors*
Kelle Sisung, *Associate Developmental Editor*

Mary Beth Trimper, *Production Director*
Evi Seoud, *Assistant Production Manager*
Mary Kelley, *Production Assistant*

Benita L. Spight, *Manager, Data Entry Services*
Gwendolyn S. Tucker, *Data Entry Supervisor*
Beverly Jendrowski, *Senior Data Entry Associate*
Nancy Jakubiak, *Data Entry Associate*

Cynthia Baldwin, *Art Director*
Barbara J. Yarrow, *Graphic Services Supervisor*
Mary Krzewinski, *Cover and Page Designer*
Willie F. Mathis, *Camera Operator*

Front cover photographs: (left to right): Volume 1: Confucius, Mohandas (Mahatma) Gandhi, Nnamdi Azikiwe, Moshe Dayan; Volume 2: Winston Churchill, Augustus Caesar, Mikhail Gorbachev, Elizabeth I; Volume 3: Cardinal Richelieu, Margaret Thatcher, Napoleon, Nicholas II; Volume 4: Clara Barton, José Batlle, Frederick Douglass, Dwight D. Eisenhower; Volume 5: Sitting Bull, Abraham Lincoln, Pancho Villa, Malcolm X.

∞™ This book is printed on acid-free paper that meets the minimum requirements of American National Standard for Information Sciences—Permanence Paper for Printed Library Materials, ANSI Z39.48-1984.

♲ This book is printed on recycled paper that meets Environmental Protection Agency standards.

Copyright © 1994
Gale Research Inc.
835 Penobscot Building
Detroit, MI 48226

ISBN 0-8103-8408-6 (5-volume set)
ISBN 0-8103-8409-4 (Volume 1)
ISBN 0-8103-8410-8 (Volume 2)
ISBN 0-8103-8411-6 (Volume 3)
ISBN 0-8103-8412-4 (Volume 4)
ISBN 0-8103-8413-2 (Volume 5)

Printed in the United States of America by Gale Research Inc.
Published simultaneously in the United Kingdom
by Gale Research International Limited
(An affiliated company of Gale Research Inc.)

I(T)P™

The trademark ITP is used under license.
10 9 8 7 6 5 4 3 2 1

CONTENTS—VOLUMES 2 & 3

CONTENTS—VOLUME 1

CONTENTS—VOLUMES 4 & 5

PREFACE

During this project's gestation, the United States went to war in the Gulf, a world superpower dissolved, the Berlin Wall came down, and we watched with horror as reports of "ethnic cleansing" brought atrocities from the former Yugoslavia into our living rooms. In the three-and-a-half years since this project began in 1990, the world changed. Every day, history was written and rewritten.

While these changes took place around the world, in the United States our very notion of history was changing. With minorities soon to comprise one third of the public-school population, educators have become aware that minority students were often learning a history that either excluded them entirely or chronicled their story from the majority's point of view. The new emphasis on multiculturalism has led to concerns that the traditional emphasis on Western civilization is "Eurocentric" and not as meaningful—and perhaps even damaging—for minority students. At the same time, women, whose roles in traditional history texts have not often been portrayed prominently, have set out to excavate a past that has been buried for hundreds of years.

Needless to say, it is an extraordinary challenge to tell the stories of world leaders, and thus compile a world history, in a time of such undisputed change.

Selection Criteria

Historic World Leaders is a five-volume set of over 620 biographical sketches. Volume 1 contains 155 entries on leaders from the Middle East, Africa, Asia, and the Pacific; Volume 2 contains 151 entries covering the letters A-K from Europe; Volume 3 contains 129 entries covering the letters L-Z from Europe; Volume 4 contains 94 entries covering the letters A-L from North and South America; and Volume 5 contains 93 entries covering the letters M-Z from North and South America.

We set out to profile as many leaders not typically covered in existing series as possible. This posed an interesting problem for two reasons: (1) Europe *has* wielded inordinate influence on the modern world and (2) in general women have traditionally not held positions of comparable power and influence to men, thus women's achievements have often not had as far-reaching consequences as those, say, of a Frederick the Great or a Napoleon. There are, however, countless examples of minority and women leaders whose accomplishments had profound effects on history.

Given these circumstances, in determining who takes a seat in this set, we have come to embrace an imbalance. This is not an imbalance in the stature of the individuals featured, nor in the magnitude of their achievements, but rather a discrepancy in the size of the mountains they moved. Hence, Rose Schneiderman takes her place beside Malcolm X who takes his place beside Joseph Stalin. Collectively, the entries reveal the history of power, but they also reveal the imbalance of opportunity that determined what size mountain any given culture has allowed certain individuals to push against.

Obviously, the greatest task in a project of this kind is finalizing the list of candidates for inclusion. In addition to combing through a plethora of historical documents, we have relied most heavily on input from our contributors, the majority of whom work daily in college classrooms around the world, bringing history alive for young people. *Historic World Leaders* became a unique opportunity for them to write in a style and tone they believed would best engage and educate students like their own. Additionally, a group of librarians and high school teachers assisted in the final determination of leaders included in *Historic World Leaders* by offering valuable input. Our collective aim has been to create a set—replete with the requisite number of larger-than-life characters, ample bloodshed, and the extremes of human virtue—that would be suitable, and *enjoyable,* for high school and college history students as well as anyone interested in the lives of world leaders.

Before we could even entertain suggestions of individuals to be included, we were forced to set down certain criteria in order to manageably limit the number of possible candidates. Aware that a necessary limitation in the number of profiles that could be included required some arbitrary decisions as to what constitutes a world leader, our goal was to make this a set of books about people who were activists and governing leaders. By and large, these five volumes feature people who stormed the barricades; they are people who made the rules by which others lived; and they are people who broke and changed just such rules. Given the limitations of space, with few exceptions, this set *does not cover leaders who are still active.* Nor does it attempt to cover leaders in the arts, industry, exploration, medicine, or philosophy. It is, however, a testament to the influence of these fields that the names of writers, artists, philosophers, and others appear throughout the biographies in *Historic World Leaders,* inextricably bound to the power holders and history of their times.

Features

In addition to a full-length biographical profile of approximately four to ten pages each, most biographical sketches include the following:

- a photograph or line drawing of the biographee
- a short description of why the leader is notable
- a quote by or about the leader that succinctly sums up his or her accomplishments, personality, and/or historical standing
- "vital statistics," such as personal name variations, birth and death facts, family information, and names of political or royal predecessors and successors
- a brief chronology that presents highlights in the leader's life
- boldfaced names within the text to indicate that an entire entry on a particular person exists elsewhere in the set
- a list of sources used to compile the entry
- suggestions for further reading

Special Entries Included

In an effort to include as many leaders as possible, the series features many joint and collective entries that chronicle the lives of those leaders linked by circumstance and/or ideology. These entries include:

- "Post-Stalin Soviet Leaders" in volume 3, which includes Yuri Andropov, Leonid Brezhnev, Nikolai Bulganin, Konstantin Chernenko, Alexei Kosygin, Georgi Malenkov, and Viacheslav Molotov;
- "The Mississippi Freedom Democratic Party and the Civil Rights Movement in Mississippi" in volume 5, which includes Fannie Lou Hamer, Robert Clark, Medgar Evans, Aaron Henry, Henry Kirksey, Robert Moses, and James Meredith;

- "American Secretaries of State" in volume 5, which includes Cordell Hull, John Foster Dulles, William Seward, Henry Kissinger, Dean Acheson, Dean Risk, and John Hay;

- "The Song Sisters" in volume 1, which includes Song Meiling (Madame Chiang Kai-shek), Song Qingling (Madame Sun Yat-sen), and Song Ailing (Madame Kong);

- "Jiang Qing and the Gang of Four" in volume 1, which includes Yao Wenyuan, Zhang Chun-quiao, Wang Hongwen, and Jiang Qing; and

- "La Flesche Family" in volume 4, which includes Susette La Flesche, Susan La Flesche, and Francis La Flesche.

In addition to these collective entries, many leaders' entries contain sidebars that summarize the lives and achievements of related personages. For example, Agrippina the Elder is included within Agrippina the Younger's entry; Queen Nefertiti is included within Akhnaten's entry; Puyi is included within Cixi's entry; Rasputin is included in Nicholas II's entry; Waldemar IV is included within Margaret of Denmark's entry; and Coretta Scott King and Martin Luther King, Sr. are both included within Martin Luther King, Jr.'s entry. Thus, while there are over 620 full-length biographies, the total number of leaders featured in the series is over 640.

To keep up with the increased interest in the history of the Eastern bloc nations, we call your attention to the leaders and overviews included in: "Walter Ulbricht and the Creation of East Germany," "Janos Kádár and the Rise and Fall of Communism in Postwar Hungary," and "Klement Gottwald and the Rise of Communist Power in Czechoslovakia." *Historic World Leaders* also features Czech leaders Alexander Dubcek, Jan Masaryk, and Thomas Masaryk, Polish Communist leader Wladyslaw Gomulka, and the machinations of Soviet secret police chief Lavrenti Beria.

As this set of books has been designed with students in mind, we have included a number of entries that we hope will hold particular appeal and inspiration for young people. These include: "Chicago 7" in volume 4 (Rennie Davis, David Dellinger, John Froines, Tom Hayden, Abbie Hoffman, Jerry Rubin, Bobby Seale, and Lee Weiner); "Young Turks" in volume 3 (Mustafa Kemal, Enver Pasha, Talat Pasha, and Cemal Pasha); and "Stephen of Cloyes" in volume 3, which illuminates the lesser known Children's Crusade that took place in the Middle Ages amidst the work of more widely known crusaders. Alongside entries about Augustus Caesar, Mao Zedong, Atahualpa, Catherine the Great, and Adolf Hitler, students will find little-told stories of resistance leaders, such as Irene Harand (see "Irene Harand and the Austrian Resistance to Nazism" in volume 2), Herbert Baum (see "Herbert Baum and Jewish Anti-Nazi Resistance Leaders" in volume 2), and Dietrich Bonhoeffer (see "Leaders of the German Resistance to Hitler" in volume 3). We feel these entries are of particular importance, as so often those leaders who fought against the horrors of the Third Reich are relegated to history's footnotes. The Harand entry features a Chronology of Bigotry, sadly relevant in an age of increased gender and sexual discrimination and racial and religious intolerance.

Additional Features

Despite quixotic efforts, there will of course be a number of individuals who have not found a paragraph of their own. It is our hope that the Leader Chronologies in Appendix A of volumes 1, 3, and 5 (e.g., holy Roman emperors, prime ministers of Italy, and the popes) will help to counterbalance these inevitable omissions. Each list either shows the history of rulers within that country or chronicles another area of interest, such as popes or the spelling variations of Chinese names (Pinyin vs. Wade-Giles). Appendix B (in volumes 1, 3, and 5) includes a set of maps to add geographic relevance to the biographies. The three indexes (also in volumes 1, 3, and 5) give readers detailed access to key subjects, people, and places. And, finally, volume 5 includes an A to Z list of all featured leaders found in the five-volume set.

Acknowledgments

We would be remiss were we not to extend a special acknowledgment to the nearly two hundred contributors—each noted on the first page of each biographical sketch—who helped define and author this project.

The aforementioned librarians and high school teachers should be thanked here as well. First the librarians: Nancy Bard, Thomas Jefferson High School for Science and Technology, Alexandria, VA;

Charles A. Bayne, formerly with Montgomery County Schools, Rockville, MD; Sharon Greiger, Mt. Prospect Public Library, Mt. Prospect, IL; Robert Kirsch, Lake Forest High School, Lake Forest, IL; and Pam Spencer, Thomas Jefferson High School for Science and Technology, Alexandria, VA. Also the high school teachers: John Bovberg, Fountain Valley High School, Fountain Valley, CA; Caroline Gecan, Thomas Jefferson High School for Science and Technology, Alexandria, VA; John Sandeen, Minot High School, Minot, ND; and Barbara Miller, chair, National Council for Social Studies in Colorado. We hope that the resulting text is one that library patrons and students of history across the country will use, enjoy, and question.

We must also thank Christine Nasso, Dedria Bryfonski, and Amy Marcaccio of Gale Research, who helped get the project off the ground, and Lawrence Baker—despite a maze of highwires—who gently lowered it back to earth.

Further thanks go to Gale developmental acrobats Peg Bessette, Jane Hoehner, Leslie Joseph, Allison McNeill, Rebecca Nelson, and Kelle Sisung. Freelance support came from copyeditors Ann Harrison and Melinda Clynes, proofreaders Michael Paré and Linda Quigley, and indexer-extraordinaire Theresa Murray and her group of indexers and helpers: Mark Coyle, Barbara Farabaugh, Nancy Guenther, Mary Kuhn, Elizabeth Markowitz, and Janice Moore. Fast illustration research and production was turned in by George Hobart and M. Rudolph Vetter. And, finally, kudos to Marco DiVita at The Graphix Group, whose layout suggestions, typesetting work, and patience were above and beyond the call of duty.

World events happen in real time. However, our understanding of them, through the writing of history, is an evolving process in which new details surface, myths are debunked, and truths are called into question. It is our hope that as students read these fascinating biographies, they will see their own beliefs and experiences reflected in the stories of world leaders, that they will come to see their own places in the making of history.

Anne Commire
Editor

Deborah Klezmer
Associate Editor

CREDITS

Most photographs and line drawings appearing in *Historic World Leaders* are in the public domain. All other illustrations were received from the following sources.

Volumes 2 & 3: Europe

Stanley Baldwin: p. 71, courtesy of Library of Congress; **Margaret Beaufort:** p. 86, illumination from the Louterell Psalter; **Willy Brandt:** p. 134, courtesy of Library of Congress; **Catherine Breshkovsky:** p. 136, courtesy of USSR State Archival Fund; **Brian Boru:** p. 144, courtesy of Library of Congress; **Charles XII of Sweden:** p. 225, courtesy of Nationalmuseum, Stockholm; **Christian IV of Denmark:** p. 230, painting by van Mandern; **Winston Churchill:** p. 253 and p. 254, courtesy of Library of Congress; **Georges Clemenceau:** p. 269, courtesy of Library of Congress; **Michael Collins:** p. 287, courtesy of Library of Congress; **Christopher Columbus:** p. 289, engraving from the Capriolo portrait; p. 291 and p. 292, courtesy of Library of Congress; **Hernán Cortés:** p. 300, courtesy of Library of Congress; **Oliver Cromwell:** p. 304, from the portrait by Sir Peter Lely; p. 306, courtesy of Library of Congress; **Georges Jacques Danton:** p. 314, from the painting in the Musée Carnavalet; **Anton Denikin:** p. 327, courtesy of Library of Congress; **Benjamin Disraeli:** p. 341, portrait by Sir J. E. Millais; **Anthony Eden:** p. 366, courtesy of Library of Congress; **Edward VII:** p. 386, courtesy of Library of Congress; **Eleanor of Aquitaine:** p. 388, courtesy of Library of Congress; **Elizabeth I:** p. 392, portrait by Marcus Gheeraerts the Younger; p. 394, courtesy of Library of Congress; **Francis Joseph I of Austria:** p. 435, portrait by Franz Russ; **Elizabeth Garrett Anderson,** p. 475, courtesy of Library of Congress; **Charles de Gaulle,** p. 484, courtesy of Library of Congress; **Wladyslaw Gomulka,** p. 505, courtesy of Library of Congress.

Douglas Haig: p. 564, courtesy of Imperial War Museum; **Irene Harand:** p. 579, courtesy of University of North Carolina Press; **Henry VIII:** p. 621, courtesy of Library of Congress; **Adolf Hitler:** p. 632 and p. 634, courtesy of Library of Congress; **Hitler's Generals:** p. 639 and p. 640, courtesy of Library of Congress; **Joseph Joffre:** p. 683, courtesy of Library of Congress; **Alexander Kerensky:** p. 720, courtesy of USSR State Archival Fund; **Nikita Khruschev:** p. 726, courtesy of Library of Congress; **Tadeusz Kosciuszko:** p. 739, courtesy of Polish Library, London; p. 742, courtesy of Library of Congress; **Lajos Kossuth:** p. 744 and p. 748, courtesy of Library of Congress; **Mikhail Kutuzov:** p. 751, courtesy of Library of Congress; **Marquis de La Fayette:** p. 755, courtesy of Library of Congress; **Pierre Laval:** p. 760, courtesy of Library of Congress; **V. I. Lenin:** p. 772, courtesy of USSR State Archival Fund;

Leopold II: p. 781, courtesy of Belgian State Tourist Office; **Louis XIV:** p. 804, courtesy of Caisse Nationale des Monuments Historiques et des Sites, Paris; **Louis XVI:** p. 809, courtesy of Château de Versailles; **St. Ignatius Loyola:** p. 814, portrait attributed to Juan de Roelas, c. 1622; **Erich Ludendorff:** p. 822, courtesy of Library of Congress; **Rosa Luxemburg:** p. 828, courtesy of Library of Congress; **Harold Macmillan:** p. 843, courtesy of British Information Services; **Marcus Aurelius:** p. 852, relief in the Museo dei Conservatori, Rome; **Jan Masaryk:** p. 891, courtesy of Czechoslovak News Agency; **Matilda of Tuscany:** p. 899, from a fresco at Verona; **Maximilian I, Holy Roman Emperor:** p. 907, portrait by Albrecht Dürer, Kunsthistorisches Museum, Vienna; **Jules Mazarin:** p. 912, engraving by Robert Nanteuil; **Catherine de' Medici:** p. 921, from a portrait by Clouet at Chantilly; **Helmuth von Moltke:** p. 944, courtesy of Library of Congress; **Bernard Montgomery:** p. 948, courtesy of Library of Congress; **Benito Mussolini:** p. 960, courtesy of Library of Congress.

Napoleon I: p. 971, from the painting by David; p. 974, courtesy of Library of Congress; **Nero:** p. 990, courtesy of Library of Congress; **Florence Nightingale:** p. 1010, courtesy of Library of Congress; **Ignace Jan Paderewski:** p. 1030, courtesy of Library of Congress; **Emmeline Pankhurst:** p. 1036, courtesy of Library of Congress; **Peter the Great:** p. 1072, from a painting by Carl Moor; **Philip II, of Spain:** p. 1078, from a portrait by Titian in the Corsini Gallery, Rome; **Jozef Pilsudski:** p. 1090, courtesy of Library of Congress; **William Pitt, the Elder:** p. 1092, courtesy of Library of Congress; **William Pitt, the Younger:** p. 1096, from a painting by Thomas Gainsborough; **Francisco Pizarro:** p. 1111, courtesy of Library of Congress; **Post-Stalin Soviet Leaders:** p. 1118, p. 1120, p. 1122, p. 1123, and p. 1124, courtesy of Library of Congress; **Grigori Potemkin:** p. 1126, portrait by Lampi; **Walter Raleigh:** p. 1134, engraving from a painting by Antonio More; p. 1137, courtesy of Library of Congress; **Erwin Rommel:** p. 1172, courtesy of Library of Congress; **Rosika Schwimmer:** p. 1193 and p. 1195, courtesy of Library of Congress; **Wladyslaw Sikorski:** p. 1205, courtesy of U.S. Information Service; **Josef Stalin:** p. 1221, courtesy of Library of Congress; **Teresa of Avila:** p. 1240, courtesy of Convento de Carmelitas Descalzas de Santa Teresa, Seville, Spain; **Margaret Thatcher:** p. 1248, courtesy of Library of Congress; **Marshal Tito:** p. 1261, courtesy of Library of Congress; **Victoria:** p. 1293, courtesy of British Information Services; 1296, courtesy of Library of Congress; **Albert von Wallenstein:** p. 1303, portrait by Anthony Van Dyck, Nationalmuseum, Munich; **Arthur Wellesley Wellington:** p. 1318, courtesy of Library of Congress; **Harold Wilson:** p. 1355, courtesy of Library of Congress.

TIMELINE—EUROPE

c. 3500–c. 1400 B.C.	Minoan civilization flourishes on Crete.
c. 1400–c. 1100 B.C.	Mainland Greeks absorb the Minoan Culture and build the Mycenaean civilization.
c. 1000 B.C.	Dorian invasions plunge Greece into a Dark Age.
594 B.C.	**Solon's** economic reforms become foundation for democracy in Athens.
561–528 B.C.	Rule of tyrant Peisistratus brings prosperity to Athens.
560 B.C.	Peloponnesian League, led by Sparta, is formed.
492–479 B.C.	Persian Wars; **Leonidas I** becomes the advance guard and defender of the Greeks at the Pass of Thermopylae.
461–430 B.C.	Under **Pericles,** Athens enjoys a cultural flowering.
431–404 B.C.	Peloponnesian War; Sparta wins struggle with Athens for supremacy in Greece.
358 B.C.	Breakup of Athenian confederacy.
356–338 B.C.	Philip of Macedon conquers and unites Greece; **Demosthenes** delivers his "First Philippic."
336–323 B.C.	**Alexander the Great** creates a vast empire which is divided after his death, but Greek culture continues to spread.
264–241 B.C.	First Punic War: Romans intervene at Messina.
219–202 B.C.	Second Punic War: Romans conquer Iberian Peninsula during war with Carthage; subsequently occupy territory, dividing it into provinces.
214–205 B.C.	First Macedonian War marks initial step in Rome's conquest of Greece.
200–146 B.C.	Rome gradually brings Greece under domination.
102 B.C.	**Julius Caesar** born.
72–71 B.C.	Spartacus leads revolts in Italy (Gladiatorial War).
60 B.C.	**Pompey** allies with Crassus and **Caesar** in First Triumvirate.

58–51 B.C.	Romans conquer Gaul.
56 B.C.	First Triumvirate reaffirmed; **Cicero** begins philosophical writing.
55 B.C.	Romans invade Britain.
52 B.C.	Revolt of Vercingetorix.
49–48 B.C.	**Caesar** crosses the Rubicon; defeats Pompey in Civil War.
47 B.C.	**Caesar** victorious in Egypt; **Cleopatra** installed as ruler.
44 B.C.	**Caesar** assassinated; **Octavian (Augustus)** made his heir.
42 B.C.	Octavian becomes part of Rome's "Second Triumvirate" with Marc Antony and Lepidus; **Livia** and family flee after Republican forces lose Battle of Philippi.
35–33 B.C.	Roman campaigns in Dalmatia.
31–30 B.C.	Roman Civil War: **Octavian (Augustus)** v. Antony and **Cleopatra; Augustus Caesar's** victory in the Battle of Actium makes Greece part of the Roman Empire.
27–25 B.C.	Roman campaigns in Spain.
c. 6 B.C.	**Jesus of Nazareth** born.
A.D. 6	Illyrian revolt; Judaean revolt.
14	**Tiberius** begins reign.
33	**Jesus of Nazareth** executed; **Agrippina the Elder** dies in exile.
37	**Caligula** proclaimed emperor.
41	**Caligula** assassinated by a tribune of the Praetorian Guard; accession of **Claudius.**
c. 43	Romans begin conquest of British Isles; establish trading center of Londinium (present-day London).
54	**Nero** becomes Roman emperor.
59	**Agrippina the Younger** murdered at Nero's command.
60	Iceni tribal queen **Boudicca** leads revolt against Roman rule, burning Londinium.
65	**Seneca** ordered to commit suicide.
68	**Nero** kills himself to avoid disgrace and assassination; end of Julio–Claudian dynasty.
81	**Domitián** becomes emperor.
98	**Trajan** ascends imperial throne.
101–06	Dacian Wars.
116	Roman Empire reaches height of expansion.
122	Hadrian visits Britain; establishes Hadrian's Wall.
179	**Marcus Aurelius** leads Roman victory over northern tribes.
218	**Julia Maesa's** forces win civil war.
222	**Julia Soaemias** assassinated.
232	**Julia Mammaea** and Alexander Severus lead an unsuccessful Roman counter-offensive against the resurgent Persian Empire.
303–04	**Diocletian's** "Great Persecution" of Christians.
306	**Constantine I** proclaimed Roman emperor; ends persecution of Christians in Gaul, Spain, and Britain.
313	Edict of Milan: Christianity is granted legal status.

330	**Constantine the Great** establishes the Byzantine Empire in the East.
398	**John Chrysostom** is consecrated Bishop of Constantinople.
c. 400	Invasions by Germanic peoples ends stability in Iberian provinces.
410	Sack of Rome.
419	Visigoths establish kingdom in Iberia.
451	**Attila** leads Huns into Western Europe.
476	Collapse of Roman power in Western Europe.
500s	Slav groups settle in the area of present-day Czech Republic.
c. 500	In Merovingian kingdom, Franks led by **Clovis** unite much of Gaul; Anglo-Saxon kingdoms are founded in area of modern England.
507–11	*Pactus Legis Salicae* ("The Salic Law") drawn up and promulgated; Clovis dies.
c. 528	Monastery of Monte Cassino founded by **Benedict of Nursia;** beginning of monasticism in the West.
565–610	Greece is overrun by Slavs and Avars.
569–72	Lombards invade and control much of northern Italy.
584	Francia's Chilperic assassinated; **Fredegund** gives birth to Chlothar (later Chlothar II).
593	Pope **Gregory the Great** writes *Dialogues.*
687	Pepin III's victory at Tertry.
711	Muslims from North Africa conquer Iberian Peninsula and expand northward.
732	**Charles Martel** victorious at the Battle of Poitiers.
751–54	Pepin the Short unites Frankish domains, founding Carolingian kingdom; invades Italy and defeats Lombards; donates Roman territory to pope, providing nucleus for Papal States.
772	Saxon wars begin.
793–1066	Age of Viking raiding, trading, and colonizing expeditions.
800s	Moravian Empire is formed by the Slav Czechs of Bohemia and Moravia, and the Slovaks of Slovakia.
800	**Charlemagne** crowned emperor of the Romans; expands Carolingian empire to include area of modern France, Germany, northern Italy, Belgium, Luxembourg, and Netherlands; Godfred rules as first Danish king.
829	Ansgar, a Frankish monk, arrives in Sweden; his missionary activity sparks the gradual Christianization of Scandinavia.
842	Muslims begin raid on Italy, sacking Rome, and eventually gaining control of Sicily.
843	Treaty of Verdun partitions **Charlemagne's** empire.
c. 850–1000	Discovery of Iceland, Greenland, and Vinland (North America).
851	Danes winter in England; sack Canterbury and London; Ethelwulf defeats Danes.
862	The Rus, under semi-legendary Rurik, establishes the principality of Novgorod in Russia.
871	Danes occupy London.
872	**Alfred the Great** proclaimed king of all Anglo-Saxons; Harald Fairhair becomes first supreme ruler of Norway.
c. 882	Kiev replaces Novgorod as the center of the Russian state.
886	Siege of Paris by Vikings; **Alfred** recaptures London from Danes.

896	Magyars settle in middle Danube basin in present-day Hungary; soon extend Hungarian state to frontiers which endure until 1918; end of the Danish invasions.
900s	Slav tribes of the Vistula and Oder basins are united under the Piasts, founders of the Polish state; Moravian Empire collapses under German and Magyar attacks; Bohemia and Moravia come under the rule of a native Bohemian dynasty, the Premyslid.
925	**Wenceslas** becomes king of Bohemia.
935–985	Harald Bluetooth unites various kingdoms of Denmark.
962–64	**Otto I** anointed emperor by the pope, constituting Holy Roman Empire (Germany) as successor state to Western Roman Empire; Otto remains in Italy to suppress risings.
985–1014	Danish king Sven I defeats the Norwegians and Swedes and conquers England.
987–96	Hugh Capet reigns as first Capetian king of Western Franks.
988	Russia converts to Christianity through the efforts of the Byzantine Church.
995–1000	**Olaf Tryggvason** assumes power in Norway; defeated by alliance of Danish and Swedish kings and Norwegian jarl at Battle of Svold.
1014	**Brian Boru** defeats Norse in Ireland at Battle of Clontarf.
1016	Danes led by **Canute** conquer England.
1016–30	Olaf II completes the unification of Norway.
1017–35	Sven's son **Canute the Great** becomes king of Denmark, Norway, and England.
1018	**Stephen I** of Hungary and Basil II of Byzantium defeat Bulgars, opening way for pilgrims to Jerusalem.
c. 1031	Central authority breaks down in Muslim Spain as result of civil war.
1033	Norwegian Revolt.
1040	Duncan I killed; **MacBeth** inaugurated as king of Scots.
1042	Anglo-Saxon rule restored.
1046	**Harald III Hardraade,** considered last of the Viking kings, becomes co-king of Norway with his nephew Magnus I the Good.
1066	Norman Conquest: **William I the Conqueror,** claiming English throne, invades England and defeats his rival at Battle of Hastings.
1075	Investiture controversy: **Gregory VII** excommunicates Holy Roman Emperor Henry IV but is driven into exile following Henry's invasion of Italy.
1077	Henry IV in penitence at **Matilda of Tuscany's** Canossa.
1088	Odo of Cluny elected pope as **Urban II.**
1094	**Rodrigo Díaz de Vivar (El Cid),** Spanish soldier of fortune, joins Muslims, conquers Valencia and becomes its ruler.
1096	First Crusade begins.
1097–98	**Godfrey of Bouillon** captures Nicaea and Antioch.
1116	**Bernard** founds monastery at Clairvaux.
1122	Diet of Worms ends investiture controversy with compromise that maintains authority of church over Holy Roman Empire.
1127	Kingdom of Two Sicilies created out of territory conquered by Norman invaders in southern Italy and Sicily.
1152	**Frederick I (Barbarossa)** elected king of Germany; attempts to reassert control over rebellious German princes.

1154	**Henry II** and **Eleanor of Aquitaine** crowned king and queen of England.
1155	**Frederick Barbarossa** crowned king of Italy and Holy Roman Emperor; Arnold of Brescia forced to flee Rome.
1158–62	**Frederick Barbarossa** moves against Italy; takes Lombard cities, including Milan.
1169	Norman troops invade Ireland, establishing English dominion; **Henry II** divides Continental possessions among his sons.
1170	**Thomas à Becket** murdered in cathedral by Henry II's knights.
1178	Diet of Spires gives Bavaria to Wittelsbach family.
1188	**Frederick Barbarossa** goes on Third Crusade; drowns while crossing River Salef in Cilicia.
1189	**Henry II** dies; **Richard I the Lionheart** crowned king of England.
1192–93	**Richard I** captured en route to England by Leopold of Austria.
1198–1216	Power of papacy at its height; Pope **Innocent III** excommunicates Holy Roman emperor Otto IV.
1199	**Richard Lionheart** dies; brother **John** crowned king.
1200s	Hapsburg **Rudolf I** establishes Austrian dynasty that will rule for 700 years.
1203–04	**Innocent III** launches Fourth Crusade; attacks Zara and Constantinople; fails to advance to Jerusalem.
1204	Western Europeans overthrow the Byzantine government in Constantinople and divide Greece into a number of feudal principalities.
1208	Albigensian Crusade launched by Pope **Innocent III** against sects in southern France; Interdict placed on English church.
1212	**Stephen of Cloye's** first appearance at French court to preach Children's Crusade; Muslim power in Spain crushed; Spain controlled by Aragon and independent Christian kingdoms of Castle and Leon.
1214	Interdict revoked; **King John** defeated at Battle of Bouvines by **Philip II Augustus.**
1215	Magna Carta signed by **King John;** Fourth Lateran Council decreed; leads to extensive church reforms.
1217–63	Norwegian royal power reaches height under King Haakon IV.
1226	Imperial decree grants Teutonic Knights control of Prussia.
1227	**Frederick II,** last great holy roman emperor, excommunicated by Gregory IX.
1236–40	Mongols invade Russian principalities; **Alexander Nevsky** defeats Mongols at the Battle of the Neva.
1240	With the fall of Kiev to the Tatars, Russian state is broken up.
1240–42	Mongols raid Poland and Bohemia, devastate Hungary.
1251	**Medicis** rise in Florence.
1253–78	Bohemia reaches height of power under Premysl II, extending from the Oder River to the Adriatic; after his death, Bohemia loses much of the realm to the Habsburgs of Austria.
1254	**Alfonso X** begins long pursuit of title of Holy Roman Emperor.
1254–73	Great Interregnum: nobles become dominant power in Holy Roman Empire.
1261	Byzantine government is restored, but much of Greece remains in Western European hands.
1264	**Edward I** captured by Simon de Montfort at Battle of Lewes.
1270	Edward I joins **Louis IX** of France on crusade.

1282	Danish nobles force King Erik to recognize national assembly and subordination of the king to the law; Sicilians revolt against French rule; French massacred.
1284	Wales formally annexed to England.
1293	Sweden completes conquest of Finland.
1294–98	England at war with Philip IV of France.
1301	With its native Arpad dynasty extinct, Hungary's crown passes to foreign rulers.
1305	Clement V moves papacy to Avignon in France; **Robert the Bruce** rebels in Scotland, defeats English forces.
1310	Rule of Bohemia passes to the House of Luxembourg.
1328	Under Ivan I, Moscow becomes the seat of the Metropolitan of the Russian Church and the most powerful of the Russian cities.
1332–70	Economic and political rivalry between Denmark and north German towns of the Hanseatic League erupts into open war: Denmark is the loser; League wins predominance in the Baltic.
1333–70	Under the rule of Casimir the Great, Poland enjoys a period of prosperity.
1337	Hundred Years' War between England and France begins.
1349–50	Bubonic plague strikes Norway; a blow to feudalism, it deprives the nobility of labor force and income.
c. 1350	Renaissance begins in Italy, spreads through Europe.
1350	Codification of Swedish national law helps unify the semiautonomous provinces.
1356	Golden Bull of 1356 reorganizes Holy Roman Empire as federation of independent kingdoms.
1377	**John Wycliffe** accused of heresy.
1378	The Great Schism creates two popes—one in Avignon, the other in Rome.
1381	Peasants' Revolt—first English popular uprising.
1386	As Poland and Lithuania join in a political union, the Jagiellonian dynasty replaces the Piast on the Polish throne.
1387–97	Margaret proclaimed queen of Norway, Sweden, and Denmark; establishes the Union of Kalmar, joins all three thrones.
1400–15	**Jan Hus,** a Czech Roman Catholic cleric, publicly advocates Church reforms; he is tried and burned as a heretic.
1410	Poles and Lithuanians defeat the Teutonic Knights at the Battle of Grunwald.
1415	**Henry V** invades France; English win at Battle of Agincourt; Burgundians occupy Paris; Charles VI of France flees.
1415–34	Rise of the Hussite movement leads to war between Hussites and Roman Catholic Germans.
1420	Treaty of Troyes signed.
1423–60	Ottoman Turks conquer the Byzantine Empire and establish domination over Greece.
1431	**Joan of Arc** captured by English and burned at stake.
1435	Treaty of Arras signed with Burgundians.
1436	**Charles VII** establishes government in Paris.
1438–39	Albert II crowned as first of Hapsburg emperors.
1442	Christopher III, king of Denmark, becomes king of Norway; initiates almost 400 years of Danish sovereignty over Norway.

1453	English expelled from all of France except Calais; end of Hundred Years' War.
1455–85	Wars of the Roses—dynastic wars fought in England by House of York to gain throne from ruling House of Lancaster.
1457	**Margaret Beaufort** gives birth to Henry Tudor (later **Henry VII**).
1461–83	Louis XI reigns as French king; expands domain.
1469	**Ferdinand II,** king of Aragon, and **Isabella I,** queen of Castile and Leon, marry; though kingdoms remain separate, they are administered jointly.
1477	First university in Scandinavia is founded at Uppsala in Sweden.
1478	Spanish Inquisition.
1480	**Ivan III** refuses to pay tribute to the Tatars, establishing the independence of the Muscovite state.
1483	English king Edward V deposed; believed killed in Tower of London.
1485	Battle of Bosworth Field; **Richard III** dies; **Henry VII** seizes throne.
1492	Jews expelled from Spain; **Columbus** discovers New World; **Lorenzo de' Medici** dies; French campaign and Treaty of Etaples.
1494–1559	**Maximilian I** begins Italian Wars.
1496	Intercursus magnus: trade agreement with Netherlands.
1497	Florence witnesses first "Bonfire of the Vanities" conducted by **Savonarola.**
1515	**Thomas Wolsey,** archbishop of York, named cardinal; becomes lord chancellor and chief minister.
1516	Charles I becomes first king of united Spain; later crowned **Charles V,** reigning over Spain and Holy Roman Empire.
1517	**Martin Luther** sparks Protestant Reformation.
1520	After execution of Swedish nationalists in the "Massacre of Stockholm," Swedish peasants, led by the nobleman **Gustav Vasa,** rebel against Danish rule; Anabaptist movement develops in Switzerland and Germany.
1522	**Hernan Cortes** appointed governor of "New Spain" by **Charles V.**
1523	Gustav Vasa elected king; Sweden secedes from Kalmar Union.
1524–25	Peasant's Revolt breaks out in Austria and southern Germany.
1526	Crowns of Bohemia and Hungary pass to the Habsburgs.
1526–1699	Turkish invaders defeat the Hungarians; Hungary is divided into three parts: center and south are under direct Turkish rule; Transylvania is semi-autonomous; Royal Hungary is ruled by the Habsburgs.
1527	Lutheran Church established in Sweden; ten years later, Denmark follows suit and forcibly introduces Lutheranism into Norway.
1528	Disputation in Berne; **Zwinglian** reforms of the Church accepted.
1534	Dispute between **Henry VIII** and pope brings about Act of Supremacy, separating Church of England from Roman Catholic Church.
1535	**Thomas More** tried and executed.
1536	**John Calvin** publishes first edition of the *Institutes of the Christian Religion.*
1537	After victorious war against Lübeck, leading city of the Hanseatic League, **Gustavus I Vasa** of Sweden ends the league's trade monopoly in the Baltic.
1540	Jesuit Order officially created by **Ignatius Loyola.**

1544–47	Schmalkaldic League, formed as alliance of Lutheran states, defeated by Holy Roman emperor **Charles V.**
1545–63	Catholic Counter-Reformation begins at Council of Trent.
1546	**Ivan IV,** the Terrible assumes the title of Tsar and consolidates the power of Moscow over other Russian cities; **Francis I** begins construction of Louvre.
1547	Brittany becomes part of French royal domains.
1548	**Zygmunt II Augustus** ascends the thrones of both Poland and Lithuania.
1551	**Francis Xavier** appointed first Jesuit provincial of the Indies province.
1554	**Mary I** marries Prince Philip of Spain; restoration of Catholic Church in England; revival of Catholic heresy laws.
1558–1603	**Elizabeth I** of England restores Protestantism.
1562–98	Wars of religion are fought between French Catholics and Protestants; **Teresa of Avila** founds St. Joseph's Convent of Discalced Carmelites.
1563–1660	Wars between Sweden and Denmark: Denmark loses northern provinces across the Sound which now separates the two nations.
1568	**William the Silent** begins first campaigns against Spanish crown; loses battles to Duke of Alva.
1571	**Philip II** of Spain, with the aid of **John of Austria,** victorious over Ottoman Turks at Lepanto.
1572	Elizabeth I intercedes to save **Mary, Queen of Scots.**
1576	**John of Austria** named governor of the Netherlands to repress Protestant rebellion.
1580	**Philip II** defeats Portugal; becomes Portuguese monarch; **Francis Drake** knighted after successful circumnavigation of the world.
1581	Russian penetration into Siberia begins.
1584	Elizabeth I discovers Throckmorton Plot; **William the Silent** assassinated.
1585–87	Elizabeth I sends English army to aid Dutch rebels against Spain; Duke of Parma completes the pacification of the southern provinces of the Netherlands (modern Belgium); **Walter Raleigh** sends out expedition and settles on Roanoke island.
1588	England defeats "Invincible" Spanish Armada of **Philip II.**
1589	**Boris Godunov** organizes Russian Church, declares Moscow "The Third Rome," the true center of Christianity.
1597	Institution of serfdom established when Russian peasants are denied the right to change their dwellings or masters.
1598	Edict of Nantes, issued by **Henry IV** of France, marks end of bloody wars of religion and grants religious freedom to Protestants.
1600s	Paris reigns as the cultural center of Europe.
1603	Death of **Boris Godunov** touches off a long struggle for power.
1611–32	Sweden becomes the dominant power in the Baltic area under **Gustavus II Adolphus,** barring Russia from the Baltic Sea.
1613	Michael, first of the Romanov dynasty, elected tsar; Peace of Knäred ends **Christian IV's** first war with Sweden.
1618	Czech nobles revolt against the Habsburgs ("Defenestration of Prague"); start of Thirty Years' War between the Protestant Union and the Catholic League in Germany.
1620	Czech nobles defeated at the Battle of the White Mountain; English Puritans, known as Pilgrims, establish American colony at Plymouth Rock.

1629	Treaty of Lübeck ends Danish war with **Ferdinand II** in Germany.
1630	Sweden joins in Thirty Years' War, defending its Baltic empire and the Lutheran faith.
1631	**Cardinal Richelieu** arranges the Treaty of Bärwalde with Sweden.
1632	While leading the victorious Swedes against the troops of the Holy Roman Emperor **Ferdinand II** led by Wallenstein, **Gustavus II Adolphus** is killed in the Battle of Lützen.
1638	First Swedish settlement in America is founded on the Delaware River.
1640	Portugal regains independence.
1642	English Parliament issues nineteen Propositions to limit king's powers; Charles I resists; war declared.
1643	**Jules Mazarin** named chief minister to Anne of Austria.
1645	Dutch legal scholar **Hugo Grotius** dies; his writings laid the basis for modern ideas about international law.
1648	Treaty of Westphalia ends Thirty Years' War; leaves Holy Roman Empire devastated; Spain loses control of Netherlands; portion of northern Germany assigned to Sweden; France emerges as Europe's leading power.
1649–60	Charles I tried and executed; **Oliver Cromwell** becomes leader of Commonwealth; Interregnum in England.
1652–54	First Dutch War between England and United Provinces.
1654	**Christina of Sweden** abdicates.
1654–67	Poland and Lithuania become embroiled in wars with the Cossacks of the Ukraine; Russia and Sweden lose large amounts of territory.
1659	Peace of the Pyrénées.
1660	**Charles II** and the Stuart family restored to the English throne; heaviest period of persecution for **George Fox** and his Quakers.
1661	**Louis XIV's** rule begins; **Jean-Baptiste Colbert** appointed minister of finances.
1663	New France (Canada) established as French colony.
1664–67	Second Dutch War between England and the United Provinces.
1667	War of Devolution.
1671	Peasant revolt in Russia is put down.
1672–74	**William III** accepts office of stadholder; Third Dutch War between England and the United Provinces.
1672–78	War between France and the United Provinces.
1676	Russo-Turkish Wars begin.
1678–81	Exclusion Crisis in England; Popish plot (fictitious) leads to hysteria and persecution of Catholics.
1682–1718	Sweden invades Norway.
1683	King **Jan Sobieski** of Poland and his army save Vienna from invading Turks and help liberate Hungary from the Turks.
1685	Charles II dies; James II succeeds; Revocation of Edict of Nantes by French king **Louis XIV** leads to mass exodus of French Protestants.
1688–89	"Glorious Revolution" brings about overthrow of James II; **William III of Orange** and wife Mary II accede to throne of England.
1689–97	War of the Grand Alliance between France and European states.

1690	James II of England defeated by **William of Orange** at Battle of the Boyne in Ireland.
1694	Bank of England created; Mary II dies.
1697–1718	**Charles XII** of Sweden spends his reign fighting the "Great Nordic War" against Denmark-Norway, Poland-Saxony and Russia; after his death, Sweden loses nearly all its overseas possessions and great power position.
1699	Turks withdraw from Hungary, whose territory comes under Habsburg rule.
1700s	Dissension increases between the Century Magyars and other elements in Hungary; attempts by the Austrian crown to improve condition of the peasantry are blocked by the landowners; in Bohemia, the crown introduces social reforms, but attempts to Germanize the Czechs provokes a revival of nationalism; Age of Enlightenment.
1701	Act of Settlement passes; James II dies while in exile.
1702	William III dies; **Queen Anne** crowned.
1702–13	**Queen Anne's** War; Great Britain gains much of France's Canadian territory; War of Spanish Succession fought against France; ended by Treaty of Utrecht.
1707	Act of Union unites England and Scotland.
1707–48	France and England compete for control of India.
1713	Pragmatic Sanction issued by Charles VI to ensure his daughter **Maria Theresa's** inheritance of Habsburg domains; **Peter the Great** transfers Russia's capital from Moscow to St. Petersburg.
1720	House of Savoy establishes Kingdom of Sardinia by uniting territories of Sardinia, Piedmont, and Savoy (modern Italian state).
1721	**Robert Walpole** forms his first government.
1729	**John Wesley** organizes Oxford Methodists.
1734	War of Polish Succession; **Eugene of Savoy** assumes command of imperial army on Rhine; **Charles III** leads Spanish invasion of Naples and Sicily; crowned king of Two Sicilies.
1740	**Frederick the Great** succeeds as king of Prussia and elector of Brandenburg; begins First Silesian War.
1740–48	War of Austrian Succession for control of Habsburg domains.
1741	Battle of Mollwitz; **Maria Theresa** is crowned queen of Hungary.
1744	Second Silesian War; Frederick II invades Bohemia, captures Prague.
1754–63	French and Indian War, between Great Britain and France over colonial territories in North America.
1756–63	Seven Years' War: France stripped of many colonial possessions; Great Britain and Prussia emerge as European powers.
1762	**Catherine the Great** usurps the Russian throne.
1772–95	Poland succumbs to three successive partitions by Russia, Prussia, and Austria.
1773–74	Misery of the peasants prompts an unsuccessful rebellion, led by Pugachev.
1775–83	American Revolution; Great Britain replaces loss of colony with control of India.
1776–79	**Marquis de Lafayette** commissioned major general in the army of the U.S.; serves in Battle of Brandywine.
1780	**Henry Grattan** demands legislative independence for Ireland; **Maria Theresa** of Austria dies; her son **Joseph II** rules alone.
1783	Spain regains Florida from Great Britain after siding with the American colonies; **Potemkin** presides over Russia's annexation of the Crimea.

1788	Louis XVI calls Estates-General into session; after reconstituting itself as National Assembly, Estates-General announces it has constitutional powers.
1789	French Revolution begins: Paris mob storms the Bastille; nobility begin to flee; Third Estate takes over Estates-General; **Robespierre** calls for liberty of the press, demands civil rights for Jews, actors, and Protestants.
1791	**Count Mirabeau** elected president of the National Assembly; **Madame Roland** opens salon at Hôtel Britannique; Louis XVI and royal family flee to Varennes; Louis signs Constitution.
1792	French Revolutionary Wars break out in Europe; Russia joins in Second Coalition against French.
1793	**Louis XVI** executed; **Robespierre** and **Jacques Danton** appointed to Committee of Public Safety; Reign of Terror begins; **Olympe de Gouges** writes *The Three Urns*, attacking Robespierre, and is guillotined.
1793–95	Spain wars against France, joining Great Britain and other nations in attempt to restore French monarchy.
1794	Poland's **Kosciuszko** rebels against the partitioning powers; Polish victory at Raclawice; Russian general **Suvorov** captures Warsaw from Polish rebels.
1796	French armies invade Italy.
1798	French military leader **Napoleon Bonaparte** deposes pope and annexes Papal States; Wolf Tone leads an unsuccessful Irish uprising against English dominion.
1800	Napoleon conquers Spain and regains Louisiana Territory; Act of Union joins England and Ireland and provides for Irish representation in British Parliament.
1801	War of Oranges; France and Spain conquer and divide Portugal; Georgians declare themselves under Russian protection, opening the way for Russian expansion in the Caucasus; **Alexander I** becomes tsar.
1802–10	**Madame De Staël** publishes works to rally opposition to Napoleon.
1803–15	Napoleonic Wars: **Napoleon** unsuccessfully invades Russia; France rules much of Continental Europe.
1804	**Napoleon** creates French Empire; has himself proclaimed emperor.
1805	**Napoleon** crowns himself king of Italy.
1806	Holy Roman Empire dissolved; Napoleon creates confederation of German states to govern other independent German kingdoms; **Pestalozzi** founds institute in Switzerland.
1807	Bombardment of Copenhagen by English forces drives Denmark into alliance with **Napoleon;** as a result of Napoleon's victory over Russia, Prussia and Austria, Poland recovers part of its lost territories.
1808	Revolt staged against pro-French policies in Spain; **Napoleon** invades Spain and names brother, Joseph Bonaparte, king; **Arthur Wellesley** (Duke of Wellington) appointed commander of a British army sent to Portugal; Battles of Rolica and Vimeiro.
1809	Sweden forced to cede Finland after defeat in 10-month war; present-day Swedish constitution is adopted, providing for separation between the king's executive power and that of parliament, and for a irremovable judiciary.
1809–14	Peninsular War: **Wellesley** commands British armies fighting in Spain and Portugal; Napoleon's forces retreat to France.
1810	After a period of internal dissension over the succession to the Swedish throne, Jean Baptiste Bernadotte, one of Napoleon's marshals, is chosen heir; eight years later, he becomes king as Charles XIV John.

1810–26	Liberal constitution for Spanish government enacted by first national Cortes in Cadiz, where rebel forces are in control; Spanish colonies in South America take advantage of turmoil in Europe and rebel; Spain loses control of major colonies.
1812	**Napoleon** invades Russia; **Kutuzov,** commander in chief of the Russian army, repels French invasion.
1812–15	War of 1812 between U.S. and Great Britain.
1813	First defeat of Napoleon's armies by a European coalition.
1814	Spanish Monarchy is reestablished under Ferdinand VII after French are driven out; Constitution abolished and Inquisition reinstituted; Sweden wins control of Norway after a short struggle with Denmark (Treaty of Kiel); brief Norwegion uprising leads to a compromise under which the two countries are to be ruled by the Swedish royal house; Norway keeps its own constituion and parliament; **Napoleon** abdicates, is exiled on the Isle of Elba; French monarchy restored; **Wellesley** made Duke of Wellington.
1814–24	Louis XVIII reigns as first king of Restoration monarchy in France.
1815	Napoleon escapes Elba and raises new army; defeated at Battle of Waterloo; Napoleon exiled on St. Helena; Congress of Vienna redefines Polish borders, but the country is in effect ruled by Russia.
1815–48	The "Age of **Metternich.**"
1817	**Elizabeth Fry** organizes Association for the Improvement of the Female Prisoners in Newgate.
1819	Spain cedes Florida and Oregon Territory to United States in return for U.S. recognition of Spanish claim to Texas.
1821	Greek War of Independence begins.
1825	Unsuccessful Decembrist Revolt in Russia indicates a growing desire for a more liberal government.
1827	Combined British-French-Russian fleet defeats the Turks in the Battle of Navarino, marking the turning point of the Greek war.
1829	**Daniel O'Connell** spearheads Irish Catholic Emancipation Act in British Parliament; **Robert Peel** introduces Catholic emancipation, angering his Party; establishes London Metropolitan Police ("Bobbies").
1829–33	Greece's independence is recognized and monarchy is established.
1830	French King Charles X forced to abdicate after liberal revolt against his reign.
1830–31	Poles rebel unsuccessfully against foreign rule.
1831	**Giuseppe Mazzini** establishes Young Italy Movement to promote unified Italy under republican government.
1832	Electoral Reform Bill awards voting rights to half of British middle-class males.
1837	**Disraeli** elected member of Parliament.
1837–1902	**Queen Victoria** reigns.
1840s	Potato famine ravages Ireland.
1844	King Otho is forced to grant a Greek constitution.
1846	Corn Laws repealed with help of **Cobden and Bright; Pius IX** elected pope.
1848	Revolutions of 1848: liberal revolts in European countries against conservative policies of monarchies; Prussia and other states grant new constitutions; in France, revolt ends with establishment of Second French Republic; German philosopher **Karl Marx** publishes *Communist Manifesto.*

1848–49	Movement for internal reform and independence from Austria comes to a head in Hungary; **Lajos Kossuth** proclaims independence, but aid from Russia enables the Habsburgs to reimpose their rule.
1848–51	Louis Napoleon (**Napoleon III**) takes office as president of Second Republic in France.
1849	Napoleon III sends French army to crush the Roman Republic.
1850	Great "Britain grants Australia limited self-government.
1852	**Camillo di Cavour** becomes prime minister of Piedmont.
1853–56	Crimean War: Great Britain joins with France and other powers to block Russian invasion of Ottoman Empire; **Florence Nightingale** arrives at Scutari.
1855	Piedmont/Sardinia enter Crimean War allied with England and France; **Lord Palmerston** becomes prime minister of Britain.
1856	Loss of Crimean War checks Russian expansion in the Balkans.
1858	Treaty of Aigun settles border dispute between Russia and China; British government takes direct control of India; agreement at Plombières between France and Piedmont/Sardinia.
1860s	Crop failures and poverty of the landless Swedish farm workers sets off an emigration wave which eventually takes 1.5 million Swedes to United States.
1860	Italian nationalist **Giuseppe Garibaldi** leads Thousand Red Shirts against kingdom of Two Sicilies.
1861	King **Victor Emmanuel II** creates kingdom of Italy; Italian parliament organized; French establish Mexican Empire under **Maximilian I; Alexander II's** reforms ease the lot of the Russian peasants.
1861–71	Wilhelm I rules in Prussia; **Otto von Bismarck** becomes prime minister.
1862–63	Greek king Otho is deposed and replaced with a Danish prince who rules as George I.
1863	**Jean Henri Dunant** begins Red Cross Movement; first workers' party founded in Germany; Poland again unsuccessfully revolts against foreign rule.
1864	Denmark loses the duchies of Schleswig and Holstein in a war with Prussia and Austria.
1864–70	**Helmuth von Moltke** plans successful operations in wars against Denmark, Austria, and France.
1864–1913	Greece extends its boundaries, principally at the expense of Turkey.
1866	Seven Weeks' War between Prussia and Austria is provoked by Prussian prime minister Bismarck; victorious Prussia excludes Austria from confederation of northern German states.
1867	British North America Act creates Dominion of Canada; dual monarchy of Austria-Hungary formed.
1869	In Spain, military revolts establish constitutional monarchy; **Paul Cullen** supports **Pius IX** and campaigns for papal infallibility at Vatican Council I.
1870	Outbreak of Franco-Prussian War; **Napoleon III** surrenders to Prussians at Sedan and is imprisoned; Piedmontese army marches into Rome, uniting it with rest of Italy.
1871	Rome becomes capital of Italy; Commune of Paris; Danish Social-Democratic Party is founded.
1871–1918	Czechs' desire for independence from Austria-Hungary mounts.
1873–74	Spanish republic established.
1873–76	**Catherine Breskovsky** initiates the "going to the people" movement to fight oppression in Russia.
1874	**Elizabeth Garrett Anderson** helps establish the London Medical College for Women.

1879	**John Henry Newman** made a cardinal by Pope Leo XIII.
1880s	Rapid industrialization of Germany begins, along with active colonization, notably in Africa; France expands its colonial empire in Africa and Indochina.
1880	**Gladstone** and Liberals defeat Conservatives in England's general election; **Charles Parnell** elected chair of Irish Parliamentary Party.
c. 1885	Belgium becomes a major colonial power in Africa.
1887	Norwegian Labor Party is founded.
1888	Kaiser **Wilhelm II** succeeds to the Prussian and German thrones; **Annie Besant** inspires strike of "match-girls" in London.
1889	Social-Democratic Party is formed in Sweden; within the decade, the important Trade Union Federation and the Consumers' Cooperative Association also founded.
1893	Social Democratic Party of Rumania is founded.
1894	French army officer Alfred Dreyfus accused of treason; court eventually overturns his conviction.
1895	**Rosa Luxemburg** establishes Social Democratic Party of the Kingdom of Lithuania and Poland.
1895–96	Italy mounts unsuccessful invasion of Ethiopia.
1897	**Millicent Garrett Fawcett** elected president of National Union of Women's Suffrage Societies.
1898	Spanish-American War.
1899	Boer War: British defeat rebels in bloody conflict in South Africa.
1903	Russia's Social Democratic party splits into two wings—the moderate Mensheviks and the revolutionary Bolsheviks; **Emmeline Pankhurst** founds the Women's Social and Political Union (W.S.P.U.).
1904	Entente Cordiale resolves differences between Britain and France over colonial territories in Africa and Far East; **Roger Casement** exposes Belgian atrocities in the Congo.
1904–05	Russo-Japanese War; Russia suffers humiliating defeat.
1905	Union with Sweden is dissolved; Norway becomes independent monarchy; Prince Carl of Denmark is elected Norway's king as Haakon VII.
1905–06	**Trotsky** leads Petersburg Soviets in failed uprising; **Nicholas II** is forced to grant a constitution and hold national elections; **Count Witte** resigns as Russian prime minister.
1906	British Labour Party, federation of trade unions and socialist societies, formed; **Keir Hardie** elected chairman of Parliamentary Labour Party.
1908	**Francis Joseph I** of Austria annexes two Turkish provinces, Bosnia and Herzegovina, causing the forces of nationalism to ultimately ignite WWI which dismembers his Empire.
1909	**Constance Markiewicz** founds the Fianna boys' movement in Dublin.
1910	**Venizelos** becomes prime minister of Greece; domestic reforms begin; Union of South Africa created by uniting Natal, Cape of Good Hope, Transvaal, and Orange Free State.
1911	Italians occupy and annex Tripoli; Germany gains Congo from France.
1913	"Bloody Sunday" in Ireland; **Rosika Schwimmer** organizes International Woman Suffrage Congress, Budapest.
1914	Archduke Ferdinand of Austria assassinated; WWI begins; **Paul von Hindenburg** returns to active duty and, together with **Erich Ludendorff,** defeats the Russians at the Battles of Tannenburg and Masurian Lakes; Joseph Joffre rallies French and British to win the Battle of the Marne.

1914–18	Three Scandinavian monarchies maintain neutrality during WWI.
1915	**Douglas Haig** appointed commander in chief of British Expeditionary Force.
1916	Easter Rebellion in Ireland (led by **Maud Gonne** among others) protests lack of home rule.
1917	Nicholas II deposed; **Alexander Kerensky's** moderate provisional government is unable to control the country and the Bolsheviks seize power; **Alexandra Kollontai** appointed People's Commissar of Social Welfare; **H. H. Allenby** appointed commander, Egyptian Expeditionary Force; captures Jerusalem.
1917–18	Greece joins the Allies in WWI and takes part in the Balkan offensive.
1917–22	Russian Revolution and Civil War.
1918	Belgian army led by **Albert I** goes on offensive; liberation of Belgium; **Ferdinand Foch** appointed to coordinate all Allied forces on Western Front, leads Allied armies to victory and presides at signing of Armistice; WWI ends; Germany sues for peace; **Wilhelm II** abdicates; German Republic proclaimed; mutiny by German sailors becomes full-scale revolt against the monarchy; Bolsheviks turn attention to winning civil war staged by anti-Bolshevik forces led by **Denikin;** Poland regains independence; **Thomas G. Masaryk** proclaims Czechoslovak independence, confirmed as president; Hungary breaks ties with Austria; Habsburgs are dethroned; **Mannherheim,** commander in chief of Finnish army, defeats Bolshevik revolution in Finland, named regent; **Pétain** named marshal of France; Woman suffrage enacted in Great Britain; **Constance Markievicz** becomes Britain's first woman MP but never holds seat.
1919	Admiral Miklos Horthy becomes regent of Hungary and rules until 1944.
1919–20	**Clemenceau** presides at Paris Peace Conference; Germany is forced to sign Treaty of Versailles which most Germans regard as humiliating; Weimar Republic in power in Germany; **Adolf Hitler** joins German Workers' Party, which becomes the National Socialist (Nazi) Party; women granted right to vote in Italy; Russo-Polish War.
1919–22	Awarding of Turkish Smyrna to Greece provokes a war between the two countries, which Turkey wins.
1919–38	Czechoslovakia flourishes but is troubled by dissatisfactions among its many minority groups.
1920	Ireland is granted home rule; Northern Ireland created; **Sikorski** takes command of the Polish Third Army, which is instrumental in liberation of eastern Poland from Soviet forces.
1920–23	**Fridjtof Nansen** takes on refugee and displaced persons relief work.
1921	**Benito Mussolini** organizes Fascist Party in Italy; Four-Power Pacific Treaty among United States, France, Great Britain, and Japan recognizes their respective spheres of influence in Pacific; **Lenin** launches New Economic Policy (NEP), relaxing government control in many areas; **Lloyd-George** approves Irish Treaty leading to independence.
1922	Mussolini's Fascists stage march on Rome, topple legitimate government, made head of state; Irish Parliament accepts Treaty; **Eamon de Valera** resigns as leader of Parliament; **Michael Collins** ambushed.
1923	After Treaty of Lausanne, large numbers of Greeks in Turkey and Turks in Greece are resettled; **Adolf Hitler** serves jail term resulting from Munich Beer Hall Putsch; writes *Mein Kamp;* French and Belgian forces occupy the Ruhr industrial district of Germany, triggering the Great Inflation.
1923–25	Following a military coup, Spain is governed by military dictatorship under **Miguel Primo de Rivera.**
1923–29	**Gustav Stresemann** becomes Germany's foreign minister, tries to restore Germany to a position of international respectability.

1924	Mussolini seizes dictatorial power following walkout (over **Matteoti** crisis) by non-Fascist members of Chamber of Deputies; New constitution unites Russia, the Ukraine, Belorussia, and Transcaucasia into the Union of Soviet Socialist Republics; republic is established in Greece; England's general election results in Conservative victory; second ministry of **Stanley Baldwin** formed.
1925	Hitler organizes Nazi Party; SS formed; **Hindenburg** elected president.
1926	**Jozef Pilsudski** becomes virtual dictator of Poland; after his death in 1935, his military collaborators rule the country; Spanish labor movement established.
1927	**Marshal Pétain** proposes a chain of forts for defense of France, eventually known as the Maginot Line.
1928	Kellogg-Briand Pact is signed; multilateral treaty renounces war; **Stalin** becomes undisputed leader of Communist Party; first of the Five Year Plans initiated, designed to transform the USSR into an industrial power.
1929	Britain's Labour Party wins election; second **Ramsey MacDonald** Cabinet formed.
1929–30	Crash of New York Stock Exchange and beginning of Depression.
1930s	Great Britain, France, and Germany hit hard by Great Depression; Nazi Party gains strength in German Reichstag in 1930 and in 1932 elections.
1930	London Naval Treaty signed, limiting number of warships for major powers; **Irene Harand** helps found Austrian People's party; Nazis win 111,000 votes in Austrian parliamentary elections.
1931	Statute of Westminster grants autonomous government to Great Britain's former colonial possessions and creates British Commonwealth.
1931–39	Second Spanish republic established; King **Alfonso** deposed; new constitution grants universal suffrage, national Cortes, and reduced role of church. In first election held for Cortes (1933), rightist factions, including Carlists and Fascists, gain over 40 percent of seats.
1933	Hitler named chancellor of Germany; Nazis take control; all opposition parties banned; civil rights suspended; operation of concentration camps begins for political opponents, Jews, and others.
1935	Nuremberg Laws officially strip German Jews of most civil rights; Germany reoccupies Rhineland; Italy invades and annexes Ethiopia; Greek monarchy is restored under George II.
1936	Hitler remilitarizes the Rhineland; Nazis succeed in destroying most illegal Socialist and Communist cell organizations; **Edward VIII** abdicates.
1936–38	Stalin carries out widespread purges within Communist Party.
1936–39	Start of Civil War in Spain between conservative right and leftist factions; Madrid falls to rightists.
1937–40	British prime minister, **Neville Chamberlain,** attempts policy of appeasement toward Nazi Germany.
1938	Nazis invade Austria; Munich Pact provides for gradual German occupation of Czechoslovakia's Sudetenland; **Beria** named chief of Soviet secret police.
1939	World War II begins; Hitler nullifies Munich pact by invading Czechoslovakia and Poland; **Paderewski** appointed president of exiled Free Polish government; Pact of Steel between Italy and Nazi Germany cements alliance; Italy occupies Albania; Denmark signs nonaggression pact, is invaded by Nazi forces; Stalin brings USSR into war as ally of Nazi Germany.
1940	Germans invade Paris; Fall of France; Germans occupy three-fifths of France; **Pétain** establishes authoritarian French State at Vichy; **Pierre Laval** chosen minister of state; **Leon Blum** imprisoned by Vichy government; Hitler invades Norway; **Vidkun Quisling** serves as self-proclaimed Norwegian head of state; Sweden remains neutral; **Francisco Franco** organizes totalitarian government in Spain; **Winston Churchill** replaces **Neville Chamberlain** as prime minister.

1941	German attack on Soviet Union unleashes merciless ideological war of annihilation against "Jewish Bolshevism"; German Jews subjected to forced labor; German Jewish population forced to wear Star of David in public; Hungary joins the Axis; Axis powers occupy Greece.
1941–45	**Queen Wilhelmina** encourages Dutch resistance through radio broadcasts from Britain.
1942	**Bernard Montgomery** appointed to head the 8th Army in North Africa; Battle of El Alamein; **Baum** Group burns down part of anti-Bolshevik exhibition "The Soviet Paradise" in Berlin's Lustgarten.
1943	Warsaw Ghetto uprising; after failures in North Africa campaigns, Italy invaded by Allied forces by way of Sicily; **Karl Dönitz** becomes commander in chief of German navy; "White Rose" student conspiracy in Munich fails; **Hans and Sophie Scholl** executed.
1944	**Charles de Gaulle** returns to Paris with armies of liberation; becomes head of Provisional Government; liberation of Paris and Vichy.
1944–45	Liberation of Greece is followed by a short-lived civil war between moderate and Communist factions; Soviet troops rout Germans in Poland, Hungary, and most of Czechoslovakia and occupy all three countries; Poland's area is reduced and its borders are shifted westward.
1945	Germany invaded by Allied armies; **Gördeler** and **Bonhoeffer** attempt assassination of Hitler; **Mussolini** executed by Partisans; **Hitler** commits suicide in Berlin; liberation of concentration camps; collapse of Third Reich; WWII ends in Europe; Germany split into occupation zones; Yalta and Potsdam conferences establish Russian spheres of influence in Europe and Asia.
1945–54	Defeat at Dien Bien Phu results in French withdrawal from Indochina.
1946	Spain denied entry to United Nations; Republican government is organized in Italy after abolition of monarchy, new constitution enacted; France enacts new constitution, forming Fourth Republic; Greek monarchy is restored causing civil unrest once again; Sweden, Norway, and Denmark join United Nations; **Trygve Lie** elected secretary-general.
1946–47	Soviet Union's control of Eastern Europe leads to increasing East-West tensions and beginning of Cold War.
1947	Spanish government is reorganized as monarchy, with **Francisco Franco** designated as chief of state for life; meeting of Big Four (U.S., USSR, Great Britain, and France) on divided Germany's economic future; India granted independence from Great Britain; People's Republic of Rumania proclaimed; Truman Doctrine pledges U.S. support in Greek struggle against Communist guerrillas.
1947–48	Russian support enables Communists to seize power in the Eastern European countries; **Klement Gottwald** becomes president of Czechoslovakia; **Jan Masaryk** dies mysteriously.
1948–49	Increasing tensions with U.S. over divided Germany result in Soviet blockade of West Berlin; U.S. supplies city by airlift.
1948–52	Defection of Yugoslavia from the Soviet bloc provokes extensive purges in Eastern Europe's Communist Parties.
1949	Formal inauguration of the Republic of Ireland; Federal Republic of Germany (West Germany) created from U.S., British, and French occupation zones; **Konrad Adenauer** elected its first chancellor; Communist guerrillas defeated in Greece; NATO (North Atlantic Treaty Organization) founded; Norway and Denmark become members of NATO, Sweden does not.
1949–71	**Walter Ulbricht** is unchallenged leader of the German Democratic Republic (East Germany).
1950–52	Soviet pacts declaring friendship and economic collaboration are signed with Communist China.

1951	Greece joins NATO.
1952	Nordic Council for economic, social, and cultural cooperation is ratified by Denmark, Norway, Sweden, and Iceland; Finland joins four years later.
1953	Death of Stalin leads to a more moderate Soviet policy, both at home and abroad; Lie retired as secretary-general; succeeded by **Dag Hammarskjöld.**
1954	Italy regains Trieste and part of adjoining territory, remainder awarded to Yugoslavia; eight-year Algerian War begins.
1955	**Nikita Khrushchev** emerges as the most powerful man in the Soviet Union.
1956	At 20th Congress of the Communist Party, excesses of Stalin regime are denounced; Poland's economic and political ills lead to change of leadership and a measure of independence from Soviet Russia; Hungarian revolution suppressed by Soviet troops; **Janos Kádár** appointed head of new, Soviet-backed government to replace regime of **Imre Nagy;** France and Great Britain send troops to Egypt during Suez crisis.
1956–65	Poland, Czechoslovakia, and Hungary attempt to improve economic conditions while attempting to acquire some independence in cultural and economic areas.
1957	**Anthony Eden** resigns as prime minister because of health and political damage from Suez crisis, is succeeded by **Harold Macmillan;** Treaty of Rome establishes European Economic Community; Haakon VII of Norway dies after long reign; Soviets launch Sputnik I; space race begins.
1958	French settlers in Algiers riot, bringing about election of **Charles de Gaulle** as French premier and approval of new constitution; Pius XII dies; Roncalli elected pope as **John XXIII.**
1961	Denmark and Norway apply for membership in the European Economic Community; Sweden applies for a form of associate membership; **Sakharov** attempts to prevent Soviet nuclear testing; Soviets construct Berlin Wall.
1962	Algeria granted independence.
1962–63	Cuban missile crisis.
1963	USSR signs the Nuclear Test-Ban Treaty with Great Britain; fighting between Greek and Turkish Cypriots leads to threats of intervention in the island's affairs by Greece and Turkey.
1964	Khrushchev ousted in Russia; **Leonid Brezhnev** named chairman of the Presidium, Aleksei Kosygin chairman of the Council of Ministers; tensions reduced in Greece by UN peacekeeping force sent to Cyprus.
1966	In face of growing unrest, **Francisco Franco** grants new, more liberal constitution in Spain.
1967	Military junta takes over Greek government; Constantine flees to Italy.
1968	**Alexander Dubcek** introduces liberal reforms in Czechoslovakia known as Prague Spring; Soviet troops invade; Dubcek ousted.
1969	**Franco** names Juan Carlos as successor in Spain; **Willy Brandt** becomes chancellor of Germany.
1970	Great Britain allowed to join Common Market; **Harold Wilson** resigns as prime minister following defeat of Labour Party; riots at Gdansk in Poland; **Gomulka** resigns.
1972	**Nixon** visits China and USSR, pursues policy of détente.
1972–74	Unrest in Northern Ireland leads to direct British rule.
1973	East and West Germany establish diplomatic relations; Brezhnev and Nixon meet and sign treaty to limit nuclear war.
1974	British Parliament building hit by IRA terrorist bomb; West German chancellor **Willy Brandt** resigns; **Ceausescu** becomes president of Rumania.

1976	Communist becomes speaker of Italian Chamber of Deputies, culminating alliances between Christian Democrats and leftists begun in early 1960s.
1977	Spain holds first free elections since outbreak of Civil War; Italy ends status of Roman Catholicism as state religion.
1978	Constitutional monarchy established by popular vote in Spain; former Italian president Aldo Moro kidnapped by terrorists; Italy's first socialist premier takes office.
1979	**Margaret Thatcher** becomes Britain's first woman prime minister; Lord Mountbatten killed by IRA bomb; terrorist bomb explodes in Italian Senate chambers; Soviet-backed coup in Afghanistan.
1980s	Election of former UN Secretary General **Kurt Waldheim** as president of Austria strikes controversy because of his service in German army in WWII.
1980	Death of **Tito** in Yugoslavia ends era of Non-Aligned leadership; major labor unrest in Poland.
1981	Socialist François Mitterrand elected president of France; attempted coup by Spanish civil guardsmen fails.
1982	Falkland Islands War; Poland bans labor movement Solidarity.
1985	**Gorbachev** becomes leader of Soviets; Reagan-Gorbachev summit in Geneva, first US-USSR meeting in six years.
1986	Nuclear accident at Chernobyl; **Sakharov** released from exile in Gorky.
1987	United States and USSR sign treaty to eliminate intermediate range nuclear missiles.
1988	Ethnic violence in Armenia and Azerbaijan; Gorbachev becomes president of Soviet Union.
1989	Destruction of Berlin Wall; German reunification; Rumanian revolution overthrows **Ceausescu;** Margaret Thatcher completes unbroken term of 10 years in office, longest for British prime minister in this century.
1990	Lithuania declares independence from Soviet Union.
1991	Disintegration of Soviet Union; Gorbachev resigns.

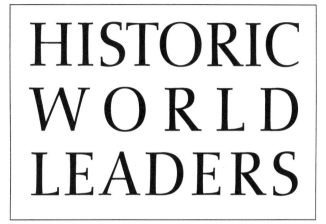

HISTORIC WORLD LEADERS

Abd-Al-Rahman III

(891–961)

Tenth-century ruler of Muslim Spain, who restored the power of the Umayyad dynasty
and was the first monarch of al-Andalus to adopt the title of caliph.

"His were those qualities of resoluteness, daring and candour which characterize leaders of men in all ages."

PHILIP K. HITTI

Abd-al-Rahman III, who ruled al-Andalus, or Islamic Spain, from 912 until his death in 961, was the most powerful ruler in Western Europe during the tenth çentury. He built a powerful war fleet and raised great armies, which he sent against Christian and Muslim enemies alike. For its size and prosperity, his capital city of Córdoba was rivaled only by Constantinople and Baghdad and it became, under his patronage, a major center of artistic and intellectual activity. The greatness of Abd-al-Rahman's rule did not survive him, however, and the Andalusian state fragmented early in the 11th century.

Al-Andalus had its beginning in the eighth century, when Muslim Berbers from North Africa invaded the Iberian Peninsula. In one decisive encounter in 711, the Berbers destroyed the Christian Visigothic kingdom which had dominated Spain since the collapse of Roman power 300 years before. After this initial conquest came other Berbers, soon joined by Arabs from the east, who sought to expand the area of Islamic domination throughout the peninsula and even into modern France. Following their defeat by **Charles Martel** at Poitiers in 732, the Muslims withdrew back into

Name variations: Abdurrahman III, Abd ar-Rahmān, Abd-al-Rahman al-Nasir (the Defender); several different spellings are in common use. Born on January 7, 891, in Córdoba, Spain; died on October 15, 961, in Medina Azahara, Spain; son of Muhammad and Muzna (María); married: Murchana and others; children: (sons) Abu-l-Walid Hisham, Abu-l-'Asi al-Hakam, Ubayd Allah, Abd al-Chabbar, Abd al-Malik, Sulayman, Abd Allah al-Zahid; (daughters) names not recorded. Predecessor: Abd Allah. Successor: Al-Hakam II.

Contributed by Stephen Webre, Professor of History, Louisiana Tech University, Ruston, Louisiana

CHRONOLOGY

Spain, where they eventually consolidated themselves in the east and south, leaving the northwest in Christian hands.

Islamic Spain was at first a remote province of the Arab empire which rose to dominance in the Middle East and North Africa during the century following the Prophet **Muhammad**'s death in 632. This empire, whose capital was initially at Damascus and later moved to Baghdad, was ruled by a series of *caliphs,* who claimed to be heirs to the Prophet's secular authority. Al-Andalus was in theory subordinate to the caliphate, but the great distance which lay between them, as well as instability within the empire itself, permitted it to develop separately. A major change occurred in 756 when Abd-al-Rahman I triumphed in a power struggle and established his capital at Córdoba. The new ruler assumed the title of *emir,* which, although often translated as "king," referred more precisely to a military commander subject to the caliph's authority.

Abd-al-Rahman I (756–788) was one of the few surviving princes of the Umayyad dynasty, a family which had occupied the caliphate from 661 until 750, when it was driven from power and nearly exterminated by the rival Abbasids. The bad blood between these two distant branches of the Prophet's family ensured that the Andalusian *emirs,* although they gave formal recognition to their Baghdad cousins' status, did not take orders from them. Under Abd-al-Rahman I and his successors, Spain became effectively independent of the rest of the Islamic world. The Umayyads consolidated their power on the peninsula and, by the time of Abd-al-Rahman II (822–852), the land was unified, prosperous, and efficiently governed. Following the latter's death, however, the emirate fell upon hard times. There was constant feuding among elements of al-Andalus's diverse population, which included a dominant Arab minority,

itself divided along tribal lines; a substantial Berber component, Muslim in religion but resentful of Arab control; a large number of Muwallads, or Spanish converts to Islam; a similarly large number of Mozarabs, or Spaniards who adopted the Arabic language and customs but remained Christian; and a small but influential Jewish population. A particular source of trouble were the ambitious warlords who governed the marches (borders), the thinly-populated frontier zones between al-Andalus and the Christian North.

By the time Abd-al-Rahman III inherited the throne in 912, al-Andalus was in turmoil and the emir's power was effectively restricted to the area immediately surrounding Córdoba. The new ruler's grandfather and immediate predecessor, the emir Abd Allah (888–912), was so distrustful of those around him that he had two of his own sons murdered when he suspected them of plotting against him. These crimes eliminated two candidates for the succession and opened the way for Abd-al-Rahman to be designated heir to the throne.

According to the accounts of medieval Arab historians, Abd-al-Rahman III was born at Córdoba on January 7, 891. His father was Prince Muhammad, one of the murdered sons of Abd Allah, and his mother is said to have been a Christian slave called Muzna, or Maria, who may have been of Frankish origin, although some sources suggest she was a Basque. The new emir's paternal grandmother was also a Christian, a princess of Navarre. Reflecting his mixed ancestry, Abd-al-Rahman III was of fair complexion and had blonde or red hair, which he is said to have dyed black to match that of his Arab courtiers. As a youth, Abd-al-Rahman was already admired at court for his good looks, his wit, and his courage. As emir after 912, he would call upon these qualities, as well as upon his political skill and ruthlessness, to revive the fortunes of the Umayyad monarchy.

Abd-al-Rahman III took vigorous action to restore Umayyad authority in al-Andalus. Resistance in the provincial centers of Écija, Elvira, Jaén, Archidona, and Seville was crushed during 912 and 913. The new ruler also continued his predecessors' long struggle against the Muwallad rebel leader Umar ibn-Hafsun, a descendant of Visigothic nobility who, beginning in 883, had gradually built his own independent zone of control in the south around Málaga. From his ancient mountain fortress at Bobastro, ibn-Hafsun appealed for support to disaffected Muslims and Christians alike. His reported conversion from Islam to the faith of his ancestors during the 890s may have cost ibn-Hafsun some of his Muslim followers, but he successfully resisted efforts to defeat him until his death in 917. His sons held out after him and were not subdued finally until 928. There is a story that, when Abd-al-Rahman entered Bobastro, he ordered his old enemy's remains disinterred and exposed on the road to Córdoba as a lesson to other potential rebels and apostates.

Once the Hafsun family was defeated, two other rebellious Muwallad households, the Marwan of Badajoz and the Kasi of the upper Ebro valley, capitulated as well. In 932, the old Visigothic capital of Toledo, traditional center of Christian life in the Arab region, was finally retaken after remaining virtually independent for some years. With Toledo's fall, Abd-al-Rahman III had succeeded in reuniting al-Andalus under his own firm hand. By that time, he had also taken an audacious political step which redefined his relationship not only to his own subjects, but to the rest of the Islamic world as well.

He Adopts Title of Caliph

On January 16, 929, Abd-al-Rahman III adopted the title of caliph, a move which placed him on an equal footing with the Abbasid ruler of Baghdad. Traditional enemies of the Abbasids, the Umayyad sovereigns of al-Andalus had never accepted the dictates of Baghdad, but they had, heretofore, honored the formal principle of Islamic unity under a single caliph. Until Abd-al-Rahman's proclamation, Friday prayers in Spanish mosques always invoked the name of the Abbasid incumbent; from now on they would exalt the Cordoban ruler instead.

The assumption of the caliphate, which elevated Abd-al-Rahman III's status farther above that of his subjects and made him the ultimate authority in religious as well as political matters, was in part a response to a similar move by an energetic new dynasty in North Africa, the Fatimids. This family, which claimed descent from the Prophet Muhammad's daughter Fatima, had proclaimed its own caliphate in Morocco in 909. Because the Abbasids in Baghdad were currently in decline, while Fatimid influence was on the increase, Abd-al-Rahman sought to reassert his own family's historic claim to dominion in the Arab world. Fearful of a Fatimid invasion, the caliph of Córdoba occupied a number of positions on the North African coast, including Ceuta in 931 and Tangier in 951, but the expected assault never occurred. Instead, the Fatimids turned their attention to the eastern Mediterranean, ultimately taking control of Egypt and establishing their capital at Cairo.

Abd-al-Rahman III's suspicion of his fellow Arabs influenced his approach to Christian powers. In 949, he exchanged envoys with the Byzantine court at Constantinople, which shared his misgivings and was in a position to pressure the Abbasids and Fatimids from the east. These diplomatic contacts appear to have continued throughout the tenth century, although little came of them. Abd-al-Rahman also sought a treaty of friendship with the German emperor **Otto the Great** (936–973), but the historical record is incomplete and the final determination is unknown.

The most important foreign policy concern for Abd-al-Rahman was the emergence of Christian kingdoms on his northern frontier. By the early tenth century, thanks in part to internal disorders in al-Andalus, new Christian monarchies had consolidated territorial control around Oviedo and León in the northwest and around Pamplona in the Basque country at the foot of the Pyrenees. The former area became the kingdom of León, while the latter became the kingdom of Navarre. In addition, Christian settlement moving south into the sparsely inhabited borderlands between the Ebro and Duero rivers created a new region known as Castile, after the many castles which dotted the militarized landscape. Formally vassals of the kings of León, the counts of Castile struggled against their dominance and eventually became major players in peninsular warfare and diplomacy themselves.

In the early years, while Abd-al-Rahman III was preoccupied with trying to restore control over his own subjects, Ordoño II (914–924) of León, with the support of the Navarrese ruler Sancho Garcés (905–926), invaded La Rioja, a Muslim-occupied corridor along the Ebro between Navarre and Castile. On September 4, 917, Ordoño defeated Abd-al-Rahman's forces at San Esteban de Gormaz, on the Duero near Osma. Christian pressure increased against key Muslim strongholds during 918 and 919, causing Abd-al-Rahman to pull away from his quarrels at home and take personal charge of the northern front. In the summer of 920, the emir recaptured several of his lost positions and, in a major engagement, scattered the Christian forces at a place traditionally referred to as Valdejunquera on July 26.

Abd-al-Rahman was confident that the Christian threat had been dealt with, but Ordoño and Sancho Garcés were unsubdued and they returned immediately to the offensive. In April 924, learning that Ordoño had died, the Muslim ruler set out to isolate and punish the king of Navarre, invading the north and sacking Pamplona in July. The victorious emir then returned to Córdoba, once again satisfied that he had secured his northern frontier.

During a lull in Christian activity afforded by an internal struggle for the Leonese crown, Abd-al-Rahman III completed the work of subjugating his own domestic enemies, an achievement symbolized by his 929 decision to adopt the title of caliph. Hostilities erupted again, however, with the accession in León of Ramiro II (930–951), a younger son of Ordoño II. A bold and ruthless leader who had consolidated his own power by blinding his brother and three male cousins, Ramiro quickly renewed his father's attacks in the south. An effort to relieve Toledo in 932 failed, but the Christian monarch made significant advances in both the Duero and Ebro valleys.

Determined to punish León once and for all, Abd-al-Rahman III planned a new campaign for 939, but it ended in disaster, in spite of Arab materiel superiority. Marching northward in July at the head of an army said to number more than 100,000, the caliph encountered Ramiro II outside of Simancas, near Valladolid, where the Christian ruler had drawn up a smaller force made up of Leonese, Navarrese, and Castilian levies. Fighting went on inconclusively for several days until August 1, when Ramiro led a daring assault that broke the Muslim lines and set Abd-al-Rahman's troops to flight.

Following his loss at Simancas—a second defeat at Alhándega, south of Salamanca, which some historians mention, probably never happened—Abd-al-Rahman III resolved never again to take personal command of troops in battle. Islamic pressure on the southern frontiers of León and Navarre consequently lessened, but, except for some Christian settlement activity south of the Duero, Ramiro II was unable to pursue his new advantage because of a quarrel with his own ally and vassal, Count Fernán González of Castile (923–970), who declared his independence in 943. The struggle with Castile, along with the succession dispute which erupted in León upon Ramiro's death in 951, made it easy for Abd-al-Rahman to manipulate the Christian states through diplomacy and intrigue. He pursued this policy for the remaining years of his reign.

Court Is Moved to Medina Azahara

The final decade of Abd-al-Rahman III's long rule was relatively quiet. Order was by that time restored within his own realm, and the frontier between al-Andalus and the Christian kingdoms was more stable and secure than it had been in years. In addition, Abd-al-Rahman's own power and prestige had grown impressively, both at home and abroad. The growth of the state bureaucracy, along with the adoption of symbols of rulership similar to those used by the Byzantine emperors, increased the isolation of the ruler from his subjects. A major step in this process occurred when the caliph moved his court from crowded central Córdoba to Medina Azahara, a newly built palace complex in the nearby countryside. According to a medieval Arab source, construction of this sumptuous self-contained community, which began in 936, consumed one-third of the caliphate's substantial annual revenues and required some 40 years to complete. From the time Abd-al-Rahman took up residence at Medina Azahara in 945, he lived in great luxury among his concubines, children, servants, ministers, and courtiers. Foreign visitors reported that the caliphal court outshown by far its contemporaries in Western Europe.

Neither devout nor fanatical, Abd-al-Rahman III sought to control, not destroy, his Christian neighbors; likewise, he did not persecute his Christian and Jewish subjects, as long as they refrained from challenging his authority. At court, he surrounded himself with men of talent, regardless of their religion. The caliph employed Christian bureaucrats and his personal physician was the Jew Hasdai ibn Shaprut, who, we are told, contributed to the success of Abd-al-Rahman's Leonese policy when he cured Sancho the Fat (Sancho I, 956–958, 960–966) of a serious obesity problem and thus enabled him to regain the throne from which he had been deposed, supposedly because of his inability to mount a horse. A patron of learning like other Umayyad rulers, Abd-al-Rahman welcomed to his court scholars from all over the known world. With his support, the university at Córdoba gained a reputation as the most advanced center of learning in Western Europe, especially in medicine, mathematics, and astronomy. Students flocked to it from both Muslim and Christian countries.

Despite his sophistication, tolerance, and love of learning, Abd-al-Rahman III was, first and last, a despot. He understood the political uses of cruelty and could be ruthless when he believed the situation warranted. Upon returning from his defeat at Simancas in 939, the caliph ordered 300 of his officers crucified outside the gates of Córdoba for having failed him on the field of battle. Even members of Abd-al-Rahman's own family were subject to brutal retaliation when he suspected defiance or betrayal. In 921, he had two of his uncles executed on charges of conspiracy. Years later, in 950, when one of the caliph's own sons,

Abd Allah al-Zahid, was accused of plotting against him, Abd-al-Rahman ordered the unfortunate prince brought into his presence and commanded his throat to be cut while he watched.

Abd-al-Rahman III was a complex personality. Learned and refined, he was tolerant and appreciative of cultural differences, but he was also a ruthless politician who was capable of astounding brutality. Both talented and lucky, he applied political skill to the restoration of the power and prosperity of the Islamic state in southern Spain, and he had the good fortune to live long enough to consolidate his achievements. His reign was the longest yet in the history of Islam, and he is remembered as the greatest of all of Spain's Muslim rulers. Unfortunately, the government of al-Andalus, like other medieval monarchies, depended too heavily on the personal qualities of the individual ruler, and Abd-al-Rahman's achievements did not long survive his death. His son, the cultured al-Hakam II (961–976), was an effective ruler, but after him came the child Hisham II (976–1013), whose extreme youth and weakness of character made possible the virtual dictatorship of the *hajib*, or chief minister, a post which came to be dominated by the ambitious Amirid family. The caliphate rapidly lost prestige and it ceased to exist entirely in 1031, when al-Andalus splintered into a collection of 23 petty states, known as *taifa* kingdoms.

One may doubt that Abd-al-Rahman III foresaw so rapid an end to the Umayyad caliphate, but there is evidence that he appreciated the paradoxes of power. It is recorded that in 961, as he lay dying at his splendid Medina Azahara, Abd-al-Rahman declared that, in all of his 70 years, he had known only 14 days free of worry.

SOURCES:

Hitti, Philip K. *History of the Arabs: From the Earliest Times to the Present.* 5th ed. Macmillan, 1956.

Lévi-Provençal, Évariste. *Le califat umaiyade de Cordoue, 912–1031.* Maisonneuve, 1950.

O'Callaghan, Joseph F. *A History of Medieval Spain.* Cornell University Press, 1975.

FURTHER READING:

Collins, Roger. *Early Medieval Spain: Unity in Diversity, 400–1000.* St. Martin's, 1983.

Watt, W. Montgomery, with Pierre Cachia. *A History of Islamic Spain.* Edinburgh University Press, 1965.

Konrad Adenauer

(1876–1967)

Politician who led the fledgling Federal Republic of Germany through its first difficult years after World War II, presided over its economic recovery, and insured its reacceptance in the family of democratic nations.

Born Konrad Hermann Joseph Adenauer on January 5, 1876, in Cologne, Germany; died in Rhöndorf, Federal Republic of Germany, April 19, 1967; son of Johann Konrad Adenauer (a former soldier and district court clerk) and Helene Scharfenberg Adenauer (daughter of a bank officer); married: Emma Weyer, 1904 (died October 1916); married: Auguste Zinnser, August 25, 1919; children: (first marriage) Konrad, Max, and Ria; (second marriage) Georg, Paul, Libet, and Lotte.

Born in Cologne in the western German Rhineland less than five years after Germany united, Konrad Adenauer rose from middle-class beginnings in a nonpolitical family to become the longest serving democratic political leader in modern German history. He was the third son in a Roman Catholic family, and he was followed by two sisters. Adenauer's father, a modestly paid civil servant, made sure all three of his sons received a good education. Each went through secondary school, and each attended a university as well. Adenauer attended the Apostel Gymnasium (high school for classical subjects) in Cologne, where he did little to distinguish himself either positively or negatively from his classmates. When he graduated in 1894, his family lacked the resources to send him immediately to join his two brothers in university studies. Instead, he went to work in a Cologne bank.

But he stayed only two weeks. The boring errands he had to run for the bank officials showed him exactly how far he would get without money or further education; fortunately, his father found a scholarship for him from a local foundation. In 1894, Adenauer began studying law at the Univer-

"Never lie, not even in politics, because you can never remember all the things you've said. Never attack anyone who isn't present to defend himself. But when he's there, tear into him. Bring up the unpleasant things right away!"

KONRAD ADENAUER

Contributed by Daniel Emmett Rogers, Assistant Professor of History, University of South Alabama, Mobile, Alabama

sity of Freiburg, in the southwest corner of Germany. The law has always been the single best path to a career in the German civil service, although at the time Adenauer may have dreamed of entering private practice in his home region. He later moved to the University of Munich and finally to the University of Bonn, near Cologne, where he successfully completed his studies after six years. His schooling should have been interrupted for military service when he was 20, but the army found his lungs and chest too weak. Adenauer passed the bar exam in 1901 but with only a "satisfactory" grade. In the following years, he worked first in the Cologne prosecutor's office, then beginning in 1902 for a private firm headed by Hermann Kausen. This was to be Adenauer's entrée into politics, for Kausen led the Center Party delegates in the Cologne city council.

The Center Party was a political movement representing Germany's Catholics. They felt discriminated against because of the policies of the Protestant Prussians who had led the unification of Germany. The Catholics used the Center Party as a rallying point to oppose the attacks upon themselves during the 1870s by German chancellor **Otto von Bismarck**. The Center Party remained one of the most important parties in German politics until 1933, and it dominated certain Catholic regions of Germany, especially Adenauer's Rhineland. Adenauer joined the Party after becoming a lawyer; in 1906, when a seat on the city council fell vacant, he persuaded his employer to support him for the post. With Kausen's support, Adenauer won the seat in an election by the city council members. He was the youngest member. A political career that would last six decades (but not without interruption) had begun.

Adenauer started a family of his own in 1904 when he married Emma Weyer, the daughter of a wealthy Cologne family. Emma's family provided useful connections for a young politician: the mayor of Cologne, an uncle by marriage, made Adenauer his deputy in 1909. When the uncle was away on official business, Adenauer would act in his place, bringing himself to the attention of both the politicians and populace of Cologne. At home, he raised his children strictly, in accordance with the views of the Germany of his age; his sons, for instance, were given the close-cropped haircut typical for young Prussians of the day, even though as a Catholic Rhinelander, Adenauer usually frowned upon most things Prussian. He lived simply and forced his family to do likewise; for example, he used city automobiles for public business, but otherwise rode on public transportation.

CHRONOLOGY

1876	Adenauer born
1917	Elected mayor of Cologne
1919	Revolutionary uprisings throughout Germany; democratic Weimar Republic formed
1933	Hitler became chancellor of Germany; Adenauer forced out as mayor of Cologne
1939	Hitler began WWII by attacking Poland
1944	Attempt on Hitler's life; Adenauer arrested in the dragnet that followed
1945	Appointed mayor of Cologne by U.S.; fired by British; joined new Christian Democratic Union
1946	Took control of CDU in British zone
1948	Led constitution-drafting body for West Germany
1949	Elected first chancellor of Federal Republic of Germany
1955	Federal Republic regained almost total sovereignty
1963	Concluded Franco-German friendship treaty; resigned as chancellor
1967	Died on April 19 at age 91

Elected Youngest Mayor in Prussian Germany

On June 28, 1914, the heir to the Austrian throne, Archduke Francis Ferdinand, was assassinated in Sarajevo, Bosnia. A little more than a month later, World War I began. Adenauer was quickly put in charge of Cologne's food supplies, a task that proved vital: Germany could not feed itself when blockaded by enemy navies. While the war lasted until 1918, the years 1916–17 proved the most decisive for Adenauer personally. First, in October 1916, his wife Emma died. She had been weak since the birth of her first son, and fell victim finally to kidney failure. Then, in March 1917, Adenauer was involved in a severe automobile accident that permanently altered his facial appearance, giving him a somewhat Oriental look for the rest of his life. While recovering in the hospital, he received the biggest news of his political career: on September 18, 1917, the Cologne city council elected him to replace his uncle as mayor by the overwhelming vote of 52-0 with two abstentions. At the age of 41, Adenauer was the youngest mayor in all of the Prussian territories of Germany.

Germany won the war on the eastern front in 1918 by forcing newly Communist Russia to surrender. Later that year, Germany tried to achieve the same results on the western front in France, but, despite an advance that came close to reaching Paris, the Germans soon began a slow retreat. By November 1918, German Emperor **Wilhelm II** (William II) had abdicated, an armistice was signed, and a revolution appeared imminent in Germany. Cologne—now Adenauer's Cologne—was one of the major metropolitan areas of Germany. It was bound to feel more acutely than most areas the effects of revolution against the old imperial government, the armed forces, and the war. Adenauer had his hands full dealing with crowds of mutinous soldiers and sailors and with military authorities who wanted to deal harshly with them. He successfully calmed both sides, sparing Cologne the horrible fighting between revolutionaries and the forces of "order" that Berlin and Munich suffered in 1918 and 1919.

In the 1920s, Adenauer became moderately well known throughout Germany. The "Weimar Republic," the era named for the city in which Germany's democratic, liberal constitution was drafted in 1919, afforded more opportunities for elected, rather than royally appointed, officials to attract notice. As a rising figure within the Center Party and mayor of Germany's then third largest city, Adenauer was a natural candidate for higher office. In 1920, he became chairman of the Prussian State Council, something akin to the senate in an American state legislature, except that Prussia still dominated Germany as no American state could dominate the U.S., since it had around 42 million of Germany's 62 million inhabitants. As much as Adenauer detested Prussian dominance of his native Rhineland province, and as much as he wanted more influence for the Rhineland, he opposed plans made by some (and supported by Germany's former French enemies) to detach the Rhineland from the rest of Prussia and Germany. His energies as mayor of Cologne from 1917 to 1933 were instead devoted to founding a university for Cologne, to creating a green ring of trees and fields around the city, and to promoting projects such as bridges across the Rhine that were necessary for daily life in a city approaching a million residents.

His work as mayor, as president of the Prussian State Council, and as a leader in the Center Party led to serious consideration of Adenauer for the post of chancellor ("prime minister") of Germany in 1926. In May of that year, the government fell over the highly charged issue of what colors the flag for Germany should be (those of the old empire or those of the new republic). Adenauer was approached and asked to form a new government. Though he had refused a similar offer in May 1921, now he seriously considered the offer; traveling to Berlin, he entered into discussions about the composition of a possible government.

But the maelstrom of party politics in the confused, often chaotic, capital was too much for any one man to overcome, no matter how successful in his home city, without risking his entire career. Under the Weimar constitution, it was far too difficult to build a successful coalition of parties to form a government, and far too easy to topple it once it managed to take office. So Adenauer again declined the chance at the highest political office in Germany. He returned home on the train from Berlin, apparently content at age 50 to finish his political life as mayor of Cologne. And why not? In a republic in which national governments came and went in less than a year, Adenauer realized, in the words of German chancellor and foreign minister **Gustav Stresemann,** that "mayors in Germany are, second only to the great industrialists, really the kings in today's Germany."

Adenauer remarried on August 25, 1919. His new wife, Auguste ("Gusti") Zinnser, was 19 years his junior; together they produced four additional children. He would need family and friends to provide important refuge during Germany's National Socialist years. In March 1933, less than two months after **Adolf Hitler** was called to power to solve the problem of an ungovernable Germany, the Nazis forced Adenauer out of office as they consolidated power. After a vain attempt to appeal to Nazi leader **Hermann Göring** to be readmitted to office, Adenauer had to flee from Cologne with his family; moves he had made in previous years to restrain Nazi violence and propaganda had not been forgotten.

Unlike many other German politicians, he decided not to leave Germany, but to practice "inner emigration," in effect to fade quietly away into apolitical retirement. After a period of living just outside Berlin, and then in a monastery closer to Cologne, he moved his family to the small town of Rhöndorf, on the Rhine opposite and just south of Bonn, where he built the house in which he would spend the remainder of his life.

Adenauer did not take an active role in opposing Hitler. True enough, he did know some of the main conspirators in the plot to kill Hitler on July 20, 1944, and he was arrested twice, once following the 1944 attempt on Hitler. But his family was too large and his sons too exposed as draftees in the German army for him to risk outright opposition. When taken into custody in August 1944, he escaped, only to be recaptured when the Gestapo imprisoned his wife Gusti and forced her to reveal his whereabouts. Adenauer's imprisonment made inroads on his health, and he was not released until November 26, 1944. For ultimate redemption he needed only to wait a few more months, for in March 1945 American soldiers seized a bridgehead at Remagen, just south of his home at Rhöndorf, and crossed the Rhine. Soon they came looking for Adenauer, asking him to resume his old office as mayor of Cologne.

He refused. His sons still served in the German army, and Hitler would shortly order one collaborating mayor murdered by commandos who had parachuted behind American lines. But Adenauer agreed to act as an advisor to the Americans on restoring public services and order to bombed-out Cologne, until, in May 1945, the military defeat of Germany allowed him to resume the office of mayor—but only as an appointee of the occupying Americans. Adenauer set about diligently trying to restore gas, water, and electricity and to begin the daunting task of clearing mountains of rubble. Politically, he made a fateful decision in September 1945: instead of rejoining his old party, the mainly Catholic Center, he sided with a new party, the Christian Democratic Union. The CDU sought to bridge the differences between Protestants and Catholics in an effort to bring Christian principles to bear in renewing Germany.

Adenauer might have ended his active life happily as mayor of a rebuilding Cologne. After all, in 1946 he was 70 years old and not in the best of health. Fate, or personal differences, intervened. The local British military governor, who had replaced the American commander in July 1945, disliked Adenauer's haughty style and thought he was too old to apply himself energetically to the task of getting Cologne on its feet. He fired Adenauer in October 1945. This dismissal marked a turning point. At the time, he felt humiliated by being cast out of office (once by the Nazis and once by the British, as he later remarked), but now he had the free time to devote to gaining the leadership of the CDU.

In January 1946, Adenauer appeared at a meeting of the Party for the British zone of Germany. Since the CDU was new, no one present was certain about the formalities of leadership. Adenauer seized the moment. He walked to the chairman's seat, proclaimed himself chair by right of seniority, and proceeded to conduct the meeting. He was not challenged (although others there had fancied themselves the CDU's leader), and later he won official recognition as permanent chair of the CDU for the British zone. It was his base for a meteoric rise to power.

Takes Office as West German Chancellor

Adenauer avoided cumbersome government office, preferring instead to try to lead the CDU to dominance against its main rival, the revived Social Democratic Party (SPD). His first true commitment came in 1948 when he accepted appointment to the Parliamentary Council, a body the three Western Allies (France, Great Britain, and the United States) had convoked to write a constitution for a semisovereign West German state. Adenauer, as head of the strong CDU, was elected chairman of the Parliamentary Council. The constitution he helped draft provided for a federal system, with powers divided between the national and state governments and with fundamental rights guaranteed. The constitution was issued in May 1949, and the first parliamentary elections were held in August 1949. Adenauer's CDU barely surpassed the SPD. In the long negotiations that followed, Adenauer cobbled together a coalition of his CDU with several small parties. In September 1949, he took office as the first democratic chancellor Germany had seen in two decades. But it was only for the western part of Germany; the Soviet zone of occupation in the east formed the communist German Democratic Republic in October 1949.

As chancellor, Adenauer had two overriding goals: regaining sovereignty for the new Federal Republic of Germany and restoring its economy. Although the Allies had allowed the Federal Republic a constitution and internal self-government, they still occupied the country and reserved certain powers to themselves. Almost immediately Adenauer pried some measure of respect and sovereignty from the Western Allies; at a meeting with the three Allied High Commissioners in September 1949, for example, he resolutely strode onto a carpet on which the three men were also standing, indicating his intention of being treated as an equal. Soon thereafter, in November 1949, he won Allied agreement to stop the dismantling of German industrial plants as punishment for starting the Second World War.

Adenauer did not surround himself with talented colleagues as his cabinet members, presiding instead over what his political enemies called a "chancellor democracy," something on the order of a one-man government. One gifted cabinet member—whom Adenauer disliked intensely—was economics minister Ludwig Erhard, an economics professor whose free-market policies turned the Federal Republic into Western Europe's economic powerhouse in the 1950s. Adenauer left economics mostly to Erhard and concentrated on diplomacy. In 1955, Adenauer won almost total sovereignty from the Western Allies; but, against strong internal opposition, he placated these same Allies by rearming Germany within NATO as a hedge against Communist expansion. He then visited Moscow in September 1955 and traded German diplomatic recognition of the Soviet Union for the return of prisoners of war the Soviets had held for over a decade. The result was an unheard-of gratitude from German voters, who in 1957 gave the CDU an absolute majority for the first and only time in German parliamentary history.

Adenauer's later years were not so distinguished, as he held onto power into his late 80s. In 1962, he aroused fears of antidemocratic sentiments when his government jailed the editor of a newsmagazine that had published secrets unflattering to the German military. He ended his career in 1963 with a flourish, however. He signed a treaty of friendship with Germany's long-time enemy France, and accompanied the young American president **John Kennedy** on his famous trip to divided Berlin. Adenauer retired to Rhöndorf in October 1963, turning the chancellery over unwillingly to Erhard, whom by now he detested. The last few years of his life were devoted to his hobbies, painting and rose-gardening, and to writing his memoirs. He died at the age of 91 in 1967, mourned by most of the leaders of the free world, who came to the Cologne Cathedral for the funeral of the man who had given Germans back some of the pride the Hitler era had so recently taken from them.

SOURCES:

Prittie, Terrence. *Konrad Adenauer, 1876–1967*. Cowles, 1971.

Schwarz, Hans-Peter. *Adenauer: Der Aufstieg, 1876–1952*. Deutsche Verlags-Anstalt, 1986.

Weymar, Paul. *Adenauer: His Authorized Biography*. Dutton, 1957.

FURTHER READING:

Adenauer, Konrad. *Memoirs, 1945–1953*. Regnery, 1966.

Hiscocks, Richard. *The Adenauer Era*. Lippincott, 1967.

Wighton, Charles. *Adenauer: Democratic Dictator*. Muller, 1963.

Agrippina the Younger

(A.D. 15–59)

Niece and fourth wife of Emperor Claudius, who was suspected of having him and his son assassinated to secure the throne for her own son Nero—through whom she hoped to dominate Rome.

"In public, Agrippina was austere and often arrogant. Her private life was chaste—unless power was to be gained. Her passion to acquire money was unbounded. She wanted it as a stepping-stone to supremacy."

TACITUS

O n her mother's side, Agrippina was the great-granddaughter of **Augustus,** who molded the Roman Empire from the ashes of the Roman Republic. Her father Germanicus was the nephew and designated heir of Augustus's successor **Tiberius.** In the year A.D. 20, Germanicus met an untimely death. Agrippina undoubtedly retained childhood memories of the subsequent mistreatment suffered by her mother and older brothers at the hands of Emperor Tiberius, who was only a stepson of Augustus. She would have learned at her mother's knee to despise "usurpers" who were not actually of Augustus's line. Historians have long suspected that a childhood spent steeped in fear and resentment warped Agrippina's brother Caligula. Perhaps it also drove Agrippina in her determination to rule rather than suffer the whims of a ruler.

Her mother Agrippina the Elder was a model of the old-fashioned Roman wife and mother, except for her practice of accompanying her husband on his military tours, even those which took him to the frontiers of the Roman world. In A.D. 15, the younger Agrippina was born in a camp on the frontier with the German tribes.

Name variations: Julia Agrippina; sometimes called Agrippina Minor (the Younger) to distinguish her from her mother Vipsania Agrippina, sometimes called Agrippina Major (the Elder.) Pronunciation: Agri-PEEN-a. Born in A.D. 15; died in A.D. 59; daughter of Germanicus and Agrippina the Elder; sister of Caligula; married: Cnaeus Domitius Ahenobarbus (father of Nero); married: Claudius (her paternal uncle, emperor of Rome); children: Nero (emperor of Rome).

Contributed by Phyllis Culham, Department of History, United States Naval Academy, Annapolis, Maryland

CHRONOLOGY

(Following her later marriage to Claudius, Agrippina the Younger would award special municipal honors to the village growing on the site.)

At 33, Germanicus, a son of Emperor Tiberius's younger brother, was the most attractive and popular member of the imperial family. When he died after a brief and undiagnosed illness while touring the eastern Mediterranean provinces, the Roman people were convinced that Tiberius had ordered his assassination out of jealousy and fear. Agrippina the Elder was also certain that Tiberius was responsible for her husband's death. The four-year-old Agrippina, brought to meet her mother at Tarracina, south of Rome, to accompany Germanicus's ashes on their journey home, could not have remembered her father or her austere mother well. The agonizing public procession to Rome, however, through crowds running wild with grief and anger at the death of their favorite, surely left an indelible impression. Her mother's dignified but clearly heartfelt grief caught the imagination of the Roman people and won popular esteem for the widow and her children. If Tiberius had not felt jealous and uneasy earlier, he now had good cause for worry.

Agrippina the Elder was too ambitious to spend the rest of her life in quiet widowhood with her children. Her relationship to Tiberius was further complicated by her status: as a granddaughter of Augustus, she was naturally heir to political connections and influence, making any second husband an automatic threat to Tiberius's plans for the succession. In such a thoroughly political household, it is likely that the young Agrippina would have been aware of the trial of her father's accused assassin (who ended inquiries by committing suicide) and of the deepening, public hostility between her mother and Emperor Tiberius, who had not even come to the ceremony when Germanicus's ashes were placed in the tomb of Augustus. Attending state dinners, Agrippina the Elder ostentatiously took precautions against poison in her dishes. In A.D. 26, she finally asked Tiberius for permission to remarry; Tiberius neglected to reply.

Modern historians of Rome are more inclined than their ancient counterparts to believe that the model matron Agrippina the Elder was aggressor, as well as victim, and that she was providing aid and support to Tiberius's enemies even if she wasn't actively plotting against him. In a move to reduce the family's potential for making alliances, Tiberius decided that Agrippina the·Younger would marry the much older Cnaeus Domitius Ahenobarbus in A.D. 28. (Betrothal of 13-year-old girls, with marriage to follow shortly, was common among Romans.) Suetonius described Agrippina's new husband as a "wholly despicable character" who was "remarkably dishonest."

Agrippina was only 14 when her mother and oldest brother were arrested in A.D. 29 and exiled to prison islands. Though her second brother had supplied evidence against them, he was the next to be arrested; held in the imperial palace, he was starved to death. As for the third brother, Caligula, Tiberius alternated between ignoring and honoring him. In A.D. 33, Agrippina the Elder starved herself to death, while her son Caligula's portrait was put on coins.

Tiberius Dies; Nero Is Born

The year A.D. 37 saw the death of Tiberius, the accession to the throne of Caligula, and the birth of Agrippina the Younger's only child, **Nero.** But if Agrippina thought she was finally safe, she was wrong. Initially, Caligula heaped honors upon his sisters, as only they and he had survived childhood diseases and Tiberius's hatred. Receiving all of the privileges and public honors previously reserved for Vestal Virgins, the three sisters were included in the annual vows of allegiance to the emperor; their portraits were also put on coins. Caligula was especially devoted to his sister Drusilla who died in A.D. 38.

Disaster soon struck when in A.D. 39 the imperial family visited and inspected the armies on the Rhine frontier. While they were still in the north, Caligula became convinced that both of his two surviving sisters were involved in a love affair and a conspiracy against him with Drusilla's widower, Marcus Aemilius Lepidus. Though it seems unlikely that both sisters were dallying with Lepidus, it is possible that Lepidus and the two women had decided that Caligula was becoming unstable and an increasing threat to them. In any case, after retrieving his oldest brother's ashes from the prison island of Ponti, Caligula sent Agrippina into exile there. Suetonius believed that he was planning to execute his two sisters at the time of his death. Miriam Griffin has observed astutely that Agrippina's "childhood and youth would have warped the most sanguine nature, as her prospects fluctuated between extremes." In A.D. 41, she had to breathe a sigh of relief at the assassination of her brother Caligula and applaud the accession of a crippled, elderly paternal uncle who was not descended from Augustus. The new emperor **Claudius** recalled her and her only surviving sister from exile.

Agrippina's son Nero had been left in near poverty during her exile, when Caligula used the excuse of her husband's death to seize most of their assets. Although Claudius returned the property taken from the two sisters, mere prosperity and imperial connections were not enough for Agrippina. She immediately tried to raise the stakes. Gossip reported that her first target was the extremely wealthy and well-born Servius Sulpicius Galba, but he escaped Agrippina's matrimonial snares and survived to later succeed Nero as emperor. She had apparently arranged a marriage with another rich senator, Gaius Sallustius Passienus Crispus, by the time of his death in A.D. 47, despite the fact that he was already married to her sister-in-law Domitia. Agrippina and Nero were remembered generously in Crispus's will, but rumors that she had poisoned him were probably inspired by her later treatment of Claudius and Britannicus.

Agrippina's campaign to become imperial consort might well have preceded the scandal which led to the suicide of Emperor Claudius's third wife, Messallina, in A.D. 47. Messallina had favored sending Agrippina's sole surviving sister Livilla back into exile, and Agrippina was thought in some quarters to have been flirting with her uncle in order to obtain protection against Messallina. Also, Messallina was apparently worried about Nero's popularity as a descendant of both Augustus and Germanicus, who was still fondly remembered. By the time Messallina was apprehended in a plot to put her lover on the throne and murder Claudius, Agrippina had already made friends in the court and was ready to make her move.

Claudius's prestige had been badly damaged by the scandal. He desperately needed a public relations triumph. As always in matters of serious business, Claudius consulted his chief executive secretary, a freedman named Pallas who was devoted to Agrippina (many, in fact, believed they were lovers). He and others of Agrippina's party in the court convinced Claudius that what he needed was Agrippina. Marriage between uncle and niece was considered incestuous in Rome, and it took a senatorial decree to legalize the marriage. Still, Agrippina was of the bloodline of Augustus and was popularly idolized as the daughter of Germanicus. Her son Nero could be adopted to secure the survival of the dynasty, since Claudius's own son Britannicus was not past the high mortality years of childhood. In A.D. 49, Agrippina and her uncle Claudius were married.

Griffin describes how Agrippina "had achieved this dominant position for her son and herself by a web of political alliances," which included Claudius's chief secretary and bookkeeper Pallas, his doctor Xenophon, and Afranius Burrus, the new head of the Praetorian Guard (the imperial bodyguard), who owed his promotion to Agrippina. Neither ancient nor modern historians of Rome have doubted that Agrippina had her eye on securing the throne for Nero from the very day of the marriage—if not earlier—and Dio Cassius's observation seems to bear that out: "As soon as Agrippina had come to live in the palace she gained complete control over Claudius."

Agrippina did not, however, concentrate on advancing her son to the point of neglecting herself. She was the only living woman to receive the title Augusta since Livia, the wife of Augustus, and Livia had not been allowed to use the name during Augustus's lifetime. Levick describes Agrippina's conduct in the court of Claudius: "Certainly from 51 onwards she appeared at ceremonial occasions in a gold-threaded military cloak, and on a tribunal (distinct from that of her husband, however), greeted ambassadors." Roman men's full nomenclature usually included a reference to their fathers, as in "son of Marcus." One official religious record listed Nero as "son of Agrippina" before putting in the usual reference to his father. Tacitus said that Narcissus, another of Claudius's influential freedman-secretaries, tried to warn others about Agrippina's plans: "There is nothing she will not sacrifice to imperial ambition—neither decency, nor honour, nor chastity." Writes Dio: "No one attempted in any way to check Agrippina; indeed, she had more power than Claudius himself."

In A.D. 50, Nero became the adoptive son of Claudius as well, sealing the fate of Claudius and his son Britannicus, though Agrippina could afford to wait for the most opportune moment. Claudius probably feared the results if he were to exclude a grandson of Germanicus from the succession, and

Agrippina the Younger's determination and ambition could well have been molded upon her mother's example. In camp on the Rhine from A.D. 14 through A.D. 16 with her children, Agrippina the Elder shamed one group of mutineers with whom her husband Germanicus had been unable to cope. On another occasion, when Germanicus was away from the base, a rumor swept the region that an overwhelming force of Germans was on the way. It was Agrippina who stopped the soldiers from destroying the bridge over the Rhine to halt the putative invasion. Tacitus even claimed that Tiberius became jealous of her influence over the men in the Rhine legions because "in those days this great-hearted woman acted as commander. She herself dispensed clothes to needy sol-

he certainly needed loyal military commanders rising through the ranks. While Claudius undoubtedly hoped that the adoption would secure the loyalty of both Nero and those who adored Germanicus, hindsight certainly revealed his error. The last months of his life were characterized by disputes with Agrippina over the advancement of Nero and Britannicus. Tacitus reports that Agrippina became afraid when she heard Claudius mutter while drunk that "it was his destiny first to endure his wives' misdeeds and then to punish them." Events were rapidly escalating. Custom dictated that Britannicus would assume a toga and be considered a man early in the spring of A.D. 55.

But in A.D. 54, the 64-year-old, gouty, always frail Claudius died. His contemporaries simply assumed that he was poisoned by Agrippina, and recent scholars have largely shared their conviction. Claudius's death was particularly timely in that he had survived long enough to award formal honors and recognition to Nero, who had used those years to make himself more popular and better known (as well as simply becoming older and more qualified to rule), yet Claudius died before Britannicus could be set on the same track. Britannicus did not live to assume a man's toga; he died shortly after attending a dinner party with the rest of the imperial family—an event that no one thought a coincidence.

Tacitus claimed that Agrippina foresaw the end to all her plotting. Having consulted astrologers about Nero's prospects several years before, she had been told that Nero would become emperor but kill his mother. She supposedly replied, "Let him kill me—provided he becomes Emperor." Nero tried to justify her subsequent murder after the fact by claiming that she intended to rule Rome using him as her puppet, and his speech to the senate, as reported in Tacitus, might well have put it fairly: "She had wanted to be co-ruler—to receive oaths of allegiance from the Guard, and to subject senate and public to the same humiliation [of swearing allegiance to a woman]."

Seneca Tutors Nero

Given those claims, it is ironic that Tacitus and others ascribe the good aspects of Nero's reign to Agrippina. She had already had Lucius Annaeus **Seneca,** the noted Stoic rhetorician and philosopher, recalled from exile and made Nero's tutor. After Nero became emperor, she encouraged Seneca and Burrus, the commander of the Praetorian Guard, to function as virtual regents. Unfortunately for her, she had made a mistake rather like that of Claudius. Seneca and Burrus thought it their duty to act for the good of their emperor, and they believed that charge, in turn, required them to ease Agrippina out before her blatant attempts to assert power evoked hostility against her son and the dynasty itself. In one dramatic incident at the end of A.D. 54, she attempted to join Nero on his dais to receive ambassadors from Armenia. Even Claudius had made her sit on a separate throne when receiving. Seneca and Burrus nudged Nero into stepping down to greet her in an apparent gesture of respect, which allowed him to escort her to a separate, lower seat.

The power and influence she had sought for so long continued to wane through the next year. Seneca and Burrus encouraged Nero in an affair with a woman of low birth of whom Agrippina did not approve. They favored anything which reduced his mother's influence over him. While they convinced Nero to dismiss his mother's partisan Pallas from his powerful administrative post, they were not implacably hostile to Agrippina. As Griffin has commented, "It was not the intention of Seneca and Burrus that Agrippina be removed from the scene. Their influence over Nero depended largely on the fact that they provided a refuge from her tactless and arrogant demands."

Gossip had it that Agrippina had even tried to seduce Nero in order to hold his loyalty and might have succeeded. In any case, Nero understood better than Burrus and Seneca that while Agrippina might be killed, she would never be quietly subdued. Having been separated from his mother in early childhood, as an older child and

diers and dressed the wounded.... Agrippina's position in the army already seemed to outshine generals and commanding officers." No wonder that friends who warned her to flee Tiberius after Germanicus's death advised her to place herself in the protection of the legions on the Rhine; had she left Rome as a fugitive, she probably could have inspired a rebellion against Tiberius in northern Gaul. For most Romans, her single, contented marriage and the number of her children recalled their supposedly more simple and virtuous republican past. Her ambition for her children and her determination to leave no wrong to her family unavenged were also models of a traditionally Roman strength. ■

adolescent Nero had been her partner in deadly conspiracy. He had acquired his political morality from her. Agrippina and her son understood each other well; she began taking preemptive doses of antidotes against common poisons.

When Nero first began to plan Agrippina's death, Burrus kept Nero's confidence by agreeing to carry out his plan if there were actual evidence that she was conspiring against her son. While such evidence did not surface, the issue did not go away. Nero called in Seneca and Burrus for emergency counsel after another plot to kill Agrippina in the preplanned collapse of a pleasure boat failed. Agrippina swam to shore, and Nero was terrified of his mother's wrath. Whereas Burrus and Seneca conceded that an angry Agrippina who knew that her son was her deathly enemy could not safely be left alive, they escaped actual complicity in Agrippina's murder by warning Nero that the Praetorians probably would not follow orders to kill her. After all, not only was she descended from Augustus and Germanicus, but she had selected many of the Guard's officers for their positions. Thus, Nero was forced to call in a contingent from the navy to stab his mother in the bedroom of her villa.

Among Agrippina's lasting accomplishments was her recall of Seneca from exile. She provided him residence in Rome and the financial resources which facilitated his completion of many works of significant influence on the Stoic tradi-

tion. She also left her own memoirs and, though they do not survive today, Tacitus used them extensively in constructing his picture of the reigns of the final Julio-Claudians. Nero, who had believed himself incapable of living with Agrippina, found that he was unable to live happily without her. Regardless of her private life and motives, Agrippina tried to ensure that Nero governed well and observed the proprieties. Tacitus characterized the rest of his reign: "Then he plunged into the wildest improprieties, which vestiges of respect for his mother had hitherto not indeed repressed, but at least impeded." Perhaps Nero's notorious misconduct was an effort to find distraction or a respite from guilt. Dio reported that he frequently saw his mother's ghost and rarely had a good night's sleep.

SOURCES:

Dio Cassius. *Dio's Roman History.* Putnam, Vol. 7, 1924, Vol. 8, 1925.

Suetonius. *The Twelve Caesars.* Penguin, 1957.

Tacitus. *The Annals of Imperial Rome.* Penguin, 1971.

FURTHER READING:

Balsdon, J. P. V. D. *Roman Women.* Barnes & Noble, 1962.

Griffin, Miriam T. *Nero: The End of a Dynasty.* Yale University Press, 1985.

Levick, Barbara. *Claudius.* Yale University Press, 1990.

Albert I

(1875–1934)

King of Belgium, whose determined leadership brought his small country through the great crisis of World War I.

Born on April 8, 1875, in Brussels, Belgium; died on February 17, 1934; son of Philip, Count of Flanders (brother of King Leopold II of Belgium) and Princess Marie of Hohenzollern-Sigmaringen; married: Duchess Elizabeth of Bavaria, 1900; children: two sons, one daughter. Predecessor: his uncle, Leopold II. Successor: his son, Leopold III.

Albert I, king of Belgium from 1909 to 1934, became one of the most respected European monarchs of his time due to his leadership in World War I. Ironically, though his family background was entirely German and he was married to a German princess, Albert led his country's heroic defense against German attack. Just as ironically, the warrior-king of World War I had seemed a quiet, scholarly, and even shy figure in the years before the war.

The Kingdom of Belgium was still a new country at the start of the 20th century. Following the Napoleonic wars, the Congress of Vienna in 1815 had put this part of Europe into a newly created Kingdom of the Netherlands under a Dutch ruler. Designed to help guard Europe against a new French attack, the large kingdom brought the Belgians unwillingly together with the Dutch.

In 1830, the Belgians revolted against their foreign ruler, and the following year a new Kingdom of Belgium was created under the Coburg dynasty. The Coburgs came from southeastern Germany; as the most important members of the new ruling dynasty of Belgium, they chose their marriage partners from families of similar rank in

"In the course of … 1914, King Albert was transformed from an apparently colorless, if well-intentioned, sovereign into a bold and resolute leader of men, the symbol of little Belgium's stand against a powerful and ruthless invader."

THEO ARONSON

Contributed by Neil Heyman, Professor of History, San Diego State University, San Diego, California

Germany. Because it stood as a strategic area affecting the interests of several great powers—France, Prussia, and Great Britain—Belgium was given a neutral status guaranteed by international treaty in 1839.

In the late 19th century, tiny Belgium played only a secondary role in Europe. When France and Prussia went to war in 1870, both sides respected Belgian neutrality. The small country became heavily industrialized, and, under King **Leopold II,** who ruled from 1865 to 1909, it became a great colonial power. Leopold sponsored a private company to explore and take possession of the Congo region in Central Africa.

The prosperous kingdom had its troubles. One difficulty was the internal tension caused by the rise of a Socialist Party and disputes over how much of the population should be entitled to vote. Another problem was the division of the population into French-speaking Walloons and Dutch-speaking Flemings.

Albert was born in Brussels on April 8, 1875. Because his uncle, King Leopold II, had no living male children, Albert became an heir to the crown in 1891 when his older brother died. The death of Albert's father, Count **Philip of Flanders,** in 1905 and the death of King Leopold II in 1909 placed Albert on the throne.

A tall young man with a heavy, awkward body, thick eyeglasses, and a shy manner, Albert seemed an unlikely figure to rule effectively. Educated as a soldier, he never looked comfortable in his army uniform. He had married Princess Elizabeth of Bavaria in 1900, and together they had immersed themselves in a number of unusual activities: yoga, mountain climbing, charity work among the poor.

When Albert became king in 1909, he faced serious difficulties. The reputation of the monarchy was severely hurt by the behavior of Leopold who had often overstepped his constitutional powers, acting more like an unlimited monarch than Belgian law allowed. After taking control of the Congo in Central Africa, Leopold damaged the reputation of his country through the brutal policy he pursued toward the native population there. Even though the Congo had been Leopold's private possession, in 1908 it became a Belgian colony. A second dilemma for Albert was growing opposition to the very idea of a monarchy in Belgium. The Belgian Socialist Party, which was increasing its voting strength, stood as a stronghold for republican feeling. If it came to power, the monarchy itself might be abolished. Finally, war clouds were forming. Belgium was still a neutral

country with its status guaranteed by the Great Powers. Nonetheless, growing tensions among the Great Powers made Belgium's position a dangerous one. A glance at the map showed that a future war between Germany and France made it likely that these foreign powers might invade Belgium, because its geographic position offered important advantages as a military base.

In fact, before 1914 the French had considered moving into Belgium upon the outbreak of a war, but they had rejected the idea. On the other hand, Germany's plans for a future war depended upon a drive into Belgium. Facing France to the west and Russia to the east, German military leaders had developed "the Schlieffen Plan," in which France would be attacked and defeated first. Because France's eastern border was heavily defended, the Germans decided to launch the most important part of their offensive through Belgium.

Some observers close to Albert saw hints of his abilities as a leader as soon as he became king. Although he insisted "I am a constitutional monarch," he attended meetings of the Belgian cabinet, influenced government policy, and made a special effort to bridge the gap between Walloons and Flemings. For example, he was the first Belgian monarch to take his oath of office in Flemish as well as French. When his cousin, **Wilhelm II** of Germany, visited Belgium in 1910 and criticized Albert for accepting the limits of a constitutional ruler, Albert hotly defended the Belgian system: "My country and I, we make our policy together."

In 1913, when Albert returned the visit, staying at the palace at Potsdam outside Berlin,

Wilhelm reminded him of their family ties. Albert's mother had been a princess of the Hohenzollerns, the same family that ruled Germany. Wilhelm and his generals spoke of an inevitable war with France and the equally inevitable victory of the German army. Albert saw this as a means of pressing him to cooperate with Germany's plans and continued to insist that Belgium would defend itself against attack from any foreign country. When the crisis came in August 1914, the shy young king took decisive control of the situation. He rejected the German demand to be allowed passage through Belgium; Belgium, true to its word, would fight invasion.

Albert Leads Belgian Military

For the next four years, Albert also became the country's military leader. As king, he was formally head of the armed forces—a responsibility he exercised in fact as well as title. Showing determination, good judgment, and military talent, he pulled the Belgian army back into the fortified port of Antwerp at the start of the war, then retreated westward in October 1914. The powerful German army overran Belgium, but Albert and his small army managed to hold a small chunk of territory in the northwest. While Albert and his wife lived in the small coastal town of La Panne, the Belgian army defended 20 square miles of Belgian territory between the Yser River and the French border. He considered it vital to keep at least some part of Belgium free of enemy occupation during the war.

The king's heroic and determined leadership during the fighting was matched by the activities of his wife Elizabeth. Some of the highest ranking commanders on the German side were her relatives. Nonetheless, she nursed wounded Belgian soldiers and stood beside her husband as a symbol of the Belgian war effort.

While the king commanded the army, he spent much of his time visiting his small army in its trenches. His popularity grew as word spread that the royal family were living a simple life in a tiny house only a few miles from the front. On one visit to his troops, he had asked them about their needs. When they asked him what he desired, he answered simply: "I should like to go back to Brussels."

With great determination, Albert worked to maintain an independent Belgium with its own policy. He refused to be dominated by his powerful wartime allies Britain and France, rejecting calls for the Belgian army to participate in the bloody offensives that cost the Allies millions of lives on the western front. He also rejected military operations that would add to the destruction of Belgian territory.

Under Albert's direction, the Belgian government took the lead in trying to end the war with a compromise peace. Seeing little hope for a decisive victory in the war, he disregarded the advice of Belgian cabinet members who wanted him to start claiming territory as the fruit of a future peace treaty. In general, Albert avoided identifying Belgian's war aims with those of Britain, France, and (later) the United States. Those countries, he claimed, wanted to defeat Germany; Belgium only wished to be free again.

A Hero's Welcome in Britain

To the rest of the world, Albert did not seem a reluctant warrior. He seemed instead to be an uncomplicated hero. In July 1918, during the final summer of the war, he and his wife, Queen Elizabeth, made a rare trip away from Belgian territory. Visiting London to help celebrate the silver wedding anniversary of the British king and queen (George V and Mary), the Belgian rulers were greeted with a storm of admiration when they appeared in public. They were cheered, as one observer put it, "as I have not heard cheering before."

In the closing weeks of the fighting, Albert took command of a group of field armies composed of French, Belgian, and British units, and he now permitted Belgian forces to go on the attack. Along with his queen, the monarch made a dramatic return to his liberated country. On November 22, 1918, he entered the capital city of Brussels in the midst of popular rejoicing. The prewar threats to end the monarchy had all but disappeared; even Socialist leaders now supported the monarchy as a symbol of the nation.

Albert returned to his life as peacetime monarch, but only after a dramatic foreign tour in which he was welcomed in the United States. Americans, like other peoples who had fought against Germany, never understood the limited role that Albert had set for Belgium in pursuing the war. They greeted the Belgian king as a victorious hero of the Allied side.

Quickly repairing the damage done by the war, Belgium returned to its pre-1914 prosperity. However, the longstanding internal tensions between Flemings and Walloons continued. The Belgian king went back to his family life and his wealth of hobbies, including such dangerous activities as mountain climbing. As he grew older, Albert claimed to fear a lingering death. Instead, on February 17, 1934, the king lost his life in a climbing accident near the Belgian city of Namur.

SOURCES:

Aronson, Theo. *Defiant Dynasty: The Coburgs of Belgium.* Bobbs-Merrill, 1968.

———. *Crowns in Conflict: The Triumph and the Tragedy of European Monarchy, 1910–1918.* John Murray, 1986.

FURTHER READING:

Helmreich, Jonathan E. *Belgium and Europe: A Study in Small Power Diplomacy.* Mouton, 1976.

Kossmann, E. H. *The Low Countries, 1780–1940.* Clarendon Press, 1978.

Schmitt, Bernadotte E. and Harold C. Verdeler. *The World in the Crucible, 1914–1919.* Harper, 1984.

Alexander the Great

(356–323 B.C.)

Macedonian king, who subdued the Greek city-states
and the Persian Empire, and ventured into India,
spreading Greek civilization in his wake.

*Name variations: Alexander III.
Born in 356 B.C. in Pella; died
in 323 B.C. at Babylon, buried at
Alexandria in a golden coffin;
numerous wives and children,
including the most famous
Princess Roxana. Predecessor:
Philip II of Macedonia.
Successor: son, Alexander IV.*

"The period 336-323 B.C. is inevitably designated the age of Alexander," writes A. B.
Bosworth. "With equal justice the period
might be termed the age of Philip." Indeed,
Alexander the Great's conquests have been interpreted as a phase, albeit the most significant, of
Macedonian imperial expansion. Viewed from this
perspective, the legacy of Alexander's father and
mother were of immense importance in laying the
foundation for Alexander's success.

Macedonia was a Greek city-state on the
fringe of Ancient Greece's classical greatness. The
Macedonians were considered, by their southern
neighbors, the more barbarous of the Hellenistic
peoples. The Macedonian Kingdom, however, was
in disarray and dissolution in 359 B.C. when Philip
II came to power. After solidifying his position in
Macedonia, he then proceeded to establish the
military, financial, and economic basis for a Macedonian Empire. Further, Philip strengthened his
hold on the kingship through marriage and military might. His army was perhaps one of the most
important legacies to his son. Its effectiveness was
developed in the 20 years of continuous campaigning, during which Philip defeated his northern

*"At his death [Alexander] had subdued the
largest tract of the earth's surface ever to be conquered by a single individual ... and ruled as
overlord, emperor or king from Mount Olym-
pus to the Himalayas."*

JOHN KEEGAN

*Contributed by Paul Dickson, Doctoral candidate, University of Guelph,
Guelph, Ontario, Canada*

neighbors and successively brought the great Greek city-states of Athens, Sparta, and Thebes under Macedonian domination. The result was an army whose leadership was based on ability as well as noble birth and whose tactical organization enabled it to defeat its enemies through sheer brute force. Used in combination with some of the best-led and organized cavalry in the Greek world and supported by the populous and wealthy Macedonian state, Philip's army proved to be a nearly unbeatable force.

A man of immense energy and ambition, Philip married often but usually for political gain. Nevertheless, the match that produced Alexander was one of equals. The strong-willed and formidable Olympias was as wily and ambitious as Philip. She was also given to eccentric religious beliefs, worshipping Dionysus, the god of natural forces. She imbued her son with an almost mystical veneration for the gods of strength and power such as Hercules and Dionysus. Soon after their union, however, Philip married again and Olympias fell into disfavor at court. Olympias was thus left to raise the boy in a manner she thought befitting a Greek prince.

Tutored by Aristotle

Alexander emerged as a man of sharp contrasts. His education ranged from a physically demanding training in the arts of athletics and war to an elite education which included tutoring at the hands of the eminent Greek philosopher Aristotle. The result was a lithe, athletic man who, while not physically imposing, revealed remarkable powers of endurance, magnified by an imposing character and unbreakable will. Alexander's contrasting physical features—the soft moist eyes, slight flush, sharp nose, fierce expression, and loud and harsh voice—reflected the emotional extremes of a man capable of both overwhelming generosity and violent outbursts of temper. Similarly, the man who became an acknowledged master of the art of war was strongly influenced by epic stories of his heroic ancestors and contemporary Greek philosophers. Indeed, one of the most significant aspects of his education was how readily his brilliant intellect was sparked by the Homeric tales of Troy in the *Iliad*. Tales of the glory of Greece complemented his religious beliefs, and his desire to spread the benefits of Greek civilization as he perceived them may have been an important factor in fueling his desire for conquest.

Alexander's brash arrogance and belief in his abilities was soon borne out by fact. By the age of 16, he was acting as Philip's regent, managing the

CHRONOLOGY

359 B.C.	Philip assumed power in Macedonia
356 B.C.	Alexander born
342 B.C.	Aristotle became Alexander's tutor
340 B.C.	Alexander's first military campaign, acting as his father's regent
336 B.C.	Philip assassinated
335 B.C.	Alexander suppressed a rebellion by Thebes against Macedonian rule
334 B.C.	Began his first campaign against the Persian Empire; defeated Persian army at Battle of Granicus
333 B.C.	Persian army defeated at Battle of Issus (Pinarus River)
332 B.C.	City of Tyre besieged and destroyed
331 B.C.	Alexandria founded after conquest of Egypt; Alexander defeated Persians in Battle of Gaugamela
327 B.C.	Formalized conquest of Northwest frontier with marriage to Roxana; began invasion of India
324 B.C.	Returned to Persian Gulf to subdue Arabia
323 B.C.	Died from fever and drink

daily business of the kingdom, while the Macedonian King continued his military campaigning. Alexander also campaigned with his father, battling northern tribesmen who resisted Macedonian overlordship. His capabilities were such that in 339 B.C., at the age of 17, he commanded a section of the Macedonian army in battle with the respected forces of Thebes and allegedly played no small part in their defeat. He maintained his claim as crown prince by continuing to play a significant role in Macedonian military, diplomatic, and political events.

The first threat to Alexander's position as successor to the Macedonian crown came, ironically, from Philip himself. Philip married again in 337 B.C., and his new wife was determined to bear an heir to the throne. Intrigue followed, and Olympias was gradually alienated from the royal court, culminating in a confrontation in which father and son drew swords on each other in defense of their relative loyalties. Olympias and Alexander withdrew from the court in a self-imposed exile. For close to a year tension and insecurity marked the relationship between Alexander and his father until the threat to their positions from pretenders who wished to see them both deposed became so great that an accommodation was reached. Alexander was persuaded to return to the royal household, and Olympias's grievances were eased, although not erased, through the dynastic marriage of her brother to a member of the Macedonian royal family. Yearlong preparations were to culminate in a huge state wedding in 336 B.C., a symbolic end to the feuding of the past months.

Alexander Claims the Throne

But the intended celebration was not to be. Philip was assassinated by a bitter young noble, a victim of the dynastic machinations that surrounded the Macedonian court. Some suspicion naturally fell on Alexander and Olympias, and, while subsequent events did not bear this out, many view the assassination as the natural outgrowth of Alexander's passion for power. Regardless, Philip's murder, as Bosworth observes, precipitated a crisis, for "Alexander's position was strong but far from unassailable." Alexander took swift action to simultaneously avenge his father's death and to solidify his own claim to the throne. The Macedonian throne was essentially an elective position; if a claimant could gather enough support from the nobility—support which was revealed in the form of donning armor and brandishing weapons as a sign of a willingness to shed blood for their "candidate"—then his would be the strongest position. Alexander's decisiveness, however, quickly blunted the opposition. Most potential rivals, real and imagined, were murdered, in what John Keegan describes as "a common practice in Alexander's world, a policy of prudence in a society where the sword spoke more mightily than the law." Nevertheless, Alexander revealed his shrewd political sense, sparing some potential claimants, preferring instead to keep his enemies to a minimum.

The "politics of succession" would plague Alexander until his death, but he had secured his position to the degree that he was able to begin the fulfillment of his broader dream of war and conquest. The year 335 B.C. was the first of a decade-long campaign which would bring the known world under Macedonian domination. In the aftermath of Philip's death, both northern border tribes and several Greek city-states attempted to rebel against Macedonian overlordship. Alexander's first campaigns were directed against the traditional tribal enemies to the north and northwest of Macedonia. In successive battles during the spring of 335 B.C., tribe after tribe was totally defeated by the overwhelming combination of the Macedonian infantry *phalanx*, a solid wedge of highly disciplined men bristling with pikes some five meters in length, and her cavalry. Macedonian military might, Philip's legacy to Alexander, so cowed the enemies to the north that no further threat from these tribes was recorded during the remainder of Alexander's reign.

Alexander had not finished his northern campaign when news arrived that the Greek city-state of Thebes had expelled the Macedonian garrison from its territory. Once again, Alexander moved swiftly and ruthlessly to forestall a general rebellion among the Greek cities. He marched his army of 30,000 infantry and 3,000 cavalry the 250 miles south to the end of the Greek peninsula, far faster than anyone believed was possible. Alexander's speedy arrival forestalled the gathering together of Theban allies and left the city's defenders alone and greatly outnumbered. Thebes, however, was still a significant military power and the city was well fortified. Few Greek observers expected it to be an easy campaign for the Macedonians. Alexander waited but two days. Attacking on the third day, he led his Macedonians and some Greek allies in a brutal attack which, despite a desperate resistance by the Thebans, resulted in the capture and virtual massacre of 6,000 of the city's defenders. Rather than allowing the traditional slaughter of the inhabitants, Alexander showed some mercy, enslaving the 30,000 Thebans and razing the city to the ground. Historian Nicholas Hammond understates the impact: "The capture in a few hours and the elimination of the strongest military state in Greece had an immediate effect on the other Greek dissidents." The Greek city-states subsequently aligned themselves with the Macedonian Empire or remained neutral for the foreseeable future.

The Campaign Against the Persians

Having consolidated his hold on Greece and the Balkan peninsula by the fall of 335 B.C., effectively securing his base, Alexander immediately finalized plans for a spring offensive against the traditional Greek enemy, the Persian Empire, part of an ongoing war begun by his father. Philip's armies were already secured on the shores of Asia Minor. In the spring of 334 B.C., Alexander joined the vanguard, bringing the Macedonian Greek forces to a total strength of some 40,000 infantry and 5,000 cavalry. He quickly sought battle with the local Persian commander, a Greek mercenary named Memnon, who led a force largely composed of Greek mercenaries and Persian cavalry. The Persian force was positioned on the banks of the Granicus River and appeared poised to defeat the

Macedonian army as it crossed. Alexander, however, seized the initiative and recklessly charged the Persians at the strongest point in their line, scattering the cavalry and slaughtering the exposed mercenary infantry. "The battle," notes Keegan, "was to set the stereotype of Alexandrian generalship: precipitate, apparently reckless and highly personal." Alexander led the cavalry charges himself, seemingly oblivious to danger; his horse was killed under him and a sword swipe cleaved the crest of his helmet. Confident in the superiority of his troops and his own will, he used a combination of brute force, intuitive timing, and a superior strategic and tactical sense to inflict defeat after defeat. His army was strengthened and imbued with extreme confidence by Alexander's courageous example. At the age of 22, Alexander enjoyed the full confidence and loyalty of his army and was poised to leave his historical mark.

After consolidating his grip on western Asia Minor, Alexander proceeded to secure the conquest of the rest of the area which forms modern Turkey. He was faced with two threats: hill tribes in the interior and Persian-controlled cities on the coast. Splitting his forces, Alexander dealt with them simultaneously and was successful on both fronts. In April 333 B.C., his army was reunited and ready to undertake further conquests. His next aim was to secure the northern and eastern Mediterranean coasts, a region known as Cilicia (southern gateway to Syria and Egypt; western gateway into the center of the Persian Empire, modern-day Iran). Mountain passes, however, were the key to passage through Cilicia and Alexander was forced to deal with these in turn. While he was so engaged, the Persian emperor Darius III began a slow march with 140,000 men, toward the Macedonian forces, determined to bring the young King to battle. Darius crossed into Cilicia uncontested and found himself, due to a precipitous move south by Alexander's forces, between the Macedonian army and its supply line. The situation favored Darius; he could choose the time and place of the battle, and the Macedonians had no choice but to seek battle or starve.

Alexander, however, who was as eager as Darius to begin the contest, did the unexpected. He marched straight for the Persian encampment on the Pinarus River and arrived within a day and a half. Once again, the Persians hoped that their positioning would slow the Macedonian charge; Alexander took it as a sign of their lack of will to fight. Taking advantage of the surprise his early arrival had caused, Alexander placed his forces so that his strengths faced the Persian's weakest points. Darius was unable to bring his superior

numbers to bear and the issue was thus decided between relatively equal forces. Having negated the Persian's main advantage, Alexander's army engaged the Persians, coordinating infantry and cavalry attacks along the line. The victory in what became known as the Battle of Issus was gained, however, by the charge of the Macedonian infantry phalanx, led by Alexander, against the Persian center. The Persians broke before the brute force and will of this array although the near death of Alexander almost marred the victory. His life was saved only by the timely intervention of his bodyguard, who hewed off the sword arm of an uncomfortably close, scimitar-wielding Persian. Fearing for his own life, Darius fled the field, a move which precipitated the final collapse and subsequent slaughter of his army. The Emperor's entourage of wives, daughters, and concubines was captured, and the western half of the Persian Empire lay open before Alexander.

Alexander's genius as a statesman and leader was revealed in the aftermath of this great victory. He maintained discipline among his troops, sparing the countryside, but generously rewarded his loyal followers with wreaths and honors. He also recognized the autonomy of local authorities, exacting taxes and tributes but allowing the peoples to retain customs and organizations which were familiar to them. The Macedonian imperial burden was thus a light one and often beneficial compared to the heavy Persian yoke. Because of his Greek cultural heritage and his lenient treatment of the conquered, Alexander was able to win the respect and cooperation of the local inhabitants and left a lasting impression of his rule; this leniency also secured his flanks and rear for further advances.

Alexander determined to conquer the remainder of the Persian Empire, rejecting Darius's offer to recognize the subjugation of the western Empire in exchange for peace. Indeed, Alexander spent the years 332 and 331 B.C. destroying Persian naval power in the Mediterranean through a succession of sieges and battles aimed at her naval bases in Asia Minor, culminating in the destruction of Tyre, the strongest port in the area, after a bloody seven-month seige. He followed these victories with the conquest of Egypt in 331 B.C., founding Alexandria, "greatest of his 'Alexander' cities." The climax of his campaign was now upon him. Darius, secure in the eastern Empire, had raised another great host, said to have comprised 200,000 infantry and 40,000 of the finest cavalry found in his Empire; other estimates put the army at one million. Against this Persian force stood Alexander's 50,000 infantry and cavalry. Nevertheless, on hearing of the movement of the Persians,

Alexander eagerly readied his army for what he believed would be the decisive battle.

The subsequent Battle of Gaugamela in October 331 B.C. destroyed the Persian army—it has been estimated that 40,000 Persians died—and shattered Darius's kingship. He fled the field for the last time and ten months later was dead at the hands of his own countrymen. In the wake of the collapse of the centuries-old Persian Empire, Alexander proclaimed himself "Lord of Asia." He now put the loyalty of his Macedonian and Greek followers to the test. Having defeated the traditional Persian enemy, would they follow him to further conquests in the East and into India? Alexander's oratory and reputation won over the men who had been campaigning far from home for some three-and-a-half years. From Mesopotamia, Alexander's army pressed on into Afghanistan, establishing a new political and administrative order in the far corners of the old Persian Empire. He proved his adeptness and adaptability, pursuing the numerous Afghani tribes and closing on the Hindu-Kush range, the "gateway to India." He plunged into India, sending the oldest of his Macedonians home and exacting pledges from the remainder to serve for the rest of the war. Thus prepared, he fought successive battles and mounted sieges against Indian princes and *satraps* ("governors"), always being drawn further east by ambition and curiosity. In 329 B.C., he subdued the Scythians and over the next two years fought his way to the Indus River. He solidified his hold on Sogdiana in modern-day Afghanistan through marriage to the Princess Roxana. His conquests in India peaked in 326 B.C. with the Battle of the Hydaspes River.

Despite successive and continuous victories, Alexander's relations with his followers became increasingly difficult. He deterred real and imagined pretenders to his throne through several executions of prominent followers who had fallen out of favor. His army had slowly wearied of the endless campaigning and in 326 B.C. refused to continue; only Alexander's hold on their loyalty prevented a full-scale rebellion, but he was forced to march his army home. Unsated, however, Alexander turned his attention to the conquest of the Arabian peninsula and further consolidation of his Empire. In 324 B.C., while planning his campaigns from his base in Babylon, the former capital of the Persian Empire, the 33-year-old Alexander succumbed to fever and drink. His body was eventually buried in a gold coffin in Alexandria. His Empire was divided between his former generals, but without his will to hold it together, quickly disintegrated. His legacy, and legend, lived on.

SOURCES:

Bosworth, A. B. *Alexander the Great and the Hellenistic World.* New York, 1966.

———. *Conquest and Empire: The Reign of Alexander the Great.* Cambridge University Press, 1988.

Griffith, G. T., ed. *Alexander the Great: The Main Problems.* Cambridge University Press, 1966.

Hammond, N. G. L. *Alexander the Great: King, Commander and Statesman.* Noyes Press, 1980.

Keegan, John. "Alexander the Great and Heroic Leadership," in *The Mask of Command.* London: Jonathan Cape, 1987.

FURTHER READING:

Jouguet, Pierre. *Alexander the Great and the Hellenistic World: Macedonian Imperialism and the Hellenization of the East.* [1928] Ares Publishers, 1978.

Alexander I

(1777–1825)

Russian Tsar who defeated Napoleon and attempted to bring constitutional reforms to his country.

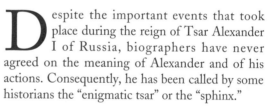

"You are right in holding that the evil comes both from the higher officials and from the poor selections of lower officials. But where can you get them? I am unable to choose fifty-two governors, and there are needed thousands."

TSAR ALEXANDER

Despite the important events that took place during the reign of Tsar Alexander I of Russia, biographers have never agreed on the meaning of Alexander and of his actions. Consequently, he has been called by some historians the "enigmatic tsar" or the "sphinx."

The difficult nature of Alexander's personality can perhaps be traced to the tense circumstances surrounding his childhood. During the long reign of his grandmother, the Empress **Catherine II, the Great** (1762–96), the question arose about who would succeed her as ruler of Russia. Relations between the Empress and her son Paul, the heir apparent, were stormy and mutually distrusting. Rumors linked Catherine with the suspicious deaths of Paul's father Tsar Peter III in 1762 and another claimant to the throne, Ivan VI, in 1764. To make matters worse, rumors circulated that Catherine wanted to disinherit Paul and name Paul's son Alexander as heir apparent.

As a young boy, Alexander walked the line between his dueling relatives. In front of Catherine, he would sincerely support his grandmother's ideas about governing Russia according to the popular 18th-century principles of Enlightenment.

Contributed by David Katz, A.M., Harvard University, Cambridge, Massachusetts

Born on December 12, 1777 (dates are according to the Julian calendar, in use in Imperial Russia, which was 12 days behind the Gregorian calendar); died on November 19, 1825; son of Tsar Paul I and Maria Feodorovna (née Sophia of Württemberg); grandson of Catherine the Great; married: Princess Luisa of Baden, 1793. Predecessor: Paul I. Successor: Nicholas I.

25

Originating from France, the Enlightenment spoke of the importance of ruling in a lawful and orderly fashion. These ideas would eventually inspire the American Revolution in 1776 and the French Revolution in 1789. In front of Paul, Alexander would patiently listen to his father's open expressions of hatred against Catherine's rule. "This self-mastery and this faculty of concealing his feelings were the fundamental traits of Alexander's character throughout his life," noted Alexander's physician in 1823. This skill of diplomacy was later used when he negotiated one-on-one with the great leaders of Europe: Napoleon of France and Metternich of Austria. Though he tried to remain neutral in the intrigues between his grandmother and father, Alexander could not escape the politics of the Russian court.

Since Catherine wanted to cultivate Alexander as a potential heir, she personally took charge of his education. To this end, she kept the boy away from his parents and imported a French-speaking tutor from Switzerland by the name of La Harpe. Teacher and student soon formed a close friendship that would last for many years. Alexander grew to enjoy an Enlightenment education that stressed the importance of equal rights; so much so that he was rumored to be disappointed that his Empress-grandmother did not do more to provide for the general liberty of all subjects by establishing a constitution or bill of rights for Russia. Unfortunately, Alexander's education did not include any experience in governing the Empire; Catherine never commissioned him to occupy any official position within the Russian government.

Such a free-spirited upbringing contrasted sharply with life at Gatchina, a suburb of St. Petersburg (then the capital of Russia), where Alexander's father kept his main residence. Partially out of spite for his mother's predilections and fashions, Grand Duke Paul distrusted anything French, preferring instead to run a very harsh household modeled on the strict military discipline of the powerful neighboring German state of Prussia. In the palace of the Grand Duke, Alexander had to stand witness when the slightest mistake by a servant or soldier would result in punishment by lashing. Nonetheless, Alexander absorbed this trait from his father and would later earn the nickname "the parading tsar," because of his love for military display.

When Alexander reached 16, Catherine arranged his marriage to the German Princess Luisa of Baden, who then took the Russian name Elizaveta or Elizabeth. One of his longtime friends Prince Czartoryski observed that from this point on, Alexander never had the time to finish a book because the Russian court was a "fatiguing, yet idle" way of life in which one was "constantly busy in doing nothing."

But Catherine the Great died unexpectedly in 1796, before she could finalize any changes in the status of the heir apparent, and Paul began his short and turbulent rule (1796–1801) as tsar. One of his first acts was to change the law of succession (1797). Nobles and courtiers could no longer conspire about whom to make the next tsar because the first-born male would automatically become heir apparent. Thus, Alexander would inherit a position that he longed to forsake. He would have preferred to retire to one of the royal estates with his new wife or travel abroad to live in the German Rhine valley (his wife's homeland) where he could continue his studies as an amateur naturalist. Alexander once wrote that a man of "ordinary capabilities" like himself would have quite a difficult time being tsar. But his tyrannical father would never hear of Alexander abdicating his responsibility.

A violent temper and rumors of mental instability won Tsar Paul many enemies. Count Nikita P. Panin, a prominent noble, suggested that Paul be retired from his official duties. When Paul refused to abdicate, he was strangled by a group of officers in the course of an 1801 palace revolution. Although Alexander had been involved in the conspiracy, he thought the conspirators intended only to force his father to abdicate, not to kill him.

Alexander Ascends to the Throne

Upon ascending the throne, Alexander declared that he wanted to rule Russia in the "spirit and wisdom" of his grandmother's philosophy; he envisioned sweeping reforms. In theory, Russia was governed by the tsar, who had supreme or autocratic power over every aspect of government. Several institutions known as the Senate and the Colleges, the members of which were tsar appointed, assisted in governing. Instead, Alexander wanted to give Russia a constitution that would guarantee the rights of every Russian citizen and outline responsibilities of a new government with elected representatives. He even sought the advice of the U.S. president, **Thomas Jefferson,** on how to establish such a constitution. It was reported that the new Tsar walked the streets of the capital unaccompanied and spoke with his subjects as equals. To discuss proposals for reform, Alexander and his close friends formed the Unofficial Committee, whose meetings were often held over coffee in an informal setting at the Winter Palace (the tsar's residence in St. Petersburg). During the two years of its activity, the Unofficial Committee provided the young and inexperienced Alexander with practical knowledge. One of the first issues that the Committee tackled was the reorganization of the government. Alexander wanted his administration to operate in an orderly fashion as opposed to the often chaotic and overlapping Collegiate system. To this end, he established in 1802 eight ministries with clearly defined jurisdictions: War, Navy, Foreign Affairs, Internal Affairs, Commerce, Finance, Education, and Justice.

The final details of how the ministries would absorb the duties of the former Colleges were worked on by one of Alexander's most brilliant advisors, Michael M. Speransky. This ministerial organization was to last in almost unchanged form until the Russian Revolution of 1917. Speransky worked out a system whereby the Senate would preserve its duties as a sort of high court, and Russia would receive a legislature with two houses: the State Council, whose members were appointed by the tsar, and the *Duma* (assembly), whose members were to be elected. An elected *Duma* in Russia, however, was not installed until the revolutionary turmoil of 1905. But Speransky was a better lawmaker than a politician, and he made many enemies in high levels of government who would force his dismissal in 1812.

Alexander and his Unofficial Committee became a forum for two other major reforms during the early part of his reign: educational and economic. To provide trained personnel, he increased the number of schools at all levels. According to the charter of 1804, the Russian Empire would now include—in addition to its three existing universities—three new schools: the Universities of St. Petersburg, Kazan and Kharkov, which have

lasted to the present day. The agricultural economy was also in need of reform. At the turn of the 19th century, about 5% of Russia's 40 million people lived in cities; the rest of the population was primarily engaged in farming. About half of Russia's farmers were peasants who rented small lots from the Russian government and the imperial family; the rest were serfs, a type of indentured servant, farming for a landlord who then sold most of the harvest for personal profit. Serfdom has been compared in severity to the system of plantations and slavery in the United States before the Civil War. Alexander wanted to free all farmers, allow them to own their land, and give them freedom of movement. According to his manifesto of 1803, a landlord was given the right to allow serfs to buy freedom and land for their own development. Nevertheless, in the years before the complete abolishment of serfdom in 1861, this measure freed only about 115,000 serfs or a little less than 1% of the total indentured population.

Since Alexander failed in these initial years to publish a constitution for Russia and to quickly free all serfs, his efforts for reform may come across as insincere. In the opinion of his critics, he was a man who jealously guarded his autocratic privilege and did not truly intend to help Russia with a constitution. They point to his establishing press censorship in 1804 and secret police in 1805 to spy against those who disagreed with his use of power.

Nicholas M. Karamzin, a contemporary of Alexander and the first great historian of modern Russia, attacked Alexander by arguing that the former Collegiate system had been a more satisfactory governing body than the newly formed ministerial government, which he saw as being too bureaucratic. Though the shortcomings of his reign were many, Alexander did take his responsibility as tsar very seriously. Originally, he planned to give Russia a stable and fair political system and only afterwards, abdicate and return to private life; but a variety of circumstances prevented him from fulfilling that dream.

At War with Napoleon

The rapid domination of Europe by France's emperor, **Napoleon,** began to alarm Alexander and his allies—Austria and Prussia. During the battles of Austerlitz (present-day Slavkov in the Czech Republic) in 1805 and Friedland in 1807, Russia suffered tragic losses. Napoleon, however, felt that his armies were too exhausted to pursue the retreating Russian armies. So in 1807, Alexander and Napoleon negotiated the treaty of Tilsit. Using his skills as a diplomat, Alexander convinced Napoleon that Russia was the faithful and loyal ally of France: "The union of France with Russia has been constantly the object of my wishes…." Overwhelmed and flattered, Napoleon thought Alexander's friendship to be genuine. The Tsar then persuaded the French Emperor to make no demands on Russia other than participation in Napoleon's Continental System of trade, which forbade any commerce with Napoleon's longtime rival, England. According to the peace treaty, France and her allies would withdraw from Russia, while Russia would gain the Polish city of Bia-lystok. At home, many considered Alexander's new alliance with Napoleon a disaster. Russia's economy was anchored on strong commercial ties with England, which consumed large volumes of Russian products such as wheat, wool, and iron. But Alexander correctly concluded that he had "gained time." Russia would need as much time as possible to regroup its armies for the future conflict with Napoleon's Empire.

Inevitably, Russia had to relax its observance of the stifling Continental System as it slowly resumed trade with England, and relations with France soured. In 1812, when Napoleon invaded Russia, Alexander rushed to rally his people to their country's defense. After Napoleon had captured Moscow, in the heart of Russia, Alexander proclaimed:

> Russia will not surrender the treasures of her laws, her religion, and independence. She is ready to shed the last drop of her blood in their defense.

His skill as an inspiring leader was instrumental in winning the necessary human and financial support from his Russian subjects to destroy Napoleon. Instead of driving Napoleon out of Russia, the Tsar decided to go further: to pursue him back to France, if necessary. The Russians scorched everything in Napoleon's path of advance—even Moscow was burned—to prevent the French from benefiting from anything Russian. Weakened by the winter cold and the continual Russian guerilla warfare, Napoleon's armies eventually retreated from Moscow. In the ensuing chase of the French, Alexander's armies saved not only Russia, but the rest of Europe, from continued Napoleonic aggression. After capturing Paris, Alexander required that Napoleon surrender and abdicate.

Alexander Sponsors Holy Alliance

Alexander's victorious march through Europe had a profound effect on him; he turned to mysticism and religion as guiding principles for restoring peace and order in Russia and Europe. In 1817, he appointed a fellow mystic and president of the Russian Bible Society, Prince Alexander N. Golytsin, as minister of education. Even after the Tsar's death in 1825, rumors would circulate that he had not really died, but had escaped to Siberia under the name Fyodor Kuzmich to live the ascetic life of a monk. In Europe, Alexander was the key to the formation in 1815 of the Holy Alliance, a union of Christian monarchs dedicated to protecting the general peace and the legitimacy of ruling monarchs against revolutionary turmoil. He described this alliance as a sort of United Nations:

> When peace is made, a new treaty should … lay down a sort of new code of international law which, being sanctioned by the greater part of the European States, would, if violated by any one of them, bind the others to turn against the offender and make good the evil he has committed.

Although most European states joined the Holy Alliance, they did not treat it seriously. Instead, the Congress of Vienna and the Quintuple Alliance of Austria, England, France, Prussia, and Russia, became the effective means for restoring order after the collapse of Napoleon's Europe.

In foreign relations, Alexander eagerly promoted constitutional government and respect for the law. When Russia took Finland from Sweden in 1809, Alexander kept Finnish laws almost intact. He also expressed his approval that the new king of France, Louis XVIII, was a constitutional monarch. After the Napoleonic wars ended, Alexander supported the efforts of Poland, now under Russian rule, to establish its own constitution and parliament (*sejm*). Sometimes, however, Alexander found that a straightforward application of his principles of foreign policy was impossible, if not contradictory. When Greece was fighting in the early 1820s for its independence from the Ottoman Empire (Turkey), Alexander, on the one hand, sympathized as a member of the Holy Alliance with his Christian comrades in Greece against their Muslim oppressors, the Ottoman Turks. On the other hand, out of his respect for law and order, Alexander felt that the Greeks were out of line in revolting because the revolutionaries were breaking the laws of the Ottoman Empire.

After the Napoleonic wars, when Alexander again turned his attention to internal Russian affairs, the momentum behind his reforms slowed in comparison to the earlier years. During the last decade of his reign, he entrusted General Alexis A. Arakcheev to act as his primary minister in directing the government. Frustrated with the opposition to his reforms, Alexander preferred to focus on foreign affairs, an area in which he met with his greatest success. Though he had stepped back from governing, he was well aware of what was happening in domestic affairs. Arakcheev's powers were extensive, but he was no dictator; rather, he was an obedient servant whose only work ethic was to satisfy the wishes of his master.

The major domestic program of Alexander's later years concentrated on founding military colonies. Since the Russian treasury could no longer maintain the large armies necessary to preserve Russia's dominance in international relations, Alexander settled soldiers, along with their families, as farmers on homesteads. This early attempt at state socialism might have worked if Alexander had not placed such emphasis on making the military settlements profitable. The organization of these colonies reflected the Tsar's personality: his orientation to frugality and discipline. In light of the strict regimen of training, the soldiers did not have the energy to make the colonies self-sufficient, providing for their own food and uniforms. The burdens placed upon the colonists were so great that this system rapidly declined after the Tsar's death.

Traditionally, historical accounts of Alexander's reign are divided into two parts: liberal (1801–15) and conservative (1816–25). Based on his hesitation to grant an immediate constitution, one group of historians concludes that weakness and timidity allowed the liberal half of Alexander's rule to slide into a more conservative, reactionary period. Another line of criticism asserts that Alexander's efforts at liberal reform were aimed at winning popular support. Yet another evaluation proposes that the issue is not whether Alexander was timid or hollow, but rather that Alexander soon learned that his office as supreme autocrat of Russia was incapable of speedily implementing reforms. Even as late as 1820, Alexander was still asking a friend and advisor to present him with a tentative draft for a Russian constitution.

During this last half of Alexander's reign, many of the officers who had served abroad during the Napoleonic wars brought back with them admiration for liberal constitutional government. To fight off the onslaught of the Napoleonic armies, Russia had to unite in new ways. Tolstoy's novel *War and Peace* is an excellent account of the spirit that brought landlord, military officer, peasant, and serf together on a national scale to fight a common enemy. Through this newfound unity, the liberal ideas of returning soldiers trickled down to other levels of society. But no constitution ever appeared, and the officer corps grew impatient. Since Alexander was not moving fast enough to

enact liberal reforms, many of these soldiers were instrumental in founding secret societies to expedite the process; some advocated overthrowing the present autocratic regime. Alexander knew about the activities of these societies through his secret police, but took no action out of sympathy, perhaps, for their ideas.

Since Alexander's marriage with Elizabeth produced only one daughter, who had died in infancy, by the law of succession his eldest brother Constantine was to inherit the throne. But Constantine abdicated his responsibilities to the next brother in line, Nicholas. Perhaps to avoid intrigue at court, Alexander kept the abdication of Constantine a secret. So when Alexander died suddenly on November 19, 1825, just before his 48th birthday, confusion ensued regarding succession. The secret societies took this opportunity to stage a revolution for a more liberal government. Unlike the palace revolution of 1801, in which the leading strata of society united in their effort to depose the hated regime of Tsar Paul I, the much more popular regime of Alexander I did not inflame widespread discontent. Thus, about a month after Alexander's death, Nicholas was able to find the support to take firm control as the next tsar. **Nicholas I** quickly repressed the rebels, or Decembrists as they were called, after their ill-fated revolution. But the rift in Russian society between the more conservative elements who supported the rule of Alexander and Nicholas and those who were more liberally inclined toward greater reforms continued to grow.

SOURCES:

Czartoryski, Adam. *Memoirs of Prince Adam Czartoryski and His Correspondence with Alexander I.* 2 vols. Edited by A. Gielgud. London: Remmington & Co., 1888.

Eroshkin, Nikolai P. *Istoriia gosudarstvennykh uchrezhdenii dorevoliutsionnoi Rossii.* Moscow, 1983.

Flynn, James T. *The University Reform of Tsar Alexander I, 1802–1835.* Catholic University of America Press, 1988.

Karamzin, Nikolai M. *Karamzin's Memoir on Ancient and Modern Russia.* Translated by R. Pipes. Atheneum, 1986.

Kliuchevskii, Vasilii O. *Sochineniia: kurs russkoi istorii.* Vol. 5. Moscow, 1958.

Kornilov, Alexander. *Modern Russian History.* Vol. 1. Translated by A.S. Kaun. Knopf, 1948.

McConnell, Allen. *Tsar Alexander I: Paternalistic Reformer.* Crowell, 1970.

Raeff, Michael. *Michael Speransky: Statesman of Imperial Russia, 1772–1839.* The Hague, 1957.

Walsh, Warren B., ed. *Readings in Russian History.* Vol. II. Syracuse University Press, 1963.

Wortman, Richard. "Images of Rule and Problems of Gender in the Upbringing of Paul I and Alexander I," in *Imperial Russia, 1700–1917.* Edited by E. Mendelsohn & M. Shatz. Northern Illinois University Press, 1988.

FURTHER READING:

Almedingen, Edith. *Emperor Alexander I.* London, 1964.

Mikhailovich, Nicholas, Grand Duke of Russia, ed. *Scenes of Russian Court Life, Being the Correspondence of Alexander I with his Sister Catherine.* Translated by H. Havelock. Jarrolds Ltd. (n.d.).

Paleologue, Maurice. *The Enigmatic Tsar: The Life of Alexander I.* London, 1938.

Tolstoy, Lev N. *War and Peace.*

Alexander II

(1818–1881)

Emperor of Russia known as the "tsar liberator," who emancipated the serfs in 1861 and instituted the first legal and political reforms in an effort to modernize Russia.

"It is better to abolish serfdom from above than to await the time when it will begin to abolish itself from below."

TSAR ALEXANDER II

Born in the Chudov Monastery in the Moscow *Kremlin* (citadel) on April 29, 1818, Alexander Nikolayevich Romanov was the eldest son of Grand Duke Nicholas Pavlovich, later Tsar **Nicholas I** (1825–55), and Charlotte, daughter of King Frederick III of Prussia and sister of Wilhelm I, the future Kaiser of Germany. Alexander had six siblings: Konstantin, Maria, Olga, Alexandra, Nicholas, and Michael.

When Captain Karl Karlovich Merder, the founder of a Moscow military school, became his tutor, the six-year-old Alexander's formal education began. During his ten-year tenure, Merder stressed martial discipline and values. Eventually, Alexander's mother entrusted his intellectual and moral development to the humanitarian and liberal poet and translator, Vasily Andreyevich Zhukovsky, who introduced Alexander to the classics, history and letters. Merder, Zhukovsky and Tsar Nicholas I all stressed a military demeanor and the Russian tradition of autocracy. But Alexander, a rather indolent boy of ordinary intelligence, obtained from Zhukovsky a romantic sensibility that he retained throughout his life.

Born April 29, 1818, in the Chudov Monastery in the Kremlin of Moscow, Russia; died by assassination in St. Petersburg, Russia, on March 13, 1881; son of Tsar Nicholas I of Russia and Charlotte (daughter of King Frederick William III of Prussia); married: Maria Alexandrovna (née Princess Wilhelmina Marie of Hesse-Darmstadt), April 16, 1841 (died 1880); married: Catherine Dolgruky, July 18, 1880; children: Alexandra, Nicholas, Alexander III, Vladimir, Alexis, Maria, Sergius, and Paul. Predecessor: Nicholas I. Successor: son Alexander III.

Contributed by Phillip E. Koerper, Professor of History, Jacksonville State University, Jacksonville, Alabama

1818	Born in the Chudov Monastery, Kremlin
1837	Toured 30 Russian provinces; first Romanov to visit Western Siberia
1855	Succeeded to throne on the death of his father
1856	Treaty of Paris; forced to accept defeat in the Crimean War
1861	Emancipation Act freed the serfs
1864	Statutes reformed the judiciary and local governments
1866	Karakazov failed in attempt to assassinate the Tsar
1872	Alexander joined the League of the Three Emperors
1877–78	Russo-Turkish War; Congress of Berlin
1880	Empress died at Cannes; Alexander married Catherine Dolgruky in a morganatic marriage
1881	Assassinated by "People's Will" after signing a constitutional proclamation

In 1837 and 1838, Alexander was sent on trips through the 30 provinces of the Russian Empire. As the first emperor to visit Siberia, he became aware of the penal camps and the abject poverty of his own people. But the trips were not all gloomy. While on a grand tour of Europe in 1838—a trip customarily used to provide the final polish to a future sovereign—he met and fell in love with the 14-year-old Princess Wilhelmina in the German principality of Hesse-Darmstadt. Although Nicholas, who hoped to gain a more prestigious dynastic marriage for Alexander, opposed their desire to marry, Alexander refused to bend and his father reluctantly accepted the union. Arriving in Russia in 1840, Wilhelmina was rebaptized into the orthodox Church as Maria Alexandrovna, and married her prince on April 16, 1841. Their alliance produced eight children: Alexandra, Nicholas, Alexander III, Vladimir, Alexis, Maria, Sergius and Paul. The couple remained in love until the latter half of the reign when Alexander took Princess Catherine Dolgruky as his mistress; he married her 40 days after the death of Empress Maria Alexandrovna in 1880.

Shortly after his first marriage, Alexander's dominating and authoritative father began a careful preparation of his son for his eventual succession. Nicholas appointed the young prince to the Council of Ministers, the Finance Committee, and other imperial councils. Alexander was also appointed Chancellor of Helsingfors University in Finland, a member of the Holy Synod, and chairman of a secret committee to study the problems of serfdom. In 1848, he succeeded his uncle as chief of all military schools and colleges and was placed in command of the Guard and Grenadier regiments. During his father's prolonged absences from the capitol, Alexander served as regent and presided over the state council. On several occasions, Nicholas utilized him as a member of diplomatic missions to Europe.

Alexander Succeeds Nicolas

When Nicholas I died of a severe cold on March 2, 1855, and Alexander Nikolayevich became Alexander II, Tsar of all the Russians, his country was still mired in the unfinished Crimean War. He had inherited an empty treasury, an exhausted nation, a formidable alliance against him, and a growing awareness of the immensity of Russia's coming defeat. Thus, when Sevastopol fell to the forces opposing Russia, Alexander quickly entered into negotiations, and the Treaty of Paris was signed on March 30, 1856. But Alexander was unhappy with the terms of the treaty, particularly the demilitarization of the Black Sea which was an embarrassing low point in Russia's international prestige.

Alexander's formal coronation took place on August 26, 1856, beneath the humiliating cloud generated by the Treaty of Paris. The defeat in the war indicated to the Emperor that fundamental social and political change could no longer be avoided. But his course as a reforming sovereign is difficult to explain. Alexander's policies were not due to training or instinct; although he was a gentler, more tolerant and flexible ruler than his father, Alexander's background did not suggest that he would become a reformer. There is, however, ample evidence that he shared Nicholas's political views, particularly his admiration for autocratic government. Because Alexander's policies and reforms were not uniformly progressive, it is difficult to assess his sympathy and involvement in the reforming movements and changes of his reign. The most obvious reasons for his change of mind were the technological and military deficiencies that became apparent during the Crimean War. He had also realized that the only way to prevent peasant uprisings and revolutionary radicalism was a massive reform of domestic affairs, industrial growth, and a coherent, successful foreign policy.

In foreign affairs, Alexander and his chief advisor, General Alexander Gorchakov, tried to achieve a diplomatic improvement with France in 1857 through a personal meeting with **Napoleon**

III. The effort proved to be a failure when France took a favorable position toward an 1863 anti-Russian rebellion in Poland. Following the fall of the Second French Empire in 1870, Alexander drew closer to Germany and Austria, and in 1872, they (Kaiser Wilhelm, **Francis Joseph I** of Austria, and Alexander) formed the League of the Three Emperors. This alliance eventually collapsed at the end of the decade when Alexander, influenced by Pan-Slavic pressures, accepted a Turkish challenge in 1877 which developed into the Russo-Turkish War. After some initial defeats, Russia eventually triumphed but saw her gains scaled back by the Western powers at the Congress of Berlin in 1878. Although Alexander and the Russian public were dissatisfied with the settlement, Alexander continued his alliance with Germany and Austria. But, by the end of his reign, Russia was once again diplomatically isolated from European affairs.

Alexander's reign, notwithstanding his foreign policy shortcomings, was remarkable for its imperial expansion. Following the sale of Alaska to the United States in 1867, Russian commanders, on their own initiative and despite Gorchakov's protests, began to expand along the East and Central-Asian frontiers. Because communications were so poor over the great distances, Alexander and Gorchakov could do little more than accept the acquisitions after the fact. Between 1860 and 1876, Russian officers annexed the central Asian Khanates of Khiva, Bokhara, and Kokand. They acquired land in the Amur-Ussuri region from China by 1860 and founded Vladivostok as the far-eastern capital in the same year. In 1881, the remainder of the land east of the Caspian Sea was added to the Empire. Russia also received Sakhalin Island from the Japanese in 1875 in exchange for the remaining Kurile Islands. The acquisition of these possessions during Alexander's reign helped provide an economic base for Russia's industrial expansion, growth of capitalism, and the necessity of improved communications.

Emancipation Act Frees Serfs

But Alexander realized that domestic affairs needed the lion's share of attention and reform. The most critical internal problem concerned the serfs. Declaring in a reception at Moscow on April 12, 1856, that "it is better to abolish serfdom from above than to await the time when it will begin to abolish itself from below," Alexander had opened discussions for reforming their conditions shortly after the Crimean War had been concluded; in 1856, he appointed a secret committee to prepare recommendations for emancipation while battling the delaying tactics of the nobles and conservative

elements opposing the reform. An editorial commission appointed in 1859 and composed of Grand Duke Constantine, Prince Sergei Lanskoi, Nicholas Milyutin, Vladimir Cherkasky, and Yuri Samarin presented a plan to Alexander's State Council a year later. There were difficult debates over issues of whether serfs should be emancipated with land, the size of land parcels, and compensation for the nobles. Alexander, as he would do in other reform proposals, fought resolutely for his emancipation plan and ultimately used his authority to overrule his opponents. On March 3, 1861, he signed the Emancipation Act which freed about 25 million serfs with immediate legal rights and modest allotments of land that they had worked before 1861. A long and complicated redemption plan to compensate the nobles confused the serfs who believed the nobles were misleading them on the actual terms of the decree. The newly emancipated serfs were often unable to complete the redemption payments, and they were additionally restricted by the new rigid system of village governance. Although emancipation was a progressive step by Alexander, it did not end the desperate poverty of the serfs, and it helped undermine the already weak economic base of the Russian state.

The emancipation of the serfs ended the landlords' rights to dispense justice and created new problems for local administration in all areas of life. Alexander supported a massive overhaul of many archaic Russian administrative institutions. On January 13, 1864, the second great reform, the Zemstvo Law, was issued to establish district and provincial councils (*Zemstvos*) elected under an elaborate system dividing voters into classes which insured peasant representation in the councils. This extended role in local self-government throughout the country improved health care, local industries, roads, communications, agricultural methods, schools, and literacy. On December 2, 1864, Alexander issued a decree to reform the legal and judicial process. Completely overhauling the courts, the reforms introduced a jury system, public debate of cases, and equality of all classes before the law.

These major reforms were rapidly followed by others: more academic freedom for universities, the abolition of corporal punishment, municipal self-government, restructuring of the secondary school system, and elective justices of the peace. Alexander's minister of war introduced universal military service on a democratic basis and abolished the privileges previously held by the nobility.

An Attempted Assassination

But Alexander's reforms failed to produce the rapid social and economic growth that he had hoped they would achieve. After 1866, he gradually abandoned his liberal and reform program, partly as a result of the Polish rebellion of 1863–64. In addition, the profound disappointment of the peasants and radical intellectuals in the reforms led to widespread social unrest and even violence. A struggle developed between his government and the dedicated revolutionary elements that had been organizing even as he passed his reforms. On April 4, 1866, a deranged student, Dmitri V. Karakazov, fired several shots at Alexander in an inept effort to assassinate the Tsar. Frightened and angry over the incident, Alexander moved steadily toward a reactionary response to the radicals. Several treason trials were held, and the police were given broad powers to keep order. These responses undermined Alexander's relationship with the Russian intellectuals, and the trials gave exposure to the radical cause. In the 1870s, the populists—known as *Narodniki*—tried unsuccessfully to influence the peasants through propaganda. The failure of the radicals to reach the masses led to conspiratorial plans. One group, the People's Will Party, placed a death sentence on Alexander and established a two-year campaign to assassinate him.

Numerous attempts were made on Alexander's life. Following a bombing of the imperial palace in February 1880, Alexander created a Supreme Commission under the chairmanship of Count Michael Loris-Melikov to combat terrorism. Loris-Melikov utilized police controls to eliminate the radicals, but at the same time he proposed concessions to the public. Promoted to minister of interior, Loris-Melikov's plan would have created a national commission with elected representatives of the Russian people. He was not creating a legislature but envisioned seating the elected delegates as consultative and advisory members within the Council of State. Known as the "Loris-Melikov Constitution," this plan could have been the beginning of constitutional reform in Russia. On March 13, 1881, Alexander hesitantly signed the proclamation giving his conditional approval to Loris-Melikov's plan. Later that morning, as Alexander rode through the streets of St. Petersburg, members of the People's Will Party hurled a bomb at his carriage. The Tsar was uninjured, but when he left his coach to attend to a wounded guard, a second bomb was thrown that shattered both of his legs. At his request, Alexander was taken on a police sleigh to the Winter Palace to die that same day. On the site of the assassination, the Church of the Spilled Blood was erected in his memory.

The significance of the life and reign of Alexander II was his realization that major change was imperative if Russia was to survive. His reforms, both in what they accomplished and in what they failed to accomplish, carry the stamp of his tolerance, creativity, and character. Despite his relapse into reaction, he produced the most significant reforms in the history of tsarist Russia. Alexander III, his successor, dismissed the Loris-Melikov proposal and enacted measures to reverse the work of his father.

SOURCES:

Almedingen, E. M. *The Emperor Alexander II.* Bodley Head, 1962.

Harcave, Sidney. *Years of the Golden Cockerel: The Last Romanov Tsars, 1814–1917.* Macmillan, 1968.

Mosse, Werner E. *Alexander II and the Modernization of Russia.* English Universities Press, 1958.

Pereira, N. G. O. *Tsar-Liberator: Alexander II of Russia, 1818–1881.* Oriental Research Partners, 1983.

Walkin, Jacob. *The Rise of Democracy in Pre-Revolutionary Russia: Political and Social Institutions Under the Last Three Czars.* Praeger, 1962.

FURTHER READING:

Broido, Vera. *Apostles into Terrorists: Women and the Revolutionary Movement in the Russia of Alexander II.* Viking, 1977.

Footman, David. *The Alexander Conspiracy.* Library Press, 1974.

Graham, Stephen. *A Life of Alexander II: Tsar of Russia.* Yale University Press, 1935.

Seton-Watson, H. *The Decline of Imperial Russia, 1855–1914.* Praeger, 1952.

Alfonso X

(1221–1284)

Thirteenth-century ruler of Castile and León, who is best remembered for his support for learning, literature, and the arts.

"It has been well said of Alfonso X that he would have had more success in any other role than that of a king."

Roger Bigelow Merriman

In Spanish history, the 13th century witnessed the high point of the Reconquista, in which Christian rulers from the north fought to win back territories lost since Muslim invaders first entered the Iberian peninsula in 711. Shortly after the important Christian victory at Las Navas de Tolosa (1212), Ferdinand III (1217–52) came to the throne of Castile, which he united with that of León in 1230. When Christian armies pushed deep into Muslim Andalusia, Ferdinand took the lead, conquering Córdoba (1236), Jaén (1246), and Murcia (1247). By the time Seville fell in 1248, the only independent Moorish kingdom left on the peninsula was Granada, but its emir ("ruler") acknowledged himself a vassal of the Castilian monarch. Ferdinand planned further conquests, including the Berber stronghold in North Africa, but he died in 1252 before he was able to carry them out.

According to tradition, Ferdinand called his son and heir Prince Alfonso to his deathbed. He was leaving him, either in full possession or in vassalage, all the territory which had once been lost to the Moors. "If you ... keep it in the state I bequeath to you," the dying ruler said, "you are a

Contributed by Stephen Webre, Professor of History, Louisiana Tech University, Ruston, Louisiana

Name variations: Known also as Alfonso el Sabio (the Wise, or Learned). Born on November 23, 1221, in Toledo; died on April 24, 1284, in Seville; son of King Ferdinand III of Castile and Beatrice of Swabia; married: Violante of Aragon; children: (sons) Fernando (de la Cerda), Sancho, Pedro, Juan, Jaime, Enrique, and Alonso (el Niño, illegitimate); (daughters) Berenguela, Isabel, Eleanor, Violante, and Beatriz (illegitimate). Predecessor: Ferdinand III. Successor: Sancho IV.

king as good as I; and if you gain more by your own efforts, you are better than I; and if you lose any of it, you are not as good as I." Like his father, the young man who became King Alfonso X of Castile and León, would reign for many years, but he would not be as powerful or successful a ruler as Ferdinand. The new king came to be known as Alfonso el Sabio, which is usually translated Alfonso the Wise, although some historians prefer to call him Alfonso the Learned. The latter is probably more appropriate, because Alfonso owed the title more to his love of learning than to his modest talent for politics and government.

The son of Ferdinand III and Beatrice of Swabia, Alfonso was born in Toledo on November 23, 1221. As was customary for royal children at the time, he spent most of his youth away from court in the company of nurses and tutors. The future Learned King must have had excellent teachers, because he demonstrated early in life a great interest in literature, science, the law, art, and music. However, scholarly and artistic pursuits could not be a full-time occupation for a monarch's son in medieval Castile, a society perpetually on a war footing. Alfonso must also be a soldier; he was trained in the code of chivalry as well as in the arts of war, and he began to travel with his father's armies at an early age. In 1247, Ferdinand placed him in charge of the force which occupied Murcia. The following year, Alfonso joined the king for the final assault on Seville.

After he assumed the throne, Alfonso sought to consolidate his father's victories in the south. In general, his policy was to displace the Muslim inhabitants by introducing large numbers of Christian settlers, but this was not possible everywhere.

The Mudéjar, or Muslim, presence in the population continued to be important, and there were frequent revolts. Several towns, including Jerez, Arcos de la Frontera, Lebrija, and Medina Sidonia, took arms against the king early in his reign, but they surrendered in 1254 when Alfonso agreed that Muslims could retain their property in exchange for accepting Christian garrisons in their communities. Such arrangements did not guarantee internal peace, however. Not all of the Learned King's enemies were Mudéjares, and discontented Christians sometimes allied with Muslims to defy royal authority. In 1255, for example, Alfonso's brother Enrique rose against him with the support of the Muslim ruler of Niebla. Eventually defeated, Enrique fled to Tunis.

In preparation to carry out the invasion of North Africa that Ferdinand was planning before he died, Alfonso sent his fleet to raid the Moroccan coast in September 1260. He also seized Cádiz in 1260 and Niebla in 1262, but when he called upon his vassal Emir Ibn al-Ahmar of Granada to hand over Gibraltar and Tarifa, the emir refused and incited a general rebellion, which broke out all over southern Spain in 1264. Major centers, such as Seville and Córdoba, remained loyal, but a number of towns rose up, including many which had rebelled ten years earlier. When the king invaded Granada itself in 1265, Ibn al-Ahmar quickly sued for terms and renewed his oath of fealty. Even so, the emir remained alert for future opportunities to challenge Alfonso.

In spite of his internal difficulties and his failure to carry out the invasion of Africa, the Learned King adopted an aggressive foreign policy toward his Christian neighbors. Shortly after coming to the throne, Alfonso claimed lordship over Navarre. The Navarrese ruler, King Thibault II (1253–70), eventually became Alfonso's vassal, but the relationship brought Castile no advantage and it was dissolved in 1274, when the throne of Navarre was united with that of France. The Learned King also resurrected an old claim to the Algarve in southern Portugal, but with no greater success. In 1253, the Portuguese sovereign Afonso III (1245–79) agreed to marry Alfonso of Castile's illegitimate daughter Beatriz in return for recognition of his sovereignty in the disputed territory.

Before Alfonso's time Castilian rulers were too preoccupied with the Reconquista to involve themselves in matters outside the Iberian peninsula. Ferdinand III's victories had won for Castile the reputation of a significant military power, however, and its new king had ambitions to match. A great-great-grandson of **Henry II** of England, Alfonso laid claim to Gascony in 1253 when local nobles sought his assistance against their current sovereign, Henry III (1216–72). In spite of reports that the Castilian king contemplated invading England with an army of Christians and Moors, nothing came of this episode. As in the Algarve, Alfonso renounced his alleged rights in return for a marital alliance, giving his daughter Eleanor to the future **Edward I** in 1254.

The King Aims To Be Holy Roman Emperor

As a result of such abortive schemes of territorial expansion, Alfonso X became known at home and abroad for projects which were hastily conceived and set in motion, and which produced no concrete benefits for him or for his subjects. The Learned King's chief personal ambition was to be elected Holy Roman Emperor. Related to the Hohenstaufen family through his mother Beatrice of Swabia, Alfonso declared his candidacy following the death of Conrad IV. He was supported by the antipapal Ghibelline faction in Italy, which meant that Pope Alexander IV and his successors opposed him. In 1257, the seven electors, having been bribed generously, voted narrowly in Alfonso's favor over Richard of Cornwall, brother of Henry III of England. Problems at home made it impossible for the Castilian king to travel to Germany, but his rival Richard did turn up in Aix-la-Chapelle, where he had himself crowned and was recognized by some parties as emperor.

In spite of Alfonso's election and Richard's imposture, the imperial throne remained officially vacant for several years. The king continued to press his claim at great expense to the Castilian treasury, and a contemporary remarked that the amount of money spent on the matter was "almost unbelievable, … it was necessary for [Alfonso] to ask the men of his realm for services and to impose unaccustomed tributes on them." The Learned King's fruitless but expensive pursuit of a crown which promised no benefit to Castile inspired discontent at home. It would help bring on the domestic political problems which plagued Alfonso throughout the later years of his reign.

To meet his expenses, Alfonso X resorted more than once to new taxes and to debasing the currency, both of which were unpopular. At the same time, the monarch provoked opposition by continuing Ferdinand III's effort to substitute a single system of laws for the many traditional *fueros,* or local customs, which prevailed throughout the kingdom. Between 1256 and 1265, Alfonso sponsored the compilation of the *Siete partidas* ("Seven Divisions of Law"), a general law code based on the Roman tradition and designed to be the standard for the application of royal justice in all jurisdictions. The Learned King was also responsible for the so-called *Fuero real,* a model code of private, or municipal, law intended to create a uniform legal regimen for cities and towns, which was granted to a number of municipalities as early as 1255.

Alfonso's legal reforms were resisted, especially by the nobility and the towns which stood to lose valued privileges. The opposition movement, which found its champion in the king's brother Felipe, also attracted the interest of Ibn al-Ahmar of Granada, who seldom missed a chance to create difficulties for his Castilian rival. At the Cortes (parliament) held at Burgos in 1272, Alfonso abandoned his project and reconfirmed all of the traditional *fueros.* Felipe and some of the nobles, refusing at first to be mollified, fled to Granada, but the king granted their additional demands and pardoned their defiance. The monarch reversed himself so completely because he desperately needed funds to revive his quest for the imperial crown. Richard of Cornwall died in 1272, and the Castilian king wanted to travel to Germany to urge his own claim in person. Alfonso's capitulation at Burgos won him a grant of taxes from the towns, and in 1274 he even arranged for the new emir of Granada, Muhammad II (1273–1302), to help finance his candidacy.

In December 1274, after 17 years of delays, Alfonso finally set off on his "journey to the empire," but he was on a fool's errand. The electors had already awarded the disputed throne to **Rudolf I, of Habsburg,** and when the Castilian candidate met with Pope Gregory X in Beaucaire, France, in May 1275, he was told to go home and stop meddling in imperial affairs. Meanwhile, Alfonso's absence from Castile encouraged Muhammad II to break the peace, with the support of Emir Abu Yusuf of Morocco. Beginning in May, North African and Granadan troops began destructive raids into southern Castile, threatening the regions around Jaén and Córdoba.

Alfonso's eldest son and heir Fernando de la Cerda took to the field to repel the invasion, but he became ill and died on July 25, 1275, whereupon a younger son, Sancho, assumed command. In the meantime, the Castilians suffered several military reverses, including a severe defeat at Écija on September 7. When King Alfonso returned to Spain, he took advantage of a growing rivalry between the two emirs to negotiate a withdrawal of all Muslim troops. Abu Yusuf invaded Spain again in 1277, but this time Muhammad sided with the Christians and the Moroccans eventually pulled out.

His kingdom had survived two Moroccan invasions, but Alfonso now found himself caught in a domestic crisis which would last until the end of his life. The death of Fernando de la Cerda created a gap in the succession, and in 1278 the Cortes of Segovia voted to set aside the claims of the deceased's two minor sons, Alfonso and Fernando, in favor of that of Prince Sancho, his younger brother. The decision had broad support from the towns and the nobility and King Alfonso accepted it with some reluctance, but it caused problems in his own household and in Castile's foreign relations. Angered by the disinheritance of her grandsons, Alfonso's queen Violante of Aragon departed for her homeland, accompanied by Fernando's widow Blanche of France and the two boys. Violante's brother, Pedro III of Aragón, supported Sancho and ordered the young princes imprisoned, but Blanche's brother, Philip III (the Bold) of France, took quite a different view. The French monarch pressured Alfonso to correct the injustice done to his nephews.

Alfonso proposed to create a separate vassal kingdom at Jaén for Fernando's son, Alfonso de la Cerda, but both Sancho and the French king rejected the idea. The situation called for a clever and able politician, something the Learned King had seldom been. Hurt deeply by the estrangement of his wife and grandchildren, he was now less likely to handle the crisis wisely. At the Cortes of Seville in 1281, Alfonso recklessly angered the towns by proposing once again to tamper with the currency, and infuriated Prince Sancho by proposing to reopen negotiations with France on the rights of Fernando's children. When Sancho objected, Alfonso threatened to disinherit him, whereupon the Prince is reported to have said, "The time will come when you will wish you had not said that."

With broad support from the towns and the nobility, and from Queen Violante, who must have acted solely from spite, Prince Sancho rose in rebellion and summoned his own Cortes, which met at Valladolid in April 1282, and voted to depose Alfonso and install Sancho in his place. The rebel prince accepted the government of Castile and León, but declined to call himself king as long as his father lived. Alfonso took refuge in Seville, one of the few places which remained loyal and where the only member of his family who joined him was his illegitimate daughter Beatriz, the dowager queen of Portugal. Unable to win assistance from Christian rulers, Alfonso turned to his old enemy, Abu Yusuf of Morocco, who took the Learned King's crown in pawn for a large cash loan. The emir crossed into Spain during the summer and raided and plundered in the region of Córdoba.

As the fighting persisted, Sancho's coalition began to weaken. Some of his supporters, including his own brothers, aspired to carve out kingdoms of their own, while others sought to play the prince against his father to see which would offer the greater reward. Tiring of the struggle, Sancho suggested a reconciliation, but Alfonso became ill and died at Seville on April 4, 1284, without forgiving him. Two wills the late monarch had drawn up to disinherit Sancho in favor of Alfonso de la Cerda were set aside, and the erstwhile rebel assumed the throne in his own right as Sancho IV (r. 1284–95).

A Patron of the Arts, and a Poet

It is fortunate that Alfonso the Learned's historical reputation does not depend upon his performance as a ruler, which was less than brilliant. Rather, he is remembered today for his enthusiastic patronage of learning and the arts. At centers in Seville and Burgos, and especially in Toledo, he gathered the best minds of his time and employed them in the translation of Arabic manuscripts, effecting a massive transfer of knowledge and ideas from the East to the West. What distinguished Alfonso's cultural project from similar ones of his day, such as that of **Frederick II** of Sicily (Holy Roman Emperor, 1215–50), was that he made Castilian, rather than Latin, the principal medium of record and communication.

In favoring the language of the masses over that of the Western cultural elite, Alfonso not only made scientific and literary works accessible to a wider audience, but also laid the foundation for the modern national language that we today call Spanish. The choice of the vernacular, however, was probably not due to a desire to achieve such grand ends, but rather to the weak status of Latin scholarship in Castile and to the fact that the bulk of the translation work was done by persons for whom Latin held no special importance, that is, by Arabs and Jews. The Learned King was remarkably free of cultural prejudice or religious fanaticism in this regard, and it is estimated that almost three-fourths of the work on scientific manuscripts was done by Jewish translators. Later rulers would be less tolerant.

Much of the scientific production of Alfonso's court was in the fields of astronomy, which held a particular fascination for the Learned King. One of his greatest projects was the so-called *Tablas alfonsinas* ("Alfonsine Tables"), a chart of planetary and stellar movements calculated on the meridian of Toledo, which remained in wide use in Europe for several centuries and which largely accounted for Alfonso's contemporary reputation as a man of great erudition. The *Tablas* were based not only on recorded Arab data, but on new observations carried out on Alfonso's orders. The king participated personally in measurements made at Toledo in 1260. The court scholars also produced the *Libros del saber de astronomía* ("Books of Astronomical Knowledge"), completed about 1276, a collection of 15 translated Arabic treatises which, among other things, proposed revisions of the Ptolemaic system. The line between science and magic was a thin one in the Middle Ages and the Learned King also patronized work in astrology. There survives a work known as the *Lapidario* (1276), which describes the occult powers of precious stones in relation to the signs of the zodiac.

In addition to the work of compiling and transmitting Oriental knowledge, Alfonso also promoted the study and codification of law, a field in which he drew far more heavily upon Spain's Roman and Germanic heritage than upon Arabic traditions. As noted above, one of the Learned King's political goals was the imposition of a single legal system throughout his realm. His *Siete partidas,* although not in force during his lifetime, was not only a systematic code of law but also a syllabus for the serious study of jurisprudence. It has had a powerful influence on the legal systems of all Spanish-speaking lands and of such widely scattered jurisdictions as the Philippines and the states of the American Southwest.

The output of the Alfonsine court included also original works, composed in the Christian tradition. In the field of historiography, Alfonso sponsored two major projects, the *Crónica general de España* ("General Chronicle of Spain"), an account of Spanish history from the earliest days to the death of Ferdinand III and the first significant historical work to be written in the Castilian language, and the *Grande e general estoria* ("Great and General History"), never completed, which the monarch intended as a history of the world to complement the *Crónica general.* The *Estoria* drew heavily on the Holy Bible as a source and involved the translation of extensive portions of scripture into the vernacular at a time when such translations were prohibited in other Catholic lands.

There is evidence that the king played an important role not only in the conceptualization of the historical works produced under his patronage, but also in their composition. As a literary figure in his own right, however, Alfonso owes his greatest fame to his poetry, which he wrote not in Castilian, but in Galician, a dialect of Portuguese much favored by the troubadours of his day. The *Cántigas de Santa María* is a collection of more than 400 hymns of praise to the Virgin Mary, most of which are thought to be by the monarch's own hand. The Learned King also wrote profane verse, including love poems and satirical pieces. A man of broad interests who apparently believed in the need to have a good time, even in periods of crisis, Alfonso commissioned near the end of his life the *Libro de ajedrez, dados y tablas* ("Book of Chess, Dice, and Backgammon," 1283), based on an Arabic text and considered today an important source on leisure activities in the Middle Ages.

While emphasizing the value and long-term significance of Alfonso the Learned's cultural and scientific contributions, it is important to maintain them in historical perspective. Many of his projects, among them the legal reforms, merely continued initiatives begun in the time of his father Ferdinand III, who was the first Castilian monarch to issue official documents in the vernacular. Also (and this will sound familiar to modern scholars), there was a significant gap between the material resources devoted to the preservation and dissemination of knowledge and those dedicated to other royal priorities. There is an accounting which indicates that, while the *Tablas alfonsinas* cost 400,000 escudos to prepare, the Learned King spent 25 times that amount on his pursuit of the title of Holy Roman Emperor.

SOURCES:

Keller, John Esten. *Alfonso X, El Sabio.* Twayne, 1967.

Marquez-Villanueva, Francisco and Carlos Alberto Vega, eds. *Alfonso X of Castile: The Learned King (1221–1284).* Department of Romance Languages and Literatures of Harvard University, 1990.

Merriman, Roger Bigelow. *The Rise of the Spanish Empire in the Old World, and in the New.* Vol. 1. *The Middle Ages.* Macmillan, 1918.

O'Callaghan, Joseph F. *A History of Medieval Spain.* Cornell University Press, 1975.

Proctor, Evelyn S. *Alfonso X of Castile, Patron of Literature, and Learning.* Clarendon, 1951.

FURTHER READING:

Ballesteros y Baretta, Antonio. *Alfonso el Sabio.* Salvat, 1963.

Hillgarth, J. N. *The Spanish Kingdoms, 1250–1516.* 2 vols. Clarendon, 1976.

Alfred the Great

(848–c. 900)

West Saxon king and first king of England, who conquered the Danish Vikings and in the process was able
to unite, for the first time, all the Anglo-Saxon people
under one ruler.

*Name variations: originally the
Teutonic (Germanic) Æ was
used, Aelfred; this had the value
of a short a sound before the 11th
century, but was later dropped
from common usage. Born at
Wantage in Wessex, England, in
848; died c. 900; fifth son of
Ethelwulf (a West Saxon king):
married: Elswitha, 868;
children: two sons, three
daughters. Predecessors: Egbert,
Ethelwulf. Successor: Edward.*

When the Angles, the Jutes, and the Saxons stormed into what is now the
British Isles between A.D. 400 and 450,
no one could have predicted that these fierce
tribesmen would first conquer and then quickly
integrate into the society of the local Britons to
create a highly cultured civilization which would
last until the Norman Conquest of 1066. Much of
the success of that civilization has been attributed,
in fact and in tradition, to the wisdom and talent of
Alfred, the only king in English history with the
title "The Great" associated with his name.

Young Alfred grew up in an England
divided among small, independent states. The
areas known as Northumbria, Mercia, and East
Anglica were under the control of the Angles. The
Jutes ruled Kent. The Saxons, Alfred's people,
ruled Essex, Sussex, and the state which was destined to control the entire island, Wessex. Only
the Picts, who came from Ireland and lived in the
north, and the Britons, who were the original
inhabitants of the island and lived in the southwest, were free from Anglo-Saxon control.

Alfred was the grandson of Egbert, a great
king of Wessex who had come out of exile in

*"Great as a warrior, he was yet greater as a
statesman, greater still as a saint, greatest of all
as a man of letters."*

EDWARD CONYBEARE

*Contributed by Alison F. Dacey, M.A. in history, Lakehead University,
Thunder Bay, Ontario, Canada*

France around 800 to take back his territory from the king of Mercia. There were constant battles among these Germanic tribes for land and power, although an uneasy peace was sometimes achieved when the kings of each state were equally strong.

Even though these small kingdoms often opposed each other politically, they were of one religious faith. In 590, Pope **Gregory I** had initiated a gentle conversion of England which was so successful that all men considered themselves members of a spiritual kingdom which, for the most part, took precedence over any local or racial distinctions among people. Each king owed his allegiance to the pope, and therefore it is not surprising, despite the horrors of the Danish invasions, that Alfred, then a boy of four, was sent to Rome to seek the pope's blessing on behalf of his father.

There has been much speculation as to the effect the visit to the pope had on young Alfred. Pope Leo IV received the boy as warmly as he had welcomed other sons of European kings and emperors. He also invested the boy with the insignia of a Roman consul and that the pomp and splendor of the ceremony would remain with Alfred all his life. It is thought that Alfred imitated this ceremony in Rome many years later when he presented his own grandson Athelstan, then aged four, with a red cloak and a shining sword. It is interesting that the honor bestowed on young Alfred had been mistaken for a coronation ceremony by 12th century historians, because, it is thought, they wanted to increase the power of the pope by declaring that popes traditionally held the power to crown kings. Historians certainly believe that Alfred was influenced intellectually and emotionally by the beauty of the architecture, art, and music of Rome. After returning from Italy as a boy of five or six, Alfred was so aware of the beauty in the world around him that he was induced to memorize a magnificent book. The Welsh monk Asser relates the story in his *Life of King Alfred:*

> Now it chanced a certain day that his Mother showed to him and to his brothers a book of Saxon poetry, which she held in her hand, and said, "I will give this book to that one among you who shall the most quickly learn it." … [Alfred] took the book from her hand and went to his master, and read it: and when he had read it he brought it back to his Mother and repeated it to her.

From his earliest years, Alfred loved the lyrical poetry of his people and the literature written in his own tongue. With a lifelong love of learning, he was determined to encourage others to love it as well.

CHRONOLOGY

848	Alfred born at Wantage
851	Danes wintered in England; sacked Canterbury and London; battle of Aclea; Ethelwulf defeated Danes
853	Alfred visited Rome; kings of Kent and Surrey killed by Danes
858	Ethelwulf died; son Ethelbald made king
860	Ethelbald died; brother Ethelbert made king
864	Men of Kent attempted to buy safety from Danes; Kent ravaged
866	Ethelbert died; brother Ethelred made king; Danes invaded East Anglia
869–70	Second Danish invasions of Northumbria and East Anglia
871	Battle of Ashdown; Danes occupied London
872	Alfred proclaimed king of all Anglo-Saxons
872–80	Danes invaded Wessex; Alfred forced into hiding; Danes pushed into East Anglia
880–82	Alfred created navy; defeated Danes at sea
886	Seige of Paris by Vikings; Alfred restored London
896	End of the Danish invasions
900	Alfred died; son Edward made king

However insulated Alfred was as a boy in his father's court, the Danish raids took their toll on his family. His father had fought many battles against the Norsemen, and because of his efforts, and perhaps a bit of luck, Wessex remained free from domination. The raids began in 787 and the people of England were becoming morbidly accustomed to the seasonal terror. Henry of Huntington describes the demoralizing effect these assaults had on the Anglo-Saxons in Edward Conybeare's *Alfred in the Chroniclers:*

> When the English Kings were hasting to meet them in the East … a breathless scout would run in saying, "Sir King, whither marchest thou. The heathen have landed in the South, a countless fleet…. " Yea, and that very day another would come running: "Sir King … A fearsome host has come to shore in the West. If ye face them not speedily they will hold that ye flee, and will be on your rear with fire and sword." Again on the morrow would dash up yet another, saying, " … In the North have the Danes made a raid…. Even now are they sweeping off your goods, tossing your

babes on their spear points, dishonouring your wives, and haling them to captivity."

It is not surprising that many of the Anglo-Saxon kings gave up hope of ever defending themselves against the Danes and fled with their families to continental Europe. And there must have been great despair among the Anglo-Saxon people when it was noted in 851 "this year did the heathen folk, for the first time, bide over winter."

The Battle of Ashdown

Many of Alfred's brothers, upon claiming their right to the throne, fought and died defending Wessex from Danish invasion. On the slopes of Ashdown in 871, the most famous battle was fought which revealed, in a curious way, the striking characteristics of the last two royal brothers. The warrior qualities of the 16-year-old Alfred contrasted with and yet perfectly complemented the piousness of his brother, King Ethelred. The following story is related with few variations in chronicles, confirming the essence, if not the facts. Early in the morning, the two brothers were attending Mass when a soldier came running in crying that the Danes had gathered their forces on the hill at Ashdown and were awaiting first light to attack. Alfred rose up from his prayers to organize his army. Ethelred, however, refused to put duty to men ahead of duty to God; he remained at Mass. Alfred rushed out to the field with his army and stood facing the Danes. As both sides waited, he was keenly aware of the Danish advantage: his forces were at the bottom of a long slope; his army would be fighting uphill. Though he was loath to begin the battle without his brother the king, the Danish warriors were shouting taunts and jeers. Alfred could not risk losing the advantage of the first strike. The battle was fierce and bloody. Then a roar went up from Alfred's army as King Ethelred plunged into the battle, sword flying among the enemy. The Danes retreated and the Saxons gave chase far from the field and into the night. It was a Danish ruse to pretend retreat then turn in strength on the opposing forces, but in this battle that was not the case. Dozens of men on both sides were slain, but Alfred's army was triumphant. During the next 14 days, many battles were fought; in one of these, King Ethelred was slain.

A.D. 871 was known as the year of the battles. Alfred—now crowned king by the Anglo-Saxon governing body, the Witan—had been successful in repelling the attacks. There came a time when the Danes were too strong, however; they arrived in terrific numbers and landed in force throughout the island. The Anglo-Saxons could no longer fight effectively against them. They overran even the county of Wessex, and by 878 Alfred was forced into hiding at Athelney with a few loyal supporters.

Athelney was a natural place for a fortress. There was a large hill surrounded by marshland in dry seasons, and when the water was high, as Alfred found it, a kind of wilderness moat was formed. From this lonely place, Alfred built up his army, raided the Danish settlements for equipment, and visited the Anglo-Saxon villagers for food. Tradition says that Alfred, disguised, came into a poor cowherd's hut. The wife fed him and gave him shelter, asking only that he keep watch over her loaves baking on the open hearth. Lost in thought, Alfred carelessly let the loaves burn. The wife, incensed, sternly chastised him on his thoughtlessness and boxed his ears. Apparently, the next day Alfred came to the woman in full royal regalia and accompanied by his men to apologize for his misdeed. Many ballads have been written about this episode, and people still make "King Alfred's cakes"—paper logs soaked in chemicals which burn colorfully in fire.

Alfred's presence gave hope to the people; by 880, he was driving the Danes out of Wessex and winning back his kingdom. Sensitive to the predicament of his soldier-farmers, he invented the first militia. By dividing each community into two sections and rotating the periods of service, he was able to maintain an army in times of need, without endangering the crops or the families left on the farms. Alfred is also credited with forming the first navy, because he realized that the Danes had to be fought on the sea as well if his people were to succeed in defending themselves. It was a common practice then to bribe the enemy to prevent attacks, although one could never be sure whether the bribe would be accepted or for how long such a peace would last. It is thought that Alfred bought time during this period in order to build up his army and his navy.

Alfred Wins Peace with Danes

After much fighting and loss of life, Alfred managed to sue for peace with King Gutrum, one of the most ruthless Danish warriors. This settlement attested to Alfred's popularity, because Gutrum's reputation as recorded in Conybeare's *Alfred in the Chroniclers* was savage, and few people believed that any peace was truly possible.

On them therefore came a brute beast in man's shape, King Gutrum, to wit, brutal and ferocious toward each and all, who with sword and axe wrought his bestial will. Nay, he spared not even such as threw themselves at his feet…. And piteous was the slaughter that might be seen. There lay they in each road and street and crossway old men with hoar and reverend locks butchered at their own doors; young men headless, handless, footless; matrons foully dishonoured in the open street and maidens with them; children stricken through with spears; all exposed to every eye and trodden under every foot.

Despite opposition, Alfred supported Gutrum's decision to become a Christian; he even acted as Gutrum's godfather and gave him a new name, Athelstan. Alfred won a peace which in effect divided the country into two kingdoms—that of the Anglo-Saxons and that of the Danes. Alfred and Gutrum settled on a system of laws. The Danes were to abide by their own customs in their territory which became known as the Danelaw, and the areas controlled by the Anglo-Saxons were under Alfred's law. Alfred was dubbed "The Truth-Teller," as he assembled sensible laws and rules of behavior in order to establish a codified system for all the English. Historian Charles Plummer notes that even though the laws were a compilation from many sources, our understanding of them is limited because only "a very small part of Anglo-Saxon life and institution is to be found in the laws, which imply a whole body of unwritten custom." Although these customs have been lost to us, Alfred caused a substantial body of literature to be written during these times, as well as translations made of earlier writings, and through these writings we can often glean what daily life must have been like for ninth-century people. For example, Alfred is acclaimed for having invented the civil structure of England, including the divisions of shires, hundreds, and tithings. He also created the first judicial system which involved a network of traveling judges who carried out the law when it was not possible for citizens to travel to Alfred's court.

Fosters Religious Scholarship Education

Although Alfred's early victories seemed to suggest that he was a practical rather than a philosophical man, it is clear from a number of sources that he was also committed to religious scholarship and education. We gain a fuller appreciation of the man through his translations of Latin works. Here Asser describes how the king first became interested in translation:

We were one day sitting together in the royal chamber and were holding converse upon diverse topics, as our wont was, it chanced that I repeated to him a quotation from a certain book. And when he had listened attentively to this with all his ears and had carefully pondered it in the deep of his mind, suddenly he showed a little book which he carried constantly in the fold of his cloak. In it were written the Daily Course, and certain psalms and some prayers which he had read in his youth, and he commanded that I should write that quotation in the same little book.

Asser tells us that he began a new book for the king as there was no space to write in the old one; he also encouraged the king to add other quotations. This new book, the beginning of the king's education, became Alfred's *Enchiridion* or handbook, growing larger and larger as Alfred collected extracts from historical writings, or from the writings of the church fathers, or some Anglo-Saxon poetry.

Alfred went on to translate into Anglo-Saxon the *Dialogues of Gregory the Great, the Bibliotheca* (a collection of Latin authors), *Orosius Universal History, Gregory's Pastoral Care, Æsops Fables, and Bede's Ecclesiastical History of the English Nation.* In his prefaces to the various works and comments within the text we come to understand Alfred the scholar. For example, in translating the Latin Bible, the *Vulgate,* Alfred adds his own admonition to the Golden Rule ("Do unto others as you would have them do unto you"): "By this one law any one may know how he ought to judge another; he needs no other law book." And again, in this translation of Boethius's *Consolation of Philosophy,* when Boethius says, "Thou knowest that ambition never was my mistress, though I did desire materials for carrying out my task," Alfred adds that his task was to

virtuously and fittingly administer the authority committed to me. Now no man … can … administer government, unless he have fit tools and the raw materials to work upon…. And a king's raw material and instrument of rule are a well-peopled land, and he must have men of prayer, men of war, and men of work…. Without these tools he cannot perform any of the tasks entrusted to him.

Alfred not only studied diligently, but he began the first court schools in England. His own children, girls as well as boys, attended, along with the children of the local nobility, and the cost was borne by Alfred. He intended that all "freeborn youth" should have the opportunity to learn to read and write English, and that those who had the talent to go further ought to be taught Latin as well.

Because the Viking invasions destroyed many monasteries, their manuscripts were lost and their scholars killed, and it was difficult to find academics who could teach. Alfred encouraged men from all over the known world to come to his court. He also attempted to establish monasteries again as centers for prayer and learning. Alfred, however, was less successful in this than in any of his endeavors. Though he was generous financially, there were too few men left, after the years of aggression, and those who were left were too rich to find monastic life attractive. Alfred gained a measure of peace in his later years. By 896, with the Danish invasions over, he was able to devote more time to his writings. It is not known for certain how he died, but only that death came on October 26, probably in the year 900, when Alfred was 52 years old. His great legacy to the English people can be illustrated through the body of recorded historical evidence as well as through the traditions which surround his life and character. His goal was to "live worthily as long as I lived; and after my life to leave to them that should come after my memory in good works." It is clear that he accomplished this in a grand manner.

SOURCES:

Conybeare, Edward. *Alfred in the Chronicles.* W. Heffer and Sons, 1914.
Jane, L. C. *Asser's Life of King Alfred.* Chatto & Windus, 1908. Plummer, Charles. *The Life and Times of Alfred the Great.* Haskell House, 1902.
Stevenson, William Henry. *Asser's Life of King Alfred.* Clarendon Press, 1904.

FURTHER READING:

Clemoes, Peter, and Kathleen Hughes, eds. *England Before the Conquest.* Cambridge University Press, 1971.
Duckell, Eleanor Shipley. *Alfred the Great.* University of Chicago Press, 1956.
Giles, J. A., et al. *Memorials of King Alfred.* Burt Franklin, 1969.
Helm, Peter J. *Alfred the Great.* Robert Hale, 1963.
Lees, Beatrice Adelaide. *Alfred the Great: The Truth Teller Maker of England, 848–899.* Lemma, 1972.
Mapp, Alf J., Jr. *The Golden Dragon: Alfred the Great and his Times.* Open Court, 1974.
Woodruff, Douglas. *The Life and Times of Alfred the Great.* Weidenfeld & Nicolson, 1974.

Edmund H. H. Allenby

(1861–1936)

British general, who in 1918 crushed the Turkish southwestern front in the most spectacular theater victory of World War I.

"Surprise, mobility and concentration were the keynotes of Allenby's victories, backed by relentless determination in the pursuit."

DAVID L. BULLOCK
ALLENBY'S WAR

Edmund Henry Hynman Allenby was born April 23, 1861, into a family of northern English extraction with property interests in Lincolnshire and Felixstowe, East Anglia, England. The Allenbys had belonged to the Lincolnshire gentry for at least three-and-a-half centuries. Edmund's father Hynman Allenby, who had married Catherine Anne Cane in 1859, was a country squire. Thus, Edmund was introduced from an early age to riding, shooting, fishing, boating, swimming, and the nearby forests.

In 1875, the young Allenby attended a new East Anglian public school, Haileybury. He was, according to contemporary accounts, a large, quiet, ruddy-faced boy who was thorough in his studies and imbued with an inner sensitivity. Scarcely three years later, his father died and the family decided Edmund should take the examinations for the Indian Civil Service. After failing these twice, he tested for a place at the Royal Military Academy, Sandhurst, in 1889, and was ranked fifth out of the 110 successful applicants. After nearly a year, he graduated 12th in his class and was gazetted as a junior officer in the 6th Inniskilling

Name variation: Field Marshal Viscount Edmund H.H. Allenby; nicknamed "the Bull." Born April 23, 1861, at Brackenhurst Hall near Southwell, Nottinghamshire, England; died on May 14, 1936; son of Hynman (a country gentleman claiming an ancestral connection to the cavalry leader Oliver Cromwell) and Catherine Anne (Cane) Allenby; married: Mabel Chapman, 1895; children: Horace Michael Hynman (killed on the western front, 1917).

Contributed by David L. Bullock, Ph.D. candidate, Kansas State University, Manhattan, Kansas

Dragoons, beginning his career at age 21 on active service in South Africa.

Allenby had been popular as a cadet, but he had not been so at the expense of his responsibilities. Superiors had already taken note of his maturity. As a soldier, he quickly adapted to life on patrol. After seven years, he was made regimental adjutant and contemporaries noticed he was becoming more serious as well as strict. In fact, fellow officers nicknamed him "Apple-pie"; it was intended not only as an obvious play on his surname, but as a derisive reference to his correctness.

In 1890, the regiment transferred to England, and Allenby served as adjutant for three years in Brighton. After failing his first exam for the relatively new and innovative Staff College at Camberly, he passed in 1895 and became the first cavalry officer to be admitted through the competitive process the following year. He left the college in 1897 as a major, but not before marrying Mabel Chapman after a whirlwind courtship. His wife shared his interests in birds and flowers and, during the course of their long and happy years together, adapted herself to his career. Thirteen months after the wedding their one child, Horace Michael Hynman, was born.

In 1898, Allenby was posted to Ireland as brigade-major where he would stay for a year and a half before his regiment was dispatched to South Africa to fight in the Anglo-Boer War (1899–

1902). The Boers were farmers of Dutch extraction who were rebelling against British rule; on horseback, these crack marksmen made formidable opponents. One letter to his wife illustrated Allenby's frame of mind as he prepared to be sent abroad:

> I am coming to the conclusion that I have too happy a life at home to make a really good soldier. I catch myself often half-hoping that the war may be won by the time we arrive, so that I may get back quick.

Nevertheless, war found him at the age of 40 in his element. Previous experience in South Africa enabled him to avoid ambushes set by the enemy, while personal daring and a natural flair for independent operations brought him rapid recognition. From 1901–02, as he served as a column commander, London war correspondents carried his story home to the British public. Very few officers would leave the Boer War with reputations intact; Allenby left with his reputation enhanced.

Further, he had learned many valuable lessons. He had been particularly impressed by Lord Robert's dashing and resourceful relief of the town of Kimberley which had been surrounded by the Boers. But he had also seen how generals exhausted their cavalry through indecisive movements, how detached forces had been left unsupported. He learned firsthand that a defeated enemy had to be ruthlessly pursued or he would recover to fight again. Subordinate officers had to be carefully handpicked and then trusted and let alone to do their work unhindered.

In 1902, Allenby returned to England, having been decorated, promoted to brevet-colonel, and elevated to the command of the 5th Lancers. He held this assignment for three years before being put in charge of the 4th Cavalry Brigade as a brigadier general. Making major general in 1909 at the age of 48, he received the office of inspector general of cavalry the following year. A new and important stage in Allenby's life had begun.

As inspector general, Allenby had to reach a tough decision regarding the role of cavalry in future conflict. Debating the Boer War and the Russo-Japanese War (1904–05), proponents of the cavalry seemed evenly divided between those who supported the age-old spirit of the charge and those who believed the only role left to horsemen was as mounted infantry. Allenby tried to steer a middle course, accepting the new techniques of firepower while preserving the older tradition of shock.

Overall, he put the critical years before World War I to constructive use. These years were a time of alliance building among the European nations. Britain joined France and Russia in security arrangements against Germany and Austria-Hungary. Prophetically, Allenby studied the topography of northern France and insisted on exercises which gave the British cavalry practice in retreating.

When the First World War started in August 1914, a British expeditionary force was sent across the English Channel to help France defend against the Germans who were advancing across the length of the western front. Commanding the cavalry division, Allenby skillfully participated in the retreat from Mons to the Marne River. By the end of the year, he was leading two cavalry divisions organized into a corps.

By 1915, however, there was little for cavalry to do on the western front. Mobility had gone. Both sides had dug themselves into immense systems of defensive trenches that were costly and nearly impossible to attack and overcome. Throughout most of 1915, Allenby commanded the 5th Corps as a part of the British defensive line. Already known as "the Bull" by the cavalry, due to his size, perseverance, and ever-shortening temper, he also became known as "the Bull" throughout the British Army. Such a temperament was needed; the casualty attrition in 1915 was the worst the world had ever seen, and it was but a foretaste of what would come.

Near the end of the year, Allenby was promoted to commander of the 3rd Army. He would remain with the 3rd Army until late spring of 1917. Unfortunately, he found that the post was a political one, and he never felt comfortable with his old Staff College classmate, now British supreme commander **Douglas Haig.** Allenby repeatedly argued, to no avail, for short artillery bombardments followed by rapid surprise attacks by the infantry. It was as head of the 3rd Army that he participated in the terrible battles of the Somme in 1916.

Allenby's swansong on the western front was at the battle of Arras in April 1917. The planning for the action had taken six months. His offensive was coordinated with British First Army's attack at Vimy and French attacks along the Aisne River. In the end, Allenby pierced the German line, but the spring thaw had turned the Arras area into such a quagmire that he was unable to move fast enough to exploit his gains.

He Takes Command in the Middle East

It was also during April that British General Sir Archibald Murray was defeated at the battle of Sec-ond Gaza in the Middle East and the Imperial General Staff recommended Allenby as his replacement. For a commander still agonizing over the lost victory at Arras, the reassignment seemed to be a demotion to an overseas sideshow. But the Imperial General Staff and the prime minister, **David Lloyd George,** had other ideas for Edmund Allenby. First, the British Egyptian Expeditionary Force (EEF) contained a large proportion of cavalry and Allenby was a cavalry general. Second, the command in Egypt would be a relatively independent one requiring self-initiative, and in this Allenby excelled. Third, it had to be admitted that Allenby had never worked comfortably with Haig. Lloyd George stressed that he considered the Middle Eastern theater second only to the stalemated western front in strategic importance. If Germany's ally, the (Turkish) Ottoman Empire, could be knocked out of the war, the result could have a positive bearing on events in Europe. Lloyd George argued that the British people—tired, their morale lowered—needed victories, and Allenby was to supply these in the Middle East. The Prime Minister ordered Allenby to capture Jerusalem "as a Christmas present for the British nation."

Allenby assumed command of the EEF at midnight, June 28, 1917. The EEF was a mixed force comprised of almost every nationality in the British Empire Commonwealth. Personnel from all corners of the British Isles merged with personnel from Australia and New Zealand (ANZACs), India, South Africa, and the West Indies. Britain's allies, France and Italy, sent small detachments in support of this new crusade in the Holy Land. Arab forces in revolt against the Ottoman Empire also participated farther to the south in Arabia. An Arab Northern Army had formed, inspired by the legendary **T. E. Lawrence** and led by the charismatic Emir **Faisal.**

Allenby found his new command demoralized by two defeats at Gaza but excellent fighting material nonetheless. Not only were the men veterans, they had not suffered the debilitating losses of the western front. His first actions included a tour of his primary combat units and the relocation of General Headquarters from Cairo to the border of Egypt and Palestine where he could be in touch with the front lines. According to the *Australian Official History:*

> He went through the hot, dusty camps of his army like a strong, fresh, reviving wind. He would dash up in his car to a Light Horse regiment, shake hands with a few officers, inspect hurriedly … and be gone in a few minutes…. [H]is imperious bearing, radiated an impression of tremendous resolu-

tion, quick decision and steely discipline. Troops who caught only one fleeting glimpse of him felt that here at last was a man with the natural qualities of a great driving commander.

Allenby's first major victory was the battle of Third Gaza. He had spent the summer of 1917 planning, organizing reinforcements, and deceiving the Turks and their German leaders and advisors into believing yet another assault would be launched on Gaza along the Mediterranean coastline. Instead, the EEF made a surprise attack on the opposite, eastern, part of the Turkish line at the desert town of Beersheba, October 31, 1917. After capturing the valuable water supplies in the town, his cavalry—supported by infantry and artillery—rolled up the enemy line in flank. Gaza, which had halted the British advance for nine months, was abandoned to the EEF.

The second part of his Jerusalem campaign ended in the capture of the Holy City on the morning of December 9, 1917. Allenby had pursued his enemy so that they were never fully able to recover. In the meantime, crack Turkish units had been combined with small German detachments into a new Army Group, code-named "Yilderim" ("lightning") under the command of German Field Marshal Erich von Falkenhayn. But "Yilderim's" planning had been faulty in design and execution, and Allenby never gave his enemy the space to halt and effectively regroup. The campaign had been no mean feat: EEF logistics had been severely strained by seasonal rains and the march through the mountains.

In retrospect, 1917 had been a decisive year. The United States had joined Britain and France, and Germany had beaten Russia. Revolution and civil war followed hard on the heels of the Russian defeat. As a result, Germany was able to transfer considerable resources to the western front in an effort to crush the French and British before the Americans could arrive in force. An anxious General Staff pulled Allenby's best troops back to Europe. In exchange, he was given raw recruits.

Defeats Three Turkish Armies

It would be September 1918 before the EEF was ready to assume another offensive. Allenby had spent the spring and summer training and reorganizing his new units and in establishing air superiority over his Turkish-German enemy. Above all, he tricked his opponents into believing a campaign would unfold against their forces in the Jordan Valley.

When he struck on September 19, Allenby had obtained a five-to-one numerical advantage in the coastal sector where he had always intended his main blow to fall. The Turks were surprised and overwhelmed as EEF infantry opened a huge gap in their lines. Cavalry galloped through and spread out in the rear of the Turkish-German armies. As the enemy tried to fall back, Allenby directed his air force to engage their columns in the mountain passes. Within days, three Turkish armies had been destroyed in the most successful theaterwide victory of World War I.

Appropriately enough, the campaign had been fought over the plains of Megiddo, the biblical location of Armageddon. But it did not end there. Damascus fell to Arab and EEF forces on October 1, and the heartland of the Ottoman Empire was threatened by the end of the month. On October 31, the Turks sued for peace; an armistice followed on the western front a few days later.

Though Allenby's rewards and recognition were heady, he would have to wait until 1919 to collect. He was thanked by both houses of Parliament, awarded a large cash benefit, and the following year was promoted to field marshal and created viscount. From 1919 to 1925, he served in Egypt as special high commissioner. Unfortunately, the position was more political than he found to his taste. Egyptian nationalists were pressing for freedom from Britain and rioting and conspiracy were in the air. Complications arising from the local situation caused him to seek retirement from governmental service in 1925. Thereafter, Field-Marshal Viscount Allenby led a quiet and uneventful life, dying 11 years later. He was cremated and his remains laid to rest in Westminster Abbey, London, alongside so many other of Britain's heroes.

SOURCES:

Bullock, David L. *Allenby's War: The Palestine-Arabian Campaigns, 1916–1918.* Blandford Press, 1988.

Gardner, Brian. *Allenby of Arabia: Lawrence's General.* Coward-McCann, 1966.

Wavell, Field-Marshal Viscount A. P. Wavell. *Allenby: Soldier and Statesman.* Harrap, 1946.

FURTHER READING:

Falls, Cyril. *Armageddon 1918.* Weidenfeld & Nicolson, 1964.

Heyman, Holger H., and Neil M. Heyman. *Biographical Dictionary of World War I.* Greenwood Press, 1982.

Savage, Raymond. *Allenby of Armageddon: A Record of the Career and Campaigns of Field-Marshal Viscount Allenby, GCB, GCMG.* Diamond Press, 1925.

Wavel, Field-Marshal Earl Wavell. *The Palestine Campaigns.* 3rd ed. Constable, 1954.

Windrow, Martin, and Francis K. Mason. *A Concise Dictionary of Military Biography: Two Hundred of the Most Significant Names in Land Warfare, 10th–20th Century.* Purnell, 1975.

Queen Anne

(1665–1714)

Last of England's ill-starred Stuart monarchs, who contributed to the settlement of a century of religious warfare and laid the foundation for England's Golden Age in world history.

"As I know my heart to be entirely English, I can very sincerely assure you that there is not one thing you can expect or desire of me which I shall not be ready to do for the happiness or prosperity of England."

QUEEN ANNE,
ADDRESS TO HER
FIRST PARLIAMENT

The world took little notice on February 6, 1665, when Anne Hyde, wife of James, Duke of York, gave birth to a baby girl. The new arrival, christened Anne, was quickly dispatched to the royal nursery. No one would have guessed that she would one day inherit the English throne, for although Anne was undeniably of royal blood, she was far removed from the line of Stuart succession.

Anne's uncle, King **Charles II,** spent his youth exiled in France after the English Civil War (1642–49) wrested the throne from the Stuart family and sent his father Charles I to the execution block. In 1660, Charles II was restored to the English throne. Having already proved his fertility by siring several bastard children, everyone expected that Charles and his queen, Catherine of Braganza, would provide an heir to the throne. Should Charles die without a legitimate heir, the throne would pass to his younger brother—Anne's father—James, duke of York. But James scandalized the court in 1660 when he secretly married Anne Hyde. Although her father, Sir Edward Hyde, had faithfully served Charles II as lord chancellor, the Hydes were commoners—not suitable

Born in 1665; died in 1714; daughter of James, Duke of York (later James II) and Anne Hyde; married: Prince George of Denmark, 1683; children: 17, none of whom survived to adulthood. Predecessor: William III (1688–1702). Successor: George I (1714–27).

Contributed by Kimberly K. Estep, Ph.D. in History, Auburn University, Auburn, Alabama

royal marriage partners. The new duchess of York quickly produced several children, but only two survived to adulthood: Mary (born 1662) and Anne.

In accordance with aristocratic childrearing practices of the day, the Lady Anne was brought up in a royal nursery where she could be groomed in courtly manners and kept secluded from the adults at court. As a result, Anne's relationship with her parents was formal and constrained. She referred to her father as "the Duke," or later "the King," and once admitted that she could not recall from memory how her mother had looked. Anne's relationship with her parents became even more distant when they converted to Roman Catholicism in 1669. The ravages of the Civil War had convinced most Englishmen that their monarchs must be members of the Church of England. Since the Test Act (1673) barred non-Anglicans from political and military office, James was dismissed from all government appointments because of his conversion. Political realities dictated that Mary and Anne, against their father's wishes, remain firmly in the hand of their Anglican tutors, where they became fervent defenders of the Protestant faith.

Two years after Anne Hyde's untimely death in 1671, James married 15-year-old Mary of Modena, a Catholic princess from Italy, causing an uproar in Parliament. Most of the country was resigned to James's eventual succession, convinced that he would soon be followed by his Anglican daughters, Mary and Anne. The possibility of a new Catholic heir set off a wave of anti-Catholic hysteria. By 1678, rumors of a fiendish "Popish Plot" warned that English Catholics, under orders from the pope, were planning to murder Charles and replace him with James. The scandal was perpetuated by a roguish liar, Titus Oates, who testified in Parliament about leaders of the plot. Charles himself was skeptical about its existence, but before Oates was finally discredited, several prominent Catholics were sent to their deaths.

In the aftermath of the plot, a political movement arose aimed at excluding James from the throne, under the direction of a group of men who were derisively referred to as Whigs, a name given to Scottish outlaws. They in turn called their opponents Tories, or Irish rebels. The party labels lasted beyond the unsuccessful Exclusion Crisis, and bickering between the two political parties blighted later reigns.

It was imperative that suitable Protestant mates be found for Mary and Anne. In 1677, Mary had married the Dutch prince **William of Orange,** a Lutheran. Negotiations with a cousin, Prince George of Denmark, for Anne's hand resulted in their marriage in 1683. Younger brother of the king of Denmark and a respectable Lutheran, George spent the rest of his life in England, but he remained in the background, amusing himself by building model ships and drinking heavily. Nevertheless, he was an affectionate and loyal husband and earned Anne's undying love and devotion.

Anne's greatest emotional attachment was to Sarah Jennings Churchill (later Duchess of Marlborough). Sarah was strong-willed, vivacious, and blunt, and Anne, who tended to be shy and reticent, was irresistibly drawn to her. Clinging to Sarah for emotional support, Anne's devotion made her a perfect vehicle for Sarah's ambition. In a note to Sarah apologizing for James's initial refusal to give her a position in Anne's household, Anne revealed her characteristic insecurity:

> I will try once more, be he never so angry; but oh do not let this take away your kindness from me, for I assure you 'tis the greatest trouble in the world to me and I am sure you have not met a faithfuller friend on earth nor that loves you better, than I do.

When Charles II died in 1685 and James II succeeded to the throne, Anne became heir presumptive behind her sister Mary, who now resided in Holland and had failed to conceive in eight years of marriage to William of Orange. Mary of Modena had also failed to produce a male heir in 12 years of marriage to James II, and many assumed her childbearing years were over. Anne, five months pregnant at James's coronation, seemed to hold the key to the future of the Stuart family. She became a rallying point for militant Anglicans, who opposed James's pro-Catholic policies.

James II exacerbated fears that he intended to reestablish Catholicism in England by handing down a Declaration of Indulgence, which allowed non-Anglicans to hold public office. He also launched a campaign to remove strong anti-Catholic Anglicans from all government positions, including Anne's own household. The final straw for many Anglicans was the announcement that Mary of Modena was pregnant. When she gave birth to a healthy son, James Edward, on June 10, 1688, Anne vigorously denied that the child was her stepmother's at all. Consequently, a rumor began to circulate that Mary of Modena had faked her pregnancy and that the baby had been smuggled into the royal bedchamber in a warming pan. In reality, it would have been all but impossible for Mary to have pulled off such a ruse, as the birth was almost a public event, attended by members of the royal family as well as important figures of state. Anne's refusal to believe that Mary had borne a child probably stemmed in part from Anne's own frustrations in childbearing. Anne's first child had been stillborn, and two later pregnancies had ended in miscarriages. In 1687, smallpox claimed the lives of her two daughters, Mary and Anne Sophia.

The birth and panic wrought by James Edward, the new Prince of Wales, prompted many prominent Anglicans to begin negotiating with William of Orange to install King James's Protestant daughter Mary on the throne. Anne and Sarah Churchill played a part in the negotiations, and when William finally landed on the shores of England, Anne deserted the court and fled incognito into the country. On hearing of his daughter's flight, James was devastated: "God help me," he was reported to have cried, "even my children have forsaken me." Before William reached London, James's own officers began to desert, and James fled to France. The bloodless nature of the transfer of power caused Englishmen to hail William's arrival as the "Glorious Revolution." Loyalists to James, called Jacobites, awaited an opportunity to bring James back to the throne.

William and Mary Rule England

In the revolution settlement, William and Mary were proclaimed joint rulers of England, Scotland, and Ireland. At William's insistence, he was made coequal with Mary, and should Mary predecease him, William was to be made sole monarch of England. Although Anne reluctantly agreed to this settlement, she later referred to it bitterly as her "abdication."

The unique political circumstances of the Glorious Revolution fostered a change in the structure of politics. Loyalty to the "Crown" became more abstract and less vested in the person of the monarch, and so a kind of "loyal opposition" to the monarch emerged, centered around the heir apparent, and continued to shape British politics throughout the 18th century. Drifting into opposition to William and Mary soon after the revolution settlement was made, Anne attracted a number of politicians to her camp who looked forward to reaping the benefits of office as soon as she succeeded to the throne.

Antipathy between Anne and the new monarchs centered around the volatile issues of succession, money, and the Churchills. William resented and feared Anne's hereditary claim to the throne and tried to keep Anne financially dependent on his own generosity; she was given no share of her father's personal estates and no guaranteed personal income. The most humiliating treatment Anne received from William and Mary was their insistence that she end her friendship with the duke and duchess of Marlborough. When she bluntly refused to part with Sarah, Anne's husband was relieved of all his government offices. Outraged, Anne left the Palace of Whitehall, assuring Sarah: "I am more yours than can be expressed and had rather live in a cottage with you than Reign Empress of the world without you." In her letters, Anne referred venomously to William as "that Monster" or "that Dutch abortive." An atmosphere of outright hostility persisted between Anne and William until, in 1694, Mary died suddenly of smallpox. Both were devastated by their loss, however, and Anne and William reached an uneasy truce that lasted for the rest of his reign.

By 1700, Anne was already something of an invalid. Plagued by poor health since childhood, she suffered from a "defluxion," or soreness and watering, of the eyes that made reading and writing difficult. By the time she was 35, she had undergone 17 pregnancies, most of which had ended in miscarriage, and in 1700 her last remaining child, an 11-year-old son, died. Anne began showing signs of physical decline, complaining of gout, rheumatism, and weakness in the legs. England faced the possibility of having no Protestant heir to the throne after William and Anne. Determined to limit the royal succession to Protestant heirs, Parliament passed the Act of Settlement in 1701, which made Sophia, dowager Electress of Hanover and granddaughter of **James I** (1603–25), heir should Anne and William die without issue. At least 52 Catholic descendants with a better claim were passed over.

Anne Becomes Queen

In 1702, the last remaining obstacle between Anne and the English throne was removed when William III died. But the new queen, prematurely aged at 37, had to be carried to her coronation. In spite of her precarious physical condition, Anne took an active role in government and during her 12-year reign, England flourished and gained stature in world politics.

Traditionally, Anne has been portrayed as a weak, easily manipulated ruler, but compared to the other Stuart monarchs, she showed remarkable political savvy. Vigorously defending her prerogatives as queen, she was adept at the use of "backstairs intrigue" and took her constitutional role as Defender of the Faith seriously. The Tory party played upon her strong Anglican bias to curry royal favor by taking up the battle cry of "the Church in Danger." In spite of her Tory bias, Anne distrusted the whole idea of political parties. She valued moderation and sought to create "mixed ministries" made up of men chosen for service and merit.

Two weeks after Anne's coronation, England declared war on France. **Louis XIV** had dominated European affairs for half a century and now intended to place his grandson, Philip of Anjou, on the throne of Spain, after the Spanish king had died without heir. England determined to put a check on Louis's aggression, which threatened to upset Europe's delicate balance of power. When Louis was told, he jokingly replied, "It means I'm growing old when ladies declare war on me." Louis's overconfidence was soon deflated by a series of setbacks on the field.

The War of Spanish Succession catapulted Sarah's husband **John Churchill,** the duke of Marlborough, into the international spotlight. An able military strategist, Marlborough routed the French at the Battle of Blenheim (1704) and continued to achieve surprising gains against them throughout the war. While Marlborough served as Anne's emissary abroad, another old friend, Sydney Godolphin, served Anne at home as Lord Treasurer. A nominal Tory, Godolphin was an able financier and administrator whose first loyalty was to Anne. The junior member of Anne's inner circle of ministers was Robert Harley, another moderate Tory. Harley was indispensable to Anne because of his ability to manage the House of Commons and to preserve good relations between Anne and her parliaments.

Sarah Churchill's relationship with Anne began deteriorating soon after Anne's succession. An ardent Whig, Sarah's tactless insistence on converting Anne to her point of view did little to endear her to the new queen; she had also become lax in her attendance at court. In her absence, Anne began to turn more and more for solace and support to Abigail Hill Masham. A poor relation of Sarah's, Abigail had been given a position in Anne's household at Sarah's request, and she proved attentive and eager to please. When Sarah discovered that she had been supplanted as royal favorite, she was furious "to see a woman whom I raised out of the Dust put on such a Superior air." When Anne's relationship with the Marlboroughs degenerated into constant bickering, she finally dismissed Sarah from her court appointments in 1711.

The most enduring achievement of Anne's reign came in 1707 with the formal union of England and Scotland. Although the two countries had been ruled by the same monarch since 1603, they had maintained separate parliaments. The union was very popular at home, but it opened up renewed problems with France. In early 1708, Louis XIV sent a French fleet commanded by Anne's half-brother James Edward to Scotland. The "Pretended Prince of Wales," now 20 years old, was anxious for an opportunity to reclaim his father's kingdom. But the Pretender never landed in Scotland, forced to retreat by the English fleet under Admiral George Byng.

The invasion scare played into the hands of the Whigs, who accused the Tories of closet Jacobitism. The Whig party, led by a powerful five-man faction called the Whig *Junto,* used popular fear of Catholic invasion to force Anne's hand in political appointments and successfully forced Harley out of office by exploiting an espionage scandal involving one of his clerks. They overplayed their hand, however, when they openly attacked a High Church clergyman, Henry Sacheverell. Preaching a sermon against "occasional conformists" (non-Anglicans who attended Anglican services once or twice a year in order to keep their government appointments), Sacheverell called them "these crafty, faithless, and insidious persons who can creep to our altars and partake of our sacraments." Even Anne agreed that his sermon was stupidly inflammatory, but when the Whigs impeached him—suspending him from preaching for three years and publicly burning his sermon—Anne felt they had gone too far. Turning the Whig *Junto* out of office, she replaced them with Tories. She also dismissed Godolphin and replaced him with Harley, who, along with his protégé Henry St. John, directed government policy during the last years of Anne's reign.

Harley and St. John immediately began secret negotiations with France to end what had become a protracted, expensive war. Although most were thoroughly tired of the war, the Whigs refused to end the struggle without removing Philip of Anjou from the Spanish throne, a goal which seemed progressively more unreachable. The Treaty of Utrecht recognized Philip as King Philip V of Spain, but recompensed England with several naval bases from which England was able to establish naval supremacy during the 18th century. When it was presented to the House of Lords for ratification in 1713 and the Whigs engineered a political maneuver to defeat it, Anne created 12 new peers to outvote the Whig bloc.

During the final months of Anne's life, Harley and St. John split the ministry. Anne dismissed Harley, throwing the government into confusion. As Anne's health continued to deteriorate, the country began to prepare for her successor. The Electress Sophia of Hanover had died that summer, leaving her son, George Ludwig, as heir. Known to harbor a deep dislike for her Hanoverian relations, Anne had been maddeningly vague about her intentions regarding James Edward, the Pretender, in her will. Many feared Anne's death would bring another Catholic invasion from France.

As Anne lay on her deathbed, doctors tried every horrifying remedy known to 18th-century medicine. They bled her, blistered her skin with hot irons, covered her feet with garlic, and shaved her head bare—all to no avail. When Anne died on the morning of August 1, 1714, a frantic search through her papers revealed no mention of her successor, and the Hanoverian George I succeeded peacefully, in spite of a brief Jacobite rising in 1715.

Anne presided over a nation that was coming into its own in the 18th century. The Glorious Revolution had put an end to abuse of monarchical authority by putting a parliamentary check on the sovereign. Militarily, England was entering its prime. The 18th century saw England emerge as the world's greatest maritime power. This century also brought financial success. Bolstered by her formidable navy, England dominated markets worldwide and acquired a prosperous overseas empire. Anne's primary contribution to this century of achievement was a reign marked by moderation and stability. In Queen Anne's reign, England finally found resolution to the turmoils that had plagued her for 150 years and looked forward to a century of confidence and Enlightenment.

SOURCES:

Curtis, Gila. *The Life and Times of Queen Anne.* Weidenfeld & Nicholson, 1972.

Gregg, Edward. *Queen Anne.* Routledge & Kegan Paul, 1980.

Holmes, Geoffrey. *British Politics in the Age of Anne.* Rev. ed. Hambledon Press, 1987.

FURTHER READING:

Brown, Beatrice Curtis. *The Letters and Diplomatic Instructions of Queen Anne.* Cassell, 1968.

Trevelyan, G. M. *England Under Queen Anne.* 3 vols. London, 1930–34.

Anthony Ashley-Cooper, 7th Earl of Shaftsbury

(1801–1885)

British philanthropist, politician, humanitarian, and social reformer, who championed improvements in living and working conditions, better treatment of the insane, education of the poor, moral improvement, and establishment of standards for health and safety.

Name variations: The eldest son of the Earl of Shaftsbury takes the courtesy title, Lord Ashley, while remaining a commoner; the 7th Earl used the family name of Ashley-Cooper, though his children and some grandchildren used only Ashley; descendants have since resumed Ashley-Cooper. Born April 28, 1801, at 24 Grosvenor Square in London; died October 1, 1885, at Folkstone; son of 6th Earl of Shaftsbury and Anne Spencer-Churchill (daughter of the Duke of Marlborough); married: Lady Emily "Minnie" Cowper (daughter of the Earl and Countess Cowper), June 10, 1839; children: (six sons) Anthony (MP for Hull and 8th Earl of Shaftsbury), Francis, Maurice, Evelyn, Lionel, and Cecil; (four daughters) Vea (godchild to Queen Victoria), Mary, Constance, and Edith.

Anthony Ashley-Cooper was born at the Shaftsbury London town house in Grosvenor Square on April 28, 1801. He was the fourth child and eldest son of Cropley Ashley-Cooper (later the 6th earl of Shaftsbury) and Anne Spencer-Churchill, daughter of the duke of Marlborough. Of the nine children in the family, the three sisters came first and were followed by six sons in succession. The Ashley-Coopers were a distinguished family which had been involved in public life for generations holding ancient Cooper lands in Hampshire and those descended from the Ashleys in Dorset. The rivers which meet in Charleston, South Carolina, bear the family names and witness to the influence of a 17th-century ancestor. The "A" in CABAL, the small group which dominated English politics under **Charles II** and whose acronym has since entered the English language, was derived from the Ashley-Cooper who became the 1st earl of Shaftsbury.

Anthony's childhood was a particularly significant one. It was unpleasant and occasionally traumatic, but it seems to have developed in him a genuine sympathy for suffering in others. His father could be selfish, coldhearted, and domineer-

"...Place me rather on the dust heap or in the dung hole than his factory!"

Lord Shaftsbury,
on Touring a Factory
in Bolton (1844)

Contributed by Richard Francis Spall, Jr., Associate Professor of History, Ohio Wesleyan University, Delaware, Ohio

54

ing. His mother, whom he described as "a fiend," was primarily concerned with high society, and the children were neglected, deprived of food and affection, and left to the servants to rear. Anthony's childhood was of such severity and complete absence of parental affection that in 1828 he recorded in his diary his prayer "that no family hereafter may endure from its parents what we endured."

It was Maria Millis, one of the servants, who met his daily needs and afforded the little boy the love which he craved. Millis had been a servant at Blenheim Palace while Lady Anne was growing up and became housekeeper at the residence in Grosvenor Square where she provided Anthony with affection and instructed him in the Evangelical religion in which she believed. At the age of seven, Anthony was separated from Millis and packed off to boarding school in Chiswick. Manor School was a place for sons of the nobility; it was expensive, exclusive, and excruciating. Pupils were subjected to both cold and hunger while being intellectually challenged. Anthony cried when forced to return after holidays and in adulthood recollected the school was: "bad, wicked, filthy; and the treatment was starvation and cruelty." Not long after going to Chiswick, Maria Millis died, and the lad was devastated by the loss. She left to him a gold watch which he cherished the rest of his life, saying it had been given to him "by the best friend I ever had in this world."

In 1811, when Cropley Ashley-Cooper succeeded his elder brother as the 6th earl of Shaftsbury, Anthony took on the courtesy title of the eldest son, Lord Ashley. His father soon opened up the great house at Wimborne St. Giles in Dorset, the place which Ashley would come to regard as home. In 1813, Ashley was transferred to Harrow School where he boarded with the headmaster, George Butler, a man who set high standards of character and conduct. With the other boys at the school, Ashley attended the parish church in Harrow where the vicar's Evangelicalism fostered Ashley's own. One event at Harrow foreshadowed Ashley's career as a reformer; he apparently shamed local authorities into cleaning up a foul pond known as Duck Puddle. At the age of 14, Ashley witnessed a pauper's funeral as a group of drunken pallbearers came over Harrow Hill singing, staggering, and cursing. Jakelegged, the men let the coffin fall, spilling its contents. Ashley said it was from that moment that he dedicated his life to the cause of the poor and friendless.

Removing him from the sixth form at Harrow the following year, Ashley's father sent him to board with a clergyman at Eckington in Der-

CHRONOLOGY

1826	Entered Parliament as MP for Woodstock at age 25
1827	Appointed to select committee on Pauper Lunatics and Lunatic Asylums
1830	Elected MP for Dorchester
1831	Returned as county member for Dorset at ruinous expense
1833	Began work for factory acts on Sadler Committee
1842	Convinced Parliament to pass Ashley Mines Act
1846	Took Chiltern Hundreds over support of Corn Law repeal
1847	Returned for Bath; Ten Hours Act adopted
1848	Began seven-year tenure on Board of Health
1851	Entered House of Lords as Earl of Shaftsbury
1867	Worked to extend and renew factory acts

byshire where Ashley spent three years in idleness without work to do or books to read. Eventually, Lord Bathurst convinced Lord Shaftsbury that the boy ought to be sent to university; so in January of 1819, Ashley entered Christ Church at Oxford. Among his classmates were his distant cousin Edward Pusey, who would later lead the Tractarians, and George Howard, Lord Morpeth (later earl of Carlisle). The summer of 1820 which he spent with Morpeth at Castle Howard was one of the happiest times of Ashley's life. Though as a noble he was not required to take examinations, Ashley determined to "challenge honours" and in 1822 earned a first in classics after a *viva voce* (oral) examination before John Keble who was later leader of the Oxford Movement. After coming down from Oxford, Ashley's father forbade him from living at either St. Giles or at Grosvenor Square. As was the custom for young gentlemen, he was sent off on grand tour, spending two years abroad beginning in late 1823, during which time he decided that, "Politics seem my destination."

Ashley Enters House of Commons

In 1826, Ashley entered the House of Commons as Tory MP for Woodstock, a pocket borough of the duke of Marlborough, where he supported the Liverpool Ministry. The next year, he refused office under Prime Minister George Canning out of respect for "Dukey," his friend the **Duke of Wellington** and Canning's rival, but he did accept appointment to the select committee on Pauper

Lunatics and Lunatic Asylums. While visiting madhouses, Ashley was appalled at the treatment of the insane. In "crib cases," lunatics were chained in straw-filled frames so as to be unable to move for months on end. The "bath of surprise," in which cold water was poured on inmates, was frequently employed, and the "circular swing," in which the victim was spun until loss of consciousness, was still in use. Ashley proposed remedial measures, and the County Asylum Bill and Madhouse Bill were adopted, allowing local officials to establish lunatic asylums, conferring powers of licensure and inspection, and establishing a Lunacy Commission on which Ashley served the rest of his life.

When Wellington became prime minister in 1828, he appointed Ashley to the India Board where he became an outspoken opponent of *Suttee*, the Hindu practice in which widows threw themselves, or were thrown, upon the funeral pyres of their husbands. He was uncomfortable, however, with imperialism and said of India, "I would protect and train it unto its riper years, and then give it, like a full grown son, free action and absolute Independence." Ashley was glad to serve on the India Board for he needed the salary as his father provided him with an allowance only £100 greater than when he had been an undergraduate.

Anxious to marry and an incurable romantic, Ashley courted Lady Emily Cowper, daughter of Earl Cowper and Lady Emily Cowper, and known as "Minnie" so as not to confuse her with her mother. Though married to the earl, her mother had long been the mistress of **Lord Palmerston** (whom she later married after being widowed) and many contemporaries believed that Minnie was Palmerston's daughter—a suspicion which surviving portraits do not dispel. Lord Ashley and Minnie Cowper were married in June 1839 at St. George's in Hanover Square.

In the general elections of 1830 and 1831, Ashley was returned for Dorchester, but when the member for Dorset died in 1831, Ashley determined to stand for the more prestigious county seat as a candidate opposed to parliamentary reform. Although Ashley won the election by 36 votes, he had amassed £15,000 in pub and other campaign debts which he could not afford.

Lord Ashley is best known for his championing of factory legislation and, in particular, the Ten Hours Bill, but he came to lead the factory regulation effort in an unplanned and unexpected way. In the industrial north of England, and especially in Yorkshire, agitations had begun to limit the hours of labor for women and children. Various "short time" committees were formed, led by John Wood, Richard Oatsler, and George Bull. In December 1831, Michael Sadler introduced a Ten Hours Bill and was appointed to chair a select committee to study the matter. The passage of the Reform Act of 1832 led shortly to a general election in which Sadler lost his seat, and so another had to be found to lead the effort in Parliament. Following a meeting of Short Time Committees in Bradford in early 1833, Lord Ashley was approached. From the south of England, an aristocrat, and heir to landed estates and incomes, Ashley seemed an unlikely choice, and he had little knowledge or interest in the issue. But he had a reputation for sympathy with the unfortunate, a paternalist inclination, and an Evangelical moral imperative. After "meditation and prayer," Ashley accepted the invitation before a meeting of the Society for the Improvement of the Condition of Factory Children "as a matter of conscience," knowing that championing such a cause would likely mean forfeiting a career in high office.

Factory Regulation Legislation Passes

It was Ashley then who led the Sadler Committee which took evidence from scores of witnesses on conditions in the mills. A Royal Commission was established to study the matter in hopes of discrediting the findings of the select committee, but instead they confirmed them. Ashley's proposal to prohibit employment of children under nine years of age, limit the hours of those less than 13 years old to ten per day, and allow for inspection of factories to enforce compliance became law in the Factory Act of 1833.

Ashley was high-strung, introverted, and extremely sensitive. He took personally what was said in the cut and thrust of parliamentary debate with the result that he was frequently alienated from his colleagues. Though invited to take offices under **Robert Peel**, whom he described as "an iceberg with a slight thaw at the surface," he refused. Ashley suffered from severe bouts of paralyzing depression throughout his life, but these were interrupted by periods of furious activity and near exaltation such as that in 1833. He was plagued too by chronic dyspepsia and periodic ringing in the ears. It was his religious faith and ventilation through his diaries which sustained him.

After 1835, Ashley seems to have deepened and sharpened his low church, Evangelical religious views. He joined and helped organize several Evangelical societies with goals of social and moral reform, and he became increasingly hostile to high church opinions and Tractarians (advocates of the

Oxford Movement led by **Cardinal Newman,** who sought to prove that the doctrines of the Anglican Church were similar to those of Rome), whom he regarded as virtually crypto-Catholics. He became deeply concerned for the spiritual and physical health of working-class children, and began in the 1840s to work for legislation to protect the "climbing boys" employed by chimney sweeps. As a member of the Royal Commission on Children's Employment, Ashley was taken on tours to see living and working conditions of poor children by the London physician Southwood Smith. He worked to get women and children out of the mines on health and safety grounds but also upon moral ones, as women often worked in the mines, as men did, naked from the waist up. The Ashley Mines Act became law in August 1842.

In 1845, Ashley introduced a bill to regulate the labor of children in the calico-printing industry which was enacted. He advocated as well the adoption of new laws to improve regulation of lunatic asylums, require construction of new ones, improve record keeping, and make more stringent the certification process. His father opposed these measures in the House of Lords, but they were enacted nonetheless. Ashley also served on the newly established Railway Commission as its chairman during this period.

The agitation led by **Richard Cobden** and **John Bright** for repeal of the Corn Laws took on new meaning when Ireland faced famine in late 1845. Ashley's support of repeal angered his Dorset constituents, most of whom were landholders. He determined, therefore, to take the Chiltern Hundreds, the method for resigning one's seat, in 1846, and remained out of Parliament until elected for Bath late the next year. With Ashley out of Parliament, it was John Fielden who introduced the Ten Hours Bill in early 1847 with which Ashley had become so closely associated. Becoming law in June, the bill limited to ten the hours of labor for women and children in the textile industry. Mill owners soon discovered they could get around the law by means of a relay system of work breaks. Ashley recognized the problem and supported a compromise position, to the dismay of his old short-time allies, of extending the workday to ten and a half hours but prohibiting the relay system.

He Becomes Earl of Shaftsbury

Ashley's career in the House of Commons came to an end in 1851 when he became the 7th earl of Shaftsbury upon the death of his father. Four years earlier, he had been appointed to the Board of Health and did much to improve health and sanitation, particularly during the cholera epidemic. As a sabbatarian, he supported closing laws despite opposition from workers who felt that their hard-won leisure time was wasted if things were closed on Sunday. When Palmerston became prime minister, Ashley was successful in urging upon his stepfather-in-law the appointment of low church bishops. During Palmerston's second ministry when a suitable monarch was being sought for Greece, King Leopold I of Belgium suggested Lord Shaftsbury. Shaftsbury had declined the offer of a knighthood by Aberdeen in 1854 and did so again in 1861 apparently upon financial grounds. His father had left massive debts. When Palmerston renewed the offer in 1862 and agreed to cover the costs, Ashley accepted the Garter.

In the late 1860s, Shaftsbury worked to renew and extend factory acts. His humanitarian work eased the grief which he felt over the loss of his wife in 1868. He took considerable interest in slum clearance and construction of working-class housing. Shaftsbury Park, a housing project of 1,200 units at Battersea, was named for him, and at Wimborne St. Giles, he built a model low-rent village. He was prominent too in the Ragged Schools movement which provided free education to poor and orphaned children. An aristocrat and paternalist, Shaftsbury did not support parliamentary reform in 1867. He also opposed the adoption of the secret ballot in 1872 but worked to avoid a constitutional clash between the Lords and Commons over the issue. He disliked **Gladstone,** whom he thought "mad" and reckless in reform, and distrusted **Disraeli,** whom he thought "bad" in character and motive; of Gladstone's resumption of office in 1880, he commented, "Nothing will surpass the ignorance, the meanness, and the unpatriotic policy of the new holders of office." He opposed Gladstone's Reform Bill in 1884, and, anxious to avoid a confrontation between the Houses of Parliament, supported separating out the issue of redistribution of seats in a Redistribution Bill.

Failing health prevented Shaftsbury from attending the closing debates on the 1884 Reform Bill or the Redistribution Bill of 1885. In July of 1885, Shaftsbury left for Folkstone in the hopes that the sea air might aid his recovery, but the end was near. The dean of Westminster offered Shaftsbury burial in Westminster Abbey among England's great and good, but he replied, "no—St. Giles, St.Giles." With his children gathered round, death came on the afternoon of October 1 at Folkstone. According to his wish, he was buried at St. Giles in Dorset. But the life of this great humanitarian and reformer, who never held cabinet office, was honored at a funeral in Westminster Abbey by a grateful nation.

SOURCES:

Battiscombe, *Georgina. Shaftsbury: The Great Reformer. 1801–1885.* Houghton, 1975.

Driver, Cecil. *Tory Radical: The Life of Richard Oastler.* Octagon, 1970.

Hodder, Edwin. *The Life and Work of the 7th Earl of Shaftsbury.* Cassell, 1887.

Parliamentary Papers. 1831–32, vol. XV, and 1842, vols. XV-XVII.

FURTHER READING:

Best, Geoffrey. *Mid-Victorian Britain.* Schocken, 1972.

———. *Shaftsbury.* Batsford, 1964.

Hammand, J. L., and Barbara Hammand. *Shaftsbury.* Constable, 1923.

Midwinter, E. C. *Victorian Social Reform.* Longmans, 1968.

Reader, W. J. *Life in Victorian England.* Capricorn, 1967.

Attila

(C. 370/400–453)

Hunnish leader, who achieved status that rivaled all barbarian predecessors and led his warriors in a series of bloody campaigns that nearly destroyed the foundations of Western Christendom.

"…it is no more paradox to say that indirectly the king of the Huns contributed, more perhaps than any other historical personage, toward the creation of that mighty factor in the politics of medieval Italy, the Pope-king of Rome."

THOMAS HODGKIN

The Huns, as a tribe, entered the pages of European history sometime in the fourth century. No professional historian, past or present, will state with any certitude when or where these people first appeared, but they constituted a decisive factor in the Early Middle Ages. Although initial reports speak of Hunnish attacks on the Alans in the area of the Don River about 376, the first instance of their historical impact was on the battlefield at Adrianople in 378, when a force of Goths—hitherto unable to confront the Romans—with Hunnic cavalry in support, slaughtered a Roman army and, in the doing, changed the nature of warfare for the next millennium and a half.

Archaeological evidence is scarce, but what little there is, together with the evidence of language, seems to point to eastern Asia, the Altaic plateau, as the place where the Huns coalesced into a definable entity. Their language appears to be similar to that of the Turks and the Finns and is sometimes labeled Finno-Ugric, Finno-Turkic, or Altaic.

Nomadic, the Huns traveled almost exclusively on horseback, using the smaller Mongolian ponies, a hardy breed. The Huns have been called

Name variations: Attila the Hun. Pronunciation: ATT-eh-lah. Born between 370 and 400; died in 453; married: Princess Honoria, 450; married: Ildico, 453. Predecessors: Mundich and Octar, Rua. Successors: sons (unnamed).

Contributed by H. L. Oerter, Professor of History, Emeritus, Miami University, Oxford, Ohio

CHRONOLOGY

two were followed by Rua, who led the "nation" until his death in 434. His successor, Attila, ruled jointly with his brother Bleda until 445, when Attila killed Bleda.

No portrait of Attila is known to exist. He is, however, described by more than one reporter as a man of about normal height for a Hun: short. He had a snub nose, small eyes, and a disconcerting stare that frightened most at whom he looked. We know that he was bearded, since the historian Priscus related that the chieftain's beard was "sprinkled with gray" when he met him in 449. This is one of the few opportunities we have to speculate about the possible birthdate of Attila. Maenchen-Helfen, one of the most recent writers to study the Huns in any depth, is of the opinion that Attila must have been born well before the year 400. Since he died in 453, of causes generally associated with age and high living, we may assume that he was well over 53 years of age at that time, and that he had been perceptibly slowing down in the years immediately prior to his death.

The mentality of the Hunnic king/chieftain is difficult to fathom, but it would seem that he observed and learned rapidly. He also had a high regard for men or women who seemed to possess unusual spiritual qualities. It is reported that several times he not only spared such people, but paid close attention to what they had to say. Despite this "better side" to his nature, Attila was, and remained, a ruthless, untutored but natural leader of fighting men, one who was able to engender boundless enthusiasm and devotion among his followers. Flawed leaders did not live very long in the Hunnic culture.

An appreciation of Hunnic society is difficult to establish. Few scholars have devoted serious study to it, and Maenchen-Helfen's conclusions are tentative: he suggests that societal divisions among the Huns were not great and reports that some students have intimated that rank depended on military prowess. Maenchen-Helfen quotes Ennodius (an early sixth-century prelate from Gaul, who was bishop of Pavia) in his *Panegyric on Theodoric*, who said that the man who killed the most enemies had the highest rank. Ennodius spoke of Bulgars in this passage, but in another he equated the Bulgar practices with those of the Huns, and he may have been accurate.

In any case, Attila, whether well-born (as some have intimated) or not, managed to scramble to the top of the Hunnic military and political pyramid and to survive for at least 19 years while casting a lengthening shadow over the Christian portions of the European continent and portions

"ugly," "ferocious," and "awe-inspiring," along with other deprecating descriptors. Only one early recorder has anything nice to say about them, and his evidence is sometimes considered "tainted" by years of close association.

Since they existed by hunting and gathering, using flocks of sheep as their traveling supply of food and leather, the Huns may be considered predatory. All who encountered them and survived would agree. Conducting their warfare with a merciless efficiency, they took few prisoners and showed no pity. Some early reporters state that the Huns virtually lived on horseback, dismounting only when absolutely necessary.

The historical character of Attila appeared with no preparatory signs. He followed a series of Hunnic chieftains of varying degrees of ferocity and efficiency. Among those whose names appear in documents of the period were the brothers Mundich and Octar; they led the tribal nation in the early fifth century, when the Huns moved into the area of Pannonia Secunda, or what is now known as eastern Austria, western Hungary, and portions of northern Yugoslavia (Croatia). These

of Africa. The domination of Europe by the Huns lasted for some 73 years, from Adrianople to the so-called "Mauriac" fields.

Military Tactics of the Huns

Ammianus Marcellinus, a Roman historian of the late fourth century, writing from personal observation, described the military tactics of the Huns as though they were inspirational rather than disciplined. He reported that they would approach their enemies in a fury while making savage noises. Since they were lightly equipped, they could dash into groups of the enemy, slashing with sword, spear, short bow, or a curiously fashioned rope not unlike the lariat, with which they could tangle an opponent while hacking him to death. Weaponry was personal and consisted of anything the Hunnic warrior could acquire, either from traders or dead victims. Fighting skill was individual and highly developed. Speed and courage were the principal factors, coupled with their notorious savagery and superb horsemanship.

As nomads, the Huns had no manufacturing skills and obtained their supplies in the form of booty. Such types of wandering cultures seldom stayed in any place for any appreciable time and, accordingly, never developed those traits acquired by societies that had settled down. Weapons, then, might be swords taken from dead Persians, Eastern or Western Romans, Ostrogoths, Visigoths, or any of the numerous forces the Huns met and defeated in the more than two generations of their dominance.

One of Attila's first moves as chieftain or king of the Huns was to establish his dominance over all possible opponents in what is now Eastern Europe. The Eastern Romans had, at an earlier date, concluded a treaty with Rua which required the emperor to render an annual tribute of 350 pounds of gold to the Huns. This payment had not been forthcoming on a regular basis, so Attila doubled the sum and required 700 pounds. It was paid beginning in 435, under the terms of the Peace of Margus.

In North Africa, the Vandals (a Germanic tribe which had crossed the Mediterranean at what is now Gibraltar, taking Roman territory in present-day Tunisia) moved against Egypt in 440. This threatened the food supply of Constantinople and its subsidiary areas, since Egypt was at that time the granary for the Middle East. This diversion required the Eastern Empire to concentrate its resources in the direction of Egypt and enabled Attila to disregard an existing truce between Huns and the Eastern Empire. He moved freely along the Danube River, against Roman fortifications on both banks, attacking and reducing outposts, towns, and cities as far as present-day Sofia, well south of the Danube.

It was shortly after this campaign that Attila killed his brother. Following a short period of relative inactivity, Attila moved against a tribe known as the Acatziri (Forest People) to the east of the Hunnic base in Pannonia. After subjugating them in 448, he turned his attention to the West.

The Roman general Aetius had enjoyed many successes in the northern part of Gaul (France and Belgium). At one point in his life, he had lived in the Hunnic camps, reportedly as a hostage. He had become closely acquainted with Attila, learning the Hunnic language and many of the customs. The friendship between Aetius and Attila has been remarked by many historians. At some time in 449 the two were estranged. Some reports state that it was over the disposition of gold and silver plate that was supposed to have been turned over to Attila. Aetius, however, after a brief period in which he had lost favor with the Western Roman court in Italy, had traveled to Gaul where he once again resumed duties of high governmental and military responsibility.

It was at about this time—450—that Attila sent word to the Roman court in Italy claiming Princess Honoria in marriage. His claim was addressed to her brother Valentinian III, although Galla Placidia, their mother, seems to have been the actual regnant. When his claim was rejected out of hand (as he doubtless knew it would be), Attila negotiated with King Gaiseric of the Vandals to secure his flanks in the south, then moved north and west against Western Europe, pillaging, raping, and burning a wide swath of destruction west of the Rhine Valley, well into Belgica Secunda. Among the cities laid waste were Reims, Cambrai, Tournai, Metz, Arras, Cologne (Köln) and Trier.

Aetius was able to raise only a small force from the Roman army, but he took them north from Italy and with the help of the Roman governor of Auvergne secured the services of the Visigoths under their king, Theodoric. When the two moved to the relief of the city of Orleans, under siege by the Huns, Attila withdrew from that area. He also would have attacked Troyes, but its bishop, a saintly person named Lupus, interceded and asked Attila to spare the town and its holy places. Attila agreed but told the bishop that he would have to accompany him.

Attila Leads Huns into Western Europe

The Huns then marched toward the Rhine Valley. Aetius and Theodoric pursued and found Attila in the valley of the Marne River in July of the year 451. Aetius was able to move his forces into a position where the Huns were on less favorable ground and the two armies closed in combat. The action was intense. Theodoric was killed and Aetius had his horse slain, but Attila's forces were badly mauled and he wisely chose to withdraw. The site of the battle has been bitterly contested among historians and has been variously identified as Châlons-sur-Marne or Mery-sur-Seine, among others. The Latin designation translates as "the Mauriac fields," and it is usually referred to in this fashion in order to avoid dispute.

The son of Theodoric, Thorismund, returned to his kingdom in order to protect himself and his inheritance from rapacious relatives. This precluded a massive pursuit of the defeated Huns and may have enabled Attila to escape without further trouble. Before leaving the Rhine Valley, Attila released Bishop Lupus, telling him to go home to his people and pray for him.

In the spring of 452, Attila, having made a partial recovery from his defeat, gathered his forces and moved through passes in the Julian Alps in vengeance against the Romans in Italy. He took and destroyed the proud city of Aquileia at the northern end of the Adriatic, then proceeded to threaten, enter, and destroy several northern Italian cities and towns, including Vicenza, Verona, Brescia, and Bergamo. He also occupied Milan.

All other solutions failing, Pope Leo I, a Roman of senatorial rank, came north and approached Attila, who received him on the banks of the Mincio River in northern Italy, near present-day Piacenza. Attila's affinity for holy men served Leo in good stead. After detailed conversations, Attila agreed to withdraw and led his forces out of Italy up into Pannonia, thereby establishing Pope Leo as Christianity's champion.

The following year an aging Attila took still another wife. She was young and, according to reports, "comely." Her name was Ildico and she was Hunnish. The wedding took place in a large wooden building and involved a heavy feast with an excessive amount of drinking. Attila was finally able to get to his bedroom, where he collapsed on his bed, lying on his back. He frequently suffered from a bleeding nose, especially after heavy drink-ing, and it happened then. Unable to rouse himself, he literally drowned in his own blood, his new heavily-veiled bride sitting there uncomprehending. When his followers finally discovered the body, it was too late. The bride was not accused of complicity and the bereaved warriors feasted again, then took the body of their fallen King away and buried him secretly in much the same fashion as other chieftains of that period. The burial site has never been found.

Careers such as that of Attila the Hun breed legends, and it is not easy to separate fact from fancy. However, much of historical fact can be verified in the numerous accounts of the military campaigns of Attila and some of his predecessors. The Huns burst on Europe like a swarm of locusts, spreading terror and chaos wherever they went for over two generations. Attila was the last and most destructive of the Hunnic chieftains.

The battle of Adrianople in 378 established the superiority of horsemen over foot soldiers insofar as the military practitioners of that period could perceive. This was reinforced by the succeeding victories of the Hunnish horsemen. This conclusion, whether right or wrong, affected tactical considerations for over 1,000 years and created the conditions whereby society was organized and directed to support the man on horseback whose life was dedicated to the profession of arms, presumably in defense of property and religion. Not until the development of gunpowder and the introduction of firearms onto the battlefield was this notion questioned—and even then it took the better part of two centuries to effect a change.

SOURCES:

Brion, Marcel. *Attila, the Scourge of God.* McBride, 1929.

Maenchen-Helfen, Otto J. *The World of the Huns: Studies in Their History and Culture.* Edited by Max Knight. University of California Press, 1973.

Thompson, E. A. *A History of Attila and the Huns.* Greenwood Press, 1975 (reprint).

FURTHER READING:

Bury, J. B. *The Invasion of Europe by the Barbarians.* Russell & Russell, 1963.

Goffart, Walter A. *Barbarians and Romans, AD 418–584: The Politics of Accommodation.* Princeton University Press, 1980.

Hodgkin, Thomas. *Italy and Her Invaders.* Vol. II. 8 vols. Oxford: Clarendon Press, 1894.

Previté-Orton, C. W. *The Shorter Cambridge Medieval History.* Vol. I. 2 vols. Cambridge University Press, 1971.

Augustus

(63 B.C.–A.D. 14)

First and greatest of the Roman emperors, who transformed the Empire into a dictatorship while maintaining the outward trappings of the Republic, thus staving off collapse and guaranteeing its survival for nearly 500 years.

"This ruler, Augustus, who truly deserves the title 'Averter of Evil,' is the Caesar who lulled the storms which thundered everywhere, who healed the ills common to the Greeks and barbarians alike."

PHILO OF ALEXANDRIA

Cold, calculating, and extraordinarily ambitious, Augustus made himself master of the Roman world. In his long reign as its first emperor, he transformed the state into a monarchy while maintaining the outward forms of a republic, a brilliant feat of statesmanship that enabled the Roman Empire to survive another five centuries after he came to the throne. His work of consolidation crowned the centuries of territorial expansion that had preceded him and made the Roman Empire a viable, functioning political organism. A patron of the arts, he presided over what has since come to be considered the Golden Age of Roman Civilization.

Of middle height (five-foot-six by report), Augustus was handsome with blondish hair and a strong "Roman" nose but with poor teeth and badly spotted skin. Possessing the dignified bearing so much esteemed among the early Romans, he held the respect and devotion of the Roman people throughout his long reign. Constantly overworking and often seriously ill, he ate sparingly, lived simply and quietly, and devoted himself to the care of his health. A womanizer in his youth, he became less so after his marriage to **Livia,** a

Name variations: Caesar Augustus; Octavian; Caius Julius Caesar Octavianus after his adoption as the son and heir of Julius Caesar. Born Caius (or Gaius) Octavianus (or Octavius) on September 23, 63 B.C.; died on August 19, A.D. 14; son of Gaius Octavius (a native of Velitrae to the north of Rome) and Atia (a niece of Julius Caesar); married: Claudia (stepdaughter of Marc Antony; divorced); married: Scribonia; married: Livia Drusilla (whose son Tiberius by a previous marriage became his heir and successor); children: (second marriage) daughter, Julia.

Contributed by R.H. Hewsen, Professor of History, Glassboro State College, Glassboro, New Jersey

and to the common people of Rome. Taking the advice of **Cicero,** Octavian took the army that Caesar had raised at his own expense and placed it at the disposal of the senate.

After Caesar's assassination, Marc Antony had been all-powerful in Rome. But the senate feared him, and, realizing that he was in danger, Antony seized public funds and headed to Cisalpine Gaul (northern Italy) with the legions at his disposal. Immediately, the senate declared him a public enemy and—with no one else to turn to—gave Octavian, still a boy, full command of the Roman Army to protect the city.

Leading his troops against Antony, Octavian defeated him at Mutina (present-day Modena) on April 21, 43 B.C., but Antony escaped to the south of Gaul (France), where he took refuge with the local governor, Lepidus, together with whom he raised a new army. Octavian, realizing that an alliance with Antony would be better than a civil war, called upon the senate to reverse its declaration of Antony as public enemy. When the senate refused, Octavian crossed the River Rubicon and marched on the capital. Upon his arrival, the senate gave way to his demands.

The Triumvirate Gains Power

Fearing civil war, the senate enacted legislation granting extraordinary powers to the three new strongmen, Octavian, Antony, and Lepidus, who thereby formed a triumvirate which was legally empowered to govern the Empire for five years. Immediately, the triumvirs launched a bloodbath to rid the capital of the "enemies of Rome." Three hundred senators and over 2,000 knights were slain (among the victims was Cicero, executed on December 7, 43 B.C.). To fight Cassius and Brutus, the surviving assassins of Julius Caesar, an army was dispatched to Macedonia, where two successful battles were fought at Philippi. After the first, Cassius committed suicide. After the second, Brutus followed suit. The murder of Julius Caesar had been avenged.

In October of 40 B.C., weary of civil war and fearing another, the triumvirs divided the Roman world between them: Octavian received Europe; Antony the East; and Lepidus the African provinces. To further deter trouble with Antony, Octavian gave his own sister Octavia as Antony's wife. But, although Antony sired children by her, the marriage remained purely political.

At this time, the admiral Sextus Pompeius was still in command of the seas around Italy. Octavian was forced to recognize him as ruler of

woman of the highest birth. Fond of ball-playing, horseback riding, and gambling, most of his time was devoted to every aspect of statecraft. As a military leader, Augustus has been characterized as a coward, and a psychosomatic cause has been postulated for his frequent illnesses on the eve of battle that prevented him from seeing action.

Born Caius Octavianus (Octavian) in 63 B.C., he was only four when his father died. First raised by his stepfather, L. Marcius Philippus, Octavian was then taken up by his mother's uncle, the famous Roman general, statesman, and dictator **Julius Caesar,** who used his influence to see his nephew appointed to the college of priests when Octavian was scarcely 17. The following year, Octavian joined Caesar on his Spanish campaign, where he displayed good sense and discretion in handling the tasks assigned him, after which he was sent to Apollonia in Epirus to complete his education. It was there, in 44 B.C., that he learned of Caesar's assassination and that Caesar's will made him son and heir. Returning to Italy, Octavian quickly assumed control of Caesar's private fortune, saw to the probate of his will, and personally attended to the distribution of his various legacies, including the monies left to Caesar's veterans

the islands of Sicily, Corsica, and Sardenia, though he was little better than a pirate and constantly interfered with the shipment of grain to Italy. Hoping to exercise some influence over Sextus, Octavian then married Scribonia, a divorcee older than himself who was the sister of Sextus's father-in-law. Scribonia provided Octavian with his only child Julia, after which he immediately divorced her. Sextus resumed his piracy. To defeat him, Octavian needed ships and thus entered into an arrangement with Antony, who needed troops for his war on Parthia. Octavian received 120 ships in return for the loan of four legions.

Wishing to retain power at the end of the designated five years (43–38 B.C.), Octavian arranged to have the triumvirate renewed for yet another five. During this time, Octavian's fleet, commanded by Marcus Agrippa, defeated Sextus Pompeius, whose piratical acts came to an end. After this brief war, some of the soldiers rebelled, demanding special bonuses, but Octavian dealt firmly with them, thereby asserting the government's control over the armed forces of the Empire. Lepidus by now had gradually lost his role in this government but would be allowed to remain as Pontifex Maximus (High Priest) until his death in 13 B.C., at which time the triumvirate would come to an end.

On January 13, 38 B.C., Octavian married Livia Drusilla, taking her from a previous husband by whom she had had a small son, and by whom she was once again pregnant. The following year, in a personal affront to Octavian, Antony married his paramour, Queen **Cleopatra** of Egypt, while still married to Octavian's sister Octavia. Antony's intention to rule with Cleopatra as joint-sovereigns over his share of the Empire soon became clear. Octavian and the senate turned against him. And a new civil war, so long avoided, was now inevitable.

In an attempt to avoid criticism, since much of his power was based on his guarantee that there would be no such war, Octavian cleverly declared war only on Egypt, whose queen was providing Antony with her navy and footing most of the bills for their grandiose dreams. This move was doubly clever on Octavian's part, for there was now an enormous psychological stake at risk for Antony's supporters who were being required, in effect, to support a foreign country at war with their beloved Rome. Granted dictatorial powers to deal with the emergency in October 31 B.C., Octavian sped to Greece with an army and a fleet. On September 2, 30 B.C., Octavian defeated Antony at the Battle of Actium, after which Antony and Cleopatra committed suicide. Egypt became a Roman province. Octavian became master of the Roman World.

Octavian Becomes Augustus

Antony's son by his first wife Fulvia and his two sons by Cleopatra were executed (as was Caesarion, Caesar's son by Cleopatra and his only child). Selene, Antony's daughter by Cleopatra, was married off to Octavian's friend King Juba II of Mauritania (Morocco). Fearing assassination if he remained dictator, Octavian renounced his extraordinary powers and proclaimed the restoration of the Republic (28 B.C.). It is doubtful, however, that he really intended to relinquish the total power he held, knowing it was necessary to keep the Empire from dissolving into another civil war that might destroy it completely. A new system had to be developed, and, over the years, step by step, Octavian crafted a dramatically new form of government. At first, he continued to hold the consulship but in 27 B.C. offered to step down, whereupon a grateful senate gave him supreme power for ten years, granted him the unprecedented title *augustus,* and decreed that the month of Sextilius should henceforth be known as "Augustus" (August), as once before it had renamed the previous month "Julius" (July) in honor of Caesar. Basing himself on the proconsular power that allowed him to continue commanding the army, Augustus, as Octavian must now be called, gradually developed what became the office of the Roman emperor, leaving the two consular posts to be held by new, younger men seeking political advancement. In 23 B.C., the senate accorded him the tribunal power for life (even though he had declined the position and the title, which were long associated with the defense of the rights of the common people and were not supposed to be held by a nobleman). In 19 B.C., the senate granted Augustus the consular power, again without the position or title, and seven years later, after the death of Lepidus, appointed him High Priest. Finally, although he refused the position of censor, Augustus acted in that capacity also, conducting a census in 8 B.C. and yet another before he died.

Though the Roman constitution was unwritten, there were certain understandings between the articulate elite of the capital and the Roman government that legitimized political power. Most important of these was the utter rejection by the Romans of the concept of a Roman king. After the overthrow in 510 B.C. of their seventh king, the semi-legendary Tarquin the Proud, the Romans maintained the fiction that the state remained a republic, even though it passed ever more frequently under the domination of individual strongmen. Julius Caesar, for example, had been assassinated by members of the senate devoted to the Republic on the mere suspicion that he wished to set himself up as king. Thus, Augustus's greatest achievement was the way in which he forever altered this constitution, placing the power in the hands of a single man without openly violating the basic understanding that the Romans were a free people, governed by the senate and never again to be subjected to the rule of a king. Not even the insanest of the "mad" emperors (**Caligula, Nero,** etc.) dared to assume the royal title, for to have done so would have ended the legitimacy of the emperor ipso facto and would have opened the way to his legal overthrow.

The emperor was not an emperor in our sense of the term (i.e., a kind of super king), but rather his position, as formulated by Augustus, embodied the sum of the powers granted to him through the various titles and offices accorded him by the senate. The emperor was—above all else—the commander in chief of the armed forces (which was the ultimate reason why no woman could aspire to the throne). He was also, however, *princeps,* "first citizen or president of the Republic." Again, he was *augustus,* "awesome," a title of religious significance which passed to Augustus's successors and signified their role as his heirs. He was also *Caesar,* the name of the family to which Julius Caesar belonged and so, in time, the heir to the first five emperors, who were all of that illustrious house. The emperor too, was *pater patriae,* "father of the fatherland," and hence the embodiment of the patriotic feelings of Republican Rome. He was *pontifex maximus,* "chief bridge-builder," the title of the High Priest of the Roman faith and so the supreme head of the state religion. Finally, as *divus,* "divinity," he was, at least potentially, in the Latin West (and actually so in the hellenized East), a divinity on earth destined to join the gods upon his earthly demise. In addition to all of this, Augustus adopted the technique, already known in the Republic, of holding the power of an office without holding the office itself.

Thus, while rejecting the title *rex,* "king," the Romans allowed the emperor to accumulate, through his various titles and by means of their theocratic political theory, far more power than any Roman king had possessed before the Republic and more than the typical Hellenistic kings of the Middle East had ever envisioned. The emperor came to possess every power imaginable save the one power possessed by a king alone: the right to be unconditionally succeeded by his flesh and blood. Though the emperor might designate his heir and even nominate his son for the position, the emperorship was never presumed to be ipso facto hereditary and this one lacuna in the imperial powers proved to be a major problem in Roman political affairs that was never fully resolved. Ultimately, no one was emperor unless he had the approval of the senate, the acclamation of the army, or the acceptance of the people—although, to be sure, the support of the one was usually sufficient to garner the support of the other two. Augustus saved the crumbling Roman Republic by transmuting it into a monarchy hidden behind a carefully maintained republican facade, but, although he arranged for his position to remain hereditary in his own extended family, this only lasted until the death of Nero 54 years after his own.

Augustus ruled, in effect, through what has been called a "discreet autocracy" backed by the army. Although he did not invent the practice of giving gifts of wine and grain to the population and regaling them with magnificent shows, under his rule these were both systematized and expanded until they became part of the government's stock in trade in dealing with the capital's population—the notorious "bread and circuses." Although the majority of Rome's upper class accepted his "dictatorial republic" without examining the implications too closely (and the grateful senate heaped him with titles), many of the old republicans remained hostile to the new order, and Augustus lived constantly in fear of sedition.

As master of Rome, Augustus lived a most unpretentious life in a modest but tastefully appointed house on the Palatine Hill that was not even new when he acquired it. To protect the emperor, he developed a private imperial army called the Praetorian Guard, loyal directly to him alone. Because of the great size of the senate, he formed around himself a smaller body of special "friends of the emperor," from among whom he selected an even smaller group to act as an advisory council. Chief among his advisors was the general and admiral Marcus Agrippa, whose aid had been indispensable in Augustus's rise to power; Augustus gave in marriage his daughter Julia to Agrippa's son Marcellus, who was the heir apparent when Augustus fell dangerously ill in 23 B.C. Second to Agrippa in influence was the plutocrat Maecenas, famed as a patron of arts and letters, who managed Augustus's affairs at Rome when the emperor was absent from the city, suppressed sedition for him, and served as his confidant, go-between and messenger on countless occasions in every conceivable affair.

A major achievement of Augustus's reign was his transformation of the equestrian order or knights, the lower level of the old upper class, into a systematically organized body from which judges, officials, and civil employees were drawn. Augustus also expanded the role of the central government in justice, gradually instituting a senatorial court and an imperial court (at the latter of which he was the judge), both of which served as supreme courts of appeal for the cases brought before them. He revived the earlier post of Prefect of the City, to manage its food supply, established a corps of urban cohorts that served as an embryonic police force, and formed a body of freedmen assisted by slaves who served as a fire brigade. Despite his own not-terribly-edifying example, he was also concerned with public morality. Believing, like many Romans, that this could be amended through legislation, he sponsored the passage of laws making adultery a criminal offence, permitting freeborn citizens to marry former slaves, and imposing penalties on unmarried persons and married couples who had no children.

Outside of Rome and Italy, Augustus engaged in a major work of consolidation. With little faith in the ability of Greeks and other easterners to govern themselves without supervision, he allowed the different provinces to continue to be administered in different ways and allowed the traditionally free cities of the East to maintain their local privileges while retaining ultimate power securely in the hands of Rome. Grateful for the peace he brought, cities and towns all over the Empire took his title augustus (and its Greek translation *sebaste*) as their names: e.g., Augusta Vindelicorum (Augsburg, Germany), Augusta Praetoria (Aosta, Italy), Caesaraugusta (Saragossa, Spain).

As emperor, he pursued a cautious foreign policy. With little inclination toward the military life, he was chary of war and, while ever mindful of Roman interests, generally shied away from anything that might warrant extensive military activity. The final conquest of Spain, however, was completed by Augustus, who uncharacteristically spent three years (27–25 B.C.) in the field there. The Danubian lands of Rhaetia, Noricum, Illyricum, and Pannonia were added to the Empire as new provinces, and the main part of the Kingdom of Judea was annexed in A.D. 6. Deliberate expansion in Germany, on the other hand, proved unsuccessful, and all attempts to extend the frontier from the Rhine to the Elbe failed. In A.D. 9, the defeat of Roman general Quinctilus Varro and the annihilation of the three legions under his command by the German chieftain Arminius (Hermann) set the northeastern Roman frontier along the Rhine for the rest of its history. To the east of the Empire lay the hellenized, and relatively weak but troublesome, Parthians. No serious threat to Rome, they could make trouble among the smaller states that acted as buffers between the two empires, and Augustus was never free of concerns in the East.

Though Augustus proudly boasted that he had found Rome a city of brick and left it a city of marble, most of the celebrated remains of ancient Rome were built either before his time or after it. While he erected numerous temples in the city and rebuilt or restored dozens of others, his most remarkable structures were the Forum of Augustus, with its temple of Mars the Avenger and its 108 statues; the Temple of Apollo on the Palatine hill, with its Greek and Latin libraries; his magnificent tomb; and the great Ara Pacis *Augusti,* "the Altar of the Augustan Peace," an open-air shrine whose magnificent friezes represent the finest Roman sculptures of the age.

Augustus Encourages Writers

Although Augustus did not hold court in the manner of later Roman emperors or Asiatic kings, he was, like his friend Maecenas, a patron of the arts. He both encouraged and subsidized many writers, thereby contributing to the establishment of his era as the Golden Age of Roman civilization. Of the great Roman men of letters who stand out in Augustus's time, Virgil, Horace, Livy, Tibullus, Propertius, and Ovid are the most remarkable. To these may be added the name of Strabo, whose description of the known world represents the summit reached by descriptive geography in antiquity. Of these writers, the poet Virgil was certainly the finest, and his masterpiece the *Aeneid,* immortalizing the origin of Rome and glorifying Roman traditions, virtues, and values, also served to glorify the achievements and vision of Emperor Augustus.

Augustus's declining years were pained, as one by one the young men of his family, whom he had hoped would succeed him, died; his daughter Julia, and her daughter the younger Julia, were both exiled because of immorality; and there were major revolts in Illyria and Judea in A.D. 6, both of which challenged the myth of the beneficial nature of the Roman Peace. The disaster in Germany occurred but three years later. Ultimately, Augustus fell back upon Livia for consolation as he began to fail. It was her son **Tiberius** by her previous marriage who became the emperor's virtual coruler after A.D. 4, and it was he who succeeded him when Augustus died at Nola after catching a chill while sailing at night in the month that still bears his name.

Emperor Augustus was one of the greatest rulers in world history—a statesman without peer, whose administrative reorganization of the Roman Empire was a work of political and legislative genius. Taking a faltering republic, which for all its faults had the genuine devotion of its best citizens, Augustus devised a method of rule that, however dictatorial, never openly trod upon the ideals and traditions that Rome held dear. Cordial and accessible, his absolute rule was conducted with careful attention to public opinion as represented by the senate, and, though he brooked no public opposition, he allowed everyone in his entourage to express their views freely. While during the early years of his rise he had sometimes been ruthless, even cruel, his 41 years as ruler revealed a different nature, and clemency, even kindness, marked his rule. In later generations, his memory was handed down as the model for all future Roman emperors but—save for the "five good emperors" of the second century— few came anywhere close to being the statesman he had been. When Augustus came to the Roman world, it was a faltering republic built on sand. He left it a mighty empire founded on rock.

SOURCES:

Augustus Caesar. *Res Gestae.* P. A. Brunt & J. M. Moore, 1967.

Suetonius. *Lives of the Twelve Caesars.* Loeb Classical Library.

FURTHER READING:

Earl, Donald. *The Age of Augustus.* Exeter Books, 1980.

Grant, Michael. *The Twelve Caesars.* Scribner, 1975.

Powell, Henry Thompson. *Rome in the Augustan Age.* University of Oklahoma Press, 1962.

Stanley Baldwin

(1867–1947)

British prime minister and dominant political leader for much of the interwar period, who led England through such crises as the General Strike of 1926 and the abdication of Edward VIII in 1936.

Always listed among the most beloved of Britain's prime ministers, Stanley Baldwin was undoubtedly one of the most skillful as well. "He was the most formidable politician I ever have known in public life," said **Winston Churchill.** Baldwin's famous lethargy was something of a mask, used to hide impulsive, emotional, and exhausting spurts of nervous energy. During periods of strain, he performed well though not easily. When he sought to address a crisis, such as the General Strike of 1926 or the Abdication Crisis of 1936, he did so with great dexterity. But when he chose to be apathetic, as he was in the wake of Hitler's rearmament, he endangered his own nation. In his periods of both strength and weakness, he possessed a sense of the popular sentiment that bordered on the uncanny.

At the peak of his power, his fellow Englishmen saw him as Mr. John Bull personified. Almost appearing to be the stereotypical Englishman, Baldwin was a stocky man, of medium height, with shaggy eyebrows and sandy hair parted in the middle. The first British prime minister to master the technique of speaking over the radio, he used his soothing voice to great effect. His tastes were

Born on August 7, 1867, at Lower Park, Bewdley, Worcestershire; died on December 14, 1947, at Astley Hall, Worcestershire; son of Alfred (an ironmaster) and Louisa (Macdonald) Baldwin; married: Lucy Ridsdale, September 1892; children: Diana, Lorna, Margot, Oliver (Labour member of Parliament; governor of the Leeward Islands), Betty, Arthur.

Contributed by Justus D. Doenecke, Professor of History, New College of the University of South Florida, Sarasota, Florida

CHRONOLOGY

1908	Elected to Parliament; seat held until his resignation in 1937
1916	Lloyd George became prime minister; Baldwin chosen as parliamentary secretary
1917	Chosen joint financial secretary to the treasury; held office until 1921
1920	Member of the Privy Council
1921	President of Board of Trade
1922	Unionists withdrew support from Lloyd George, resulting in Bonar Law as prime minister
1923	Baldwin replaced Bonar Law
1924	General election resulted in Conservative victory; second Baldwin ministry formed
1926	General Strike; Imperial Conference
1927	Trade Disputes Act passed
1929	Labour party wins election
1935	Reorganization of the cabinet; Baldwin again prime minister
1936	George V died; Edward VIII became king, then abdicated; Spanish Civil War broke out
1937	Baldwin stepped down; Neville Chamberlain became prime minister

always those of the middle class for which he spoke. Smoking his pipe, watching cricket, taking long walks in the British countryside, reading popular British authors from all periods of history, he resembled nothing so much as a sturdy countryman. His chief desires, he said, were "to read the books I want; to live a decent life; to keep pigs." But one should make no mistake, as noted by historian A. J. P. Taylor: "His simple exterior concealed a skillful political operator."

Stanley Baldwin was born at Bewdley, a quiet old town on the Severn River about 25 miles from Birmingham. His father Alfred, the descendant of Shropshire yeomen, was chairman of Baldwins, Ltd., one of Britain's great ironworks, and the Great Western Railway. His mother Louisa, a semi-invalid, was half Welsh, half Highland Scot, ancestry that, said Baldwin, created "the odd, erratic creature that is me." She was the daughter of a Methodist minister and aunt of author Rudyard Kipling. An only child, young Stanley was raised in an atmosphere of piety, frugality, and wealth. He attended Hawtrey's preparatory school, Harrow, and Trinity College, Cambridge. Though he had a love of reading that never left him, he always remained an indifferent student.

His early career, both in and out of politics, was far from spectacular. Upon graduating from Cambridge in 1885, he entered his father's iron business, where he made it his business to know personally every workman in the foundry. Never an aggressive capitalist, he once said that a man who made a quick million ought not to be in the House of Lords but in prison. In 1919, he attacked a Parliament dominated, he claimed, by "a group of hardfaced men who looked as if they had done well out of the war."

Baldwin was a resident of Wilden, where his father had built a church, school, and vicarage. "I lived in a backwater," he once reminisced. In 1906—after serving as parish and county councillor, magistrate, and justice of the peace—he ran as Conservative candidate for Parliament from Kiddermaster, a town noted for its carpet manufacture. He advocated a protective tariff while opposing home rule for Ireland, the secularization of the schools, and disestablishment of the Welsh church. He lost amid a general Liberal landslide. Yet when his father, who had a parliamentary seat from the West Division of Worcester, suddenly died in 1908, Baldwin succeeded him without opposition and held the seat for close to 30 years.

In the House of Commons, Baldwin at first attracted little attention. Between 1908 and the outbreak of World War I, he spoke only five times, the first in opposition to an eight-hour law for coal miners. Yet he was soon perceived as a man of substance. Notes biographer G. M. Young: "Patience, good humor and an unexpected readiness in answering questions are gifts to which the House of Commons always responds."

Late in 1916, when Andrew Bonar Law, a friend of the Baldwin family, entered the War Cabinet of **David Lloyd George** as chancellor of the exchequer, he took on Baldwin as his parliamentary secretary. From 1917 to 1921, Baldwin was joint financial secretary to the treasury, an onerous job involving the drafting of detailed reports on all wartime spending. In 1920, he became a privy councillor. The Great War had made its mark on the budding administrator. Baldwin had wanted to enlist but, at age 47, was too old. Appalled by the waste and misery of the conflict, he said that it only revealed "how thin is the crust of civilization on which this generation is walking."

In July 1921, Baldwin entered Lloyd George's coalition cabinet as the unobtrusive president of the Board of Trade. However, he soon found the prime minister too untrustworthy and volatile. He was seldom consulted on policy issues, even industrial ones. When in September 1922, "the Welsh wizard" sent British troops to the Dardanelles in the famous Chanak affair, Baldwin was quick to voice his opposition. He suspected Lloyd George of fomenting a Christian war against the Muslim Turks, after which the prime minister would call a general election that would ensure his power for several more years. In a famous speech at the Carlton Club given on October 19, Baldwin called upon his fellow Conservatives to leave the Lloyd George coalition (composed of Conservatives and those Liberals who had broken with former prime minister Herbert Asquith). Were the Conservatives to continue backing Lloyd George, the party would be "smashed to atoms and lost in ruins." The speech carried the Conservative party. Said American journalist John Gunther, "The lumbering tortoise tripped the bright sharp fox." Bonar Law became prime minister and Baldwin chancellor of the exchequer. During the subsequent campaign of October 1922, Lloyd George remarked that Conservative standard-bearer Bonar Law was "honest to the verge of simplicity." Baldwin retorted, "By God, that is what we are looking for."

The November elections resulted in a Conservative victory, confirming Law and Baldwin in their posts. Baldwin's major task was to settle the American debt accumulated during the war. Traveling to Washington to negotiate with American secretary of the treasury Andrew Mellon, he brought back an agreement that pledged to make payments for 62 years. Bonar Law, already furious, found his anger compounded when Baldwin publicly insulted his creditors as a bunch of midwestern "hicks," thereby making any reduction unlikely. Ultimately the cabinet confirmed Baldwin's terms.

Baldwin Named Prime Minister

When, on May 22, 1923, illness forced the resignation of Bonar Law, King George V chose Baldwin prime minister. Baldwin's main rival was the unabashed imperialist George Curzon, foreign secretary and a peer. Curzon took the decision badly, saying of Baldwin: "Not even a public figure. A man of no experience. And of the utmost insignificance." Said the *New Statesman*, "Not half the electors of Great Britain, we suppose, had ever heard his name until this week." But, writes historian Alfred F. Havighurst, "The man on the street

recognized in Baldwin one of his own kind." A colleague noted that Baldwin deliberately tried to be as little like Lloyd George as possible: "plain instead of brilliant; steady instead of restless; soberly truthful instead of romantic and imaginative; English and not Welsh." Baldwin deliberately cultivated the image of the successful gentleman farmer—pipe, baggy clothes, simplicity of taste and manner. To a nation increasingly composed of city-dwellers, he echoed the confidence of the British countryside: "I speak not as the man in the street even, but as a man in the field-path, a much simpler person steeped in tradition and impervious to new ideas."

Baldwin's short-lived government had only one achievement to its credit: a housing act fostered by Minister of Health **Neville Chamberlain.** Faced with increasing unemployment, the new prime minister saw economic salvation lying in a protective tariff. Like most steel manufacturers, he trusted in the sufficiency of the home market. Believing it dishonest to break with Britain's free trade tradition without endorsement from the populace, Baldwin dissolved the Parliament and

Stanley Baldwin liked his image of a common, gentleman farmer, one who enjoyed his baggy clothes and a good pipe.

called for a general election. However, he misjudged popular sympathy. On December 6, 1923, Conservatives experienced heavy losses, and for over seven months the Labour Party was in power.

Another election, held on October 29, 1923, resulted in a huge Conservative victory—some 227 seats in the House of Commons. Baldwin had called for a "sane, commonsense government, not carried away by revolutionary theories or harebrained schemes.... We cannot afford the luxury of academic socialists or revolutionary agitation." He again became prime minister, this time for over four years.

On paper, his cabinet had the most impressive assemblage of Tory talent in a century: Curzon as president of the council (1924–25); former prime minister Arthur Balfour in the same post (1925–29); Winston Churchill, who had just defected from the Liberal Party, as chancellor of the exchequer; F. E. Smith, the earl of Birkenhead, as secretary of state for India; Austen Chamberlain as foreign secretary; and Neville Chamberlain as minister of health.

With Baldwin's approval, in 1925 Churchill returned Britain to the gold standard, but the nation's severe unemployment remained. Despite such nostrums, the fundamental problem lay in a quite different direction: the preeminence of old export stables—coal, steel, cotton, wool, and ships—that the world no longer desired. Addressing this ailment took more talent than Baldwin—or any of his rivals—would ever possess.

Baldwin's greatest crisis came with the General Strike of May 1926. During the previous year, owners of the coal mines had announced that wages must be cut in the less profitable mines. By far the largest industry, it had long been the symbol of class struggle. A million miners protested, supported by the railroad unions, who promised to handle no coal in case of a strike. Fearing a tie-up of the entire British economy, Baldwin consented to subsidize the coal industry to preserve prevailing wages and the seven-hour day.

On March 11, 1926, a royal commission made its recommendations on the matter. Headed by Sir Herbert Samuel, the commission recommended nationalization of mining royalties and the retention of the seven-hour day, both of which the owners opposed. Yet a reduction in wages was the commission's only immediate demand. "Not a penny off the pay, not an hour on the day" was the miners' reply. Baldwin did not press for the immediate adoption of the report, but faltered instead. A procrastinator by nature, he feared the wrath of the owners and foolishly tried to frighten the miners with the prospect of unemployment. On May 1, the owners declared a lockout.

On May 4, the trade unions began to strike in support of the miners. Workers in the iron, steel, building, and railroad industries stopped work. Baldwin denounced the strike as an attempt "to set up an alternative government" and summoned British people to resist. At the same time, he sought to keep the nation as calm as possible, no easy task amid such government firebrands as Churchill. He enlisted thousands of special constables and called for volunteers to deliver food. In a broadcast to his countrymen on May 8, he said: "I am a man of peace. I am longing, and looking and praying for peace. But I will not surrender the safety and the security of the British Constitution." In private, he said, "We must wait for the strike to wear itself out." Inside of eight days the strike was broken. Although Baldwin was personally on the verge of collapse, he emerged with his prestige at its height. To many, he was the savior of his nation. Said the *Spectator:* "The British people have taken him upon their shoulder and lifted him into a position such as no Prime Minister has occupied since the days of William Pitt."

There had been no violence involved, though the embittered miners kept up their struggle before drifting back to work. Their hours were uniformly increased to seven and a half, and in some places wages were cut. Many mines, particularly in South Wales, were totally abandoned. Baldwin called the mine operators "stupid," but his own efforts at conciliation were perfunctory and brief. There was no follow-through. The general strike revealed him as calmly upholding the supremacy of the state; the coal strike showed him listless and partial to the owners. Moreover, he acquiesced in the extremist Trade Disputes and Trade Union Act of 1927, which outlawed general and sympathetic strikes, made workers' contribution to political parties optional, and forbade the unionization of new civil servants.

In foreign affairs, Baldwin reversed the more militant position of the Labour government, including the Geneva protocol that provided for the compulsory arbitration of all disputes. Spearheaded by Foreign Secretary Austen Chamberlain, Britain as a nation participated in the Locarno treaties of 1925, a series of agreements that included mutual guarantees of Germany's western borders. In 1926, the Imperial Conference was held, linking the self-governing dominions to the British crown. But here it is Curzon, not Baldwin, who deserves the greatest credit.

72

Under Baldwin's premiership, a number of measures were passed reforming local government and extending housing, though these were really Neville Chamberlain's doing. In 1928, Parliament extended the franchise to women on the same terms as men. In all of these measures, however, both foreign and domestic, Baldwin had only passing concern.

Baldwin defended his style of leadership in 1928, when—speaking at Yarmouth—he said, "It is not wise in a democracy to go too far in front of public opinion. The British people are slow to make up their minds on a new question but they are thinking and thinking hard." Little wonder the Conservative Party watchword was "Safety First!," based on a motoring campaign of the Ministry of Transport.

On May 30, 1929, with unemployment over one million, Labour returned to power. Baldwin had little ability and less desire to hurt the Labour government of **Ramsay MacDonald**. But, as leader of the Conservative Party, Baldwin took on two major press moguls. Max Aitken, Lord Beaverbrook, was an erstwhile political kingmaker and something of a political voyeur. Harold Sidney Harmsworth, Lord Rothermere, was known as the Hearst of England. Both had their pet causes. Beaverbrook stressed what he called Empire Free Trade, that is commercial preference with the British Empire; Rothermere opposed any political concessions on India and was Baldwin's bitter personal enemy as well. On March 17, 1931, in a fiery speech at London's Queen's Hall, Baldwin used the phrasing of his cousin Rudyard Kipling in attacking both publishing lords by name: "What the proprietorship of these papers is aiming at is power without responsibility, the prerogative of the harlot throughout the ages."

In 1925, Baldwin had appointed Edward Wood, Lord Irwin and later Lord Halifax, as Viceroy of India. Both in and out of office, Baldwin had backed a lenient India policy, including Irwin's pledge, made in 1929, of full dominion status. He even bucked Churchill, who resigned from the shadow cabinet over the issue. He said after one Churchill address, "I felt that if George III had been endowed with the tongue of Edmund Burke, he might have made such a speech."

In August 1931, the Labour government collapsed and its prime minister, Ramsay MacDonald, became the leader of a national coalition government. Baldwin told George V that he would gladly sacrifice "party interests for the sake of the country." He became lord president of the council, a post that could mean anything or nothing. Here he exercised great influence both over the cabinet and the Conservative Party. An election held that October confirmed the new arrangement.

At the time, the unemployment rate was 2.8 million; Wales experienced a jobless rate of 34%, Scotland 26%. Though MacDonald dominated the limelight, Baldwin was the real power. Describing his new quarters at 11 Downing Street, he said, "It was very comfortable, and I could always keep my eye on the Prime Minister." In reality, he served as MacDonald's father-confessor, though he never encroached on the prime minister's formal prerogatives. In March 1932, he helped spearhead import duties and in July and August, he presided with patience and good humor over the imperial economic conference at Ottawa. Both events marked the return to protectionism, causing Herbert Samuel and other free-trade Liberals to resign from the government.

On the question of rearmament, Baldwin appeared apathetic. His first major statement, made on November 10, 1932, was most pessimistic. He told the Commons, "The bomber will always get through," adding, "The only defense is offense, which means that you have to kill more women and children more quickly than the enemy if you want to save yourselves."

Even though Hitler became Germany's chancellor in January 1933 and soon instituted major rearmament, Baldwin expressed little concern. In July 1934, he did tell the Commons, "The old frontiers are gone. When you think of the defense of England you no longer think of the chalk cliffs of Dover; you think of the Rhine." Yet, in introducing a small measure of rearmament, he sounded no alarm. Indeed, in November 1934, he declared, "It is not the case that Germany is rapidly approaching equality with us." Only in May 1935 did he concede that his estimate of British air strength had been "completely wrong."

On June 7, 1935, the aging and infirm MacDonald stepped down, and Stanley Baldwin began his third stretch as prime minister. Within two weeks, the Anglo-German naval agreement was concluded, by which Germany agreed to construct no more than 35% of British tonnage. In August, under the prodding of Baldwin and MacDonald, Parliament passed the Government of India Act, giving that nation more self-government.

A few weeks after Baldwin took office, the results of a peace poll were released. Covering 37.9% of the electorate and conducted by the League of Nations Union, the survey indicated that the great mass of English people favored League membership, mutual reduction of armaments, prohibition of the private manufacture of munitions, and—in case of aggression—economic measures to prevent it. Of the 11.5 million polled, some 4 million voiced either indifference or opposition to military sanctions. Baldwin had originally opposed both the poll and collective security itself. Without Germany and Italy in the League and without knowledge of United States policy, he would not—he said—pledge the service of the British navy to any coercive peace measures. Once the results of the poll were announced, however, Baldwin hailed the League as the "sheet-anchor" of British policy. At the same time, he said to the Peace Society, "I give you my word that there will be no great armaments."

In the general elections of November 14, 1935, Baldwin's ministry (which continued to call itself the National Government) won a strong victory, thanks to widespread support of its foreign policy. But trouble soon came. On September 11 of that year, just before Mussolini's invasion of Ethiopia, Sir Samuel Hoare, British foreign secretary, had given a vigorous speech at Geneva in which he implied that Britain would impose sanctions on Italy. Baldwin called *Il Duce* a savage. Yet, believing that "real sanctions mean war," he endorsed penalties that excluded the vital resource of oil.

In December, Hoare and **Pierre Laval,** temporarily France's premier as well as foreign minister, sought in private to settle the Ethiopian crisis by allowing Italian dictator **Benito Mussolini** to annex two-thirds of that nation. Though Baldwin did not trust Laval, he had said to Hoare, "Keep us out of war, Sam. We are not yet ready for it." The British public was outraged, though Baldwin declared before the House of Commons: "My lips are not yet unsealed, but if these troubles were over and I could make a full case I guarantee there is not a man that would go into the lobby against us." Yet within two weeks, Baldwin forced Hoare's resignation, and there was acute danger of war in the Mediterranean. Baldwin's reputation took the sharpest plunge of his entire career, with scars from the fiasco remaining visible for most of the following year. In the end, however, Britain shrank from levying crucial oil sanctions and the crisis blew over.

Hitler Invades the Rhineland

Hitler's invasion of the Rhineland, an event that took place on March 7, 1936, placed Baldwin even more on the defensive. He confessed, with tears in his eyes, that Britain lacked the armed forces to adhere to the Locarno pact and stop German aggression. Moreover, he said, public opinion would be opposed.

In November 1936, Baldwin publicly recalled an important by-election that took place several years earlier. In East Fulham, a district in London, the Conservative candidate, who advocated strong British defenses, lost to a Labourite who accused him of preparing for war. It was hard for him to find a more clear-cut indication of Britain's desire for peace. Baldwin said in a speech that would pursue him to his dying day:

> Supposing I had gone to the country and said that Germany was rearming and that we must rearm, does anybody think that this pacific democracy would have rallied to that cry at that moment? I cannot think of anything that would have made the loss of the election from my point of view more certain.

In 1936, Baldwin belatedly but systematically instituted rearmament, though his endorsement of a hands-off policy in the Spanish Civil War simply encouraged the blatant intervention of Germany and Italy in that conflict. Domestically the economic situation had greatly improved, with unemployment much reduced.

The Prime Minister's last great crisis came in 1936, when he forced a king of England to abdicate his throne. On January 20, George V died and his eldest son Edward VIII became monarch. Edward was handsome, charming, and extremely popular. His coronation seemed a matter of course, that is until Baldwin discovered that the king sought to marry Mrs. Wallis Simpson. An American citizen, stemming from what people in her hometown of Baltimore might consider lesser gentry, Mrs. Simpson had divorced one husband and was in the process of divorcing another. By telling the new king of the negative opinion among both the British Isles and the dominions, Baldwin convinced Edward VIII to abdicate in favor of his brother George VI. "When I was a little boy in Worcestershire reading history books," he said whimsically, "I never thought I should have to interfere between a King and his Mistress." One commentator, in paying Baldwin tribute, wrote: "It was like one of the great chess games—yet only one man could have played it. If it had gone wrong, could anything have saved the monarchy?"

Aging and exhausted, suffering increasingly from asthma and deafness, on May 28, 1937, the 70-year-old Baldwin relinquished the premiership to Neville Chamberlain. Created an earl, he was seldom consulted and took no further part in politics. He died on December 14, 1947, at his home, Astley Hall, in Worcestershire.

SOURCES:

Baldwin, Arthur. *My Father: The True Story.* Allen & Unwin, 1955.

Hyde, H. Montgomery. *Baldwin: The Unexpected Prime Minister.* R. Hart-Davis, 1973.

Jenkins, Roy. *Baldwin.* Collins, 1987.

Middlemas, Keith, and John Barnes. *Baldwin: A Biography.* Macmillan, 1970.

Young, G. M. *Stanley Baldwin.* R. Hart-Davis, 1982.

Young, Kenneth. *Baldwin.* Weidenfeld & Nicolson, 1976.

FURTHER READING:

Mowat, Charles Loch. *Britain Between the Wars, 1918–1940.* University of Chicago Press, 1955.

Raymond, John, ed. *The Baldwin Age.* Eyre & Spottiswoode, 1960.

Taylor, A. J. P. *English History, 1914–1944.* Oxford University Press, 1965.

Herbert Baum

(1912–1942)
and Jewish Anti-Nazi Resistance Leaders

German Jewish resistance leader in Berlin, who in 1933 started to organize a group of mostly Jewish anti-Nazis who maintained links with all major underground groups in the German capital, strengthening the morale of a Berlin Jewish community being deported to death camps in the East.

Herbert Baum born on February 10, 1912, in Moschin/Posen, Germany; died of torture in Berlin, June 11, 1942; married: Marianne Cohn (executed at the Plötzensee penitentiary on August 18, 1942).

Jewish Anti-Nazi Resistance Leaders: Mordecai Anielewicz, Yeheskel Atlas, Marianne Baum, Edith Fraenkel, David Frankfurter, Herschel Grynszpan, Yehiel Grynszpan, Hella Hirsch, Helmut Hirsch, Marianne Joachim, Martin Kochmann, Sala Kochmann, Abba Kovner, Lotte Rotholz, Manfred Stern, and Otto Strasser.

Except for the messianic Bar Kochba uprising of A.D. 132–135, the idea of self-defense and resistance played a relatively small role in Jewish history during the almost 2,000 years that elapsed between the Roman destruction of Jerusalem in A.D. 70 and the 20th century. These political and military catastrophes, which brought on the destruction of ancient Israel as a sovereign state, led to the dispersion of the majority of the Jewish population throughout the civilized world. Powerless and unwilling to accept the religion of the Christian majority, the best they could hope for was to be protected by a tolerant king or emperor. By the end of the Middle Ages, many of Europe's Jews found themselves confined to ghettoes, a minority that was either tolerated by rulers who deemed their skills economically valuable for their states, or one that often found itself persecuted in bloody pogroms, singled out as a destructive alien presence in a Christian society.

With the French revolution of 1789 and the appearance of democratic institutions in Europe in the 19th century, ghetto walls were literally knocked down and full civil rights, particularly in Western Europe, were guaranteed to Jews and

"Let us not go as sheep to slaughter! It is true that we are weak and defenseless, but resistance is the only reply to the enemy! Brothers! It is better to fall as free fighters than to live by the grace of the murderers. Resist! To the last breath."

ABBA KOVNER
TO JEWISH PIONEER YOUTH GROUP
VILNA GHETTO (1942)

Contributed by John Haag, Associate Professor of History, University of Georgia, Athens, Georgia

other minorities. In Great Britain, France, Germany, Austria-Hungary, and other European constitutional states, Jews began to fully participate in the economic, political, and intellectual life of their nations. Many Jewish soldiers proudly served in their nations' armed forces. Discrimination against Jews remained in some countries (in Germany only Jews who converted to Christianity stood a chance of becoming university professors or officers in the armed forces), but in the first years of the 20th century it appeared that a new age of enlightenment was at hand—an era in which all remaining religious and ethnic prejudices would soon vanish.

While most Jews in Western Europe were willing to be accepted by the imperfect but improving societies in which they lived, small but influential groups of intellectuals from assimilated Jewish backgrounds rebelled against both the religious traditions of their families and the dominant capitalistic ideals of their immediate environment. These intellectuals, whether in Berlin, Vienna, or Paris, were attracted to the powerful message of **Karl Marx** and other socialist thinkers, whose books envisioned a world free from age-old scourges of poverty, exploitation, and war. Marx, too, was born into an assimilated German-Jewish family, and for radical German-Jewish intellectuals—many of whom were indifferent to Judaism as a religion and regarded themselves as culturally German—acceptance of Marxist concepts of class struggle and secular redemption meant another milestone on the road to full acceptance into the modern world.

In Eastern Europe as well, Jewish intellectuals and many of the impoverished masses saw the road to a better future in terms of socialism. Large numbers of Jews in Poland and other Eastern European nations were also attracted to Zionism, which held that only by creating a Jewish Homeland in Palestine would the sufferings of their people finally end. Both Marxist and Zionist ideologies were militant ideologies that were essentially optimistic in tone, holding that a bright new future was close at hand. Both belief systems condemned what members of both movements saw as the passivity and political indifference of traditional Jewish attitudes, which they were convinced had been the inevitable result of a totally outmoded "ghetto mentality."

The First World War led to mixed results for Europe's Jews. Toward its conclusion, in 1917, the British Government pleased Zionists by declaring itself in favor of a Jewish National Home in Palestine. In Russia, two revolutions that same year cheered Jews and radical Marxists alike by first toppling the anti-Semitic tsarist regime and

then creating the Bolshevik dictatorship led by **Vladimir Lenin,** a non-Jew, and **Leon Trotsky,** who was of assimilated Jewish background.

Meanwhile, in a briefly independent Ukraine, bloody pogroms led to the deaths of many thousands of Jews, while in newly independent Poland and defeated Hungary the Jewish minorities often suffered from harshly discriminatory legislation. In Germany, the humiliating WWI military defeat in November 1918 quickly unleashed a bitter spirit of recrimination and a search for the "subversive un-German" forces that had brought on a national catastrophe. Even though 12,000 German-Jewish soldiers had died defending the Fatherland, anti-Semitic demagogues, including an obscure Austrian living in Munich named **Adolf Hitler,** found the perfect scapegoat for Germany's woes in its Jewish minority. Hitler accused Jews of spreading the "poison" of Marxism and treasonously "stabbing Germany in the back" by engaging in profiteering and spreading defeatist and pacifistic ideas on the homefront.

In the late 1920s, the great majority of Germany's Jewish population of about 500,000 regarded themselves as solid, respected citizens of a nation that offered them the security in which they could carry on their careers and raise their children. Most thought of themselves as "German citizens of the Jewish faith" and were thoroughly assimilated to German culture and values. The May 1928 parliamentary election comforted Jews because the most rabid anti-Semites in Germany, Hitler's Nazis, made a poor showing, receiving 810,000 votes, 2.6% of the total. But even in the late 1920s some of Germany's Jews disagreed with the optimism of the assimilationist majority, whose political affiliations ranged from democratic socialism to moderate conservatism. A tiny minority of probably less than 15,000 activists regarded themselves as Zionists—but even among these only a handful of stalwart members felt equal to the hardships of emigrating to Palestine (in 1928 only 12 from Germany chose to go there).

Another minority of German Jews found themselves attracted to the powerful secular faith centered in Moscow and joined the German Communist Party (KPD). Although the great majority of Germany's Jewish population were urban middle-class professionals and unsympathetic to the ideals of a Communist revolution, some Jews (perhaps one-fifth of the total), who had been born in Poland or Russia, were not German citizens and made their livings as blue-collar wage earners, craftsmen, or peddlers. Some among this Jewish proletariat listened favorably to the KPD propaganda, which argued that neither bourgeois assimilation nor Zionism would end poverty and banish the intolerance of anti-Semitism, but that only a total economic, social, and cultural revolution, such as was being achieved in the Soviet Union, could create a world free of prejudice and discrimination. These beliefs were particularly attractive to Jewish intellectuals whose religious faith had crumbled but who still believed that all could be redeemed if only the next phase of history—the destruction of capitalism and the creation of a universal socialist society—was achieved. Indeed, one of the founders of the KPD, **Rosa Luxemburg,** who was murdered in 1919, had been born into a Polish-Jewish family.

Hitler Heads the German Reich

German Jews were as shocked as most other Germans when Adolf Hitler was appointed chancellor of the German Reich on January 30, 1933. Starting in March 1933, the rapid creation of a brutal dictatorship by Hitler and his National Socialist Party, as well as a Nazi-inspired boycott of Jewish businesses, created a mood of panic among many Jews, and about 53,000 fled Germany in 1933. But when the anti-Jewish terror was moderated somewhat, a significant number (about 16,000) returned from abroad. The organization that spoke for German Jews, the *Reichsvertretung der deutschen Juden,* counseled patience and urged its members to continue to be loyal to German authorities. The majority of the German Jewish population heeded this call. Jews loyal to either Zionist, Social Democratic, or Communist beliefs had little choice but to view the terrors of Nazism as an opportunity to test their ideals. The Zionist organizations grew rapidly, concentrating on preparing Jews, particularly the young and those with financial assets, to emigrate as quickly as possible to Palestine. Most endangered in the new Nazi state were those German Jews who before Hitler's seizure of power had been active in either the Social Democratic or Communist parties. More than any other group of German Jews in the early years of the Hitler dictatorship, these individuals suffered the most from Nazi repression.

Although the German Communists had made some efforts to prepare for the time when a Fascist dictatorship ruled Germany, when that moment actually came they were grievously unprepared. In March 1933, KPD leadership was decapitated when the leader of the party, Ernst Thälmann, was captured by the Nazis. Known to the rank-and-file as "Teddy," Thälmann would be killed at Buchenwald in 1944. While underground cells (units) started to operate almost immediately, their effectiveness varied from place to place, and by 1936 the Gestapo had been able to ferret out and destroy the great majority of such conspiratorial units. From the start of the Nazi dictatorship, Jews with socialist political beliefs were customarily treated with a brutality that far exceeded that meted out to their non-Jewish comrades. The first concentration camps, which included Dachau near Munich and Oranienburg near Berlin, were rapidly filled in the spring of 1933 by individuals whose political beliefs were anathema to the Nazis.

While Germany's Jews prayed for their situation to improve, Jews and other anti-Nazis outside of Germany worked to help those still living in Germany, as well as to weaken and possibly hasten the collapse of the Nazi regime. Social Democratic, Communist, and other political foes of Hitler set up headquarters in Paris and Prague to train agents for missions in Germany and to lobby for governmental action against the Nazis. In the United States, an anti-Nazi boycott movement began in April 1933, with the goal of applying sufficient economic pressure to force the Nazis to stop persecuting Germany's Jewish population, or perhaps even toppling the regime itself. When it became clear that Hitler would not respond to such measures, new and more dramatic methods of alerting the world to the Nazi menace appeared on the scene. On July 3, 1936, the Hungarian-born Czech Jewish journalist Stefan Lux (1888–1936) committed suicide on the crowded assembly floor of the League of Nations in Geneva. Besides his dramatic gesture, he left behind letters pleading with the world's leaders to organize a system of collective security against the threat posed by Nazi Germany, which he described as a government composed "without exception of real criminals."

Other Jewish activists believed that killing the aggressor would send a more powerful message than would killing themselves. On February 4, 1936, a Croatian-born Jewish medical student named David Frankfurter (1909–82) shot and killed Wilhelm Gustloff, leader of Switzerland's Nazi movement. After surrendering himself to the Swiss police, Frankfurter stated that his aim in killing Gustloff was to warn the world of the dangers of Nazi aggression and subversion. He was sentenced to 18 years' imprisonment. Helmut Hirsch was much less fortunate. A German-Jewish student of architecture who fled to Prague after the Nazis came to power, Hirsch vowed to prove that Jews had the courage to take up arms against Nazism. In Prague, Hirsch met Otto Strasser, a deadly foe of Hitler who believed Hirsch capable of carrying out a mission in the heart of Germany to kill the notorious anti-Semite Julius Streicher or possibly even Hitler. But the plot was poorly organized and Hirsch was arrested soon after crossing the frontier. Despite international protests, he was convicted by the Nazi People's Court and beheaded at Berlin's Plötzensee penitentiary on June 4, 1937.

Probably the most dramatic instance of world Jewish solidarity against Nazism and Fascism before World War II took place in Spain from 1936 to 1939, a time when Spain was torn apart by a bloody civil war. Supported by massive amounts of military aid from Nazi Germany and Fascist Italy, the rebel General **Francisco Franco** came close to seizing control of Spain in the final months of 1936. But the heroic defense of the city of Madrid in November and December of that year succeeded in part because of the appearance of International Brigades of volunteers who risked—and in many instances lost—their lives fighting in defense of the threatened Spanish Republic. Among the leaders of the International Brigades were many Jews, including General Manfred Stern, who founded and commanded the XI Thälmann Brigade of volunteers from Germany and Austria. At least 6,000 Jewish volunteers from over 50 countries fought in various units of the International Brigades; of these, about 500 came from German-speaking countries, most of which were by 1938 under Nazi rule.

Polish Jews Are Deported

A final and tragic act of Jewish defiance before the onset of World War II took place in 1938. In October, the Nazi regime began to deport to Poland large numbers of the almost 57,000 Polish Jews living in the Reich. The situation was compounded by the fact that Poland, whose dictatorial government was also anti-Semitic, had recently decreed that Polish citizens living abroad who had not visited Poland for five consecutive years would be deprived of their citizenship. This act of blatant discrimination meant that many of those Jews deported from Germany would not be accepted by Polish authorities. As a result, over 5,000 expelled Polish-Jewish refugees from Germany were forced in late October 1938 to live in horrible conditions in the village of Zbaszyn, in a no-man's-land just over the Polish side of the frontier. When a young man named Herschel Grynszpan (1921–1943?), who had fled Germany to Paris in 1936, learned that his parents had been deported to Zbaszyn, he vowed to make the Nazis pay for their cruelty and also to make a dramatic statement concerning Jewish rights. On November 7, 1938, Grynszpan went to the German Embassy in Paris with the intention of assassinating the ambassador; instead, he shot and killed a junior diplomat named Ernst vom Rath (ironically, vom Rath was known to be critical of Nazi policies). The diplomat's death provided the Nazis with a pretext for the bloody pogrom known as *Kristallnacht* ("Night of the Broken Glass"), which resulted in scores of Jewish deaths and immense destruction of property.

It was in this complex political and cultural environment that a small group of Berlin Jews defied the Nazi regime for almost a decade before the group was destroyed in 1942. Herbert Baum was the man largely responsible for their actions. He was born in 1912 into a poor Jewish family in the province of Posen (today Poznan in Poland), but a few years later the family moved to Berlin. There he joined Jewish youth organizations, including the German-Jewish Youth Community (DJJG) and the League of Jewish Youth (Ring). In both groups Baum quickly displayed strong qualities of leadership, but their vaguely idealistic bourgeois ideology soon seemed inadequate to him as the twin specters of Nazism and unemployment loomed on the German horizon. By 1931 he had become a member of the Communist Youth Organization and soon was regarded as a promising Communist activist. He met his wife Marianne in the Communist Youth movement and both were deeply convinced that only the creation of a Communist society would free Germany of the evils of capitalism and anti-Semitism. While most Berlin Jews quietly prayed for better times after Hitler came to power, Herbert Baum and his small circle of Communist activists openly defied the Nazis by building a complex, multitiered cell apparatus and distributing leaflets calling for an overthrow of the regime. As early as July 1934, Baum participated in a successful "action" that disseminated anti-Nazi propaganda to a Berlin populace that still included large numbers of passive anti-Nazis whose morale needed encouragement.

After the Nazi intelligence services succeeded in destroying most Communist and Social Democratic underground cells in 1936 and 1937, the Baum group remained virtually isolated in Berlin, and was ordered by the Communist leadership abroad to maintain itself as an exclusively Jewish organization in order to safeguard both itself and other still-existing resistance cells from Nazi infiltration. But while most members of the group were sympathetic to Zionist ideals, Baum and the inner circle of the organization were orthodox Communists for whom the writings of Marx, Engels, Lenin and Stalin were political wisdom incarnate. His iron devotion to the wisdom of the party's leadership even made it possible for him to accept the correctness of the Hitler-Stalin Pact of

August 1939—an event that prompted many Communists to quit the Party. Without denying his Jewish background, Baum believed that after the fall of Hitler Jews might still be able to live in a renewed German culture purged of Nazi racial hatred, and that as a German and a Communist temporarily transformed into a racial pariah he had a grave responsibility to help bring about this historical turnabout. It is significant that he never attempted to flee Germany or secure a visa in order to emigrate; although they doubtless had an idea of the fate that awaited them, the Baum group believed they had a duty to remain in Germany to hasten the pace of revolutionary change.

Baum's Group Destroys Goebbels Exhibit

By 1940, Baum, who worked as an electrician at the Siemens Electrical Motor Plant, had like most Jewish males remaining in Germany become a slave laborer (the first decree authorizing certain types of Jewish forced labor was issued as early as December 20, 1938). But the hardship of slave labor was merely a prelude to what was to follow. In September 1941, German Jews were forced to wear a Star of David on their clothing in public. Then, on October 18, the final catastrophe began. A group of 1,013 men, women, and children, the first of what would eventually be 180 Jewish transports, left Berlin for the East and death. In the midst of fear and confusion among Berlin's Jews, Baum and his circle prided themselves on their realism, fully recognizing that their actions were essentially symbolic and could not by themselves topple a regime built on terror as well as propaganda. But symbols are powerful weapons, and there is little doubt that the partial destruction by arson of the **Joseph Goebbels** propaganda exhibit ("The Soviet Paradise") in Berlin on May 18, 1942, was a significant psychological blow to the inner circles of the Nazi leadership. The German press was forbidden to publish any stories about the event, and so the German people were never officially informed that a small but well-organized resistance circle of Jewish Communists had destroyed a major Nazi propaganda show more than nine years after the Nazis came to power in Germany.

By this time, Germany's Jewish population had been reduced by emigration, suicide, and deportation to death camps from over 500,000 in 1933 to slightly over 100,000. Their mood was generally one of despair and resignation, not surprising given the fact that almost a decade of discrimination and persecution had inflicted a massive psychological toll. In the midst of this demoralization, in addition to the Baum group, there existed at least seven smaller illegal Jewish resistance organizations ready and willing to undertake acts of resistance. The growing confidence of Baum and his comrades on the eve of their exhibition attack could be seen in their ability to establish contacts with French, Belgian, and Dutch slave laborers at the Siemens plant where Baum and many of his group worked. The attack succeeded at least in part because Baum could count on the crucial support of Werner Steinbrink (1917–42) and Hildegard Jadamowitz (1916–42), two non-Jewish Communists who secured authentic documents, enabling them to pose as members of the Criminal Police (*Kripo*). A chemist, Steinbrink was able to secure incendiary materials for torching the Goebbels exhibit.

Goebbels, the regime's brilliantly unscrupulous propaganda chief, had designed the exhibition to keep the German fighting spirit at a fever pitch by documenting the evils of "Jewish Bolshevism." After major military defeats at the gates of Moscow and Leningrad in the closing months of the previous year, a new Nazi military offensive was under way on Soviet territory and the elaborate exhibition in Berlin's Lustgarten was one way to keep the homefront ideologically primed to support a war-to-the-death on the eastern front. That part of the exhibition could be destroyed by a Jewish resistance unit in the capital of the Greater German Reich proved a severe propaganda defeat for Goebbels, for even though the destruction was not reported in press or radio, virtually the entire population knew about the incendiary act within a few days. But the powerful Nazi intelligence and police system was determined to destroy men and women who, though numerically weak in numbers and resources, had been bold and resourceful enough to achieve such a significant propaganda victory.

On May 22, 1942, Herbert and Marianne Baum were arrested, as were most of the leading members of his group. Herbert Baum was tortured and taken to the Siemens plant to identify fellow workers who had joined in the arson plot, but he refused to reveal anything. On June 11, his frustrated Nazi captors murdered him (the Gestapo simply informed the trial prosecution staff that Baum had "committed suicide"). The trial of the Baum group's leaders resulted in a verdict that was a foregone conclusion—death by decapitation. The sentence was carried out on August 18 at Plötzensee penitentiary in Berlin. Executed were Marianne Baum, Joachim Franke, Hildegard Jadamowitz, Heinz Joachim, Sala Kochmann, Hans-Georg Mannaberg, Gerhard Meyer, Werner Steinbrink, and Irene Walther. Franke, Jadamowitz, Mannaberg, and Steinbrink were all non-Jewish German Communists who had cooperated with the Baum group, and whose actions were deemed equally treasonous by a Nazi court. Sala Kochmann tried to kill herself during interrogation because of the intense torture used to make her reveal information, but was only able to fracture her spine. She was carried both to the trial and to her execution on a stretcher.

The fate of other Baum group members was decided in two other trials. The first of these resulted in indictments on October 21, with sentences rendered on December 10, 1942. All but three of the defendants were sentenced to death. Executed on March 4, 1943 were, among others, Marianne Joachim and Siegbert Rotholz. Of the three who escaped death sentences, all of whom were women, Lotte Rotholz received a sentence of eight years' imprisonment but did not survive the war, having been sent to Auschwitz extermination camp. Edith Fraenkel and Hella Hirsch received sentences of five and three years respectively, but they too were killed at Auschwitz in 1944. The final trial of Baum group members took place in June 1943. By then the battle of Stalingrad had taken place, and with the Third Reich fighting for its very existence the regime, and its Nazified system of justice, decided it no longer needed to show a merciful face. All of the defendants were found guilty and condemned to death, with sentences carried out on September 7, 1943; Martin Kochmann was among those executed. Of the 31 members of the group (not counting Herbert Baum) who died during the war, 22 were executed by decapitation, while nine died in death camps.

Only five members of the Baum group, Ellen Compart, Alfred Eisenstadter, Charlotte and Richard Holzer, and Rita Resnik-Meyer (Zocher), survived the war. Their oral testimony, as well as the Nazi court documentation, provides a picture of extraordinary courage in the midst of terror and demoralization. There were other, smaller, and less effective Jewish resistance groups in Nazi Germany, who also shared the daily dangers of carrying out conspiratorial work. Because most of these groups pledged allegiance to various forms of Marxian socialism, which was already a harshly punishable offense for the German "Aryan" population, the risks they took were made all the greater. It has been estimated that about 2,000 Jewish men and women were either members of exclusively Jewish resistance groups or worked with non-Jews in various clandestine political activities in Nazi Germany during the years 1933 through 1945. This number—given that the German-Jewish community in these years had a disproportionately high number of older people and was led by an elite that hoped to adapt itself to the Nazi dictatorship through compromise and emigration—strongly suggests that a younger generation had appeared on the scene that would live, and die, not passively but resiliently in the face of adversity, courageously defying and resisting oppression.

The courage exhibited in Berlin by the Baum group would be repeated by other Jewish individuals or organizations many times during World War II in other parts of Nazi-occupied Europe. The Nazi conquest of Poland in September 1939 added a huge Jewish population of almost 2 million people to an expanded German Reich, while the conquest of France, Belgium, and the Netherlands in the spring of 1940 placed almost 600,000 more Jews under German control. While Polish Jews were often brutally treated from the very start of the occupation, Jewish communities both in Poland and in the German-occupied nations of Western Europe generally believed that their best hope for surviving was to accept the new situation as best they could, work hard at their daily tasks, and let their group interests be represented by German-approved Jewish Councils (*Judenräte*). The most radical elements within the Jewish community, the Communists, remained politically quiescent from September 1939 through June 1941 because during this period the party line was dictated by the Soviet Union's desire not to antagonize its new "friend," Nazi Germany. Consequently, during this period there was little evidence of organized resistance to Nazi rule from within Europe's Jewish communities.

Hitler's invasion of the Soviet Union, which began on June 22, 1941, radically changed the situation of Europe's Jews. This was an ideological war between two totalitarian states, and for the Nazis any restraints that had inhibited their desire for a "final solution of the Jewish question" were now swept away. Throughout the summer and fall of 1941, special mobile SS murder squads (*Einsatzgruppen*) on the eastern front killed 1,400,000 Jews. By December 1941, the killing process had become "industrialized" when the first death camp using gas vans went into operation in Chelmno in western Poland near the city of Lodz. Throughout 1942, more death camps were set up in Poland: Belzec, Sobibor, and Treblinka. The infamous extermination camp of Auschwitz (Oswiecim) near the Polish city of Cracow, which began in 1940 as a concentration camp for Poles, after June 1941 received large numbers of Soviet prisoners of war. Auschwitz was actually a system of camps: Auschwitz I contained prisoners and administrative offices; Auschwitz II (Birkenau) was the death camp and included four gas chambers, while

Auschwitz III (Monowitz) was a huge industrial slave labor camp where synthetic rubber was produced at the I.G. Farben Buna factory complex.

Because the Nazis took great pains to hide their systematic process of exterminating all Jews under their control, many Jews even in occupied Europe refused to believe that such plans were being carried out. Many continued their belief that Jews were being "resettled" in the German-occupied territories of occupied Poland and the Soviet Union, and that even Hitler would, or could, not carry out such horrendous deeds in the middle of a war when, at the very least, Jewish slave labor would prove valuable for the Nazi war effort. The various *Judenräte* continued to cooperate with the German authorities, hoping that somehow things would improve and that, while clearly many individual Jews would suffer terribly and perish, the Jewish people would survive the war and live to see the day when the Allies defeated Hitler. But by early 1942, a small but growing minority of Jews in both Eastern and Western Europe began to detect ominous signs of a new Nazi policy regarding the Jews, one of total annihilation. Though the Nazi leadership had hoped to keep their operations secret, as a few individuals escaped from death camps in 1942 young Jewish activists began calling for active resistance to the Nazis.

In occupied Polish and Soviet territory, young Zionists as well as Communists and other Jewish political factions began in December 1941 to draw up plans for armed resistance. In Vilna on January 1, 1942, Abba Kovner (1918–88) proclaimed a manifesto that called on the Jews of Lithuania to resist the Nazis and, if need be, die with pride while offering armed resistance. This was the first time that the killing of Jews by *Einsatzgruppen* was analyzed in terms of an overall master plan for the destruction of the Jewish people. Although the numbers of volunteers remained small, and virtually no weapons were on hand, on January 21, 1942, a Jewish combat unit called the United Partisan Organization was founded in Vilna. This organization remained intact and survived the end of the Vilna ghetto in the summer of 1943, fighting alongside Soviet partisans as a distinct Jewish combat unit under Kovner's command. In the Lithuanian city of Kovno (Kaunas), Jews formed resistance cells soon after the Nazis occupied the city in June 1941, but not until 1943 were Communists and Zionists able to unite to form a General Jewish Fighting Organization, which enabled 350 Jews to escape the ghetto in order to join partisan units in nearby forests and villages.

In occupied Poland, two rebellions in the Bialystok ghetto in February and August 1943 made clear that while the virtually unarmed Jews stood no chance of winning, at least here they would no longer permit the Germans to ship them to death camps without a final, bitter armed struggle. Without weapons, Jewish resistance groups almost invariably found their situation in the ghetto to be a militarily hopeless one. Only by working together with Soviet partisan units, which were often relatively well armed, did they stand a chance of effectively fighting the Germans. This was certainly true in the career of Yeheskel Atlas (1913–42), a Polish-Jewish resistance leader who had trained to be a physician. After the destruction of the Derechin ghetto in July 1942, Atlas organized a Jewish partisan unit of 120 which was subordinated to a Soviet partisan battalion. By August, Atlas's unit had attacked Derechin and killed 44 German policemen, and soon went on to launch another attack in which more than 30 Germans died. Also able to destroy a strategic bridge and blow up a train, the Atlas group played an important role in a partisan attack in October that killed 127 Germans, captured 75, and seized significant amounts of weaponry. Atlas died in action on December 5, 1942, much mourned by his fellow partisans.

From 1942 to 1944, 27 Jewish partisan units came into existence. One of the most important was commanded by Yehiel Grynszpan and consisted largely of individuals who had escaped deportation to the Sobibor death camp in 1942. Operating out of the Parczew forest near Lublin, this unit received weapons from the Polish underground as well as supplies from Soviet airdrops and grew in size from 50 to 120 while carrying on raids against German police stations and communications lines. In Yugoslavia, which had the most important partisan movement of all Nazi-occupied nations, Jewish partisans played a significant role even though Jews were a tiny minority in the country and most had been killed by the Nazis by the end of 1942. **Marshal Tito,** leader of the partisans, had many close Jewish friends and advisors, including his prewar comrade and jailmate Mosa Pijade. A total of 1,318 Yugoslavian-Jewish partisans died in battle and ten of them received the nation's highest award, the National Hero decoration. In the Slovak national uprising of 1944, Jewish partisan participation was also significant; the 1,566 Jewish partisans represented about ten percent of the total number of partisans fighting the Germans in Slovakia.

Meanwhile, Jewish prisoners were active in resistance organizations in concentration camps and even in death camps. In 1943 a resistance movement that included Jews was created at the Buchenwald concentration camp; called the International Underground Committee, it concentrated on sabotaging armaments produced at the camp. At the Treblinka death camp at least 50 prisoners spent more than six months organizing a rebellion which broke out on August 2, 1943. Though the original plan to seize the camp had to be abandoned, during the uprising virtually the entire camp went up in flames and the Nazis plowed over the ruins. Of the 700 prisoners who tried to escape, about 70 lived to see the day of liberation. Another uprising, at the Sobibor death camp on October 14, 1943, resulted in the deaths of ten SS guards and the escape of several dozen prisoners, some of whom were able to join Jewish partisan units in the area. A final death-camp rebellion took place on October 6 and 7, 1944, at Auschwitz II (Birkenau) when a special crematorium detachment of prisoners used explosives provided by female Jewish prisoners working at a nearby factory to kill several SS men and destroy one of the crematoria. In this instance all of the rebels fell in battle or were later executed.

Jews Fight Back in the Warsaw Ghetto

The most dramatic instance of Jewish resistance to the Nazis during World War II took place during the Warsaw Ghetto uprising of 1943. As soon as Warsaw, Poland, was conquered in late September 1939, harsh measures were taken against the city's Jews, but since the Polish population was also treated in a brutal fashion by their German conquerors few Jews could imagine their ultimate fate. By October 1940, all of Warsaw's Jews had been herded into a ghetto, in which an average room contained 13 people. With no jobs for over 60% of the working-age population, and a daily food allocation per capita of only 184 calories, it was clear that the Nazi plan for the ghetto's population was one of death through starvation and disease. In October 1941 the German authorities decreed that leaving the ghetto without permission was an offense punishable by death. By summer 1942, inhumane conditions in the ghetto had led to the deaths of more than 100,000 of its inhabitants. Deciding that the time had come to start liquidating the ghetto, the Germans deported about 300,000 of its residents from July 22 until September 13, 1942. The great majority of those seized were taken to Treblinka, where they were killed.

Soon after the deportations began, on July 28 a Jewish Fighting Organization (ZOB) was founded by several of the Zionist youth movements active in the ghetto. At first it was weak, virtually without weapons, and unable to establish contacts with the Polish underground, the Home Army. Able to do little to prevent the deportation of friends and relatives, it felt abandoned by the non-Jewish Polish resistance movement outside the ghetto walls. By October, however, the morale of ZOB members was boosted when more factions joined the organization, as well as by the small amounts of weapons from the Home Army that had been smuggled into the ghetto. Training for future German assaults on the ghetto now took place under the leadership of Mordecai Anielewicz (1919–43), and when the Germans resumed their policy of deportations on January 18, 1943, they were met by a small but determined Jewish resistance group. One ZOB unit broke into a column of Jews being marched to the assembly point from which they would be shipped out of the ghetto, and at an agreed-upon signal they confronted the German guards in a face-to-face battle. Although many of the ZOB were killed, the Jews scattered in all directions, and within days a change of mood had taken hold of the ghetto. Encouraged by four days of fierce street fighting—the first in occupied Poland—most Jews now felt emboldened to refuse to show up for "resettlement," hiding instead in newly built bunkers and other improvised hiding places. Frustrated in their efforts, the German authorities halted for the time being their efforts to deport Jews from the ghetto.

The temporary German retreat from the Warsaw ghetto in January 1943 buoyed Jewish spirits despite the continuing material privations. Civilians who had previously been skeptical or fearful of the idea of armed resistance now embraced it as their only hope for salvation. On April 19, 1943, the eve of Passover and the day before Hitler's 54th birthday, about 2,100 German soldiers and policemen entered the ghetto. They found its center deserted, for the entire population now accepted the resistance strategy of their underground fighters, a force of about 750 poorly armed young men and women. The resistance members were all young (only a few were over 30), had neither military training nor battle experience, and were armed with little more than pistols (they had only one machine gun). On the first day of their ghetto operation, the Nazis were forced to withdraw after having lost a tank and an armored vehicle to Molotov cocktails. The German commander, SS-Major General Jürgen Stroop, chosen by Reichsführer-SS **Heinrich Himmler** for his experience in antipartisan warfare, replaced a predecessor deemed inadequate for the task of pacifying an important urban ghetto.

For several days after April 19, bitter house-to-house fighting took place in the ghetto, frustrating the Germans because their Jewish foes usually managed to escape off the roofs of buildings and then retreat to the relative safety of their prepared bunkers. In a report of April 23 to Himmler, Stroop noted that some of the bunkers had been constructed in a "most artful" fashion and tried to explain the slow progress of his operation as a result of "the cunning ways in which the Jews and bandits behave." Changing his strategy, Stroop then ordered that the ghetto be systematically burned down building by building. This approach turned the Nazi sweep of the ghetto into a bunker war in which the Jews were forced to retreat into their deep shelters. Despite heat and lack of air, food, and water, most of the Jewish resisters survived until forced to surrender because of gas bombs. A major Nazi victory took place on May 8 when ZOB headquarters on 18 Mila Street was captured. It was here that the uprising's commander, Mordecai Anielewicz, and a large number of his staff were killed in action. On April 23 Anielewicz had written his own epitaph in a letter to a ZOB officer serving outside the ghetto:

> Peace be with you, my dear friend; perhaps we shall still meet again. The main thing is that my life's dream has been realized: I have lived to see Jewish defense in the ghetto in all its greatness and glory.

The Jews of Warsaw fought and died alone, since all attempts by the Polish underground to assist them failed, and the several air raids by the Soviet Air Force on the ghetto area were of little military significance. On May 16, 1943, Stroop reported to Himmler that the fighting had ended and that "the Jewish quarter of Warsaw no longer exists." In the same report, it was noted that 56,065 Jews had been captured or "definitely destroyed," while admitting to only 16 dead and 85 wounded on the German side. To symbolize the Nazi victory, Stroop ordered the destruction of the Great Synagogue (which was situated outside the ghetto, now largely a pile of rubble). Even after May 16 hundreds of Jews remained in what was left of their bunkers, and they would emerge at night in search of food and water. While the Germans would continue to patrol the area and capture Jews, miraculously some survived until the summer of 1944, when they participated in another Warsaw tragedy, the great Polish Warsaw uprising of August–October 1944.

The Impact of the Uprising

Despite its failure, the Warsaw ghetto uprising of April–May 1943 made a significant impact on both Jews and non-Jews. As the first example of an urban uprising in Nazi-occupied Europe, Warsaw's Jews showed how a general rebellion could hold out for weeks if the fighters had the support of a populace willing to provide places of refuge as well as moral encouragement. Objectively viewed, the uprising was of minor military significance, tying down relatively few German men and supplies, and it was doomed from the start given that the German force's firepower exceeded that of the ghetto fighters by a ratio of at least 100 to 1. But in moral and psychological terms the martyrdom of young Jewish men and women fighting to the death against the Nazis marked a turning point in modern Jewish history, announcing to the world that a revival of the ancient Hebrew tradition of armed struggle was at hand.

Jews in other parts of Nazi-occupied Europe were deeply moved when they heard about the uprising in the Warsaw ghetto. In France, many Jews joined the general Resistance Movement (15% of French Resistance membership was Jewish, even though only about 1% of France's population were Jews). A number of distinctly Jewish resistance movements appeared in France, including one calling itself the Jewish Army, which was particularly active in the southern part of the country. In Belgium, a strong Jewish resistance movement carried out many missions, including a spectacular attack in April 1943 on a train carrying Jews to Auschwitz, a successful action that enabled several hundred Jews to escape.

In free countries, Jews served as members of regular armed forces units, but in British-controlled Palestine as early as 1940 the occupying authorities permitted the formation of separate Jewish ground crews for the Royal Air Force and similar auxiliary forces. About 3,000 Jewish volunteers served in the British forces in Greece in 1941; of these, about 100 were killed in action while about 1,700 became German prisoners of war. In 1942 a Palestine Regiment was authorized, but since it included Arab as well as Jewish volunteers it proved unpopular. Not until the final stages of World War II, in September 1944, did the British create a Jewish Brigade Group, which was the only Jewish military formation in World War II to fight under the Zionist flag as its official standard. Five thousand served in this unit, which saw action on the Italian front in April 1945, sustaining about 250 casualties.

An elite group of Jewish military volunteers were those Palestinians who became parachutists and in 1944 were dropped into German-controlled territories as part of Allied intelligence and spearhead plans. From about 250 volunteers, 110 finished their training and of these 37 were dropped into enemy territory in Italy, Austria, Hungary,

Slovakia, Rumania, and Yugoslavia. Twelve of the parachutists were captured by the Nazis, and seven of these were executed. Several of the executed parachutists were women, including Hungarian-born Hannah Senesh (Szenes) and Slovak-born Haviva Reik. The full story of Jewish resistance to tyranny in World War II is a complex one, and much remains to be researched and written. Facing overwhelming odds, the members of the Jewish resistance movements in World War II could often do little more than somehow find inspiration from the words of the song of the Vilna partisans, "Oh, never say that you have reached the very end."

SOURCES:

Bauer, Yehuda. *A History of the Holocaust.* Franklin Watts, 1982.

Brothers, Eric. "On the Anti-Fascist Resistance of German Jews," in *Leo Baeck Institute Year Book.* Vol. 32. 1987: pp. 369–382.

Gutman, Israel, ed. *Encyclopedia of the Holocaust.* 4 vols. Macmillan, 1990.

The Jewish Quarter of Warsaw is No More! The Stroop Report. Pantheon, 1979.

Laska, Vera, ed. *Women in the Resistance and in the Holocaust: The Voices of Eyewitnesses.* Greenwood Press, 1983.

Marrus, Michael R., ed. *Jewish Resistance to the Holocaust,* Meckler, 1989.

Suhl, Yuri, ed. *They Fought Back: The Story of the Jewish Resistance in Nazi Europe.* Crown, 1976.

FURTHER READING:

Biale, David. *Power and Powerlessness in Jewish History.* Schocken Books, 1986.

Crome, Len. *Unbroken: Resistance and Survival in the Concentration Camps.* Schocken, 1988.

Edelheit, Abraham J., and Hershel Edelheit. *Bibliography on Holocaust Literature.* 2 vols. Westview Press, 1986, 1990.

Hoffmann, Peter. *The History of the German Resistance 1933–1945.* MIT Press, 1977.

Arno Lustiger, "German and Austrian Jews in the International Brigade," in *Leo Baeck Institute Book, Year.* Vol. 35, 1990: pp. 297–320.

Sargent, Betty. "The Desperate Mission of Stefan Lux," in *Georgia Review.* Vol. 43. No. 4. Winter, 1989: pp. 693–707.

Margaret Beaufort

(1443–1509)

Queen dowager and mother of Henry VII, who was instrumental in his rise to power during the Wars of the Roses.

Born in 1443; died in 1509; daughter of John Beaufort, Duke of Somerset; great-granddaughter of John of Gaunt, Duke of Lancaster; great-great-granddaughter of King Edward III; married: Edmund Tudor, earl of Richmond, 1455 (died 1456); married: Henry Stafford, 1461 (died 1471); married: Thomas, Lord Stanley, 1483; children: Henry Tudor (later Henry VII).

M argaret Beaufort lived during one of the most turbulent times in English history: the age of the Wars of the Roses. Two powerful families, the Yorks (symbolized by a white rose) and the Lancasters (symbolized by a red rose), were immersed in schemes, murders, and battles as they fought for the throne of England. As the great-granddaughter of John of Gaunt, Duke of Lancaster, Margaret Beaufort was part of this great struggle. But Beaufort survived the violent conflicts of the war and went on to become the matriarch of one of England's most prominent royal dynasties. Her son **Henry VII,** took the throne in 1485, becoming the first of the Tudor monarchs who would rule England until 1603.

Born in 1443, the only surviving child of John Beaufort, duke of Somerset, Margaret became a rich heiress at the age of eight upon her father's death. The Lancastrian king Henry VI bestowed wardship of the girl on his half-brother Edmund Tudor, earl of Richmond; his brother Jasper, earl of Pembroke; and a Welsh clerk of the wardrobe, Owen Tudor. The new arrangements changed the course of Margaret's future. As a small child, she had been engaged to John de la

"Of marvellous gentleness she was unto all folk, but specially unto her own, whom she loved and trusted tenderly."

JOHN FISHER,
BISHOP OF ROCHESTER

Contributed by Kimberly K. Estep, Ph.D. in History, Auburn University, Auburn, Alabama

Pole, son of the duke of Suffolk, but when informed of the change in custody arrangements, eight-year-old Margaret sought the advice of a trusted older woman who suggested she pray to St. Nicholas for guidance. Margaret stayed awake praying that very night, until "about four o'clock in the morning one appeared to her arrayed like a bishop, and naming unto her Edmund Tudor, bade her take him as her husband."

Ready to obey her heavenly visitor, Margaret agreed to the match, but the wedding was postponed until she reached the more mature age of 12 in 1455. Alas, Edmund Tudor, 13 years her senior, died in November of the following year, leaving his 13-year-old wife seven months pregnant. Margaret moved to Pembroke Castle, home of her brother-in-law Jasper, where on January 28, 1457, she gave birth to a son, Henry Tudor.

A small and sickly infant, in an age when over half of all children died before five, Henry was given little hope for survival. But the young countess of Richmond showed her son untiring care, and young Henry survived—only to face even greater danger with the changing fortunes of the Lancastrian clan in the Wars of the Roses. In 1461, Yorkist king Edward IV successfully took the throne after having the Lancastrian Henry VI imprisoned as a lunatic. Pembroke castle was confiscated and given to a Yorkist sympathizer, and Henry's wardship sold to another Yorkist, Lord Herbert of Raglan. Although it was doubtless very painful for Margaret to be separated from her five-year-old son, at least Henry's welfare was assured. Intending for Henry to marry their daughter Maud, Lord Herbert took great care to ensure his safety and education.

In 1461, Margaret married another distant cousin of royal ancestry named Henry Stafford. Whether or not she held feelings of affection for her new husband remains unknown, but as a propertied young widow, with Jasper Tudor no longer in favor, she needed a male protector. This marriage lasted until Stafford's death ten years later, but Margaret never conceived again. Henry Tudor would be her only child, and she poured out all her love, attention, and ambition on him, obsessed with securing his "glory and well-doing."

Though Henry VI briefly regained the throne in 1470, the Yorks again seized the reigns of government after the Battle of Tewkesbury in 1471, forcing the hand of disaster upon the Lancastrian line. At 15, Henry Tudor suddenly became the only surviving male of the House of Lancaster, "the only imp now left of Henry VI's blood." Consequently, Henry's life was in great

CHRONOLOGY

1443 Henry VI succeeded to English throne; Margaret Beaufort born

1455 Married Edmund Tudor

1457 Henry Tudor born

1461 Edward IV took power; Margaret married Henry Stafford

1470–71 Henry VI briefly back in power

1471 Battle of Tewkesbury; Edward IV back on throne; Jasper and Henry Tudor fled to Brittany

1483 Edward IV died; crown seized by Richard III; Margaret married Thomas, Lord Stanley

1485 Henry Tudor returned to England; Battle of Bosworth; Henry assumed the throne as Henry VII

1509 Henry VII died; succeeded by Henry VIII; Margaret Beaufort died

danger from Yorkist plots, so his enterprising uncle Jasper spirited him out of England in June of 1471 and settled the boy in Brittany.

Margaret Works for Return of Her Son

For the next 12 years, though Margaret Beaufort did not see her beloved son, she never tired in her efforts to secure his return. At first, her attempts centered on convincing the House of York that Henry represented no real threat to their interest. But Edward IV died suddenly in 1483, before she could gain his goodwill. Edward left two young sons behind, the eldest of whom was crowned Edward V. Their uncle, Edward IV's brother Richard, was not content with his position in 13-year-old Edward V's regency, however, and seized power, imprisoning his two nephews in the Tower while declaring them illegitimate. Eventually, the two Yorkist heirs were quietly murdered, and Richard was crowned **Richard III.** After the coup, Henry Tudor became the only living rival to the English throne.

Following Richard III's usurpation, Margaret began plotting in earnest to secure the overthrow of the Yorks and the return of her son, this time to claim his right to the English Crown. She married again, this time to Thomas, Lord Stanley, the head of a powerful Yorkist family. The first obstacle Margaret faced was to convince her husband and his family to support her son in a coup against Richard, a delicate task which took her two years to accomplish. In the meantime, she set out to make an agreement with Edward IV's widow Elizabeth Woodville. After Edward's death, Elizabeth had been treated unmercifully by Richard. Along with the murder of her two sons, Richard had declared Elizabeth's marriage invalid and stripped her of her dower rights. Elizabeth and her five daughters had fled into hiding at Westminster, when Margaret approached her with an interesting offer. Through a trusted messenger, Margaret proposed to marry her son Henry to Elizabeth's eldest daughter, Elizabeth of York, in return for the queen's promise of the support from the Woodville clan in Henry's bid for power. This union of the Lancastrian heir with the Yorkist heiress would bring with it a promise for the end of the destructive family quarrel which had cost so many royal lives. Elizabeth quickly pledged her support—not only would the plan provide her an opportunity to regain her rights as Edward IV's widow, but it also promised revenge against her unscrupulous brother-in-law Richard III.

Contributing a large portion of her personal fortune to the scheme, Margaret sent messengers to canvass disaffected aristocratic families for further support; she also personally convinced the duke of Buckingham, formerly a staunch Yorkist, to back the scheme. All went well until September 1483 when Richard uncovered the plot and executed Buckingham for treason. Surprisingly, Richard dealt more leniently with Margaret; unwilling to antagonize her husband's powerful family, Richard confiscated Margaret's personal property and transferred it to her husband, warning him to keep his wife under strict observation to prevent her further plotting against the king. Less surprisingly, Lord Stanley did a rather ineffective job keeping Margaret under control. Forced to work more discreetly, she nevertheless continued her efforts on her son's behalf.

Henry Is Crowned, Marries Elizabeth of York

Finally, by the summer of 1485, all was ready for Henry Tudor's return. In August, he landed in South Wales, defeating Richard's army at the Battle of Bosworth. Richard himself did not survive the battle, and Henry emerged as undisputed heir to the throne. As he was crowned Henry VII, it is recorded that his mother wept continually, overjoyed to see her son "the king crowned in all that great triumph and glory," but fearful that "in that prosperity … the greater it was, the more she dreaded adversity." Fortunately, her fears proved to be unfounded; three months later, Henry married Elizabeth of York, thus uniting two royal houses locked so long in a blood feud.

Margaret also profited materially from her son's rise in fortune. Henry VII's first Parliament conferred upon her the rights and privileges of a "sole person, not wife nor covert of any husband," allowing her personal control over her extensive properties "in as large a form as any woman now may do within the realm." As "my Lady the King's mother," she had the right to sign herself Margaret R. and in court held the place of honorary Queen Dowager. Henry also gave his mother the wardship of Edward Stafford, son of her late ally, the duke of Buckingham, whose welfare she guarded as carefully as if he were her own son. The support of the Stanleys at Bosworth having been a deciding factor in the outcome of the battle, Lord Stanley was also rewarded with the Earldom of Derby.

With her son's fortune secure, Margaret Beaufort, now countess of Richmond and Derby, retired from her active role in politics and turned her talents to overseeing the royal household. She devised a series of ordinances related to the lying-in of the queen—a crucial element in the continuation of England's peace and prosperity—and supervised the running of the royal nursery. When not making her somewhat imposing presence known at court, she occupied herself with the administration of her vast estates and the education of the young duke of Buckingham. She became renowned as a patroness of the University of Cambridge and as a great benefactor to the poor.

Next to Henry, the most important thing in Margaret's life was her faith, and her interests in charity and education sprang from deep religious convictions. A devout woman, she spent several hours a day in prayer and meditation, hearing at least four Masses a day on her knees. "My Lady the King's mother" was also known to observe fast days meticulously and even to wear a hair shirt to mortify the flesh on occasion. To ensure that the Church had a well-trained clergy, she spent lavishly on colleges and universities.

Margaret lived to see her granddaughter and namesake become queen of Scotland when the 12-year-old Margaret married the king of Scotland, James IV, in 1502. Margaret also lived long enough to see her only surviving grandson become king of England. His father Henry VII, exhausted by the arduous supervision of every detail of government, began complaining of ill-health by his mid-40s. Two great personal tragedies—the loss of his eldest son in 1502 and of his beloved wife in 1503—hastened his decline. He died six years later, in 1509, "of a consuming sickness," at the age of 52, leaving a stable and solvent throne to his 18-year-old son **Henry VIII.**

Margaret, who had remained healthy and active for 66 years, did not long survive her beloved son. Traveling to London in 1509 to see her grandson crowned, she died there in July. Her lifelong friend, John Fisher, bishop of Rochester, preached the funeral service at her Requiem Mass. He spoke movingly of her great contribution to all of England, especially to

the poor creatures that were wont to receive her alms; … the students of both the Universities, to whom she was as a mother; all the learned men of England, to whom she was a very patroness; all the virtuous and devout persons, to whom she was as a loving sister; … all the good priests and clerics, to whom she was a true defendress; all the noble men and women, to whom she was a mirror, an example of honour; all the common people of this realm, for whom she was in their causes a common mediatrix, and took right great pleasure for them.

In an age when women were excluded from virtually all roles of responsibility and leadership, Margaret Beaufort stands out as a bold and courageous personality, who used the limited means at her disposal to leave her mark on the world and to give birth to a dynasty.

SOURCES:

Levine, Mortimer. *Tudor Dynastic Problems: 1460–1571.* Allen and Unwin, 1973.

Mackie, J. D. *The Earlier Tudors: 1485–1558.* Clarendon Press, 1966.

Plowden, Alison. *Tudor Women: Queens and Commoners.* Atheneum, 1979.

St. Aubyn, Giles. *The Year of Three Kings: 1483.* Atheneum, 1983.

Thomas Becket

(1118–1170)

Chancellor and archbishop of Canterbury, who first supported then vied with the dynamic English king Henry II over the balance of power between state and Church in England.

Name variations: Thomas à Becket. Born on December 21, 1118, in London; died on December 29, 1170, in Canterbury; son of Gilbert Becket and Matilda (or Roesa) Becket. Predecessor: Theobald of Bec (1138–61). Successor: Richard of Dover (1174–84).

O f Norman ancestry, Thomas Becket was born in London, the son of Gilbert and Matilda (or Roesa) Becket. Though the family surname probably derives from the Norman place name *bec*, meaning "brook," his contemporaries and biographers called him Thomas of London.

A prosperous London citizen, Gilbert Becket may have been a merchant and seems to have held land investments. He also served for a term as sheriff of London. Thomas and his three sisters, Agnes, Roheise (or Rose), and Mary, thus grew up in comfortable circumstances. In his early years, his mother probably cared for him. She was noted for introducing him to religious devotions and encouraging him in his studies.

Although he probably began elementary education as young boy in London, Thomas started his formal schooling at age ten when his parents sent him to the boarding school at the Augustinian priory of Merton located at Surrey not far from London. His curriculum followed the traditional medieval course of grammar, rhetoric, and logic. In his teens, Thomas returned to Lon-

"Proud, forceful, stubborn, fond of good food and wine, more given to luxury and display than asceticism, he had been a thoroughgoing man of the world until his consecration as archbishop."

RICHARD WINSTON

Contributed by Karen Gould, Ph.D., Consultant in Medieval and Renaissance Manuscripts, Austin, Texas

don to complete his basic education at one of the city's grammar schools.

When Thomas Becket was around 18 years old, he journeyed to Paris to continue advanced studies. During the mid-1130s, Paris was one of the leading intellectual centers in Europe. Though the formal organization of the university was yet to come, many famous teachers such as Peter Abelard and their pupils congregated at the cathedral schools. Little information survives about Thomas's brief stay in Paris. He was not a great scholar, but his studies would have acquainted him with methods of disputation and the most current theological and philosophical issues.

Changes in his family's circumstances curtailed his schooling and brought Becket back to London when he was about 21. His mother, for whom he had great affection, had died, and his father was having financial difficulties. For a few years, Becket was associated with the household of Norman nobleman Richer de l'Aigle, and he served as a clerk to a London citizen and banker, Osbert Huitdeniers.

Becket was a handsome young man, tall with fair complexion, dark hair, and a prominent aquiline nose. He also was quite intelligent. With his talents as well as his family's associations, he was able to obtain a place in the household of Theobald, the archbishop of Canterbury. Being a clerk on his staff was a great opportunity. The archbishopric of Canterbury was the highest Church office in England and therefore had important connections with the royal court as well as the Church hierarchy in Europe. During Theobald's episcopacy, his household was filled with men of keen intellectual abilities, notably John of Salisbury.

Although no precise record of Becket's duties and activities are available, he likely served as a secretary and administrator of the archbishop's properties, and then was sent abroad for about a year to study law at Bologna in Italy and Auxerre in France. Eventually, he became a close and trusted associate of Archbishop Theobald and was promoted to archdeacon, the highest rank in the household. During this period of service, Becket thus became well acquainted with Church affairs in England and on the continent.

In 1154, Henry of Anjou became **Henry II**, king of England, through the inheritance of his mother Matilda, the daughter and only surviving heir of the English king Henry I. Though the new king was just 21, as duke of Normandy, count of Anjou, and duke of Aquitaine, he was already ruler of significant continental territories in western

CHRONOLOGY

1118	Thomas Becket born
1133	Henry of Anjou, future Henry II born
1135	Henry I died; Stephen of Blois coronated
1138	Theobald of Bec elected archbishop of Canterbury
1143	Thomas Becket entered household of Theobald
1152	Henry of Anjou married Eleanor of Aquitaine
1154	Stephen of Blois died; Henry II ascended throne
1155	Thomas Becket became chancellor of England
1159	Pope Alexander III elected
1161	Theobald, Archbishop of Canterbury, died
1162	Thomas Becket elected and consecrated as archbishop of Canterbury
1164	Council of Clarendon and Constitutions of Clarendon; Council of Northampton; Becket went into exile
1170	Henry the Young King coronated; Thomas Becket returned to Canterbury; murdered in the cathedral

France. He was also recently married to **Eleanor of Aquitaine,** one of the most remarkable and powerful women of her time. Henry II thus reigned not just over England but over the extensive Angevin Empire that extended across both sides of the English Channel.

Henry II faced a difficult task in governing England. During the 15 years of civil war between two claimants to the English throne, Stephen of Blois and Matilda of Anjou, that preceded Henry II's accession, the English barons had gained power at the expense of the centralized governmental institutions that **William the Conqueror** and Henry I had instituted. But Henry II was well equipped to restore and strengthen the prerogatives of the monarchy: he was quick, intelligent, learned, and determined. He was also temperamental and unpredictable. He needed men to serve him who were capable of matching his energy as well as securing and increasing his royal power.

Becket Serves as Chancellor

Archbishop Theobald recommended his young protégé to become Henry II's chancellor, and Becket assumed his new duties in 1155 shortly after Henry II's coronation. Although technically the office of chancellor made Becket the King's secretary as keeper of the royal seal and head of king's chapel, Becket became an influential royal official. He and the king became close associates, and Henry entrusted Becket with important advisory and administrative duties.

Thomas Becket served as chancellor of England for seven years, from 1155 to 1162. Besides the routine duties he performed, such as supervising the exchequer, overseeing vacant holdings for the king, and acting as an itinerant justice, Becket was instrumental in several important missions for King Henry II. Traveling to Paris, he arranged the marriage of Henry II's heir, the Young Henry, with Margaret of France, daughter of King Louis VII. Both the dynastic marriage alliance and Margaret's dowry of a key territory in France were significant results of Becket's diplomatic efforts. He also participated in Henry II's continental campaigns to secure the French territories of Anjou and Maine in 1156, and to support claims through Henry's wife, Eleanor of Aquitaine, to the county of Toulouse in 1159.

As chancellor, Becket's life was devoted to affairs of the royal court. He maintained a large household with a lavish lifestyle. He was often in the company of Henry II, enjoying the courtly pleasures of hunting, hawking, and entertaining with sumptuous feasts. The young Henry was entrusted to Becket to be raised and groomed for his future royal duties.

When Theobald died in 1161, Thomas Becket's life took a very different turn. For about a year, Henry II left the archbishopric of Canterbury vacant. By 1162, Henry determined that a new archbishop should be named, in part because he wanted to arrange a coronation to ensure the succession of his heir, Henry the Young King. Henry decided that Thomas Becket should become archbishop of Canterbury, and he pressured the ecclesiastical chapter at Canterbury to insure Becket's election.

Henry II undoubtedly anticipated that Thomas Becket would continue to act in the interest of the king's policies and thus bring about a cooperative union between church and state. Becket, however, took his new position seriously and devoutly. From his education in canon law and his experience as archdeacon of Canterbury, he knew that reform Church policy not only insisted that Church affairs be conducted without secular interference but also argued that the spiritual powers of the Church took precedence over the temporal powers of the state. Thus, Becket resigned his chancellorship and submitted himself to acts of penance to atone for his worldly life at the court. Most important, he began to act in the interest of the Church by enforcing revenue producing rights to property held by the archbishopric of Canterbury.

His new attitude set him on a collision course with Henry II. While Becket staunchly upheld traditional privileges of the Church, Henry II was trying to centralize his royal administration; he wanted to include the English Church in one legal, judicial, and financial system headed by the monarchy.

Conflict Arises Between the Archbishop and the King

Within a year after Becket's consecration as archbishop, he and Henry II became involved in a major dispute over the issue of "benefit of clergy." When a member of the clergy committed a crime, his trial occurred within the jurisdiction of religious courts under canon law. Henry II believed that these felons, if found guilty, should then be tried in secular courts and punished accordingly. The Church argued that such a policy put these individuals in double jeopardy and that Church law operated in a separate sphere from the secular legal system. The ensuing conflict over this issue unfolded at two levels. On the one hand, it represented the clash of two people of strong wills and beliefs, Thomas Becket and Henry II. On the other hand, it symbolized the fundamental issues of power and autonomy for Church and state.

Henry II raised the issue of jurisdiction over "criminous clerks" at the Council of Westminster in October 1163. Thomas Becket immediately perceived its threat to the Church's power; supported by most of the English bishops, he opposed Henry's proposal. In the following months, in an effort to reach a compromise, Becket modified his position slightly. However, Henry II pressed his case by insisting that the ancient customs be committed to writing. The document known as the Constitutions of Clarendon, which was drawn up at the Council of Clarendon in January 1164, embodied not only royal authority over ecclesiastics who had been convicted of secular crimes in ecclesiastical courts but also other provisions such as royal limitation on appeals of English churchmen to the papacy. Although Becket initially opposed this starkly written imposition of royal over ecclesiastical powers, he again vacillated in his position during the following months, while his relationship with Henry II continued to deteriorate. Finally, after another direct confrontation with Henry II at the Council of Northampton in October 1164, a disguised Becket fled to the continent.

Under the protection of King Louis VII of France, he remained in exile for six years. Most of the time, Becket resided at the Cistercian abbey at Pontigny where he readily adopted the austere lifestyle of the Cistercian monks. He spent much of his time studying the Bible, theology, and canon law, while he continued to argue his position through correspondence to Pope Alexander III, to other English bishops, and to Henry II. In these letters, Becket asserted his stand even more forcefully, thus making compromise more difficult.

By 1169, all parties involved in this dispute were at a point of exasperation. Pope Alexander III, who had gained a firmer political position, urged Henry to reach a settlement with Becket. Several times during 1169 personal meetings between the archbishop and the king took place in France. In each case, however, Thomas Becket and Henry II failed to find a satisfactory resolution. Becket refused to accept Henry's terms without adding the conditional phrase "saving liberty of the Church." Henry would not give the kiss of peace to symbolize their accord.

Then, on June 14, 1170, in the presence of most of the English bishops and with Roger, Archbishop of York, officiating, Henry II went ahead with the coronation ceremony at Westminster Abbey of Henry the Young King. Thomas Becket was outraged. Only the archbishop of Canterbury as primate of England had the privilege of crowning the English king. Despite this additional affront, Thomas Becket and Henry II met in July 1170 and seemed to come closer to resolving their differences. As their apparent reconciliation continued during the following months, Becket decided to return to Canterbury. He arrived in early November.

Asserting his authority as archbishop, he excommunicated all the bishops who had participated in the coronation of Henry the Young King. Then he publicly repeated these sentences of excommunication at Christmas Mass in Canterbury Cathedral. When Henry II, who was celebrating the Christmas season in Normandy, heard this news, he flew into a rage. Turning to his dinner guests, he furiously demanded, "Will no one rid me of the turbulent priest?" Four knights took him at his word. Immediately leaving Henry's court, they crossed the channel, arrived at Canterbury on the evening of December 29, 1170, and brutally murdered Thomas Becket while he was celebrating vespers in the cathedral.

Thomas Becket's influence on the English Church continued long after his death. In the matter of Church and royal policy, his martyrdom seemed in the short run to be a victory for his cause. Henry II had to perform various acts of penance. Most important, he was forced to renounce the Constitutions of Clarendon. In practical terms, however, tension eased between Henry II and the English Church. Henry was able, in gradual and subtle ways, to extend royal control over the Church in England. The destruction of Becket's shrine in 1538, soon after **Henry VIII** confirmed himself as head of the Church of England, seemed to symbolize the culminating break from the Church in Rome.

Canonized in 1173, the martyred saint inspired people from all walks of life. Through veneration of Becket, many miracles were believed to have been worked. His shrine at Canterbury became one of the most popular pilgrimage sites in Europe. Geoffrey Chaucer's masterpiece, *The Canterbury Tales,* evokes the spirit of the Canterbury pilgrims.

From an historical perspective, Thomas Becket remains a fascinating enigma. The stark contrast in behavior between his earlier life through his tenure as chancellor and his actions as archbishop of Canterbury is as puzzling in modern times as it undoubtedly was to Henry II. Some historians have judged Thomas Becket a failure because his stubbornness and inability to compromise exacerbated the conflict between Henry II and the English Church. Other historians view the contradictions in Becket's stance as evidence of his devotion to duty required of the different positions he held. Becket's life is significant because the personal drama of his situation reflected major issues raised by the emergence of national states and the role of the Church and religion in an increasingly secular world.

SOURCES:

Barlow, Frank. *Thomas Becket.* University of California Press, 1986.

Knowles, Dom David. "Archbishop Thomas Becket: A Character Study," in *The Historian and Character.* Cambridge University Press, 1963.

———. *Thomas Becket.* Stanford University Press, 1971.

Winston, Richard. *Thomas Becket.* Knopf, 1967.

FURTHER READING:

Brooke, Z. N. *The English Church and the Papacy.* Cambridge University Press, 1931.

Kelly, *Amy. Eleanor of Aquitaine and the Four Kings.* Harvard University Press, 1950.

Warren, W. L. *Henry II.* University of California Press, 1973.

Benedict of Nursia

(c. 480–c. 547)

Italian hermit and monk, who founded Monte Cassino and, with his Rule, became the most influential director of monastic life for all of the Middle Ages.

Founder of the great Italian monastery at Monte Cassino, Saint Benedict was admired as a miracle-worker in his own lifetime, yet we know little about him. Like many figures in early Christian history, he became the subject not of biographies, detailing the events of his mortal life, but of hagiographies, detailing the events of his divine life with tales destined to strike contemporary ears as ludicrously unlikely. The only summary of his life to have survived the 15 intervening centuries is Pope **Gregory the Great**'s *Dialogues*, written in 593. Though Gregory is known as a normally level-headed, shrewd man— and one of the great administrators of the early Catholic Church—on the subject of Benedict he lost his usual self-restraint, depicting a much larger-than-life individual. From this historically untrustworthy but entertaining source, from Benedict's monastic Rule, and from circumstantial surrounding evidence, we can nevertheless piece together something of Benedict's life.

Born to a wealthy family about the year 480 in the north Italian village of Nursia, Benedict was the twin of a sister who would later become a nun,

"From the seventh century onwards the Benedictines brought both Christianity and civilization to much of Europe, Cruce, libro et atro, *as the tag ran, with cross, book, and plough."*

Esther DeWaal

Contributed by Patrick Allitt, Assistant Professor of History, Emory University, Atlanta, Georgia

Saint Scholastica. According to Gregory, from Benedict's very childhood:

> He carried the heart of an old man. His demeanour indeed surpassing his age, he gave himself to no disport or pleasure, but living here upon earth he despised the world.

At 16, this sober young man traveled to Rome to undertake his formal education, but upon seeing "many of his fellow students falling headlong into vice he stepped back from the threshold of the world in which he had just set foot," and decided to devote himself to God, rather than to the world. His plan was to live reclusively in a cave, and he was helped in this project by the kindly monk Romanus who gave him a robe and fed him covertly with bread from his own meager portion. Lowering the bread down a cliffside to Benedict's isolated cave, Romanus would ring a bell to announce its arrival.

Though Satan, writes Gregory, spitefully broke the bell, he couldn't break Benedict's will. The Devil tried to distract him, first by appearing in the form of a blackbird, then by reminding Benedict of a beautiful woman he had once known. This vision and the "violent temptation" it provoked were almost too much for the hermit who, aided by a patch of nettles and briars, managed to recover his self-control by a classic early Christian maneuver:

> Throwing his garment aside he flung himself into the sharp thorns and stinging nettles. There he rolled and tossed until his whole body was in pain and covered with blood. Yet, once he had conquered pleasure through suffering, his torn and bleeding skin served to drain the poison of temptation from his body. Before long, the pain that was burning his whole body had put out the fires of evil in his heart.

So great was this victory over temptation, continues Gregory, that Benedict never again felt any sexual temptation, becoming one of many prominent figures in early Catholic history to regard sex as demonic and chastity as close to godliness.

In the third year of Benedict's hermit life, God appeared to a local priest on Easter, telling him to seek out the holy man, discuss spiritual matters, then provide him with a good dinner. A group of local shepherds later discovered the cave and, seeing Benedict dressed in wild skins, at first mistook him for a beast. Later recognizing his wisdom,

CHRONOLOGY

410	Sack of Rome
476	Collapse of Roman power in Western Europe
c. 480	Birth of Benedict
c. 528	Monastery of Monte Cassino founded: Benedict wrote the *Rule*
546	Totila the Goth captured Rome
c. 547	Traditional dating of Benedict's death
587–89	Lombard invasion and destruction of Monte Cassino
593	Pope Gregory the Great wrote *Dialogues,* including his life of Benedict
720	Monte Cassino refounded by Petronax
1943	Battle of Monte Cassino

they reformed their moral lives according to his instructions, and when a local abbot died, his monks—a group of backsliders by Gregory's account—asked Benedict to be their new leader. He came to them reluctantly and, as he had warned, proved a stern master; indeed, he was so stern that the monks tried to poison him. A miracle saved him, however, and Benedict left their monastery in disgust, returning to his hermit's cave.

Many admiring Christian men began gathering around him and, seeing that they had genuine need of his help, Benedict organized them into 12 small "monasteries" of about 12 members each. When a monk in one of these groups was not attending to his prayers, Benedict spied the Devil in the form of a black boy leading the man away from his meditations. Benedict whacked the monk on the head with his staff, after which the monk reformed. Gregory writes: "It was as if that ancient Enemy [the Devil] had been struck by the blow himself and was afraid to domineer over the monk's thoughts any longer." Not only was Benedict able to accomplish a dozen miracles, but with Benedict's blessings his noble assistant Maurus walked on water, rescuing another young monk who had fallen into the nearby lake.

After various trials and temptations, Benedict moved to Monte Cassino, a hilltop site on the main road between Rome and Naples on which stood a temple to Apollo. Destroying the icons of this pagan cult, he cut down the sacred groves around it, building instead a chapel dedicated to Saint Martin and another to John the Baptist.

According to Gregory, by preaching in the neighborhood, Benedict managed to convert the local people to Christianity while he fended off repeated attacks by the Devil who appeared—not in disguise but in his full, horrible reality—breathing fire and smoke, cursing, and trying to sabotage the monk's labors.

By about 493, the Ostrogoths under the leadership of Theodoric, one of the successive invaders to overrun the western Roman Empire, had occupied most of Italy. Though Emperor **Justinian** drove them back in the mid-sixth century, under King Totila (541–52) the Ostrogoths advanced again. While marching past Monte Cassino during one of his campaigns, Totila asked to be received by Benedict. At first, the ruler dressed up his sword-bearer Riggo in his own kingly robes to test Benedict's powers, but Benedict saw through the ruse at once. Totila was so impressed with Benedict at their meeting that he reportedly fell down prostrate in his presence. Urging him to cease his warfare, Benedict raised Totila but told him that he was "the cause of many evils," adding, "You have nine more years to rule and in the tenth year you will die." Gregory reports that from then on "Totila was less cruel"; still, he perished in the tenth year just the same.

In the last years of Benedict's life, a vision allegedly foretold of the monastery falling into barbarian hands. He confided this vision to Theoprobus, a nobleman who had joined the monastery, and added that only because of his own persuasion had God agreed to spare the monks' lives. Having also foreseen his own death, he notified his monks and, in about the year 547, died of a fever. Some monks not at his deathbed saw a glittering, carpeted road to heaven along which he was to pass. The monastery was overrun and destroyed in 589 by Duke Zotto, one of the Lombards who next overran Italy just as Benedict had foretold. Monte Cassino was not rebuilt until 720, some 130 years later.

As the late Roman Empire, headquartered at Constantinople, began losing its grip on Western Europe in the sixth century, monasticism offered an appealing sanctuary to men of Benedict's generation who were trying to escape a life of chronic warfare. Influential throughout much of Europe, the Celtic monasteries organized by the nomadic Saint Columbanus (c. 540–615) and others made fierce demands on their monks, exacting lives of heroic self-sacrifice and turning away from the hierarchical organization of pope, bishops, and priests. Moreover, their severity drew talented individuals whom the Church could otherwise have used in its search for a permanent niche in the post-Roman world of rival barbarian kingdoms.

The Development of Benedict's Rule

According to tradition, monks escaping from Monte Cassino during the Lombard invasions brought the original version of Benedict's Rule to Pope Gregory the Great (590–604); Gregory was delighted to learn of Benedict's experiments which seemed to him more temperate, more adaptable to the hierarchical church, and a sounder basis for monasticism in troubled times. This Rule, the system of life Benedict had organized for his monastery, was distinguished for both its common sense and its ability to keep monks detached from daily cares without drawing them completely away from the everyday world. Declaring the Rule "remarkable for its discretion and clarity of language," Gregory remarked that "anyone who wants to know more about his life and character can discover in his Rule exactly what he was like as abbot, for his life could not have differed from his teaching." Many early copies of the Rule have survived to the present, and it remains one of relatively few sixth-century documents that we can confidently say has come to us almost unchanged from the original. In 9,000 words, divided into a prologue and 73 chapters, Benedict deals with the aims of monastic life, how such a life shall be carried out, and how monks should understand their tasks in their self-sufficient communities.

The Celtic abbots, and the then-influential "Rule of the Master" used in some monasteries (from which Benedict took some precepts), emphasized harsh discipline and advocated that novices find and become disciples of a holy man who was above reproach or challenge. Benedict by contrast wrote extensively of the relationships *between* the monks in community, saying that they were "brothers bound in love to each other." In his Rule, writes Esther DeWaal, the abbot "is expected not to be infallible or omniscient, but a man who will exercise his discretion as the circumstances demand." Benedict had in mind small communities of about 12 monks, though as the Benedictines became a wealthy, powerful, and populous order, the Rule was later adapted to much larger groups. Scholars have speculated on the social composition of his monasteries; it seems likely that many high-born and wealthy men were attracted to him, partly because of Benedict's prestige as a miracle-worker and partly because, writes T.F. Lindsay:

> All slaves, and all members of other classes bound to the cultivation of the soil or to hereditary civic duties, found it extremely difficult to escape from their obligations and enter religious life.

While there may have been some serfs in his monasteries—since one section of the Rule deals with their admission—all the men mentioned by name in the *Dialogues* were well-born, and it seems unlikely that class distinctions were completely obliterated within the monastery's walls.

As far as we know, Benedict was never ordained into the priesthood, and his Rule makes no distinction between laymen and clergy; the assumption that a monk would also be an ordained priest did not develop until later in the Middle Ages. Regarding idleness as "the enemy of the soul," he believed that monks should have a well-structured day and be busy at all times. Among other things Benedict required them to gather in the oratory eight times each day, beginning at 2:30 A.M. for the service of Vigils, followed at intervals of a few hours by Lauds, Prime (at sunrise), Terce, Sext, Nones, Vespers, and Compline (at dusk). The other hours of the day were spent in farming or other manual work (six hours), spiritual reading (four hours), eating one big meal (no red meat allowed, but a pint of wine per man every day), and sleeping. Not intellectually rigorous, the Rule made provision for those capable of higher learning but did not insist on it, showing a steady awareness of the variation in men's abilities and inclinations. The monks were to make use of craftsmen's skills as they found them. However, as cited by Lindsay:

> If any of them be puffed up by reason of his knowledge of his craft, in that he seemeth to confer some benefit on the Monastery, let such an one be taken from it, and not exercise it again, unless, perchance, when he hath humbled himself, the Abbot bid him work at it anew.

A suitable monk would be designated *cellarer* ("domestic manager"); another, gate-porter; a third, novice-master; while one chosen for his special virtues would serve as abbot. Appointed for life, according to D. H. Turner, the abbot was supposed to be "a living example of the rule, ever mindful that on the day of judgement he would have to give account for the souls committed to him."

There were two ways to become a Benedictine: as a child, if parents gave their son to a monastery, or as an adult making the decision for himself. An adult postulant (one seeking admission) would ritually be refused admission four or five times before being admitted even to the guest house. Once admitted, the novice-master would then show him what the monastic life entailed, providing several opportunities for him to accept or reject the rigors of the Rule. Only if he stayed this course could he stand in the chapel, or oratory, and take the vows of stability, conversion of manners, and obedience.

Section five of the Rule dealt with obedience, section six with silence, and section seven with humility, but the bulk of the Rule—dealing with holy office and practical matters—steered, as Paul Johnson observed, "a middle way between severity and decency." Monks were to be

> properly and warmly clad, with two tunics and cowls each; and they were issued with a mattress, a woollen blanket, under-blanket and pillow, shoes, stockings, girdle, knife, pen, and writing tablets, needle and handkerchiefs. Otherwise no property was to be held individually ... and beds were to be searched frequently for private possessions.

Ultimately, the Rule became the basis for all Catholic monks, though this reform took several hundred years to fully institute. In 817, Louis the Pious, ruler of the Carolingian Empire, and his spiritual director Benedict of Aniane issued an edict, the "Capitula of Aachen," to all monks, which required them to follow the Rule of Saint Benedict; this ruling contributed to the Rule's spread through much of northwestern Europe. The *Regularis Concordia* of Winchester (970) had the same effect in England. By the tenth century, however, many Benedictines believed that monasticism had deviated from the ways of its founder. Certainly the intellectual, literary, artistic, and sometimes political power which the Benedictines wielded were not powers that Benedict (who had never set up any centralized authority nor thought in terms of an *order* of Benedictines) had foreseen or coveted. In consequence, successive Benedictine reform movements took place, giving rise to the Cistercian, Cluniac, and other orders of Benedictines, each of which tried to revive primitive Benedictine monasticism by emphasizing certain aspects of the Rule.

Constantly in existence since the eighth century, Benedict's monastery at Monte Cassino became the site of one of the bloodiest battles in the Second World War. A natural defensive site, it was fortified by German armies trying to prevent the Anglo-American advance toward Rome. Bombarded by artillery and aircraft, the monastery was subject to repeated infantry assaults, resulting in enormous casualty rates on both sides and the reduction of the buildings to rubble. Mercifully, the monastery was painstakingly restored to its former condition following the war. Excavations which preceded the rebuilding also brought to light what may have been the tomb of Benedict and his sister Scholastica; the human remains were placed beneath the altar in the new monastery church.

SOURCES:

Chapman, Dom John. *Saint Bernard and the Sixth Century.* Greenwood, 1971 (originally 1929).

DeWaal, Esther. *Seeking God: The Way of Saint Benedict.* Liturgical Press, 1984.

Gregory the Great, Saint. *Dialogues.* Fathers of the Church, 1959 (originally c. 594).

Lindsay, T. F. *Saint Benedict: His Life and Work.* London: Burns and Oates, 1949.

FURTHER READING:

Hilpisch, Stephanus. *Benedictinism Through the Centuries.* St. John's Abbey Press, 1958.

Johnson, Paul. *A History of Christianity.* Atheneum, 1979.

Turner, D. H., *et al. The Benedictines in Britain.* George Braziller, 1980.

Lavrenti Beria

(1899–1953)

Chief of the Soviet secret police during the dictatorship of Joseph Stalin, who made a bold but fatally unsuccessful attempt to take power over the Soviet political system following Stalin's death.

"Beria ... the very embodiment of terror and torture."

ROBERT CONQUEST

Name variations: Lavrenty. Pronunciation: Ber-EE-ah. Born Lavrenti Pavlovich Beria on March 29, 1899, in the village of Merkheuli in the Georgian region of the Russian Empire; died in Moscow sometime between late June and the end of December 1953; married in 1929; one son. Predecessor: Nikolai Ezhov. Successor: Ivan Serov.

As one of **Joseph Stalin**'s most important lieutenants, Lavrenti Beria directed the secret police apparatus of the Soviet Union, playing a crucial role in maintaining Stalin's dictatorship during the purges of the 1930s, World War II, and the years after. But when Stalin died in 1953, Beria maneuvered to seize power. Ironically, his rapid success in gaining support led to his execution by several of his competitors. Beria's death in 1953 was a final episode of violence among the men at the top of the Soviet political system.

Lavrenti Beria rose to power during a brutal era in which drastic changes took place in Russian life. Following the Russian Revolution of November 1917, **V.I. Lenin** and other Bolshevik leaders consolidated their power over most of the areas that had been ruled by the tsar. This meant restoring Russian control, based in Moscow, over regions inhabited by non-Russian nationalities. Such areas had escaped central control during the turmoil that followed the year of the Revolution. The process was completed by 1922 with the formation of the Soviet Union, a new state dominated by the Russians.

Contributed by Neil Heyman, Professor of History, San Diego State University, San Diego, California.

After Joseph Stalin rose to dictatorial power in 1929, he struck at men and women he saw as real or potential enemies. This era of purges claimed millions of victims, from Stalin's former colleagues at the top of the Party to ordinary Soviet citizens. Both the process of consolidating control over minority areas and the purges of the 1930s depended upon the institution of the secret police. This organization was founded under the name of the *Cheka* during the era of the Revolution and Civil War, and was later called the OGPU and the NKVD. To run the secret police, Stalin depended upon loyal lieutenants who were willing to use unlimited violence and brutality against their fellow Soviet citizens. Lavrenti Beria served Stalin longer than any of the dictator's secret police chiefs.

Born on March 29, 1899, the son of a Georgian peasant, Beria left his small village of Merkheuli for the nearby city of Sukhum while he was still a boy. There he lived with a merchant's family and worked in the shop to support himself while going to high school. At the age of 15, he left for the oil center of Baku where he hoped to study engineering. At the technical college at Baku, Beria was drawn into a Marxist study circle; he read Lenin's writings, participated in heated discussions over the philosophy of **Karl Marx,** and followed the great events of World War I.

Volunteering for the army in the summer of 1917, he was sent to the Rumanian front where troops were still well-disciplined, despite the turmoil and chaos affecting army units elsewhere. Perhaps Beria had been instructed by superiors in the Marxist organizations in the Caucasus to help spread unrest in the army. It is also possible that Beria had not made up his mind what political position to take, or that he was willing to defend the Provisional Government set up following the overthrow of Tsar **Nicholas II** in March.

Whichever, Beria seemed strongly inclined to Marxism by the close of 1917, and signs of the future secret policeman now appeared. The young man, only 18 years old, volunteered to become a Bolshevik spy in Georgia. That region of the Caucasus was now under the control of the Menshevik Party, a moderate Marxist group who were rivals to the Bolsheviks. Over the next several years, his activities as a spy led to his arrest, imprisonment, and expulsion from Georgia.

In 1921, Beria joined the *Cheka,* and over the next ten years, he rose rapidly. By the spring of that year, all parts of the Caucasus—Georgia, Armenia, and Azerbaijan—were under Soviet control. In 1922, they were combined into the Transcaucasian Soviet Socialist Republic. Beria was named head of the *Cheka* in Georgia that year, and he made a name for himself in crushing nationalists who opposed the newly established Soviet system there.

Looking more like a teacher or office worker than a secret police leader, Beria wore pince-nez glasses, a business suit, and a gray hat. Nonetheless, he soon came to the attention of Soviet Communist Party leader Joseph Stalin. Stalin like Beria was a native of the region near the Caucasus mountains known as Georgia, and he appreciated a subordinate who was brutal enough to bring this area under Moscow's control.

In November 1931, the dictator promoted Beria to chief of the Communist Party in Georgia. In this important post, Beria had immense opportunities to please Stalin, transforming Stalin's birthplace at Gori into a giant monument to the Soviet dictator. He rewrote the historical record of Stalin's past as a young revolutionary in the Caucasus to add luster to the dictator's reputation. When the great purges began to strike Soviet society in the middle of the 1930s, Beria carried them out with gusto in the region around the Caucasus.

Beria Rises to Power in Secret Police

In the summer of 1938, Stalin placed Beria at the center of Soviet power by making him deputy to Nikolai Yezhov, the head of the Soviet secret police. Stalin may have thought that the purges were spreading too rapidly and causing too much disruption in Soviet life. In any case, the Soviet leader had no desire to see Yezhov become too powerful. By the close of the year, Beria formally replaced Yezhov, who was imprisoned and never heard from again.

Under Beria, the vast complex of labor camps established in the 1930s was reshaped. Under Yezhov, prisoners had died in huge numbers from deliberate mistreatment. Under Beria, prison labor was still exploited brutally, but this was now done with a sense of planning. The GULAG, the great network of forced labor camps, now became a carefully run economic enterprise, not just a series of locales where "enemies of the state" were worked to death.

Beria's power expanded in visible ways. In 1938, he joined the Soviet Communist Party Central Committee. A year later, he was named a candidate (non-voting) member of the Politburo, the small policy making body at the top of the Communist Party. No other leader of the secret police had reached such high positions in the Party. When he filled Stalin's household with his own appointees from Georgia, the Soviet dictator was surrounded by people from his home region, but they were individuals assigned by Beria.

The outbreak of World War II in 1939 saw the continued growth of Beria's importance. His security troops carried out the grisly task of executing 15,000 captured Polish officers at Katyn near the city of Smolensk in 1940. When Hitler attacked the Soviet Union in 1941, Beria was placed at the center of the national war effort. Along with Stalin and three other Party leaders—**Viacheslav Molotov,** Klement Voroshilov, and **Georgi Malenkov**—he was named to the State Defense Committee, the nation's war cabinet. Beria's main task was to maintain domestic order in the Soviet Union during the war. A brutal example of his methods was the expulsion of eight minority peoples from their native lands. Groups like the Volga Germans and Crimean Tartars were moved to distant parts of the Soviet Union because Beria thought they might cooperate with the invading Nazi armies.

The higher Beria rose, the more stories spread of his personal cruelty and the abuse of his immense powers. Contemporaries like **Nikita Khrushchev** recorded tales that he enjoyed torturing and executing political prisoners with his own hands. He boasted to Khrushchev in 1939 of his ability to torture an individual into saying anything Beria desired: "Let me have him for one night, and I'll have him confessing he's the king of England." Rumors spread through Soviet society that he used his powers as head of the secret police to kidnap and rape young girls without fear of punishment.

Beria's power seemed to reach a peak in the years following World War II. Put in charge of the development of Soviet atomic weapons, he became a full member of the Communist Party Politburo. Nonetheless, his power rested on his ties to Stalin. In the years between 1945 and 1953, Stalin grew increasingly suspicious of the circle of high-ranking lieutenants around him, including Beria. He encouraged conflict among powerful figures like Beria, Andrei Zhdanov, and Malenkov. Following World War II, for example, Stalin exploded with rage at the household Beria had carefully arranged for him, demanding: "Why am I surrounded by Georgians?" The removal of all his Georgian servants was a perilous sign for Beria. At the start of 1953, there was another danger signal. When a number of high-ranking physicians, including doctors responsible for the health of top Party officials, were accused of deliberately murdering their patients, the accusation struck at Beria, since it raised questions about why this deadly "doctors' plot" had not been uncovered earlier. Stalin's death in early March 1953 ended immediate threats to his lieutenants, but the close of the dictator's life marked the start of a period of turmoil in the country. Supreme power was now something one of Stalin's lieutenants might seize. But which one?

Beria seemed in an advantageous position. He controlled the secret police with its links to all parts of Soviet society. His frontier guards and security forces provided him with a large private army. The network of forced labor camps he had set up since the 1930s played a key role in the Soviet economy. Beria perhaps thought of seizing power at once, using his security forces to take control of the capital city of Moscow right after Stalin's death. Security troops gathered near the Kremlin, but in the end Beria decided to hold back. Perhaps he thought he needed more support among the nation's key institutions in order to take power and to hold on to it.

Over the next four months, a new Beria appeared. He became a spokesman for reform in the same areas where his own policies had long been so brutal. In his speech at Stalin's funeral, for example, he mentioned the need to respect the legal rights of Soviet citizens. In another remarkable turnaround, he promoted the authority of non-Russian leaders in the minority areas of the Soviet Union.

Beria's success alarmed the other competitors for power like Malenkov and Khrushchev. His march upward stopped suddenly when they combined against him. It is still uncertain how Beria's rivals removed the secret police leader from the power struggle. He was arrested in late June, and official announcements described his trial and execution in December 1953. In versions of the story sometimes told by Khrushchev, Beria was so dangerous that his fellow Party leaders killed him with their own hands as soon as he was toppled from power in June 1953.

Beria's reputation had to be destroyed as well. When his trial and execution were officially announced in December, Soviet *Pravda* readers were told that the secret police chief had always been a traitor to the Communist Party, that his work against the Revolution had supposedly begun back in 1919, and that he had allegedly been caught at the last moment trying to end the control of the Party in order to restore capitalism.

The remaining competitors to succeed Stalin fought fiercely against one another after Beria's death. Nonetheless, losers were now deprived of their political offices, their right to live in Moscow, and the privilege of remaining in the public eye. Beria was the last to pay with his life for his failed lunge for power.

SOURCES:

McNeal, Robert H. *Stalin: Man and Ruler*. Macmillan, 1988.

Talbott, Strobe, ed. and trans. *Khrushchev Remembers*. Little, Brown, 1970.

Wittlin, Thaddeus. *Commissar: The Life and Death of Lavrenty Pavlovich Beria*. Macmillan, 1972.

FURTHER READING:

Brzezinski, *Zbigniew K. The Permanent Purge: Politics in Soviet Totalitarianism*. Harvard University Press, 1956.

Conquest, Robert. *The Nation Killers: The Soviet Deportation of Nationalities*. Macmillan, 1970.

———. *Power and Policy in the U.S.S.R.: The Study of Soviet Dynastics*. St. Martin's Press, 1962.

McNeal, Robert H. *The Bolshevik Tradition: Lenin, Stalin, Khrushchev, Brezhnev*. 2nd ed. Prentice-Hall, 1975.

Bernard
of Clairvaux

(1090–1153)

Theologian, mystic, monk, and dominant figure in the Christian history of the first half of the 12th century, under whose guidance the Cistercian order grew from one to 340 monasteries.

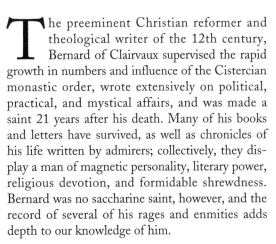

"To recount [St. Bernard's] career would be to write a history of Europe during his time."

MARSHALL BALDWIN

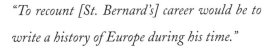he preeminent Christian reformer and theological writer of the 12th century, Bernard of Clairvaux supervised the rapid growth in numbers and influence of the Cistercian monastic order, wrote extensively on political, practical, and mystical affairs, and was made a saint 21 years after his death. Many of his books and letters have survived, as well as chronicles of his life written by admirers; collectively, they display a man of magnetic personality, literary power, religious devotion, and formidable shrewdness. Bernard was no saccharine saint, however, and the record of several of his rages and enmities adds depth to our knowledge of him.

Little is known of his youth, but like most male saints he had to overcome the "temptations of the flesh" at an early stage; his many biographers attempted to explain his methods. "On one occasion," said one of them, "he threw himself into a pond of icy water to calm the tempest of his passions after he had allowed himself to exchange admiring glances with a girl who was passing."

Bernard comes into clearer focus when we learn of his decision to join the monks of Citeaux in northeastern France. Founded about 12 years

Name variations: Saint Bernard. Born third of seven children in 1090 in Fontaines les Dijon, France; died in 1153; son of Tescelin Sor (a Dijon knight) and Aleth of Montbard. Predecessors: The saints, especially, St. Benedict, on whom he modeled his conduct. Successors: The Cistercian monks.

Contributed by Patrick Allitt, Assistant Professor of History, Emory University, Atlanta, Georgia

previously, Citeaux was located in a wilderness where its monks—the first Cistercians—had pledged themselves to renew the austere life which St. Benedict had outlined in his *Rule* (written about 527). Under the leadership of St. Stephen Harding, an Englishman who sought contemplative solitude, the abbey was deliberately sited away from other settlements.

Bernard declined the chance to go to Cluny—a more famous establishment—"because I am a thing of flesh and blood, sold unto the slavery of sin. I was conscious that my weak character needed a strong medicine." Most of the "black monks" at Cluny had long since abandoned the rigors of primitive Benedictinism and become wealthy and easygoing, especially those of noble birth. Although an expression of earlier reforms, the century-old Cluny now stood for "power, authority, centralization, law," noted Thomas Merton. "Its grandeur, the lavishness of its liturgy, the vastness of its monastic empire were the outward expression of the rule of Christ the King in His Church." One of Bernard's cousins, Robert of Chatillon, tried the austere Cistercian life for a while but then opted for Cluny instead, and one of the earliest of Bernard's surviving letters is his plea for Robert to return. "The soul is not fattened out of frying pans" Bernard warned his cousin. "Pepper, ginger, cumin, sage and all the thousand other spices may please the palate but they inflame lust. And would you make your safety depend on such things?"

Bernard's arrival at Citeaux—along with 30 male friends and relatives who had decided to share his vocation—seems to have made continua-

tion of the Cistercian experiment in organized austerity possible. Containing only 13 members when he arrived, Citeaux was on the brink of dissolution. After Bernard's novitiate, Stephen Harding sent him to found another monastery at Clairvaux on the river Aube in the Champagne country, about 70 miles away. On this new venture, he was accompanied by his brothers Gerard, Guy, and Andrew and his Uncle Gaudry. At first Clairvaux was no more than a cluster of huts with a makeshift infirmary where Bernard intermittently suffered from what one biographer describes as "chronic gastritis developing into a pyloric ulcer, accompanied by neuralgia, stomach spasms and cramps, intestinal difficulties, and asthenia." Habitually undernourished, he was sick throughout much of his life but retained a prodigious capacity for hard work.

Clairvaux itself was chronically poor in the early years, relying solely on charitable donations. Only when the nearby Bishop of Chalons-sur-Marne, William of Champeaux, took over provisioning of the community was it assured of a future. The Cistercians were able not merely to survive but to prosper; their heroic austerity won converts throughout Europe and the rapid rise of the order under Bernard's direction began. Implicitly a threat to the older Benedictines, tension between the two orders, while never absent, was alleviated by Bernard's friendship with Peter the Venerable, the abbot of Cluny.

Bernard was a gifted and prolific writer and dictated hundreds of letters to his secretaries. Many of his letters survive, as well as a dozen books, including the great *86 Sermons on the Song of Songs,* begun in 1135 and still unfinished at the time of his death. Writing the majority of these works in response to requests or orders from his superiors, who had early recognized his great intellectual and organizational gifts, he showed a talent, said biographer Jean Leclercq, for "such diverse literary genres as satire, descriptive portraits, the aphorism, the parable, the liturgical office, legends of hagiography, the epistle, the sermon, the treatise, and the biblical commentary." He was deeply learned in the Bible, paraphrased it extensively, and offered biblical illustrations to reinforce his message.

A recurrent theme in his letters and tracts was that contemplation and meditation are superior to action. Although in an imperfect world action is unavoidable, it is ultimately inferior, as it clouds man's awareness of God. Bernard believed that freedom for man consisted of perfect attunement with God, rather than absence of external restraints. Thus the outward hardships of monastic life, the suffering, the confinement, and the sensual self-restraint, all contributed not to confinement but to liberation.

Ironically, Bernard's understanding of Christian mystery, eloquently described in his letters and tracts, helped spread his reputation and prevented him from living the meditative life he described as ideal. As his fame grew, he was summoned away from Clairvaux ever more frequently to arbitrate disputes in the Church and among the secular rulers of Europe. Following a disputed papal election in 1130, for example, it was Bernard's influence which enabled one of the two rival candidates, Innocent II, to lay claim to St. Peter's throne.

The Conflict with Abélard

In 1139–40, Bernard came into conflict with Peter Abélard (1079–1142), who was probably his closest intellectual match. Abélard was already a legendary figure. As a young teacher, he had fallen in love with his pupil Heloise, niece of Canon Fulbert of Notre Dame de Paris; they had had a child and married in secret. Fulbert, learning of their affair, had hired thugs who castrated Abélard, after which Heloise was sent into a convent but kept up a correspondence with her lover on spiritual affairs. Abélard fled from Paris and became a monk of St. Denis. He then wrote *Summi Boni,* a treatise on the Holy Trinity, but saw it condemned as heresy in 1121. Despite these setbacks, his intellectual and administrative skills led him to rise to prominence yet again, first as an abbot, then once more as a teacher at the University of Paris from 1136.

In Paris, Abélard taught on questions of God, redemption, faith, sin, and grace, not heretically but at least in ways which challenged current orthodoxy. In particular, he tried to approach the mystery of the Holy Trinity—one of the most complicated subjects in the history of theology—in a rationalistic way. When Bernard, a man as intellectually conservative as Abélard was swashbuckling, learned of Abélard's teaching, he wrote a *Treatise Against the Errors of Abélard* which became part of a long, acrimonious exchange of views. "Master Abélard," said Bernard, "is a monk without a rule, a prelate without responsibility; he is neither in order nor of an Order. He argues about faith against the faith; he assails law against the law…. Raw and inexperienced listeners hardly finished with their dialectics … are introduced by him to the mystery of the Holy Trinity, to the Holy of Holies, to the chamber of the King, and to him who is shrouded in darkness." Part of Bernard's indignation may have sprung from his awareness that in Abélard "everything is put quite differently from what we have been accustomed to hear." Abélard is recognized today as one of the first scholastics, upon whose work the great medieval theologians Albertus Magnus and Thomas Aquinas built. From our vantage point it is a novelty to find scholasticism (itself now a byword for formalism) condemned by Bernard as daringly modern and unconventional.

The two men finally arranged to stage a formal dispute at a bishops' meeting in Sens, June 1140. Abélard arrived expecting to debate. But the night before, Bernard, who had come early by design, had arranged with the bishops to treat Abélard as a man accused of heresy, who was merely being given the opportunity to defend himself. Abélard took offense, refused to speak at all, and appealed Bernard's maneuver to the Pope. The malicious tone of Bernard's letters in this controversy, and his devious use of influence to get Abélard condemned before the debate began, show him at his worst, though he was to use the same methods in 1148 in another theological dispute with Gilbert de la Porrée. Defeated and discredited at Rome before he could reach it, Abélard suffered the public burning of his books and was confined for the rest of his life to the monastery of Cluny (though he is supposed to have been reconciled with Bernard before his death, two years later, in 1142).

One of the most vivid indications of the spread of Cistercian influence under Bernard is that one of their number, Bernard Paganelli, became pope in 1145, taking the name of Eugenius III. This man had lived under Bernard's instruction for ten years at Clairvaux before becoming abbot of Tre Fontane near Rome, on Bernard's recommendation. When he became pope, accordingly, Bernard gained a position of massive influence in western Christendom and he wrote to Eugenius: "Men are saying it is not you but I who am the Pope, and from all sides they are flocking to me with their suits." In a book entitled *De Consideratione ad Eugenium Papam,* he warned his old protégé of the worldly dangers he would face as pope, but showed also that he had an accurate grasp of papal responsibilities and opportunities.

Bernard Preaches the Second Crusade

During Eugenius's pontificate Bernard preached the Second Crusade. The First Crusade—50 years prior—had won early successes against Saracen armies but the crusaders' kingdom in the Holy Land was now under attack: Edessa, the crusaders' stronghold near Jerusalem, fell to the Saracen leader Zengi in 1144. King Louis VII of France wanted Bernard to inspire a new effort to reclaim the Holy Land for Latin (Catholic) Christianity. Bernard refused at first but succumbed when Louis persuaded the Pope of the plan's merits. He preached a powerful crusade sermon at Vezelay, France, on Palm Sunday 1146, and then in other parts of France and Germany. Further, in a circular letter sent to those he could not address in person, Bernard described the crusade as a form of pilgrimage, a chance granted to this generation by God to redeem themselves and make amends for their sins. Bernard said he hoped that Christians from all walks of life, including even "murderers, thieves, adulterers, perjurers," united in their zeal against the Muslims, would sweep across Europe to victory. As for the Eastern Christians of the Byzantine Empire, whose lands the crusaders would cross and whose cooperation was vital, Bernard believed that here was an opportunity for the reunification of a divided Christendom. His enthusiasm got the better of his political judgment, however, and his prospective idea of the crusade was sheer utopianism.

Crusading fervor was always an unreliable emotion in medieval Europe. One of its first fruits this time was the rabidly anti-Jewish preaching of a Cistercian monk named Rudolph (or Rasul) in Germany, a man whom Bernard denounced in disgust. "Is it not a far better triumph for the Church to convince and convert the Jews than to put them all to the sword?" asked Bernard in a letter to the archbishop of Mainz. The Jews, he said were "descendants of our fathers, to whose number belonged, according to the flesh, the Christ who is blessed for all ages."

The anti-Jewish monk was a portent of things to come. The different groups comprising the crusader army, especially the French and German contingents, were constantly at each other's throats and, as Thomas Merton aptly summarized: "The whole history of the campaign is one of treachery and murder." Disease, defeat, and starvation led to successive military catastrophes; nothing was gained. As stragglers made their way back from the Holy Land, many criticized Bernard himself for the machinery in motion.

Bernard accepted part of the blame: "I promised peace and there has been no peace. I promised good things and behold there has only been trouble. It is as if I had been rash or fickle.... Why has God ignored our fasts and turned a deaf ear to our prayers?" Comparing the crusaders' situation to that of the Children of Israel in the Old Testament, however, his first recommendation to the pope after the disaster was that the crusaders should try again, rather than accept defeat. God, he believed, having chastised them for their sins, would now grant them victory. Fortunately his advice was not followed (or at least not straightaway). Even Bernard's most sympathetic biographers have had to admit that the crusade left a stain on his reputation. Bruno James puts it this way:

> Bernard himself was quite incapable of understanding how anyone could undertake the crusade for any but the highest motive and apparently quite unaware of the danger inherent in the promiscuous recruitment of all the riff-raff of Europe.

Another aspect of Bernard's interest in crusades was his composition of a handbook for the Knights Templars, "The Praises of the New Knighthood." This order of Crusading Knights (founded in 1119) had the job of fighting for the Holy Land and policing it once it was won. "To fight in a Holy War is to become an instrument of divine justice, re-establishing the order violated by sin"; such was Bernard's assumption. The Templars would be the antithesis of secular knights, he added: "Lions in battle, they are lambs at home." Living with monastic discipline they were to obey their superior at all times and own everything in common.

> Gentle to orphans and widows, they are terrible to the proud and truculent. God has chosen these men from the strong men of the most distant parts of the earth, to serve him and to guard the most holy sepulchre of Christ.

The sordid history of the Knights was a sad deviation from Bernard's eulogy almost from the start; once again, he was indulging more in wishful thinking than political realism.

When Bernard died in 1153, miracles were reported almost at once at the site of his tomb. His intellectual influence among Christians remained immense thereafter, though most emphasized his mystical theology and doctrine on contemplation more than his role as a Christian warrior. Even among the Protestant reformers of the 16th century, he was admired. **Martin Luther** said: "Bernard surpasses all the other doctors of the Church," and **John Calvin** declared that "the Abbot Bernard speaks in the language of the truth itself." Saint Bernard of Clairvaux was made a Doctor of the Church in 1830, was the subject of Pope Pius XII's encyclical letter *Doctor Mellifluus* in 1953, and has remained one of the most closely studied and widely admired figures in Christian history.

SOURCES:

Baldwin, Marshall. *The Medieval Papacy in Action.* Macmillan, 1940.

James, Bruno. *Saint Bernard of Clairvaux.* Harper, 1957.

Leclercq, Jean. *Bernard of Clairvaux and the Cistercian Spirit.* Cistercian Publications, 1976.

Merton, Thomas. *The Last of the Fathers: Saint Bernard of Clairvaux and the Encyclical Letter, Doctor Mellifluus.* Greenwood, 1954.

Metford, J. C. *Dictionary of Christian Lore and Legend.* Thames & Hudson, 1983.

Williams, Watkin. *Saint Bernard of Clairvaux.* Manchester University Press, 1935.

FURTHER READING:

Gilson, Etienne. *The Mystical Theology of Saint Bernard.* Macmillan, 1940.

Pennington, M. Basil, ed. *Saint Bernard of Clairvaux.* Cistercian Publications, 1977.

Runciman, Steven. *A History of the Crusades.* Cambridge University Press, 1954.

Annie Besant

(1847–1933)

British radical, who used her forceful personality and outstanding talent as a speaker, journalist, and organizer on behalf of agnosticism, birth control, science, socialism, trade unionism, educational reform, theosophy, and Indian nationalism.

Pronunciation: BEZ'nt. Born Annie Wood in London, England, on October 1, 1847; died in Madras, India, on September 20, 1933; married: Frank Besant (a clergyman in the Church of England) in 1867; children: (son) Arthur Digby; (daughter) Mabel; (wards) brothers Krishnamurti and Nityananda Naryaniah.

Annie Besant had a remarkably varied career. The rapid succession of her enthusiasms prompted her biographer Arthur H. Nethercot to describe her as having nine lives, with four of her lives devoted to India. A revision of his categories to emphasize her busy middle years might identify a different nine lives: as the devoutly Christian clergyman's wife, the outspoken atheist who espoused a secular religion of humanity, the birth control crusader who seized public attention during a dramatic court trial, the student and teacher of the natural sciences, the socialist agitator, the patron of a strike by unskilled women workers, the educational reformer at the London School Board, the theosophist believer in the occult, and (overlapping with the long theosophist phase), the friend of Indian nationalism. She also supported controversial feminist reforms such as equal rights for women in marriage and divorce and voting in parliamentary elections, advocated a republican form of government in Britain, and condemned racism and imperialism.

Annie Besant was born on October 1, 1847, as Annie Wood, the daughter of a middle-class family living in London although mostly Irish in

"I was denounced as an agitator, a firebrand, and … all orthodox society turned up at me its most respectable nose."

ANNIE BESANT

Contributed by David M. Fahey, Professor of History, Miami University, Oxford, Ohio

origin. Her father, who died when she was only five, had been trained as a physician but followed a business career with moderate success. Her mother, who struggled to make a living for the family by keeping a boardinghouse for Harrow schoolboys, was happy to let Ellen Marryat, sister of the novelist, raise her young daughter for eight years (1855–63).

During this formative period, Annie Wood developed a strong commitment to evangelical Christianity that contrasted with the unconventionally liberal religious views of her parents. Her biographers agree that she remained passionately religious despite her repudiation of Christianity in her mid-20s. She acknowledged in her memoirs—Autobiographical *Sketches* (1885) and Autobiography (1893)—the attraction of quasi-religious martyrdom.

In 1867, Annie Wood married the young Church of England clergyman Frank Besant (whose brother Walter later became a popular novelist). Never a happy marriage, it broke down when Annie Besant developed doubts about Christianity. In 1873, she rejected her old faith altogether, and she and her husband agreed to a legal separation. He retained custody of their son, she of their daughter.

Champions Radical Causes

From 1873 to 1888, Annie Besant found secular outlets for her religious (and highly combative) temperament. In an age that valued public platform oratory, she stood out as a speaker before both friendly and hostile audiences. She also was an effective writer, contributing to periodicals and editing them, as well as publishing numerous pamphlets and books, often reprints of periodical articles. Championing many radical causes intended to protect civil liberties and improve the lot of ordinary working-class people, she was a courageous, hardworking woman with a flair for the dramatic, an outspoken fighter for what she considered right, always insistent on freedom of expression. Her notoriety cost her dearly. As a result of her advocacy of birth control (and rendering of methodical instructions), a judge transferred custody of her daughter to her estranged husband. Supposedly, Annie Besant was an unfit mother.

At first her approach was individualist and libertarian, later collectivist and socialist. In 1874, she joined the atheist or agnostic National Secular Society and began to write for its official journal, the *National Reformer,* often under the pen name of Ajax and served as coeditor, 1881–87. In 1877,

CHRONOLOGY

1874	Joined National Secular Society, an atheist or agnostic organization
1875	Theosophical Society founded in the United States
1877	Prosecuted (with Charles Bradlaugh) under Obscene Publications Act
1880	Bradlaugh elected to Parliament; not allowed to take his seat until 1886 because of his atheism
1885	Besant joined socialist Fabian Society
1888	Inspired strike of "match-girls" in London; elected as member of London School Board
1889	Contributed to *Fabian Essays;* converted to theosophy by Russian mystic Helena Blavatsky
1893	Visited India; later made it her permanent home
1907	Elected president of Theosophical Society
1913	Became active in Indian politics
1916–17	Exiled to a remote district in India
1917	Elected president of Indian National Congress

together with Charles Bradlaugh, she was prosecuted under the Obscene Publications Act when their Freethought Publishing Company reprinted Charles Knowlton's *Fruits of Philosophy,* a book first published in the United States in 1832, which described methods of contraception. Through her eloquent defense, Besant acquired a national reputation. Although the trial ended with a guilty verdict, a higher court reversed the decision on a technicality. Shortly after the trial, Besant published her own short book advocating the use of contraception. In 1879–83, she studied for a University of London degree in the natural sciences and delivered popular lectures on science. She never got her degree, perhaps because of the prejudice of an examiner.

Dissatisfied with her old individualistic radicalism, Besant moved toward socialism. She published articles sympathetic toward socialism in *Our Corner,* a periodical which she edited from 1883 to 1888. In 1885, she joined the Fabian Society, a moderate socialist propaganda organization. She was one of the authors of the celebrated *Fabian Essays* published four years later under George Bernard Shaw's editorship. By then, she had shifted her allegiance to a Marxist political party, the Social Democratic Federation, although she never accepted Marxism itself.

Always a defender of personal liberty, she organized the Socialist Defence Association in 1886 in support of the right to hold public meetings and parades and helped found the Law and Liberty League in 1887 after the London police suppressed the "Bloody Sunday" demonstration at Trafalgar Square. During 1887–88, she edited the League's short-lived journal, *The Link*. In 1888, one of her articles inspired a successful strike by the "match-girls" at a London factory, a dramatic early triumph of the "new unionism" of unskilled workers. The Matchmakers' Union chose her as honorary secretary.

In 1888, Besant won election to the powerful London School Board as a candidate of a local alliance called the Progressive Party. She served on the board until 1891 as the representative of the working-class East End district of Tower Hamlets. She fought successfully to provide schoolchildren with free lunches and medical inspection and employees of companies holding board contracts with trade union-scale wages.

Heads Theosophical Society

Although historians remember Annie Besant most for her secular causes—particularly her efforts on behalf of birth control—her most sustained commitment was overtly religious. In 1889, she met the central figure in theosophy, Helena Petrovna Blavatsky, a Russian mystic who died two years later. Converted in 1889, Besant became Madame Blavatsky's successor, in effect, a priestess and prophetess in the occult sect of theosophy. She lectured on theosophy in Europe, America, Australia, and India. In 1907, she became president of the Theosophical Society.

Like many other intellectuals of her time, Besant rejected both traditional Christianity and the mechanistic philosophy often identified with science; she searched instead through psychic and mystic methods for a hidden reality more profound than what the senses could perceive. Theosophy did not demand adherence to a rigid body of doctrine. For Besant, theosophy provided a connection between the individual and the cosmos, between past, present, and future. It claimed to offer assurance that justice ultimately would prevail and that progress was inevitable, as well as a reconciliation of modern science with mysterious Hindu and Buddhist lore from India and Tibet. Theosophist sages said that they had received revelations from all-wise Masters, some of them describing the numerous previous incarnations of leading members, and even reported astral travel, for instance, to Mars.

Besant's conversion to theosophy horrified old friends like Bradlaugh and Shaw. Critics denounced theosophist revelations as frauds and sneered at the quarrels and scandals that beset the Theosophical Society as well as the esoteric beliefs and ritual practices embraced by the adherents of theosophy. Even Krishnamurti, the young Indian whom Besant brought up to lead the society (and all humankind) as a kind of messiah, ultimately rejected theosophy as an organized sect. The Theosophical Society survived continuing controversy and still exists.

As a result of the Theosophical Society locating its international headquarters at Adyar, near Madras in south India, and Besant establishing her home there (and at the holy city of Benares), she became involved in another cause, India. She developed close relations with some Indian reformers. In 1898, for instance, she founded the Central Hindu College in Benares (which evolved into a university and granted her an honorary doctorate). Accepting Hindu traditions, Central Hindu College admitted only male students. Besant later organized a Central Hindu Girls' School. Her respect for the ancient Brahmanical heritage, although pleasing upper-caste Indians, frequently irritated lower-caste ones, and her assumption that Hindi should be the national language offended Tamil-speakers in Madras.

In 1913, Besant entered politics with a series of lectures published as Wake Up, India. In the following year, she started two English-language newspapers in Madras, the weekly *Commonweal* and the daily *New India*. She hoped to replace British imperial rule with Indian self-government, with the same status as Canada, a Dominion within the British Empire–Commonwealth. In 1916, she organized the All-India Home Rule League, as a supplement to the principal nationalist organization, the Indian National Congress. Worried about political unrest during the First World War, the British governor of Madras interned Besant for three months in 1917. She was exiled to a remote district. Shortly after her release, the Indian National Congress elected Besant as its president, a largely honorary position. Within a couple of years, she was eclipsed in Indian politics by a more radical leader, **Mohandas Gandhi.** In the wake of a massacre of Indian civilians ordered by a British general at Amritsar, Gandhi answered the limited concessions that the British Government offered in 1919 with massive civil disobedience campaigns. Besant believed that the British proposals provided a basis for discussion and feared that civil disobedience might lead to widespread bloodshed. Most Indian nationalists accepted Gandhi as their leader.

Although Besant continued to write, speak, and organize on behalf of home rule, she had become a marginal figure in Indian politics long before her death on September 20, 1933.

Contemporaries and biographers have pointed out that Besant's various "lives" often were intertwined with an alliance with a much-admired man. Sometimes these were romantic relationships but apparently none of them was sexually consummated. Most notably, Charles Bradlaugh, president of the National Secular Society, was her partner in arousing atheist militancy and in encouraging birth control. Probably Bradlaugh and Besant would have married, but her estranged husband would not allow a divorce. The unscrupulous Dr. Edward Aveling (later the common-law husband of **Karl Marx**'s daughter Eleanor) was involved with Besant when she was studying at the University of London for a science degree. The playwright George Bernard Shaw flirted with her during her Fabian socialist days. When she supported the more extreme Social Democratic Federation, the journalist Herbert Burrows became her companion. The newspaper editor W. T. Stead was a staunch friend during her trade union and London School Board period. The controversial C. W. Leadbeater was a close associate in theosophy. Besant was always loyal, reluctant to acknowledge the faults of her friends, even those of the notorious Leadbeater who repeatedly had been accused of immorality with young boys.

The interpretation of her complicated career as that of a woman whose enthusiasms reflected the interests of one male friend after another was dismissed by Besant as sexist. "The moment a man uses a woman's sex to discredit her arguments," she commented, "the thoughtful reader knows that he is unable to answer the arguments themselves." Although Rosemary Dinnage—who wrote Besant's most recent book-length biography—endorsed the interpretation, biographer Laura Oren argued that "all the changes [in Besant's beliefs], up to and including Theosophy as an intellectual doctrine, can be understood as part of a development." In other words, a kind of logic directed the movement. Oren points out that many of Besant's contemporaries made similar transformations, for instance, from an individualist critique of the status quo to socialism and from hostility to religion to conversion to a new religion. What made Besant's shifts from one cause to another so famous (or infamous) was her genius as a propagandist on behalf of her various crusades, her high visibility in public life after the obscenity trial of 1877, and her sex.

SOURCES:

Dinnage, Rosemary. *Annie Besant.* Penguin, 1986.

Irschick, Eugene F. *Politics and Social Conflict in South India: The Non-Brahman Movement and Tamil Separatism, 1916–1929.* University of California Press, 1969.

Nethercot, Arthur H. *The First Five Lives of Annie Besant.* University of Chicago Press. 1961.

———. *The Last Four Lives of Annie Besant.* University of Chicago Press, 1963.

Oppenheim, Janet. "The Odyssey of Annie Besant," in *History Today.* Vol. 39. September 1989, pps. 12–18.

Oren, Laura. *Biographical Dictionary of Modern British Radicals.* Edited by Joseph O. Baylen and Norman J. Gossman. Vol. 3. 1870-1914. Harvester Wheatsheaf, 1988.

Rubinstein, David. *Dictionary of Labour Biography.* Edited by Joyce M. Bellamy and John Saville. Vol. 4. Macmillan, 1977.

FURTHER READING:

Ausubel, Herman. *In Hard Times: Reformers among the Late Victorians.* Columbia University Press, 1960.

Blavatsky, Helena Petrovna. *The Secret Doctrine: the Synthesis of Science, Religion and Philosophy.* Theosophical Publishing Company, 1888 (and subsequent editions).

Campbell, Bruce F. *Ancient Wisdom Revived: A History of the Theosophical Movement.* University of California Press, 1980.

Chandrasekhar, Sripati. *"A Dirty Filthy Book": The Writings of Charles Knowlton and Annie Besant on Reproductive Physiology and Birth Control and an Account of the Bradlaugh-Besant Trial.* University of California Press, 1981.

Melton, J. Gordon, ed. *Annie Besant: The Atheist Years.* Garland, 1990.

Saville, John, ed. *A Selection of the Political and Social Pamphlets of Annie Besant 1874–1890.* Augustus M. Kelley, 1970.

Taylor, Anne. *Annie Besant.* Oxford University Press, 1992.

Otto von Bismarck

(1815–1898)

German chancellor, who provoked and won three quick wars against Denmark, Austria, and France to create the conservative imperial Germany in 1871.

Born Count Otto von Bismarck on April 1, 1815; died on July 30, 1898; son of Ferdinand (a Prussian noble) and Wilhelmine Mencken Bismarck; married: Johanna von Puttkamer in 1847; children: Maria, (1848), Herbert (1849), and Wilhelm (1851).

In 1815, the year Otto von Bismarck was born, Europe's diplomats convened at the Congress of Vienna. Led by Austria's foreign minister, **Klemens Metternich,** they were trying to put their traditional conservative world back together after years of upheaval caused by the French Revolution and Napoleonic wars. Having been subjugated by the French, Prussian advisors were attempting to restore the strength and dignity of the monarchy that **Frederick the Great** had established a half-century earlier.

Throughout Europe, the liberals were promoting nationalism and industrialization, while conservatives associated democracy with anarchy and republicanism. Eventually that ideological struggle would erupt into revolution, and the king of Prussia would be compelled by the liberals to grant his people a constitution. It would be Otto von Bismarck, however, a conservative Prussian aristocrat, who would unify Germany and spend the last 20 years of his political life trying to control his creation.

Bismarck represented the twin pillars of the Prussian state—the aristocracy and the bureaucracy. His father, an easygoing *Junker* ("Prussian

"The great issues of the day will not be settled by speeches and majority votes ... but by blood and iron."

BISMARCK

Contributed by David R. Stevenson, Professor of History, University of Nebraska-Kearney, Kearney, Nebraska

noble"), enjoyed the country life; his mother was the driving force who planned her son's future with meticulous care. Intensely ambitious and taking advantage of her family connections, Wilhelmine Mencken abruptly ended young Bismarck's early childhood on the family estates to send him to Berlin for schooling in preparation for a career in the Prussian civil service. As Bismarck would say later, his mother gave him everything but love.

After enduring the rigorous *Gymnasium* ("secondary school"), topped off by a year of university-level law training at Gottingen, the adolescent Bismarck rebelled. Drinking heavily, he engaged in many duels with sword—a practice common among university students—then left the university to return to Berlin, where he eventually passed the necessary examinations to enter the civil service. Finding the Prussian civil service more disagreeable than school, however, Bismarck quit and joined the army. When he found the army even more stultifying, he resigned from all government work and returned home.

Bismarck was ripe for change. When his mother died in 1839, the lonely Junker farmer was befriended by strict Christians of a Pomeranian Pietist sect. Not only was he introduced to doctrinally strict conservative Christian faith, but he was introduced to Johanna Puttkamer who became his wife in 1847—a 40-year union that provided emotional security and produced three children.

With religious conversion and domestic tranquillity came a renewed sense of political purpose. Leopold von Gerlach (1791–1860), an ultra-conservative Junker noble, took charge of Bismarck's political education and introduced him to the royal court of King Frederick William IV. At this time, however, the struggle between liberals and conservatives erupted into revolution. In February of 1848, the French overthrew their monarch; in March, the Austrians expelled Metternich, the architect of the Congress of Vienna; and Prussia's King Frederick William IV was compelled to grant his people a constitution. By the middle of that year, a parliament was convened in Frankfurt to unify the many states along the lines of the American republic. When the 1848 revolution threatened all Prussian conservatism, von Gerlach persuaded Bismarck to reenter government service to defend the monarchy.

Bismarck attended the Frankfurt Parliament and was dismayed by the fractious debate that he witnessed. Making his conservative opinions known in speeches and in print, he was appointed official envoy to the *Bundestag* ("Federal Diet") in 1851. Rising rapidly through the diplomatic service, he was appointed ambassador to St. Petersburg (Russia) in 1859.

CHRONOLOGY

1815	Congress of Vienna shaped Central Europe and German *Burschenshaft* movement
1840–61	Reign of Frederick William IV
1848	February revolution in France triggered European-wide revolutions; Frankfurt Parliament convened
1851	Bismarck appointed Prussian envoy to **BUNDESTAG**
1859	Appointed ambassador to St. Petersburg
1864	Provoked war over Schleswig and Holstein; Prussia and Austria defeated Denmark
1866	Defeated Austria at Sadowa
1867	Prussia created a North German Confederation
1870	France declared war with Prussia
1871	German empire created; Wilhelm I became kaiser
1872	Diplomatic alliance between Wilhelm I, Francis Joseph of Austria, and Alexander II of Russia; Bismarck initiated *Kulturkampf*
1878	Congress of Berlin
1879	Dual Alliance between Germany and Austria-Hungary
1879–80	Bismarck broke with National Liberal party
1882	Triple Alliance, Germany, Italy, and Austria-Hungary
1890	Dismissed by Wilhelm II
1891	Elected to Reichstag at 76

But the Prussian monarchy had fallen on hard times. The success of a monarchy depends upon the health of the monarch, and Frederick William's mental powers were disintegrating. In 1858, he had no choice but to turn over the administration of government to his brother; in 1861, at the advanced age of 64, his brother became Wilhelm I, king of Prussia.

In the meantime, the revolutionary heirs of 1848 were busy. Even though the liberals had been subdued in France and suppressed throughout Central Europe, they believed correctly that the future was on their side. In France, the great Napoleon's nephew, calling himself Emperor **Napoleon III,** seized power by overthrowing his own republican government in 1851. But the French liberals were able to preserve their democratic institutions at home and persuade the Emperor to promote nationalism abroad.

As liberalism survived in France and prospered in Queen **Victoria**'s England, Prussian liberals wanted to limit the power of the Hohenzollern monarchy. In 1862, facing a new and inexperienced king, liberal legislators attempted to gain control of the government by claiming a constitutional right to control the entire government budget, including the military budget which historically had been administered by the king.

King Wilhelm I objected. Like his royal ancestors, he believed the army to be the personal property of the king. Unlike most of his predecessors, however, Wilhelm fancied himself a military man and wore his uniform every day of his adult life. As the king's younger brother, he had never expected to rule. Ill-prepared for dealing with legislators, accustomed to giving orders, he would not back down. When it became apparent that the liberals would not back down either, there was a major constitutional crisis. With the government careening toward civil war and the king considering abdication, it was apparent to everyone that something had to be done.

King Appoints Bismarck Chief Minister

Recognizing that the king needed a tough advocate to protect the monarchy's interests, royal advisors convinced a reluctant Wilhelm to recall Bismarck from St. Petersburg. On September 22, 1862, King Wilhelm at last relented and consented to appoint Bismarck as chief minister. For the next three decades, Bismarck would serve the Hohenzollern monarchy as its "minister president" (1862–67), as chancellor of Prussia (1867–71), and as chancellor of Germany (1871–90).

Bismarck's strategy on the budget crisis was simple: refuse to compromise with the legislature and collect the taxes anyway. Conservatives and liberals alike were shocked. After all, had not **Charles I** of England tried the same thing, provoking a civil war that cost him his crown in 1645 and his head in 1649? Had not **Louis XVI** of France tried essentially the same thing just 70 years earlier (1789–93) with the same result?

To all this Bismarck replied that Prussians were not English or French. He argued that they were "good Germans" who would pay their taxes because they revered their king more than they respected their legislature. As for those few intrepid souls who ventured to stop paying taxes, his officials arrested and punished them with efficiency.

Even though most Germans obediently paid their taxes, the Prussian legislature declared the whole process to be illegal and refused to ratify the entire government budget. In 1863, Bismarck shored up his position with the king and most Germans by joining the Russians in brutally repressing a Polish revolt. In doing this, he proved that he would resort to military force to crush rebels, but he still could not persuade the liberals to back down on the budget question.

It was in this context that Bismarck provoked the first two of his short successful wars. For several years Denmark and Prussia had disputed the ownership of two provinces, Schleswig and Holstein. By isolating Denmark diplomatically and keeping England and France from assisting her, Bismarck provoked Denmark into attacking Prussia in 1864. The Prussian army, headed by General **Helmuth von Moltke,** quickly dispatched the overmatched Danes. Bismarck had now demonstrated that the army deserved financial support, yet the Prussian liberals were still not impressed and again refused to approve the budget. The deadlock continued. When the legislature withheld approval in 1865, even the law-abiding conservatives were becoming nervous and angry.

Bismarck upped the ante. He had thoughtfully included Austria in his postwar plan to administer the two provinces, and in 1866 he goaded Austria into attacking Prussia. Bismarck had isolated Austria diplomatically, taking advantage of Russia's anger against Austria from the Crimean War (1854–56) and France's recent victory over Austria during the Italian unification (1859–61). The Prussian army again rose to the occasion to demolish the Austrians at Sadowa on July 3, 1866. Bismarck had once more demonstrated that the army deserved financial support. This time the Prussian liberals caved in and approved five years of budget expenditures. Although their *ex post facto* approval was moot since the money had long since been collected and spent, the liberals' dedication to constitutional principle had been broken.

Bismarck was not home free. Transforming themselves into National Liberals, the Prussian liberals embarrassed Bismarck by declaring him their leader *(Führer)*, one who would promote their liberal cause of German national unification. Scholars still debate the degree to which Bismarck was converted to their cause. In his memoirs, aided by hindsight, he declared that he had planned to unify Germany.

Bismarck's third war, the Franco-Prussian War (1870–71), was definitely caused by the other side. Unlike the Danes and the Austrians, the French emperor required little manipulation. Haunted by Victor Hugo's cruel nickname of "Napoleon the Little," beleaguered by a sour economy at home, humiliated by the Mexican dethronement and execution of their emperor **Maximilian** (whom France had supported), and anxious about the spreading Prussian influence in western and southern Germany after the Austrian war, Napoleon III needed a dramatic military victory to rescue his regime. When a minor member of the Hohenzollern extended family was offered the throne of Spain, Napoleon insisted that Wilhelm force his relative to withdraw his candidacy. Bismarck edited Napoleon's telegram to Wilhelm to seem even more insulting than it was intended to be. On July 13, 1870, Bismarck published the infamous Ems Dispatch and provoked Napoleon to declare war against Prussia. For the third time in less than a decade, General von Moltke's army obliterated its opposition. The Prussians destroyed the entire French army on September 2 at Sedan and even captured Emperor Napoleon himself.

Modern Germany Is Born

Modern Germany was born on January 18, 1871. Bismarck had saved the Prussian monarchy by uniting Germany. He arranged the coronation of his sovereign at the Versailles Palace, built 200 years earlier by Europe's grandest "Sun King" himself (Louis XIV). For the next 18 years, Bismarck was the most powerful leader in Europe. Unfortunately, this did not guarantee a smooth political life in his own country.

Bismarck devoted the remainder of his political life to restraining the German nation he had done so much to bring into being. He feared the spread of nationalism. Perceiving the dangerously unlimited aspirations of the new industrializing democratic nation states, he dreaded the prospect of Germany joining the parade. He intuitively knew that Germany would provoke bigger wars that would invariably arouse the rest of Europe to form coalitions. He feared that either successful German national expansion or successful anti-German resistance would overwhelm his beloved Prussia and destroy the conservative Christian social order that he had worked so hard to preserve.

Imperial Germany was not a totalitarian dictatorship. Although the "Iron Chancellor," as Bismarck came to be called, was responsible only to his sovereign and could administer through an obedient bureaucracy, he still had to govern in accordance with laws enacted by the legislature.

Bismarck's political method, which was called *Realpolitik* ("politics of realism"), was to identify a target, isolate it, and rally the other forces in the system against it to cripple it—not destroy it. Before German unification, Bismarck had identified liberalism, isolated it through military success, and crippled it, but he did not destroy it. He needed liberalism to combat the conservative opponents of unification. In foreign policy, he had successively isolated each opponent before going to war. After each war, he reconciled his former opponent. He merely wounded Denmark and prevented his generals from killing Austria, but he permanently alienated France when he was unable to prevent his generals from annexing Alsace-Lorraine.

After unification, Bismarck selected the Roman Catholic Center Party to be his target. Escalating the political rhetoric in January 28, 1872, he invoked the *Kulturkampf* ("struggle between state and church") against the Roman Catholic Church. While Bismarck was taking advantage of secular hostility against Pope **Pius IX**'s proclamation of Papal Infallibility (Vatican 1, 1870), and Protestant German antagonism against Catholic Austrians and Poles inside the new Reich, his real enemy was the German Center Party. From 1871 to 1879, this political party occupied the position of dissent analogous to that held by the liberals in the previous decade. The Center party was headed by Ludwig Windthorst (1812–91) about whom Bismarck said, "Two things keep me going, the love for my wife and the hatred for this puny little man."

In the sphere of foreign policy, Bismarck, whose own career had been launched by three quick glorious little wars, believed that peace was necessary because war could reshuffle the alliances to jeopardize Germany's current supremacy. He sponsored international conferences to promote peace. Convening the Congress of Berlin in the summer of 1878, he declared that he was merely "the honest broker" who wanted nothing for Germany beyond the preservation of the diplomatic status quo in Europe and the fair distribution of colonies in Africa. Taking the noble high road throughout the next decade, Bismarck volunteered to mediate international disputes all over the world.

But there was the selfish side called *Realpolitik*. Bismarck needed a target around which to rally Europe's peaceful forces, and selected France to be the scapegoat. Capitalizing on France's thirst for revenge over losing Alsace-Lorraine, he played upon European fears of a perpetual French Revolution and a revived Bonapartism. Bismarck then settled down to devote himself to making treaties with all of France's possible allies: in 1879, a Dual Alliance between Germany and Austria; in 1881, three Emperors League with Germany, Austria-Hungary, and Russia; in 1882, a Triple Alliance among Germany, Austria-Hungary, and Italy; in 1887, the Reinsurance Treaty between Germany and Russia. Since England was not in an alliance-making mood, Bismarck tried to discourage Germans from building a navy or developing colonies which would compete with England. Although imperialistic Germans would plunge their country into the colonial race in the middle of the 1880s, they did so without Bismarck's blessing; they had to wait until after his departure for their navy to be built to support them.

Bismarck discovered to his chagrin that success in foreign policy did not translate into success in domestic policy. At the end of 1870s, the burning domestic issues were religion and economics. The *Kulturkampf* was failing. Its enthusiastic administrator, atheist Adalbert Falk, attacked all religious organizations with equal fervor. Consequently, the *Kulturkampf* not only alienated the Catholic Germans, most of whom wanted to be patriotic citizens of the Reich, but it also antagonized the Protestants, many of whom were Prussian Lutheran Conservatives. Bismarck himself had never been comfortable with the *Kulturkampf* secularists, and he was angered when they started waging war against all conservative Christians. In 1878, when the zealous Pope Pius IX died and was replaced by the diplomatic Pope Leo XIII, Bismarck stopped enforcing the antireligious legislation against the German Catholics. He fired Falk and let the campaign die. In 1887, Bismarck persuaded Pope Leo XIII to command Windthorst and the Center Party to cease fighting for a political abolition and settle for the government's bureaucratic dissolution of the *Kulturkampf.*

More importantly, Bismarck was dissatisfied with the National Liberals' economic policy. He was learning that the laissez-faire (free trade, free enterprise) economic policy pursued by England was not good for Germany. Free trade was hurting both the new class of industrialists in the West and the traditional Junker agriculturists in Prussia. While Bismarck cared little for the industrialists who were nevertheless providing the military muscle Germany needed, he cared a great deal for his fellow Prussian farmers who were being economically devastated by foreign imports of American grain.

In 1879, therefore, Bismarck changed course. Dropping the Roman Catholics, he discovered a new target: socialists. In the late 19th century, socialism was basically the Marxist revolutionary movement which began in the 1848 turmoil, the same revolutionary force that the 20th century would know as communism.

The year before, there had been two attempts to assassinate Emperor Wilhelm. The second was perpetrated by a terrorist affiliated with the socialist movement. Using this as a pretext, Bismarck outlawed the Social Democratic Party. This party not only represented the urban working classes, but it contained the hard-core remnant of the 1860s Prussian liberals and the 1870s National Liberals who remembered the constitutional crisis and opposed Bismarck's administrative power.

In 1879, then, Bismarck formally broke with the National Liberals who had been his allies since unification. He repudiated free trade and instituted tariffs to protect west German industry and east German agriculture. This meant that he now forged a new political alliance with his old enemies, the Catholic Center Party, and his old friends, the Prussian Conservatives. Bismarck was always more comfortable with conservatives than with liberals.

Develops Social Welfare Programs

This conservative alliance provided the base for Bismarck's crowning domestic achievement, his comprehensive social insurance program. He developed the European world's first elaborate social welfare program to prevent the workers from turning socialist to grab political power in the 1880s. In 1883–84, Bismarck enacted the first state-mandated health and accident insurance programs for workers. In 1889, he completed the enterprise by adding disability and old-age insurance. In tune with the conservative paternalism of feudal Prussia and over the opposition of the laissez-faire liberal business interests of western Germany, he made the employers bear the monetary brunt. Long after his treaties were broken and the national alliances superseded, Bismarck's social insurance program stood as a monument of government responsibility and control.

While Bismarck was renowned and respected for his foreign policy triumphs, he remained a prophet without honor in his own country. His political base was never solid. As long as Wilhelm I reigned, Bismarck was secure in his office as chancellor, but his political position never took root in the legislature or in public sentiment. When Kaiser Wilhelm I died on March 9, 1888, Bismarck's position was in jeopardy. Wilhelm's son Frederick III was married to Queen Victoria's daughter, Augusta, and both despised the chancellor. And when Frederick died on June 15, having reigned for less than 100 days, Bismarck's position was doomed. Frederick's son, **Wilhelm II** (1859–1941), was determined to be his own master.

Bismarck tried to rule the new kaiser the way he had the old one. But, after a little more than a year, the collision came over renewing the Reinsurance Treaty which Bismarck treasured as essential to good German-Russian relations and which the kaiser denigrated as unnecessary because of his personal dynastic relationship with the Romanov family. In March of 1890, the young kaiser ordered his chancellor to rescind the antisocialist laws. Bismarck refused and was dismissed on March 20, 1890.

In retirement Bismarck condemned every move that Wilhelm and his government made. Elected to the Reichstag in 1891, he started working closely with a newspaper and tried vainly to meddle in politics. But his wife's death on November 27, 1894, slowed him down. Although the government and high society honored the old man four months later on his 80th birthday (April 1, 1895), he fired his last shot on October 24, 1896, when he published the contents of the unrenewed Reinsurance Treaty. Cantankerous to the last, he died peacefully on July 30, 1898.

Bismarck lived and died for the Prussian social system as it was enshrined in the monarch. He prospered by the monarchy and perished by the monarchy. He unified Germany to preserve Prussia, but thus enabled Prussia to grow and dominate Germany. He stabilized Europe to preserve the Prussianized Germany, but thus enabled Germany to dominate Europe. At each step, he discerned that he was contributing to the destruction of feudal, agrarian, conservative, Christian Prussia. He was the perhaps the first person to foresee what would happen when Germany, armed with Prussian power, threw off the shackles of Prussian self-discipline.

SOURCES:

Anderson, Eugene N. *Social and Political Conflict in Prussia*. Lincoln, Nebraska, 1954.

Eyck, Erich. *Bismarck and the German Empire*. Macmillan, 1958.

Hamerow, Theodore S. *The Social Foundations of German Unification*. Princeton, Vols. 1, 2, 1969–72.

Hayes, Carlton J. H. *Its Historical Evolution of Modern Nationalism*. New York, 1931.

Holborn, Hajo. *History of Modern Germany*. New York, Vols. 1, 2, 3, 1959–69.

Kohn, Hans. *The Idea of Nationalism A Study in its Origins and Background*. New York, 1944.

Langer, William L. *European Alliance and Alignments 1871–90*. Harper, 1931.

Pflanze, Otto. *Bismarck and the Development of Germany*. Princeton, Vol. 1, 1963; Vols. 2, 3, 1990.

Raff, Dieter. *A History of Germany*. St. Martin's Press, 1988.

Sempell, Charlotte. *Otto von Bismarck*. Twayne, 1972.

Stern, Fritz. *Gold and Iron*. New York, 1977.

Taylor, A. J. P. *Bismarck*. Knopf, 1955.

Léon Blum

(1872–1950)

Three-time prime minister, who was the first socialist and the first Jew to lead a French government, carrying out a domestic reform program in late 1930s comparable to the New Deal in the United States.

Pronunciation: Surname pronounced "bloom." Born on April 9, 1872, in Paris; died on March 30, 1950, in Paris; married: Lise Bloch, 1896 (died 1931); married: Thérèse Pereyra, 1932 (died 1938); married: Jeanne Levilliers Humbert, 1943; children: (first marriage) one son.

A distinguished literary critic and attorney in the years before World War I, Léon Blum stood at the center of French intellectual and political life during the first half of the 20th century. War in 1914 brought Blum a high office in the government, and the postwar period saw him become the leader of the French Socialist Party. From that position he came to govern France and to be persecuted during World War II for his actions in power.

When Léon Blum was born in Paris on April 9, 1872, France had just been defeated by the German states led by Prussia. Nonetheless, his native country remained one the great centers of European cultural life where a talented young man could rise to fame as an intellectual. France also was emerging as one of the centers of European industry, an event accompanied by a growing socialist movement. Blum was to play an important role in all three areas: the continuing conflict between France and Germany, the achievements of French intellectual life, and the growing role of socialism on the French political scene.

Blum was the son of a family of French Jews who had moved from Alsace, near the German

"When a man grows troubled, he has only to think of humanity."

LÉON BLUM

Contributed by Neil Heyman, Professor of History, San Diego State University, San Diego, California

border, to Paris in the 1840s. His father was a ribbon merchant whose business prospered enough to put the family in the upper middle class. But an important influence on the young man was his grandmother. A bookseller near the law courts, she fostered in him a fervent enthusiasm for the French Revolution of 1789. Although he did not remain religious as an adult, Blum received Jewish religious training, and he staunchly defended his Jewish heritage when he was attacked by anti-Semitic political opponents. He claimed the tenets of Judaism gave him a special impetus to create a just society.

Blum was a brilliant student in a society where intellectual gifts were highly valued. He studied at the lycée Henri IV, one of the most famous high schools in Paris, and entered the École Normale Supérieure, a highly prestigious college devoted to training the country's most talented students to become teachers. Apparently finding the idea of becoming a teacher unappealing, however, Blum deliberately neglected his work. He concentrated instead on his social life and followed his real interests to work on several literary journals. With no apparent regrets, he failed his exams at the École twice and was dropped from the program.

He put his talents to use in acquiring both a law degree and a degree in liberal arts. In the mid-1890s, he began a dual career, working as a government lawyer while achieving success as a writer and literary critic. In his legal work, he served in the elite *Conseil d'Etat* ("Council of State"), the branch of government that dealt with suits between the government and individual citizens. His legal post gave him the income to support his work as a writer. Although he was a fine writer, Blum soon discovered that his greatest accomplishments came as a critic. A friend and supporter of cultural giants like André Gide, he became an influential literary reviewer and essayist writing for the journal *La Revue blanche*.

Helps Defend Dreyfus

During the 1890s, Blum was attracted to the Socialist Party as a result of two factors. First, he became a close friend and protege of Jean Jaurès, the central figure of French socialism around the turn of the century. A graduate of the École Normale, Jaurès was a brilliant speaker and charismatic leader whose greatest achievement was to hold together the different factions—some radical, some moderate—of the growing socialist movement. The second factor was "the Dreyfus Affair," in which Frenchmen of the Right and Left con-

CHRONOLOGY

1896	Entered *Conseil d'Etat*
1897	Joined pro-Dreyfus side in Dreyfus Affair
1899	Dreyfus pardoned
1914	Jaurès assassinated; outbreak of WWI; Blum became cabinet secretary to Marcel Sembat
1919	Elected to French Parliament
1920	Split in French Socialist Party at Tours
1933	Hitler came to power in Germany
1934	Stavisky Riots
1936	Rhineland crisis; First Popular Front government; Spanish Civil War
1938	Second Popular Front government
1939	WWII broke out
1940	Fall of France; Blum imprisoned by Vichy government
1942	Riom Trial
1943	Blum taken to captivity in Germany
1945	End of WWII; Blum freed
1946–47	Special ambassador to U.S.; last term as prime minister

fronted each other. The guilt or innocence of Captain Alfred Dreyfus in face of a charge of treason was the immediate issue. The possibility that Dreyfus had been convicted by army officials who deliberately used falsified evidence created a deep split in the French population. It involved the independent role of the army in France, the country's willingness to support the democratic political system, and the threat of right-wing dictatorship. Blum put his legal talents to work as a member of the team defending Dreyfus, who was pardoned in 1899.

Like most Europeans, Blum found that his life took a new turn in World War I when his friend and mentor, Jean Jaurès, was assassinated by a right-wing fanatic just as the war began. For the first time, leaders of the Socialist Party entered a French government, and one of these men, Marcel Sembat—a friend of Jaurès—asked Blum to serve as his chief assistant. Between 1914 and 1916, Blum dealt with the problems of mobilizing France's economy, participated in high-level negotiations with France's allies, and helped direct the war effort. Seeing France's leaders in action convinced him that he had more than enough talent for a political career himself.

But the end of the war led to a crisis in French Socialism. When the Revolution of 1917 brought the Bolsheviks to power in Russia, the Russian Communists moved to create a new international organization of militant left-wing political parties, a "Third International." An earlier "Second International," composed mostly of moderate socialist parties, had collapsed when war broke out in 1914. The Third International was intended to pull members away from more moderate socialist parties and to form them into new communist parties. In postwar France, hit by economic problems, the Socialist Party had grown with the new membership of 100,000 young workers. The mass of the French Socialist Party favored adopting the formulas of the Third International, that is making the Party into a communist party. This was the decision taken at the Tours Socialist Congress in December 1920.

In this bitter atmosphere, Blum emerged as the leader of moderate French socialism. He admired the Russian revolution in many ways, but he rejected the Russian model for France's circumstances. He said farewell to those French socialists who went over to communism, and he insisted on defending the Jaurès legacy and democratic tradition of French socialism. "Someone," he noted, "must guard the old house."

Blum's party soon regained most of its old membership. Nonetheless, during the 1920s and the early '30s, it remained far distant from power. Since Blum refused to join in coalition cabinets (governments formed with the support of several different political parties), he remained in political opposition. Like Jaurès before 1914, however, he succeeded in holding together a socialist party containing a number of squabbling groups. Blum was now an intellectual who had become a political figure. This combination struck some observers as odd. In 1920, one noted that he seemed to represent "the revolution in pearl-gray gloves," and his parliamentary speeches were said to resemble "the music of Mozart."

In 1933 and 1934, however, the challenges facing France changed. In January 1933, **Adolf Hitler** came to power in Germany. In February 1934, a scandal in the French government concerning official ties to a crooked financier named Serge Stavisky led to massive riots in the streets of Paris by right-wing groups. It now seemed possible that France might see its government overthrown and replaced by some form of Fascist dictatorship. The parties of the left and center came together in a "Popular Front." Blum himself experienced the dangerous bitterness affecting French political life; in February 1936, he was dragged from his car and attacked by a group of right-wing students in the center of Paris.

Leads Popular Front Government

Coming to power as the head of a Popular Front government in June 1936, Blum was the *premier* ("prime minister") of France for the next 13 months. It was an era of turmoil at home and increasing danger abroad. From the moment he took office, Blum was plunged into a series of crises. His first challenge came from his natural allies. France's factory workers had celebrated the victory of the Popular Front by seizing factories and calling for concessions from their employers. Their demands included collective bargaining, paid vacations, and a 40-hour week. Blum brought together leaders of business and labor at the Hotel Matignon in Paris. In the background, there was news of a million French workers on strike. With Blum acting as mediator, the two sides agreed on a sweeping reform program.

Several issues placed a cloud over Blum's success. France's economic problems, including high unemployment, continued. He was attacked from the left for stopping short of basic changes in French society; he was attacked from the right for going too far. Blum's own description of his middle way in 1936 and 1937 stressed the need to prevent deeper splits in French society: more bitterness might bring on civil war.

In foreign affairs, Blum inherited a dark situation that quickly grew worse. Less than three months before the Popular Front's victory, Hitler had sent the German army into the Rhineland. Although a part of Germany, the 1919 peace treaty had forbidden the Germans from placing any of their military power into this important border region. Hitler's success humiliated and endangered France, whose government had stood by helplessly. Blum responded to the growing threat from Germany by starting a program of rearmament. This meant abandoning a long-held socialist policy in France of promoting disarmament.

On another French border, a second danger emerged the month after Blum took office. Military forces led by General **Francisco Franco** revolted against the government of Spain. That government, like Blum's in France, was a Popular Front coalition. When Blum began to aid the Madrid government (the Loyalists) with arms, he quickly faced objections on two fronts. The British government favored a policy of nonintervention, that is a refusal to let either side in the Spanish war get military help from the outside. Within France, the Radical Party—one of Blum's political partners in the Popular Front—also pushed for nonintervention. Blum reluctantly agreed, even though Hitler and Benito Mussolini openly provided aid to Franco and the rebels. Nonintervention quickly came to mean a bar to outside help for the Loyalists only.

Blum's government fell in June 1937. Although he briefly held office at the head of a second Popular Front government in 1938, his years in power were over.

The outbreak of war brought tragedy and humiliation to France and placed Blum in deadly danger. The German offensive of May–June 1940 led to the occupation of northern France, the fall of the French Third Republic, and the installation of a pro-German government at Vichy under Marshal **Philippe Pétain.** The groups on the French right that had been defeated at the time of the Dreyfus trial now seemed to be in power, thanks to the shock of the German victory.

Arrested by Vichy authorities in September 1940, Blum was held in a Vichy prison until 1943. During this time, he and other former government leaders were tried at the city of Riom by a Vichy court. Facing accusations that he had failed to prepare France for a future war by his concessions to the workers in 1936, Blum defended himself with great skill, but his safety no longer depended upon the legal system.

As the war turned against Hitler, Blum and other captive French leaders were deported to Germany as political hostages. Blum survived two years at the concentration camp at Buchenwald.

Although he was held as a special prisoner and not physically mistreated, he was never far from the possibility of execution. In August 1944, American newspapers carried accounts of his death.

In the closing days of the war, Blum and other prisoners were carried southward away from the liberating armies. Blum, his wife, and the others in a convoy of 150 prisoners were freed in northern Italy by the American army.

Despite his age and his wartime experiences, Blum returned to active political life in France. Serving as a special ambassador to the United States in 1946, he obtained economic assistance to help in France's postwar recovery. He also became prime minister one final time in the winter of 1946–47. The prominent socialist leader died in Paris on March 30, 1950, only a few days before his 78th birthday. Noted Clement Atlee, "He was the most remarkable Socialist of his generation and an admirable leader of free men."

SOURCES:

Colton, Joel. *Léon Blum: Humanist in Politics.* MIT Press, 1966.

Joll, James. *Three Intellectuals in Politics.* Pantheon, 1960.

Logue, William. *Léon Blum: The Formative Years, 1872–1914.* Northern Illinois University Press, 1973.

FURTHER READING:

Goldberg, Harvey. *The Life of Jean Jaurès.* University of Wisconsin Press, 1962.

Jackson, Julian. *The Popular Front in France: Defending Democracy, 1934–38.* Cambridge University Press, 1988.

Lacouture, Jean. *Léon Blum.* Holmes & Meier, 1982.

Lichtheim, George. *Marxism in Modern France.* Columbia University Press, 1966.

Wright, Gordon. *France in Modern Times: From the Enlightenment to the Present.* 3rd ed. Norton, 1981.

Lucrezia Borgia

(1480–1519)

Duchess of Ferrara, renowned poisoner and political schemer who, in actuality, was a pawn in the intrigues of her father and brother.

Name variations: Lucretia. Born in Rome, Italy, on April 18, 1480; died at Ferrara, Italy, on June 24, 1519; daughter of Cardinal Rodrigo Borgia (later Pope Alexander VI) and his mistress Vannozza [Vanezza] Cattanei; married: Giovanni Sforza of Milan, June 12, 1493 (marriage annulled, December 27, 1498); married: Alfonso of Aragon, duke of Bisceglie, July 21, 1498 (murdered in 1500); married: Alfonso d'Este, duke of Ferrara, February 2, 1502; children: Giovanni (reputedly by Pedro Caldes), Rodrigo (with second husband, Alfonso of Aragon); Ercole II, Ippolito, Alessandro, Eleanora, Francesco (all with third husband, Alfonso d'Este).

Lucrezia Borgia was born into the Renaissance world of Italy (1320–1520), a time when artists, sculptors, architects, scientists, and others rose to prominence. She was also born into one of the most notorious families in world history. Reputed to be evil, violent, and politically conniving, the Borgias were interested in claiming as much control of Italy as they could. And they were very successful.

Their prosperity was facilitated by the fact that Italy was not a unified nation but rather a collection of papal states, republics, duchies, and kingdoms organized around an urban center and the surrounding countryside, each with its own ruler. Although these individual states were powerful, their rulers were more inclined to fight each other than to band together against such enemy countries as France or Spain.

Italy desperately needed to unify and strengthen itself. Having lost much of its sea trade to France, Spain, and England, the Mediterranean was no longer the main site of commercial activity. Through the right political maneuvers, influential alliances could be formed and a great deal of power gained. It was a time of political turmoil and lethal intrigue; many political problems were solved by killing the person seen as the source of irritation. The males in the Borgia family followed the trend.

Lucrezia Borgia was the daughter of Cardinal Rodrigo Borgia, later to become Pope Alexander VI, and his mistress Vannozza Cattanei, who was also the mother of Lucrezia's two older brothers, Cesare and Giovanni. The job of raising Lucrezia, however, was given to Rodrigo's cousin, the widow Adriana daMila. While living in a palace in Rome, Lucrezia was educated at the Convent of St. Sixtus on Via Appia. Described as being slender, she was of medium height, with light-blue/green eyes and golden hair, which she later bleached to maintain its goldenness. A painting by Pinturicchio, "Disputation of Saint Catherine," is said to be modeled after her, depicting a slender young woman with wavy, blonde hair cascading down her back.

The young girl was no more than 11 when she was first affected by the political ambitions of her father Rodrigo and her brother, Cesare. Desiring an alliance with Spain, they arranged a marriage contract between Lucrezia and the lord of Val d'Agora in Valencia; her dowry was set at 100,000 ducats. But two months later, the contract was mysteriously annulled without explanation. Historians assume that Rodrigo, who had instigated the annulment, had formed a new alliance involving his dynastic ambitions; he then arranged a marriage contract with another Spaniard, 15-year-old Don Gaspare, son of Count Averse in the Kingdom of Naples. This too was annulled that same year. The vacillating Rodrigo had decided it was more important to be aligned with the Sforza family of Milan.

The groom-to-be was the conceited, well-educated Giovanni Sforza, a 27-year-old with a fierce temper. He, too, stood to profit. Prior to his marriage to Lucrezia, Giovanni was only the lord of an insignificant Adriatic fishing town. Afterward, he would be a close relation to one of Italy's most powerful families. Having been elevated from cardinal to Pope Alexander VI, Rodrigo, the prospective father-in-law, had become even more powerful. During the Italian Renaissance, the papacy was treated as a lucrative and powerful prize for any family that could gain control of it. Marrying the pope's daughter would strengthen Giovanni's hold on his inheritance over the state of Pesaro. In addition, Giovanni's uncle, Ludovico Sforza, the ruler of Milan, took note of Giovanni after his engagement and offered him a lucrative command in the Milanese army. Through his generosity, Ludovico hoped to gain an ally in the Borgia camp.

CHRONOLOGY

1480   Born in Rome

1493   Married to Giovanni Sforza

1497   Giovanni fled to Pesaro; Lucrezia withdrew to the Convent of San Sisto; marriage annulled

1498   Married to Alfonso of Aragon

1500   Alfonso murdered

1502   Married Alfonso d'Este, duke of Ferrara

1519   Died at age 39

So the 13-year-old Lucrezia was married to Giovanni Sforza on June 12, 1493, in a sumptuous wedding with a retinue of 500 ladies. The wedding feast featured poetry readings and comedy performances, followed by gifts of jewels, gold and silver objects, brocade, rings, and gold table settings. The pope and other religious leaders reportedly threw food into the ladies' low-cut bodices, but bawdy behavior was not unusual in that time.

By the time she was 17, Lucrezia was said to be tired of her husband, claiming he often neglected her. Giovanni had his own grievances. Reportedly weary of the political intrigue of the Vatican and the arrogance of Lucrezia's brothers, he may also have heard that Cesare Borgia was considering ways to eliminate him. Now preferring a closer alliance with Naples than Milan, Lucrezia's father and brother made plans to have the marriage annulled, claiming that Giovanni was impotent, that the marriage had never been consummated. Giovanni implored his uncle to intercede, but Ludovico, who had brought about the invasion of Italy by Charles VIII of France—an invasion that almost toppled Rodrigo from the papacy—was unwilling to do anything that would further provoke the pope. Sensing danger, Giovanni fled to Pesaro in the spring of 1497; Lucrezia withdrew to the Convent of San Sisto in Rome.

During the annulment process, statements from both camps served to hold the litigants up for social ridicule. Indignant over the charges of his impotency, Giovanni insinuated that Lucrezia's father and brother wanted Lucrezia for themselves. These accusations led to rumors about possible incestuous behavior that haunted Lucrezia throughout her life. In return for the right to keep the sizable dowry his wife had brought to the marriage, Giovanni reluctantly capitulated and signed a confession of impotency.

Cesare and Rodrigo then chose 17-year-old Alfonso of Aragon, the duke of Bisceglie and son of the late king of Naples, as Lucrezia's next husband; Rodrigo sent his trusted Spanish chamberlain Pedro Caldes to carry out the marriage negotiations. But by the time her first marriage was officially annulled on December 27, 1497, Lucrezia was six months pregnant. This created more grist for the Italian rumor mill. Some speculated that Pedro Caldes was the child's father, others pointed to Rodrigo or Cesare. As a result of this scandal, Pedro was stabbed to death and thrown into the Tiber River along with one of Lucrezia's maids. Three months later, she gave birth to her son Giovanni, who was later legitimized by Rodrigo. Some scholars believe that Giovanni was actually a brother of Lucrezia's, although his parentage will probably never be known.

Alfonso of Aragon was reputed to be a handsome youth, with fine manners. The proxy wedding occurred on June 29, 1498, with the actual wedding on July 21. A wedding feast, similar to that of Lucrezia's first marriage, was celebrated with plays and masquerades, but the marriage was brief. Only a year later, political changes were once again stirring. Sensing that his alliance with the Borgias was no longer needed, Alfonso fled from Rome but was persuaded by Lucrezia to rejoin her and the pope at Nepi, where she was invested as governor of Spoleto. Lucrezia was again pregnant, and on November 1, 1499, gave birth to a son, naming him Rodrigo after her father.

Alfonso of Aragon Is Murdered

On the evening of July 15, 1500, while returning home to the Vatican, Alfonso was attacked by hired killers and stabbed in the head, right arm, and leg. Lucrezia cared for him, called for doctors, and arranged for armed guards both day and night; she even prepared his food, fearing that someone might poison him. But on August 18, as Alfonso was still recovering, Cesare reputedly came to him and whispered in his ear that "what was not finished at breakfast would be complete by dinner." Returning to Alfonso's room later that day, Cesare ordered everyone out and directed his strongman to strangle Lucrezia's young husband. Alfonso's executioner later confessed that Rodrigo had ordered the murder, but few believed his story.

Left a widow at the age of 20, Lucrezia spent most of her time weeping over the loss of her husband. Tired of watching her mourn, her father and brother sent her to Nepi in the Etruscan Hills. On her return to Rome in November 1500, she began assisting her father as a sort of papal secretary,

often opening and responding to his mail when he was not in residence.

Italian society continued to feast on Borgia gossip at Lucrezia's expense. There were rumors that she frequently danced until late at night with her brother Cesare at his infamous parties at the Vatican. Whether or not she deserved this speculation is debatable, since many contemporaries commented on her reserve and piety. Some historians have suggested that she and Pope Alexander were guests at dinners her brother hosted but left before revelries began. Others feel she may have been an innocent victim of the hatred directed toward her father and brother.

Casting about for new alliances, Cesare and Rodrigo's attention now turned to the 24-year-old widower Alfonso d'Este, eldest son of Ercole d'Este, duke of Ferrara. Cesare wanted to conquer the Romagna region, and therefore needed an alliance with the duchy of Ferrara—an important military power strategically placed between the Romagna and the Venetian Republic. Not surprisingly, neither Alfonso d'Este nor his father was too happy at the prospect of a wife whose first husband had been ridiculed as impotent and whose second husband had been murdered. In addition, the d'Este family was the oldest ruling family in Italy and considered the Borgia family upstarts, not in the same class.

But politics once again determined Lucrezia's married life. While the main powers of Italy, fearing the control it would give Rodrigo's papacy, roared in opposition, King Louis XII of France advised his ally, Ercole, to consent to the marriage. Further prodding came from another quarter. Rodrigo, as Pope Alexander VI, threatened to depose Ercole if he did not consent to the marriage. Ercole finally agreed, but in return he demanded a large dowry; reduction of his annual tribute to the Church; the position of archpriest of St. Peter's for his son, Cardinal Ippolito d'Este; and receipt of the cities of Cento and Pieve, along with the harbor of Cesenatico.

Lucrezia was eager for the marriage, for she regarded Rome as a prison and thought she would have a better chance of leading her own life away from her ambitious father and brother. She wrote often to her future father-in-law, who at one time was considering marrying her if Alfonso did not. Since this was clearly an arranged marriage, Ercole's envoys checked at court to ensure that Lucrezia's trousseau would bring to this third marriage as much as the dowry of 100,000 ducats accompanying her first marriage. With one dress alone costing 15,000 ducats, the envoys were assured that the total value of the trousseau would easily equal 100,000 ducats. In addition, Lucrezia would be taking along jewels, furniture, and a table service of silver and gold.

Lucrezia Travels to Wed Third Husband

On December 30, 1501, the proxy marriage was held at the Vatican, and in early January, Lucrezia left Rome on her approximately 220-mile trip to Ferrara, adorned in her colors of yellow and brown, with 150 mules carrying her baggage carts. She and her retinue of 1,000 were entertained at every city along the way. As the bridal party approached Ferrara, a disguised Alfonso rode out to catch a glimpse of Lucrezia; he was so pleased that he spent several hours in conversation with her, then returned home for the official welcome.

On February 2, 1502, the actual wedding ceremony was held with both Lucrezia and Alfonso in full regalia. Lucrezia wore black velvet with a cape of gold brocade trimmed with ermine, a net of gold and diamonds on her hair, and a necklace of rubies and pearls. Alfonso was dressed in red velvet, with even his horse attired in crimson and gold. Lucrezia had married a man who not only was interested in artillery, tournaments, dogs and horses, but who also played the viol and made pottery. He was also known for his cruelty, stinginess, and eccentricity.

The people of Ferrara adored Lucrezia, praising her for her beauty and "inner grace of personality." Avoiding political machinations, she became a notable patron of the arts. Content to socialize with artists, courtiers, poets, and citizens of the Renaissance court, she helped make Ferrara a center for artists and writers. A lock of golden hair, given by her to the poet Pietro Bembo, can today be found in the Ambrosian Library in Milan, along with letters she wrote to him in the gallant manner of the day.

In 1503, Rodrigo died, along with many of Cesare's plans. Since Lucrezia had not yet borne any children for Alfonso, the king of France suggested to Ercole that he should seek an annulment of the marriage. The idea was discarded because both Ercole and his son Alfonso were by this time fond of Lucrezia; in addition, they did not want to repay her dowry. Finally, some stability appeared in Lucrezia's life. When Ercole died in 1505, she and Alfonso became the reigning duke and duchess of Ferrara. She requested that Giovanni, her illegitimate son, come live with her. When he was old enough to come to court, he was always introduced as her brother.

Lucrezia had several children by Alfonso d'Este. Although two died in infancy, one was stillborn, and there were at least two miscarriages, the couple had five children who survived infancy: Ercole II (b. 1508), Ippolito (b. 1509), Alessandro (b. 1514), Eleanora (b. 1515), and Francesco (b. 1516). Of these, only Ercole and Ippolito survived into adulthood.

In 1512, Lucrezia began to lead a retired life, perhaps caused by news of the death of Rodrigo, her son by Alfonso of Aragon. Though separated from her son, she had made sure he was well taken care of, selecting his governess, his tutor, and the stewards to oversee his duchy of Bisceglie (which he had inherited from his father). She began to spend more time in her apartments or in nearby convents, becoming withdrawn and ill-humored. Turning more and more to religion, piety, and charitable works, she took to wearing a hairshirt under her embroidered gowns as a form of penance. As the years progressed, her body thickened, and she was said to age greatly. She was also plagued by spells of melancholy. On June 14, 1519, while giving birth to a stillborn girl, she developed a debilitating fever. She died ten days later at the age of 39. A few days before her death, she wrote a letter to Pope Leo X asking his blessing and commending her husband and children to him.

Lucrezia Borgia was often accused of being frivolous and heartless, yet an examination of her life reveals that such assessments were not always deserved. Indeed, much of the innuendo about her illegitimate child and alleged incestuous behavior may have been in retaliation for the evil deeds committed by her father Rodrigo and brother Cesare (who also murdered their brother Giovanni). Many historians view her as a political pawn whose marriages were used to further the ambitions of both her father and her brother. Lucrezia was very much a product of her times, accepting these ambitions and their consequences for the good of the family.

SOURCES:

Avery, Catherine B. *The New Century Italian Renaissance Encyclopedia.* Meredith, 1972.

Chamberlain, E. R. *The Fall of the House of Borgia.* Dial Press, 1974.

Cloulas, Ivan. *The Borgias.* Translated by Gilda Roberts. Watts, 1989.

Fusero, Clemente. *The Borgias.* Translated by Peter Green. Praeger, 1972.

Guicciardini, Francesco. *The History of Italy.* Translated by Sidney Alexander. Macmillan, 1969.

Latour, Anny. *The Borgias.* Translated by Neil Mann. Abelard-Schuman, 1966.

Boudicca

(A.D. 26/30–62)

Icenian warrior queen, who led the Britons in an historic rebellion against Roman rule, stunning the overconfident Empire and claiming the lives of an estimated 70,000 Romans and provincials.

Name variations: Boudica (the popular spelling, Boadicea, was derived from an error in an influential Renaissance manuscript). Born perhaps between A.D. 26 and 30; died c. 62; daughter of a royal family; married: Prasutagus; children: two daughters.

Proclaiming himself the "first to bring the barbarian peoples across the Ocean under the sway of the Roman People," Emperor Claudius invaded Britain in A.D. 43, extending his Empire to the western limits of the known world and conquering tribe upon tribe of Britons. Some submitted without disturbance and were proclaimed allies, others fought and were destroyed. At that time, Boudicca's people, descendants of the Celtics, were living as a fairly secluded, culturally underdeveloped tribe near present-day Norfolk and north Suffolk, England. Little is known about the Iceni up until the period of the Roman invasion—when they took their place among the tribes who quietly submitted.

Archaeological discoveries point toward the possibility, written of by Caesar, that there existed both a lesser and greater Icenian tribe; or, perhaps, that there was a threefold division which allowed for three different royal centers. It appears that a center did exist near Norwich close to the later Roman town *Venta Icenorum,* "marketplace of the Iceni." Archaeologists have confirmed that the Icenian culture was dominated by the horse and chariot (evidenced in part, by coins stamped with

"It has been remarked more than once that at the hands of the Romans the weak had no rights. Momentarily under Boudica, the Britons ... had ceased to be the weak."

ANTONIA FRASER

Contributed by Deborah Klezmer, Associate Editor, Historic World Leaders

pictures of galloping horses). Such chariots were probably light, wicker vehicles—a far cry from the armored cart with scythes protruding from its wheels, in which Boudicca is so often represented.

Despite the scarcity of information, it is apparent that though the Iceni had voluntarily submitted to Roman rule, they were a courageous people with no intention of relinquishing their right to defense. In A.D. 47, the Romans disarmed the tribes in their newly acquired territories—even those considered allies—and the Iceni were particularly bitter to see their submission thus rewarded. They were joined by neighboring tribes who fought under their leadership in an unsuccessful rebellion thought to have taken place in A.D. 49 or 50. Following the uprising, Prasutagus emerges from history as client king of the tribe, though it remains unknown whether he was ruling at the time of the rebellion or came into power in its wake. Among the speculation concerning his life and rule, only two factors can be substantiated: (1) that sometime before the rebellion he had married a woman of royal birth named Boudicca; (2) that in A.D. 59 or 60, he died.

Prasutagus passed away without male heirs, and though he did not leave the kingdom to Boudicca, she was entrusted with the regency on behalf of his two daughters; but the regency was the least of the family's problems. Having been renowned for his wealth, Prasutagus left his lands and personal properties jointly to his daughters and Emperor Nero, hoping that by leaving a large portion of his wealth to the emperor, he had safeguarded his family's inheritance and assured the tribe's continuation as a client state (an ally of Rome rather than a conquered province).

His will, however, was not regarded favorably by the local Roman administration. Procurator Catus Decianus, the chief financial administrator of the British province, sent men to seize the king's estate and all his wealth. Roman historian Tacitus reports that "kingdom and household alike were plundered like prizes of war." Iceni chiefs were deprived of their hereditary lands; their new queen, Boudicca, was flogged; and her two daughters, heiresses to the kingdom, were raped by Roman slaves. Tacitus continues: "These outrages and the fear of worse … moved the Iceni to arms." But it appears there must have been other contributing factors to the monumental revolt that followed—if for no other reason than that other tribes (for whom the abuse of the Iceni royal family was of less consequence) joined forces with Boudicca and her people. Most likely, the chief reasons for the revolt were financial exploitation and land appropriation by the Romans, with

CHRONOLOGY

55 B.C.	Caesar's first invasion of Britain
A.D. 43	Roman invasion under Aulus Plautius; Emperor Claudius traveled to Britain to receive the surrender
49	*Colonia* at Camulodunum founded (Essex)
59 OR 60	King Prasutagus died
60 OR 61	Icenian (Britons) revolted
c. 62	Boudicca possibly ingested poison

Decianus calling in loans which the client kings had thought were gifts.

Boudicca Leads Revolt

Regardless of the motivations, the rebellion that followed Prasutagus's death was the most historically significant opposition the Romans would face from the Britons, not because of its size, which was formidable, or the amount of blood spilled, which was considerable, but rather because it was led by a woman. It is ironic that our only accounts of Boudicca's revolt come from her sworn enemies, the Romans. Tacitus wrote of the rebellion in both his *Agricola* (A.D. 98) and *Annals* (written 15–20 years later), as did Dio Cassius in about A.D. 163. Though each of these accounts was written considerably after the event, those of Tacitus are generally regarded with more favor because his father-in-law, Julius Agricola, was a member of the governor's staff in Britain, and he fought in the campaign as a junior officer.

Though it remains uncertain which other tribes heeded Boudicca's call to arms, it is clear that the Trinovantes of Camulodunum (present-day Colchester) fought alongside the Iceni. The Romans had set up a *colonia,* a settlement of Roman army veterans, on their land, designed to help civilize what they considered the rude British. The largest Roman temple in Britain, the Temple of Claudius, was erected there, with a bronze statue of the emperor in front of the entrance steps. The large income needed to support what Tacitus termed a "blatant stronghold of alien rule" was drawn from the Trinovantes' local taxes. The *colonia* sparked great resentment from the Britons, as did the Roman veteran settlers who "drove the Trinovantes from their homes and land, and called them prisoners and slaves." Thus, it is no surprise that, nursing grievances of their own, the displaced tribe took up arms with the Iceni. Equally unsurprising is the first town targeted for the attack.

According to Dio Cassius, as Boudicca finished addressing her troops on the eve of the rout, she released a rabbit from the folds of her dress "as a species of divination." When it was spied running "in the auspicious direction," a favorable omen for the uprising was said to have befallen the troops. Then, sometime in A.D. 60 or 61, Queen Boudicca's rebel forces of 120,000 headed for the Roman *colonia* at Camulodunum.

The Roman settlers in the bush were the first to be brutally attacked and killed, and as Boudicca headed south, word spread quickly of her approach. Tacitus reports that Camulodunum itself issued unheeded warnings of what was soon to come:

> Delirious women chanted of destruction at hand. They cried that in the local senate-house outlandish yells had been heard; the theatre had echoed with shrieks; and at the mouth of the Thames a phantom settlement had been seen in ruins. A blood-red colour was the sea, too, and shapes like human corpses left by the ebb-tide were interpreted hopefully by the Britons and with terror by the settlers.

Meanwhile, elsewhere in Britain, Suetonius Paulinus, the Roman governor, was attacking the Druids and rebels on the island of Anglesey. With their governor absent, the veterans of the *colonia* turned to Procurator Decianus for help. Not taking the threat with the seriousness it would shortly demand, he sent 200 poorly armed men—all of whom were eventually killed when the rebels sacked Camulodunum. This grave oversight had occurred for the same reason that Boudicca's army was to find the *colonia* defenseless; the Romans did not think it possible that the Britons could rise up, attack a city, and massacre its inhabitants. Not only did Decianus fail to send further reinforcements while there was still time, but the women, children, and elderly of the town were not evacuated.

Boudicca surrounded Camulodunum, then burned the town of Roman excesses to the ground. One area alone withstood the holocaust—the temple. There, those who had managed to escape the fire held out against the queen for two days before the temple was taken by storm and those remaining were slaughtered. The rebels spared nothing in Camulodunum, desecrating even the Roman cemetery. The Romans received word that the rebel army had risen with a vengeance; not only had the Britons leveled their *colonia*, but "moreover," notes Dio, "all this ruin was brought upon

[them] by a woman, a fact which in itself caused them the greatest shame."

The commander of the nearest Roman legion, the 9th, rushed his troops (estimated at 2,000) toward Camulodunum to stop the army in its tracks. But such an event only allowed the queen an opportunity to prove that her forces were not a leaderless mob. The legionaries were destroyed in a carefully planned ambush, convincing the rebels that they could take on battle-hardened troops and succeed. Elated by this enormous triumph, the Iceni army headed toward the defenseless Londinium (present-day London), then a Roman center of business spread over 30 acres with, prior to the queen's arrival, approximately 30,000 inhabitants.

When news reached Suetonius of the rebels' destination, the governor headed for Londinium, managing to cross the 250 miles to the town before the queen's troops. Upon his arrival, he assessed the city: it was not fortified, it had no walls, it could not be defended. Consequently, Suetonius decided to abandon Londinium to the enemy. Said Tacitus, "He decided to save the whole situation by the sacrifice of a single city." While the inhabitants, all civilian, pleaded not to be left unprotected, Suetonius, "unmoved by tears and prayers" signaled for departure, and the Roman cavalry left the city of Londinium to its bloody fate. Many tried to leave with him, and Tacitus reports that those strong enough to keep up were given a place. Left behind were the women, the old, the young, and any too attached to their city and shops to leave. "Never before or since," wrote Tacitus, "has Britain ever been in a more disturbed and perilous state."

Today, wherever archaeologists dig in London, they find a red and black layer of burned ash and soot, testifying to the destruction wreaked upon the city by the queen's growing forces. Amidst all other unanswered questions concerning her life, one thing about Boudicca is certain—the attacks she led were ruthless. The Britons did not believe in taking prisoners; rather, said Tacitus, "they could not wait to cut throats, hang, burn, and crucify—as though avenging, in advance, the retribution that was on its way." Dio, on the other hand, was not so sparing with details of the torture:

> The worst and most bestial atrocity committed by their captors was the following. They hung up naked the noblest and most distinguished women and then cut off their breasts ... ; afterwards they impaled the women on sharp skewers run lengthwise through the entire body.

But Dio's account was recorded more than 100 years after the rebellion, and it is probable that he took certain liberties of the pen to engage his readers' imaginations. Regardless, the outcome of the attack is certain; Londinium and any still-remaining inhabitants were thoroughly destroyed.

Verulamium (present-day St. Albans) suffered a similar fate, before Boudicca followed Suetonius into the Roman military zone, hoping to deal the decisive blow. The location of the Iceni's last battle is still unknown. Tacitus notes that on the battlefield, Suetonius's men had woods behind them and open country in front of them, but he never names the spot. Roman forces may have numbered around 1,200, while Boudicca's army numbered over 100,000 (Dio Cassius cites 25 million).

Prior to sending her troops into battle, Tacitus tells us that Boudicca

drove round the tribes in a chariot with her daughters in front of her. "We British are used to woman commanders in war" she cried. "I am not fighting for my kingdom and wealth now. I am fighting as an ordinary person for my lost freedom, my bruised body, and my outraged daughters. Nowadays Roman rapacity does not even spare our bodies. Old people are killed, virgins raped. But the gods will grant us the vengeance we deserve. The Roman divisions which dared to fight us are annihilated. The others cower in their camps, or watch for a chance to escape. They will never face the din and roar of our thousands, much less the shock of our onslaught."

This speech, set in the queen's mouth by Tacitus, has become entangled with Dio's equally suspect physical description to construct the popular image of Boudicca, the Warrior Queen:

She was very tall, the glance of her eye most fierce; her voice harsh. A great mass of the reddest hair fell down to her hips. Around her neck was a large golden necklace, and she always wore a tunic of many colours over which she fastened a thick cloak with a broach. Her appearance was terrifying.

Even if the Icenian queen never actually delivered the speech recorded by Tacitus, it does display the confidence with which the rebel forces evidently entered their final battle. So certain were they of triumph, that they pulled their oxcarts, peopled with their wives and families, in position at the rear of the battlefield in order for their loved ones to sit as ringside spectators at the massacre.

Britons Are Massacred

And a massacre it was. Victory, however, did not belong to the queen. When her army charged the Roman line, the Romans showered them with two volleys of several thousand javelins—seven feet long with three-foot iron points—enough to cut down a number of Boudicca's forces, none of whom had the benefit of body armor. Confronted by the front line of Romans, charging with sword and shield, the Britons' superior numbers actually worked to their disadvantage, because, as they fell back upon themselves, they were unable to properly engage their long swords. The Roman cavalry worked around their flanks, then the packed rear ranks broke in retreat. But there was nowhere to flee; they had blocked their own escape with the oxcarts from which their families witnessed the slaying. Driven back and pinned against the carts, the Britons were ruthlessly slaughtered—even when trying to surrender—along with their women, children, and baggage animals. According to Tacitus, 80,000 Britons were massacred in the battle, with the Romans losing only 400 men.

It is unlikely that Boudicca died on the battlefield, but rather, wrote Tacitus, she later poisoned herself. Oddly enough, the legendary image which succeeds her is one unstained by the violence of her revolts; it will never be known whether she actually climbed down off her chariot to spill Roman blood with her own hands. The fate of her unnamed daughters, like so much about the queen, remains a mystery. As for her people, the cost of their glorious hour was immense. Having neglected their own crops with aspirations of seizing Roman supplies, they suffered a terrible famine. Whereas their mighty rebellion had not served to stop the Romans, it simply ensured that the Romans would take greater precautions against such uprisings in the future, making Boudicca's revolt the last of its kind. Under Roman rule, many of the remaining Iceni were transported, others enslaved.

SOURCES:

Blair, Peter Hunter. *Roman Britain and Early England: 55 B.C.–A.D. 871.* Norton, 1963.

Cottrell, Leonard. *A Guide to Roman Britain.* Chilton, 1966.

Fraser, Antonia. *Boadicea's Chariot.* Weidenfeld & Nicolson, 1988.

Welch, George Patrick. *Britannia.* Wesleyan University Press, 1963.

Wood, Michael. *In Search of the Dark Ages.* Facts on File, 1987.

Willy Brandt

(1913–1992)

Mayor of West Berlin, leader of German Social Democratic Party, foreign minister and chancellor of Germany, who received the Nobel Peace Prize for normalizing relations with the Eastern European countries which Nazi Germany had terrorized.

Pronunciation: Villy Brahnt. Born Herbert Ernst Karl Frahm in Lübeck on December 18, 1913; died of cancer in October 1992; adopted name Willy Brandt in March 1933; illegitimate son of an absent father and a salesclerk mother; married: Carlota Thorkildsen, 1941 (separated 1943); married: Rut Hansen, 1948 (divorced 1980); married: Brigitte Seebacher, 1988; children: (first marriage) daughter Nina; (second marriage) Peter, Lars, and Matthias.

When Willy Brandt gave his "Speech on the State of the Nation" as German chancellor in January 1970, he said his report must "necessarily deal with the problem of partition." He added that "we shall never cease to work on the problem, which has been a subject of international political preoccupation since the end of the war, under the label 'German question.'" Twenty years later, when the Berlin Wall was being breached, Brandt proclaimed "what belongs together must grow together." The proclamation became prophecy: within a few months, East Germany had become part of the western state. That reunification was credited mainly to his conservative rival, Helmut Kohl, but many feel Brandt had contributed more than Kohl to solving the "German question" by helping to make Germany a normal nation-state within a less hostile Europe. When Brandt died of cancer in 1992, *Time* magazine eulogized: "More than anyone else, it was Willy Brandt who rehabilitated his country, who helped it earn unification when the opportunity so suddenly presented itself."

Brandt's early life showed little prospect of his later role as a world leader. Born illegitimately

Contributed by Dieter K. Buse, Professor of History, Laurentian University, Sudbury, Ontario, Canada

as Herbert Ernst Frahm (a name he would use for the first 30 years of his life), Brandt came from a working-class family in the small northern German city of Lübeck. For many years he did not know the identity of his father. His mother worked as a salesclerk, and Brandt later remembered being a lonely child cared for by a neighbor. A believer in self-development and social justice, his mother participated in left-wing politics; his grandfather, with whom Brandt lived from age five, was even more influential. Through him, Brandt learned the values of the German labor movement, its Social Democratic Party, and its trade unions. Concepts of class conflict and social justice were ingrained early. As one biographer has suggested, perhaps Brandt found a substitute for family life in the socialist youth groups. Later, he would credit the influence of his family's membership in Social Democracy and unionism: " I was born into socialism, so to speak."

By his own admission, Brandt "had many friends but no one who was really close to me." He shared carefree days camping and hiking with other socialist youth and became a Socialist Party member by age 16, organizing and speaking on its behalf. When the working-class youth won a scholarship to a middle-class school, his studies went well, but Brandt chose to examine topics such as the history of socialism. Politics became an early passion.

Sponsored by Julius Leber, Brandt became a full member of the German Social Democratic Party (SPD) in 1930. As editor of the Lübeck party paper, Leber played an important role in the SPD. A good speaker with solid worker contacts despite his intellectual background, Leber tried to bring middle-class youth into the SPD to help defend a German republic threatened by Nazis and Communists. For his efforts, he was branded a "rightist," but he served as a role model for Brandt who claimed they stood "in the same relationship … as a son to his father."

He Adopts New Name

When Brandt broke ideologically with Leber over the tactics which the SPD employed in fighting Nazism, he followed the splinter group that became the Socialist Workers' Party (SAP) in 1931. Brandt lost his job as a journalist with Leber's paper, as well as the promise of future financial support for university studies. Although stifled by the dull work of a shipping clerk, he learned much about seaport workers and made important contacts with Scandinavians. Between 1931 and 1933, Brandt led the youth section of the

CHRONOLOGY

1929	Joined the Social Democratic Party of Germany
1931	Joined the Socialist Workers' Party
1933	Fled to Scandinavia from Hitler's Germany
1936	Traveled incognito in Germany
1942	Appointed head of Norwegian-Swedish Press Bureau
1945	Returned to Berlin as Norwegian press correspondent
1954	Became head of Berlin SPD caucus
1957	Appointed governing mayor of Berlin
1964	Named chairperson of SPD
1966	Named German foreign minister
1969	Became chancellor of Germany
1971	Awarded Nobel Peace Prize
1974	Resigned as chancellor
1976	Became president of Socialist International
1977	Named chairperson, North-South Commission
1992	Died of cancer at age 78

SAP, working against Nazism, first openly, then secretly. When the Nazis took power under Hitler, they immediately tried to arrest liberals and socialists; left-wing parties were soon outlawed. In March 1933, while he secretly attended a Party meeting in Dresden, he dropped the name Herbert Frahm and adopted the name Willy Brandt, which he would keep. In another shift, he contacted Communists to resist Nazism. By taking the identity of a person who had been arrested, Brandt was able to escape to Oslo.

In exile, Brandt became a professional journalist and earned his living translating and writing. The work meshed well with his socialist and anti-Nazi efforts. Norway delighted him; he quickly learned Norwegian, and he became part of its labor movement. Unlike other refugees, he did not remain an outsider. He learned a more pragmatic social democracy: less theory and more tolerance for differing viewpoints. Brandt collected funds for other refugees and helped colleagues who had been arrested in Berlin. He still thought revolutionary socialism provided the answer to Germany's problems, but his radicalism was being tempered by Scandinavian moderation.

As a leader of his Party's youth wing, Brandt became known and trusted by many socialists. He traveled incognito to Berlin during 1936 to help coordinate underground activities. Party leaders sent him to report on the Spanish Civil War. He had, in his own words, "overcome my original left-socialist position, not its revolutionary elan, but its dogmatic narrowness."

After war broke out in 1939, Brandt faced new dangers. The Nazi regime had taken away his citizenship in 1938. When the German military occupied Norway in early 1940, Brandt might have tried to escape to Sweden. Instead, he put on a Norwegian uniform and let himself be interned. (Later, he would be accused of having fought against his own countrymen.) When the German occupiers freed what they thought was a Norwegian, Brandt made his way to Sweden, and again worked as a journalist and socialist, fostering a democratic post-Nazi Germany and Europe. His proposals and contacts brought him to the attention of other resistance leaders as well as the Allies, who were looking for Germans to replace Nazi leaders at war's end.

While in Scandinavia in 1941, Brandt had married a woman nine years his senior who had already given birth to his daughter. Separation and divorce followed in 1943, partly because Brandt sought the company of other women.

In 1945, when Brandt returned to Germany as a Norwegian reporter, he witnessed the destruction in his country. Although he did not approve when the Allies gave Germany's eastern territories to Poland, he did agree with the Nuremberg trials of Germany's war criminals. He arrived in Berlin in 1947 as Norwegian press attaché; in early 1948 he accepted a job with the SPD as liaison officer. Then, just as his personal life had become more stable by a second marriage and more children, his political career took a new course.

In the western part of Berlin, occupied by the victorious Allied powers of the United States, France, and England, Social Democracy had established itself by 1947 as the leading political party. Ernst Reuter became the SPD mayor and Brandt his protégé. Staunchly anti-Communist, Reuter opposed the national SPD leader Kurt Schumacher who tried to keep a distance from the Allies in order to maintain German unity. Brandt may have learned some anti-Communist rhetoric from Reuter during the Soviet blockade of West Berlin in 1948. By 1949, Brandt, with Reuter's support, became one of the 11 Berlin representatives in the new West German parliament in Bonn. From this base, he moved toward leadership posts in his Party.

The road to the top of the SPD proved to be long and difficult. Tactical differences and factional infighting abounded over relations with the Allies, coalition with the conservative Christian Democrats, and the Party's policies on property and education. At various Party conferences, Brandt came to know the regional leaders but tried not to offend any. In 1954, he still could not muster the votes for election to national executive, though Berliners strongly supported the SPD. When Brandt became head of the Berlin house of representatives, he continued his ambiguous stance on many Party policies—except that of rearmament. His vagueness, historian Barbara Marshall claims, can "be explained by his renewed attempt to be elected to the main SPD's executive committee." Others suggest he was "realistic."

Named Mayor of Berlin

In 1956, angry crowds gathered to vent their frustration when the Soviets crushed the Hungarian uprising. With the Soviet military occupying the Eastern sector of Berlin, easily seen from the Western sector, the Berliners might have rioted. When Brandt took over a mass meeting and had the crowd vent their frustrations by singing folksongs, his popularity increased. At the next elections, he was easily voted mayor. Continuing to serve as leader of the Berlin SPD, he not only had a large public following but had carefully cultivated young Party members. The Soviet threats to take over or blockade the city necessitated contacts with the Americans and forced Brandt onto the international political stage. Ticker-tape parades in New York as well as visits to Geneva and London made him a very visible politician; he was the "German Kennedy": youthful, energetic, with a pretty and pregnant wife at his side. Seeing in him a well-known personality, a capable and calculating tactician, the Social Democrats made him their candidate for chancellor of the country.

In 1961, his campaign—marred by personal smears from the opposition—failed to unseat the wily conservative **Konrad Adenauer.** But before Brandt had time for the personal depression which usually accompanied his defeats, the Soviets and East Germans built a wall to stop emigration from east to west via Berlin. While the conservative papers were accusing the West of "doing nothing," Brandt again helped calm an agitated populace.

The end of 1961 and much of 1962 found Brandt frustrated at not becoming chancellor.

Informing his Party that he would not necessarily be its candidate for chancellor again, he resigned his parliamentary seat to focus on Berlin. Though he had acquired a reputation for drinking and womanizing, support for him and for his Party in Berlin's 1962 elections helped him rebound.

By this time, he began to develop policies which made him not merely a Party politician but a world leader. Brandt had been rethinking the situation in Europe. Like Kennedy, who stood beside Brandt when giving his "I am a Berliner" speech, Brandt began to see the necessity of accepting the international situation. Change might come through cooperating with the Eastern bloc instead of trying to oppose it. Brandt's phrase "transformation by getting closer" hinted at what would become *Ostpolitik,* a new Eastern policy.

While basking in the glory of close relations with Kennedy, Brandt moved up in the SPD. Behind the scenes, Herbert Wehner and Fritz Erler were important in his bid to become Party leader. They controlled the Party organization and the parliamentary caucus. In 1964, at a special conference, Brandt attained the Party chairmanship and became candidate for chancellor for 1965. However, in that election the smear campaign went beyond accusations about his lifestyle to claims that he had betrayed national interests. Brandt was personally hurt by the attacks and suffered another depression. But his fast recovery from his second defeat demonstrated his ambitions as well as his strengths. He later stated that he experienced 1965 as a turning point, "Since then the decisions which I had to make were easier, because ... they no longer had to do with what one can become but rather with what one wants to do." Ambition gave way to purpose.

Brandt's Party, which had moderated its socialist policies, appeared to have reached a plateau. Despite having renounced Marxism in 1959 and having distanced itself from the Communists, the Party seemed unable to make the jump to power. Yet behind the scenes the SPD slowly shifted from a workers' to a popular party. As prosperity retreated before the recession of 1966, its demands for social and institutional reforms were finally heard by the public. Adenauer's successor Ludwig Erhard proved incapable of managing the government, directing the economy, and stemming the increasing far-left and far-right critiques of Germany. The ruling coalition of liberals and conservatives fell apart. While Wehner and Helmut Schmidt opted for continuity, the Christian Democratic-Social Democratic "great coalition," in which Brandt became foreign minister, was supposedly the cabinet of reconciliation between Germany's conservative and social-reform parties. Brandt only reluctantly joined the ministry, but he immediately led the march toward a new foreign policy.

Brandt's life had prepared him to see Germany from an international perspective. With Jean Monnet of France, he wanted to work toward a united states of Europe in which peace and prosperity would become the norm. He had good connections with Western leaders and soon built ties to the Soviets. Most important, he advocated acceptance of the self-interest of all other states, including East Germany. Acknowledging the existence of Eastern states and recognizing their existing borders, he felt, would begin to normalize diplomatic relations in Central Europe.

Between 1967 and 1969, Brandt encountered great difficulties in trying to implement an alteration of postwar German foreign policy. That policy, known as the "Hallstein" doctrine, had aimed at isolating the East German state and breaking diplomatic relations with any country which recognized it. Confrontation and sabotage had been the basic principles.

The internal situation hardly seemed better. In 1968, student radicals closed the universities and demanded direct democracy. They wanted Nazi criminals exposed and the elitist educational system opened. They pointed to the disparities between rich and poor. Because the "great coalition" had left such a small liberal and nationalist opposition in parliament, the students, many of whom admired Brandt for his anti-Fascist past, advocated an opposition "beyond parliament." Brandt and the SPD had difficulties because the Party leaders were cautious and the conservatives reluctant to make social changes.

By 1969, Brandt and other Social Democrats wanted to abandon their uncomfortable coalition with the conservatives. In the elections of that year, the SPD, claiming credit for bringing Germany up-to-date internationally, won just enough seats to combine with the liberals. Brandt could form his own government. When he became chancellor, Brandt confidently announced: "We do not stand at the end of our democracy, we are only just beginning." In two cabinets between 1969 and 1974, he would consolidate *Ostpolitik* and initiate internal reforms.

If the institutions proved difficult to change, Brandt and the succeeding Schmidt governments did create a renewed Germany. The rest of the world stopped asking whether the second German democracy would collapse. The fear of a revival of Nazism declined as the country increasingly began to acknowledge its past. The shift had been made

West German chancellor Willy Brandt makes a point at a 1973 press conference.

ern neighbor. Through visits to Eastern Germany, Brandt demonstrated the desire for national unity which was not at the cost of peace in Europe. He would later state that he had never attained anything by himself, but his personal friendship with the Soviet leader **Leonid Brezhnev,** his steadfastness despite conservative slander, and his ability to coordinate efforts with the Western Allies were decisive. Brandt worked toward and achieved the rehabilitation of Germany internationally; the Nobel Peace Prize awarded to him in 1971 recognized that contribution.

In internal matters, he was neither as successful nor as decisive. Cabinet members fought over the degree of state intervention in the economy, and Party members disapproved of harsh measures employed by provincial governments which opposed terrorism but also stifled legitimate dissenters. Workers demanded a share of the benefits of prosperity. Even during his second term, Brandt could achieve few significant reforms. With pressures from the Party, an oil crisis which increased economic problems, and finally the discovery of an East German spy within his own office, Brandt resigned in 1974.

Out of office at age 60, he hardly retired. Within a year, he increased the SPD's international contacts; within two years, he became president of the Socialist International. His European initiatives for normalization of state relations would become global. In conjunction with such credible Social Democratic leaders as Sweden's Olof Palme and Portugal's Mario Soares, he encouraged human rights. In 1977, as head of the North-South commission, he helped write a report which made the plight of the Third World better known. He acted, as he had previously on the diplomatic scene, as a kind of conscience to the industrialized world.

By the time Brandt retired from leadership of the Social Democratic Party in 1988, he had helped make that party an integral part of the normal political landscape within Germany. He had brought Germany respect as a modern state, and in the end his approach to the German question reaped the reward of the reunification of his country.

to the Party which had not led a government since 1930, yet it soon proved Social Democrats could run a state as well as conservatives. Normality had descended upon Germany, and other countries noted the decline of right radicalism and the state's successes at opposing terrorism. Brandt's major contribution was not to foster a dramatic change of institutions but to encourage an alteration of attitudes.

Nobel Peace Prize Awarded

If Brandt had merely presided over the process of Germany's internal normalization, he would have to be remembered as a significant German leader. However, he also presided over the consolidation of *Ostpolitik.* Between 1970 and 1971, four treaties were negotiated: with the Soviet Union, with Poland, with East Germany, and an international agreement on Berlin. Borders were recognized, nonaggression principles written into treaties, and contacts with Germans behind the Wall improved. In Warsaw, Brandt symbolically knelt and acknowledged Germany's crimes against its east-

SOURCES:

Bolesch, Hermann O., and Hans D. Leicht. *Willy Brandt: A Portrait of the German Chancellor.* Horst Erdmann, 1971.

Brandt, Willy. *In Exile: Essays, Reflections and Letters, 1933–1947.* Owald Wolff. 1973.

———. *People and Politics: The Years 1960–1975.* Collins, 1978.

Harpprecht, Klaus. *Willy Brandt: Portrait and Self-Portrait.* Nash Publishing, 1971.

Marshall, Barbara. *Willy Brandt.* Cardinal, 1990.

Prittie, Terence. *Willy Brandt: Portrait of a Statesman.* Weidenfeld & Nicolson, 1974.

FURTHER READING:

Brandt, Willy. *My Life in Politics.* Viking, 1992.

Catherine Breshkovsky

(1844–1934)

The only Russian revolutionist whose adulthood spanned the entire revolutionary period—from the early 1860s to 1917—and whose lifework was devoted entirely to the welfare of the peasants.

Name variations: Ekaterina or Katerina Breshkovskoi. Pronunciation: BRESH-kawf-skee. Born Ekaterina Constantinovna Breshko-Breshkovskaia on January 1844; died in 1934; daughter of Constantine Mikhailovich Verigo (an aristocrat) and Olga Ivanovna; married: Nikolai Breshko-Breshkovsky (a landowner); children: one son, Nicholas.

Born to Olga Ivanovna and Constantine Mikhailovich Verigo, Catherine Breshkovsky would often remark later in life, "I had wonderful parents; if there is anything good in me, I owe it all to them." From her father, she inherited frankness, good-heartedness, and a short temper; from her mother—a woman of gentility—she received an education from Bible stories. Her parents never whipped the children, never allowed a word of profanity. But in her childhood, Breshkovsky preferred solitude. In her memoirs, she would later explain that her tendency toward withdrawal sprang from feelings of being unwanted as a child; she recalled her mother saying once: "When you were born, I detested you so much…. My other children behave like typical children, Katia is like a whirlwind." Known as a violent and furious child, Breshkovsky's habitual withdrawal led to sudden and frequent disappearances that drove her governess insane: "Breshkovsky is a spider," she would scream.

As a child, Breshkovsky scrutinized events, people, even her own behavior, and could not accept personal failure. Often confused between the accepted evils of the culture around her and

"To look upon the face of this silver-haired apostle is like receiving a benediction."

KELLOGG DURLAND,
BOSTON TRANSCRIPT

Contributed by John Jovan Markovic, Assistant Professor of History, Andrews University, Berrien Springs, Michigan

what she thought to be right and humane, she snuck peasant friends into her wealthy home—a tendency for which she was scolded. She could not understand why it was unacceptable to bring a peasant friend into her home, while it was acceptable to see a child hungry, dirty, and in rags. Whipped and exiled for trivial infractions, serfs were treated like chattel; their wives and daughters were used as concubines, their children often taken away and sold.

The lot of the serfs horrified Breshkovsky. She would run off to the serfs' huts, eat with them, confide in them, and listen to stories of their plight. Although her father treated his serfs exceptionally well, she was still dismayed by the contrast between the living conditions of the hut and of her own home. Thus, the young aristocrat developed a strong desire to rectify social wrongs. Bearing witness to the life of the serfs transformed her into a merciless fighter for peasants' rights. Throughout her entire life, when she herself was in dire need, Breshkovsky was giving away food, money, and clothing to the poor and destitute.

Interested in the realities of life, she was a fervent reader, with little interest in fiction. At the age of nine, she read the entire *History of Russia* by N. A. Karamzin. Many years later, she admitted with trepidation to her son Nicholas—a successful novelist—that she would most likely skip many pages of his books for lack of interest in fictional works. They were two opposites: she was a revolutionist; he was a liberal without much sympathy for the outlaws.

Seventeen when Tsar **Alexander II** issued the Emancipation Act in 1861, Breshkovsky was soon aware that it did little to improve the peasants' anguish and misery. Since her father was a government-appointed arbiter for the district, she was exposed to heartrending scenes, the sobbing of wives, the whipping and crippling of men. In spite of the suffering, peasants clung to the belief that the Tsar would soon issue the real Manifesto. Although rumors were spread that the corrupt officials substituted the false document for the real one, the peasants did not believe that the Tsar, their Little Father, would betray them.

Two years later, at 19, Breshkovsky, her mother, and sister left for St. Petersburg. On the train, a young prince—a favorite of the Tsar—returning from an official visit to Siberia accidentally entered their compartment. He spoke with fiery zeal about Russia's future now that Tsar Alexander had issued a series of reforms. The prince was Peter Kropotkin, who later became a revolutionary anarchist. Breshkovsky interpreted the incident as providential.

CHRONOLOGY

1855	Alexander II ascended the Russian throne
1861	Emancipation Act issued
1863–70	Period of "Great reforms"
1873–76	Start of the "going to the people" movement
1881	Assassination of Alexander II
1891	Trans-Siberian Railway construction began
1903	Second Congress of the Social Democratic Party convened; party split into two factions: Bolsheviks and Mensheviks
1905	"Bloody Sunday" in St. Petersburg
1914	Outbreak of World War I
1917	Nicholas II abdicated; Provisional Government assumed power; Lenin returned to Russia; Bolsheviks seized power
1918	World War I ended
1918–21	Civil War fought Russia
1924	Lenin died
1928	Stalin introduced the First Five Year Plan and collectivization of agriculture
1936-38	Great Purges began

While in St. Petersburg, she joined the circles of liberal-minded young nobility, attending classes of higher education (though it was illegal for females to pursue higher education). But when her mother took ill, she returned home and opened a boarding school for girls, the earnings from which helped her teach peasant children free of charge. Always independent in spirit, at the age of 25, she arranged a marriage with a broad-minded young nobleman, Nikolai Breshko-Breshkovsky. Marriages of "convenience" were not then uncommon among the radical Russian youth. The law required direct supervision of females by the nearest male kin; in order to break away from their often abusive fathers, many female revolutionists married close friends. Ordinarily, the couples would part the day after the wedding, sometimes never to see each other again.

Breshkovsky and her husband stayed in their district, however, where they opened a school and a cooperative bank for the peasants. But a desire to engage in more meaningful activities took Breshkovsky to Kiev. There, she was invited to join a group of radicals on their way to the United

States to establish a socialist colony. "Never," she replied, "how can we leave Russia now, when there is much of importance to be done here?" Instead, she began searching for companions, "students not only of books but of life."

Conflict Between Motherhood and Revolutionist

Four years after her marriage, Breshkovsky faced one of her greatest challenges: she decided to devote herself, and everything she owned, to the cause of the revolution. Her husband and family begged the pregnant Breshkovsky to stay and pursue reforms in their own district, urging her to consider the needs of the child. Convinced that "the call of the greatest and gravest duty" bade her leave everything and everyone behind, with great pain she left her parents and husband. Before the winter of 1873–74 was over, she gave birth to a boy, whom she promptly entrusted to her sister-in-law. The separation from her son would last 23 years. "The conflict between my love for the child and my love for the revolution and for the freedom of Russia robbed me of many a night's sleep," she wrote. "I knew that I could not be a mother and still be a revolutionist."

In the spring of 1874, thousands of young educated idealists left their homes and classrooms to go to the countryside and live with the peasants. In July, Breshkovsky and her two companions, Masha (Mariia) Kalenkina and Iakov Stefanovich, left for the Ukrainian villages. This "going to the people" movement was born of the belief that once the peasants heard the socialist "gospel," they would rise and overthrow the yoke of oppression.

Breshkovsky's clear, strong voice, her choice of concepts and words that peasants could relate to, and her sincerity impressed the peasants everywhere. Dumbfounded in the presence of someone who could read, they held a printed page with reverence, and gathered in great crowds to listen to her. However, when the revolutionists singled out the Tsar as the primary cause for their oppression, the peasants refused to believe them, and many immediately dispersed. Breshkovsky often compared the tsarist regime with evil forces. Since, to the peasants, the mention of the Tsar and the devil in the same breath was scandalous, some visited local authorities to report such "subversion."

Disguised as peasants, and with false internal passports, Breshkovsky and her comrades were continually on the run from the police. In one of the villages, she and Masha Kalenkina took up lodging with a peasant family. There, one of the family's girls—having snooped through their belongings—confided to neighbor friends that the strangers had literature and maps. The news eventually reached the local chief of police who immediately confronted Breshkovsky and asked for her papers. She told him that she was a peasant woman from a northern Russian province. But in the course of interrogation, he tried to take her by the chin as nobility and officials then did to the serfs; instinctively, she backed off, inadvertently revealing that she was of aristocratic descent. The chief was elated, for the arrest of an important revolutionist meant a respectable reward from his superiors.

First Woman Condemned to Hard Labor

In October 1877, Breshkovsky was taken to St. Petersburg and brought before the court. The famous Trial of the 193 lasted several months. Female prisoners typically received light sentences, but Breshkovsky's arrogant refusal to submit to the authority of the tsarist court was her undoing. The first woman in Russia to be condemned to hard labor, she was sent to work in the mines at Kara, far east of Lake Baikal, in Siberia. After a stay of ten months, she was marched to Barguzin, a small prison town on the east shore of Lake Baikal.

Breshkovsky's later writings indicate that at Barguzin, she was condemned to the "torture" of enforced idleness. Forbidden to teach or meet with other prisoners, she nevertheless befriended three students in exile. With the help of a native guide, the four of them escaped the town, walking some 600 miles eastward across the mountains before the police caught up with them. Because of the strict order from St. Petersburg to capture Catherine Breshkovsky, the police were tenacious, and the attempted escape cost her four more years of hard labor at Kara. After Kara, she was marched again, this time 1,000 miles south to Selenginsk.

In Selenginsk, she met George Kennan who was collecting material for his book *Siberia and the Exile System*. After eight years in Selenginsk, Breshkovsky was permitted to travel within Siberia, allowing her to befriend some important individuals. Then, in 1896, her term of Siberian exile at last expired, leaving her free to return to Western Russia, though not to St. Petersburg.

Upon her return, Breshkovsky faced a new world. Her parents and husband had passed away. Brought up as an aristocrat, her 23-year-old son Nicholas snubbed his revolutionist mother. The peasants had changed, too, having matured politically. Believing them nearly ready for revolution,

Breshkovsky began another missionary journey into the Russian countryside. For eight years the railway compartments were her home. As the name Catherine Breshkovsky disappeared from Western Russia, people talked instead of *Babushka* ("grandma").

During these years, she coached the peasants and organized underground circles and terrorist attacks on government officials, though this work placed her on the list of the most wanted political criminals. She also helped establish the Socialist Revolutionary Party. In May of 1903, she left Russia via Odessa and Vienna to Geneva. The following year, she arrived in the United States to seek help for her cause.

Speaking in New York, Boston, Chicago, and other major cities, she was received everywhere with enthusiasm. She stressed the strength of the revolutionary movement in Russia and appealed for both moral and material help. She reassured audiences that the Russian peasant had demonstrated that he was able to manage his own future and argued that, in only four decades since 1861, he had cast off the blind faith in the tsar and learned of his own worth. The most significant change, she stressed, was the peasants' ability to read and understand political issues. After her speech in Philadelphia, approximately 2,000 exhilarated Russian immigrants sang and shouted while carrying her around on their shoulders.

Shortly after her return to Russia, the government—with help from agent Evno F. Azeff—caught up with Breshkovsky and arrested her. Azeff, a well-known and much-trusted revolutionist, had infiltrated the Socialist Revolutionary Party to the very top. The list of charges against Breshkovsky was so long that it took the court clerk an hour to read it. Were it not for friends from abroad who pressured the Russian government, and the government's reluctance to create a martyr, Babushka most likely would have received the death sentence. An American friend came from the United States and begged government officials to release her. They would not.

Free at Last

The government considered the 66-year-old woman a dangerous prisoner. A journalist reported that on her way out of court, she was escorted by a police officer in front of her carrying a naked sword and ten armed officers behind. By April 1910, she was making her second journey to Siberia. Sent to a small island in the Lena River,

some 200 miles north of Lake Baikal, she was allowed limited correspondence with a few close friends, many of them outside Russia. For some time, the public in Western Russia heard little of her, until—in the winter of 1913–14—the newspapers reported that the 70-year-old prisoner had escaped from her place of exile. This time, the government sent 50 armed men to bring her back to face 16 months of incarceration. Following the first Russian Revolution in February 1917, she was freed.

The newly formed Provisional Government sent Catherine Breshkovsky a special invitation to return to Petrograd (formerly St. Petersburg) from her place of exile. Upon arrival in Moscow, she was placed in the deposed Tsar's state coach, receiving a military escort and royal treatment. At the railroad station in Petrograd, the crowd nearly stormed the station, trying to see and touch Babushka. She later wrote, "I do not think that anywhere in the world there ever was a bride who received so many flowers." **Alexander Kerensky,** then Secretary of Justice, addressed the crowd: "Comrades, the Grandmother of the Russian Revolution has returned at last to a free country." Breshkovsky truly deserved the title; no other Russian revolutionist, male or female, had lived through the entire revolutionary period from the early 1860s to 1917. Her lifelong service to the cause of Russian peasantry extended from the cruel reign of **Nicholas I** to the ruthless rule of **Joseph Stalin.** Little did Kerensky know, however, that the Bolshevik coup d'état in October of 1917 would eventually exile both him and Breshkovsky from their "free" country.

Following the October 1917 Revolution, Breshkovsky remained in Russia, actively involved in the political struggle against the Bolsheviks, but in December of 1918—as the Civil War was consuming Russia—she was forced to leave. For the third time, she traveled east, across Siberia, this time not into Siberian exile but exile abroad. After she reached Japan in 1919, she left for the United States. From there, she moved to Czechoslovakia in 1924. In Prague, under extreme conditions, she continued to fight the oppressive Bolshevik regime. Her struggle for the Russian peasant did not stop with her exile; she continued working among the Carpatian Russians who lived in the territories then part of post-war Czechoslovakia. Breshkovsky's real strength of persuasion was not so much in her ability to charm and speak, as in her living example. After living in France for a short time, she returned to Czechoslovakia where she died at the age of 90.

SOURCES:

Blackwell, Alice Stone, ed. *Little Grandmother of the Russian Revolution.* Little, Brown, 1919.

Breshkovskaia, Ekaterina. "1917-yi god," in *Novyi Zhurnal (The New Review).* Vol. 38, 1954: pp. 191–206.

Kerensky, Alexander. "Catherine Breshkovsky (1844–1934)," in *The Slavonic and East European Review.* Vol. 13. No. 38. January 1935: pp. 428–431.

———. "Kak ia khodila v narod," in *Novyi Zhurnal (The New Review).* Vol. 62, 1960: pp. 176–210.

———. "Rannie gody E. K. Breshkovskoi," in *Novyi Zhurnal (The New Review)*, Vol. 60, 1960: pp. 179–195.

FURTHER READING:

Arkhangelsky, V. G. Katerina *Breshkovskaya.* Prague, 1938.

Hutchinson, Lincoln, ed. *Hidden Springs of the Russian Revolution: Personal Memoirs of Katerina Breshkovskaia.* Stanford University Press, 1931.

Maxwell, Margaret. *Narodniki Women: Russian Women Who Sacrificed Themselves for the Dream of Freedom.* Pergamon, 1990.

Brian Boru

(c. 941–1014)

First overlord of all Ireland, whose reign marked the earliest attempt to develop a centralized monarchy in Ireland and ensure freedom from Viking domination.

"The death of Brian Boru at the battle of Clontarf in 1014 marked the end of the most successful attempt to establish a kingdom of Ireland. King Brian, obscure in origin and without the kind of respectable ancestry admired by the conservative Irish, had forced his way through a succession of usurpations to the kingship of Ireland."

J. F. LYDON

Brian Boru ruled in Ireland during the late 10th and early 11th century, a time when the historical often verged on the legendary. The numerous legends and stories that have been written about his exploits make tracing the real, historical Brian difficult. His origins are obscure, and there is precious little known about him until he succeeded his brother as king of Thomond, one of the numerous petty kingdoms into which Ireland was divided in the mid-10th century. By the time of his death, Brian Boru had succeeded in securing recognition of his status as high-king, and had become the first overlord of all Ireland. While he worked hard to consolidate his rule over all the petty Irish kingdoms, the union he created ran too much against Irish traditions, and after his death it crumbled and split apart. His achievement, however, lived on in popular memory.

The Ireland into which Brian was born was changing. Traditionally, the country had consisted more or less of five provinces or kingdoms—Munster, Connacht, Leinster, Ulster, and Meath—which were composed themselves of smaller petty kingdoms organized around clans, whose importance and influence rose and declined with the per-

Contributed by Douglas C. Jansen, Ph.D. in Medieval History, University of Texas, Austin, Texas

Name variations: Brian Borowe, Brian Bóruma, Brian Boroma, Brian Bórumha; also Brian macCennetich, Brian macCennétig (Irish). Born c. 941 at Bórumha (near modern Killeloe); died in the battle of Clontarf on April 23, 1014; son of Kennedy (Cennétig), king of the Dál Cais; married: Gormfallith (Gormflaith), mother of Sitric king of Dublin; married: Dub Choblaig, daughter of the king of Connacht (died 1009); children: (sons) Murchad, Domhnall, Tadhg, Donnchad; (daughter) Sadbh. Descendants: The O'Brien dynasty of Irish kings, including Tairrdelbach (Turloch) Ua Briain, high-king (1072–86) and Muirchertach Ua Briain, high-king (1088–1119). Predecessor: Kennedy son of Lorcán. Successor: Donnchad macBrian.

altered the traditional political structure, for the ability of a king to protect his people became as important as his ancestry. For centuries, the Uí Néill kings had both: their dynasty had been hereditary high-kings for generations, and they had been the most effective defenders of Ireland against the depredations of the Vikings. In the late tenth century, however, the Uí Néill lost their advantage to Brian Boru, who used the disruptions caused by the Vikings' presence to unseat the Uí Néill kings and make the high-kingship a reality for the first time in Irish history.

Brian Boru was born into the family of Dál Cais, an aristocratic dynasty of Thomond (Munster), around 941. He was a younger son of Kennedy son of Lorcán, and undoubtedly was reared steeped in the conservative legal and social traditions of tenth-century Ireland, traditions that emphasized the military role of the nobility. His early years were filled with losses that often afflict those who engage constantly in war. When he was only two years old, his grandfather was killed by Norse Vikings; his father died in 951 when Brian was about ten. Even though the Dál Cais were only petty kings, in the 950s and 960s the sons of Kennedy took the lead against the Vikings in southern Ireland. The activities of Brian and his elder brother, Mathgamain, and their struggle against the nearby Viking menace at Limerick show the strength of Brian's personality and illustrate the ambition and persistence that would eventually propel him to the high-kingship.

After the death of their father, Mathgamain and Brian took up the struggle against the powerful Danish force headquartered in Limerick. Outnumbered by the Danes, they conducted a hit-and-run war against the invaders, with no quarter given on either side. Refusing to submit to the kings of Limerick, they retreated into the forests and wilderness of Dál Cais, where their people lived in caves and hidden huts, and even in the knotty wet roots of trees. Eventually, Mathgamain tired of this existence and agreed to a truce with Ivar, king of Limerick, but Brian refused to participate. Angry with Mathgamain for making a truce with the enemy and unable to do so himself, Brian fell back deeper into the wilderness. He and those few men who followed him fought on unceasingly, ambushing and attacking the enemy whenever they could, killing them in twos or threes or fives. Brian and his men persisted with their guerilla warfare until it was reported that only 15 of his followers were left alive.

According to the author of the *War of the Gaedhil with the Gaill*, a somewhat dubious literary account written over a century after Brian's death,

sonality and leadership abilities of their individual kings. The authority of these kings, and the overkings who ruled the five greater kingdoms, was severely restricted by very conservative, separatist-oriented customs. These customs and the law codes they engendered gave a king the right to conduct "foreign" relations and make war, but it limited a king's ability to interfere in the domestic affairs of his own nobility.

Before Brian became high-king in the early 11th century, the position was one of fictional power. The men who held the title rarely exercised the authority they claimed, that is, ultimate authority over all of Ireland. The high-kingship had rested for three centuries in the hands of the Uí Néill dynasty whose power base was in northern Ireland, in the kingdoms of Ulster and Meath. In the early ninth century, Viking raiders from Norway and Denmark pillaged their way through the island, eventually establishing forts at places like Wexford, Waterford, Limerick, and Dublin, from which they controlled the surrounding countryside. The Vikings' intrusion into Irish society

the two brothers met and argued. Mathgamain lamented all those who had gone to their graves following Brian, but Brian bitterly responded to Mathgamain's pity, implying that Mathgamain had betrayed his inheritance. Maintaining that their grandfather would never have made a truce with the invaders as Mathgamain had done with the king of Limerick, Brian defended his decision to refuse peace. He argued angrily that it was hereditary for all the Dál Cais to die as their fathers had done before them. It was not natural that they should submit to insult or contempt, and there was no honor in abandoning their inheritance, either to invaders or to other Irish. An assembly of the kingdom was called to decide on peace or war, and Brian's side won the day. The Dál Cais would expel the foreigners from their land. Although this account may be a later literary invention, it is possible to see in this conflict Brian's persistence and his inability to compromise.

The brothers gathered allies from around Thomond and Connacht and in 967 met and defeated the Limerick Vikings in the battle of Sulcoit. There was no sparing the defeated Scandinavians. Marching to Limerick, Brian and Mathgamain sacked the fort, burned the town that had grown up around it, killed or enslaved the town's inhabitants, and drove Ivar overseas. Mathgamain, in his victory over the men of Limerick, was acknowledged as the king of Munster, but not without opposition. Maelmuad, king of Desmond (southern Munster) and rival for the Munster kingship, succeeded in having Mathgamain treacherously murdered in 976.

In a period of two years (976–78), as chief of the Dál Cais and the self-appointed avenger of his brother, Brian defeated yet another incursion by the Vikings of Limerick, and in the battle of Belach Lechta (978), met and defeated Maelmuad and the men of Desmond. According to the accounts, 1,200 of Maelmuad's men fell in the battle. Now king of Munster, Brian consolidated his triumph by marrying his daughter, Sadbh, to Maelmuad's son, Cian. In the years following, Brian worked persistently to consolidate his gains in Munster and subjugate neighboring kings. He was eminently successful and showed himself able to protect his lands and the people under his rule. By the end of the tenth century, he had become the preeminent power in southern Ireland and forced the region's kings to recognize his supremacy.

The growth of Brian's power and, indeed, even his overlordship of southern Ireland were not fulfilled without a struggle. The high-king, Maelseachlinn II, contested Brian's claims to southern provinces, and the two kings launched raids against each other throughout the 980s and 990s. In 984, Brian marshaled his forces and constructed a fleet of 300 boats on the River Shannon, sailing them up to Loch Ree. From the lake, he and his fleet ravaged much of Maelseachlinn's territory of Meath. Maelseachlinn retaliated the next year by burning a region under Brian's control. And so it went until in 997 the two kings met on the shore of Loch Ree and agreed to a truce which divided Ireland between them. Maelseachlinn II, faced with Brian's growing power, recognized his authority over the southern half of the island.

After signing this truce, Brian could work to extend his authority over those areas in southern Ireland that still held out against him—Leinster and Dublin—without fear of attack from the northern clans. At Glen Mama in 999, he fought a great battle against Dublin Vikings and the men of Leinster. The Viking king escaped but could find no refuge, and so was forced to submit to Brian's mercy. Brian accepted the king's submission, accepted his hostages, and placed Dublin under the rule of a new king of his own choosing.

Brian Boru Becomes High-King

With Dublin finally subdued, Brian turned his ambition to the high-kingship. Maelseachlinn and the other northern kings had become alarmed by Brian's growing power, so in 1001 they tried to check him by building a boom across the River Shannon against the Munstermen. Brian responded by launching raids against the king of Connacht and Maelseachlinn, both of whom were forced to give Brian hostages and recognize his superiority. Thus, in 1002, Brian Boru had replaced Maelseachlinn as high-king and broken a long historical tradition. No longer would the high-kingship be the hereditary domain of the Uí Néill; after Brian's reign, the high-kingship would go to the king who was the strongest and most capable of protecting his position.

Perhaps in conscious emulation of earlier kings like Charlemagne, Alfred the Great, and Otto the Great, of whom he would certainly have had knowledge, Brian adopted a strategy designed to consolidate his power, strengthen the position he had worked so hard to achieve, and unify the island under his control. He was already over 60 years old, and it appears that he was looking toward strengthening Ireland for his descendants. He had roads and bridges built, harbors constructed, new churches erected and old ones repaired. Significantly, like his Saxon predecessor in England, Alfred the Great, he also built

King Brian before the Battle of Clontarf.

siastical overlordship over the English Church. He also clarified his perception of his position as high-king when he gave the church 20 ounces of gold and had the gift recorded as having been given "in the presence of Brian, emperor of the Irish." By choosing to use the term "emperor," with its weighty implications of sovereignty and authority, Brian was trying to strengthen a traditionally weak high-kingship, perhaps to make Ireland's kingship resemble other Western monarchies.

Brian's usurpation of the high-kingship from Maelseachlinn II and the Uí Néill, his attempt to centralize Irish government, and his attempt to enhance the authority of the high-king—in effect, his attempt to unify Ireland under himself and his successors—was such a break with Irish political tradition that it could not last. The men of Leinster and the men of Dublin, with promises of support from Vikings from the Orkneys and the Isle of Man, rebelled against Brian's authority.

In the summer of 1013, Brian gathered his entire force to put down the rebellion. He and his eldest son Murchad split the army into two parts: Murchad led half the army through Leinster, plundering the kingdom as he went. Brian took the other half, and marched by a different route to meet Murchad outside Dublin. Reunited, Brian's army besieged the Leinstermen, who had fled within the city, and the Dublin Vikings to no avail. Around Christmas, Brian lifted his siege and returned home.

Sitric, the king of Dublin, at the encouragement of his mother, Gormflaith, who had once been Brian's wife but had been spurned by her husband, sought help against the high-king from other sources. He enlisted the aid of Sigurd, the powerful Norse jarl of the Orkneys, and of Brodir, a Viking chieftain on the Isle of Man, by promising each the overlordship of Ireland if the campaign proved successful. These outsiders were to land on Palm Sunday 1014 and march with the men of Dublin and Leinster against Brian. With his widespread sources of information, Brian learned of these plans and began to marshal his own forces. His army, composed mostly of Munstermen but containing elements from kingdoms throughout the island, set out for Dublin to meet the rebels and invaders. The battle scene was set.

The Mighty Battle at Clontarf

According to a rather incredible literary account written over a century later, the sky was full of omens in the days before the battle, indicating the slaughter that was to follow. Norse accounts report

fortresses throughout Munster as defensive bulwarks against possible enemy incursions. Recognizing the importance of an educated clergy, not only for the salvation of peoples' souls but for the promotion of effective government, he encouraged and emphasized learning and attempted to raise Irish culture to the glorious levels it had attained in the seventh and eighth centuries.

Traditionally, a high-king of Ireland was limited in his ability to interfere in the domestic disputes of his subject kings. Brian, however, while respecting tradition, also seems to have encroached upon tradition. After 1002, he acted more like an emperor than a high-king. In 1005, he subdued the last unconquered resisting kingdom, Ulster, and made a progress throughout the island to show his power and position. He even made a circuit of the north and stayed for a week at the church and monastery of Armagh, which was the most important religious center in Ireland. There he attempted to centralize religious affairs by recognizing the ecclesiastical overlordship of the abbot of Armagh over the whole Irish Church, much as the Archbishop of Canterbury was recognized to have eccle-

showers of blood, flights of savage ravens, and axes battling spears in midair. Irish chronicles recorded that before the battle Brian had visions that foretold his impending death. Obviously these portents are difficult to believe, but it is clear from all accounts that both sides fully understood the importance of the upcoming battle. It was to be a battle to determine whether the Irish would rule themselves or whether they would be dominated by Scandinavian conquerors. On the morning of Good Friday, April 23, 1014, the rebel host—which accordingly to the *Annals of the Four Masters* consisted of over 1,000 warriors in coats of mail—armed itself and marched out of Dublin. The two armies met on a battlefield called Clontarf, just outside Dublin (today a Dublin suburb).

According to the chronicler of the battle, Brian refused to fight on a holy day for religious reasons and, choosing to remain behind the battle lines in a headquarters tent to pray for success, gave command to his son, Murchad. More likely, Brian declined active participation in the battle because of his age; he was 73 and too old to fight. While he was as involved in strategy and tactics as was possible, he conceded the strenuous leadership of the battle to his son. Thus, on a cold and blustery spring day, the two forces met. The wind was so fierce, it is reported, that the blood shed by Danish warriors sprayed into the eyes of the Irish. Battle raged from dawn to almost dusk, and as the day progressed the death toll became staggering. Of the enemy many, including Sigurd and the king of Leinster, were killed. Of Brian's forces, his son Murchad, his grandson Tordelbach, and numerous others were killed as they fought the rebels and invaders.

Toward the end of the day, when the tide had turned against the invaders, Brodir, chief of the Manx Vikings, a savage fighter whose black hair was so long he had to tuck it in his belt, broke through the king's guards and began to slash at the elderly Brian, finally killing him by burying his axe deep in Brian's skull. Reportedly, Brodir, having done this, called out in a loud voice, "Now let man tell man that Brodir felled Brian!"

While the Leinstermen and Dublin Vikings lost the battle of Clontarf, it was a Pyrrhic victory for the men of Munster. Brian had been killed, and Murchad, his most likely successor, had also perished in the battle. The kingship of the Dál Cais, and by extension the kingship of Munster fell to Brian's younger son, Donnchad, who was ill-suited to claim his father's position or authority. While he was a contender for the high-kingship, he never attained the position of his father, and the political situation in Ireland returned to the more traditional separatist norm. Brian's attempt at high-kingship was ambitious and ultimately unsuccessful, but it produced a vision of Irish unity.

SOURCES:

Hennessy, William M., ed. *Annals of Ulster.* Vol. 1. Dublin: Her Majesty's Stationary Office, 1887.

———. *Chronicum Scotorum (A Chronicle of Irish Affairs).* Rolls Series, London, 1866.

Mac Airt, Sean, ed. & tr. *Annals of Inisfallen.* Dublin Institute for Advanced Studies, 1951.

O'Donovan, John, ed. *Annals of the Kingdom of Ireland by the Four Masters.* Dublin: Hodges, Smith, 1856.

FURTHER READING:

Curtis, Edmund. *A History of Ireland.* 6th ed. Barnes and Noble, 1950.

D'alton, Rev. Edward Alfred. *History of Ireland from the Earliest Times to the Present Day.* Gresham Publishing Company, 1913.

Green, Alice Stopford. *History of the Irish State to 1014.* Macmillan, 1925.

Lydon, J. F. *The Lordship of Ireland in the Middle Ages.* Gill and Macmillan, 1972.

Otway-Ruthven, A. J. *A History of Medieval Ireland.* 2nd ed. Ernest Benn, 1980.

Robert Bruce

(1274–1329)

King of Scots, who came to the throne by usurpation but went on to lead Scotland's fight for independence against England, stablizing the Scottish monarchy and nation.

Name variations: Robert I of Scotland, Robert the Bruce. Born at Turnberry castle on July 11, 1274; died at Cardross on June 7, 1329; buried in Dunfermline Abbey; son of Robert Bruce and Marjorie of Carrick; married: Isabella of Mar; married: Elizabeth de Burgh; children: (first marriage) Marjorie; (second marriage) David, John, Matilda, and Margaret. Predecessor: John Balliol (1292–96). Successor: David II (1329–71).

On July 11, 1274, Robert Bruce was born at Turnberry castle, the remains of which can still be seen perched on a cliff overlooking the Firth of Clyde. Known in the later years of his reign as "Good King Robert," Bruce helped restore the Scottish realm and monarchy to a strong position after ten years of civil and foreign war, while securing the recognition of Scottish independence from the English crown and the papacy.

The eldest son of Robert, who was the sixth of that name, and Marjorie, the countess of Carrick, the young Robert Bruce is absent from the historical record from the time of his birth until 1286 when he and his father witnessed a charter. He again disappears from 1286 to 1292 but would have likely received the traditional education accorded the son of a nobleman, which at that time laid heavy emphasis upon military skills, horsemanship, and proficiency in arms.

Little territorial difference existed between Bruce's Scotland and that of today. In 1266, Norway had ceded the Western Isles to Scotland, and there had been a well-established, if permeable, border with England since 1237. But within this

"At length it pleased God ... to restore us to liberty ... by our most serene prince, king, and lord Robert, who, for the delivering of his people's and his own rightful inheritance from the enemy's hand, did ... undergo all manner of toil, fatigue, hardship and hazard."

THE DECLARATION
OF ARBROATH (1320)

Contributed by Russell Andrew McDonald, Ph.D., University of Guelph, Guelph, Ontario, Canada

compact territory lived a racial and linguistic medley of peoples, of whom the Scots formed only one part. The highlands and Western Islands were strongly Gaelic in both race and speech, with the Norse heritage still felt; in the south, in Lothian, the Anglo-Saxon and English inheritance was strong. And wherever the Anglo-Norman aristocracy had settled in the 12th and 13th centuries, French culture and language had taken root. Robert Bruce would have known and spoken English, French, and Gaelic. Yet, despite this heterogeneity, there remained a sense of Scottish unity that found its greatest expression in the monarchy—which had by the 13th century emerged as a stable European type of kingship—and in the development by 1286 of the *communitas regni Scotie* ("the community of the Realm of Scotland"), that is, the whole body of free subjects of the crown.

But during Robert Bruce's youth this Scottish identity came into great peril when on a dark, rainy night in March 1286, King Alexander III fell from his horse and broke his neck. The heir apparent was a small girl who died shortly thereafter in October of 1290, and those who felt entitled to the throne submitted their claims to **Edward I** of England, who first insisted that he be recognized as feudal suzerain of Scotland by all competitors (there were over a dozen). The two frontrunners were Robert Bruce "the Competitor" (young Robert's grandfather), and John Balliol, both of whom claimed descent from David of Huntingdon, the youngest brother of two previous kings of Scots, Malcolm IV and William the Lion. After much deliberation, Edward I chose John Balliol to be king of Scots in November of 1292. Earlier in the month, when Robert Bruce the Competitor had resigned his claims to the throne to his son and heirs, Robert Bruce's father had resigned the earldom of Carrick to his 18-year-old son. Consequently, the events of the years 1291–92 no doubt firmly impressed upon Bruce his family's claims to the throne.

The middle years of the 1290s were crucial for Bruce. In 1295, his grandfather died, and because of his father's lack of interest in Scottish political affairs, the younger Robert became the virtual head of the household. In the same year, he married Isabella of Mar, but his wife died a few months after the birth of their daughter Marjorie. Meanwhile, tensions between England and Scotland escalated until March of 1296 when the displacement of King **John** by a Scottish council and a Scottish alliance with France drove King Edward to declare war against John. By August, John had submitted to Edward, and the English king received the homage and fealty of many Scottish

CHRONOLOGY

1274	Born at Turnberry castle
1286	Alexander III of Scotland died
1291–92	Edward I of England arbitrated Scottish succession; John Balliol appointed king
1296	Balliol deposed by Edward I
1297	Popular uprisings against English led by William Wallace
1298	Edward I defeated Scots at battle of Falkirk
1300	Robert Bruce and John Comyn appointed joint Guardians
1302	Bruce resigned Guardianship and returned to Edward's favor
1305	Wallace captured and executed in London
1306	Bruce killed Comyn; had himself enthroned at Scone; excommunicated by pope; defeated by English and forced to flee Scotland
1307	Began recovery of lands from the English; Edward I died
1309	Bruce held first parliament at St. Andrews
1314	Bruce and Scots defeated English at battle of Bannockburn near Stirling
1315	Edward Bruce invaded Ireland to open second front
1320	Scots sent "Declaration of Arbroath" to the pope
1328	Treaty of Edinburgh-Northampton recognized Robert Bruce as king of Scots, and Scotland as an independent country
1329	Bruce died at Cardross; succeeded by son David

nobles, including the Bruces. When Robert Bruce's father reminded Edward of an earlier promise of the throne, the English king retorted, "Have we nothing else to do than win kingdoms for you?" In the fall, Edward returned to England, leaving the government of Scotland in the hands of English administrators. But Scotland had not been subdued.

By May of 1297, there were already uprisings against English rule, led by a knight named William Wallace. Bruce meanwhile headed a revolt in his own earldom of Carrick. It remains an open question as to why, having until now proven loyal to Edward I, Bruce suddenly changed sides. Were his sights already set on the throne? Historians cannot decide. Perhaps he was merely joining his countrymen; as he himself reportedly remarked, "No man holds his own flesh and blood in hatred and I am no exception. I must join my own people and the nation in which I was born."

In September of 1297, the Scots, led by Wallace, defeated the English at the battle of Stirling Bridge. It is not known whether Bruce was present, but it is clear that Wallace was fighting in the name of the deposed King John. In the victory's aftermath, Wallace was made Guardian (in the name of King John), and Edward I once again prepared for war.

Gathering an enormous force of cavalry, footsoldiers, and archers, Edward headed north in the summer of 1298. When they met the Scots at Falkirk on July 22, the English forces overwhelmed their opponents. Wallace escaped but resigned the Guardianship almost immediately, and the position then fell jointly upon the shoulders of Robert Bruce and John Comyn the Red of Badenoch, who was related to the Balliols by marriage. Theirs proved an uneasy alliance, since Bruce and Balliol were old rivals, and since the Guardians still acted in the name of King John. So, Bruce resigned in 1300. His decision may also have had something to do with English campaigns in his earldom, and with Scottish negotiations with the papacy to see John Balliol released from papal custody. A Balliol restoration would have boded ill for the Bruce family's claims to the throne. By 1302, Bruce had submitted to Edward I and was back in the English king's favor. Motives for his switch of allegiance remain puzzling, with the most likely explanation, according to G. W. S. Barrow, being his "growing disgust and frustration with a struggle which threatened to exalt the Balliols at the expense of his family's power and position." The politically ambitious, expedient side of Bruce's character cannot, however, be overlooked. Following his submission, he married Elizabeth de Burgh, daughter of the powerful earl of Ulster and one of King Edward's staunchest supporters.

Murder in the Church at Dumfries

Edward invaded Scotland again in May 1303, making armed progress throughout the realm. In March of the following year, he held a Parliament at St. Andrews and most of the nobility and important men of Scotland returned to his favor. When Stirling castle fell to the English in July— and when Wallace was betrayed, taken to London, tried, and executed as a traitor (August 1305)— Edward could well have imagined that his troubles in Scotland were over. Then on February 10, 1306, Bruce met John Comyn at the Franciscan church in Dumfries. The contents of their conversation remain a mystery, but the meeting resulted in a

quarrel which ended with Bruce and his companions slaying Comyn. Though the murder apparently was not premeditated, it forced Bruce's hand, and in a hastily arranged ceremony on March 25, he was enthroned at Scone. He was, by almost any standard, a usurper. Hearing the news, Edward went into paroxysms of rage, the pope excommunicated Bruce for committing murder in a church, and Bruce now had to face the wrath of the Comyns and their allies. Thus, civil war with the Comyns and Balliols and war with England were Bruce's short-term legacy.

Twice defeated by the English during the summer of 1306, Bruce again disappears from the record until early 1307; his activities during this interval are one of the great mysteries of Scottish history. Most likely he fled to the Western Isles, but he may have ventured as far afield as Ireland, the Orkneys, or Norway. The story of his hiding in a cave and gaining new hope while watching a spider's repeated attempts to spin a web did not arise until the 18th century and is certainly apocryphal. Regardless of Bruce's whereabouts, Edward took gruesome vengeance upon his followers: the bishop of St. Andrews and the bishop of Glasgow were held in irons; Bruce's brother Nigel was captured and hanged; and Bruce's wife and daughter were imprisoned in iron cages.

Despite such reverses, in January of 1307 Bruce returned to Scotland. Again disaster ensued. His brothers Thomas and Alexander were captured and executed, and Bruce was forced to flee into the hills. Then, after overcoming several attempts on his life by treachery, he and his band of followers defeated the English at Glen Trool. Edward I died on July 7, 1307, striving to the last to destroy his Scottish enemy, and from that moment on the tide turned in Bruce's favor, for Edward's son and successor Edward II was a poor soldier and an even poorer statesman. From 1307 to 1309, Bruce enjoyed an amazing military recovery, transforming himself from a hunted fugitive to the ruler of two-thirds of Scotland. His initial success came in the civil war during which John Comyn was finally routed and his lands wasted with fire and sword, leaving Bruce free for the task of winning back his kingdom from the English. He finally began acting like a national monarch: his first surviving acts of government date from 1308, and in 1309 he held his first parliament at St. Andrews, which was concerned primarily with legitimizing his kingship. Nevertheless, much work would need to be done to justify his title "King of Scots."

From 1310 to 1314, Bruce's rule was established throughout Scotland. Although he was master of the north of Scotland, the English strongholds in the south still had to be captured and destroyed. This was achieved through avoiding pitched battles, using instead guerilla warfare and surprise tactics (as at Perth in 1313 when Bruce waded waist-deep in icy water across the moat to scale the wall). Whenever strongholds were captured, their defenses were torn down to prevent the English from using them in the future. By the summer of 1313, only Lothian was outside of Bruce's control, and in the spring of 1314 Edinburgh castle was captured by a daring assault up the cliff face. This left Stirling, which was due to surrender by midsummer if not relieved, and several other castles in the south.

It was this agreement between the commander of the garrison at Stirling castle and Robert's brother Edward which led to direct confrontation between Robert Bruce and Edward II. The English king could not ignore this challenge, and in June of 1314 he invaded Scotland with some 15,000 infantry and 2,500 knights. Edward was met near Stirling by Bruce, who commanded about 8,000 men, mostly infantry. An incident that occurred on the day before the battle foreshadowed its outcome. Sir Henry de Bohun, part of an English scouting party, spotted a lone figure on a grey palfrey (saddle horse), armed with a hand axe and wearing a helmet surmounted by a gold crown—it was Robert Bruce … unguarded. The opportunity to vanquish the king of Scots in personal combat did not come often to a knight, and Bruce's biographer recorded what happened next:

> Together charged they galloping.
> Sir Henry missed the noble king!
> And he, that in his stirrups stood,
> Lifted his axe, so sharp and good,
> And such a mighty stroke he aimed
> That neither hat nor helmet stemmed
> The force of that mighty blow.
> Down did the bold Sir Henry go.
> The hand-axe shaft was broke in two.
> His skull was almost cleft right through.

When his generals chastised him for risking his life in single combat, the king ignored the rebuke: "But for his hand-axe made great woe/ That had been broken by the blow!"

The following day, June 24, 1314, after a restless night spent on the damp ground surrounding Bannockburn, the flower of English chivalry was defeated by a ragged army of Scots footsoldiers led by their king. King Edward II barely escaped from the fray—so quickly had he been spirited off that the royal seal and shield were left behind—

and the English king and his small bodyguard were pursued so fiercely it was said none of the English dared to stop, even to make water. A chronicler at Lanercost in northern England wrote: "After the aforesaid victory, Robert the Bruce was commonly called king of Scotland by all men, because he had acquired Scotland by force of arms."

In one sense this was true. At a Parliament in November 1314, Bruce disinherited any who did not support him, thus ending the civil war for his lifetime. In another sense, however, Bannockburn was relatively unimportant, since Edward II and the papacy still refused to recognize him as king of Scots. Military campaigns continued: the Scots raided northern England, and in 1315 Bruce's brother Edward opened a second front by invading Ireland. In 1316, Bruce also suffered another personal tragedy when his pregnant daughter Marjorie was killed in a horse accident, though the baby was successfully delivered from her dead body. It was this child, Robert Stewart, who would succeed to the throne in 1371 as the first Stewart monarch of Scotland.

Kings of England and Scotland Sign a Truce

The year 1320, then, saw Bruce little further advanced in his goal of recognition. Reluctant to recognize as king someone who had murdered his rival in a church, the papacy renewed his excommunication in 1319–20. As early as 1316, the pope had sent several letters addressed to "Robert Bruce, acting as King of Scots." "There are," replied the king, "several gentlemen in Scotland who have the name of Robert Bruce," and returned the correspondence unopened. In an effort to gain the papacy's support for their king, the nobility and the "community of the realm" of Scotland sent a long, impassioned letter to the pope. Known as the "Declaration of Arbroath," it was designed to do three things: to prove the Scots were fighting a just war against unjust English aggression—"it is not glory, it is not riches, neither is it honours, but it is liberty alone that we fight and contend for"; to justify Robert's kingship; and to ask the pope to urge Edward II to leave the Scots in peace. Their plea, however, had little effect, and from 1320 to 1323 the raids on England continued. The English king himself was nearly captured on one occasion in late 1322. Finally, in 1323, due in large measure to internal trouble in England, Edward II and King Robert signed a 13-year truce, marking the first real break in hostilities in 27 years. Still, the truce made no mention of Bruce being recognized by the English as the rightful king of Scots.

The following year, a son named David was born to Bruce and his wife, and at a Parliament in 1326 the boy would be designated heir to the throne. The truce of 1323 allowed Bruce to turn his attention toward his realm. Although he was not known for innovations in government, he restored a stable administration and was renowned for his evenhanded distribution of justice.

In 1327, the deposition of Edward II by **Edward III** set in motion a series of events that led to a treaty with England, the recognition of Scottish independence, and the acknowledgment of Bruce's kingship. The Scots considered that this nullified the 1323 treaty and again began cross-border raiding. After an abortive expedition against Scotland, in 1328 the English finally recognized both Scotland's independence and Bruce's kingship in the treaty of Edinburgh-Northampton, which was cemented by the marriage of Edward III's sister to Bruce's son David. The treaty and marriage marked the culmination of Robert Bruce's career and represented the fruit of his 20-year struggle against England.

By the time the treaty was signed, King Robert was already in ill health. In early 1329, he had retired to his home at Cardross (near Dumbarton on the Clyde) and had decided to undertake a pilgrimage to the shrine of St. Ninian at Whithorn. On April 1, 1329, he reached his objective and returned to Cardross, his health failing. After a moving speech to the comrades gathered at his bedside, King Robert I of Scotland died on June 7, 1329, just short of his 55th birthday, never having received the news that the papacy had finally recognized him as legitimate king of Scots.

In accordance with his wishes, his heart was removed, embalmed, and carried by Sir James Douglas on crusade, while the king's body was taken to Dunfermline Abbey for burial. On March 25, 1330, Sir James was killed in battle against the Muslims in Spain. When his body was recovered, the king's heart was still in its silver casket around his neck. Both the heart of Robert Bruce and the bones of Sir James were eventually brought back to Scotland, and legend says that Bruce's heart was interred at Melrose Abbey in the borders.

Although not above criticism for his actions in the early 1300s when he seized the throne, Robert I was one of the great kings of medieval Europe. He kept the cause of Scottish independence alive, and it is a fitting tribute to his work that he died in a kingdom that was both independent and at peace. Under his successor, Bruce's five-year-old son David (II), the Scottish cause once again entered trying times.

SOURCES:

Barbour, John. *The Bruce*. Edited and translated by A. A. H. Douglas. William MacLellan, 1964.

Barrow, G. W. S. *Robert Bruce and the Community of the Realm of Scotland*. 2nd ed. Edinburgh University Press, 1976.

———. "Robert the Bruce, 1329–1979," in *History Today* 29. 1979: pp. 808–15.

Dickinson, W. C. *Scotland from the Earliest Times to 1603*. Revised and edited by A. A. M. Duncan. Clarendon Press, 1977.

Grant, A. *Independence and Nationhood Scotland 1306–1469*. New History of Scotland, vol. 3. Edward Arnold, 1984.

FURTHER READING:

Fisherm, A. "A Patriot for Whom? Wallace and Bruce, Scotland's Uneasy Heroes" in *History Today* 39. February 1989.

Nicholson, R. *Scotland: The Later Middle Ages*. Edinburgh History of Scotland, vol. 2. Oliver and Boyd, 1974.

Scott, R. McNair. *Robert the Bruce, King of Scots*. Peter Bedrick Books, 1989.

Edmund Burke

(1727–1797)

Irish-born statesman and prominent political philosopher, who opposed British taxation of the American colonies and worked for the causes of economical reform, abolition of the slave trade, and political autonomy for Ireland.

"It is not, what a lawyer tells me I may do; but what humanity, reason, and justice, tell me I ought to do."

EDMUND BURKE

Political and constitutional developments frequently dominated mid- and late-18th-century Great Britain and Ireland. As a member of Parliament and political philosopher, Edmund Burke was intimately involved with some of the most significant changes that occurred during his lifetime.

Born in his parents' home in Dublin, Ireland, on January 12, 1729, Edmund Burke was the second son of 15 children born to Richard Burke and Mary Nagle; only four of the children survived to adulthood. Edmund's father was a successful attorney in Dublin, and an Irish Protestant, while his mother came from a Roman Catholic family, of which one branch descended from the poet Edmund Spenser. Of solid Irish stock, the Burkes could trace their ancestry to the late 12th century. But Burke's health through those early years was also delicate, and his parents feared he was afflicted with consumption.

As was the case for many middle-class children in this era, Burke received his earliest education from his mother. While a young child, he made a number of regular visits to his grandfather

Born on January 12, 1727, in family home, Dublin, Ireland; died at Beaconsfield estate, Buckinghamshire, England, on July 9, 1797; second surviving son of Richard Burke and Mary Nagle; married: Jane Nugent; two sons (died during Burke's lifetime).

Contributed by Donna Beaudin, Ph.D. candidate in History, University of Guelph, Guelph, Ontario, Canada

in County Cork, in the south of Ireland, where, according to biographer Peter Burke:

> amid the memories hanging around the ruins of Kilcolman, he first thirsted for the historic knowledge which was to throw such power and prophetic force into his reasoning and his language.

His first formal schooling consisted of five years attendance at the village school of Glanworth where he acquired some rudimentary Latin. From there, he was sent to Ballitore Academy with his brothers in 1741, at a distance of 28 miles from Dublin. Burke's instructor at this academy was Abraham Shackleton, a Yorkshire Quaker. Burke spent three important years here: a lifelong friendship with Shackleton's son Richard was begun, and Burke increased his toleration of the religious faiths of others.

From the Quaker-run academy, Burke proceeded to Trinity College, Dublin, in April 1744, where he remained until 1750. Within two years of arrival, he was a scholar of the house and had received prizes for proficiency in the classics. While at Trinity, he read in logic, rhetoric, composition, moral philosophy, history, and physics. In line with his great interest in historical studies, he founded the college's Historical Society in April 1747. He also wrote poetry and developed an early dislike of the logic branch of philosophy. By February 1748, Burke had graduated a bachelor of arts. It was during his years at Trinity that he actively wrote and edited literary works for the first time. His earliest pamphlets were of a socio-philosophical nature. Into the spring of 1748, Burke edited *The Reformer*, a weekly paper much influenced by the work of Joseph Addison and Richard Steele. Though Burke wanted to make his living by writing, his father intended him for the legal profession. Thus, in 1747, before completion of his undergraduate degree, he was enrolled at Middle Temple, London (one of the four great Inns of Court), where he would study law.

Arriving in London in 1750, Burke commenced his legal studies, but the law as a profession held no appeal for him. Nor did he perceive it to be a lucrative career choice. Though he remained with the Temple through the early 1750s, his health declined, and he made no real effort to apply himself; he preferred to read and study literature. His angry father promptly withdrew Burke's living allowance.

He continued to write and to publish—"A Vindication of Natural Society" (1756) and "The Sublime and Beautiful" (1757)—and attended debates at the Robin Hood Society's meetings and at the Grecian Coffee-house. He used such outings to improve his oratorical skills by learning from the speaking of others. While recovering his health in the winter of 1756–57, Burke married his physician's daughter Jane Nugent, a Presbyterian from Bath. Though married to a nonconformist, this did little to shift Burke's support away from the political claims of Catholics. His life is testimony to the pervasive nature of religion in 18th-century life and society.

Burke was something of a romantic, and his marriage was a happy one. Their first son Richard was born in 1758. A second son was baptized Christopher but died in infancy. Richard quickly became the pride of his parents, especially of his father. In 1758, the Burke family moved to their newly acquired estate in Buckinghamshire. Originally called Gregories, it soon came to be known as Beaconsfield; it was here that Burke could live a regular domestic life while indulging his interests in agricultural improvement. Shortly after marrying, Burke had begun work on an abridged history of England but had stopped when he heard that David Hume was working on a similar project. During this busy period, Burke developed lasting friendships with actor David Garrick, portraitist Joshua Reynolds, and literary critic and essayist Samuel Johnson. Burke's editorial efforts continued, anonymously, with the *Annual Register,* the first volume of which appeared in 1759. He continued to be secretly involved with the journal until 1791, at an editorial wage of £100 per year.

Elected to House of Commons

Burke came to the attention of the first earl of Charlemont, and a lasting friendship developed. Gradually, Burke became part of the political world that he had merely watched from a distance. In the early 1760s, he was part of the political retinue which accompanied the earl of Halifax to Ireland to administer its government. This accorded neatly with Burke's own views on how a nation should be governed. He despaired of popular democracy and the system of political parties, and advocated responsible aristocratic government as essential to the proper ordering of the world. Burke's stay in Ireland amounted to less than two years, and after he returned to England he was voted a pension from the Irish Treasury. He continued to be noticed by political figures and, in 1765, was made private secretary to the marquis of Rockingham, current First Lord of the Treasury and, therefore, effectively prime minister. Just before Christmas of that year, as a convinced Whig who believed more in men than in measures, Burke secured election to the House of Commons. The year, however, was not without its misfortunes: his elder brother Garret died, which meant that Burke was now heir to his father's property in Ireland. Burke's association with Ireland went beyond the realm of landowning; he also became patron of painter James Barry and poet George Crabbe.

As a politician, Burke tended to work behind the scenes and continued to advise Lord Rockingham on the state of affairs in Ireland. But there were several factors which initially hampered his career: (1) he was not a political opportunist; (2) he had to withstand scandalous accusations made by the duke of Newcastle, who was in political opposition; (3) his generosity often exceeded his financial capacity to give; and (4) his skillful orations were delivered with an Irish accent. While some repeatedly reminded him that he was a novus *homo* ("a new man"), Burke was not ashamed of his origins. Further, his level of thought and analysis went beyond that of most of his fellow members of Par-

liament, and this limited his parliamentary power for a time. Burke was better at anticipating than his contemporaries. He supported the principles of commercial trade and realized as early as 1767 that the imperial Parliament would not be successful at collecting duties on American trade and commerce. As a political prophet and philosopher, he incurred the jealousy of those who sought to keep him out of high political office, though he was widely recognized as "the brain of the Whigs."

A career in politics did not preclude time to pursue his writing activities and, in some ways, 1770 marked a peak in Burke's writing career. In the spring, he published *Thoughts on the Causes of the Present Discontents* which addressed Bolingbroke's position as presented in *The Patriot King.* In this work, Burke outlined a constitutional policy for the Whigs which was "truly English" and had a rejuvenating effect on the party. In the House of Commons, he had no rival nor equal as a speaker. Both his style of oratory and his physical appearance were striking. Relatively tall, about five-foot-ten, Edmund Burke had a muscular, compact build and was usually recognizable in Parliament by his bob-style wig and his spectacles. Biographer Robert Murray concludes that:

> He possessed the highest quality of the orator—the gift of the perfect, the deathless, phrase.... The eloquence of Burke was characterized by a lofty and philosophical speculation.

It was during this decade, the 1770s, that Burke established his reputation as an orator and statesman. In 1772, he was approached by the East India Company and asked to be their agent. Though tempted by the offer, Burke declined it. The company, however, remained a dominant element in his political life, and he opposed Lord North's attempts to regulate it on the grounds that the Crown was independent of parliamentary control and, by extension, so was the East India Company since it had been created solely by royal charter.

Another prominent issue in Burke's career concerned the American colonies. In the mid-1770s, he spoke against proposals to tax the colonies and to regulate the government of Massachusetts. He did not dispute that the imperial government had the right to take such actions, but he did question the worthiness of such rights. To make his point, Burke delivered two impassioned speeches in the House of Commons: one dwelt on the matter of American taxation by duties and the other urged a reconciliation between the imperial

Parliament and the colonies. When the American War for Independence did come, Burke opposed it; he perceived it a danger to the liberties of the colonies and, therefore, of all English subjects.

During the American Revolution, Burke campaigned for other causes, including economic reform and the condition of Ireland's Catholic population. In opposition to increasing calls for parliamentary reform, which he saw as a risky, dangerous experiment, Burke introduced a bill for economic reform into the Commons in February 1780. He proposed a reformation of the king's household, of some placemen automatically holding a seat in the House of Commons, and of the salaries and perquisites of certain public offices. In this last group was included Burke's future position as paymaster of the forces in 1782. The bill and speech were among Burke's finest efforts and became one of the main planks of the Rockingham Whigs' platform but, like nearly all opposition-generated bills, it was doomed to fail until the Whigs took office in 1782. Excluded from the cabinet because he was often difficult to deal with, Burke was made a member of the Privy Council, as well as paymaster of the armed forces. Once a member of the government, Burke set about reforming his own office.

After a brief period out of office after the death of the marquis of Rockingham, Burke became paymaster in the Fox-North government. He continued to write, especially legislative proposals, for the Whigs. For Charles James Fox, Burke drafted an India Bill. Along with others, Burke was concerned with the administration of the East India Company and with the governance of India. He spoke strongly on these concerns in the Commons:

> Our Indian government is in its best state a grievance. It is necessary that the correctives should be uncommonly vigorous; and the work of men, sanguine, warm, and even impassioned in the cause. But it is an arduous thing to plead against abuses of power which originates [sic] from your own country, and affects those whom we are used to consider as strangers.

Clearly, the focus of Burke's political energies had shifted from the now-independent American states to what he perceived to be the misgovernance of India. To this end, he believed that the governor-general of India/Bengal, **Warren Hastings,** was responsible and should be impeached. Burke was to play a significant role in the impeachment process. On May 10, 1787, he accused Hastings, at the bar in the House of Lords, of nearly 20 instances of high crimes and misdemeanors; Hastings went on to face only four of the original charges levied against him. When the trial began on February 13, 1788, Burke's opening speech lasted five days. The power and indignation which he put into this speech took its toll on his health and kept him from the trial for approximately two months. The Hastings impeachment trial lasted seven years. Near its conclusion, in 1794, Burke made a nine-day speech justifying the proceedings. Though he perceived prosecution as his duty, Burke had not been certain that Hastings would be convicted and was present at Hastings's acquittal.

Publishes Famous Work on French Revolution

The French Revolution, which began in 1789, was the most conspicuous development to coincide with Burke's career. On this subject, Burke "spoke and acted like a visionary." In the next year, he published *Reflections on the French Revolution* as a warning to fellow English subjects and admirers that the loss of monarchy and liberty could also occur in England, as it had in France, if preventive action was not taken. This most famous of his works went into an 11th printing before the year ended and served to create an English reaction to the Revolution.

Even more dramatic was his reaction concerning the 1791 bill for a constitution for what would become Upper and Lower Canada. Philosophically a conservative but never a Tory (which carried the taints of Jacobitism and absolutism), Burke disagreed vehemently with Fox and the majority of the Whig party. This alienation culminated in Burke's 1791 crossing of the floor of the House of Commons to sit with the Tories between Treasurer Henry Dundas and **William Pitt the Younger.** Burke did not see his behavior as politically inconsistent, though some of his contemporaries did.

Edmund Burke continued to be politically active into his mid-60s: he published on the issues of opposition political conduct, the coming war with France, and the policies of England's allies. He also made his political separation from the Whigs final by seceding from the Whig Club. But during the early to mid-1790s, his private sufferings dwarfed his political life. In February 1792, his friend Joshua Reynolds, the portraitist, died and left Burke the executor of his will and the guardian of Reynold's niece. Burke's own niece Mary French came to live at Beaconsfield after the 1790 death of his sister Juliana Burke French. In August of the same year, his friend of longest standing, Richard Shackleton, also died. These were blows to Burke, but they paled in the face of the grief he experienced at the death of his unmarried brother Richard in February 1794, and the premature death of his son Richard, in August, from consumption.

After his son's death, life for the aged Burke became little more than drudgery (he had retired from politics two months earlier). He began to spend most of his time in the country, particularly at his Buckinghamshire estate. In 1796, he opened a neighborhood school for foreign and immigrant children who would not otherwise have been educated. In early 1797, his health began to decline measurably, and he journeyed to Bath to take the healing waters. He stayed there four months before returning to Beaconsfield where he died, of internal abscesses, shortly after midnight on July 9, 1797. Though Charles James Fox proposed to the House of Commons that Burke be interred, with public honors, in Westminster Abbey, Burke's own will stipulated that he be buried in the yard of the parish church of Beaconsfield; this was done on July 15, 1797. That his pallbearers were leaders of the old Whig party is a testimony to the esteem and respect in which Edmund Burke had been held during his lifetime.

SOURCES:

Burke, Peter. *The Public and Domestic Life of the Right Hon. Edmund Burke.* Nathaniel Cook, 1854.

Murray, Robert H. *Edmund Burke: A Biography.* Oxford University Press, 1931.

FURTHER READING:

Chapman, Gerald W. *Edmund Burke: The Practical Imagination.* Harvard University Press, 1967.

Magnus, Sir P. M. *Edmund Burke.* J. Murray, 1931.

Julius Caesar

(102–44 B.C.)

Military and political leader of Rome, who brought about the end of the Roman Republic and laid the foundations for the Roman Empire.

Name variations: Gaius Julius Caesar. Born on July 13, 102 B.C.; murdered on March 15, 44 B.C.; married: Cornelia (daughter of Cinna), 84 B.C.; married: Pompeia (granddaughter of Sulla), 67 B.C. (divorced 62 B.C.). Descendant: Augustus, first emperor of the Roman Empire.

Gaius Julius Caesar was born into one of the original *patrician* (upper-class) families of Rome. Although aristocratic, the family was of modest means and relatively undistinguished in political and military accomplishment. Detailed information about Julius Caesar's early life is lacking, but it appears he received an excellent education from the tutor-freedman Marcus Antonius Gnipho, a master of Greek and Latin rhetoric. While a sound grounding in rhetorical training was vital to any Roman hoping to participate in the political life of Rome, it was the marriage of Caesar's aunt Julia to Dictator Gaius Marius that propelled the young Caesar into politics. As a result of Julia's efforts, Marius planned to name her nephew Caesar the *flamen Dialis* (priest of Jupiter). Despite Caesar's previous plans to marry the daughter of a wealthy *equestrian* (business-class) family, he married Cornelia, daughter of the consul Lucius Cornelius Cinna, to fulfill the requirement that the *flamen* marry a patrician. Because of Marius's changing political fortunes, however, Caesar was never appointed *flamen*.

When Marius, Cinna, and the *populares* (an alliance of liberal senatorials and equestri-

"I came, I saw, I conquered."

GAIUS JULIUS CAESAR

Contributed by Peter L. Viscusi, Professor of History, Central Missouri State University, Warrensburg, Missouri

ans) were finally driven from power in 82 B.C., Rome fell under the control of the dictator **Sulla** and the *optimates* (conservative landowning senatorials). To force Caesar's disassociation from the previous regime, Sulla insisted he divorce Cornelia. Others, similarly ordered, had obeyed. Caesar refused, however, and chose to avoid arrest by hiding in the Sabine country. During this period, Caesar contracted malaria. In his absence, his mother's family interceded with Sulla, gaining a pardon for him, after which he returned to Rome and became a soldier.

As the son of a senator, Caesar immediately became an officer and was assigned to the staff of Marcus Minucius Thermus, the *propraetor* (governor) of the Roman province of Asia. In 80 B.C., Thermus honored Caesar with the *corona civica* (oak wreath) for his conspicuous bravery in the taking of the Greek city Mytilene. Caesar continued his military service in 78 B.C. with the proconsul (provincial governor) Publius Servilius Vatia in the war against the Cilician pirates.

With news of Sulla's death, Caesar returned to Rome to prepare himself for a political career. In 77 B.C., he prosecuted a leading Sullan associate, Gnaeus Cornelius Dolabella (consul in 81 B.C.), for extortion; although Dolabella was acquitted, Caesar had enhanced his own reputation as an orator. In an effort to further improve his oratorical skills, he traveled to Rhodes to attend the lectures of rhetorician Apollonius Molon but was captured south of Miletus and held for ransom by pirates. Upon his release, Caesar led troops against his former captors and defeated them.

Returning to Rhodes, Caesar's daring was tested again when Mithridates, king of Pontus, invaded the province of Asia in 74 B.C. On his own initiative and without orders, Caesar crossed from Rhodes to Asia Minor, took command of local troops, and expelled the enemy. While serving in Rhodes, he received word that he had been co-opted in 73 B.C. into the college of *pontifices* (priests) in Rome—a particularly significant honor and a clear indication that Rome's aristocracy recognized Caesar as having important political connections. With the standard prerequisites to power in place—good birth, excellent oratorical skills, and bravery and success in war—Caesar turned full attention to his political career.

Roman politics of the first century B.C. was polarized between the *optimate* and *populare* factions. The city-state of Rome had been undergoing tremendous administrative stress since 189 B.C. when she gained de facto control of the Mediter-

CHRONOLOGY

102 B.C.	Caesar born
73 B.C.	Co-opted Pontifex
69 B.C.	Made quaestor under the governor of Farther Spain
65 B.C.	Elected *Curule Aedile*
63 B.C.	Chosen *Pontifex Maximus*
62 B.C.	Chosen praetor
61 B.C.	Chosen propraetor of Farther Spain
59 B.C.	Made consul; proconsular governor of Cisalpine Gaul (with Illyricum) and Transalpine Gaul
55 B.C.	Invasion of Britain
53 B.C.	Battle of Carrhae in Mesopotamia; Crassus died
52 B.C.	Revolt of Vercingetorix
49 B.C.	Crossed the Rubicon; elected dictator
48 B.C.	Victorious over Pompey at Pharsalus
47 B.C.	Victorious in Egypt; Cleopatra installed as ruler; Caesar defeated Pharnaces in Asia Minor
45 B.C.	Dictator for life
44 B.C.	Refused diadem offered by Mark Antony; murdered

ranean. Roman politics evolved into a series of violent political and military struggles for control of the state. Political advancement depended on military *gloria* (fame) and on large sums of money which the rising politician could use to alternately threaten or bribe the electorate. Politicians borrowed heavily to participate in the party strife and hoped to repay their debts by obtaining important governorships and preying upon the provincials. The depredations and extortion practiced by Roman governors were, therefore, a direct result of the Roman political system.

Given the parameters of Roman politics, Caesar was not only well suited but also well prepared to be an important participant. Frequently described by writers of the time as "fond of elegance and luxury," he was known for an extravagant lifestyle which Roman historian Suetonius tells us included a collection of "gems, carvings, statues, and pictures by early artists," despite the tremendous debt required to finance his political activity. Caesar commissioned the building of an expensive villa on Lake Nemi only to have it torn down upon completion because it did not suit him. Known for his generosity, he gave expensive gifts to friends. With such freespending ways, Caesar did not shrink from bribing officials and the voters of Rome.

In 73 B.C., the Romans elected Caesar one of the 24 military tribunes, his first elected office. Elected *quaestor* (junior magistrate) in 69 B.C., he gave public funeral orations honoring his recently deceased aunt Julia and his wife Cornelia. According to Suetonius, Caesar took the opportunity in his oration to glorify his family:

> The family of my aunt Julia is descended by her mother from the kings, and on her father's side is akin to the immortal Gods.... Our stock therefore has at once the sanctity of kings, and the claim to reverence which attaches to the Gods.

Seeing the tide of politics change, Caesar allied himself with Marcus Licinius Crassus, reputed to be the wealthiest man in Rome, and married Pompeia, the granddaughter of Sulla. In 65 B.C., Caesar was elected *Curule Aedile* along with the *optimate* Marcus Calpurnius Bibulus. Although both men spent large sums to present the public games, Caesar could not be outspent; he sponsored gladiatorial games of unprecedented proportion to honor his father who had died 20 years earlier. When popular election was restored in 63 B.C. for the position of *Pontifex Maximus* (head of the college of priests), Caesar was elected after heavy bribery. In the following year, when the women's religious ritual honoring the *Bona Dea* (goddess of chastity and fertility) was held at Caesar's home, Publius Clodius Pulcher committed sacrilege by witnessing the ceremonies disguised as a woman. As a result of this scandal, Caesar divorced Pompeia saying, according to Suetonius, "I maintain that the members of my family should be free from suspicion as well as from accusation."

Following his election to the position of *praetor* (senior magistrate), Caesar went to the province of Farther Spain as governor. According to the historian Appian, he was 25 million denarii in debt when he left for his province but returned with enough money to pay his creditors and to stand for and be elected consul for 59 B.C. Bibulus was once again Caesar's colleague in this office. When Bibulus tried to stop Caesar's *populare*-supported legislative program by the announcement of "ill-omens," Caesar ignored him and forced his legislation through the assembly. According to Suetonius, people began to joke that things were now being done "in the consulship of Julius and Caesar, instead of Bibulus and Caesar."

The First Triumvirate Is Formed

When Gnaeus Pompeius Magnus (**Pompey**) returned from the East and his war against Mithridates, Caesar formed an informal alliance with Pompey and the wealthy Crassus to control the Roman state. This alliance, formed in 60 B.C. and known as the First Triumvirate, was no small accomplishment as Pompey and Crassus viewed each other with suspicion. As consul, Caesar provided the legislative support both Pompey and Crassus needed. In exchange, they helped Caesar obtain Cisalpine Gaul (with Illyricum) and Transalpine Gaul as his proconsular provinces. Anxious to take up proconsular duties with the possibility for military fame, Caesar left for Gaul even before his term as consul was completed.

A cause for war with the Gallic tribes was not long in coming. The Helvetii wanted to migrate to Aquitaine and so asked Caesar for permission to cross a small portion of Roman provincial territory. Caesar, realizing that the Helvetii intended to cross the Roman frontier with or without his permission, saw this as an opportunity to enhance his military reputation. He not only repelled the Helvetii but aided the Aedui and the Sequani in defeating the Helvetii. Soon various Gallic tribes appealed to Caesar for military aid against the German Ariovistus, the leader of the Suebi. By defeating Ariovistus and his allies, the Roman legions then controlled all of central and northern Gaul. To prevent the Gauls from receiving aid from the Britons, Caesar invaded Britain in 55 B.C. and again in 54 B.C. Although Caesar's occupation of southern Britain was brief, it marked the beginning of Roman interest in the island. Because of increasing resentment toward the Romans in Gaul, the Belgae rose in revolt under their leader Ambiorix and other Gallic tribes rose under Vercingetorix. After several hard-fought campaigns, Caesar and his troops had quelled the rebellion by 51 B.C.

During Caesar's Gallic campaigns, Pompey and Crassus reverted to their bickering in Rome. In 56 B.C., Crassus, Pompey, and 120 senators went to meet with Caesar to reach a new understanding at Luca, a town just inside the province of Cisalpine Gaul. There, the three political leaders decided that Crassus and Pompey would be consuls for 55 B.C. and that their proconsular commands were to be for five years. Caesar's proconsular command was extended for an additional four years. This renewed alliance, however, proved short-lived. Pompey distanced himself from Caesar after Pompey's wife Julia (Caesar's daughter) died in 54 B.C. Anxious to take up his proconsular command in Syria and to participate in an expected war with Parthia, Crassus left Rome soon after his election as consul. Not as able a military commander as Caesar, Crassus died in 53 B.C. shortly after the Roman defeat at the Battle of Carrhae.

With Crassus removed from Roman politics, the *optimates* turned to Pompey for leadership, hoping to see Caesar superseded in his command. When Caesar was once again a private citizen, they planned to prosecute him for illegal acts committed during his consulship with Bibulus. Caesar countered these moves by paying huge bribes to buy the support of the consul Lucius Aemilius Paullus and the tribune Gaius Scribonius Curio. According to Appian, Caesar "bought the neutrality of Paullus for 1500 talents and the assistance of Curio with a still larger sum because he knew that the latter was heavily burdened with debt."

Caesar Crosses the Rubicon

Despite calls for mutual disarmament, Rome was clearly moving toward civil war. Realizing the *optimates* would never compromise with him, Caesar began the civil war on January 10, 49 B.C., when he crossed the Rubicon into Italy, a small shallow river that separated Italy from Cisalpine Gaul. In an attempt to reach the East where Rome had most of her troops stationed, Caesar and his men hastened to the port of Brundisium on the southeast coast of Italy. Pompey, however, reached the seaport first and rallied Roman forces in the eastern provinces to come to his aid against Caesar.

In a relatively short period of time, Caesar defeated his *optimate* enemies. While Caesarian forces defeated Pompey's troops in Spain, Caesar defeated Pompey himself in Greece at the Battle of Pharsalus. Before he could be captured, however, Pompey fled to Egypt where he was taken captive and beheaded by Ptolemy XII, a claimant to the Egyptian throne. Arriving in Egypt, Caesar claimed the right to judge who was Egypt's rightful ruler—Ptolemy or **Cleopatra**. Ptolemy, resentful of such interference, led an armed uprising against Caesar's Roman troops. Caesar, however, defeated Ptolemy and placed Cleopatra on the Egyptian throne.

Taking advantage of the Roman preoccupation with Egyptian politics, Pharnaces (son of Mithridates) attempted to conquer Pontus. But Caesar swiftly responded to the threat, totally defeating Pharnaces within five days of his arrival in Asia Minor. This short, decisive campaign prompted Caesar to write a brief but succinct description of events to a friend in Rome: "I came, I saw, I conquered."

As the victor in the civil war, Caesar instituted a number of reforms. His economic reforms included a reduction in the number of people eligible for free grain from 320,000 to 150,000, the discontinuation of old equestrian-controlled system of tax-farming in the Roman province of Asia, and, in an effort to relieve the extreme unemployment among the Roman poor, the mandate that Romans had to employ one free man for every two slaves who worked the great estates of Italy. As an important first step toward political reform, the membership of the senate was increased from its traditional number of 300 members to 900 with the admission of Gallic chieftains and various other supporters of Caesar. Caesar had succeeded in making himself simultaneously consul, proconsul, perpetual dictator, and *pontifex maximus,* while possessing the powers of a censor and a tribune. This was a tremendous and unprecedented concentration of political and military power in the hands of one individual.

Now without a rival, Caesar enhanced his position to such a degree that he began to flirt with assuming godlike attributes: the Roman month of Quintilis was renamed July and a temple dedicated to Venus, the divine ancestor of the Julians, was erected. In addition, Caesar's portrait appeared on the obverse of coins, an honor previously reserved for the gods. Finally, he wore a purple toga at all times which some scholars have said resembled the kind used to clothe the statues of the gods.

Caesar held such an exalted position in the state that he sat rather than stood in the presence of the senate, and witnesses in court were required to swear by his *genius* (guardian spirit). Many in Rome had reason to believe that he wanted to establish a Hellenistic-style monarchy. Marcus Antonius (Mark Antony), Caesar's consular colleague, even tried to place a diadem (Greek crown) on Caesar's head—perhaps in an attempt to test public opinion. In any case, Caesar was wise enough to refuse the offered crown.

Regardless of their political persuasion, everyone in Rome recognized Caesar's impressive character. A multitalented man of great daring, he was courageous and self-confident. Suetonius describes Caesar in his later years:

> He is said to have been tall of stature, with a fair complexion, shapely limbs, a somewhat full face, and keen black eyes; sound of health, except that towards the end he was subject to sudden fainting fits and to nightmare as well. He was twice attacked by the falling sickness during his campaigns. He was somewhat overnice in the care of

his person, being not only carefully trimmed and shaved, but even having superfluous hair plucked out, as some have charged; while his baldness was a disfigurement which troubled him greatly, since he found that it was often the subject of the gibes of his detractors. Because of it he used to comb forward his scanty locks from the crown of his head, and of all the honours voted him by the senate and people there was none which he received or made use of more gladly than the privilege of wearing a laurel wreath at all times.

The overwhelming control Caesar exercised over virtually every aspect of Roman life drove approximately 60 of his aristocratic opponents to participate in an assassination plot. Although many of these men were former followers of Pompey, a majority of them were of Caesar's own faction. Even Decimus Brutus, a man named in Caesar's will as an alternate heir, was among the plotters. Caesar, having completed preparations for a war with Parthia to avenge the Roman defeat under Crassus, planned to bid a formal farewell to the senate on the Ides (the 15th) of March. Upon his entrance into the senate, the conspirators set upon him with daggers, stabbing him 23 times. After Caesar's death, all in the senate, conspirators and nonconspirators alike, fled to their homes.

A short time later, the senators reconvened to discuss their course of action. If the senate sided with the conspirators, declaring Caesar a tyrant, such a position would mean that all of his acts would be declared illegal, for which the senate would have to face the anger of Caesar's soldiers. If, however, the senate sided with Caesar's faction, it would mean declaring that Caesar had been a legal magistrate all along, making the assassins enemies of Rome. In the end, despite the inconsistency, the senators ratified Caesar's acts, voted him a public funeral, and declared an amnesty for the conspirators.

While successful in eliminating Caesar, his enemies would prove unable to reverse the constitutional course he had set for Rome. The Roman Republic would not be a republic much longer. Although few realized it, Rome had already begun the process of transforming itself into the Roman Empire.

SOURCES:

Caesar, Gaius Julius. *The Gallic War.*

Gelzer, Matthias. *Caesar: Politician and Statesman.* Harvard University Press, 1968.

Suetonius. *Lives of the Caesars.*

FURTHER READING:

Balsdon, J. P. V. D. *Julius Caesar: A Political Biography.* Atheneum, 1967.

Grant, Michael. *Julius Caesar.* McGraw-Hill, 1969.

Kahn, Arthur D. *The Education of Julius Caesar.* Schocken, 1986.

Yavetz, Zwi. *Julius Caesar and His Public Image.* Cornell University Press, 1983.

Caligula

(A.D. 12–41)

Third Roman emperor and "mad" tyrant, who was noted for megalomania and cruelty.

"Nature produced [Caligula] merely to show how far supreme vice, when combined with supreme power, could go."

SENECA

The Roman world had every reason to expect great things from Caligula. His father Germanicus, adopted son of Emperor **Tiberius,** was a popular military commander who seemed marked as the Emperor's successor; his mother **Agrippina the Elder** was the granddaughter of the first Roman emperor **Augustus.**

One of the earliest references to Caligula's childhood appears in a letter written by Augustus to Agrippina, who was then staying with Germanicus at a military camp on the Rhine. Evidently, the two-year-old Caligula had been separated from his parents, possibly for some 18 months, and in this correspondence Augustus referred to travel arrangements for the boy so that he would be united with his mother. Following his arrival at the camps, his parents reportedly outfitted him in a miniature soldier's uniform and military boots, and the child became a mascot for the troops, earning the Latin nickname for "Little Boots." Thus, the future emperor, born Gaius Julius Caesar Germanicus, acquired the name "Caligula."

About three months into Caligula's stay, Augustus died and the troops rebelled. Despite Germanicus's popularity, the ensuing commotion

Contributed by Sylvia Gray Kaplan, Adjunct Faculty, Humanities, Marylhurst College, Marylhurst, Oregon

Name variations: Gaius Caligula; (as emperor) Gaius Caesar Augustus Germanicus. Born Gaius Julius Caesar Germanicus at Antium (present-day Anzio in Italy) in the year A.D. 12; assassinated by a tribune of the Praetorian Guard in A.D. 41; son of Germanicus (who was the adopted son of the Emperor Tiberius) and Agrippina the Elder (granddaughter of Augustus); married: Junia Claudilla (died); married: Livia Orestilla (divorced); married: Lollia Paulina (divorced); married: Milonia Caesonia (murdered with Caligula); children: Julia Drusilla by Caesonia. Predecessor: Tiburius. Successor: Claudius.

placed him in jeopardy. Fearing for her family's safety, Agrippina prepared to leave the camp with her son. But as the two set out, some of the soldiers apparently had a change of heart. Ashamed of their behavior, they begged the family to remain, prompting Suetonius, a biographer of the early second century, to note, "the mere sight of little Gaius unquestionably calmed them down." Taking advantage of the situation to regain some control, Germanicus conceded that Caligula—the camp darling—could stay, but he sent Agrippina on her way since she was about to give birth. Though Caligula was undoubtedly too young to remember these events, the story of his turning back the rebellion became both family and Roman legend.

When Germanicus celebrated the defeat of the Germans with his "triumph" (a glorious victory parade in Rome), Caligula once again experienced the adulation of crowds as he rode in the chariot alongside his father. Soon after, Germanicus left for the Middle East where he was posted to new military duties—accompanied again by his family, including the five-year-old Caligula. Although given overriding authority in the east, Germanicus was challenged by Piso, the governor of Syria, who had been appointed by Tiberius. In A.D. 19, after a quarrel with Piso, the 33-year-old Germanicus suddenly fell ill and died. Poisoning was suspected. Undoubtedly, the death of his father remained strong in Caligula's memory, as well as the mournful journey home.

A few years later, Caligula's two older brothers celebrated the rituals of manhood and were both appointed to important public offices before legally acceptable ages. This privilege seemed a preparation for possible future emperorship. But conflict soon erupted between the house of Germanicus and Emperor Tiberius. The two brothers were accused of treasonous activities, and Agrip-

pina was placed under house arrest. Caligula—still deemed too young to constitute a threat—was sent to live with **Livia,** mother of Tiberius and honored widow of Augustus.

At 17, Caligula made his first public appearance, delivering the funeral oration for Livia in A.D. 29. Though Livia and Tiberius had quarrelled in the last years of her life, she had evidently retained a moderating influence over him, for after her death, Agrippina and one of her sons were banished to islands and mistreated, while the other implicated son was imprisoned in Rome. Soon, all were dead.

Caligula was sent to live with his grandmother Antonia, where he spent the best years of his life. But in A.D. 32, Tiberius ordered Caligula to join him on his island of Capri. For the next five years—which, according to the ancient records, were among the most degenerate of Tiberius's life—Caligula lived with the Emperor. Although his mother and brothers had died as a result of Tiberius's orders, Caligula survived by acting unaffected.

On Capri, Caligula assumed the toga of manhood and married Junia Claudilla, the woman Tiberius had selected for him. He was appointed augur for the priesthood and he held a *quaestorship* (public office) for one year. Although Tiberius refrained from committing himself to an heir-designate, these privileges gave Caligula reason for hope. According to Suetonius, Tiberius expressed his hesitation about Caligula, fearful that he was "nursing a viper for the Roman people." There remained two other possible contenders for the throne: Tiberius's grandson Gemellus, who was too young, and the family "fool," **CLAUDIUS.** However, Macro, the powerful prefect of the Praetorian Guard (elite troops who protected the emperor), considered Caligula the best bet and gave his support accordingly.

Tiberius died in A.D. 37. Before the contents of Tiberius's will were even read to the senate, with the help of Macro Caligula secured the formal allegiance of both the senate and the troops. Remembering Germanicus and expecting a joyful rule under his young son, the people celebrated. "Gaius' accession seemed to the Roman people—one might almost say, to the whole world—like a dream come true," wrote Suetonius, despite rumors declaring Caligula an accomplice in Tiberius's death.

Caligula Becomes Emperor

In his will, Tiberius had merely left Caligula an equal heir with his young grandson—no doubt a deliberate ambiguity. But the senate proclaimed the will null and void, declaring Tiberius mentally incompetent. Then, the senate officially handed on to Caligula the powers of the emperorship formerly held by Augustus and Tiberius. Caligula was 24 years old.

At the beginning of his reign, Caligula journeyed to the islands where his mother and brother had died and returned with their ashes for proper burial. He decreed great honors for his sisters Drusilla, Julia, and **Agrippina:** they were included in oaths, and on coins they personified "Security," "Peace," and "Prosperity." He elevated his "foolish" uncle Claudius, later the succeeding emperor, to his first public office. As the family of Germanicus had received sympathy for its sufferings at the hand of Tiberius, these actions were interpreted favorably by the Roman people.

Other immediate and popular acts seemed to confirm the blessings of his rule. Caligula released exiles, announced the end of the treason trials that had marked the last years of Tiberius's reign, and gave generous amounts of money to the Praetorian Guard and to the people of Rome. He reinstated games and theatrical shows which Tiberius had minimized. He delivered an accession speech, condemning the wrongs done under Tiberius and promising to show proper respect for the senate. This speech was so popular that the senate decreed it should be read aloud annually.

This auspicious beginning was short lived. It may be that the strains of his turbulent childhood, caused by the extremes of adulation and mortal danger and his nonchalant facade toward the sufferings of his family, had begun to take their toll. Suetonius wrote: "So much for the emperor; the rest of this history must deal with the monster." Only a few months into his reign, Caligula fell ill, almost reaching the point of death. As he recovered, he began to demonstrate the arbitrary cruelty for which he became so famous.

While some scholars have argued that his illness brought about the transformation, others like Philo (an Alexandrian Jew who met Caligula) have suggested that he merely began "openly displaying the savagery which he had concealed under a cloak of hypocrisy." Philo further notes that during Caligula's days with Tiberius, "eccentricity and crazy tendencies were appearing, and [Caligula] preserved no logicality in either his words or his actions." In fact, traces of the excesses which would become more pronounced could be discerned from the very beginning of his rule.

Perhaps it was only the moderating hand of Macro that had restrained him from showing his aberrant mental state sooner. But when Caligula recovered from his illness, he killed three of the people closest to him: Macro (because he gave Caligula unwanted advice); Tiberius Gemellus, the young grandson of Tiberius (who was considered a threat to his rule); and his father-in-law (for allegedly wishing Caligula dead). Upon hearing of a man who had vowed to give his own life in order that the emperor recover, Caligula insisted he carry out his vow. Slaves paraded the unfortunate man through the streets, then hurled him off an embankment to his death.

All the ancient sources speak of Caligula's cruelty. To demonstrate his character, Suetonius enumerates both minor malicious tricks and gross cruelties. For instance, Caligula removed canopies at the hottest time of day during the games, forbidding people to leave. He fed criminals, rather than butcher's meat, to wild animals in the arena. He made fathers attend their sons' executions and in one case invited the father to dine with him immediately afterward in jovial company. According to Suetonius, "he frequently had trials by torture held in his presence while he was eating or otherwise enjoying himself." One of his favorite sayings was: "Make him feel that he is dying!" His daughter Drusilla's violent temper convinced him of his own paternity: "While still an infant she would try to scratch her little playmates' faces and eyes."

Caligula, unlike his predecessors, interpreted his position as emperor in terms of ability to do whatever he wanted whenever he wanted. He admonished his grandmother Antonia, "bear in mind that I can treat anyone exactly as I please." When, during a banquet, he suddenly burst out laughing and was asked to share the joke, he replied, "It occurred to me that I have only to give one nod and both your throats will be cut on the spot!" Likewise, he taunted his lovers as he kissed them, saying, "And this beautiful throat will be cut whenever I please."

Many of Caligula's actions were more capricious than cruel. He made dignified senators run along with his chariot for miles or wait in short linen tunics at the head or foot of his couch. He treated his favorite horse, Incitatus, with more honor than he showed to the most honorable citizens in Rome, providing a marble and ivory stall, a jeweled collar, and special slaves to care for him. Allegedly, he intended to appoint the horse as consul, the most prestigious senatorial position in Rome.

When Philo headed a delegation to the Emperor on a mission of utmost importance to the Jews, his audience was granted during Caligula's distracted inspection of several mansions. Philo's opponents were allowed to mock him for his Jewish beliefs during the interview. Remarked the horrified Philo, "Indeed, the whole affair was a farce."

Although Caligula's new emphasis on games was greeted with pleasure by the people, by any standard it was excessive. Third-century historian Dio Cassius writes that the emperor required some sort of entertainment every day, and Philo confirms that "the festivities … went on by day and night, in private houses and in public places alike, and continued without a break for the first seven months [of Caligula's rule]." "In less than a year," Suetonius tells us, "he squandered Tiberius' entire fortune of 27 million gold pieces, and an enormous amount of other treasure besides."

When his sister Drusilla died, Caligula "made it a capital offence to laugh, to bathe, or to dine with one's parents, wives, or children while the period of public mourning lasted," writes Suetonius. Though in the Roman past only **Julius Caesar** and Augustus had been deified, Caligula deified Drusilla, setting up a shrine for her complete with priests, and gave her the name "Panthea" to show that she had the qualities of all goddesses. Ancient sources unanimously condemn Caligula's action as aberrant.

One example of Caligula's extravagant behavior is the three-mile bridge he had built near the Bay of Naples. Requisitioning all available ships (causing a shortage of grain in the cities), he anchored them together and built a road over them, complete with rest stops and running water. After donning the breastplate of **Alexander the Great** and other finery, he rode back and forth across the bridge with troops and cavalry. According to Suetonius, one explanation for the project was to mock a prediction once given by an astrologer: "As for Gaius, he has no more chance of becoming emperor than of riding a horse dryshod across the Gulf of Baiae."

The "Invasion" of Britain

Perhaps Caligula's greatest fiasco was his military adventure in the north. This included a trip to the Rhine, a long stay in Lugdunum (Lyons), where he raised funds from wealthy Gauls by nefarious means, and an "invasion" of Britain. In the latter case, he arranged all his forces across the channel from Britain—including catapults and war machines—as if for battle. He then set out to sea in a warship, after which he quickly returned to shore. The troops could not understand his intentions and confusion reigned until he gave the order to charge, telling the soldiers to pick up seashells off the seashore. Caligula styled this action a great military victory and counted the seashells as "spoils from the ocean." When he returned to Rome, he took with him a few Gaulish deserters and made the tallest of them dye their hair and learn a few German words. These were the "Germans" he had conquered.

Caligula displayed his megalomania both by petty actions and by a full-blown claim to godhood. In the eastern part of the Empire, it was customary for people to worship their rulers as gods, but in Roman culture no living man could be considered a god. Augustus and Tiberius had been careful not to accept divine honors. Caligula, however, built a shrine on the Palatine containing a life-size golden image of himself. The statue's clothes were changed daily to correspond to whatever the emperor was wearing. He appointed priests, and daily they made sacrifices of exotic animals to him.

Claiming a special closeness to the god Jupiter Capitolinus, Caligula built a house next to Jupiter's temple in order to live closer to his "brother." He put on wigs and costumes to impersonate different gods and at times carried on conversations with them. Dio records an incident when, as Caligula claimed to be conversing with the moon, he asked a companion if he could see the goddess: "The other, trembling as in awe, kept his eyes fixed on the ground and answered in a half whisper: 'Only you gods, master, may behold one another.'" This man became one of Caligula's most trusted friends.

Caligula notoriously offended the Jewish nation by insisting that his own statue be set in the most sacred spot in their temple, the Holy of Holies, and that sacrifices be made to him there. This command was in opposition to the most basic tenets of Judaism. For the Jews, to obey would have been equal to defying the one and living God, not to mention trampling on their most cherished customs. Many were ready to die rather than obey the emperor. The governor of Syria—responsible for carrying out the command but understanding the sacrilege involved and the danger of revolt—purposely prolonged the process of constructing the statue in order to avoid erecting it. Ultimately, Agrippa, a Jewish companion of Caligula, persuaded him on the basis of friendship to rescind the order.

Although various scholarly attempts have been made to explain Caligula's actions as rational, it may simply be that he was insane. The following assessment by Suetonius has been echoed by other ancient historians as well:

> Gaius was, in fact, sick both physically and mentally. In his boyhood, he suffered from epilepsy.... He was well aware that he had mental trouble, and sometimes proposed taking a leave of absence from Rome to clear his brain.

Several plots to end his rule were formed and discovered before the conspirators could carry out their plans, including one involving his own sisters. In that particular case, he banished his sisters to exile and executed the other participants. In A.D. 41, however, a successful conspiracy was carried out by a tribune of the Praetorian Guard who held both personal and public grievances against the emperor. "Thus Gaius," writes Dio, "after doing in three years, nine months, and twenty-eight days all that has been related, learned by actual experience that he was not a god." Hatred for Caligula was so great, in fact, that after he had been assassinated, his wife Caesonia was killed as well, and his daughter Drusilla's "brains were dashed out against a wall."

There are really no accomplishments worth mentioning to counterbalance the negatives of Caligula's brief rule. Some scholars have questioned whether the ancient authors were biased or merely prone to sensationalism. Even allowing for some error and exaggeration, the accounts generally confirm one another. As it turned out, the governmental structure of the Empire was strong enough to hold together despite this glitch in its fortunes. There is no doubt, however, that Caligula was one of the most malevolent emperors ever to hold that title in Rome.

SOURCES:

Balsdon, J. P. V. D. "Gaius," in *Oxford Classical Dictionary*. Oxford: Oxford University Press, 1970.

Barrett, Anthony A. *Caligula: The Corruption of Power*. London: Simon & Schuster, 1989.

Dio Cassius. *Dio's Roman History*. Translated by Earnest Cary. 9 vols. Harvard University Press, 1968.

Ferrill, Arthur. *Caligula: Emperor of Rome*. Thames & Hudson, 1991.

Philo. *Legatio ad Gaium*. Edited and translated by E. Mary Smallwood. E. J. Brill, 1961.

Suetonius. "Gaius (Caligula)," in *The Twelve Caesars*. Translated by Robert Graves. Viking Penguin, 1986.

FURTHER READING:

Balsdon, J. P. V. D. *The Emperor Gaius (Caligula)*. Oxford, 1934.

John Calvin

(1509–1564)

Theologian, preacher and Reformation leader, whose stern interpretation of scripture was the basis of the church developed at Geneva which became the center of the growing Protestant movement "Calvinism."

Born Jean Cauvin on July 10, 1509; died May 27, 1564; son of Gérard Cauvin (a lawyer) and Jeanne Lefranc; married: Idelette Bure, 1540; children: one child, died in infancy. Successor: (as director of Genevan Church) Théodore de Beza.

John Calvin was perhaps the most influential of all religious leaders of the Protestant Reformation in 16th-century Europe. Though a contemporary of the famous **Martin Luther,** Calvin was 26 years his junior and had developed some important theological differences. Significantly, Calvin's stern, "puritanical" interpretations brought a renewed vigor to Luther's Reformation. "Calvinism," as he established it at his base of Geneva, was adaptable to the current social and political changes in European society. And, under his tireless direction, Geneva became the cosmopolitan focus of an effective and far-reaching evangelism to which many Protestant churches today owe their birth.

Calvin was born Jean Cauvin in Noyon, France, on July 10, 1509. His father Gérard Cauvin was an ambitious lawyer; his mother Jeanne Lefranc was the daughter of a fairly well-to-do innkeeper. At an early age, Calvin was sent by his father to the University of Paris with the intention that he would one day enter the priesthood. But in 1528, his father ordered him for practical reasons to switch his emphasis from theology to law. This Calvin obligingly obeyed, leaving Paris for the

"If I may say so, I have wanted to do well, my sins have always displeased me and the fear of God has been in my heart."

JOHN CALVIN,
APPROACHING HIS DEATH

Contributed by Alan James, Ph.D., University of Manchester, Manchester, England

University of Orléans and, later, for Brouges. Although he had already developed a passion for theology, Calvin embraced the study of law.

In 1531, Calvin published his first book which eloquently demonstrated his potential as an intellectual and promised a bright career. But the death of his father, earlier that year, was to change his life drastically. Returning to Paris, Calvin was now free to indulge his humanist and theological interests. The precocious Calvin, who already displayed a distinct moral uprightness, came to accept fully the intellectual premise of God's omnipotence and felt a personal challenge to be an instrument of God's will. To accompany these convictions, by 1533 he had converted from Catholicism to Protestantism. Thereafter, he pursued religious study with a renewed sense of purpose and focus. As a result, he reacted increasingly to opposition with a feverish temper, completely assured of his divine inspiration.

To escape royal persecution for his new religious affiliation, Calvin left France in 1534 and traveled under the assumed name Martianus Lucianius. In Basel, he met similar-minded men and in 1536 published the first edition of his magnum opus, the *Institutes of the Christian Religion.* Though he was continually to revise this work until 1559, the first appearance of the *Institutes* gave Protestant theology the thorough and lucid expression that it so dearly needed and marked Calvin as a religious leader of some significance and authority. In it, one can find the essentials of Calvinist thought.

For Calvin, the only spiritual authority was scripture, both the New Testament and the rigid law of the Old Testament. According to his interpretation, a natural corollary of God's omnipotence was the conviction that God had determined, from the beginning of time, who was to be saved and who was to be damned. All people, he felt, were sinful by nature and unequal to the task of meriting redemption, or even of fully knowing God. It was through God's inexplicable mercy that the Elect were saved.

Though this concept of predestination was to be stressed by some later "Calvinists," Calvin felt simply that the purpose of life was to strive to know or understand God as well as possible and then to follow God's will. This could only be done through faith, by which people pursue union with God's earthly manifestation, Christ. With this faith, then, all people were required to strive to live a moral lifestyle, not as an assurance, but out of hope that they were among the Elect chosen by their omnipresent God. In this active pursuit Calvin was

CHRONOLOGY

1509	Calvin born
1517	Martin Luther nailed 95 theses to door of a Wittenburg church
1536	Calvin published first edition of the *Institutes of the Christian Religion;* journeyed to Geneva for first time
1538	Banished from Geneva along with Guillaume Farel
1541	Returned to Geneva
1545	Council of Trent
1546	Martin Luther died
1564	Calvin died

severe, and the church that he would model was to be an instrument of strict moral discipline.

One evening in June 1536, when Calvin stopped in Geneva to spend the night, he fully intended to continue on his journey the following day. But the local evangelical preacher, Guillaume Farel, had another idea. He convinced Calvin that it was his duty to God to remain where he was most needed. The task at hand: expelling the remnants of Catholicism from the city, which had recently won its independence from its ecclesiastical overlord. Thus, despite his distaste for his surroundings and for the politics of his newly adopted city, Calvin would primarily focus his ministry on Geneva for the rest of his life.

Together Farel and Calvin directed the Reformation in Geneva hoping, as part of a total moral reform, to fully establish Protestantism and to eliminate frivolous indulgence. Within a couple of years, both were expelled for their moral strictures and their encouragement of French immigration. For Calvin, this simply meant freedom from the burden of politics and ministry. Happily, he went to Strassburg where he taught at an academy, preached, and developed his ideas on the nature of the ideal Christian church.

Perhaps for the good of his health, perhaps to soften his dour manner and impatience, Calvin's friends in Strassburg urged him to marry. In August 1540, choosing a chaste and sensible candidate, he married a widow of one of his converts, Idelette Bure, who brought to the marriage a son and a daughter. Unfortunately for the couple, their only child together died shortly after birth in 1542. After Idelette died seven years later, Calvin never remarried. Little is known of their lives together, though Calvin's relations with women were not entirely warm. Indeed, typically, it was women who most vociferously opposed his moral reforms.

Calvin Returns to Geneva

Yet it was with his calling, not with women, that he was always preoccupied; in 1541, he returned reluctantly to Geneva in response to a call from the now floundering church. After receiving assurances that he would be given the freedom he felt was necessary to build God's earthly kingdom, he soon organized the local church government with his *Ecclesiastical Ordinances*. With these, he began to develop a well-regulated social network within a morally disciplined society.

Despite considerable opposition within the city, Calvin's influence grew steadily as he defeated theological and political opponents alike. In 1553, Michael Servetus, a theologian traveling incognito to avoid persecution for his almost universally scandalous religious ideas, came to Geneva in spite of Calvin's earlier warnings. When Calvin recognized his heretical foe sitting within the crowd listening to one of his sermons, he promptly had Servetus arrested and put on trial. As the "Defender of the Faith," Calvin demanded his execution and was supported in this by the city government. On October 27, 1553, Servetus was burned alive for heresy.

Soon Calvin overcame most remaining opposition to his plans, and in 1555 the Consistory, which acted as a sort of moral court, was accepted and given effective powers by the city. Henceforth, moral discipline was strictly enforced. Taverns were closed and replaced with *abbayes* in which patrons were closely scrutinized for signs of excess. Indeed, throughout Geneva, citizens monitored each other's behavior, ready to report any sort of wrongdoing. In this spirit of mutual recrimination, a strict moral order—based on Calvin's particular vision of truth—was built. To modern sensibilities the extremes which Calvin's Geneva reached in its enforcement of narrow moral values are thoroughly distasteful, but they stand as a constant warning against the institutionalization of fanatical righteousness. Calvin associated himself with godliness and truth in every battle, religious or otherwise. Thus, for him, to tolerate opposition

of any kind was to tolerate evil. Though Calvin was particularly willing to enforce his will, it must be remembered that he was not entirely unlike his 16th-century contemporaries in their intolerance of dissent.

Despite his influence and implacable will, Calvin was unassuming physically. Though thin and pallid, he was brilliant and had boundless energy. These gifts he directed to much more than simple moral reform. Constantly preaching and writing, he involved himself in all aspects of Genevan affairs including education, trade, diplomacy, and even sanitation.

In 1559, he established the Genevan Academy (now the University of Geneva) for the training of clergy. Calvin was not interested in Geneva alone, but also with spreading the Reform movement abroad, especially within his native France. Under his direction, Geneva became a haven for persecuted Protestants and the unofficial center of growing Protestant movements in places as far removed as Scotland.

But Calvin's incessant activity was his undoing. In 1558, he had suffered an attack of pleurisy, and later, after delivering a sermon, began to cough blood. By 1563, he was effectively bedridden. Yet Calvin remained true to his moral standards and dutifully bound to his ethic of hard work, determined to continue his work in whatever manner possible. On May 27, 1564, he died of pulmonary tuberculosis.

SOURCES:

Elton, G. R. *Reformation Europe: 1517–1559.* Fontana Press, 1963.

Hunt, R. N. Carew. *Calvin.* Centenary Press, 1933.

McNeill, J. T. *The History and Character of Calvinism.* Oxford University Press, 1954.

Parker, T. H. L. *John Calvin: A Biography.* J. M. Dent, 1975.

FURTHER READING:

Hancock, Ralph C. *Calvin and the Foundations of Modern Politics.* Cornell University Press, 1989.

Harkness, G. *John Calvin: The Man and his Ethics.* Abingdon, 1958.

MacKinnon, James. *Calvin and the Reformation.* Russell & Russell, 1962.

Wendel, F. *Calvin: The Origins and Development of his Religious Thoughts.* Translated by P. Mairet. Harper, 1963.

Canute I, the Great

(c. 995/998–1035)

Viking king, who united the English and Danish people of England and was the first since the fall of Rome to rule over all of England.

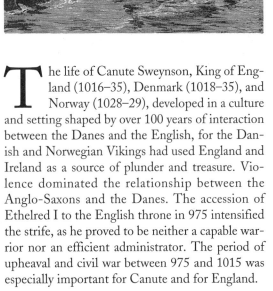

"He was ... far and away the greatest lord of the Viking world, and so a natural center for loyalty for English Scandinavians, and a guarantee of peace to his English subjects."

CHRISTOPHER BROOKE

The life of Canute Sweynson, King of England (1016–35), Denmark (1018–35), and Norway (1028–29), developed in a culture and setting shaped by over 100 years of interaction between the Danes and the English, for the Danish and Norwegian Vikings had used England and Ireland as a source of plunder and treasure. Violence dominated the relationship between the Anglo-Saxons and the Danes. The accession of Ethelred I to the English throne in 975 intensified the strife, as he proved to be neither a capable warrior nor an efficient administrator. The period of upheaval and civil war between 975 and 1015 was especially important for Canute and for England.

Inhabitants called the northeast section of England the Danelaw. This was the largest Viking settlement, a region occupied by Danes for over 100 years. By 975, the local English population had accepted the presence of these foreigners; indeed, English and Danish intermarriage was not uncommon. In this Viking settlement, the tribal leaders laid the groundwork for a Viking king to unite them.

Descended from the Shieldings, a long line of kings, Canute was also reputed by the Viking

Name variations: Translations of Viking runes phonetically indicate that Knut is proper, but the Anglicized versions—Cnut, Canute—are more popular. Pronounced: Ke-NOOT. Born Canute Sweynson between 995 and 998; died at Shaftesbury on November 12, 1035; son of Sweyn Haraldson (king of Denmark) and Gunhild (a Polish princess and sister to Duke, later King, Boleslav Chrobry); married: Aelfgifu of Aelfhelm; married: Emma (widow of the English king Ethelred), 1017; children: (first marriage) Harald Harefoot and Sweyn; (second marriage) Harthacanute and Gunhild. Predecessor: Ethelred the Unready in England, Harald Sweynson in Denmark, and Olaf Haraldson in Norway. Successors: son Harald Harefoot in England and Denmark.

Contributed by E. Lanier Clark, Assistant Professor of History, Albany State College, Albany, Georgia

sagas to be descended from the Knytling dynasty, adding to his prestige. His grandfather was Harald Bluetooth, and his father Sweyn Haraldson, both kings of Denmark. When Canute was born (c. 995/998), his father was in the process of conquering more areas of England under Ethelred's rule. Canute's mother Gunhild was a Polish princess and sister to Duke (later King) Boleslav Chrobry. Gunhild became Sweyn's consort and mistress. Though they had no formal marriage arrangement, Sweyn made their sons, Harald and Canute, his heirs.

Details of Canute's early life remain unclear because no written record exists. When the King married Sigrid the Haughty (the widow of King Eric of Sweden) in order to cement an alliance with Sweden, Gunhild had to leave Sweyn's court. Evidently, Gunhild took Canute—then no more than two or three years old—to the court of her brother. Though his childhood is shrouded in mystery, evidence points to a foster father, Thorkil the Tall, a distant cousin and brother to Earl Sigvaldi of Jomburg. Thorkil had also served as second-in-command to Sweyn on several raids during the years preceding Canute's birth.

Between 994 and 1007, Sweyn led a constant barrage of raids upon the beleaguered kingdom of England. Canute's brother Harald served as regent during the father's absence from Denmark. Sweyn resumed these attacks in 1009, and Canute appeared for the first time with his father in 1013. In that year, Canute held the fleet camp at Gainsborough in northeastern England while his father subdued all of northern and eastern England. Even London, which had lost no battles to the Vikings, submitted to Sweyn's authority, and in January 1014, Ethelred fled to Normandy and the court of his brother-in-law, Duke Richard.

On February 3, 1014, Sweyn's death, following a brief illness, set a number of events in motion. His elder son Harald received the crown of Denmark, while Sweyn's host ("army") at Gainsborough acknowledged Canute as his father's successor in England. Unfortunately, Canute needed the acceptance of both English and Danish nobles to claim the English throne. Though untested, the 20-year-old Canute must have displayed great promise or the Viking host would not have followed him.

Although they had given hostages to insure their submission to Sweyn and his son, the English nobles conspired with their exiled King. In April, Ethelred returned and gathered a large army to drive Canute from England. Realizing he could not hope for victory, Canute withdrew in May, taking revenge upon his unfortunate hostages. By his hasty retreat, Canute lost the Danelaw. He arrived in Denmark to find his brother in firm command with no interest in redividing the inheritance. Though both brothers agreed to assist each other in their endeavors to secure their kingdoms, Canute's claim remained more tenuous.

The following year, Canute (with assistance from another brother, Earl Eric, regent of Norway, and his foster father Thorkil) led an army which overran English territories of Wessex and Mercia. While this force was in England, Olaf Haraldson (the Stout), in the absence of Eric, began his quest to gain the throne of Norway. Because of his preoccupation with England, Canute could not spare Eric to return to defend Norway and would have to wait 15 more years for his chance to bring Norway under his sway.

Though Ethelred and his son, Saxon King Edmund Ironside, were no match for Canute, the Eadric of Mercia's change in allegiance gave Canute a significant edge. In the fall of 1015, Ethelred lost Wessex; in early 1016, Northumbria surrendered and was placed under the control of Earl Eric of Norway; by April, Canute was planning his attack on London. Before he could launch the assault, however, Ethelred died on April 23. Though in choosing a new king the English witan ("council of nobles") usually selected a successor in the line of Alfred of Wessex; they evidently had some powers of discretion. Before May's end, when over three-fourths of the kingdom had submitted to the Dane, many magnates and ecclesiastical leaders had met to designate Canute as their choice. At the same time, a similar body in London declared for Ethelred's son Edmund—an act which could only prolong the violence.

Using Mercia as a source of provisions, Canute besieged London over the course of the summer. In the fall, he led an attack on East Anglia, despite having to simultaneously besiege London. On October 18, 1016, Edmund's army found the Danes at Ashingdon and—against the advice of Eadric—attacked Canute's army. Edmund lost decisively. With England by then too exhausted to continue raising armies for him, Edmund's councillors suggested a division of England with peace. The "Compact of Olney" followed, dividing England into two sections: Edmund received Wessex while Canute held London, Mercia, and Northumbria. Edmund agreed in addition to levy a *Danegeld* ("tax") upon his lands to support Canute's army. Each ruler made the other his heir and exchanged oaths of friendship.

Canute Gains Undisputed Control of England

Edmund died on November 30, however, leaving Canute in undisputed control of England. For the first time in seven years, peace returned to the country, and at the Christmas celebration in London all of England's nobles recognized Canute as England's king.

Not wishing to destroy the existing social order, Canute made England the center of a growing empire, governing the kingdom with the advice of English as well as Danish nobles. The new king would need strong English support for a stable rule, yet he brought with him from Scandinavia the custom of allowing considerable freedom to nobles. Indebted to his Danish and Norwegian nobles who had shown him strong support, he raised several Scandinavians to high court positions, while depending most heavily upon Earl Eric of Norway and his foster father Thorkil. To compensate for the loss of Norway in 1016, he made Eric the Earl of Northumbria. Thorkil became Earl of East Anglia and Canute's regent in Denmark in the King's absence. Canute also utilized the Mercian Eadric, despite Eadric's history of shifting allegiances; the Archbishop of York, Wulfstan II; and the newly made Earl Godwin of Devon. The use of such English councillors clearly indicated Canute's desire to rule the kingdom in the manner of his Anglo-Saxon predecessors.

Confirming the existing system, Canute's first act as king was to divide the kingdom into four great earldoms. While Eric, Eadric, and Thorkil held the above-mentioned positions, Canute held Wessex for himself, developing a division of power and land that would later provide a base for resistance by other such nobles against future kings. In addition to this system, Canute established a series of lesser earldoms along the Scottish, Welsh, and Cornish marches to protect those regions from raiders.

In July 1017, Canute married Emma, the widow of Ethelred. He had as well a consort in Denmark, Aelfgifu of Aelfhelm, with whom he had initiated a relationship in 1013 while holding charge of the fleet at Gainsborough. His marriage to Aelfgifu was after the Danish custom and not one sanctioned within the Christian church; together they had two sons, Harald Harefoot and Sweyn. When Canute then married Emma, a precondition was that the sons of their marriage would stand in line for the English throne before Canute's older sons or Emma's sons by Ethelred. The royal couple would eventually have two children, a boy, Harthacanute, and a girl, Gunhild, who later married Prince Henry of Germany.

During 1018, Canute sent most of his Scandinavian host back to Denmark. With the remaining 3,000 men, he established an elite bodyguard, which became the core of his army, and stationed these soldiers at strategic points around the kingdom. The defense of the peace against both English offenders and Danish raiders rested upon this force. In the summer his brother Harald died without heirs. Then in October, Archbishop Wulfstan drafted a law code for Canute; it reinforced the idea that Canute was ruling as an English successor to the line of Alfred of Wessex, thus making his rule more palatable to his English subjects.

Canute returned to Denmark in 1019 to establish a firm claim to the throne, but, regarding England as not yet stabilized, he did not remain long in his homeland. After making Thorkil his regent in Denmark in the spring of 1020, Canute journeyed back to London to contend with a plot led by the Earl of Devon whom he replaced with Godwin of Devon.

Among the problems Canute faced during his rule was the conflict between his Christian and pagan followers. In England, he ruled as a most Christian king, ordering his nobles to follow the advice of the bishops and abbots and having the holy relics of the martyred Archbishop Aelfheah transferred from London to Canterbury in June 1023. His outlawing of Thorkil, a determined pagan, in 1021, may also have been a concession to the Christian church in England; Thorkil was reconciled to Canute two years later but never returned to England. This period also found the King endowing many churches and rebuilding monasteries to secure the goodwill of the Church.

After Thorkil's fall from grace, Canute used his brother-in-law, Earl Ulf, and his Danish consort, Aelfgifu, to enforce the laws and collect the taxes in Denmark. He named Sweyn, his son by Aelfgifu, regent though the power resided with Earl Ulf and Aelfgifu. In 1023, Canute sent Harthacanute, his son by Emma, to the Danish court to learn Danish customs as would befit a future king of Denmark.

That same year, he began pressing his claims to Norway in opposition to King Olaf Haraldson the Stout. With Earl Eric of Norway dead, no one else could contest Canute's claim, and if Olaf meant to hold the kingdom, Canute said, then he would do so as a vassal to Canute—an idea which Olaf rejected. In preparation for the forthcoming war, Canute was able to forge an alliance with the Holy Roman Emperor Conrad the Salic. This alliance added some disputed territory to Canute's southern Danish border and gave Conrad support against dissident Slavs in the eastern part of his realm. This treaty also freed Canute from the worry of intervention by Conrad should an invasion of Norway be necessary.

By the autumn of 1025, Canute was in Denmark preparing a fleet and army for war. With large sums of money in hand, he also employed bribery as a means to change the loyalties of some Norwegian nobles. Six months later, Canute traveled to England, leaving Harthacanute as regent under the guidance of Earl Ulf. Unfortunately, Ulf's ambition outran his common sense; heavy-handed in ruling the Danes, he provoked some to rebel against the regent and declare their support for Olaf. Ulf even went so far as to declare Harthacanute king before an assembly of Danish nobles.

That summer Canute returned to Denmark with a large English force to suppress the rebellion and to press a war against Olaf. In the former act, Canute was successful, even forgiving Ulf; in the latter, however, Canute was defeated in battle September 1026 at the mouth of the Holy River. It was, however, a pyrrhic victory for Olaf. Badly outnumbered, he was forced to flee to Sweden for the winter.

During the war, Earl Ulf was assassinated in a church, and for this Canute had to repay the Church in Denmark and the widow, his sister. With this deed weighing on his mind, in 1027 Canute proclaimed that he would make a pilgrimage to Rome and ask forgiveness of the pope, John XIX, hoping that such a trip would repair the strain put on his relationship with the Roman Catholic Church by the murder of Earl Ulf. The trip would also offer Canute an opportunity to confer with the Holy Roman Emperor Conrad face to face.

Arriving in Rome near the end of March, Canute attended a Church synod at the Lateran Palace and requested a reduction in fees for the *palia* of English archbishops, to which the Pope consented under the condition of a more regular payment of Peter's pence. In addition, Canute managed to obtain lower charges for pilgrims at inns along the route from England through Burgundy, as well as a promise for better protection for English pilgrims traveling through that region.

His business concluded in Rome, Canute returned to Denmark quickly, perhaps fearing a renewal of hostilities with the spring thaw. Fortunately, Denmark was quiet enough to allow him to return to England in late 1027 to deal with Scottish raiders. With a large army, Canute forced King Malcolm of Scotland and Earl **Macbeth** to render homage.

By 1028, the English ruler was back in Denmark to pursue his conquest of Norway. He encountered little resistance when he finally invaded. Advancing through the kingdom, he summoned the assemblies of minor nobles, the franklins, who swore faith and gave hostages. At the *Ere-thing* ("council meeting") in Throndheim, the franklins declared him the true king of Norway. At that meeting, many lords rendered homage to and received enlarged fiefs ("estates") from Canute.

A Meeting of the Nobles

In 1028, for the only time in his life, Canute called an imperial meeting at Nidaros, where the nobles from all three parts of his kingdom met. Creating a system of vassal earls and kings, he named his nephew, Haakon, earl of Norway and vice-regent while he made Harthacanute king of Denmark, with his foster brother Harald Thorkilson as chief advisor. As long as Canute reigned with an easy hand, his Norwegian nobles remained loyal. But when Aelfgifu, as regent for Harthacanute in Denmark and Norway, ruled with a heavy hand in Canute's name, the nobles of Norway began to turn away.

In 1029, Canute was again in England with his eastern portions of the kingdom once more secure. Unfortunately, his nephew Haakon perished during a storm in January 1030 and in his place Canute appointed Kalf Arnesson as vice-regent; his son Sweyn was named earl of Norway.

King Malcolm of Scotland renewed his homage during the year 1031, while many Welsh lords apparently submitted to Canute's overlordship as well. Yet the Empire had already grown too large for one man to rule easily. By 1033, problems were developing in Norway; Aelfgifu's rule had grown burdensome to Norwegian nobles, many of whom spoke of bringing Olaf Haraldson back. In the face of their growing rebellion, in 1035 Canute planned to travel again to Denmark in part to finalize the arrangements for a marriage between his daughter, Gunhild, and the son of Emperor Conrad, the future Henry III.

But the trip never took place. Following a period of illness, Canute died on November 12, 1035, at Shaftesbury while on an inspection tour of England; his remains were buried at Winchester. In the *Anglo-Saxon Chronicle,* the writer reported jaundice as the cause of death. During his 19-year reign, Canute had provided peace for England, as well as freedom from the savage raids which had marked his predecessor's reigns. His children did not long survive his death. Harthacanute reigned briefly as king of the entire realm but did not possess his father's strength or abilities. Harald also ruled briefly, but the great Anglo-Danish Empire depended upon a vigorous personality such as Canute. By 1040, the Empire was an idea of the past and in 1042, another Anglo-Saxon king, Edward the Confessor (son of Ethelred II), ascended the throne.

SOURCES:

Larson, Laurence Marcellus. *Canute the Great, c. 995–1035, and the Rise of Danish Imperialism During the Viking Age.* Putnam, 1912.

Loyn, H. R. *The Vikings in Britain.* St. Martin's Press, 1977.

FURTHER READING:

Brooke, Christopher. *From Alfred to Henry III, 871–1272.* Norton, 1961.

Garmonsway, G. N. *Canute and His Empire.* University College Press, 1964.

Roger Casement

(1864–1916)

Irish nationalist and British consular official, whose attempt to secure aid from Germany in the struggle for Irish independence led to his execution by the British for the crime of high treason.

Born Roger David Casement on September 1, 1864; executed on August 3, 1916; youngest son of a Protestant Irish father and Catholic Irish mother; never married; no children.

Born on September 1, 1864, in Kingstown, Ireland, to a Protestant father and Catholic mother, Roger David Casement was heir to two radically different traditions in Ireland. As the son of a landed Protestant gentleman, Casement had definite cultural links to England that the majority of his poorer Catholic countrymen did not. Yet as the son of a Catholic, Casement's heritage was bound up with that of Irish men and women who had fought English Protestant rule in their country for hundreds of years.

Casement was the youngest of four children; his sister, Nina, was eight years his elder, and his brothers Thomas and Charles were one and three years older, respectively. In 1868, when Casement was barely four, his Catholic mother had all her children secretly baptized into the Catholic faith. Unknown to the children's father and probably little understood by the children themselves, the baptism took place while the family was vacationing in North Wales. But Casement thought of himself as a Protestant for most of his life, converting to Catholicism only shortly before his death.

The event that most shaped Casement's childhood was the death of his mother in 1873.

"I have known no one who was so stirred at the thought of injustice and wrong, whether it was in Africa, America or Ireland. I have not met his equal for courtesy or kindliness or generosity…. I do not expect to meet his like again."

BULMER HOBSON

Contributed by Colleen Carpenter Cullinan, Ph.D. candidate, University of Chicago Divinity School, Chicago, Illinois

Nine at the time, the boy was deeply shaken by the loss. His father moved the children to the family estate, Magherintemple House, where Casement stayed for only a short time before being sent off to boarding school. Not quite four years later, Casement's father also died. Now orphans, the children were taken in by relatives. For the most part, Casement and his sister stayed with their mother's sister, Grace Bannister, and her family, while Charles and Thomas remained with their uncle, John Casement.

Grace and Edward Bannister lived in Liverpool, England, with their three children. Like her sister, Grace had married a Protestant, but she had converted to her husband's religion and raised her children and her sister's children in the Protestant faith. It is rumored, however, that Grace was only nominally Protestant, that she provided a quietly Catholic environment for the children. A seeming proof of this can be found in the eventual conversion of both Casement and Gertrude Bannister, one of Grace's own children.

Casement thrived in his aunt's home and was adored by his cousins. Although she was nine years younger, Gertrude was his favorite. In a pleasing baritone, Casement would sing traditional Irish songs for her and spin Irish fairy tales. He also loved to read, especially history and poetry, and there is evidence that even as a teenager living in England, he was interested in the Irish nationalist cause. Not only did he devour books on Ireland, but he is said to have covered the walls of his room with political cartoons that dealt with the issue. Despite his nationalist leanings, however, he did not return to Ireland when he finished school. Instead, after a brief and unhappy apprenticeship as a junior office clerk at the Elder Dempster Shipping Company, Casement embarked on the first of many voyages to Africa.

His first position, in 1883, was as purser on board the SS *Bonny,* an Elder Dempster ship that traded with West Africa. Making four round-trips aboard the *Bonny* over the following year, he became completely enamored of the African continent. In 1884, he began to serve with the International Association, a Belgian-run group of national committees seeking to bring European civilization to the Congo. **Leopold II** of Belgium had recently taken over the association, which was soon to become an entirely Belgian operation. Casement worked primarily as a surveyor, exploring land previously unknown to the Europeans and often making friends with native Africans along the way. One of his supervisors reported in despair that Casement refused to haggle over prices with the natives, and that he "would rather give 20 rods, for

one thing, than bargain and beat down to 12 rods, the proper price."

In 1890, Casement left the Belgian Congo, having become more and more uncomfortable with an enterprise that was no longer international but strictly Belgian. While working briefly as a surveyor for a railroad company, he met Captain Korzeniowski, a young Polish ship worker who would later become known as author Joseph Conrad. Conrad's experience in the Congo formed the basis for his famous and haunting work, *Heart of Darkness.* Casement does not figure in that work, despite its autobiographical cast; in fact, Conrad spoke of his meeting with Casement as one of his few good experiences in the Congo.

In 1892, Casement, at long last, found himself working for the British. The Niger Coast Protectorate employed him as a surveyor, and enlisted him with a great variety of other tasks, including that of the acting director-generalship of customs. Casement's interactions with the natives were not always friendly during these survey expeditions; at one point, he was surrounded by shouting warriors and only rescued when a native woman intervened. Casement spent three years in Niger, and though he was usually quite busy with surveys and other work, he still found time to write. Poetry was one of his great loves, and he also tried his hand at

CHRONOLOGY

1864	Casement born
1867	Irish rebellion failed against British rule
1868	Casement secretly baptized into Catholicism
1883	Journeyed to Africa
1895	Became a British consul
1899–1902	British war against the Boers in South Africa
1904	Casement exposed Belgian atrocities in the Congo
1906	Became a consul in South America
1909	Promoted to consul-general of Brazil
1910	George V succeeded Edward VII as king
1912	Casement published Putumayo Report; knighted
1914	Archduke Ferdinand of Austria assassinated; World War I began
1916	Casement converted to Catholicism
1916	Executed

short stories. Unlike his friend Conrad, however, Casement's skills as a creative writer were never to be recognized (and were not, in fact, particularly worthy of recognition).

Appointed Consul by Foreign Office

But in 1895, when Casement returned to Britain briefly on leave, he discovered that his reports from Niger had been published as a Parliamentary White Paper. Casement had become a public figure, and the Foreign Office scrambled to claim him as an employee. He was appointed consul to the port of Lorenco Marques in Portuguese East Africa, near what is now South Africa. His primary task was to protect British subjects and promote British interests, but an additional duty involved overseeing the political situation in the area, which was to erupt within a few years into the Boer War.

Casement was unhappy in Lorenco Marques; it was a miserably inadequate, run-down place, and the climate disagreed with his health. Further, used to the free life of exploration, he hated consular routine. He wrote that he dreaded:

> to be forced as I now am to interview anyone, whether black, white or Indian, who calls throughout the long day at this consulate, often upon trifling business or in quest of unimportant details, sometimes being even compelled to rise from bed when ill, to listen to a drunken sailor's complaint, or the appeal to my charity of a distressed British subject.

Casement grew ill and returned to England to recover. When he found to his dismay that the Foreign Office expected him to return to his hated post, he delayed and detoured on his way back to Lorenco Marques until told by a doctor to return to England immediately for an operation. Thus ended Casement's first round of consular service. Despite his unhappiness at the work, the Foreign Office found him to be, for the most part, a capable, hard-working, clever, and confident representative of the British government.

He was sent in 1898 to West Africa, where he had once worked for the Belgians, in order to investigate claims of ill-treatment of British subjects. He spent the next several years documenting grossly illegal and vicious treatment of the natives by the Belgians. Interested only in extracting as much rubber as possible, as quickly as possible, from the Upper Congo, Belgium had employed terrorist methods in order to force natives to work. In the process, they had reduced populations by 80% and more. In one area, the number of natives had fallen in ten years from about 5,000 to 352. The Belgians claimed that sleeping sickness was killing the natives, and while the disease did indeed kill great numbers of people, the huge declines in population had more to do with the extreme labor the people were forced into, the rough punishments inflicted when rubber quotas were not met, the lack of proper food, and the ever-present fear of Belgian overseers. Many natives were mutilated by Belgian soldiers, losing hands or feet as punishment for minor or even imagined wrongs. Casement documented beatings, floggings, imprisonments, mutilations, and other forms of mistreatment to such an extent that he himself was horrified.

> The daily agony of an entire people unrolled itself in all the repulsive terrifying details.... I verily believe I saw those hunted women clutching their children and flying panic-stricken to the bush; the blood flowing from those quivering black bodies as the hippopotamus hide whip struck and struck again; the savage soldiery rushing hither and thither among burning villages; the ghastly tally of severed hands.

Casement's report, when published in England in 1904, did not cause quite the sensation one might have expected. Leopold of Belgium denied everything, and Casement was portrayed by the Belgians as being in the pay of British rubber companies. Nevertheless, there were calls for an international investigation of the Congo. Casement was greatly disappointed that the British Foreign Office did not back up his charges to the fullest extent their own records would have allowed, but political considerations of the time did not allow such a step.

Casement took a leave of absence that almost turned into an early retirement. It was fully two years later that the Foreign Office was able to convince him to take up the post of consul in Santos, Brazil. In 1908, he was promoted to consul-general of Brazil and moved to Rio de Janeiro. Rumors of atrocities associated with yet another rubber company came to his attention, and Casement once more embarked on an exhaustive inquiry. His 1912 Putumayo Report exposed the cruel and exploitative treatment of Brazilian Indians by a Peruvian company and set a precedent for the British Consulate to intervene on behalf of native peoples. Until the Putumayo Report, it had been possible to think of events in the Congo as a strange aberration in colonial practices; now it was becoming clearer that abuse of colonized countries and natives was a serious problem.

Taking an extended medical leave of absence, Casement returned to Britain when his report was published. He had been knighted on his return to Britain, in recognition of the extraordinary work that led to the Putumayo Report. His health had never been good, and he was seriously considering retirement.

His Involvement with Irish Nationalists

Now Sir Roger Casement went to Ireland and quickly became involved with Irish nationalists. Casement was an effective speaker and fundraiser for the Irish Volunteers, and when Britain and Germany went to war in 1914, he saw a new way to put pressure on the British. He called on the Irish public to support Germany while he conceived a plan for an uprising. His intentions: to recruit Irish soldiers who had fought for Great Britain and had been captured by Germany. Traveling to Germany, Casement was well received by German leaders who promised to help him in raising an Irish Brigade. Germany even issued a declaration in favor of Irish independence—which Britain, of course, ignored.

Casement's recruiting efforts among captured soldiers did not go well: he soon discovered that German offers of assistance were hardly more than ploys to keep the English busy with worries of German troops in Ireland. Casement had been promised that 200,000 rifles, along with German officers and soldiers, would accompany him and the Irish Brigade back to Ireland. As things turned out, there were no Germans heading for Ireland and only one-tenth of the promised rifles. Since Irish leaders had planned an uprising based on projected German assistance, they decided to go ahead without it. Knowing such an uprising would fail miserably, Casement attempted to return in time to stop it, convincing the Germans to bring him to Ireland by U-boat. He also knew that his activities in Germany were well known to the British, and that he would be subject to arrest for treason if he were to return to Ireland (which still was British territory). Still, he made the desperate effort to return home and prevent a hopeless civil war. British Intelligence was aware of his impending arrival, and Casement was captured shortly after he landed on Irish soil.

Immediately imprisoned, Casement was soon brought to England for trial. In his final speech from the dock, he stated unequivocally that he had never sought to aid the king's enemies, but only his own country—Ireland; how can a man, he asked, be condemned for treason on such grounds?

His pleas to be tried in Ireland and judged by Irishmen went unheard, and he was condemned for treason by an English jury in an English court. Despite appeals on his behalf from many quarters, he was sentenced to hang.

For a brief time, there was hope of a reprieve of the death sentence from the Crown. However, Casement's diaries had been discovered by this time and copies circulated to King George V, members of Parliament—anyone with influence. The diaries revealed that Casement was a practicing homosexual and had been for many years. The shock and scandal accompanying this revelation precluded any possibility of a reprieve.

In Casement's last weeks in prison, he acknowledged his lifelong semi-association with the Catholic Church by formally converting. As he explained shortly before his death, he had always been looking for something, and "in Protestant coldness I could not find it, but I saw it in the faces of the Irish. Now I know what it was I loved in them: the chivalry of Christ speaking through human eyes." Thus, Casement died a Catholic. Brought to the scaffold on August 3, 1916, he was said to have met death calmly. The hangman described him as "the bravest man it fell to my unhappy lot to execute."

Casement's story, it would appear, is a contradictory one. After years of faithful service to the British Empire, he suddenly becomes enamored of Ireland and betrays Britain for this new love. Yet that is an overly simplified version of what happened, and is, in effect, wrong. Casement saw, in his service of the Empire, a service in the name of *both* Ireland and England, and it is certain that he had always valued his Irish heritage. His interest in Irish nationalism was nothing new in 1913; it was, however, the first time that he had had the chance to act on his beliefs. His attempt to work with Germany was not in contradiction to his previous work, but in keeping with his efforts to struggle against oppression. In Africa, in Brazil, and in Ireland, Casement saw colonial powers being abused; for his efforts in Africa and Brazil, he was hailed as a hero. It was only when he tried to awaken the British to their own failings that he was pronounced a traitor. Casement, then, died as he had lived: in service to his country.

SOURCES:

Inglis, Brian. *Roger Casement.* London: Hodder and Stoughton, 1973.

Sawyer, Roger. *Roger Casement: The Flawed Hero.* London: Routledge and Kegan Paul, 1984.

FURTHER READING:

Gwynn, D. *The Life and Death of Roger Casement.* London: Jonathan Cape, 1930.

Mackey, H. O. *The Life and Times of Roger Casement.* Dublin: C. J. Fallon, 1954.

————. *Roger Casement: The Secret History of the Forged Diaries.* Dublin: Apollo, 1962.

Reid, B. L. *The Lives of Roger Casement.* Yale University Press, 1976.

Catherine II, the Great

(1729–1796)

Autocratic, astute, and dynamic empress who—guided by the teachings of the Enlightenment—ruled Russia during a period of unprecedented political growth.

In 1773, Catherine the Great arranged for the marriage of the Grand Duke Paul, her son and heir, to the German princess, Wilhemina of Hesse-Darmstadt. This happy marriage ended three years later with the princess's death in childbirth. Catherine then imported another German princess for her son, Sophia Dorothea of Württemburg. Fearing that the newlyweds would become a center of opposition if her political rivals chose to rally around them, Catherine arranged that their activities be closely monitored; the young couple were retired to a palace outside the capital of St. Petersburg where they spent most of their time until the end of Catherine's reign. The Grand Duke and Duchess resented the Empress for removing them from participation in governmental affairs, and Catherine, having lived through similar circumstances, understood their frustration. She too had come from Germany to marry into the royal family of Russia, only to become a victim of intrigues which isolated her from life in the Russian court.

From an early age, Catherine's political astuteness had been evident. By studying her family tree, the young Princess Sophia (as she was

Born Sophia Augusta Fredericka, Princess of Anhalt-Zerbst, a small principality in Germany, on April 21, 1729; died on November 6, 1796, in St. Petersburg; daughter of Christian August, prince of Anhalt-Zerbst, and Johanna Elizabeth (from the family of Holstein-Gottorp, which ruled the Duchy of Holstein in Germany); first cousin to King Gustavus III of Sweden; married: second cousin Peter Fyodorvich (Peter III), 1744; children: Paul, Anne, Aleksey Bobrinksy. Predecessor: Peter III. Successor: her son, Paul I.

Contributed by David Katz, A.M., Harvard University, Cambridge, Massachusetts

known as a child) observed her connections with other royal families and came to an important conclusion: "This idea of a crown began running in my head then like a tune, and has been running a lot in it ever since." Her father was Prince Christian August of Anhalt-Zerbst; her mother was Johanna Elizabeth, whose family ruled the Duchy of Holstein. Although Sophia's parents did not control vast land and wealth, her mother's family was well-connected with some of the great royal families of Europe. Though small in size, the Duchy of Holstein-Gottorp was strategically placed between Denmark and Germany, on the eastern coast of the Baltic Sea, and thus could exert influence in the region as competing powers wrestled for control of the Baltic and Northern Europe. But Sophia's parents had no particular plans for her. She would write later that her father "saw her very seldom," and her mother "did not bother much about me." Her childhood was spent in the Prussian city of Stettin, where her father kept busy with

official duties as governor. Sophia was raised speaking both French and German.

In 1744, Sophia and her mother Johanna received an invitation to visit the court of Empress Elizabeth of Russia; as she said goodbye to her father and tutor, the young girl was unaware that she would never see them again. The purpose of the invitation was to arrange for the marriage between Sophia and Grand Duke Peter Fyodorovich, heir to the Russian throne who has been cited in one source as a "hare-brained zany." Upon the announcement of the engagement, Sophia converted from the Lutheran faith of her homeland to the Orthodox faith of Russia, and thenceforth was known by her Russian name, Catherine. She would later recall in her memoirs: "To tell the truth I believe that the Crown of Russia attracted me more than his person."

During these early years, Catherine learned how to survive Russian politics by practicing neutrality:

> I decided to humour the Grand Duke's confidence in order that he should at least consider me as a loyal friend to whom he could say anything without risk.... As a matter of fact, I tried to be as charming as possible to everyone and studied every opportunity to win the affection of those whom I suspected of being in the slightest degree ill-disposed towards me.... It pleased me when I realized that I was daily winning the affection of the public.

Speedily adapting to Russian ways and eager to learn the language, she would jump out of bed in the middle of the night and "while everyone was still asleep" would learn "by heart all the lessons."

Her mother's intrigues with **Frederick the Great,** King of Prussia, did not help Catherine win approval in the eyes of Empress Elizabeth, however. When it was discovered that Frederick had asked Johanna to intercede secretly on behalf of Prussian interests at the Russian court, she was promptly banished from Russia in 1745. Mother and daughter never saw each other again. Catherine's private life became the domain of diplomats and courtiers; any letters to her family had to be sent through the College of Foreign Affairs. As a Grand Duchess, Catherine was a potential rival for the Empress Elizabeth, and it was deemed necessary to isolate her further. She later noted that "all those who were suspected in the slightest" of any affection or attachment were "either exiled or dismissed, and their number was not small."

Although the young bride would have been ready to accept her new husband "had he been capable of affection or willing to show any," Peter openly bragged to her of his sexual exploits with other women. It is no surprise then that Catherine also found love outside marriage; by most accounts she had 12 lovers in her lifetime. Contemporaries viewed her actions as a sign of moral laxness, but Catherine defended her behavior: "God is my judge that I did not take them out of looseness, to which I have no inclination." Catherine and Peter came to tolerate each other's extramarital relations. Peter kept his bedroom at a distance from hers, which facilitated her relations with her first lover, Sergius Saltykov, a Russian noble.

It was during this time that Catherine gave birth in 1754 to her son Paul. A rather important point of controversy arose over the identity of Paul's biological father—Peter Fyodorich or Sergius Saltykov—endangering her son's claim to the throne. After Catherine's death, Paul tried unsuccessfully to burn all copies of his mother's memoirs, which hinted that his father might have been Saltykov. Catherine's next lover was Stanislaw Poniatowski, a Polish nobleman. Together they had one child, Anne, who died in her second year. Catherine would later use her considerable Russian influence in Polish politics to get Poniatowski elected king of Poland.

Catherine was an avid reader: "I read anything that came my way." The writings of Plutarch, Tacitus, Machiavelli, and Montesquieu caught her attention, while she actively corresponded with Voltaire. As part of an 18th-century intellectual movement called the Enlightenment which taught reliance on reason over passion, Frenchmen Montesquieu and Voltaire insisted that logic prevail over old-fashioned traditions. All people were entitled to certain basic civil rights. It was the duty of governments to devise rational means to secure and increase the welfare of its citizens.

Peter meanwhile was becoming unpopular. An intense admirer of Frederick the Great, Peter's predilection for Prussian ways was especially irksome as Russia was then at war with Prussia. The Imperial Guard particularly resented Peter's introduction of Prussian uniforms and drills. Talk circulated about plans to pass over Peter in favor of his son Paul, with Catherine as regent. But when Elizabeth died in late 1761, Peter succeeded as Emperor Peter III.

Peter immediately ended the European phase of the Seven Years' War (known as the French and Indian War in America) by declaring peace with Prussia even though Russian armies were in a position to pursue further victories. The new Emperor also took to publicly disowning his wife. At this time, Catherine's lover was Gregory G. Orlov, who—along with his four brothers—was an influential leader among the élite guard regiments. It was with Orlov that Catherine gave birth in 1762 to another son who became known as Aleksey Bobrinksy. When the Orlov brothers orchestrated a plan to remove the unpopular Emperor, Catherine marched at the head of the army that arrested her husband. Peter was confined with his violin, his dog, his slave, and his mistress.

A Coup Elevates Catherine to the Throne

Since the seizure of St. Petersburg was sufficient to wrest control from the supposedly all-powerful Emperor, Catherine was then crowned as Catherine II, Empress of Russia. Then, just a few days after his arrest, at a drunken dinner attended by Orlov, Peter III was carried out dead; although no evidence has been found to substantiate the claim, suspicions suggested that Catherine planned the murder. The ease of the bloodless coup of June 1762 illustrates not only Catherine's political acumen, but also the instability or weakness of autocratic rulers in Russian history.

To secure her position and to appeal to the conservative elements in Russian society who opposed rapid change, Catherine maintained a strong interest in Orthodox rites to emphasize her advocacy of traditional Russian ways. Although in name Catherine was empress and absolute ruler of Russia, she was not an all-powerful ruler. In a decree of 1764, which appointed Prince Alexander A. Vyazemsky as procurator-general (a position roughly equivalent to prime minister), Catherine advised him that "in the senate you will find two parties.... You must not respect either one or the other side, but must treat each courteously and impartially, ... and progress with firm steps by the shortest route to the truth." Vyazemsky so faithfully managed Catherine's wishes that he remained in office until his death almost 30 years later.

The atmosphere at Catherine's court was relaxed but industrious. The Empress rose at five or six in the morning and, after coffee, kept four secretaries busy during a 15-hour work day; she preferred to work in informal, modest dress except on ceremonial occasions. Later in her reign, her figure grew much fuller, and she preferred a comfortable light gown over the tightly corseted dresses of the court.

The Instruction Is Published

Catherine received early fame with the publication of the *Instruction* (*Nakaz*), which describes her ideal government for Russia. Her manifesto shares many 18th-century ideas. From Montesquieu, she borrowed the importance of the moral behavior of government officials; from the Italian jurist Beccaria, notions about criminal justice; sections from her *Instruction* even reflect the views on taxes and trade of the English economist Adam Smith.

It is interesting to note the resemblance between the *Instruction* and other political documents from this period. The fundamental documents of the United States are as much a product of the Enlightenment as Catherine's celebrated tract. The Bill of Rights insists that: "Congress shall make no law respecting an establishment of religion, or prohibiting the free exercise thereof…. Cruel and unusual punishments [shall not be] inflicted." One can see sentiments in the *Instruction*:

> Permission to believe according to one's own faith softens even the hardest hearts … , stifling those disputes detrimental to the tranquility of the state…. The use of torture is repugnant to a healthy and natural mind…. We [rulers] were created for our people…. For God forbid that after this legislation is finished any nation on earth should be more just and, consequently, more flourishing.

Shortly after the appearance of the *Instruction* in 1767, Catherine called forth representatives of all classes (except the serfs) to form a legislative commission to codify and simplify Russian laws and to apprise her of the needs of the country. In one clause of the *Instruction*, Catherine stated that land can be best cultivated by those who are free and own their land. Many of her contemporaries interpreted such a declaration as a sign of Catherine's commitment to the abolition of serfdom, a system by which many peasant farmers had to fulfill onerous obligations of forced labor for their landlords. But the provincial gentry upon whom she still depended insisted on serfdom, and Catherine claimed it was necessary to give in to their demands: "One is barely allowed to admit [serfs] are men like ourselves."

Despite her disclaimers, Catherine was instrumental in strengthening serfdom. During her reign girls were sold for 10 rubles, and she gifted various noblemen with over 800,000 peasants; one of her later decrees also legalized serfdom in the Ukraine. Moreover, though Catherine was an Enlightened ruler, she did not necessarily believe democracy was the best form of government. She prefaced her celebrated *Instruction* with the observation that:

> an extensive Empire demands absolute Power in the Person who rules it: it is necessary that [quick] Dispatch in the Decision of Affairs sent from distant places compensate for the Delay occasioned by their remoteness…. It is better to obey the Laws under the direction of one Master, than to be subject to the Wills of many.

Catherine hinted at her fear that one group of nobility, without sincere intentions, could come to dominate all others in government. Autocratic government, she maintained, was the best for Russia: "What is the Object of absolute Government? Certainly not to deprive the People of their natural Liberty, but to direct their Conduct in such manner that the greatest good may be derived."

The Legislative Commission was adjourned, however, because of the impending war with Turkey. The Sultan of the Turkish Empire became apprehensive about the predominance of Russian influence in neighboring Poland. Catherine had succeeded in making the Polish king, Stanislaw Poniatowski, a pliant agent of Russian wishes. In 1768, war erupted when Polish nobles rebelled and formed the Confederation of the Bar, which opposed Russian influence over the king. The fighting spilled over into Turkey, which promptly declared war on Russia in hopes of reestablishing its sphere of influence in Poland. But Turkey was defeated both on land and sea, and in the Treaty of Kuchuk Kainarji of 1774, Russia gained permanent access to the Black Sea. Austria and Prussia were also alarmed by the growing Russian control of Eastern European affairs. To ensure equal influence in the region, it was decided to partition off parts of Poland (First Partition) to all three powers—Austria, Prussia and Russia. (Poland lost about one-third of her territory and one-half of her inhabitants.)

The end of hostilities came none too soon for Russia. Troops had to be amassed against Emilian Pugachev, leader of a massive rebellion against Russian authority in the eastern perimeters of the Empire. By pretending to be Catherine's dead husband Peter III, Pugachev was laying claim to the Russian throne. His appeal was directed toward serfs, factory peasants, Cossacks, and other minority groups which felt mistreated and cheated by their Russian masters.

As Catherine realized the danger, her temper erupted at her generals who could not subdue the first wave of Pugachev's revolt. It became imperative for her to win the support of significant segments of her Empire's eastern flank before Pugachev's appeal could penetrate further. The livelihood of the towns and the local gentry depended on the success of loyal government forces. To win support, Catherine focused on their concerns, reassuring the nobility and townspeople that their safety and welfare were the ultimate goals of her government. As troops continued to move east, the rebellion was subdued by late 1774.

To prevent further outbreaks, Catherine published her "Statute (*uchrezhdenie*) of 1775 on Provincial Government." She wrote in the preamble that her intention was to put an end to "neglect of duty, arbitrariness and chicanery" in provincial government. The provinces of Russia were largely governed through agents appointed directly by the central government in St. Petersburg; to aid these officials in the reform of Russian provincial government, the new statute called for the assistance of local gentry and townspeople in governing themselves through newly created elective offices.

Catherine published another major reform in 1785; the "Charters (*gramota*) to the Nobility and Towns" reaffirmed the freedom of the nobility to leave state service and guaranteed their right to own land. Prior to Catherine and Peter's reigns, the special privileges of the Russian gentry had been contingent upon a career in state service, either as civil servants or as soldiers. The "Charters to the Nobility" also emphasized property as a defining characteristic. Only nobles who owned a minimum of land and only those town merchants who possessed a minimum of assets could enjoy the special privileges of their class, such as exemption from taxes and the right to vote in local elections. Along with the emancipation of serfs in 1861 and the constitution of 1905, Catherine's "Charter of 1785" was a landmark in Russian civil rights and political development.

Earlier in 1774, Catherine had appointed Prince **Gregory A. Potemkin** adjutant general, an official title for the Empress's lovers. But this affair was to be different from others: after the end of their romantic relations, Potemkin continued to play a prominent role in Russian politics and foreign policy until his death in 1791.

Theories about the importance of a large population were popular in the 18th century, and Catherine believed that the greater the population, the greater the strength of the Russian Empire. At the beginning of her reign, some 20 million people lived in Russia; by the end of her reign, she had extended the borders of the Russian Empire to include some 36 million. She began active plans to colonize vast southern regions of Russia. Farmers from other countries were invited to settle in these unpopulated lands. Bulgarians, Germans, Greeks, Jews, and Rumanians made up a large number of these immigrants. Colonists in the southern regions along the Black Sea were given the right to free movement, a right denied to serf farmers to the north. But many serfs achieved their freedom by escaping to the southern regions where their labor was in high demand.

Potemkin played a prominent role in the economic development of the southern half of the Russian Empire. During his tenure in these regions, Catherine and Emperor **Joseph II** of Austria visited Potemkin, where he led them on a grand tour of all the improvements he had completed. Prior to the visit, Potemkin had ordered that counterfeit villages be erected with favorable facades to make them appear prosperous to his two distinguished guests. From this effort was coined the phrase "Potemkin villages" to mean any impressive facade that hides something undesirable. Many of Potemkin's efforts did result in genuine development, however. The cities of Kherson and Sebastopol, founded by Potemkin, exist to this day. He also founded the city of Ekaterinoslav (now Dnipropetrovsk) in honor of the Empress.

Turkey, however, had plans to reconquer the Black Sea region from southern Russia. When late in 1787 Turkey declared war, Russia once again severely defeated its neighbor to the south. By 1792, the Peace of Jassy was signed, reaffirming Russia's presence along the Black Sea. It also brought an end to the kingdom of Poland. Although Poniatowski had pleaded with Catherine to allow a new constitution that could revitalize Poland and prevent an imminent rebellion of Poles against their foreign masters, she dismissed his proposal. After defeating the Polish rebels, Russia partitioned the rest of Poland among its neighbors, Prussia and Austria. Catherine justified her annexations by claiming it was Russia's historical destiny to reclaim lands that were once Russian. Clearly, the modern-day peoples of the region, the Poles, the Belorussians, the Ukrainians, would disagree that their lands ever "belonged" to Russia.

Domestic Accomplishments

The growth of the Russian Empire, both through internal development and external expansion, brought a need for a more extensive school system which could widen the pool of educated personnel to fill new government offices. Russians primarily received their education through private tutors. Catherine set up a commission in 1782 under the direction of her current favorite Peter A. Zavadovskii. By the end of her reign, this commission increased the number of grade schools in Russia from 50 to about 550 with at least one high school in each province. In St. Petersburg today one can visit the buildings of the Smolny Institute, which was founded by Catherine as a high school for young women from gentry families.

Two other architectural monuments commissioned under Catherine's reign are still noticeable landmarks in modern St. Petersburg. The Hermitage or west wing of the Winter Palace was finished under her direction. In tribute to the reforming spirit of **Peter the Great,** Catherine invited the French sculptor Etienne Falconnet to cast a large statue of the Emperor on horseback, which was later immortalized in the poem "Bronze Horseman" by the Russian poet Alexander S. Pushkin.

Catherine directly participated in the literary and intellectual life of Russian society. She sponsored and edited the journal *Vsyakaya vsyachina* (*All Kinds of Things*) in 1769, which inspired Nikolai I. Novikov (1744–1818) to create the first original Russian satire. Her patronage of the arts inspired two great literary figures of 18th-century Russia. As a government bureaucrat, Denis I. Fonvizin (1745–92) criticized Russia's current tendency for French mannerisms. Gavril R. Derzhavin's (1743–1816) series of poems, "Felitsa," serve as an ode to Catherine and the rule of reason.

Despite her liberal sentiments, Catherine did not warmly receive the news of the American Revolution of 1776 or the French Revolution in the 1790s. These struggles were an abomination to her sense of justice and order. The French revolutionaries had strayed from "legitimate authority" and from "every good moral doctrine"; the execution of their king **Louis XVI** by guillotine particularly outraged Catherine as the epitome of violence which "exceeded all bounds." As for the America's War for Independence, Catherine remarked that "rather than sign the separation of thirteen States [of America].... I would have shot myself."

After the French Revolution, she became increasingly concerned that the destructive fury would spread to Russia. She began to take stern measures against any one who would question her authority. Now finding Novikov's politics to be too liberal and a threat to the autocratic nature of her government, she had him jailed. In 1790, when Alexander N. Radishchev published his *Journey from St. Petersburg to Moscow* in which he discussed the horrors of serfdom and blamed the Empress for its continued existence, he too was jailed. Catherine felt that his criticism was harsh and seditious. Among those imprisoned was the Polish general **Tadeusz Kosciuszko,** who had fought on the side of the colonists in the American Revolu-

tion before returning to free his native Poland from foreign rulers.

Regardless of Catherine's lessening tolerance, the last years of her reign marked a growing variety of opposing opinions. When she lifted the ban on owning a private printing press, the publication of books flourished. During the last ten years of her reign, over 3,000 books were published, surpassing any previous decade in Russian history. Stimulated by Catherine's laws and writings, Russian society matured intellectually as the forum for public debate expanded. Newly founded Masonic lodges offered to civic-minded individuals the first meeting ground for public discussions that were not under government sponsorship.

Even after the French Revolution turned Catherine further away from democratic reform, she still respected the principles of liberty and read to her grandson, much to the irritation of her son Paul, the Declaration of the Rights of Man. Catherine decided to see personally to the education of young Alexander (the future **Alexander I**), hoping that he would serve the Russian State with principles she held dear.

Indeed, near the end of her reign, plans were afoot to skip over Paul in favor of Alexander, but Catherine suffered a stroke before she could publish an edict depriving Paul of the throne. After spending one day unconscious, she died on November 6, 1796. Paul had his mother buried next to Peter in St. Petersburg.

SOURCES:

Alexander, John T. *Catherine the Great, Life and Legend.* Oxford University Press, 1989.

De Madariaga, Isabel. *Russia in the Age of Catherine the Great.* Yale University Press, 1981.

Dukes, Paul. *The Making of Russian Absolutism. 1613–1801.* London: Longman, 1990.

Kliuchevskii, Vasilli O. *Kurs russkoi istorii.* Vol. 5. Moscow, 1958.

Kornilov, Alexander. *Modern Russian History.* Translated by A. Kaun. Knopf, 1948.

Mendelsohn, Ezra, and Marshall S. Shatz, eds. *Imperial Russia, 1700–1917.* Northern Illinois University Press, 1988.

Raeff, Marc, ed. *Catherine the Great: A Profile.* Hill & Wang, 1972.

———. *Understanding Imperial Russia.* Translated by A. Goldhammer. Columbia University Press, 1984.

Riasanovsky, Nicholas V. *A History of Russia.* 4th ed. Oxford University Press, 1984.

Troyat, Henri. *Catherine the Great.* Translated by J. Pinkham. Dutton, 1980.

Camillo di Cavour

(1810–1861)

Italian aristocrat, whose masterful manipulation of both the European diplomatic system and Italian revolutionary movements placed Italy on the path toward unification.

"The greatness of Cavour is like the greatness of Bismarck … it consists not in the undeviating pursuit of a ruthless master plan … but in the infinite suppleness with which he adapted his policy and his objectives to every changing circumstance."

L. C. B. SEAMAN

"Italy," quipped the Austrian statesman **Klemens von Metternich** in 1815, "is a geographic expression." Like Germany, Italy until late in the 19th century was not a single nation, united under a single government, but a series of smaller states, each ruled by petty monarchs reluctant to relinquish control of their limited realms.

The largest state in Italy—the Kingdom of Naples, which occupied the southern half of the Italian peninsula—was ruled by a former French family that had taken control of the area in the late Middle Ages. Between this kingdom and the small states of northern Italy lay the Papal States, remnants of the feudal power of the papacy many centuries before. To Italian nationalists who dreamed of uniting their country under a single government, the most daunting task, in highly Catholic Italy, was removing the Papal States from the papal control.

In the early 19th century, still another obstacle to unification emerged. During the late 1700s, the French emperor **Napoleon Bonaparte** had invaded large sections of Italy, declaring himself the king of Italy and making the Italian peninsula a virtual French province. After Napoleon's armies

Name variations: Count Cavour. Pronunciation: Cah-MEE-loh Dee CAH-vore. Born on August 10, 1810, in Turin; died on June 6, 1861, in Turin; son of the Marquis Michele Antonio di Cavour and Adele de Sellon; unmarried; no children.

Contributed by Niles R. Holt, Professor of History, Illinois State University, Normal-Bloomington, Illinois

1805–15   Italian Peninsula under the control of French Emperor Napoleon Bonaparte, the "king" of Italy

1814–15   Congress of Vienna awarded parts of northeastern Italy to Austria

1831   Charles Albert became king of Piedmont

1849   Piedmontese army suffered crushing defeat to Austrian forces in Battle of Custoza; Charles Albert abdicated in favor of Victor Emmanuel II

1859   Austrian troops driven from parts of northeastern Italy by Napoleon III

1860–61   Red Shirts of Guiseppe Garibaldi took control of the Kingdom of Naples

1866   Austria lost Seven Weeks' War to Prussia; relinquished control of remaining Italian land

1870   Napoleon III abdicated after defeat in Franco-Prussian war; Piedmontese army marched into Rome and united it with the rest of Italy

were defeated at Waterloo, Belgium, in 1815, the diplomatic conclave named the Congress of Vienna tried to protect Italy from future French encroachment. Responsibility for the area was given to Austria. Austrian troops occupied, and built fortresses in, the northeastern Italian states of Lombardy and Venetia.

The *Risorgimento* ("the Resurrection") was the name given to the popular movement in Italy which attempted to unite the country, beginning in 1815. The first group to embrace this goal was the *Carbonari* ("charcoal burners"), secret revolutionary sects which taught that Italy should be united only through liberal revolutions to overthrow existing monarchs. The intellectual and emotional prophet of Italian nationalism, the fiery revolutionary **Guiseppe Mazzini,** lamented the Carbonari's lack of militance and founded his own Europeanwide organization, Young Italy. Mazzini's revolutionary ideas were supported by **Guiseppe Garibaldi,** a southern Italian peasant whose armies fought to bring down the monarchy of the Kingdom of Naples. Later, Italians would remember Mazzini and Garibaldi as the heroes of their struggle for national independence.

Less attention would fall on Camillo di Cavour, an aristocratic statesman whose specialty was diplomacy. A less exciting figure than the Romantic revolutionary Mazzini or the humble and magnanimous Garibaldi, Cavour nevertheless was the individual most responsible for the even-

tual unification of his country. His clever, shrewd diplomacy harnessed the energy of Italian revolutionaries and made the divided Italian people an object of interest and sympathy among the Great Powers of Europe, setting Italy on the path to eventual unification in 1870.

Born into a northern Italian noble family, Cavour grew to adulthood during a time when Italy was changing from French rule to the control of the Austrian ruling family, the Habsburgs. His parents, who had served the Bonapartes in northern Italy, were forced to shift loyalties. Only with some difficulty were they able to ingratiate themselves with the Habsburgs. They also became political servants of the House of Savoy, the ruling family of the important state of Savoy-Piedmont, in northwest Italy. The Cavour family's ties to the House of Savoy proved to be important: Piedmont, which shared a common border with France, would eventually prove to be the Italian state most independent of Austrian control or influence.

Cavour's parents tried to inculcate into their son a proper respect for the Piedmontese monarch they served, but the independent and spoiled schoolboy rebelled against such conservative ideas. "Study bores me," he complained. "What can I do? It is not my fault." When he was ten, his parents enrolled him in a military school in his native city of Turin, in northern Italy. His duties included working as a page for Charles Albert, son of the king. The young Cavour poisoned his relationship with Charles Albert—a coolness between them that would last for 20 years—by his scandalous behavior at court, including his public complaints that the uniform he was forced to wear was demeaning. It reminded him, he said, of servants' "livery."

Most alarming to Cavour's parents was his choice of best friends, including the baron Severino Cassio, a liberal who favored replacing the absolute monarchs of northern Italy with constitutional governments and parliaments, and the similarly minded Marchesa Anna Schiaffino-Giustiniani, wife of a high municipal official in Genoa.

Upon graduation from military school in 1826, Cavour served as a lawyer in the area of Milan. The work bored him; he found the military life to be "half barracks and half monastery." When friends suggested that he join them on a vacation trip through France and Britain, Cavour took a leave of absence from lawyering. He was highly impressed with the government and society of Britain, which he thought superior to the social and political life of the other great European power that he knew well, Austria. He came to admire the parliamentary systems of both France and Britain, and he marveled at the "openness" of university lectures and political meetings.

Cavour believed that the examples of France and Britain proved that successful government depended on a "golden mean," or an avoidance of the extremes of revolution or absolute monarchy. Returning to Italy, he proclaimed himself willing to act as a "realistic monarchist" who believed that the best opportunity to unite Italy would be provided by an enlightened monarch, a monarch who was willing to reform his government and give his subjects a voice in governing themselves through a parliamentary system. "If I were the chief minister," he boasted to friends, "Austria would tremble and the world would be astonished."

Cavour Wins Seat in Government

That "reforming monarchy" proved to be the government of Cavour's own Piedmont. During 1848, when revolutions swept across Europe, the Piedmontese monarch Charles Albert issued his people a constitution, voluntarily placing limits on his power and establishing a Piedmontese parliament. Cavour successfully ran for a seat in the parliament, where he occupied a political middle ground between monarchists and revolutionaries. Described as "squat, rotund, and ebullient," he proved to be a persuasive speaker.

Cavour was one of several parliamentary members who urged Charles Albert to use the events of 1848 to attack Austria, in hopes that the Austrian monarchy, embroiled in its own revolution, would relinquish control of northeast Italy. The Piedmontese attack went badly; Austria won an easy victory, and Charles Albert was forced to abdicate in favor of his son **Victor Emmanuel II.** Cavour had won the new king's attention, however, and in 1850 he was appointed minister of agriculture. A few months later, he was promoted to minister of finance.

When the king appointed Cavour as prime minister in 1852, events were set in motion which would place Italy on the road to unification. As the leading political figure in Piedmont, Cavour boldly moved to raise the "Italian question" with the great military powers of Europe. Since Piedmont, with its small army, could not unify Italy on its own efforts, the aid of one or more of the Great Powers of Europe was essential.

Cavour's diplomacy was the highest form of *Realpolitik,* a term often applied to the diplomacy of the German chancellor **Otto von Bismarck.** Literally meaning "realistic politics," *Realpolitik*

signified a hard-nosed or a realistic attitude toward diplomacy; cleverness and determination were assets to its practitioners. For Cavour, *Realpolitik* meant that he would exploit the splits among the European great powers, while portraying himself to the world as the bulwark against the agents of "anarchy and chaos"—Italian revolutionaries such as Mazzini.

There was, seemingly, no logical reason for Piedmont to become involved in the Crimean War of 1854–55 that pitted France and Britain against Russia. The war was the result of British and French complaints that the Russian government was bullying the government of the Ottoman Empire, or Turkey. Yet when Austria hesitated to become involved in the war, Cavour saw an opportunity. With characteristic boldness, he declared that the Piedmontese army would fight alongside the armies of Britain and France. Piedmont earned the gratitude of those countries, while Austria, which eventually joined the alliance against Russia, was made to appear hesitant and untrustworthy. The Austrian government realized the cleverness of Cavour's diplomacy: the Piedmontese entry into the Crimean War, observed one Austrian diplomat, was "a pistol shot pointed directly at the head of Austria."

At the peace conference (Peace of Paris) which followed the war, Cavour worked to make Italy an object of sympathy and to transform the "Italian question" into a European issue. He also established a personal friendship with the French emperor **Napoleon III** (a nephew of Napoleon Bonaparte), who observed that it was a "formidable task to make a great state out of a small one." As a young man, Napoleon III had sympathized with the aspirations of Italian nationalists; during the 1830s, he had personally led attempted revolutions in Italy—all of them unsuccessful.

The Cavour-Napoleon III friendship bore fruit. In 1858, the two met secretly in Plombières, France. Knowing that the Emperor wanted to reassert French influence in Italy, Cavour convinced Napoleon III to use French troops to force Austria from the Italian peninsula. To buy the cooperation of the Emperor, Piedmont transferred to France sovereignty over Nice and Savoy, territories which bordered France.

Although French troops were victorious in battles with Austrian forces in northern Italy, the appearance of French troops in the Italian peninsula alarmed the other great powers. In order to declare a victory over Austria and lay the groundwork for withdrawing French troops from Italy, Napoleon III sought a meeting at Villafranca with

Victor Emmanuel, the king of Piedmont. Shocked that his monarch had agreed to end the French intervention before all of northeastern Italy had been cleared of Austrian troops, Cavour resigned. It was one of two occasions on which he resigned; both times, Victor Emmanuel refused to accept the resignation. Cavour the diplomatic planner had become indispensable for the cause of Italian unification.

Aware that the other Great Powers of Europe were uneasy over the rapidly changing events in Italy, Cavour continued to portray Piedmont as a moderate nation which was steering a course between radical revolutionaries such as Mazzini and reactionary Italian monarchies which opposed unification. Stung by rumors that he was "Napoleon III's lackey" and that Piedmont had become an instrument of French diplomacy, Cavour strongly opposed Napoleon III's suggestion that the French army might be used to overthrow the Kingdom of Naples.

That task—of liberating southern Italy from its monarchy—fell to Garibaldi. Leading a ragtag, ill-armed collection of small farmers named the Red Shirts, Garibaldi became an Italian national hero when he overwhelmed the monarchy in 1860. Garibaldi's only outside help from a Great Power had come from England, which had used its navy to protect Garibaldi's army when it sought refuge on the island of Sicily.

When a victorious Garibaldi marched north to the Papal States, however, Cavour, fearing that Napoleon III might intervene to protect the papal interests, ordered the Piedmontese army to march through the Papal States and stop him. In the process, Piedmont took control of much of the land in the Papal States. A rivalry had been clearly established between Cavour and Garibaldi. Yet Garibaldi, who sought no political power, later offered the conquered Kingdom of Naples to Piedmont, on the condition that it be made part of a unified Italy—and not simply an addition to a glorified Piedmont.

Italy Proclaimed United

In 1861, Italy was proclaimed united, with the exceptions of the state of Venetia, under Austrian control in northeastern Italy, and the city of Rome, which was the last of the pope's "temporal possessions." Victor Emmanuel was proclaimed emperor, and Cavour was named the nation's prime minister. He did not serve long; he died the same year, allegedly muttering, on his death bed, that "Italy is made, all is safe."

Austria was driven from Venetia as a result of the Seven Weeks' War between Prussia and Austria in 1866. During the war, Piedmont fulfilled a prior promise to Prussia and used its troops to attack Austrian fortresses in southern Austria. The attacks forced Austria to keep parts of its army in the south, away from the fighting with Prussia. In gratitude, a victorious Prussia forced Austrian troops to withdraw from all of Italy. If Cavour had been alive, he would have heartily approved.

Bringing the city of Rome into a united Italy proved more complicated. Pope **Pius IX,** who had ascended to the papal office in 1846 with the reputation of being an Italian nationalist, became more wary of unification after an attempted revolution in Rome in 1848. Although the Pope had threatened to excommunicate any Italian citizens who tried to take control of papal lands, the real protector of the city of Rome was the French emperor Napoleon III. Envisioning himself as a defender of Catholic interests in Europe, Napoleon III threatened war against any Italian government which attempted to annex the Holy City.

Following Cavour's practice of biding his time and waiting for helpful developments in European diplomacy, the Piedmontese government waited until 1870, when the French emperor declared war on Prussia. Napoleon III became a Prussian prisoner early in the war and abdicated. With his abdication, the path was clear for the Piedmontese army to march into Rome—and to proclaim a united Italy.

The Italy created by Cavour was not without problems. It was divided economically; the wealthy industrial north looked suspiciously at the south, which had an economy consisting mainly of small farms. The "religious problem" would persist for decades; the split between the pope and the government of highly Catholic Italy was not officially ended until the 1920s.

Cavour is often compared to the German statesman Otto von Bismarck, a fellow aristocrat whose diplomacy led to the unification of his country. Yet there is a significant difference between the two. Bismarck, a devoted believer in absolute monarchies, was determined to keep a united Germany from having a true parliamentary government; he saw all things "liberal" as anathema. In contrast, Cavour insisted that a parliamentary government in Piedmont was a prerequisite for that state to unite Italy. In Italy, unification and parliamentary government were achieved together, largely because of Cavour's influence; in Germany, chances for a true parliamentary system were destroyed by unification.

SOURCES:

Cadogan, Edward. *Makers of Modern History: Three Types: Louis Napoleon, Cavour, Bismarck.* Kinnikat Press, 1970 (reprint of 1905 edition).

Coppa, Frank J. *Camillo de Cavour.* Twayne, 1973.

Smith, Denis Mack. *Cavour and Garibaldi: A Study in Political Conflict.* Cambridge, England: Cambridge University Press, 1954.

Whyte, Arthur J. B. *The Political Life and Letters of Cavour, 1848–1861.* Oxford University Press, 1930.

FURTHER READING:

Smith, Denis Mack. *Victor Emmanuel, Cavour, and the Risorgimento.* Oxford University Press, 1971.

Thayer, William R. *The Life and Times of Cavour.* 2 vols. H. Fertig, 1914.

Whyte, Arthur J. B. *The Early Life and Letters of Cavour, 1810–1848.* Oxford University Press, 1925 (reprinted by Greenwood Press, 1970).

Nicolae Ceausescu

(1918–1989)

Rumanian leader whose attempts to fuse nationalism and communism to make his country internationally respected and economically self-sufficient resulted in such an increasingly brutal despotism that the Rumanians overthrew his regime.

Pronunciation: Chaow-u-SESH-coo or Shaow-CHESS-coo. Born on January 26, 1918, at Scornicesti, Rumania; died on December 25, 1989; son of Andruta and Alexandra Ceausescu; married: Elena Petrescu, 1944; children: two sons, Valentin and Nicolae (popularly known as Nicu), and one daughter, Zoia. Predecessor: Gheorghe Gheorghiu-Dej. Successor: The National Salvation headed by Ion Iliescu.

O n January 26, 1918, at Scornicesti, a small Rumanian village 100 miles west of Bucharest, Alexandra Ceausescu gave birth to Nicolae, the third of her ten children. Nicolae's father Andruta eked out a living for his family on a small farm, but his constant drunkenness greatly distressed his family; he once shocked the village when, in an inebriated state, he mistakenly gave Nicolae's name to another of his sons.

Little is known of the family roots or of Nicolae's childhood. His paternal name is a Rumanianized form of *Ceaus,* a Turkish word for a low rank in the Ottoman army or a government informer; Andruta Ceausescu may have been the local police informer. Farming held no appeal for the young Nicolae; he was also an unsuccessful—if compliant—pupil and left school at the age of 11, barely literate. A distinct stammer, which worsened noticeably under stress and plagued him throughout his life, may have influenced his poor academic performance. Ceausescu's physical appearance continued to handicap him. As an adult, he was short and awkward, with a personality as rigid as his gestures.

"People like me come only once in five hundred years."

NICOLAE CEAUSESCU

Contributed by Robert Frank Forrest, Assistant Professor of History, McNeese State University, Lake Charles, Louisiana

Given Ceausescu's meager education and distaste for farming, his parents apprenticed him in 1929 to a cobbler in Bucharest, the capital city of Rumania. Several of his siblings also migrated to Bucharest where they found economic security and escaped their father's abusiveness. Those who knew Ceausescu at that time describe him as an angry, violent youth who—while living with his married sister, Niculina, whose husband was also a cobbler—regularly shirked his apprentice duties to attend the street demonstrations that characterized the city's political life during the early 1930s.

Having sided with the victorious Allies during World War I, Rumania was rewarded at the Paris Peace Conference in 1919 with territories from Austria-Hungary (Transylvania and Bukovina), Bulgaria (southern Dobruja), and Russia (Bessarabia) that more than doubled prewar Rumania's population and area. Between 1918 and 1928, King Ferdinand and the conservative National Liberal Party, headed by a wealthy noble family named Bratianu, controlled Rumanian politics and centralized most government activity in Bucharest to the detriment of Rumania's large minority population, especially the Hungarians. Then Rumania briefly flirted with democracy until Carol II assumed control in 1930 and implemented an increasingly authoritarian regime. University-trained bureaucrats performed the day-to-day tasks of governing the country, but the politicians and bureaucrats were notorious for their corruption and nepotism.

Fascism flourished along with the Great Depression in Rumania during the 1930s. The Rumanian fascists or Iron Guard—gangs of street brawlers led by Corneliu Zelea Codreanu—had an anti-Semitic, xenophobic attitude in common with West European fascists. Unlike their Nazi colleagues, however, they were fanatically devoted to Orthodox Christianity. Rumania's Communists posed a greater symbolic than real threat for the Iron Guard. Although they frequently demonstrated in the streets of Bucharest after 1930, the Communists had little popular support, even before the government banned their Party in April 1924, because throughout the interwar years they complied with Moscow's order to advocate returning Bessarabia to the Soviet Union.

Bucharest in the 1930s certainly offered unhappy young men such as Nicolae Ceausescu ample opportunities to vent their frustrations. It is unclear how, when, and why Ceausescu chose communism over other forms of political involvement. His brother Marin, who also lived in Bucharest as a cobbler's apprentice, belonged to a Communist front, anti-fascist committee. Nicolae seems to

CHRONOLOGY

1893	Social Democratic Party of Rumania founded
1910	Party reorganized after it had become inactive
1918	Ceausescu born; World War I ended
1919	Greater Rumania created
1924	Rumanian Communist Party banned
1933	Ceausescu's first involvement in Communist activities
1936	Prison terms began that lasted until June 1944
1947	Peoples' Republic of Rumania proclaimed
1952	Ceausescu reached inner circle of power
1965	Became Rumania's Communist leader
1969	Convening of the 10th Congress of the Rumanian Communist Party
1974	Ceausescu became president of Rumania
1989	Revolution overthrew Ceausescu

have become associated with this group and probably joined the government-banned Union of Communist Youth (UCY) in 1933. On November 23 of that year, the police briefly jailed Ceausescu for street brawling, possibly in connection with a political demonstration. But Ceausescu played no role in the 1934 strike of railroad workers in the Bucharest suburb of Gravita organized by Gheorghe Gheorghiu-Dej, who was also a cobbler before the railroad employed him.

Ceausescu's political activism on behalf of Communism accelerated after the government crushed the Gravita strike. The police arrested him three times between June and September 1934 for engaging in Communist activities. On his release, the judge remanded this "dangerous Communist agitator" into his parent's custody and ordered him to report daily to the local post office. Soon violating the terms of parole, Ceausescu slipped back into Bucharest where he worked for the Union of Communist Youth until an informer helped the police to apprehend him again in early 1936. The state tried him, along with several other Communists, in May at Brasov. When the defendants marched out of the courtroom in protest, Ceausescu obtained considerable media attention by hurling insults at the judge. That outburst added an extra six months to his sentence, and he remained in Doftana prison until December 8, 1938.

Doftana prison, jokingly referred to at the time as the Marxist University of Rumania, was where the government imprisoned its Communists. All of the Rumanian Communist Party's (RCP) leaders, including Gheorghiu-Dej, were already there. Although the leaders found Ceausescu boring, devoid of humor, and ignorant of Marxism, his commitment to Marxism and hero-worship of Gheorghiu-Dej and Stalin impressed them, and they decided to tutor him in Marxism-Leninism, French, history, and geography. They also let him divide the contents of their parcels among all the prisoners and take care of their minor needs. Soon after the authorities released Ceausescu from prison, he became a secretary of the Central Committee of the Union of Communist Youth.

After World War II began on September 1, 1939, King Carol II's regime failed to prevent the partitioning of Greater Rumania. First Stalin retrieved Bessarabia and seized northern Bukovina; shortly thereafter, Bulgaria repossessed the southern Dobruja; and then, on August 30, 1940, the fascist dictators awarded two-fifths of Transylvania to Hungary. When the right-radical Marshal Ion Antonescu assumed control of the Rumanian government and united with the Axis (Germany and its allies), King Carol fled the country and his son Michael V ascended the throne.

But the man whom police had designated "a person dangerous to public order" rode out most of the war tucked safely away in prison. A Bucharest court had convicted Ceausescu in absentia for having become general secretary of the UCY. Captured and returned to prison in July of 1940, he remained there for four years in much greater safety than those Communists who had avoided arrest. During his imprisonment, Ceausescu moved closer to Gheorghiu-Dej by bringing his meals to him, shining his shoes, sleeping outside his door, and seeing that his leader's wishes were executed. In return, Gheorghiu-Dej gave Ceausescu extra money to purchase food and bribe the guards.

When Ceausescu was released in June 1944, he was still just a minor member of the Rumanian Communist Party and played no role in the August 23 *coup d'état* that overthrew Marshall Antonescu's government. The Rumanians now fought with the U.S.S.R. against Hitler for the remainder of the war, for which Stalin awarded them a portion of Transylvania lost to Hungary in 1940. Ceausescu's first significant action was to write three articles for the Party newspaper *Scînteia* in late September and early October. Since he was still barely literate, the newspaper's editor has reported that the articles required extensive editing. It was also at this time that Ceausescu married Elena Petrescu, a woman from a peasant background who had flunked out of school at the age of 11.

Promotions within a Leninist Party depended heavily on personal ties and loyalty to a member of the ruling elite and Gheorghiu-Dej was Ceausescu's patron. Following the Rumanian Communist Party's Congress on October 16, 1945, its first since 1924, Ceausescu became a member of the Central Committee over the objections of Ana Pauker, Gheorghiu-Dej's rival for control of the RCP. Pauker led a group of Rumanian Communists who, after spending the war in the Soviet Union, had returned to Rumania with the Red Army. In November 1947, one month before the People's Republic of Rumania replaced the monarchy and forced King Michael to abdicate, Ceausescu became the Party secretary for Oltenia, which includes Scorniçesti. Charged with preparing the town for elections scheduled for November 1947 and with overseeing the progress of collectivizing agricultural land in the district, Ceausescu had problems in Oltenia. First an angry crowd of peasants protested collectivization by overturning his chauffeur-driven car. Later, in the village of Slatina, either Ceausescu or his driver stabbed a bank manager to death for refusing to contribute money to the local RCP campaign fund. Despite this incident, the RCP had Ceausescu elected to the Grand National Assembly in March 1948.

Suffering a temporary setback in February 1948 when the RCP merged with the Socialists to form the Rumanian Workers' Party (RWP), Ceausescu was demoted to a candidate member of the Central Committee to make room for the Socialists. But by 1949, Gheorghiu-Dej was winning his power struggle with Ana Pauker for control of the RWP, and Ceausescu profited from the victory. First, in March 1949 Ceausescu became a deputy minister of agriculture. A year later, Gheorghiu-Dej sent him to the Ministry of Armed Forces with the rank of major general to supervise the political indoctrination of the Rumanian army.

Reaches the Inner Circle of Power

Hard work, total commitment to Stalinism, and unswerving loyalty to Gheorghiu-Dej, most notably in the form of speeches attacking Ana Pauker and her supporters, paid off for Ceausescu by 1952. In May of that year, just one month before Pauker's faction was purged, Gheorghiu-Dej reappointed Ceausescu to full membership on the Central Committee, plus a membership on the short-lived Organization Bureau (*Orgburo*, 1950–53), which had been created to oversee Party organizations and discipline. Ceausescu had now reached the inner circle of power in Communist Rumania, a fact underlined in March 1953 when he became a member of the small Rumanian delegation that attended Stalin's funeral in Moscow. Two years later, Gheorghiu-Dej gave Ceausescu the task of increasing Party membership.

In 1958, when **Nikita Khrushchev** withdrew all Soviet troops from Rumania, Gheorghiu-Dej announced that Rumania's Stalinist program of rapid heavy industrialization would be broadened to make Rumania more self-sufficient. Collectivization of agriculture, which had been halted in 1951, was also to be resumed. These measures precipitated a quarrel with the Soviet Union, which was abandoning Stalinism's national autarky (economic independence) in favor of using the Council of Mutual Economic Assistance (Comecon) to economically develop Eastern Europe as a whole. This disagreement, plus the 1962 Cuban Missile Crisis, persuaded Gheorghiu-Dej that Rumania need not follow Russia's leaders unquestioningly. Showing an openness to the West, Rumania gradually became more independent of the Soviet Union.

But Gheorghiu-Dej died suddenly from cancer on March 20, 1965, without having designated a successor. Some of the Party leaders, who were personally unable to succeed Gheorghiu-Dej but certain that they could control the youthful Ceausescu, secured his selection as first secretary of the RWP on March 22. Relatively unknown and ridiculed by Party intellectuals for his inelegance, Ceausescu reluctantly participated in a collective leadership that included the popular reformer Ion Gheorghe Maurer as prime minister. Between 1965 and 1971, the ambitious and revengeful Ceausescu outmaneuvered his colleagues by shrewdly pursuing domestic and foreign policies designed to make him the unrivaled ruler of Rumania.

The RWP's Politburo favored continuing Gheorghiu-Dej's less authoritarian tendencies, and Ceausescu enhanced his popularity among Rumanians and the RWP by publicly endorsing this position between March and July 1965 when the 9th Party Congress convened in Bucharest. A new constitution promulgated at the 9th Congress, which renamed the RWP the Communist Party of Rumania (RCP), helped Ceausescu weaken his rivals. Replacing the 12-member Politburo with a 15-member Presidium, it divided Rumania into 40 regional subdivisions rather than 16. Ceausescu

not only appointed his supporters to these new positions, but he also persuaded the RCP to prohibit individuals from simultaneously holding important Party and political offices. The immediate benefit Ceausescu derived from this rule was to force the powerful Alexandru Draghici to resign as head of the Ministry of Internal Affairs (which also had made him head of the *Securitate*, the secret police) to accept a seat on the Presidium.

By 1967, Ceausescu felt strong enough to rescind this rule, becoming president of the State Council in addition to first secretary of the RCP. The next year at the April 22 Plenum (general assembly) of the Central Committee, he seized complete control of the RCP by attacking the earlier conduct of his rivals and expelling Draghici from the Party. The 10th Party Congress, held during August 1969, accepted Ceausescu's criticisms of the RCP's Old Guard and excluded all but two of them from the Central Committee.

During these years, Ceausescu carefully fostered his popularity among the Rumanian masses and intellectuals by continuing to espouse freedom of expression in place of *Securitate* arbitrariness and to pursue Gheorghiu-Dej's nationalist, primarily anti-Soviet foreign policy that seemed to be turning Rumania into another nonaligned socialist state like Yugoslavia. Between 1966 and 1971, Ceausescu's foreign policy placed himself and Rumania at the center of Cold War diplomacy, and he offered to mediate the Sino-Soviet and the Arab-Israeli conflicts. Although a member of the Warsaw Pact, he denounced and boycotted the Soviet's 1968 invasion of Czechoslovakia. Ceausescu privately detested Czechoslovakia's liberal reforms and publicly exaggerated the threat of a similar Soviet invasion of Rumania to win support at home and abroad for his regime.

Personal Dictatorship, Family Dynasty

The popularity Ceausescu derived from his foreign policy failed to encourage him to seek a personal relationship with the Rumanian people based on shared goals. Instead, between 1969 and 1974, he created a personal dictatorship for himself. The turning point seems to have been his 1971 state visit to the People's Republic of China, North Vietnam, and North Korea. After returning from Asia, Ceausescu increasingly sought to legitimize his rule by associating himself with figures from Rumania's past who had struggled to unite the Rumanians and to liberate them from foreign domination. He also started to elevate his wife Elena into political prominence, something that was unheard of in the Communist world. After receiving an unearned Ph.D. in chemistry, she—along with her husband—was hailed as a great genius in an attempt to equate both of them with the university-educated bureaucrats who had governed Rumania until the Communists seized power in 1945. They also sought to turn their family into the first Communist dynasty during the 1980s by grooming the favorite son, Nicu, to succeed his father. Other members of the family received high offices, while in 1974, 1980, and 1985, Ceausescu had himself elected president of Rumania, a post which gave him control of both the Party and the state.

Armed with complete power, he began to impose his vision of the ideal Communist society on the Rumanians: rapid heavy industrialization *à la* Stalin, pursuit of puritanism concerning individual and family life, and systematization, which was designed to destroy the last vestiges of bourgeois mentality by housing the entire population in concrete high-rise apartment buildings and demolishing churches. Ceausescu chose Bucharest as the showplace of systematization, especially after an earthquake severely damaged the city in 1977. In the 1980s, he bulldozed an entire district in the center of Bucharest and replaced it with the Victory of Socialism Boulevard, which was lined with high-rise apartment buildings for his favorites and dominated at one end by the People's Palace, the largest building in the world. Both the boulevard and the People's Palace were unfinished when he was overthrown in 1989.

While systematization progressed at ever greater cost, Ceausescu's economic policy failed due to poor investments, often made with the assistance of foreign loans. To repay the loans, Ceausescu drastically reduced imports in the early 1980s and increased exports, especially of agricultural products. In addition to food, he deprived the Rumanians of such basic necessities as heat and electricity. Until 1989, his privileged *Securitate* kept him in power, but between December 15 and 25 the Rumanian people, with the help of the army, overthrew his regime. After a summary trial, he and Elena were executed on December 25, 1989.

SOURCES:

Behr, Edward. *Kiss the Hand You Cannot Bite: The Rise and Fall of the Ceausescus.* Villard, 1991.

Codrescu, Andrei. *A Hole in the Flag: A Romanian Exile's Story of Return and Revolution.* Morrow, 1991.

Dima, Nicholas. "Nicolae Ceausescu of Communist Romania: A Portrait of Power," in *The Journal of Social, Political and Economic Studies* 13 (Winter 1988): 429–34.

Fischer, Mary Ellen. *Nicolae Ceausescu: A Study in Political Leadership.* Lynne Rienner Publishers, 1989.

Fischer-Galati, Stephen. *Twentieth Century Rumania.* 2nd ed. Columbia University Press, 1991.

Galloway, George, and Bob Wylie. *Downfall: The Ceausescus and the Romanian Revolution.* Futura Publications, 1991.

FURTHER READING:

Gilberg, Trond. *Nationalism and Communism in Romania: The Rise and Fall of Ceausescu's Personal Dictatorship.* Westview Press, 1990.

Nelson, Daniel N. *Romanian Politics in the Ceausescu Era.* Gordon and Breach Science Publishers, 1988.

Sweeney, John. *The Life and Evil Times of Nicolae Ceausescu.* Hutchinson, 1991.

Neville Chamberlain

(1869–1940)

British prime minister from 1937 to 1940, who initially won recognition as a social reformer until his name became lastingly associated with the appeasement of Nazi Germany.

"The Prime Minister sometimes reminds me of the Stuart Kings— he is clear and upright but inelastic."

R.A. BUTLER
ON NEVILLE CHAMBERLAIN

As an administrator, Neville Chamberlain was outstanding. Entering Parliament at age 50, until 1937 he excelled in every office entrusted to him. As prime minister, he had a strong sense of duty, led the cabinet with a firm hand, and hoped above all to foster domestic reform. It was, however, in statecraft that he failed. Having infinite confidence in his own wisdom, he refused to listen to knowledgeable advisers and hence endangered his nation by a series of fatal blunders. A genuinely good, if rigid, man in an evil age, he could not cope with the sinister or the irrational.

The tall, gaunt man with blue eyes was known for his efficiency, clarity, and resoluteness. Until his last fatal illness, he was physically tireless, although his demeanor was one of shy dignity. Lacking any sense of charm, he was reserved to the point of humorlessness with his half-brother Austen commenting, "It is his coldness which kills." Beneath the tough exterior lay an exceptionally sensitive man who unfortunately treated all criticism as a personal affront. Though denounced by **David Lloyd George** as possessing "a retail mind" in dealing with "wholesale problems," he

Born Arthur Neville Chamberlain on March 18, 1869, in Edgbaston, England; died on November 9, 1940, at Highfield Park, Heckfield; son of Joseph Chamberlain (British statesman) and Florence Kendrick; married: Annie Vere Cole, January 1911; children: Dorothy, Frank. Predecessor: Stanley Baldwin. Successor: Winston Churchill.

Contributed by Justus D. Doenecke, Professor of History, New College of the University of South Florida, Sarasota, Florida

CHRONOLOGY

1914	England declared war on Germany
1915	Lord Mayor of Birmingham
1916	Director general of national service
1918	Chamberlain elected to Parliament
1921	Irish treaty
1922	Appointed postmaster general
1923	Minister of health, chancellor of the exchequer
1937	Became prime minister
1938	German occupied Austria; Chamberlain made three trips to Germany
1939	Germany seized Prague, invaded Poland; Chamberlain announced that Britain was at war with Germany; tendered resignation as prime minister

was surprisingly urbane, well read in Shakespeare and the classics, widely traveled, and an expert on orchids, birds, and butterflies.

Born in Edgbaston, a suburb of Birmingham, Chamberlain said shortly after becoming prime minister, "Although I cannot boast of my forbears, I am yet prouder of being descended from those respectable tradesmen than if my ancestors had worn shining armor and carried great swords." His father, Joseph Chamberlain, was one of the most dynamic Englishmen of his day, not only as a leading industrialist, but as the mayor of Birmingham (1873–76), the president of the Board of Trade (1880–85), and the colonial secretary (1895–1903). Chamberlain's mother died when he was six, and the boy was raised by two paternal aunts, Caroline and Clara.

Unlike his half-brother Austen, who was groomed for politics, he was steered toward business, studying commerce, metallurgy, and engineering design at Mason College (later converted into the University of Birmingham). In 1890, after working for a firm of accountants, he was sent at age 21 to the island of Andros in the Bahamas where his task was to develop some 20,000 acres of sisal, a fleshy plant used in making rope. Though Chamberlain labored for seven years, the task was futile, the soil too thin. In his isolation, he read profusely, but his traits of shyness and reserve were reinforced. Still, the experience gave him confidence.

In 1897, after £80,000 of family money was lost in the venture, Chamberlain returned to a business career in Birmingham. His field of endeavor: the copper brass industry. A model employer and an outstanding figure in the industrial life of the city, he fostered hospitals, schools, the territorial army, and was soon attracted to local politics. Like his father, he began his political career as a member of the city council, to which he was elected in 1911; in 1915, he became lord mayor. Making his mark in urban planning and in the establishment of a municipal savings bank, he was—even more than his father—a man of Birmingham, and no Conservative politician of his generation understood local government as well as he. In 1915, Chamberlain was appointed to the national Central Control Board, in charge of liquor traffic. In all his posts his concern centered on domestic reform.

He might have spent his entire life in the Midlands had not Prime Minister David Lloyd George appointed him director general of National Service in December 1916. Though his job was to secure voluntary recruitment of labor for war industries, the prime minister failed to give him the needed authority, and Chamberlain chose inferior personnel. Facing other handicaps, including few contacts, the lack of a parliament or cabinet seat, and no apprenticeship in government on the national level, he found little opportunity to distinguish himself and resigned his post after seven months. Embittered, Chamberlain returned to Birmingham. In December 1917, his young cousin Norman died in No Man's Land on the front, sparking an abhorrence of war Chamberlain would harbor the rest of his life.

In 1918, with the nation in a mood of retrenchment, he was elected to Parliament as Conservative member for the strongly conservative Ladywood district of Birmingham. Chamberlain supported the Lloyd George coalition, but—feeling himself once burned by the prime minister—would not accept any cabinet post. He chaired several departmental committees and, in December 1921, backed the treaty granting Ireland dominion status as the Irish Free State.

Then, in October 1922, an outright Conservative administration was formed first under Bonar Law, then under **Stanley Baldwin,** and Chamberlain rose quickly, holding four posts within little over a year: postmaster general; paymaster general; minister of health, where he secured a major housing bill; and chancellor of the exchequer, in which his time of service was so short he never presented a budget. His competence in all these positions made him indispensable to any Conservative ministry.

After an interim in 1924, in which **Ramsey MacDonald** formed a Labour government, Chamberlain served in Baldwin's second ministry as minister of health. The office was the great love of his life. Here he sought to make his reputation as a "radical Conservative," one who would combine the ethos of self-help and social reform. According to biographer Ian MacLeod, Chamberlain carried out "one of the most far-reaching and complicated programmes of legislation any Minister had attempted before or since." Historian A. J. P. Taylor found him "the most effective social reformer of the interwar years."

In the general election of May 1929, Chamberlain was returned from Edgbaston, a seat he held until his death. Because his party was out of power, he performed several tasks for Baldwin, including serving as chairman of the Conservative's central office. In the financial crisis of August 1931, it was Chamberlain who first represented the Conservatives in the negotiations leading to the coalition government (Baldwin was abroad at the time).

Once the new government was established, MacDonald appointed Chamberlain to his old post at the Ministry of Health. When the government was reorganized as a result of the November election, Chamberlain again became chancellor of the exchequer, this time holding the post five and a half years amid economic depression. Acting on the best financial advice of the time, he followed a policy of stern deflation and drastic economy, giving the impression that he was executing policy without due sympathy for the human misery it involved. He fostered a revenue tariff of ten percent, which was enacted in 1932, and thereby adopted the tariff cause popularized by his father, ending 86 years of free trade. Promoting the Ottawa Imperial Economic Conference of 1932 which granted commercial preference within the Empire, he was also responsible for the Unemployment Act of 1934, which reformed the relief system. **Winston Churchill,** himself out of power, called Chamberlain "the pack horse" of the administration. In 1934, he announced that Britain was finished with *Bleak House* and could now enjoy *Great Expectations.* He was able to reduce the income tax, and restore a cut in unemployment benefits and half a cut in government salaries.

Chamberlain Becomes Prime Minister

In May 1937, Chamberlain became prime minister when Baldwin, worn down by the position, decided to step down. Of necessity, he became increasingly involved in foreign policy. Distrusting the foreign office, he placed great stock in personal diplomacy and adhered to the views of military theorist B. H. Liddell Hart, seeing no need for a large professional army as he believed that the war of the future would be won by a small, professional, mechanized force. British participation on the European continent would be limited to air and sea power.

His policy was dominated by three axioms: the "decadence" of France, the hostility of the Soviet Union, and the reality of German power. "On the whole," he said during a holiday in the Black Forest in 1930, "I loathe Germans," an attitude developed during the Boer War and reinforced by World War I. Never a defender of Nazism, he privately called **Adolf Hitler** "a lunatic" and "half mad," felt propaganda minister Joseph Goebbels possessed "a vulgar common little mind," and found diplomat Joachim von Ribbentrop "so stupid, so shallow, so self-centered and self-satisfied, so totally devoid of intellectual capacity that he never seems to take in what is said to him." Moreover, said Chamberlain, "I am horrified by the German behavior to the Jews." In the fall of 1934, he went so far as to say, "The *fons and origo* of all our European troubles and anxieties is Germany."

Yet, Chamberlain was determined to avoid war with Germany, finding neither Britain nor its ally France ready. Hence he turned to direct negotiation with German chancellor Adolf Hitler while, at the same time, seeking to enlist the support of Italian dictator **Benito Mussolini.** *Il Duce*'s support for General **Francisco Franco**'s insurgents in Spain, however, aborted any such negotiations. Contrary to myth, Chamberlain saw Mussolini's invasion of Ethiopia as "barbarous." At the outset of the crisis, he supported oil sanctions, but once Emperor **Haile Selassie** had fled, he called the continuation of economic pressure "the very midsummer of madness."

By the spring of 1938, Germany was threatening Czechoslovakia over the status of three and a half million German-speaking occupants of the Sudetenland. Since 1925, France had entered into a mutual assistance treaty with Czechoslovakia; both countries promised to lend each other immediate aid and assistance in case one were attacked. Britain, however, was not bound by any commitment apart from a general guarantee of assistance embodied in Article 16 of the League of Nations Covenant. On March 24, 1938, Chamberlain claimed that if war broke out over Czechoslovakia: "It would be well within the bound of probability that other countries besides those which were parties to the original dispute would almost immediately become involved." Yet Chamberlain saw no British interest in Czech independence, felt it unjust that three million Germans remained within its borders, and believed that at any rate Britain could not aid that nation.

Toward the end of August, he persuaded Lord Runciman, past president of the board of trade, to journey to Prague to mediate the crisis. Though the Czechs accepted Runciman's solution—home rule for the Sudeten areas on the model of the Swiss cantons—the Sudeten leaders broke off negotiations while Hitler called for an autonomous Sudeten province within the Czech state.

Hitler Makes Proposal to Chamberlain

On September 14, Chamberlain proposed a personal meeting with Hitler, who immediately accepted, and on the following day, the prime minister traveled to Berchtesgaden, a town close to the Austrian border. This time Hitler demanded that Germany receive directly all areas in which over 50% of the inhabitants were Sudeten Germans and promised to restrain from hostilities if Britain concurred.

Upon return to London, Chamberlain met with the cabinet and the two major French leaders—Prime Minister Edouard Daladier and Foreign Minister Georges Bonnet. Both governments presented to Eduard Benes, president of Czechoslovakia, their final decision: any territory populated by over 50% Sudeten inhabitants must be ceded directly to Germany. For Czechoslovakia to accept meant giving up its line of fortifications, relinquishing some 800,000 Czechoslovakians, and in substance surrendering the independence of the Czech state; yet, realizing that any resistance would have had to be made alone, it concurred.

On September 22, Chamberlain went to Germany again, this time to meet Hitler at Godesberg, a town on the Rhine. He announced acceptance of Hitler's Berchtesgaden terms by Britain, France, and Czechoslovakia, telling the German Führer that the arrangements for transfer of territory had already been worked out. Hitler, denouncing these arrangements as dilatory, insisted on immediate evacuation by the Czechs. In a particularly humiliating demand, he called for a triumphal advance of German forces and the withdrawal, with all installations intact, of Czech troops. On the following day, Hitler appeared to make a slight concession, for he established a deadline of October 1, the very day he had sched-

uled an attack under the code name Operation Green. He also said that plebiscites in certain additional areas could be held in November. The conference had ended in deadlock.

Chamberlain was inclined to accept the Gotesberg memorandum as a basis of negotiation, but his cabinet, British public opinion, and the French government found the terms impossible. The Czechs refused indignantly. Even then, the prime minister did not give up his hopes for peace. On September 26, he sent Sir Horace Wilson, his industrial adviser, to Germany with a letter suggesting that German and Czech representatives should meet to consider how best to cede Sudeten territory. Wilson also conveyed Chamberlain's warning that "If, in pursuit of her treaty obligations, France became actively engaged in hostilities against Germany, the United Kingdom would feel responsible to support her." Hitler retorted, "It is Tuesday today and by next Monday we shall be at war." On the next day, Chamberlain called for a four-power conference—composed of Britain, France, Germany, and Italy—to resolve the dispute.

The height of Chamberlain's despair came on the 27th, when—in a flat, tired voice—he broadcast to the nation: "How horrible, fantastic, incredible it is that we should be digging trenches and trying on gas-masks here because of a quarrel in a far-away country between people of whom we know nothing."

The 28th of September saw Chamberlain reporting pessimistically to the House of Commons that all chances for peace had been exhausted. Yet, as the speech was nearing its end, the prime minister received a note passed by his foreign minister Lord Halifax announcing that Hitler had invited him, along with Mussolini and Daladier, to Munich the following day. Chamberlain told a much-relieved House, "I need not say what my answer will be."

Sudeten Territory Treaty Signed

The conference at Munich was a brief one, lasting only 14 hours. In a treaty signed at 2:00 A.M. on September 30, the participants agreed to divide the Sudeten territory into four zones, which the German army would occupy progressively between October 1 and 7. The determination of a fifth zone, to be occupied by the 10th, was left to an international commission that included the four signatories plus Czechoslovakia. The four powers agreed to guarantee Czechoslovakia's new borders, although the remaining fragment of a state was truncated indeed. It had lost its defenses, most of its industrial resources, and one-third of its population; it had also forfeited its treaty with France and Russia. Later that same morning, Chamberlain and Hitler signed a statement declaring that the agreement was "symbolic of the desire of our two peoples never to go to war again."

Chamberlain returned to London that night, welcomed by throngs of cheering people. From his window in Downing Street, he echoed a phrase used by **Disraeli** upon returning from Germany 60 years previously. But the words of the prime minister would soon come back to haunt him: "This is the second time in our history that there has come back from Germany to Downing Street peace with honor. I believe it is peace in our time."

Then in November 1938, the infamous *Kristallnacht* (night of the broken glass) took place, in which the Nazis looted 7,500 Jewish shops in Czechoslovakia, burned 175 synagogues, and transported over 20,000 Jews to concentration camps. Early in 1939, Hitler prepared for the destruction of Czechoslovakia. After encouraging the Slovaks to separate from the Czech Republic, Hitler alleged that "disturbances" existed inside the country and, at 6:00 A.M. of March 15, ordered troops across the Czech frontier. Pushing through howling wind and snow, German-mechanized columns completed the occupation in one day. That evening, Hitler arrived in Prague and proclaimed a protectorate. Britain and France did nothing, and Chamberlain declared that the disruption of the Czech state by the Slovak secession had nullified the Munich agreement. Five days before Hitler invaded, Chamberlain had told the Commons, "Europe is settling down to a period of tranquillity." Just after Hitler's move, he seemed little disturbed.

But Chamberlain knew the fragile peace was obviously in shambles. Under the prodding of Lord Halifax, hitherto a leading appeaser, he warned Hitler on March 17 in a speech given at Birmingham. Here he confessed that his policy of appeasement had been "wantonly shattered." If Hitler, he said, was attempting to "dominate the world by force," Britain would "take part to the uttermost of its power in resisting such a challenge."

On March 31, in the wake of German threats to Poland, Chamberlain told the Commons that Britain and France would give all support in their power to that state if its independence were threatened while negotiations were in process, and on April 13 Rumania and Greece were included in the British guarantee. On April 27, Britain took the unprecedented step of introducing peacetime conscription. Yet, as noted by Churchill and Lloyd George, Britain had no means of fulfilling its pledges without a Soviet alliance. Chamberlain's overtures to the Soviet Union to form an anti-Hitler alliance proved tentative and half-hearted; in that fatal August, Britain and France dithered in their military negotiations with Moscow. On the 23rd, the Nazi-Soviet Pact was signed.

At 11:15 A.M. on September 3, 1939—two days after German armies invaded Poland—Chamberlain broadcast from 10 Downing: "This country is at war with Germany.... Right will prevail." That noon, in addressing the parliament, he said, "Everything that I have worked for, everything that I have hoped for, everything that I have believed in during my public life has crashed in ruin." Five hours later, France, too, had declared war on Germany.

In the fall of 1939, Chamberlain spurned any effort at a negotiated peace, saying: "Past experience has shown that no reliance can be placed upon the promises of the present German Government." Any peace, the prime minister believed, must involve disarmament, restoration of frontiers, and protection of Jews and Austrians. Britain might assist Germany economically and make colonial concessions, but—according to Chamberlain's secretary John Conville—"Hitler himself shall play no part in the proposed new order."

Until the spring of 1940, little action took place in the West. American journalists called the conflict "the phony war," the Germans referred to it as the *Sitzkrieg*, and Chamberlain himself called it the "twilight war." There were only minor clashes on the Franco-German frontier. Though U-boat attacks on Allied shipping began the first day, many months passed before enemy air raiders bombed London. Chamberlain mocked the lack of German activity, declaring on April 4, "Hitler has missed the bus"—a favorite Chamberlain phrase.

All changed just five days later when Germany invaded Norway and Denmark. Seeking to rescue Norway by landing small units at such places as Narvik and Bergen, England met with defeat. Though the responsibility for the Norwegian campaign fell on First Lord of the Admiralty Churchill, who accepted it unflinchingly, the odium fell on Chamberlain. On May 7 and 8, when the House of Commons debated withdrawal from Norway, Chamberlain was subject to bitter attack from leading members of the Labour and Liberal parties. Some Conservative back-benchers attacked as well, with Leo Amery quoting the words by which **Oliver Cromwell** had dismissed the Long Parliament: "You have sat too long here for any good you have been doing. Depart, I say, and let us have done with you. In the name of God, go!"

The government's majority fell from 200 to 80, and a poll taken May 9 and 10 found that only 22% approved of Chamberlain's continuing in office. Told on May 10 that Labour ministers still refused to serve under him, he tendered his resignation. In his last broadcast as prime minister, he said that it had become apparent that essential unity could only be secured "under another prime minister." When Winston Churchill assumed the post, he offered Chamberlain the exchequer, but Chamberlain declined, joining the government instead as lord president of the Council and remaining leader of the Conservative Party.

In August, he experienced an unsuccessful operation for cancer and on October 1 resigned from the War Cabinet. Refusing an earldom and the Order of the Garter, he preferred to die "plain Mr. Chamberlain like my father before me." On November 9, 1940, the eve of his passing, he spoke bitterly of the press accounts of his resignation; not one of them, he noted in his diary, "shows the slightest sign of sympathy for the man or even any comprehension that there may be a human tragedy somewhere in the background."

SOURCES:

Dilks, David. *Neville Chamberlain*. Vol. I: *Pioneering and Reform*, 1869–1929. Cambridge University Press, 1984.

Feiling, Keith. *The Life of Neville Chamberlain*. Macmillan, 1946.

Hyde, H. Montgomery. *Neville Chamberlain*. Weidenfeld & Nicolson, 1976.

Macleod, Iain. *Neville Chamberlain*. Atheneum, 1962.

Rock, William R. *Neville Chamberlain*. Twayne, 1969.

FURTHER READING:

Charmley, *John. Chamberlain and the Lost Peace*. Hodder & Stoughton, 1989.

Colvin, Ian. *The Chamberlain Cabinet*. Taplinger, 1971.

Gilbert, Martin, and Richard Gott. *The Appeasers*. Houghton Mifflin, 1963.

———. *The Roots of Appeasement*. New American Library. 1966.

Rock, William R. *Chamberlain and Roosevelt: British Foreign Policy in the United States, 1937–1940*. Ohio State University Press, 1988.

Charlemagne

(c. 742–814)

King of the Franks, who was renowned for the force of his sword, his concern for justice and the Church, a revival of learning and culture in Western Europe, and the creation of an ordered Empire in the early part of the Middle Ages.

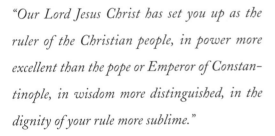

"Our Lord Jesus Christ has set you up as the ruler of the Christian people, in power more excellent than the pope or Emperor of Constantinople, in wisdom more distinguished, in the dignity of your rule more sublime."

ALCUIN
TO CHARLEMAGNE

At the end of January 814, Charles the Great, called "most serene Majesty, crowned by God, Emperor great and pacific, governing the Roman Empire and by God's mercy king of the Franks and of the Lombards," died at his favorite palace in Aachen, in what is now Germany. He was 71 years old, an advanced age by the standards of the day, and he had ruled as king of the Franks for 46 years and as emperor of the Romans for 13 years.

When Charles the Great—commonly known as Charlemagne from the Latin form of his name *Carolus Magnus*—was born in about 742, the map of Europe bore little resemblance to the Europe of today. The Roman Empire had given way in the later fifth century to the so-called Germanic successor states. One of the most important of these states was that of the Franks, a people who inhabited the Rhineland region of northern Europe. The various tribes of the Franks had been united by the aggressive king **Clovis** (d. 511), but by the late seventh and early eighth century their kings (known as the Merovingians) had become little more than figureheads or puppets; the real power was held by an official known as the Mayor

Contributed by Russell Andrew McDonald, Ph.D., University of Guelph, Guelph, Ontario, Canada

Name variations: Charles I of France, Charles the Great, St. Charles, Karl der Grosse. Born c. 742; died on January 28, 814; buried in Aachen; son of Pepin, King of the Franks, and Bertrada; married: the daughter of Desiderius, king of the Lombards; married: Hildigard; married: Fastrada; married: Liutgard; children: (second marriage) Charles, Pepin, Louis, and others. Predecessor: Pepin the Short. Successor: Louis the Pious.

CHRONOLOGY

c. 742	Charlemagne born
751	Pepin the Short crowned as king of Franks; Childeric III deposed
768	Pepin's land divided between Charlemagne and his brother Carloman who ruled as joint kings
771	Carloman died; Charlemagne became sole king of Franks
772	Saxon wars began
773–74	Campaigns against Lombards led by Desiderius in northern Italy
778	Spanish expedition; defeat at Roncevaux
786	First campaign against Bretons
790s	Construction of Palace at Aachen
791	Campaigns against Avars began
800	Charlemagne crowned emperor of the Romans
806	Divided lands among his sons
810	Campaigned against Godefrid, king of the Northmen
813	Recognized as emperor by Byzantines; son Louis crowned as emperor of the Romans
814	Charlemagne died
c. 829–36	Einhard wrote the *Vita Caroli* (*Life of Charlemagne*)
843	Treaty of Verdun; Charlemagne's Empire partitioned

of the Palace. It was this position which Charlemagne's grandfather **Charles Martel** had filled, and which his father Pepin the Short also held. In 751, when Charlemagne was only about nine, a remarkable occurrence took place. The pope, Stephen II, deposed King Childeric, thus ending the Merovingian line, and anointed Charlemagne's father as king of the Franks. When Pepin died in 768, following Frankish custom he was succeeded by his two sons, Charles and Carloman, who became joint kings.

Of Charlemagne's boyhood until 768 little is known. Even Einhard, his biographer, who had lived through the reign and began to compose his *Life of Charlemagne* (*Vita Caroli*) some 15 years after Charles's death, lamented that, "it would be foolish for me to write about Charlemagne's birth and childhood … for nothing is set down in writing about this and nobody can be found still alive who claims to have any personal knowledge of these matters." But despite the scarcity of direct information, something may still be said about these years. Einhard recorded that in his later life Charlemagne "spent much of his time on horseback and out hunting, which came naturally to him." It seems very likely that Charlemagne would have practiced the sport as a boy, since hunting was a common pastime of the medieval nobility, and it also sharpened the skills necessary to become a successful warrior.

But while he would have spent a good deal of time out-of-doors in his youth, there is nothing to suggest that Charlemagne was taught reading and writing. During most of the Middle Ages, these skills were uncommon among everyone except members of the Church. Einhard recorded that Charlemagne tried to learn to read and write, and that "he used to keep writing tablets and notebooks under the pillows on his bed, so that he could try his hand at forming letters during his leisure moments." But, Einhard added, "although he tried very hard, he had begun too late in life and he made little progress." Charlemagne was also a devout Christian, as he had been brought up in this faith since his childhood. Einhard wrote that the ruler went to church in the morning and at night with great regularity, and he had probably received some rudimentary instruction on religion when he was young, perhaps from a cleric in his father's household.

By the time he was about ten, Charlemagne was being groomed for power and began to play a role in his father's kingdom. In 753, he was sent to accompany the pope to St. Denis, near Paris, and in 761 he accompanied his father on a campaign in Aquitaine, in southwest France. When Pepin died in 768, the 26-year-old Charlemagne was well prepared to take over the responsibilities and rigors that medieval kingship entailed.

Since the brothers, ruling as joint kings, did not get along, it was probably fortunate for the Frankish state that Carloman died prematurely in 771. Charles ignored the young son of his brother and accepted the allegiance of many of his brother's most important supporters. His power now ran throughout most of what is modern France and Germany, and this action demonstrates Charlemagne's opportunism as well as his ability to act promptly and decisively, a characteristic which he displayed over and over again throughout his long reign.

Charlemagne was first and foremost a warrior, like all of his ancestors and particularly his grandfather Charles Martel, and so he naturally looked beyond the bounds of his inherited kingdom. In 773, he answered a papal appeal to defend

Rome from the Lombards, another of the Germanic peoples to settle in and around the Roman Empire. Between 774 and 776, Charlemagne campaigned against the Lombard king Desiderius, eventually capturing him at Pavia and bringing northern Italy under his sway. In 781, he saw his son Pepin anointed as king of Italy by the pope, and a campaign in 786 extended his authority over southern Italy as well.

Since he was a Christian ruler, Charlemagne felt that it was his divine vocation to spread the Christian faith. To the north and west of his kingdom there lay the Saxon tribesmen, still pagan, who often harassed his borders. Believing that it was his duty to conquer these people for the glory of God, in order to save their souls and in order to protect his Empire, Charlemagne tirelessly campaigned against the Saxons from 772 until 804. In the first campaign, he destroyed Irminsul, the sacred tree which was the symbol of Saxon pagan religion. Subsequent campaigns saw the destruction of Saxon harvests; the deportation of men, women, and children in 794, 797, and 798; forced baptisms; conversions at swordpoint; and, in a horrible moment after a rebellion in 782, the beheading of some 5,000 Saxons at Verden. Eventually, the Saxons could resist no longer, and they too became incorporated within the Frankish realm. These campaigns showed Charlemagne's skill as a leader and his zeal as a Christian monarch; they also revealed the ruthlessness which was an essential component of early medieval kingship.

Although the Saxons were Charlemagne's main concern, he embarked on many other campaigns during his reign. In the north and east, as he advanced further into Saxon lands, he and his armies encountered other tribes of peoples, like the Avars, the Wends, and the Slavs. But his battles were not all fought in the east. In 778, he crossed the Pyrénées into Spain and engaged the Muslims, suffering a defeat at Roncevaux. This disaster formed the basis for the 12th-century *Song of Roland,* one of the later medieval legends which formed around the figure of Charlemagne. In 786, he campaigned for the first time against the Bretons in the west of France. In the first part of the ninth century, a new threat emerged: the Northmen. In 808, Charlemagne fought against Godefrid, their king, and in 810, when he was nearly 70, Charlemagne responded vigorously to an invading fleet of ships by gathering a huge army and marching to meet the Northmen. But Godefrid was murdered before Charlemagne arrived; this was the last of the campaigns which had characterized Charles's reign for some 40 years.

To be a successful king throughout most of the Middle Ages one had to be a successful warrior. As both a warrior and a general, Charlemagne certainly lived up to medieval expectations, and he showed considerable skill in his campaigns. Einhard idealized the King's military abilities:

> These [wars] were directed by Charlemagne with such skill that anyone who studies them may well wonder which he ought to admire most, the King's endurance in time of travail, or his good fortune.... He never withdrew from an enterprise which he had once begun and was determined to see through to the end; and danger never deterred him.

Once Charles had drastically expanded his kingdom, he was faced with the problem of administering the vast realm in an age when travel was hazardous and slow, roads were few, and messages traveled as fast as a man or a horse could carry them. In addition to being a consummate warrior, Charles was also concerned that his realm should run smoothly, that disorder should be suppressed, that justice should be done, that criminals should be punished, and that the Church should be fostered and protected. In early medieval times, administration hinged upon the royal court, and the royal court was wherever the king was: this meant it was constantly on the move from one great rural estate to the next. But in the 790s, Charlemagne began the construction of a royal palace at Aachen in what is now Germany, the church of which can still be seen today. The interior districts of Charles's kingdom were ruled by counts, and the border regions were administered by margraves ("military governors"). Since the real problem was how to ensure the loyalty of these officers, Charles created an official known as the *missi dominici.* Two men, one a churchman and one a noble, were sent out to survey a part of the kingdom, to carry the king's orders, and above all to keep an eye on the counts. While the system worked well as long as Charles loomed in the background, historians agree that he did not succeed in creating any institutions which would allow a weaker monarch to control the huge kingdom of the Franks.

Charlemagne imposed laws on all of the various peoples making up his realm by decrees called *capitularies.* They dealt with all sorts of matters, including military service, management of royal estates, and the Church; there was even one titled "On Scribes—That They Should Not Write Corruptly." Above all, Charlemagne was convinced that he ruled by "the grace of God," and he took for granted his ability to govern the affairs of the Church as well as the realm. He was extremely active in the reform of the Church: he regulated life in the monasteries, imposed his will upon the local church as well as the bishops and archbishops, and established missionary activity among the Saxons in the wake of his campaigns.

Scholars Come to the Court

One of Charlemagne's great ambitions was to rekindle the light of learning and knowledge in his vast Empire. Historians cannot be certain what motivated him, but his considerations were probably at least partly practical, since an effective government required some officials who could read and write. However, Charlemagne himself, as portrayed by Einhard, appears genuinely curious, a man who entertained a desire and enthusiasm for knowledge. In the 780s and 790s, Charlemagne succeeded in attracting to his court the leading scholars of Europe. The chief of them was the Saxon Alcuin (d. 804) from York, but they came also from Italy, Spain, Germany, and Ireland. For 15 years, Alcuin ran a school in Charlemagne's palace. The king was an avid pupil and is said to have understood both Greek and Latin, though he never mastered letters. He was also careful to preserve some Germanic culture and learning, and even began a grammar of his native tongue.

The main concern of the scholars, however, was with language and the copying of manuscripts (books had to be copied by hand until around 1500). Although lacking in originality, the latter was very important: more than 90% of the works from ancient Rome which survive today exist in their earliest form in a manuscript from Charlemagne's time. Without the work of these industrious copyists throughout his realm, almost all of the great works of classical literature would be unknown today.

Another important innovation was a major reform in handwriting. The script used around the time of Charlemagne's birth was almost illegible. All of the letters ran into one another in a scrawled form and books written in this script were difficult to copy. During Charles's reign a new form of writing was developed in which the letters and words were separated from one another. It was revived during the Italian Renaissance and forms the basis for modern lower-case letters. On the whole, the light kindled by Charlemagne's efforts was not very bright, and historians debate almost endlessly over whether or not this revival of learning should be called a "Carolingian Renaissance." But if the creative achievement of this period was slight, the copying of manuscripts was of great importance for the future of the Middle Ages, the Italian Renaissance, and modern times.

Charles Is Crowned Roman Emperor

For both medieval and modern people alike, however, the climax of Charlemagne's reign and the symbol of his domination of Western Europe was his coronation as Roman emperor in St. Peter's Basilica in Rome on Christmas day, A.D. 800. In 799, Pope Leo III had been attacked in the streets of Rome, beaten, and imprisoned. Eventually, he escaped and made his way to Charlemagne's court. The king sent him back to Rome with a force of warriors, and then, a year later, arrived himself in mid-December to settle the case. At a council on December 23, the Pope took an oath to clear his name. Then, on Christmas Day, as the king rose from prayer, the Pope produced a crown and placed it upon Charles's head, while the people in the church cried, "To Charles Augustus, crowned by God, great and peace-giving emperor, life and victory." There is still a great controversy over whether the Pope or Charlemagne was responsible for engineering the coronation. Einhard declared that Charles "would not have entered the cathedral that day at all … if he had known in advance what the Pope was planning to do," but other sources flatly contradict this statement. Whatever the case, the title added little to Charlemagne's actual power, but it did open a new phase of diplomatic relations with the Byzantine (Roman) emperors at Constantinople who regarded Charles's assumption of the imperial title as a challenge and an insult to their own position. It was not until 813, after a series of campaigns against the Byzantines in Italy, that the emperor Michael I finally accepted Charles's use of the title.

Einhard recorded that Charles was strong and well built; he was tall in stature and dignified in appearance, but his stomach was "a trifle too heavy." He took delight in outdoor activities such as hunting, and he seems to have particularly enjoyed swimming and bathing in the thermal springs, often with a crowd of attendants and bodyguards. Einhard also wrote that he always wore the Frankish national dress, and that he "hated the clothes of other countries, no matter how becoming they might be." In addition to being a conscientious ruler, Charlemagne was a devoted family man. According to his biographer, "he paid such attention to the upbringing of his sons and daughters that he never sat down to table without them," and his devotion to his daughters was such that he kept them with him in his household throughout his entire life instead of giving them in marriage.

From 801 until his death in 814, Charles remained actively engaged in the administration of his realm. Some new campaigns were launched, although the king seldom took part now; negotiations with the Byzantine court took place until 813; and, beginning in 806, Charles began to make arrangements for the succession. In that year, he proposed a tripartite division of the Empire among his three sons, Pepin, Charles, and Louis the Pious. By 811, sons Pepin and Charles had died; thus, in 813, in a magnificent ceremony at the palace at Aachen, the great magnates of the realm gathered and watched as Charles "placed the crown on Louis' head and ordered that he should be called Emperor and Augustus."

After a teary parting from his son, Charlemagne was reputed to have spent his remaining months in prayer and almsgiving, as well as reading and correcting Gospel books, but Einhard stated that he had merely gone hunting. Then, on January 21, 814, after one of his favorite thermal baths, he was "attacked by a sharp fever" and took to his bed. He soon developed a pain in his side, and seven days later, having received Communion, he died at nine o'clock in the morning. Einhard recorded many portents which supposedly marked the approach of his death, including eclipses and earthquakes. Charlemagne was buried in his chapel at Aachen, and over his tomb was placed a portrait with the inscription:

> Beneath this stone lies the body of Charles the Great, the Christian Emperor, who greatly expanded the kingdom of the Franks and reigned successfully for forty-seven years. He died when

more than seventy years old in the year of the Lord 814 … on 28 January.

Without doubt *Carolus Magnus*—Charlemagne, Charles the Great, Karl der Grosse—was one of the great figures of medieval Europe. His reign was viewed as a "Golden Age," and he was regarded as one of the Nine Worthies, along with Abraham and Julius Caesar. A warrior-king, he was immortalized and idealized in poetry, song, and story as a hero of Christian Europe, and in 1165 Frederick Barbarossa even had him canonized as St. Charles. For centuries after his death, the leading monarchs of Western Europe went out of their way to claim they were continuing his work and to link their dynasties with his name. But although Charlemagne is often regarded as the "Father of Europe," within a generation his mighty Empire was shattered by the Treaty of Verdun (843).

SOURCES:

Bullough, D. *The Age of Charlemagne.* 2nd ed. Paul Elek, 1973.

Duckett, E. S. *Carolingian Portraits: A Study in the Ninth Century.* University of Michigan Press, 1962.

Einhard, and Notker the Stammerer. *Two Lives of Charlemagne.* Translated by L. Thorpe. Penguin (reprint), 1969.

Grant, M. *Dawn of the Middle Ages.* Bonanza Books, 1986.

Tierney, B., and S. Painter. *Western Europe in the Middle Ages, 300–1475.* 4th ed. Knopf, 1983.

FURTHER READING:

Chamberlin, E. R. *Charlemagne, Emperor of the Western World.* Grafton, 1986.

Fichtenau, H. *The Carolingian Empire.* Translated by P. Munz. Harper, 1964.

Holmes, G., ed. *The Oxford Illustrated History of Medieval Europe.* Oxford University Press, 1988.

Charles II

(1630–1685)

King of England, Scotland and Ireland, who returned to the restored Stuart throne after exile and charted a political path between the extremes of theology and faction.

Name variations: Merry King. Born May 29, 1630, at St. James Palace, London; died in London in 1685; eldest surviving son of Charles I and Henrietta Maria; married: Catherine Braganza of Portugal, 1662; children: fathered 14 illegitimate children but only one, James, Duke of Monmouth, played any role in politics. Predecessors: James I, Charles I. Successor: James II.

Great Britain enjoys an unparalleled reputation for political stability. In terms of continuous constitutional development unbroken by revolutionary upheaval, the British government is the world's oldest, dating its origins from the Glorious Revolution (1688–89). The constitutional settlement—a balanced government of crown, lords, and commons—grew out of the turmoil of the "seventeenth century crisis." The four decades preceding the Glorious Revolution saw England send one Stuart king (Charles I) to the scaffold, two others into exile (Charles II and his brother, James II); a republican interregnum; the Anglican Church deposed, then restored; the House of Lords disfranchised, then reinstated; and the House of Commons expand its authority at the expense of crown and lords. Amidst all these disruptions, the reign of the restored Stuart king, Charles II, stands as an island of relative calm.

Known in British history as the Restoration period, Charles II's reign produced a cultural flowering, the furthering of scientific inquiry, and, in the 1680s, rapid economic growth. Rejecting the rigid morality and austerity imposed on them by Puritanism, the English reveled in the new relaxed

"'Tis True, that when the nation has been so long mad, after so many changes and revolutions, ... we might with reason have expected God should have sent us the worst of tyrants.... But He was so gracious as to send us our own King to redeem the nation from all the infamy it had undergone and to restore it to all it had lost."

SIR RICHARD BULSTRODE
ON CHARLES II

Contributed by D. K. R. Crosswell, Lecturer, National University of Singapore, Singapore.

atmosphere that accompanied the collapse of the Commonwealth's republican experiment. Restoration literature and comedies—cynical, urbane, and sensual—mirror exactly the new mentality. The charming, tolerant, and bawdy plays also reflect the personality and tastes of Charles II, the "Merry Monarch."

The eldest surviving son of Charles I and his French wife Henrietta Maria, Charles II began life on May 29, 1630, at St. James Palace, London. Dark-featured, the infant more resembled his French Bourbon mother's line than the Scottish Stuarts. At age eight, his father invested Charles as Knight of the Garter, gave the prince his own household, and placed the earl of Newcastle in charge of his son's education. Neglecting disciplined study, Newcastle wanted the future king to lead an active, masculine life. "I would not have you too studious," Newcastle instructed his charge, "for too much contemplation spoils action." Given to music and dance, Charles excelled as a fencer and horseman. A precocious and self-indulgent youth, he developed at an early age the laziness and moral evasiveness that marked his adult personality.

Not quite as Newcastle envisioned, Charles received his education in the bitter school of experience. In 1642, civil war erupted in England between the royalist forces and their Puritan-Parliamentarian opponents. At age 15, Charles, as Prince of Wales, raised forces in the west of England before joining the Queen in France. While in the French court, he resisted all efforts of his mother and his favorite sister, Henrietta Anne, duchess d'Orléans, to convert him to Roman Catholicism. In 1648, he returned to Britain in a desperate but vain bid to save his father. After the king's execution in January 1649, Scotland and Ireland rose in rebellion, proclaiming Charles king. **Oliver Cromwell,** Puritan commander and future Lord Protector of the Commonwealth, crushed the Irish. Scotland proved a more difficult problem.

Charles Flees After Cromwell Victory

Charles took up residence in Scotland and accepted the strident anti-Catholic and anti-Anglican Presbyterian Covenant. Cromwell moved against Scotland in 1650, defeating the Scottish army at Dunbar on September 3. Crowned king of Scotland at Scone on January 1, 1651, Charles invaded England in the hope of rallying English royalists while relieving pressure on Scotland. Cromwell followed Charles's forces, bringing them to battle at Worcester, a year to the day after Dunbar. Worcester, Cromwell's greatest victory, decisively ended the civil war, leaving him

CHRONOLOGY

1642–51	English Civil War
1645	Battle of Naseby; Charles fled to France
1648	Returned to Britain
1649	Charles I executed; Ireland and Scotland declared for Charles
1649-59	Oliver Cromwell named Lord Protector of England's "Commonwealth and Free State"
1650	Battle of Dunbar
1651	Battle of Worcester; Charles's dramatic flight to France
1651–60	Exiled in France, Germany, and the Spanish Netherlands
1660	Breda Declaration; restoration of Stuart monarchy
1660–85	Charles II crowned king of England, Scotland, and Ireland
1665–74	Anglo-Dutch Wars
1685	Charles II died in London

general master of the three realms of England, Scotland, and Ireland. For the next six weeks, Charles led the life of a fugitive. After a number of close calls, he made a sensational escape to France.

Although his quixotic adventures added luster to his reputation, the dispossessed king entertained few prospects. Backed by the Rump Parliament and the army, Cromwell seemed invincible. Without resources and surrounded by adventurers and hangers-on, Charles slipped into a hedonistic world of excess. "When he found his struggles doomed to failure," wrote Madame de Motteville, confidant to Queen Henrietta, "[Charles] sank into indifference and bore the ills of poverty with reckless nonchalance, snatching at whatever pleasures came in his way, even those of the most degraded kind." "He is so much given to pleasure," intoned Edward Hyde, distinguished historian and Charles's chancellor in exile, "that if he stays [in Paris] he will be undone."

Since France curried England's active support against Spain, the presence of the Stuart claimant to the throne in Paris proved politically embarrassing. Sent packing, the vagabond king set up his court at Cologne, in Germany. When England entered the war alongside France, Charles saw an opportunity and allied himself with Spain. He persuaded his brother James, Duke of York, to relinquish his French command and come over to the Spanish. James took control of some Anglo-

Irish regiments in the Spanish service. The shift in policy accomplished little since bankrupt Spain could ill afford subsidies for either Charles's disreputable court or his impotent little army.

Deep in debt and ignored by continental princes, Charles took solace in news of Cromwell's death in September 1658. Traveling incognito, Charles made his way to Fuentarrabia, site of the peace conference which ended the Franco-Spanish War (Treaty of the Pyrénées). Employing his considerable charm and dressed in his best set of clothes—an old threadbare French suit—Charles solicited backing for his restoration. As always, he also tried to contrive a dynastic match for himself, even offering to marry the niece of **Cardinal Mazarin,** French first minister. Politely rebuffed on all counts, Charles returned to Brussels, capital of the Spanish Netherlands and seat of his peripatetic court.

Meanwhile, events in England moved rapidly. Taken together, the unpopularity of the rule of the army, the ebbing of ideological fervor, the growing sense even among republicans of the corruption of Puritanism by power, and the death of Cromwell led to the collapse of the Protectorate in May 1659. A succession of governments—the restored Rump Parliament (May–October); a "Committee of Safety" dominated by senior military men (October-Christmas); a "rump" Rump Parliament (Christmas–mid-February)—foundered trying to preserve the republican coalition.

George Monck, one of Cromwell's ablest generals and commander in Scotland, ended the chaos. Asserting "the freedom and rights of [the] three kingdoms from arbitrary and tyrannical usurpation," "Old George" marched his army toward London, arriving on February 3. A conservative republican, Monck, fearing a swing toward radicalism, favored the restoration of legitimate monarchy over the anarchy of another civil war. Two weeks after his arrival, he called a "free parliament"—the remnant of the Long Parliament as it stood in December 1648. The movement toward a Stuart restoration now proved irresistible.

With Breda Declaration, King Returns from Exile

The Long Parliament sat long enough to vote itself out of existence and call elections for a Convention Parliament. Anticipating a shift toward a royalist settlement, Charles acted. Amazed by the remarkable reversal of his fortunes—none of which can be attributed to any of Charles's actions or those of his royalist supporters—the uncrowned and exiled king of England fled across the frontier from the Spanish Netherlands to Breda in the Netherlands. (England and Spain remained at war.) From here, he issued his famous Breda Declaration, one of the most cleverly conceived manifestos in English constitutional history.

The work of Hyde, the declaration offered all things to all factions. Charles expressed his own desire for a general amnesty, compensated resolution of land disputes, full payment of money owed the army, and "liberty to tender consciences" in religious matters. Posturing as defender of the "ancient constitution" and parliamentary privileges, he unloaded the divisive problems—retribution against republican opponents, compensation for royalist supporters, and religion—onto Parliament. The declaration simultaneously proclaimed, "by the laws of God and man," the restoration of "King, Peers (Lords) and people to their just, ancient and fundamental rights." Claiming absolute sovereignty for the king and promising to uphold the Protestant faith, the Breda Declaration offered a constitutional settlement that the supporters of Parliament and congregationalists (Presbyterian and Protestant Nonconformists) could accept. With the actual terms left to a "free Parliament," the declaration served as the provisional basis for the restoration. Invited home, Charles crossed the English Channel on May 25. Ironically, he sailed in the ship-of-the-line *Naseby,* pride of the Commonwealth navy and bearer of the name of Cromwell's victory over Charles I.

On his 30th birthday—May 29, 1660—Charles entered London "with a triumph [parade] of above twenty thousand horse and foot; brandishing their swords and shouting inexpressible joy; the ways strewn with flowers, the bells ringing, the streets hung with tapestry, fountains running with wine." As another contemporary noted, "never … in history [had a] monarchy, laid aside at the expense of so much blood, returned without the sheading of one drop." Confronted with this outpouring of affection, Charles wryly proclaimed himself a fool for staying away so long.

The king's London reception illustrated that neither republicanism nor Puritanism had taken root in England during the 17-year interregnum. The Parliament elected in 1661—known as the Cavalier Parliament because of its royalist, Anglican, and landed-gentry membership—restored king, House of Lords, and the Church of England. The tide of royalism assured the unconditional restoration of sovereignty to the Crown. Even with the concessions made by Charles I in 1640–41—end of prerogative courts and controls on royal revenue—the king's formal powers remained immense. He empowered or dismissed Parliament at will, and no mechanism existed to call it independently if the monarch ignored the Triennial Act which required the summoning of Parliament at least once every three years. The king also controlled foreign policy. In an unprecedented step, the Cavalier Parliament granted Charles the right to maintain a standing army in peacetime, providing he paid its maintenance. With his government centered on Hyde (now the earl of Clarendon) and Monck (created duke of Albemarle), Charles inaugurated a reign he hoped would bring the political stability all segments of British society desired.

The Cavalier Parliament (1661–79), viewing the Convention's work incomplete, extended its authority, particularly over questions of religion. In 1662, the king issued his first Declaration of Indulgence, promising suspension of laws against nonmilitant dissenters, including Roman Catholics. His efforts miscarried in the face of fierce parliamentary and popular opposition. Ignoring the king's pleas for toleration, Parliament moved aggressively, limiting the political and civil, as well as religious, rights of all but Anglicans. The Corporation Act (1661) allowed for the removal of objectionable officials from municipal and local administrations. Various other legislation imposed limits on the press and freedom of assembly. The Act of Uniformity (1662), a Conventicles Act (1664), and Five Mile Act (1665) established controls over religious practices and education. Known collectively, and somewhat misleadingly, as the Clarendon Code, the Anglican settlement underlined both the limits on Charles's power and the continuing importance of religion.

Doubts emerged about Charles's religious leanings. His licentiousness ruled out Puritanism; his domestic and foreign policies led some to question the king's commitment to Protestantism. Charles's marriage to a Catholic princess, Catherine Braganza of Portugal, in 1662, and the conversions to Catholicism of his favorite mistress, Barbara Villiers, duchess of Cleveland, and his brother and heir apparent, the duke of York, all fed rumors the king had changed his religion. All the conflicts that punctuated Charles's reign—over the constitutional settlement, foreign policy, and the succession—rotated around religious issues.

Restoration of economic and foreign policy—the Navigation Acts of 1660 and 1663 and the second Anglo-Dutch war (1665–67)—followed the designs laid down during the Commonwealth. Charles reasoned a popular war against the Dutch would unite the nation and the commercial elite behind the throne while deflecting Parliament from pursuing its Anglican settlement. Full of optimism, he told Parliament in 1664: "I have a fleet now at sea worthy of the English nation and not inferior to any that hath set out in any age." At first the war went well. After seizing winning naval victories in 1665 (Lowestoft) and 1666 (North Forelands), the year 1667 saw England suffer its worst defeat at sea. Dutch admiral Michiel de Ruyter sailed unchallenged into the Thames Estuary and attacked the English fleet at anchor, sinking four ships before retreating undamaged with the enemy flagship *Royal Charles* (formerly *Naseby*) in tow. "As dreadful a spectacle as ever Englishmen saw," lamented a commentator, "and a dishonour never to be wiped out." A product of negligence and maladministration, the Chatham disaster, coupled with the Great Plague of 1665 and the Fire of London in 1666, forced England to sue for peace.

Treaty of Dover Signed with Louis XIV

Charles deflected blame by dismissing his trusted old advisor, Clarendon. He then embarked upon an even more ambitious foreign policy. In May 1670, Charles signed the Treaty of Dover with his cousin **Louis XIV** of France. In exchange for subsidies and promises of territorial gains, Charles pledged to join France in a war of aggression against the Netherlands. The secret provisions of the treaty committed the king to announce his conversion to Catholicism. If the change produced armed resistance in staunchly anti-French and anti-Catholic England, Louis would intervene with troops. The treaty also pulled England out of a powerful anti-French alliance of Protestant powers (England, the Netherlands, Sweden). A victory over the Netherlands would remove the stain of the 1667 defeat, badly damage England's chief commercial and naval rival, and win a large cash indemnity. If England pried a larger share of European and world trade from the Dutch, Charles's financial position would improve because much of his income derived from customs duties. Together, French subsidies and improved revenue would free the king from reliance upon Parliament. He could then assert his own religious settlement independent of Parliament. Charles made sure the conversion clause of the treaty remained a closely guarded secret.

The bold policy ended in abject failure. In March 1672, while the Cavalier Parliament stood adjourned, Charles declared war and issued his second Declaration of Indulgence. Charles's diplomatic about-face aided Louis in his Grand Design, but for England the war went badly. When Parliament reconvened in February 1673, the king desperately needed money. The House of Commons forced Charles to withdraw the Declaration of Indulgence and passed the Test Act, which specified that only Anglicans could hold state offices. Hopelessly compromised by his secret deal with Louis and without financial resources, the king suffered the indignity of seeing the duke of York surrender his post as commander of the fleet because of his Catholic religion. Confronted by widespread opposition, Charles sought a separate peace with the Netherlands (Treaty of Westminster, January 1674).

His foreign policy a debacle, Charles surrendered the day-to-day running of government to the earl of Danby. Believing that "God [would] never damn a man for allowing himself a little pleasure," the king turned from affairs of state to the conduct of his many sexual affairs. One courtier described the king as:

> inferior to none, either in shape or air; his wit was pleasant; his disposition easy and affable; his soul … was compassionate … and tender even to excess…. [H]is heart was often the dupe, but oftener the slave, of his attachments.

His attachments proved many. Only two of his many mistresses meddled in politics: Cleveland and Louise de Kérouaille, duchess of Portsmouth. Charles fathered at least 14 illegitimate children but only one, James, duke of Monmouth, played any role in politics. On balance, his inattention to duty did the King more harm than his amours.

Ironically, Charles's inability to father a legitimate child produced the severest storm of his political life. In the absence of a legitimate heir, his brother James, duke of York, would succeed to the throne. James's second marriage, to Mary of Modena, increased the likelihood of a Catholic line of succession. Where Charles possessed no rigid doctrines, political or religious, and displayed an ability to adapt to changing situations, his brother was rigid in his views and unbendingly authoritarian.

A number of rumors surfaced placing James at the center of conspiracies to kill the king and ensure the Catholic succession. The bizarre Popish Plot of 1678, hatched by an Anglican clergyman and former Jesuit novice by the name of Titus Oates, produced a national hysteria. Parliament issued a decree announcing:

> there hath been, and still is, a damnable and hellish Plot, contrived and carried on by the Popish recusants for the assassinating and murdering the King, and for subverting the government, and rooting out and destroying the Protestant religion.

The mysterious murder of a London magistrate who heard evidence in the case supported Oates's claims.

Feeding on the frenzy, Parliament impeached Danby. In April 1679, the Commons introduced the Exclusion Act, prohibiting James from succeeding to the throne. Refusing to accept the imposition of any conditions upon royal power, Charles dissolved the Cavalier Parliament in July. The elections in August and September 1679 saw the embryonic origins of English political parties: Tory in support of the Crown, court, and Church of England; Whigs in support of parliamentary power and limited religious toleration. To appease the opposition, the king sent James out of the country and accepted the earl of Shaftesbury and other partisan Whigs—men he loathed—into the government.

Between 1679 and 1681, Charles nearly lost control of the government. Three general elections furnished three truculent Parliaments. The situation in 1681 reminded many of 1640–41. Taking advantage of the dread of renewed civil war, Charles dissolved his last Parliament. As the king well knew, the Crown and the landed gentry remained united in their determination to avoid a repeat of the chaos of civil war and dictatorship. Reminiscent of 1660, a royalist reaction swept the country in 1682, allowing the king to rule alone, without Whigs in his government or the consent of Parliament.

Other than religion, the single most damaging limitation on royal action lay in the area of finance. Imprudent where money and morals were concerned, Charles II could not refuse office seekers and petitioners. When he returned from exile, the Exchequer had slightly more than £11 in reserve. Although he repudiated the Protectorate's debt, Charles soon built his own. Parliament granted him an income of £1,200,000 but revenue collected rarely approached that figure. By the time this gap narrowed, the king's debt had multiplied and his credit correspondingly fell. The king's prestige, not to mention his power, sank.

The royal finances improved during the first half of the 1680s. With England at peace, Charles no longer had to call Parliament to plead his case for money. Economies made in defense spending could be redirected. The archaic and ramshackle royal administration gave way to a more centralized bureaucracy. A prosperous England produced greater revenue which could then be more efficiently collected and spent. To assure his independence from Parliament, Charles signed another secret subsidies treaty with Louis XIV. At long last, Charles ruled over the kind of England—peaceful and prosperous—he had always sought. But he did not have long to bask in his successes. Charles II died at sunrise on February 6, 1685, but not before he took the last rites of the Catholic religion. On his deathbed he made good on his promise to cousin Louis.

While Charles II did not solve the great issues of the "seventeenth century crisis," the tensions between king and Parliament, Anglicanism and the dissenters, and court and country did not boil over in civil war. England wanted political stability and an end to civil strife and changing regimes. All this Charles's 25-year reign provided.

SOURCES:

Bryant, Sir Arthur. *King Charles the Second.* London. 1931.

Hutton, Ronald. *The Restoration.* Oxford, 1985.

Ogg, David. *England in the Reign of Charles II.* New ed. New York, 1984.

FURTHER READING:

Bliss, Robert. *Restoration England, 1660–1688.* London, 1985.

Fraser, Lady Antonia. *Royal Charles and the Restoration.* London, 1979.

Charles III

(1716–1788)

King of Two Sicilies and of Spain, who is considered one of Europe's 18th-century "Enlightened Despots," and is remembered for the assistance he provided to the 13 American colonies during their struggle for independence against Great Britain.

Name variations: Known as Don Carlos in his youth, he was King Charles IV of the Two Sicilies and King Charles III of Spain. Born January 20, 1716, in Madrid, Spain; died on December 12, 1788, in San Lorenzo del Escorial, Spain; son of King Philip V of Spain and Elizabeth Farnese; married: Maria Amalia of Saxony; children: (sons) Philip, Charles, Ferdinand; (daughters) Maria Louisa and four others. Descendant: Juan Carlos I, the present king of Spain. Predecessor: Ferdinand VI. Successor: Charles IV.

A troubled time for European monarchies in general, the 18th century opened in Spain with the death of King Charles II (1665–1700), last feeble remnant of the once powerful Spanish Habsburgs. Having no direct heir, Charles was succeeded by his great nephew Philip of Anjou, grandson of King **Louis XIV** of France. As Philip V (1700–46), Anjou became the first Bourbon monarch of Spain, and his accession provoked the War of the Spanish Succession (1701–13), when Louis's European rivals, Great Britain and the Netherlands, sided with Austria in an unsuccessful attempt to install the Habsburg claimant Archduke Charles instead. The Treaty of Utrecht (1713) confirmed the Bourbon succession, but Philip had to renounce his own claim to the French throne. He was also compelled to surrender Spain's possessions in Italy and the Netherlands to his Austrian rival, who in 1711 had become Holy Roman Emperor as Charles VI.

This agreement was supposed to restore stability in Europe, but it was followed instead by a series of crises and wars, caused in part by uncertainty about the succession in several other countries. Louis XIV died in 1715, leaving the French

"In his desire to remodel outworn institutions and to promote the welfare of his people by wise legislation he was a true prince of the Enlightenment; in his jealous retention of authority and his impatience at opposition he was a true despot."

GEOFFREY BRUUN

Contributed by Stephen Webre, Professor of History, Louisiana Tech University, Ruston, Louisiana

throne to his five-year-old great-grandson (Louis XV, 1715–74). In the Empire, Charles VI failed to produce a male heir and he now sought to secure the rights of his daughter **Maria Theresa,** although Austria had no tradition of female succession. Meanwhile, Queen **Anne** of England was aging and childless, and several old Italian dynasties were nearing extinction.

In these years of difficulty for ruling households, the new king of Spain enjoyed one great political advantage. Although he was emotionally unstable and suffered throughout his life from bouts of mental illness, Philip V was physically robust, and he had the good fortune to father five sons, four of whom outlived him. Three of his sons would follow him to the throne, and one of them, Charles III (1759–88), would prove to be one of the ablest rulers in Spanish history, although in his youth no one had thought it likely that he would ever be king at all.

The prince who eventually became King Charles III was Philip's third son, and the first by his second wife Elizabeth Farnese. Born in Madrid on January 20, 1716, he was christened Don Carlos, and was generally known by that name until he inherited the Spanish throne more than 40 years later. Because Philip already had two living sons by his marriage to Maria Louisa of Savoy, he and Elizabeth sought suitable employment for Don Carlos somewhere other than in Spain. Their preference was in the northern Italian duchies of Tuscany and Parma, where the once great Medici and Farnese dynasties were about to die out. Elizabeth was related to both families, so the royal couple aggressively advanced their son's candidacy to inherit them. Don Carlos never inherited in Tuscany, but in 1731 he did become duke of Parma, when the last Farnese died. Emperor Charles VI, who feared for his own recent acquisitions in Milan and Naples, initially opposed a Bourbon presence in Italy, but he dropped his objection when Philip V agreed to recognize the succession in Austria of Maria Theresa and her descendants.

Don Carlos's rule in Parma was brief. In 1733, he saw a better opportunity when the War of the Polish Succession broke out. Spain and Austria backed rival claimants to the crown of Poland, and the brief moment of amity between the two powers came to an end. When Philip V sent troops to attack the Emperor's position in Lombardy, the 18-year-old Don Carlos assumed command of a second Spanish force, which headed south to capture Naples and Sicily. At Palermo in July 1734, he was crowned king of the Two Sicilies, an arrangement confirmed four years later by the Treaty of Vienna. In compensation for this territorial loss,

CHRONOLOGY

1731	Recognized as duke of Parma
1734	Led Spanish invasion of Naples and Sicily, crowned king of Two Sicilies
1759	Became king of Spain upon death of Ferdinand VI
1761	Signed Family Compact with France
1767	Expelled Jesuits from Spain and its empire
1779	Intervened in War for American Independence

the Emperor received Parma, which Don Carlos happily abandoned in exchange for a kingdom of his own. Philip and Elizabeth were satisfied that their son was now appropriately and honorably employed.

As King Charles IV of the Two Sicilies (that is, of Naples and Sicily), Don Carlos presided for 25 years (1734–59) over a government considered in its day to be efficient and forward-looking. Serious, intelligent, and honest, the new monarch was more interested in domestic reforms than in foreign military adventures. Inspired by the idea of absolutist, or centralized, monarchy associated most commonly with his famous ancestor Louis XIV, as well as by the French Enlightenment and its emphasis on reason, the new ruler set out to remake Neapolitan institutions. In particular, he attacked the privileges of the Roman Catholic clergy and, although himself a devout Catholic, he responded to Church resistance by enacting tough anticlerical measures. Don Carlos's years in southern Italy were prosperous ones. He was popular with the people and there is a story that in 1759, when he departed Naples to assume the Spanish throne, crowds of weeping subjects gathered at the wharf to bid him farewell.

He Begins 30-Year Reign in Spain

By the time he sailed for Barcelona to become king of Spain, Don Carlos had known for years that he would someday wear his father's crown. In 1724, for reasons still little understood but probably related to his mental condition, Philip V had abdicated in favor of his eldest son, who became King Luis I at the age of 16. Only months after his accession, however, Luis died, so Philip ended his brief retirement and returned to the throne, where he remained until his own death in 1746. When Philip died, he was succeeded by his second son and Don Carlos's only surviving half-brother, Ferdinand VI. Because Ferdinand and his queen, Barbara of Braganza, had no children, the succession passed next to the sons of Elizabeth Farnese, of whom Don Carlos was the eldest.

In preparation for his eventual move to Spain, the Neapolitan king was careful to secure the rights of his own sons in southern Italy. As a result of the War of the Austrian Succession (1740–48), Parma changed hands again, being this time awarded to Don Carlos's younger brother Don Felipe, who then renounced any claim he might have to the Two Sicilies. When Ferdinand VI finally died in 1759, Don Carlos declared his second son, Don Carlos Antonio, to be his own heir in Spain, while the Kingdom of Naples passed to his third son, Don Fernando. (Carlos and Fernando had an older brother named Felipe, but he was mentally retarded and, therefore, excluded from the succession.)

As King Charles III, Don Carlos ruled Spain for almost three decades until his death in 1788. It is reported that his reputation for probity and justice preceded him from Naples, and that his Spanish subjects greeted him with enthusiasm upon his arrival. Charles did not fit the traditional image of a king, however. Contemporaries described him as physically unimpressive, as stoop-shouldered, toothless, and poorly dressed. An intensely private person, he disliked ceremony, preferring to spend his time in administrative routine. Charles was a devoted family man, and when his wife of more than 20 years, Maria Amalia of Saxony, died shortly after his accession in Spain, he felt the loss so deeply that he never remarried.

Charles III was determined to give his new kingdom the same reformist leadership he had shown in Italy. Years of neglectful rulers and failed policies had left Spain, once the wealthiest and mightiest of Western powers, in economic decline and military weakness, a situation made worse by the Seven Years' War (1756–63), in which Great Britain and France were engaged at the time of Charles's accession. The new monarch attempted at first to remain neutral in this conflict, but British assaults on Spanish interests in the New World, along with Charles's own Francophile sympathies, led him finally to intervene. In 1761, he signed the Family Compact with his Bourbon cousin Louis XV, and in January 1762, he declared war on Great Britain.

Spain's brief involvement in the Seven Years' War was costly. It left the Spanish government deeply in debt, and it brought complicated territorial changes which weakened Spain's strategic position. The British navy seized the important colonial ports of Manila in the Philippines and Havana in Cuba, and to get them back Charles III had to agree in the Treaty of Paris (1763) to the cession to Great Britain of Florida, which controlled access to the shipping lanes for American treasure. In partial compensation for Spain's losses, France handed over Louisiana, but that territory, although vast, was unprofitable and difficult to defend.

After the war, Charles III reorganized his government, promoting two Italians to powerful positions, the Genoese Jerónimo, marquis of Grimaldi, as minister of state, and the Sicilian Leopoldo de Gregorio, marquis of Squilacci, as minister of finance and war. Squilacci, whom the Spanish called "Equilache," was of humble origins but had much in common with Charles, whom he had previously served in Naples. Both monarch and minister were simple, businesslike men who scorned finery and pretense. In addition, neither of them was sentimentally attached to traditional Spanish institutions. Although born in Spain, Charles had spent his adult life in Italy and had learned the craft of kingship there. He was, in many ways, as much an outsider as his servant.

Unrest Culminates in Madrid Riot

Confident of his royal master's support, Squilacci set out to modernize and centralize the Spanish state by undermining the traditional privileges of the nobility, the clergy, and the towns. He also hoped to increase economic productivity by lifting regulations and abolishing monopolies, while at the same time increasing government revenues through simpler taxes with fewer exemptions and tougher collection policies. These innovations offended almost every interest in Spain, and it did not help that their author was a foreigner, or that they came at a time of repeated crop failures. Disturbances in 1764 in a number of localities marked the beginning of a wave of popular unrest, which culminated in March 1766 in a major riot in Madrid. Fearing for his own safety, the monarch fled the capital. Charles ultimately agreed to the rioters' demands and shipped the unpopular minister back to Italy.

Historians consider the so-called "Esquilache Riot" a turning point in Charles III's reign. Squilacci's fall permitted the rise to power of Pedro Pablo de Abarca y Bolea, count of Aranda, leader of an antiforeign party among the Spanish nobility. After 1766, Aranda became in effect Charles's chief minister. As a grandee, or high-ranking noble, he had little sympathy for the king's absolutist ideas, but, like Charles, he was an admirer of the French Enlightenment—in fact,

Aranda was a friend of Voltaire's. The king and his chief minister, therefore, agreed on administrative and economic reforms, and Aranda supported the initiatives championed by such economic modernizers as Gaspar Melchor de Jovellanos and Pedro Pérez y Rodríguez, count of Campomanes.

As another consequence of the riot, in 1767 Charles ordered the expulsion from Spain and its possessions of the Jesuit fathers, whom nationalist nobles, such as Aranda, had blamed for the violence. The king had his own reasons for this measure, which was not popular in Spain or the colonies. The Society of Jesus was wealthy, powerful, and international, and Charles saw it as a threat to the consolidation of royal power at the national level. In fact his fellow monarchs, the kings of Portugal and France, had already driven the Jesuits from their own realms.

Charles III's economic policies were inspired by the ideas of the French physiocrats and by Scottish economist Adam Smith's free trade critique of mercantilism. The king sought to increase agricultural productivity by selling off village common lands to individual proprietors and by canceling the monopoly grazing rights of the tiny group of privileged sheepraisers known as the Mesta. To promote an increase in trade with the American colonies, Charles in 1778 abolished the exclusive rights once enjoyed by the powerful merchant cliques of Seville and Cádiz. He also attempted to promote the development of manufacturing in Spain by erecting trade barriers designed to exclude foreign competition. Convinced of the value of new ideas, Charles worked to reform Spain's universities, and he encouraged the establishment both at home and in the colonies of so-called "economic societies," local learned associations which disseminated practical information such as modern agricultural techniques.

"Enlightened Despots" Undertake Reforms

Charles III's various reformist initiatives represented one of the most sweeping and energetic domestic programs ever undertaken by a Spanish monarch, and his record of major changes is probably exceeded only by that of **Isabella and Ferdinand** in the late 15th century. Charles's massive effort to modernize Spain won him a place in history among Europe's "Enlightened Despots," a group of contemporary reforming rulers which included Frederick the Great of Prussia (1740–86), **Catherine the Great** of Russia (1762–96), and **Joseph II** of Austria (1780–90). Although Charles had in common with his fellow monarchs a concern for efficient administration,

economic development, and elementary social justice, his notion of political reform, like theirs, sought only to increase the power of the king. However enlightened they may have been, the "Enlightened Despots" were genuinely despots, and none of them felt the least sympathy for the ideas of constitutionalism and representative government which were gaining ground in both Europe and America in their day.

Some of the Bourbon reforms yielded beneficial results, but others met strong resistance, failed to retain royal interest, or simply turned out in ways that those who had conceived them had not expected. To be fair, many of these experiments lacked sufficient time to prove themselves, because foreign crises had a way of diverting the government's attention and altering its priorities. In particular, the War of American Independence (1775–83) presented Spain with both an opportunity and a challenge. In 1779, Charles III followed France in intervening against Great Britain, but, unlike the French, he declined to ally himself directly with the rebellious colonies, because he feared the effect of their example on his own overseas possessions. During the fighting in America, Louisiana governor Bernardo de Gálvez captured Florida, which was returned to Spanish sovereignty by the Treaty of Paris (1783). Although Spain benefited from the war in some respects, the expense involved interfered with domestic reforms. For example, it was not possible to follow through with tax rate reductions designed to stimulate manufacturing, because of the negative impact such decreases might have had on needed revenues.

Even before the American war, a quarrel at court over policy toward Great Britain had led to the fall of Aranda, whom in 1773 Charles III sent in thinly disguised exile to France as Spanish ambassador. In Aranda's place, José Moñino y Redondo, count of Floridablanca, rose to power and influence. In 1776, Floridablanca became minister of state, replacing Charles's longtime associate Grimaldi who now returned to Italy, and he continued to serve the king until the latter's death. In contrast to Aranda, the new minister was a strong royalist, but he was a reformer, too. He was responsible for some important innovations in the administration of justice and, with royal support, he worked to limit the power and activities of the Spanish Inquisition.

Always jealous of his powers and prerogatives, Charles III became more inflexible during the 1780s. Nevertheless, by the time of his death of fever in 1788, he could look back with some satisfaction on his accomplishments. As historian Olwen Hufton summarized Charles's career, whatever failures or shortcomings there may have been, it can be said that "Spain, very cautiously … was moving into the eighteenth century." Of course, that century was nearly over, and it would end with the explosion of the French Revolution, whose popular excesses spread fear throughout the courts of Europe. In Spain, Charles's son and heir, Charles IV (1788–1808), abandoned reformism and became an embittered reactionary. Arrested with his family in 1808 when **Napoleon Bonaparte** captured Madrid, he would end his days a prisoner in France, while his kingdom descended into bloody guerrilla warfare and his American empire disintegrated. For Spain, Hufton wrote, the upheaval north of the Pyrenees became truly the "fall of snow on blossoming trees."

SOURCES:

Bruun, Geoffrey. *The Enlightened Despots*. Henry Holt, 1929.

Hargreaves-Mawdsley, W. N. *Eighteenth-Century Spain, 1700–1788: A Political, Diplomatic and Institutional History*. Macmillan, 1979.

Hufton, Olwen. *Europe: Privilege and Protest, 1730–1789*. Cornell University Press, 1980.

Petrie, Sir Charles. *King Charles III of Spain: An Enlightened Despot*. John Day, 1971.

FURTHER READING:

Addison, Joseph. *Charles the Third of Spain*. B.H. Blackwell, 1900.

Herr, Richard. *The Eighteenth-Century Revolution in Spain*. Princeton University Press, 1958.

Lynch, John. *Bourbon Spain, 1700–1808*. Basil Blackwell, 1989.

Charles V

(1500–1558)

Habsburg Holy Roman Emperor and king of Spain, who ruled territories larger than Charlemagne's—including vast tracts of Germany, Italy, the Netherlands, Central Europe, North Africa, and the Americas.

"Charles V carried the Hapsburg dynasty to the height of its greatness…. [H]e created a world Empire dependent for the first time in history … on a dynastic theory and unity of faith."

KARL BRANDI

Born on February 24, 1500, Charles V became the ruler of one of the largest empires the world has ever seen. His territories consisted of the ancestral Habsburg family estates; the Spanish Empire; the kingdoms of Germany, Hungary, Bohemia, Naples, and Sicily; the duchy of Milan; the Netherlands; and possessions in North Africa and the Americas. One awestruck Englishman observed that the Spanish king was "the most potent Monarch of Christendome, who in his hands holds the Mines of Wars' sinews—money—and hath now got a command so wide, that out of his Dominions the Sunne can neither rise nor set." Indeed, even without "counting the Habsburg lands, Charles owned roughly twice as much of Europe as **Francis I**," the Valois king of France.

Charles V dominated the stage of European and world politics from 1516 until his death in 1558. A man of enormous military talent, he endeared himself to his soldiers, and eventually even his Spanish subjects, by his courage and love of action. Next to him, Francis I and **Henry VIII** of England—his principal rivals—were but minor players on the political chessboard of Europe.

Contributed by Glenn Feldman, Ph.D. candidate in History, Auburn University, Auburn, Alabama

Name variations: Charles I of Spain. Born February 24, 1500, in Ghent, the Netherlands; died on September 21, 1558, in San Jeronimo de Yuste, Spain; son of Philip I the Handsome, King of Castile, and Joanna the Mad; married: Isabella of Portugal; children: Philip II and Don John of Austria (illegitimate). Descendants: Louis XIV of France. Predecessors: Emperor Maximilian I Habsburg and Mary of Burgundy, King Ferdinand II and Queen Isabella of Spain. Successors: Philip II and Emperor Ferdinand I.

When Charles was only six, his father died, and the young boy was transported to the household of an aunt to be raised. Charles spent his early years between two mentors who differed widely in character and opinion. His aunt Margaret of Austria, regent of the Netherlands, and his chamberlain, Sieur de Chievres, clashed often. Since both exercised great influence on the young Habsburg prince, it "taught him that authorities may clash," one historian has observed, "and that however great one's sense of reverence one must often neglect the counsels of age and decide for oneself." Charles's guardians also assigned a priest, Adrian of Utrecht (who would later become Pope Adrian VI), to serve as the prince's spiritual guide. The young Habsburg enjoyed hunting, music, singing, art, and architecture. Yet he despised learning Latin, Greek, or any other ancient language.

At 15, Charles became ruler of the Netherlands. In 1516, upon his grandfather's death, he inherited Spain and her vast empire. A year later, when he visited Spain, the immature monarch brought with him a coterie of Flemish advisers, which led to much resentment among the Castilians. Although he stayed until 1520, he was young, unsure of himself, and utterly unfamiliar with the language or customs of his proud Spanish subjects. Spain, and especially the province of Castile, however, remained the heart of his far-flung realm for the remainder of his life.

Due to the influence of the Habsburg dynasty and a loan of 850,000 florins of bribe money from the wealthy Jacob Fugger banking syndicate, Charles gained the critical election in 1519 as Holy Roman Emperor. His election came at the expense of the young and dashing Francis I and the robust Henry VIII and initiated a rivalry between the three young kings that was to last for the balance of their natural lives.

In 1520, Castile erupted in the Revolt of the *Comuneros* (shareholders) over resentment of the Flemish influence at Charles's court. The emperor, in Germany at the time, had left Adrian behind as Spanish regent. Upon his return, Charles brutally crushed the rebellion and executed over 270 people. Yet curiously from that time on, Charles became primarily a "Spanish king," and the people of Spain adopted him with an uncompromising affection.

Martin Luther Initiates Protestant Reformation

When Charles was only 17, an obscure German monk named **Martin Luther** nailed his *95 Theses* to a Catholic church door in Wittenberg. In his now-famous attack on the Church, Luther listed his grievances with Roman Catholicism and initiated the Protestant Reformation in Europe. Occupied by the bitterly fought election as Emperor and by the *Comuneros'* revolt, Charles neglected Luther as an insignificant heretic during the critical years of 1517 to 1521 when the Lutheran movement gained much momentum, especially in Germany and the Netherlands.

In 1521, Charles summoned the truculent Luther before the Imperial Diet at Worms to explain himself. In an epic face-to-face confrontation with the emperor, the German priest refused to budge on his controversial views. Charles, in turn, rejected Luther's doctrine and thereafter considered him a heretic beyond the scope of rehabilitation:

> [I]t is a great provocation that a single monk of erring opinions should rise up against the Faith that Christendom has practised for a thousand years, and would teach us that all Christians ... have been in error. Therefore I am determined to pledge for this cause all my realms, my friends, my body, my life and my soul ... to defend the Catholic Faith.

War with France over Italy broke out in 1521. Spain and France had begun fighting over the rich and divided Italian principalities as early as

1499 when **Ferdinand II** of Aragon had defeated Louis XII of France. In those early Italian Wars, Gonsalvo de Cordoba, *el Gran Capitan,* helped forge his reputation for invincibility and that of the Spanish infantry. In fact, Spain's famed land troops did not lose a pitched battle for 150 years.

But Francis I threatened Italy. In 1515, he had triumphantly defeated Massimiliano Sforza, duke of Milan, at the Battle of Marignano. Pope Leo X and Charles V came to the aid of Sforza; the result was the tremendous victory of Spanish forces over the French at Pavia in 1525. Francis was humiliated when he was captured and removed to Madrid as a prisoner for over a year. In 1526, he agreed to leave his two sons as hostages and married Eleanor, Charles's sister and the dowager queen of Portugal. Once safely home, Francis ignobly repudiated the terms of the treaty he had signed in Madrid, and ransomed his sons for 2 million florins.

Also in 1521, a young and handsome noble lawyer from Spain had led a group of 600 Spanish adventurers against the immense Aztec Empire in Mexico. Ignoring an order from Cuba's governor not to sail, **Hernán Cortés** spurred his men forward by burning their ships—their only route of escape—once they had landed on the Yucatan peninsula. Cortés's astounding feat won tremendous lands and wealth for his Spanish sovereign.

In Europe, **Suleiman I** (the Magnificent), sultan of the Ottoman Empire from 1520, challenged Charles's authority in the Mediterranean as well as the Habsburg possessions in Central Europe. In 1526, the Turks killed King Louis of Hungary and Bohemia, and Charles V inherited these thrones also. He married Isabella of Portugal in the same year.

Meanwhile in Italy, Pope Clement VII joined Francis I and Henry VIII in the League of Cognac to oppose Charles's imperial ambitions on the peninsula. Charles's Spanish and German troops, angered by repeated delays in the payment of their wages, brutally sacked the holy city of Rome in 1527. This action at once demonstrated the massive power at Charles's disposal and also the innate limitations on the ability of 16th-century monarchs to fully control their soldiers. Clement, who had been locked away in a tower for his own safety, was horrified and quickly came to terms with Charles, as did Henry. Deserted by his allies, Francis was also forced to make peace by 1529.

When the Turks continued to menace Europe, most of Christendom's desperate rulers turned to Charles V for protection. In 1529, and again three years later, Charles's imperial forces united with his brother's, Ferdinand I, to defeat the Turks before the very gates of Vienna.

Charles Is Crowned Holy Roman Emperor

With their hostilities behind them, Clement VII crowned Charles as Holy Roman Emperor at Bologna in 1530. Negotiations continued between the emperor and those of his subjects who had embraced the Protestant faith—but to no avail. The Protestants offered an explanation of their doctrine in the Confession of Augsburg, and the Catholics countered with the Confutation. Meanwhile Luther, forced to defend himself, became even more radical in his views.

Francisco Pizarro, an illegitimate ex-indentured servant, won for Charles V one of Spain's most spectacular victories when he conquered the fabled Inca Empire in 1533. Landing on the Pacific coast of Peru with just "180 men, 37 horses and two cannons," the intrepid Pizarro accomplished one of the most incredible coups of all time. The enormous wealth of the Incas was to fuel Spanish foreign policy well into the 17th century.

At Tunis, the Emperor triumphantly captured a Turkish stronghold and became the hero of all Christendom when he liberated thousands of Christians who had been held prisoner by the Turks. A year later, Charles appeared before the College of Cardinals and Pope Paul III in Rome to challenge Francis I and to decide the fate of Italy through personal combat. Francis, who fancied himself a chivalrous knight throughout his entire reign, abruptly refused. Charles then invaded Provence, but operations bogged down and Paul III interceded, bringing about a temporary truce in 1538.

That same year, Charles rushed to Ghent to quash a rebellion of local elites under the rule of his sister, Mary of Hungary. Again the Emperor exhibited little tolerance for challenges to his authority as he executed 13 of the rebels. Several years later, in 1541, Charles suffered a major disappointment when a large-scale amphibious assault on the Ottoman base of Algiers had to be aborted due to inclement weather.

Charles vacillated in 1542 between renouncing his claim to Milan in the interest of peace with Francis I or bequeathing the duchy to his son **Philip II.** In the end, he decided on Philip, and a fresh war between the houses of Habsburg and Valois began. Charles defeated the French king, and then agreed on terms. Instrumental in his decision to bestow Milan on Philip instead of on his Valois rival was the advice of his Venetian ambassador, Don Diego Mendoza:

> Milan is the gateway to Italy. Let it but once fall into the hands of the French and all your friends in the peninsula will desert you.

Finally in 1543, Paul III convened the long-awaited Council of Trent to reform the Roman Catholic Church from within. The council ended with a basic reaffirmation of Catholic doctrine—but with a decidedly more tolerant tone. Still, the troubles between Protestants and Catholics in Europe were only in their infancy. Charles's enemies, the German Protestant princes, sought collective protection from the Spanish colossus by banding together in an elaborate alliance known as the Schmalkaldic League. Historian Royall Tyler observes:

> Charles had seen the bloodshed, chaos and ruin that followed upon the overthrow of the Old Religion in parts of Germany; also the atrocities committed by the Anabaptists, there and in the Low Countries.... He believed that to burn a few heretics would be a lesser evil than what he had witnessed and what still might follow.

Accordingly in 1547, Charles V won arguably his greatest victory as 70,000 imperial soldiers annihilated the forces of the German Protestant princes at Muhlberg. Although hostilities ended for a time, by 1551 the German princes had found another ally in the new king of France, Henry II. One German elector even came dangerously close to capturing the emperor himself.

After Muhlberg, Charles V concentrated more and more of his foreign policy on marriage rather than war. In 1554, his labors were rewarded when he brought elusive England into the Spanish orbit by marrying his son Philip II to the Catholic English queen, **Mary Tudor.** (Parliament would refuse to recognize Philip as an independent monarch, and when no heirs were born by the time of Mary's death in 1558, all of the emperor's work would be for naught.)

By 1555, Charles was seriously considering abdication and retirement. Philip was of sufficient age and maturity to rule, and the enormous strain of directing such a massive empire had clearly taken its toll on Charles. In America, the Spaniards had established courts of law in eight colonies as well as three universities. Tons of silver from the mines of Potosi and Mexican and Peruvian gold and gems were streaming into Spanish ports aboard giant galleons. Charles had firmly consolidated the Spanish hold on an area "eight times the size of Castile, inhabited by one-fifth of the world's population."

Finally in January 1556, Charles V abdicated the bulk of his vast possessions in favor of Philip II and retired to a monastery at San Jeronimo de Yuste in Spain, having bestowed the prestigious title of Holy Roman Emperor and the traditional Habsburg feudal properties on his younger brother, Ferdinand I. On September 21, 1558, clutching a crucifix, Charles V died in Spain.

Although some scholars have pointed to the inconclusive events of his last years as signs of a failure on Charles's part, such a position is hardly tenable. Charles ruled vast and disparate territories for 40 years, added immensely to his possessions by unparalleled successes in the New World, and kept Spain at the very pinnacle of world power, a position she did not relinquish for 100 years. Although his efforts against the Turks were not completed, he had preserved Christendom far better than any of his peers. Through his memorable victories at Pavia and Muhlberg, he thoroughly dominated Francis I and Henry VIII, his closest rivals for Western hegemony. Charles's final years, spent largely as an adviser to his son, were not in vain. Just one year before he died, Philip decisively ended more than a half century of Habsburg-Valois conflict over Italy by demolishing the French at St. Quentin and concluding a peace which preserved Spain's preeminence at Cateau-Cambrêsis in 1559. Fittingly enough, in 1571 another son of Charles V, **Don John of Austria,** settled old Habsburg accounts by crushing the Turks in one of the world's great naval battles at Lepanto.

SOURCES:

Brandi, Karl. *The Emperor Charles V: The Growth and Destiny of a Man and of a World Empire.* Knopf, 1939.

Kohn, George C. *Dictionary of Wars.* Anchor Press, 1986.

Parker, Geoffrey. *Philip II.* Little, Brown, 1978.

von Schwarzenfeld, Gertrude. *Charles V: Father of Europe.* Henry Regnery, 1957.

Tyler, Royall. *The Emperor Charles the Fifth.* Allen & Unwin, 1956.

FURTHER READING:

Dominguez Ortiz, Antonio. *The Golden Age of Spain.* Basic Books, 1971.

Merriman, Roger B. *The Rise of the Spanish Empire in the Old World and in the New: Volume III, The Emperor.* Macmillan, 1925.

Charles VII

(1402–1461)

King of France, who lived for a decade in exile, was restored to his throne largely through the exertions of Joan of Arc, and who expelled the English from French soil, ending the Hundred Years' War.

"Physically and mentally, Charles was a weakling, a graceless degenerate."

EDOUARD PERROY

Historians have often portrayed Charles VII as one of France's worst kings: a weak, indolent, and deceitful man. The character flaws he exhibited were doubtless linked to the circumstances of his early life. He was born in 1402, the fourth son of Charles VI "the Mad" and Isabeau of Bavaria, known throughout Europe for her scandalous, profligate lifestyle. Since all of the sons of this union were weak and sickly, by 1417 young Charles was their only surviving son. Given the title duke of Touraine, he was declared the *Dauphin*, or heir to the French throne. Charles VI also made him "lieutenant-general of the king" and set him up with his own staff and advisors.

Since 1337, France had been locked in war with England over the French crown. In 1328, when Charles IV (the Fair), the last of the direct Capetian line, had died without a male heir, English king **Edward III** had claimed the French throne through his mother Isabella, Charles IV's sister. The French had denied Edward's claim (the royal succession, they insisted, could be traced only through the male line) and installed Philip of Valois, a distant cousin, on the throne as Philip VI (1328–50). When Edward III invaded France to

Born in 1402; died in 1461; fourth son of Charles VI "the Mad" and Isabeau of Bavaria; married: Marie of Anjou; children: Louis XI and others. Successor: Louis XI.

Contributed by Kimberly K. Estep, Ph.D. in History, Auburn University, Auburn, Alabama

221

CHRONOLOGY

1415	English won Battle of Agincourt; Burgundians occupied Paris; Charles fled
1420	Treaty of Troyes signed; Charles disinherited
1422	Charles VI died; Charles started calling himself Charles VII
1429	Joan of Arc appeared; siege of Orleans lifted; Charles crowned at Rheims
1435	Treaty of Arras signed with Burgundians
1436	Charles VII set up government in Paris
1453	English expelled from all of France except Calais; end of Hundred Years' War

take the throne by force, he touched off a devastating conflict that lasted over 100 years.

The Hundred Years' War had been fought sporadically. Though the English won most of the set battles, they were never able to take complete control of France. But the conflict broke out with renewed fury during the reign of Charles VI, when the young English king **Henry V** invaded France, renewing Edward III's old claim. The French fared badly in this phase of the war. French morale reached an all-time low when the English defeated France's best cavalry troops at the Battle of Agincourt in 1415.

In this time of crisis, Charles VI (cursed with recurring bouts of insanity), stood by helplessly as the English pushed further into France. His son Charles, the *Dauphin*, still in his early teens, also provided no leadership in this struggle, but in fact played into the hands of the English. In 1417, young Charles quarreled with his mother, cut off her allowance, and banished her from her estates. Fleeing Paris, Isabeau fashioned an alliance with the duke of Burgundy, John the Fearless. Technically vassals of the king of France, by the 15th century the dukes of Burgundy had become more wealthy and powerful than the king himself. When Isabeau and John the Fearless set up a rival government, they were welcomed as heroes by the people of Paris, where John the Fearless claimed title as the de facto king of France. The young Dauphin was persuaded by his supporters to lay siege to Paris, but when his troops dispersed once they got inside the city, Charles withdrew, leaving his supporters to be massacred by the pro-Burgundian mobs.

In spite of his power, John the Fearless knew that he did not have the resources to stop the English advance, so he resolved to negotiate with the

Dauphin to unite their forces against the invader. In September of 1419, both sides met on a bridge at Montereau. Discussions between the two groups became heated, and Charles's men suddenly fell upon John the Fearless, stabbing him to death. Most of France was outraged by the incident, and the northern provinces defected from the Dauphin's cause. Now, against a rapidly approaching English army, Charles could count on the support only of the central and southern parts of the realm.

By 1420, there appeared little chance that the French crown would survive the English onslaught. In a brief period of lucidity, Charles VI took frantic steps to protect himself. He offered his daughter Michelle to the new duke of Burgundy, Philip the Good. This did not prevent Philip, however, from uniting with Henry V in a pact to overthrow the Dauphin. In a last-ditch effort to save his own head, Charles VI negotiated the Treaty of Troyes (1420) with Henry V. According to the treaty, Henry would marry Charles VI's last remaining daughter, Catherine. Upon Charles VI's death, Henry V would inherit the French throne, and until that time he would act as regent of France. The young Dauphin was repudiated, disinherited, and banished from the kingdom "for his horrible crimes and misdeeds." His mother Isabeau declared that he was not the son of Charles VI at all, but a bastard of undisclosed patrimony.

After the treaty was signed, France was divided. The north and east (including Paris) accepted the treaty and supported the duke of Burgundy. The Dauphin fled to the South, where his partisans were strongest, and set up his own court at Bourges. In the north, active guerilla warfare against the English raged in the countryside for some time, but it eventually quieted when liberation was not forthcoming. When the Dauphin's strongest force suffered a crushing defeat at Verneuil in 1424, most of the people lost heart and became resigned to the new government. Charles did nothing to encourage his loyalists. Timid and apathetic, he gave up personal command of his army after 1422 and thereafter called off many planned campaigns. Hoping to be put back in power through diplomacy, he did little to regain his inheritance by force.

The Dauphin's entourage continually engaged in quarrels, intrigues, and plots. His favorites took advantage of him and sponged off the funds he gathered through taxing the loyal provinces. Although practically destitute, Charles spent what little resources he had on fine clothes and lavish entertainment. He was referred to disparagingly as the *Roi de Bourges* ("King of

Bourges"), where he sat, seemingly frozen, waiting for a change in his fate. His golden opportunity came in 1422 when Henry V fell sick and died on August 31, leaving behind an eight-month-old son. Less than two months later, Charles VI died, at the age of 54. Although Charles began referring to himself as Charles VII, he remained at Bourges, gloomy, despondent and filled with self-doubt.

Before his death, Henry V had entrusted the regency of France to his brother John, duke of Bedford. Continuing a push to gain control of all of France in the name of England's new infant king Henry VI, by 1428 Bedford was able to move against the city of Orléans, which was considered the strategic key to central France. Throughout that summer Bedford moved troops, materials and supplies in preparation for a siege. Receiving word of Bedford's preparations, the Dauphin sent troops to intercept a convoy transporting barrels of salt fish. But, in what became known as the "Day of the Herrings," the French army was beaten back by a significantly outnumbered English force. Charles's supporters looked on in dismay as the English continued to descend upon Orléans. Since it was widely believed that the fall of Orléans would guarantee total victory for the English, Charles began to make preparations to withdraw; he considered fleeing to Dauphine, or Castile, or even to Scotland.

Joan of Arc Leads Army; Dauphine Crowned

In 1429, in the wake of this widespread despair, a young peasant girl, **Joan of Arc,** made her way to Charles's court at Bourges. She claimed to have heard the voices of God's messengers telling her to seek out the Dauphin and persuade him to lead his forces to relieve Orléans. Charles would then be crowned at the ancient site of Rheims, from which he would emerge to drive the English completely from French soil. Joan's sincere conviction and the desperate nature of Charles's fortunes convinced him to follow her advice. With Joan at their head, Charles's forces marched forthwith to Orléans, where they decisively beat the English and recaptured the town. Plagued by sickness and low on supplies, the English were an easy target for Charles's fresh, well-fed army. The relief of Orléans was the turning point in the war. After almost a century of defeat, France had finally proved it could beat the English in battle. And the Dauphin, at the age of 27, was finally crowned at Rheims as Charles VII.

The same year saw an awakening of French nationalism. Many who had accepted the Treaty of Troyes because it promised an end to the destructive war were fed up with the English, who had brought further devastation. Leading the French army to continued victory over the next two years, Joan of Arc declared their mission a holy crusade, and persuaded Charles to encourage moral, godly behavior among the troops. Drinking and gambling were prohibited; the camp followers were sent home. Support for Charles's cause grew steadily, and the English were gradually pushed back towards the Channel. Finally captured in 1431 by a Burgundian soldier, Joan of Arc was delivered to the English, who put her on trial for heresy. Not surprisingly, she was convicted and sentenced to be burned at the stake. When Charles did not intervene, Joan was publicly burned on May 28, 1431, and Charles returned to his old ways.

By now everyone in France, even the Parisians, had become tired of the English occupation, but Paris still remained fiercely loyal to the duke of Burgundy. If Charles could hope to reclaim his capital, he would have to reconcile with Philip the Good. For his part, Philip was disappointed with his lot after Troyes. He had allied with the English for two main reasons: to avenge his father's death and to put himself in a position of power as the "tutor" of the new sovereign. After Henry V's death, Philip had been given no part in the regency. In the wake of Charles VII's victories over the English, Philip began looking for his best opportunity to shed the English alliance. Negotiations began by the end of 1432 but dragged on slowly, as neither side wished to make any real concessions. In order to avoid looking like a turncoat, Philip included the English in the negotiations, but when the British refused to relinquish their claim to the French Crown, Philip decided to come to terms without them. In September 1435, Philip and Charles signed the Treaty of Arras. In exchange for his support, Charles granted Philip possession of the territories he already occupied and exempted him from paying homage for his French fiefs during Charles's lifetime. Charles also sent an entourage to apologize publicly for the death of John the Fearless, and he promised to punish those responsible, to erect monuments in John's memory, and to have masses said for his soul. In return, Charles gained overnight the allegiance of all territories loyal to Burgundy.

The English troops were rapidly cleared from all of France except Normandy and Guienne. In April 1436, when royal troops entered Paris, Charles VII set up his first real administration. He was able to retain the best elements of the Valois and Burgundian administrations, which earned him the nickname "the Well Served." The two greatest changes brought about during Charles's reign were permanent taxation and military reform. The upheavals of war enabled Charles to dispense with the consent of the provincial assemblies to levy the *gabelle* (a salt tax) and the taille (a head tax). He divided the country into four areas for collecting taxes. Royal revenues jumped to an unprecedented two million livres per year. Although the power of the crown under Charles VII remained limited, French kings acquired considerable power to raise money.

Military reforms were made necessary when unemployed soldiers began rampaging the countryside. These *fleecers* terrified an already impoverished population, and forced Charles to put the military under more direct regulation. He created a permanent standing army paid by the king, which consisted of 20 companies of elite cavalry (200 lances to a company, six men on horseback to a *lance)*. These men received better and more regular pay. Charles's administration also created an infantry composed of "free archers"—men exempted from taxation and trained in their spare time to use a bow.

The End of the Hundred Years' War

Fighting broke out anew in 1441. The English war effort suffered at this period while a strong peace party urged Henry VI to withdraw from France. French armies decisively beat the English out of some of their strongholds. In May 1444, a temporary truce was devised through the marriage of Henry VI (now a young man of 23) to Charles VII's niece, Margaret of Anjou. A meeting to conclude a peace treaty was promised but never materialized. During 1445, Charles was jolted out of his lethargy by his new royal mistress, Agnes Sorel, who persuaded him to take up arms to expel the English completely. In an intense 12-month campaign, the French captured Normandy and, in August 1452, moved into Guienne. In 1453, the English army briefly reconquered Guienne, but by October Charles's forces had forced the English to surrender unconditionally. The English retained possession of the port town of Calais. The only way the French army could have reached it would have been through the territory of the duke of Burgundy. Rather than agitate the duke, Charles declared France reclaimed. No real peace treaty was ever drawn up, but hostilities between the French and the English ceased for 116 years.

Once the war was over, Charles set out to rehabilitate his image. He commissioned a new inquiry into Joan of Arc, which overturned the verdict of the English court and declared her a good and faithful Catholic. Charles benefited from the widespread hatred of the English, emerging from the struggle as the symbol of the nation. The financial difficulties of the postwar era forced the nobility and clergy to rely more heavily upon the King's pleasure.

The Hundred Years' War left France ravaged and scarred, and the countryside had still not recovered from its effects at Charles's death in 1461. The duke of Burgundy remained a powerful competitor, but Charles was able to keep him out of positions of real authority. As Charles's life neared its end, however, Philip's opportunity arose. In 1456, Charles's son, the future Louis XI, quarreled with his father and left the court to become the protégé of the duke of Burgundy.

SOURCES:

Allmand, Christopher. *The Hundred Years' War: England and France at War c.1300–c.1450*. Cambridge: Cambridge University Press, 1988.

Goubert, Pierre. *The Course of French History*. Translated by Maarten Ultie. Franklin Watts, 1988.

Lewis, P. S. *Essays in Later Medieval French History*. London: Hambledon Press, 1985.

Perroy, Edouard. *The Hundred Years' War*. London: Eyre & Spottiswoode, 1959.

FURTHER READING:

Lewis, P. S. *The Recovery of France in the Fifteenth Century*. Harper, 1971.

Sackville-West, Victoria. *Saint Joan of Arc*. G. K. Hall, 1984.

Tuchman, Barbara. *A Distant Mirror: The Calamitous 14th Century*. Knopf, 1984.

Charles XII of Sweden

(1687–1718)

Swedish king and one of the greatest soldiers of his day, who led his armies in the "Great Northern War" in defense of the Swedish "Baltic Empire."

"The sword makes the best conditions, it always means what it says."

CHARLES XII OF SWEDEN

He is remembered by history as the last of the royal adventurers, a monarch who—sword in hand—risked his life in battle at the head of his regiments. Posterity has hailed him as a great commander and warlord, a hero in the medieval mold. But he is also remembered as the king who led Sweden into a war that lasted over 20 years and which ended ultimately in Sweden's fall from her position as a great European power.

Charles XII, of the House of Vasa, was born on June 17, 1687, in Stockholm Castle. As the firstborn son and heir to the throne, the future king had a happy and secure childhood. His education was carefully planned in its emphasis on the military arts and the complexities of European politics. His father, Charles XI, was concerned that his son should be trained to rule as an absolute and enlightened monarch, and that nothing should sway him from his foremost duty, which was the defense and welfare of his subjects and kingdom.

Charles quickly grew to kingly stature. Close to six feet tall, of a slim and wiry build, he had deep blue eyes and fair brown hair. His features were marked by a strong jaw and a broad nose. Parental worries that he might grow up sickly soon van-

Contributed by Kevin Cramer, Ph.D. candidate in history, Harvard University, Cambridge, Massachusetts

Name variations: Carl, of the royal House of Vasa; nicknamed the Swedish Meteor. Born on June 17, 1687; killed at seige of Frederiksten, November 30, 1718 [some sources cite December 11]; son of Charles XI and Princess Ulrika Eleonora of Denmark; never married, no known children. Successor: Queen Ulrika Eleonora (sister).

CHRONOLOGY

ished as the young prince hardened his body for the vicissitudes of warfare by many hours on horseback, hunting the bears and wolves of Sweden's fir forests.

That Charles might be expected to fight in defense of his kingdom was not an unreasonable supposition. Sweden owed her position as a great power to the territorial gains she had made as a consequence of the Treaty of Westphalia in 1648, which ended the Thirty Years' War. Partially as a result of the victories of King **Gustavus Adolfus,** Sweden emerged as a guarantor of the peace and had received valuable lands in northern Germany. Sweden also ruled the Baltic provinces of Livonia, Estonia, and Ingria on the southern littoral (coastal region) of the Gulf of Finland.

A glance at a map, circa 1700, shows plainly that Sweden was a power in northern Europe by virtue of her control of these territories. This "Baltic Empire" enabled her to oversee the valuable trade in grain, timber, hides, and ore that flowed from Eastern Europe to the markets of the Atlantic. Sweden's Baltic holdings also made a tempting target for the designs of the ambitious rulers of Denmark, Russia, Prussia, and Saxony. Charles XII's career would be the story of the battles to maintain Sweden's Baltic position on which her great power was based.

After his father's death in late 1697, the 15-year-old prince was crowned king in December of 1697. Though a minor, he was not restrained by a regency, and he pursued his father's absolutist policies with diligence, paying particular attention to the military reforms initiated by the late ruler.

By 1698, Charles had a firm grip on the reins of power, and he turned his attention to the threat of Danish bellicosity and Russian expansion along the Baltic under **Peter the Great.** Both Denmark and Russia looked to an alliance with Augustus II, ruler of Saxony and the elected king of Poland.

The "Great Northern War" Begins

This threatening combination became reality in the spring of 1700, when Frederick IV of Denmark invaded Schleswig, menacing the Duchy of Holstein-Gottorp, an ally of Sweden. In February, Saxon troops had invaded Swedish Livonia. The "Great Northern War" had begun.

With characteristic speed and resolve, Charles assembled his army and fleet and daringly landed in Denmark at the head of his troops in July. By August, Copenhagen had been blockaded and Frederick was brought to terms at the Peace of Travendal. Charles had his first victory. He was 18 years old.

Charles now looked to the east, seeking to punish the "treachery" of Augustus, who had besieged the Livonian port of Riga. Diplomacy was not congenial to the headstrong King, and his advisors were helpless to change his mind once it was decided. Sweden's resources were extremely limited, and the decision not to negotiate with a willing Saxony after Travendal was a serious error. But Charles had declared upon leaving Stockholm: "I have resolved never to begin an unrighteous war; but I have also resolved never to finish a righteous war till I have utterly crushed my enemies."

Charles landed in the Gulf of Riga in October 1700 and relieved Riga. Intimidated, Augustus withdrew into winter quarters. Then Charles marched to deal with the Russians. In November, the Swedish regiments, some 11,000 men, arrived at the fortress of Narva after a long trek through heavy snow and rain. Charles's army confronted 40,000 Russians. The next day, Charles led his men in a surprise morning attack in a driving snowstorm. Shouting their battle cry, "With God's help!," the Swedes drove the Tsar's men in a panic from their trenches. Many drowned as a bridge across the river Narova collapsed.

This famous victory, fought at long odds, established Charles as a military genius. The young warrior King now loomed large in the councils of Europe's crowned heads. So balanced were the opposing forces in the War of the Spanish Succession that Sweden's intervention on either side would have been decisive. But Charles was not to be diverted from his "righteous war." Above all, he felt it was his primary duty to defend Swedish territory. This meant the defeat of Denmark, Russia, and Saxony, and the pacification of Poland.

With the Russians temporarily cowed, Charles briskly made preparations to deal with Saxony. Having received information that Augustus had concluded an alliance with Tsar Peter, Charles decided on quick action. Accordingly, he and his Swedes descended on Courland in a spectacular amphibious assault across the river Dvina in July 1701, scattering the Saxons in surprised retreat. The Duchy of Courland was occupied, and Charles made ready for a renewal of the campaign in the spring of 1702. He was determined that Augustus should be stripped of his Polish crown.

Throughout the summer of 1702, Charles chased the Saxon army south, winning a dramatic victory at Kliszow and capturing Cracow and Warsaw. Yet a decisive decision over Augustus eluded him. In the spring of 1703, Charles marched north from Warsaw along the Vistula, capturing the key fortress of Thorn in October. He was now in a strong position in Poland, and in February he forced the Polish Diet to deprive Augustus of his throne and elect the Swedish candidate, Stanislas Lesczynski.

During the winter of 1705–06, Charles's marched east in pursuit of the Russian-Saxon army. When the Russians retreated beyond the river Niemen, Courland and Lithuania were freed from the immediate threat of invasion. Charles's diplomatic and military advisors counseled him to advance to the Baltic and recover the territories that Peter had seized. Charles, however, was adamant that Saxony should be brought decisively to heel and Poland secured. He acknowledged that, "we may be a long time on this side of the Baltic."

By July 1706, Charles's army had entered Silesia. With the Saxons retreating before him, by September Charles reached the Saxon capital of Dresden. He then forced Augustus to relinquish the Polish crown, to give up his alliance with the Tsar, and to provide winter quarters for the Swedish forces. These conditions were embodied in the Treaty of Altranstädt, which marked the zenith of Charles's prestige and influence in Europe. France, Prussia, Britain, and Austria vied for his favor. But Charles wanted to avoid entanglement in the War of the Spanish Succession. Convinced that the immediate threat to Sweden was to the east, he planned an invasion of Russia aimed at the capture of Moscow. Narva had caused the King to seriously underestimate Russian martial prowess, and he believed that only a decisive victory would free Sweden from the Russian menace.

The Campaign Against Russia

In August 1707, Charles led his fit and rested regiments eastward out of Saxony. This began a long and exhausting war of maneuver, march and counter-march across the vast plains of Poland. The Russians ravaged the land as they retreated, and the Swedish soldiers were hard pressed to find food and forage in the desolate countryside. In January 1708, the Swedes reached the Niemen.

By July, Charles had pursued the Russians to Mohilev on the river Dnieper, but he had still not been able to engage the bulk of the Russian army. The Swedish forces were exhausted, short of supplies, and laid low by disease. In September, Charles had no choice but to turn south into the Ukraine, where he hoped to find much-needed supplies and allies. Bogged down by wet weather, his supply train from the Baltic had never arrived, and his army was dwindling along the line of the tortuous march. One of the King's officers wrote in his diary, "… hunger and want will drive us out."

Charles now hoped to establish winter quarters in the Ukraine and gain allies among the restive Cossack princes, who chafed under Muscovite rule. It was a turning point in the campaign in Russia, an acknowledgment by Charles that the road to Moscow was blocked and that the decisive battle still eluded him.

The Russians had managed to precede the Swedes into the region, and the countryside was as ravaged as before. Also, the winter of 1708–09 was incomparably severe. Thousands of men and horses died from this "cold beyond description," and many more were maimed by frostbite. Charles and his army faced a desperate situation. However, by the spring of 1709, Charles felt he had some reason for optimism. With Cossack help, the supply situation had improved, and Charles prepared to draw the Russians into a decisive engagement by laying seige to the fortress of Poltava, which commanded the main road through Kharkov to Moscow. Although he did not have enough men for a proper seige, Charles hoped to lure the Tsar into battle. He also hoped for the timely arrival of the Polish Crown Army under King Stanislas, as the Swedes would be badly outnumbered by the Russians.

The battle of Poltava began at dawn in July 1709. Weeks earlier, on his birthday, Charles had been shot in the foot. As he could not ride, he was forced to observe the battle from a stretcher. Consequently, the Swedish command was divided, which would have disastrous results.

The Swedish attack against the Russian fortified camp north of Poltava went badly from the start. The Russians were entrenched and their guns decimated the already thin ranks of the advancing Swedes. A Swedish attempt to outflank the Russians to the northwest failed dismally and broke up in disorder. The main body facing the Russian redoubts (barriers) became divided and was forced to break off the attack. Very quickly, the Swedish attack collapsed and Charles's men were in full retreat toward the south, leaving behind 7,000 dead and 3,000 prisoners.

The wounded and feverish King now faced a difficult decision. Should he stay with what remained of his army and try to retreat into Poland, or should he make his way ahead of the main body, to raise another force? He decided, reluctantly, on the latter course, but found his way blocked to the west. He traveled by coach, with a small guard, south through the domains of the Cossacks toward the Ottoman Empire. In the meantime, the remnants of his army had surrendered.

The impact of Poltava had an immediate effect on European politics. The anti-Swedish coalition revived, and Tsar Peter was free to renew his march into Poland and the Baltic provinces. In July, Charles found himself a "guest" of the Porte (the government of the Ottoman Empire), enduring a gilded exile in the Bessarabian town of Bender. Russian and Saxon troops blocked his return to Poland, and he would not contemplate a return to Sweden by sea, fearing capture.

Charles spent these "lazy dog days" in Turkey trying to bring the Sultan into the war with Russia and corresponding with his ministers in Stockholm on all manner of domestic affairs of the kingdom. He was determined that a relief army be raised and sent to Poland, in hopes that he might reach it and renew the war against Sweden's enemies. He categorically rejected all appeals for negotiation.

Charles was ultimately unsuccessful in his efforts to persuade the Sultan to sustain his war with Russia, and peace between the two empires was concluded in 1711. Between 1709 and 1713, the Danes had besieged Bremen, and the Saxons and Russians had invaded Swedish Pomerania. With Swedish fortunes at such a low ebb, King Charles had become somewhat of a diplomatic liability to the Sultan. In 1713, the local khan attacked the Swedish compound in Bender and narrowly missed capturing the King.

In the meantime, the Treaty of Utrecht had ended the War of Spanish Succession, and the ensuing peace in central Europe made it safe for Charles to travel through the Habsburg domains. German Emperor Charles VI extended every courtesy to the wandering monarch, believing that Charles and Sweden could be useful as a brake on the expansionary aims of the north German princes.

The epic "ride to Stralsund" began on September 20, 1714, with Charles traveling incognito as "Captain Peter Frisk." Covering almost 1,300 miles in two weeks, Charles and his small party reached Stralsund in Swedish Pomerania on November 11.

Stralsund came under seige by the Danes and Prussians in the winter of 1715, and the weakened Swedes could not hold the town, despite Charles's valiant efforts. On December 22, 1715, Charles left the burning and ruined port ahead of the Prussians, arriving in Sweden by a small boat on Christmas Eve. He immediately began organizing another campaign and raising another army. He did not return to Stockholm, the capital he had last seen 15 years earlier.

An invasion of the Danish possession of Norway was now contemplated, as a means to divert Denmark from a descent on Sweden's southern provinces. The attack was launched in February of 1716 and was basically successful in preventing the assault on Scania, even though by June the army had pulled back to its starting positions. The anti-Swedish coalition was increasingly infirm, as Tsar Peter withdrew his troops in reaction to Danish and Prussian refusal to allow Russian troops to enter Wismar. Russian power was pushing uncomfortably westward.

Charles now settled into his headquarters and "court" in the small town of Lund in Scania. He devoted his time to the continuing economic and fiscal reorganization of his kingdom, attempting to distribute the burdens of the war more fairly. The Swedish people were tired of the war and longed for peace. This period, known as the "Gortzian time," after Charles's chief minister Baron Gortz, was marked by increasing austerity, a debased coinage, and the introduction of conscription. Clearly, Sweden was very close to the end of her tether.

Diplomatically, Charles had two choices: peace with Russia or peace with Denmark, in order to concentrate Sweden's dwindling resources on one enemy or the other. Charles favored negotiation with Russia, as he was pessimistic about an attack in the eastern Baltic. Gortz also supported this position. Consequently, Charles began planning another attack into Norway and raising a new army. He hoped operations in Norway would train the recruits for Continental operations, through which he would try to bring Denmark, Hanover, and Prussia to the table to negotiate a "tolerable peace."

In late summer of 1718, Charles led his newly recruited regiments into southern Norway, aiming at the capture of Kristiana and Bergen. He exhorted his officers at the beginning of his last campaign: "Our parties must be told to act in the old manner, to attack the enemy without pausing to reflect whether the enemy is stronger or weaker. They must breakthrough with sword in hand." Militarily, this was his last throw of the dice.

The initial phase of the attack aimed at clearing access to the road network leading to Kristiana, along the east coast of Kristianfjord. These roads were blocked by the fortress of Frederiksten. By the end of November, Charles was directing the seige, personally supervising the engineers as they pushed their trenches closer to the walls. In the late evening of November 30, 1718, the King was inspecting the seige works, the trenches lit by a full moon and the glare of torches on the fortress walls. As he lay prone on a parapet facing a Norwegian outwork, he was struck in the head by an enemy bullet. He died instantly. His last words to his officers had been, "Do not be afraid." He was 32 years old.

Charles XII's career has been problematic for historians, especially in Sweden. Was he a vainglorious adventurer who had led Sweden to ruin, or was he a "patriot-king" in the mold of Gustavus Adolfus, who defended his kingdom and its honor and glory till he too fell on the battlefield? There is no doubt that Charles was stubborn and rigidly devoted to a personal code of honor that found the double-dealing of diplomacy distasteful. Yet war was not his only passion. He was an enthusiastic and informed patron of the arts and was very interested in building and architecture. He spent much of his time planning the modernization of his kingdom, surrounded as it was by greedy neighbors. He honestly believed that his solemn duty as king would not permit him to cede any of Sweden's territories in a "bad peace." However, Sweden did not have the resources to defend her Baltic Empire against the rising power of Russia and Prussia. Charles's epic campaigns in the wildernesses of Poland and Russia kept the wolves from the door for much longer than could have been expected. Sweden's only hope, ultimately, had lain in a crushing victory over Peter the Great's Russia. That had been Charles's aim from the start. Yet that hope had died in the heat and dust of Poltava.

SOURCES:

Bain, R. Nisbet. *Charles XII and the Collapse of the Swedish Empire.* Putnam, 1895.

Bengtsson, Frans G. *The Life of Charles XII, King of Sweden, 1697–1718.* [1935]. Translated by Naomi Walford. London: Macmillan, 1960.

Godley, Eveline. *Charles XII of Sweden: A Study in Kingship.* London: Collins, 1928.

Hatton, R. M. *Charles XII of Sweden.* London: Weidenfeld & Nicolson, 1968.

FURTHER READING:

Klingspor, Carl Gustafson. *Charles the Twelfth King of Sweden.* Translated by John A. Gade. Houghton Mifflin, 1916.

Roberts, Michael. *The Swedish Imperial Experience, 1560–1718.* Cambridge: Cambridge University Press, 1979.

Scott, Franklin D. *Sweden: The Nation's History.* Southern Illinois University Press, 1988.

Voltaire. *The History of Charles XII of Sweden.* [1731] Translated by Antonia White. London: Folio Society, 1976.

Christian IV

(1577–1648)

Denmark's most renowned king, who led his country through a period of political and cultural ascendancy but also mired it in a costly war against Sweden and the devastating Thirty Years' War in Germany.

Born at Frederiksborg Castle in Hillerod, Denmark, on April 12, 1577; died in February 1648; son of Frederick II (king of Denmark and Norway) and Sophia of Mecklenburg; married: Anna Catherine of Brandenburg (died 1612); married: Kirsten Munk; children: (first marriage) Frederick; (second marriage) twelve. Predecessor: Frederick II. Successor: His son, Frederick III.

At Frederiksborg Castle in Hillerod, Denmark, the future Christian IV was born on April 12, 1577, to Frederick II, king of Denmark and Norway, and Sophia of Mecklenburg. The young boy was given an intense education typical of other European princes. Among his many subjects, he was instructed in the art of fencing, dancing, military command, and navigation; he also studied Latin, German, French, and Italian. In 1588, when the 11-year-old Christian's father died, the young prince became king. He would have to wait until 1596, however, until he reached 19—the age of majority—for his coronation and the start of his personal rule. Meanwhile, Denmark was governed by a regency from the *rigsraad* ("privy council"), the very body which Christian IV would later battle for his political authority.

In 1597, Christian IV married Anna Catherine of Brandenburg. Though she died in 1612, she bore him a son and heir, the future King Frederick III. Three years later, Christian remarried, this time to a Danish woman named Kirsten Munk who was to bear him 12 children. But Christian eventually banished his second wife from

Contributed by Alan M. James, Ph.D., University of Manchester, Manchester, England

230

the court for having committed adultery. Considering Christian's own reputation for promiscuity, this charge was, at the very least, incongruous.

Yet Christian's personal life was much more renowned for his gambling and heavy drinking. An English visitor to the Danish court once noted, "Such is the life of that king, to drink all day and lye with a whore every night." And such was the influence of Christian's personality that the customary heavy drinking of the Danish court became fashionable among other Protestant princes in Germany. Nevertheless, Christian IV attended to matters of much more seriousness, and his influence went well beyond mere indulgence.

Throughout his career, his greatest concern was the protection and invigoration of the power of his crown. The aristocracy in Denmark had put itself in an enviable political position with respect to the monarchy. The *rigsraad*, which was dominated by the wealthy landowning nobility, held extensive powers, including the right to approve extraordinary taxes and the right to veto the declaration of war. Moreover, the regency government prior to 1596 had been reasonably successful in the management of finances, and landowners generally benefited handsomely from an overall prosperity in Denmark. Thus, from the outset of his personal rule, Christian was challenged to defend his authority against a powerful and wealthy nobility.

Christian IV undertook many projects toward the commercial invigoration of the realm. Yet he realized that to develop his financial strength was the most effective method of preserving his political independence; of his many different activities, the sound management of his personal finances was to be his most resounding success. Through land speculation (with many interests in north Germany) and by lending money, he accrued a vast personal fortune. In this way, he was able to bind much of the Danish nobility to him politically as, for example, from 1618 to 1624 (a time of economic crisis) when he provided much needed capital. It was his wealth (or, his "ten tons of gold," as it was called) and the corresponding political independence that it afforded him that was to make Christian IV one of the most powerful figures in early 17th-century Europe.

Crucial to Christian's personal finances was the control of narrow Danish waterways that gave the only access in and out of the Baltic Sea. Where the Sound is narrowest, the Danes had erected a number of castles, including one at Elsinore (Helsingör), as elaborate tollbooths on one of Europe's busiest channels. For 428 years, ships had to pay Sound dues ("a toll") and dip their flag as they passed the castle. Much to the chagrin of neighboring countries, whenever Denmark needed revenue, it raised the tolls. In 1599, Christian headed to North Cape: in part, to exploit Danish holdings in the far north of Norway; in part, to prevent the discovery of a northerly sea route to northern Russia, which could bypass the Sound and weaken Danish control. Any such opening threatened both Denmark and Christian personally.

At this time, Sweden clearly presented the greatest challenge to Denmark. Up to 1570 (the Treaty of Stettin), Sweden had struggled to escape Danish overlordship. Now, Sweden's growing military strength (including direct involvement in the eastern Baltic) actively threatened Danish dominance. Equally, an increasing Swedish presence (especially from 1606–09) jeopardized Denmark's presence in Norway. Despite the Danish Council's desire to maintain peace with Sweden and to pursue an isolationist foreign policy with respect to the maelstrom of European politics, Christian spent a considerable amount of money preparing for war. He built up a significant naval force and fortified important cities and fortresses along the Swedish frontier.

Denmark Declares War on Sweden

Finally, on April 4, 1611, Christian had his way, and Denmark declared war on Sweden. Very

CHRONOLOGY

1577	Born at Frederiksborg Castle
1588	Frederick II died; Christian acceded to the throne
1596	Reached age of majority; personal rule began
1611	Gustavus Adolphus succeeded Charles IX of Sweden
1613	Peace of Knäred ended Christian's first war with Sweden
1618	Start of Thirty Years' War between the Protestant Union and the Catholic League in Germany
1626	Christian suffered defeat against Catholic forces at Lutter-am-Barenberg
1629	Treaty of Lübeck ended Danish war with Ferdinand II in Germany
1645	Peace of Bromsbero ended Christian's second war with Sweden
1648	Christian IV died; Peace of Westphalia ended Thirty Years' War

quickly, the important holding of Kalmar fell to the Danes. By October, upon the death of the Swedish king Charles IX, it appeared that a precarious situation would be inherited by his successor, the illustrious **Gustavus Adolphus.** Over the next two years, Denmark continued to fight Sweden to protect its powerful interests in the Baltic and in the north. And, The Dutch (The Netherlands), in whose interest it was to stabilize the Baltic and ultimately to free the Sound from the Danish monopoly, intervened to end the fighting and act as intermediaries between the belligerents. At the Peace of Knäred (January 1613), Sweden agreed to renounce its expansionist intentions and to pay exacting reparations to Christian personally.

Thus Christian IV was in a very favorable position. Having successfully controlled Danish foreign policy and established himself as a military figure of some note, he now enjoyed unprecedented fortune and independence. Yet his influence was not restricted to the Baltic. King Christian IV was also the Duke of Holstein, and as such he held a great deal of influence among the other Lutheran princes of Germany. Thus, the Dutch and their allies increasingly hoped to involve this wealthy and newly powerful force in the Protestant struggle on behalf of **Frederick V** of the Palatinate against the emperor **Ferdinand II** and Catholic hegemony ("influence") in Germany.

In 1624, when Gustavus Adolphus was invited to lead an allied army against the forces of the Catholic emperor, Ferdinand II, Christian perceived this as a threat to his position. Thus, in January 1625, he rashly offered to raise and lead an army himself. This he did over the protests of his Council and without securing the necessary assurance of support from his allies. Assuming the role of Defender of the Protestant Faith, he led an army of about 20,000 mercenary soldiers south in June of that year.

At the time, it looked as if the Danish invasion of Germany would be straightforward. Yet unbeknownst to Christian, Ferdinand II had brought into his employ the wealthy **Albrecht von Wallenstein** who had assembled an army of his own of about 30,000 men. Threatened by this additional force, Christian was compelled to withdraw.

Catholic Forces Defeat Christian

In this way, the King lost much of his international support, but at the Hague Convention in December of 1625, the English and the Dutch agreed to continue to back Christian's army. The next year, at a time when Wallenstein was distracted, Christian invaded again; by August he had set forth from Wolfenbuttel. After days of heavy fighting in the rain at Lutter-am-Barenberg, Christian was soundly defeated, losing half his men and artillery. After this disastrous defeat, Denmark was left vulnerable to foreign invasion. In a strangely matter-of-fact tone, however, Christian's diary entry for August 26, 1626, reads simply: "Fought with the enemy and lost. The same day I went to Wolfenbuttel."

Thereafter, Christian's fortunes did not improve greatly, whereas Wallenstein met with many successes against the Protestant forces, including a decisive rout of Christian's army at Wolgast in September 1628. While awaiting Christian's surrender, Wallenstein invaded and occupied the entire Jutland peninsula, enabling Ferdinand to issue enormous demands (Edict of Restitution). Christian was to renounce any claims to territory in Germany, cede all of Jutland, and pay overwhelming reparations. And, for their support of Christian, the dukes of Mecklenburg were stripped of their titles; these were given to Wallenstein.

All this, Christian and the Protestant cause could not allow. Thus, even Sweden joined in a defensive alliance with the King early in 1629. Together, these reluctant allies successfully defended Straslund against Wallenstein in 1628. But Denmark was desperate for peace and reentered negotiations with Ferdinand II. By the Treaty of Lübeck of May 1629, Christian was allowed to regain his lost territories. Nevertheless, his military failures left him exhausted and utterly discredited.

This Danish phase of the Thirty Years' War cost Christian, and Denmark, enormously. The forests of Jutland had been devastated, finances were drained, and the resentful population was forced to pay the occupying imperial army for which they suffered greatly. Heavy taxation, epidemic disease, and a bad harvest added to the people's misery. Personally, Christian no longer had the luxury of his fortune. Yet his ambitions were not satisfied, and he hoped to consolidate his position and to continue to spend on defense.

The Council was willing to raise more money for its King, but it insisted that it control the collection and distribution. Initially, Christian was furious with any such attempt to restrict his authority and demanded an unconditional offer, even threatening to refuse to abide by the peace with Ferdinand II. Since further war would have been devastating, the Council agreed. By 1637, however, Christian had spent the new funds and was forced to accept that the aristocracy would have significant control over the administration of taxes. To counter this dependence, Christian attempted to extract more revenue from the Sound tolls. Not surprisingly, this antagonized Sweden, whose power had grown notably after successful intervention in Europe from 1630. Once again Denmark was in serious danger.

To make matters worse, Christian again interfered in German affairs. He managed to persuade Ferdinand II to use him as the mediator between the German Empire and Sweden. If necessary, Christian suggested that he might even join forces with the Empire. In exchange, Christian hoped to gain control of Hamburg and the mouth of the Elbe, which his naval forces blockaded early in 1643. At the same time, Christian made overtures to Poland, Russia, and the German Emperor about an offensive alliance that he hoped to direct against Sweden. Under such provocation and pressure, Sweden declared war on Denmark on May 25, 1643.

Soon the Swedish forces that were in Bohemia headed toward Denmark, and in 1644 Jutland again was easily overrun. In a disastrous naval battle, in which the Dutch intervened on Sweden's behalf, Christian lost an eye. He also lost the islands of Oesel and Gotland. By the Peace of Bromsbero (August 25, 1645), Sweden won almost complete exemption from the Sound tolls. Moreover, Sweden was given important territory on its side of the Sound, effectively ending Denmark's exclusive control of the straits and its status as a major European power.

The withdrawal of Swedish forces was followed by renewed harvest failure and plague in Denmark from 1647 to 1651. The population fell by almost 20% in this period of general suffering. In February 1648, Christian died a broken man, conceding military defeat to his neighbors and political defeat to the aristocrats of his country. Indeed, his son had to bargain for months just to secure his election to the throne.

Although Christian IV failed in his attempts to be a great military leader, he was an industrious king who tried to epitomize the ideal of the Renaissance prince. He concerned himself with the minutest details in the administration of his country (not simply with military and naval hardware). He personally set Denmark's mercantilist policies and founded companies. His interests were varied, and as a result he brought many of the early Renaissance cultural influences to Denmark. Numerous cities were founded and built under Christian IV, including Kristiania (modern-day Oslo). He is even credited with considerable architectural achievement. Moreover, he subsidized students and built a residential college for university students in Copenhagen. Notes historian Palle Lauring:

> He worked and he gave orders. More than 3,000 letters originating from his own hand have been preserved. He was indefatigable. Nothing escaped his attention and he poked his nose into everything. He ruled his two kingdoms rather in the manner of a careful country squire, and completed one building after another in the manner of an efficient building contractor.

Thus, despite his military failures and their destructive legacy, Christian IV personally brought Denmark into the politics of Europe as a major power and led it through a period of greatness. He was a leader of tremendous influence, and he remains one of Denmark's most popular kings.

SOURCES:

Lauring, Palle. *A History of the Kingdom of Denmark.* Translated by David Hohnen. Høst and Søn, 1963.

Parker, Geoffrey. *Europe in Crisis: 1598–1648.* Cornell University Press, 1979.

Petersen, E. Ladewig. "Finance and the Growth of Absolutism: Some Aspects of the European Integration of Seventeenth-Century Denmark," in *Europe and Scandinavia: Aspects of the Process of Integration in the Seventeenth Century.* Edited by G. Rystad. Scandinavia University Books, 1983: pp. 33-49.

———. "The Danish Intermezzo," in *The Thirty Years' War.* Edited by Geoffrey Parker. Military Heritage Press, 1987.

Christina
of Sweden

(1626–1689)

Queen of Lutheran Sweden, who abdicated at the height of Sweden's power during the Thirty Years' War, converted to Catholicism, and spent the second half of her life in Rome.

Born in 1626; died and buried in St. Peter's, in Rome, in 1689; daughter of Gustavus II Adolphus, King of Sweden, and Maria Eleanora Hohenzollern of Brandenberg; unmarried and with no heirs. Predecessor: Gustavus Adolphus. Successor: her cousin, Charles X.

Queen Christina is one of the most unusual monarchs in European history. Inheriting her throne at the age of six, she was raised by brilliant tutors to face a complex and dangerous political world. Intellectually gifted, with a highly complex personality, she confounded her advisors first by refusing to marry, then by voluntarily surrendering her throne, and finally by converting to Catholicism in an age of bitter religious warfare, although her Swedish kingdom was then leader of the Protestant powers. The 1933 movie *Queen Christina,* starring Greta Garbo, which made the queen's name familiar to 20th-century audiences is entirely misleading about the historical Queen Christina, but it is not alone; she has been the subject of extravagant praise from some observers and detestation from others—so much so, that reliable information in English has remained the exception rather than the rule.

Christina was the daughter of King **Gustavus II Adolphus,** one of the great military heroes of Swedish history. Entering the Thirty Years' War in 1630 when the "Protestant Cause" was at its lowest ebb, Gustavus Adolphus won a succession of sweeping victories over the armies of the Catholic

"She made a triumphal progress through Europe, entering Spanish Brussels amid wild merrymaking, until she reached Innsbruck. There Christina of Sweden was officially received into the Roman Catholic Church with pomp and ceremony, and the whole Catholic world rejoiced at the conversion of its greatest enemy."

Eric Elstob

Contributed by Patrick Allitt, Assistant Professor of History, Emory University, Atlanta, Georgia

Holy Roman Empire, culminating in the triumphs of Breitenfeld (1631) and Lützen (1632). At this second battle, however, Gustavus was killed, and although his generals fought on through the following two decades, none could quite match him for strategic daring or tactical elan. At his death Christina, his only child, inherited his throne. For the immediate future, power went to her regent, Axel Oxenstierna, a brilliant politician who continued Gustavus's active policy in northern Europe. He negotiated favorable terms for Sweden in its war against Denmark, settled at Bromsebro in 1644. By winning title to extensive south Baltic lands and ports for Sweden in the general pacification of Westphalia (1648), Oxenstierna showed unmistakably that Christina's Sweden had become the major power of northern Europe.

Not until December 1644, her 18th birthday, did Christina become queen in her own right, though by then she had been attending meetings of the Regency Council for two years. In the meantime, Oxenstierna had taken her away from her mentally unbalanced mother and put her education in the hands of Johannes Matthiae, a broadminded and widely learned man, who gave her a thorough grounding in history, philosophy, theology, and the sciences, in accordance with her father's early orders that she should be raised like a boy. Matthiae nourished in her a passion for philosophy and whetted her intellectual appetite, preparing for the days when she would be one of the chief patrons of European intellectual life. She became a confident speaker of French, German, Latin, Spanish, and Italian, but her written works—letters, aphorisms, and an autobiography—suggest that, although she was surely bright, she was not the genius whom flattering courtiers described in their dedications.

As she matured, Sweden faced domestic and international crises. In the late 1640s, Swedish statesmen watched anxiously as a revolution overthrew the English monarchy and beheaded King Charles I. In Paris, the *Fronde* rebellion came close to unseating the French monarchy, and the boy-king **Louis XIV** had to flee for his life. Revolutions in these and other parts of Europe alarmed Oxenstierna, and he feared that the high taxes he had levied for war and for Christina's court expenses might spark a peasant revolt at home. In 1650, Sweden's representative assembly, the Diet, met at a time of widespread hunger following a poor harvest and protested against the power and privileges of the aristocracy, the price of food, and the costs of a foreign policy from which ordinary Swedes gained nothing. The Diet also argued that Oxenstierna's policy of giving away crown lands, in the

CHRONOLOGY

1626	Christina born
1632	Gustavus Adolphus died at Lützen
1644	Regency ended
1648	Treaty of Westphalia signed
1650	*Protestation* of the Swedish diet
1651	Christina's first declaration of intent to abdicate
1654	Abdicated; self-exile from Sweden; converted to Catholicism
1657	Naples conspiracy and the murder of Monaldesco
1659	Christina created her salon at the Palazzo Riario
1689	Died and buried in St. Peter's in Rome

hope that they would yield more revenue when taxed than when farmed, benefited none but the aristocracy.

Noting the Diet's formal *Protestation*, Oxenstierna tried to curb Christina's lavish tastes in art, architecture, and music when she began to rule in her own right—one of several sources of tension between the old servant and his new mistress. She, however, scorned Oxenstierna's efforts at frugality and defied him by giving large gifts of lands to returning veterans when the long series of wars came to an end. As the leading historian of Sweden, Michael Roberts, notes: "She had neither interest in, nor grasp of, finance; and after 1652 seems to have been cynically indifferent to the distresses of a crown she had already decided to renounce." She also rewarded her favorites, such as Magnus De la Gardie, lavishly and tactlessly, and angered Oxenstierna further by introducing men into the royal council whom he thought unsuitable but could no longer oppose.

Every 17th-century European monarchy had to think about and plan for the succession. The presence of a queen made matrimonial diplomacy even more hazardous and more necessary than usual because the wrong husband could be politically disastrous. As an adolescent Christina was in love with, and planned to marry, her cousin Charles (the future Charles X), with whom she was educated at Stegeborg Castle. The attraction was mutual and led him to hope for a throne. But as she matured Christina's ardor cooled. Though she kept alive the possibility of a marriage to Charles, it was more as a tactic to secure the succession than from affection. Her Council of Regents and her Parliament were also eager to assure a politically suitable royal marriage of this kind, which could eventuate in the birth of heirs.

But once she was queen in fact as well as in name, Christina was in no hurry to tie the knot. Like Queen **Elizabeth I** of England a generation earlier, she realized that the promise of her hand in marriage was a more potent instrument than marriage itself. Once wed, her power would probably decline, whereas the hope of it beforehand would keep Charles, and other possible suitors, guessing as to her intentions and assure her dominance. Meanwhile, she endured rumors which alleged that she was involved in a lesbian affair with her friend Countess Ebba Sparre.

After lengthy disputes with her councillors, she agreed in 1649 to the principle that *if* she married it would be to Charles, but added that she could not be compelled to marry at all. She was more eager to have Charles formally recognized as her heir. Since the two of them were nearly contemporaries, it was unlikely that Charles would enjoy a long reign after her. In the meantime, he had to skulk on his estates where, according to the court gossip of the day, he spent much of his time in a drunken stupor.

Christina Converts to Catholicism

Christina was therefore still unmarried when, in 1651, she told Parliament of her intention to abdicate. A collective cry of dismay from the Swedish statesmen delayed her, but in 1654 she renewed the project and this time carried it out, leaving Sweden permanently in June of that year, and traveling to the Spanish Netherlands. From there, traveling in fine style and assured (as it then seemed) of a lifelong income from her Swedish estates, she went to Innsbruck in Austria, and during her stay openly declared her conversion to Roman Catholicism. To nearly all Swedes her conversion, even more than her abdication, appeared as a horrific form of betrayal. In this age of bitter, protracted religious wars, in which Lutheran Sweden had been pitted for 30 years against the Catholic Empire, a conversion of this sort seemed not so much an act of personal conscience as a symbolic declaration of allegiance to the enemy. Why she took these steps has always been a mystery, and has continued to be the subject of a keen dispute among Swedish historians. Her often-voiced conviction that women were unsuited to rule may have played a part in the decision, but religious conviction was probably more decisive.

Generations of historians have also debated the exact sequence of events and causes surrounding this amazing set of actions. While still in Sweden, Christina had been secretive about her interest in Catholicism, because of its politically volatile implications. She had certainly been strongly impressed by the Catholic French ambassador to her court, Chanut, and by the French philosopher Rene Descartes, also a dedicated Catholic, who spent the last year of his life at her court in Stockholm (he died there of pneumonia in 1650). Next she had encountered Antonio Macedo, who was a Jesuit priest posing as the Portuguese ambassador's interpreter. Christina had several conversations with Macedo and told him that she would welcome the chance to discuss Catholicism with more members of his order. When he hurried to Rome with this news, the Father General of the order responded by sending two learned Jesuit professors, Fathers Malines and Casati, also incognito, to her court. After winning her notice by their pose as Italian noblemen, they quickly recognized that she was a thoughtful and gifted person, "a twenty five year old sovereign so entirely removed from human conceit and with such a deep appreciation of true values that she might have been brought up in the very spirit of moral philosophy." They recalled later that "our main efforts were to prove that our sacred beliefs were beyond reason, yet that they did not conflict with reason. The queen, meanwhile, shrewdly absorbed the substance of our arguments; otherwise we should have needed a great deal of time to make our point."

Christina may have converted as early as 1652, more than a year before her abdication, but if so she did it secretly. When she went to the Netherlands in 1654, she was still accompanied by a retinue which included a Lutheran chaplain. But while there, he died and was not replaced. Christina, meanwhile, gained a reputation in those years, 1654 and 1655, for having a caustic and dismissive attitude towards all forms of Christianity, which may have been a smokescreen to allay suspicions of her conversion. At any rate, after her open confession of her new faith, scandalous tales of her atheism died away. On the other hand scurrilous rumors of her real motives, printed in an avalanche of hostile and lurid pamphlets, were to follow her to the grave and to mislead historians in the ensuing three centuries.

Arriving at Rome in high style after her stately progress through Europe, she took up residence in the Farnese Palace, alarmed Pope Alexander VII by meeting him in a red dress (the color usually reserved for Roman prostitutes) and entertained lavishly, but with little outward sign of religious fervor. Her home quickly became a salon, where intellectuals, cardinals, and noblemen met, and it inevitably became the focus of political intrigues. Despite Christina's lack of outward piety, she was the most prominent convert of the century, and Rome countered Protestant taunts with an avalanche of its own propaganda, singing her praises. She declared that other European princes should follow her lead and end the Reformation rift which had divided Europe for the last 150 years, but none did so.

Charles X, her successor in Sweden, gained a crown sooner than he had dared hope. He proved an effective—and sternly Protestant—monarch, carrying on the policy which Gustavus Adolphus had initiated, of gaining conquests in what is now Poland and North Germany, on the south shore of the Baltic. One pamphleteer noted that while the Pope had gained one lamb in Queen Christina he had lost an entire flock in Poland at the hands of Charles. Lands and tax revenues from this area strengthened the monarchy in its continuing conflict with the aristocracy, and facilitated the paradox of Sweden, a nation of very small population and indigenous resources, remaining a major European power for the best part of a century.

As for Christina, the second half of her life saw her embroiled in the complex politics of baroque Rome, in which she gained the greatest possible leverage from her royal position and felt constrained only by lack of money. When she arrived, the city was one of the focal points of a conflict between pro-French and pro-Spanish factions: France and Spain themselves were at war. At first the common view was that she was pro-Spanish, but her old friend Chanut reassured his master, **Cardinal Mazarin,** Louis XIV's chief minister, that this was not true. Sure enough, the early months of 1656 bore witness to a gradual deterioration of Christina's courtesy towards the Spanish ambassadors and her cultivation of French envoys and diplomats. She recognized that France was becoming the dominant power in Europe and that it could better serve her interests than any other nation. Among other things her income had fallen precipitously despite her precautions at the time of abdication. Since less than a quarter of the anticipated revenue was coming to her from her Swedish estates, she hoped Mazarin might offer her a substitute. In late 1656, therefore, she traveled to Paris and was again accorded a sumptuous royal welcome; she then settled down to debating with Mazarin the possibility that she might be made queen of Naples. The Kingdom of Naples, constituting what is now southern Italy, was then in Spanish hands, and making it an independent, pro-French monarchy was one of the central aims of Mazarin's diplomacy. Christina seemed a likely candidate for monarch, and the two of them signed an accord at Compiegne which drew up a timetable for the achievement of this plan.

The Marquis Is Murdered

The expedition of conquest, prepared in secrecy, was due to sail from Marseilles to Naples in February 1657, but French military commitments elsewhere led to a delay. Christina returned from Italy to France and urged Mazarin to hurry, lest he lose the element of surprise. Sure enough, an Italian member of her own entourage whom she had treated lavishly in the past but who now felt slighted, the Marquis of Monaldesco, warned the Spanish Viceroy in Naples of the impending attack. The Viceroy prepared his fortifications to repel it, and Mazarin canceled the expedition. In a fury of disappointment and rage, Christina retaliated against Monaldesco, whose mail she had intercepted, by having his throat cut in her presence at Fontainbleau Palace, despite his agonized pleas for mercy. News of this bloody act, undertaken while she was a foreign king's guest and in his house, undermined her reputation and nullified the Neapolitan scheme altogether. She had fatally underestimated its consequences for her future. Some pamphlets appeared on the streets of Paris which said Monaldesco had been her lover and that she had killed him to keep the fact a secret; others added that he was just one in a long line of murdered lovers. These allegations were groundless, but the killing was politically inept, especially for a woman who prided herself on her Machiavellian skills and diplomatic tact. In 1659, France and Spain signed the Treaty of the Pyrénées and any lingering hopes of a Neapolitan kingdom for Christina fizzled.

From then on Mazarin would make no more schemes with her and Pope Alexander VII now referred to her as "a woman born a barbarian, barbarously brought up, and living with barbarous thoughts." She returned to Rome without further hope of political power but was still resourceful enough to create one of the most refined and brilliant salons in Europe at the Palazzo Riario. For 30 more years, she remained the great anomaly in Europe, a skilled and talented queen without a realm. A circle of friends and retainers still surrounded her, led by Cardinal Azzolino, who did everything he could to repair her tarnished reputation but was careful always to answer her passionately loving letters in a tone of cold severity, lest further scandal attach itself to her name.

Unable to break the habits of a lifetime, she remained an inveterate intriguer (including an effort to become queen of Poland, and a plan to have Azzolino elected pope) but died in 1689 without making any further impact on the course of events. Without the backing of another monarchy, she lacked the resources for further expeditions, and her Swedish successor, Charles X, himself an ally of France, was careful to do nothing to encourage her. Vatican dismay at the Monaldesco affair had cooled sufficiently after 30 years that Christina the eminent convert could be given the final honor, by Pope Innocent XI, of burial in St. Peter's.

SOURCES:

Elstob, Eric. *Sweden: A Political and Cultural History*. Rowman & Littlefield, 1979.

Masson, Georgina. *Queen Christina*. London: Secker & Warburg, 1968.

Roberts, Michael. *Essays in Swedish History*. University of Minnesota Press, 1967.

Scott, Franklin D. *Sweden: The Nation's History*. University of Minnesota Press, 1977.

Stolpe, Sven. *Christina of Sweden*. Macmillan, 1966.

Weibull, Curt. *Christina of Sweden*. Bonniers: Svenska Bokforlaget, 1966.

John Chrysostom

(c. 344/354–407)

Father of the Eastern Church and patriarch of Constantinople, whose uncompromising reforms brought him into conflict with authorities and caused his eventual exile.

"Glory be to God for all things. I will never cease saying this, whatever befalls me."

JOHN CHRYSOSTOM

Antioch had been founded in 300 B.C. by Seleucus, a Greek general from **Alexander the Great**'s army. Although a Greek-speaking city where Greek influence was predominant, Antioch also hosted a sizable Jewish community. The town was strategically located between the mountains in northern Syria, which paralleled the coastline, and the Orontes River, which flowed into the Mediterranean Sea. Twenty miles from the sea, Antioch had access by river to the port city of Seleucia Pieria on the Mediterranean coast and by land to the north-south trade routes from Phoenicia to Asia Minor and the east-west routes to the Tigris-Euphrates valley. It was also surrounded by a fertile plain north and east of the city, which provided food for an estimated population of 150,000 to 300,000. Moreover, from Daphne's springs, located five miles from the city on a high plateau, two aqueducts brought an abundant supply of water to the public baths, fountains, and homes.

During Roman rule, Antioch was the official residence for the Roman governor of Syria, and the Emperor Julian had lived there while preparing his campaign against Persia. With the spread of Christianity, missionaries had visited Antioch

Name variations: John of Constantinople; it was not until the 6th century that the surname Chrysostom, which means "golden-mouth" in Greek, was given to him. Pronunciation: KRIS-es-tum. Born in Antioch sometime between 344 and 354; died in exile on September 14, 407; son of Secundus (a high-ranking military officer in the Roman army of Syria) and Anthusa.

Contributed by Branan Becknell, Ph.D. candidate, Miami University of Ohio, Oxford, Ohio

239

quite early; the very name "Christian" was first given to the disciples of Jesus who lived in Antioch during the first century. Thus, when John Chrysostom lived in Antioch during the fourth century, the Christian community, which lived side by side in this ancient city with their pagan and Jewish neighbors, possessed a rich tradition of nearly 200 years.

Sometime between 344 and 354, John was born to his mother Anthusa and his father Secundus, a high-ranking military officer in the Roman army of Syria who died not long after. Devoutly accepting the Christian teachings of the time which discouraged remarriage, the 20-year-old Anthusa dedicated her life to raising her son. She gained the praise of Christians and pagans alike who admired her example of marital faithfulness long after her husband's death.

Undoubtedly, her ardent enthusiasm for religious piety strongly influenced John's own development. Anthusa spared no expense for her son's future law career; he studied public speaking with the famous rhetorician Libanius. During the reign of the Roman Emperor Julian (361-63), Libanius was not only the Emperor's personal friend, but he was also deeply involved in Julian's movement to revive the worship of the old Greek and Roman gods. Trained under the best teachers of his time,

John's natural gifts were well developed. As Church historian Sozomen reports, Libanius acknowledged on his deathbed that his successor "would have been John had not the Christians taken him from us."

According to historian Palladius, the 18-year-old John "revolted against the professors of verbosities." He was a "man in intellect, he delighted in divine learning." Under the religious training of Bishop Meletius, John entered the class of catechumens and was baptized during the Easter season, probably around 368–70. The delay of John's Christian baptism was not unusual. The practice of infant baptism was not well established, and since many believed that sins committed after baptism would not be forgiven, they put off this rite until just before death. Later in his own ministry, John would attack this custom, teaching that God would forgive more than one sin after baptism. Although innovative, this teaching was offensive, even among his friends.

After his decision to "exercise himself in the sacred books and to practice philosophy according to the law of the Church," Sozomen informs us that John attended a school in Antioch which was taught by Diodore of Tarsus. According to the ecclesiastical historian Socrates, Diodore "limited his attention to the literal sense of scripture, avoiding that which was mystical." In contrast to the allegorical method of interpreting the Bible which was popular at that time, Diodore emphasized the historical-grammatical interpretation of the Bible. Adopted by John throughout his life, this methodology may be credited for the "practical" nature of his sermons, which unwaveringly stress the moral improvement of the hearer. This is not to say that John rejected allegory altogether, but he only allowed an allegorical interpretation when the biblical text gave good reason for doing so.

Although most of his former friends thought that John's new life of study, prayer, and fasting was anti-social, Sozomen credited John with persuading two of his former classmates, who had also studied with Libanius, to follow his example. And so Theodore and Maximus, who both became bishops in the Church, joined John in studying with Diodore. (Years later, however, Theodore became the father of Nestorianism, a heresy teaching that the human and divine natures in Jesus were separate, which was condemned by the Council of Ephesus in 431.)

Three years after his baptism, still living at home while studying and practicing a disciplined life, John was made a lector or reader by Meletius. Yet John was not satisfied; he wanted to demonstrate even greater self-discipline. In the first part of his famous treatise entitled *On the Priesthood,* John recounts that his closest friend Basil wanted to become a monk while John was still pursuing a law career. Even when John had begun his religious studies, Basil further challenged him in his zeal for spiritual matters; he thought that they should leave their homes in order to live with the monks. When John shared this plan with his mother, however, she strongly objected:

> I beg one favor do not plunge me into a second widowhood; nor revive the grief which is now laid to rest: wait for my death: it may be in a little while I shall depart.

John did not join the monks until his mother died.

When John and Basil heard a rumor that the people of the Church were going to force them to become bishops, a practice which was common at the time, both agreed to follow the same course whether it be to flee or to suffer the ordination by the Church. When the day came to ordain Basil, he "resented being seized" and resisted. Told that John, who was "more hot tempered," had consented to his ordination, yielding "very mildly to the judgment of the Fathers," Basil agreed to do likewise. Basil learned later, to his great grief, that John had escaped and, to his great shock, that John had participated in the deception. Against all of Basil's accusations, John defended his actions.

> For great is the value of deceit, provided it be not introduced with a mischievous intention. In fact, action of this kind ought not to be called deceit, but rather a kind of good management, cleverness and skill, capable of finding out ways where resources fail, and making up for the defects of the mind.

John argued that "pious frauds" were legitimate if the intention was well meant; he justified this position by an appeal to strategy in war, the conduct of doctors, some examples from the Old Testament, and even from the life of the Apostle **Paul.** For John, the deception of Basil was necessary because he believed that Basil would make a good bishop, while he would not.

According to some, this account of Basil did not really happen. They suggest that it was simply a literary device, providing the background for John's theme of the importance of the priesthood. Others accept this story as historically true, for it would be hard to imagine that John, who strongly wrote

against the practice of seeking the priesthood on one's own initiative, would even pretend to be a candidate for ordination, if in fact he were not. According to John's own standards, the intention of such a pious fiction would convict him of blatant pride. And since they are in the same context, the questionable authenticity of Basil's story also throws John's account of his mother into doubt as well. Perhaps it is best to conclude that the chronology of John's early life is uncertain. But in these two accounts John's love for his mother, passion for argument, and his youthful idealism are portrayed.

For the next four years, John lived with an old hermit in the nearby mountains. Following that, he spent two years alone in a cave, studying "the covenants of Christ"; he also practiced extreme forms of self-denial, which both ruined his health and changed the course of his life. Wrote Palladius:

> Two years spent without lying down by night or day deadened his gastric organs, and the functions of the kidneys were impaired by the cold. As he could not doctor himself, he returned to the haven of the Church.

When John returned to Antioch, he resumed his duties as reader in the Church. According to the historian Socrates, John also composed his book *Against the Jews* at this time. In a series of eight sermons delivered before the Jewish New Year of Rosh Hashanah, John vehemently attacked the customs of the *Judaizers* in his church. These were Christians who either still kept parts of the law, participated in the Jewish holidays, followed the Jewish calendar for determining the date of Easter, or sought out the Jews for magic amulets and cures. In response to what John perceived as Jewish proselytizing, he used all of his rhetorical powers to completely denigrate not only Judaism, but also the Jews as individuals.

> No Jew adores God! Who says so? The Son of God says so. For he said: "If you were to know my Father, you would also know me. But you know neither me nor do you know my Father." Could I produce a witness more trustworthy than the Son of God? If, then, the Jews fail to know the Father, if they crucified the Son, if they thrust off the help of the Spirit, who should not make bold to declare plainly that the synagogue is a dwelling of demons? God is not worshipped there.

John vilified the Jews as drunkards, harlots, greedy, deceitful, murderers, and lawbreakers. Some have even traced the anti-Semitism that continues to flourish to these sermons. Yet it should be remembered that these sermons were addressed to a Christian audience in order to reclaim their own straying members. John was concerned with defending the deity of Christ, which is the main religious difference between Christianity and Judaism. Most would agree that his use of Greek rhetoric, which stressed hyperbole and left nothing good to be said about an opponent, was a cultural practice of his day that certainly was not designed for balanced judgment.

John's impassioned advocacy for the Church was appreciated by many. Church historian Socrates stated that Meletius "conferred on him the rank of deacon," probably in 381. During this time, John protested in his book *On the Priesthood* that the "safety of the Church" was being ruined by the current practice of making bishops from unworthy men. He felt a bishop should be even more holy than a monk. "For as great as the distance between a king and a commoner," the duties of the bishop are extremely more demanding than those of the monk.

> But if any one who has devoted himself to whole multitudes, and has been compelled to bear the sins of many, has remained steadfast and firm, guiding his soul in the midst of the storm as if he were in a calm, he is the man to be justly applauded and admired of all, for he has shown sufficient proof of personal manliness.

Having been given more responsibility, the bishop will be judged by a stricter standard than other Christians. In essence, this high view of the priesthood, found in his early work, foreshadows the reforms which John would implement later in his career. In the same year of 381, Meletius died while attending the Council of Constantinople, and it was under the new bishop Flavian that John was ordained to the priesthood in 386.

When Emperor Theodosius I announced a heavy tax, perhaps in 387, the people of Antioch rioted: an angry crowd destroyed the public baths, attacked the governor's home, and the statues of the Emperor and his wife were dragged through the streets of the city. After the Roman governor quelled the disturbance, the people's anger turned to fear, anticipating slavery, torture, and death. Many were imprisoned and executed, even before the Emperor was notified. Under these circumstances, John preached roughly 21 sermons, entitled *The Homilies on the Statues*. In the third homily, John announced that Bishop Flavian (who had gone to plead for mercy from a furious Theodosius), had "gone to snatch so great a multitude

from the wrath of the Emperor." While waiting to hear word, John delivered a series of sermons which were designed to challenge the Christians to forsake their evil ways and to "persevere continually in virtue." Speaking against the covetous practices of the rich, John taught that "what is beyond our wants, is superfluous and useless." And "the rich man is not one who is in possession of much, but one who gives much." While awaiting the Emperor's judgment, John spoke on such themes as wealth, poverty, repentance, prayer, swearing, oaths, and virtue, sustaining his congregation with both rebukes and encouragements.

> I proclaim, both loudly and distinctly, that if we become changed, and bestow some care upon our souls, and desist from iniquity, nothing will be unpleasant or painful.

With the return of Flavian, John celebrated the good news on Easter Sunday that the Emperor had magnanimously pardoned the people of Antioch. He closed his sermons by praising "God's loving kindness towards the city," because the people were "stimulated to piety" by everything that happened.

John Is Consecrated Bishop of Constantinople

In 397, Nectarius, the Bishop of Constantinople, died. This episcopal office was very important because Constantinople was the imperial capital for the Eastern part of the Roman Empire. Hearing of John's reputation, Sozomen said that the clergy and the people were "unanimous in electing" him, and their "choice was approved by the emperor." The Emperor sent Asterius, "the general of the East," to escort John to Constantinople. Thinking that John's departure from Antioch might provoke a riot among his followers, Asterius cunningly requested that John meet him in a church outside the walls of the city. When John arrived, Asterius made him get into his chariot, and John was carried to Constantinople without being consulted. Theophilus, the Bishop of Alexandria, opposed John's selection, but Eutropius, the minister of the Emperor, used threats until Theophilus finally yielded. And so on February 26, 398, John was consecrated Bishop of Constantinople.

According to Sozomen, John immediately instituted reforms for the clergy, expelling some for blatant corruption. In contrast to the luxury of his predecessor, John lived a simple life and spent the bulk of his income on the poor. Establishing hospitals and boldly preaching on the importance of giving alms, he also condemned the practice of priests who lived with women called "spiritual sisters." John's boldness was unlimited. For example, Gainas, one of the Gothic generals, had asked the Emperor to let the Arians have a church building inside the city. Arianism, a sect of Christianity, taught that there was a time when Jesus had been created by God, the Father; this contradicted the orthodox position, gradually affirmed in the Council of Nicaea (325) and the Council of Constantinople (381), that Jesus eternally shared the same substance with the Father. John encouraged Gainas to be content with the churches which they already had outside the city. Despite John's direct speech, Gainas started a second rebellion, which was eventually defeated.

Although beloved for his preaching, John's actions began to make him many powerful enemies. In January of 401, he went to neighboring Ephesus to investigate the charges that some of the bishops had purchased their positions with money. After a period of several months, he deposed six bishops and ordained new ones. While most praised him for this action, the deposed bishops argued that John had changed the "rights of the ordained, contrary to the ancestral laws." Meanwhile, Severian, who had been preaching in Constantinople in John's absence, won the favor of the Empress Eudoxia (wife of Arcadius). Sozomen maintains that when John heard that Severian had preached sermons only to please the people, he "was filled with jealousy." When an argument broke out between Severian and an overbearing friend of John's named Serapion, John expelled Severian from the city. Only the earnest entreaties of Eudoxia were finally able to bring about a temporary and uneasy reconciliation. John eventually lost the goodwill of Eudoxia as well; after hearing one of his sermons on Elijah in the Old Testament, Eudoxia thought that John had compared her to the wicked Jezebel.

Born a slave, made a eunuch, and owned by several masters, Eutropius entered the lowest ranks of the imperial chamberlains. He served Theodosius and gradually won the confidence of Theodosius's son, the Emperor Arcadius. Eutropius consolidated his power by eliminating his potential rivals and by dominating the weak will of Arcadius. When some of his opponents fled to the church for sanctuary, Eutropius passed a law which prevented the Church from protecting fugitives from the State. However, Eutropius experienced a complete reversal of fortune after he was unable to put down a rebellion against Arcadius. Both Gainas and Eudoxia succeeded in having him banished for his failure. Fearing further reprisals, Eutropius ran to the church and appealed to John to save his life.

Refusing to deliver Eutropius to the soldiers, John persuaded Arcadius to uphold the right of the Church to grant sanctuary. As the next day was Sunday, John preached a sermon on the vanity of riches while the fallen Eutropius was meekly holding the altar for all to see. John used this occasion to dramatize his lesson of "self-control."

> Fear not the devices of a potentate, but fear the power of sin. No man will do thee harm, if you do not deal a blow to yourself. If you have not sin, ten thousand swords may threaten you, but God will snatch you away out of their reach but if you have sin, even should you be in paradise you will be cast out.

Although John also taught the importance of forgiveness, his enemies complained that John had used more "rebuke" than compassion on Eutropius. When Eutropius fled the shelter of the church, agents of the king found him, and he was later beheaded. But John boldly proclaimed that the Church was the surest refuge for the soul, and "if he had not abandoned the Church he would not have been surrendered."

With the passing of Eutropius and Gainas, the power of Eudoxia over her husband waxed even stronger. When John again delivered a sermon "against the vices to which females are peculiarly prone," Sozomen said that Eudoxia still "imagined" that John was preaching against her, and "the enemies of the bishop did not fail to report his discourse in this sense to the empress." After she complained to the emperor, a council was quickly gathered. In addition, Bishop Theophilus of Alexandria had new cause to resent John, because John had given shelter to some monks whom Theophilus hated. Consequently, Theophilus hurried to Constantinople and the Emperor housed him in the palace. In the nearby suburb of Chalcedon, Severian, along with John's enemies and the bishops that John had deposed, joined an assembly of 36 bishops, most of whom came from Egypt with Theophilus. Three times John refused to answer the summons to appear before this council because his judges were both his accusers and enemies. Ignoring his appeal for another council, the Synod of the Oak condemned John in 403. Arcadius ratified the decision, and three days later John was hurried out of the capital with a military escort. Historian Theodoret credited an earthquake for terrifying Eudoxia into canceling his exile, but Sozomen and Socrates attributed John's return to the fierce protests of the people who were ecstatic upon John's return to Constantinople. His popularity dissolved any hurts which his enemies wished to inflict.

For two months, John and Eudoxia were on friendly terms. But when a silver statue of Eudoxia was dedicated near the church, John protested against the loud noise during his sermon with the provocative remark: "Again Herodias is raging, again she is dancing, again she demands the head of John on a platter." John's enemies delighted in reporting this latest offense against Eudoxia, for he had clearly compared Eudoxia to the immoral Herodias in the New Testament. When Arcadius prohibited John from entering his church, John proceeded to continue the Easter baptismal services in the baths of Constans. But armed soldiers broke up the service and, wrote Palladius, the "baptismal waters ran red." After two assassination attempts against John had failed, the city was in an uproar. Finally, Arcadius signed a decree, and John left Constantinople for the last time on June 24, 404.

Exiled to Cucusus, where his enemies hoped that the cold climate or the marauding Isaurians who lived nearby might soon kill him, John prospered for three years, and many of his letters have survived from this period. In response to his suffering, John wrote *None Can Harm Him Who Does Not Injure Himself* in order to encourage his friend Olympias. According to Cardinal **John Henry Newman,** John had a "sunniness of mind, all his own." As an eternal optimist, he "was ever forgetting his enemies in his friends." During his sojourn in Cucusus, John stayed in touch with his friends, engaged in missionary projects, and even raised money to alleviate a famine in his area. He was so active that once again his enemies determined to kill him by inches. Arcadius signed a new order which exiled John to Pityus. Under the torture of forced marches, John finally collapsed in Comana, nearly 350 miles from Cucusus, and died on September 14, 407, after saying his usual prayer, "Glory be to God for all things."

Leaving a large literary legacy and given the title "Doctor of the Church," John's sincerity and fiery preaching earned him the nickname Chrysostom ("golden-mouth"). His reforms as well as his uncompromising boldness made him a martyr of the pulpit.

SOURCES:

Palladius. "Dialogue on the Life of St. John Chrysostom," in *Ancient Christian Writers.* Translated by Robert T. Meyer. Vol. 45. Newman Press, 1985.

Schaff, Philip, and Henry Wace, eds. *A Select Library of Nicene and Post-Nicene Fathers of the Christian Church.* Vols. II and III. Eerdman, 1989.

FURTHER READING:

Baur, Chrysostom. *John Chrysostom and His Time.* 2 vols. Translated by Sister M. Gonzaga. Christian Classics, 1960–61.

Newman, John Henry. *Essays and Sketches.* Volume III. Longmans, Green, 1948.

Quasten, Johannes. *Patrology.* Vol. III. Christian Classics, 1984.

Wilken, Robert L. *John Chrysostom and the Jews.* University of California Press, 1983.

John Churchill, 1st Duke of Marlborough

(1650–1722)

British statesman and general, who guided the Grand Alliance against Louis XIV of France during the War of the Spanish Succession while winning some of the most renowned battles in European history.

During the English Civil War (1642–51), when a West Country lawyer by the name of Winston Churchill took up arms in defense of crown and his Anglican church, his fortunes fell along with those he championed. Facing destitution, the Royalist cavalry captain and his wife Elizabeth took refuge with her mother, the staunch Parliamentarian Lady Eleanor Drake. On May 26, 1650, while living under Lady Drake's roof, Asche House in Devonshire, Elizabeth gave birth to a son, John.

John Churchill, the future 1st duke of Marlborough, spent his first ten years in difficult circumstances. His Royalist father entertained few prospects. The Drake family did enjoy a measure of social prestige. The century before, it had produced the great Elizabethan admiral, Sir **Francis Drake.** Through marriage, the Drakes were related to the Villiers family. George Villiers, the duke of Buckingham and the most infamous rake of the period, had been the intimate friend of both James I and Charles I. But during the Puritan Commonwealth, such affiliations offered no advantage. A childhood spent in genteel poverty taught young John to venerate the established

Name variations: Marquis of Blandford, Reichfürst (Imperial Prince) von Mindelheim, Baron Churchill of Aysmouth (1682–85), Baron Churchill of Sandridge (1685–89), Earl of Marlborough (1689–1702). Born on May 26, 1650, at Asche House in Devonshire, England; died at Windsor Lodge in London in 1722; son of Sir Winston Churchill (a West Country lawyer) and Elizabeth (daughter of Lady Eleanor Drake); married: Sarah Jennings, c. 1677. Predecessors: Sir Francis Drake, Sir Winston Churchill (father). Successors: Sir Winston Churchill.

Contributed by D. K. R. Crosswell, Lecturer, National University of Singapore, Singapore

245

CHRONOLOGY

1666	Entered service of Duke of York
1672–78	Served in the Dutch War
1679–82	Exiled to Brussels and Scotland with the Duke of York
1685	Succession of James II; battle of Sedgemoor
1688	Defected to William III
1689–97	War of the Grand Alliance
1693	Imprisoned in Tower of London
1701–13	War of the Spanish Succession
1702	Named captain-general
1704	Battle of Blenheim
1706	Battle of Ramillies; conquest of the Spanish Netherlands
1708	Battle of Oudenarde; siege of Lille
1709	Battle of Malplaquet
1712–14	Removed from office; exiled in Germany
1722	Died at Windsor Lodge, London

church and the House of Stuart, to mask his personal political feelings, and to appreciate the value of money. These traits composed the core of his psychological makeup and motivated his actions at pivotal junctures in his life.

The Stuart Restoration in 1660 produced an immediate improvement in the Churchill family fortunes. Elected a member of Parliament for Weymouth, Winston Churchill took his seat in the Convention Parliament in 1661. Making a mark for himself in Parliament, he quickly earned an entrée to **Charles II**'s court and substantial royal preferments. In 1662, Winston Churchill became commissioner for Irish Land Claims and the following year obtained a knighthood and a posting in London.

John Churchill attended the Free School in Dublin in 1662 and then spent the next two years studying at the distinguished St. Paul's School in London. Aside from being conventional for the day, historians known little about his education other than the fact he carefully read *De Re Militari*, the work of the great Roman military thinker Vegetius.

Of the many paths to fame and success that existed in the 17th and 18th centuries, the boudoir and the battlefield numbered among the most traveled. John Churchill's rise followed these routes. His social climb can be attributed in part to his physical assets. "About middle height, and the best figure in the world," observed Sicco van Goslinga, "his features without a fault, fine, sparking eyes, good teeth, and his complexion ... the fairer sex might envy: in brief ... one of the handsomest men ever seen." Add grace of manner, affable charm, tact, and ruthless ambition, and the combination practically assured social success— especially in the permissive society of Restoration England. Still, one could not expect to rise far without connections and the patronage of highly placed people. John Churchill enjoyed both, owing to the women in his life: first through his older sister Arabella; then his lover and second cousin once removed Barbara Villiers, the duchess of Cleveland; and finally his wife, Sarah Jennings.

At age 17, Arabella received a coveted position in the household of the duchess of York. Not long afterward, she became the duke of York's favored mistress. Through Arabella's connections in court, John Churchill secured the post of page to the duke of York; the 16-year-old courtier looked forward to a promising career.

For a young man with limited means but good connections, no better way existed to improve his fortunes than the military; on September 14, 1667, the duke of York secured a commission for his page in the regiment of Foot Guards. The next year, Churchill journeyed to Tangier where he served as a "gentleman volunteer" for better than two years.

Returning to court in 1671, John Churchill renewed his acquaintance with the duchess of Cleveland, the king's preferred mistress. Described by a Victorian period historian as "not only the most beautiful but ... also the most licentious ... of women," Barbara Villiers shared her favors with Charles II, her Guards officer cousin, and many others. The King once caught them *en flagrant délit* but dismissed the transgression saying "you do it to get your bread." The material gifts the duchess bestowed upon John Churchill furthered his career: in 1672, she paid for his promotion to captain and in 1674 made him a present of £4,500, a princely sum he shrewdly invested. She also gave him a daughter, one of her numerous illegitimate progeny.

In 1672, England joined France in a war of aggression against the Netherlands. Churchill saw action at sea, serving on the duke of York's flagship at the battle of Solebay. The next year, he joined the English forces fighting in the Low Countries, and at the siege of Maastrict (June 17–July 8, 1673), saved the life of the English commander and illegitimate son of Charles II, the duke of

Monmouth. For his gallantry, **Louis XIV** of France awarded Churchill with a colonelcy and command of an English regiment in the French service. He then had the chance to study the art of war from the master, the French commander the Marshal vicomte de Turenne. Churchill duly received promotion to lieutenant colonel of the Duke of York Regiment and in 1677 an English colonelcy. A year later, he gained the rank of brigadier general, but the Dutch War ended before he could take command.

Sometime in the winter of 1677–78, Churchill secretly married 18-year-old Sarah Jennings. A stunning beauty with a stormy disposition, she also made her ascent through connections in the duke of York's court. Friend and confidante to the duke's daughter, Princess **Anne,** Sarah Jennings had conducted a clandestine romance with Churchill since 1675. A bona fide love match, the union lasted 44 years; a considerable share of the praise and blame for Marlborough's rise and fall must be attributed to his fiery and formidable wife.

In 1678, Churchill accompanied his old friend and rising politician Sidney Godolphin as diplomatic envoy to the Hague. His first nationally important duty, the Hague mission inaugurated Churchill's career as a diplomat. When an anti-Catholic backlash forced the duke of York into exile (1679–82), first in Brussels and then in Scotland, Churchill earned the appreciation of his patron by sharing the ordeal. On a number of occasions, he served as confidential agent between Charles II and his brother and between them and their French cousin and benefactor Louis XIV. For his efforts on behalf the Stuart dynasty, Churchill received a Scottish peerage as baron of Aysmouth and colonelcy of the Royal Dragoons. Restored to London, he escorted Prince George of Denmark to England for his marriage to Anne.

Both John and Sarah Churchill enjoyed high favor at court. On the accession of James II in 1685, the king sent Churchill to Versailles to inform Louis XIV. Upon his return, James showered his favorite with honors: an English peerage (Baron Churchill of Sandridge), Lord of the (King's) Bedchamber, and governor of the Hudson Bay Company. When his former commander, the duke of Monmouth, contested the throne and invaded the west of England, James II appointed Churchill second-in-command of the royal forces with the rank of major general. Largely owing to Churchill's administrative ability and tactical skill, the Monmouth Rebellion collapsed at the battle of Sedgemoor. As reported in the London Gazette (July 18, 1685), Churchill "performed his part with all the courage and gallantry imaginable."

Churchill's strong Protestant beliefs proved stronger than his gratitude to his Catholic king. As he explained to Lord Galway in 1685 while on his mission to Louis XIV, "if the king should attempt to change our religion, I will instantly quit his service." As opposition to James II's Catholicizing and arbitrary policies mounted, Churchill vacillated and sent overtures to **William of Orange** (husband to James's Protestant daughter and heir Mary) in the Netherlands. When William landed a powerful Dutch force at Torbey, James promoted Churchill to lieutenant general (November 7, 1688) in command of the Royalist forces. Facing battle, Churchill slipped away in the middle of the night and joined the Orangist forces. The trickle of defections to William became a torrent after Churchill's opportunistic departure. Churchill had betrayed the man to whom he owed virtually everything. Ambition, as much as religious feeling, lay at the heart of his duplicity.

In the coronation honors (April 1689), William and Mary awarded Churchill with the title Earl of Marlborough; he also entered the government as member of the Privy Council. When England joined the Netherlands and the Grand Alliance in war against France (1689–97), Marlborough accepted a command in Flanders. While the campaign brought little success, Marlborough won commendation from the supreme commander, the prince of Waldeck, who remarked that Churchill had displayed in a single campaign greater military aptitude than most generals exhibit in a lifetime. Later that year, Churchill rapidly and efficiently raised and moved forces to Ireland where the fortresses of Cork and Kinsale fell after short sieges.

Despite all the honors and wealth, Marlborough remained unsatisfied. He wanted a dukedom, elevation to Knight of the Order of the Garter, and appointment as master-general of the Ordnance. Seeking to convince both the reigning and exiled king of England of his fealty, and maneuvering to be on the winning side whatever the turn of events, Marlborough served William while conspiring with James. Meanwhile Sarah's scheming on Anne's behalf earned Queen Mary's enmity. After criticizing the King for bestowing appointments on Dutch officers, Marlborough's refusal of a command in 1692, unless he commanded all English forces in Flanders, produced an explosion.

Charged with High Treason, He Goes to Tower of London

In January 1693, Marlborough lost all his posts and offices. The following year, he went to the

Tower of London on charges of high treason. Although he won release, he remained out of favor at court until the death of his implacable foe Queen Mary in 1695 and unemployed for the duration of the war. A reconciliation with William finally occurred in 1698—the earl's seat on the Privy Council, his military rank, and his colonelcies were restored.

William III devoted his life to combatting the aggrandizement of Louis XIV. As the 17th century drew to an end, a general European war loomed over the issue of the succession to the Spanish throne. The king wanted to revive the Grand Alliance of England, the Netherlands, and Austria. William and Marlborough both agreed on the adoption of a continental strategy linking England to European allies. On May 31, 1701, William made Marlborough Ambassador-Extraordinary and Plenipotentiary with the right to "conceive treaties without reference, if need be, to King and Parliament." On September 7, the three powers formally entered into alliance. William III never lived to see the outbreak of the war he dreaded—he died in March 1702 and England declared war on France on May 4.

For Marlborough the succession of Anne to the throne produced a deluge of honors, offices, and titles: Knight of the Garter, master-general of Ordnance, and commander of all English forces. For the next nine years, Marlborough exerted a vast concentration of power. At home, no ministry could stand without his support. The earl of Godolphin, his old friend, headed the treasury and, in effect, acted as prime minister at Marlborough's behest. The key to Marlborough's political influence lay with the degree of leverage Sarah exerted over Queen Anne. In foreign relations, Marlborough assumed the role of William III. A virtual unknown, he struggled to surmount the competing interests and jealousies of the coalition states. In his role of commander in chief, he administered the English armies as well as led them in the field. As "supreme commander," Marlborough directly commanded the English and Dutch armies as well as allied and auxiliary forces within his theatre of operations.

The campaigns of 1702 and 1703 represent Marlborough's apprenticeship as a commander. While conducting conventional maneuver and siege operations, Marlborough outgeneraled French commanders of far greater experience. Anxious to conduct a static defensive strategy, the Dutch repeatedly vetoed Marlborough's offensive schemes. Nonetheless, the capture of Liège in October 1702 and successes along the Meuse in 1703 left the coalition armies in an excellent position for the next campaigning season.

Sandwiched between these two campaigns Marlborough received a long sought after honor and a crushing blow. He gained a personal triumph on December 14, 1702—a dukedom and a large annuity. Two months later a personal tragedy befell him—his eldest and only surviving son died of smallpox.

During the winter of 1703–04, the Grand Alliance's situation deteriorated. The ardor of the German states for war waned. When Bavaria entered the war on France's side, one French army reinforced Bavaria while another prepared to follow. In Vienna, the hard-pressed Emperor Leopold I faced a multifronted war in Germany and Italy and a serious rebellion in Hungary. In London, Marlborough and Godolphin's moderate Tory administration faced attacks from extreme Tories and Whigs alike.

Marching to the Battle of Blenheim

Recognizing that only bold action could retrieve the situation, Marlborough conceived the most daring military strategy of his age, an audacious combination of political deception and strategic execution. The previous year's campaign had left him in a strong position to develop operations up the Moselle. On May 2, the Dutch Estates-General (parliament) approved just such a line of attack. In a letter to Godolphin on April 29, 1704, Marlborough outlined a more ambitious scheme:

> My intentions are to march with all the English to Coblentz [at the confluence of the Moselle and Rhine] and to declare that I intend to campaign on the Moselle. But, when I come there, to write to the Dutch States that I think it absolutely necessary for the saving of the Empire to march with the troops under my command and to join with those that are in Germany that are in Her Majesty's and the Dutch pay, in order to take measures with [the Imperial forces] for the speedy reduction of the Elector of Bavaria.

The plan revolved around reinforcing the imperial armies in south Germany and destroying the Franco-Bavarian army before the other French army under Marshal comte de Tallard could intervene. It also required he deceive his Dutch allies. "I am very sensible that I take a great deal upon me," he confided in Godolphin two days later. "But should I act otherwise, the Empire would be undone, and consequently the Confederation."

On May 19, the coalition army moved southward with 21,000 troops. A week later, Marlborough reached Coblentz. He then crossed the Rhine, linking up with Hanoverian and Brandenburg reinforcements. A large French covering force under Marshal duc de Villeroi shadowed Marlborough and screened the Moselle. When the coalition force continued up the Rhine, Villeroi decided Marlborough intended to move against Strasbourg and Alsace. Villeroi's halt (June 3–7) allowed Marlborough to cross two obstacles—the Rivers Main and Neckar. Only on June 6, when he could no longer be recalled, did Marlborough inform the Dutch of his plans. On June 22, Marlborough united with the imperial commander, Louis of Baden, just north of Ulm in the Danube valley. A week later Marlborough combined with another Imperial force under Prince **Eugene of Savoy.** In what amounted to a lightning thrust for the period, the coalition army marched over 250 miles in five weeks.

The march required administrative planning of unparalleled complexity. His staff established advance depots so when the troops arrived at the preselected point, "the soldiers had nothing to do but pitch their tents, boil their kettles and lie down to rest." At Heidelburg, a new pair of shoes awaited each man. "Surely never was such a march carried on with more order and regularity," remarked Captain Parker, an English officer, "and with less fatigue to man and horse." Called "the old corporal" by his men, Marlborough took genuine care of his troops. Not only had he completed the march, Marlborough brought his polyglot army into the theater of war in remarkably good shape. By comparison, the French army lost a third of its strength from desertion and straggling.

Concentrating the coalition forces between the converging enemy armies, Marlborough brought the Franco-Bavarian army to battle at Blenheim on August 13. The duke conducted the battle in what emerged as his characteristic fashion: attack the enemy flanks to draw off his attention and reserves; then unleash a smashing combined cavalry-infantry assault in the center. Although outnumbered in men (52,000 to 56,000) and outgunned (66 cannon to 90), Marlborough and Eugene inflicted 34,000 casualties on the Franco-Bavarian armies. "[I] heard of armies being beaten," observed Captain Parker, "but never of one taken." In a single afternoon, Marlborough reversed the tide of the war, crushed French ambitions in Central Europe, and revived the morale of the Grand Alliance. Blenheim established Marlborough as one of the great commanders in history.

None of Marlborough's later triumphs— Ramillies, Oudenarde, Malplaquet—approached the scale of Blenheim. In 1705, Marlborough resumed operations in Flanders. Determined never to be left exposed as in 1704, the Dutch kept Marlborough on a tight leash. After several missed opportunities in 1705, Marlborough's tenacity paid dividends the following year when he routed Villeroi at Ramillies (May 23, 1706). Moving quickly to exploit his victory, Marlborough seized Brussels, Antwerp, and most of the Spanish Netherlands.

A period of frustration followed a year of startling achievements. The French scored a remarkable success early in 1708, surging across the Scheldt River and cutting Marlborough's direct communications to England through Ostend. Although many of Marlborough's gains after Ramillies were lost, he refused to surrender the strategic initiative. Instead of retreating, he executed a daring counterthrust, interposing himself across the French communications. The coalition army marched 50 miles in 60 hours, an astounding feat for the period. Upon hearing that Marlborough had executed the advance, the French co-commander, Marshal duc de Vendôme, exclaimed "if they are there, the Devil must have carried them ... such marching is impossible." Ignoring the counsels of the experienced Vendôme, the duke of Burgundy, Louis XIV's grandson, accepted battle at Oudenarde (July 11, 1708). Illustrating a remarkable ability to improvise and a keen sense of terrain, Marlborough won another renowned victory. In addition to regaining the territories lost in the opening of the campaign, Marlborough went on to conduct a masterpiece in siegecraft at Lille. After a bloody siege lasting three and an a half months, France's greatest fortress fell on December 9, 1708.

Following the disasters of Oudenarde and Lille, Louis sued for peace. When French overtures produced no result, Louis fielded a magnificent army of 90,000 in Flanders under Marshal duc de Villars. Pursuing an active campaign, Villars drew Marlborough and Prince Eugene into battle at Malplaquet. The two largest armies assembled in the Western world to that date (Marlborough had 100,000; Villars 90,000) engaged in the hardest-fought battle of the War of the Spanish Succession. Although the French surrendered the field, they inflicted 24,000 casualties on the allied forces (they lost 12,000). A tactical victory for Marlborough, the battle of Malplaquet was the bloodiest battle of the early modern period in European history, not to be matched until the battle of Borodino in 1812 during the Napoleonic Wars.

After the horror of Malplaquet, neither side evidenced any enthusiasm for open battle. The campaigns of 1710–11 returned to a contest of maneuver and minor sieges. In 1711, Marlborough demonstrated his pure martial mastery of maneuver and siege warfare. Repeatedly deceiving Villars, he forced the *Non Plus Ultra* line, thought to be impassable, without the loss of a single man. Later that year, he took the fortress of Bouchain, despite being virtually encircled by a larger French army.

Between campaign seasons (armies of the period did not fight in winter or early spring), Marlborough put down the sword and took up his duties as statesman. As the focal point of the anti-French coalition, he induced the member states of the Grand Alliance to continue the war. He scored a noteworthy success of personal diplomacy when he traveled all the way to Saxony in eastern Germany in April 1707 to dissuade the Swedish king, **Charles XII,** from intervening in the war in Germany. In 1706 and again in 1709 and 1710, Marlborough used his influence to undercut compromise settlements. Although his enormous military abilities cannot be questioned, Marborough could not escape the natural lethargy of 18th-century positional warfare. As a commander, he could not decisively defeat France; as a statesman, he bears a major responsibility for the war's prolongation.

Handling the intransigent Dutch or divisive German princes proved easy in comparison to Queen Anne and British political factions. All his battlefield glory could not isolate Marlborough from being undermined by party intrigues. Tory opposition to the continental war forced Marlborough and Godolphin into the arms of the Whigs. Sarah Churchill, a committed Whig, lost her influence over the queen, who bore a strong dislike of the Whig leadership. The breach between Sarah and Anne became final when, during the thanksgiving service in celebration of Marlborough's victory at Lille, the Duchess hissed at the queen to be quiet before the assembled grandees of the realm. Anne dismissed Sarah from her many offices and the two old friends never met again. After the general election of 1710, the queen ousted Godolphin and his Whig supporters. Isolated and at odds with the new government over the terms of the peace being offered to France, Marlborough was removed from command of the army and lost his offices amidst charges of misuse of public money. When the House of Commons condemned him for misappropriation of funds, the Marlboroughs went into exile.

After two years abroad, Anne secretly invited Marlborough to return. He arrived on August 1, 1714, the day Anne died. In his first official act, the new king George I signed a decree restoring Marlborough to his posts as captain-general, master-general of the Ordnance, and colonel of the Guards. But poor health prevented the duke from regaining his commanding position in the administration. Bouts of sickness, devastating personal losses, and monumental family disputes marked his last years. The death of his beloved daughter Anne led to a paralytic stroke on May 28, 1716. Another stroke followed that November and, after several relapses, he died at Windsor Lodge, London, on June 16, 1722.

Napoleon described Marlborough as a commander whose mind was not solely centered on the battlefield; "He fought and negotiated; he was at once a captain and a diplomatist." While Marlborough's political and diplomatic careers ended in frustration, Great Britain never produced a greater general. In assessing Marlborough as a commander, it must be remembered he never possessed freedom of action. Only in the Blenheim campaign, when he consciously misdirected allies and enemy alike, could he conduct war according to his own discrimination. Constrained by the attrition strategy of the Grand Alliance, he demonstrated a unique inclination for offensive operations climaxing in pitched battle. Between Dutch obstructions and the limitations imposed by the very nature of the mode of warfare of the period, Marlborough's accomplishments are all the more impressive.

A century and a half after Marlborough's death, the Churchill family produced another historic figure. Born in Blenheim Palace, Sir **Winston Churchill** led Great Britain to victory during World War II. Like Marlborough, Sir Winston Churchill emerged as the greatest Englishman of his day. In an ironic twist of history, one Churchill played a central role in Britain's rise to great power standing while another presided over its demise.

SOURCES:

Chandler, David. *Marlborough as Military Commander.* London, 1972.

Churchill, Winston. *Marlborough: His Life and Times.* 6 vols. London, 1933–38.

FURTHER READING:

Barnett, Correlli. *The First Churchill: Marlborough, Soldier and Statesman.* New York, 1974.

Winston Churchill

(1874–1965)

British statesman who served in Parliament for more than 60 years, held most of the high offices of Great Britain, served twice as prime minister, and personified democratic values and determination against tyranny as Britain's leader during most of World War II.

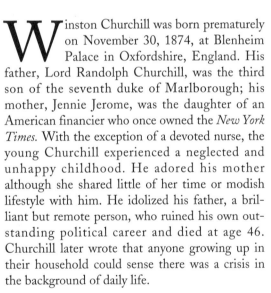

"I have nothing to offer but blood, toil, tears and sweat.'"

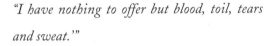

Winston Churchill was born prematurely on November 30, 1874, at Blenheim Palace in Oxfordshire, England. His father, Lord Randolph Churchill, was the third son of the seventh duke of Marlborough; his mother, Jennie Jerome, was the daughter of an American financier who once owned the *New York Times*. With the exception of a devoted nurse, the young Churchill experienced a neglected and unhappy childhood. He adored his mother although she shared little of her time or modish lifestyle with him. He idolized his father, a brilliant but remote person, who ruined his own outstanding political career and died at age 46. Churchill later wrote that anyone growing up in their household could sense there was a crisis in the background of daily life.

After a dispassionate preparatory schooling, Churchill entered Harrow School which emphasized the classics. Having no aptitude for mathematics, Latin, or Greek, he loathed school. He later wrote that he was considered a dunce because he could only learn English, but that he did learn the "essential structure of the ordinary English sentence—which is a noble thing." His conspicu-

Born Winston Leonard Spencer Churchill on November 30, 1874, at Blenheim Palace, Oxfordshire, England; died in London, England, on January 24, 1965; son of Lord Randolph Churchill (a British politician) and Jennie Jerome (daughter of an American financier); direct descendant of British nobility (Marlborough); married: Clementine Ogilvy Hozier; children: Randolph (a journalist and author who had an undistinguished record in politics), Sarah (an actress), Mary, Diana, Marigold (died at age three). Predecessor: Neville Chamberlain. Successor: Anthony Eden.

Contributed by Phillip E. Koerper, Professor of History, Jacksonville State University, Jacksonville, Alabama

251

CHRONOLOGY

In the spring of 1896, Churchill's 4th Hussars were stationed at Bangalore, India. While serving in the 1897 expedition against the Pathans in Northwest India, his accounts written for the London *Daily Telegraph* became the basis for his first book, *The Story of the Malakand Field Force* (1898). That same year, Churchill was attached to the 21st Lancers in Egypt, served during **Sir Horatio H. Kitchener**'s conquest of the Sudan, and played a distinguished role in the great cavalry charge at the Battle of Omdurman. Once again, his newspaper accounts were incorporated into a book, *The River War* (1899). Often critical of tactics and leadership, his books made many enemies among professional soldiers like Kitchener, who disliked Churchill's combining soldiering and journalism. Resigning his commission in 1899 to devote himself to politics, Churchill made an unsuccessful attempt to enter Parliament as a Conservative candidate.

War Hero Churchill Elected to Parliament

When the Anglo-Boer war broke out in 1899, Churchill went to South Africa as a war correspondent for the *London Morning Post*. Acting more as a soldier than as a correspondent, he was captured while defending a British armored train. During his stay at a prison camp in Pretoria, he made a daring escape and with a £25 reward posted for his capture, traveled through Portuguese East Africa to Natal. The accounts of his escape made him an international celebrity. His books about the Boer War and a lecture tour of the United States with Mark Twain provided him with money to renew his political goals. Returning to England as a military hero, he ran successfully in 1900 as a Conservative in the district of Oldham, Lancashire.

Churchill made his first speech in the House of Commons in February 1901. From the very beginning, he was a notable figure in the House but a speech defect and difficulty with impromptu debate made speaking an ordeal that he eventually overcame. His progressive sympathies clashed with his party, and he changed his political allegiance by joining the Liberal Party. When the Liberal majority formed the cabinet in 1905, Churchill was appointed undersecretary of state for colonies. In 1908, while campaigning in Dundee, Scotland, he met and married Clementine Hozier. Theirs was a marriage of constant affection that produced stability and happiness during his turbulent career. He trusted her completely, told her everything, and accepted her counsel for more than half a century. In those years, first as president of the Board of Trade (1908–10) then as Home secretary

ous lack of success at Harrow led to his father's decision to enter him into a military career. After passing the entrance examination to the Sandhurst Royal Military Academy on his third attempt, he seriously applied himself and graduated 20th in a class of 130. Commissioned as a second lieutenant in the 4th Queen's Own Hussars in 1895, he immediately used his first leave to serve as an observer with the Spanish army in Cuba. Combining his desire for military action with his talent for journalism, Churchill was hired to send reports from Cuba by the London newspaper, the *Daily Graphic*. While in Cuba, on his 21st birthday, he received his baptism of fire during an attack.

(1910–11), he authored legislation that reformed prisons, regulated wages and hours, and helped establish a social security system for the elderly.

In 1911, Churchill was appointed First Lord of the Admiralty. Believing in the possibility of war with Germany, he had the Royal Navy ready for action in 1914; in the spring of 1915, however, he was demoted to the minor post of chancellor of the Duchy of Lancaster because of his sponsorship of the disastrous Gallipoli campaign, which was an effort to drive Turkey out of the war. In 1916, he resigned this position to serve in the 6th Royal Scots Fusiliers as a lieutenant colonel on the Western Front. When **David Lloyd George** became prime minister in 1917, he recalled the energetic Churchill to the cabinet as minister of munitions. After the armistice in 1918, Churchill served as secretary of state for war (1918–21) and as colonial secretary (1921–22). Still haunted by the shadow of the Gallipoli disaster, he was defeated in the general election of 1922.

During the two years out of Parliament, Churchill resumed his love of landscape painting and worked laying bricks while renovating his new estate called Chartwell, in Kent. Having strengthened his reputation as a writer with the biography of his father *Lord Randolph Churchill* (1906), he began his excellent four-volume account of the war, *The World Crisis* (1923–29). During these years, Churchill gradually moved back toward the Conservative Party and, after winning a seat from the district of Epping in 1924, was appointed chancellor of the Exchequer by Prime Minister **Stanley Baldwin.** During the five years at the Exchequer, he restored Britain to the gold standard, alienated the labor movement by helping crush the general strike of 1926, and lost power along with his party during the onset of the great world depression.

Between 1929 and 1939, Churchill did not hold cabinet office. In addition to his painting, writing, and work on Chartwell Manor, he con-

stantly warned the nation about the sinister ambitions of Nazi Germany and the lack of diplomatic resolve and weak military preparedness of Britain. In 1938, he denounced Prime Minister **Neville Chamberlain**'s Munich Agreement which attempted to avert war with Germany by giving up a portion of Czechoslovakia. Churchill questioned the belief that British security could be achieved "by throwing a small state to the wolves" and called the agreement "a total and unmitigated defeat." The appeasement policy toward Germany ultimately failed, and two days after Chamberlain declared war (September 1, 1939), he invited Churchill to again serve as First Lord of the Admiralty. A jubilant navy message relayed throughout the fleet proclaimed "Winston is back!"

Speeches Inspire British Defiance

The Chamberlain government finally lost the confidence of the British public when the Germans attacked Norway. On May 10, 1940, the day that Germany launched their surprise invasion of Belgium and Holland, Chamberlain resigned and advised King George VI to appoint Churchill as prime minister. With the Labour and Liberal Party leaders agreeing to a wartime coalition government, Churchill later wrote that his "life had been but a preparation for this hour." In his first statement to the House of Commons on May 13,

1940, he offered them nothing "but blood, toil, tears, and sweat." During the next five years, Churchill went forward with courage, hope, and determination while supervising every aspect of the war effort. Utilizing his great oratorical skills in Parliament and over the radio, he inspired a defiance in the British people during the darkest days of their history. In his initial speech to Parliament, he had gone on to say:

> You ask, what is our aim? I can answer in one word: It is victory, victory at all costs, victory in spite of all terror, victory however long and hard the road may be; for without victory there is no survival.

In June 1940, Churchill urged the people to be resolute and stand firm so that "if the British Empire and its commonwealth last for a thousand years, men will still say: 'This was their finest hour.'" In expounding the nation's gratitude for the Royal Air Force's victory over the German Air Force during the Battle of Britain, Churchill in 1940 said that "Never in the field of human conflict was so much owed by so many to so few." But earlier in the year when the people had rejoiced over the successful evacuation of nearly 340,000 men from Dunkirk on the French coast, he had grimly reminded them: "Wars are not won by evacuations." Anticipating the fall of France in

June 1940, he explained to the British that they would be fighting Germany alone and proclaimed:

> We shall defend our island, whatever the cost may be, we shall fight on the beaches, we shall fight on the landing grounds, we shall fight in the fields and in the streets, we shall fight in the hills; we shall never surrender

In addition to his inspiring speeches and resolute attitude, Churchill presided over every aspect of the war effort, holding direct control over the formulation of policy and the conduct of military operations. When the United States entered the war in December 1941, he and President **Franklin D. Roosevelt** planned many of the allied military campaigns. He supported **Charles de Gaulle** as a "man of destiny" and as the spokesman of the "Free French" forces who had fled to Britain. When Germany ignored their nonaggression treaty and attacked the Soviet Union in June 1941, Churchill defended his offer of alliance to the Soviets by saying: "If Hitler invaded Hell I would make at least a favorable reference to the Devil in the House of Commons." He journeyed without complaint between Roosevelt and Stalin to coordinate the alliance's operations and policies. Aging, he traveled at the expense of his health to major conferences in Washington, D.C., Cairo, Casablanca, Moscow, Teheran, Yalta, and Potsdam. Following the second Cairo Conference in December 1943, Churchill's physical exhaustion led to pneumonia. As he lay gravely ill, everyone from king to commoner was concerned, and Britain had, for the first time since Churchill became prime minister, shown signs of faltering. Although his recovery was rapid, his convalescence was not completed until mid-January 1944. Following the surrender of Germany in May 1945, Churchill took an active role in the celebrations in London, but he wrote that there was a serious foreboding in his heart about the future of European relations with Russia.

Churchill had furnished both the British people and the people of the free world with determined and inspiring leadership during the most dangerous years of the war. But as the war had progressed towards a positive conclusion, he had tried at the Teheran and Yalta Conferences to impress upon Roosevelt and his own nation the dangers posed by certain Soviet policies and actions. Reduced to representing a war-weary nation as junior partner in the alliance with the Americans and Soviets, Churchill could not persuade Roosevelt to heed his warnings. Then, in one of the most striking reversals in political history, Churchill's Conservative Party was soundly defeated by the Labour Party in the general election in July 1945. Rather than a personal vote of censure against Churchill, the defeat was probably a reaction against 20 years of Conservative rule, a desire for social reconstruction, and uncertainty about the aggressive international policies espoused by the Conservatives. He easily won a seat in his new district of Woodford, Essex, which he held for the last 19 years he spent in Parliament. He resigned as prime minister immediately, and Clement Attlee formed the new Labour Government.

Warns of Soviet Threat

Churchill, as leader of the opposition from 1945 until 1951, continued to enjoy a worldwide reputation and warned the Western democracies to stand firm in the face of the growing threat of the Soviet Union. Speaking at Westminister College in Fulton, Missouri, on March 5, 1946, he warned of an "iron curtain" that was descending across Europe, separating the areas under Soviet control from the "free world." Churchill's speeches created a storm of protest and controversy in the West, but events soon confirmed his views of world events and the rapidly developing "cold war."

During his six years as opposition leader, Churchill devoted his free time to his painting and writing. His many paintings were exhibited regularly at the Royal Academy of Art. His six-volume *The Second World War* (1948–53) won him the Nobel Prize for Literature in 1953. Politically, Churchill worked to revitalize the Conservative Party, and in the general election in 1950 he cut deeply into Labour's majority. Another election was called for October 25, 1951, and Churchill appealed to the British public to give him the "last big prize" he would seek to win. The Conservatives won a narrow victory and Churchill, at age 76, was returned as prime minister.

Because of the poor economy and the small majority held by the Conservatives, it was Churchill's iron will and stature that kept them in power. In April 1953, Queen Elizabeth II conferred on him the Knighthood of the Order of the Garter, and he became Sir Winston Churchill. In July, he suffered a stroke but continued in office for nearly two more years. On April 5, 1955, Churchill resigned, but he refused the peerage usually given to retiring prime ministers and continued to serve the district of Woodford in the House of Commons until shortly before his death. He was succeeded as prime minister by his longtime friend, **Anthony Eden.**

Churchill's last decade was relatively tranquil. He continued to paint and write. He bred race horses and devoted more time to Chartwell which was a working farm. On April 9, 1963, the U.S. Congress made him an honorary American citizen, and President **John F. Kennedy** remarked that during the war Churchill had "mobilized the English language and sent it into battle."

During his illustrious career in the military, in journalism and in politics, Churchill found the time to write over 40 volumes. The publication of *The History of the English Speaking People* (four volumes, 1956–58) was the last of his writings which included a novel, *Savrola* (1900), *Marlborough: His Life and Time* (four volumes, 1933–38), *A Roving Commission: My Early Life* (1930), and *Thoughts and Adventures* (1932). Churchill also left hundreds of paintings and even wrote a short book on the subject, *Painting as a Pastime* (1948).

Sir Winston Churchill died on January 24, 1965, two months after his 90th birthday. He helped to plan his own funeral which he had named "Operation Hope Not." The entire world paid its reverence and tribute in the most splendid state funeral ever held for a British commoner. He was buried beside his parents in the family section in the churchyard at Bladon, near Blenheim Palace.

SOURCES:

Gilbert, Martin, ed. *Churchill.* Prentice-Hall, 1967.

James, Robert Rhodes, ed. *Winston S. Churchill: His Complete Speeches 1897–1963.* 8 vols. Chelsea House, 1974.

Payne, Robert. *The Great Man: A Portrait of Winston Churchill.* Coward, McCann and Geoghegan, 1974.

Pelling, Henry. *Winston Churchill.* Dutton, 1974.

Schoenfeld, Maxwell P. *Sir Winston Churchill: His Life and Times.* Dryden Press, 1973.

FURTHER READING:

Bonham-Carter, Violet. *Winston Churchill: An Intimate Biography.* Harcourt, 1965.

Churchill, Randolph S., and Martin Gilbert. *Winston S. Churchill.* 8 vols. Houghton, 1966–88.

Churchill, Winston S. *A Roving Commission: My Early Life.* Scribner, 1930.

———. *The Second World War.* 6 vols. Houghton, 1948–1953.

Lewin, Ronald. *Churchill as Warlord.* Stein & Day, 1973.

Manchester, William. *The Last Lion: Winston Churchill.* 2 vols. Little, Brown, 1983–88.

Moran, Lord. *Churchill: Taken From the Diaries of Lord Moran 1940–1965.* Houghton, 1966.

Wheeler-Bennett, John, ed. *Action This Day: Working With Churchill,* St. Martin's Press, 1969.

Cicero

(106–43 B.C.)

Orator, politician, and philosopher, who struggled to steady the Roman Republic as it slid toward Empire.

"Cicero made the Romans see how great is the charm eloquence confers on what is good ... if it is well expressed."

PLUTARCH

Marcus Tullius Cicero was the elder son of a wealthy but undistinguished Roman of equestrian status from the Italian town of Arpinum. Little is known of his family before Marcus (hereafter, merely "Cicero") rose to fame, except that it was distantly related by marriage to the war hero, C. Marius (also from Arpinum), and that it bore an unusual *cognomen*. The name Cicero meant "chick-pea," and it is alleged that it was adopted because an ancestor had sported a pronounced dent (about the size of a chick-pea) in his nose. Cicero (born 106 B.C.) and his younger brother Quintus (born 102 B.C.) were close from childhood, maintaining the same friends and associates. Despite their mutual fondness for each other, the two had very different aptitudes: Cicero excelled at rhetoric and politics and was the intellectual of the family, while Quintus inherited most of the family's military ability and its share of practical, administrative horse sense. The brothers were educated together (along with two cousins) in Rome and Greece, with an eye to escaping the obscurity of Arpinum. Far from home and parents, Cicero was as much a father as an older brother, a role he would continue to assume throughout his life.

Contributed by William Greenwalt, Associate Professor of Classical History, Santa Clara University, Santa Clara, California

Name variations: Marcus Tullius Cicero. Eldest of two sons born in 106 B.C.; died in 43 B.C.; son of a Roman equestrian from the Italian town of Arpinum; married: Terentia, 76 B.C. (divorced 46 B.C.); married: Publilia; children: (first marriage) daughter Tullia, who died in childbirth; son, Marcus.

of Pontus) erupted into outright rebellion, and then to a civil war among the Romans themselves (pitting the liberal Marius and his faction, the Populares, against the conservative L. Cornelius Sulla and his supporters, the *Optimates*). Sulla's rise to dictatorial authority temporarily brought peace to Rome, but at a huge cost, for besides those who died fighting, thousands more were proscribed, that is, executed after having been publicly named as undesirables. Even after order was restored, the mood in Rome remained somber.

It was an awkward time for an aspiring lawyer (especially one who deeply respected the freedoms associated with the traditional Roman Republic), but through it all, Cicero steeped himself in the legal heritage of Rome. He emerged from his studies and gained his first real recognition with the successful defense of Sextus Roscius Amerinus, in the course of which he not only dispelled a trumped-up charge of parricide, but also attacked a close associate of the reigning dictator, Sulla. At the time, one could vanish for lesser offenses, so Cicero (his brother and his cousins) escaped any potential political ramifications and pursued his professional training by traveling to Athens and Rhodes for the study of rhetoric and philosophy. During his stay, he studied with some of the most famous teachers of the day—Antiochus of Ascalon, Xenocles of Adramyttium, Dionysius of Magnesia, Menippus of Caria, and especially with the polymath, Poseidonius of Rhodes.

Cicero Begins His Political Career

After Sulla's death and with his intellectual curiosity momentarily sated, Cicero returned to Rome. There, without the strong hand of Sulla to suppress them, political rivalries once again exploded into violence. Most noteworthy of these disturbances: in Spain, the renegade Marian, Quintus Sertorius, waged a guerrilla war against the Optimate faction (80–72 B.C.), until Pompeius Magnus (hereafter, "**Pompey**") mopped up the conflict after arranging for Sertorius's assassination; and, in Italy, Spartacus (a slave trained in the gladiatorial schools of Capua) escaped to lead a slave revolt (72–71 B.C.). Thus, in a climate polluted by constant disorder, Cicero began his political career— the first of his family to seek office in Rome. His debut was impressive, for the people elected him to the offices of quaestor and praetor at the youngest ages legally possible. Clearly, his magnificent rhetorical style scored heavily with the electorate. In between these political victories, he enjoyed a well-publicized triumph in the successful prosecution of the ex-governor of Sicily, C. Verres, on

As a youth, he displayed a love of language, and even turned his hand to the writing of epic poetry. Nevertheless, his attention to words would soon serve him as a means to a political career, and he would avidly seek an oratorical education. Before doing so, however, he understood the need for some practical military training, for Roman magistrates wielded military as well as political authority, and no Roman voter would support a candidate without army experience. Cicero's soldiering, nonetheless, was the briefest possible. During the Social War in 90–89 B.C. (when Rome fought to reassert its power over rebellious Italian subjects), he served on the staff of Pompeius Strabo, and discovered that army life was not to his liking. Thereafter, even as a magistrate, when Cicero could avoid military responsibilities, he inevitably did so.

After his short-lived military service, Cicero made his way to Rome to study rhetoric and law at the side of Q. Mucius Scaevola, the leading legal authority of the day. The 80s were a troubled time in Roman history, with the Social War giving way first to a conflict in the East where a bevy of provincial complaints (championed by Mithridates

charges of provincial extortion. Verres's unexpected conviction (although guilty, Verres had many powerful friends—and the Roman courts were notoriously corruptible), established Cicero virtually overnight as Rome's most effective lawyer. Thereafter, Rome's politicians grudgingly admitted that this vigorous orator was a figure to be reckoned with, even if he was a man of no family from their blue-nosed perspective.

Cicero became what the Romans called a *novus homo* (new man)—that is, his family had never held any of Rome's most prestigious magistracies. Although a free Republic in theory, Rome had in fact been dominated by a small circle of elite families for a long time (although the composition of this circle gradually changed). These families did everything possible to keep others out of office, so as to insure their unique influence. As such, the odds were long against anyone new reaching high office. It was to Cicero's credit that he beat the odds, eventually attaining the consulship (the loftiest annual post) in 63 B.C. (the first *novus homo* to reach this office since 94). This noteworthy achievement was only somewhat tainted by the fact that Cicero defeated a slate of unexceptional—or in one case, downright dangerous—rivals.

Cicero proved his mettle as consul, deftly outmaneuvering his colleague (Rome annually elected two consuls) in his attempt to maintain Rome's precarious security. In 63 B.C., two major threats loomed over the state. The first concerned Pompey, who was engaged in a final showdown with Mithridates in the East, and who thus had a large army under his command. The last general to wield such power had been Sulla, and every Roman knew that Sulla had returned to Italy to dictatorial domination. No one knew exactly how Pompey would act, but in 63 B.C. everyone intrigued against all possibilities. The second menace was Lucius Sergius Catiline. This reckless demagogue began his career under Sulla and worked his way through the lower magistracies, although not without scandal. Before 63 B.C., he had twice run for the consulship, and twice been defeated—the second time by Cicero (which Catiline considered a grave insult, since Cicero's origins were so obscure). When Catiline ran for the office a third time in 63 B.C., Cicero openly opposed him. Again Catiline lost. Infuriated, Catiline turned to outright rebellion, attempting to seize by force what the ballot had denied. Making common cause with those who resented the status quo, and counting on his previous connections with such figures as Marcus Crassus and the up-and-coming **Julius Caesar,** Catiline mounted a serious threat. He proved, however, indiscreet in his planning, so that many of his former friends, including Caesar, quit his association. Catching wind of the plot, Cicero carefully collected a wealth of evidence with which to confront his opponent. In November, Cicero's case came together, and he began to rail against Catiline's treason in a series of famous orations. His rhetoric drove Catiline from the city to Etruria, where his premature, revolutionary call to arms was crushed. Some of Catiline's well-placed supporters (including one of the sitting praetors), however, were captured in the city, along with conclusive evidence of Catiline's sedition. Considering the gravity of the situation, and encouraged by the senate, Cicero executed these manifestly guilty traitors, albeit without holding a trial. Few at the time objected, but this procedural indiscretion would eventually cost Cicero dearly.

With the collapse of this insurrection, Cicero was a hero—and he reveled in the extravagant honors then lavished. Before long, however, and much to his dismay, other issues intruded and Cicero's success relegated to yesterday's news. Yet, he had difficulty letting go of his one shining moment. His self-promotions (he even begged poets and historians to glorify his "salvation of the Republic") took such epic proportions that others began to snicker whenever he brought up the issue.

In such fashion, the times left Cicero behind. When Pompey returned to Italy, he proved less ruthless than Sulla. Instead of turning his army against the city, he disbanded it as a show of good faith, while clearly expecting his unrivaled military reputation to give him the necessary *auctoritas* to overshadow the running of the state. Pompey hoped to dominate Rome, because he had much business he wanted passed into law—including significant rewards for his decommissioned soldiers and an official acceptance of the hundreds of administrative decisions he had unilaterally approved while in the East. Without the immediate support of his legions, however, Pompey's expectations proved misguided. He had many enemies in Rome, especially Marcus Cato, who saw their chance to humble the man they recognized as the greatest martial threat to the Republic since Sulla. Though Cicero attempted to win Pompey as an intimate political ally, Pompey was reluctant to associate too closely with Cicero, both because many in Rome had already begun to see Cicero as slightly ridiculous, and because Pompey believed that his success must come with a wooing of Rome's old families, most of which still chafed at Cicero's *novus homo* status. A political stalemate resulted and, with every passing day, Pompey's opposition proved that he was a far better general than an effective political infighter. Thus, as the 60s waned, so did Pompey's reputation. Cato's faction alienated others, too. Chief among these was Crassus, Rome's richest citizen and patron of business interests—not all of which Cato thought savory. As months of frustration stretched into years, Caesar approached Pompey and Crassus with a political proposal: in return for their help in his bid for the consulship, he promised to pass into law everything which they had been unable to get past Cato's filibuster.

First Triumvirate Is Born

Thus, the First Triumvirate was born; Caesar won the consulship (59 B.C.) and delivered on his promises, although he did so by invoking violence. The Triumvirate constituted an illegal junta, but one which proved expedient for its members. As long as the three remained loyal to their mutual interests, they collectively ruled Rome and made a mockery of its free political institutions. Caesar came to be identified as the most dangerous of the three because of his willingness to employ violence, and eventually because of his striking military conquest of Transalpine Gaul. Until Gaul established Caesar's military reputation, few suspected that he might become another Marius, Sulla, or Pompey. Nevertheless, Caesar's success provided the enemies of the Triumvirate with a means to disrupt its unity, for, as his reputation grew, so did Pompey's jealousy. Cicero was one of those who sought to win Pompey away from the Triumvirate, but without success, primarily because in 58 and 57 B.C. Cicero was fighting for his own political survival.

One of the great personal rivalries of Cicero's life was that with Publius Clodius, another in a long line of budding demagogues, whom Cicero had once angered by testifying against him at a criminal trial. Since that confrontation, Clodius hounded Cicero at every opportunity. In 58 B.C., with Caesar's initial support (quickly withdrawn as Clodius became too extreme to handle), Clodius challenged as unconstitutional Cicero's execution of Catiline's supporters in 63 B.C. Clodius successfully bullied a law through the Plebeian Assembly which effectively exiled Cicero, after which Clodius continued his vendetta by destroying much of Cicero's private property. Cicero remained in exile for about 18 months, until Pompey, thinking Cicero might be useful if his own rivalry with Caesar flared, effected his recall.

In Rome, Cicero strove to strengthen his political ties with Pompey, but his hopes were dashed in 56 B.C. when Caesar outmaneuvered all opponents of the Triumvirate with a compromise, temporarily shoring up its internal disputes. With this development, Cicero entered a semiretirement devoted chiefly to the pursuit of philosophy. For about five years, he thus occupied himself, although he occasionally made public appearances out of gratitude to Pompey (for his recall) and others. One bright spot during this period was Cicero's election to the position of *augur,* one of the public-religious posts so coveted by Rome's elite. Also during this period, he emerged to participate in a real media event: unfortunately, however, despite a vivacious defense, Cicero could not obtain Titus Annius Milo's pardon for the murder of Clodius (52 B.C.).

Even with this failure, by 51 B.C. Cicero was encouraged about the Republic's prospects since Pompey and Caesar were again obviously on the outs. Thus, with growing optimism, Cicero accepted a governorship of Cilicia in 51–50 B.C., but as a result he was away from Rome when the showdown between Pompey and Caesar worked its way toward open confrontation. When war came in 49 B.C., Cicero joined Pompey (although without much enthusiasm), notwithstanding Caesar's attempts to win him as an ally. (It is an irony of history that Caesar, one of the men Cicero least trusted throughout his career, was the only contemporary to appreciate fully Cicero's political value.) When Caesar defeated Pompey in 48 B.C., he pardoned Cicero, displaying a mercy toward defeated opponents few others in Rome ever showed. Again, Cicero retreated into philosophy.

The 40s were as cruel to Cicero privately as the previous decade had been publicly. In 46 B.C., he divorced Terentia, his spirited wife of 30 years, allegedly for her disloyalty during the war of 49–48 B.C. Subsequently, he married the young and rich Publilia, whom he soon divorced (45 B.C.) for her lack of sympathy over the passing of his beloved daughter Tullia, who died in childbirth. This tragedy devastated Cicero, as we know from his poignant letters (still extant) written shortly after Tullia's death.

With Caesar's assassination in 44 B.C., Cicero's hopes for a free Republic were again buoyed, and he reentered the political arena. Far from seeing freedom restored, however, there quickly developed another civil war between Caesar's assassins and those who revered his memory. These latter were led by Caesar's two top lieutenants—Mark Antony and Marcus Aemilius Lepidus, but Caesar's surprising posthumous adoption of his grandnephew Octavian as son and heir introduced a third significant figure into the Caesarian camp. Cicero, who thought that the Republic's future lay with the destruction of the Caesarian faction, attempted to play these men against one another. Unfortunately, he misread the men with whom he was dealing. Thinking Antony the most dangerous, Cicero helped sponsor the rise of Octavian. He reasoned that he could exploit this 18-year-old nonentity until Antony fell, after which Octavian himself could be discarded. Octavian, however, proved more adept at the subsequent intrigues. Strutting his "naivete," while pretending to revere men like Cicero as his models, Octavian (soon to be Caesar Augustus) gained extraordinary concessions from the senate (44–43 B.C.), including the command of an army with which he promised to track down Antony. During this period, Cicero viciously attacked Antony in his *Philippics*, claiming that the latter had been guilty of every imaginable vice. Not surprisingly, Antony took offense. When Antony then cut the deal with Octavian and Lepidus which created the Second Triumvirate, Cicero became a marked man. By the end of 43 B.C., the Second Triumvirate (which unlike its predecessor, was empowered as a constitutional entity to "stabilize" the state) resorted to the terror of proscriptions so ruthlessly employed by Sulla. At Antony's insistence, Cicero headed the list of those who would die. In December, Antony's executioners butchered Cicero and his brother.

Cicero was the foremost Latin prose author of his day—and his reputation is well deserved, as his extant work makes abundantly clear. Regardless of prose medium, his style was balanced, polished, lucid, and where appropriate, wickedly humorous. His chief faults lay in his vanity and susceptibility to flattery—perhaps occupational hazards for politicians. Although the power of his rhetoric has inspired generations to esteem traditional Republican virtues, it remains a tragedy that he had little impact on the decline of his own Republic. Why this was so is quite simple: Cicero was an outsider in an insider's world, a moderate in an age of extremism, and a wordsmith in an age of warlords.

SOURCES:

Cicero. *Selected Letters.* Penguin Classics, 1989.
———. *Selected Political Speeches.* Penguin Classics, 1969.
———. *Selected Works.* Penguin Classics, 1960.
Plutarch. "Life of Cicero," in *Fall of the Roman Republic.* Penguin Classics, 1958.
Sallust. *Conspiracy of Catiline.* Penguin Classics, 1963.

FURTHER READING:

Habicht, C. *Cicero the Politician.* Johns Hopkins University Press, 1989.
Stockton, D. *Cicero: A Political Biography.* Oxford University Press, 1989.
Wood, N. *Cicero's Social and Political Thought: An Introduction.* University of California Press, 1991.

Claudius

(10 B.C.–A.D. 54)

Neglected, handicapped historian from the imperial Julio-Claudian family, who became the fourth Roman emperor by a historical quirk.

Name as emperor: Tiberius Claudius Caesar Augustus Germanicus. Born Tiberius Claudius Nero in Lugdunum (modern-day Lyons, France) in 10 B.C.; died A.D. 54; son of Drusus the Elder (son of Livia) and Antonia the Younger (daughter of Augustus' sister Octavia and Marc Antony); married: Plautia Urgulanilla (divorced); married: Aelia Paetina (divorced); married: Valeria Messalina (executed); married: Agrippina the Younger; children: Drusus by Urgulanilla; Claudia Antonia by Aelia Paetina; Octavia and Brittanicus by Messalina; Nero, son of Agrippina, by adoption. Predecessor: Gaius Caligula. Successor: Nero.

Claudius was born into the most powerful aristocratic family of his time: the Julio-Claudians, from which five Roman emperors derived. The paternal grandson of **Livia,** wife of Emperor Augustus, the great founder of imperial Rome, Claudius was also the maternal grandson of Augustus's sister Octavia and Marc Antony, Augustus's great rival and the famed lover of the Egyptian queen **Cleopatra.**

In spite of these brilliant origins, Claudius did not experience a privileged childhood, for he was afflicted with a physical disability, now believed to have been cerebral palsy. The biographer Suetonius, writing about 70 years after Claudius's death, records that he was often a sickly child. His head and hands shook slightly, his right foot dragged when he walked, he stuttered when he spoke, and he was known to slobber when angry or excited. He was, as a result, treated as if he were mentally and socially deficient for much of his life. His father Drusus died when he was just a baby, leaving his mother Antonia to refer to their son as "a monster, a man whom Nature had not finished but had merely begun." Antonia used Claudius as a standard of foolishness, remarking of another, "he is a bigger fool even than my son Claudius."

"Instead of keeping quiet about his stupidity, Claudius explained in a number of short speeches that it had been a mere mask assumed for the benefit of [Caligula] and that he owed both life and throne to it."

SUETONIUS

Contributed by Sylvia Gray Kaplan, Adjunct Faculty, Humanities, Marylhurst College, Marylhurst, Oregon

Suetonius records correspondence from Augustus to Livia that betrayed an ambivalence concerning Claudius:

> As you suggested, I have now discussed with Tiberius what we should do about your grandson Claudius at the coming Games of Mars.... The question is whether he has—shall I say?—full command of all his senses. If so, I can see nothing against sending him through the same degrees of office as his brother; but should he be deemed physically and mentally deficient, the public (which always likes to scoff and mock at such things) must not be given a chance of laughing at him and us.... I have no objection to his taking charge of the priests' banquet at the Festival of Mars, if he lets his relative, the son of Silvanus, stand by to see that he does not make a fool of himself. But I am against his watching the Games in the Circus from the imperial box, where the eyes of the whole audience would be on him.

In another letter: "How on earth anyone who talks so confusedly can nevertheless speak in public with such clearness, saying all that needs to be said, I simply do not understand."

As Suetonius observes, Augustus eventually decided to keep Claudius out of the public eye as much as possible. For the customarily important rite of manhood when a boy could begin wearing the toga, Claudius was given only a hushed-up ceremony in the middle of the night, and instead of presiding at the games with the rest of the imperial family—an occasion when the public could feast their eyes on royalty—Claudius was confined, supposedly because of ill health.

Claudius's uncle **Tiberius,** successor of Augustus, adhered to the same policy. Claudius, now an adult and vainly hoping that the change of ruler might mean a new opportunity for him to be involved in public life, asked if he might receive a state office. Tiberius sent him the regalia for the office of consul but gave him no accompanying authority. When Claudius persisted in requesting the duties of office as well, Tiberius answered that the gold pieces he had sent were meant to be spent on toys for the Saturnalia, a festival where proper roles were temporarily reversed. The implication, of course, was that his nephew was unfit for any public office.

With the usual political avenues of action closed to him, Claudius turned to the writing of history. While still a boy, with the encouragement of the great historian Livy and some assistance from another scholar, Claudius wrote a history of Rome beginning with the death of Julius Caesar. On the advice of his mother and grandmother,

CHRONOLOGY

10 B.C.	Born at Lugdunum
9 B.C.	Father died
A.D. 14	First Roman emperor, Augustus died; Tiberius began his reign
37	Tiberius died; Caligula began his reign
41	Caligula assassinated; Claudius proclaimed emperor by the Praetorian Guard
43	Claudius invaded Britain
44	Celebrated his triumph
48	Messalina "married" Silius; they and their fellow conspirators executed
49	Claudius married his niece Agrippina the Younger, mother of Nero
53	Nero married Claudius's daughter Octavia
54	Claudius died and was deified; Nero began his reign

however, his account prudently skipped the years of the Second Triumvirate—the period when Augustus ruthlessly eliminated his enemies. Claudius was given the privilege of reading publicly from some of this work, but as so often happened, he was unable to make a dignified public appearance. Suetonius wrote that during this occasion a fat man joined the audience and broke several benches when he sat down. Everyone laughed, but "even when silence had been restored Claudius could not help recalling the sight and going off into peals of laughter."

Claudius continued his scholarly pursuits through his years of enforced idleness, writing a twenty-volume history of the Etruscans and an eight-volume history of the Carthaginians. He later continued adding to his history of Rome when he became emperor, but a professional reader gave the public presentations.

Claudius did not confine his scholarly activities merely to history. He wrote an autobiography and a treatise on dicing (games with dice). He learned Greek and could quote from Homer extensively. Noting certain problems with Latin spelling in his studies, he proposed adding three letters to the alphabet to resolve the difficulties. As emperor, he used his imperial authority to decree these letters into effect. According to Suetonius, though the letters had by his time fallen again into disuse, they could still be seen on public buildings and in certain books.

When not enjoying scholarly pursuits, Claudius consorted with people from the nonaristocratic classes—gambling, drinking, and womanizing. He learned to place his trust in those who were personally loyal, particularly his own freedmen who still had social obligations toward him, several of whom he relied on both for friendship and administering his household. Despite the royal family's negative assessment of him, certain people did see a worthwhile side to him. For instance, the Equestrians, people from the second-highest group of social standing, chose Claudius on two different occasions to represent them on a mission to the consuls. **Caligula** chose him for his first colleague as consul, and in this way Claudius finally embarked on his political career in his late 40s. Thereafter, Caligula often appointed Claudius to take his place in presiding at the games; even so, Claudius often remained the butt of jokes and was continually subjected to small humiliations.

Through a Quirk, He Becomes Emperor

At age 50, he became emperor by a quirk. Soon after members of the Praetorian Guard assassinated Caligula, some of them discovered Claudius hiding behind a curtain in the royal palace, trembling in fear that because of his royal blood, he too would be assassinated. Since the main task of this elite body was to guard the emperor—and they were paid more than other soldiers to do so—it behooved them to find one. Furthermore, the Praetorian Guard had a special attachment to Claudius's family, for the name of his brother Germanicus, formerly a focus for their loyalty, still retained a charismatic aura for the men. All ancient sources agree that the soldiers took Claudius from behind his curtain to their camp, and once there he was persuaded to claim the authority of the emperor.

Up to this point, emperors had formally been appointed by the senate without coercion. Now that the unpredictable and cruel Caligula had been disposed of, the senate understandably looked back with longing to Republican days when its own role had truly been one of power. Opposing the emperorship of Claudius, it sent messages pleading that he hand the government back and allow the law to determine who would rule Rome. Claudius, pressured by the Praetorian Guard, refused. According to the Jewish historian Josephus, he sent this answer to the senate:

> In the first place ... it was against his will that he had been carried off by the soldiers; at the same time he considered it both unjust to betray such

devoted supporters and unsafe to abandon the fortune which had befallen him, for the mere fact of having received the imperial title entailed risks.... He would govern the empire as a virtuous ruler and not as a tyrant.

Essentially, Claudius received the emperorship because he had immediate and powerful military support in the Praetorian Guard, whereas the senate had none to speak of. When this became apparent to the senators, they gave their official blessing to Claudius in interest of their own survival, and any lingering hope of returning to a Republican form of government was lost to the Roman Empire forever.

Once formally established as emperor, Claudius began working to gain broad support for his rule. His first action was to grant amnesty to any and all who had opposed his reign and to recall exiles who had been unfairly deported by Caligula. The only people he punished were Caligula's direct assassins, holding that they had also intended to assassinate him; whether or not this was true, and regardless of the previous emperor's erratic behavior, Claudius's claim to authority was based on his blood relationship to Caligula. Furthermore, those who assassinated emperors could not be rewarded.

Attempting to repair the breach with the senate by following procedural forms, Claudius also participated in the senate himself, encouraging senators to speak their minds. The following lively speech addressed to the senate, betrayed his frustration with their relationship:

> If you want to take more time to consider the matter at greater leisure, take it, so long as you remember that, in whatever order you are called, you must state your own view. For, Conscript Fathers, it is altogether unbecoming to the majesty of this body to have one man alone, the consul designate, state his view here, copying it word for word from the motion of the consuls; and the rest of you utter but one word, "I agree," and leave saying "Well, we spoke."

In an effort to place his claim to authority on a more charismatic basis, in the year A.D. 43 Claudius engaged in a conquest of Britain to gain both military glory and the goodwill of the senate. **Julius Caesar** almost a century before had invaded Britain, and Rome had established treaties with various tribes and exacted tribute ever since. Recently, however, anti-Roman rumblings had been heard.

Ordering his army to take Britain, Claudius then made a personal appearance just in time to claim the victory over a major tribe as his own. He returned to Rome and celebrated a "triumph"—a victory procession traditionally granted only to the greatest commanders for the most outstanding victories. There had been no triumphs celebrated since the time of Augustus, and it appears that this victory did enhance Claudius's prestige.

His Accomplishments Make Him Popular

In fact, even without the conquest, and despite resentment from the senatorial class, Claudius seems to have been quite popular with the Roman people. Dependent to some degree on their support, he seems to have been mindful of his subjects' needs and sympathetic to their problems. One event which demonstrated his concern took place as he sat in court dispensing justice. The city of Rome had grown quickly and the populace had become dependent on the government to supply them with their daily bread. The supply was threatened, and people felt desperate. An angry mob attacked the Emperor in court, pelting him with dry bread crusts and demanding bread. Rather than punish them for their effrontery, Claudius listened to their grievances and began offering insurance for ships which would make the daring voyage to procure grain in midwinter. Those who built new grain ships were rewarded, while Claudius also took long-range action to protect the grain supply. He enlarged the harbor of Ostia, the port nearest Rome, to provide a larger and better anchorage for ships, and he constructed granaries there to ensure a back-up source in times of scarcity. Though his grand, 11-year scheme to generate farm land nearer Rome by draining the Fucine Lake proved unsuccessful and Claudius was criticized for his foolish waste, the idea proved worthy nearly 2,000 years later, when the task was successfully accomplished.

To provide more fresh water, Claudius built two famous aqueducts, the Aqua Claudia and the Anio Novus. Like his other major building projects, these were practical in nature; they put people to work, enhanced the livability of Rome, and added to the Emperor's popularity.

Claudius is also known for certain "enlightened" legislation which he brought to the senate for approval. One remaining inscription for instance announces legislation enacted to protect tenants from landlords who wanted to tear down buildings for profit and speculation; another famous law protected slaves who, when abandoned by their masters to die on a certain island in the Tiber River, could not be reenslaved if they survived; still another law allowed women to make their own property decisions unless they were under guardianship of their fathers or former slaveowners. Though by our standards not all his legislation can be termed "humanitarian," clearly Claudius acted with a concern for individuals and a desire to promote justice.

Claudius displayed a marked concern for his subjects in the provinces as well. In Gaul, he built roads and an aqueduct. In the east, he provided relief after earthquakes, restored various buildings, and protected the privileges of particular groups. He also established colonies of Roman citizens in strategic areas around the Empire. In one letter still extant, Claudius addresses a conflict between Jews and other Alexandrians in Egypt, demonstrating a knowledge of these faraway issues and consideration for both sides:

> On the one hand, the Alexandrians show themselves forbearing and kindly toward the Jews, who for many years have dwelt in the same city, and dishonor none of the rights observed by them in the worship of their god but allow them to observe their customs … which customs I also, after hearing both sides, have confirmed. And, on the other hand, I explicitly order the Jews not to agitate for more privileges than they formerly possessed, and in the future not to send out a separate embassy as if they lived in a separate city, a thing unprecedented.

Claudius was also noted (and criticized) for granting citizenship to certain favored provincial towns and peoples. In a speech to the senate recorded on a bronze tablet, he went a step further, advocating that prominent citizens from "civilized" Gallic townships be permitted into the senate at Rome. Such actions naturally brought Claudius widespread provincial support, but if his gestures served his own interests, they also demonstrated a broad concern for the well-being of all his subjects.

Regardless, Claudius was never able to overcome the fact that he had taken power by force against the will of the senate. And the senatorial resentment went even beyond this. Third-century historian Cassius Dio noted that the Emperor often behaved inappropriately, not having been groomed for public service. Sickly and subject to "terrors" as a child, he consequently acted in ways which seemed cowardly; having spent much of his leisure time with people from the lower classes, he therefore often acted plebian; burdened with visible handicaps, he learned to act foolish in self-defense. Claudius was not in any way deficient of intellect, but he claimed in later life that the only reason he had survived Caligula's reign was that he had assumed a mask of stupidity: "He owed both life and throne to it." As a result, despite his accomplishments, he never acquired the refinement and acculturation that the aristocratic class expected in a Roman ruler.

It is also possible that the senatorial class resented Claudius's reliance on his freedmen to perform the most important administrative tasks in his regime. Suetonius listed the various "departments" and the particular freedmen who were responsible for them, leading some scholars to hold that Claudius was innovating and centralizing his rule in a rationalized manner, and leading others more recently to conclude that he was merely relying upon those men he trusted the most, those who were most loyal. Above all, ancient historians criticized him for being easily manipulated. Several deaths of prominent people, for instance, were allegedly machinated by his wives and freedmen working in concert who skillfully played on Claudius's greatest fears, deceiving him into ordering executions without fully examining the issues.

Claudius's freedmen generally proved loyal; if only the same could be said for his wives. Messalina was allegedly involved in a treasonous plot and went so far as to publicly celebrate a marriage to Gaius Silius, a senator who entertained hopes of taking over the empire. When those involved in the conspiracy, several of them senators, were caught, they were summarily executed. When Messalina begged for special mercy, Claudius's powerful freedman Narcissus exercised the authority Claudius had delegated to him, ordering that she be slain before Claudius could relent. (This gripping story is related in *The Annals* of the historian Tacitus, a contemporary of Suetonius.)

A few months after the conspiracy, Claudius was persuaded to marry his niece **Agrippina the Younger.** Tacitus describes this remarkable woman as "the daughter of a great commander and the sister, wife, and mother of emperors." Using the lever-age of her position, Agrippina gradually built herself a power base in the court; she saw to it that men loyal to her were appointed to key positions and persuaded Claudius to adopt her son **Nero** as his own. When Nero reached 16, and his chief potential rival for the throne—Claudius's son **Brittanicus**—was still too young to rule, Claudius died.

Most accounts agree that Agrippina poisoned Claudius by feeding him a plump, juicy, lethal mushroom from her own plate, and he died during the night. The official version released by the court, however, was that Claudius died the next day about noon, having just been entertained by comic actors. Agrippina successfully arranged for Nero to be proclaimed emperor immediately after the announcement of Claudius's death.

Overall Claudius received mixed reviews from the ancient historians who recorded his good intentions and attempts to rule justly, while highlighting his vulnerabilities and failings. It is symbolic, however, that after his death Claudius was deified—declared a god by the senate. He was the only Julio-Claudian emperor besides Augustus to receive this honor.

SOURCES:

Cassius Dio. *Dio's Roman History.* Translated by Earnest Cary. 9 vols. Harvard University Press, 1968.

Levick, Barbara. *Claudius.* Yale University Press, 1990.

Suetonius. *The Twelve Caesars.* Translated by Robert Graves. Viking Penguin, 1986.

Tacitus. *The Annals of Imperial Rome.* Translated by Michael Grant. Viking Penguin, 1987.

FURTHER READING:

Graves, Robert. *I, Claudius.* Modern Library, 1937.

Momigliano, Arnaldo. *Claudius: The Emperor and his Achievement.* Translated by G. W. D. Hogarth. Greenwood Press, 1981.

Scramuzza, V. M. *The Emperor Claudius.* Harvard University Press, 1940.

Georges Clemenceau

(1841–1929)

French statesman and journalist, whose drama-ladened 50-year career in politics was crowned by his leadership during the last year of the First World War and his presidency of the Paris Peace Conference, which wrote the Treaty of Versailles.

"My foreign policy and my domestic policy are one. Domestic policy, I make war; foreign policy, I make war. Always, I make war ... and I shall continue to the last quarter of an hour, for the last quarter of an hour will be ours."

GEORGES CLEMENCEAU

Georges Clemenceau was France's most famous political figure between the mid-19th and mid-20th centuries. He was a man of unbreakable will and pile-driving energy whose personality abounded in striking contrasts. A British general, Sir Edward Spears, who knew personally a host of leaders in both the First and Second World Wars, remembered him as "the toughest, the hardest, and perhaps the most cruel" man he ever met. Clemenceau exercised a brilliant wit at the expense of everyone and was served by an extraordinary verbal facility which made him one of the greatest public speakers of his day as well as a much-read (and feared) newspaper columnist.

His rough exterior and public image as "the Tiger," however, concealed a sensitive spirit containing, as Joseph Reinach once remarked, "the soul of an artist." Clemenceau was highly cultured and well read, especially in the Greek and Roman classics, philosophy, and anthropology. He loved art passionately, was an early supporter of the Impressionists, and a friend of many artists of the time, above all of Claude Monet, whose water lily series he encouraged and convinced the French government to display permanently at the

Name variations: nicknamed "The Tiger." Pronunciation: Clay-ma-só. Born in Mouilleron-en-Pareds (Vendée) on September 28, 1841; died on November 24, 1929, in Paris; son of Benjamin and Emma (Gautreau) Clemenceau; married: Mary Elizabeth Plummer (an American), June 23, 1869 (divorced, March 1892); children: Madeleine Clemenceau-Jacquemaire (a writer), Thérèse, Michel (a businessman, politician).

Contributed by David S. Newhall, Distinguished Professor of the Humanities, Centre College, Danville, Kentucky.

Orangerie in the Tuileries Gardens. He was capable of thoughtful small attentions, made and kept a large number of friends, was generous (and often careless) with money, loved animals, and loved to hunt. Although he was a proud man who made a host of enemies—as he once cracked, "If you have no enemies it's because you've done nothing"—he was totally without airs and cared nothing for the trappings of office. Even as premier, he continued to live in a modest book-lined, curio-filled apartment (now a small museum) at 8, rue Franklin, in the Passy district of Paris.

Georges-Eugène-Benjamin Clemenceau was born on September 28, 1841, in the home of his maternal grandfather in Mouilleron-en-Pareds, a village in the Vendée, a region on the French coast just south of Brittany. The Vendée had been the site of terrible civil wars during the French Revolution and Napoleonic period (1789–1815) and was famous for its tough peasantry and conservatism—Catholic and monarchist. The Clemenceaus, however, were prominent landowners and physicians who were Republicans. Georges's father Benjamin was twice arrested and once nearly deported to Algeria by the regime of **Napoleon III** (1852–70) because of his views, persecutions which deeply impressed the boy. His mother Emma Gautreau,

daughter of an estate manager, was a Protestant and likewise of Republican lineage. Georges thus inherited his life's work in politics: the creation and defense of a republic for France—which came to pass with the Third Republic, 1870–1940.

Clemenceau was the eldest son and second of six children (three sons, three daughters). His childhood was spent largely in Nantes, where his father practiced medicine before retiring in the 1860s to the Château de l'Aubraie (near Chantonnay, Vendée), which the family had acquired by marriage soon after the Revolution. There he tended his properties and lived as a virtual recluse. Georges was educated at home, at a small private school, and at the lycée in Nantes. Following family tradition, he then earned a medical degree by preparing at a school of medicine and pharmacology in Nantes (1858–61) and completing his work at the University of Paris in 1865.

As a student, he was very bright but impulsive, impertinent, and hard to control. He became involved in political activities while in Paris, wrote for ephemeral reviews, and once was jailed for two months for organizing a Republican demonstration. He was for a time much influenced by Auguste Blanqui (1805–81), a famous Republican conspirator, but Blanqui ultimately rejected him as a recruit. Shortly before he received his degree, his suit for the hand of Hortense Kestner (who later married Charles Floquet, a future premier) also was rejected. Reacting to these disappointments, he left for the United States, apparently at first intending to settle.

While in the United States (1865–69), he lived in New York, active but rather unfocused, working as a physician for awhile but also writing about the American political scene for a Paris paper, *Le Temps,* and teaching riding and French at Miss Aiken's School for Young Ladies in Stamford, Connecticut. There he met a pupil, Mary Elizabeth Plummer, orphaned daughter of a Wisconsin dentist, whose guardian, a wealthy New York businessman, finally consented to their civil marriage (June 23, 1869). By now, having "grown a bit older and … if not more modest, at least more moderate," as he wrote to a friend, he decided to settle again in France. But a year after he and Mary returned to l'Aubraie, the Franco-Prussian War (1870–71) began, and he headed to Paris to serve as a doctor and participate in overthrowing the regime of Napoleon III, who had been captured at Sédan.

The Third Republic was proclaimed on September 4, 1870, and carried on the war against the invading Germans. Paris was besieged, and Clemenceau was named (and later elected) mayor

of a radical district, Montmartre. When the siege finally forced the Republic to sue for peace (January 28, 1871), Clemenceau was elected to the National Assembly, which felt compelled to accept the loss of Alsace and part of Lorraine and the payment of a heavy indemnity; he was one of the 107 deputies who voted against the treaty, although he admitted years later that his heart, not his head, had dictated his vote. On March 18, powerful radical forces in Paris—fearing that the conservative assembly would now restore a monarchy—revolted and lynched two generals, reacting to the government's attempt to capture cannons they were holding. The uprising began in Montmartre, where Clemenceau was nearly lynched himself while trying to rescue the generals. He was driven from his city office and resigned from the assembly, but he participated in attempts to mediate between the government and the radicals, who had proclaimed Paris an independent city (the Commune), before the revolt was crushed in May.

Returning to Montmartre in July, he failed to win reelection to the assembly but did gain a seat on the Paris City Council, where he served until 1876, rising to the presidency in late 1875. Meanwhile, he practiced medicine among the poor of Montmartre, fought a successful duel with an officer who had insulted him over the events of March 18 (he became famous as a dueler with pistols or swords), and earned triumphant election

from Montmartre to the new Chamber of Deputies in 1876, thus relaunching his career in national politics. With that he moved his wife and children—Madeleine (1870), Thérèse (1872), Michel (1873)—to Paris. He was reelected in 1877 and 1881 from Montmartre, in 1885 from the Var, a region on the Mediterranean around Toulon, and 1889 from Draguignan (Var). By 1880, when he founded a newspaper, *La Justice*, he was emerging as the leader of the Radical (or "Radical-Socialist") Republicans.

In this role, he waged war on the ministries of the day, run by moderate Republicans nicknamed "the Opportunists." He pushed such causes as unemployment and old age insurance, nationalization of railroads and utilities, rights for labor unions, the income tax, free public education exempt from religious influence, separation of church and state, abolition of the (conservative) Senate, and opposition to imperialist ventures overseas. Much of this program was eventually enacted but well after the turn of the century. As leader of up to a quarter of the deputies and gifted with wit and skill as a debater, he was much feared by his opponents. He helped to defeat ministry after ministry—such as Gambetta (1881), Freycinet (1882, 1892), Ferry (1885), Rouvier (1887), Tirard (1888)—but his foes always kept him excluded from power as being too radical and untamable. And in 1893, they defeated him at the polls.

Georges Clemenceau was known as one of the greatest public speakers of his way.

Back in 1886, he had helped General Georges Boulanger become minister of war in order to reform and "republicanize" the army. Boulanger, however, built a noisy following in order to try to take over the government. Clemenceau turned against him as a public danger. Boulanger's movement collapsed in 1889, but many of his followers bitterly blamed Clemenceau for deserting him. When the Panama Canal Company failed in 1892 and evidence surfaced that politicians had taken bribes to support it, Clemenceau became a target; a leading briber, Cornelius Herz, had been his friend and had invested for a time in *La Justice*. No evidence was ever found to prove he had taken bribes, but a band of ex-Boulangists now charged that he was in the pay of England. Their "evidence" turned out to be forged (the Norton trial), but in a wild election campaign they managed to persuade enough of his constituents to ensure his defeat (1893).

Alone now (he had divorced his wife for adultery in March 1892, although he himself was far from innocent) and fighting through early bouts of discouragement, he began to write almost daily columns for *La Justice* and other papers, notably the *Dépêche de Toulouse*. Over the years, he published 17 books of articles selected from the several thousand he wrote. A majority of them were on political subjects, but many treated social problems, city and village (especially Vendée) life, art, and literature. For good measure, he added a novel, *Les plus forts* (*The Strongest*, 1898), and a one-act play, "*Le voile du bonheur*" ("*The Veil of Happiness*," 1901).

His Involvement in the Dreyfus Affair

In October 1897, he gave up the struggle to keep La Justice afloat and joined the newly founded *L'Aurore* (*The Dawn*), which almost immediately became a leading advocate of a retrial for a Jewish officer, Captain Alfred Dreyfus, who had been convicted in 1894—partly on forged evidence—of spying for Germany and sentenced to life on Devil's Island. For over two years, Clemenceau wrote almost daily articles on the greatest court case of modern times. Some 666 of them were later published in seven volumes which are one of the monuments of crusading journalism. When the famed novelist Émile Zola denounced in *L'Aurore* (January 13, 1898) the acquittal of Major Charles Esterhazy, the real traitor, and accused the army and the government of a cover-up, it was Clemenceau who suggested that the title be changed from "An Open Letter to the President" to the sensational "J'accuse …!" And he and his

brother Albert, a prominent lawyer, defended *L'Aurore* at Zola's trial for libel (February 7–23), which drew world attention. Dreyfus finally was retried but was reconvicted. A now embarrassed government pressed him to accept a pardon; wanting outright victory, Clemenceau only reluctantly agreed to urge him to accept it and abruptly resigned from *L'Aurore*. (In 1906, Dreyfus was officially declared innocent upon review.)

After writing a weekly, *Le Bloc*, by himself for a year (1901–02), he was prevailed upon to run for the Senate from the Var, having been impressed by the Senate's defense of the Republic during the Boulanger and Dreyfus affairs. He was elected in 1902 and 1909 and was a power in the Senate from the day he arrived. From 1903 to 1906, he was also back at *L'Aurore* as editor in chief and daily columnist. He strongly supported the anticlerical campaign against the Roman Catholic Church's political power which culminated in the separation of church and state (1905). His speeches and articles and energy brought him at last (at age 65) into the government, first as minister of the interior in Jean Sarrien's cabinet (1906) and then as premier himself, heading what proved to be the Third Republic's second longest-lived ministry (1906–09).

He announced an ambitious program. Results by comparison were disappointing, although a ministry of labor was created, the Western Railway was nationalized, railway workers received pensions, miners got an eight-hour day, the regime governing separation of church and state was installed, and the Chamber passed an income-tax bill. Relations with labor and the newly unified "revolutionary" Socialist party (which under Jean Jaurès had replaced Clemenceau's Radical-Socialists as the core left-wing party) were strife-ridden, however, especially because these years marked the height of anarcho-syndicalism in the union movement and the beginnings of attempts to unionize public employees (which Clemenceau opposed). A vast movement in the distressed vineyards of the south in 1907 due to collapsed wine prices also disturbed public order. Clemenceau adopted a firm line against violence, which brought charges that he had become a hard-faced reactionary, charges which gained credibility because of his fierce energy, impatience with subordinates, and confrontational attitudes in Parliament. By 1909, however, the unions were beginning to moderate their behavior. Meanwhile, in foreign affairs, he sought to strengthen ties with Great Britain and Russia to counterbalance Germany and Austria-Hungary, with both of whom he kept reasonably good relations even during his intervention in Morocco (1907–08) to protect French and Western interests and during the great Balkan crisis

(1908–09) caused by Austria's annexation of Bosnia from the Ottoman Empire. But he left office shrouded in gloom about the future prospects of European peace.

Having accumulated enough enemies, he lost a sudden vote of confidence on July 20, 1909, and was more than glad to be free again. In 1910, he made a well-paid lecture tour in Argentina, Brazil, and Uruguay, and in 1913 founded a new paper, *L'Homme Libre* (*The Free Man*). When the First World War began (1914), he apparently hoped he would be called to the helm again, but instead he was excluded from the top post; in turn, he would not accept a lesser one. He became the government's harshest critic and a prime target of the Censorship; when in early October 1914 they banned his paper for a week for revealing grave deficiencies in the medical service, he answered with a "new" paper, *L'Homme Enchainé* (*The Chained Man*). There, and as chairman of the powerful Senate committees on foreign affairs and the army, he pressed the government relentlessly for answers and for a better-organized conduct of the war by France and the Allies. Regarded as a dangerous, boat-rocking malcontent, every day brought him hate mail. But as he once wrote: "It is a noble thing to love one's country. It is even nobler to serve it, at the risk of being misunderstood, by warning it of its errors."

His Wartime Leadership

On November 16, 1917, at the Allies' darkest hour (with the Italians reeling from defeat at Caporetto, the Bolsheviks taking over Russia, the French discouraged and bled-out, the British army drowning in mud at Ypres, and the United States still many months from having a strong army in France), President Raymond Poincaré—a foe whose election Clemenceau had opposed in 1913—summoned the 76-year-old Clemenceau as a last resort. Clemenceau remarked to a new cabinet member, "If you knew, my dear friend, what France expects of us, you would be appalled." Over the next year, until the November 11th Armistice in 1918, his unflagging energy and iron will played a critical role in pulling France and the Allies through to victory. Dozens of times, he toured the front's most forward positions restoring confidence. He played a key role in securing better cooperation among the Allies, notably in the naming of General **Ferdinand Foch** as commander in chief. He vigorously prosecuted traitors and had Joseph Caillaux, a top politician and leader of the "peace" forces, arrested on subversion charges which sent a message to both friends and foes. He ran a virtual dictatorship, yet he did so only with Parliament's consent and without requesting special powers—a striking example of effective wartime leadership in a democracy.

He was the last survivor of "the 107" of 1871 when he announced the return of Alsace-Lorraine at the Armistice. He went on to preside at the Paris Peace Conference (1919), history's largest such gathering, and continued his work despite an assassination attempt on February 19 which left him carrying a bullet in his chest. A tough but not unreasonable negotiator, he sought above all to prevent a future German aggression. He believed that the best guarantee of peace would be solidarity among Great Britain, Italy, the United States, and France until Germany had mended her ways. He gave up his demand to occupy permanently German land west of the Rhine when **Woodrow Wilson** and **David Lloyd George** promised him treaties of alliance, and later was shocked when the U.S. Senate and the British Parliament refused to ratify the agreements and retreated to isolationism. He wanted no injustice done to the Germans, but warned:

> as for persuading them that we are just toward them, that's something else. I believe we can find a way to spare the world a German aggression for a long time; but the German mind will not change so quickly.

Although he hated the Germans (if not German culture), he did not think that taking vengeance would work; to those in France who thought him too easy on Germany, he replied: "Over there, no matter what, are sixty million men we must get along with." But the price of peace would have to be vigilance: "Life itself condemns us to it."

To worldwide surprise, on January 16, 1920, he was defeated for the presidency of France (a largely ceremonial post). Economic discontent, his numerous enemies, age, and anticlerical views all contributed. Having already decided to leave the premiership and the Senate, he retired. After trips to Egypt (1920) and South Asia (1920–21), he made a lecture tour in the U.S. (1922), during which he pleaded against isolationism. He was hailed as a great hero of the war, but his warnings of future trouble with aggression went unheeded. In his 80s now, he still managed to write a two-volume philosophy (*In the Evening of My Thought*), a short life of the ancient Greek orator-statesman Demosthenes, a study of Claude Monet's paintings, and a book of essays on controversies pertaining to the First World War (*Grandeur and Misery of Victory*) which he finished four days before his death. He died of uremia and complications of diabetes on November 24, 1929. He had forbidden a national funeral and at his request was buried in a nameless grave beside his father at Le Colombier, a farm near the village of Mouchamps (Vendée).

SOURCES:

Clemenceau, Georges. *Sur la démocratie. Neuf conférences de Clemenceau rapportées par Maurice Ségard.* Librairie Larousse, 1930.

France. *Journal Officiel, Sénat, Débats parlementaires.* Oct. 11, 1919: pp. 1619, 1621–22.

Krebs, Albert. "Le secret de Clemenceau, revélé par les souvenirs de'Auguste Scheurer-Kestner," in *Société industrielle de Mulhouse: Bulletin trimestrial.* No. 735 (1969), p. 84.

Lémery, Henry. "Clemenceau comme je l'ai vu," in *Histoire de notre temps.* No. 6 (1968), p. 175.

L'Homme Enchaîné, Aug. 30, 1915.

Mantoux, Paul, ed. *Les délibérations du Conseil des Quatre (24 mars–28 juin 1919).* Notes de l'Officier Interprête Paul Mantoux. 2v. Editions du Centre national de la recherche scientifique, 1955, 1:43.

Newhall, David S. *Clemenceau: A Life at War.* The Edwin Mellen Press, 1991.

Reinach, Joseph. *Histoire de l'Affaire Dreyfus.* Vol 5. La Revue blanche, 1901–11.

Spears, Sir Edward L. *Assignment to Catastrophe.* Vol 2. Heinemann, 1954.

FURTHER READING:

Brogan, D. W. *The Development of Modern France.* New and rev. ed. Hamish Hamilton, 1967.

Clemenceau, Georges. *Grandeur and Misery of Victory.* Translated by F. M. Atkinson. Harcourt, 1930.

Ellis, Jack D. *The Early Life of Georges Clemenceau, 1841–1893.* Regents Press of Kansas, 1980.

Martet, Jean. *Georges Clemenceau.* Translated by Milton Waldman. Longmans, 1930.

Watson, D. R. *Georges Clemenceau: A Political Biography.* Eyre Methuen, 1974.

Wright, Gordon. *France in Modern Times.* 4th ed. Norton, 1987.

Clovis I

(466–511)

Frankish king of the Merovingian line, who established Frankish power over Roman Gaul, and whose conversion to orthodox Christianity secured great advantages over possible rivals, gaining complete cooperation of orthodox clergy.

"Clovis's most significant achievement was not the conquest of large parts of Gaul but the elimination of all rivals to his kingship."

EDWARD JAMES

The Germanic peoples who entered the Roman Empire over a period of centuries—encountering and overcoming existing social, political, and military institutions—underwent many changes. The Franks were the product of some of these changes. One of their greatest kings, Clovis I, who inherited his throne when only 15, was more than a product of his times: he was a remarkably successful, single-minded, and ruthless leader who made full use of Romanized institutions and Germanic custom in solidifying and expanding the power and territory he inherited from his father, Childeric.

The Franks were not included among the tribes or "nations" enumerated by the Roman and Greek historians who saw and described the early Germans. The result of a coalition of some Germanic peoples who settled in the Rhine Valley, the Franks developed distinctive weapons (i.e., the Francobard—a battle axe), their own dialect (now known as Early Frankish), and an ability to adapt to changing conditions. Because their war chieftains wore their hair long (possibly daring enemies to approach and take hold of it during battle), they became known as the "Long-Haired Kings."

Contributed by H. L. Oerter, Professor of History, Emeritus, Miami University, Oxford, Ohio

Name variations: Chlodovechs; Clodovic. Probable date of birth, 466; died in 511; son of King Childeric; descendant of Merovech, "legendary" king of Franks, from whom Merovingian line takes its name; married: Clotilda (Chlothilde, Chrotechildis; a Burgundian princess); children: (four; each inherited portion of kingdom) Theodoric, Chlodomer, Childebert, Chlothar.

border) in 1653, complete with Roman, Byzantine, Hunnic, and Germanic articles in gold, bejeweled, and with coins and seals which clearly indicated the identity of the body. It is thought that Childeric died in 481 or 482.

The rule of Clovis over the Salian Franks was noteworthy for several reasons: he acquired and improved on the power and position he inherited from Childeric; he effected a union of Salian and Ripuarian Franks; he obtained, by conquest or diplomacy, lands and peoples of adjacent "kingdoms" including Gauls, Alemanni, Thuringians, Armoricans (Bretons), and Visigoths, creating a kingdom that included much of what is today France, Belgium, and Netherlands, as well as parts of western Germany.

Many of his predecessors, in the act of conquest, either expelled or slaughtered the inhabitants of areas they acquired by war. Clovis did not. He seems to have made a conscious effort to include these conquered peoples under his rule, thereby gaining taxpaying subjects together with the products of their industry. One of the results of this policy was a distinct change in social and political practices among the Franks, who adopted many Roman or Gallo-Roman ways.

The reign of Clovis may be seen as a period of considerable warfare. It also marks the foundations of the early French nation. Not all of the innovations were intentional; it is more likely that they were incidental to the desire to avoid unnecessary conflict which could dilute Clovis's almost single-minded objective of acquisition and subjugation of neighboring peoples and lands. To this end, Clovis affected Roman dress and manners when useful, authorized the drafting of laws based on Roman models, and adopted the religion of the majority of his new subjects: orthodox Christianity.

The first of his conquests was the area under the rule of Syagrius, reportedly a Gallo-Roman who ruled the remnants of Roman Gaul. The 20-year-old Clovis defeated the forces of Syagrius (mostly Germanic warriors) near the site of present-day Soissons, forcing Syagrius to flee to the protection of Alaric II, king of the Visigoths, located in the south of what is now France. But on demand, Alaric quickly surrendered Syagrius, and Clovis secretly had the defeated king executed.

A Germanic tribe called the Thuringians lived in a large area to the northeast of the Gallo-Roman and Frankish-controlled lands. Clovis's next target was a smaller group of Thuringians who had settled in the middle-Rhine Valley; he defeated them in 491.

Roman Gaul, and parts of the Rhine Valley and lands north and west of that river, had been infiltrated by Germanic peoples for several centuries since the time of **Julius Caesar.** By the fifth century, those people who had become known as Franks had settled down in two distinct groupings in the Rhine Valley. To the northwest, in the area known today as Belgium and the Netherlands, the so-called *Salian Franks* held sway. The adjectival descriptor of *Salian* was given by Romans and referred to the source of their economic power: the salt flats near the mouth of the Rhine and the North Sea shores. Salt was a precious commodity in those days. Further up-river were the *Ripuarian Franks,* related through language, custom, and probably intermarriage. Their name was also derived from the Latin and signified that they lived on the river banks.

The first so-called king of the Salian Franks, named Merovech (Merovecs, Merovic, Meroveus), received his power from at least two sources: descent from a tribal hero and confirmation of his leadership by a Roman or Roman-appointed official in northern Gaul. Probably a war chieftain who wore his hair long and braided in the Frankish-Germanic manner, Merovech's descendants became known as Merovingians. The first of these was presumably Clovis's father Childeric I, whose richly appointed grave was discovered in Tournai (located in present-day Belgium near the French

Sometime after the Thuringian conquest, Clovis's representatives, while visiting the Burgundian kingdom (to the southeast), discovered Princess Clotilde, one of two surviving daughters of a king named Chilperic, who had been killed by his brother Gundobad (or Gundobald). Since the brother had also drowned Clotilda's mother, the princess was in danger. But when the emissaries saw Clotilda and remarked on her beauty and intelligence to Clovis, he persuaded Gundobad to approve her removal to his kingdom, where she married the Frankish ruler and became his queen.

Clovis Converts to Orthodox Christianity

Now Clotilda was orthodox Christian. In fact, the bulk of the Gallo-Roman population was orthodox Christian. But many of the Germanic peoples already living within what had been the Roman Empire were Arian Christians. Adjudicated a heresy by the Council of Nicaea in A.D. 325, Arianism rejected the doctrine of the Trinity and held that Christ was mortal. Orthodox Christianity in the fifth and sixth centuries believed in a Triune God and the Deity of Jesus Christ and was followed by those who looked to Rome and to Constantinople for their religious leadership. (A later break between Rome and the East would produce the divisions known as Catholic and Greek Orthodox.) In the time of Clovis, orthodoxy prevailed in most of western Christendom, excepting the area inhabited by the Visigoths and some Ostrogothic remnants in Italy. Bringing with her orthodox Christian clergy, Clotilda lost little time working on her mate to convince him of the error of his ways. But it was not until Clovis encountered the Germanic tribe known as the Alemanni that he made any overt gesture in favor of Christianity.

Occupying an area which today would include much of the Upper Rhine Valley, a sizable group of the Alemanni had begun to press westward. In an effort to halt that expansion, Clovis, with his Salian Franks and newly allied Ripuarian Franks, moved into the valley of the Moselle River to a place called Tolbiacum where they met a large force of Alemanni. According to Gregory, the late sixth-century bishop of Tours who wrote the history of the Franks, Clovis's forces were in danger of defeat when he called upon the God of his queen to help him, promising to convert to Christianity if he won. At that point, the Alemanni broke and ran. Since Clovis was apparently a man of his word, he began immediate arrangements with Remigius (Remi), orthodox bishop of Rheims, and along with some 3,000 of his warriors, was baptized in a ceremony at Rheims on

Christmas day, in the year 496 (or 497 or 506). (The Christmas date may be the forerunner of the Frankish tradition to accomplish great things on that day.) It was this same bishop who had written to Clovis in 481–82, praising him for continuation of his father's policies and recommending that he follow the advice of his Christian bishops.

The conversion to orthodox Christianity gave Clovis a decided advantage over all other candidates for high positions in western Christendom. The bulk of the population in the Christian West was not Germanic but Roman and Gallo-Roman. Encouraged by the clergy, they gave their loyalty to Clovis and his descendants, first as orthodox Christians, then as Catholics. The mastery gained by Clovis over the Armoricans was diplomatic rather than military. Armorica was the name given by the Romans to the coastal district of western Gaul which included much of the peninsula of Brittany and portions of what is now Normandy, Anjou, and Maine from the Seine to the Loire rivers. It is doubtful that even Clovis could have conquered the Armoricans, since their history was one of rugged independence. The success of Clovis in this matter is both surprising and decisive, the more so since it gave him positional advantage for his next step, which was subjugation of the Visigothic kingdom in southern Gaul.

The Visigoth campaign was relatively lengthy. The most decisive battle took place in 507 at Vouillé, near Poitiers, where King Alaric II was killed. Although some further fighting was necessary to complete the task, the death of Alaric sealed the fate of the kingdom and ensured Clovis an unchallenged future.

He Promulgates the Salic Law

With the Visigoths out of the way, Clovis could concentrate on cleanup. He authorized the drafting and promulgation of the *Pactus Legis Salicae,* the Salic (or Salian) Law which was to govern the Franks for centuries to come. This is roughly the same period which saw the production of Justinian's Code in Byzantium—the Eastern Roman Empire. The Burgundians, too, had worked at the fashioning of a law code to govern the kingdom. The accomplishment of Clovis in culminating his rule of some 30 years with the publication of the Salic Law is equal in importance with his territorial acquisitions and his religious alignment. When Clovis died at age 55 in the year 511, his death set another precedent: he was interred in Paris, presaging the position that city was to hold in the future for France.

His was a charismatic leadership. The military victories, the political achievements, the social advances which witnessed the differing peoples—Germanic, Gallic, and Roman—settling and living in close proximity and in relative peace, laid the groundwork for the later Holy Roman Empire and the concept of a unified state that included many cultural and linguistic differences.

There can be little doubt that Clovis was a blunt, direct, forceful leader, who had good counsel and listened to it. He benefited from the advice of men who were older and more experienced than he. It is also obvious that he possessed an instinctive flair for doing the right thing at the right time. Even though, following a strong Germanic tradition, he divided his kingdom among four surviving sons when he died, the precedent for unification was there and it manifested itself several times in the centuries ahead. The Belgian historian, Pirenne, has said that without Mohammed (the prophet of Islam) there would have been no Charlemagne (also king of the Franks). It is entirely probable that without Clovis there would also have been no Charlemagne.

SOURCES:

Geary, Patrick J. *Before France and Germany: The Creation and Transformation of the Merovingian World.* Oxford University Press, 1988.

Gregory, Bishop of Tours. *History of the Franks. Selections,* translated by Ernest Brehaut. Octagon Books, 1965 (Columbia University Press, 1916).

James, Edward. *The Origins of France: From Clovis to the Capetians, 500–1000.* St. Martin's Press, 1982.

FURTHER READING:

Bachrach, Bernard S. *Merovingian Military Organization.* University of Minnesota Press, 1972.

Bury, J. B. *The Invasion of Europe by the Barbarians.* Norton, 1967.

Lasko, Peter. *The Kingdom of the Franks: North-west Europe before Charlemagne.* McGraw-Hill, 1971.

Sergeant, Lewis. *The Franks.* Putnam, 1898.

de Sismondi, J. C. L. Simonde. *The French Under the Merovingians and the Carlovingians.* Translated by William Bellingham. London: W. & T. Piper, 1850 (1975).

Wallace-Hadrill, J. M. *The Long-Haired Kings: And Other Studies in Frankish History.* London: Methuen, 1962.

Zollner, Erich. *Geschichte der Franken Bis zur Mitte des 6. Jahrhunderts.* Munich: C. H. Beck Verlag, 1970.

Richard Cobden

(1804–1865)
and

John Bright

(1811–1889)

Political partners, who both embodied and strove to attain the political, social, and economic goals of the Northern urban industrial middle class, especially the economic doctrine of free trade.

"Bright and Cobden were the two leading representatives of the emergence of the manufacturing class as a force in English politics after the Reform Act of 1832. Both believed in the middle class as more valuable to a civilised community than an aristocracy bred in martial traditions."

ISAAC SAUNDERS LEADAM

Forging a political partnership that lasted from 1839 to 1865, Richard Cobden and John Bright became the most prominent spokesmen for the Anti-Corn Law League, a pressure group that agitated for the abolition of import tariffs on foreign foodstuffs as the preliminary to complete free trade in all commodities. The League and its spokesmen stood for what Tory politician **Benjamin Disraeli** called "the Manchester School," an economic doctrine that advocated a totally free market with only the minimum of government regulation, a political system favorable to middle-class business interests, and a social system in which middle-class values predominated.

Richard Cobden, the senior member of this political partnership, was born on June 3, 1804, near Midhurst, Sussex, in the South of England, where his family had been small farmers since the late 16th century. His father "was a man of soft and affectionate disposition," as Cobden's biographer, John Morley, put it, "but wholly without the energy of affairs…. Poverty oozed in with gentle swiftness, and lay about him like a dull cloak for the rest of his life." His mother, a much stronger figure, kept a village shop to support the family until her death in 1825.

Contributed by Denis Paz, Professor of History, Clemson University, Clemson, South Carolina

Richard Cobden (above) was born on June 3, 1804, on a farm near Midhurst, Sussex; died in London on April 2, 1865; son of William Cobden (a small farmer) and Millicent Amber; married: Catherine Anne Williams; children: two sons and five daughters.

John Bright was born on November 16, 1811, at Rochdale, Lancashire; died at Rochdale on March 27, 1889; son of Jacob Bright (a bookkeeper and cotton spinner) and Martha Wood (a tradesman's daughter); married: Elizabeth Priestman; married: Margaret Elizabeth Leatham; children: (first marriage) one daughter, (second marriage) four sons and three daughters. Descendants: John Albert Bright and William Leatham Bright, Liberal Party members of Parliament.

Learning business as a clerk in his uncle's London muslin and calico warehouse in 1819, Cobden later worked as a traveling salesman. In 1828, he went into partnership with some other calico salesmen; within three years, the partnership was printing its own calicos. In the following year, Cobden moved from London to Manchester and seemed destined for prosperity in the business world.

Even while a clerk, Cobden had educated himself in economics, and his first pamphlets, published in 1835 and 1836, marked him as an able writer. In those pamphlets, as well as in his unsuccessful 1837 election campaign as member of Parliament (MP) for Stockport, a cotton town in Cheshire near Manchester, Cobden sketched the outlines of beliefs that he was to hold to his death: free trade, a noninterventionist foreign policy, the vote for middle-class males, and the separation of church and state. At the end of 1838, Cobden joined the recently formed Anti-Corn Law League, and invited **John Bright,** to join early in 1839.

John Bright, the son of a Lancashire cotton spinner, was born at Rochdale on November 16, 1811. After studying at schools belonging to his family's Quaker denomination, he helped manage the family cotton mill and went into partnership with his brothers; his business and religious experiences led him to develop an interest in politics and economics. His first public speeches were in support of temperance, and he became a lifelong abstainer from alcohol in 1839. During the 1830s, he also became active in opposition to church rates: local property taxes levied for the upkeep of Anglican parish church buildings. As Quakers, Bright's family refused to pay these taxes, his father had property confiscated for refusal to pay, and he himself vigorously agitated for their abolition. Lastly, Bright became interested in state-supported nonsectarian elementary education for children who worked in factories. It was on this issue that Bright first made Cobden's acquaintance, asking the latter to speak in a public meeting on the subject at Rochdale. Their friendship ripened, and, in 1839, Cobden invited Bright to join the Anti-Corn Law League.

The goal of the Anti-Corn Law League pressure group was the abolition of import duties on foreign grain and the promotion of free trade in all commodities. Headquartered in Manchester, the center of British cotton manufacturing, the league came to stand for the economic and political aspirations of the industrial middle classes, which went beyond simple tariffs. Opening the domestic market to foreign farm produce, the league hoped to reduce the economic and political power of the agricultural landed gentry classes,

which still dominated Britain in the early 19th century. By arguing that repeal of the corn laws would lead to a fall in the price of food, the league hoped to convince the working classes that their interests were best served by following middle-class leadership rather than by organizing labor unions or agitating for the vote. The league's long-range goal was to promote free trade in all commodities, for it believed that British manufacturers could beat their competitors for world markets if tariffs were eliminated.

For the following eight years, from 1839 to 1846, Cobden and Bright cooperated in advancing the goals of the league. Working in two ways, the league sought to convert public opinion to free trade by means of public meetings, demonstrations, and pamphlet propaganda; it also sought to exert pressure on politicians by means of electing free traders to Parliament.

In an age without television, radio, and film, public meetings represented a major source of popular entertainment. Males attended to enjoy the oratory and to see famous people. (It was not considered ladylike for women to attend public meetings, unless the meetings were primarily religious in purpose.) League rallies were especially exciting because they were often the scene of debates (and fights) between middle-class free traders and Chartists, supporters of a working-class movement that advocated universal manhood suffrage. Cobden and Bright became the leading public spokesmen for the league, speaking at public rallies throughout Britain. Both men had the knack of casting complicated economic principles in simple, easy-to-understand language; together, they made the most effective propaganda and agitational team in the history of 19th-century oratory. In their teamwork, Cobden specialized in stating the case for free trade, while Bright specialized in destroying the arguments of opponents.

Both Gain Seats in Parliament

The league also engaged in electoral pressure by helping its supporters register to vote, quizzing the economic views of candidates for public office, and supporting candidates who pledged themselves to free trade. Cobden was one of the first league free traders to be elected to Parliament, representing Stockport from 1841 to 1847. Bright joined him in the House of Commons as M.P. for Durham, 1843 to 1847. Together, they proved formidable debaters and effective exponents of the economic doctrine. The Conservative prime minister, Sir **Robert Peel,** gradually came to accept the validity of the free-trade argument, but not until the Irish Potato

Famine of 1845 provided him with a need for action was he able to announce his conversion. Although Peel brought about a repeal of the corn laws in 1846, his supporters—drawn as they were from the landed interest—repudiated his leadership and voted him out of office. In his last speech as prime minister, Peel declared that the man chiefly responsible for the coming of free trade was Richard Cobden, "a man who, acting … from pure and disinterested motives, has advocated their cause with untiring energy, and by appeals to reason, expressed by an eloquence the more to be admired because it was unaffected and unadorned."

Both Cobden and Bright suffered personal losses in their service to the Anti-Corn League. When Bright's first wife died in 1841, after less than two years of marriage, Cobden convinced him to forget his grief in work for the league. (Bright married a second time in 1847, after the corn laws had been abolished.) Cobden's marriage in 1840 produced a large and happy family; but, in order to devote most of his time to league activities, he had given charge of his business interests to his elder brother who was as bad a businessman as their father. By 1845, Cobden's affairs were in disarray, and he was on the verge of bankruptcy. Bright organized a public subscription that raised enough money to pay off Cobden's debts, buy him a small farm, and invest in the Illinois Central Railway Company.

The political partnership continued for 19 more years, until Cobden's death in 1865. Both sat in Parliament almost uninterruptedly during the period, Cobden representing the heavily industrialized West Riding of Yorkshire (1847–57) and Rochdale (1859–65), and Bright representing Manchester (1847–57) and Birmingham (1857–89).

Cobden was a visionary who believed that free trade, if it could be spread throughout the world, would inaugurate universal peace. "There is no human event that has happened in the world more calculated to promote the enduring interests of humanity than the establishment of the principle of free trade," he declared. "[W]e have a principle established now which is eternal in its truth and universal in its application. It is a world's revolution and nothing else." Becoming an international missionary for free trade, his greatest success came in 1860 when he negotiated the Cobden-Chevalier Treaty, establishing free trade between Britain and France.

Advocates for Noninterference

Cobden and Bright also believed in peace through negotiation and in noninterference in the affairs of other countries. This view challenged the more traditional British diplomatic policy of interfering in the affairs of other states to preserve the balance of power. During the American Civil War (1861–65), they defended the Northern cause against those who wanted Britain to support the Confederacy, on the grounds that the South's support for slavery outweighed the North's support for protective tariffs against British goods. They opposed the Crimean War (1853–56), in which Britain and France supported the Turkish Empire against Russia for control of the Black Sea. The two men believed that Britain had not exhausted a negotiated settlement before going to war, and they contended that Turkish brutality toward its minority populations negated British support. Bright warned of the human costs of war in a speech accounted one of the most brilliant in the history of Victorian oratory.

> I am certain that many homes in England in which there now exists a fond hope that the distant one may return—many such homes may be rendered desolate when the next mail shall arrive. The Angel of Death has been abroad throughout the land; you may almost hear the beating of his wings…. [H]e takes his victims from the castle of the noble, the mansion of the wealthy, and the cottage of the poor and the lowly, and it is on behalf of all these classes that I make this solemn appeal.

Their opposition to the war in the face of public war fever led to their defeat in the election of 1857.

In domestic matters, Cobden and Bright tirelessly campaigned for reforms dear to the hearts of middle-class manufacturers. They supported the enfranchising of more males from the middle class and the upper reaches of the working class, and thus took an active role in the debates over the Reform Act of 1867 (legislation which did just that). They opposed government subsidies for the Church of England, advocated equal rights for dissenters from the Established Church (supporting the right of Jews to sit in the House of Commons), and even went so far as to call for the separation of church and state. True to the interests of their class, they opposed legislation to limit the working day for factory workers, arguing that the state had no business interfering in the relationship between employer and employee. They stood for peace abroad, the retrenchment of government spending, the reduction of taxes, and the reform of British institutions so as to increase the political power of the middle classes.

Cobden, whose health had never been robust, died of respiratory failure on April 2, 1865. Bright, present at the deathbed, was devastated by the unexpected loss; at the memorial in the House of Commons he wept and could only say, "He has been my friend and as my brother for more than twenty years, and I did not know how much I loved him till I found that I had lost him."

Bright's public life lasted for another 22 years. In foreign matters, he retained his beliefs in peace, free trade, and negotiated diplomacy. Although never as visionary as Cobden—for instance, he never rejected the abstract principle of warfare—Bright believed that Britain should pursue the policy of neutrality. "Force," he once declared, "is not a remedy." Thus he opposed British involvement in the Russo-Turkish War of 1876–78 and in the Egyptian civil war of 1881–82. He also opposed the spread of the British Empire in the 1870s and 1880s, especially during the foreign secretaryship of the marquess of Salisbury, a man who believed strongly in balance-of-power diplomacy.

In domestic affairs, however, Bright grew increasingly conservative. He continued to support civil rights for dissenters from the Church of England, arguing that even atheists should have the right to sit in Parliament, and to call for the separation of church and state, playing a prominent role in the debates over the disestablishment of the state Church of Ireland in 1869. But he gradually ended his activities for parliamentary reform, reversed his earlier support for women's suffrage, and came to oppose home rule for Ireland. He accepted an office in **William Ewart Gladstone**'s ministry in 1868, and again in the 1880s, which contrasts with Cobden's refusal of office when **Lord Palmerston** had offered it in 1860.

Bright maintained an active public life until 1887. He died on March 27, 1889, of diabetes and Bright's Disease. Although in his later years Bright had become the personification of middle-class industrial liberalism in the eyes of many, he was not as successful in effecting political change alone as he had been in partnership with Cobden. Most 20th-century historians accept the verdict of Justin McCarthy, a Victorian journalist and political commentator.

> There was, in Mr. Bright's nature, a certain amount of Conservatism which showed itself clearly enough the moment the particular reforms which he thought necessary were carried; Mr. Cobden would have gone on advancing in the direction of reform as long as he lived…. Not much difference, to be sure, was ever to be noticed between them in public affairs. But when there was any difference, even of speculative opinion, Mr. Cobden went further than Mr. Bright along the path of Radicalism.

SOURCES:

Leadam, Isaac Saunders. "John Bright" in *Dictionary of National Biography.* Vol. XXII. Oxford University Press, 1901.

Trevelyan, George Macaulay. *The Life of John Bright.* Houghton, 1913.

Morley, John. *The Life of Richard Cobden.* 2 vols. Macmillan, 1906.

Read, Donald. *Cobden and Bright: A Victorian Political Partnership.* St. Martin's Press, 1968.

FURTHER READING:

Ausubel, Herman. *John Bright, Victorian Reformer.* John Wiley & Sons, 1966.

Edsall, Nicholas C. *Richard Cobden, Independent Radical.* Harvard University Press, 1986.

McCord, Norman. *The Anti-Corn Law League, 1838–1846.* 2nd ed. Unwin University Books, 1968.

Jean-Baptiste Colbert

(1619–1683)

French statesman who, during his 20-year career as a civil servant/courtier, introduced mercantilism to France and was Louis XIV's most important minister.

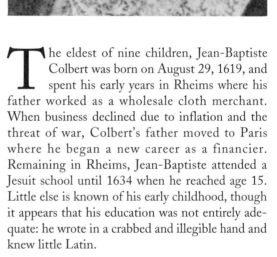

"There are many reasons why great things should not be undertaken, but they do not fail to produce great effects when sustained."

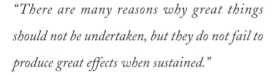

The eldest of nine children, Jean-Baptiste Colbert was born on August 29, 1619, and spent his early years in Rheims where his father worked as a wholesale cloth merchant. When business declined due to inflation and the threat of war, Colbert's father moved to Paris where he began a new career as a financier. Remaining in Rheims, Jean-Baptiste attended a Jesuit school until 1634 when he reached age 15. Little else is known of his early childhood, though it appears that his education was not entirely adequate: he wrote in a crabbed and illegible hand and knew little Latin.

After leaving school, Colbert acquired on-the-job training by working first as a financier's apprentice in Lyons and later as a notary in Paris. His real career as a civil servant began in 1640 when he became a *commissaire ordinaire des guerres* ("war commissioner"). Traveling widely, he inspected garrisons, counted troops, and oversaw equipment and materials. Even at this early stage, Colbert exhibited what historian Ines Murat described as "a firm, precise, and assiduous turn of mind." In 1643, he married a rich heiress, Marie Charon. Although she bore him nine children, vir-

Born on August 29, 1619, at Rheims; died in Paris on September 6, 1683; eldest son of a cloth merchant/financier; married: Marie Charon, 1643; children: three daughters, six sons.

Contributed by Margaret McIntyre, Ph.D. candidate, University of Guelph, Guelph, Ontario, Canada

CHRONOLOGY

1624	Richelieu's ministry began
1635	France declared war on Spain
1638	Mazarin entered Richelieu's service
1640	Colbert appointed war commissioner
1643	Louis XIII died; accession of Louis XIV under regency of Anne of Austria
1648	Treaty of Westphalia; the Fronde (to 1653)
1651	Colbert entered Mazarin's service (age 32)
1654	Louis XIV crowned at Rheims
1661	Mazarin died; Louis XIV's rule began; Fouquet arrested; Colbert appointed minister of finances
1664	Appointed superintendent of buildings
1665	Became comptroller-general of finances and superintendent of commerce
1669	Appointed secretary of state
1672	France declared war on United Provinces; Louvois became minister of war
1675	Revolts in Brittany and Bordeaux against taxation
1678	Treaty of Nijmwegen
1683	Colbert died at age 64

tually nothing is known of her character or of their married life. Colbert's career, as always, was to take precedence over his personal affairs. His determination and hard work were rewarded in 1645 when he became the assistant to the war minister, Michel Le Tellier.

When Louis XIII died on May 14, 1643, the heir to the throne was a six-year-old boy whose mother Anne of Austria became regent. Due to the heavy responsibilities of government, she relied upon **Jules Mazarin,** a man who had served under **Cardinal Richelieu** during Louis XIII's reign. Some historians have concluded that Mazarin and Anne of Austria were lovers and that he became **Louis XIV**'s "unofficial" stepfather, although there is no substantial evidence to support this conclusion. In any case, during the minority of Louis XIV, Mazarin was dominant as the young king's advisor, mentor, and guardian.

Colbert's work for Le Tellier increasingly involved him in governmental affairs, especially from 1648 when France was embroiled in a series of rebellions known as the Fronde—a direct result of war with France's traditional rival, Spain. Heavy taxes and high interest payments not only left the French monarchy bankrupt but alienated the majority of the population, including the nobility, who resented the continual harassment from government tax collectors for money. During the rebellions of the Fronde, which continued for five years, the focus of animosity centered on Mazarin. By 1651, he was forced to flee to Germany for his personal safety.

Colbert, in his capacity as assistant to Le Tellier, had met Mazarin and had come to act as a go-between for the two ministers. In 1651, Mazarin asked Le Tellier to release Colbert from his duties in order to secure the assistant's services for himself. Colbert became indispensable to Mazarin. As his agent, he was entrusted with the minister's personal and private affairs as well as his business ventures and financial arrangements. When Mazarin returned to Paris in 1653 after the Fronde had been crushed, Colbert's compensation for services rendered accumulated. By the time of Mazarin's death on March 9, 1661, Colbert was already Baron de Seigneley, Secretary of the Orders of the Queen and Counselor of the King. Through the sale of ecclesiastical and government offices, he also built up a considerable personal fortune.

After Mazarin's death, the 23-year-old Louis XIV took control of the government and was determined from the outset to maintain that control within the crown; there were to be no chief ministers such as Richelieu and Mazarin. Instead, the king chose men from the officeholding class to be his principal advisors and ministers. Three men were chosen to assist him in his High Council: Le Tellier, as minister of war; Hugues de Lionne, as minister of foreign affairs; and Nicolas Fouquet, who became finance minister. Appointed Intendant of Finances, Colbert was immediately charged by Louis XIV to audit Fouquet's finances. Historians have concluded that Colbert, in his quest for more power, convinced the king that Fouquet was not only mismanaging the crown's finances but was enriching himself at the crown's expense. It was also rumored that Fouquet was plotting to reintroduce the Fronde and seize power.

Consequently, on September 5, 1661, Fouquet was arrested on charges of treason and fraud. In order to ensure Fouquet's destruction, Colbert created a judicial body to try him, the Chambre de Justice. After a three-year trial, Fouquet was eventually found not guilty of treason but guilty of fraud and sentenced to life imprisonment. Appointed minister of finance after Fouquet's fall, Colbert became Louis XIV's most trusted and most important minister; by the time of his death, he was responsible for virtually every government portfolio except the ministries of war and foreign affairs. In 1664, he was appointed superintendent of buildings, in 1665, he became superintendent-general of commerce, and in 1669, he was named secretary of state in charge of the navy, galleys, commerce and horse-raising.

He worked harmoniously with the king although his financial policies, nepotism, and cold demeanor did not win him many friends. Madame de Sevigne nicknamed him "The North" because of his hard and glacial temperament. Another contemporary described him as:

> Insensible to satire, deaf to threats, incapable of fear and of pity, concealing beneath a phlegmatic exterior a hot and impatient nature; though before deciding he asks advice with care and in good faith, he then executes despotically and crushes all opposition.

In spite of his faults, Colbert held the king's confidence and was entrusted with the upbringing of two of Louis's illegitimate children. His main concern, however, was to reform royal finances and glorify the King.

His Quest for Reform

Colbert's financial policies, while effective for the first decade of his career, were bitterly hated by financial circles. The Chambre de Justice continued to take action against other accused financiers and was successful in recovering over 100,000,000 livres for the government. Historian Charles Cole has concluded that "of all Colbert's financial preoccupations, the greatest was that of raising revenue by taxation, and of all taxes the *taille* seems to have interested him most." The taille was a head tax of which certain individuals—nobles, clergy, some officials, and towns—were exempt. As such, the heaviest burden of taxation fell upon those least able to pay: the peasantry. While Colbert wished to redress this inequity, he was never successful in doing so. In addition, the taxation system in France was disorganized and corrupt to the extent that more than half of the money collected did not reach the royal treasury. Colbert's goal was to reform the tax system or, as historian Andrew Trout notes, "to introduce system into a chaotic administration."

This quest for reform characterized the first 11 years of Colbert's ministry. Not only did he desire a revised tax system, but he also worked to unify the various law codes of the country; to implement urban reform through widening streets and enforcing sanitation regulations; to nationalize weights, measures, roads, and rivers; and to rebuild crown finances through the creation of new monopolies. As superintendent of buildings, Colbert undertook the supervision of Louis XIV's palace at Versailles, as well as encouraging artists, musicians, and writers to create works which would glorify the king. His efforts in all of these areas were largely successful until 1672 when war was declared against Holland. This was the turning point of Colbert's political career and one which brought to the fore his only serious rival for the king's confidence, the marquis de Louvois, son of Colbert's old employer, Le Tellier.

Although Colbert supported Louis XIV's decision to wage war on the United Provinces, his reasons for doing so differed from those of the king. Since the Treaty of Westphalia in 1648, Louis XIV maintained an animosity towards the Dutch not only because of their commercial and naval power but because they had frustrated his attempts to annex and dominate the Spanish Netherlands. Louis's political and dynastic aims were complemented by Colbert's economic goals. Much of Colbert's support for the war was due to his economic theories which have come to be known as mercantilism. Most historians now agree that Colbert did not invent mercantilism nor was he an innovator in economic theory. Mercantilist ideas had been in existence since the 16th century, but Colbert's contribution was to coordinate these various theories and attempt to put them into practice.

Colbert's goal was to make France strong and wealthy. He believed that the strength of the state depended upon its finances. In its broadest terms, mercantilism was a system of government intervention in economic affairs that was intended to promote national prosperity and increase the power of the state. The purpose of this intervention was not only to expand the volume of manufacturing and trade but also to bring more money into the royal treasury in order to enable the king to wage war more effectively and efficiently. As such, Colbert sought to increase the supply of money by attracting it from other lands through encouraging exports, keeping money in the country by reducing imports, and, finally, by encouraging existing internal commerce and industry through establishing new trades or manufacturing that appeared likely to succeed.

To Colbert, commerce was essential to the well-being of the state, but the success of commerce in one country could only be achieved at the expense of other nations. Thus, commerce was a "continual and bitter war between nations, for economic advantages." In his own words, Colbert claimed that: "Commerce is the well-spring of finance, and finance is the sinew of war." And, in his opinion, the greatest threat to the economic success of France came from the Dutch. Consequently, when Louis XIV declared his intentions to wage war against the United Provinces, Colbert gave him a hearty approval.

War with Dutch Drains Treasury

Unfortunately for Colbert, however, the war was not a success. In spite of his efforts to keep the royal treasury financially afloat, within four years from the onset of hostilities in 1672, the budget deficit had risen from 8 million to 24 million livres. Colbert attempted to raise revenue by imposing fines, and new and extraordinary taxes, by increasing the sale price of government offices, and by creating new offices. These measures, however, only served to decrease his already waning popularity. In 1675, popular revolts against the imposition of new taxes broke out in Brittany and Bordeaux. When peace was finally achieved through the Treaty of Nijmwegen in 1678 not only was Colbert's balanced budget utterly destroyed, but his "economic war" against the Dutch had failed. In addition, his influence with the king was overshadowed by Louvois. From 1680 it was the policies of Louvois, rather than those of Colbert, that the king chose to follow.

Nevertheless, Colbert continued to work his usual 12- to 16-hour days. In addition to being paid a huge salary, he also received numerous gifts and favors from the king so that by the time of his death his personal fortune was thought to be worth over 10 million livres. He owned several lands, estates, and châteaux, and he entertained the king on several occasions at his favorite residence at Sceaux. Colbert also spent much of his time seeking status, favors, and positions for the various members of his family. For his sons, uncles, and cousins, he obtained several important government and ecclesiastical posts while he arranged advantageous marriages for his daughters, all of whom became duchesses. His only distraction from work was his library. A confirmed bibliophile, Colbert collected over 17,000 books and manuscripts, and he had a particular affection for Oriental works. Many historians, however, have concluded that his interest in books was acquisitive rather than literary.

Most of Colbert's ideas and opinions were derived from economic and financial motivations. Although he was a Catholic, he advocated toleration for Protestants and Jews because it was good for the economy. His single-mindedness led him to dislike anyone or any group of people whom he felt was unproductive. Thus, in Colbert's opinion, the clergy were a drain on the economy because they did not marry and raise families that would eventually pay taxes. Likewise, any profession that did not serve the king's purposes was derided. Hence, lawyers, beggars, officers, and tavern-keepers were "idlers" and useless. He sympathized with the plight of the peasants only because he believed they should not be so oppressed that they could not pay their taxes. In all, Colbert's policies and personality did nothing to endear him to either the general populace or the middle or upper classes; for much of his life, he could not go out at night without an armed escort.

Losing favor with the king took its toll on his health. Throughout his life, Colbert suffered from gastric troubles and gout. In August 1683, he fell ill, and on September 2, he was given the last rites. A letter from Louis XIV expressing hope for a speedy recovery did nothing to rouse his spirits, and on September 6, 1683, Colbert died of kidney stones at the age of 64.

SOURCES:

Cole, Charles Woolsey. *Colbert and a Century of French Mercantilism.* Archon, 1964.

Murat, Ines. *Colbert.* University Press of Virginia, 1984.

Trout, Andrew. *Jean-Baptiste Colbert.* Twayne, 1978.

FURTHER READING:

Lodge, Eleanor. *Sully, Colbert and Turgot: A Chapter in French Economic History.* Kennikat Press, 1931.

Michael Collins

(1890–1922)

Irish nationalist, who fought in the Easter Rising of 1916 and conducted a guerrilla campaign that helped drive England to negotiate a treaty with Ireland offering limited sovereignty.

"Michael Collins was the man who fought the Black and Tan terror for twelve months, until England was forced to offer terms."

ARTHUR GRIFFITH

Born near Sam's Cross, a small village in County Cork, Ireland, on either the 16th or the 18th of October 1890, Michael Collins was the youngest of eight children. His father was 75 years old when he was born. The Collins family lived on a moderate-sized farm, covering somewhere between 60 and 80 acres. Being the youngest of so many, Mike Collins was a spoiled child; he was also a physically active and combative boy. Rough sports appealed to him, but so did sitting at the feet of his older relatives, listening to stories of Ireland's past. He was a hard worker on the farm and quick at school. From the age of five, he walked two miles daily to the Lisavaird National School; his teacher later recalled that Collins was exceptionally observant, very good at math, and had "more than a normal interest in things appertaining to the welfare of his country." Perhaps some of this interest in politics and the relationship between England and Ireland had grown while Collins listened to family tales of the Great Famine (1860s) and other episodes in Ireland's long and often tragic history. England had controlled Ireland for centuries, brutally oppressing the Irish, first through warfare and confiscation of land and later through a legal system

Born near Sam's Cross in County Cork, Ireland, on October 16 or 18, 1890; ambushed and killed at Beal na mBlath on August 22, 1922; last son of a large farming family; never married; no children.

Contributed by Colleen Carpenter Cullinan, Ph.D. candidate, University of Chicago Divinity School, Chicago, Illinois

known as the Penal Laws. Agitation for Irish independence had been growing over the previous century, but it still seemed unattainable.

After completing elementary school, Collins went on to prepare for the civil service exam at a secondary school in Clonakilty. Entering the civil service, most probably in England, seemed to be the only career available. The family farm had already passed to his eldest brother, and there was not much work available in Cork. But Clonakilty was too far away from home for him to walk there daily, so Collins spent weeknights with his older sister, Margaret O'Driscoll, and her family. Since Margaret's husband published a small newspaper, Collins eagerly became involved with the family business. As a reporter and typist, he preferred to focus his attention on sporting news.

In 1906, after passing the civil service exam, Collins traveled to London to take a job with the Post Office Savings Bank, moving in with his sister Johanna who was also working in the civil service. There was a solid, active Irish minority community in London, including Collins's best friend, Jack Hurley. Quickly becoming involved with Sinn Fein, an Irish political party working for Irish independence, Collins also became a member of the Gaelic Athletic Association. The GAA sponsored Irish sports such as hurling and Irish football and discouraged its members from participating in British sports such as soccer or rugby. Collins belonged to the Geraldine Club of the GAA, and served as its secretary from 1909 to 1915. The Geraldine Club was in fact an abysmal team: Collins reputation as a solid player but poor loser was probably exacerbated by playing for years with a team that rarely if ever won.

In 1909, Collins joined the Irish Republican Brotherhood, a secret organization dedicated to making Ireland a free nation through armed rebellion. The IRB's specific embracing of the possibility—indeed, the eventual necessity—of violent uprising was problematic for many of the more moderate nationalists, such as most members of Sinn Fein. Although Collins stayed involved with Sinn Fein, he came to see the moderates as too patient, too willing to accept British rule. Rising quickly within the ranks of the IRB, he was soon treasurer for the entire south of England district of the Brotherhood.

With the outbreak of World War I in 1914, Irishmen in England had to face the possibility of conscription to fight in the war. Collins briefly debated moving to the United States, where his brother Patrick lived, but eventually decided to return to Ireland. In 1916, he quit his job in London and told his employers that he was going to "join up." Naturally, they thought he was about to join the British army, but in fact he meant that he was returning to Ireland to join the Irish Volunteer Force in its planned rebellion against Britain.

The Easter Rising and Its Aftermath

The Irish looked at Britain's involvement in World War I as an opportunity to achieve independence. Using the logic that "the enemy of my enemy is my friend," the Irish attempted to enlist Germany's help in the endeavor. **Roger Casement** traveled to Germany in quest of arms and men but was captured aboard a German submarine on his way back to Ireland. The plot was thus exposed, and the rebellion planned for Easter Sunday, 1916, was hastily called off. IRB leaders realized, however, that even if they didn't go ahead with the rebellion, the English had discovered too much about who they were and what their plans were, and they were probably going to be arrested anyway. Accordingly, the rebellion was rescheduled for Easter Monday—but by then, confusion and contrary orders and expectations had doomed the effort.

During the Easter Rising, Michael Collins was part of the group of rebels who took over the General Post Office in Dublin and occupied it for almost a week. But the GPO could not stand up to the incendiary shells that the British began launching on Friday, and the rebels surrendered. By this time, a good part of Dublin had been destroyed in the fighting, and 262 civilians had been killed. In comparison, only 141 British soldiers and 62 rebels died. The citizens of Dublin were outraged at the foolishness and destruction caused by the ill-timed rebellion and lined the streets to pelt the prisoners with rotten fruit and vegetables as they were led away.

But the British response to the rebellion soon turned Irish hearts in favor of the rebels. The British arrested over twice as many people as had actually participated in the Easter Rising and deported many of them. When 16 of the leaders were executed, they were immediately hailed as martyrs to the cause of Irish freedom. Michael Collins spent the rest of 1916 in prison in England, becoming one of the acknowledged leaders of the prisoners. Public support for the imprisoned rebels and those unjustly arrested grew stronger throughout the year, and Collins was released with many others near Christmas.

Back in Ireland, Collins worked on putting the crumbled remnants of the IRB back together. Ostensibly, he was working for a charitable organization, the Irish National Aid and Volunteers' Dependents' Fund, which raised money to help the families of those rebels still in prison, but in fact he used that position and its requirement that he travel throughout the country in order to work for the IRB. He also spent time campaigning for Sinn Fein candidates at elections and eventually was asked to run himself. He won handily but was not nearly as interested in serving as an elected official as he was in organizing prison breaks. He freed several rebels in the spring of 1919, including **Eamon de Valera,** later to be Ireland's first president.

Later that same year, Collins was formally appointed Director of Intelligence of the Irish Volunteers. This was the beginning of his career as an urban guerrilla. The skills once noted by his elementary school teacher—gifts for mathematics and observation—were called into play as Collins became a master of organization and military tactics. He set up an elaborate escape network throughout Dublin that served many a rebel well as the British embarked on sweeps of buildings and sometimes neighborhoods in search of identifiable nationalists. Collins organized the smuggling of arms and the detailed functioning of his intelligence-gathering workers, and also embarked on a campaign of assassinations of British police officers and public officials. He was a wanted man and feared by the police.

By 1920, murders of policemen and constables were such a common occurrence that many men were resigning in order to save their lives. It is said that over 200 officers a month were leaving their jobs, while murders and firebombings were only increasing. The British brought in a new security force, known as the "Black and Tans" because of their uniforms. Many were poorly

trained, and most were certainly not ready for the hatred and violence they encountered in Ireland. The Black and Tans were soon out of control, embarrassing the British government and catching the attention of the world at large.

Anglo-Irish Treaty Is Signed

By November of 1920, the British were desperate to get control of the situation and began to talk about offering Ireland limited freedom. They also sent in members of their Secret Service to try to capture Collins and his coworkers. But Collins appeared unstoppable, and his men were murdering most of Britain's finest agents. After many false starts, peace talks were begun in London, with Collins as one of the Irish representatives. Britain had said from the outset that they would consent to anything short of an independent Irish Republic; the Irish, unfortunately, could return home with no less than that. Discussions about the content of the Anglo-Irish Treaty raged back and forth over the course of many weeks, with the Irish delegation finally deciding to accept less in the hope that they would be able to press for more

Michael Collins delivers a St. Patrick's Day speech in Cork in favor of the present Irish Treaty and the Irish Republican Government, less than five months before he was gunned down in 1922.

after the treaty was signed. In fact, that is exactly what happened: over the course of the years following the adoption of the treaty, Ireland unilaterally modified it again and again until, in 1949, the Republic of Ireland was formally born.

In 1921, however, they would have to settle for the Irish Free State, with ties to England that were weaker yet still uncomfortable. Collins remarked upon signing the Treaty that he had just signed his death warrant, little knowing that he spoke prophetically. When the Irish delegation returned to Dublin and submitted the treaty to the *Dail* (Irish Parliament), they were roundly condemned. When the *Dail* voted to accept the treaty as it stood, Eamon de Valera resigned. Collins was called a traitor and began to receive death threats. Once again, Ireland became the province of terrorists and guerrilla fighters—only now, instead of Collins organizing them, he was their target.

On the 22d of August 1922, less than a year after the passage of the treaty by the *Dail,* Collins and several colleagues were ambushed as they drove to Cork. As machine-gun fire sprayed over their car, Collins insisted that they stop and fight. After a fierce battle, Collins saw two figures running away up the road. He left his protected position behind the armored car and ran forward into the road before dropping to the ground to fire at the escaping ambushers. He got off several shots before a bullet struck him in the head. He died within minutes.

Michael Collins had been a ruthless terrorist, yet in his work in negotiating the treaty he had begun to show true statesmanship. It is possible that he could have become one of the great leaders of the Irish Free State as it moved towards full independence. Instead, he died the victim of nameless men who hated the Treaty, could not see in it the eventual possibility of true Irish nationalism, and so struck down one of their own. Some might have seen it as a fitting end that a terrorist died at the hands of other terrorists, but the majority of the Irish people saw it as a true loss. They knew that Collins had been instrumental in driving the British to compromise, and they believed he would have continued to play a role in driving the British off Irish soil forever.

SOURCES:

Dwyer, T. Ryle. *Michael Collins: The Man Who Won the War.* Mercier Press, 1990.

O'Broin, Leon. *Michael Collins.* Macmillan, 1980.

FURTHER READING:

Coogan, Tim Pat. *The Man Who Made Ireland: The Life and Death of Michael Collins.* Roberts Rinehart, 1992.

Forester, Margery. *Michael Collins: The Lost Leader.* London, 1971.

O'Connor, Frank. *The Big Fellow: Michael Collins and the Irish Revolution.* Dublin, 1965.

Taylor, Rex. *Michael Collins.* London, 1958.

Christopher Columbus

(1451–1506)

Genoese navigator and explorer who, under Spanish auspices, planned and led the first successful discovery of the New World in 1492.

W hen Christopher Columbus was born in Genoa, Italy, in 1451, there was no exact knowledge as to the size of the earth and the width of the ocean off the continent of Europe. Trade for spices and jewels with Asia, or the Indies as it was called, had been carried on by land extending over thousands of miles. But it was about this time that the Mohammedan Turks took control of Asia Minor and the Balkans and put a stop to it.

Columbus first went to sea when he was nine or ten years old, making several Mediterranean voyages. Years later, while on a voyage in 1476, he was wounded in a battle at sea off the coast of Portugal. Though his Genoese ship was sunk, he swam to shore, and remained in Portugal for about ten years. He and his brother Bartholomew engaged in chartmaking, and he married the daughter of a Portuguese officer, governor of an island near Madeira, who had been successfully engaged in the sea trade and passed on much of his knowledge and experience. (The marriage was brief. His wife died in 1483, leaving Columbus with one son, Diego.)

Name variations: Originally Cristoforo Columbo (Italian), Don Cristóbal Colón (Spanish title). Born sometime between August–October 1451, in Genoa, Italy; died May 20, 1506; son of a master cloth weaver of Genoa; married: Felipa Perestrello e Moniz; children: Don Diego Colón (legitimate), Ferdinand Columbus (illegitimate). Descendants: Dukes of Veragua.

Contributed by Joseph C. Kiger, Editor in Chief, International Encyclopedia of Learned Societies and Academies, University of Mississippi, University, Mississippi

At that time, Portugal was the leading seafaring nation of Europe, carrying out voyages further and further south down the coast of Africa. The ultimate goal was to reach the Indies by sailing around Africa. Columbus began to develop the idea of reaching the Indies by sailing due west across the Ocean Sea. Despite a variety of arguments that favored continuing the attempt to reach the Indies by sailing around Africa, Columbus pressed the king of Portugal for financial aid in the enlisting of men and outfitting of ships. Rebuffed by the Portuguese monarch, he then carried his case to the Spanish court of King **Ferdinand** and Queen **Isabella.** In 1492, he was successful in his suit. Along with financial aid, it was agreed that Columbus and his descendants would be awarded the title Admiral of the Ocean Sea, made governor of the lands he discovered, and granted a percentage of the profits to be obtained from them. The Spanish monarchs, of course, were also to reap significant financial rewards. In addition to the monetary rewards, a desire to advance the Christian religion was undoubtedly shared by Columbus and Queen Isabella, since both were deeply committed to Christianity.

Columbus Sets Sail

On the morning of August 3, 1492, Columbus set sail west with approximately 100 men aboard three ships. Despite the misgivings and restlessness of his crew, he kept on for 37 days. Finally, on October 12, 1492, the present-day island of San Salvador was sighted and possession was taken in the name of the Spanish sovereigns. About 100 days were spent in exploring; then Columbus and his crew touched on the islands off Cuba and Hispaniola. Believing that he had reached the outskirts of the Indies, he was unaware that he had discovered the "New World"—the Americas. Consequently, a great deal of time was spent in searching for gold and other treasures expected to be found there. Although some gold was eventually obtained from the native Indians, by January 1493, with one of the ships sunk on a reef, Columbus decided to return to Spain. Leaving about 40 men behind in a fort which had been built in Hispaniola, the explorer sailed home in the two remaining ships. His booty: a few Indians, along with such native items as belts, aprons, bracelets, and some gold. When the ships landed in Spain on March 15, 1493, news of the successful voyage spread rapidly, and Columbus made a triumphant journey to Barcelona to be received at the Spanish court. Ferdinand and Isabella loaded him with honors and even acted as godparents for two of the Indians who were baptized into the Christian faith.

A measure of the esteem in which Columbus was now held is attested to by the size of the fleet which he commanded on his second expedition to the New World. Consisting of 17 ships, some 1,200 men, and supplies for six months, this fleet set sail from Cadiz on September 25, 1493. Upon reaching Hispaniola in November, Columbus discovered that the men who had been left behind had been killed by the Indians and that the fort had been destroyed. Although a new fort was constructed, from this point on things went from bad to worse. The Spaniards became sick and unruly, and the food and supplies began to run low. Thereupon, Columbus dispatched 12 ships for resupplies back to Spain, along with a cargo of native plants, parrots, 26 Indians, and a small amount of gold that had been collected. He then continued his explorations, touching on Cuba and Jamaica, but found little gold. When he returned to the fort in 1494, the ships had arrived from Spain with new supplies. But in their attempts to obtain gold, the Spanish settlers in Hispaniola had become increasingly unruly, dissatisfied, and barbarous in their treatment of the Indians. Though Columbus stayed on in Hispaniola, he was unsuccessful in imposing order and eventually decided to return to Spain in 1496.

Though Ferdinand and Isabella received Columbus, in the absence of expected wealth, his reception was noticeably tepid. Nevertheless, the Spanish monarchs agreed to a third voyage and put eight ships at his disposal. In 1498, Columbus had three of the ships sail directly for the settlement at Hispaniola while he and the other ships explored

the area to the south. He reached the island of Trinidad before sailing north and reached Hispaniola on August 31, 1498. Upon landing at what had become the small city called Santo Domingo, he found that a rebellion against his authority had occurred. When word of the many complaints against Columbus and his lieutenants reached Spain, an official, Bobadilla, was sent to investigate the matter. Bobadilla had Columbus chained and thrown into prison for eventual return to Spain in October 1500. Columbus remonstrated to Ferdinand and Isabella that he had crushed several rebellions in maintaining their interests and insisted that Bobadilla had been lied to and taken in by his enemies. The monarchs eventually freed Columbus and received him on December 15, 1500, assuring him that justice would be done. Ferdinand and Isabella later solved the matter by appointing a new governor for Hispaniola and allowing Columbus to continue his exploring. In March 1502, they authorized his fourth and last voyage.

On May 9, 1502, he departed from Spain with four ships. Upon his arrival in Hispaniola in late June, Columbus, who had been forbidden to land in Santo Domingo by the new governor, had to search for another safe anchorage in the face of an impending hurricane. Successfully riding it out, he engaged in a fruitless attempt to discover some strait or passage which could eventually carry him to the Indies. On June 25, 1503, he reached Jamaica. By this time, his ships were completely unseaworthy and were beached to serve as housing for the explorers. Two men were dispatched in a canoe to Hispaniola, which was only about 100 miles from Jamaica, in hopes of obtaining a rescue ship. Though the men arrived safely in Hispaniola in a short period of time, Columbus and the

The ships of Christopher Columbus.

Christopher Columbus explains his discovery of America to King Ferdinand and Queen Isabella.

unsettled when Columbus died on May 20, 1506. Thus, the king compensated his heirs. His son, Don Diego Colón, assumed the title of Admiral and in 1509 was appointed governor of Hispaniola. His grandson, Don Luis Colón, was later awarded the Duchy of Veragua.

Christopher Columbus's remains were nearly as widely traveled as the man himself. Differing conclusions can be drawn as to where his tomb is located. From Vallodolid in Spain, where he died, his remains were taken to Seville, also in Spain, then to Santo Domingo in Hispaniola, and then back to Seville. Somewhat later, parts of his remains were taken to Genoa in Italy and others to Pavia, also in Italy.

Columbus's chief claim to fame rests on the fact that, despite all obstacles, he led in the first successful discovery of the New World. Yet, it is one of the major ironies of history that this New World was not named for him but rather for a relatively obscure Florentine seaman named Amerigo Vespucci. Why? Because in 1508, two years after the death of Columbus, a geographer and mapmaker named Martin Waldseemuller, who was an admirer of Vespucci, announced that Amerigo had discovered this part of the world and therefore it should be named America. The suggestion took hold and appeared on the new maps, and thus we still refer to the lands that Columbus discovered as the Americas.

[In 1992, the proposed hoopla for the 500th Anniversary of Columbus's discovery soon found itself mired in controversy. Celebrants viewed Columbus as one who brought an advanced civilization to the New World, altering science, geography, philosophy, law, and government. Others argued that an advanced civilization was already there—that all Columbus brought to the New World was disease, greed, and the eventual slaughter or enslavement of the indigenous peoples and their cultures. "For too long, the American myth demonized or ignored the people whom Columbus encountered on these shores," wrote Paul Gray in *Time* magazine. "Must people now replace this with a new myth that simply demonizes Columbus?"—Ed.]

remaining men in his party were forced to wait about a year before a rescue ship was reluctantly dispatched by the new governor. During this period, Columbus had to put down another rebellion among his followers and at the same time keep a tolerable peace with the Indians. In any case, he set sail for Spain on September 12, 1504, but hardly anyone took notice of his arrival at the end of November.

Queen Isabella Dies

Now 53 years old and in very poor health, Columbus was suffering from malaria, arthritis, and a serious inflammation of both eyes. To add to his woes, Queen Isabella, the monarch who had been the most sympathetic to his plans, died on November 26, 1504. Although Columbus had become a relatively wealthy man from the colonial profits that had begun flowing to him, he felt that the Spanish monarchs had not completely lived up to the terms of their contract. King Ferdinand took no action on Columbus's pleas for restitution and tried to settle matters by offering to award him a grant of land in Spain, which the admiral refused. Matters were still

SOURCES:

Gray, Paul. "The Trouble with Columbus," in *Time* magazine. October 7, 1991.

Irving, Washington. *The Life and Voyages of Christopher Columbus.* Edited by John Harmon McElroy. Twayne, 1981.

Morison, Samuel Eliot. *Admiral of the Ocean Sea, A Life of Christopher Columbus.* Little, Brown, 1942.

FURTHER READING:

Colón, Ferdinand. *The Life of the Admiral Christopher Columbus By His Son Ferdinand.* Translated and annotated by Benjamin Keen. Rutgers University Press, 1959.

The Journal of Christopher Columbus. Translated by Cecil Jane, Clarkson N. Potter, 1960.

Constantine I

(285–337)

The first Christian emperor of the Roman Empire, who founded Constantinople and is credited with the very existence of the later Roman Empire.

Name variation: (full imperial name) Flavius Valerius Aurelius Constantinus Magnus. Born Flavius Valerius Constantinus on February 27, 285, at Naissus; son of Constantius Chlorus and Helena; married: Fausta; children: four sons. Predecessor: Maximinus. Successor: Constantine II.

In about 285, Constantine was born at Naissus in Dacia Ripensis to Constantius Chlorus and his wife or companion Helena. By the time Constantine was eight, **Diocletian** had established the unprecedented collegial imperial system in which the two Roman emperors, known as the Augustii, each adopted an unrelated man, called a Caesar, to serve as an associate emperor. Should Diocletian and his colleague Maximian then abdicate their offices, the Caesars would advance to be the Augustii, choosing new Caesars to replace themselves. But the system suffered. Since the Caesars had no vested interest in the well-being of the Augustii, intermarriage and a form of taking hostages were employed to ensure the cooperation of the Caesars by invoking self-interest. In 293, Constantius was declared Caesar and his son Constantine was admitted to the court of Diocletian as one such hostage to guarantee his father's loyalty.

As a young man, Constantine was described as "matched by none in grace and beauty of form, or in tallness, and so surpassing his contemporaries in personal strength that he struck terror into them." He distinguished himself serving against the Persians under his father's fellow Caesar

"My own desire is, for the common good of the world and the advantage of all mankind, that the people should enjoy a life of peace and undisturbed concord."

CONSTANTINE

Contributed by Steven L. Tuck, Ph.D. candidate in Classical Art and Archaeology, University of Michigan, Ann Arbor, Michigan

Galerius. As a reward, he was appointed tribunus militum of the first class. The expedition against the Persians resulted in the conquest, and transfer to the Romans, of Iberia, Armenia, and Mesopotamia.

Constantine's worth as a hostage increased with the abdication of Diocletian and Maximian and the accession of his father Constantius and Galerius as emperors in 305. Now only one step away from the throne, the threat to his life increased the longer he was held by his father's rival. After many appeals by Constantius and many near attempts on his life, he was finally allowed to rejoin his father in 306, reaching Boulogne just in time to accompany Constantius to Britain on his expedition against the Picts. Constantine was present at his father's death at York on July 25, 306, and before dying Constantius declared his son as his successor. The legions proclaimed Constantine emperor and the barbarian auxilleries, led by the king of the Alemanni, acknowledged him.

In a letter to Galerius, Constantine protested that he had not sought the crown, but had instead been pressed by the troops, and he solicited acknowledgment as Augustus, coequal with Galerius. Recognizing Constantine as ruler of the countries beyond the Alps, but with the title of Caesar only, Galerius conferred the superior title of Augustus on his own son Severus.

The Empire enjoyed only a short peace. Galerius's absence from Rome probably encouraged the rebellion of October 28, 306, which resulted in Maxentius, the son of Maximian, seizing the throne. Informed of his son's move, Maximian left his retirement to reassume the title Augustus. Their actions meant war with Galerius and his son Severus. Though Severus entered Italy with a powerful force, he was besieged in Ravenna, surrendered, and was put to death by Maxentius.

To replace Severus, in 307 Galerius chose C. Valerius Licinianus Licinius as Augustus, while Maximin Daia, an imperial guard who had been made a Caesar, was likewise proclaimed Augustus by his troops in Syria and Egypt. In following year, the Roman Empire thus obeyed six masters: Galerius, Licinius, and Maximin Daia in the East; and Maximian, Maxentius and Constantine in the West. The union of the Western Augusti was cemented by the marriage of Constantine to Fausta, daughter of Maximian, at the same occasion when Maximian and his son Maxentius acknowledged Constantine as Augustus. Before long Maximian was forced by disagreements to flee from Maxentius and to take refuge with Constantine. Once more Maximian abdicated the

throne, but while Constantine was on campaign Maximian began plotting with his son to overthrow him. Constantine discovered the rebellion and pursued Maximian to Marseilles where he besieged the town. The inhabitants gave up Maximian and Constantine quelled the rebellion. Despite his status as Constantine's father-in-law, Maximian was put to death in 309. Constantine's authority was now secure in Britain, Gaul, and the recently acquired Spain.

Maxentius, however, was gathering a large force in Italy with which to invade Gaul. But Constantine, with a large veteran army and many German auxilleries, secured the loyalty of more of his subjects by ordering a stop to the persecutions of the Christians in his dominions. He then crossed the Alps into Italy, inflicting defeats on Maxentius's forces at Turin and Verona. On October 28, 312, at a battle fought outside Rome, Maxentius was finally defeated, his forces routed, and he himself drowned in the Tiber as he was driven off the Milvian Bridge—six years from the day that his rebellion had brought him to power. Constantine, now emperor of the entire West, added Italy and Africa to his holdings, and entered Rome.

He did much to try to restore peace to the city by disbanding the Praetorian Guard, who had become a political force of their own in the Empire. As an elite body of troops who guarded the emperor, they frequently chose his successor.

He also imposed a heavy tax on the senators and their families and accepted the title of Pontifex Maximus—chief priest of Rome.

After Emperor Galerius's death in 311, Licinius had taken over his domains. He was then involved in a war with Maximin Daia who was defeated in several battles and died at Tarsus in Cilicia in 313. Now Licinius was ruler of the Eastern Empire while Constantine was ruler of the West.

Edict Legalizes Christian Worship in Empire

In February 313, Constantine issued what would become known as the Edict of Milan. It formally ended the great Christian persecution begun by Diocletian. The edict legalized Christian worship in the Empire and authorized the restitution of church property. The profession of Christianity was no longer a capital offense.

The following year, war broke out between the emperors over territories they mutually claimed. When a victorious Constantine was ceded Illyricum, Pannonia, and Greece, he strengthened their alliance by giving Licinius the hand of his sister Constantina.

During the ensuing nine years of peace, Constantine reformed the administration of the Western Empire. He developed the hierarchical system of state dignitaries established by Diocletian. The coinage was reformed with new gold and silver currencies which helped to reestablish a monetary economy to replace the barter economy which had sprung up during Diocletian's reign when money was scarce.

The military administration was entirely separated from the civil administration and two supreme commanders were appointed: the Master of the Cavalry and the Master of the Infantry. The number of legions was reduced and the size of the army increased, while a central reserve of crack troops was created to act as a rapid-deployment force. When the borders of the Empire were threatened, they could now be reinforced without removing the replacements from other border posts. The increase of the army and bureaucracy, however, brought about various oppressive taxes which were unequally assessed and caused many revolts.

In 323, Constantine declared war against Licinius, who was then advanced in years but whose forces were at least equal to his opponent's. The first battle took place near Adrianople on July 3, 323, with each emperor leading a force of over 100,000 men. Licinius was routed, his fortified camp taken, and he fled to Byzantium. Aided by his son Crispus who commanded the navy, Constantine laid siege, once again forcing Licinius to flee. After a final defeat at Chrysopolis, Licinius surrendered. He was put to death a short time later, despite the intercession of his wife Constantina, Constantine's sister. Licinius's reign was declared an usurpation and his laws were declared void. Constantine was now sole ruler of the Roman Empire.

But in 324, personal upheaval marred imperial peace. Constantine's wife Fausta and his eldest son Crispus were accused of high treason, arrested, and put to death. Licinius Caesar, son of the emperor Licinius and Constantina, was also accused and suffered the same fate. Many others were implicated in the plot and executed.

Second Capital Founded at Constantinople

The same year, Constantine made a bold decision. After moving his court between a number of different cities to better control the Empire, he founded a second capital, in addition to Rome, from which to rule. Constantine situated the new capital of Constantinople at the ancient Greek city of Byzantium on the strategic Bosphorus strait between Europe and Asia. Possessed with an excellent harbor, the site could be defended from land and sea, and was accessible to both the Asian and German frontiers as well as the population centers of coastal Asia Minor and Syria. Though Rome remained the superior of the two at least nominally, Constantinople soon became the metropolis from which the Empire would survive to dominate the Middle Ages. The dedication of Constantinople took place on May 11, 330. Most of the festivities were held in a new marble-paved, oval forum surrounded by a two-story marble portico, in the middle of which stood a porphyry column bearing a gilt statue of the emperor. At the ceremonies' close, a parade of soldiers in dress uniform—bearing white candles and escorting a wagon containing a golden statue of the Fortune of Constantinople—moved into the hippodrome where Constantine hailed the image and decreed that the celebration would be continued annually.

Constantine sponsored one of the most massive building campaigns in Roman history, and a great amount of it was directed at the Christian church, for which Constantine was the major patron. Crediting his victory at the Milvian Bridge to divine intercession, he had the Greek letters *chi-rho* (X-P) symbol of Christianity painted on his armies' shields, helmets, and standards. After his victory, he did not just legalize Christianity but actively promoted it, leaving the most visible testament to his service to the faith in the churches he built.

In addition to the number of round, central-plan churches founded or rebuilt by Constantine, there was a new form of church created which more easily accommodated the growing numbers of worshipers: the basilica. In pagan Rome, the basilica was not a religious building type; it was a public hall used to accommodate large numbers of people. Constantine previously had one built as his audience hall in his capital at Trier and one as a secular building in Rome. This form "spiritualized" by Constantine's church foundations became the archetype for a Christian church in the Western tradition.

Constantine took an active interest in the running of the church as well. While he did not involve himself with doctrinal or theological problems, he was aware of the different sects that Christianity had—even then—spawned, and he supported the unity of the church. In 325, he sponsored the Council of Nicaea, a conference of 220 bishops that formulated the Nicene Creed and attempted to deal with Arius and other advocates of what would become known as the Arian heresy. At the Council of Nicaea, Bishop Eusebius reported that Constantine "proceeded through the midst of the assembly like some heavenly Angel of God, clothed in a garment which glittered as though radiant with light."

For the remainder of his reign, Constantine was concerned with two threats. The first was the external threat posed by the constant pressures on the borders of the Empire. After campaigning along the Danube (326–29) to secure that frontier, he dealt with Persia in the east (335–37) and Shapur who wished to recover his predecessor's losses. Still, the second threat was perhaps the greater of the two: the internal strife caused by succession and the desire for power.

Constantine attempted to make provisions for after his death. By 333 his three surviving sons had been elevated to the rank of Caesar along with two of his nephews. He hoped that by dividing the Empire among them, he might present each with the opportunity to share power, rather than grant it to two and deny the others. It was a miscalculation which would be solved by bloodshed after his death.

Taken ill shortly after Easter in 337, Constantine traveled to Nicomedia and there Bishop Eusebius baptized him. He died on the Feast of Pentecost, May 22, 337. Having long since prepared for his death, he had constructed the Church of the Holy Apostles in Constantinople as a final resting place. Inside the church were 12 sarcophagi, one for each of the apostles, and in the midst of them, Constantine had a sumptuous sarcophagus prepared for himself. His body was placed in a golden coffin draped with imperial purple to lie in state in the main audience hall of the palace in Constantinople. A military guard escorted the body to the Church of the Holy Apostles where he was laid to rest. His burial place immediately became a place of pilgrimage.

SOURCES:

Barnes, Timothy D. C*onstantine and Eusebius.* Harvard University Press, 1981.

Bowder, Diana. *The Age of Constantine and Julian.* Barnes & Noble, 1978.

MacMullen, Ramsay. *Constantine.* Dial Press, 1969.

FURTHER READING:

Baynes, N. H. *Constantine the Great and the Christian Church.* 2nd ed. Oxford University Press, 1972.

Eusebius. *Vita Constantinii.*

Jones, A. H. M. *Constantine and the Conversion of Europe.* 2nd ed. 1972.

Hernán Cortés

(c. 1484–1547)

Conqueror of the Aztec empire, who helped to establish the economy and social relations of colonial Mexico.

Name variations: Due to the lack of any fixed orthography in the Europe of his time, Cortés's first name appears as "Hernán," "Fernán," "Hernándo," and "Fernando." Born around 1484 in the town of Medellín in Spain; died on December 2, 1547; son of an impoverished minor nobleman named Martín Cortés de Monroy; married: Catalina Xuárez.

Born some time around 1484 in the town of Medellín on the banks of Spain's Guadiana River, Hernán Cortés was the son of an impoverished minor nobleman named Martín Cortés de Monroy. As an *hidalgo*, or lesser aristocrat without titled lands, Martín Cortés de Monroy ranked well below the titled counts, dukes, marquises, and other *grandes* of Spain. There was little which he, himself, could provide his son, other than an exalted sense of family honor.

From the time of his birth until the time of his departure for the Americas in 1504, nothing is absolutely certain concerning the life of Hernán Cortés. Some chroniclers of that period wrote that Cortés enrolled at the University of Salamanca, eventually receiving a bachelor of law degree. It is far more likely, given his father's relative poverty, that he spent a year in a notary's office in Valladolid. As a trained notary, Cortés would have been familiar with some of the details of Spanish law since notaries were responsible for drawing up wills and all sorts of business and matrimonial contracts. This training in Spanish legalism made Cortés one of the most educated of the conquistadors, and it made him a man who was able to jus-

"We were always victorious and killed great numbers of the enemy, for every day a multitude of people came to join our forces."

HERNAN CORTÉS

Contributed by Abel A. Alves, Ph.D., Ball State University, Muncie, Indiana

tify his conquest of the Aztec empire on the basis of Spanish legal precedent.

After whatever legal training he did receive, Cortés initially planned to serve in the Italian Wars being fought by Spain in that period. For reasons that will never be known, he changed his mind, and, in 1504, left for the recently discovered Americas. Today historians only can speculate as to his precise motivation, but, as with later European emigrants, the hope of a better life beckoned.

Cortés arrived on the Caribbean island of Hispaniola, where the first permanent Spanish settlement of Santo Domingo had been founded by Christopher Columbus's brother Bartholomew in 1496. Soon after his arrival he was made a notary of the recently founded town of Azúa. He served there for five or six years, until, in 1511, he accompanied Diego Velázquez in his conquest of Cuba. He started life on Cuba as Governor Velázquez's secretary, and in 1514 he built a house in Santiago de Cuba, where he settled with Catalina Xuárez, whom he may have been reluctant to marry. Though some report that he was happy with Catalina, others paint a less idyllic scene. A friend of Catalina's named María Hernández later recounted that Cortés physically abused Catalina, and that Catalina told her that some morning she would be found dead. Bernal Díaz, who later soldiered with Cortés in Mexico, wrote that even though Cortés had a worthy number of conquered Indians who labored for him in a system of tribute payment called *encomienda,* he and his wife lived well beyond their means and were in debt: "He spent on his person, on finery for his newly married wife, and on entertaining guests who had come to stay with him." In a society which valued ostentation and the sharing of one's wealth with one's followers, Cortés was trying to live as a great nobleman. Twice he served as *alcalde mayor* (governor) of Santiago, and entertaining throngs of people at his table would have been a way to cement alliances. In the long run, his expenditures proved to be a sound investment, but they may have contributed to frictions with Catalina, who brought no great wealth to the marriage.

Opportunity struck in 1518, when Velázquez appointed Cortés to head the third expedition to explore the newly discovered Mexican coast. When Velázquez drew up his instructions on October 23, Cortés was given permission only to explore the Mexican coast and trade, but he used all his skill as a notary to create a legal loophole which would allow him to take any measures conforming to "the service of God and their highnesses" in the event of an unexpected emergency.

CHRONOLOGY

1504	Arrived on the Caribbean island of Hispaniola
1511	Aided Diego Velázquez in the conquest of Cuba
1519	Met the Aztec *tlatoani* Moctezuma II
1520	Spaniards and their Tlaxcalan allies retreated from Tenochtitlán
1521	Aztecs surrendered to Cortés
1522	Appointed governor of "New Spain" by Charles V
1524–26	Honduras expedition proved futile
1530	Made *Marqués del Valle de Oaxaca*
1540	Retired to Spain
1547	Died on December 2

Cortés knew that he now had the room to maneuver as he saw fit.

He left Santiago on November 18, 1518. Purchasing provisions on other Caribbean islands, Cortés's fleet reached the Yucatán channel on February 18, 1519. He had 11 ships and over 500 soldiers of fortune and sailors, including his chief lieutenants Diego de Ordaz, Gonzalo de Sandoval, Cristóbal de Olid, and Pedro de Alvarado. Among the common adventurers was the future chronicler Bernal Díaz del Castillo.

After arriving on the coast of the Yucatán, Cortés and these men proceeded to Tabasco. Along the way, he had dealings with the coastal Maya Indians, demonstrating a diplomatic ability which would serve him well vis-à-vis the Aztec empire. He also acquired the slave Malintzin, or Malinche, as a valuable translator. Malintzin, who was soon baptized Doña Marina, spoke Mayan and her native Aztec language, Nahuatl. By all accounts, she quickly learned Spanish as well. She gained a great deal of respect among the patriarchal conquistadors, both as Cortés's avowed lover on the expedition, and as a woman who, according to Bernal Díaz, "betrayed no weakness."

The Founding of Veracruz

Through the Indians of Tabasco and Doña Marina, Cortés learned of the powerful Aztec tributary union of the interior. This led to his setting sail for the region which the Spaniards would dub Villa Rica de la Veracruz (Rich Town of the True Cross). There Cortés and his men founded a city,

Hernán Cortés faces the Tlascalans in 1519.

making themselves its voting citizens, or *vecinos.* In actuality, Veracruz was nothing but a set of foundations mapping out the intended structures which symbolized civilization to the Spaniards: a church, a marketplace, and a pillory and gallows. In search of improved social standing, he and his men were also self-proclaimed missionaries of the gospel: hence the new town's name, embracing both material and spiritual ends.

It was in the Veracruz region that Cortés first encountered actual representatives of the Aztec empire. Gifts were exchanged, and Cortés inquired concerning the Aztecs' chief city and its "chief speaker," or *tlatoani,* **Moctezuma II.** In actuality the Aztec "empire" was a forced confederacy which created new enemies with every conquest. The Aztecs believed that the very existence of the universe was dependent on sacrificing the precious hearts of warriors to the sun, and this led to the fighting of "flower wars" in which the taking of captives was far more vital than the outright slaying of enemies on the battlefield. Aztec victory in the flower wars meant that the vanquished would pay regular tribute, including sacrificial humans, but that they could continue to rule themselves as they otherwise chose. The tribute served as a basis of wealth for the Aztecs' magnificent city of Tenochtitlán, but it also served as a source of hatred among those upon whom the Aztecs preyed. When Cortés's small force of

Spaniards finally reached Tenochtitlán, it would be bolstered by thousands of Amerindian allies who impatiently had awaited an opportunity to topple Aztec might. Cortés's genius lay in his ability to manipulate these circumstances with the aid of his translator Doña Marina.

Before leaving Veracruz, Cortés acted to legitimize his cause in the eyes of King Charles I of Spain (who was also the Holy Roman Emperor **Charles V** of the Germanies). He wrote at least one letter detailing the founding of Veracruz as an act by men loyal to the Crown, who only desired to repudiate the self-interested Velázquez by placing themselves directly under royal authority as voting townsmen. To demonstrate his sincerity, Cortés sent this letter to Spain with all the gold and jewels brought as gifts by Moctezuma's envoys, and with the traditional royal fifth of booty acquired thus far. Then Cortés scuttled all the ships, except for the one needed to return to Spain with Cortés's gifts and representatives. The march inland proceeded with no possibility of retreat remaining.

On the march, Cortés and his men developed an image of themselves as knights-errant sent by God to save the indigenous population of Mexico from the brutalities of the Aztec empire and the "demons" who demanded human sacrifice. Stopping at a number of Amerindian towns, the Spanish noted fine masonry, skillfully woven cloth, irrigated and fertile fields, but, according to Bernal

Díaz, they were "greatly shocked" by the presence of pyramid temples with "walls and altars all splashed with blood and the victims' hearts laid out before the idols." They would use these aspects of Mexican Indian culture to justify their own bloody massacres, starting with the Tlaxcalan campaign.

Upon arriving at Tlaxcala, Cortés and his conquistadors were faced with massive opposition. In a battle fought September 5, 1519, one Spaniard died, while 60 were wounded. The conquistadors lost heart at this point, blaming Cortés for scuttling their ships and eliminating all chance of escape. According to Bernal Díaz, Cortés convinced his men to remain steadfast by means of a speech, saying:

> If God helps us, far more will be said in future history books about our exploits than has ever been said about those of the past. For, I repeat, all our labours are devoted to the service of God and our great Emperor Charles.

When 17 emissaries from the Tlaxcalan captain Xicotencatl appeared to be spies, Cortés returned them to their lord with the hands of some and the thumbs of others cut off. After this, for whatever reason, Xicotencatl chose to deal with Cortés, appearing at his quarters and vehemently denouncing the oppression of the Aztecs and their *tlatoani* Moctezuma. When Cortés left Tlaxcala to continue his march to Tenochtitlán, he had 1,000 Tlaxcalan allies with him, but this doubling of his forces did not prevent his panicking on the way at the important religious center of Cholula. Fearing rumors of another attack, Cortés staged a massacre of Cholulan warriors as they gathered unprepared in a plaza. Despite his brave words, a sense of overwhelming odds and encirclement was beginning to wreak havoc with Cortés's nerves.

Since, on the coast, Cortés had exchanged gestures of peaceful diplomacy with Moctezuma's emissaries, on November 8, 1519, Moctezuma II received Cortés in Tenochtitlán as the ambassador of the Holy Roman Emperor Charles V. It also is known that the wonders of Cortés's guns and horses piqued the *tlatoani*'s curiosity. However, Moctezuma was not the only one to be left in awe at the accoutrements of a strange and alien culture. In his second letter to Charles V, Cortés described the Aztec capital of Tenochtitlán as a city full of markets, commerce, shops, and very wide main streets. He was amazed by the agricultural abundance and variety which he saw, and he concluded by admitting his confusion that a non-Christian and "barbarous" people could live such a civilized existence:

I will say only that these people live almost like those in Spain, and in as much harmony and order as there, and considering that they are barbarous and so far from the knowledge of God and cut off from all civilized nations, it is truly remarkable to see what they have achieved in all things.

Cortés told Moctezuma that Charles V wanted to make Catholic Christians of the Aztecs, thereby saving the souls of his new vassals. Moctezuma listened politely, presented gifts to these men who still appeared to be ambassadors, and then provided them with lodging. Cortés, fearing the fact that he was surrounded by Aztec warriors, took the *tlatoani* captive in his palace. According to Cortés, Moctezuma willingly submitted to Spanish authority. This seems unlikely, however, just as it seems unlikely that he took the Spaniards for gods (after all, Spanish men and horses already had been slain). Both Bernal Díaz and Cortés stated that Moctezuma was treated honorably, but he proved a worthless hostage. The tlatoani was an elected position, and, as Moctezuma had been captured, the leading Aztec nobles elected a new *tlatoani* to rid their city of men who now clearly were seen as invaders.

At this time, Cortés also had to contend with more than 1,000 Spaniards sent by Velázquez to take him prisoner since the Cuban governor feared that Cortés had reached beyond the authority delegated to him. While he was absent from Tenochtitlán in a successful attempt to convert Velázquez's forces, his lieutenant Pedro de Alvarado ordered a massacre of unarmed Aztec priests and warriors as they celebrated a feast in honor of their god Huitzilopochtli. Upon returning to Tenochtitlán, Cortés found that he immediately had to bid a hasty retreat. In the process, Moctezuma either was slain by his own people as he pleaded for peace, or was strangled at Cortés's order (Spanish and Aztec sources differ on this point). On the night of July 10, 1520, *la noche triste* (the sad night), Cortés led his men out of Tenochtitlán, with thousands of hostile Aztec warriors flanking him on all sides. According to Bernal Díaz, "Here Cortés showed himself the brave man that he was," but casualties were still high on the retreat. It appears that the Aztecs rejected their unwillingness to kill outright, learning from Spanish practice. Of some 1,300 Spaniards and well over 2,000 Tlaxcalans, more than 860 Spaniards and 1,000 Tlaxcalans were killed and sacrificed.

Knowing well that if he returned to Cuba a failure Velázquez would easily imprison him,

Cortés successfully rallied his forces for an assault on Tenochtitlán by means of protracted siege. In this venture, he was aided by an unseen ally, for while the Spaniards were still in the city, a black man in Cortés's party had contracted smallpox, a disease quite common to Europeans and Africans but unknown to native Americans. Without immunities, the population of Tenochtitlán was decimated by the disease. In fact, smallpox took the life of the immediate successor to Moctezuma's title, Cuitláhuac, and he was replaced during the siege by the last *tlatoani*, Cuauhtémoc.

The Aztecs Surrender

In late April 1521, the final struggle for Tenochtitlán began. This time Cortés was joined by thousands of Amerindians who finally saw an opportunity to overthrow Aztec dominance. Fighting now proceeded from street to street and house to house, destroying the once proud city and its people. Cortés later wrote Charles V that he tried repeatedly to persuade the Aztecs to surrender, but nothing could alter their will to resist. In his own words, "We could not but be saddened by their determination to die." Finally, on August 23, 1521, Cuauhtémoc and his starving people surrendered in the ruins of their city.

Tenochtitlán was rebuilt as Mexico City, and Cortés rewarded his followers by distributing the labor of conquered Amerindian peasants in the system known as *encomienda*. The Spaniards thereby replaced Aztec dominance with their own brand of imperialism, but Cortés did conceive of it as an imperialism with rules and limits. To him, *encomienda* was a system which required limits so that peasants were allowed time to produce food and goods for their own upkeep. Calling Mexico "New Spain," Cortés envisioned an ordered land where Amerindian peasants served both Spanish and Amerindian lords, with his chief native American allies and relatives of Moctezuma, upon their baptism, being granted *encomiendas* like Spaniards. New Spain was to be a society with classes, but race did not prevent the Amerindian nobility from being recognized as an elite. Intermarriage was encouraged early on, and Cortés himself recognized and provided for the illegitimate son he had by Doña Marina; since he could not marry her (his wife Catalina arrived in New Spain three months after Tenochtitlán's fall), he provided for Marina's marriage to his lieutenant Juan Jaramillo. Then, soon after her arrival, Catalina died under mysterious circumstances, discoloration being found on her throat. Servants murmured of murder and allegations were raised, but Cortés never was prosecuted formally.

On October 15, 1522, Charles V officially appointed Cortés the governor of New Spain, thereby legitimizing all of Cortés's maneuvers against his immediate superior Velázquez. Two years later, in 1524, Cortés decided to march to Honduras to quash a rebellion against his rule—one which was initiated by Cristóbal de Olid, the very same lieutenant he had sent to subdue Honduras. The Honduras expedition was a parody of Cortés's previous success. Cristóbal de Olid was dead and his faction defeated before Cortés's arrival on the coast of Hibueras. On the way there, Cortés seemingly learned of a plot by his hostage Cuauhtémoc to initiate an Indian revolt. This led to Cortés's execution of the last *tlatoani* on the road to Honduras, though Aztec sources accuse Cortés of having no evidence of a planned revolt and simply wishing to be rid of this legitimate ruler of his people. In any event, after being racked by hunger and suffering, the remnants of this futile expedition returned to Mexico City in June 1526. There, Cortés discovered that his followers had put down a revolt led by the old Velázquez faction among his conquistadors—a group which had felt cheated at the distribution of the spoils of victory. The tone of Cortés's fifth and final letter to Charles V describes a man chastened and chastised, who no longer believed that he was capable of moving heaven and earth by the good graces of his God. He wrote of his being a man who feared that the emperor would dispossess him of all his newfound wealth and glory; and of his desire to return to his native Spain, but in a state "so that I shall not arrive … begging for alms."

A few days after his return to Mexico City, the royal judge Luis Ponce de León arrived to conduct a *residencia*, suspending Cortés from the office of governor during the proceedings. The Spanish residencia was both an audit of accounts and an inquiry into the doings of royal officials. Above all else, it was the chief means by which the crown retained its control over men who hoped to maintain their status and wealth in Spanish society. Frustrated by the interminable investigations, Cortés decided to seek redress before the emperor in person, setting sail for Spain in March 1528. There he married Doña Juana de Zúñiga, a woman of old noble lineage who added to his standing in a way the humble Catalina Xuárez never could have. Eventually he had three daughters and a son by Doña Juana—the son, Don Martín, inheriting the lion's share of what his father had to bestow. In Spain, Charles V confirmed the personal wealth Cortés had acquired as conqueror of New Spain and bestowed upon him the title of *Marqués del Valle de Oaxaca,* but he did not reappoint him as governor. When Hernán Cortés returned to Mexico in 1530, he was able to enjoy his wealth, which was considerable, but he saw political power placed in the hands of university-trained bureaucrats and noblemen from old families.

Stripped of political authority, Cortés found solace in the fact that he had acquired status, wealth, and an inheritable title. Not only did he collect tribute in the form of gold dust, textiles, maize, poultry, and other goods, but he also engaged in the wholesaling of tribute he collected, diversifying his business activities so as not to suffer an irreparable loss in any one area. In the Oaxaca and Michoacán districts he used forced labor to pan gold, and in the Taxco area he mined silver. Cortés also raised a large number of cattle and hogs, as well as growing grain, fruits, and vegetables on large diversified estates called *haciendas*. Near Tehuantepec he had herds of approximately 10,000 wild cattle which supplied tallow and hides for export to Panama and Peru. By 1528, he was worth some 500,000 gold pesos, and by the time of his death in 1547, he was still receiving some 30,000 gold pesos annually in *encomienda* tribute payments.

Cortés retired to Spain in 1540. The very next year he joined a royal expedition against Moslem Algiers, losing a great deal of his investment, but not his life, when the fleet was destroyed by a storm. Then the old warrior lived out his remaining years following the court of Charles V on its endless peregrinations. He died on December 2, 1547, and his last desire was to be interred where he had first met Moctezuma II, and where he later had tried to make amends for his deceptions. According to his secretary Francisco López de Gómara:

> Cortés founded a hospital in Mexico [the *Hospital de Jesús*], where in his will he directed that his bones be sent…. He ordered a school built there, and a nunnery at Coyoacán. He endowed each of these foundations with four thousand ducats a year (the rent of his houses in Mexico), and two thousand more toward the support of the pupils.

A self-made *grande,* he performed the acts of charity and social reciprocity expected of a Spanish marquis. In his life, Cortés had used the tension inherent in the Aztec empire to help bring about its downfall. In his death, he confirmed his acceptance of the social order espoused by the Spanish empire. His life's ambition had been to be recognized and honored within his own culture. In this, Cortés succeeded.

SOURCES:

Clendinnen, Inga. "'Fierce and Unnatural Cruelty': Cortés and the Conquest of Mexico," in *Representations 33* (Winter 1991).

Cortés, Hernán. *Letters from Mexico.* Translated and edited by Anthony Pagden. Yale University Press, 1986.

Díaz, Bernal. *The Conquest of New Spain.* Translated by J. M. Cohen. Penguin, 1963.

Keen, Benjamin, and Mark Wasserman. *A History of Latin America.* 3rd ed. 1988.

Lacroix, Jorge Gurría. *Itinerary of Hernán Cortés.* 2nd ed. Ediciones Euroamericanas, 1973.

López de Gómara, Francisco. *Cortés: The Life of the Conqueror by His Secretary.* Translated and edited by Lesley Byrd Simpson. University of California Press, 1964.

McAlister, Lyle N. *Spain and Portugal in the New World, 1492–1700.* University of Minnesota Press, 1984.

Wagner, Henry R. *The Rise of Fernando Cortés.* Kraus, 1969.

White, Jon Manchip. *Cortés and the Downfall of the Aztec Empire: A Study in the Conflict of Cultures.* Hamish Hamilton, 1971.

Oliver Cromwell

(1599–1658)

General and statesman, who led the forces of Parliament in victories over King Charles I during the English Civil War, advocated the King's trial and execution, and ruled the newly established Commonwealth and Protectorate until his death.

Born on April 25, 1599, in Huntingdon in the parish of Hartford; died at Whitehall on September 3, 1658; son of Richard and Elizabeth (Steward) Cromwell, farmers and landowners; educated at Cambridge in mathematics and civil law; married: Elizabeth Bourchier, 1620; children: (four sons) Robert, Oliver, Richard, and Henry; (four daughters) Bridget, Elizabeth, Mary, and Frances. Successor: Richard Cromwell (1626–1712).

Oliver Cromwell was born at the beginning of an era when both England and Europe were entering a stage of transition that would create the modern constellation of nation states. It was during the upheavals of the 17th century that England would build the foundation for its emergence as the first industrialized and expansionist power in Europe.

The elements of this transformation are diverse and complicated. The English Civil War, the Restoration, and the "Glorious Revolution" of 1688 all formed a sequence of political, economic, social, and intellectual developments that moved hesitantly toward the structure of the modern state as recognized today. Constitutional guarantees of rights, property, legal equality, and restriction of royal power evolved to eliminate many of the abuses of arbitrary rule associated with the "divine right of kings." The effective and practical division of powers between the executive and legislative arms of government was considered. Freedom of conscience and religious toleration remained tendentious sources of social discord, but it was granted that religious freedom was an issue that could not be ignored. Perhaps most significant was

"Religion was not the first thing contested for, but God brought it to that issue at last … and at last it proved that which was most dear to us."

OLIVER CROMWELL

Contributed by Kevin C. Cramer, Ph.D. candidate in History, Harvard University, Cambridge, Massachusetts

the final emergence of Parliament as the acknowledged source of power, consent, and revenue in the realm, representing a spectrum of interests and rights that not only restrained royal power but judged and confirmed it as well. This was the most portentous consequence of the civil war, and therein lies the historical importance of Oliver Cromwell as the preeminent soldier and statesman of Parliament.

Cromwell's youth and early adult years saw a period when the prerogatives of the king as an absolute ruler were being increasingly called into question in England. When **James I,** the first Stuart king of England, took the throne in 1603, his reign was characterized by struggles with Parliament over control of revenue and the levying of taxes, as well as divisive debates over the Protestant identity of the nation between sectarians like the Puritans and the leaders of the royalist Church of England.

Cromwell would come to manhood during these struggles. He was born into a moderately wealthy family of gentleman farmers whose Protestant faith was buttressed by the fact that much of their land had been acquired in the expropriation of Church property under **Henry VIII** in the 16th century. His early schooling reflected a sectarian Protestant militancy. These beliefs were further reinforced when the young Cromwell went to Cambridge and attended the Puritan Sidney Sussex College. He did not earn a degree, however, and returned home after a year when his father died in 1617. Cromwell was now a landowner, a farmer, a man of means with local status. He married in 1620, and in 1628 was elected to the House of Commons.

By the time he was 30, Oliver Cromwell had been shaped in the mold that was characteristic of the parliamentary opponents of the king. Brought up in the sectarian Protestantism that resisted the centralizing conformism of the Church of England, he was also a landowner and a local magistrate in municipal government, as well as a member of Parliament. Conflict with a monarchy intent on preserving and enlarging its powers was all but inevitable. Within Parliament, Cromwell, and other men like him, would find a forum and an alternative in resistance to the king. What made Cromwell such a formidable opponent was his belief in the righteousness of his cause, and his single minded devotion to the service of God.

King **Charles I,** who succeeded his father James in 1625, pursued his father's policies as he attempted to assert the autonomy of the monarchy from Parliament's restraints. Determined to rule

CHRONOLOGY

1628	Elected to House of Commons
1641	Rebellion in Ireland; "Grand Remonstrance" passed by Parliament; Charles I fled London
1642	First battle of Civil War; Cromwell led a regiment
1644	Decisive victory over Charles at Marston Moor
1645	Parliament formed "New Model Army"; rout of King's army at Naseby under leadership of Cromwell and Fairfax
1646	Royalist army surrendered at Oxford; Charles imprisoned
1647	Under Cromwell, army asserted control over Parliament; Charles escaped to Scotland
1648	Cromwell defeated royalist invasion from Scotland
1649	Charles I executed; England declared a republic; as commander-in-chief of army, Cromwell suppressed Irish rebellion
1650	Defeated Charles II and Scots at Dunbar
1651	Defeated last royalist army at Worcester; Charles II escaped to France; Navigation Acts passed; war with Dutch
1653	Cromwell named "Lord Protector"
1654	Peace with Netherlands; war with Spain
1655	Rule of "Major-Generals"; royalist uprisings
1657	Alliance with France against Spain
1658	Cromwell died; succeeded by eldest son Richard
1660	Restoration: Charles II restored to throne

without hindrance, he dismissed Parliament in 1629, beginning 11 years of "personal rule." It is in this period that the conflict between king and Parliament deepened, with both sides articulating and refining their arguments. The core of the debate, as always, was the struggle over control of revenue and the levying of taxes. Parliament would not grant Charles the revenue he demanded unless he acknowledged the autonomy, privileges, and powers of Parliament. This the king would not do. Stalemate. During the next 11 years, Charles would finance his reign by forced loans, the sale of offices and titles, confiscation of noble property, arbitrary—and in Parliament's view—illegal customs duties and taxes, and loans from Catholic France. None of these expedients was very popular. However, by 1640, the king had reached the end of his fiscal rope and was forced to summon

Lt. Gen. Oliver Cromwell leads his cavalry in the Battle of Marston Moor in 1644.

Parliament. When Oliver Cromwell was elected to the House of Commons from Cambridge, the great struggle began.

Cromwell Backs Government Reform

Cromwell was firmly on the side backing significant reform in the way England was governed. Along with the parliamentary leader John Pym, Cromwell supported four major demands made on the King: (1) the arbitrary power of the royal courts was to be abolished; (2) customs duties and taxes levied without Parliament's consent were to be judged illegal; (3) the arbitrary imposition on town corporations to support the navy, "ship money," was also to be made illegal; and (4) a "Triennial Act" was to provide that the king must summon Parliament every three years.

One vital question was left open. In 1641, the Irish were in rebellion, and the issue became whether king or Parliament should control the army raised to suppress the revolt. This debate gave rise to the "Grand Remonstrance," a bill of particular grievances against the king, authored mainly by Pym. Cromwell supported this measure, which passed the Commons by 11 votes, though many of the royalists were absent.

On January 4, 1642, attempting to regain control of his recalcitrant Parliament, Charles personally led 400 soldiers to Westminster to arrest Pym, Cromwell, and the other leaders of the opposition. However, Pym and his followers managed to escape. The break with the king was now irreparable and both sides began to raise troops and prepare for war.

The first battle of the Civil War was a minor skirmish at Edgehill on October 23, 1642. Though Cromwell led a regiment of cavalry, he did not play a major role in the outcome, which was inconclusive. It was apparent, however, at this early stage that the cavalry of the king's forces, led by Prince Rupert, was far superior to that of Parliament's. The horsemen under Cromwell would gradually gain experience under his cool and disciplined leadership, and Cromwell's "Ironsides" would soon win respect and renown.

On July 2, 1644, the two sides confronted each other in force at Marston Moor in the north of England. Cromwell, now a lieutenant general, shared the command of Parliament's forces with Lord Fairfax. At a key point in the struggle, Cromwell led his cavalry in a brilliant charge against the royalist flank and center, routing Rupert's formidable troops. The battle ended in a decisive victory for Parliament, and Charles had to give up any hope of securing control of northern England.

Elsewhere, the war ground on in stalemate. Parliament controlled London, with its vital resources of men, money, and supplies, and the

HISTORIC WORLD LEADERS

rich counties of the southeast. The king, based at Oxford, controlled the poorer areas of the west and southwest. Neither side seemed to be able to bring the war to a decisive conclusion by force of arms. At the end of 1644, Cromwell supported a measure that aimed at ending this stalemate. He believed that military efficiency, and ultimately victory, could be gained through a thorough reorganization of the army. Thus, the "New Model Army" would come into being.

The New Model Army marched on its first campaign in early 1645, and under the command of Cromwell and Fairfax won a decisive victory over the king's army at Naseby on June 14, 1645; the king's men were driven from the field in a rout, and a vast haul of supplies, coin, and jewels was taken. The last viable military force available to Charles had been destroyed. Parliament had won its most important military victory. For the rest of the campaigning season, the king's forces were pursued and destroyed, and most of the remaining royalist strongholds were besieged and captured. In May 1646, Charles escaped to Scotland, where he was held a prisoner. When the last royalist stronghold at Oxford surrendered on June 24, the Civil War was over.

But military victory, however decisive, did not solve the question of a constitutional and political settlement. The religious question was also rearing its head. The New Model Army supported a militant "Independency" which believed in the autonomy of local Protestant congregations from civil authority and looked to Cromwell as its leader. A new battle was shaping up in Parliament where "freedom of conscience" was beginning to mean freedom from royal or government power.

Parliament tried to negotiate with Charles in an attempt to construct a constitutional settlement that would confirm the church structure of the Independents and give Parliament control of the army and navy. Charles rejected these terms, and in frustration the Scots surrendered the king to Parliament in early 1647.

The moderate and conservative factions within Parliament—the "Presbyterians"—feared the religious militancy of the Independents and the autonomy of the army; they wanted either to disband the army, or send it to turbulent Ireland. In this atmosphere of unrest, the Presbyterians began to look toward the king as a figure of authority and unity. In April of 1647, the army mutinied, demanding back pay and a redress of their grievances by Parliament.

This soldiers' revolt became a general uprising in May, when Parliament tried to disband the army. The army leaders—the "Agitators"—refused to disband and seized the king from his house arrest at Holmby. Sympathizing with the army's demands, Cromwell tried to mediate the dispute, well aware that if Parliament continued to alienate the army, it played into the king's hands and threatened the gains of the victory at Naseby. By holding the king, the army could continue to press its demands.

Occupying London in August, the army tried to force Parliament and the king to accede to its demands as embodied in "The Agreement of the People," which also outlined significant limitations on royal power. Cromwell knew that these proposals meant major constitutional change, yet he also felt that civil order required the retention of the monarchy.

Cromwell tried to work out a compromise, but all roads to compromise were blocked when Charles escaped to the Isle of Wight in November 1647. Could this king be allowed to keep his throne? His intransigence and escape alienated his supporters in Parliament and gave more weight to the radical demands for his arrest and execution. An end to the Stuart monarchy would effectively put power in the hands of the army and its leader, Oliver Cromwell.

The Independents continued to fear an alliance between the royalists and the Presbyterian faction in Parliament. This consideration weighed on Cromwell, as he decided finally that any compromise with the king that allowed him to keep his throne was a threat to civil order and the "godly rule" of the nation under the protection of the army. When Cromwell ordered the forceful removal of all Presbyterian-royalist members of Commons in December 1648, it became known as "Pride's Purge."

The King Is Put on Trial

In January 1649, King Charles I was put on trial in Commons as a tyrant who had failed in his obligation to respect the property, powers, and rights of the lords and gentry in Parliament who constituted the "nation." With Cromwell's unwavering support and insistence, the sentence of death was delivered on January 27, 1649. Declaring himself a "martyr of the people," the king was beheaded on January 30. In February, Commons abolished the House of Lords and the office of king. On May 19, England was declared a republic, a "Commonwealth or Free State."

Though a "Rump Parliament" remained after the purge of 1648, real executive power in the new government resided in the Council of State, where Cromwell, as commander of the army, wielded much influence. This power grew with his military victories over Irish and Scottish revolts. In 1651, he defeated a royalist invasion under Charles II at Worcester, driving the king into exile in France. By 1652, Cromwell had effectively eliminated any internal and external threats to the new Commonwealth.

However, the constitutional structure still remained in flux. How were powers to be divided? What would be the function and form of Parliament? How would religious toleration be enacted? Outside of England's borders, how was the Protestant cause to be advanced against the Catholic powers of Europe? How could England expand commercially and compete militarily with France, Spain, and the Netherlands? None of these questions, except perhaps the latter, would be resolved satisfactorily during Cromwell's rule.

England was drifting toward authoritarian rule. Commercial, military, and bureaucratic modernization did not necessarily mean enlightened progress toward democratic government. In April 1653, Cromwell dismissed what remained of Parliament with the words, "You are no Parliament … I will put an end to your sitting." The Council of State was also abolished. Though Cromwell believed he had removed the last obstacle to constitutional reform, actually he created the foundation of a military dictatorship, with the army as the main pillar of the state.

Cromwell Installed as Lord Protector

Government was in the hands of the "godly." In the "Rule of the Saints," the army nominated the members of the new Parliament. This body submitted a draft of a written constitution, "The Instrument of Government." Cromwell would be "Lord Protector," holding wide executive powers at the head of a reconstituted Council of State. On December 16, 1653, Cromwell was officially installed as Lord Protector of the Commonwealth at Westminster. However, Cromwell felt that the Council of State impeded effective rule and reform, and he proposed a modification of the Instrument that would divide power between the authority of one person and Parliament. The Instrument, no matter how modified, was satisfactory to almost no one and the opposition of dismissed MPs, royalists, Presbyterians, as well as continued rebellion in Ireland and Scotland, made consensus impossible. In January 1655, Cromwell again dismissed Parliament.

Domestic unrest and royalist uprisings inspired the division of the realm into 11 military districts, governed by "major-generals." In 1657, an abortive attempt on Cromwell's life prompted the "Humble Petition and Advice," a proposal which advocated the de facto re-creation of the monarchy with Cromwell as "king." On June 26, 1657, with royal pomp and splendor, Cromwell was newly created Lord Protector. But the traditional stability of monarchy could not easily be replaced, and no comprehensive constitutional alternative had been achieved.

By 1658, Cromwell's England was in a position of military, and potentially economic, advantage in Europe and in the Atlantic trade, but there was growing resentment at home of increased taxation and the coercive enforcement of militant Puritan morality. Until Cromwell's death in 1658, England was governed by the force of his personality and beliefs and the conviction of the righteousness of his rule. Yet despite his belief in a divine sanction of resistance to tyranny, the Lord Protector, as dictator, could not establish stable, constitutional government as long as the army remained the sole pillar of the Commonwealth, the creation of the parliamentary victory in the Civil War. This victory also effectively "politicized" the issue of religion in England, and there developed a popular reaction against the sectarian bias of the rule of the major generals, and a resistance to puritanism in general as a fundamental *raison d'etat*. Oliver Cromwell, despite his integrity and convictions, could not overcome these paradoxes and contradictions, and that remains the main theme of his life. His achievements, however, were substantial. His biographer Charles Firth writes a fitting closure to Cromwell's life: "Yet he had achieved great things. Thanks to his sword absolute monarchy failed to take root in English soil."

SOURCES:

Firth, Charles. *Oliver Cromwell and the Rule of the Puritans in England.* Putnam, 1906.

Gardiner. Samuel Rawson. *Oliver Cromwell.* Longmans, Green, 1901.

Hill, Christopher. *God's Englishman: Oliver Cromwell and the English Revolution.* Dial, 1970.

Howell, Roger, Jr. *Cromwell.* Hutchinson, 1977.

Young, Peter. *Oliver Cromwell and his Times.* Severn House, 1962.

FURTHER READING:

Hill, Christopher. *The Century of Revolution, 1603–1714.* Sphere Books, 1969.

Morrill, John. *Oliver Cromwell and the English Revolution.* Longmans, 1990.

Paul, Robert S. *The Lord Protector: Religion and Politics in the Life of Oliver Cromwell.* Lutterworth Press, 1955.

Paul Cullen

(1803–1878)

First-ever Irish cardinal, who fundamentally shaped modern Irish Catholicism by bringing its church, its hierarchy, and its practices firmly in line with the Vatican's teachings.

"Fervently sincere, single-minded, devout, unflinching, distrustful of culture, a Catholic and nothing but a Catholic, domineering yet obedient, [Tally] represented the militant temper of his church."

TIMES
(OBITUARY)

Born on April 29, 1803, on the 76-acre farm called Prospect in the parish of Narraghmore, County Carlow, Paul Cullen was one of 16 children (six were from his father's first marriage). During the late 18th century, the penal laws which had long been imposed on Catholics in both Great Britain and Ireland were beginning to be relaxed, if not removed. In the south of Ireland, Catholic families took advantage of this relaxation and began to buy land formerly reserved for Protestants. Hugh Cullen owned about 700 acres when his son Paul was born. This gave him the status of strong Catholic farmer, a class that greatly influenced 19th-century Irish society. They were fervent in their Catholicism and fearful of social unrest. Their fear of unrest came from the human and material losses they suffered during the rising of the republican United Irishmen in 1798, and their fervent Catholicism provided financial support for the Church and younger sons for the priesthood.

Even though the Cullens and others of their class were virulently anti-Protestant, young Paul Cullen was sent to the Quaker school in nearby Ballitore because (1) it provided the best education available in the area; and (2) the Quakers had

Name variations: Cardinal Cullen, Cardinal San Pietro in Montorio. Born on April 29, 1803, at Prospect, Narraghmore parish, County Carlow; died on October 24, 1878, in Dublin; son of Hugh Cullen and Mary Maher; ordained 1829. Predecessors: (as rector of the Irish College in Rome) Christopher Boylan, 1832; (as archbishop of Armagh and primate of Ireland) William Crolly, 1849; (as archbishop of Dublin) Daniel Murray, 1852. Successors: (as rector) Tobias Kirby, 1849; (in Armagh) Joseph Dixon, 1852; (in Dublin) Edward McCabe, 1878.

Contributed by Patrick F. Tally, University of Wisconsin, Madison, Wisconsin

CHRONOLOGY

1821	Arrived in Rome to enter Propaganda College
1829	Ordained and appointed chair of Greek and Oriental languages at Propaganda College; British Parliament granted Catholic Emancipation
1832	Appointed rector of the Irish College in Rome
1845–50	Great Irish Potato Famine
1849	Appointed archbishop of Armagh and primate of Ireland
1850	Convoked the Synod of Thurles as Apostolic Delegate to Ireland
1852	Transferred to the Dublin Archdiocese
1864	Organized the political National Association to compete with the Fenians
1866	Elevated to the rank of cardinal
1869	Gave support to Pius IX and campaign for papal infallibility at Vatican Council I
1871	Protestant Church of Ireland disestablished
1878	Died in Dublin

aided Hugh Cullen during the anarchy of the rising. In all, the Cullen clan sent nine of its members to this school, where the famous political philosopher **Edmund Burke** had received the rudiments of his training.

In 1816, at the age of 13, Cullen entered Carlow College as a boarder. His natural academic gifts were soon recognized by his professors, many of whom would later hold prominent positions in the hierarchy of the Irish Catholic Church. On the recommendation of his godfather, James Maher, Cullen's family decided that the talented Paul should follow this strong-minded uncle to Rome. Ten years older, Maher was just completing his theological studies when the 17-year-old Paul arrived in Rome early in 1821 to enter Propaganda College.

It was the end of the pontificate of Pius VII, the pope who had stood up to **Napoleon.** The romantic hero of conservative Europe, Pius was revered as a symbol of all that was worth preserving in the tumultuous 19th century. In the atmosphere following Napoleon's defeat, the Eternal City was once again alive. Scholars flocked to its colleges, libraries, galleries, and museums, and the royalty and aristocracy of Europe streamed to the city, especially for the great religious holidays. As a young man from rural Ireland, Cullen was enthralled by the dynamic life of Rome and by its great baroque churches filled with the spirit of the Counter-Reformation.

The grandeur of the liturgical observances, the magnificent processions, the rich dress, and notable personages had a profound impact on the young seminarian from Ireland where, due to the lingering effect of the penal laws and local tradition, Catholic worship was held without pomp and ceremony. Amid the triumphalism of Pius's reign and that of his successor Leo XII, the young Cullen formed his lifelong system of religious and ecclesiastical beliefs. He wholeheartedly supported the religious, ecclesiastical, and political conservatism of Leo XII (1823–29), Gregory XVI (1831–46), and **Pius IX** (1846–78). This support stemmed from Cullen's natural conservatism and his adherence to the Ultramontane belief that the pope truly was the universal pontiff, the focal point of Catholicism to whom all Catholics owed obedience.

While Cullen was a student, **Daniel O'Connell**'s campaign to emancipate Irish Catholics was making rapid progress. Recognizing his intelligence, the Vatican asked Cullen to keep them abreast of developments back home. But Ireland was not the foremost thing on Cullen's mind for he was preparing to defend his doctoral dissertation. On September 11, 1828, Cullen brilliantly defended his 224 theses before an audience which included Leo XII, the Cardinal Prefect of Propaganda, the future Gregory XVI, and nine other cardinals. Writing to his father, Cullen reported proudly that, "Your son was the first among Irishmen who attempted to show his skill in theology in the presence of the Vicar of Christ." The Pope was so impressed that he personally conferred on Cullen the doctor's cap. To Cullen's delight, the Pope and others in the Vatican hierarchy then took him into their confidence on the affairs of the Irish Church. This spurred Cullen to begin an in-depth study of developments in Ireland about which he knew little.

Sometime in 1829 or 1830, Cullen was ordained a priest and appointed to the chairs of Greek and Oriental languages in the College of Propaganda. At this time, Europe was rocked by a series of political revolts. The anticlerical beliefs held by many of the liberals prominent in these revolutions frightened Cullen. Of special concern was the threat posed to the papacy's temporal possessions by the Young Italy movement founded by **Giuseppe Mazzini** in 1831. Holding to the Ultramontane belief in absolute papal supremacy, Cullen saw the liberal nationalist challenge to the papacy as a threat to Catholicism itself. From then on, Cullen was wary of all types of political agitation, especially ones led by oath-bound secret societies like Young Italy.

In February 1832, he was made vice rector of the Irish College in Rome and became rector when his predecessor died in June of that same year. The college, reestablished in 1826 after having been a barracks during the Napoleonic occupation, was in poor shape. Owing to his dedication, growing influence, and powerful personality, Cullen was soon able to build up the college's enrollment and endowment. He expected the Irish College to be instrumental in helping to bring Ireland into the Ultramontane camp. Under the strong guiding hands of Cullen and his vice rector and eventual successor Tobias Kirby, the college was dedicated to molding young Irish priests who would then return home and lead in the reshaping of the Irish Catholic Church. Cullen was so committed that he passed up more prestigious job offers (i.e. bishop of Charleston, South Carolina) to remain at the head of the college, enforcing a rigid discipline.

His Influence in the Vatican Increases

Papal authorities saw in Cullen a kindred soul, and his influence in the Vatican grew. In the 1830s, when the Irish bishops became aware of Cullen's influence, they began to seek his assistance, and Cullen acted as their agent in transactions with the apostolic. Both parties benefited from this relationship. The bishops gained an influential representative at the nucleus of the Church, and Cullen both expanded his knowledge of Ireland and obtained information on Irish churchmen that would prove useful when he returned to Ireland in the 1850s as Apostolic Delegate.

But the Irish bishops fell into two camps which Cullen perceived as Gallican. First enunciated by the French Church in the 17th century, Gallicanism was the antithesis of the Ultramontanism. Gallicanism claimed limited autonomy from papal authority for national churches in alliance with national governments. One group of Irish bishops, the old Gallicans or "Castle bishops," allied themselves with the crown—as opposed to the pope—even though the Irish crown was worn by the Protestant monarch of Great Britain. The other group, the new Gallicans, were nationalists who, while fervently opposing the British government and professing loyalty to the Holy See, resented taking direction from Rome. They wanted the Church to be free to identify with the liberal and national movements sweeping over Europe, movements that the Pope and Cullen feared. These clerics, led by John MacHale, the archbishop of Tuam, were deeply involved in

Daniel O'Connell's drive to repeal the Union of Great Britain and Ireland, and did not wish to be told by a conservative Pope to stay out of politics.

Three great issues divided the Irish hierarchy during the years Cullen acted as agent in Rome. The divisions concerned the proper Catholic response to (1) the 1831 government legislation which established a national system of secular primary education in Ireland; (2) the Charitable Bequests Act of 1844 which reformed charity laws; and (3) the nondenominational Queen's Colleges which were established in Belfast, Cork, and Galway in 1845. During the tumult following each of these contentious acts of Parliament, many bishops—especially the nationalists—solicited Cullen's and the Vatican's support.

The old Gallicans argued that the Catholics of Ireland would benefit from the educational and charitable institutions established by these acts. The followers of MacHale objected to the National Schools and Queen's Colleges as being either "godless" or establishments of proselytizing Protestantism. These bishops saw the three pieces of legislation as attempts by imperial Britain to encroach on the Irish Catholic Church and community. Cullen, like the MacHaleites, opposed all this legislation and gave support to these nationalist clerics. His opposition to these measures, however, stemmed not from a nationalist dislike of the British but from his passionate Ultramontanism. In Cullen's eyes, schools, colleges, and charity boards controlled by the government and aided by the old Gallicans threatened to undermine whatever hold the papacy still had on overwhelmingly Catholic Ireland. Cullen believed such institutions would spread heretical ideas and make it that much harder for him to succeed in his nascent campaign to bring Ireland under Vatican discipline.

Pope Appoints Cullen Archbishop

In 1849, while still negotiating to save Propaganda College from the forces of Mazzini that had captured Rome during the revolutions of 1848, Cullen was given a chance to carry his crusade to Ireland. During Holy Week of that year, William Crolly, archbishop of Armagh and primate of Ireland, died. Passing over the three candidates nominated, the pope appointed Cullen archbishop in December of 1849. After his consecration in Rome in January of 1850, he landed in Ireland in May. Meanwhile, in April, he had been made Apostolic Delegate and ordered by the pope to convoke a national synod as soon as he arrived in Ireland. An assembly of all the bishops and abbots in the land had not been held in Ireland since the 12th century. This gathering was intended not only to strengthen the ties between Ireland and Rome but also to bring the bishops together in hopes of ending episcopal divisions.

When the synod was convoked at Thurles on August 22, 1850, the split over the Queen's Colleges was papered over but remained. Cullen succeeded in securing near unanimous approval of the papal recommendation to establish a Catholic university to compete with the "godless colleges," but his proposal both to forbid priests to accept posts in these colleges and to exhort Catholic parents not to enroll their children passed by only two votes. Although this confrontation provided much drama, it was the no less contentious but less fought-over decisions which had a greater impact on the Church and the nature of Irish Catholicism.

At Thurles, Cullen strongly pushed for major changes in religious practice. At his request, decrees were passed which mandated that the sacraments of baptism, marriage, and confession take place in the church building and not at the recipient's home. These dictums were part of a reform policy begun by Cullen in Armagh and continued when he was transferred to the Dublin archdiocese in 1852. This program sought to make Irish religious practice more respectable by having it conform to Vatican teaching which centered worship in the parish church. Cullen introduced church-centered Roman devotional practices like the novena, benediction, and 40-hours adoration of the Blessed Sacrament. He also endeavored to move some traditional Irish practices, like the stations of the cross, from lay people's houses into the confines of a church or chapel. Wakes, patterns, and pilgrimages, popular religious customs that could not be brought inside a church building, were discouraged and eventually replaced by church funerals and other respectable devotions.

In this drive, Cullen put himself at odds with his former nationalist allies. Many of these bishops, especially those in the West where churches and priests were thin, preferred the traditional outdoor Irish customs to what they saw as foreign innovations. In 1853, the antipathy of the MacHaleites increased when Cullen prohibited the clergy in the Diocese of Dublin from participating in public political movements. He thought clergy should spend their time strengthening the faith of their congregations rather than participating in ill-fated movements to topple the British government. Although he opposed this government because as a Protestant power it was a threat to the faith of the Catholic population, he found revolutionary nationalist movements a greater threat—one that could lead Catholics to secularism and anticlericalism.

But in 1859, Cullen had no such qualms about his clergy being involved in the organization of the Irish Brigade which went to Rome to help defend the pope's forces in the Papal States against the invading Italian nationalist armies. Cullen's opposition was not to political activity per se but to movements that were secretive and/or potentially revolutionary. In the 1860s, he denounced and opposed the Fenian brotherhood because it was a secret society pledged to obtaining Irish independence through violent revolution. Meanwhile, in 1864, Cullen founded the National Association to press for limited rights for tenant farmers, the disestablishment of the Protestant Church of Ireland, and government endowment of the Catholic University. It was basically a program which sought to strengthen the position of the Catholics vis-a-vis the Protestants whether it be in economic, religious, or educational terms.

Cullen saw the nationalist struggle in denominational terms. By becoming more Catholic, the Irish would set themselves apart from their British rulers. He did not want to destroy the British Empire but rather to build an Irish one based on Catholicism. His political goal was to strengthen the position of Catholics within Ireland and the Empire. To this end, he aided in pressuring **William Gladstone**'s Liberal government to pass some conciliatory measures. In 1870, a Land Act granting fixity of tenure and free sale to Irish tenant farmers was passed, and the Church of Ireland was disestablished in 1871. With the power of the government no longer supporting the Church of Ireland, Cullen, who was now a cardinal, continued his drive to make the reformed Catholic Church the true national Church of Ireland.

Because of his influence with the Vatican and knowledge of the Irish clergy, Cullen was able to have most vacated bishoprics filled to his liking, thereby gaining unprecedented control over the Irish Church. During his tenure (1849–78), Catholicism began to touch every part of Irish life. The number of priests, nuns, and teaching brothers doubled and there was a tremendous spate of church, convent, and school building. Religious institutions spread the Ultramontane Catholicism into every corner of the land and to the emigrant communities overseas. The great bulk of Irish men and women became Catholics in practice as well as in name, their Catholicism an integral part of being Irish. Whether they remained at home or emigrated to foreign shores, they no longer identified themselves as "Irish" but as "Irish Catholics."

Throughout his life, Cullen remained an adamant Ultramontanist. For his service in the cause, in June of 1866, he became the first Irishman raised to the rank of prince of the Church, taking the title of Cardinal San Pietro in Montorio. At the Vatican Council I in 1869, he was the main author of the document promulgating the dogma of papal infallibility. In 1875, he again presided over a national synod at Maynooth. This synod confirmed Cullen's influence over the Irish Church by reinforcing the mandates of Thurles to further Romanize Irish religious practice. In February of 1878, Cullen received the news of Pius IX's death. Pio Nino had been pope longer than Cullen had been a bishop, and Cullen, faithful servant of Rome, departed Ireland to pay his last respects. But Cullen arrived in Rome too late to participate in the election of a former Propaganda classmate to papacy as Leo XIII. Soon after his return to Ireland, the 75-year-old Cullen, working until the end, died on October 24, 1878, in his office on Eccles Street, Dublin.

SOURCES:

Bowen, Desmond. *Paul Cardinal Cullen and the Shaping of Modern Irish Catholicism.* Gill & Macmillian, 1983.

Corish, Patrick. *The Irish Catholic Experience: A Historical Survey,* Michael Glazier, 1985.

Larkin, Emmet. *The Making of the Roman Catholic Church in Ireland, 1850–1860.* University of North Carolina Press, 1980.

FURTHER READING:

Comerford, R. V. *The Fenians in Context: Irish Politics and Society 1848–82.* Humanities Press, 1985.

Larkin, Emmet. *The Consolidation of the Roman Catholic Church, 1860–70.* University of North Carolina Press, 1987.

Norman, E. R. *The Catholic Church and Ireland in the Age of Rebellion, 1859–1873.* Cornell University Press, 1965.

Georges-Jacques Danton

(1759–1794)

Lawyer, orator, Jacobin leader, and member of the first Committee of Public Safety, who helped defeat absolutism and create the First French Republic in 1792.

Born on October 26, 1759, in Arcis-sur-Aube, a small town southwest of Paris; guillotined in 1794; married: Gabrielle Charpentier (daughter of an innkeeper), 1787; children: several.

Georges-Jacques Danton was born on October 26, 1759, in Arcis, a small town on the river Aube, to the southwest of Paris. In 1762, his father died and Georges was raised by his mother and a devoted uncle. Exhibiting a brash and impetuous personality, in 1771 the 13-year-old was sent by his mother to the city of Troyes, located a short distance to the south of Arcis, to be more closely supervised and educated by the order of clergy known as the Oratorians.

The Oratorians had been founded in the 17th century by a close friend of the mathematician and philosopher René Descartes. Descartes's rationalism displaced revelation as an acceptable tool of human inquiry, and revelation was a major underpinning of absolutism (the theory that absolute power should be in the hands of one or more rulers). This antiabsolutist spirit of Cartesian rationalism permeated the educational philosophy of the Oratorians, and it infected Georges as well.

The most famous member of the Oratorians was Father Quesnel, the 17th-century Jansenist theologian. The Jansenists also attacked traditional Roman Catholic theology, as well as absolutism, and as a result, they were excommunicated in

"My name is in the Pantheon of history ... and the people will respect my head after it has been guillotined."

GEORGES-JACQUES DANTON

Contributed by Joseph Tempesta, Associate Professor of History, Ithaca College, Ithaca, New York

314

1713. Though they were not Jansenists, the Oratorians were sympathetic to their antiabsolutist spirit; Georges also learned to sympathize with these Jansenist views.

The democratic spirit of the Enlightenment was the third major influence on the Oratorians; it was reflected in the rules which governed the order. Their superiors were required to heed the majority will of the members of the order, and their curriculum consisted of Enlightenment science, economics, and political science. By the time he left the Oratorians in 1780 at age 21, Georges was familiar with Voltaire, Rousseau, and the other philosophers; he had learned to abhor absolutism, so much so that he acquired the sobriquet, "the republican." Danton the revolutionary was born.

In 1780, Danton went to Paris, and by 1784, he was a lawyer. Three years later, he married Gabrielle Charpentier, the 24-year-old daughter of the keeper of an inn which he and other lawyers frequented. The couple loved each other deeply and had several children. Their life together, however, would soon be interrupted by the cataclysmic events which overwhelmed France at the end of the decade.

By 1787, the French economy had completely collapsed: landless, jobless, and homeless people poured into the major cities from rural areas. The people had grown to hate the tax exemptions and the opulent life style of the clergy (the First Estate) and the nobility (the Second Estate). Comprising less than ten of the French population, the First and Second Estates held most of the political power. The Third Estate (middle class, city workers, and peasants) comprised more than 90% of the population and held no political power. These conditions would lead to the French Revolution, and Danton would play a major role in it.

At the end of the decade, when **Louis XVI** attempted to avoid the approaching revolution by appeasing the population, he convened the representative assembly of France, the Estates-General, which had not been convened since 1614. In May 1789, the Estates-General—made up of the First, Second, and Third Estates—met at Versailles. When the Third Estate demanded a total transformation of the economic, social, and political life of the nation, the King resisted. Thus, on June 17, the Third Estate declared itself to be the National Assembly and the only body representing France. This revolutionary act effectively abolished the Estates-General.

On June 20, in an attempt to defeat this revolution, the king locked the members of the

National Assembly out of their meeting place. Undaunted, they withdrew into the royal indoor tennis court at Versailles and took an oath not to adjourn until they had written a constitution for France. On June 27, Louis XVI appeared to capitulate and ordered the first two estates of the old Estates-General to join the National Assembly.

In reality, Louis had no intention of surrendering so easily. During the rest of June and the beginning of July, he brought royal troops from outlying areas of France into Versailles and Paris, hoping to use them against the National Assembly. Then on July 11, he dismissed Jacques Necker, a popular reform-minded minister. This dismissal and the increasing presence of royal troops ignited Paris.

In 1789, Paris had been divided into 60 electoral districts, and each sent representatives to the Estates-General. Danton and his wife had settled in one of these districts, the Cordelier. Because the Cordelier was a poor working-class district, most of the people in it did not have the right to vote; they were known as passive citizens. Those in the district who could vote were known as the active citizens. These people were mostly small shopkeepers of very meager means. For this reason, the Cordelier attracted the most radical players in the French Revolution. In particular, it attracted editors of revolutionary newspapers such as Jean-Paul Marat and Camille Desmoulins. The residents of the Cordelier called for radical reforms such as universal male suffrage and the abolition of the monarchy.

Parisians Storm the Bastille

When news reached Paris of Necker's dismissal, Danton delivered an impassioned speech on July 13 to the restive residents of the Cordelier district. He warned them that "an army of 30,000 [royal] soldiers stood ready to descend on Paris ... and massacre its inhabitants." With this, the Cordeliers joined the thousands of Parisians who were roaming the city looking for arms. Encouraged by Desmoulins and Danton, the next day, July 14, 1789, they all stormed the Bastille.

The attack on the Bastille ushered in the violent phase of the Revolution which spread to other parts of France. To stem it, on July 16 Louis XVI reappointed Necker. In August, the National Assembly promulgated the Declaration of The Rights of Man, along with the August Decrees which officially ended serfdom, noble privileges, and the Old Regime in France. For his part in the events during the summer of 1789, Danton was elected president of the Cordelier Club in October.

By then, with food shortages in Paris growing acute, the king made his Second Appeal, summoning more troops to Versailles and Paris. This situation was made more explosive on October 1 when Louis held a banquet at Versailles, during which his guests toasted the king but did not toast the nation and ended by stepping on the new revolutionary flag.

On October 3, Marat and Danton urged the Parisian mob to bring the king back to Paris so that he could be watched. On October 6, thousands of Parisian women and children, hungry and desperate, marched to Versailles and escorted the king and his family back to Paris. Placed in the Tuileries Palace, they were now prisoners of the Parisian revolutionaries. A day later, the National Assembly, which was now called the Constituent Assembly because its function was to write a new constitution for France, also moved to Paris.

In May 1790, Danton joined the Jacobins, the most influential radical political club in Paris, where he met the Jacobin leader, **Maximilian Robespierre.** Until 1794, the two would have an immeasurable impact on the French Revolution. In 1790, his political star rising rapidly, Danton was also elected to the municipal government of Paris.

In 1791, Danton again had the opportunity to play to the mob and influence the Revolution. In April, the king hoped to spend Easter in Saint-Cloud, a town north of Paris. As Louis and his queen **Marie-Antoinette** prepared to leave Paris by coach, the Parisians, who feared that the royal family might flee France, blocked their way. To protect the king, the Parisian National Guard, commanded by the **Marquis de Lafayette,** arrived to keep order and permit the departure. Danton also arrived and talked some Cordeliers members of the National Guard into disobeying Lafayette and turning the coach back. The royal family returned to the Tuileries. Louis XVI was now determined to escape France.

Two months later, in June 1791, Louis and his family did make an attempt to escape, leaving behind a letter to the nation in which he condemned the Revolution and attacked the Jacobins for their radicalism. The royal family was on its way to Austria to ask Emperor Leopold II, Marie-Antoinette's brother, to invade France and crush the Revolution. Recognized, however, at the town of Verennes in Lorraine, the royal family were returned to Paris on June 24. The city greeted them with a silence that presaged their doom.

The Constituent Assembly did not immediately depose Louis XVI because it had nearly completed work on a new constitution which severely limited the king's power. Deposing the king would surely destroy the assembly's work and might invite intervention by European monarchs to save Louis. The Parisian mob, on the other hand, now rallied behind Danton, Robespierre, and the Jacobins who demanded that Louis be dethroned and tried for treason and that a republic be established.

On July 16, 1791, the Cordeliers and Jacobins carried a petition containing these demands to the Champ-de-Mars so that thousands of Parisians gathered there could sign it. These republicans intended to present this petition to the assembly. When the throng arrived at the Champ-de-Mars, they found two suspicious characters in hiding. Believing them to be spies for the king, the mob hanged them. Lafayette and the National Guard rushed to the Champ-de-Mars and, in the process of restoring order, fired into the mob and dispersed it. The assembly imposed martial law on Paris for the next several weeks and ordered the arrest of radical leaders, including Danton who fled to England and escaped arrest.

By September, the assembly promulgated the Constitution of 1791 which Louis accepted. Its work completed, the Constituent Assembly passed out of existence. On October 1, the new Legislative Assembly, as called for in the new constitution, met to govern the country. But the country was about to erupt again.

The new constitution abolished absolutism and placed the king under the rule of law. It severely limited the franchise, however, by maintaining the distinction between active and passive citizens; it also prohibited unions and strikes, placing all political power in the hands of the wealthy middle class. The majority of the population now felt betrayed by this constitution. This betrayal, the Massacre at the Champ-de-Mars, and the king's attempted flight combined to make for an explosive atmosphere. By the end of September, Danton returned to France and stood ready to lead the crowd again.

National Assembly Declares War on Austria

The political faction in the National Assembly (the Girondins) which wished to preserve the constitutional arrangements of 1791 sought to divert another popular uprising by involving France in a foreign war. They reasoned that this would rally the people behind the country and would give the new political order time to take root. The king welcomed a war in the hopes of losing it so that the monarchs of Europe would invade France and restore absolutism. In contrast, the republican Jacobins wanted to eliminate the king and the bourgeois Constitution of 1791; they also believed that the country was ill prepared for war. Though Danton and Robespierre spoke out strongly against war, their fulminations were ignored, and on April 20, 1792, the National Assembly declared war on Austria. Prussia soon joined Austria against France.

From the start, the war went badly. By April 30, French troops led by General Dumouriez invaded Belgium; but in the face of Prussian resistance, several French generals and their regiments deserted en masse and went over to the Prussians. On all fronts the French army collapsed. On July 11, the assembly declared the country to be in danger (*patrie endanger*) as the fear of invasion increased. In the midst of this hysteria, 20,000 Federes (National Guardsmen from areas of France outside of Paris) began descending upon Paris to celebrate Bastille Day. On July 14, 1792, several hundred *Federes* from Marseilles marched into Paris singing a new marching song soon to become the French national anthem, the "Marseillaise." The Cordeliers housed the *Federes,* and Danton and the Jacobins planned to use them in an insurrection to topple the government and establish a republic.

On August 1, the commander of the invading Prussian army unwittingly aided the insurrectionists. He issued a manifesto ordering the French to restore Louis XVI to his former position as absolute ruler of France and threatened Paris with total destruction if any harm came to the king. The manifesto angered the insurrectionists, and Danton urged them to issue an ultimatum to the assembly. They gave the assembly until August 9 to depose the king and establish a republic, or the king would be attacked in the Tuileries.

On August 10, the Parisians attacked the Tuileries and the king took refuge in the National Assembly. The royal guard defended the palace, but after hundreds of soldiers and attackers were killed, the king gave the order to surrender. The insurrectionists proclaimed the creation of the Revolutionary Paris Commune. The assembly was forced to recognize it and its demands that the monarchy be suspended, that the King be brought to trial for treason, and that a new National Assembly be elected by universal manhood suffrage. In place of the monarchy, a Provisory Executive Council of six was established. Danton was named minister of justice on this council, which dictated policy to the assembly and actually conducted the affairs of state. Danton had gotten his republic.

Throughout August, as the Commune arrested enemies of the insurrection, the war continued to go badly. On September 2, news arrived in Paris that Verdun was about to fall. Danton immediately issued a call for all able-bodied French citizens to come to Paris to form battalions to defend Verdun. Before they set off for Verdun, concerned about leaving enemies of the state behind to attack their loved ones, the volunteers went into prisons and murdered prisoners. In four days in Paris alone, more than 1,100 prisoners, including 150 children from a reformatory, were butchered. The violence spread to the rest of France. While many others (such as Jean-Paul Marat) must be held chiefly responsible for the September Massacres, because his incendiary speeches inflamed the population during this time of danger to France, Danton must be held responsible as well. The Revolution had turned violent at the time that Danton was at the crest of his popularity.

On September 20, 1792, the new National Convention was elected to replace the old Legislative Assembly, and Danton, Marat, Robespierre, and Desmoulins were elected to it. On September 21, Danton's nationwide call to arms resulted in a French victory at Valmy. At Verdun, the French army under Dumouriez stopped the Prussians under the duke of Brunswick. On that same day, the monarchy was abolished and "Year I of The First French Republic" was declared by the new National Convention.

On December 3, 1792, Louis XVI was brought to trial before the National Convention. On January 21, he was guillotined in the Place de la Revolution. Danton voted for his execution.

In February, the western portions of France (the Vendee) revolted in support of a return to monarchy and against a new conscription; food shortages grew more acute, and on all fronts the war went badly. General Dumouriez, now fighting in the Netherlands, planned to march on Paris and take over the government in order to end this chaos and political warfare in the National Convention. When his troops refused to follow, General Dumouriez and several of his officers defected to the Austrians. In the face of these disasters, on April 6 Danton and the Jacobins maneuvered the convention into creating the Committee of Public Safety. Danton was elected as one of the first nine members of the committee.

At first, Danton worked tirelessly on the committee, but then his energies flagged. Gabrielle had died in March in childbirth, and though he remarried in June, Danton was so grief stricken that his interest in the Revolution waned. Spending more and more time at home with his new wife and children, he began missing meetings of the Committee of Public Safety and the Jacobins Club. Because of his absences, when the convention elected a new committee on July 10, it excluded Danton. In October, Danton returned home to Arcis-sur-Aube.

Reign of Terror Begins

Three days after Danton was ousted from the Committee of Public Safety, Charlotte Corday murdered the popular Jean-Paul Marat while he sat in his bathtub. Corday was a self-styled enemy of the radicals such as Marat and the Jacobins. This deed inflamed the mob and the Committee of Public Safety, and they began a systematic purge of the convention and society at large. They arrested anyone, including members of the convention, whom they branded an enemy of the state. Moving cruelly against the Revolution in the west, they slaughtered thousands of Vendeans. On September 5, 1793, the Convention passed The Law of Suspects which facilitated the execution of "enemies of the state." The Reign of Terror had begun.

This was a dangerous time for Danton to retire from the Revolution. When he left Paris, he created a power vacuum which was filled by radical upstarts who hoped to eliminate old-timers such as Danton and take over the Revolution. These new players, led by Jacques Hebert, the new president of the Cordeliers, accused Danton of antirevolutionary activities.

In November 1793, Danton returned to Paris to defend himself in the convention. At first, Robespierre, who was now a member of the Committee of Public Safety, remained loyal. They made a formidable pair; they defeated Hebert's attack, and he fell from power. Hebert was arrested and executed in 1794. By this time, however, in keeping with his change of heart after Gabrielle's death, Danton began advocating an end to the Reign of Terror. In fact, on March 28, while reflecting on the Terror's butchery, Danton stated that "it is better to be guillotined than to guillotine." Robespierre considered Danton's new attitude to be a threat to the Committee of Public Safety and turned on him.

On March 31, Danton was arrested for crimes against the Revolution. He was accused of having supported General Dumouriez's plan to march on Paris in 1792 and of having bribed the duke of Brunswick into retreating at Valmy, so as to prevent the French army from capturing a large portion of the Prussian army. Finally, Danton was accused of having profited from the Revolution. There was no evidence to prove any of these changes.

The trial began on April 2. For three days, Danton defended himself brilliantly, but by the last day of the trial his voice had given out. Nevertheless, because the convention did not allow him to call witnesses against him, Danton was sentenced to be guillotined on April 5.

During the night in prison on April 4, Danton comforted his friends, including Desmoulins, condemned along with him. On April 5, Danton and his companions were transported to the guillotine by cart. Danton insisted upon being executed last so that he could continue to comfort his friends. When his turn came, he told his executioner, "above all, don't forget to show my head to the people, it is well worth a look," and died bravely.

At the start of his trial, Danton was asked where he lived. His response could serve as his epitaph: "I live nowhere but my name is in the Pantheon of history ... and the people will respect my head after it has been guillotined." France now reveres Georges-Jacques Danton as one of its great patriots.

SOURCES:

Gershoy, L. *The French Revolution and Napoleon*. Appleton Century Crofts, 1964.

Hampson, N. *Danton*. Holmes & Meier, 1978.

Hérissay, J. *Cet excellent M. Danton*. Librairie Artheme Fayard, 1960.

Palmer, R. R. *Twelve Who Ruled*. Atheneum, 1965.

Soboul, A. *The French Revolution*. Vintage, 1975.

Thompson, J. M. *The French Revolution*. Oxford University Press, 1966.

FURTHER READING:

Dwyerm F. *Georges Danton*. Chelsea House, 1978.

Wendel, H. *Danton*. Yale University Press, 1935.

HISTORIC WORLD LEADERS

Eamon de Valera

(1882–1975)

Soldier in the 1916 Easter Rebellion, who rose to prominence as Ireland's leading spokesman for independence, triumphantly leading his country for decades and becoming the first president of Ireland.

"Our whole struggle is to get Ireland out of the cage in which the selfish statecraft of England would confine her—to get Ireland back into the free world."

EAMON DE VALERA

E amon de Valera, the famous and respected Irish leader, was in fact an American; both his parents were immigrants to the United States. His mother Katherine (Kate) Coll came from Ireland; his father Vivion Juan de Valera came from Spain. Their son Edward (he changed his name to its Gaelic form, Eamon, as an adult) was born on October 14, 1882, in the middle of Manhattan. Vivion de Valera had never been a healthy man, and he soon left New York City in search of a healthier climate and cleaner air. Though he had planned to return to his wife and son, he died in the spring of 1885. Widowed and penniless, Kate de Valera was forced to find a fellow Irish immigrant to care for her son while she worked as a domestic.

But Kate worried about the conditions in which her son was growing up. The city was nothing like the Irish countryside of her childhood, and Edward was without the company and security of a large, extended family. A solution soon presented itself. Kate's brother Ned, who had come to America shortly after she had made the long journey, was planning to return home. If Edward were to travel with his uncle, he could safely reach the Coll

Born Edward de Valera on October 14, 1882; died on August 29, 1975; son of Vivion Juan de Valera (Spanish) and Katherine (Kate) Coll (Irish); married: Sinead Flanagan, 1910; children: seven (two daughters and five sons).

Contributed by Colleen Carpenter Cullinan, Ph.D. candidate, University of Chicago Divinity School, Chicago, Illinois

By the time Edward finished elementary school at the age of 12, he knew that his prospects of a career in Ireland were limited. Preferring not to end up a farm laborer like the rest of his family, he wrote to his Aunt Hannie, who had since joined his mother in America, and pleaded with her to convince his mother to bring him to New York. When nothing came of this, Edward turned to improving his schoolwork. He managed to convince the Colls that he wanted to attend Christian Brothers high school in Charleville, despite the fact that this meant a seven-mile walk each way. Studying diligently, he ended up winning a scholarship to Blackrock College, Dublin. He was able to continue his studies at Royal University by winning another scholarship in 1902.

De Valera began to teach to supplement his scholarship income, and on graduation, turned to teaching full-time. He joined the Gaelic League in 1908, an organization devoted to Irish national history (as opposed to the purely British history that was taught in Irish schools of the time) and to the preservation and spread of Gaelic, Ireland's dying native language. Taking the Gaelic form of his name, Eamon, de Valera was never again known as Eddie or Edward. Sinead Flanagan, a popular and politically active member of the Gaelic League, was one of his teachers. De Valera soon fell in love with the vibrant, dedicated woman, and they were married on January 8, 1910. Insisting that the ceremony be performed in Gaelic, they had to teach the priest the proper words.

He Joins the Irish Volunteers

As de Valera became more and more involved in the Gaelic League, his dedication to the Irish language led to a passion for an independent Ireland. Yoked unwillingly to Britain by the Act of Union in the year 1801, Ireland had never really ceased the struggle for freedom. Turning his attention from language revival to political action and the possibility of war, de Valera decided in 1913 to join the Irish Volunteers, a military organization nominally independent and dedicated simply to law and order. Though his company was trained by a soldier of the British Army, the Volunteers were in truth being led by the Irish Republican Brotherhood (IRB), a secret organization dedicated to expelling the British from Ireland by force. De Valera rose quickly in the Volunteers, eventually commanding a battalion and being persuaded to take the oath that bound him to the IRB.

By 1915, plans for an uprising against Britain were taking shape. Preparations were made throughout the year. But just as Irish readiness was

home and be cared for by his grandmother. Thus, Edward left the United States at the age of four.

The Coll home was slightly north of the rural village of Bruree, in County Limerick. The first night that the young boy spent in Ireland was in a home typical of those built before the Great Famine of the mid-19th century—one room, with a fire at one end, and a single window and door. The walls were mud and the roof, thatched. This was certainly a change from the apartments of New York City. The next day, however, Edward and the Colls—his grandmother, his Uncle Pat and Aunt Hannie—moved into housing built by the Liberal government of the time, known as an agricultural laborer's cottage. Though the cottage was a definite improvement, it still bespoke the poverty of the Irish peasants. There was a kitchen, two small bedrooms, and a loft above that was reached by a ladder. While sleeping in the loft, Edward once took a bad fall down the ladder.

At the age of six, he was judged old enough to walk the mile to school alone, and so began his education at the National School of Bruree. Known as Eddie Coll, his attendance at school was unfortunately irregular, as duties at home and around the farm kept him occupied from an early age. When his grandmother died in 1895, an even larger share of work fell to him. His Uncle Pat was a strict man, who made sure Eddie was never idle enough to indulge in sports.

becoming a reality, rumors spread that the British were about to disband the Volunteers, shut down the Gaelic League, and take over trade union buildings. Fearing that a crackdown would come before the uprising, preparations were hurried, and at noon of Easter Monday, 1916, the ill-fated military escapade began. Confusion and contrary orders doomed the effort. A group of rebels occupied the General Post Office in Dublin for almost a week, but the building could not stand up to the incendiary shells that the British began launching on Friday, and the rebels surrendered. A good part of Dublin was destroyed in the fighting, and 262 civilians were killed. In comparison, only 141 British soldiers and 62 rebels died. De Valera was commandant of the last Irish unit to surrender at the end of the week. He was also one of the last of the rebels to stand trial. Though he expected to be sentenced to death, public outrage at the numerous executions had mounted by the time he was brought before the court. Instead, he was given a life term, along with one other commandant, Thomas Ashe, and deported to Dartmoor Prison in England. The following year, in the midst of a de Valera-led prison strike, for apparently unrelated reasons, the British government suddenly decided to free the Irish prisoners.

Now an Irish hero thanks to his role in the Easter Rising, de Valera ran for Parliament and won easily; he was also soon elected to the presidency of Sinn Fein, the Irish nationalist political party. In 1919, Sinn Fein decided to abandon the British Parliament altogether and set up an independent Irish Parliament, known as the *Dail Eireann*. The Dail promptly adopted a declaration of independence and reaffirmed the establishment of an Irish republic (first announced during the 1916 Easter Rebellion). Elected *Priomh Aire* ("prime minister") of the Dail, de Valera promptly began a tour of the United States, gathering support for the independent Irish nation. Although Britain had not recognized Ireland's new government, de Valera was hoping that international pressure could be brought to bear.

After a year in the United States, de Valera returned to Ireland and to negotiations with the British on the precise status of the British-Irish relationship. The British feared that their national security would be gravely compromised were Ireland to become truly independent, and there was the additional problem that the six northernmost counties of Ireland, which were primarily Protestant and pro-British, had no interest at all in Irish independence. Indeed, they feared it; just as the Catholics of Ireland suffered discrimination under Protestant British rule, the Protestants of North-

ern Ireland feared they would fare the same were they to be a minority in an Irish Republic. De Valera did not travel to Britain for the 1921 negotiations, preferring not to be forced personally into the compromises that he knew the negotiators would face. In fact, de Valera resigned in 1922 when the Dail approved a separation treaty that he thought inadequate.

De Valera Founds His Own Party

De Valera's career appeared to be at an end; he was 30 years old; Ireland was independent, and he had voluntarily stepped down from the Dail. He retained his presidency of Sinn Fein, however, and was so dissatisfied with the Treaty that he remained active in politics. For the next four years, de Valera struggled within Sinn Fein, but in 1926, he abandoned the party and founded his own, Fianna Fail. Immediately successful, it was soon the largest party in the Dail. In 1932, the Fianna Fail members of the Dail formed a coalition government with members of the Labour party, and de Valera was elected president of the Executive Council—in effect, the equivalent of his former status as prime minister. This was only ten years after he had resigned.

De Valera's government systematically fought the burdensome conditions of the Separation Treaty, primarily by claiming to be a sovereign state and ignoring aspects of the treaty that would undermine that claim. The Dail consistently passed legislation that undermined or invalidated aspects of the treaty, and within five years, the Irish Free State was—in fact as well as name—a free state, and not a dependent of Britain.

By the late 1930s, the stirrings of war were once again being felt across the European continent. De Valera was determined that Ireland should remain neutral, both due to the fact that Ireland had little to no military capability and that it would truly demonstrate Ireland's independence to remain neutral in a war that Britain was involved in. However, the Irish neutrality was certainly sympathetic toward Britain, and it took all of de Valera's diplomatic skill to maintain that friendship while giving Germany no excuse to attack Ireland. Ireland secretly cooperated with Britain, and later with the United States, but stopped short of entering the war.

The decade following the war was a tumultuous one for both de Valera and Ireland. He and his party were in and out of power throughout the late 1940s and 1950s, and in 1959, de Valera was elected president of the Republic of Ireland. His duties now were not so much political as ceremonial, and he welcomed many foreign dignitaries to Ireland. In 1964, de Valera was invited to the United States by President **Lyndon Johnson** and asked to address a joint session of Congress. Though 81 years old and blind, he spoke for nearly a half hour and was well received. He ran for a second term in 1966 and won a close election. It was during this term that Ireland formally entered the European Economic Community (EEC).

Since the Irish constitution prevented him from seeking a third term as president, de Valera stepped down in 1973, at the age of 91. Having outlived most of his friends and family, he entered a nursing home outside of Dublin, where he died on August 29, 1975.

SOURCES:

Dwyer, T. Ryle. *Eamon de Valera.* Dublin: 1980.

Earl of Longford, and Thomas O'Neill. *Eamon de Valera.* Dublin: 1970.

FURTHER READING:

MacManus, M. J. *Eamon de Valera.* Dublin: 1957.

Moynihan, Maurice, ed. *Speeches and Statements by Eamon de Valera, 1917–1973.* Dublin: 1980.

Demosthenes

(384–322 B.C.)

The greatest orator of antiquity, who was a defender of the democratic freedoms of Ancient Greece against the invading barbarian armies of the Macedonian king, Philip II, and his successor, Alexander the Great.

"Demosthenes now made it his one business to arouse the Athenian to a sense of their danger."

CHARLES ADAMS

Demosthenes was an unlikely prospect to become a leading defender of Greek ideals. Born in 384 B.C. in the city-state of Athens, he was a weak, physically awkward youth at a time when strength and gymnastic ability were worshipped. When his father died in 376 B.C., much of the family estate was embezzled by unscrupulous executors. Fortunately, Demosthenes' mother was strong-minded and intelligent, and completely thorough in her understanding of what was necessary for success in the Greek world. Though relatively impoverished, she ensured that Demosthenes was well-educated.

During his adolescence, with long hours of study, Demosthenes became particularly proficient in rhetoric, which was the highly regarded art of speechmaking and debate. By 366 B.C., he had mastered his speechcraft to the extent that he was able to study law under **Isaeus,** one of Greek civilization's most famous lawyers.

Being adept in Athenian law and its courtroom presentation was a pathway to success and influence in ancient Athens. Under the democratic traditions originally established in Athenian courts, citizens involved in lawsuits or contests

Born in 384 B.C. in the city-state of Athens; committed suicide by poison in 322 B.C.

Contributed by Scott A. McLean, Ph.D. in history, University of Guelph, Guelph, Ontario, Canada

were required to plead their point of view in court personally. However, as the city-state's politics and economics became more sophisticated and the systems of laws became more complex, it was recognized that being represented in court by an expert in law was not only expedient but desirable. This gave lawyers an obvious source of income and influence; it also meant that lawyers learned to speak for both the powerful and the weak.

Demosthenes had a gift for the rhetoric of the courtroom. He could analyze issues deeply and present his arguments forcefully and convincingly. This was especially important for the type of courtroom drama which might unfold in ancient Greece; it was often not so much a question of who was right or wrong as it was who could best embarrass or humiliate his opponent. In this regard Demosthenes was master. In many of his greatest works of oratory, including On the Crown, his speeches crackle with abuse—from bitter remarks and name-calling to more subtle forms of sarcasm.

As his years of experience in the law courts lengthened, Demosthenes' devotion to the Athenian democratic ideal and his ability to dramatically illustrate his beliefs in carefully crafted speeches became well-known to many Athenians, especially those of political influence and wealth. As in our society today, politics was a special calling in the ancient Greek world that appealed to lawyers and the students of the law. It would have been surprising, indeed, if Demosthenes had not begun to use his talents in the service of his government.

One of his earliest appointments was to the *ecclesia*, the Athenian popular assembly. To understand the importance of this political body, one must remember that the early Greek systems of democracy had developed around the independent existence of cities. These city-states usually consisted of the environs of the city: the buildings, outlying farms, countryside, small villages, a coastal region, and a defendable harbor. As these city-states acted much like sovereign nations, all the major decisions that affected the prosperity of the municipalities, and even their existence at a time of war, were made by the *ecclesia*. But unlike today, where political party allegiance is relatively firm and unwavering, the Greek party or alliance structure of the popular assembly was fluid and shifting. This meant that an orator such as Demosthenes could greatly influence the outcome of any decisions being made by the *ecclesia* by using strong argument, whether right or wrong, to convince those around him.

Demosthenes reached his political maturity during a volatile period in the history of Athens. From 377 B.C., Athens had been the leader of a group of allied city-states, the Second Athenian Confederacy, which was held together by the economic and military strength of Athens and philosophically united by a constitution that promoted economic security and peaceful coexistence. The union was mainly between the island states and the northern coastal states.

At age 24 in the year 360 B.C., Demosthenes was called upon by his government to serve a brief time in the Athenian fleet. As befitted his status, he was appointed *trierarch* ("commander") of a warship, a position which allowed him to see firsthand the prosperity and benefits of the Athenian alliance. However, upon his return to the *ecclesia*, Demosthenes would also bear witness to the subtle but increasing disintegration of Athens's economic and political hegemony ("influence") over the region.

In 358 B.C., a small group of allied northern city-states withdrew from the Athenian confederacy. These states were convinced by their own prosperity to pursue an independent trade direction, some even being tempted to reestablish direct commerce with Persian dependencies on the Asia Minor coast. These actions angered the government of Athens, for not only were they an affront to its leadership, but Persia was an ancient enemy of the Greek states. For the "rebel" states to trade with the Persian dependencies was, in the eyes of Athens, to formally accept the loss to the Persian Empire of these once-Greek colonies in Asia Minor.

Responding aggressively to the breakup of their confederacy, the Athenians attempted to regain the seceding states by the use of force. But after three fruitless years of bloody and expensive war, Athens had to recognize their independence. Demosthenes shared with all Athenians the loss of prestige and political influence that the defeat underscored.

The disruption within the Second Athenian Confederacy could not have come at a worse time. In the northern state of Macedon (roughly between present-day Greece and the ex-Yugoslavian republic of Macedonia), a new ruler, Philip II, was consolidating and expanding his power. Within seven years of his ascension to the Macedonian throne, Philip's powerful army was on a successful march of conquest south along the Greek peninsula. This was a much greater threat than the internecine squabbles between city-states. The Macedonians' monarchial government and imperial outlook was in direct and deadly conflict with the concept of Greek city-state democracy.

His "First Philippic" Warns Athenians

Demosthenes, with his understanding of political power and his experience in the navy, realized the danger that Philip posed. The orator had tried early on to arouse the Athenian assembly against the Macedonians. In 351 B.C., he delivered his "First Philippic" warning the Athenians of the dangers of inaction. But at that time Athens was suffering in the war against the northern seceding states and there seemed to be little stomach for expanding the war effort to include the then remote Macedonians. Still, Demosthenes persevered in his arguments, for he judged Philip II to be a warrior with an insatiable appetite for glory, power and riches. He worried that Philip would prevent the peace of Northern Greece from ever being restored, and that the northern unrest would dangerously threaten Athens's traditional sphere of political and economic influence.

Respected as he was, Demosthenes could not fully martial the *ecclesia* to establish a war footing against Philip. The danger was deemed too remote. Classical historian Charles Adams summarizes some of Demosthenes' recorded arguments:

> [H]e denounces the indifference of the people, the unwillingness of the rich to tax themselves to support the fleet, and of the masses to serve in person; he warns them that if Philip gains control of the North, there will be nothing to hinder his intervening in the troubled affairs in north-central Greece, and even moving upon Athens.

Most pointedly, Demosthenes warns the *ecclesia* of the "irreconcilable hostility between an irresponsible monarchy and a free democracy." Although the *ecclesia* did respond with the calling up of some troops, a domestic crisis on the nearby island of Euboea distracted the attention of Athens, and the momentum generated by Demosthenes' efforts was lost.

Indeed, the politics of the times became increasingly complex as fighting broke out in north-central Greece among a number of city-states over the control of the Apollo shrine at Delphi. Thebes, the leading city involved, was unable to reestablish its influence over the area and called to Philip II to aid them in this quest. Now Athens feared that the armies of Macedonia would make their way directly into central Greece.

To confound the issue further, Philip had sent a messenger to Athens announcing that he wished to cement a peace accord between the Macedonian Empire and Athens. As a leading member of the embassy, Demosthenes was sent to discuss a possible treaty. The fact that he was in the delegation was indicative of how sensitive Athens was to his position on the danger of Philip's expanding Empire. Demosthenes hoped to create a treaty in which Philip would recognize Greek sovereignty among the northern central city-states and would not seek to consolidate his power over this area. But Demosthenes hoped in vain, and the Peace of Philocrates, signed in 346 B.C., ensured peace only within Athens.

Philip's armies continued moving south into positions of strength. Where he could negotiate position, he did. Where he could not negotiate, his large armies took what they needed. Within five years of the treaty, Philip, through negotiation and threat, had set up a complex series of alliances and treaties that gave the Macedonians hegemony over north and central Greece, and effective control over almost all of Hellas (Greece) by 338 B.C.

Throughout the five years that followed the signing of the Peace of Philocrates, Demosthenes continued to struggle to rally Athens against the Macedonians. Initially, his efforts were dismissed as blatant warmongering. A peace had been signed with Philip, and Philip was following the treaty to the letter. However, as Philip's influence grew, so did suspicions over the Macedonian's intentions for all of Greece.

Demosthenes Speaks Out; Philip Crushes Athens

Demosthenes' speeches began to be received as expressions of statesmanship and Greek ideals;

they also were published in order to reach the widest possible audience. Traveling throughout Greece, his missions contributed to the creation of an anti-Macedonian alliance between city-states, which even included the membership of a now-disenchanted Thebes. Open warfare between the alliance and the Macedonian forces broke out at the Battle of Charonea in 338 B.C. When Philip crushed Athens and its allies, Demosthenes delivered the eulogy of the 1,000 Athenian soldiers killed at the battle. Probably out of his respect for Athens's still sizable navy, Philip's peace terms were unexpectedly moderate, though they caused the dissolution of the Athenian confederacy and the recognition of Macedonian dominance over Greece.

While on the surface Demosthenes seemed to acquiesce to Athens's fate, behind the scenes he was fighting to maintain underground resistance to move against Philip when the time was ripe. Though it left him open to criticism, he even went so far as to negotiate with Greece's ancient enemy Persia to help fund an insurrection. Demosthenes and his followers believed that their moment had arrived in 336 B.C. when Philip was assassinated. However, his consolidated Empire passed unimpeded into the hands of his son, Alexander, later to be known as **Alexander the Great,** who suppressed the rebellion that followed with a ruthlessness that leveled Thebes.

Demosthenes lost his influential leadership role after the battle and, though he remained in politics, his career went into eclipse for a decade. In 324 B.C., he was exiled from Athens over charges of embezzling city funds, but due to the disfavor in which anti-Macedons were held in that time, it is difficult to say whether he was guilty or framed for the crime.

In 323 B.C., after Alexander the Great's sudden death, Demosthenes found himself recalled from exile when Athens formed the Hellenic League, a movement to expel the Macedonian forces from Greece. This independence movement was short-lived as Athens was defeated by land and sea in 322 B.C. by Alexander's successor, Antipater, and Demosthenes and other Athenian patriots fled the city. Cornered by the soldiers of Antipater upon the nearby island of Calaria, Demosthenes committed suicide by poison to escape his arrest.

Having devoted half a century to the political struggles and turmoil of Athens, Demosthenes had been hailed—in the words of historian D. Brendan Nagle—as "heroic patriot defending Athens' liberty against tyranny" and denounced as "a blind chauvinist fighting against the tide of the times." Perhaps clearer than either epitaph would be Demosthenes' recognition as a practical, shrewd politician, gifted with the talent of oratory, and consistent in his fearless defense to preserve the Greek democratic ideals that he felt represented true justice.

SOURCES:

Adams, Charles. *Demosthenes and His Influence.* New York: Cooper Square Publishers, 1963.

Nagle, D. Brendan. *The Ancient World, A Social and Cultural History.* Prentice-Hall, 1979.

Pearson, Lionel. *The Art of Demosthenes.* Scholars Press, 1981.

Robinson, Charles Alexander. *Ancient History.* Macmillan, 1967.

FURTHER READING:

Bury, J. B., and Russell Meiggs. *A History of Greece to the Death of Alexander the Great.* St. Martin's Press, 1975.

Webster, T. B. L. *Athenian Culture and Society.* University of California Press, 1973.

Anton Denikin

(1872–1947)

Leader of the White Volunteer Army which in 1919, during the Russian Civil War, nearly succeeded in defeating the "Red" Bolshevik forces.

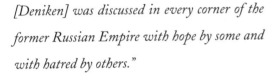

[Deniken] was discussed in every corner of the former Russian Empire with hope by some and with hatred by others."

DIMITRY V. LEHOVICH

Anton Ivanovich Denikin was born on December 7, 1872, in Warsaw Province, a section of Poland that had been absorbed by the Russian Empire in the 18th century. His father Ivan Denikin (1807–85) had been born a serf in Saratov Province, Russia, yet had worked himself up to the rank of major in the Russian frontier guards. Two years after retiring in 1869, Ivan married a poor Catholic seamstress, Elizaveta Vrjesinski (1843–1916), who was supporting her aged father.

The pension of a retired major was not sufficient to support the family in circumstances other than abject poverty; even so, Ivan Denikin always had a charitable hand for others in need. Anton, an only child, was technically a Russian-Polish "half-breed," but his father's commitment to Russian patriotism and the Russian Orthodox Church provided the boy with a path eagerly followed. Indeed, at age 70, Deniken's father volunteered to fight in the Russo-Turkish War (1877–78), and it seems clear that from an early age young Denikin had determined to become a soldier.

As a student, Anton Denikin was capable, if not brilliant, and was admitted to secondary school

Born Anton Ivanovich Denikin on December 4, 1872, at Shpetal Dolnyi village near the city of Wloclawek in Warsaw Province, Russian Poland; died near Ann Arbor, Michigan, on August 7, 1947; son of Ivan Efimovich and Elizaveta Fedorovna (Vrjesinski) Denikin; married: Xenia Vasilievna Chizh, January 1918; children: one daughter, Marina.

Contributed by David Bullock, Ph.D. candidate in history, Kansas State University, Manhattan, Kansas

at age nine. Four years later, after the death of his father, he began tutoring younger boys so that the family could earn a tiny additional income. He became a proficient swimmer and athlete, and local soldiers taught him how to use a rifle.

At 18, Denikin began a course at the Kiev Junker School, a military college from which he graduated in 1892. As a newly commissioned officer, an ensign, he was posted to the 2nd Field Artillery Brigade. During this initial assignment, Denikin prepared to take the entry examinations for the Academy of the General Staff, which he passed in 1895.

Life at the Academy in the Russian capital of St. Petersburg opened new vistas for this provincial young man in his early 20s. He met members of the intelligentsia, had occasion to read politically "subversive" left-wing material, and was able to contact persons from most walks of life and from all social classes. So much interested him outside the Academy that he graduated at the bottom of his class.

Due to an injustice in bureaucratic procedure, over which he petitioned Tsar **Nicholas II,** Denikin was not able to assume a position as an officer of the General Staff until 1902. Therefore,

in 1900, he returned to his old artillery brigade in Warsaw Province and waited.

Finally, in 1902, he was transferred to the General Staff and was rotated through a series of positions considered beneficial for the development of his career. Serving at the lowest level as a squad leader in an infantry regiment, he was then attached to the headquarters of the 2nd Cavalry Corps, acquiring experience in each of the main branches of the army: artillery, infantry, and cavalry.

A captain in 1904 when the Japanese made a surprise attack on the Russian fleet at Port Arthur in the Far East, Denikin immediately volunteered for frontline duty and, according to Dimitry Lehovich, soon "acquired a reputation for personal bravery and for ability to make a quick assessment of combat situations." Action suited him better than staff work. In November, he distinguished himself during hand-to-hand attacks at Tsinchentchen and again the following year during a large cavalry raid behind enemy lines. In the course of the Russo-Japanese War, Denikin served with the border guards, the Trans-Baikal Cossacks, the Ural Trans-Baikal Division, and with the mounted troops of 2nd Army, rising to the rank of colonel.

Despite Denikin's personal success, the fate of the Russian military was tragic. Inadequate logistics and incompetent leadership robbed the gallant Russian soldiery of victory. Political unrest among soldiers and workers spilled over into the Revolution of 1905. After the war, it took Denikin one month to cross Russia from the Far East to St. Petersburg via the Trans-Siberian Railroad. At times, he and his traveling companions exchanged fire with revolutionary mobs as he made his way back to the 2nd Cavalry Corps near Warsaw.

By spring 1906, order had been restored to Russia. Before the close of the previous year, Tsar Nicholas II had proclaimed his October Manifesto which was an attempt to compromise with political dissidents by providing Russia with a parliament, or *duma.* For a military officer, Denikin's political views were atypically a little left of center; he welcomed the Manifesto and a constitutional monarchy and advocated major political reforms.

Militarily, it was also time for self-examination. From 1906 to 1913, Russian authorities replaced over half of the officer corps with abler men. Denikin introduced reforms while on the staff of the 57th Reserve Brigade at Saratov and as commander of the 17th Arkangelogorodsk Regiment near Kiev. Unfortunately, while progress was measurable, domestic discontent and the march of international events were not to give Russia the time she needed to enter the 20th century.

Politically, the Tsar's government never was able to achieve a working relationship with the *Duma*. Radical left-oriented parties continued to grow, including the Social Revolutionaries, the Mensheviks, and the Bolsheviks. In 1911, terrorists assassinated the Russian premier, Peter Stolypin, thereby ending perhaps the best opportunity for a compromise between *Duma* and Tsar. Two wars broke out in southeastern Europe in 1912 and 1913, and Russia was embroiled more deeply into the dangerously entangled web of European diplomacy. Finally, in 1914, the assassination of Franz Ferdinand, the heir to the Austro-Hungarian throne, pushed Europe into the First World War.

During the course of the four-year-long cataclysm, the Allies (Russia, France, Great Britain, Belgium, and Serbia) fought against the Central Powers (Germany, Austria-Hungary, and the Ottoman Empire). Italy, Rumania, and the United States would join the Allies, respectively in 1915, 1916, and 1917, and Bulgaria would follow the Central Powers in 1915. The Russians found themselves fighting each of the Central Powers along the length of the Eastern Front.

Despite a few glorious moments, the Russian road was one of successive defeat—from the 1914 disaster at Tannenburg to the 1917 revolutions and the 1918 Civil War. The personal record of Anton Denikin, however, was laudable. In 1914, he was promoted to major-general and reorganized the staffs of 3rd and 5th Armies. Briefly attached as deputy chief of staff to Alexei Brusilov in August, he volunteered for and received a frontline assignment as commander of the 4th Rifle "Iron" Brigade, which was expanded to a division in April 1915. Looking back with hindsight, Denikin would say that his two years with the "Iron" Division were his most fulfilling. In the first months of war, he won both the Sword of St. George and the Cross of St. George, 4th Class, for bravery.

Throughout the first winter of World War I, Denikin's troops were deployed against the Austro-Hungarians in the snowy passes of the Carpathian Mountains. Not only was he able to maintain unit cohesion when so many other Russian units were breaking down, he succeeded in invading Hungary, a feat which produced accolades from every corner of the Russian army.

In the spring of 1915, Russian morale was still high, but severe munitions shortages were threatening to make it impossible to continue the war. Sensing a military opportunity, the Germans threw their main offensive against Russian Poland and the "great retreat" of 1915 began. The Tsar, contrary to the advice of his chief counselors, assumed personal command of the armed forces. The talented and respected General M.V. Alexeev was appointed his chief of staff. By the end of 1915, however, many of the original and experienced Russian soldiers had been killed and the army primarily consisted of uniformed civilians who were already showing the strains of war. Denikin had fought two exemplary engagements at Lutsk and Chartoryisk, rising to lieutenant-general in the process.

The year 1916 was a year of decision for the Russian military. In May, Brusilov led four armies into Russia's most famous offensive of the entire war. Denikin's "Iron" Division participated under General A.M. Kaledin's 8th Army and was instrumental in the breakthrough at Lutsk. In fact, Denikin was first into the town, an act of gallantry for which he would be awarded the rare Sword of St. George with Diamonds. In September, he was promoted to the command of 8th Corps and sent to help Russia's ally, Rumania. Unfortunately, after spectacular gains, the Brusilov offensive lost momentum and suffered major reverses by the end of the year.

The fatal crucible for Russia and Denikin was 1917. The Royal Family had successively discredited itself through ineptitude and scandal so that political chaos and military defeat combined to herald the downfall of Tsar Nicholas. By February, a Provisional Government was established in the capital of St. Petersburg, the name of which had already been changed to Petrograd.

Denikin Appointed Chief of Staff

While taking a decidedly left-wing political turn, the Provisional Government, under **Alexander Kerensky** as minister of war, nevertheless sought to continue the war and fulfill treaty obligations previously contracted with the Allies. Denikin was appointed chief of staff to the supreme commander, a position he would hold for two tumultuous months. This elevation was sudden and unexpected. The government sought a talented combat general who had been critical of the old regime and who had welcomed the February Revolution. The government also reasoned that Denikin's peasant origins would endear him to the people.

Summer saw the end of the Russian army. A fresh offensive, carried out with more rhetoric than energy, was bathed in blood. Discipline and morale, already at a low point, vanished. Soldiers shot their own officers and entire regiments threw down their weapons and marched home to the Bolshevik rhythm of "peace, land and bread." **V.I.**

Lenin's Bolsheviks (Communists) were already undermining the Kerensky government from within.

During these unhappy months Denikin served under a succession of supreme commanders; Alexeev, Brusilov, and finally, Lavr G. Kornilov. Denikin and Kornilov were in full agreement that discipline had to be restored in the army and civil order established in Russia. From July to October, a series of intricate political maneuvers unfolded wherein Kornilov was pitted against Kerensky, who was simultaneously at odds with members of his own government.

At the end of August, after a brief, abortive coup, Kornilov and his sympathizers, including Denikin, were arrested and imprisoned. In order to defeat Kornilov, Kerensky had armed Lenin's Bolsheviks. This act was the prelude to Kerensky's swan song as head of state. In October, Lenin—aided by **Leon Trotsky** and assorted bands of workers, soldiers, sailors, and politicos—succeeded in toppling the ramshackle remnants of governmental authority in that epoch-turning event known to history as the Russian Revolution.

In December 1917, by escaping from prison or eluding capture altogether, Denikin and several key army officers—including Kornilov and Alexeev—managed to meet in Don Cossack territory in southern Russia. There, painstakingly, the first small units of the White Volunteer Army were born. Three years of Civil War ensued during which Lenin's followers became known as "Reds," while Denikin and other opponents were called "Whites."

He Commands White Volunteer Army

The original plan of the White Volunteer Army had been to unite with the Don Cossacks and liberate Russia. Unfortunately, the Reds overran the Don so that the Whites had to retreat south into the lands of the Kuban Cossacks in the hope of obtaining allies. For several weeks during the frozen winter and early spring of 1918, the Volunteer Army fought their "Campaign of Ice" against vastly superior numbers. When Kornilov was killed in the desperate siege of Ekaterinodar in April, Denikin assumed command and led the brilliantly successful Second Kuban Campaign that summer and the North Caucasian Campaign in the autumn. By the end of the year, the Volunteer Army had grown significantly, despite its extremely heavy casualties. When the Kuban and Don Cossacks agreed to participate under a joint leader, Denikin became the commander in chief of the Armed Forces of South Russia (AFSR).

The tide of international events also had been swift. In March, the Bolsheviks had surrendered much of Russia to the Germans in the humiliating Treaty of Brest-Litovsk, and the Central Powers, in turn, had surrendered to the Allies in November. But if World War I had ended, the Russian Civil War was set to enter its most virulent phase. White armies had sprung up in northern and western Russia and in Siberia. Several of the Allies advocated limited aid to the various disparate and disunited White groups; the British and French offered military assistance to Denikin.

In the spring of 1919, Denikin decided to launch one of the most spectacular advances in military history. For six months, from May to October, the world watched, breathless, as the fate of Russia and the Communist Revolution hung in the balance. In the first weeks, the Whites captured several hundred square miles of enemy territory. Other units of the AFSR took the critical city of Tsaritsyn (later called Stalingrad).

Encouraged, Denikin issued his famous "Moscow Directive" in June. Three wings of the AFSR were to move in a massive fan-shape up the Volga in the east and to the Polish border in the west, then shift in unison toward the common goal of Moscow—the ancient capital of Russia and contemporary seat of the Red Bolshevik government. It was an ambitious thrust, yet by October, Volunteer units had reached Orel, only 200 miles south of Moscow.

That summer, Lenin had ordered the concentration of every resource against Denikin, including a special Red cavalry army led by S.M. Budenny. In October, at the critical point of Denikin's offensive, the Red cavalry struck the AFSR in flank at Voronezh and drove a deep wedge between the Volunteers and the Don Cossacks.

The White defeat rapidly became a retreat and then a rout. Disease and winter snows ravaged the remnants of Denikin's armies. Survivors were evacuated by ship from Novorossiisk to the Crimea in southern Russia in March 1920. What had begun with so much hope and promise had ended in failure. Physically and emotionally exhausted, Denikin resigned in favor of his sharpest critic, General Baron P. N. Wrangel, who reconstructed a White Russian army. After a remarkable comeback, however, the Whites were decisively defeated in November 1920 and were forced to leave Russia. Denikin's involvement in Russian public affairs ended; he would spend his final 27 years in exile.

Early in his military career Denikin had established a reputation as a skilled orator and writer, qualities that were not wasted. His earliest publications were vignettes of military life. In particular, he attacked harsh punishments and the lack of progressiveness in the officer corps. When he went into exile and retirement, he applied himself to a five-volume work concerning Russia in the First World War, the Revolution, and the Civil War. Translated into English, Volume I has been published as *The Russian Turmoil*, while Volumes II–V have been substantially abridged into one book, *The White Army*. These comprise his most valuable work, but his *The Career of a Tsarist Officer: Memoirs, 1872–1916*, published after his death, provides significant insights into the Russian imperial army.

As commander in chief, Denikin had worn tattered uniforms. In exile, his only revenue came from his many books and lectures, but this was not enough to save his family from penury. (In 1918, he had married Xenia Vasilievna Chizh; their daughter was born the following year.) During these years, the Denikins lived in England, Belgium, Hungary, and France. When the Nazis invaded Soviet Russia during World War II, he warned expatriate White Russians not to participate alongside the Germans.

After the war, the Denikins emigrated from France to the United States and lived in New York City. On August 7, 1947, at the age of 74, Denikin died while vacationing near Ann Arbor, Michigan. Originally buried in Detroit, his remains were transferred to St. Vladimir's Cemetery in Jackson, New Jersey.

Communist propagandists have claimed Denikin was a dictator and an enemy of the Russian people who was born into a family of wealthy estate-owners near Kursk. His memoirs, backed by the historical facts, prove these accusations false. On the contrary, according to Dimitry Lehovich:

> In some ways Denikin invites comparison with Robert E. Lee, who in a different period and country, also suffered defeat in a civil war and emerged from it with his honor intact and with the respect of his contemporaries and of future historians.

Indeed, until the end of his life Anton Ivanovich Denikin hoped and believed that the Russian people would one day rise up and overthrow communism. In 1991, 44 years after his death, the Communist Party was outlawed in Russia.

SOURCES:

Denikin, Anton I. *The Career of a Tsarist Officer: Memoirs, 1872–1916.* Translated by Margaret Patoski. University of Minnesota Press, 1975.

Kenez, Peter. *Civil War in South Russia, 1918: The First Year of the Volunteer Army.* University of California Press, 1971.

———. *Civil War in South Russia, 1919–1920: Defeat of the Whites.* University of California Press, 1977.

Lehovich, Dimitry V. *White Against Red: The Life of General Anton Denikin.* Norton, 1974.

FURTHER READING:

Denikin, General A. I. *The White Army.* Translated by Catherine Zvegintsov. Jonathan Cape, 1930.

Footman, David. *Civil War in Russia.* Faber and Faber, 1961.

Luckett, Richard. *The White Generals: An Account of the White Movement and the Russian Civil War.* Longman, 1971.

Mawdsley, Evan. *The Russian Civil War.* Allen & Unwin, 1987.

Stewart, George. *The White Armies of Russia: A Chronicle Counter-Revolution and Allied Intervention.* Macmillan, 1933.

Rodrigo Díaz de Vivar *"El Cid"*

(c. 1043–1099)

Castilian nobleman and military commander, who was celebrated as the national hero of Spain, led the Christian forces in several battles against the invading Muslim forces, and captured the important coastal city of Valencia.

Name variations: Ruy Díaz de Vivar (or Bibar); often called El Campeador, a Spanish term for "master of the battlefield," or El Cid, an honorific title derived from s_d, sayyid_, the Arabic word for "lord" or "master." Born in the small town of Vivar, north of Burgos, Spain, around 1043; died in Valencia on July 10, 1099; son of Diego Laínez (a distinguished Castilian soldier) and a mother of aristocratic background; married: Jimena Díaz (niece of King Alfonso VI), 1074; children: (two daughters) Cristina and María; (one son) Diego. Descendants: García IV Ramírez, king of Navarre (1134–50).

The Spain of Rodrigo Díaz was preoccupied with the reconquest of those areas of the Iberian peninsula that had fallen under Islamic control during the eighth century. Spain was not unified under one leader, but rather it was splintered into competing kingdoms and principalities, each ruled by Christians or Muslims depending on the region. At the time of Díaz's birth, Christian and Muslim had been locked in conflict for over 300 years.

Born about 1043 to parents closely connected to the warrior class of Castile, a kingdom in northern Spain ruled by Christian monarchs, Rodrigo Díaz's birthplace has been traditionally identified as the small village of Vivar which is situated north of Burgos, the ancient capital of Castile. Belonging to the lesser nobility of the region, his father Diego Laínez was a distinguished soldier whose family was linked to Laín Calvo, one of the legendary judges who—according to tradition—ruled Castile during the late ninth century. Relatives on his mother's side were loyal supporters of Fernando I, king of Castile, Leon, and Galicia. His maternal grandfather administered several important strongholds for the

"From modest origins among the aristocracy of Old Castile he so prospered that he ended his life as the independent ruler of a principality which he had won for himself in that region of eastern Spain known as the Levante, whose capital is Valencia."

RICHARD FLETCHER

Contributed by Isidro J. Rivera, Assistant Professor of Spanish, Wittenberg University, Springfield, Ohio

king. Other maternal relatives held positions of honor within the royal household. These links with the Castilian ruling dynasty gave Díaz access to an upbringing befitting a member of the nobility. Documents attest to his ability to read and write, skills that few people possessed during the Middle Ages. During his youth, it was likely that Díaz learned to ride a horse and handle a sword.

On the death of his father in 1058, Díaz was transferred to the royal household of Fernando I, king of Castile, where he became a ward of Prince Sancho, Fernando's eldest son. Under Sancho's tutelage, Rodrigo Díaz received additional education and military training. Since the political situation of the Iberian peninsula during the 11th century demanded skill in the art of war, the emphasis on military affairs would prove invaluable. Rodrigo Díaz's first contact with war occurred in 1063 during a campaign led by Sancho against Ramiro I, king of Aragon.

The death of Fernando I in 1065 brought changes to the kingdom. As eldest son, Sancho inherited the kingdom of Castile, while the remaining territories were given to Sancho's younger brothers: Alfonso received Leon, and García was given Galicia. This partition caused enormous friction within the family and was to provoke internal strife for several years to come. With Sancho's succession to the crown of Castile, Díaz acquired new status. In recognition of his military abilities, he was appointed *armiger regis* ("royal standard bearer"), a position which made Díaz responsible for the training, supervision, and command of the household guards. These troops normally guarded the royal household and formed the nucleus of the king's army. As chief commander, Díaz also functioned as the primary military advisor to Sancho, an honor reserved for a select few. And because of the official status of his position, Díaz actively joined in the important ceremonies of the court.

According to various traditional accounts, Díaz's skills as a warrior were confirmed by an incident involving a dispute between Castile and Navarre. At the center of the squabble was the border castle of Pazuengos. It was decided to settle the matter by means of single combat between representatives from both kingdoms. Díaz, representing the Castilians, emerged victorious against Jimeno Garcés, Navarre's most renowned knight. The victory earned Díaz the title of *Campeador*, a term meaning "master of the battlefield" and often given to one skilled in the art of war.

Díaz's talents proved indispensable to Sancho II, who embarked on a series of campaigns to

recover territories ruled by his brothers and rivals. The first of these campaigns was led by Díaz against the kings of Navarre and Aragon in 1067 and resulted in a victory for the forces of Castile. The following year hostilities between Alfonso and Sancho came to a head at the battle of Llantada. Although Sancho's forces were victorious, the battle failed to resolve the enmity between the two brothers. Alfonso remained in power in Leon. In 1071, Sancho and Alfonso defeated García, their brother, and seized control of Galicia. A second engagement with Alfonso proved Sancho's determination to seize total control of the region, including Leon. Castilian forces decisively routed Alfonso at the battle of Golpejera (1072). Sancho banished his brother to Toledo and was crowned king of Leon on January 12, 1072. The military leadership provided by Díaz was instrumental in establishing Sancho's supremacy in the region. The *Historia Roderici*, a chronicle of Díaz's activities, notes that: "Rodrigo bore the king's royal standard, and distinguished himself among soldiers, bettered himself thereby."

Sancho's reign was short-lived. In the fall of 1072, while participating in the siege of Zamora, Sancho was surprised by an assassin and murdered. The death of his liege brought Díaz's fortunes to an abrupt halt. Sancho's brother Alfonso, whom Díaz had earlier defeated in two crucial battles, assumed the throne of Leon-Castile and imposed significant changes in the makeup of the court. Díaz, although pledging allegiance to the new king, found himself an outsider within the new court. Alfonso VI stripped Díaz of his military offices and appointed Leonese followers to important positions within the army, among them Count García Ordóñez. But Díaz still commanded the respect of his men and other Castilian nobles. Documents from this period attest to Díaz's participation in several important court cases. And his signature on royal diplomas confirms his presence at the court of Alfonso VI, albeit with lesser standing than before. A turning point came in 1074 with his marriage to Jimena Díaz, daughter of the count of Oviedo and the niece of King Alfonso. The marriage, probably arranged by the king himself, bound Díaz to a prominent family from Asturias with blood ties to the royal dynasty. The match represented a move upward for Díaz; the setbacks that he had experienced during Alfonso's succession were gradually being undone.

Despite the marriage, Díaz's position at court remained uncertain. Unable to exercise his military skills, his prospects for recognition were diminishing. In 1079, Díaz became involved in an incident that was to prove extremely damaging to his standing within the court. While on a mission to Seville to collect tribute from its Muslim king, Díaz came upon a large group of marauders from Granada, a rival Islamic kingdom in southern Spain. When Díaz confronted the superior forces and defeated the raiders at Cabra near Seville, several influential members of Alfonso's court, who were serving as mercenaries, were captured. The most prominent of these was Count García Ordóñez, a staunch ally of King Alfonso. As was custom, Díaz demanded ransom from each of his prisoners. This action created much friction among the nobles, especially those loyal to the Ordóñez clan. Díaz by all accounts acted severely in his dealings with the Count and the other Castilian prisoners and created a serious rift between himself and those close to King Alfonso.

Diaz Is Exiled

His standing at court was further damaged by an incident two years later. During the summer of 1081, while King Alfonso was occupied with matters elsewhere, Moorish bandits from Toledo raided the castle of Gormaz, a Christian stronghold on the Duero River. Díaz rallied a group of his men and led a raid into Toledo, capturing, according to some accounts, nearly 7,000 prisoners. Díaz's retaliation, undertaken without authorization from King Alfonso, caused much consternation at court because of its political implications. At the urging of his advisors, Alfonso VI took action and ordered Díaz exiled.

Rodrigo Díaz spent the next five years as military advisor to al-Mu'tamin, the Muslim ruler of Zaragoza. His first major victory occurred during the summer of 1082. While supervising the refortification of the castle of Almenar, Díaz engaged superior forces led by Ramón Berenguer II, the count of Barcelona. The Zaragozan troops commanded by Díaz routed the attackers and captured the count along with his knights. During 1083–84, Díaz waged several minor campaigns along the eastern frontier against forces from Aragon and Lérida. With Díaz's skillful leadership, al-Mu'tamin was able to maintain firm control over an area beset by invaders from surrounding kingdoms. After the death of al-Mu'tamin in the 1085, Díaz remained loyal to his successor. Events of 1085 and 1086, however, were to affect Díaz's allegiances.

In May 1085, Toledo—an Islamic stronghold for over 300 years—fell to Alfonso's Christian forces. The following spring, Alfonso threatened several Muslim principalities, and Zaragoza came under siege by Alfonso's troops during that summer. The Muslim kingdoms, menaced by Alfonso's growing might in the region, sought assistance from the Almoravides, an Islamic fundamentalist sect based in North Africa. In October 1086, an Almoravide invasion force, led by Yusuf ibn Tashufin, crossed the Straits of Gibraltar, joined military contingents from the Muslim kingdoms of Seville, Granada, and Málaga, and advanced toward Badajoz, a city northwest of Seville. Alfonso VI withdrew his forces from the siege at Zaragoza and engaged the Almoravide army at Sagrajas, northeast of Badajoz on October 23, 1086. The North Africans overwhelmed the Christian forces and decisively halted Alfonso's rise to power.

As a consequence of this defeat, Alfonso evaluated his political relationship with Díaz and decided to reinstate the exiled vassal. In recognition of Díaz's skills as a military leader, Alfonso entrusted him with the administration of several important fortresses in Castile. The reconciliation with Alfonso was brief. In 1089, Díaz's failure to reinforce Alfonso's army during an offensive against an Almoravide force infuriated the king. Díaz's detractors seized the opportunity and leveled charges of treachery. The king decreed a second, far more severe banishment from the kingdom. Díaz's property was confiscated, and his wife and children were imprisoned briefly. All ties with the Alfonso's court were effectively cut without hope of reconciliation, leaving Díaz a man without a country once more.

Díaz set his sights on the Levante, the coastal region of eastern Spain. Without allegiance to anyone, he began to exercise force in the region. By the spring of 1090, he had exacted tribute from several cities, including Valencia, the principal stronghold of the region. Ramón Berenguer II, count of Barcelona and ruler of Catalonia, considered Díaz's actions in the Levante a threat to the balance of power in the region. In May, mounting a campaign against Díaz, Count Berenguer's army surprised Díaz's troops just south of Valencia in the forests of Tévar near present-day Teruel. Díaz's army repelled the attack and won resoundingly against the larger Catalan forces. Count Berenguer and his commanders were taken prisoners by Díaz who obtained ransom and important diplomatic concessions from Count Berenguer. By the end of 1090, Díaz had acquired dominion over most of the Levante with only Valencia remaining outside his direct control.

Valencia Surrenders

An alliance with Alfonso VI of Castile during the winter of 1090–91 brought Díaz into Castile, where he briefly supported Alfonso's campaign against the Almoravides. Full reconciliation with the king again failed to materialize during this period, and Díaz remained banished from the Castilian court. Incursions into the Valencia area by Alfonso VI during 1092 threatened Díaz's hold of the region. In response to the attacks, Díaz entered Castile and devastated the Rioja, a region in Castile held by García Ordóñez, Díaz's nemesis at court. The strategy succeeded; Alfonso withdrew his forces from the Levante, and Díaz was able to resume his domination of the region. In the summer of 1093, Díaz moved against Valencia. Positioning his forces around Valencia, he began to reduce the flow of goods into the city and gradually wore down the defenders. The tactics succeeded. After months of siege, Valencia surrendered. Díaz entered the city in triumph on June 15, 1094, and assumed sovereignty over its inhabitants.

Hispano-Arabic reaction to the fall of Valencia was immediate. Yusuf ibn Tashufin, the leader of the Almoravides, dispatched a large force to recapture the city. By early October, the Almoravide army had surrounded Valencia. Díaz's smaller forces engaged the enemy outside the city on the plain of Cuarte on October 14, 1094. When Díaz cunningly divided his troops and attacked the enemy army from two directions, the Almoravides succumbed to his tactics. It was the first defeat suffered by the Almoravide army since their arrival on Iberian soil. Boosting morale among Díaz's men, the victory ensured continuance of his rule in Valencia; Díaz spent the next years securing and defending his hold of the Levante. In alliance with Pedro I, king of Aragon and Navarre, Díaz repulsed an Almoravide invasion at Bairén during the winter of 1096–97. Resistance along the coast was subdued by Díaz with crucial victories at Almenara (1097) and at Murviedro (1098).

Rodrigo Díaz died in his bed on July 10, 1099, in Valencia. Shortly after Díaz's death, Ibn Bassam, a contemporary Arabic chronicler, declared that "this man, the scourge of his time, by his appetite for glory, by the prudent steadfastness of his character, and by his heroic bravery, was one of the miracles of God." Control of Valencia fell to Jimena, his wife, who struggled to defend what Díaz had fought so hard to possess. Three years later on the advice of Alfonso VI of Castile, Jimena evacuated Valencia and sought refuge in Castile. Many of the treasures, spoils, and possessions accumulated by Díaz were taken to the ancestral lands near Vivar. The most important item transported was the body of Díaz which Jimena reinterred near Burgos, in the Benedictine monastery of San Pedro de Cardeña. In May 1102, the Almoravides occupied Valencia, and the city remained under Muslim control until 1238 when Christian forces led by James I of Aragon recaptured it.

Díaz in time became a symbol in Spain—especially in Castile—of the valiant struggle to liberate the Iberian peninsula from Islamic control during the Middle Ages. Posterity accorded Díaz the epithet El Cid, a title derived from the Arabic word *s_d, sayyid_* meaning "lord" or "master." In Spanish literature, Díaz is the subject of the *Poema de mio Cid,* a 13th-century Castilian epic, which depicts Díaz as a loyal vassal and ardent defender of Christian Spain. But for most Spaniards, Rodrigo Díaz is the manifestation of the individual who emerges triumphant against the political adversity of his times.

SOURCES:

Fletcher, Richard. *The Quest for the Cid.* Knopf, 1989.

Menéndez Pidal, Ramón. *La España del Cid.* Espasa-Calpe, 1964 (English translation. The Cid and His Spain. John Murray, 1934).

FURTHER READING:

de Chasca, Edmund. *The Poem of the Cid.* Twayne, 1976.

O'Callaghan, Joseph F. *A History of Medieval Spain.* Cornell University Press, 1975.

Diocletian

(240–312)

Roman emperor, who reformed the entire structure of the Roman Empire after years of civil war, social strife, and barbarian invasions.

Marcus Aurelius is often considered to be the last emperor of the *Pax Romana* or Peace of Rome. After his death in 180, the Empire slipped into a period of civil war and economic decline that severely damaged Roman society. The period of 235–84 was especially chaotic as a succession of 21 Roman generals, known as the "Barracks Emperors," seized the imperial throne. One after another they gathered their armies and marched on the city of Rome. Some of these leaders genuinely tried to restore peace, while others were simply greedy. The armies and the Praetorian Guard (Palace Guard) violently controlled the government. Of the 21 emperors, 13 were murdered and four died in civil war.

Economic problems were also widespread. Trade was disrupted due to the wars and lack of defense protection. Germanic tribes crossed into Roman territory in the west, and the Persians attacked in the east. The constant warfare, plus a subtle climate change causing cooler temperatures, hurt agricultural production. In addition, the coins minted by the Empire lost their value as the general-emperors put less gold in the coins used to pay their soldiers. It seemed that Rome might collapse.

Contributed by Kenneth R. Calvert, Ph.D. candidate in History, Miami University, Oxford, Ohio

"Like Augustus Diocletian may be considered as the founder of a new empire."

EDWARD GIBBON

Born in 240, Diocles knew the turmoil of Rome's hard times. His father was a freedman, neither a slave nor a citizen, and his family was poor. Diocles did, however, have an opportunity for a limited education, as his father apparently worked as a servant in the house of a senator.

His home was in the territory of Illyricum, an area north of Greece equivalent to present-day Yugoslavia. A loyal province, dedicated to the ideals of Rome, Illyricum had given many men and leaders in defense of the Empire. Diocles joined the army around the year 270.

Roman soldiers had been traditionally recruited from the poor classes of society, while the officers and generals had been noble or wealthy men using their positions to obtain political office. But Diocles joined an army that was changing. The armies would no longer accept inexperienced generals, allowing men from the lower classes the opportunity to become leaders of the powerful Roman legions. By 260, noblemen had lost the exclusive right to lead the armies of Rome.

Diocles soon became a general. The earliest account of him is as commander of a large unit of troops in Moesia (modern Bulgaria). Calm, patient, and self-controlled, he was a fervent believer in traditional Roman religion and wanted to live up to the virtues of past Roman leaders. As various other generals seized and lost control of power, Diocles watched and waited. Though not highly educated, he had a practical approach to organization and a bright, alert mind. These characteristics allowed him to understand Rome's problems and devise a cautious rise to power.

In 284, when the emperor Numerian was assassinated, Diocles—now an imperial general—executed those thought to be responsible. Although there is some doubt concerning the involvement of Numerian's brother in the plot, Diocles personally executed him in front of the gathered legions and used the event to have himself proclaimed emperor. At the age of 40, promising his soldiers gold for their support, he took his imperial name: Gaius Aurelius Valerius Diocletianus.

In 285, Diocletian strengthened his power, using friendships made with other generals from Illyricum. That spring, he fought a major battle and came close to losing, until his rival Carinus was murdered. When the leaderless army agreed to join with Diocletian's forces, he became the undisputed ruler of Rome. Using the humane rule of Marcus Aurelius as his model, he first made a sacrifice to the gods in thanksgiving for his victory. Then, assuring Carinus's supporters that they were safe, which was unusual during a period of such

CHRONOLOGY

240	Born in Dalmatia/Illyricum
270	Joined the military
284	Hailed as emperor of Rome
284–305	Rome divided into new provinces
286–95	Diocletian fought border wars
293	Created the "Rule of Four"
294–301	Established economic reforms
298	Defeated the Persians
303–04	"Great Persecution" of Christians
304–05	Diocletian became ill and retired
308	Temporarily returned to politics
312	Died at home of natural causes

bloodshed, he sent messengers to announce a new era of peace and reconciliation.

As emperor, he immediately began to change Rome. He took the unheard-of step of becoming emperor without the senate's approval; his trust of politicians was less than his trust of military men. Diocletian also began pursuing a war against the Germanic tribes in an attempt to establish permanent stability for Rome's government and borders.

He Reorganizes the Government

It is in the reorganization of the government that Diocletian made his most dramatic innovations. For an emperor to adopt a young man as a son to succeed him was not unusual. However, Diocletian adopted Maximian, an experienced general who was only several years younger than himself. Maximian was made *Caesar*, a position second only to Diocletian's office of *Augustus*. By sharing authority, Diocletian would have a second in command who was both powerful and loyal. Unfortunately this arrangement fell apart in 285 when a revolt erupted in Gaul (France) and Britain, led by Carausis. To strengthen Maximian's rule, Diocletian gave him complete imperial authority over the Western Roman Empire. Maximian and Diocletian were now coemperors; the documents of the time call them "brothers."

Diocletian also began to restructure other areas of government. By doubling the provinces of

Rome from 50 to 100 and assigning administrators who worked only for the emperor, he made the new dioceses smaller and easier to govern. Past governors had been relatively independent, while some provinces were controlled by senatorial administration. With the government of the Empire becoming more unified and efficient, Diocletian was creating a huge military camp. The administration of this nascent organization occupied most of his time.

Another of Diocletian's innovations was the establishment of Nicomedia as his capital. This village, located in Asia Minor (Turkey), was made into a royal city meant to rival Rome. In the same way, Maximian established his capital in the city of Milan in northern Italy. These new centers gave each emperor an established headquarters, drawing the focus of the Empire away from the old capital: the city of Rome.

Rome had been the prize in past attempts to seize power; it had also been the home of the corrupt dealings of many senators and politicians. The new capitals of Nicomedia and Milan provided better administration and safety; they also sent the message that the center of the Roman Empire was no longer in a city, but wherever the emperor made his home.

In 287, Diocletian secured the border with Persia through diplomatic means. Three years later, he defeated the German invaders in the border area nearest his home of Illyricum and held a celebration in Milan to honor his success. It was at this gathering that the religious element of his reign became more evident. The peace which the two emperors had brought to the Empire was called *Concordia Deorum* or the Peace of God. It was an age of renewed belief in the old religious ideals of Rome.

Equating himself with Jupiter (the leading Roman god) and Maximian with Hercules (the ancient Greek hero), he had their birthdays celebrated during the yearly festivals of these gods. In the *Panegyric to Maximian*, Diocletian claims: "Jupiter rules heaven and Hercules pacifies the earth: just as, in all great enterprises, it is Diocletian who directs … and you (Maximian) who carry them out." Diocletian began to elevate himself in authority and in symbol by having himself carried above the heads of the people. When a person came to see the emperor, he or she now poured a libation to Diocletian, as if to a god. He also built elaborate palaces for himself, his family, and Maximian. With long hallways and high doors, the palaces emphasized the new opulence of the emperor and established a sense of awe in the minds of those who visited.

To ensure that the Empire would continue in peace and that the political process would be stabilized, Diocletian established the *Tetrarchy* or Rule of Four. He crowned two Caesars (junior emperors)—one for himself and one for Maximian—who were second in command and next in line to become the rulers of the eastern and western halves of the Empire. In this way, Diocletian tried to eliminate all doubt about who would be the next rulers of Rome.

In the West, the new Caesar was Marcus Flavius Constantius (the father of Constantine). In the East, Diocletian crowned Gaius Galerius. Both men were military leaders, and all four rulers now had armies with equal strength, containing military units which were constantly interchanged. None of the leaders was allowed to glory in his own victories but had to share all honors with the others. Diocletian and Galerius fought side by side while Maximian and Constantius shared the long-awaited victories in Britain against Carausius. This was not four separate governments but an empire ruled by a united "brotherhood," with Diocletian as its leader. Aurelius Victor says of their partnership: "They looked up to (Diocletian) as to a father, or as one would to a mighty god."

Between 293 and 295, Diocletian fought more battles against German tribes, further strengthening the border defenses. But another important military campaign, accompanied by Galerius, was against the Persians. A new Persian Empire had been emerging under the leader Shapur. In 296, Shapur broke the treaties of 287 and marched into Rome's territories, badly defeating Galerius early in the war. To make things worse, a revolt broke out in Egypt against an unfair tax levied by a weak Roman governor. Marching part of his army to Alexandria in Egypt, Diocletian besieged the city, while Galerius worked to restore the troops facing the Persians. Fortunately, the Persians did not pursue their initial victories, and in 298 the Egyptian revolt was also destroyed.

That same year, Diocletian inducted up to 25,000 fresh troops from the Germanic borders to renew the effort against Persia. The old method of defense had been the use of a thin line of fortresses with small garrisons of soldiers along the border. Now Diocletian built more defensible forts with large groupings of cavalry and fast-moving infantry who could quickly intercept invaders. Years later Zosimus would describe this defense saying: "The frontiers were everywhere dotted with cities, forts and towers, and the whole of the army set along them…. [I]t was impossible for the barbarians to break through." In 298, Galerius defeated the Persians in a battle near Erzerum in Syria; when Diocletian convinced the enemy to give up hopes of victory the following year, a treaty was signed between the two empires providing stability in the East.

The tax revolts in Egypt were clear evidence of the need for Diocletian's economic and tax reforms. From 294 onward, he had been creating these reforms to support the growing administration and an army that now numbered 500,000. Since the coinage of the Empire had lost much of its value, Diocletian began making new coins and establishing new Empirewide standards for minting money. To improve taxation, a new census was made of each province, resulting in a tremendous increase in the wealth of Diocletian's government. Funds were drawn from all areas, even Italy which had previously been exempt.

Economic reforms were implemented by price-fixing and government control in the marketplace. The most important of these actions was the Law of Maximum Prices which established the highest price to be charged on items such as foods, raw material, clothing, transport, and wages. Prices on education and private tutors were also included. This decree, along with taxation and further economic controls, made it possible to support the Empire and its army. But the drawbacks were immediate.

Wealthier people found ways to avoid paying taxes so the lower classes bore the weight of this burden. Also, the size of the system was too great even for Diocletian's administration to handle. Many laws went unenforced, and a large black market grew parallel to the Empire's controlled economy. People also resented government interference in their jobs and property.

Along with the reforms, the legal system grew to such proportions that laws regulated even the personal matters of the individual. Laws regarding marriage and religion, some of which had always been present, were strengthened. In his role as *Dominus et Deus* or Lord and God, Diocletian was creating controls over all aspects of life in the Empire.

In 296, he approved official attacks against the new religion called Manichaeism. Singled out for allegedly being involved in the Egyptian revolt and its Persian origins, this group was considered a religion of traitors. But there were other reasons as well. In his reforms, Diocletian was trying to create a unified society. Part of that unity was a return to the ancient gods who had made Rome an empire. Thus any religion which attacked these gods or Roman belief was suspect. Manichaeism was one such religion; the other major faith was Christianity.

Christians Are Persecuted

Although Christianity had existed in the Empire for almost 300 years, it was still subjected to constant persecution. At the intense urging of Galerius, Diocletian passed an edict in 303 against the Christians. The fact that Diocletian's own wife is said to have been a follower of this faith makes this decision difficult to comprehend. In addition, Christians had built a welfare system to feed the poor. Again, the decision to persecute seemed illogical, especially after years of work to establish peace. The persecution, however, fits Diocletian's plan for unity. Christianity preached against Rome's gods and had drawn thousands of people away from temples operating throughout the Empire. The Christians also rejected the idea of proclaiming the emperor Lord and God, as only **Jesus** was worthy of such titles.

At first only the churches were attacked. Buildings were to be burned along with the Christian scriptures. Christians who refused to sacrifice to the gods lost all civil rights: some were arrested, some executed. Others were weeded out of the royal household. A split arose among Christians as many gave in to the authorities while others stood in defiance.

The persecution intensified later in 303 when a new edict went out to arrest all clergy, who were then tortured, imprisoned, and burned. As with all such prisoners, the Christians were also thrown to the lions or the gladiators of the Empire's coliseums. An example of the extreme nature of the persecution came in Phrygia (Iraq) where an entire Christian town was destroyed, along with its men, women, and children. The pressure continued throughout Diocletian's reign until it eased in 306. Persecution did not end until **Constantine** made Christianity legal in 313 with the Edict of Milan.

In 303, when Diocletian visited the city of Rome for the first time, he held a celebration there in honor of his 20 years of rule. Only a year later, he became ill and retired from public life, forcing Maximian to retire as well. With Constantius and Galerius the new emperors, the first transition from one set of emperors to the next had taken place. Diocletian, who had ruled longer than any emperor since Marcus Aurelius, retired to his old home in Illyricum and grew cabbages. But Diocletian's reforms for succession were not completely successful, and in 308 Galerius requested his aid in thwarting various leaders attempting to take control, including the old Maximian. Indeed, the civil strife that had broken out eventually allowed a new emperor, named Constantine, to emerge.

In 312, Diocletian died at home of natural causes. His restructuring of the government was an astounding achievement which had brought the Roman Empire back from the edge of destruction. Emperors would use his ideas for another century in the West and until 1453, in the form of Byzantium, in the East.

SOURCES:

Barnes, Timothy. *The New Empire of Diocletian and Constantine.* Harvard University Press, 1982.

Frend, W. H. C. *Martyrdom and Persecution in the Early Church.* Baker Book House, 1981.

Gibbon, Edward. *The Decline and Fall of the Roman Empire.* Edited by D. M. Low. Harcourt, Brace, 1960.

Williams, Stephen. *Diocletian and the Roman Recovery.* Methuen, 1985.

FURTHER READING:

Brauer, George C. *The Age of the Soldier Emperors.* Noyes Press, 1975.

Grant, Michael. *The Roman Emperors.* Scribner, 1985.

Jones, A. H. M. *The Later Roman Empire.* 2 vols. Basil Blackwell, 1964.

Benjamin Disraeli

(1804–1881)

Politician and founder of the British Empire, who modernized his county's Conservative Party and committed it to democracy and social reform.

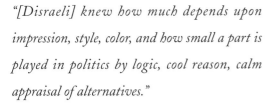

"[Disraeli] knew how much depends upon impression, style, color, and how small a part is played in politics by logic, cool reason, calm appraisal of alternatives."

ROBERT BLAKE

Pronunciation: Dis-RAY-lee. Name variations: Lord Beaconsfield, Earl of Beaconsfield. Born on December 21, 1804; died in 1881; son of Isaac Disraeli (a respected man of letters) and Maria Besevi (descendent of a Spanish Jewish family forced into exile by the Spanish government's persecution of Jews); married: Mary Anne Lewis, August 28, 1838 (died 1872); no children.

Few politicians seemed less likely to be successful at their chosen occupation than Benjamin Disraeli, who was in many ways an "outsider" in his own Party. He was born into a Jewish family which traced its lineage back to ancient Spain and Italy. Yet Disraeli aspired to be the political leader of a country whose Parliament did not even seat Jewish members until 1858. He set his sights on becoming leader of the Conservative Party, a Party whose leaders were largely "country gentlemen" landowners who did not look kindly on ambitious middle-class challengers such as Disraeli. British Conservatives, who placed great importance on "respectability," were alarmed by the colorful and flamboyant Disraeli.

Disraeli made his successful "climb up the greasy pole," as he termed it, through a combination of circumstances and his own abilities. When he was 12, his father, who had quarreled with the authorities of their synagogue, was convinced by a Christian friend to allow Disraeli, his sister, and two young brothers to be baptized into the Church of England. Until 1848, members of Parliament took an oath of office "on the faith of a true Christian." Baptized into the Anglican church, Disraeli encountered no such barrier.

Contributed by Niles Holt, Professor of History, Illinois State University, Normal-Bloomington, Illinois

CHRONOLOGY

1832	Electoral Reform Bill awarded right to vote to half of British middle-class males
1837	Disraeli elected member of Parliament
1837–1902	Queen Victoria reigned
1846	Corn Laws repealed
1851	Disraeli appointed chancellor of the exchequer
1867	Electoral Reform Bill, passed by Disraeli's Conservatives, awarded right to vote to remainder of middle-class males
1868	Elected prime minister
1874–80	Elected prime minister
1875	British purchased half of Suez Canal shares from Khedive of Egypt
1876	Disraeli made final speech in the House of Commons; Victoria appointed him first Earl of Beaconsfield
1877	Russo-Turkish War and Treaty of San Stefano
1881	Disraeli died

Disraeli grew up in a financially comfortable family. In 1817, his father inherited a considerable sum of money from his mother, and the family moved into a large house in the Bloomsbury section of London, where many lawyers and financiers lived. As a child, Disraeli was able to visit the British Museum just around the corner, but he often preferred to spend his time among the books in his father's home library. He later remembered that he liked "to play" at being a member of Parliament.

His family's financial position allowed them to send him to small private schools, including a Unitarian school, where he showed more interest in "ideas than schoolwork" and excelled in self-defense and riding. There are conflicting stories as to whether he was a sociable student, popular with his classmates, or a superior-acting boy with a sharp tongue.

With his father pressing him to become a lawyer, Disraeli accepted his first job as clerk in a law firm when he was 17. There he attracted considerable notice—deliberately, it appears. His outlandish clothes, ruffled shirt, curly black hair, and rings on both hands made him the center of attention. His reputation as a foppish dresser was increased when one woman testified that he appeared at a party in green velvet trousers and a

black shirt; the story became so widespread that Disraeli later swore to the editor of a newspaper that he had never owned a pair of green velvet trousers in his life.

In time, Disraeli became a regular at fashionable parties, where his elegance and wit made him a popular figure. One contemporary insisted that "no party goes down without him," and an American who met him described him as "the most wonderful talker" he had ever met. Disraeli suffered financial losses when he attempted to establish a new daily newspaper named the *Representative*, but he gained a minor literary reputation with his novel *Vivian Grey* (1826), the story of a "clever" but ambitious young man who attempts to rise in society but finds only unhappiness as a result.

Although he declared to another politician as early as 1834 that he wanted to be prime minister, his political career did not go smoothly. After three unsuccessful attempts to win a parliamentary seat, including twice as an "independent radical," Disraeli finally won a seat in 1837. He chose to join the Conservative Party, which was dominated by the agricultural interests of the British nobility, rather than the Liberal Party, which represented industrial and commercial interests.

Disraeli was far from beloved in his chosen Party. The problem was not so much anti-Semitism—although *Vivian Grey* was attacked by one critic as something written by a middle-class Jew who merely "affected good breeding" and showed "shameful puffery." Instead, Disraeli was hindered by a widespread impression that he was ambitious, impulsive, eccentric, and not entirely trustworthy.

One wit remarked that "he always seems to speak in a burlesque … with his tongue in his cheek." He was criticized for unfairly lampooning in *Vivian Grey* a friend of his father's who had also been his partner in the failed *Representative* project; he was also criticized for his affair with the wife of Sir Francis Sykes, and for his continuing problems with financial debts resulting from failed investments in South American mines.

Even his marriage to a wealthy widow in 1838 contributed to his reputation as calculating and ambitious. The marriage made it possible for Disraeli to buy a large estate and play the role of country gentleman. Yet he conceded that it was not a "love match," adding that "I may commit many follies in life, but I never intend to marry for love." Eventually, the marriage matured into a relationship of real affection, and he was devastated when his wife died in 1872.

A hostile reception even greeted his maiden speech in the House of Commons (the elected, or "lower," house of Parliament), where members responded with jeers to his elaborate manner of speaking and his outrageous style of dress. When Conservatives won the election of 1841 and the Party leader **Robert Peel** became prime minister, Disraeli was not offered a seat in the Cabinet. Disappointed, he gravitated to a wing of the Conservatives termed Young England, an informal group opposed to the iron discipline of Peel.

The Potato Blight and the Corn Laws

A national crisis in the mid-1840s brought the members of Young England to prominence. Beginning in the late 1830s, a crop disease, the Potato Blight, spread throughout Scotland and Ireland, two areas where potatoes were staples of the diets. Demand for other kinds of food in the British Isles quickly exceeded the supply, but it became impossible to import affordable food because of the Corn Laws.

According to the Corn Laws, the greater the shortage of food within Britain, the higher the tariff to be placed on food imported from abroad. In effect, during times when food was in short supply, the Corn Laws drove food prices even higher, guaranteeing that the nobility, who owned most agricultural land (and provided the major financial and electoral support of the Conservative Party), would make a financial killing.

Most of the opposition Liberal Party favored repeal of the Corn Laws, since their supporters were mostly industrialists and middle-class businessmen who wanted to sell British manufactured goods throughout Europe. They preferred free trade to protectionism. For Peel, however, the choice was between supporting his Party or saving large numbers of people from starvation. He chose the latter, rounding up just enough parliamentary votes from his fellow Conservatives to join with the opposition Liberals in repealing the Corn Laws in 1846.

The Repeal of the Corn Laws destroyed Peel's career, forcing him to leave the Conservative Party, and function—for the rest of his political life—as a leader of a small third party. One of his greatest critics was Disraeli, who was convinced that he would rise in party politics only if the current Conservative leadership fell from power. He insisted that "agriculture must always prevail over manufacturers."

But Disraeli realized that there was no future for his Party in being the representatives of only the nobility. Conceding that England was rapidly industrializing—by the mid-19th century it was the most industrialized nation in the world, or what proud British citizens termed the "Workshop of the World"—he worked to broaden the electoral base of the Conservatives. "Toryism is worn out," he declared. The Liberals had given half of the middle-class males the right to vote in 1832; Disraeli proposed that the Conservatives commit themselves to gaining the franchise (vote) for the remaining middle-class males, and then reap their reward at the polls.

Many of his fellow Conservatives were even more surprised at the other social group Disraeli proposed to woo—the working class. In a novel entitled *Sybil* (1845), Disraeli sympathized with the workers in the early British factories, who often labored long hours, six days a week, at low pay and in unsafe working conditions. *Sybil* portrayed an Industrial Revolution which brought extreme wealth and extreme poverty; he charged that it unfairly placed long working hours, and an "earnings burden," on women and children. Britain, Disraeli wrote, had become two nations, "the nation of The Rich and the nation of The Poor … between which there is no social intercourse and no sympathy; they are as ignorant of each other's habits, thoughts, and feelings as if they are dwellers in different time zones or inhabitants of different planets."

In *Sybil*, Disraeli gave the first hints of his plans to undercut the Liberals, who had portrayed themselves as the party of reform but who refused to help the workers form labor unions. If Conservatives extended the franchise to all middle-class males, and passed laws allowing workers to form labor unions, Disraeli believed that his Party would certainly benefit in future elections. The key was to convince voters that the Conservative Party was no backward, obstructionist group, opposing all change, but was instead the party of social concern and careful, thoughtful change:

> In any country change is constant and the real question is not whether you should resist change which is inevitable, but whether that change should be carried out in deference to the manners, the customs and laws, and the traditions of a people or whether it should be carried out in deference to abstract principles and arbitrary and general doctrines.

In 1851, Disraeli was finally appointed to the Cabinet as chancellor of the exchequer; the prime ministership was his by the late 1860s. In his two terms as prime minister, in 1868 and from 1874 to 1880, he clashed with **William Glad-**

stone, the leader of the Liberal Party. During the late 1867s and late 1870s, when the Conservatives won elections, Disraeli was prime minister. When the Liberals were victorious, Gladstone held that office. It is hard to imagine a greater contrast of personalities: Gladstone, moralistic and very serious, thought Disraeli was too glib and shallow, and he did not appreciate Disraeli's playful, and often sarcastic, eloquence. The rivalry between these two men was obvious as early as 1865 and 1866, when Gladstone's Liberals proposed to expand the electorate to include all middle-class males. After such a bill was rejected, Disraeli took a "leap in the dark" and introduced a remarkably similar bill as the Electoral Reform Bill of 1867. He became a hero in his Party by passing it with Conservative support and declaring that the Conservatives were the true party of reform.

Although he was disappointed that more middle-class voters did not support his Party in ensuing elections, Disraeli used the office of prime minister to convince the British Parliament to pass legislation regulating factories and workshops and expanding the rights of workers to form labor unions. The maximum number of hours women might be required to work in factories per week was limited to slightly more than 50. Helping him in many of these efforts was Queen **Victoria,** who far preferred Disraeli to Gladstone. As *prime* minister, Disraeli was officially the main minister of the queen—although, by British tradition, the prime minister really represented the majority party in Parliament. He met with Queen Victoria frequently and charmed her, arguing that everyone likes flattery and "when you come to royalty, you should lay it on with a trowel." The queen, in turn, complained, in "Dear Dizzy" letters, that Gladstone treated her like an institution or a "schoolgirl," while Disraeli treated her like an authentic woman.

British Empire Expands

One of Disraeli's most significant discoveries was that voters gloried in seeing their country exert its power in other parts of the world. Disraeli pursued an active foreign policy, particularly in expanding the British Empire. The Empire grew so large that by the end of the century, newspapers proudly boasted that "the sun never sets on the British Empire"—meaning that wherever the sun shone at any one time, there was a British colony.

Disraeli convinced Parliament to vote Queen Victoria the new title of Empress of India. When the spendthrift Khedive Ismail, ruler of Egypt, became nearly bankrupt, Disraeli arranged to buy the Khedive's half-share in the Suez canal in 1875, setting the stage for Britain to take complete control of the canal. Gladstone had no interest in acquiring a large Empire, and he had even less affection for the Ottoman Empire (Turkey), which he believed was responsible for massacres of Bulgarians and Armenians. In contrast, Disraeli believed that it was important to support the Ottoman Empire against Russian expansion, and he was one of many European statesmen who cried foul when Russia went to war with the Ottoman Empire in 1877.

When Russia won the war and Tsar **Alexander II** imposed a harsh treaty on Turkey (the Treaty of San Stefano), Disraeli called for an international conference to "back the Russians down." The result was the Congress of Berlin of 1878, at which Disraeli and other European leaders such as the German Chancellor **Otto von Bismarck** worked to "secure peace with honor." Disraeli's performance as a diplomat at Berlin drew from Bismarck the admiring (and anti-Semitic) comment, "That old Jew, he is a real man!" When Russia agreed to soften the Treaty of San Stefano, Disraeli returned to Britain as a national hero.

Problems in Ireland caused Disraeli and Gladstone to clash again. Ireland had been conquered by English soldiers beginning in the Middle Ages, and much of its land was taken by British landlords during the 1600s. As a result, Irish revolts were frequent. Gladstone attempted to appease Ireland through economic and church reforms; he also tried to create some measure of self-rule in Ireland. Disraeli completely rejected this approach, arguing that the revolts were caused by small groups of conspirators who would be encouraged by concessions. Arrest and suppress the conspirators, argued Disraeli, and peace would follow. On August 11, 1876, Disraeli made his final speech in the House of Commons. The next day, Queen Victoria appointed him the first earl of Beaconsfield. As a new member of the British nobility he had the right to sit in the upper house of Parliament, the House of Lords.

When he died in 1881, he left a legacy of a transformed and modernized Conservative Party. The Liberal Party would decline, early in the 20th century, to third-party status. But Disraeli's Party of "measured reform" survived and continued as one of the two major British political parties throughout the 20th century.

SOURCES:

Blake, Robert. *Disraeli.* St. Martin's Press, 1966.

Disraeli, Benjamin. *Lord Beaconsfield's Letters, 1830-1852.* Edited by Ralph Disraeli. Murray, 1886.

Froud, James A. *Lord Beaconsfield.* Books for Libraries Press, 1971.

Jerman, B. R. *The Young Disraeli.* Princeton University Press, 1960.

FURTHER READING:

Aronson, Theo. *Victoria and Disraeli.* Macmillan, 1978.

Davis, Richard W. *Disraeli.* Little, Brown, 1976.

Hibbert, Christopher. *Disraeli and His World.* Thames & Hudson, 1978.

Levine, Richard A. *Benjamin Disraeli.* Twayne, 1968.

Maurois, Andre. *Disraeli: A Picture of the Victorian Age.* Translated by Hamish Miles. Appleton, 1928.

Pearson, Hesketh. *Dizzy: The Life and Personality of Benjamin Disraeli, the Earl of Beaconsfield.* Harper, 1951.

Domitián

(A.D. 51–96)

Emperor of Rome, who centralized the control of the government in the emperor's hands and attempted to rule without senatorial interference.

Name variations: Titus Flavius Domitianus. Born in Rome on October 24, A.D. 51; assassinated on September 18, A.D. 96; son of Vespasian (Titus Flavius Vespasianus); married: Domitia. Predecessor: His brother, Titus (A.D. 79–81). Successor: Nerva (A.D. 96–98).

Domitián was born into the Flavian family of Rome on October 24 A.D. 51, one month before his father Vespasian, a friend to Emperor Nero, was to assume a consulship. As his mother died while he was still very young, Domitián was raised by his nurse Phyllis, and, according to Suetonius, passed his youth in "great poverty and infamy," while Titus, his elder brother by ten years, was fortunate enough to acquire his education at the imperial court. It seems unlikely, however, that Vespasian would not have provided for the education of his younger son. Domitián lost what little family contact he had when Titus began his military career in A.D. 56, traveling to Germany and Britain. But Domitián's isolation as a child would later give way to a strong sense of self-reliance.

Fast-moving political and military events in Rome put Vespasian on the path to becoming emperor in A.D. 69 and cast Domitián in a new role. When Nero died in A.D. 68, first Galba (June A.D. 68–January 69) and then Otho (January–March) claimed the imperial throne; although their reigns were brief, they contributed greatly to the instability of the time by establishing the

"He used to say that the lot of princes was most unhappy, since when they discovered a conspiracy, no one believed them unless they had been killed."

SUETONIUS

Contributed by Peter L. Viscusi, Professor of History, Central Missouri State University, Warrensburg, Missouri

precedent that individual legionary generals might aspire to the throne. By April A.D. 69, Vitellius exercised the imperial power. When word reached Rome that the legions in the eastern provinces had hailed the Flavian Vespasian as emperor, Flavian family members in the capital were endangered. Seeking refuge in the Temple of Jupiter Capitolinus, the Flavians were besieged by Vitellius's forces who set fire to the sacred building. In the ensuing confusion, Domitián narrowly escaped by dressing as a follower of the Egyptian goddess Isis.

But the Flavian cause was triumphant in December and, as Vespasian had not yet reached Rome, the 18-year-old Domitián was granted important governmental powers despite his lack of experience. Acting as the Flavian family representative in Rome while his father and brother were occupied with the Jewish War in Judaea, the young man had no illusions concerning his position. He did, however, rise to the occasion. Quick to recognize that the civil wars and the accompanying disruption of food supplies had seriously depleted the cattle herds of Italy, Domitián issued an edict that no cattle be sacrificed to the gods. Although this was not a permanent solution to the problem, it displayed Domitián's early interest in economic matters and his concern for the well-being of the Italian economy. With the arrival of Vespasian and Titus, Domitián's importance somewhat receded. Bestowing honors upon both sons, Vespasian made it clear that the elder and more experienced Titus was his intended successor.

When Vespasian died ten years later, Titus— "the delight and darling of the human race," according to Suetonius—succeeded his father, reigning a brief two years before Domitián ascended the throne. Suetonius describes Domitián as "tall of stature, with a modest expression and a high colour. His eyes were large, but his sight was somewhat dim. He was handsome and graceful too, especially when a young man, and indeed in his whole body with the exception of his feet, the toes of which were somewhat cramped." He was in addition "so sensitive about his baldness, that he regarded it as a personal insult if anyone else was twitted with that defect in jest or in earnest."

He Addresses Economic Problems

Once Domitián became emperor in A.D. 81, he set about addressing the economic difficulties of Italy and her empire, the most pressing of which concerned the lack of balance in Italian agriculture. The overemphasis on wine production adversely affected grain production, forcing the government to import more and more grain from the provinces;

CHRONOLOGY

A.D. 51	Born on October 24
81	Became emperor
84	Roman coinage reformed
89	Revolt of Saturninus
96	Domitián assassinated

the Italian wine trade, in turn, was then faced with intense competition. Wines from the Greek East dominated the eastern markets while the inexpensive wines from Spain dominated the markets in the West, leaving few markets open to the Italians. The problem had escalated during the civil war and remained largely unaddressed until Domitián's reign.

Realizing that he had to deal with the complex issue of agricultural trade on an Empire-wide scale, the Emperor issued an edict "forbidding anyone to plant more vines in Italy and ordering that the vineyards in the provinces be cut down, or but half of them at most be left standing; but he did not persist in carrying out the measure." Recognizing the need to be flexible, Domitián "did not persist" in those provinces with special circumstances; despite these exceptions, he expected the edict to be enforced even on imperial estates. One inscription even records an edict that forbade the planting of new vineyards on imperial estates in Africa; there were probably other laws pertaining to other provinces but none have survived. It appears that such edicts remained in force until the reign of the emperor Probus (A.D. 276–82).

To stimulate trade and commerce throughout the Empire, Domitián initiated a great number of projects. In Rome, he followed Vespasian's policy of providing more commercial space for merchants but expanded this program by building and repairing warehouses for the storage and sale of eastern goods, especially perfumes and spices. In Egypt, he ordered work performed on the canal, connecting the Nile to Alexandria, and appointed a competent staff to control and extend the government monopolies of papyrus production, the quarrying of building materials, and the mining of mineral ores. Meanwhile, throughout the Empire, the Roman army continued to build bridges and extend the road system.

Recognizing that a healthy economy would demand a healthy coinage, Domitián affected an unseen but nonetheless important economic change by reversing the policy of his predecessors and increasing the gold and silver content of his coins. His coinage reform, however, was later undone by Emperor **Trajan** and his successors when they melted down Domitián's coins and once more debased the coinage.

Despite his efforts to bring about economic prosperity, Domitián faced military challenges to Roman authority. Along the Danube, the province of Dacia raided the province of Moesia in A.D. 85, causing widespread destruction in the Roman-controlled territories. Roman troops fought a holding action until Domitián arranged for reinforcements to be sent to the area. The conflict continued for four years until the Romans defeated the Dacians at Tapae in A.D. 89, and Domitián arranged for a peace treaty with the Dacian king, Decebalus.

In Upper Germany, where the barbarian Chatti were actively attacking Roman positions, Domitián organized a defense system that was both defensive and offensive. Along the frontier, he built small earthen forts manned with auxiliary troops, separated by wooden watchtowers on stone foundations; farther back, he built stone forts manned with legionary soldiers. A system of roads linked all the forts together. As the result of an abortive revolt in January of A.D. 89 led by L. Antonius Saturninus, governor of Upper Germany, Domitián administratively reorganized the region, turning Upper and Lower Germany into Roman provinces the following year.

Constructs Temples, Commemorates Minerva

In addition to concerns about the economy and military, Domitián maintained an active interest in religion, instituting a major program to construct new temples and renew older ones dedicated to the various gods and goddesses of Rome. Minerva, his favorite goddess, was commemorated in a variety of manners and portrayed on most of the coins issued during this time; Domitián even created a new legion, naming it the I Minervia, despite the people's expectation that it be named Domitiána or Flavia. A traditionalist, he revived ancient Roman religious customs, including the practice (dating from the time of **Augustus**) of sending embassies to the Delphic Oracle.

In order to maximize the collection of taxes and tribute to pay for his military campaigns and building programs, Domitián prosecuted people for tax evasion. In exchange for religious liberty, the Jews paid a special tax to the Romans. Although many of the early Christians were ethnically Jewish, they refused to pay the Jewish tax because they were not Jewish by belief. The Romans—never clear on the religious distinctions between the Christians and the Jews—looked upon the early Christians as Jews and as tax-dodgers.

Compounding his religious difficulties with the Christians, Domitián, according to Suetonius and Dio Cassius, wanted to institute emperor worship through his use of the title *dominus et deus* (lord and god). Although both historians cite Domitián's use of *dominus et deus,* this unique title cannot be found in any inscription, record, or official source. While it is true that the poets Statius, Martial, and Juvenal used this title in connection with Domitián's name, they may have been trying to curry favor with the emperor as a patron.

Throughout his reign, Domitián did not have a very good working relationship with the Roman senate, primarily because he failed to show the senators the "appropriate" deference they demanded. He did in fact view the senate as indecisive, the senators as ineffective. Suetonius describes Domitián's reserved manners:

> Whenever he had leisure he amused himself with playing at dice, even on working days and in the morning hours. He went to the bath before the end of the forenoon and lunched to the point of satiety, so that at dinner he rarely took anything except a Matian apple and a moderate amount of wine from a jug. He gave numerous and generous banquets, but usually ended them early; in no case did he protract them beyond sunset, or follow them by a drinking bout. In fact, he did nothing until the hour for retiring except walk alone in a retired place.

Because these moderate habits were not what people had come to expect of emperors, most senators interpreted Domitián's actions as aloof and arrogant.

If senatorial opinion of Domitián was less than favorable before, it did not improve with his attempts to bring honesty and efficiency into government. The emperor's desire for an accountable government did not stop with his appointment of provincial governors but went on to include his sending imperial curators to audit the financial records of major municipalities in the provinces. In an effort to maintain an honest administration, he encouraged *delatores* (informers) to report on the illegal activities of senators and others. Even after his death—despite Domitián's sometimes brutal treatment of his enemies—his administration of the Empire was not condemned by his successors, because so many of them had cooperated and/or participated in its operation either as administrators or as *delatores*.

But Domitián's reign was not free of assassination plots or cruel retribution against such plotters. As he did not avoid confrontation and controversy, the emperor acquired a considerable number of enemies; senatorial feelings of rejection led some to conspiracy. Despite the existence of plots against his life, when Domitián moved against his enemies, he was often called a tyrant. Suetonius quotes him as saying, the "lot of princes was most unhappy, since when they discovered a conspiracy, no one believed them unless they had been killed."

On September 18, 96, Domitián fell victim of a conspiracy that included members of his family (his wife Domitia, whom he had married in A.D. 70), staff, government, and the senate (among whom was his successor Nerva, who was not a relative). According to Suetonius:

The people received the news of his death with indifference, but the soldiers were greatly grieved and at once attempted to call him the Deified Domitian; while they were prepared also to avenge him, had they not lacked leaders. This, however, they did accomplish a little later by most insistently demanding the execution of his murderers. The senators on the contrary were so overjoyed, that they raced to fill the House, where they did not refrain from assailing the dead emperor with the most insulting and stinging kind of outcries.

Domitián was an emperor who was both a bold innovator and a product of his imperial office. He successfully intervened in the economy of the Empire and produced a soundly based financial system. On the frontiers, his policies enabled the Empire to maintain a strong defensive posture, making it better able to resist an increasing number of barbarian incursions. He improved upon the efforts of his imperial predecessors and centralized the control of the Roman government in his own hands. The exalted position of the emperor reached its culmination in the powerful person of Domitián, while growth in the efficiency of the imperial government and the emperor's claims to supremacy over the state turned the senatorial class against him and ultimately caused his downfall.

SOURCES:

Gsell, Stephane. *Essai sur le regne de l'empereur Domitien.* Thorin, 1894.

Suetonius. *Lives of the Caesars.*

Tacitus. *Histories.*

FURTHER READING:

Henderson, B. W. *Five Roman Emperors.* Cambridge University Press, 1927.

Jones, Brian W. *Domitián and the Senatorial Order.* American Philosophical Society, 1979.

Scott, Kenneth. *The Imperial Cult under the Flavians.* Kohlhammer, 1936.

Sir Francis Drake

(1538/45–1596)

To some a pirate, to others a patriot, this adventurer is remembered for his menacing of Spanish and Portuguese interests worldwide, for his important role in the defeat of the Spanish Armada, and as the first Englishman to circumnavigate the earth.

Born in Tavistock, Devon, somewhere between 1538 and 1545; died on January 28, 1596; son of Edmund Drake; married: Mary Newman, July 4, 1569 (died January 1583); married: Elizabeth Sydenham, 1584 or 1585; no children.

Details about Francis Drake's birth and upbringing are incomplete. His father was named Edmund, his mother's maiden name was Mylwaye, but neither her first name nor the exact date of the seaman's birth is known. Estimates regarding his date of birth at Tavistock use 1540 as a midpoint. Edmund and his wife had 12 children, of whom Francis was the oldest. Legend has it that Edmund was forced to flee to Kent due to religious persecution of his Protestant beliefs, but the most recent scholarship suggests that Edmund was, in fact, fleeing the law, for he was indicted on two counts of theft in 1548.

The family settled in Kent, where they made their home in the hull of a ship. Drake thus developed a familiarity with ships and the water at an early age. It is unclear when his mother died, but it appears that Edmund became a widower within a few years after the birth of his 12th child. Unable to provide for them all, he seems to have sent most of those who survived to their teens to sea. Drake was apprenticed to a vessel engaged primarily in coastal trade, where his education in the art of navigation began. So loyally and efficiently did he fulfill his duties that the boat's owner, dying without heirs, willed the boat to his apprentice.

Contributed by Maureen P. O'Connor, Ph.D. candidate in History, Harvard University, Cambridge, Massachusetts

"The wind commands me away. Our ship is under sail. God grant that we may live in his fear as the enemy may have cause to say that God doth fight for Her Majesty as well abroad as at home."

SIR FRANCIS DRAKE

Ever ambitious, Drake sold the boat within a short time and relocated to Plymouth, where he found work with his cousin, John Hawkins, thereby setting his life on an adventurous course. A trading voyage of 1566–67 involved him in the slave trade and took him to the Spanish Caribbean colonies for the first time. Late in 1567, Drake again sailed to the New World, commanding one of six ships gathered by Hawkins for illicit trade in areas controlled by Spain and Portugal. This mission ran into trouble at San Juan d'Ulua, where the Spaniards violated an agreement and attacked the English, who were trying to resupply their ships for the Atlantic crossing. Only two ships returned to home waters. Already a devout Protestant, Drake carried an intense hatred of Spain and Catholicism for the rest of his life.

In 1570 and 1571, Drake twice returned to the Caribbean to reconnoiter the region, preparing for a larger foray into the "Spanish lake," which he led out of Plymouth in May 1572. With two ships, he spread panic in the Spanish Caribbean colonies. Drake and his men captured Nombre de Dios and huge quantities of silver, but an injury he received caused the group to withdraw to sea before much treasure had been collected. They proceeded to Cartagena where they boarded a large ship in the harbor as the town's residents looked on helplessly. In an attempt to capture Spanish treasures as they traveled out of the jungle, Drake began to work in conjunction with escaped black slaves, known as *cimarrones*. His new allies detested the Spanish as much as Drake and were very familiar with the routes Spain used to transport valuable shipments across the isthmus of Panama. With the *cimarrones*, Drake saw for the first time the Pacific Ocean, the sight of his future exploits. The raiding party did manage to trap a part of the Spanish silver convoy, more than enough wealth to make Drake's voyage a financial success. This was, however, leavened by personal loss; his brother John Drake, left behind with the ship, was killed by Spaniards, one of the 200 to 300 Englishmen lost on the trip. Satisfied that the expedition had been successful in punishing the Spanish and in enriching the voyage's English investors, Drake set sail for England, reaching Plymouth on August 9, 1573.

How Drake occupied himself for the next few years is not well documented. He was involved in an expedition which the earl of Essex led to Ireland in 1575. Drake benefited from the patronage of two great haters of Spain within Elizabeth's court, the earl of Leicester and Sir Francis Walsingham, the secretary of state. The aid of these powerful men undoubtedly helped make possible the now-famous journey undertaken by the adven-

CHRONOLOGY

1566–67	Drake's first trip to the Caribbean
1575	Expedition to Ireland with the Earl of Essex
1577–80	Circumnavigated the globe
1581–85	Elected member of Parliament; knighted by Queen Elizabeth
1585–86	Attacked Spanish possessions in the Caribbean
1587	Successfully raided Iberian coast
1588	Instrumental in English defeat of the Spanish Armada
1589	Disappointing "counter-armada" aimed at Iberian coast
1593	Elected member of Parliament
1596	Died at sea of dysentery

turer in 1577. Queen **Elizabeth** was an unnamed investor in the expedition, which was organized in great secrecy. The crew hired to man the vessels was deliberately misled as to the destination and nature of the voyage. Ostensibly, it was a trading mission to the Mediterranean; in fact, its motives were to profit by plunder elsewhere, at once irritating Spain and turning a profit.

Drake Sets Sail on Famous Journey

Four ships sailed from Plymouth on December 13, 1577, alongside Drake's command ship the *Pelican*. Nearly three years later, Drake would return with only one ship, the renamed *Pelican* (now the *Golden Hind*). The *Swan* and *Christopher* were deliberately scuttled at different times before the Straits of Magellan, the *Marigold* was lost at sea, and the *Elizabeth* turned back for England after becoming separated from the *Golden Hind* on the Pacific side of the Straits. The route took Drake and his men from Plymouth to the Moroccan Pacific coast, where local Muslims attacked them; on to the Cape Verde Islands, where they resupplied themselves and captured two Portuguese vessels (one of which carried a Portuguese pilot most useful to Drake); and from thence to the Brazilian coast.

Traveling southwest down the east coast of South America, the ships touched shore in Montevideo's bay in April 1778, and then in mid-May reached a place the sailors named Point Desire, where they found ample supplies of food and fresh water. Over a fortnight later, the ships set sail once more, anchoring in mid-June at Port St. Julian, their last stop before the Straits of Magellan. There they encountered troubles from within and without. The exterior threat came from unfriendly local Indians, who killed two Englishmen but then retreated upon experiencing the effects of European firearms. The trouble from within came in the shape of Thomas Doughty, one of several adventurous gentlemen accompanying the trip, who, due to aloofness from social inferiors, tended only to get in the way of the ships' operations. Drake received a number of complaints from his crew about Doughty's conduct and placed him under some form of arrest. When matters came to a head at Port St. Julian, Drake charged Doughty with treasonous attempts to overthrow the voyage commissioned to further the Queen's interests. In proceedings of questionable legality, the accused was tried, found guilty, and beheaded. This did not, however, end all dissent among the voyagers.

The pared-down force of three ships entered the Straits of Magellan on August 20, 1778, and reached the Pacific Ocean 17 days later, on the 6th of September. More trouble met them. Heavy storms battered the ships, first sinking the *Marigold*, and later causing the *Golden Hind* and *Elizabeth* to permanently lose sight of each other on October 7. The command ship was blown down to Cape Horn, where on the 24th of the same month, the crew saw sun for the first time in weeks and confirmed what Drake had suspected in passing through the Straits of Magellan—that the southern border of the Straits was in fact formed by an archipelago, not by a huge continent erroneously labeled *Terra Australis*. This was an important contribution to geographical knowledge of the day.

Anxious to find the *Elizabeth*, Drake headed for 30 degrees latitude on the Chilean coast, where Captain John Wynter was to direct his ship were it to become separated from Drake's vessel. But at this point, whether it was the captain, master, or crew's decision may never be determined, the *Elizabeth* had ignored its orders and was safely within the strait, headed to the Atlantic. It arrived in England on June 2, 1579. After a stop at Mocha Island, the *Golden Hind* captured a large trading ship in the port of Valparaiso, and then the town itself. The Englishmen proceeded up the coast, capturing a few trading vessels and a minor port town. Drake's trip failed to yield great treasure until on March 1, 1579, the *Golden Hind* overtook and overpowered the *Nuestra Senora de la concepcion* (also known as the *Cacafuego*), a Spanish ship brimming with gold, silver, and jewels. Though this was not the last prize that Drake took on the trip, it was certainly the richest. Drake's last call in

New Spain was at Gualtulco, where he and his men destroyed a small port. Having extracted both material reward and revenge from the New World, Drake was finally ready to return to England.

To risk returning through the Straits of Magellan and alerting Spanish and Portuguese forces would be to court disaster. Presented with the choice of crossing the Pacific or seeking the fabled Strait of Anian through the North American continent, Drake chose the latter. In either case he would have to rely upon extremely undependable maps. From mid-April to mid-June, the ship was out of sight of landfall, finally anchoring in the near-vicinity of San Francisco Bay. In the month spent there in reprovisioning and repairing, the crew established friendly relations with the natives. Drake no longer believed in the existence of the isthmus through North America and realized that a trans-Pacific crossing must be undertaken; thus, on July 23, the *Golden Hind* sailed west for over two months before sighting land.

The ship passed the Caroline Islands but did not stop, due to the aggressiveness of the natives, and finally landed in the Philippines, where fresh water and food were taken on. From there Drake proceeded to the Moluccas, also known as the Spice Islands, where Baab, the sultan of Ternate, who had no great love of Spain and Portugal, treated the English visitors with respect and supplied their ship with food. Drake also managed to acquire six tons of cloves, an extremely precious spice in his time. After a five-day visit, he left the sultan with promises to send an English expedition back to the island within two years. The crew spent almost a month on what they named Crab Island in order to perform necessary repairs before the long journey home. After visits to Timor and Java, on March 26, 1580, Drake made a direct line to the Cape of Good Hope, hoping to steer clear of main Portuguese trading routes, and crossed the Indian Ocean in under two months. At Sierra Leone, on the African Atlantic coast, the ship stopped for fresh water and food for a mere two days and promptly resumed its homeward journey. The *Golden Hind* sailed into Plymouth Sound on September 26.

Knighted by Queen Elizabeth

Initially, theirs was not the triumphant return one might have expected. The arrival was kept secret from all but a few for several days until the political climate became known. Upon a summons from Queen Elizabeth, Drake led an armed convoy to deliver a sampling of the treasures to the monarch and, in a private interview, regaled her with stories of his adventures. The voyage made Drake a wealthy, extremely famous, and esteemed man; the queen knighted him on April 1, 1581. That same year, he was sent to Parliament where he sat in the Commons until 1585. He also performed a range of other civic duties. When Drake's first wife died in early 1583, he married a wealthy young woman, Elizabeth Sydenham, in the winter of 1584–85.

As Drake lived the sedentary life of an English country gentleman, tensions between England and Spain grew worse. When **Philip II** of Spain impounded all British shipping in his harbors without warning, Elizabeth resolved to send troops to the Protestants in the Netherlands and to send Drake on a reprisal mission against Spanish possessions. Receiving his commission in July 1585, Drake set sail with 25 ships on September 14. Ten months later, the expedition returned, having captured Santiago, Santo Domingo, before heading to Florida to sack St. Augustine. Drake then paid a visit to an English colony on Roanoke Island. Because the settlers were fast running out of supplies, Drake decided to return to England with the fleet.

In April of 1587, the queen gave her knight a new assignment: to harass shipping passing into and out of the ports of Spain and Portugal. Taking the port of Cadiz completely by surprise, Drake sailed unimpeded into the harbor, destroyed an ample amount of shipping, and occupied Cape Vincent; from there he was able to significantly reduce the amount of supplies shipped from the Mediterranean to the Lisbon area. After a side trip to the Azores where he managed to capture a handsome prize, Drake returned once more to England, having seriously set back Philip of Spain's plans to assemble an armada against England. Back at home, Drake unceasingly preached the need for naval preparedness against certain attack from Spain. Prone to stay on the offensive, the admiral proposed to send a large fleet toward Spain to preempt their attack. But other voices prevailed and the navy was kept in home waters.

The Spanish assault came in July 1588. In the series of encounters in which the English drove off the Spanish, Drake was second in command to the Lord-Admiral, Howard of Effingham. Though the English ships were outnumbered, they were compensated by certain advantages in mobility and arms. In the sea battles which stretched from the 21st to the 29th, Drake managed to capture the *Rosario*, the command ship of one Spanish squadron, and to acquit himself favorably in leading his forces against the enemy. But Drake was rarely free from controversy of some kind, and this was no exception; once the Spanish threat was gone, he and Sir Martin Frobisher fell to fighting over the *Rosario's* booty, which involved a considerable amount of money.

Queen Elizabeth sent forth what amounted to a counter-armada the following spring under Drake and Sir John Norris, consisting of an estimated 180 ships. The fleet scattered before it even made it to Spain, and first attacked Corunna, where they failed to capture the town or any Spanish shipping. Next, the expedition made an unsuccessful attempt to capture Lisbon. When the weather denied the remains of the armada from reaching the Azores, the ships made their way back to England, having lost at least several thousand men. For the first time and on the most sizable expedition of his life, Sir Francis Drake failed to fulfil his mission.

Drake lived in Devon for the next few years and returned to Parliament in 1593. He lobbied hard for internal improvements to Plymouth and served as Devon's deputy lord lieutenant. His lust for adventure at sea, however, never ebbed. When Queen Elizabeth once more offered him a commission, he did not hesitate to abandon dry land and accepted joint command with Sir John Hawkins. The queen funded the majority of this joint stock operation, consisting of 27 ships carrying approximately 2,500 men, which left Plymouth in August 1595 bound for the Caribbean to annoy Spain. Attempts to capture Grand Canary and San Juan failed. The force took its frustration out on Rio de la Hacha and neighboring towns, Santa Marta, and Nombre de Dios, setting them all on fire. An effort to march overland to Panama proved short- lived. As though to signal the bad luck that followed this mission, the dysentery which had afflicted Drake for some while took a serious turn. He died aboard ship, off the island of Puerto Bello, on the 28th of January 1596 and was buried at sea the following day.

SOURCES:

Sugden, John. *Sir Francis Drake,* Barrie & Jenkins, 1990.
Wilson, Derek. *The World Encompassed: Drake's Great Voyage 1577–1580.* Hamish Hamilton, 1977.

FURTHER READING:

Thomson, George Malcolm. *Sir Francis Drake.* Morrow, 1972.
Thrower, Norman J. W. *Sir Francis Drake and the Famous Voyage, 1577–1580.* University of California Press, 1984.

Alexander Dubcek

(1921–1992)

Czechoslovakian leader, whose failed attempt to loosen the Communist grip on his nation became known as the "Prague Spring."

Pronunciation: DOOB-check. Born November 27, 1921, in Uhrovec, Slovakia; son of Stefan Dubcek; married: Anna Ondrisova, November 1945. Predecessor: Antonin Novotny. Successor: Gustav Husak.

"A hero against his will" is the way one writer has described Alexander Dubcek. Born into a Slovakian-Communist family and educated at Moscow, Dubcek became the symbol of both Czechoslovakian nationalism and freedom of speech during the "Prague Spring" of 1968. His attempts to create a "Socialism with a Human Face" were met with hostility by the Soviet government, which, together with the armies of other Communist-Eastern European nations, invaded Czechoslovakia in the summer of 1968.

Dubcek and his family had become Communists because of circumstances in his own country in his youth. Until the end of World War I, the people of Czechoslovakia were part of the Austro-Hungarian Empire, ruled by a German-speaking family, the Habsburgs. Alexander's father Stefan was a member of a socialist cell group opposing that monarchy. In 1910, the family emigrated to the United States, but returned to their native soil when conditions were not to their liking. They found significant changes in their native country. The Austro-Hungarian Empire had collapsed at the end of the war, and its individual nationalities had been granted independence in the peace set-

"That they should have done this to me, after I have dedicated my whole life to cooperation with the Soviet Union, is the great tragedy of my life."

ALEXANDER DUBCEK

Contributed by Niles Holt, Professor of History, Illinois State University, Normal-Bloomington, Illinois

tlements which followed. The Czechs and Slovaks had been thrown together into a single government, originally spelled "Czecho-Slovakia" to indicate that it contained two separate nationalities. Alexander Dubcek was born in 1921, only a year after his family's return.

Within the new government, the Slovaks were unequal partners. Since the Czechs had more experience working within the bureaucracy of the old Austro-Hungarian Empire, they dominated the new government. **Thomas G. Masaryk,** Czechoslovakia's founding father and first president, believed that the Czechs were inexperienced and less capable of governing. Resentment over such treatment increased communism's appeal for Stefan Dubcek. In 1925, he moved his family to Russia where they lived near other Czechoslovakian Communists. It was also in Russia that Alexander attended high school and met the Slovak woman he would later marry. These where the years in which Joseph Stalin's forced industrialization was begun, a brutal and intense process which made Russia, by World War II, the major industrial power in Europe. Many potential opponents of Stalin were "purged"—imprisoned or executed.

When the Dubceks finally returned to Slovakia in 1938, the Munich Peace Conference was awarding the northern half of Czechoslovakia to **Adolf Hitler.** Slovakia, in the southern half, was allowed to function as an autonomous puppet state to the Nazi regime. Opposing Nazism, Stefan Dubcek joined the banned Communist Party of Slovakia. In 1944, during World War II, he participated in a Slovakian national revolt against Nazism. His son Alexander joined a partisan brigade and was twice wounded.

Although Czechoslovakia, like almost all of Eastern Europe, was liberated from German occupation by the Soviet army, it was treated differently from its neighbors by the Soviet government. A major reason was that Czechoslovakia in the 1930s stood alone among the countries of Eastern Europe in adopting a diplomacy friendly to the Soviet Union; in 1935, it had signed a mutual assistance pact with the Soviet government.

As a result, from 1945 through 1948 the Czechoslovakian government was allowed to chart its own course with little Soviet interference. Elections were held in 1946 (in which the Communist Party gained more votes than any other party), and a parliamentary system took root. That changed in 1948, when the Czechoslovakian Communist Party took over in a coup d'état. Some non-Communist citizens, such as **Jan Masaryk,** the son of the ex-President, died under mysterious circum-

CHRONOLOGY

1917	Bolshevik (Communist) Revolution in Russia
1918	Collapse of Austro-Hungarian Empire; Czechoslovakia created, with Thomas Masaryk as first president
1921	Dubcek born in Slovakia
1925	Family moved to Russia
1938	Munich Peace Conference awarded half of Czechoslovakia to Hitler's Germany; Dubcek family returned to Czechoslovakia
1944	Dubcek twice wounded as partisan while fighting Nazis
1946	Cold War began
1948	Communists took over Czechoslovakian government in coup d'état
1955–58	Dubcek attended Communist Party school in Moscow
1956	Khrushchev denounced Stalin in speech to 20th Soviet Party Congress
1968	Dubcek became first secretary of Czech Communist Party; his reforms brought about Prague Spring; invasion of Czechoslovakia
1969	Dubcek replaced by Husak
1992	Died following an automobile accident

stances; many Czechoslovakians were convinced that foul play was involved.

Hailing the Communist takeover as a "great milestone in our history," Alexander Dubcek became a Communist Party functionary, first in Trencin and later in Bratislava. From 1955 through 1958, he attended a Party school in Moscow, studying communist economic and management techniques and graduating with top grades. The year he returned from Moscow, he was made leading Secretary of the Bratislava Communist Party. He rose through the ranks steadily, becoming, by 1962, a member of the central committee of the Czechoslovakian Communist Party.

In the Cold War which followed World War II, the European continent was divided by what British Prime Minister **Winston Churchill** called an "iron curtain," an invisible line separating Communist and non-Communist Europe. Western Europe became allied with the United States through the North Atlantic Treaty Organization (NATO). The Soviet Union responded by creating the Warsaw Pact, a military alliance tying the armies of Communist-Eastern European nations to the Soviet Union. There were signs, however, that nationalism was a threat to Communist unity in Eastern Europe—that a "socialist pluralism" would emerge, in which each Eastern European nation would fashion its own version of Communism. In two cases—riots in East Germany in 1953 and open rebellion in Hungary in 1956—popular discontent turned into open revolt. Speaking privately to friends, Dubcek questioned why it was necessary to send Soviet tanks to suppress the revolt in Hungary.

Even within the Kremlin there were signs of change. Within three years of Stalin's death in 1953, the new ruler of the Soviet Union, **Nikita Khrushchev**, was denouncing the brutalities of Stalinism in a speech to the 20th Soviet Party Congress. Although there were signs of "de-Stalinization" in various Eastern European countries, there was no such development in Czechoslovakia: the government chose to ignore Khrushchev's speech. The Czechoslovakian government of Antonin Novotny even tried to ignore the fact that Stalin's body had been removed from a place of honor near the Kremlin.

Loyally Communist, Dubcek still could not ignore what he thought was mistreatment of colleagues. When a fellow Slovakian leader named Karol Smidke died in disgrace in 1952—outlawed from the Communist Party—no party functionary could be found to deliver a eulogy at the funeral. In an act of courage, Dubcek volunteered, calling Smidke a "great leader and a true revolutionary." Later he said publicly that the country's centralized government and economy were not producing "economic results."

In 1967, Alexander Dubcek rose to speak at a Czechoslovakian Communist conference. He criticized the government of Novotny for running a centralized government which ignored the interests of the Slovaks. He spoke of "loopholes and shortcomings in the economic tools," and he argued that Slovakia was being cheated on economic matters, particularly investments. His speech did not go unnoticed; he became a hero to many Slovaks, who thought that Novotny was "high-handed" in his treatment of them. He also gained the attention of reformers who sought changes in the Marxist-based economy of their country.

Dubcek Gains Power

On January 5, 1968, Novotny was replaced as first secretary of the Czechoslovakian Communist Party by Dubcek. Some historians believe that the change was engineered by the Soviet leader **Leonid Brezhnev,** who may have regarded Novotny as too resistant to change. If so, Brezhnev may not have understood the extent to which Dubcek's supporters wanted political and economic reform in their country.

But neither, it appears, did Dubcek. Shortly after his election, he was briefed on the excesses of the Stalinist period in his country and Russia. He was astounded: "How is it possible," he asked, "for Communists to behave this way?" He did not favor democracy—he thought that his country's politics from 1945 through 1948 was too chaotic—but he wanted greater freedoms. "The party," he declared, "was created for the workers. It exists to serve them and its main political force is for the workers. The party does not have a life of its own, above or outside society." As an example for other government bureaucrats, he eschewed riding to work in the traditional limousine. He and his family continued to live in their modest five-room house in Bratislava; during the week, he lived in an apartment in the capital city of Prague, within walking distance of his office.

In February 1968, restrictions were lifted on the press and an "Action-Program" of economic decentralization announced. Some victims of the Stalinist era were "rehabilitated." On March 22, it was announced the Novotny had resigned from the central committee. His supporters waited uneasily for the purge that traditionally followed such a change; none came.

The "Prague Spring" Begins

What followed has gone down in history as "Prague Spring." From the country's newspapers and magazines came a torrent of anti-Communist and anti-Soviet stories. One story reported that Czechoslovakia was being forced to pay more for oil that it bought from the Soviet Union than did another (non-Communist) country, Italy. A number of Czechoslovakian intellectuals urged Dubcek, in a document named the "2,000 Words," to begin further liberalizing the government.

The response from the Soviet Union was alarm. Looking back, it appears that a wise course might have been for the Soviet Union to remain uninvolved, since Dubcek's "Socialism with a Human Face" had the potential for making Communism a popular and patriotic cause. Soviet leaders, however, worried that "Prague Spring" might result in Czechoslovakian withdrawal from the Warsaw Pact. Soviet newspapers denounced "the antisocialist and counterrevolutionary forces" in Czechoslovakia. Brezhnev ominously warned that when socialism was threatened, it became "a problem not only for people of the country concerned, but a common problem and concern for all social-ist countries."

The leaders of two other Eastern European nations, **Wladyslaw Gomulka** of Poland and **Walter Ulbricht** of East Germany, were particularly prominent in calling for military intervention. In a "Warsaw Letter" of July 1968, the leaders of five Eastern European nations opposed democratization in Czechoslovakia and worried that the country might not be able to defend its borders against West Germany.

Most likely, there was no consensus in Moscow on what to do. Dubeck was, after all, a committed Communist, and there may have been hope that he could control matters. Dubcek later observed that "neither then, nor in the period since, have I ever thought of myself as being in any way antiSoviet."

Troops Invade Czechoslovakia

In June 1968, on only one month's notice, troops of Warsaw Pact nations began military maneuvers within Czechoslovakia. When Dubcek and Brezhnev met at Cierna between July 29 and August 2, the Czechoslovakian leader made minor concessions to the Soviet leader. When the maneuvers were completed in August, however, Soviet troops did not leave the country. On the morning of August 20, Dubcek was awakened by a phone call from a trusted aide. The military forces of other Warsaw Pact nations, he was told, had crossed the borders of his country. Eventually, Czechoslovakia would be occupied by 29 divisions, 7,500 tanks, and 1,000 airplanes—with the announced goal of "promoting international proletarian solidarity." Dubcek resisted calls that he appear on television and urge armed resistance; he believed that the task of a responsible statesmen was to solve such problems with negotiations. He did say, however, that the invasion damaged the "international Communist movement."

The next day, Dubeck and his advisers were abducted from Prague and taken to Moscow. Rumors of Soviet threats swept the country, including a threat to annex Czechoslovakia to the Soviet Union. Because of anti-Soviet demonstrations, hostile comments shouted by the citizens at passing Soviet army officers, and anti-Soviet speeches on Czechoslovakian television (the Soviets were slow to take control of the media), it is possible the Kremlin began to have second thoughts about the invasion. There may have been hope that Dubcek could still bring the situation under control.

Within four days, Dubcek was returned to Czechoslovakia. In a sorrowful and emotional speech, in which he had to stop several times to recover his composure, he asked his fellow countrymen to refrain from "provocative acts." He announced "temporary" measures to lessen the trend toward free speech, but he held out the hope that soon foreign troops might withdraw from his country's soil.

Events had clearly moved beyond his control. In January 1969, a young Czechoslovakian, Jan Palach, burned himself to death in Prague, leaving a note that asked for the end of censorship and the restoration of a free press. A total of 800,000 people lined the streets for Palach's funeral procession. Demonstrators appeared on the streets of Prague, demanding the return of the "Prague Spring."

Dubcek, reported to be close to a nervous breakdown, was further damaged by the "hockey incident." On March 28, 1969, the Czechoslovakian hockey team played the team of the Soviet Union in the second game of the world hockey championship at Stockholm. Pro-Czechoslovakian signs appeared in the crowd, with messages such as "Russians, Your Tanks Won't Help You This Time." When Czechoslovakia won the game, a crowd in Prague attacked the local offices of the Soviet airline, breaking windows and carrying furniture into the street for a bonfire.

Rumors swept Prague that Brezhnev had ordered Dubcek to resign. The Soviet media began referring to Dubeck as a "renegade and traitor." On April 3, 1969, Dubeck appeared on television, saying that he was resigning in order to preserve the possibility of continuing "our policies." Though his replacement, Gustav Husak, was a fellow reformer, he now referred to Dubcek's ideas as a "perversion of socialist principles," and soon began a systematic purging of Dubcek supporters from the party, government, and press.

Forced to resign from the Czechoslovakian Communist Party, Dubeck was sent to Turkey as ambassador. The experience was humiliating; major decisions were made by the staff, and he was excluded from real responsibilities. Within six months, he was returned to Czechoslovakia and given a job as a forestry inspector. While living in his small house in Bratislava, he could not have avoided noticing the banner, hung in a nearby village, that read "Death to Dubeck." Though he rejected suggestions from the Czechoslovakian Central Committee of the Communist Party that he say in public that "Prague Spring" had been a mistake, he continued to consider himself a Communist.

Unlike the victims of the Stalinist era, Dubcek survived. When the Cold War began to fade in the late 1980s, he reemerged into public life, began to give interviews to journalists, and was elected chair of the Czechoslovakian national assembly. Some writers noticed a similarity between his ideas and the ideas of **Mikhail Gorbachev,** the Soviet leader whose ideas of *glasnost* and *perestroika* marked the beginning of major changes in the Soviet system. After a brief bid at Czechoslovakia's presidency in late 1989 which he lost to Vaclav Havel, Dubcek became the largely symbolic president of Parliament. He died on November 7, 1992, one week after his chauffeur-driven BMW skidded off a rain-slick highway southeast of Prague and plunged into a gorge.

Events, and not his own choice, had made Dubcek a symbol of his people's yearnings for freedom and reform. "Where Socialism is concerned," he declared, "in the end the people must reign; they cannot be the object of a reign." When he was asked what he remembered of "Prague Spring," he replied, without hesitation, "the people began to trust us."

SOURCES:

Dubcek, Alexander, and Andras Sugar. *Dubcek Speaks.* Tauris, 1990.

Navazelskis, Ina L. *Alexander Dubcek.* Chelsea House, 1990.

Shawcross, William. *Dubcek.* London: Weidenfeld & Nicolson, 1970.

Tigrid, Pavel. *Why Dubcek Fell.* London: MacDonald, 1969.

FURTHER READING:

Schwartz, Harry. *Prague's 200 Days.* London: Pall Mall, 1969.

Windsor, Philip, and Adam Roberts. *Czechoslovakia 1968.* London: Chatto & Windus, 1969.

Zeman, Z. A. B. *Prague Spring.* London: Penguin, 1969.

Jean Henri Dunant

(1828–1910)

Swiss merchant who, as a witness to the cruelties of the battle of Solferino, made public the inefficiency of the sanitary organizations in wartime and developed a vision for a relief society of trained volunteers that resulted in the founding of the Red Cross.

"Would it not be possible, in time of peace and quiet, to form relief societies for the purpose of having care given to the wounded in wartime by zealous, devoted and thoroughly qualified volunteers?"

JEAN HENRI DUNANT

Jean Henri Dunant was born on May 8, 1828, in Geneva, Switzerland, to parents who belonged to the nobility. Combining Christian faith with a strong sense of charity, humanity, and justice, his parents taught their young son to respect and support those in need. He often accompanied his mother on her visits to the poor and sick in Geneva's suburbs, visits to dark streets that he would later recall as his first encounters with misfortune and misery. In these early years, the mother's generosity passed to the son, whose enthusiasm for improvement would accompany him throughout his life.

During his first years of adulthood, Dunant focused his efforts on the promotion of the Young Men's Christian Association (YMCA). Founded in 1844 by London merchant George Williams, the YMCA had quickly spread to the Continent and subsequently to the United States and Canada. Eight years later, Dunant was among the cofounders of the YMCA in Geneva. He promoted (and in 1855 succeeded in) the unification of the various YMCA groups that existed in Europe and overseas.

Name variation: Jean Henry Dunant. Born in Geneva, Switzerland, on May 8, 1828; died on October 30, 1910, in Heiden, Switzerland; son of Jean Jacques Dunant (patrician and a member of the Representative Council of Geneva).

Contributed by Susanne Peter-Kubli, Historian, Wädenswil, Switzerland

CHRONOLOGY

1828	Born in Geneva, Switzerland
1853–59	Head of a joint-stock company in Algeria
1859	Business trip to Northern Italy
1862	*Un Souvenir de Solferino* printed
1863	Foundation of the Red Cross Movement
1864	Geneva Convention
1867	Declared bankruptcy; resigned from the Committee of the Red Cross; several years of poverty and humiliation followed, and he left Switzerland
1887	Returned to Heiden in the state of Appenzell, Switzerland; friends promoted his rehabilitation
1901	Awarded the first Nobel Peace Prize
1910	Died in Heiden, Switzerland

Dunant's professional career began as a merchant and banker, an occupation that led him to Algeria from 1853–59. More than 20 years earlier, in 1830, Algeria had been conquered by France, and since then many young adventurers had sought their fortunes there. Dunant had similar intentions. He opened his own business of corn-mills and marble quarries, financed by influential citizens of Geneva. Though he had acquired French citizenship in 1858, he continued to be harassed by the colonial bureaucracy in Algeria. To stop these impediments, he planned to speak to French emperor Napoleon III, personally.

In his leisure hours, Dunant observed the manners and habits of the North African people, praising their hospitality, codes of honor, and chivalry—qualities that, he believed, were deficient in the European nations. Devoting some time to reading, he was deeply impressed by Harriet Beecher Stowe's *Uncle Tom's Cabin* and spoke strongly against slavery as it was practiced in the north of Africa. He especially condemned the transatlantic slave trade to the United States and remained perplexed by American members of the YMCA who tolerated what he considered the blatant violation of the message of Christianity.

Dunant Sees Battlefield Tragedy at Solferino

In the summer of 1859, Dunant traveled to Italy. His suitcase contained a written homage to Napoleon III who, in alliance with Sardinia, was waging a war on Austria. On June 24, the two armies met at Solferino, a few miles west of the city of Mantua. The ensuing battle—though of small strategic or political significance—was one of the most devastating battles fought in terms of casualties. Nearly 40,000 wounded men begged for help on the battlefield at the fighting's end. Dunant, known as "the man in white" because of his tropical outfit, was attempting to arrange his meeting with Napoleon, but found himself instead witnessing the shocking scene:

> Some, who had gaping wounds already beginning to show infection, were almost crazed with suffering. They begged to be put out of their misery, and writhed with faces distorted in the grip of the death-struggle. There were poor fellows who had not only been hit by bullets or knocked down by shell splinters, but whose arms and legs had been broken by artillery wheels passing over them.

Realizing that thousands of lives would be lost within the following days due to a lack of surgeons, medication, nurses, bandages, and food, Dunant headed for the French headquarters and successfully persuaded Marshal MacMahon to liberate all captive Austrian surgeons so that they might be allowed to tend their wounded. Three days later, permission was officially granted by Emperor Napoleon. Meanwhile, churches and private houses of nearby Castiglione were transformed into hospitals. But the number of convoys of wounded increased to such proportions that:

> the local authorities, the townspeople, and the troops left in Castiglione, were absolutely incapable of dealing with all the suffering. Scenes as tragic as those of the day before, though of a very different sort, began to take place. There was water and food, but even so, men died of hunger and thirst; there was plenty of lint, but there were not enough hands to dress wounds; most of the army doctors had to go on to Cavriana, there was a shortage of medical orderlies, and at this critical time no help was to be had.

With the assistance of Don Lorenzo Barzizza, priest of Castiglione, Dunant gathered several hundred women who were willing to act as nurses, cooks, and laundresses to help the wounded—regardless of their background or nationality. *Tutti fratelli* (all brothers) became the slogan that helped save hundreds of lives.

Dunant tirelessly tended the wounded, organized supplies, and wrote letters to military headquarters, as well as to personal friends in Geneva, asking them to send clothes, bandages, medication, camomile to cleanse the wounds, and tobacco (to offer a distraction to the wounded and dying). After two weeks of immense struggle, Dunant left Castiglione, exhausted. In Milano, and later in his hometown Geneva, news of his efforts spread rapidly. High-ranking families invited him to their homes and palaces. Wherever he went, he was celebrated as a great benefactor to humanity.

To improve his business in Algeria, Dunant then moved to Paris, where memories of the wounded and dying continued to haunt him. In three years' time, he wrote and published an account of these last days of June 1859. In 1862, *Un Souvenir de Solferino* (*A Memory of Solferino*) was printed in Geneva at the author's expense and distributed among his friends and the courts in Europe. *Solferino* immediately attracted a wide circle of readers; within a few years, it was translated into 12 languages. Generals and field-marshals, along with princes and dukes, expressed their willingness to support Dunant's plan to improve the care of wounded soldiers.

One of the first to compliment him on his book was the lawyer Gustave Moynier of Geneva. Dunant, Moynier, and three other friends—the "Committee of Five," as they were called—drew up a memorandum, calling for an international conference to inquire into "the means of providing for the Inadequacy of the Sanitary Service of Armies in the Field." The memorandum suggested a solution: the institutionalization of a committee designed to answer the needs of troops wounded in battle. After the International Congress of Welfare in Berlin was called off, the Committee of Five decided to bring its cause before the Congress of Statistics which was to take place in Berlin.

One of Dunant's great admirers was the surgeon-mayor Doctor Basting who had translated *Solferino* into Dutch and who, like Dunant, would be participating in the congress. When they met for the first time, Dunant and Basting immediately discovered mutual interests and became close friends. Indeed, together with Basting, Dunant rewrote the memorandum only a few days before the opening of the congress, adding aspects which would be of the utmost importance. He requested that "the Governments of Europe agree that for the future the military staff and attendants, together with the officially recognized volunteer ambulance corps, be regarded as neutrals by the belligerents."

Committee of the Red Cross Is Founded

The Congress of Statistics in Berlin proved a big success for Dunant, and delegates of various European countries were invited to an International Congress in Geneva set for October 26, 1863. But Dunant's decision to alter the memorandum without consulting the other members of the Committee of Five led to a cool reception back in Geneva. Moynier, especially, reproved Dunant for his impetuosity and sought to curb it by appointing Dunant as secretary of the congress over which Moynier was to preside.

From October 26–29, 36 delegates of 16 countries discussed the issues promoted and presented by the Committee of Five. They passed a resolution consisting of ten articles and four recommendations. In times of peace, the various National Committees would store up requisites and enlist and train a Volunteer Ambulance Corps. It was also decided:

> In times of war, the committees of the belligerent nations shall furnish the needful supplies to their respective armies. They will organize their Volunteer Ambulance Corps and arrange with the military authorities as to the places where the wounded are to receive attention…. The volunteer assistants will be placed under the orders of the military chiefs, and all shall wear, as a distinctive badge, a red cross on a white ground.

Among the points recommended were: the expressed protection by the government; the neutralization of the Ambulance Corps; and the adoption of a common flag for ambulances and hospitals. Thus, in October of 1863, part of Dunant's dream had come true. The Committee of the Red Cross was founded. The following year, in the Geneva Convention of 1864, the recommendations expressed were fully accepted and integrated into the resolutions. A first, important step toward a new humanitarian international law had been taken.

But as Dunant's star as the promoter of the Red Cross was rising, his career as a merchant and banker was coming to a crushing finale. Devoting himself to his humanitarian work, he had neglected his business obligations for years. The honors that were paid to him could not avert financial bankruptcy and the loss of his reputation. Expelled by his hometown Geneva, and hunted by creditors, Dunant thought it best to leave Switzerland. Even more devastating was his resignation from the Committee of the Red Cross. The other members, Gustave Moynier among them, no longer considered the bankrupt Dunant of value to their cause. Upon discovering years later that Dunant was still using the letterhead of the Red Cross for his correspondence, Moynier sharply rebuked him. Thus, one of Dunant's earliest supporters openly turned into his enemy.

Dunant then spent several years in Paris, where his work with the Red Cross had kept him in high esteem with both the royal family and the aristocracy. Acquaintances, however, became fewer as news of his financial breakdown spread. Still, in Paris, Dunant was more than welcome as an expert in organizing the French Red Cross. In the war of 1870–71, France was heavily defeated at Sedan by a superior German army. Napoleon III was taken prisoner by the Prussians. After the defeat, France proclaimed the downfall of the monarchy and the inauguration of the Third Republic. Following his release, Napoleon lived in exile in England, where he would then die in 1871.

Unexpectedly, Dunant's efforts were supported by the exiled emperor. Dunant was provided with financial aid for the *Alliance Universelle de l'ordre et de civilisation,* an institution founded to help the victims of the Siege of Paris and of the Civil War in France. Moreover, he was given a house in Paris to use as a home as well as an office. With brighter prospects in mind, in August of 1872 he went to England to win supporters for his new mission to institute a convention for prisoners of war. This enterprise proved quite successful. Among those who complimented him on the recent undertakings was **Florence Nightingale,** "the lady with the lamp," who had been working as a volunteer nurse during the Crimean War, 1853–56. Devastated by the poor conditions of the military hospitals and the lack of properly trained nurses, Nightingale reorganized military as well as civilian nursing in Britain.

This short period of recognition, however, could not prevent Dunant's slow drift into oblivion. In Europe, Gustave Moynier was celebrated as the founder of the Red Cross, while Dunant gradually lost what had been his hallmarks—his energy and his faith in humanity. He traveled in Europe, taking odd jobs offered to him by old friends, living on their generosity and a small annual pension of 1,200 Swiss francs provided by his family in Geneva.

In 1887, Dunant, prematurely aged and in poor health, moved to Heiden, Switzerland. There, in the hospital where he was treated for his various ailments, he lived a secluded life; few visitors ever broke the monotony and the silence of his room. Likewise, there were not many whom the former "Samaritan of Europe" wished to see. He had become pessimistic and distrustful. No longer hunted or offended, he began to recover his mental stability and was glad for the peaceful retreat in Heiden. A religious man, he spent most of his time speculating on Genesis and Salvation, considering their impact on human evolution.

One friend who remained loyal, despite Dunant's failure, was Rudolf Mueller from Stuttgart, Germany. When, in 1892, an International Congress of the Red Cross was about to take place in Rome, Italy, Mueller published an article in a German newspaper, recalling the beginnings of the Red Cross and referring to Dunant as its founder and promoter. Yet it was not until 1895 that Dunant again became a topic for the public in Europe.

Suddenly, after being presumed dead, Dunant was surrounded by previous and newly won admirers. Swiss journalist George Baumberger's article in a German magazine had revealed that Dunant was indeed alive but living a lonely life of poverty. Baumberger finished his article with an appeal to the readers that, in anyway possible, they support Dunant—a man who had done much for others and asked nothing for himself. Letters of sympathy and encouragement were sent to Dunant, often including money, to make his later years more comfortable. His biographer, Rudolf Mueller, reestablished Dunant's reputation by reminding his audiences of Dunant's situation in many speeches. Mueller and other friends vehemently fought the rumors that *Solferino* had not been written by Dunant but by a French officer. Dunant knew of these allegations, and freely admitted that in order to correctly record the military details he had consulted army officials; otherwise, *Solferino* had been completely his own doing.

In 1896, a Dunant fund was started, primarily to enable the "Father of the Red Cross" to live in dignity. In December 1901, the Nobel Committee awarded Dunant with its first Peace Prize, an honor which he shared with Frenchman Frederic Passy. From his hometown Geneva, the International Committee of the Red Cross sent the following message:

> There is no man who more deserves this honour, for it was you, forty years ago, who set on foot the international organization for the relief of the wounded on the battlefield. Without you, the Red Cross, the supreme humanitarian achievement of the nineteenth century, would probably never have been undertaken.

One honor seemed to follow another, and, in 1903, the degree of Doctor honoris causa was conferred upon Dunant by the Faculty of Medicine of the University of Heidelberg, Germany.

On October 30, 1910, 82-year-old Jean Henri Dunant died peacefully in the hospital in Heiden. According to his own wishes, he was buried in Zurich.

SOURCES:

de Lisle, Arnold. *The Story of the Red Cross Movement.* London: The Banner, 1904.

Dunant, Henry. *A Memory of Solferino.* Geneva: International Committee of the Red Cross, 1986.

Heudtlass, Willy. J. *Henry Dunant, Gruender des Roten Kreuzes, Urheber der Genfer Konvention, Eine Biographie.* Stuttgart: Kohlhammer, 1977.

FURTHER READING:

Huber, Max. *The Red Cross, Principles and Problems.* Geneva: A. Kundig Press, 1942.

Willemin, Georges, and Roger Heacock. "The International Committee of the Red Cross," in *International Organization and the Evolution of World Society.* Vol. 2. Martin Nijhoff, 1984.

Anthony Eden

(1897–1977)

British statesman, who served in Parliament for more than 50 years, held several high offices of Great Britain, and served a short tenure as prime minister during the Cold War era.

Name variations: First Earl of Avon. Born Robert Anthony Eden on June 12, 1897, at Windlestone Hall near Bishop Auckland, Durham, England; died in Alvediston, Wiltshire, England, on January 14, 1977; son of William Eden (baronet and country gentleman) and Sybil Frances Grey; married: Beatrice Helen Beckett (marriage dissolved, 1950); married: Clarissa Anne (daughter of Major John Spencer Churchill and Lady Gwendeline Spencer Churchill); children, (first marriage) two sons, Simon (killed with the Royal Air Force in 1945 in Burma) and Nicholas. Predecessor: Winston S. Churchill. Successor: Harold Macmillan, succeeded as prime minister on January 10, 1957, when Eden resigned over ill health and the Suez Canal crisis.

Anthony Eden (who never used his first name Robert) was born the third of four sons to Sir William Eden, baronet and country gentleman, and Sybil Frances Grey, grandniece of the former prime minister, the Second Earl Grey. Through both sides of his family, Eden was closely associated with the British landed governing class.

Educated at home by a governess, Eden then attended Sandroyd Preparatory School near Cobden, Surrey. He spent four years at Eton and was in his final year when World War I commenced. In September 1915, he joined the 21st battalion of the King's Royal Rifle Corps, served at the 1916 Battle of the Somme in France, and was appointed battalion adjutant. He was gassed at the Battle of Ypres, and, in June 1917, received the Military Cross for rescuing a wounded sergeant while under German fire. During the war, Eden lost two brothers in combat, yet he served for three years on the western front, becoming the youngest brigade-major in the British army before returning to civilian life in 1919.

Following the tradition of his ancestors, Eden entered Christ Church College, Oxford,

"I do not believe that we can make progress in European appeasement ... if we allow the impression to gain currency abroad that we yield to constant pressure."

ANTHONY EDEN

Contributed by Phillip E. Koerper, Professor of History, Jacksonville State University, Jacksonville, Alabama

where he studied Oriental languages. Able to use French as a second language, he obtained first-class honors in 1922 in Arabic and Persian. Although he took no interest in the politics of the Oxford Political Union, Eden did occasionally speak on behalf of the Conservative Party in Oxfordshire. Choosing to forgo the usual career of a linguist in the diplomatic service when he left Oxford, Eden embarked on a career in politics, losing as a Conservative candidate for the seat in Spennymoor, Durham, in the November 1922 general election.

But the following year, he easily won the seat for the constituency of Warwick and Leamington. On November 5, 1923, in mid-election, he married Beatrice Beckett at St. Margaret's, Westminster and, following a brief honeymoon, returned to his successful campaign. Eden's maiden speech in the House of Commons on February 9, 1924, was a spirited call for a Royal Air Force capable of defending the country; thus, he immediately established his reputation in foreign policy and defense—areas that would always be associated with his career.

Appointed parliamentary undersecretary to the home secretary, Godfred Locker-Lampson, in the government of Prime Minister **Stanley Baldwin** in early 1925, Eden represented the *Yorkshire Post* at the Imperial Press Conference in Melbourne, Australia. En route home, he visited several countries, further establishing his credentials in foreign policy and providing material for his first book *Places In the Sun* (1926).

Recognized as a favorite of Baldwin, Eden rose rapidly in the Conservative Party's leadership. He moved to the Foreign Office with Locker-Lampson in 1926 and in July was named parliamentary private secretary to Foreign Secretary Austin Chamberlain. Although these were secondary positions, Eden profited from the foreign policy experience and the close relationship with both Baldwin and Chamberlain.

In 1929, Labour won the general election and **Ramsay MacDonald** became prime minister. Eden, who won reelection, was out of office until MacDonald formed the coalition National Government in August 1931 to face Britain's economic crisis. Serving as undersecretary at the foreign office under Lord Reading, and later under Sir John Simon, Eden gained prominence and valuable expertise during the World Disarmament Conference of 1932–34 in Geneva, and the Manchukuo crisis in China (when Japan attempted to set up a puppet state in Manchuria with **Henry P'u Yi** as regent). In January 1934, he

CHRONOLOGY

1915	Promoted to second lieutenant, King's Royal Rifle Corps, WWI
1917	Gassed in combat; won the Military Cross
1923	Won Parliament seat in by-election in Warwick and Leamington as a Conservative
1926–29	Parliamentary private secretary to the secretary of state for colonies
1931–33	Undersecretary of state for foreign affairs
1935–38	Appointed foreign secretary; resigned to protest Chamberlain's appeasement of the fascists
1939–40	Secretary of state for dominion affairs; war secretary under Churchill
1940–45	Foreign secretary under Churchill
1942–45	Leader of the House of Commons
1945–51	Deputy leader of the Opposition
1951–55	Foreign secretary and deputy prime minister; elected prime minister and first lord of the treasury
1956	Crisis created by Nasser's seizure of the Suez Canal
1957	Resigned as prime minister because of health and political damage from Suez crisis
1961	Entered House of Lords as the Earl of Avon

was appointed Lord Privy Seal by MacDonald. During this period of diplomatic activity, Eden held talks with **Adolf Hitler in Berlin,** Eduard Benes in Prague, and **Benito Mussolini** at Stresa. In January 1935, Eden endorsed the Saar plebiscite favoring reunification with Germany, and in April he became the first foreign diplomat to be received by **Joseph Stalin** in Moscow. Then Baldwin succeeded MacDonald as prime minister in June 1935, and the new foreign secretary was Sir Samuel Hoare. Eden joined the cabinet as minister for the League of Nations without portfolio; in this position, he was extremely critical of Mussolini's dispute with Ethiopia and championed a collective security approach by the League of Nations in international conflicts.

At 38, Eden Becomes Foreign Secretary

Eden tirelessly traveled about Europe trying to mobilize support for Ethiopia. On June 24, 1935, he visited Mussolini, but his conciliatory proposals were rebuffed by the dictator. In October, Mus-

British Foreign secretary Anthony Eden aboard a tank with the divisional commander of a British Armoured division during a big scale exercise in 1942.

the prime minister's appeasement of Nazi Germany and Fascist Italy. In light of Chamberlain's tendency to bypass Eden in policy decisions, and the decision to open negotiations with Mussolini on his terms, Eden resigned on February 20, 1938. Wrote a Chamberlain critic, **Winston S. Churchill:**

> There seemed one young figure standing up against long, dismal, drawling tides of drift and surrender ... but he seemed ... to embody the life-hope of the British nation.... Now he was gone.

Following his resignation from the Cabinet, Eden was unwilling to join the outright opposition to Chamberlain's appeasement policy. He also refused to form a dissident faction in Parliament but did deliver several speeches and wrote a book, **Foreign Affairs** (1939), explaining his foreign policy views. The obstinate demands made by the Fascist dictators soon strengthened his position. When Britain finally declared war on Germany on September 3, 1939, Eden briefly rejoined his old military regiment. Under pressure, Chamberlain was forced to add Churchill to a small reorganized War Cabinet, and Eden was appointed secretary of state for dominion affairs.

Churchill succeeded Chamberlain as prime minister on May 10, 1940, and he appointed Eden secretary of state for war. Eden inspected British forces in the Middle East and attended conferences in Egypt and Turkey. When Lord Halifax became ambassador to the United States in December 1940, Churchill once again appointed Eden to the vacant position of foreign secretary—a post he would hold until 1945 while also serving as the leader of the House of Commons from 1942–45.

Eden was a tireless foreign secretary during the war years. He made numerous trips to the United States, the Middle East, Europe, Russia, and Canada, conferring on wartime strategy and postwar policy. He persuaded Portugal to permit the use of the Azores for convoy defense, brought Russia and Poland briefly together in 1941, attended most of the major summit conferences, and convinced Churchill to follow the policy of a regency rather than an immediate restoration of the monarchy in Greece. On many issues, he and Churchill maintained serious differences that resulted in sharp disagreements over such matters as Churchill's reluctance to open the "second front," Eden's belief that **Charles de Gaulle**'s French Committee of National Liberation should

solini's army invaded Ethiopia. On December 13, 1935, Hoare and the French foreign secretary **Pierre Laval** agreed to a partition of Ethiopia that awarded about two-thirds of the country to Mussolini. Public opinion about the agreement in Britain forced Hoare to resign, and Baldwin summoned Eden home from Geneva to assume the position of foreign secretary on December 22, 1935. At 38, Eden became the youngest foreign secretary since Lord Granville in 1791.

During the 26 months that Eden held the position, Hitler reoccupied the Rhineland, Mussolini conquered Ethiopia, the Spanish Civil War continued, and the League of Nations was forced to accept the failure of its economic sanctions against Italy. Meanwhile, **Neville Chamberlain** had replaced Baldwin as prime minister in May 1937. Although he retained Eden as foreign secretary, Chamberlain followed his own initiatives in foreign policy. Concluding that France was unwilling—and Britain unprepared—to face the European dictators, he chose to follow a policy of appeasement.

At first, Eden reluctantly supported Chamberlain, but differences could not be avoided over

HISTORIC WORLD LEADERS

have received stronger support, and Eden's growing doubts toward the war's end about Stalin's intentions. Relations between Eden and Churchill were often strained, but—despite Eden's belief that Churchill's treatment of him was unfair—they privately admired and respected each other and managed to end the war with a harmonious relationship.

But the war ended on a sad note for Eden. The Yalta Conference in January 1945 resulted in a Russian dominance in Eastern Europe. In April, President **Franklin D. Roosevelt** died in Warm Springs, Georgia. After attending the funeral, Eden remained to attend the San Francisco Conference on the United Nations and missed the "Victory In Europe" celebrations in Britain. Suffering from a duodenal ulcer, he played virtually no role in the general election in which Churchill and the Conservatives were heavily defeated. Six days earlier, he had received confirmation that his elder son Simon had perished in the air war over Burma.

Eden served as Churchill's deputy leader in the Shadow Cabinet from 1945 to 1951 and helped direct the parliamentary tactics used by the opposition to Prime Minister Clement Attlee's Labour Government. Both Eden and Churchill were forceful spokesmen against the Soviet Union's military buildup in Eastern Europe, the failure of Attlee's government to take a position on the rearmament of Germany, the decline of British air power, and the nationalization program instituted by the Labour Party. Eden did support the American Marshall Plan to rebuild Europe and the British Government's decision to send naval forces to Korea in support of United Nations' policies.

In the election of 1950, the Conservatives were narrowly defeated by the Labour Party, but Eden won his seat easily. Realizing that the Conservatives might soon return to power, Eden—who had been bipartisan in his relations with Labour Foreign Secretary Ernest Bevin—became more critical of Bevin's successor Henry Morrison. He openly attacked Labour's opposition to the Schuman Plan, its handling of the Iranian oil crisis in 1951, and its general policy towards Egypt.

The Conservatives returned to power under Churchill's last ministry in the general election of October 25, 1951, and Eden was both appointed foreign secretary again and designated as deputy prime minister. This term as foreign secretary was distinguished by Eden's successes in negotiating solutions for several volatile issues. He was instrumental in settling the Anglo-Iranian oil dispute, solving the Italian-Yugoslavian conflict over Trieste, helping France conclude the prolonged war in Indochina, establishing of the Southeast Asia Treaty Organization (SEATO), and facilitating West Germany's entry into the North Atlantic Treaty Organization (NATO).

In 1950, Eden had his marriage dissolved on the grounds of desertion. Beatrice Eden, who had always disliked playing the role of politician's wife, had left him in 1947 during a trip to the United States. On August 14, 1952, Eden married Clarissa Anne Spencer Churchill, a niece of Winston Churchill. During the following year, Eden suffered a major health setback that led to jaundice and three operations involving his gallbladder. The elderly Churchill took over the Foreign Office during his illness. Eden's health was never the same again, but as Churchill's heir apparent, he returned to his duties.

Eden became prime minister and first lord of the treasury on April 6, 1955, following Churchill's resignation due to his age and health. Great expectations were held for Eden's ministry and things started well. With the economy booming and unemployment low, he introduced a tax-cutting budget and quickly called for an election on May 26, 1955. His Conservative Party increased its majority in the House of Commons from 17 to 60 seats. During the campaign, he was the first British prime minister to utilize television as a campaign tool. His slogan, a "property-owning democracy," and face-to-face unscripted television appearances, impressed the British voters.

By 1956, he was confronted with a series of financial and economic difficulties. Inflationary pressures grew stronger, and unemployment increased. Wages and prices continued to rise, while gold and dollar reserves declined. Because imports increased and exports decreased, Eden raised the bank rates and placed restrictions on imports from the dollar market areas. After a few months, economic growth expanded and slight gains were registered in industrial production.

Foreign policy monopolized Eden's premiership. He attended a July 1955 summit conference in Geneva and hosted a state visit the following April by Soviet leaders **Nikita S. Khrushchev** and **Nikolai A. Bulganin.** But it was the Middle East that ultimately dominated Eden's attention and led to his greatest crisis.

The Suez Crisis Erupts

In July 1954, as foreign secretary, Eden had negotiated the Anglo-Egyptian Treaty for the removal of British troops from the Suez Canal Zone with Egyptian president Colonel **Gamal Abdel Nassar.**

Eden's attempt to establish military alliances with the Arab nations, however, led to Nassar's denunciation of Britain's efforts and his decision to purchase aircraft and weapons from the Soviet bloc nations. Then on March 1, 1956, King Hussain of Jordan dismissed General Sir John Bagot Glubb, British commander of the Jordanian Arab Legion, and Eden concluded that Nassar was behind the dismissal. When the United States—angry over the growing Soviet influence in Egypt—canceled a proposed loan for the construction of the Aswan Dam, Nassar retaliated on July 26, 1956, by seizing and nationalizing the Suez Canal.

Eden and French Premier Guy Mollet held several conferences and made several proposals that were rejected by Egypt. The failure of negotiations led to an Anglo-Franco aerial bombardment of Egypt on October 31, two days after Israel had launched an attack toward the canal. On November 5, British and French airborne troops landed in Port Said and advanced over 20 miles along the canal causeway. The following day, all of the combatants agreed to a cease-fire, and a United Nations peacekeeping force soon took control.

In London, Eden had faced a stormy session in the House of Commons where he was accused of ignoring the United States, circumventing the United Nations, alienating the Commonwealth nations, and risking a wider military conflict. He argued that the Anglo-Franco intervention had ended the conflict between Israel and Egypt and forced the United Nations to involve itself in the problems of the Middle East. Although public opinion generally supported Eden's decision to invade Egypt, support faded quickly when Egypt retained control of the canal.

During the Suez crisis, Eden had been stricken with an abnormally high fever and had collapsed on October 5 from bile duct problems. Using drugs and sleeping very little, he persevered through the crisis and on November 21 flew to Jamaica to recuperate. He returned to London on December 14 to find his Conservative Party in disarray. On January 9, 1957, his doctors announced that he should no longer carry the heavy burdens of office. That evening Eden met with Queen Elizabeth, submitted his resignation, and resigned his parliamentary seat for Warwick and Leamington two days later.

Despite poor health, Eden lived 20 years past retirement. Having been knighted in 1954, he was elevated to the peerage as the First Earl of Avon in 1961. He occasionally published articles on foreign policy and spoke in the House of Lords but was never again active in politics. His memoirs were published in three volumes: *Full Circle* (1960), *Facing the Dictators* (1962), and *The Reckoning* (1965). In addition, he wrote a brief work on diplomacy, *Towards Peace In Indochina* (1966), and a nostalgic memoir about his youthful days, *Another World: 1897-1917* (1976). After a long struggle with cancer, Eden died on January 14, 1977, at Alvediston, his country home in Wiltshire.

SOURCES:

Astor, Sidney. *Anthony Eden*. St. Martin's Press, 1976.

Campbell-Johnson, Alan. *Eden: The Making of a Statesman*. Greenwood Press, 1976.

Carlton, David. *Anthony Eden: A Biography*. Allen Lane, 1981.

Pike, E. Royston. *Britain's Prime Ministers From Walpole to Wilson*. Odhams, 1968.

Van Thal, Herbert, ed. *The Prime Ministers From Sir Robert Walpole to Edward Heath*. Stein & Day, 1975.

FURTHER READING:

Barker, Elizabeth. *Churchill and Eden at War*. St. Martin's Press, 1978.

Churchill, Winston S. *The Second World War*. 6 vols. Houghton, 1948–1953.

Eden, Anthony. *Facing the Dictators*. Houghton, 1962.

———. *Full Circle*. Houghton, 1960.

———. *The Reckoning*. Houghton, 1965.

James, Robert Rhodes. *Anthony Eden: A Biography*. McGraw-Hill, 1987.

Edward I

(1239–1307)

A belligerent and tough-minded English king, who tried to conquer Wales and Scotland and devoted his life to ruinously expensive warfare.

"As a young man he escap[ed] a great stone which crashed down from the vault ... upon the seat he had been occupying; in Palestine he survived the murderous attack of the assassin; ... in Paris the lightning passed over his shoulder and slew two of his attendants.... Even illness seemed to pass him by and his last years found him as vigorous and upright as a palm tree."

L. F. SALZMAN

Most of the qualities which won praise for Edward I in his time make him seem odious today. He was ambitious, unscrupulous, merciless with his enemies, devoted nearly all his life to warfare, and monetarily squeezed his subjects to pay for his incessant campaigning. Twice married and father of 17 children, he was survived by few of them, and his successor, Edward II, undid by incompetence most of Edward I's achievements.

Edward was the first son of King Henry III, who ruled England from 1216 to 1272. By the time Edward's birth in 1239, nearly 200 years had passed since the Norman Conquest of 1066. The Normans, at first racially and culturally distinct from the English, had now come to share much of their heritage and outlook. Edward was named in honor of Edward the Confessor, a pre-Norman English king whom his father had honored as a saint and who, like his father, had been weak and self-indulgent. Despite his personal piety and integrity, Henry III burdened England with unpopular foreign favorites who enjoyed extravagant royal patronage while the English people reluctantly footed the bill.

Contributed by Patrick Allitt, Assistant Professor of History, Emory University, Atlanta, Georgia

Born in 1239; died in 1307; son of King Henry III of England and Eleanor of Provence; married: Eleanor of Castile (daughter of Alfonso X; died 1290); married: Margaret of France (died 1317); children: seventeen. Predecessor: Henry III. Successor: Edward II.

CHRONOLOGY

1239	Edward born
1264	Captured by Simon de Montfort at Battle of Lewes
1265	Defeated and killed Simon at Battle of Evesham
1270	Joined Louis IX of France on crusade
1272	Survived assassination attempt; Henry III died
1274	Edward returned to England; crowned
1277	First Welsh war
1282–83	Second Welsh war
1286–89	Long visit to Gascony
1291	The Great Cause (arbitration of Scottish throne)
1294–98	War against Philip IV of France
1296	Scottish wars
1297	Confirmation of the Charters
1306	Robert Bruce rebelled in Scotland
1307	Edward I died

We know little of Edward's upbringing, other than that it took place in a pious household and that he attended mass three times each day. At 15, for dynastic reasons, his father married him to **Eleanor,** daughter of **Alfonso X** of Castile, and gave him the territory of Gascony in southwestern France, along with large territories in Britain and Ireland. Gascony was the only remaining part of France in British hands (the rest had been lost by Edward's incompetent grandfather King **John**), and Edward was destined to spend several years of his reign in Gascony fighting its lawless grandees.

In 1254, Henry III accepted the throne of Sicily from Pope Innocent IV on behalf of a younger son, but he soon found himself unable to meet the costs of fighting for it as the Pope had required. Henry incurred immense debts and the threat of excommunication, which finally delivered him and his 19-year-old heir Edward into the hands of a council of barons. Led by Simon de Montfort, earl of Leicester, and Henry's brother Richard, earl of Cornwall, the barons believed that Henry's incompetence made it necessary for them to take a large permanent role in the affairs of the kingdom. Edward was so impressed by his Uncle Simon that for a short time, while the king was abroad in 1260, he joined in opposition to his father. But Henry

regained his son's loyalty when he sailed home; from then on Edward and Simon de Montfort, who felt betrayed, were sworn enemies.

Despite Simon's continued insistence that he was simply trying to remove the king's false advisors and assure a decent government for England, civil war broke out. At the 1264 Battle of Lewes, Henry was captured and had to hand over Edward as a hostage. Edward escaped from a relaxed captivity, however, raised a new army, and defeated Simon at the Battle of Evesham in 1265. Edward's men hacked Simon's body to pieces and threw it to the dogs. In later years, popular tradition venerated Simon de Montfort as a champion of Englishmen's liberties despite his challenge to the king and his own grand ambitions.

Nevertheless, Edward had recovered some of the dignity of the monarchy and was now king in all but name. But like many of his ancestors, he was attracted to the crusades, and with King—later Saint—**Louis IX** of France, took part in the eighth and last crusade, leaving England in 1270. Their adversary, Sultan Baibars, was a former military slave who had assassinated the previous sultan and undertaken a Muslim crusade of his own against Mediterranean Christianity. The expedition had hardly begun before King Louis died of a plague at Tunis and his successor made a truce with the Emir of Tunis and then sailed home. Edward was determined to press on to the Holy Land even without his expected French allies and declared:

> By the blood of God, though all my fellow soldiers and countrymen desert me, I will enter Acre with Forvin, the groom of my palfrey, and I will keep my word and my oath to the death.

He arrived, but with too few soldiers to reverse Baibars's conquests. Apart from relieving the siege of Acre, a crusader stronghold which was about to surrender, and a few skirmishing raids (in one of which he exterminated the entire Muslim population of Nazareth), his crusade came to an inconclusive end, other than to magnify his growing reputation for warfare.

Unable to prevail, Edward signed a compromise treaty with the sultan in 1272 and prepared to return home, but was stabbed by an assassin wielding a poisoned dagger. Seemingly on the point of death, he recovered with eerie speed once a surgeon had cut away the affected area, and by the autumn of that year was well enough to be jousting in Sicily. There he learned of his father's death and his own uncontested accession to the throne, though he did not set foot back in England until another two years had passed, years spent in Gascony, visiting the pope, and jousting with other princes. Edward never lost interest in crusading, however, and again "took the cross" (pledged to go on crusade) in 1287. But the distractions of his kingship and the disastrous surrender of Acre in 1291 meant that neither he nor any other Western Christians resumed the quixotic crusader quest.

Edward Goes to War Against Wales and Scotland

Edward is probably best remembered for his wars against Scotland and Wales, the "Celtic Fringe" of Britain. Wales was at that time poor, internally divided, and an ancient rival of England. The southern part was the stronghold of the "Marcher" lords, loyal to the English king but free to do much as they pleased in the face of a hostile Welsh population; the north was an independent principality ruled by Llewelyn ap Gruffudd and a source of frequent raiding into England. Edward I, who had failed to tame Welsh raiders on his border estates as a young man, decided to rid himself of this chronic problem once and for all: he would conquer Wales and set up a permanent occupation, based around a string of castles and linked by good roads. First, he gained papal support for his plan: the pope agreed that any Welshman who took up arms against Edward would be automatically excommunicated. Then, to justify the war, a clerk of Archbishop Pecham of Canterbury wrote a "racist diatribe" against the Welsh. In time-honored style, this made the enemy appear as wicked as possible so that its destruction would seem, in the consciences of the perpetrators, all but an act of charity. According to clerk's manifesto:

> The Welsh were "Trojan debris" swept into the wooded savagery of Cambria under the guidance of the Devil. Their sexual promiscuity was notorious; they spent their lives in theft and rapine, or sloth; they were so depraved that only a few had learned to till the soil. Only the mild forbearance of the English kings had prevented the English from long ago blotting out the existence and memory of this "detestable people."

Edward carried out his war of conquest in 1282 with far more determination and manpower than he had shown in a first Welsh campaign of 1277; squeezing Llewelyn's forces into the Snowdon mountain range, he beat them into submission. After Llewelyn's death in 1282, Edward pursued his brother Dafydd, captured him the following year, and had him hanged, drawn, and quartered.

> The villain's head was bound with iron, lest it should fall to pieces from putrefaction, and set conspicuously upon a long spear shaft for the mockery of London.

The conquest of Wales was now complete. English law replaced Welsh, and Edward shared the spoils among his faithful Welsh barons but took the precaution of maintaining and enlarging his castles there. Built by a Savoyard architect, those at Conway, Harlech, and Caernarvon remain standing today as vivid symbols of Edward's imperious rule.

Scotland proved a much tougher nut to crack, and Edward died without fulfilling his ambition of conquest. One of his many nicknames was "Hammer of the Scots" and, according to legend, he once swore an oath that he would never spend two nights in the same place until he had subdued the northern kingdom. His involvement began in 1291 after the Scottish royal family had died out in a series of accidents: King Alexander III fell off a cliff while riding on a stormy night, and his daughter "The Maid of Norway" died in 1290 in a shipwreck. Edward claimed to be ultimate feudal overlord of Scotland, but faced 13 immediate competitors for the throne; he summoned them all to meet him at Norham on the Anglo-Scottish border in 1291. The debate which followed, remembered as the Great Cause, culminated in Edward selecting John Balliol as king. Balliol owned lands in England as well as Scotland, and Edward soon showed that he expected a high degree of subordination from the king he had helped create. When Balliol balked and tried to enlist French aid against him, Edward launched another war of aggression which won victories at Berwick and Dunbar and soon overcame all Scottish resistance. He then removed the "Stone of Destiny" on which Scottish kings were traditionally crowned at Scone and took it to Westminster Abbey, a pointed insult to the Scots and a symbolic declaration that he intended to rule directly from now on.

His illusion of complete victory did not last long. In 1297, **Robert Bruce,** grandson of one of the 13 claimants, rebelled, and his rebellion gathered force by the adhesion of William Wallace and Andrew Moray, popular Scottish patriots. Though they defeated a badly led English army at Stirling Bridge in 1297, they paid the price the following year when a more disciplined English force, led by Edward himself, overpowered them at the Battle of Falkirk. Years of warfare ensued before most of the Scots rebels made terms with Edward in 1304; Wallace, who refused to conciliate, was captured and dismembered as gruesomely as Dafydd ap Gruffudd had been. The Scots committed counter-atrocities; for example, they cut up the body of Hugh Cressingham, a very fat royal official whom they captured at Stirling Bridge, and distributed the parts as mementoes of victory.

This long Scottish war yielded little in the way of tangible booty; English barons were correspondingly reluctant to fight in it, and every campaign was marked by mass desertions. The armies in the early years of Edward I's reign took the form of armored knights on horseback advancing with the aid of archers and infantrymen on foot. Cavalry cannot operate well in swampy conditions of the sort common in Scotland, however, and after Stirling Bridge the English knights recognized the need, at times, to dismount. Many historians think that the long campaigns against Scotland acted as a training ground for the English wars against France in the mid-14th century in which the English bowmen paved the way for massive victories, above all at Crecy (1346). Edward does not seem to have been an innovative battlefield general; his real strength lay in logistics, bringing together large forces, supplying and reinforcing them well by land and sea, and prevailing through superior numbers and discipline on the battlefield.

His Actions Toward English Jews

The English population had a long tradition of hating foreigners or any other social outsiders; one group which they particularly disliked and distrusted was the Jews, about whom baseless rumors of ritual child-murder and torture circulated. Sporadic bursts of anti-Jewish rioting and synagogue-burning had disfigured urban life over the previous 200 years—at times rising to mass killings, as had happened at the coronation of **Richard I, the Lionheart** in 1189. To monarchs with ambitious military plans, wealthy Jews were useful, however, because they were willing to lend money at interest, which Christian laws forbade. The kings had therefore extended some protection to Jews who could help them. Henry III and Edward I both extorted money from wealthy English Jews, impoverishing them in the process, but then, as growing numbers of Italian traders and bankers began visiting England, turned to this new source of money instead. In 1275, Edward prohibited Jews from practicing usury, and ordered that all Jews older than seven should wear two broad yellow cloth stripes on their clothes for easy identification. In 1290, he expelled the entire Jewish population from England, possibly at the urging of his mother Eleanor of Provence, who had always hated and feared them. An estimated 16,000 were forced to leave, most heading for Paris. Edward then asserted the right to collect all debts owed to the Jews and sold their houses and property at a profit. England next permitted Jews to enter only when, in the English Revolution of the 1640s and 1650s, the monarchy had been abolished.

The search for money to pay for his military adventures continued, but Edward, who is remembered for many constructive administrative reforms, was generally seeking ways to undo his subjects' purse strings rather than acting as a new Justinian, as some historians later claimed. His unceasing quest for more money could have unforeseen consequences; a large tax assessment in Wales, 1294, for example, led to a renewed rebellion, this time with popular rather than noble leadership. Though Edward quelled it too and carried on his ambitious castle-building program, the most distinguished of his castles—Beaumaris on the island of Anglesy—could never be finished for lack of funds. Even the stupendously rich Ricciardi family of Florence, which financed Edward's campaigns through the 1280s, was bankrupt by the mid-1290s, and no comparable financial dynasty was willing to take its place. Shortage of money at last provoked a constitutional crisis in 1297, intensified for Edward by the fact that the king of France had seized his possessions in Gascony. At a Parliamentary gathering in Salisbury, the earl of Norfolk, Roger Bigod, flatly told Edward that he would not go with him on campaign to Gascony. According to the chroniclers, Edward said: "By God, O Earl, either you go or you hang." Bigod did not back down but answered; "By the same oath, O King, I shall neither go nor hang."

The king found that his army, made up of barons and their retainers, refused to serve because of its anger over taxation and seizures of food supplies. Determined to fight for Gascony in any case, he set sail with what small force he could gather. The Battle of Stirling Bridge disaster took place while he was abroad and, with the kingdom in turmoil, the king's ministers and the baronial opposition finally reached an agreement. This agreement, the Confirmation of the Charters, ended several punitive taxes and signaled Edward's willingness to reconfirm the Magna Carta (written 80 years previously) as the basis for his relations with the barons.

In the last years of his reign, Edward continued to incur huge debts, but this time he decided to accept them rather than face the political unpopularity of trying to pay them off: he let his fraudulent but efficient treasurer, Walter Langton, absorb most of the blame, and Langton was thrown to the wolves when Edward died. In the 19th and early 20th centuries, historians believed that Edward I was in effect a great constitutional monarch who had laid the foundations of the modern monarchy. More recent historians are skeptical and see his innovations simply as desperate measures to use traditional money-raising methods in innovative ways to keep his wars going.

Nearly all the later years of Edward I's reign were devoted to fighting against the Scots. When Edward died en route to Scotland in 1307, the campaign for that year was called off, though it would resume under his successor Edward II and lead to a shattering defeat for the English at Bannockburn in 1314. In his biography of Edward I, Michael Prestwich writes:

> One story has it that he asked that at his death his body should be boiled until the bones were clean of flesh; the rattling skeleton should then be carried north on every expedition against the Scots. Perhaps more credible is his wish that his heart should be taken to the Holy Land and that his executors should pay the wages of a hundred knights for a year on crusade.

In any event, he was buried simply in Westminster Abbey, leaving the throne to a far less gifted son, Edward II. Like all medieval kings, Edward I had had to worry perpetually about the succession of a son but had little confidence in the feeble young man who took his place on the throne.

SOURCES:

Chancellor, John. *The Life and Times of Edward I.* Weidenfeld & Nicolson, 1981.

Herbert, Trevor, and Gareth E. Jones, eds. *Edward I and Wales.* University of Wales Press, 1988.

Johnson, Paul. *A History of the English People.* Harper, 1985.

Prestwich, Michael. *Edward I.* Methuen, 1988.

———. *The Three Edwards.* St. Martin's Press, 1980.

Salzman, L. F. *Edward I. Constable,* 1968.

Seymour, William. *Battles in Britain and their Political Background Volume 1, 1066–1547.* Sidgwick & Jackson, 1975.

Edward III

(1312–1377)

English king, who ruled for 50 years—waging war on the Scots, beginning the Hundred Years' War with France, winning victories at Crécy and Poitiers—and whose reign saw the evolution of Parliament, and the ravaging of England by the Black Death.

Born Edward of Windsor on November 13, 1312; died on June 21, 1377; buried in Westminster Abbey; son of King Edward II and Isabella; married: Philippa of Hainault, 1328; children: 12, including Edward the Black Prince (died 1376), Lionel Duke of Clarence (died 1368), and John of Gaunt (died 1399). Predecessor: Edward II (1307–27). Successor: Richard II (1377–99).

King Edward III, who ruled England for 50 years in the 14th century, was one of the greatest English monarchs. Waging fierce campaigns against the Scots and French, he was internationally renowned for his skill as a chivalrous warrior, an honor he shared with his eldest son **Edward, the Black Prince.** The later years of his reign were marked by Parliament's coming of age, the horrible effects of the Black Death, domestic tension, and a lonely death.

Edward of Windsor was born on November 13, 1312, at Windsor Castle, the first-born son of King Edward II and his French queen, Isabella, who was the daughter of the French king, Philip IV. Edward's birth was greeted with much rejoicing by the people, for they had little else about which to rejoice.

England was in deep turmoil in the early years of the 14th century. Edward's father had ascended the throne upon the death of the great **Edward I** (the "Hammer of the Scots") in 1307 and had soon proven himself to be an incapable ruler. Edward II had surrounded himself with favorites at court, offending the sensibilities of his nobles, and it was in the middle of a crisis over one

Contributed by Russell Andrew McDonald, Ph.D., University of Guelph, Guelph, Ontario, Canada

"Indeed, this king among all other kings and princes of the world had been glorious, gracious, merciful and magnificent, and was called par excellence 'Most Gracious' for his pre-eminent and outstanding grace."

THOMAS OF WALSINGHAM

such favorite, Piers Gaveston, that Isabella gave birth to Edward, about whom little is heard for the next 12 years. In 1314, the English suffered a humiliating defeat at the hands of the Scots led by **Robert Bruce** at Bannockburn; in 1315, there was a series of agrarian crises; and in 1322, an eight-year seesaw battle between the king and some of his nobles over more royal favorites finally ended in victory for Edward II. In the same year, the ten-year-old Edward of Windsor was called to take his place as earl of Chester in Parliament; from then on, his attendance was regular.

The king's tendency to support royal favorites led to the 1326 invasion of England by his wife Isabella and Roger Mortimer. Despite rumors that Isabella had taken Mortimer as a lover while in Paris, nearly all support for Edward II evaporated; in Parliament, during January of 1327, the king was deposed as the nobles swore homage to his son, acclaiming the 14-year-old Edward king. The reign of King Edward III formally began on January 25, 1327; he was knighted by Henry of Lancaster on February 1 and crowned the same day in Westminster Abbey. One chronicler recorded that after the crown was placed upon his head, "those who saw marvelled that such a slip of a lad, who had never worn a crown before, could manage to wear one of such size and weight." The fate of his father remains something of a mystery. Although rumors circulated that he was living in Scotland, it is more likely that he was murdered in September of 1327 without his son's knowledge and buried at Gloucester abbey.

In January of 1328, Edward married Philippa of Hainault at York; she was to be his queen for nearly 40 years. The royal couple celebrated the birth of their firstborn son, Edward of Woodstock, the future Black Prince, in June of 1330.

Although Edward III's succession promised an end to the abuses of his father's reign, the young king's regency council was quickly shoved aside by Isabella and Mortimer, so that he was, to quote one chronicler, "not ruling, nor yet well ruled." This state of affairs persisted until October of 1330, when the 17-year-old Edward III attempted a daring coup. Late on the night of October 19, Edward and some of his loyal knights entered a secret passage below Nottingham castle, where Isabella and Mortimer were staying. Bursting into Mortimer's chambers, they seized him and carried him away. While announcing the arrests the next morning, Edward declared that Mortimer and Isabella were guilty of maladministration and that henceforth he would govern for himself. Following a trial before his peers in Parliament, Mortimer

CHRONOLOGY

1307	Edward I died; succeeded by Edward II
1312	Edward of Windsor born
1314	Scots defeated the English at Bannockburn
1327	Edward II deposed; his son became Edward III
1330	Broke away from tutelage of Isabella and Roger Mortimer; Mortimer executed; Edward of Woodstock, the Black Prince, born
1333–36	Scottish campaigns
1337	Outbreak of war with France
1346	English victorious over French at Crécy and over the Scots at Neville's Cross; David II of Scotland captured
1348	Order of the Garter founded
1348–50	Black Death ravaged England
1356	English victorious over French at Poitiers; King John of France taken prisoner
1360	Treaty of Brétigny
1369	Queen Philippa died
1376	"Good Parliament" dismissed King's advisors; Edward the Black Prince died
1377	Edward III died; succeeded by his 10-year-old grandson Richard

was hanged as a common criminal on November 29; Isabella, let off with a lighter sentence, was provided a comfortable pension on which to retire.

During the next several years, Edward managed to restore law and order to the land, make peace with his nobility, and give himself over to the pursuit of tournaments and the joust before facing the prospect of war with the Scots. In 1332, Edward Balliol, son of Scotland's king John Balliol and one of those disinherited by Robert Bruce after the Battle of Bannockburn, attempted to claim the throne of Scotland for himself. In this effort, he had the covert backing of Edward III who raised a large army in 1333. On July 19, his army crushed the Scots at the Battle of Halidon Hill, and within a year the king of Scots, David II (1329–71), was forced to flee to France. Resistance to Balliol and the English continued in David's absence, however, so that Edward was forced to launch another campaign in 1335 with the largest army assembled in many years. Scottish chronicler Andrew Wyntoun wrote: "In the face of his might, none but children in their games would answer openly that they were the men of king David." Between 1333 and 1337, Edward III led four campaigns in Scotland that were expensive but did not constitute failure. Indeed, the victory at Halidon erased the humiliation of Bannockburn, and Edward was revealed as a capable military leader, setting a new tone for his reign.

The Hundred Years' War Begins

But as important as they were, the wars with Scotland formed merely a prelude to the wars with France that were to prove the dominating characteristic of Edward's reign. Since the days of **William the Conqueror,** the kings of England had held land in France. This cross-channel "empire" reached its peak under **Henry II,** and although **King John** lost Normandy, the king of England still held considerable land in southwestern France (Gascony) in the time of Edward III. It was this land—a boon to the English king and a thorn in the side of the French king—which sparked the war. In 1336, King Philip VI of France declared Edward's hold on Gascony forfeited for allegedly harboring a French fugitive at his court. Edward responded in October of 1337, replying that he would prosecute his right to the throne of France— a claim which had lain dormant for nine years but had arisen with the 1328 death of France's King Charles IV without a male heir. Edward's claim to the French throne passed through his mother Isabella, but since the crown was deemed unable to pass through the female line, Philip had been enthroned nearly ten years earlier. The war which began in earnest during the spring of 1338 would last for over 100 years and is accordingly called the Hundred Years' War, though it did not represent continuous hostilities for that length of time.

Initially faced with a crisis over financing the fighting, by 1346 the English under Edward's leadership had defeated the French in the naval battle of Sluys (1340) and the Battle of Crécy in August 1346. At Crécy, Edward watched the battle while the right wing of the English forces was commanded by his 16-year-old son, Edward the Black Prince. In the heat of the battle the young prince was unhorsed. According to Jean Froissart, the chief chronicler of these wars, when several nobles sent a messenger to the King requesting reinforcements, Edward replied:

> Go back ... to those who have sent you and tell them not to send for me again today, as long as my son is alive. Give them my command to let the boy win his spurs, for if God has so ordained

it, I wish the day to be his and the honour to go to him and to those in whose charge I have placed him.

Following this victory, the king turned his attention to the port of Calais, and after a year-long siege, it too fell to him in August of 1347; the English had also won a notable victory in 1346 over the Scots at Neville's Cross, capturing King David II of Scotland and sending him to an 11-year captivity in the Tower of London.

The year 1348 saw the zenith of Edward III's prestige both at home and abroad. He was 35 years old, at the height of his martial powers, the most chivalrous and successful warrior in Christendom, and when he returned home victorious from the Continent his country welcomed him. "The folk thought a new sun was rising over England, for the abundance of peace, the plenty of possessions, and the glory of victory," wrote Thomas of Walsingham, a monk of St. Albans. There were celebrations and tournaments throughout the land. Early in the year, Edward was offered the title of Holy Roman Emperor, which he wisely declined; in August, he established the Order of the Garter, a fellowship of knights modeled on the legends of King Arthur and the Knights of the Round Table who were bound to support one another, serve their lord faithfully, and uphold the cause of right.

The Black Death was marching across Europe at the same time. Contemporary writers recorded the horror of the deadly Plague, which was seen as God's punishment:

> All England suffered from this sore affliction so that scarce one in ten of either sex survived. As the graveyards were not big enough, fields were chosen where the dead might be buried.

In September of 1348, Edward's 15-year-old daughter Joanna succumbed to the pestilence at Bordeaux, leaving the king—in his own words— "pierced by the shafts of sorrow." By November, the Plague had reached London. Although relatively few nobles died as a result, it carried off between 20 and 50% of the English population and periodically returned, as in 1361–62. Government ground to a halt—Parliament was dissolved in January of 1349. In the aftermath of the pestilence, the war with France languished and Edward's government had to institute unpopular wage and price controls to deal with mounting social and economic problems that would eventually erupt in the 1381 Peasants' Revolt.

When war with France broke out again in 1355, Edward took little part in the actual campaigning, leaving this task to his son the Black Prince. In September of the following year, Edward won yet another crushing victory at the Battle of Poitiers. The French king John the Good was captured and Edward's prestige grew even greater: at home, England was peaceful and recovering from the Black Death, while France was without a king and devastated both by the campaigns that had taken place there and by the ravages of the Plague. After an abortive attempt to have himself crowned king of France at Rheims in 1359–60, Edward came to terms with the French in the Treaty of Brétigny, whereby he became lord of a third of France. It was a great victory, further enhancing his reputation. The chronicler Jean le Bel wrote, "when the noble Edward gained England in his youth, nobody thought much of the English…. Now they are the finest and most daring warriors known to man."

Throughout the 1360s, Edward began to relax his grip on public affairs. On his 50th birthday in 1362 he made all of his sons great territorial magnates in a grand ceremony: the Black Prince became prince of Aquitaine; Lionel of Antwerp became duke of Clarence; Edmund of Langley became earl of Cambridge; and John of Gaunt had been made earl of Lancaster sometime earlier. It was on his sons that many of the king's duties devolved, with the Black Prince campaigning in Aquitaine, the Iberian peninsula, and in France when hostilities broke out again in the late 1360s. While the king's image was no less glorious than that of the 1340s and 1350s, it was now less publicly displayed. Edward took less interest in administrative affairs and devoted his attentions to the kingly pursuits of hawking, hunting, supervising building projects throughout his realm, and presiding over his magnificent court.

By the late 1360s, the reign began to take a downturn; perhaps, as some historians have suggested, Edward had simply ruled too long for his own reputation. In 1368, his son Lionel of Clarence died, followed in 1369 by Edward's beloved Queen Philippa who had been a loyal counsellor to Edward throughout their life together, often acting as a calming influence upon his formidable Plantagenet temper. Many years earlier, after the capture of Calais in 1347, Edward was prepared to execute the six burghers handed over to him as hostages until the pregnant Philippa threw herself to her knees before him, begging his mercy upon them. Though this account may be apocryphal, Froissart recorded:

The king remained silent for a time, looking at his gentle wife as she knelt in tears before him. His heart was softened, for he would not willingly have distressed her in the state she was in.…

After her death, Edward's condition quickly deteriorated, and he began losing control of the realm he had governed so ably for over 40 years. Although his son John of Gaunt took over the reins, he was not trusted by the nobility as his father had been, and he soon retired from public life. The aging Edward was again surrounded by a select group of courtiers, much as he had been in his youth. Notable among these hangers-on was Alice Perrers, Edward's companion and mistress who was given lavish gifts of jewelry, clothes, and property.

By 1376, Parliament had seen enough of these royal favorites and from April until July, the "Good Parliament" attacked these advisors; many members of the king's government were dismissed, including Alice. A Council of Nine was set up to advise the king, but before the Parliament was over another tragedy had struck the aged monarch: after a lengthy illness, his eldest son Edward the Black Prince died on June 8, 1376. There was international grief at his passing. Froissart called him "the flower of the world's knighthood … and the most successful soldier of his age." The Black Prince was buried at Canterbury cathedral, where his finely wrought tomb, inscribed with mottoes of chivalry, can still be seen today. At Christmas of 1376, Edward held a great feast at Westminster during which Richard, the Black Prince's son, was invested by the king and presented to his nobles as successor to the throne. On Edward's death he would succeed as King Richard II.

The Cultural Achievements of His Reign

Although the second part of Edward's reign has been seen as a disappointment by some historians, many cultural achievements date from this period. A great patron of building, Edward launched many new projects throughout his realm, particularly at Windsor and Westminster. At Cambridge, the king endowed King's Hall. It was during his reign that the first version of William Langland's allegory *Piers Plowman* was produced and Geoffrey Chaucer began to write. It was also during Edward's reign that Parliament matured and began to function effectively in every sphere of administration, justice, and politics, buttressing royal authority and making possible the vast mobilization of resources.

Having been in ill health for some time, possibly since as early as 1372, King Edward had suffered a number of strokes that rendered him feeble in mind and body, and following Christmas of 1376 he lapsed again into illness. Although he recovered enough to travel to Windsor in April to celebrate his Jubilee, the king died on June 21, 1377, having been little more than a bystander to the events of the last years of his reign. One chronicler recorded that he died almost alone, with only a priest to offer absolution and with his mistress Alice Perrers at his bedside:

> When she realized that he had lost the power of speech and that his eyes had dulled ... quickly that shameless doxy dragged the rings from his fingers and left.

The priest offered the dying king a crucifix, and he reportedly "took it with great reverence, kissing it devoutly ... with tears pouring from his eyes." Froissart, however, recorded that "to witness and hear the grief of the people, their sobs and screams and lamentations on that day, would have rended anyone's heart."

The king's body was embalmed and taken for burial to Westminster Abbey, where it was laid "between our ancestors of famous memory Kings of England, where we have chosen our royal sepulture," beside Queen Philippa. The stylized tomb effigy of gilt bronze, which can still be seen today, shows Edward's long face, long straight nose, and flowing hair and beard, more an image of the glorious early years of the reign than the lonely, tense, last years. Thomas of Walsingham wrote: "This king among all other kings and princes of the world had been glorious, gracious, merciful and magnificent, and was called *par excellence* 'Most Gracious' for his pre-eminent and outstanding grace," but also noted, "it should be remarked that just as at first both grace and prosperity made Edward III renowned and illustrious, so in his old age and declining years ... that good fortune diminished; and many misfortunes and difficulties arose."

While the reign of Edward III was certainly one of contrasts, there can be no doubt that he united the aristocracy, was a glorious warrior who achieved notable military victories, and—if he did not weld England into a nation—he certainly brought the ingredients for nationhood together during his 50-year reign.

SOURCES:

Froissart, J. *Chronicles*. Translated by G. Brereton. Penguin, 1968.

Hallam, E., ed. *Four Gothic Kings: Henry III, Edward I, Edward II, Edward III—Seen Through the Eyes of Their Contemporaries*.

Harvey, J. *The Plantagenets*. Fontana Library, 1967.

Packe, M. *King Edward III*. Ark, 1985.

Tuck, A. *Crown and Nobility, 1272–1461*. Barnes and Noble, 1986. Weidenfeld & Nicolson, 1987.

FURTHER READING:

Cannon, J., and R. Griffiths. *The Oxford Illustrated History of the British Monarchy*. Oxford University Press, 1988.

Keen, M. *England in the Later Middle Ages*. Routledge, 1973.

Longman, W. *The History of the Life and Times of Edward III*. 2 vols. Longmans, 1869.

McKisack, M. *The Fourteenth Century*. Oxford University Press. 1959.

Waugh, S. *England in the Reign of Edward III*. Cambridge University Press, 1991.

Edward, the Black Prince

(1330–1376)

Most chivalrous knight and successful military leader in the 14th century, who won the initial stages of the Hundred Years' War for England.

"We shall willingly attend on the appointed day at Paris, since the King of France sends for us, but it will be with our helmet on our head, and accompanied by sixty thousand men."

EDWARD, THE BLACK PRINCE

O n June 15, 1330, at Woodstock in Oxfordshire, Philippa, the wife of **Edward III,** king of England, gave birth to a son whom she named Edward. In his lifetime, this son was known as Edward of Woodstock, and, as heir to the throne, the Prince of Wales. However, Edward of Woodstock is best known to history as the Black Prince, a title which English and French chroniclers bestowed upon him to celebrate his deeds in the Hundred Years' War.

Edward spent the early part of his life in the constant and loving care of his mother. In 1341, Philippa donated money to Oxford University and founded Queens College where Edward was educated. This was the 14th century, however, the era in which the Plantagenet dynasty in England claimed the French crown and French lands. As a result, the Hundred Years' War broke out, which coincided with and dominated the life of Edward, the Black Prince, cutting short his idyllic existence in England. At the tender age of 15, in June 1346, in order to test his son's mettle, King Edward III placed the young heir in partial command of a force which invaded Normandy.

Name variations: Edward Plantagenet; Edward, the Prince of Wales; Edward of Woodstock. Born in Woodstock, Oxfordshire, England, in 1330; died of dysentery in 1376; eldest son of King Edward III and Philippa; married: Joan, Countess of Kent, 1361; children: Edward and Richard (only Richard survived childhood). Descendants: Richard II.

Contributed by Joseph Tempesta, Associate Professor, Ithaca College, Ithaca, New York

Although simmering for years, the Hundred Years' War ignited officially in 1328, when King Charles IV of France died. France would not accept the French king's only child, a daughter, as its monarch. Though Charles's sister Isabella was the mother of Edward III of England, France would also not accept the English king as its monarch. Eventually, France chose Philip of Valois, first cousin to Charles, who became Philip VI. Since Edward III was a nephew to the deceased French king, he believed that he had a stronger blood claim to the French throne. This dynastic controversy led to the Hundred Years' War.

In June 1346, the English launched an armada of 1,000 ships, carrying 30,000 men, and invaded Normandy. The 15-year-old Black Prince was given command of an advance troop of invaders. By the end of June, he and his invaders had captured the city of Caen. A month later, they moved northeast from Caen, crossed the Somme, and occupied high ground above the city of Crecy. On August 26, 1346, 50,000 French troops attacked the English force, which numbered some 17,000.

The English were well positioned, and the French tactics were antiquated. As a result, the French suffered a great defeat at the Battle of Crecy. The key to the English victory was their use of the longbow, which had been developed by the Welsh. As the French attacked the English positions, the Welsh longbowmen rained volleys of arrows upon the French knights and broke up their charging cavalry formations. By the end of the battle, the French had lost over 5,000 knights and the English 300. It was said that the flower of French chivalry perished at Crecy.

In the battle, the Black Prince deployed his forces brilliantly; though only 16, he fought sword to sword and his courage never flagged. At battle's end, Edward III stood before his son and proclaimed, "You are worthy to be king." The blind king of Bohemia, an ally of the French, had been slain in the battle, after he insisted upon being led into the thick of the fray. Edward, the Black Prince, adopted the motto of the courageous, slain monarch. To this day, "*ich dien*" ("I serve") is the motto of the Prince of Wales.

After the great victory, some in the English forces wanted to march on Paris, but Paris was too well fortified. In order to guarantee a retreat to England should this become necessary, Edward III decided instead to take the city of Calais on the English Channel. Arriving at Calais in September 1346, the English army attacked the city for the next several months. In July 1347, the city finally surrendered when Edward III received a volunteer delegation of six prominent citizens of Calais. At first, Edward intended to hang the burgers; eventually, he showed them mercy, accepted the surrender of Calais, and did not sack the city. Calais became an important stronghold and commercial center for England for years thereafter. After this phase of the Hundred Years' War, the Black Prince and Edward III returned to England.

In 1350, in return for bribes, the governor of Calais planned to turn the city over to the French king. Informed of this treachery, the Black Prince and Edward III crossed the Channel and occupied the city. The French eventually attacked in 1350. The English forces emerged from Calais, surprised the French, and repulsed them. During the fighting, when King Edward found himself isolated and surrounded by French forces, the Black Prince led a charge to rescue his father.

A year later, in the Channel, the Black Prince led the English fleet against the Spanish fleet which had been raiding Flanders. At the battle of Espagnols Sur Mer, the English defeated the Spanish. In gunwale-to-gunwale combat, the Black Prince fought fiercely and was a major reason for this English victory. By 1350, the Black Prince had gained a reputation as the most courageous and chivalrous knight in Europe. It appeared that England had a worthy successor to Edward III.

The Triumph of the Black Prince

In 1355, fighting between England and France again intensified. In September, the Black Prince landed in Bordeaux at the head of English forces numbering 6,000. With impunity, he raided towns throughout Gascony and Aquitaine. Finally, in June 1356, French forces numbering 16,000 attacked the English at the city of Poitiers. The Battle of Poitiers was the Black Prince's finest hour. Standing at the head of his troops, urging them on when they despaired in the face of the vast French army, he fought with an inspiring ferocity. By the end of the battle, having lost only 60 knights, the English had slain 2,500 French knights and 5,000 ordinary soldiers; they had also captured 2,000 French knights, including John The Good, the king of France. The following year, the Black Prince triumphantly entered London with his captive.

In 1361, the Black Prince married Joan, the countess of Kent. Though his father had hoped that his son might choose a wife who would prove to be politically beneficial to England, Edward married for love. But the king relented and finally approved of the union. Joan and the Black Prince had two children—Edward and Richard—but only Richard would survive childhood, later becoming King Richard II on the death of Edward III.

In 1362, Edward III named his son prince of Aquitaine and feudal lord of other French lands. These territories amounted to approximately a third of the land mass of France. Because he was English, the French population and nobility reluctantly accepted the Black Prince as their feudal ruler. Within a few years, the fortunes of the prince would decline because of his ill-advised involvement in Spanish politics. In 1362, England formed an alliance with Don Pedro, the king of Castille. Since Castille bordered on Aquitaine, at the Pyrenees, the English saw this alliance as a means of preventing the French from forming an alliance with the Castillians. But such an alliance presented a threat to Aquitaine from the south.

In 1367, Don Enrique of Castille rebelled against his half-brother Don Pedro, seizing the throne of that Spanish kingdom. Because of the English alliance with Don Pedro, the Black Prince led an army across the Pyrenees and attacked the forces of Don Enrique. At first, the expedition went badly. Finally, however, at the city of Najera near the Castillian capital of Burgos, the Black Prince devastated the forces of Don Enrique, who lost some 5,000 troops while the English lost about 100. With Don Pedro restored to the throne of Castille, the English forces returned to Aquitaine in 1368.

Unfortunately for the Black Prince, the Spanish adventure proved to be extremely expensive, and his knights enjoyed very little booty from it. Further, Don Pedro, who had promised to reimburse the Black Prince for the cost of the invasion, reneged. The French knights now demanded money from the prince, whom they had only reluctantly accepted as their feudal lord. When King Edward attempted to raise money by imposing a hearth tax on the inhabitants of Aquitaine and Gascony, the nobility in these feudal states grew even angrier with him for overtaxing their subjects. In 1369, they appealed to the king of France, Charles V, and asked him to remove the Black Prince as prince of Aquitaine.

Charles V sought the advice of lawyers at the University of Bologna to ascertain whether or not the Black Prince was the vassal of the king of France, and whether or not the king of France could remove him as the prince of Aquitaine. The lawyers answered in the affirmative. Therefore, in January 1369, Charles V demanded that the Black Prince appear at Paris to answer charges brought against him by the lords of Gascony and Aquitaine.

Edward Defies French King

Not surprisingly, the Black Prince considered himself to be the vassal of the king of England for whom he had conquered Aquitaine and Gascony. Therefore, to the summons of the French king, Edward ominously responded, "We shall willingly attend on the appointed day at Paris, since the King of France sends for us, but it will be with our helmet on our head, and accompanied by sixty thousand men."

By January 1369, however, the Black Prince was dying of dysentery which he had contracted on the Spanish campaign. As a result, in February the lords of Aquitaine and Gascony renounced their fealty to the Black Prince and swore it to the king of France, and Charles V launched an invasion of Aquitaine.

The new war in Aquitaine went badly for the English because the Black Prince was too ill to command his armies personally, and because the French had improved their tactics. This phase of the Hundred Years' War is highlighted by the massacre at Limoges, an English-held city, which surrendered to the French forces without a fight. This enraged the Black Prince. As a result, he was brought before the city on a stretcher and personally commanded an attack upon Limoges. When the city fell to the English in 1370, the Black Prince ordered it to be sacked. In the ensuing slaughter, some 300 men, women, and children were killed.

In January 1371, the oldest son of the Black Prince, the six-year-old Edward, died. This was the final blow. Deathly ill, the Black Prince turned Aquitaine over to his brother, John of Gaunt, the duke of Lancaster, and boarded a ship for England. There he lived a few more years but remained mostly bedridden, while Aquitaine fell to the French. In 1376, on Trinity Sunday, after preparing for death and guaranteeing his son Richard's succession to the English throne, the Black Prince died.

For four months his body lay in state in Westminster Hall as thousands of English subjects from all classes and all parts of the realm paid their respects. The French king even ordered a Mass said in Paris. Finally, in 1376, Edward of Woodstock, the Black Prince, was buried in the Canterbury Cathedral, not far from **Thomas Becket,** whom Edward had revered throughout his life.

SOURCES:

Barber, Richard. *Life And Campaigns of The Black Prince.* St. Martin's Press, 1986.

Cole, Robert. *The Black Prince.* Hart-Davis, 1976.

Emerson, Barbara. *The Black Prince.* Weidenfeld & Nicolson, 1976.

Harvey, John. *The Black Prince And His Age.* Rowman & Littlefield, 1976.

FURTHER READING:

Hewitt, H. J. *The Black Prince's Expedition of 1355–57.* Manchester University Press, 1958.

Packe, Michael. *King Edward III.* Routledge & Kegan Paul, 1983.

Edward VII

(1841–1910)

King of England, who exercised much less direct domestic political power than his predecessors, but was an effective representative of his country in international diplomatic negotiations.

"We have always been an Aristocratic Country, and I hope we shall always remain so, as they are the mainstay of this Country, unless we become so Americanized that they are swept away."

EDWARD VII

The 20th-century British monarchy is known around the world. Instant telecommunications bring great ceremonies such as coronations, royal weddings, and jubilees to audiences of millions. King Edward VII was an important transitional figure in the development of this modern British monarchy.

Albert Edward, the second child and first son of Queen **Victoria** (1819–1901) and Prince Consort Albert of Saxe-Coburg-Gotha (1819–61), was born at St. James' Palace, London, on November 9, 1841. His older sister, Victoria the Princess Royal, had been born almost exactly a year before, and he was followed by three younger brothers and four younger sisters. "Bertie," as he was known until his accession to the throne, was made Prince of Wales within a month of his birth. His parents were consciously trying to raise the monarchy from the pleasure-seeking frivolity of their predecessors Kings George IV (1820–30) and William IV (1830–37). During those reigns, and especially during that of George IV, the monarchy sank to its modern nadir of unpopularity. George's gluttony, gambling, and mistresses so repulsed the public that talk of republicanism grew. Bertie's

Contributed by D. G. Paz, Professor of History, Clemson University, Clemson, South Carolina

Born on November 9, 1841, at St. James's Palace, London; died at Buckingham Palace, London, on May 6, 1910; son of Prince Consort Albert of Saxe-Coburg-Gotha and Queen Victoria; married: Princess Alexandra of Schleswig-Holstein-Sonderburg-Glucksburg, March 10, 1863; children: (two sons) Albert Victor (Duke of Clarence, who predeceased his father), and George (Duke of York, Prince of Wales, and King George V); (three daughters) Maud (Queen of Norway), Louise Victoria (Princess Royal and Duchess of Fife), and Princess Victoria. Descendants: Elizabeth II and the House of Mountbatten-Windsor.

parents believed that the royal family should stand as a moral example for the nation and take seriously the job of governing. Prince Albert, therefore, supervised the education of the young Prince of Wales. A studious man himself, Albert expected his son to buckle down to work, assigning him five hours a day of lessons; when Bertie was ten, these were increased to six hours a day, six days a week, supplemented by harsh physical education.

Albert wanted to teach his son to be moral, manly, and educated, yet Victoria was convinced that none of her children ever could hope to be as moral, manly, and educated as their father: "None of you can ever be proud enough of being the child of such a father who has not his equal in this world—so great, so good, so marvellous." Because Bertie, not intellectually inclined to begin with, was held to an impossibly high standard, his unhappy childhood was marked by temper tantrums and depression. "[H]e takes everything that is at hand and throws it with the greatest violence against the wall or window," his tutor reported; "or he stands in the corner stamping with his legs and screaming in the most dreadful manner." His parents interpreted these as signs of willfulness and lack of intelligence, to be corrected by increased discipline.

This regimen began to be relaxed in 1856, when Victoria and Albert took Bertie along on their state visit to the emperor **Napoleon III** at Paris. He was allowed to visit Italy on his own in 1859, and North America in the summer of 1860.

The sense of independence, the pleasure of being the center of attention, gave him a lifelong love of travel. Yet the young prince of Wales also showed an unusual sensitivity to political nuances. His North American tour plunged him into the maelstrom of ethnic and religious rivalries. In Ontario, where Irish Protestants were a strong political force, the prince deflected attempts to link loyalty to the Crown with anti-Catholicism and anti-French sentiment. In New York City, where political battles (and even riots) raged between Roman Catholic Irish and Protestant Irish, he managed to charm both sides.

Ignoring his accomplishments, Queen Victoria continued to harp on the idea that Bertie could never hope to be as good a man as his father. Bertie, however, was growing up. Sent to university, he was the first Prince of Wales in modern times to taste formal higher education, but only a taste it was. He spent two terms at Oxford and two at Cambridge, but he was isolated from the other undergraduates and never took a degree. What he really wanted to do was get proper training as a soldier. His parents had him made a colonel (despite his wish to gain promotion on his own merit), but finally agreed to give him a formal course of military training at the Curragh Camp near Dublin during the summer vacation of 1861.

Bertie, not quite 20, had already developed a few bad habits—he liked to hunt, eat rich foods, and smoke—but his fellow officers introduced him to what became a lifelong habit: sex. The British officer class, especially of elite regiments, cared little for middle-class morality and kept mistresses. While at Curragh, Bertie was introduced to the actress Nellie Clifden. The liaison lasted for about two years. When Bertie's father learned about the affair, he rushed up to Cambridge to rescue his son from danger. Victoria and Albert were worried that their attempts to rescue the monarchy from its Regency decline would be undone. Consumed by worry that the behavior of Victoria's bad uncles had reappeared in her children, Albert caught a chill in Cambridge. Returning to Windsor Castle, he worked too hard, stayed up too late, and couldn't throw off the cold. With his immune system at a low ebb, Albert fell victim to the castle's bad drains. He developed typhoid fever and died on December 14. Victoria became convinced that her husband had died from worry over Bertie's transgressions: "Bertie (I never can or shall look at him without a shudder) does not know that I know all … the disgusting details." Mother and son were eventually reconciled, but she was determined to get him out of England for the moment, and, as she and Albert had arranged, to get him married.

HISTORIC WORLD LEADERS

Following plans that the prince consort had laid down shortly before his death, Bertie was sent on a grand tour of Egypt, Palestine, and Greece, during which he climbed a pyramid and grew a beard. Of greater long-term importance, however, was his marriage to Princess Alexandra of Schleswig-Holstein-Sonderburg-Glucksburg on March 10, 1863.

The Marriage of the Prince

The marriage of the Prince of Wales and Princess Alexandra was fraught with political dangers and was not universally welcomed, either in Britain or on the Continent of Europe. Alexandra was a Danish princess; her father, Prince Christian, was the heir to the Danish throne. The problem was that the German Kingdom of Prussia, into whose royal family Bertie's eldest sister had already married, claimed the provinces of Schleswig and Holstein, which were held in a personal union by the Danish king. Rabid German nationalists wanted to take over those provinces, while Danish nationalists wanted to incorporate them into the Kingdom of Denmark. Trouble was sure to break out when Prince Christian succeeded to the throne. Victoria and Prince Albert loved Germany, sympathized with Prussian efforts to unite that country, and therefore were anxious about the Danish match. On the other hand, there existed a considerable body of public opinion that was decidedly anti-Prussian. Moreover, Princess Alexandra was desirable, and the tsar of Russia was showing an interest in her for *his* son and heir. Thus, Victoria and Albert agreed to the match despite their doubts, but only after reassuring Prussia that Bertie understood that the match was not to signal a shift in British foreign policy.

Only eight months after the marriage, Alexandra's father succeeded to the Danish throne. He bowed to public opinion by incorporating the provinces of Schleswig and Holstein into the Danish kingdom, and Prussia led other German states into war two months later. The Danish War, which lasted but five-and-a-half months, drove Alexandra to furious anti-German sentiment. For years thereafter, she refused to speak to Bertie's German relatives; when Queen Victoria finally forced her to receive them, she did so with frigid civility. During the Franco-Prussian War of 1870, she openly supported the French.

Reputed to be one of the most beautiful princesses of her day, Alexandra retained her striking looks into old age. The two came to love and respect each other, even though they were quite different personalities. Bertie believed that punctuality was a cardinal virtue, while Alexandra was chronically late. Bertie loved dinner party chitchat, while Alexandra's growing deafness led her to prefer evenings at home. The two produced a family of two sons and three daughters; then, in the detached style of the aristocracy, each followed his or her own interests.

For about 25 years after Prince Albert's death, the Prince of Wales had little to do of an official nature. Though Victoria was reconciled to him after a few years, she never trusted his judgment. She refused to share government dispatches with him, or let him represent her during her years of secluded mourning for her late consort. In 1871–72, the Liberal prime minister **William Ewart Gladstone** proposed that the Prince of Wales take up residence in Ireland as the Crown's permanent representative to that island, but Victoria would have none of it. Other prime ministers suggested that the prince assume a more regular role in taking on the public appearances that the queen had been neglecting, but again she rejected such ideas. Only when the queen began slowing down in the late 1880s did she begin sharing her secret dispatches with her son. The Prince of Wales's official duties amounted, on average, to 27 days a year of public dinners, inspecting institutions, and inaugurating buildings. He lent his name to several worthy causes (the Society of Arts and Christ's Hospital, for instance), and he was honorary colonel of several regiments.

Lacking a formal role in public affairs, the Prince of Wales spent most of his time as unofficial leader of Britain's social elite. Enjoying gossip and chitchat, he began an annual round of hunting parties at country houses, dinner parties and evenings at the theater during the London social season, and days at the races, capped by visits to the spas of Germany and the French Riviera. Most of his public activities were booked for the summer months. His London home at Marlborough House became a center for beauty, sophistication, and wit, and he gave his name to the "Edwardian Age."

It was only a matter of time before Edward began having affairs. Some were with actresses like Sarah Bernhardt, Lillie Langtry, and the Moulin-Rouge cancan dancer, La Goulue. Others were with society women such as Frances, Countess of Warwick; Mrs. Alice Keppel; and Miss Chamberlayne, the daughter of a millionaire from Cleveland. Alexandra tolerated these affairs largely because having affairs was not uncommon among the royalty and aristocracy of Europe, because neither divorce nor separation was an acceptable option, and because the Prince of Wales was a good husband and father who stood by his wife against Queen Victoria's occasional displeasure.

was too friendly to Jews. Although Bertie was an aristocrat and a gentleman, he was no snob, nor did he feel constrained by social prejudice. On several occasions, he invited men from working-class backgrounds to his home, but he did so because he had met them on political occasions and respected their acumen. Such also was the case with Jews. He was friends with Lord Nathan Rothschild, Sir Ernest Cassel, Baron Hirsch, Louis Bischoffsheim, and even the Jewish Indian Sassoon family. In this respect, he flouted the anti-Semitic practices of the European aristocracy.

Bertie's personal lifestyle combined with Queen Victoria's isolation to bring the monarchy into disrepute during the 1860s and 1870s. The Prince of Wales almost died from typhoid fever in October 1871, and the thanksgiving service for his recovery, held at St. Paul's Cathedral on February 27, 1872, saw a momentary burst of popular enthusiasm for the royal family. More common, however, were antiroyal pamphlets such as *Jon Duan* (1875), written by Thomas and Isabella Beeton of cookbook fame, and republicanism became a respectable political viewpoint. The queen's emergence from seclusion under Prime Minister **Benjamin Disraeli**'s encouragement helped to restore the popularity of royal institutions, but the Prince of Wales's own charm converted at least two prominent republicans, Sir Charles Dilke and Joseph Chamberlain, into staunch supporters of the monarchy.

He Succeeds to the Throne

Upon the death of Queen Victoria, Bertie succeeded to the throne on January 22, 1901. Symbolizing a break with the past, he chose to be known as Edward VII, thereby rejecting his mother's wish that he be known as Albert. In quick succession, the new king turned Osborne House into a naval training center, remodeled the long-disused Buckingham Palace for his permanent residence, and replaced afternoon "drawing-rooms" with evening receptions. He opened Parliament in person (for the first time since 1886), enacted a glittering coronation on August 9, 1902, conducted a series of royal visits to various parts of the country, and by means of ostentatious ceremony and dress turned the monarchy into a national pageant. The public loved it.

But what practical power was the king to wield? When Victoria had ascended the throne in 1837, lack of royal favor could prevent a politician from becoming prime minister or force a prime minister out of office. Prince Consort Albert, however, taught Victoria to support whichever prime

The Prince of Wales was good about discharging his responsibilities as a father. He especially wanted to avoid isolating his children as he had been isolated. His children had appeared very rapidly in succession: Albert Victor in 1864, George in 1865, Louise in 1867, Victoria in 1868, and Maud in 1869. The girls were given conventional educations that fitted them to marry royalty (which Louise and Maud did). As for the boys, Bertie and Alexandra sent them to sea as cadets after tutoring at home. Unfortunately, Albert Victor suffered from what his tutors called an "abnormally dormant" mind and developed a taste for unconventional sex with both men and women. His parents decided that the thing to do was get him married early. They engineered a union with a German princess, May of Teck, but Albert Victor died on January 14, 1892, only a month after becoming engaged. In retrospect, this was a good thing for the monarchy, because May went on to marry the younger brother, George, who turned out to be one of the better kings of Britain.

The Prince of Wales's lifestyle provided another source of criticism: it was charged that he

minister was in power. With the expansion of the electorate to include the masses of working men, the power of the House of Commons grew while that of the monarchy declined. Prime ministers, in 1837, had to convince the queen to accept their policies; by 1901, they informed the queen of their policies.

King Edward VII, who had no desire to see a further diminution of royal power, constantly complained that the prime minister did not keep him sufficiently informed on the deliberations of the Cabinet. But over the course of the 19th century, the monarch had lost the rights to be kept apprised of internal cabinet discussions and to consult with individual ministers independently of the prime minister, and Edward's attempts to recapture those rights were to no avail. Edward's own personality and interests, moreover, contributed to the decline of his power. First, in contrast to his mother, who was lax about the ceremonial functions of monarchy but conscientious about the paperwork, the new king loved pageantry but was bored by the dispatches and correspondence. Second, King Edward spent three months of the year abroad and the rest of the time in hunting and dinner parties; he devoted little time to the business of state. Third, although he liked army, navy, and foreign matters, he was bored by domestic and colonial issues.

Edward's influence, however, was not insignificant. His personal friendship and support, for example, kept in office Admiral Sir John Fisher, whose reforms had the effect of modernizing the Royal Navy just in time for the First World War. In foreign policy, the king was a useful and effective diplomat. The major themes in the history of British foreign policy between 1890 and the First World War were growing estrangement with Germany and, consequently, the abandonment of balance-of-power diplomacy in favor of an alliance with France and Russia. King Edward VII certainly was popular with the French people and well liked by Tsar **Nicholas II,** who was married to his niece. The king's many visits to France smoothed the way for the Anglo-French agreement, or *Entente Cordiale,* of April 8, 1904. Especially significant was his visit of May 1903, when he melted the initially frigid response of the Parisian crowd. Now, diplomatic imperatives clearly drove Britain to the *Entente:* German hostility meant that Britain needed to find an ally. The king's contribution was to create the feeling of good will that allowed the agreement to be negotiated sooner than otherwise.

Edward VII's contribution to social attitudes lay in the area of opening doors to outsiders. The king was a great aristocrat, clearly uninterested in democracy and the leveling of social distinctions. He retained his circle of plutocratic friends after he succeeded to the throne and made no effort to learn about ordinary people. Nevertheless, he spoke out in favor of racial tolerance, declaring that "because a man has a black face and a different religion from our own, there is no reason why he should be treated like a brute." Though Edward admittedly was referring to Indian nobility, not commoners, this comment represents a more enlightened attitude than that held by most other Englishmen.

Edward's bad habits began catching up with him around 1906; observers began to notice that he was short of breath, and he started to have bronchial trouble. His health was worsened in 1909 by worry over a looming constitutional crisis. In order to pay for the arms race with Germany and the newly established system of old-age pensions, the Liberal ministry of Herbert Asquith had introduced a budget with high death duties and income tax. The Conservatives used their majority in the House of Lords to reject the measure, even though the Constitution forbade the Lords from rejecting finance bills. This controversy stirred up a grave dispute over the question of whether the Lords or the Commons should prevail in a dispute between the two Houses of Parliament. Prime Minister Asquith warned the king that an election might need to be called.

The king's physicians, meanwhile, wanted him to take a vacation, and he reluctantly went to France in March 1910. He returned to London on April 27, little refreshed, to find the political world in turmoil. As his bronchitis worsened, Queen Alexandra, on holiday in Greece, was urged to return home; when she arrived in London on May 5, the king was too weak to meet her at the station. The next morning, Edward tried to carry on his work, but he collapsed after lunch and suffered several heart attacks. The queen notified his friends that he was dying and made a point of calling his mistress, Mrs. Keppel, to his side. He died shortly before midnight on May 6, 1910.

SOURCES:

Magnus, Philip. *King Edward the Seventh.* Dutton, 1964.

Middlemas, Keith. *The Life and Times of Edward VII.* Weidenfeld & Nicolson, 1972.

FURTHER READING:

Brook-Shepherd, Gordon. *Uncle of Europe: The Social and Diplomatic Life of Edward VII.* Harcourt, 1976.

Lee, Sidney. *King Edward VII, a Biography.* 2 vols. Macmillan, 1925–27.

Roby, Kinley. *The King, the Press, and the People: A Study of Edward VII.* Barrie & Jenkins, 1975.

St. Aubyn, Giles. *Edward VII, Prince and King.* Atheneum, 1979.

Eleanor of Aquitaine

(1122–1204)

Duchess of Aquitaine, the richest and largest province in 12th-century France, queen of France and later queen of England, who was one of the most powerful and fascinating figures in the medieval West.

Name variations: Alia-Anor, Alienor. Born in 1122 in either Bordeaux or Belin (both in the south of France); died at the abbey of Fontevrault, France, in 1204; daughter of William X (Duke of Aquitaine and Count of Poitou) and Anor of Chatellerault; married: Louis VII of France (divorced 1152); married: Henry II of England, 1152; children: (first marriage; two daughters) Marie and Alix; (second marriage; five sons and three daughters) William, Henry the Young King, Matilda, King Richard I, Geoffrey, Eleanor, Joan, King John. Descendants: Otto IV of Brunswick, Holy Roman Emperor; Louis IX (St. Louis) of France. Predecessor: William X of Aquitaine.

Not much is known of Eleanor's childhood in Aquitaine, though it is thought that her early years must have been marked by her father's conflicts with the Catholic Church, most especially with **Bernard of Clairvaux.** In an age distinguished by the all-pervasive influence of religion, conflicts with the Church were of profound importance, and the young Eleanor witnessed first hand the fruitlessness of rebellion. During a dispute over whether Anaclet II or Innocent II was the true pope, her father, Duke William X, supported Anaclet against the unanimous decision of the bishops of France and was excommunicated. Confronted by St. Bernard for his manifest sinfulness in continuing to support an anti-pope, the powerful and stubborn Duke William was defeated, some say by miraculous intervention. Arnauld de Bonneval writes that:

> The Duke became rigid with fear, then quivered all over and fell to the ground as though the soul had gone out of him. When his chevaliers [knights] raised him, he fell again, his face to the earth.

"Eleanor of Aquitaine steered a path through the twelfth century that might forever put the lie to the notion that women had no place in a man's world until the middle of the twentieth century."

WILLIAM W. KIBLER

Contributed by Colleen Carpenter Cullinan, Ph.D. candidate, University of Chicago, Chicago, Illinois

The arts were another important influence on her youth. Her grandfather William IX was known as William the Troubadour, and his poetry and music were a great influence in the south of France. The court of the Duke of Aquitaine became a center of culture, and Eleanor was raised to love the fine arts. Later a patron of the arts herself, Eleanor enjoyed music and tales of knights and their fair ladies throughout her life.

She was still a teenager, however, when her private life as a protected young member of a powerful family ended, and her public life, with Eleanor herself wielding power, began. Her father's death in 1137 made her, as Duke William's eldest child and sole heir since he had no sons, the Duchess of Aquitaine and Countess of Poitou. She was now a most desirable prize: the man who married her would control more of France than the king himself. Because of the fear that she would be abducted by and "married" to the first unscrupulous nobleman who heard of her father's death, the news was carried swiftly and secretly to the king of France, Louis VI, who was now Eleanor's guardian. Since the king's son and heir was unmarried at the time, Louis VI saw the perfect opportunity to extend the power of his realm. He sent his son Louis to marry Duchess Eleanor, thus linking his own lands with her vast holdings. Before the young Louis and Eleanor could return from the summer wedding, however, King Louis VI died, and Eleanor found herself queen of France at the age of 15.

The early years of Eleanor's marriage to Louis VII saw her begin to exert influence over her husband in political decisions. Louis had not been raised to be king; his elder brother Philip was the heir apparent until his sudden death in a fall from a horse in 1131. Louis had been raised for the Church and retained many of the manners and habits of mind of a monk throughout his kingship. Thus the conflicts between the Church and the French monarchy that marked the 1140s were said to be of Eleanor's making.

One dispute in particular was decidedly due to Eleanor's maneuvering. Petronille, Eleanor's younger sister, wished to marry Count Ralph of Vermandois—who already had a wife. Divorce being forbidden by the Church, Eleanor sought to have the marriage annulled. She succeeded, and the marriage of Petronille and Ralph was quickly performed. Unfortunately, Count Ralph's discarded wife was the niece of the powerful Thibaud, count of Champagne, who was outraged and sought out the pope. The pope then decided that, since Ralph failed to seek papal permission to remarry after an annulment, the marriage of

CHRONOLOGY

1137	Became Duchess of Aquitaine and Countess of Poitou; married Louis, heir to France; Louis and Eleanor crowned king and queen of France
1147	Eleanor and Louis went on crusade to Jerusalem
1152	Marriage to Louis dissolved; married Henry Count of Anjou, later king of England
1154	Henry and Eleanor crowned king and queen of England
1169	Henry divided his Continental possessions among his sons
1170	Henry the Young King crowned; Thomas Becket murdered in his cathedral by Henry II's knights
1173	Eleanor and her sons rebelled against Henry; Eleanor imprisoned
1183	Henry the Young King died
1189	Henry died; Richard crowned king of England
1199	Richard died; John crowned king
1204	Eleanor died at age 82

Petronille and Ralph was not valid. Despite what she had witnessed as a child in her father's defeat by St. Bernard, Eleanor convinced Louis to support Petronille's marriage to Ralph. Excommunications and war followed. Once again, Bernard of Clairvaux intervened. The conflict over Petronille dragged on for several years, and Louis exacerbated France's problems with the pope by interfering in the election of a bishop.

But the French monarchy had other problems: it was becoming painfully apparent that the queen of France had borne no heirs to the throne. Eleanor turned to Bernard, who gave this advice:

> Seek, my child, those things which make for peace. Cease to stir up the king against the Church and urge upon him a better course of action. If you will promise to do this, I in my turn promise to entreat the merciful Lord to grant you offspring.

Accordingly, on Eleanor's advice, Louis made peace with the Church, and in 1145 Eleanor gave birth to a daughter Marie.

Following his religious reconciliation, Louis chose to lead the Second Crusade to the Holy Land of Jerusalem as part of his penance. Eleanor joined in the pilgrimage. In Antioch, where the crusaders gathered, she met her uncle, Prince Raymond, who was only 12 years her senior. They spent long hours together, and it was to Raymond that Eleanor confessed her frustration with her marriage, "I thought I had married a king, but I find I have married a monk." Unfounded rumors linked Raymond and Eleanor romantically; it is also said that it was Raymond who first suggested to Eleanor the possibility that her marriage could be annulled on the grounds of consanguinity (blood relationship). In fact, Eleanor refused to return from the crusade with Louis, citing their close blood ties and a desire to remain in Antioch with Raymond, but she was overcome by the king and forced to return.

Eleanor Leaves Louis, Marries Henry of Anjou

Still, it was the beginning of the end. Despite a reconciliation arranged by the pope and the birth of a second daughter, Eleanor left Louis only five years later, in 1152. Her marriage was dissolved in March, and within two months she married **Henry, count of Anjou.**

Henry of Anjou was known as Henry Fitzempress, for his mother was Matilda, widow of Henry V, the Holy Roman Emperor. Although his own father Geoffrey was count of Anjou, it was his mother's family that gave Henry a claim to the throne of England. For Matilda was the daughter of Henry I of England, and her throne had been usurped by Stephen. When Henry fought Stephen for his rights as king, the 1153 Treaty of Winchester allowed Stephen to keep the kingship until his death, whereupon Henry would succeed. Stephen died in 1154. Thus, within two years, Eleanor went from being queen of France to queen of England.

It is said that Eleanor's marriage to Henry caused the next 300 years of war between France and England. Once Henry became king of England, he was not a vassal to the king of France because of his French territorial possessions of Anjou and the Aquitaine, but a king and peer of Louis. Henry controlled more of France than Louis did—and all by marrying Louis's ex-wife. Since Louis was overlord of Aquitaine, Eleanor should have obtained his permission. But knowing that Louis would never consent to her marriage to a future king of England, she ignored her feudal obligation and went ahead with her wedding. Claiming the marriage was thus invalid, the French king fought wars with the English king over custody of their mutual wife. But Louis, no match for the younger and battle-trained Henry, was eventually forced to admit defeat and acknowledge the marriage.

Eleanor no longer suffered from the twin curses of prolonged childlessness and the lack of sons. Just over a year after her marriage, she bore William in 1153. Though he died in infancy, William was followed by seven more children over the next 13 years—four of them sons. During these years, Eleanor served as regent of England when Henry was away on long trips to the Continent, taking care of his domains there. In 1168, when Henry returned full control of the duchy of Aquitaine to Eleanor, she moved there to rule her homeland. From that time on, Eleanor's interests were primarily centered around her sons; she turned her political skills and powers to their advancement, often at the expense of her husband's power.

But it wasn't just politics that interested Eleanor. Home in Aquitaine, she turned her court into a center of culture and the arts. Andreas the Chaplain, author of *De Amore,* an infamous work of courtly love, is said to have been at Eleanor's court. Further, Eleanor's daughter Marie, now the countess of Champagne, was a literary patron in her own right, commissioning courtly romances from poets such as Chretien de Troyes. Chretien's works include "Lancelot, or The Knight of the Cart," and other Arthurian romances. Some think that the woman known only as "Marie de France," who wrote many popular *lais* (story-songs), was either the countess of Champagne or else an illegitimate sister of Henry II (and thus Eleanor's sister-in-law). In either case, Marie de France and her music quite possibly enriched Eleanor's court in Aquitaine.

The arts, however, were never enough to fill Eleanor's life completely. When Henry divided his Continental possessions among his sons in 1169, she urged her husband to follow the dictates of Continental (not English) practice and have young Henry crowned in 1170. The succession to the English throne was now assured. But even though Henry the Young King had a title and a crown, he had no power and no domains of his own. The old king couldn't bear to give up ruling his lands. Three years later, all of Henry's sons, frustrated by their merely nominal titles and lack of true power, began a rebellion. They were aided by Eleanor and Louis VII, and upon his death in 1180 by his son **Philip II (Augustus),** but despite this help, the sons were roundly defeated. After almost 20 years as king, the 40-year-old Henry was still unbeatable on the battlefield.

She Again Wields Power

Henry had his wife Eleanor imprisoned in Salisbury Castle. Although she occasionally appeared in public at state occasions, she remained a prisoner until Henry died in 1189. To a woman who had traveled all across Europe, from Jerusalem to London, these years of imprisonment were perhaps the most difficult in her life. But Henry's death meant freedom. As Henry the Young King had died in 1183, Eleanor's next son **Richard**—who was known as "Coeur de Lion" (**the Lionheart**)—claimed the throne, and Eleanor once again began to wield considerable power as his trusted counselor. During Richard's ten-year reign, she arranged his marriage to Berengeria, the daughter of the king of Navarre; she quelled her son **John**'s rebellion in 1192 when Richard was out of the country; she ran England herself once word arrived that Richard was being held prisoner by Leopold, Duke of Austria, and Henry VI, the Holy Roman Emperor; and she personally oversaw the gathering of Richard's immense ransom, which she brought to his captors in Germany (the Holy Roman Empire) in the dead of winter, 1194. After Richard's return to England, Eleanor—not Richard's wife—presided as queen at a ceremonial crown-wearing at Winchester.

Richard's sudden death in 1199, due to an infected arrow wound, is said to have devastated Eleanor. Richard the Lionheart was her favorite son; now only John was left (Geoffrey had died from wounds received in a tournament in 1186). The youngest of her children and the least in terms of noble qualities, John succeeded Richard as king of England. He is remembered by chroniclers as greedy, irresponsible, selfish, and cruel. John was bright enough, certainly, to be a good king, but not inclined to use his intelligence for good ends. Still, he was Eleanor's son, and she did everything she could to ensure that he was crowned instead of Arthur, son of Geoffrey, who also claimed the throne. Richard had at one time indicated that his nephew Arthur was to be his heir, but had given up the plan when Arthur was sent to the court of the king of France to be raised. King Philip of France, of course, supported Arthur in his claim to the throne, but John defeated Arthur on the battlefield, and Eleanor coerced the noblemen of Aquitaine and her other realms into accepting John as overlord.

Despite Eleanor's best efforts to recruit and maintain support for John, he continued his practice of alienating everyone through his treachery, suspicion, and deceit. It was even rumored that he killed Arthur with his own hand and threw the body in the Seine. King Philip's continuing wars against John eventually drove him from most of his French possessions, including Maine, Anjou, Normandy, and Brittany. John even lost Château Gaillard, a castle in Normandy that Richard had designed, built, and greatly loved.

By this time, Eleanor was in her eighties. Having fought and schemed and survived for decades beyond the normal 12th-century lifespan, she finally admitted that she had grown old. The loss of Richard, and then of Richard's beloved Château, had taken its toll. Retiring to the abbey of Fontevrault, where her husband Henry and son Richard were buried, Eleanor spent her last days among the nuns there. She died in the spring of 1204, at the age of 82.

SOURCES:

Kelly, Amy. *Eleanor of Aquitaine and the Four Kings*. Harvard University Press, 1950.

Kibler, William W., ed. *Eleanor of Aquitaine: Patron and Politician*. University of Texas Press, 1976.

Pernoud, Regine. *Eleanor of Aquitaine*. Coward-McCann, 1967.

Rosenberg, Melrich V. *Eleanor of Aquitaine: Queen of the Troubadors and of the Courts of Love*. Riverside Press, 1937.

Walker, Curtis Howe. *Eleanor of Aquitaine*. University of North Carolina Press, 1950.

FURTHER READING:

Facinger, Marion. *A Study of Medieval Queenship: Capetian France, 987–1237*. University of Nebraska Press, 1968.

Goldman, James. *A Lion in Winter* (play). Random House, 1981.

Meade, Marion. *Eleanor of Aquitaine: A Biography*. Hawthorn Books, 1977.

Seward, Desmond. *Eleanor of Aquitaine*. Times Books, 1979.

Elizabeth I

(1533–1603)

Last Tudor monarch of England and arguably its most successful ruler, who presided over England's transformation from a relatively remote island to one of the most important political and maritime powers in the world.

Born September 7, 1533, at Greenwich Palace on the Thames River, England; died on March 24, 1603, at Richmond Palace, Surrey, England; daughter of Henry VIII (Tudor king of England) and Anne Boleyn; never married. Descendants: Stuart kings of England. Predecessor: Mary I. Successor: James I.

By most accounts, Elizabeth I was the most successful monarch ever to ascend an English throne. Whether this was due to good fortune or her own devices is still a subject of much debate and conjecture. Yet it is most likely that the reasons for her success lay somewhere between the two: a measure of luck combined with skill.

The Elizabethan Period was an heroic age for England. It was a time of dashing figures like Sir Walter Raleigh, Sir Francis Bacon, and the earls of Leicester and Essex. It was a time when Catholics connived on behalf of Mary Stuart, and Protestants conspired against her; when Thomas Knox thundered from his pulpit in Scotland; when the irrepressible Francis Drake met the noble Medina-Sidonia in the English Channel and decided the fate of his country; and when the dangerous duke of Parma was kept by mere inches from taking England for his uncle, Philip II of Spain. It was a time when Spain bestrode the world like a great colossus, but England began to challenge; a time of the sea-dogs, undauntable men like Hawkins, Cavendish, Grenville, and Frobisher. But most of all, it was a time when England came of age, transforming herself from a remote island backwater,

"It is difficult to convey a proper appreciation of this amazing Queen, so keenly intelligent, so effervescing ... so imperious and regal. She intoxicated Court and Country.... [N]o woman without her superlative gifts could have attempted it without disaster."

J. E. Neale

Contributed by Glenn Feldman, Ph.D. candidate in History, Auburn University, Auburn, Alabama

which was likely the next province in the mighty Spanish Empire, to a country and a people to be reckoned with. And despite the presence of the great men who were her peers, the era was dominated by a woman: Elizabeth Tudor.

Elizabeth began life at Greenwich Palace on the Thames on September 7, 1533. Her father was the legendary king **Henry VIII** and her mother was Anne Boleyn, a lady-in-waiting to Henry's first wife, Catherine of Aragon. Obsessed with producing a male heir for the Tudor dynasty, Henry gained a divorce from Catherine in 1529, but at the expense of excommunication from the Roman Catholic Church and seriously stretching ties with Spain. When Anne Boleyn, the new queen, failed to produce a male heir, she too was disposed of; this time execution on grounds of adultery was used instead of divorce. Elizabeth was only two when her mother was beheaded in May 1536.

The young Elizabeth was educated by a team of Cambridge humanists led by Roger Ascham. Under their tutelage, she studied the classics, learned both classical and modern languages, and read historical and theological works. Through her studies, Elizabeth developed her intelligence and quick wit. Her household contained over 60 musicians, and she was, during her youth, reputed to speak six languages better than her native tongue.

When Henry VIII died in 1547, Elizabeth's half-brother became King Edward VI. During his reign, the young princess became romantically involved with Thomas Seymour, Lord High Admiral. Seymour, who was jealous of his own brother Edward, protector of the realm during Edward VI's minority, envisaged himself as Elizabeth's husband. In January 1549 the king had Seymour arrested, and he, Elizabeth, and her entire household were subjected to intense rounds of interrogation. In the end, Seymour was executed.

When Edward VI died in 1553, Elizabeth's half-sister **Mary Tudor** came to the throne. Like her mother Catherine of Aragon, Mary was pro-Spanish and Catholic. Soon after being crowned, she married Philip of Spain (soon to be **Philip II**), but Parliament blocked his accession to the English throne. Mary's Catholic sympathies triggered Protestant reaction in England that led to a series of plots against her government. When Protestant leaders looked to Elizabeth as a possible Protestant replacement, the English queen—known as Bloody Mary—had her half-sister arrested and sent to the Tower of London, and later to Woodstock. Until her own accession, Elizabeth had to survive by her wits and caution.

CHRONOLOGY

1549	Implicated in failed plot of Lord Seymour against reign of Edward VI
1554	Imprisoned after Sir Thomas Wyatt's failed rebellion against Mary I
1558	Acceded to the throne of England
1572	Interceded to save Mary, Queen of Scots; sent monetary aid to the Dutch rebels
1580	Knighted Francis Drake upon his successful circumnavigation of the world
1584	Discovered Throckmorton Plot; William the Silent assassinated
1585–87	Sent English army to aid Dutch rebels against Spain
1587	Signed death warrant of Mary, Queen of Scots; began war with Spain
1588	Defeated the "Invincible" Spanish Armada
1589	Sent aid to Henry IV of France against the Catholic League and Spain
1596	Drake repulsed at Puerto Rico and died off Panama
1601	Approved the execution of the Earl of Essex

Five years later, aware that she was near death, Mary named Elizabeth to be her successor. Thus, on March 17, 1558, the last Tudor monarch of England ascended the throne. Elizabeth enjoyed special support from the residents of London and from most English Protestants, but her reign would be threatened by others. The two events which dominated her long stay in power were the execution of **Mary, Queen of Scots** and the defeat of the Spanish Armada. While they occurred within two years of one another, the final settlement in each case was a long time in coming.

The Anglican Church Is Established

The new queen disappointed some of her earliest Protestant backers by showing herself to be apolitical on the religious issue—not at all inclined toward a radical Protestant regime. The height of Elizabeth's religious compromise occurred in 1563 when the Act of the Thirty-Nine Articles established the Anglican Church. While acknowledging the church's separateness from Rome, Elizabeth retained an episcopal structure and a liturgy largely dependent on the Catholic model.

Elizabeth I, queen of England, signs the death warrant of Mary Stuart (queen of Scots).

Meanwhile, the international scene was coalescing with the domestic and religious. Spain dominated Europe and the world, but Anglo-Spanish relations had been strained by Henry VIII's divorce from Catherine of Aragon. Since 1529, matters had grown worse. The Spanish colossus, led after 1556 by Philip II, seemed intent on controlling the world. Tiny England and her queen feared for their very existence, especially since a Protestant England had become a constant source of irritation to the Spaniards. In 1566 the Dutch provinces revolted against Spanish rule, and by 1572 Elizabeth authorized subsidies to help finance the rebels. Relations also deteriorated in America. Long jealous of Spain's monopoly on New World bullion, England and other countries allowed sea-dogs such as Francis Drake and Thomas Cavendish to plunder Spanish shipping whenever they could. Beaten and very nearly killed off San Juan de Ulua in 1567, Drake had pledged a lifelong personal war against the Spanish. From 1577 to 1580, he circumnavigated the world, becoming the first man after Ferdinand Magellan to accomplish the feat. In the process, he ravaged Spanish settlements on South America's unprotected west coast. Upon his return to England, Elizabeth, who had consistently apologized to Philip for Drake's exploits, brazenly knighted the privateer aboard the *Golden Hind* at Deptford. The act enraged Philip, who decided that war had become inevitable with England.

Elizabeth and her ministers in turn were alarmed by Spanish ascendancy elsewhere. In 1580, the duke of Alva conquered Portugal and annexed its huge empire for Spain. In June 1584, the French protector of the Dutch, the duke of Anjou (Alencon) died; a month later, **William the Silent** was assassinated. By 1585, **Alessandro Farnese,** the duke of Parma, had taken over 30 rebel towns in the Low Countries, including the thriving commercial entrepot ("trading port") of Antwerp. Many in England felt that the Protestant island was next in line for annexation.

In order to keep Catholic Spain and France at bay, Elizabeth had neither married nor had she executed Mary Stuart. She had dangled the prospect of marriage in front of Philip more than once, and had kept her cousin alive so that her foes would await a peaceful Catholic succession in England.

In the fall of 1585, Elizabeth sent an English army under her favorite, the earl of Leicester, to the Low Countries. Under strict orders not to accept any titles, he immediately disobeyed his queen. The next year saw the uncovering of yet another plan to assassinate her, the Babington

The religious issue eventually reached a crisis in the person of Mary, Queen of Scots. Born Mary Stuart, a cousin of the powerful Guise family of France, Mary became queen of France in 1559 when her Valois husband, Francis II, acceded to the throne. Francis died a year later, however, and Catholic Guise ascendancy at court was replaced by the Huguenot leader, the Admiral de Coligny. In 1561, Mary returned to her native Scotland and married a Stuart cousin, Robert Darnley. Promiscuous and quite unlike her intellectual cousin Elizabeth I, Mary soon took up with an Italian court musician named David Rizzio. When Darnley had Rizzio murdered, Mary consoled herself with a new lover, the earl of Bothwell. This time Darnley was killed, and Bothwell and Mary were implicated in his murder. Opposed by the Scottish nobles and the Presbyterian minister John Knox, Mary fled to England in the face of rebellion. There, in 1567, Elizabeth placed her under house arrest for the murder of Bothwell. Mary proved to be a constant thorn in Elizabeth's side. Openly Catholic in her sympathies, and next in line for the English throne, Mary became the vortex around which a series of Catholic plots revolved.

Plot. When Mary Stuart's complicity was convincingly proven, Elizabeth signed Mary's death warrant. She was executed on February 8, 1587.

The Scottish queen's execution coincided with the advent of a more repressive Elizabeth. She utilized intelligence networks all over Europe, especially in the Spanish ports. If the spies "failed to send true advertisement of all that was being done," Elizabeth laconically said, "she caused them to be hanged." The persecution of English Catholics also spread during the 1580s. Elizabeth sent several hundred to their deaths; she subjected at least 90 unfortunates to the horrors of the wrack, the manacles, and the Scavenger's Daughter, "an iron hoop that brought together its victim's head, hands and feet, so that they were trolled up together like a ball, and so crushed that the blood sprouted out at divers parts of the bodies." Torture was administered by Thomas Norton, Richard Young, and Richard Typecliffe, the latter "an unspeakable sadist who was driven by a fanatical hatred of Catholics."

Spanish King Seeks to Invade England

Mary Stuart's execution was the signal to Philip that war had arrived. While Parma's armies mopped up Leicester in the Netherlands, Philip planned his great enterprise, the invasion of England. The plan called for 130 ships manned by 30,000 men to sail up the English Channel, rendezvous with Parma off the Flemish coast, and ferry 22,000 handpicked men to England. Almost from the beginning, things went wrong with the complicated Spanish plan. In 1587, Francis Drake launched a preemptive strike against Cadiz that "singed the beard" of Philip and delayed embarkation for another year. In the interim, the ancient marquis de Santa Cruz, an admiral of at least the ability of Drake and the natural choice to lead the enterprise, died. In his stead, Philip placed the valiant but inexperienced duke of Medina-Sidonia. To his everlasting credit, Medina-Sidonia refused command of the venture, protesting that as a land general he was unqualified to lead a naval fleet. Philip brushed his reservations aside; he needed a man of Sidonia's fame to command obedience from a large fleet with so many noble captains.

When in July of 1588 the Spanish Armada set sail for England, pandemonium reigned on the little island. Charles Howard, Lord Admiral of the English fleet, urged Elizabeth, "For the love of Jesus Christ, Madam, awake thoroughly … and draw your forces round about you." Sir Francis Drake, the legendary sea captain and also an astute judge of character, repeatedly counseled caution,

warning of the dangers of Alessandro Farnese, generally considered the foremost soldier at the head of the foremost army of his day:

> I hope in God the Prince of Parma and the Duke of Sidonia shall not shake hands this few days…. We ought much more to have regard unto Parma and his soldiers than to Sidonia and his ships.

But 1588 was destined to be England's finest hour. One of Elizabeth's greatest gifts was the ability to attract men of real talent to her standard, in war and in peace. Now from all over the globe they rushed home to defend their homeland for their beloved Gloriana: men of character like Drake, John Hawkins, and Martin Frobisher. All of Europe watched breathlessly and awaited news from the Channel. Several years after the armada sailed, Sir **Walter Raleigh** frankly admitted that Elizabeth's land forces "were of no such force to encounter an Armie like unto that, wherewith it was intended that the prince of Parma should have landed in England." In 1588, beneath the bluster of wartime rhetoric, England's soldiers knew it too.

While the Spanish set sail, the duke of Guise captured Paris in the Day of the Barricades to remove the specter of any possible French intervention. Reviewing her modest troops at Tilbury, Elizabeth stirred them by saying that although she had "the body of a weak and feeble woman," she had "the heart and stomach of a King…. I think foul scorn that Parma or Spain, or any Prince of Europe should dare to invade the borders of my realm."

A nine-day running battle ensued between the armada and 130 English vessels. The English were smaller, quicker, had longer-range firepower, and could easily outmaneuver the bulky Spanish galleons; yet they could inflict no serious damage for fear of coming within range of the grappling hooks of the Spaniards. The massive Spanish crescent pushed on inexorably up the Channel, closer and closer to Flanders and Parma's 22,000 men.

At Calais, Medina-Sidonia committed his first and last mistake. Improperly anchoring the fleet for the night, he allowed the English to send a squadron of fireships into the Spanish vessels. Fires raged, panic seized the Spaniards, then chaos as single ships broke their cables and ran for open water. The smaller Englishmen pounced on the stragglers, and, as if by divine intervention, a "Great Protestant Wind" rose to destroy any semblance of a Spanish formation. Medina-Sidonia, realizing that a rendezvous or invasion was now out of the question, did his best to save the fleet;

the armada sailed north. Storm after storm seemed to come out of nowhere to pound the galleons as they desperately tried to sail around the British isles. Nearly three months after the battle, Geoffrey Felton, secretary for Ireland, went walking on the coast of Sligo. Although the secretary had seen slaughter and bloodshed in the Irish wars, he reported that "nothing matched the spectacle" that awaited him that autumn day. "In a walk of less than five miles," he counted more than "eleven hundred Spanish corpses on the beach, washed up, bloated and decaying, by the coming tide."

Half of the armada was lost and so, temporarily, was Philip's dream of making England into a Catholic province. Although he received news of the disaster with his customary stoicism, Philip was appalled, and privately wondered why God had allowed such misfortune. Medina-Sidonia took full responsibility for the debacle, and reported to Philip simply: "The troubles and miseries we have suffered cannot be described to your Majesty. They have been greater than have been seen in any voyage before." Historian Charles Wilson writes that "few contemporaries saw it as in any sense the … decisive triumph over Spain which it seemed to be to later chroniclers.… In the wake of the brief glory of 1588 injury piled upon injury, failure upon failure," for Elizabeth. Her invasion of Spain and Portugal in April 1589 proved to be "an expensive failure. It lost six or seven thousand Dutch and English troops and won nothing." Calais fell to Spanish arms in 1595. The following year, Sir Francis Drake was repulsed at Puerto Rico and died off Panama. In 1596 and 1597, Philip used his vast resources to send two fleets greater than the original armada to invade England. Fortunately for Elizabeth, these too were scattered by storms. The war gradually degenerated until it was ended by Elizabeth's death.

At home, Elizabeth's final years were dominated by controversy surrounding one of her favorite courtiers, Robert Dudley, the earl of Essex. Two of the queen's most able ministers were the Cecils: William, Lord Burghley and his son, Robert. During the 1590s, Elizabeth struggled to keep her government solvent while cultivating her "Cult of Gloriana," a pageant of royal excess designed to overawe her subjects. Essex and the Cecils increasingly clashed. At Burghley's death, Elizabeth snubbed Essex and awarded her highest council post to Robert Cecil. Then in 1599, she granted Essex command of an expeditionary force to subdue Tyrone's Rebellion in Ireland, but he botched the job miserably. His military failure was aggravated by his refusal to follow Elizabeth's orders, and his unauthorized signing of a truce with the rebels. Upon his return to court, Elizabeth reluctantly withdrew favor and patronage from the earl. In 1601, he attempted open revolt in London, but was caught and executed on February 25.

Elizabeth's reign, while darkened by religious persecution and unsavory episodes such as the executions of Essex and Mary Stuart, was most memorable for her successes at home and against Spain. Domestically, she strengthened the Anglican Church, a notable compromise in an age of religious fanaticism. She kept government finances stable, some critics have charged, through a policy of parsimony. Yet this too was a rare accomplishment for the period. Most of all, she embodied the spirit of her people, and their determination to survive and indeed prosper in the face of enormous odds.

Her court became the cultural center of its day; her reign was a time of unparalled literary achievement. Edmund Spenser dedicated his masterpiece, *The Fairie Queen*, to Elizabeth, and drama under Shakespeare and his contemporaries was one of the distinctive achievements of the Elizabethan age. Her death in 1603 marked the end of an era and the end of the Tudor dynasty.

SOURCES:

Erickson, Carolly. *The First Elizabeth*. Summit Books, 1983.

Laughton, John Knox, ed. *The Defeat of the Spanish Armada Anno 1588*. Burt Franklin, 1971.

Neale, J. E. *Queen Elizabeth*. Harcourt, 1934.

Parker, Geoffrey. *Spain and the Netherlands, 1559–1659*. Enslow Publishers, 1979.

Somerset, Anne. *Elizabeth*. Knopf, 1991.

Wilson, Charles. *Queen Elizabeth and the Revolt of the Netherlands*. University of California Press, 1970.

FURTHER READING:

Johnson, Paul. *Elizabeth I: A Biography*. Holt, 1974.

Smith, Lacy Baldwin. *Elizabeth Tudor: Portrait of a Queen*. Little, Brown, 1975.

Eugene of Savoy

(1663–1736)

General who led the armies of Austria in victories over the French and Turks, establishing Habsburg control over Northern Italy, Hungary, Serbia, and Transylvania, and ending the Turkish threat to Central Europe.

"Either I will take Belgrade, or the Turks will take me."

PRINCE EUGENE OF SAVOY

Prince Eugene's contribution to the Habsburg Empire during the 17th and 18th centuries was far-reaching: **Frederick the Great** called him the "real Emperor" behind the Habsburg throne; **Napoleon** considered him one of the seven greatest commanders of all time. Along with his "twin marshal" **John Churchill,** Duke of Marlborough, Prince Eugene of Savoy was the nemesis of King **Louis XIV**'s dreams of French expansion in Europe. Yet Eugene's greatest service to the Habsburgs was his defeat of the Turks, which ended their centuries-long threat to Central Europe and created the Danubian Monarchy that would be the core of Austrian power until 1918. His reputation on the battlefield was mirrored in the glory of his patronage of the art and architecture of the Baroque era at its apogee, reflected in the magnificent buildings and collections of his palaces, the Belvedere, Himmelfortgasse, and the Schlosshof. In addition to being a patron of the arts, Eugene was acquainted with some of the great minds of the Age of Genius, notably Rousseau, Leibniz, and Montesquieu.

Born in Paris on October 18, 1663, Eugene came from a mixed heritage. His paternal grand-

Name variations: Prinz Eugen. Born Eugene de Savoy-Carignan in France, of the Italian House of Savoy, on October 18, 1663; died on April 21, 1736; son of Eugene Maurice (prince of Savoy-Carignan) and Olympia Mancini (niece of Cardinal Mazarin); educated for the priesthood in France, studied mathematics; never married, no children. Successor: Princess Anna Victoria of Savoy, his niece.

Contributed by Kevin Cramer, Ph.D. candidate in history, Harvard University, Cambridge, Massachusetts

1683	Vienna besieged by Turks; Eugene joined imperial army at Passau; made colonel of cavalry regiment
1687	Made field-marshal lieutenant
1694	Appointed "General in Italy"
1697	Decisively defeated Turks at Zenta
1699	Treaty of Karlowitz signed
1700	Charles II of Spain died; War of Spanish Succession began
1701	Eugene took command of army in northern Italy
1703	Made president of Imperial War Council
1706	Defeated French at Turin; appointed Viceroy of Milan
1708	Joined Marlborough in Flanders; French driven out of Spanish Netherlands
1716	Eugene defeated Turks at Peterwardein
1717	Decisively defeated Turks; Belgrade captured
1718	Peace of Passarowitz with Turks
1734	War of Polish Succession; Eugene assumed command of imperial army on Rhine
1736	Died on April 21

mother was a Bourbon who had married into the Italian House of Savoy, and his father was Eugene Maurice of Savoy. His mother Olympia Mancini was a niece of **Cardinal Mazarin,** chief minister to the young Louis XIV. Eugene's origins and childhood were shadowed by the intrigues of Versailles, where Mazarin entertained hopes of marrying his niece Olympia to the future French king; indeed, Olympia was Louis's mistress for a time, prompting rumors that Louis was actually Eugene's father.

Though little is known of his youth, Eugene was reportedly a shy, sickly, ugly child, raised mainly by his paternal grandmother. He was tutored in mathematics and evidently groomed to enter the clergy. In fact, Louis's nickname for him was the "Little Abbe." Early on, Eugene aspired to a military career (his father had served in the French army, his eldest brother Louis in the army of Baden). Thus, in 1683, when Louis rejected his request for a commission, Eugene turned in desperation to Louis's great enemy—Habsburg emperor Leopold I, who was then facing a great Turkish host ("army") outside the walls of Vienna.

On July 26, Eugene left Paris and was pursued by royal agents intent upon bringing him back. He rode south along the Rhine and Danube, finally reaching the Habsburg imperial encampment at Passau in August—his horse and purse exhausted. Taking advantage of his brother's position in the army of Baden, he was accepted as a volunteer by the Margrave Louis of Baden. Thus, as a humble messenger, Eugene began his military career, joining the imperial army that was assembling to march to the relief of besieged Vienna.

Grand Vizier Kara Mustapha, the "scourge of humanity," had led his Turkish and Hungarian forces to the gates of Vienna in July of 1683. By mid-July, Vienna was encircled. Emperor Leopold and his court had fled to Passau on the Bavarian border, and Turkish horsemen pillaged the rich Danube valley. The German princes—somewhat contrary to their usual hostility toward the Habsburgs—rallied at this infidel threat to the seat of the Holy Roman Empire. Saxons, Bavarians, Franconians, and 16,000 Poles under King **John Sobieski** marched to the relief of Vienna. On September 12, the Polish cavalry descended from the hills around Vienna and routed the Turkish forces, which left 10,000 dead and captured. It was a spectacular, decisive victory; Vienna would never again be in such danger from Constantinople.

Distinguishing himself in the relief of Vienna, Eugene attracted the notice of Emperor Leopold and Duke Charles of Lorraine, the latter presenting him with a pair of golden spurs. That December, Eugene received his first command, the Kufstein Dragoon Regiment.

Hoping to liberate Turkish-occupied Hungary and Transylvania, Leopold decided to continue the campaign against the Turks, and it was during these campaigns, under the command of Duke Charles, that Eugene gained many valuable lessons in the art of warfare. He was wounded in the capture of Buda and, in the summer of 1687, participated in the imperial advance into Transylvania and Serbia. By December, he had been promoted to field-marshal lieutenant. He was badly wounded in the 1688 siege of Belgrade, but Transylvania was largely subdued and the Hungarian crown made a hereditary possession of the Habsburgs.

In the meantime, the French were on the move, advancing their territorial claims on the Rhine frontier and in northern Italy; in the spring of 1689, Louis's forces invaded the Palatinate. To oppose Louis's ambitions, in May Leopold entered William III's "Grand Alliance" with the English and Dutch. Eugene was sent to northern Italy to engage an alliance with Savoy, his ancestral House, as second in command under General Caraffa—a position he did not relish under a soldier he despised (Caraffa had directed the persecution of Protestants in Hungary, a policy which Eugene abhorred). Now a general in the cavalry, Eugene was in command of five regiments.

The campaigns in Italy proved indecisive. After serving in a series of subordinate positions, by 1694 Eugene had been appointed general in Italy, under the nominal command of Duke Victor of Savoy. More inconclusive campaigning followed, and in 1696 Austria, Spain, France, and Savoy signed a treaty that brought an uneasy truce in northern Italy.

The Empire, however, still faced difficulties in Hungary and on the middle Danube. Eugene requested a command in rebellious Hungary, and in July of 1697 he took command of the imperial forces there with orders to hold southern Hungary and Transylvania against the resurgent Turks.

The Turks Are Routed at Zenta

The Turks had recaptured Belgrade in 1690 and now—seven years later—their army again crossed the Danube into Transylvania. Eugene advanced into southern Transylvania and met the Sultan's forces on September 11, 1697, at Zenta on the Tisza River. Boldly attacking at twilight, Eugene's men drove the routed Turks into the river, inflicting great slaughter and killing the Grand Vizier in command. Immense caches of booty, weapons, and supplies fell into the hands of the victorious Austrians. Eugene went on to lead a cavalry raid into Bosnia, which ended in the sack of Sarajevo.

The Empire had gained great prestige from Zenta, and in November Eugene was greeted in Vienna by a triumphal procession and hailed as a savior of Europe and Christendom. At the same time, he gained significant influence at the imperial court, an advent accompanied by the inevitable rise of a faction in opposition to his escalating fame and honors.

By 1699, Austria had concluded the Treaty of Karlowitz with the Turks, bringing Hungary and Transylvania firmly under imperial control. Vienna had become the center of a large Central European empire based on the Danube basin. Eugene, the major architect of this expansion, returned to a revitalized court society in Vienna as an accepted and influential member of the aristocracy and the ministerial circle around the Emperor.

With the Turkish menace subdued, the Habsburgs were free to turn their attention to the French threat. A new source of conflict was emerging in the West, as the dynastic heads of Europe anxiously awaited the death of Spain's Charles II. In November of 1700, Charles died, leaving his throne to Louis's grandson Philip of Anjou with the stipulation that he renounce any future claim to the French crown. Emperor Leopold rejected this settlement and prepared for war to support the Habsburg claim to the Spanish throne. By the spring of 1701, Eugene again found himself in Italy, facing the French forces with an ill-equipped, poorly supplied army of some 30,000 men. He resolved upon a bold plan of campaign to reconquer Milan. In one of the most audacious forced marches in the history of warfare, Eugene led his ragged soldiers on a wide swing east through the forbidding and snowy defiles of the South Tyrolean Alps to take the French by surprise, prompting Louis's rueful comment that Eugene had "violated all the precepts of warfare."

Under General Catinat, the French withdrew rapidly, giving up most of Lombardy. General Villeroy took over in September and challenged Eugene at Chiari near Milan, where Eugene defeated him and inflicted heavy losses. This initial success marked the beginning of a great popular enthusiasm for Eugene, particularly in England.

In the spring of 1702, he confronted 80,000 French with a force of a little over 30,000—many of whom were ill. The dearth of proper supplies and equipment continued, a situation made worse by the Pope's order that Italians in the countryside should deny food to the imperial soldiery. Desertion was rife. In August of 1702, Eugene was forced into a desperate attack on the French camp at Luzzara, and the result was a costly stalemate.

Following a grim winter, Eugene traveled to Vienna in January of 1703 to personally ask for more support and, if possible, to challenge the inept and corrupt ministers advising Emperor Leopold. By the summer of 1703, it was clear the Empire faced a serious crisis. The Hungarians were again in revolt, the Bavarians were again marching, and the chronic fiscal infirmity of the Austrian state was worse than ever. In a move intended to restore order and direction to the war effort, Leopold appointed Eugene president of the Imperial War Council.

An Alliance with Marlborough

The French and Bavarian incursion on the upper Danube was the immediate concern in spring of 1704. Eugene sought close cooperation with the English and Dutch forces in the Netherlands under the command of John Churchill, Duke of Marlborough, and one of history's most famed military collaborations was about to be born.

Marlborough's army set out on its epic march to the Danube on May 19, marching up the Rhine into Germany, where it joined the imperial forces under Eugene in Württemberg. Taking an instant liking to each other, the two leaders began the joint planning of the coming campaign. Then, on August 13, 1704, 52,000 Allied soldiers engaged 56,000 French and Bavarians on the heights above the tiny village of Blenheim on the Danube, north of Ulm. While Eugene's forces met and held the Bavarians, Marlborough's calvary struck the French-held center with crushing impact. At the end of the day, 11,000 French were taken prisoner, along with vast hauls of material. It was a momentous victory for the Grand Alliance, marking the first time one of Louis's vaunted armies had been destroyed in battle.

In April of 1705, Eugene returned to Italy, recognizing this region's importance as the main Habsburg bulwark against French expansion. On May 5, Leopold died and Joseph I, a staunch supporter of Eugene, ascended the Habsburg throne. Eugene planned to break the French siege of Turin over the winter, fighting a war of diversion to hold down as many French soldiers as possible. Nothing much was achieved that year, but in the summer of 1706, with his army revived by an influx of German mercenaries and English loans, Eugene advanced westward along the Po valley in a quick march that caught the French unawares. On September 6, he met the French outside the walls of Turin, the seat of his ancestral House, and inflicted a decisive defeat on them, lifting the siege. The consequences of this victory were significant; not only was Eugene's reputation as a military genius sealed, but the French defeat ended their last hopes of hegemony over the states of northern Italy and saw the beginning of Habsburg dominance in the region for the next 150 years. By the end of 1707, Eugene was able to negotiate complete French withdrawal from Italy, becoming in the process Viceroy of Milan.

Prince Eugene departed for the Netherlands in March of 1708 to join Marlborough. Eugene proposed a campaign to secure the entire Lower Rhine for the Allies, and in July the two leaders led an invasion of Flanders that culminated in the victory at Oudenarde on the Scheldt river—a victory that owed much to Eugene's meticulous planning and staff work.

With the Spanish Netherlands lost, in the spring of 1709 Louis began to seek peace. The war went on, however, as the Allies, particularly Emperor Joseph, refused to contemplate any compromise on the issue of the Spanish succession. For his part, Eugene had advised the Emperor to make peace. While demonstrating French resilience, the costly Allied victory at Malplaquet in September also encouraged the Tory peace party in England—which was to have ominous consequences for Eugene and the imperial cause.

At this point, neither side was willing to make significant concessions. The Grand Alliance, however, was showing signs of strain. Austria was bedeviled by a precarious financial situation and continued unrest in Hungary. The English were wavering in their support of the war due to the pressures of internal politics, as the Tories gained influence with Queen **Anne.**

In April of 1711, Joseph died and in October, Charles VI ascended the imperial throne. At this time the Tory ministry in England indicated its willingness to acknowledge **Philip V** as King of Spain as part of a general peace agreement. Violently opposed to a peace based on this principle, Austria sent Eugene on a mission to London in January of 1712 in the hope that he might persuade the English to stay in the war. Despite the popular enthusiasm that greeted his arrival, he made no headway against the Tory ministers and returned to the Continent to report the failure of his mission.

He at once threw himself into the preparations for a spring campaign in Flanders. There is some evidence that the English communicated information about his plans to the French. In any case, the English forces soon came under the "Restraining Orders," which limited them to a strictly defensive stance desired by the Tory government. In July of 1712, the Dutch were defeated at Denain and by October the French had retaken most of their fortified towns on the Lower Rhine, threatening Eugene's supply lines and forcing him to retreat.

Meanwhile, the English had concluded an armistice with the French. Vienna, for its part, was also forced to move toward peace, however reluctantly. Peace between France, England, and the Netherlands came with the Treaty of Utrecht in 1713. Austria came to terms with the Treaty of Rastadt in 1714. The War of the Spanish Succession was over.

But once again the eternal threat to the East, Ottoman Turkey, cast its shadow across the Danube frontier. With victories over Russia and Venice in 1711 and 1714, the Sultan again moved up the Danube. Eugene's army met the Turks on the Sava river in southern Hungary, and 30,000 Turks were killed in August's great battle of Peterwardein. Moving quickly to exploit his victory, Eugene invaded Turkish Transylvania (the Banat) and captured the fortress of Temesevar in October. He was then decorated by Clement XI, the same Pope who had denied his soldiers food in 1702. The vital frontier region of the Banat was put under Austrian administration.

Belgrade Falls to Eugene

Renewing the campaign in 1717, Eugene set his sights on the capture of the stronghold of Belgrade, which would finally secure Central Europe from the Sultan's loyalists, and by June his forces had infested the city. In August, the Turkish relief army arrived and battle was joined on the 15th. The Turks were routed and Belgrade fell to Eugene—the final crowning victory of his career. The Treaty of Passarowitz, signed in July of 1718, formally surrendered the Banat, Belgrade, and most of Serbia to Emperor Charles. The Danubian empire of the Habsburgs, created largely by Eugene's victories, was to endure for the next 200 years.

By 1720, Eugene's health was on the decline, as was his power and influence in Vienna following almost 40 years of continuous campaigning. He turned most of his energy to his books, art collections, and palace gardens, particularly at the opulent Belvedere, perhaps the finest example of "Imperial Baroque." This palace's immense grounds and gardens included an orangery, an aviary, and a zoo. Eugene also spent time hunting at his lodge, the Schlosshof, outside Vienna, frequently in the company of his mistress of many years, the Hungarian Countess Elenora Batthyany.

Though his political influence was on the wane, he worked with Emperor Charles to undermine the French and British influence in Germany by means of alliances with Russia and Prussia in 1726 and 1728, respectively. But he was also willing to entertain an accommodation with London and Paris in return for recognition of the Pragmatic Sanction of 1713, which guaranteed the succession of Emperor Charles's daughter **Maria Theresa.**

In 1733, however, Austria again found itself at war with France and Bavaria, as France supported a rival candidate to the vacant Polish throne. During the "War of the Polish Succession," Eugene, now 70, took up arms for the last time. Commanding the imperial army on the Rhine in the spring of 1734, he was forced into a defensive strategy, as Austria was without allies. When peace was made in 1735, Austria was forced to give up Naples, Sicily, and Lorraine, the latter loss a serious breach of the imperial frontier on the Rhine.

Prince Eugene of Savoy died on April 21, 1736. His body, worn out in the service of the Habsburg emperors, was buried in the Krüzkappel in St. Stephen's Cathedral in Vienna. His heart was conveyed to the Savoy family tomb in Turin.

SOURCES:

Dunn, Richard S. *The Age of Religious Wars, 1559–1715.* 2nd ed. Norton, 1979.

Evans, R. J. W. *The Making of the Habsburg Monarchy, 1550–1700.* Clarendon Press, 1979.

Frischauer, Paul. *Prince Eugene.* Translated by Amethe Smeaton, Morrow, 1934.

Henderson, Nicholas. *Prince Eugene of Savoy.* Weidenfeld & Nicolson, 1964.

McKay, Derek. *Prince Eugene of Savoy.* Thames & Hudson, 1977.

MacMunn, George. *Prince Eugene: Twin Marshal with Marlborough.* Sampson, Low, Marston, 1933.

FURTHER READING:

Kann, Robert A. *A History of the Habsburg Empire, 1526–1918.* University of California Press, 1974.

McKay, Derek, and H. M. Scott. *The Rise of the Great Powers, 1648–1815.* Longman, 1983.

Wolf, John B. *The Emergence of the Great Powers, 1685–1715.* Harper, 1951.

Alessandro Farnese

(1545–1592)

Duke of Parma, who led the Spanish suppression of the Dutch Revolt, doubled the size of Spain's holdings in the Netherlands through his conquests, and ensured Spanish rule in the southern provinces for another 129 years.

Name variations: Alesandro or Alexander Farnese, Duke of Parma. Born on August 27, 1545, in Rome, Italy; died on December 3, 1592, in Arras, France; son of Ottavio Farnese (the second Duke of Parma) and Margaret of Austria (the illegitimate daughter of Charles V, the Habsburg Holy Roman Emperor and king of Spain); married: Maria (the Portuguese infanta); children: Margherita, Ranuccio and Odoardo. Descendants: Elizabeth Farnese, wife of Philip V, mother of Spanish King Carlos III, and Philip of Bourbon. Predecessor: Don John of Austria. Successor: (disputed) Count Peter-Ernest Mansfelt and Don Pedro Enriquez, Count of Fuentes.

S erving as Spain's governor-general of the Netherlands from 1578 to 1592, Alessandro Farnese, the third duke of Parma, distinguished himself with a tolerance and restraint uncommon in his day. These qualities, combined with diplomatic acumen and military astuteness, made him Spain's most successful military leader during the Revolt of the Netherlands (1566–1648). Throughout his 15-year tenure, Farnese checked the redoubtable **William of Orange,** stymied the United Provinces, restored and cemented Spanish hegemony (dominance) in the largely Catholic southern provinces, and crowned his considerable achievements with a devastating offensive.

Farnese was born the scion of a distinguished Italian family. His great-grandfather, Pope Paul III, had created the Duchy of Parma and Piacenza in 1534, carving it out of rich papal lands for one of his sons. Originally, the family had risen to prominence in Renaissance Italy as mercenaries who served the Roman pontiffs and married well politically. One such union matched Ottavio Farnese and Margaret of Austria, an illegitimate daughter of **Charles V,** Habsburg Holy Roman

"A genius … with an almost poetic intellect … the finest soldier and most scrupulous diplomatist of his day."

JOHN L. MOTLEY

Contributed by Glenn Feldman, Ph.D. candidate in History, Auburn University, Auburn, Alabama

Emperor and king of Spain. On August 27, 1545, Margaret gave birth to a son named Alessandro.

In order to guarantee his father's questionable allegiance to the Spanish crown, the family sent the child to reside at the court of his uncle, **Philip II** of Spain. At the age of 20, Farnese journeyed to the Low Countries where his mother was serving as regent. Once there he married Maria, a princess of Portugal. After several quiet years, Farnese served Spain brilliantly at the epic naval Battle of Lepanto. With this experience, he returned to Parma but yearned for further military and political action. It was the revolt in the Netherlands that finally presented Farnese with his opportunity.

Acquired through marriage in 1506, Spain held all of the Netherlands intact and would continue to do so until the end of the Thirty Years' War in 1648. In Farnese's day, growing disaffection with the overbearing policies of Philip II, loss of privileges, and simmering religious animosities combined to trigger the 1566 armed Dutch Revolt against Habsburg rule. For seven years, Spain's notorious duke of Alva acted as governor-general of the region. Despite Spanish military victories, the period was marked by the vicious repression of Protestant rebels and "heretics" by Alva's Council of Troubles—aptly dubbed the "Council of Blood." Alva's arrest and execution of two rebel leaders did little to crush the revolt but went far toward fomenting a more rigid defiance of Philip. The executions of perhaps 12,000 other rebels effectively etched Alva's name in blood in the annals of European history.

Following Alva's recall in 1573, Philip installed his half-brother, **Don John of Austria,** hero of Lepanto, as the new ruler in the Netherlands. In 1577, Don John called upon his nephew, Alessandro Farnese, to help put down the rebellion in the Dutch provinces. The next year, Farnese distinguished himself at Gembloux as Spanish forces crushed the Dutch. Upon John of Austria's deathbed endorsement in 1578, Philip formally named 33-year-old Farnese to accede to the post of governor-general of the Netherlands.

He Negotiates Treaty of Arras

That year, Farnese captured the French-speaking provinces of the Netherlands in rapid order. Demonstrating a thorough understanding of the diverse nature of the Dutch Revolt, he negotiated a tolerant agreement with the southern Walloon provinces at the May 1579 Treaty of Arras. The treaty, his first great diplomatic success, would keep the South solidly Spanish and Catholic until

CHRONOLOGY

1571	Assisted his uncle Don John of Austria at the epic naval Battle of Lepanto
1578	Acceded to the post of Spanish governor-general of the Netherlands
1579	Negotiated the Treaty of Arras; Union of Utrecht was signed
1580	Began the offensive which captured over 30 Dutch rebel towns by 1585
1584	Francis, Duke of Anjou died; William, Prince of Orange murdered
1585	Parma completed the successful seige of Antwerp
1586–87	Decisively outfought the Earl of Leicester and the English forces in the Netherlands
1588	Missed the crucial rendezvous with the Duke of Medina-Sidonia's "Invincible" Armada
1590	Invaded France; lifted Henry of Navarre's siege of Paris
1592	Second invasion of France; again defeated Navarre, at Rouen

1714. Only one month later, Farnese struck a tremendous blow to the prestige of his most prominent rival, William, prince of Orange. On June 27, Parma's forces completed the successful seige of the powerful, walled town of Maastricht. Farnese was not to experience defeat of any kind for the next nine years.

Historians have described Alessandro Farnese in glowing terms: "able and resourceful, rich and cultivated, subtle and shrewd." Garrett Mattingly depicted him as "easily the first captain of his age." Simply put, the duke of Parma embodied both military genius and diplomatic talent. He was shrewdly tolerant in a way that contrasted sharply with previous Spanish administrators such as Alva; still, he remained the most feared and respected military strategist and tactician of his day.

At Arras, the Spanish had made several vital concessions: in return for allegiance to Philip, Spain acceded to the withdrawal of Farnese as governor and the evacuation of all foreign troops from his Army of Flanders. Left with only a pitiful remnant of mostly Walloon malcontents, Farnese—now strictly military commander in the Netherlands—avoided pitched battles and protracted sieges. Still, his policies continued to be successful.

The Walloon leaders themselves broke the impasse. Fearing an invasion from the northern Protestant provinces, and realizing the paralysis of Farnese's army without its Spanish complement, they appealed to Philip to recall both Farnese and his Spanish soldiers.

Describing this change of heart as "a miracle," Farnese spent most of 1582 regrouping his famed infantry. Farnese called his troops "asphalt soldiers ... tough, disciplined and, born to fight with the people of the Netherlands." Indeed, Spain's feared infantry did not lose a pitched battle in any theater of the world for 150 years. Both admirers and adversaries considered them the "pride of the Hapsburgs ... the defence of Christendom ... [and] the sole foundation of the Monarchy." By the following year, Farnese's preparations were complete, and he was ready to implement a strategy that would take over 30 fortified towns by 1585.

Success was instantaneous and spectacular. In July and August 1583, he took the walled towns of Dunkirk, Nieupoort, Veurne, Diksmuide, and Berges. In October, he moved his armies to the northeast and captured four large towns along the Scheldt estuary. Simultaneously, he sent a small army north to take various towns in Friesland. In the east and along the Rhine, other Dutch towns fell one after another.

For 1584, Farnese's strategy was to starve the great towns along the Scheldt into submission. Realizing their position as untenable, Aalst's English garrison sold the town in February. On April 7, Ypres surrendered after a six-month seige. Bruges soon followed suit. Dendermonde withstood one fierce Spanish assault, but it too fell in August. The next month, Farnese completed his pacification of Flanders when Ghent capitulated, and after subduing the large towns of the province of Brabant, he turned his attention to the great town of Antwerp.

Two noteworthy events took place before the Spanish invested Antwerp. The first was the June 10, 1584, death of Francis, duke of Anjou (brother of Henry III and the last Valois heir to the French throne), who had been made lord over the Netherlands by a desperate rebel States-General in 1581. Though Calvinist Holland and Zealand had protested the solicitation of a Catholic's aid, the majority of the States had hoped Francis would be able to shield the Dutch from Farnese's inexorable advance. Although Anjou had brought a French army to aid the rebels, he fared poorly against Farnese and could not prevent the Spaniards from taking five cities by 1582. The second significant event followed precisely one month after Anjou's death when an assassin killed William of Orange in his own home on the Delft. Although William too had been unable to withstand Farnese's assaults, he had been the great, spiritual leader of the rebels. His loss was considered insurmountable.

Farnese Prepares To Invade Antwerp

With the deaths of Anjou and Orange, and the remarkable success of his own campaigns, Farnese prepared to invade Antwerp in July 1584. The city—surrounded by walls five miles in circumference—was considered one of the most strongly fortified towns in Europe, as well as one of the richest. When Farnese ordered the construction of a pontoon bridge on the Scheldt below the city in order to cut Antwerp's access to the sea, Antwerp's leaders responded by opening the dikes and flooding the land held by his army. The dikes themselves remained above water, and "became the scene of bitter and bloody encounters between the picked men of the two sides." While the Spaniards enjoyed the better of these encounters, they had to brave the oncoming winter "with bare legs and empty stomachs" outside the city's gates.

Farnese meanwhile implored Philip to send more money for their survival. His letters often betrayed his frustration with his uncle's parsimony:

> The millions promised me have arrived in bits and morsels and with so many ceremonies that I haven't ten crowns at my disposal. The enterprise at Antwerp is so great and heroic that ... if your Majesty knew [it] you would estimate what we have done more highly than you do, and not forget us so utterly, leaving us to die of hunger.... God will grow weary of working miracles for us.

In early March, news of the fall of Brussels helped lift the Spanish morale. About this same time, Farnese's men finished constructing their massive bridge, an engineering miracle for its day. At 2,400 feet long, the bridge rested on piles driven 75 feet deep by a machine invented expressly for this purpose. Regarding it as "his sepulchre or his pathway into Antwerp," Farnese protected it with over 200 large cannon.

After Dutch fireships destroyed a 200-foot span of the bridge, blew up 800 Spanish troops, and nearly killed Farnese, the Spanish decided to act. On May 26, they clashed with the Dutch, English, and Scottish defenders of the city in the decisive Battle of Kowenstyn. For eight hours, over

5,000 men struggled on the slippery surface of the narrow, mile-long dike. Following a sharp engagement which favored the defenders, Farnese "descended suddenly … like a deity from the clouds," inspiring the Spaniards to rally and rout the defenders. Though the English and Scottish soldiers resisted to the last man, most were cut to ribbons. About 2,000 of Antwerp's stout defenders lost their lives in the engagement. On August 17, 1585, Antwerp fell.

Farnese and the Spanish appeared unstoppable. The deaths of Anjou and Orange had been major blows, but the fall of Antwerp was even more frightening to Protestant leaders like Queen **Elizabeth** of England. To safeguard her own interests, Elizabeth realized that she somehow had to stop Farnese in the Netherlands. For Farnese, the path lay open to sweep into the northern provinces and crush the Dutch Revolt for good. Elizabeth knew she had to act. If Farnese completed his conquest of the Protestant provinces, England might be next. On August 20, 1585, just three days after the fall of Antwerp, Elizabeth reluctantly, and with great fear, agreed to the Treaty of Nonsuch with the rebels—in effect, openly declaring war on Spain.

The English declined sovereignty over the Netherlands, but the queen sent her favorite, the earl of Leicester, to act as governor-general. By Christmas, 8,000 Englishmen were fighting in the Netherlands. There was no love lost between Protestant England and Catholic Spain. But along with this hatred also came the fear that the formidable power of Spain might swallow up England as the "ravenous Crocodile doeth the smallest fish."

Philip's reaction was fast and furious. In Spanish ports, he seized all English and Dutch shipping. He also ordered his advisers to prepare a study for the invasion of England. Meanwhile, Farnese continued to enjoy unimpeded success, concentrating his 1586 efforts along the Maas and the Rhine despite the English presence. "Sadly outgeneraled" by Farnese, Leicester gave up Grave, Meghen, Batenburg, Venlo, Neuss, and Mors; yet he consoled himself and his queen by exaggerating the losses of his nemesis. The English general had begun his defense of the Dutch by portraying Farnese as "dejected … melancholy" and "out of courage." Farnese seemed only mildly amused by this assessment when he informed Philip that the "English think they are going to do great things and already consider themselves masters of the field." The only real moment of concern for the Spanish came at Grave, where Farnese lost the hind half of his horse to a cannonball. Within a

few weeks, the duke had swept the English out of every town in the area.

The Spanish spent most of 1587 preparing for the invasion of England. Accordingly, Philip sent orders for his nephew to mass his troops on the Flanders coast. There, his strategists foresaw a rendevous between Farnese's hand-picked army and the 130 ships of the Spanish Armada. In preparation, Farnese besieged the deep-water port of Sluys in August. Despite the resistance of England's best troops and commanders, the Spaniards took the town. Soon thereafter Devanter's Anglo-Irish garrison betrayed their town to Farnese. At Zutphen, the duke engaged Leicester in the Battle of Warnsfield, defeated him, and took that town also. By now it was apparent to all that Leicester's rule in the Netherlands was "little short of a continuous disaster."

Historians since Sir **Walter Raleigh** have speculated on what might have happened if Farnese's army had ever reached England. In 1614, Raleigh wrote that the English were "of no such force to encounter an Armie like unto that." Geoffrey Parker concurred that Farnese's invasion force constituted the "cream of the most famous and formidable army in Europe…. The English were terrified of them."

Spanish Formation Is Broken

But disaster struck in the summer of 1588. England's admirals, assisted by a great "Protestant Wind," managed to break the formation of the Spaniards. The Dutch and English bottled up Farnese's transport barges in their ports and prevented the crucial rendezvous with the fleet. Rightly or not, Farnese received much of the blame for the disaster. In Spain, his prestige plummeted.

On the heels of the armada debacle, Philip decided to intervene openly in the civil war raging in France over the succession of Henry III. Accordingly, he ordered Farnese to invade France. In 1590, literally "sick to death," Farnese, at the head of a 20,000-man army, confronted Henry of Navarre near Paris and defeated the great French general, thereby lifting the seige of the city. Meanwhile, in the Netherlands, the rebels took advantage of his absence to seize Breda, their first success in over 12 years. Maurice of Nassau, the second son of William of Orange, also rose to prominence in Farnese's absence. Disregarding his uncle's urgent entreaties to continue subduing the French Protestants, Farnese rushed instead to the north of the Netherlands to turn back the rebel offensive at Nijmegen. He paused at home in July

1591 to inform the King of his disobedience. A furious Philip retaliated by slashing his nephew's economic support in order to compel his obedience. Instead of helping, this action led to the mutiny of 2,000 of Farnese's finest troops at Diest.

In August 1591, an exhausted and sick duke of Parma retired to Spa to convalesce. By November he had raised another army of 22,000 and was preparing a second French invasion. With Farnese's absence in France, Henry Navarre's military reputation and victories had been steadily growing. But all of that was to change when the two met again at Rouen in 1592. Spanish troops wounded the Frenchman, and Farnese lifted his seige despite Navarre's English allies. After Rouen, Farnese laid seige to Caudebac, where he was severely wounded. Still, the town fell. Exhausted and ill, Farnese returned to the Netherlands late in the year. He died at Arras on December 3, 1592. Farnese's death brought immediate confusion and deterioration to the Spanish position in the Netherlands. One of Spain's most brilliant lights had been extinguished.

SOURCES:

Mattingly, Garrett. *The Armada.* Riverside Press, 1959.

Motley, John L. *History of the United Netherlands.* Harper, 1900.

Parker, Geoffrey. *The Army of Flanders and the Spanish Road, 1567-1659.* Cambridge University Press, 1972.

———. *The Dutch Revolt.* Cornell University Press, 1977.

———. *Spain and the Netherlands, 1559–1659.* Enslow, 1979.

Pierson, Peter. *Philip II of Spain.* Thames & Hudson, 1975.

Thompson, S. Harrison. *Europe in the Renaissance and Reformation.* Harcourt, 1963.

Wilson, Charles. *Queen Elizabeth and the Revolt of the Netherlands.* University of California Press, 1970.

FURTHER READING:

Geyl, Peter. *The Revolt of the Netherlands, 1555–1609.* Williams and Norgate, 1932 and 1945.

Wedgwood, C. V. *William the Silent, Prince of Orange.* Yale University Press, 1944.

Millicent Garrett Fawcett

(1847–1929)

British feminist, who led the nonviolent campaign for votes for women.

"An unshakable reasonableness was evident in everything she did."

RAY STRACHEY

At the turn of the century, Millicent Garrett Fawcett was Britain's most important leader in the fight for women's suffrage. Although people today often identify the militant **Emmeline Pankhurst** and her daughters with the struggle, Fawcett contributed more than anyone else to British women obtaining the right to vote in parliamentary elections. Valuing rational thought and her own privacy, she rejected the cult of personality that surrounded more dramatic and emotional leaders.

Changing times make Fawcett appear old-fashioned, an unchanging adherent of the ideology of individual rights popular in the mid-19th century who was surprisingly conventional in many of her opinions. She seems frozen in the late 1860s, opposing free schools as undermining a healthy spirit of independence, defending the severe sexual code that prevailed among the middle classes during her youth, and glorying in an unthinking patriotism. The modern feminist Ann Oakley described Fawcett's life as "marked by monotony and by great tranquility of spirit, and by no detectable change or development in her moral philosophy or political attitudes." Significantly,

Contributed by David M. Fahey, Professor of History, Miami University, Oxford, Ohio

Name variations: after marriage, generally called Mrs. Henry Fawcett. Born Millicent Garrett in 1847 at Aldeburgh, Suffolk, England; died in London in 1929; daughter of Newson and Louisa (Dunnell) Garrett; sister of Elizabeth Garrett Anderson; married: Henry Fawcett, 1867 (died 1884); children: (one daughter) Philippa.

CHRONOLOGY

1867	Joined England's first women's suffrage committee
1882	Married Women's Property Act passed
1884	Third Reform Act enfranchised a majority of rural men
1886–1903	Fawcett active in Liberal Unionist party, opposed to Home Rule for Ireland
1897	Elected president of National Union of Women's Suffrage Societies
1901	Chaired government inquiry into conditions in concentration camps for Boer civilians
1913	National Union entered into an alliance with the Labour Party
1914–18	First World War
1918	People Act enfranchised women, age 30 and older, together with all men, age 21 and older
1919	First woman member of Parliament
1924	Received the Grand Cross of the Order of the British Empire
1928	Women enfranchised on equal basis with men
1929	First woman member of British Cabinet

nobody has bothered to write a full-length biography of this unrevolutionary suffragist since 1931 when a friend did the rather bland, official life. As a result, Fawcett is a half-forgotten giant of British reform.

Millicent Garrett was born at Aldeburgh, Suffolk, in England, on June 11, 1847, one of the younger children in a large, middle-class family. She had a close relationship with her admiring and independent-minded father, but she rejected her mother's rigidly evangelical religion. Although Milly, as she was known to family and friends, obtained very little formal schooling, she benefited from a supportive family that expected much of her. Her older sister **Elizabeth (Garrett Anderson)** set an example by becoming Britain's second woman physician.

In 1867, the 19-year-old Millicent Garrett married Henry Fawcett (who had previously proposed to her sister Elizabeth and to the prominent feminist, Bessie Rayner Parkes). Already committed before her marriage to liberal principles in politics and economics, Millicent Garrett Fawcett fully shared the interests and convictions of her husband and served for several years as his secretary. A Liberal Party member of the House of Commons, he had been blinded in a shooting accident ten years earlier. As she read what he had to read and wrote what he had to write, she acquired a political education, along with one in economics, the subject which he taught at Cambridge University. She also learned from her husband's friends, including John Stuart Mill, the most influential liberal thinker in mid-Victorian Britain.

As a young woman, Fawcett pursued many interests. Along with a novel, she wrote two books on economics, one in collaboration with her husband; worked to promote higher education for women, particularly Newnham College at Cambridge where her daughter eventually studied; and, most important, enlisted in the campaign to provide women with the vote, in her opinion the key to equality between the sexes. She also joined the first organization advocating votes for women, the London Women's Suffrage Committee.

She Becomes a Leader for Suffragists

After her husband's sudden death in 1884, leaving her a widow at age 37, she made the cause of women's suffrage her life's work. Following the death of the longtime suffrage leader Lydia Becker in 1890, Fawcett emerged as the most influential figure in Britain's small band of suffragists. When the organizations united in 1897 as the National Union of Women's Suffrage Societies, she became the first president (and served until her retirement in 1919).

Although most suffragist women supported the Liberal Party, Fawcett broke with the Liberals in 1886 out of opposition to Irish Home Rule, a proposal that Ireland enjoy political autonomy but not independence. She was active in the new breakaway Liberal Unionist Party that cooperated closely with the Conservative Party, but she never put political party over her principles. For instance, in the mid-1890s, she offended many important men in the Conservative-Liberal Unionist alliance when she tried to hound out of politics a Conservative who had seduced a young woman and then failed to marry her. In 1901, her prominence in Liberal Unionist affairs earned her an appointment to head an investigation of conditions at interment camps for Boer civilians during the South African war. Some old friends accused her of collaborating with brutal imperialism. In 1903, she broke with the Liberal Unionist party because she could not support its leader Joseph Chamberlain in his new policy of tariff reform. Fawcett remained loyal to the mid-19th-century principles of free trade and laissez-faire.

The problems confronting the suffragists were complex. Although some women could vote in local government elections (and hold office), none could vote for members of the national legislature. Influential newspapers scoffed at the notion of women voting in parliamentary elections (which might deal with questions leading to war) and feared the political role of women (i.e., making possible moral reform legislation to restrict the sale of alcoholic drink). A majority of the House of Commons, particularly Liberal Party members, probably sympathized with women's suffrage in principle, but this did not mean voting for a bill that would enfranchise women. Part of the problem was the personal opposition of turn-of-the-century Liberal leaders **William Gladstone** and Herbert Asquith. Another part of the problem was the absence of universal male suffrage. If the vote went only to those women who met the existing requirements for men, the change would likely benefit the Conservative Party by enfranchising prosperous widows but not married women. Moreover, some politicians tried to entangle the enfranchisement of any women with the more controversial reform of universal male suffrage. Finally, women's suffrage never became the central question for ordinary voters and politicians in the way that, for instance, Irish Home Rule did.

Fawcett struggled to keep her cause alive when prospects for success seemed remote. Known for her sense of humor, she never allowed herself to be discouraged: she was an inexhaustible worker who without the aid of a secretary answered all her correspondence on the day it was received. Though she detested speechmaking, she became an effective public speaker whose unemotional speeches were distinguished by the clarity of her logic. Self-reliant, she ordinarily traveled on foot to her interviews with politicians even when that meant walking for miles and, a bit old-fashioned, she refused to have a telephone in her home.

But in the early 20th century, women's suffrage could not be ignored. Beginning in 1905, the organization headed by Emmeline Pankhurst and her daughters **Christabel** and **Sylvia** adopted militant tactics: they disrupted political meetings, destroyed private and public property and, when arrested, resisted with hunger strikes. Although Fawcett and her much larger National Union rejected such tactics, the constitutional suffragists benefited from the attention that the militants provoked.

Probably some form of women's suffrage would have been enacted, sooner or later, even without the First World War, but the war of 1914–18 promoted women's suffrage in many ways. The contribution of women to the war effort converted some former antisuffragists and allowed others a pretext for a change of position that political expediency had forced. The desire to enfranchise voteless soldiers forced politicians to deal with a general enlargement of the suffrage. Prime Minister Asquith, an old enemy of women's suffrage, was replaced by the more sympathetic **David Lloyd George.** On the other hand, the war presented a brief but severe challenge to Fawcett's leadership of the National Union in 1915. She wanted to use the suffragist organization to work for military victory. In contrast, pacifist-minded officers wanted to negotiate a peace without insisting on the defeat of Germany.

Fawcett supported the compromise in 1918 that enfranchised women age 30 and older and men age 21 and older. Having succeeded in obtaining women's suffrage, she retired as president of the National Union at the beginning of 1919. Remaining active in the promotion of the status of women, she was gratified by the legislation in 1928 that gave women voting rights equal to those of men. Ironically, by this time she had resigned her membership in the National Union to protest her successor's advocacy of family allowances, subsidies paid to mothers for the upbringing of children. Fawcett also continued writing books, including one about Palestine where she had traveled with a sister. Although her religious principles remained essentially agnostic, she often attended Church of England services in her last years. In 1924, she was honored with the Grand Cross of the Order of the British Empire and became Dame Millicent Fawcett, a woman's title equivalent to a man's knighthood. Two years later, activists in the women's movement established the Fawcett Library, a collection of the materials for women's history that acquired most of her papers. (It is now located at the City of London Polytechnic.) She died at her London home on August 5, 1929.

Her only child, Philippa Garrett Fawcett (1868–1948), was a brilliant mathematics student at Newnham College, Cambridge. In 1890, refuting the notion of women's intellectual inferiority at a time when Cambridge University let women take the exams but would not award them degrees, she earned higher grades in the mathematics examination than the ablest male student. She served as principal assistant to the director of education, London County Council, from 1904 until her retirement in 1934.

SOURCES:

Banks, Oliver. *The Biographical Dictionary of British Feminists, 1880–1930.* Vol 1. New York University Press, 1985.

Fawcett, Millicent Garrett. *What I Remember.* T. Fisher Unwin, 1924.

Oakley, Ann. "Millicent Garrett Fawcett: Duty and Determination (1847–1929)," in Dale Spender, ed., *Feminist Theorists,* Pantheon Books, 1983.

Strachey, Ray (Rachel). *Millicent Garrett Fawcett.* John Murray, 1931.

FURTHER READING:

Caine, Barbara. *Victorian Feminists.* Oxford University Press, 1992.

Dodd, Kathryn. "Cultural Politics and Women's Historical Writings: The Case of Ray Strachey's *The Cause,*" in *Women's Studies International Forum.* Vol. 13 (1990): 127–137.

Harrison, Brian. *Separate Spheres: the Opposition to Woman Suffrage in Britain.* Croom Helm, 1978.

Hume, Leslie Parker. *The National Union of Women's Suffrage Societies, 1897–1914.* Garland, 1982.

Kent, Susan Kingsley. *Sex and Suffrage in Britain, 1860–1914.* Princeton University Press, 1987.

Liddington, Jill, and Jill Norris. *One Hand Tied Behind Us: The Rise of the Women's Suffrage Movement.* Virago, 1978.

Mantin, Jo. *Elizabeth Garrett Anderson.* Dutton, 1965.

Pugh, Martin. *Women's Suffrage in Britain, 1867–1928.* Historical Association, 1980.

Rubinstein, David. "Victorian Feminists: Henry and Millicent Garrett Fawcett," in Lawrence Goldman, ed., *The Blind Victorian: Henry Fawcett and British Liberalism.* Cambridge University Press, 1989.

Strachey, Ray (Rachel). *The Cause: A Short History of the Women's Movement in Great Britain.* G. Bell, 1928.

Ferdinand II

(1578–1637)

Holy Roman Emperor who sought to crush Protestantism and establish the power of the Habsburg dynasty.

"Repeatedly in the course of his life he twisted disaster into advantage, wrenched unexpected safety out of overwhelming danger, snatched victory from defeat. His contemporaries, unimpressed, commented on his astonishing luck. If it was luck it was certainly astonishing."

C. V. WEDGWOOD

F erdinand II was born July 9, 1578, at Graz in Styria. His father Charles, Archduke of Styria (southeastern Austria and Slovenia), was the youngest son of Emperor Ferdinand I, founder of the Austrian branch of the House of Habsburg. His mother Maria was the daughter of the Duke of Bavaria. Ferdinand's cousin Rudolf II was Holy Roman Emperor, King of Hungary and Bohemia (present-day Czech Republic) and Archduke of Austria. The Habsburg king of Spain was a more distant cousin ruling the Netherlands, parts of Italy, and the New World as well as Spain and Portugal. Ferdinand's life would center around his struggle to suppress the Protestant Reformation.

When Ferdinand I made a settlement with the Lutherans at the Peace of Augsburg in 1555, the 300 states that made up the Holy Roman Empire (modern Germany) had been given the right to choose between Lutheran and Catholic. In 1578, Charles of Styria had grudgingly agreed to recognize Protestant rights. By the time Charles died in 1590, the Duchies he left his son were two-thirds Protestant.

That same year, the 12-year-old Ferdinand was sent to the Jesuit college at Ingolstadt, Bavaria,

Born in Graz, Austria, in 1578; died in Vienna in 1637; son of Charles, Archduke of Styria, and Maria of Bavaria; married: Maria Anna of Bavaria; married: Eleanora Gonzaga; children: three sons and three daughters. Descendants: Ferdinand III and Austrian Habsburg dynasty. Predecessor: Emperor Matthias. Successor: Ferdinand III.

Contributed by Arthur White, Episcopal School of Acadiana, Breaux Bridge, Louisiana

while two uncles ruled in his name. Five years of Jesuit education forged the young Archduke into a dedicated servant of the Catholic Church whose amiable personality masked a will of steel. Historian C. V. Wedgwood describes him as:

> a cheerful, friendly, red-faced little man with a reassuring smile for everyone. Frank good nature beamed from his freckled countenance and short-sighted, prominent light blue eyes. Sandy-haired, stout and bustling, he presented a wholly unimpressive figure ... [but] an easier tempered man was not to be met.

In 1600, Ferdinand married his first cousin Maria Anna of Bavaria with whom he lived in placid domestic affection, raising four children in rustic happiness until her death in 1616. Family, hunting, and religion were the great passions of his life. His wife would wake in the night to find him kneeling in prayer by the bedside and would with difficulty coax him back to sleep. He said that if he had been born into a lower rank he would have wanted to be a Jesuit. Once he declared he would rather "live with his family in exile and beg his bread, to be spurned and insulted, to lose his life itself, than to stand by and suffer injury to the true Church."

When Ferdinand took up the government of Styria in 1596, he went on a pilgrimage to Loretto

and was consecrated to his tasks by Pope Clement VIII. With the blessings of the pontiff, the 18-year-old Archduke of Styria went to work. Sending Protestant preachers and teachers into exile, he demolished Protestant churches and schools, restored Catholic ones, and founded Jesuit colleges and Capuchin convents. Then he ordered Protestants to choose conversion or exile while Catholic immigrants were brought in to repopulate the country. But Ferdinand was also noted for his care for the poor and sick and his interest in the troubles of his humblest subjects.

While Ferdinand purged Styria, his ineffective uncle, Emperor Rudolf II, was overthrown as king of Bohemia and Hungary by his brother Matthias. Since Rudolf died before Matthias was elected Holy Roman Emperor, and Matthias was old and unlikely to have children, a family agreement among the Habsburgs in 1617 chose Ferdinand as heir to Matthias. He was then elected king in both Bohemia and Hungary.

The Start of the Thirty Years' War

In Bohemia, Ferdinand had to confirm the Letter of Majesty issued by Rudolf granting rights to the Protestants, but he issued ordinances against the spread of Protestantism and left the country in charge of a council led by men who opposed the Letter of Majesty. When this council found a technicality to stop construction of some Lutheran churches, a committee of Protestant nobles marched into the castle at Prague and threw two councillors out a window. This "Defenestration of Prague" on May 22, 1618, started the Thirty Years' War, and the rebellion spread from Bohemia to all of Ferdinand's lands. The Austrian Estates demanded the expulsion of the Jesuits and a Protestant church in Vienna. The Bohemians and Hungarians invaded up to the gates of Vienna.

When Matthias died in 1619 and the Electors of the Empire met in Frankfort to choose his successor, the Holy Roman Empire was a welter of semi-independent states over which the emperor had only nominal power. Ferdinand hoped to find an opportunity to restore the emperor's power and use it to restore the Catholic Church. Emperors were elected by the Seven Electors, key figures in the constitution. Although the Electors reluctantly chose Ferdinand, the election was hardly concluded when news reached Frankfort that the Bohemians had deposed Ferdinand and elected as their new king, Frederick V, Elector Palatine, leader of the German Calvinists.

As Frederick went to Prague, Ferdinand scrambled for men and money with which to reconquer his rebellious kingdoms. He quickly amassed a coalition army. In October 1619, he struck a deal with his brother-in-law Maximilian, Duke of Bavaria. As head of the Catholic League, an alliance of Catholic princes in whose name he maintained an army, Maximilian agreed to attack the rebels if Ferdinand would give him Frederick V's lands and Electoral rank. John George, the Lutheran Elector of Saxony, was willing to attack Frederick in exchange for the Bohemian province of Lusatia. Spain offered money and cooperation if it was allowed to conquer the Lower Palatinate, Frederick's richest possession which lay along the Rhine River and blocked Spanish access to the Netherlands. Although the northern half of the Netherlands had rebelled against Spain and established its independence, a truce with this Protestant Dutch Republic was about to expire.

In August 1620, the Spanish forces occupied the Lower Palatinate. At the same time the army of Maximilian's Catholic League led by Count Tilly suppressed rebellion in Austria. Then Tilly crossed into Bohemia while the Saxons invaded Lusatia. On November 8, at White Mountain just outside Prague, Tilly destroyed the rebel forces, and Frederick of the Palatinate fled while his remaining territory, the Upper Palatinate, also fell to Maximilian.

Proclaiming the crown hereditary in the House of Habsburg, Ferdinand treated Austria and Bohemia as he had treated Styria. Leaders of the rebellion were executed, the Letter of Majesty was canceled, Protestantism was outlawed, and the Jesuits were brought in. All or part of the estates of 658 families and 50 towns in Bohemia were confiscated and the lands were sold to loyal, Catholic purchasers at less than a third of their value. A new, largely foreign aristocracy took advantage of the bargains to amass enormous wealth. Eventually, in 1627, the remaining Protestants were given the choice between conversion and exile. The kingdom was now Catholic, but as C.V. Wedgwood notes, "One of the most progressive and commercialized countries in Europe had slipped back two centuries."

There were other problems. Ferdinand's victory was mortgaged to Spain and Maximilian of Bavaria. Although the Protestant powers would accept Ferdinand's victory in Bohemia, stripping Frederick V of all his lands and titles for the benefit of Bavaria was more than they could stomach. Since they considered Ferdinand's action illegal when he transferred Frederick V's electorate to Maximilian, the Protestant Electors refused to sit with this new colleague, paralyzing the constitution. The Dutch, now that war with Spain was resumed, could not accept permanent Spanish control of the Rhine and signed a treaty to help Frederick V regain his lands. While his enemies seethed, Ferdinand married his second wife, Eleanora Gonzaga of Mantua in 1622. This marriage was as happy as his first and produced two more children.

King **Christian IV** of Denmark prepared to rescue Protestantism by invading the Empire. Consequently, in 1626, Ferdinand accepted the offer of **Albrecht von Wallenstein,** who had purchased 56 Bohemian estates, to raise an army for the imperial service. By raising the army at his own expense, Wallenstein, not the Emperor, would control it.

Tilly and the army of the Catholic League defeated Christian IV of Denmark at the Battle of Lutter in 1626, but Wallenstein soon recruited and was supplying an army of 140,000 in an age when 20,000 was considered large enough for major military operations. Sweeping aside Danish resistance in 1627, Wallenstein conquered all of northern Germany. The German princes quaked in terror of this enormous army.

He Issues Edict of Restitution

When Denmark made peace at Lübeck in 1629, Ferdinand felt powerful enough to extend the policies he had applied to Styria and Bohemia to the Empire as a whole. On March 6, he issued the Edict of Restitution which ordered that all Church lands taken by Protestants since the Peace of Augsburg in 1555 must be restored. This revolutionary Edict, issued without approval by the Electors or the Diet, would have established not only Catholic control of the Empire, but imperial control of the princes as well. Many of the great princes would be ruined, and some of the strongest Protestant cities made Catholic. Dortmund, for example, would become Catholic though it had only 30 Catholics in it. Ferdinand called a Diet in 1630 to seek the election of his oldest son, Ferdinand (who would be Ferdinand III), as heir to the imperial throne. But the princes would do nothing unless Ferdinand dismissed Wallenstein and rescinded the Edict of Restitution. Although Ferdinand dismissed Wallenstein, he would not retract the Edict.

Meanwhile, **Gustavus Adolphus,** the Lutheran king of Sweden, had come to the aid of the Protestants. Landing on the Baltic coast, he quickly occupied the northeastern quarter of the Empire. He then summoned all the Protestant princes to Leipzig where they declared war against

Ferdinand unless he withdrew the Edict of Restitution.

Ferdinand's armies were melting away. Furious at his dismissal, Wallenstein cut off all supplies to the army. Since Ferdinand could not support the army without Wallenstein's wealth, the mercenary soldiers drifted away, many to join the growing forces of Sweden. The other Catholic force, Tilly's army of the Catholic League, was annihilated by Gustavus Adolphus at the Battle of Brietenfeld on September 18, 1631. Shortly thereafter, Wallenstein invited Gustavus to occupy Prague.

In the fall and winter of 1631, Gustavus conquered all of western Germany. The Spanish in the Netherlands were cut off from money and supplies. With Germany at his feet, Gustavus planned a whole new empire to replace the old one, with himself as its head.

Ferdinand was defenseless, and the only man who could help was Wallenstein. As the news rolled in of the Swedish sweep through the Empire, Ferdinand begged Wallenstein to raise a new army. But Wallenstein demanded exorbitant rewards. History does not know the secret terms Wallenstein finally accepted, but they were rumored to include an Electorate and the kingdom of Bohemia.

When fighting resumed in the spring of 1632, Wallenstein held Bohemia but did nothing to prevent Gustavus from conquering Bavaria. Finally, Gustavus and Wallenstein met in battle at Lützen on November 16, 1632. Although Wallenstein lost the battle, Gustavus Adolphus lay dead on the field.

Gustavus had shattered the Habsburgs, but after his death they revived. In Spain, the Cardinal-Infante (Philip IV's brother) planned to bring a new army from Italy to the Netherlands and wanted to cooperate with the imperial army on the way. But the imperial army under Wallenstein was as dangerous to Emperor Ferdinand—whose orders Wallenstein ignored—as to his enemies. In the council at Vienna young Ferdinand, the Emperor's son, was eager to replace Wallenstein at the head of the armies.

Officers Murder Wallenstein

Wallenstein had undermined his own popularity with the army. Executing his own men on absurd charges, he had become a hesitant and indecisive commander. Worst of all, it was clear that he was about to betray the Emperor by accepting a French offer of the Bohemian crown. In January 1634, Ferdinand signed an order to remove him. Officers loyal to the Emperor murdered Wallenstein on February 25.

The death of Wallenstein unleashed the energy of the younger generation of Habsburgs. When the Cardinal-Infante brought his army north from Italy, the young Ferdinand led the imperial army to join him. Converging on the Swedish and Protestant forces at Nördlingen in Bavaria on September 6, 1634, they slaughtered 17,000 of the enemy and captured 4,000 out of a force of only 24,000. The Emperor was hunting when the Empress brought him the news. He wept speechless tears of joy and pride.

Soon all Germany was at the feet of the Habsburg cousins. But the young Ferdinand rather than the old Ferdinand directed affairs. Young Ferdinand negotiated the Peace of Prague which canceled his father's Edict of Restitution and allowed each church to keep what it had in November of 1627. Although Ferdinand II balked at sacrificing the Edict of Restitution, his son prevailed.

With German states joining the Peace of Prague and the Habsburgs paramount once more, only France, their traditional enemy, could stand against them. On May 21, 1635, France declared war on Spain. The complex, multisided war resolved itself into a continuation of the 200-year struggle between France and the Habsburgs. As both countries were Catholic, the war ceased to be religious. Ferdinand, for whom religion was always the motive, was out of step with the times.

At an Electoral meeting at Regensburg, Ferdinand finally achieved the election of his son as heir to the imperial throne. On his journey back to Vienna, he wrote to his confessor requesting the privilege of shortening his morning devotions. Knowing he must be seriously ill, the confessor went at once to fetch him home. Ferdinand lay propped up on his pillows, smiling and cheerful, attended by his wife and daughter and comforted by the Church. He died on February 15, 1637.

Ferdinand was fortunate to die when the power of the Habsburgs was at a peak. France turned out to be a more dangerous enemy than Gustavus Adolphus. In 1643 at the Battle of Rocroi, the French destroyed the military power of Spain. Five years later in 1648, the Peace of Westphalia ended the Thirty Years' War on terms that reduced the Holy Roman Empire to a loose, largely ceremonial association of independent German states. But Ferdinand had welded Bohemia, Austria, Hungary, and Styria into a single hereditary state and had purged them of the Protestant heresy he detested. Ferdinand had been destined to be "the creator of the Austrian, not the restorer of the Holy Roman Empire."

SOURCES:

Chudoba, Bohdan. *Spain and the Empire, 1519–1641.* Octagon, 1969.

Coxe, William. *History of the House of Austria.* Vol. II. Henry G. Bohn, 1847.

Crankshaw, Edward. *The Habsburgs: Portrait of a Dynasty.* Viking, 1971.

Parker, Geoffrey. T*he Thirty Years' War.* Military Heritage Press, 1984.

Wedgwood, C. V. *The Thirty Years' War.* Anchor, 1961.

FURTHER READING:

Evans, R. J. W. *The Making of the Habsburg Monarchy, 1550–1700.* Oxford, 1979.

Konigsberger, H. G. *The Habsburgs and Europe, 1516–1660.* Cornell, 1971.

Lockyear, Roger. *Habsburg and Bourbon Europe, 1470–1720.* Longmans, 1974.

Wandruska, Adam. *The House of Habsburg.* Translated by Cathleen and Hans Epstein. Sidgwick and Jackson, 1964.

Ferdinand Foch

(1851–1929)

Commander in chief of the Allied armies in the last months of World War I, who beat off a series of desperate German offensives and then led the drive to final victory.

Pronunciation: Fawsh. Born on October 2, 1851, in Tarbes (Hautes-Pyrénées); died in Paris on March 10, 1929; buried at the Invalides near Napoleon's tomb; son of Napoléon Foch and Marie-Jacqueline-Sophie Dupré; married: Louise-Ursule-Julie Bienvenue; children: Marie (1885–1972), Anne (1887–1981), Eugène (1888), Germain (1889–1914; killed in action).

On May 11, 1871, in a large lecture hall at Metz, a city in Lorraine in eastern France, scores of young men were working intently on an entrance examination for the École Polytechnique, the famed Paris engineering school and chief source of officers for the army's technical services. Suddenly, artillery volleys began thundering over the city. The men in the room instantly knew what this meant. The salvos, from the German army of occupation, were announcing the formal signing of the Treaty of Frankfurt ending the Franco-Prussian War (1870–71), which had brought disaster and humiliation to France and her army. The very room where they were sitting was now on foreign soil, for Metz and northeastern Lorraine, plus all of Alsace, were being ceded to Germany.

"My children," the examining professor began, but he could say no more. As heads bent lower over the papers, the silence in the room was punctuated from without by more salvos and from within by sobs of grief and shame and suppressed rage. If one of the applicants, young Ferdinand Foch, had had any questions about what his life's mission would be, they vanished in that hall that

"One speaks of genius. Bah! Genius doesn't count…. In the hour of decision, when it became necessary to say the 'yes' on which thousands of lives depended, I was, and I felt it, the instrument of the divine Providence."

FERDINAND FOCH

Contributed by David S. Newhall, Professor of History, Centre College, Danville, Kentucky

day. Unlike so many men there and untold hundreds of thousands yet unborn, he would live to see the day of reckoning and the return of Alsace-Lorraine to the Motherland. More than that, he would be the leader of the Allied armies in their hour of triumph.

In short order, the site of the remaining examination was transferred to Nancy. Perhaps because of the emotional upheavals and preparatory interruptions caused by the war, Foch failed one of the tests. But the authorities relented and allowed him a makeup, which he passed, thus securing his long-desired entry to the Polytechnique. He ranked a mediocre 78th of 140 admitted, the only time in his scholastic career he stood anywhere but at or near the top.

Young Foch seemed destined for the army; from an early age, he devoured everything he could find about Napoleon and was encouraged in this direction by his family. His maternal grandfather was a professional soldier and had a sister who was the widow of one of Napoleon's generals. This great-aunt was a devotee of all things Napoleonic and continually stoked young Foch's interest. His father had been named Napoléon by Grandfather Foch in hopes he would have a military career. But the post-Napoleonic army was small, and he had to settle for being a civil servant in the Ministry of the Interior, which shunted him from post to post in or near his native Pyrénées Mountains.

Ferdinand Foch was born in Tarbes (Hautes-Pyrénées) on October 2, 1851, into a family which had lived in the region for centuries, originally as paper makers and then as wool merchants traveling into Spain. He was the sixth of seven children (of whom four grew to adulthood) born to Napoléon Foch and Marie-Jacqueline-Sophie Dupré. His older brother Gabriel became a lawyer in Tarbes and his younger brother Germain, with whom he was especially close, became a Jesuit priest—a circumstance that had repercussions later in Foch's career.

His education began in Tarbes and continued at the lycée in Rodez, where he earned baccalaureate degrees in letters (1868) and sciences (1869) and where a mathematics teacher noticed his "geometrical mind" and pointed him toward the Polytechnique. He prepared further at Jesuit colleges in St.-Étienne and Metz. The Franco-Prussian War forced him to leave Metz for St.-Étienne where his father was stationed, and where, with his permission, he enlisted. But he spent the short war in a training camp. What he had seen of the war and the army that had lost it, however, made an indelible impression. Late in life he remarked to Major Bugnet:

CHRONOLOGY

1873	Commissioned as lieutenant of artillery
1885–87	Student at the École Supérieure de Guerre
1890–92	Assigned to the General Staff; returned to it in 1894–95
1895–1901	Professor at the École Supérieure de Guerre
1904–05	Published *Principes de la guerre* and *Conduite de la guerre*
1908–11	Commandant of the École Supérieure de Guerre
1914	Commanded the XXth Corps at Morhange and Lunéville and the 9th Army at the Marne; coordinated Allied forces defending the Channel ports
1915	Commander of the Northern Army Group; bloody offensives in Artois
1916	Commanded the French armies in the Somme offensive; relieved of command
1917	Named chief of the General Staff
1918	Appointed to coordinate all Allied forces on the western front; named commander in chief; led Allied armies to victory and presided at the signing of the Armistice
1919	Tried unsuccessfully to have Germany's military frontier fixed permanently at the Rhine
1920	Appointed president of the Allied Military Committee

No one was in command. The leaders were never there! The Colonel? Good … [f]or walking in front and crying "Forward" with a cigar in his mouth. They followed him. Brave? Certainly they were brave. Very! But bravery is quite beside the point. They were soldiers, fine soldiers, but not leaders.

After a year at the Polytechnique, Foch accepted a chance to enter the training school at Fontainebleau for artillery—Napoleon's service branch. Graduating third in his class (1873), he was sent to the 24th Artillery at Tarbes. In 1876, he entered Saumur for cavalry training to perfect his horsemanship (until the war, he rode for two hours every morning) and in 1878 resumed his artillery career with an early promotion to captain. He passed through a series of provincial postings and in 1883 married Louise-Ursule-Julie Bienvenue (1860–1950), a prosperous and happy union which helped him purchase a fine country home, "Trofeunteuniou," in Brittany.

The decisive early turn in his career came in 1885 when he was sent to the recently established

École Supérieure de Guerre, reserved for especially promising officers. Graduating fourth in his class (1887), he circulated mainly through staff positions including two coveted tours on the General Staff. A marked man now, he returned to the École Supérieure as professor of military history, strategy, and general tactics (1895–1901). His influence began to extend to the whole army through the impression he made upon the elite of a generation of young officers. They found him an unforgettable lecturer: a stocky five feet, five inches tall, full-chested, bandy-legged man with a cavalryman's rolling gait and jauntily tilted cap. Light-haired, with a square, powerful jaw, he had an habitual tilt of the chin when he was not staring at the ground lost in thought. His speech was full of fire and conviction, snapping out phrases by turns clear and opaque but always accompanied by gestures whose eloquence left little doubt about what he meant.

His ideas were influenced mostly by Karl von Clauswitz's *On War* (1833) and his own studies of Napoleon and especially the Seven Weeks' (1866) and Franco-Prussian wars. Their influence came less from their (fairly modest) originality or profundity than from his ability to communicate his conviction of their truth. Besides, as he observed, "in war, a fact has priority over ideas, action over talk, execution over theory." In brief, he taught (1) the importance of willpower, especially in the commander, as the means of establishing psychological ascendancy over the enemy; (2) that one finally wins only by fighting, hence tactics are more important than strategy; (3) that final victory can only come through the offense, for which the defense is only a preparation; (4) that the offense should operate against the enemy's communications, preferably against a flank; (5) that what wins battles is shock, which derives from a combination of mass and movement; and (6) that the battle is prepared by using an "advanced guard" to find and grasp the enemy, followed by large reserves to deliver shock at the critical time and place.

Unfortunately for his reputation and the lives of hundreds of thousands of French soldiers, by 1914 fervent disciples, notably Lieutenant Colonel François Loyzeau de Grandmaison, had distorted his ideas into a rigid formula, proclaiming that the all-out offensive is the key to war and that will is more important than any material realities. It was a tragic irony that in the First World War the defense almost always won: machine guns, quick-firing artillery, barbed wire, and reinforced concrete turned those all-out offensives into carnivals of slaughter.

Foch's tenure at the École Supérieure ended abruptly in 1901, during the government's assault against the Roman Catholic Church's political influence on the army which was exhibited during the Dreyfus affair (a Jewish officer had been mistakenly convicted of treason and then prevented by embarrassed or anti-Semitic authorities from being cleared when the truth began to leak out). Foch's loyalty to the Republican regime became suspect—wholly unjustly—because he was a devout, Jesuit-educated Catholic with a Jesuit brother. Sent off to provincial commands at Laon and Vannes, his promotion to colonel was delayed until 1903. To his credit, he did not recriminate, and admonished brother officers who were talking of resigning: "You have no pluck! When war comes you will have to put up with worse things than that!" Even more to his credit, given the climate of his times, was that despite his fervent religion he did not parade his piety, was no bigot, and respected without comment the beliefs (or nonbelief) of others.

Typically, he worked hard in "exile," published the essence of his teaching in two books, and waited for his day. It came in 1907—hastened by aid from a Protestant admirer, General Millet—with a promotion to brigadier general capped by a return in triumph to the École Supérieure as commandant (1908) by order of a staunch anticlerical (no less), Premier **Georges Clemenceau.** Foch strengthened the school's methods and persuaded the government to establish an even more advanced school, the Center for High Military Studies, to train officers for field army and army group staffs. His term completed in 1911, he was promoted to *général de division* (the highest permanent rank) and in 1913 took over the crack XXth Corps, the army's spearhead in Lorraine. But for the coming of the First World War in August 1914, he soon would have retired.

The Battle of the Marne

In the first three months of the war, Foch vaulted into first place in the esteem of the French commander in chief, General **Joseph Joffre.** At the outset, the XXth Corps had charged boldly into Lorraine according to plan. The Germans retreated, then suddenly struck back at Morhange (August 20), inflicting a severe check. The corps held up well but had to withdraw with the rest of the Second Army, which it aided by a counterattack near Lunéville (August 25). Two days later, Joffre named Foch to command the Ninth Army, being formed to help stop the vast German invasion swinging down from Belgium. The Ninth successfully defended part of the French center at the crucial Battle of the Marne (September 6–9).

Foch's energy and determination helped steady his forces, which bent but did not break:

> The first day I was beaten. The last day it was a question of holding on. Yet I advanced four miles. Why? I don't know. A good deal because of my men. A little because I had the will—and then, God was there.

Once the Germans began to pull back north, he pushed them hard, something not all his subordinates were eager to do after so close a call. As he once remarked, "I am always ready to hustle people; I stick the spur into them."

Four days after the Marne, he received the cruelest blow of his life when he was informed of the deaths of his only son Germain, an infantry lieutenant, and his daughter Marie's husband, Captain Paul Bécourt.

On October 4, Joffre chose Foch to take charge of all French troops in the north to prevent the Germans from reaching the Channel ports, enveloping the Allied left, and cutting off the British from their home base. In reality, he was being called upon to coordinate the French, British, and Belgian armies there without any formal authority to do so. His instruments were (1) French reserves, which to the exasperation of Allied generals he doled out very sparingly, but—as it turned out—wisely; (2) his sensible advice offered in timely and tactful ways; and (3) his fiery spirit and iron will, which he infused into shaken commanders facing truly desperate situations. In terrible battles around Messines Ridge, Ypres, and the Yser River, the Germans were halted and the western front stabilized into a giant siege. Foch's masterful handling of multinational forces in this crisis laid the foundation for the call he received in 1918.

Formally appointed on January 6, 1915, as commander of the Northern Army Group (there were three such groups), Foch remained there until December 22, 1916, when he was relieved of command a few days after the firing of his "patron," Joffre. During those two years while directing offensives in Artois (1915) and on the Somme (1916), he tried in vain to find the key to The Breakout, some way of ending the siege. As an artilleryman, he had quickly grasped the importance of huge concentrations of guns, especially heavies, hitherto not emphasized by the French, and in general began to pay more attention to establishing material, not just moral, superiority. He also began to work toward a concept of extending offensives over wider frontages and launching them in series in order to disrupt the enemy's ability to switch reserves to plug holes or to counterattack.

His career in eclipse, he was relegated to advisory and study missions. But his appointment as chief of the General Staff (May 15, 1917)—when General **Philippe Pétain** took over from General Robert Nivelle (who had followed Joffre)—brought him part way back to the limelight as the government's chief military advisor. In late October and November, his star brightened when he went to Italy bringing some British and French divisions and firm advice to help stem the tide after the Austro-German breakthrough at Caporetto. With Russia now out of the war and the Germans hurrying troops west before American forces could make their weight felt, the Allies were on the defensive. Foch persuaded Allied leaders to create a strategic reserve force to aid the defense but also to take the offensive as soon as possible because, as he had taught, only offense finally wins and because seizing the initiative would establish the necessary moral ascendancy. Though he was put in charge of this reserve, Pétain and Douglas Haig (British), not trusting his offensive plans, refused to release any troops to it.

Allies Choose Foch as Commander in Chief

The great German offensive launched on March 21, 1918, ended these disputes. It threatened to split the front at Amiens and roll the British up to the Channel and the French back to Paris. In an emergency meeting at the village of Doullens on March 26, the Allied leaders turned to the obvious choice for a commander to hold things together: Foch. Commissioned at first merely to "coordinate" operations, he subsequently was given overall strategic direction and formally titled commander in chief (April 14), with powers later extended to Italy (May 2) and over the Belgians (September 9). On August 6, he was awarded the rank of marshal of France.

The first German drive was halted after ferocious fighting. Another followed in April against the British, with the same result. On May 27, a breakthrough against the French at the Chemin des Dames caught Foch with too many reserves held for too long in the north, where he had guessed correctly that General **Erich Ludendorff** meant to eventually deliver his main blow. Hard fighting and a timely counterattack retrieved the situation—with the Americans making their first serious appearance at Château-Thierry. Critics called for Foch's firing but to the Allied commanders and Premier Clemenceau, he had become all but irreplaceable. The tide turned for good when a German offensive in Champagne (July 15–17) stalled and then was hit by a powerful counterattack that Foch and Pétain had carefully prepared. From then until the Armistice, Foch directed an unrelenting series of alternating offensives aimed toward the Germans' supply corridors, thus forcing their tiring armies into successive withdrawals toward the frontier.

When the Germans asked for an armistice, Foch told the Allied leaders, "War is only a means to results." If Germany accepted the Allies' terms, then he believed he had no moral right to shed more blood just to win a more overwhelming victory (and more glory for himself, one could add). He drew up most of the terms the Allies presented, and presided over their signing (November 11) in his railway dining car parked near Compiègne. "It was the best day of my life.... When I saw them in front of me, on the other side of the table, I said to myself: 'There is the German Empire.' I can assure you I was a proud man!"

During the 1919 Paris Peace Conference, Foch tried by every means, even to the verge of outright disobedience, to persuade the Allied leaders to put Germany's frontier at the Rhine and mount a permanent military presence there. Clemenceau tried to oblige, but when Britain and the United States opposed this plan, he settled for a much-modified version to preserve Allied unity. Foch predicted disaster and never forgave Clemenceau and the others: "They have destroyed what I gave them. They missed their opportunity. Their treaty? I did not wish to sign it."

In the 1920s, he presided over the Allied Military Committee set up to recommend and carry out treaty-enforcement measures. The Académie Française elected him (November 21, 1918) and foreign governments showered decorations on him during ceremonial visits, including one to the United States in 1921. Dying of heart disease on March 10, 1929, he was entombed at the Invalides with Napoleon and France's other greatest soldiers.

As Allied commander in chief in 1918, Foch was served by only a tiny staff and a remarkable aide and confidante, General Maxime Weygand. Foch was more a planner and coordinator than a true commander of combined forces such as **Dwight D. Eisenhower** was in World War II, but his success laid the groundwork for inter-Allied commands. He was well versed in the military science of his time and contributed to it. Although he was a man of high intelligence, he was no true genius. What he did possess was character, concentrated most in a will and unconquerable optimism which made him all but indispensable in times of crisis. He inspired confidence and trust.

"The important thing is to have an objective, a plan, and a method," he once said. "It is to know what one wills and to do it.... But it is necessary to have learned how to think, by work and reflection. It is essential to be prepared and to continue to the end." Ferdinand Foch, a born teacher, had a certain penchant for expressing high moral sentiments; but unlike so many men, he also lived by them.

SOURCES:

Autin, Jean. *Foch ou le triomphe de la volonté*. Perrin, 1987.

Bugnet, Commandant. *Foch Talks*. Translated by Russell Green, Victor Gollancz, 1929.

Hart, B. H. Liddell. *Foch, the Man of Orleans*. Little, Brown, 1932.

Hunter, T. M. *Marshal Foch: A Study in Leadership*. Directorate of Military Training, Army Headquarters (Ottawa), 1961.

FURTHER READING:

Carver, Sir Michael, ed. *The War Lords: Military Commanders of the Twentieth Century*. Little, Brown, 1976.

Churchill, Winston S. *Great Contemporaries*. Putnam, 1937.

Earle, Edward Meade, ed. *Makers of Modern Strategy*. Princeton University Press, 1944.

Falls, Cyril. *Marshal Foch*. Blackie & Sons, 1939.

Foch, Ferdinand. *The Memoirs of Marshal Foch*. Translated by Col. T. Bentley Mott. Doubleday, Doran, 1931.

King, Jere C. *Foch Versus Clemenceau*. Harvard University Press, 1960.

George Fox

(1624–1691)

Religious leader, who founded of the Society of Friends, better known as Quakers, an English religious movement which survived heavy persecution to become a powerful influence in Anglo-American history.

"[H]e was an original, being no man's copy."

WILLIAM PENN

George Fox was born into a devoutly religious household in 1624. His parents leaned toward Puritanism, the movement within the Church of England that wished to see the Church reformed and spiritually purified. His father had earned the nickname "Righteous Christer"; his mother Mary was descended from the Lago family, famous for its martyrs. In his *Journal*, written many years later, Fox recalled:

> In my very young years I had gravity and stayedness of mind and spirit not usual in children…. When I came to eleven years of age I knew pureness and righteousness; for while a child I was taught to walk to be kept pure.

Apprenticed to a shoemaker, he learned the trades of shoemaking and shepherding, both of which sustained him in his early years of wandering, which he began in 1643 at age 19. Fox took to the road in part to seek out other religiously minded people who could answer his deepest questions about God and religion. He met and spoke with all sorts of people, including many Puritans, and experienced a spiritual transformation in

Born in July 1624 in Drayton-in-the-Clay (or Fenny Drayton), Leicestershire, in the midlands of England; died near London on January 13, 1691; married: Margaret Fell of Swarthmor Hall, 1669.

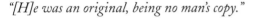

Contributed by Thomas Templeton Taylor, Assistant Professor of History, Wittenberg University, Springfield, Ohio

1647–48. Afterward he thought himself called directly by God to travel and teach.

Out of his travels arose associations with other like-minded men and women who would eventually produce the early Quaker teachings. As he later put it, the "Truth first sprang up to us to be a people of the Lord" in 1644 in Leicestershire. Groups of such Quakers gradually formed throughout central and western England (1645–50), in northern England (1651–53), and even in London, Scotland, and Ireland (1654). In these early years, Fox was not the leader of the movement, but instead one of several young preachers with no credentials other than a firm conviction that God had called them to teach a new message. They frequently challenged the authority of ministers, whom they derisively called priests. In 1649, Fox began the practice of interrupting worship services. When a minister claimed that the Scriptures were the authority for the church, Fox, who believed that the Spirit of God was the authority, jumped up and said, "No, no it is not the Scriptures." For this he spent a short time in jail, one of many such stays. He was called a "Quaker" at least as early as 1650, by a judge in Derby who was in the process of sending him to prison again.

What did Fox and his friends teach? Historian Hugh Barbour offers this edited version of Fox's own account in his *Journal*:

> I was … commanded [by God] to turn people to that inward light, spirit, and grace … I was to bring people off … from men's inventions … with their schools and colleges for making ministers of Christ … and from all their images and crosses, and sprinkling of infants, with all their holy days (so called)…. Moreover, when the Lord sent me forth into the world, he forbade me to put off my hat to any, high or low; and I was required to "thee" and "thou" all men and women, without any respect to rich or poor, great or small.

In the 1600s, such a message posed a threat to many important conventions in English society. The idea that everyone has the Truth ("Inner Light") already within him seemed to contradict the traditional Church teachings that everyone is sinful and only some will be saved. Many thought the Quaker claims to the Inner Light amounted to blasphemy. Most of the English populace believed that ministers should have a college education, but Quakers only wanted a call from God. English society expected men and women to "respect their betters" and to tip one's hat to a social superior; Quakers treated everyone equally, calling everyone "thee" and "thou." Once called to court, matters often got worse. Because of one of Jesus's sayings, Quakers refused to take oaths, even though they believed in always speaking truthfully. But not taking an oath seemed to defy the authority of the law itself.

One could not encounter a Quaker without being reminded of the differences. As a consequence, Quakers stood out more than many religious groups in their defiance of accepted practice and customs. This helps explain why so many Quakers spent so much time in jail: their critics thought Quakers challenged social stability and were as dangerous as thieves.

But Quaker leaders like Fox saw their attacks on common social conventions as symbolic of the difference between the way of the world and the way of Christ. They called these early struggles "The Lamb's War" (the Bible calls Jesus the Lamb of God), a war waged against a sinful world, fought with words and prayer rather than arms and bloodshed.

He Travels to Swarthmor Hall

By 1651, the Quakers had moved into northern England which became the great stronghold of Quakerism, while Puritanism would remain dominant in southern England. Hundreds converted in 1652 alone, including many "Seekers" and radical Puritan leaders. Later that year, Fox traveled to Swarthmor Hall, where he met Judge Thomas Fell and his wife Margaret. An advocate of religious and political reform, Judge Fell protected the Quakers in his region until his death in 1658.

Swarthmor Hall became crucially important to early Quakerism. Although Judge Fell did not convert, his young and beautiful wife did, along with most of the household. This family conversion changed the house considerably. Largely under Margaret Fell's guidance, the household became one of intimacy and extensive sharing. The children were raised as ones with the Inner Light, a light which must be nurtured daily. Influenced by Fox and others, Margaret Fell spiritualized family life in a remarkable way. In his many letters and published works, Fox extolled this household as a model for Quaker families, and Margaret as the model mother.

Swarthmor's principles deeply influenced Quaker ideas about marriage and child rearing in England and in America. Unlike Puritans who emphasized the sinfulness of children, Quakers emphasized the Inner Light. The earliest Quaker parents often assumed that because each child has this Inner Light, the parents should be passive in raising the child. Therefore some parents tended toward laxness in discipline. But Fox and Fell emphasized great parental responsibility for their children. Though the child was born with the Inner Light, it was the responsibility of the parents to nurture this light until the child had grown. Quaker families gradually became known for their love and discipline, for the tender care of their children.

Quaker marriages observed the conventions of English law. When a minister was not available, they still used the same words between groom and bride. In 1653 Fox instructed that marriages should take place in the presence of the local Meeting and with its blessing. This became very important, giving the community a say in marriages. When Fox married the widowed Margaret Fell in 1669, her family attended and affirmed their approval and belief that the marriage was God's work.

Meanwhile, Quakerism continued to spread, and Fox's stature as a leader grew steadily. In 1654, when over 60 pairs of Quakers headed into southeastern England, they received hostile receptions but also won many converts. Later that year, when Fox called all Quaker leaders to gather at Swannington in the north, hundreds came; these ministers agreed to send back reports to Swarthmor. As a result, later crusaders were more organized, filing periodic reports at Swarthmor, where they were handled by Margaret Fell. Swarthmor in effect became a center of operations, with Fell handling most of the correspondence. Although Quakers had no one official leader, it is clear that by 1655 George Fox had emerged as one of the most respected leaders within the movement.

Although Quakers frequently risked jail in these years, the early 1650s gave them much freedom at a critical time. The Puritans had just defeated King **Charles I** and the Anglicans in the English Civil War, and **Oliver Cromwell,** the most powerful Puritan, tried to be lenient toward other religious groups. Fox met Cromwell on several occasions and made a great impression on the ruler. Those who dissented from the Church of England (who were members of neither the Puritan nor the Anglican camps) were at their freest during these years. This allowed Quakerism to grow quickly, though with difficulty.

But one result of the religious warfare of the 1640s was a deep distrust of strange, new religious ideas. Public prejudice and local law still posed a great threat. Like most Quaker leaders, Fox was beaten or stoned more than once by townspeople. Arrest could be equally dangerous. In the 1600s, jail could be deadly; conditions were unsanitary and unsafe. Although Fox was almost hanged for blasphemy in 1653, death from disease posed the greatest threat.

Quaker tactics admittedly were confrontational. They sometimes entered a church and preached uninvited, denouncing the false teachings of that particular minister or church. And because they respected the Spirit in each other, they were slow to criticize a peer's tactics, even when they disagreed. Thus, though some Quakers would enter a town and walk through it naked ("going naked for a sign") to symbolize nakedness before God, other Quakers would never consider such a radical tactic. Their reluctance to criticize, however, created the appearance that all Quakers used or endorsed such methods.

While in jail, Quaker ministers wrote letters and pamphlets for publication, further spreading the Quaker message. Few criticisms of the movement went unanswered. Fox produced scores of such pamphlets and letters during his lifetime. In 1656, when Fox was imprisoned in Cornwall in the dungeon at Launceston Castle, hundreds of Quakers, many of them preachers, converged there. Fox's visitors and the meetings they organized became so numerous that the government decided to release him after eight months.

That same year, Fox traveled into western England with another Quaker leader by the name of James Nayler. Nayler was followed by a group of women that openly spoke of him as some kind of messiah. Although leaders had been reluctant to criticize the women, many doubted that *Spirit* had led them in this matter. When the women wanted Nayler to reenact Jesus's triumphant entry into Jerusalem on Palm Sunday in Bristol, Fox warned against this, but the plans proceeded anyway.

Meant to symbolize the coming of the inward Christ to all people, Nayler did not mean that he was the new messiah. But when Cromwell heard that the women leading Nayler's procession sang, "Holy, holy, holy," James Nayler was arrested. While Quakers sympathized with his suffering (he was tortured and a hole was driven through his tongue), many disowned Nayler's actions as inappropriate. Quakers expected persecution for their teachings, but not every persecution was a sign that the Quaker had been right. One immediate result of the events of 1656 was to strengthen Fox's position of moderate leadership within the movement.

Persecution of Quakers Increases

By this time the Puritan government under Oliver Cromwell was less willing to ignore Quakers. For the next few years, Quakers seldom interrupted sermons or went "naked for a sign," and Fox issued a call for the end of forced tithes ("taxes paid to the church") and for an end to persecution. Meanwhile, they strengthened their Meetings and their overseas efforts—they even sent one team to convert the pope. When Cromwell died and Puritan rule became more and more unstable, some groups openly called for the restoration of the monarchy. The Puritan government offered Fox a colonelcy which he refused, and he and other Quakers announced that they would remain neutral.

The monarchy was restored in 1660, and Charles II initially freed several hundred Quakers jailed by the Puritans. Fox, however, spent six months in jail on suspicion of hostility toward the king. And after an uprising in January 1661, 4,200 Quakers were arrested out of fear that they too were a threat. During this time, Fox, Fell, and others issued their first formal statement of pacifism, a doctrine for which Quakers have been famous ever since.

Under Charles II, and a Parliament now dominated by Anglicans, persecution grew even worse. Anglicans first pushed through the Act of Uniformity of 1662, requiring all ministers to be licensed by the Church of England and to use the Book of Common Prayer and uphold it. Because of this law, at least 2,000 ministers of various persuasions lost their positions. The later Conventicle Act hurt Quakers much more, banning all religious meetings of four or more, outside of families. Between 1660 and 1685, 11,000 to 15,000 Friends were jailed, including many leaders, Fox among them; 450 of them would die there. Puritans and Baptists also suffered, but Quakers suffered the most, because they insisted on holding their now illegal meetings in public. Arrests would be at their height in 1662–67, 1675, 1682–83, and 1685.

Early on, Quaker communities had organized themselves into Meetings, which in the 1660s Fox organized into a national network. He also helped introduce the idea of women's Meetings and men's Meetings. Such Meetings gave women unprecedented social and religious power, and helped in the spiritualization of marriage and family life. The local Meetings eventually sent representatives to the Yearly Meeting, thus giving Quakers an extensive but very democratic structure without stifling the Spirit. As the Quaker movement became more organized, new missions were sent to the West Indies, the American colonies, Holland, Scotland, and Ireland.

Despite the persecutions, Fox continued his work through the 1660s and the 1670s. Visiting North America in 1672–73, he advised **William Penn** on the establishment of a Quaker haven in what would be become Pennsylvania. After 1675, his life began to change. Following another prison stay in 1674, he had returned home to Swarthmor with his wife Margaret. There he dictated to his wife's son-in-law an autobiography, the chief source on his life from birth through 1675. By this time, he had traveled and preached for the better part of 25 years and had spent nearly six years in prisons for his faith. Most of his six years of marriage had been spent away from his wife, traveling or in jail. In 1675–77, he stayed at Swarthmor, in part due to illness, while corresponding with Quakers on both sides of the Atlantic.

At this point, Fox had literally outlived many of his former associates and persecutors. He traveled to Europe again in 1677–78, spent from late 1678 until March 1680 again at Swarthmor, and then left Swarthmor for the last time in March. The remainder of his life he spent near London—the center of all national activity—writing pamphlets, gathering information about Quaker persecutions, and drafting letters to the government seeking relief. William Penn said of him:

> He held his place in the church of God with great meekness and a most engaging humility and moderation—his authority was inward not outward, and he got it and kept it by the love of God and power of an endless life.

His wife Margaret, ten years older and also in declining health, visited him three times during his last 11 years, once managing to also visit both the dying King Charles II and his successor James

II. By the time of his death in 1691, Parliament and a new king and queen, **William** and Mary, had relaxed most of the laws used to persecute Quakers. Fox had lived long enough to see Quakers granted more freedom.

SOURCES:

The Quakers in Puritan England. Yale University Press, 1964.

Hugh, Barbour, and Arthur O. Roberts, eds. *Early Quaker Writings, 1650–1700.* Eerdmans, 1973.

Gwyn, Douglas. *Apocalypse of the Word: The Life and Message of George Fox (1824–1691).* Friends United Press, 1986.

Jones, Rufus M. *George Fox: Seeker and Friend.* Harper, 1930.

Levy, Barry. *Quakers and the American Family.* Oxford University Press, 1988.

Nickalls, John, ed. *The Journal of George Fox.* Cambridge University Press, 1952.

Francis of Assisi

(1182–1226)

Medieval Italian, who renounced the wealth of his family to live in poverty according to the teaching of Jesus; set out to reform the Catholic Church; and founded the major religious order of the Franciscans.

Born Giovanni (John) Bernardone in Assisi in 1182 (nicknamed Francesco; known in English as Francis); died at Portiuncula in 1226; son of Pietro (a wealthy merchant) and Pica Bernardone; never married.

Early in 1182, while Pietro Bernardone, one of the wealthiest men in Italy's central city of Assisi, was traveling in France on business as a cloth merchant, his wife Pica bore their eldest son Giovanni (John). Nicknamed "Francesco" ("Francis" in English) shortly after his father arrived home, the boy was evidently pampered by his indulgent parents, prompting St. Bonaventure's remark that Francis was "nurtured in vanity among the vain sons of men." A reportedly content, playful child, Francis was not much interested in school, where he learned little more than the basics of reading and writing. His father taught him French, the language of international business, and it is possible that the boy occasionally accompanied his father on business journeys to France. He also learned Latin, the primary language of the Catholic Church (all masses and Church writings were in Latin) and the language of higher education in the universities. But Francis would later describe himself as uneducated—perhaps because he never attended a university or studied theology or philosophy. Never very good at writing, as an adult he would dictate letters signed with a simple cross rather than with his name.

"Now many were not only smitten with devotion, but also kindled by yearning after the perfection of Christ, and, despising all the vanity of worldly things, followed in the footsteps of Francis."

ST. BONAVENTURE

Contributed by Colleen Carpenter Cullinan, Ph.D. candidate, University of Chicago Divinity School, Chicago, Illinois

As a young man, Francis worked in his father's store, waiting on customers and cutting cloth. An attentive salesman, he was rumored to have been flirtatious with women customers. His father was both proud of his son and ambitious on his behalf, for, though the Bernardones were not a noble family, they lived in a time when it was possible for someone with enough money and military skill to join the ranks of the nobility. Pietro's wealth could supply his son with the equipment needed to be a soldier, and with any luck Francis would distinguish himself and be knighted. Earning the title "Sir Francis," and winning glory in warfare, were accolades dreamed of by Francis, as well as by his father.

When not in his father's store, Francis spent time with a group of friends—some of whom were nobles, as he hoped to be—who greatly enjoyed their wealth and idleness. Like their counterparts in any age, rich, bored teenagers in the 12th century had the potential to be quite troublesome, and Francis caused his share of problems. He enjoyed playing practical jokes and spent money in excess. Fond of fine clothes, elaborate banquets, and long evenings of drinking and singing, he hardly resembled the mendicant preacher he was to become. Still, he was known as a generous youth, who gave liberally not only to his friends but also to the poor.

During his youth, the citizens of Assisi were subjects of German overlords. Though Germany was not then a nation, its lands formed the core of the Holy Roman Empire, which extended over much of Europe at the height of its power. In 1197, during a disputed succession of leadership, the people of Assisi took advantage of the confusion and drove out their foreign lords; surprised and encouraged by their success, they went on to attack the local Italian feudal aristocrats. It is unknown whether or not Francis, only 15 at the time, participated in these events. However, the uprising was accompanied by a swift and thorough rebuilding of Assisi's aging defenses (the town wall, for one), and it is said that Francis—later, so well known for his building skills—likely helped his town prepare to defend itself against the enemies it was undoubtedly making.

And the reprisal did come—though not for a few years. Driven from Assisi, the aristocrats fled to the neighboring, rival city of Perugia. In 1201, the rulers of Perugia, urged on by Assisi's displaced nobility, declared war on Francis's hometown, and this time it is certain that he fought. In November of 1202, at the Battle of Ponte San Giovanni, he was taken prisoner and brought back to Perugia, where he was held in prison for about a year.

CHRONOLOGY

1182	Born in Assisi
1197	Citizens of Assisi rose up against German overlords
1201	Neighboring city of Perugia declared war on Assisi
1202	Francis taken prisoner at the battle of Ponte San Giovanni
1206	Commissioned by God to repair the Church
1212	St. Clare began a women's order, following the Rule of St. Francis
1212–15	Fourth Lateran Council of the Catholic Church met and planned reforms; Francis met St. Dominic
1216	Pope Innocent III died
1219	Rule of the Franciscans approved
1223	Revised Rule of the Franciscans approved
1226	Francis of Assisi died
1228	Canonized

Though fortunate to have been held with noblemen, rather than common soldiers, Francis's already questionable health was far from aided by the year's imprisonment. Released in November of 1203 during a temporary truce (the war between Perugia and Assisi would drag on for ten years), he returned home and almost immediately fell ill. Never of robust health, his teen years of excesses and the trials of imprisonment had taken their toll. At 22, he was bedridden for weeks. And the sickness seemed to change him. Once he began to recover, his old pastimes turned uninteresting; horse riding, rich dinners, and even singing brought no pleasure. One thing, however, had not changed: Francis knew he wanted to become a knight.

His health regained, he fitted himself out with a horse and armor, and prepared to join the armies of Pope **Innocent III** who was embroiled in a dispute with German princes over who was the rightful guardian of **Frederick II,** the young successor to the throne of the Holy Roman Empire. This was a time when the pope was still a political, as well as spiritual leader, in Europe, and this was a matter of much importance. Frederick's guardian would hold immense power as the effective leader of the Empire.

Francis Has a Dream, Returns Home

But Francis never made it to Innocent's armies. Along the way, while staying overnight at the town of Spoleto, he had a dream. He dreamed that God spoke to him and challenged his belief that military glory was a route to an honorable life. Which lord would Francis serve—an army commander, or his Lord in heaven? Certain that he'd been told to return home, Francis went back to Assisi. His parents were shocked; the townspeople thought him a coward. And Francis himself was unsure as to why God wanted him back in Assisi.

With all his friends off at war, leaving him with little companionship, Francis began spending long hours in prayer at various churches and chapels around Assisi. Finally, in 1206, at the chapel of San Damiano, he received his commission from God. Kneeling in prayer before a crucifix, he heard Jesus speak to him: "Francis, go repair my house, which is falling in ruins." The chapel of San Damiano was certainly run down, as were many other churches, and Francis believed that it was God's wish for him to repair and build churches.

In contrast to his upbringing, Francis then embraced poverty. Rather than request money from his father for the rebuilding, he would beg from the townspeople. He begged not only for money and materials for the churches, but even for food for himself. Francis avoided his home, sleeping outdoors or in churches. The people of Assisi were baffled to see such a rich young man become a dirty, ill-clothed beggar, and they laughed at him when he asked for food or money. His father was profoundly embarrassed, disappointed—and furious. When Francis passed by his father's shop while begging in the streets during April of 1207, his father accosted him and dragged him before the magistrates of the city, hoping that their authority could convince his son to behave reasonably again. Francis asked that the hearing be held before the bishop, and his father agreed, assuming that Francis's behavior had been as reprehensible in the eyes of the Church as in those of secular society.

Once in the bishop's presence, Francis stripped himself of the clothing he was wearing and laid them at the bishop's feet. Then—no longer clad in anything his father had provided—Francis announced: "I have called Pietro Bernardone my father … now I will say Our Father who art in heaven, not Pietro Bernardone." The bishop covered Francis with his cloak, and Pietro was left without a son.

The following year, with Francis still intent upon rebuilding churches stone by stone, he heard a reading from the Gospel of St. Matthew during mass. This reading described Jesus sending the apostles out to preach the good news; they were to speak of Jesus and the promise of God's kingdom, and were not to bring with them any money, but to rely on the generosity of those to whom they spoke. Francis suddenly realized that rebuilding the Church did not mean fixing fallen stones and cracked mortar; it meant, instead, renewing the life and faith of the people of God by telling them clearly and simply about the life and death of Jesus. Deciding to go and preach the good news, as Jesus had told his disciples to do, Francis also decided to live in imitation of Jesus: he would care for the sick, give away what he owned, and depend on God for food and a place at night to sleep.

In his day, there were many wandering preachers. But Francis was different. He did not condemn political or Church leaders, nor did he preach the horrors of God's wrath and an impending apocalypse. Instead, he spoke about the good news of the Gospel with simplicity and joy. People listened to him, fascinated—and soon, some joined him in his life of poverty and preaching.

The first man to join Francis was Bernard of Quintavalle, a rich man who, impressed by Francis's devotion to God and his simple way of life, sold all his possessions and gave the money to the poor. Bernard became the first "Franciscan," and many others followed suit. In time, Francis decided to see if they could form a Church-approved religious order, with a Rule (like St. **Benedict**'s or St. Augustine's, detailing a monk's way of life) that would set out their purposes and manner of living. He traveled to Rome for an audience with Pope Innocent III, who was at first suspicious of this man dressed in rags who wanted permission to form a religious order.

Pope Approves Franciscan Order

But the night after his meeting with Francis, the pope dreamed that the Church of St. John Lateran—the mother Church of all Christendom—was tilting dangerously to one side and beginning to fall. Just as it was about to crash to the ground, a small man dressed in rags appeared and held up the collapsing church. Pope Innocent recognized the man as Francis and decided that perhaps he had been called to renew and restore the church. Accordingly, he met with Francis the next day and gave papal approval to preach and live together with his followers as religious brothers.

Indeed, the Franciscan brothers were not the only order inspired by Francis. A young woman of Assisi, Clare, who came from the rich and noble Offreduccio family, was so impressed by Francis and his way of life that she, too, wished to become a poor Franciscan. She ran away from home with her cousin Pacifica in 1212, and Francis met them at the chapel of Portiuncula (one of the churches he had rebuilt). There, he cut off Clare's long hair and gave her a rough tunic to wear. Both of these things were symbols of her rejection of worldly beauty and all worldly things. She and Pacifica then entered a convent. Later, Clare's younger sister Agnes joined them, and with this small beginning, the order of the "Poor Clares" was born.

Meanwhile, Francis was becoming known not only for his preaching but also for his extraordinary love for Nature and animals, as all of God's creation was dear to him. There are legends that speak of Francis taming wild animals, including a wolf at the town of Gubbio who had been threatening the townspeople and their livestock. Clearly, Francis loved God's people as well. He tried to travel to Morocco and Palestine, where Christians were fighting Muslims, with hopes of preaching peace and acting as a mediator; but his travels were stopped by sickness and shipwreck.

Back in Italy, more and more people were joining the Franciscans. Designed for a small group of men, the simple Rule of the order was not capable of dealing with thousands of men spread out all over Italy and into other countries. Francis and some of his most trusted counselors attempted to revise the Rule, but in the process much of the simplicity that Francis held so dear was lost. He was disappointed with the final Rule of the order, approved by the pope in 1223—it seemed to sacrifice too much to the worldly demands of politics and practicality, and neglected the promises of God in order to satisfy human needs for security about a place to sleep and one's next meal.

But Francis was still dedicated to the ideal of living in imitation of Christ. Late in his life, he made a pilgrimage to the mountain of La Verda, far to the north of Assisi. There he prayed to experience some of the suffering Jesus had endured on the cross. It was then that he is said to have received the stigmata, the wounds of Christ, as his healthy hands, feet and side suddenly began to bleed in the exact places where nails and a soldier's lance had pierced Jesus. For the rest of his life, he was marked by these miraculous wounds.

By this time, though, Francis's life was coming to an end. He was too ill to attend the general meeting of the Franciscans, called a Chapter meeting, in 1224, where the particulars of the new Rule were announced and put into effect. He was only in his early 40s, but his fragile health had not stood up well to a life of wandering and poverty. In 1226, at the age of 44, he died at Portiuncula, and legend has it that his sickness-ravaged body was renewed in death: his skin became pure white, his limbs supple and healthy as a young man's, and his face beautiful and unmarked by age or suffering. The wounds of Christ stood out black against his white skin, and there were those that said he looked exactly as Jesus must have in death. He was buried in Assisi, but his body was later moved to a crypt in a large, grand basilica built by one of the Franciscan brothers—a strange burial place, perhaps, for a man committed to a life of simplicity and poverty.

Francis's simplicity and goodness of life were recognized as holiness by many who knew him, and only two years after his death he was canonized (that is, declared to be a saint) by the Catholic Church. St. Francis of Assisi remains one of the most popular saints even today; his simplicity, love for life and nature, and commitment to Jesus and the Church still serve as models for Catholics.

SOURCES:

Bishop, Morris. *St. Francis of Assisi.* Little, Brown, 1974.

Bodo, Murray. *Francis: The Journey and the Dream.* St. Anthony Messenger Press, 1972.

Englebert, Omer. *St. Francis of Assisi.* Franciscan Herald Press, 1965.

FURTHER READING:

St. Bonaventure. *The Life of St. Francis; The Mirror of Perfection; The Little Flowers of St. Francis.* (All in English translation in *The Little Flowers of St. Francis*, J. M. Dent, 1944.)

Francis I

(1494–1547)

A true Renaissance monarch, who patronized the arts and letters, practiced a Machiavellian-type diplomacy, strengthened centralized rule in France, but consistently failed in his struggles with his premier rival, Charles V of Spain.

Born September 12, 1494, in Cognac, France; died on March 31, 1547, in Rambouillet, France; son of Charles Valois, Count of Angoulême, and Louise of Savoy; married: Claude de France; married: Eleanor of Portugal; children: (first marriage) Louise, Charlotte, Francis, Henry, Madeleine, Charles, Marguerite. Descendants: Henry III, Henry IV (great-nephew) and Louis XIV, kings of France. Predecessor: Louis XII. Successor: Henry II.

During the first half of the 16th century, Europe—and indeed the world—was dominated by the kings of France, Spain, and England: Francis I, **Charles V** and **Henry VIII**. While Charles V clearly eclipsed his two great rivals, his struggles with Francis I and the House of Valois over Italy formed a centerpiece of European politics during the era.

Francis was a dashing figure, a man of immense charm, humanity and a lust for life. He was daring and courageous in battle, to the point of folly. His numerous affairs both scandalized and impressed his countrymen. His compassion and leniency were uncharacteristic of the age, and he did much to improve the cultural life of his country during the Renaissance.

Yet there was a darker side to the gallant French king. He practiced a foreign policy that would have made Machiavelli proud. He broke his solemn word, and on occasion even allied with Muslim "infidels" and Protestant "heretics" to oppose Catholic Spain. He neglected to properly reward several of his best lieutenants, and as a result lost their fidelity. Finally, he became so obsessed by his futile rivalry with Charles V that he lost all

"On the whole his life was a royal progress, an upward journey of the mind and spirit."

BURKE WILKINSON

Contributed by Glenn Feldman, Ph.D. candidate in History, Auburn University, Auburn, Alabama

sense of proportion, chivalry, and financial discretion. All of this was done during the Renaissance—the twilight of chivalry in Europe. To say the least, Francis I of Valois was a complicated man.

He began life at Cognac on September 12, 1494, the son of Charles, count of Angoulême, and Louise of Savoy. While his parents were fairly obscure nobles, Francis had a strong claim to the French throne; his father was a cousin of the king of France, **Louis XII.**

Francis's childhood was remarkable for his enlightened, humanist education. His mother supervised his upbringing, and a strong bond developed between them. The young boy learned Spanish and Italian, and spent his time reading mythology, history, and literature and admiring art. His youth was equally dominated by a proper noble education in the art of war. Surrounded by young playmates, Francis learned the strategy and methods of Renaissance warfare and showed signs of precociousness at the craft.

At the age of 13, Francis left his mother's household to reside at the French court where courtiers referred to him as the *dauphin*. King Louis XII granted Francis the duchy of Valois, created from the vast estates of the House of Orleans, and in 1512, gave the 18-year-old command of a hundred lances and the army of Guyenne in a war with Spain. **Ferdinand of Aragon** had conquered and annexed the small Bourbon kingdom of Navarre in southwestern France. Although he was aided by the able Odet de Foix, seigneur de Lautrec, Francis's attempt to recover the area was a fiasco. Worse news awaited King Louis in June 1513. Swiss troops had inflicted a humiliating defeat on the French at Novara. On New Year's Eve 1514 the old king died, and on the first day of 1515 Francis I acceded to the throne of France.

Troops Rout Swiss Mercenaries

Francis's reign began auspiciously. To avenge Novara, the young king personally led an army across the Alps, clashing with the Swiss at Milan. Then at Marignano, on September 13 and 14, Francis won the greatest military triumph in what was to be his long career at arms. His troops annihilated the Swiss mercenaries hired by Maximilian Sforza, duke of Milan. Overcome by the victory, Francis ordered the Chevalier de Bayard, the most renowned soldier of his day, to knight him on the spot. An Italian observer meanwhile chronicled the Swiss retreat:

1515	Acceded to the throne of France; crushed the Swiss troops in the employ of the Sforza Duke of Milan at Marignano
1516	Signed the Concordat of Bologna with Pope Leo X
1519	Lost bid for election as Holy Roman Emperor
1521–25	Lost the First Habsburg-Valois War over Italy
1525	Crushed by the Spanish at Pavia; captured and imprisoned in Madrid for a year
1526	Formed the League of Cognac against Charles V
1526–30	Lost the Second Habsburg-Valois War over Italy
1535–38	Achieved a stalemate in the Third Habsburg-Valois War over Italy
1536	Allied with the Ottoman Turks against Spain
1542–44	Lost the Fourth Habsburg-Valois War over Italy
1544	Made the Peace of Crespy with Charles V

It was a marvel to see the routed Swiss return to Milan—one had lost an arm, another a leg, a third was maimed by the cannon. They carried one another tenderly; and seemed like the sinners whom Dante pictures in the ninth circle of the Inferno.

In the aftermath of Marignano, Francis took the duchy of Milan, and Pope Leo X ceded him Parma and Piacenza. The papacy also entered into the famous Concordat of Bologna with Francis the following year. According to the terms of the covenant, the Catholic Church in France became *Gallican;* that is, subject primarily to the authority of the French crown. The Concordat marked a high point in the struggle between *Gallicans* and *Ultramontanes* in France, those who cast their allegiance to the pope "over the mountains." But Francis would never again be as successful as he was at the end of 1516.

Flushed with these victories, Francis openly challenged Charles of Spain and Henry VIII of England for election to the vacant throne of the Holy Roman Empire. The imperial title was bitterly contested between the three young monarchs, especially between Francis and Charles. In the end, New World wealth along with an 850,000 *florin* bribe carried the day for the Spanish king of the House of Hapsburg; thus, in June 1519, Charles (who had been Charles I of Spain) was named by the German electors as Holy Roman Emperor Charles V.

In order to avenge this slight, Francis initiated the first of five Habsburg-Valois Wars over Italy. Both houses had inherited the conflict over the rich and divided Italian lands from their predecessors. In 1494, the year of Francis's birth, French and Spanish armies had collided over the question of Italy. The French, under Charles VIII, had become involved in the Angevin quest for Italian territory when they were summoned by Lodovico Sforza to team with the Milanese and Swiss to successfully overthrow Medici rule in Florence. Pope Alexander VI appealed to Ferdinand of Aragon on behalf of the Medici, and the Spanish drove the French from Italy in 1495.

The drive for Italian property had become even more byzantine by 1499. Charles VIII's successor, Louis XII, joined with Swiss troops and Ferdinand of Aragon to overthrow Sforza rule and seize Naples. A falling-out ensued between the French and Spanish monarchs, leading to overwhelming Spanish victories at Barletta, Cerignola, and Garigliano. By 1503, the Spaniards were masters of the Kingdom of the Two Sicilies (Naples and Sicily). During these wars, the 150-year invincibility of the Spanish infantry was begun under Ferdinand's *el Gran Capitan,* Gonsalvo de Cordoba.

Now, in August 1520, Francis met with Henry VIII in Calais, at the Field of the Cloth of Gold, but failed to win Henry's support for a Spanish war. Meanwhile, Charles V allied with Pope Clement VII. In late 1520, Francis covertly sponsored an assault on imperial Luxemburg by Robert de la Marck and took advantage of the revolt of the *Comuneros* ("Spanish dissidents") to occupy a defenseless Spanish Navarre for the Bourbon House of Albret. During the next four years, the war went poorly for Francis. His men won a few battles, at Parma and Fuenterrabia, but were soundly defeated at Ezquiros and Pamplona and driven out of Navarre. The Spanish invaded France proper and took Mouzan and Toulon. In Italy, Spanish arms were triumphant at Tournai, Lodi, Cremona, Genoa, and Alessandria. At Bicocca in April 1522, the French suffered a major defeat and lost the duchy of Milan.

Complete disaster awaited Francis at Pavia in February 1525. He led an army of 37,000 men against a Spanish army of equal numbers. The Spanish lost 1,000 men. Between 10 and 14,000 Frenchmen died, and many others were taken prisoner, including Francis himself. One biographer describes his capture:

> [A] stab or a shot went home: his horse quailed under him and fled. He was now on his feet, slay-ing to right and left.... In this last stand Francis seemed doomed. The enemy engulfed him.... There Francis stood, encircled, gasping bewildered, shaken, his hand pierced, his cheek [and knee] bleeding.... [T]he news ran like fire.... And soon the whole air rang ... "Vittoria, Vittoria, Espana, Espana."

Soon after this unmitigated disaster, Francis wrote his mother to assure her of his health: "All that is left to me is my honor and my life." Before a year had passed, Francis would have only his life.

The King Breaks His Word

The French king begged to be taken from Naples to Spain and was placed under house arrest in Madrid for over a year. The captivity was far from oppressive; Francis hunted regularly, enjoyed the companionship of his most illustrious comrades, and attended numerous dinners given in his honor. He gained his release in March 1526 by agreeing to relinquish all claims to Italy and by ceding the duchies of Burgundy, Flanders, and Artois. When Francis swore as a gentleman to return to captivity if he failed to live up to his end of the bargain, Charles agreed to set him free. Once back in his own realm, however, Francis declared the Treaty of Madrid to be null and void. His excuse was that he had signed the document under duress. The act was at best an example of his rapidly maturing *realpolitik;* at its worst, one lacking completely in honor.

Francis's violation made another war with Spain inevitable. To that end, he quickly prepared the Holy League of Cognac, which arrayed France, England, Milan, Venice, the papacy, and the Florentine Republic against Charles. In Spain, the emperor bitterly regretted his decision to release the French king at his word; "Pavia might as well not have happened."

But in this second Habsburg-Valois War, Charles was destined to win an even greater victory than in the first. Francis's strategy called for the simultaneous sending of two armies: one across the Alps and another across the Pyrénées. Swiss troops in the employ of Clement VII and Venice would then attack Spanish holdings on the Italian peninsula. The French would meanwhile send a fleet to take Genoa and Naples. At first all went well for Francis. Genoa fell to his talented naval commander Andrea Doria; then a French army overran most of the countryside around Milan.

But in May 1527, Charles's imperial soldiers, with their pay in arrears, mutinied and sacked the eternal city of Rome. The brutal act shocked Francis's partners. Pope Clement imprisoned himself in a tower for his own protection and was soon placed under arrest by the Spanish. He capitulated to Charles in the Treaty of Barcelona. Henry VIII, whose heart had never really been in the enterprise, also quickly came to terms. Encouraged, Charles issued a challenge of personal combat to Francis, but, as in 1526, the offer of a duel was ignored by the French king.

While the French fought on in Naples, the Spaniards advanced on all fronts. Andrea Doria, miffed at Francis's failure to reward him for his victory at Genoa, left French service for the emperor. The French effort utterly deteriorated in 1528. The Spanish won two battles at Genoa and were victorious at Aversa and Savona. By 1529, Francis, "anxious for peace," capitulated in the Treaty of Cambrai, which repeated the humiliating terms of 1526, and also called for the ransoming of Francis's two sons in Madrid at 2 million gold crowns. The pact was sealed by Francis's marriage to Charles's sister, Eleanor of Portugal. The Florentines fought on gamely until 1530 when the Spanish overwhelmed them and installed Alessandro de Medici as duke.

Francis Becomes Patron of the Arts

For six years, Francis seethed. In order to divert himself, he became an enthusiastic patron of the arts, and in the process, helped bring the Italian Renaissance to France. A pet project was the renovation of the royal palaces at Blois, Chambord, Fontainebleau, and the Louvre. Purchasing works of Michelangelo, Raphael, and Titian, Francis invited some of the finest artists of the day to come to France: men like Leonardo, Benvenuto Cellini, and Andrea del Sarto. Fond of literature, Francis corresponded with the humanist Erasmus and sponsored a royal lecture series that patronized promising scholars. He also had time for a number of affairs; two of his more noteworthy mistresses were Diane de Poitiers and Anne, duchess of Etampes.

Despite his marriage to Eleanor, by 1536 Francis could no longer contain his thirst for revenge. In February, he completed the Capitulations, an "unholy alliance" with the Muslim Turk Khair ad-Din-Barbarossa, a move which shocked and offended most Christians in Europe, even many of his longtime supporters. Though they appreciated his will to resist the Spanish colossus, there were limits: allying with "infidel" Turks to slaughter fellow Christians was considered nothing less than heresy.

But Francis was not to be deterred from what had become a quest. The papal nuncio ("papal representative") in Paris measured the French king's growing obsession for revenge with alarm. Francis's hatred of Charles had grown to such a venomous level "that he seems to make it his [exclusive] business to provoke the emperor" into war. Charles responded by flinging down the gauntlet, proposing a personal duel with Francis for the third time. Unlike the two prior challenges, the French king accepted, but Pope Paul III interceded to prevent the combat.

Undaunted, Charles launched a successful assault against Francis's Turkish ally in the Mediterranean. Spanish expeditionary forces led personally by Charles took La Goletta, liberating thousands of Christian prisoners, and soon thereafter captured Tunis. Barbarossa fled to Algiers with the remnant of his fleet. Charles then turned toward Italy, landed in Sicily in August, and advanced with ease toward the Alps.

Francis also faced attack at home. Charles launched a two-pronged invasion of France: in Provence and in northern France. The Spanish took Aix and Guise but were stopped at St. Quentin and Peronne in the north. Credit for Francis's successful defensive campaign was given to Anne de Montmorency, the French constable. Montmorency himself took to the offensive and recaptured two towns in northern France, but the Spanish replied by winning at St. Pol and Montreuil.

By 1538, both sides were financially exhausted. In one year alone, Francis spent 5.5 million livres on the war. The French king had done better in this war, but at best only a draw had been gained. Europe was in an economic depression, and Francis was forced to utilize the sale of *rentes* ("royal bonds"), offices and titles as shortsighted, stop-gap financial expedients. Peace was signed at Nice in 1538, renewing the Italian status quo once again.

In 1542, Francis finalized a treaty with Ottoman sultan **Suleiman** "the Magnificent," and declared war on Charles yet again. At first the war went well for Francis, but by 1544 he had sustained another loss against Charles. French forces took Luxemburg and laid seige to Perpignan but were soon defeated in both theaters. The campaign of 1543 went better. Francis experienced several successes in the Spanish Netherlands, but a stalemate was reached when imperial forces prevailed at Julich, Venloo, Zutphen, Cambrai, and Guelders. A joint Franco-Turkish assault on Nice was then repulsed. In Italy, Francis won a close victory at

Cerasole in April 1544 but lost two months later at Serraville.

Abruptly, the stalemate turned to a resounding Spanish victory. Charles signed a treaty with Henry VIII for a joint invasion of France, and the English took Boulogne. Meanwhile, Charles's armies captured St. Dizier, Epernay, and three other strongholds in Champagne. By September, the war was over as Francis and Charles reaffirmed the status quo at Crespy. Venice's ambassador was one of those astounded by the sudden French collapse: "Who ever would have thought that the French would allow the invaders free passage and let them devastate their country!"

The following year, Francis took out his frustrations by allying with the German Protestant "heretics" of the Schmalkaldic League against Charles. At Muhlberg, Charles recorded his greatest victory by prevailing over the Lutheran princes. Francis also vented his anger on the Waldensian heretics in his own country (followers of Peter Waldo who were reacting to clerical corruption). A brutal campaign against the Waldensians demolished 22 towns and killed 4,000 people. Perhaps feeling guilty over his Turkish and Protestant alliances, Francis posed as the model Catholic prince by instituting an index of banned books and a court of religious heresy that burned hundreds of Huguenots ("French protestants").

The Franco-Spanish dispute over Italy was finally put to rest in a seventh war, one that lasted from 1547 to 1559, and was waged by the successors of Francis and Charles. In these wars, Spanish arms were victorious for the sixth time, racking up major wins at Marciano, Siena, Naples, St. Quentin, and Gravlines. Spanish hegemony ("superiority") in Italy was cemented by the Treaty of Cateau-Cambrêsis in 1559. Ultimately frustrated by his nemesis in Madrid, Francis died of gout and liver disease at Rambouillet on March 31, 1547. At his death, the French crown was 6 million livres in debt. Ten years later, the crown declared bankruptcy.

SOURCES:

Hackett, Francis. *Francis the First.* Literary Guild, 1935.

Knecht, R. J. *Francis I.* Cambridge University Press, 1982.

Kohn, George C. *Dictionary of Wars.* Doubleday, 1986.

Wilkinson, Burke. *Francis In All His Glory.* Farrar, Straus, 1972.

FURTHER READING:

Knecht, R. J. *Francis I and Absolute Monarchy.* London Historical Association, 1969.

Seward, Desmond. *Prince of the Renaissance: The Golden Life of Francis I.* Macmillan, 1973.

Francis Joseph I

(1830–1916)

Austrian ruler who came to the throne in the midst of a revolution, died in the midst of a war, and dedicated himself to holding together his polyglot empire.

"Beloved by few, hated by few, during his later years he was respected by nearly all as the linch-pin that held the empire together."

WILLIAM M. JOHNSTON

Name variations: Franz Joseph I, Francis Joseph I of Austria. Born on August 18, 1830; died on November 21, 1916; eldest son of archduke Francis Charles (second son of the Emperor Francis I) and Sophia (daughter of Maximilian I, King of Bavaria); married: Elizabeth (his cousin), April 12, 1854; children: three daughters, one son, Rudolf. Predecessor: Ferdinand I (1793–1875). Successor: Charles I (1887–1922).

Francis Joseph, who saw as his main duty the preservation of his diverse Empire and the House of Habsburg-Lorraine, embodied—as had so many of his ancestors—the will to survive. He came to the throne in the midst of the revolutions of 1848 which erupted in Vienna, Prague, Budapest, Zagreb, Milan, and Venice and which helped to topple his predecessor Emperor Ferdinand I (1793-1875). Dubbed by his subjects "The Benign," Ferdinand was feeble in mind and sick in body and clearly unable to resolve the crises which plagued the Empire in 1848. The army, with the aid of Russia, defeated the revolutionary students and workers and virtually restored the old order. The only lasting achievement of the 1848 turmoil was the emancipation of the Austrian peasant, who had supported the crown throughout the upheaval, the dismissal of the state chancellor, Prince **Klemens von Metternich,** and the accession of 18-year-old Francis Joseph as emperor.

As the symbol of the Empire and the concern for law and order, Francis Joseph was to rule for more than 68 years. (By 1914, near the end of his reign, the Austria-Hungary Empire, the second largest state in Europe, had grown to a popu-

Contributed by Marsha and Linda Frey, Professors of History, Kansas State University and University of Montana

CHRONOLOGY

1848	Became emperor
1859	War with Piedmont and France; lost Lombardy
1866	Defeat at Königgrätz in Seven Weeks' War with Prussia; lost Venice
1867	Creation of Dual Monarchy; execution of brother, Ferdinand Maximilian
1889	Suicide of son Rudolf
1896	Death of younger brother, Archduke Karl Ludwig
1898	Assassination of wife, Empress Elizabeth
1908	Annexation of Bosnia and Herzegovina
1914	Assassination of Franz Ferdinand; onset of World War I

lation of approximately 50 million.) Although the bureaucracy and the army used German as the language of government and command, the Germans were but one of the many ethnic groups in the Empire; the largest also included Magyars, Czechs, Ruthenes, Poles, Rumanians, Serbo-Croats, Slovenes, and Italians. In an era of strong nationalistic passions, an Empire which based its rule on the sacrifice of nationalism could not and did not survive. But by the time Francis Joseph died in the midst of World War I—a war which would destroy his Empire—he had come to be venerated as a father figure.

Throughout his long reign, the responsibility for his many lands fell on his shoulders. By the end, he was quite alone: his brother **Maximilian,** emperor of Mexico, had been shot by a firing squad (1867) and his sister-in-law Carlota driven mad; his other brother, Archduke Karl Ludwig (1883–96) had drunk from the river Jordan while on a pilgrimage and died from an intestinal infection; his son and heir apparent, Count Prince Rudolf (1858–89) had killed his lover and committed suicide at a hunting lodge outside of Vienna at Mayerling; his adored wife Elizabeth (1837–98) had been stabbed to death by an anarchist; and his nephew Franz Ferdinand (1863–1914) and his morganatic wife Sophie Chotek (1868–1914) had been assassinated at Sarajevo. On learning of his wife's death, Francis Joseph remarked that "nothing has been spared me in this world." Two of the few joys of his life were his friendship with the actress Katharina Schratt and his hunting, a traditionally noble pastime.

Francis Joseph was particularly attached to the army which he thought had saved his Empire in the 1848–49 turmoil. Regarding himself throughout his life as a soldier first and foremost, he was extremely punctilious in matters of apparel and ceremony, refusing to appear in any dress other than a military uniform. Noted one of his generals: "He lives and dies for the army." After the 1852 death of his minister president, the ruthless and amoral Prince Felix Schwarzenberg, Francis Joseph never appointed another but relied, often fatally, on his own judgment. A pedantic man of mediocre mind and colorless personality, he distrusted men of intelligence and ability, preferring ministers like himself: meticulous, unimaginative, routine. Although ignorant of history, with no interest in the arts, he was a man of integrity and industry and toiled relentlessly to preserve his Empire. Rising punctually at 5 A.M., he addressed his decrees to "my peoples."

Unemotional and cold, he brutally and callously dismissed officials once they outlived their usefulness. He disliked everything progressive, modern, or liberal and shunned new inventions such as the typewriter and the telephone. Remaining wedded to tradition and traditional ideas, Francis Joseph refused to make any concessions to democratic demands. Because he believed in Divine Right governance, he thought that he was answerable to God alone. This authoritarian view of government also prompted him to interfere in ecclesiastical affairs if the interest of the state demanded it.

In further attempts to preserve his Empire, he acceded to demands for constitutional rule, for the creation of the Dual Monarchy in 1867, and for universal suffrage in Austria. The Dual Monarchy in effect created the kingdom of Hungary, east of the river Leith, and the kingdom of Austria, west of the river Leith. Each half had its own constitution and parliament, but they shared a ruler and a common ministry for finance and foreign affairs. This compromise worked to the disadvantage of the Slavs who were treated as an oppressed minority. Francis Joseph proved unable to solve the problem of oppressed minorities, a problem which ultimately led to the unravelling of the Empire and the end of the Habsburg-Lorraine dynasty's rule. Although he did agree to the establishment of constitutional governments in both Austria and Hungary, he retained a veto over all legislation.

During his rule, he encouraged extreme centralization, bureaucratic rule, and repression of liberalism. A tradition of muddling along and piecemeal concessions continued. Still his reign was a

HISTORIC WORLD LEADERS

very prosperous one; because of the establishment of a free trade area and the abolition of the serf's feudal obligations, productivity and wealth grew. In the latter part of his rule, however, Francis Joseph adopted increasingly protectionistic policies.

Vienna Is Cultural Capital

Although neither music nor art appealed to the Emperor, Vienna served as the cultural and intellectual capital of Europe during the time of Francis Joseph. It was there that luminaries such as Sigmund Freud, the playwright Arthur Schnitzler, and the poet Hugo von Hoffmansthal lived, and artists such as Arnold Schoenberg, Gustav Klimt, and Oskar Kokoschka flourished. It was there that the waltz made Vienna the world's dance capital and the "waltz king," Johann Strauss the younger, perfected that orchestral form.

In foreign policy, Francis Joseph's vacillation eroded the prestige the monarchy had earlier enjoyed. His decision to remain neutral during the Crimean War succeeded in alienating both sides in the conflict and leaving his Empire diplomatically isolated. In the 1859 war with Piedmont and France, Austria lost Lombardy and in the 1866 war with Prussia, Venice.

The Seven Weeks' War with Prussia proved a disaster; on July 3, 1866, at Königgrätz, the Prussians trounced an Austrian army, inflicting the most decisive defeat Austria suffered between the Napoleonic wars and World War I. Francis Joseph proved no match for the astute **Otto von Bismarck**, who established Prussian hegemony ("influence") in the German lands, nor for Italian premier **Camillo Cavour,** who forced the Habsburgs out of Italy. Francis Joseph, who sought to preserve his Empire intact and maintain Austrian influence in Germany and Italy, failed in all three endeavors.

After the 1866 debacle, Francis Joseph turned eastward toward the Balkans in hopes of consolidating Austria-Hungary's influence there. In 1908 the Empire annexed two Turkish provinces, Bosnia and Herzegovina. But Francis Joseph was unable to understand the forces of nationalism which would ultimately ignite World War I and cause the dismemberment of his Empire.

Austria-Hungary was determined to end the problem with the South Slavs and crush the threat from Serbia, which served as the nucleus of Slav agitation. Serbian nationalist groups aimed to destroy and dismember the Habsburg monarchy while government officials remained just as determined to eliminate this threat. Habsburg authorities attempted to subordinate Serbia by banning the importation of all Serbian livestock. Because the Serbs exported approximately 90% of their products to Austria-Hungary, economic hardship increased and resentment flared. This economic tactic backfired and ignited the "Pig War" which exacerbated relations between the two countries. Terrorist groups, such as the Black Hand, increased in strength; they disseminated propaganda, smuggled activists across the border, and assassinated government officials.

Balkan Struggle Escalates to World War

In 1914, the Black Hand, after several bungled attempts, succeeded in assassinating the heir apparent Archduke Franz Ferdinand and his wife Sophie Chotek at Sarajevo. What began as a small Balkan struggle between Serbia and Austria-Hungary escalated into a world war. After the Serbs refused to agree to the terms of the ultimatum issued by Austria-Hungary, Austria-Hungary declared war on the Serbs, who in turn looked to their protector Russia. Because of the system of entangling alliances, Russia pulled in her allies, Britain and France (the Triple Entente), and Austria-Hungary drew in hers (the Triple Alliance). Ottocar Czernin, the Austro-Hungarian foreign minister remarked about the decision to go to war: "We were bound to die. We were at liberty to choose the manner of our death and we chose the most terrible."

Nor was the Emperor under any illusion about the outcome of the war. He rightfully thought that the struggle was beyond the strength of his people, but he did not live to see his people starving and freezing, deprived of basic necessities such as flour and oil. Nor did he live to see the subsequent dissolution of his Empire, the collapse of this carefully orchestrated realm "with definite classes and calm transitions." When he died on November 21, 1916, he was succeeded by his grandnephew Charles I of Austria, who would be forced to abdicate under the armistice terms imposed by the Allied Powers one year later. World War I had destroyed the world of security which Francis Joseph epitomized and with it the dynasty which had ruled these lands for hundreds of years.

SOURCES:

Crankshaw, Edward. *The Fall of the House of Habsburg.* Penguin, 1963.

Johnston, William M. *The Austrian Mind.* University of California Press, 1972.

May, Arthur J. *The Passing of the Habsburg Monarchy.* University of Pennsylvania Press, 1966.

Taylor, A. J. P. *The Habsburg Monarchy.* University of Chicago Press, 1976.

Zweig, Stefan. *The World of Yesterday.* University of Nebraska Press, 1964.

FURTHER READING:

Jaszi, Oscar. *The Dissolution of the Habsburg Monarchy.* University of Chicago Press, 1929.

Kann, Robert A. *A History of the Habsburg Empire, 1526–1918.* University of California Press, 1977.

May, Arthur J. *The Habsburg Monarchy, 1867–1914.* Norton, 1968.

Murad, Anatol. *Franz Joseph I of Austria and his Empire.* Twayne, 1968.

Redlich, Joseph. *Emperor Francis Joseph of Austria: A Biography.* Macmillan, 1929.

Francisco Franco

(1892–1975)

General in the Spanish Civil War, who led the victorious Nationalist Army and subsequently became head or Caudillo of the Spanish state.

"Above all, Franco was a professional soldier, dedicated to the maintenance of discipline and order, with a minimal interest in constitutional forms and a paternalistic conception of his patriotic duty."

BRIAN CROZIER

No one in the small sea town of El Ferrol in northwestern Spain would have guessed that the baby boy born on December 4, 1892, would one day be head of state. El Ferrol was 375 miles from the capital, Madrid, and the family of Francisco Franco Bahamonde was respected but not overly distinguished. The parents, in fact, could scarcely have presented a greater contrast; Don Nicolás Franco was a rake, a man of the world, while his wife María del Pilar Baamonde y Pardo de Andrade was serious, austere, and devoted to the Catholic Church.

Don Nicolás had continued the Franco family tradition by serving in the Naval Administrative Corps, rising to the top of his profession before retiring in 1924. Eventually taking a mistress, he separated from the family and fathered an illegitimate child. His relationship with his second son was never happy; Don Nicolás never ceased criticizing Francisco's abilities, even after his son had become the leading political figure of Spain. Consequently, Franco adopted his mother as a role model.

The young Franco was adventurous; he also swam, went hunting, and played football. When

Born Francisco Franco Bahamonde on December 4, 1892, in El Ferrol, Spain; died on November 20, 1975; son of Don Nicolás Franco and María del Pilar Baamonde y Pardo de Andrade; married: Doña María del Carmen Polo Martínez Valdés, October 16, 1923; children: (one daughter) Carmencita.

Contributed by David L. Bullock, Ph.D. candidate, Kansas State University, Manhattan, Kansas

he was sent to the small local School of the Sacred Heart, he proved diligent and conscientious, even though he could not be called an outstanding student. At 12, he was admitted to the Naval Preparatory Academy whose graduates were destined for the upper echelons of the Spanish navy.

Unfortunately, international events conspired to cut short his anticipated naval career. In 1898, much of the navy had been sunk by the United States in the Spanish-American War. Since Spain was slow to rebuild, many ports which had relied on naval contracts were plunged into an economic recession. Not only was El Ferrol hit hard, entrance examinations for the navy were canceled in 1907. These conditions caused the young Franco to despise professional politicians whom he blamed for defeat, recession, and the decline of Spain's world status.

Frustrated, Franco passed examinations for the Toledo Infantry Academy in 1907. A small boy, who came to be nicknamed "Franquito" or "Frankie Boy," the future dictator had a difficult and unhappy passage through school. "Studious and introspective," notes George Hills, "and unwilling to follow his fellows into sexual or alcoholic experiments in the town," Franco "became

the object of malicious bullying and 'initiations.'" Performing adequately but not brilliantly, he graduated in the middle of his class in 1910. Overall, Franco had demonstrated a knack for sizing up terrain which could be suitable as a field of battle. "In later life," writes J.W.D. Trythall, "his appreciation of ground was his most remarked quality as a military commander."

Until 1912, Franco served in his home town as a second lieutenant. After twice volunteering, he was finally accepted to fight in Spanish Morocco, a transfer that would, in effect, hone his martial talent and earmark him for the primary role he would play later in the Spanish Civil War. By 1915, at age 22, he had become the youngest captain in the Spanish army. Further, he had been decorated several times and had led so many successful operations that the locals, or Moors, were convinced the *baraka* or divine blessing was with him. In 1916, however, he was severely wounded while leading a charge; subsequently decorated, he was promoted to major and transferred to Oviedo, Spain.

His next three years were relatively quiet. Franco read widely in the area of military history while romancing Carmen Polo y Martínez Valdés. Then, in 1920, he was placed second-in-command of the newly formed Spanish Foreign Legion in Morocco and had to delay plans for marriage until 1923. The Legion was modeled on the vaunted French Foreign Legion and tended to attract the same breed of men; whether ardent romantic, hard-bitten veteran or criminal, those who joined were united by a lust for adventure. The Legion motto "Long Live Death!" had been coined by its highly decorated and oft-wounded commander, José Millán Astray.

He Commands the Legion

During the next three years, Franco was continuously baptized in blood while engaging in one colonial operation after another, always against a fresh constellation of rebellious Riff tribesmen. The fighting and corresponding reprisals on both sides were swift, summary, and often involved mutilations. By 1923, he had become a living legend in contemporary Spain; promoted to lieutenant colonel, he was made commander of the Legion.

The year 1923 was also a watershed in Spanish history. Spain's involvement in Morocco had been costly and unrewarding, and the unhappy situation had produced a parliamentary regime politically paralyzed. In September, General **Miguel Primo de Rivera** set himself up as head of a Military Directory with the intention of greasing the jammed political machinery and saving the social fabric of Spain. The king, Alfonso XIII, was retained in a titular capacity.

As Spanish strategic policy devolved into withdrawal from the hinterland of Morocco and a concentration of strength along the coast, the talented leader of the Riff tribe, Abd el-Krim, overstepped himself by simultaneously attacking the forces of both France and Spain. Franco, having been promoted to full colonel, was chosen to spearhead a critical amphibious landing in Alhucemas Bay. The newspapers again cried his name as his Legion held, then defeated, superior enemy forces. As a result, he was promoted to brigadier general in 1926, the youngest in Europe.

A prestigious assignment followed as commander of the 1st Brigade of the 1st Division in Madrid under the very nose of the king. Franco was too well known, however, to feel forced into courtly ritual. Instead, he studied military history and political theory in his spare time. Perhaps because of his studies, his name became linked with the new General Military Academy which was being planned in Zaragoza. In 1928, he was appointed director. After touring French and German military schools, Franco decided to create a different and innovative Spanish academy which stressed mobility and practical field training over classroom theory. His attention to the health of his troops and, in particular, his methods in the prevention of venereal disease were clearly progressive.

In 1930, the fortunes of Spain took another abrupt and historic turn. The national economy had so declined that both the paternal dictator, Primo de Rivera, and King Alfonso were forced to leave the political arena. Shortly after, in 1931, the Spanish Republic was born. The next years were often as uncertain for Franco as they were for Spain. Extensive military reforms were put in motion and the academy was suppressed; Franco, in effect, was out of a job until 1932, when he assumed command of the 15th Infantry Brigade at Corunna. The following year, he readied the defenses of the Balaeric Islands. Neither position was likely to accelerate his career.

Finally, in 1934, he met and won the patronage of the new Minister of War, Diego Hidalgo. A promotion to major general preceded a governmental mission to crush a general worker's strike in Asturias. This he orchestrated using his old unit, the Legion, and the *Regulares* from the Army of Africa. Awarded the Knight Grand Cross of the Order of Military Merit, his name was splashed once more across every newspaper in Spain. Depending upon one's political inclinations,

Franco had become the man to hate, or the man to love.

Politics in Spain, meanwhile, had taken an increasingly bipolar turn. Dramatically, the strength of the liberal center of the new Republic was undermined by extremists of the political Left and Right. Communist youth gangs and the fascist *Falange* (Phalanx) became the street *pistoleros* of radical political groups in the Spanish Parliament. Confidence in the new Republic waned.

In February 1936, the left-wing Popular Front scored major successes in the general elections. As a result, a group of generals under Emilio Mola began planning a coup to restore law and order. General José Sanjurjo, who in 1932 had tried a similar but abortive coup and was now in self-imposed exile in Portugal, was intended to head the new *junta*. Conspiratorial eyes looked to Franco for support.

Early in 1935, Franco had been appointed commander in chief of the military forces in Morocco. Months later, he had served briefly as chief of the general staff before a left-wing shift in the government maneuvered him to the distant Canary Islands in an attempt to isolate him politically. Personally, Franco was in no hurry to compromise his career by participating in a risky coup d'état. As he had done in the political crises of 1923, 1930, and 1932, he stayed his hand. Not until he was sure Mola's counterrevolution had a reasonable chance of success did he signal he would be prepared to lead Spain's elite force, the Army of Africa, onto the Spanish mainland in an attempt to overturn the faltering Republic.

Spanish Civil War Begins

The Spanish Civil War began in July 1936. Those who would defend the remains of the Republic were aided by **Joseph Stalin**'s Soviet Union and called "Republicans," or "Loyalists." Those who sought to alter the left-wing drift were aided by **Adolf Hitler**'s Germany and **Benito Mussolini**'s Italy and called "Nationalists." From the start, Franco assumed a leading Nationalist role.

Slipping out of the Canaries by air, Franco landed in Morocco and succeeded in obtaining German and Italian help in transporting the Army of Africa across the Straits of Gibraltar. Inside Spain, the Nationalist revolt had met with varying degrees of success. Franco's first major thrust was to link with Mola's Army of the North. Fortuitously for Franco, General Sanjurjo was killed in an airplane accident while in transit to the Nationalist zone (Mola also would die, conveniently enough, in an airplane accident in 1937). By September, Nationalist forces were knocking on the gates of Madrid, and at Salamanca, Franco established his headquarters; that same month, he was named commander in chief as well as head of state or *El Caudillo.*

Beyond his excellent if sometimes overly cautious generalship, Franco's chief quality was probably his insistence on unity. No small part of the Nationalist growth had been due to Fal Condés's religious and militant militia, the Carlists, and to José Antonio Primo de Rivera's fascist Falange. In December, Franco united these potentially disparate militias, incorporating them officially into the jurisdiction of the Nationalist Army. His decree of April 1937 adopted the Falange as his official state party. Since the generals who had opened the Civil War had had no coherent political or social platform, Franco found Falange ideology useful in order to appeal to a broader base of public support.

Furthermore, Franco maintained law and order. Indeed, most foreign correspondents reported that life seemed normal behind Nationalist lines. Franco kept inflation down and instituted a basically sound fiscal policy. The Republicans were never able to obtain a commensurate level of coordination and cooperation. While Republican radicals carried out acts of violence against the clergy and Church property, Franco conducted prayer services in his army and respected Catholic rights. Consequently, in the autumn of 1937, the Nationalists received the blessing of the Vatican with all the moral support that conferred in a predominately Catholic country.

Strategically, from 1936 to 1939, Franco's Nationalists held the military initiative. While a constant pressure was maintained along the Madrid Front, Nationalist forces spent 1937 reducing Republican strongholds in northern Spain. In 1938, the Nationalists "marched to the sea," the Mediterranean Sea, virtually splitting the Republic in half. Catalonia, the last Republican bastion in northeastern Spain, fell in the spring of 1939, and Madrid and remaining Republican troops in the southeast surrendered.

The ending of the Civil War heralded a settling of scores; a half million Republicans fled to France. If the Republic had wasted little time in executing political undesirables, the Nationalists could now exact their vengeance at leisure. Over the next several years, tens of thousands of Spaniards were imprisoned and executed.

While Franco began the unification of Spain and the consolidation of his position, Europe plunged into World War II in September 1939. Franco next demonstrated a remarkable diplomatic prowess. Both Hitler and Mussolini (the Rome-Berlin Axis) had a natural expectation that as they had assisted Franco, Franco should ally himself with them against the Allies. If Spain cooperated in an Axis seizure of Gibraltar, Allied—and particularly British—strategic interests would be seriously undermined throughout the Mediterranean region.

At the Hendaye Conference in October 1940, Hitler discussed such a plan, but Franco remained adamant that Spain would need "time" to prepare for war. After protracted negotiations, Hitler grew exasperated and remarked to aides that he would rather have a few teeth pulled than meet with Franco again. Despite a continued courtship, Franco's contribution to the Axis war effort was a single division, the Blue Division, which fought in Russia for over two years. Throughout, *El Caudillo* pursued a policy of neutrality, delay, and cautious self-interest.

By the end of World War II, fascist credentials had become singularly unattractive. Franco had already taken his first step of survival into the postwar era by restricting many of the public activities of his official state party, the fascist Falange. Nevertheless, in 1946, the newly created United Nations declared that all countries should remove their ambassadors from Madrid. A political pariah, Franco's Spain seems to have been saved economically only by the assistance of **Juan Peron**'s Argentina.

U.S. Ambassador Returns to Spain

In the late 1940s, however, Franco moved with commensurate skill to rehabilitate Spain with the family of nations. Flying the banner of anticommunism during the emerging Cold War served him well. In 1950, the United States returned its ambassador and three years later the Americans were allowed four military bases in Spain. President **Dwight D. Eisenhower** personally greeted Franco in Madrid in 1959. Indeed, considering his Concordat with the pope in 1953, Franco can be said to "have arrived."

Franco is known to have said that Spain was a relatively easy country to rule. Certainly, he let little interfere with his daily routine. After a personal interview in the 1960s, Brian Crozier provided a general sketch of Franco's activities:

He works from 10 A.M. till mid-afternoon, then lunches frugally, allowing himself a single glass of wine, neither more nor less. Back at his desk at 5 or 6 P.M., he works till 10, when dinner is served. At midnight he and Doña Carmen recite the Rosary together, then he reads himself to sleep. Twice a week he grants audiences—military on Tuesdays, civil on Wednesdays.

His daily cabinet meetings were long, arduous, without rest breaks, and smoking was not permitted. Within general guidelines, ministers were given great latitude; indeed, many complained they did not know where they stood. Franco was a pragmatist, not an ideologist, who exuded an optimistic self-confidence and who revealed a knack for balancing subordinates and affairs of state. Listening to proceedings with varying degrees of interest, he became involved most actively when the military, foreign policy, the Church, the media, and labor came under discussion. Socially, he sought to strengthen the middle class.

Overall, according to historian Stanley Payne, "There is no evidence that Franco's central ideas and values—rightest, nationalist, authoritarian and Catholic—were ever altered substantially at any point in his life." Neither, it seems, were his morals, which in a personal sense remained exemplary from youth to death. Even political opposition reluctantly admitted that Franco never smoked, became drunk, or had extramarital affairs.

Among his hobbies, which included fishing, golf, painting, and horseback riding, he was most famous for his lengthy hunting excursions. He allowed himself frequent vacations, and hunting—judging by the tremendous amount of ammunition expended—seemed to be a way to let off steam. These almost legendary bouts in the countryside continued well into his 60s, which were physically vital years free of health complications. His final refuge, however, remained his wife, daughter, brother Nicolás, and only sister Pilar.

As with most leaders in authoritarian states, Franco seems to have become progressively more distant. When he toured Spain, it was in a black Rolls Royce replete with national coat-of-arms and accompanied by an entourage of red-bereted bodyguards. Movements were not published, and in urban areas police were positioned every 30 feet. Not that security measures are unusual for any head of state, but Franco spoke and laughed less. Presiding over a Spain in transition, Franco, in a very real sense, represented the end of an era; it is probable he was uncertain what his country's tomorrow would bring.

Conversely, unlike most authoritarian states, Spain prospered. The nation opened to foreign investment and tourism in 1959. A limited economic liberalism flowed, and Spain experienced an economic boom in the 1960s. Modernization and industrialization walked hand-in-hand, and by 1970 approximately 49% of the population was middle class.

Franco's rule in the 1960s continued to be authoritarian, but in 1966—prompted by student unrest—censorship was eased, and he proclaimed the Organic Law of the State. Unfortunately, the gesture included few concessions beyond minor changes in the elections to the *Cortes* (parliament). Far from creating a dynasty of his own, however, as some of his most ardent followers suggested, Franco seems to have seen himself as a temporary guiding hand. Therefore, on July 21, 1969, Prince Juan Carlos (a Bourbon and third son of Alfonso XIII) was designated Franco's successor and king of Spain. After so many years, Spain was to be returned to a limited monarchy.

Clearly, Franco was not blind that history was marching on. Spanish Morocco had won its independence in the 1950s, and Spain's petition to the United Nations for Gibraltar in the 1960s had fallen on deaf ears. By the early 1970s, the Spanish Sahara was pressing for independence.

Meanwhile, inside Spain there had been university protests, industrial disturbances in the north, separatists-terrorists (chiefly though not exclusively Basques), and even a loyal opposition group within his bureaucracy that sought to reform the system. Yet, no group believed that a change of government was possible during Franco's lifetime.

On December 20, 1973, his prime minister and closest friend, Carrero Blanco, was assassinated; in July 1974, Franco suffered an attack of thrombophlebitis, an attack that signaled a host of successive afflictions over the following 16 months: partial kidney failure, bronchial pneumonia, coagulated blood in his pharynx, pulmonary edema, bacterial peritonitis, gastric hemorrhage, endotoxic shock and finally, cardiac arrest. At one point, Franco exclaimed, "My God, what a struggle it is to die." On November 20, 1975, when relatives asked doctors to remove his support systems, the 82-year-old Franco passed into history.

During those final months, Juan Carlos prepared to ascend the throne of Spain. From 1976 to 1978, the new king managed a liberal democratization of the governmental machinery without great conflict or civil war. In the words of Stanley Payne: "Never before had the formal institutional mechanisms of an authoritarian system been used peacefully but systematically to transform the whole system from the inside out."

Scholars have struggled to place the Franco regime into its proper context. It may be that Franco took the reins of a state wracked by Civil War and through paternalistic guidance half-controlled and half-witnessed historic changes as they unfolded during his 39 years in power. Possibly, the blood and ink have not yet sufficiently dried to render balanced judgment. In any case, the final verdict must come, with time, from the hearts and minds of the Spanish people.

SOURCES:

Crozier, Brian. *Franco: A Biographical History.* Eyre & Spottiswoode, 1967.

Hills, George. *Franco: The Man and His Nation.* Robert Hale, 1967.

Payne, Stanley G. *The 1936–1975, Franco Regime:* University of Wisconsin Press, 1987.

Trythall, J. W. D. *Franco: A Biography.* Rupert Hart-Davis, 1970.

FURTHER READING:

Cortada, James W., ed. *Historical Dictionary of the Spanish Civil War, 1936–1939.* Greenwood Press, 1982.

Gallo, Max. *Spain Under Franco: A History.* Allen & Unwin, 1973.

Jackson, Gabriel. *A Concise History of the Spanish Civil War.* Thames & Hudson, 1974.

———. *The Spanish Republic and the Civil War, 1931–1939.* Princeton University Press, 1965.

Preston, Paul. *The Politics of Revenge: Fascism and the Military in Twentieth-Century Spain.* Unwin Hyman, 1990.

Fredegund

(c. 550–597)

Slave attendant turned queen, who cleared the way for her son to rule a
reunited Francia by her ruthless use of assassination as a political tool.

*"Cast all fear aside then, and let no dread of
death enter your minds, for you know full well
that all human beings are but mortal. Steel your
hearts like men."*

EXHORTATION TO HER ASSASSINS
ATTRIBUTED TO FREDEGUND

Among the enslaved women who attracted
the attention of Merovingian monarchs
while serving in the royal households, Fredegund was also among the much smaller number
who became queens, not merely concubines. She
survived political dangers which would have ended
the careers of even well-born queens and held on
to her husband's loyalty though unable to provide
him with healthy sons. Developing innovative
methods of assassination and the ability to persuade others—even monks and priests—to join her
plots, Fredegund distinguished herself by sheer
viciousness even in the midst of the spectacular
brutality of the Merovingian dynasty. By the standards of her day, she was a great success: she was
honored by her royal husband; accumulated a great
treasure chest; put her son on his throne; and even
died a natural death.

It is impossible to recover any information
about Fredegund's early life, but she must have
been in her mid-teens when she first attracted the
attention of Chilperic, king of the Soissons, while
attending his first wife Audovera. Quick to obtain
influence over him, she displaced Audovera in his
affection and in the intrigues of the court,

*Name variations: Fredegunda,
Fredegond, Fredegundis.
Pronunciation: FRED-uh-
gund. Born c. 550; died in 597;
an unfree attendant to
Chilperic's first wife Audovera;
married: Chilperic I, king of
Soissons (later called Neustria);
children: Samson, Chlodobert,
Dagobert, Theuderic, one other
(all died in early childhood),
Rigunth, Chlothar. Predecessor:
Guntram, as regent for
Chlothar II. Successor: her son,
Chlothar II.*

*Contributed by Phyllis Culham, Department of History, United States
Naval Academy, Annapolis, Maryland*

445

although Audovera had borne Chilperic three sons. As a teenaged concubine, Fredegund must have been very clever, since Merovingian queens were able to acquire political authority independent of that exercised by their husbands. As Suzanne Wemple writes:

> They could participate in assemblies and issue donations and privileges…. [T]hey received secular and ecclesiastical officials; they could also influence episcopal elections and draw upon the treasury to build a network of political loyalties.

Audovera had had plenty of time to organize a coterie of followers who could have opposed her political eclipse by a mere concubine; nevertheless, she virtually dropped out of the dynasty's history once Fredegund became the center of Chilperic's court. She is heard of only later as one of Fredegund's victims.

Fredegund's own status is difficult to discern. While Merovingian kings were certainly not given to lifelong devotion to one woman, some scholars believe that they practiced "serial monogamy." Once married, they took only concubines, not second and third wives, or they divorced one wife before acquiring the next. Others believe that they enjoyed the polygamy customarily practiced by Frankish kings. In any case, Fredegund was probably not married to Chilperic when in 567 he married Galswinth, the older sister of his sister-

in-law Brunhild, queen of Metz (later Austrasia) through her marriage to Chilperic's brother King Sigibert. As the two sisters were from the royal family of Visigothic Spain, a second marriage to a second Frankish king must have been a carefully negotiated diplomatic event with implications for Europe from the Atlantic to the Danube, since Galswinth converted from Arianism to Roman Catholicism upon her marriage to Chilperic. Surely the Visigothic king would not have sent his oldest daughter to be the second wife of the Frankish king with the smallest territory, especially if the first wife were a former slave. Fredegund must have been only a concubine at the time, or she must have been temporarily repudiated. Very temporarily, since Chilperic found Galswinth dead, strangled in bed, shortly after the wedding.

The marriage had begun happily, since, as Gregory of Tours remarked, "He loved her very dearly for she had brought a great dowry with her." Unfortunately, Gregory's account of her death is not altogether coherent. He believed that Galswinth had annoyed Chilperic with her constant jealousy of Fredegund and that Chilperic, consequently, had her strangled by a servant. Chilperic's discovery of the body seems odd in that context, but Gregory despised Fredegund and surely would have blamed her for the murder had he been able to discover any evidence to support the accusation. Whether Chilperic had Galswinth killed or Fredegund had suborned the murder and got away with it, Fredegund's powerful hold on Chilperic is clearly demonstrated. Gregory ends his account: "King Chilperic wept for the death of Galswinth, but within a few days he asked Fredegund to sleep with him again."

Contemporaries had no doubts, however, about Fredegund's role in the later events of 573. Chilperic's territorial ambitions had led him to make war on his brother Sigibert, and he was losing badly. Theudebert, one of his sons by Audovera, had been killed. Although they were under seige and in personal danger, Fredegund saved the situation when her agents approached Sigibert—just as his army was raising him triumphantly on their shields—and hacked him and his chamberlain to death with poisoned axes. Fredegund's talent for such well-timed, impressively brutal assassinations might have endeared her to Chilperic. As Wemple writes:

> Her willingness to make arrangements through her own servants for assassinations … and for handling bribes … made her a political asset to the king.

Brunhild, Sigibert's determined widow, quickly provided Fredegund the opportunity to apply her special skills on Chilperic's behalf again. Brunhild married Merovech, another son of Chilperic and Audovera, and began plotting with him to take over both kingdoms, Soissons and Metz. Brunhild had long blamed Fredegund for the death of her sister, and Fredegund began to return her hatred. Fredegund had already contracted a secret alliance with Duke Guntram Boso of Metz. Although he had been Sigibert's right-hand man, he had killed Audovera's son Theudebert, and she liked him for that reason. As an enemy of Chilperic's, Guntram Boso was able to win Merovech's confidence and lure him out of sanctuary, but Fredegund's assassins did not work so efficiently that time, and Chilperic would need to hunt down Merovech later. Nonetheless, this may have been just the kind of service which led Chilperic to depend on her. He would not have wanted to bear the opprobrium attached to conspiring with a man who had already killed one of his sons to do in another. But Fredegund could do it for him.

She did, however, still lack an important component of queenly power. Even high-born queens needed the leverage which came from having sons in the line of succession. As Janet L. Nelson notes: "A Merovingian ex-wife often cut a pathetic figure, especially if she was sonless, or if her sons quarrelled with, or pre-deceased their father." What Fredegund most needed was a healthy son to enable Chilperic and Soissons to dispense with Audovera's boys altogether. Gregory claimed that while they were besieged by Sigibert, Fredegund believed that she was dying of complications of childbirth when she bore Samson to Chilperic, and therefore wanted to have the boy killed. Presumably she did not want to leave a pawn for others to play. Chilperic refused and had Samson baptized. It must have been a great disappointment to Fredegund when the boy died shortly before his fifth birthday; with Theudebert and Merovech dead, and only Clovis in the way, Fredegund must have believed that her son had a good chance to succeed Chilperic.

She was not spared additional blows. An epidemic of lethal dysentery swept Gaul, nearly killing Chilperic and almost all the infants in that part of Francia; Fredegund's sons Chlodobert and Dagobert were among the victims. According to Gregory, Fredegund told Chilperic what the problem was:

> We still lay up treasures, we who have no one to whom we can leave them…. Now we are losing the most beautiful of our possessions! Come, then, I beg you! Let us set light to all these iniquitous tax-demands!

Their bonfire of records ended the first attempt at an orderly exchequer in Gaul, and it apparently did not strike contemporaries, including Gregory, as odd that Fredegund assumed that taxation was a greater sin than murder. Her "conversion," as it came to be known, was too late to save their youngest son, who was deeply mourned. "From this time onward," wrote Gregory, "King Chilperic was lavish in giving alms to cathedrals and churches and to the poor, too."

Never one to miss an opportunity, Fredegund promptly convinced Chilperic to send Audovera's last boy, Clovis, to a city where the dysentery was still raging. He stayed healthy, however, and joined Fredegund and Chilperic at the country estate where they were spending a month in mourning. There he made the mistake of gloating over what he would do to his enemies when he took the throne and thereby terrified Fredegund, who according to Gregory, was uncharacteristically vulnerable and deeply depressed over the loss of her own sons. Such vulnerability might have enticed her to listen to the sycophant who reported that Clovis, while sleeping with the daughter of one of her serving women, had persuaded that servant to kill Fredegund's young princes with black magic. Fredegund had the mother and daughter tortured and persuaded Chilperic to have Clovis arrested. He died in custody, and Chilperic accepted the story that he had somehow stabbed himself. In the sequel, Fredegund finally had Audovera tortured to death and the informer burned at the stake.

Fredegund bore another son, Theuderic, but similar events followed upon his death in infancy. Informers told her that he had been killed by witchcraft and that her old enemy Mummolus the Prefect was behind it. As a result she had a large number of Parisian bourgeois wives tortured until they admitted that they were witches who had associated with Mummolus; they were then beheaded, burned alive, or tortured to death. Mummolus underwent a particularly varied torture. Again demonstrating that wealth was not an end in itself, according to Gregory, Fredegund burned everything associated with little Theuderic:

> All his clothes, some of them silk and others of fur…. Any object in gold or silver was melted down in a furnace, so that nothing whatsoever remained intact to remind her of how she had mourned for her boy.

Nor did Fredegund miss the destroyed wealth. When her daughter Rigunth was sent on her abortive expedition to marry into the Visigothic dynasty, Fredegund added to the dowry Chilperic provided "a vast weight of gold and silver and many fine clothes."

Chlothar Is Born; Chilperic Assassinated

Certainly Fredegund participated with Chilperic in all he did. In his obsequious poetry addressed to Chilperic, Venantius Fortunatus described Fredegund as an important aide and support to Chilperic, ascribing the prosperity of the royal house to her. There were those who suggested, however, that Fredegund was engaged in other activities about which Chilperic knew nothing. Count Leudast spread the rumor that Gregory himself was spreading the rumor that Fredegund was having an affair with Bertram, the bishop of Bordeaux. Fredegund ordered that Count Leudast be killed by being beaten on the throat with a block of wood. The *Liber Historiae Francorum*—which was even more hostile to Fredegund than was Gregory—claimed that she had Chilperic assassinated in 584, because he had caught on to her affair with his mayor of the palace, Landeric. The chronicler Fredegar, on the other hand, believed that Brunhild was behind the assassination. Just months before the murder, Fredegund had born Chilperic a son, Chlothar. Chilperic ordered him hidden away in the countryside, apparently out of the belief that their other children had indeed been killed by enemies. Fredegund may have been pregnant again at the time of the assassination, but nothing is heard of that child later.

Whether she had planned the assassination or had been surprised by it, Fredegund's immediate situation was extremely dangerous. Seeking sanctuary in the cathedral at Paris, along with her personal treasury and her infant son, she sent a message to Chilperic's brother King Guntram, placing herself and her son Chlothar under his protection. He and her nephew-in-law King Childebert—son of her old enemies Sigibert and Brunhild—both converged on Paris. Luckily for Fredegund, Guntram got there first. Childebert's emissaries brought a simple message to Guntram: "Hand over the murderess, the woman who garrotted my aunt, the woman who killed first my father, and then my uncle, and who put my two cousins to the sword." Guntram's eventual reply demonstrated the importance of sons of royal blood to a woman without powerful family to protect her: "She has a king as her son, and she therefore cannot be surrendered."

While Fredegund was still hiding in the cathedral, she began accusing various people of theft and worse, prompting Gregory to claim: "Fredegund had no fear of God, in whose house she had sought sanctuary, and she was the prime mover in many outrages." Eventually Guntram sent her off to a manor near Rouen, where Chilperic's chieftains deposited her in the care of Bishop Melanius and set up a government under the infant Chlothar. Fredegund could hardly bear this quiet life of retirement in the countryside, since, wrote Gregory, "She was very depressed because much of her power had come to an end, and yet she considered herself a better woman than Brunhild." She persuaded her household cleric to an assassination attempt on Brunhild. When he was caught and sent back to her, she had his hands and feet cut off. For her next project she sent two clerics, armed with swords specially grooved to hold poison, after both Brunhild and Brunhild's son King Childebert. Caught along with another of her agents, they were tortured, mutilated, and killed.

Attending church in Rouen, Fredegund had a hostile encounter with an old enemy, Bishop Praetextatus, whose words Gregory reports:

> In exile and out of exile I have always been a bishop ... but when you give up your role as Queen you will be plunged into the abyss. It would be better for you to abandon your stupid malicious behavior.

As one would expect, "The Queen bore his words ill. She was extremely angry." So angry, in fact, that she had him stabbed while he said Easter Mass. After he had been carried still living to his bed, she called upon him under the pretext of offering her own doctors. Giving her one last lecture, Praetextatus died without further assistance. When a local leader came to call, expressing his opinion that she had gone too far, Fredegund offered him a hospitable drink which killed him within an hour. She attempted to assassinate Leudovald, bishop of Bayeux, for trying to bring her to justice, and sent agents to try to kill King Guntram, when he too took a strong stand against the assassination of bishops during mass.

Meanwhile, having never made it to Spain with her large dowry, Fredegund's daughter Rigunth was stranded in Toulouse where her own situation was now perilous. Though Fredegund was finally able to rescue her daughter, they were unable to live together happily. Gregory claimed that "she would often insult her mother to her face, and they often exchanged slaps and punches."

Worst of all, Rigunth repeatedly reminded her mother of her servile origins by pointing out her own royal blood. Inviting Rigunth to lean over into the treasure chest and pick out whatever she liked, Fredegund tried to break her neck with the lid. Servants pulled her off just in time to keep Rigunth from being strangled. Clearly, there was little possibility that mother and daughter could live on their manor placidly after that, and Gregory described the aftermath: "There were never-ending outbursts of temper and even fisticuffs. The main cause was Rigunth's habit of sleeping with all and sundry."

Some of Fredegund's projects in Rouen prospered, while others did not. A team of 12 more assassins sent after King Childebert were caught, and some killed themselves in prison rather than face the torture and mutilation inflicted on the others. When a blood feud between two large families in Tournai became a hazard to public safety, Fredegund warned them to stop. When they would not, she invited them to a dinner of reconciliation. As all were seated at the table, the three survivors of the original quarrel were simultaneously beheaded by axemen. The problem, quite simply, was solved.

Fredegund Becomes Regent

Most important, she convinced Guntram to bring her son to Paris for baptism (which was then routinely delayed long past infancy) and to allow her to participate in the ceremony. From there it was a short step to replace the men around Chlothar and become regent herself, although she accepted an arrangement which left Guntram as Chlothar's godfather and protector.

Naturally, she did not remain in the background during her regency. In 593, the childless Guntram died, leaving his kingdom to King Childebert and touching off war between the two surviving royal families. The *Liber Historiae Francorum* claims that Fredegund took to the field herself after Landeric fell in battle. Fredegar associated her with the 12-year-old Chlothar in describing Neustria's victories in 596: "Fredegundis and her son King Chlotar took possession of Paris and other cities after the barbarian fashion." Though Childebert's early death that same year left Brunhild vulnerable, Fredegund's own death the following year deprived her of enjoying the victory for which she had planned. She died unaware that the now aged, but heretofore astute, Brunhild would make the fatal error which would leave Fredegund's son Chlothar II the ruler of a reunited Francia.

In 612, Brunhild's grandson died, and she refused to partition the two kingdoms among his four sons or even to separate Burgundy from Austrasia again. Powerful dukes who wanted more recognition of their regional authority defected and in one campaign Chlothar reunited all of Francia, celebrating his victory by having the elderly Brunhild tied to horses and dragged to death in memory of his mother.

Nonetheless, Fredegund could not have been an altogether terrible mother, because Fredegar described her son as "strong-minded and well-read, … also a god-fearing man, … kindly disposed to all and full of piety." While it is true that Chlothar had been sent away from his mother for much of the first decade of his life, it is tempting to see Fredegund's influence in his later respect for women. Fredegar, in fact, regarded this as his main failing, commenting that he "took too much notice of the views of women young and old." Although Chlothar never witnessed Chilperic's intense and long-term devotion to Fredegund, Fredegar did think that Chlothar's love for his second wife was eccentric in its intensity. Still, Nelson insisted: "Fredegund's is probably the best-documented case of a king's passion giving his consort long-term political ascendance."

Fredegund used her ascendance not only to accumulate wealth and power but also to contribute to some of the processes which were to transform Europe: the rise of the mayors of the palace, steps taken toward the creation of an exchequer, and the union (if only temporary this time) of Francia.

SOURCES:

Fredegar. *The Fourth Book of the Chronicle of Fredegar.* Translated by J. M. Wallace-Hadrill. Nelson, 1960.

Gregory of Tours. *History of the Franks.* Translated by Lewis Thorpe. Penguin, 1974.

Liber Historiae Francorum. Translated by Bernard Bachrach. Coronado Press, 1964.

FURTHER READING:

James, Edward. *The Franks.* Basil Blackwell, 1988.

Nelson, Janet L. "Queens as Jezebels: The Careers of Brunhild and Bathhild in Merovingian History," in *Medieval Women.* Edited by Derek Baker. Basil Blackwell, 1978.

Wemple, Suzanne Fonay. *Women in Frankish Society: Marriage and the Cloister 500 to 900.* University of Pennsylvania Press, 1981.

Frederick I (Barbarossa)

(1123–1190)

King of Germany, Holy Roman Emperor, and king of Italy, who restored order in Germany, then spent 30 years trying to subdue the cities of northern Italy, with the aim of restoring the glories of the Roman Empire.

*

Name variations: Frederick I Hohenstaufen; "Barbarossa" means "Redbeard." Born Frederick, Duke of Swabia, in Weiblingen (Germany) in 1123; died by drowning on crusade in Cilicia (Asia Minor) on June 10, 1190; son of the Duke of Swabia (located in the Black Forest in southwest Germany); nephew of Emperor Conrad III; married: Beatrix of Burgundy, 1156. Predecessor: Conrad III (his uncle). Successors: Henry VI (son), Frederick II "Stupor Mundi" (grandson).

Frederick Barbarossa, first of the Hohenstaufen kings of Germany, Holy Roman Emperors, created a legend in his own lifetime. Strong, energetic, highly intelligent, an intuitive politician and superb leader of men, he was elected to leadership in Germany when that assemblage of tribal duchies was in the throes of disintegration. Through masterful use of traditional Germanic law and Roman principles of justice, charismatic leadership, skillful employment of primitive economic notions, and recourse to exceptional political solutions, he managed to bring a sense of unity to a land that had been beset with tribal animosities for centuries.

Frederick was born into a Germany of antagonistic small states, successors to the Carolingian and Ottonian eras. German geography dictated the organization. From the areas drained by the Rhine River in the west, to those of the Oder River in the east, from the shores of the North and Baltic seas in the north to the slopes of the Alps in the south, Germany was a collection of competing duchies, only vaguely associated by slightly differing dialects of an approximately common language.

"[Frederick Barbarossa] has become, as it were, the patriarch of a nation, and his memory still lives in the German heart as the personification of Germany unity."

EDWARD FREEMAN

Contributed by H. L. Oerter, Professor of History, Emeritus, Miami University, Oxford, Ohio

Using the existing feudal system, Frederick employed the notion of *vassalage:* military service in return for political protection and award of land, a two-way path of loyalty between and among fighting men who gave their services to a lord who would treat them justly. The lesser vassals protected the agricultural workers (serfs) and—in the more heavily populated areas—the artisans and tradespeople assembled in the towns. These same vassals gave military service to the lord on an annual basis. Frederick took this system and improved on it, making fuller use of the tendency for artisans and tradespeople to gather at places which were conducive to the conduct of trade. By making special grants to these cities and towns, in effect, he made the towns "vassals," too. This feudal arrangement, which slowly converted to a capital-driven system, was dominated at one extreme by the king or emperor, and at the other by the Church.

Frederick's early life was spent in preparation for the period of his rule. His father, Duke of Swabia, had given up the effort to rule and retired to a monastery in Alsace, permitting young Frederick to assume the ducal duties. Then, in 1147, his uncle, Emperor Conrad III, went on crusade. Frederick accompanied him and learned much from the tragic errors of that mismanaged effort, while escaping most of the blame.

Frederick Elected King of Germany

When Conrad III died in 1152, his only son Henry having predeceased him, Frederick was at his side and received the imperial "blessing," ostensibly designating him as heir to the throne of Germany and the Holy Roman Empire. Through judicious negotiating—give-and-take politics—Frederick managed to secure his election as king of Germany. This was the equivalent of election, also, as Holy Roman Emperor, although tradition required papal consent and coronation in a spot of the pope's choosing. The actual coronation did not take place until much later. Frederick was crowned king of Italy in Pavia in 1155, in return for his having captured the rebellious reforming monk, Arnold of Brescia, and having turned him over to the papacy for execution. The imperial coronation was accomplished at Rome in that same year.

Frederick operated on two different fronts. He worked tirelessly to organize his German fiefs (feudal estates), keeping the German nobility satisfied with concessions, honors and consultations. He also paid close attention to his rights as king of Italy and Holy Roman Emperor. In this area, he experienced difficulties, not only with recalcitrant

CHRONOLOGY

1147	Went on Second Crusade with uncle (Conrad III); Duke of Swabia abdicated; Frederick succeeded
1152	Conrad III died; Frederick elected king of Germany
1155	Arnold of Brescia forced papacy to flee Rome; Frederick crowned king of Italy and Holy Roman Emperor; captured Arnold
1157	Pope Hadrian IV and King William I of Sicily concluded agreement against Frederick; Frederick moved against Poland
1158–62	Moved against Italy; took Lombard cities, including Milan; Hadrian died, succeeded by Alexander III; Frederick ordered Milan razed; excommunicated by Alexander III
1164	Henry the Lion given leeway by Frederick
1174	Frederick's second Italian campaign; Lombards organized against him
1176	Frederick's third Italian campaign; defeated at Legnano
1177	Treaty of Venice; Frederick's excommunication revoked; peace with Lombard League.
1178	Frederick crowned king of Burgundy; Diet of Spires gave Bavaria to Wittelsbach family
1186	Urban III taken prisoner at Verona by Frederick; Henry invaded Papal States
1188	Frederick agreed to go on Third Crusade
1190	Drowned while crossing River Salef in Cilicia

Italian city-states, unaccustomed to imperial authority, but also with counties, duchies and marquisates, many of which enjoyed virtual autonomy.

In asserting his imperial authority on the Italian peninsula, Frederick undertook several different visits to the area. The first of these, in 1155, witnessed his political victory as king and as emperor. Since the time of **Charlemagne,** the office of emperor was realized when the individual first attained the crown as king of Germany, then as king of the Romans. The so-called Iron Crown of Lombardy symbolized the holding of power in the upper peninsula, and the title of king of the Romans was a convenient fiction to permit the holder to claim imperial powers and privileges.

In 1158, Frederick descended into Italy in order to assert his authority in Lombardy, where he succeeded in imposing his will on most of the cities and towns of the region. This was solidified by the Diet of Roncaglia where he confirmed ancient privileges of those cities that had submitted to his will. He also granted the first university charter, when he proclaimed the existence of the University of Bologna (1158), authorizing its students to organize.

From 1159 to 1168, in successive campaigns in Italy, Frederick's fortunes rose and fell as resistance to his will increased among his Italian "subjects" and problems arose between Frederick and Pope Alexander III, who actively worked to prevent the emperor from gaining more powers. Alexander had excommunicated Frederick in 1160. Although this did not initially affect the emperor's operations, it increasingly worked to weaken his position both in Italy and in Germany, where the papacy urged the clergy to resist him. Since Frederick had chosen and appointed many of the bishops, especially in Germany and Burgundy, he retained an advantage for a long time.

Frederick and Henry the Lion Quarrel

Part of Frederick's troubles in Germany stemmed from a long-standing quarrel between the emperor and Duke Henry the Lion, a Bavarian noble who secured appointments not only in Bavaria but also in north Germany. Henry grew powerful and became a source of many problems for the emperor and for the balance of the German nobility.

Frederick's problems in northern Italy were concentrated in the Lombard League, a collection of northern Italian cities which organized to resist his tax collectors and imperial officials, many of whom acted with excessive force and awakened distrust, suspicion and anger among the Italians. From 1162 when he succeeded in taking the city of Milan, ordering its nearly total destruction, until 1176 when the army he was leading back into Italy from Germany was met and defeated by forces of the Lombard League at Legnano (in northern Italy), Frederick's troubles multiplied. Following his military defeat, he secured a partial political victory by obtaining the recession of his excommunication, making his peace with the papacy at Venice.

While Frederick was occupied in Italy, Henry the Lion had been usurping power in the north. Instead of having him executed, Frederick managed to get Henry charged by a court of German nobles and clergy, secured his conviction at two different trials in 1178 and 1179, and had him exiled. All of Henry's lands were forfeited and the great majority of his noble peers concurred in finding him guilty of a number of charges.

The activities of Henry the Lion had nearly undone Frederick's work in northern and central Germany, and he had to set about the reorganization of the German kingdom, a task that was not completed when Frederick left to go on the Third Crusade in 1189. But before he departed, Frederick secured the German crown for his surviving son, Henry, who became the sixth of that name to sit on the German and imperial thrones, managed to have him marry Princess Constance, sole heiress to the Norman Kingdom of Sicily and southern Italy, and even had him named coemperor over strenuous objections, both lay and clerical.

Frederick's reign spanned the terms of five popes. The last of these was Clement III, who convinced him to go on the Third Crusade, in company with **Richard the Lionheart** of England and **Phillip II Augustus** of France. The German contingent, 20,000 strong, met and organized at Regensburg, on the Danube River in Bavaria, and marched along its course through Austria (in those days a Grand Duchy), Hungary, Serbia, and Bulgaria, arriving near Constantinople in the late part of 1189.

The Byzantine emperor, Isaac Angelus, had schemed against the crusaders (all Western Christians were called *Franks* at the Byzantine court). This offended Frederick and resulted in his taking Philippopolis and several nearby fortresses. Then Frederick's army began to march against Constantinople, causing Isaac to sue for peace and to promise immediate transportation to Asia Minor, one of the goals of the crusaders.

The crusaders crossed the Hellespont at Gallipoli (the western end), and Frederick was headed toward Seleucis, one of his intermediate objectives, when he drowned while attempting to cross a swiftly running river, the Salef. The body was found, thus verifying his death. He was 67 years of age.

In 43 years of ruling as duke, king, and emperor, Frederick had established himself as a most unusual ruler, employing every technique then known to gain his ends. While he was not completely successful, he earned the respect and confidence of most of his subjects. He died while on crusade, having committed himself and his Empire to the cause of the Christian Church. This was sufficient to preserve his memory in the hearts of his subjects for centuries to come. In the time of his grandson, **Frederick II,** the legend sprang up that told of Barbarossa, asleep, seated at a stone table in a cave in the mountain of Kyffhäuser, in Thuringia, his red beard continuing to grow. It is still being said that when Germany is in dire need of him, Frederick Barbarossa will come forth and lead his nation to victory.

Of more importance, however, is the fact that Frederick built a firm foundation on which the German nation was to rest. The ideas, the ideals, and the reality all appeal to the German spirit and continue to exist in one form or another. Even **Adolf Hitler** was not averse to using the Barbarossa legend to further his own objectives.

SOURCES:

Munz, Peter. *Frederick Barbarossa: A Study in Medieval Politics.* Cornell University Press, 1969.

Pacaut, Marcel. *Frederick Barbarossa.* Scribners, 1970.

Previté-Orton, C. W. *The Shorter Cambridge Medieval History.* Vol. 2. Cambridge: Cambridge at the University Press; 1971.

FURTHER READING:

Barraclough, Geoffrey. "Frederick Barbarossa and the Twelfth Century," in *History in a Changing World.* Oxford, 1955.

Jordan, Karl. *Henry the Lion: A Biography.* Oxford: Oxford University Press, 1986.

Otto I, Bishop of Freising. *The Deeds of Frederick Barbarossa.* Translated and edited by Charles C. Mierow. Columbia Records of Civilization, Sources and Studies. Columbia University Press, 1953.

Frederick II

(1194–1250)

Last great Holy Roman Emperor known as the "wonder of the world," who was locked in conflict with the papacy, but who was also renowned for his legislation and his patronage of the arts, culture, and learning.

Name variations: Stupor Mundi; Frederick II, King of the Romans, King of the Germans, Emperor of the Holy Roman Empire. Born on December 26, 1194, at Jesi in central Italy; died on December 13, 1250, buried in Palermo; son of the Emperor Henry VI (from the German house of Hohenstaufen) and Constance (a Sicilian princess; daughter of King Roger II); married: Constance (sister of Pedro II of Aragon; died 1222); married: Isabella (sister of Henry III of England); children: Henry, Conrad, Manfred. Predecessors: Henry VI (1190–97), Philip (king of Germany, 1197–1208). Successor: Conrad IV (r. 1250–54).

The life and career of Frederick II, king of Sicily, Germany, and Holy Roman Emperor, known to contemporaries as the "wonder of the world," the "scourge of the earth," and even the Antichrist, has engendered more controversy than perhaps any other ruler of the 12th or 13th centuries.

Born in December 1194 at Jesi in central Italy, Frederick II was the son of the emperor Henry VI, from the German house of Hohenstaufen, and the Sicilian princess Constance, daughter of King Roger II. Numerous rumors and considerable gossip surrounded the event, as his mother was at least 40 years old (an advanced age in the Middle Ages). One story held that the pregnancy had been faked and that a butcher's baby had been smuggled into the palace and presented as Constance's son. Other legends purport that Frederick was really the result of a liaison between the empress and a demon, while more favorable prophecies predicted that he would be the "hammer of the world."

But the prospect of the young Frederick uniting the houses of Germany and Sicily was thrown into chaos by the death of his parents before his

"Since the time of Alexander there has been no prince in Christendom such as [Frederick II], not only because of his great power, but also on account of the skill with which he dared to oppose the Pope."

FAKHR-AD-DIHN

Contributed by Russell Andrew McDonald, Ph.D., University of Guelph, Guelph, Ontario, Canada

fourth birthday and led to civil strife in both kingdoms. Although his mother had entrusted her son to the care of Pope Innocent III, it was not until 1206 that some degree of control was exercised on the child's behalf in Sicily, and it was 1209 before the pope was able to provide any security by arranging a marriage to another Constance, the sister of King Pedro II of Aragon. Wed at the age of 15—for political rather than romantic reasons—to a woman who was at least ten years his senior, Frederick and his wife would eventually develop a surprising sense of mutual affection, respect, and admiration. Years later, when Constance died in 1222, Frederick had his crown placed with her in the sepulchre, symbolizing his love.

But during the early, uncertain years, Frederick—known as the "boy of Apulia"—remained in Sicily, and, despite the political turmoil, proceeded with his education. (By the 13th century it was becoming more common for rulers to be able to read and write.) Moreover, Sicily had for centuries been a cosmopolitan kingdom where Western, Muslim, and Greek influences had mingled, producing a rich cultural heritage, and Frederick was a product of this environment. Salimbene, a 13th-century Italian Franciscan, wrote that: "He could read, write, and sing and he could compose music and songs," and "speak many different languages." Frederick is said to have been an avid student, reading history—his favorite subject—late into the night. In addition to academic pursuits, he also trained in the arts of war, as was common among the nobility. Accordingly, Frederick mastered the knightly arts, including riding and the handling of arms.

In 1210, regardless of his absence, Frederick had been elected king by some of the nobles in Germany. Despite the apprehensions of his wife as well as other influential advisors, the 17-year-old decided to take up the challenge: in 1212, he set out from Messina for Germany. As his rival, Otto of Brunswick, rushed to counter him, Frederick stayed just ahead of his enemy, prompting one contemporary writer to remark that "if Frederick had delayed three hours he never could have entered Germany." It took two more years before Otto was defeated by **Philip Augustus,** king of France, and one more year, 1215, before Frederick was crowned in an elaborate ceremony in the cathedral at Aachen. Immediately thereafter, he took the cross and promised to go on a crusade to free the Holy Land from the Muslims, who had recaptured Jerusalem from the Christians in 1187.

During the next few years, by delaying his promise to go on crusade and by relying heavily on the ecclesiastical princes (the important bishops

CHRONOLOGY

1194	Frederick II born
1198–1209	Civil strife in Germany and Sicily; Frederick entrusted to care of Pope Innocent III
1214	Rival Otto of Brunswick defeated
1215	Frederick crowned and anointed king of Germany
1220	Journeyed to Rome; crowned and anointed Holy Roman Emperor by the pope
1224	Founded University at Naples
1226	Expedition to Lombardy; conflict with papacy began
1227	Excommunicated
1228–29	Went on crusade to Holy Land; regained Jerusalem through treaty
1231	Constitutions of Melfi promulgated
1232–35	Civil strife in Germany
1239	Gregory IX renewed excommunication
1244–45	Pope fled to Lyon and deposed Frederick
1245–48	Frederick campaigned in Italy until his defeat at Parma in 1248
1250	Died in Sicily

and archbishops of his realm), Frederick worked to stabilize his northern kingdom. But as one who had been born in Italy and raised in Sicily, Frederick found Germany cold, damp, and gloomy. Although he remained there until 1220, he did so only to organize it, before turning his thoughts to Empire; he wrote in a letter: "From our earliest days ... our heart has never ceased to burn with the desire to re-establish in the position of their ancient dignity the founder of the Roman Empire and its foundress, Rome herself." This would mean turning his attention to Italy and would ultimately cause a protracted and bitter struggle between Frederick and the papacy. After securing the succession of his son Henry as king of Germany by granting the spiritual princes special privileges, in 1220 Frederick set out for Italy.

During Frederick's stay in Germany, the old pope, Innocent III, had died and been succeeded by Honorius IV. Won over by Frederick's renewed promises to go on crusade and support the liberties of the Church, the new pope crowned and anointed Frederick II as Holy Roman Emperor in November 1220 without first obtaining important concessions from him. Later that same year, Frederick returned to Sicily, where he reestablished law and order and began transforming his kingdom into a centralized and uniform state. In the course of this reorganization, in 1224 Frederick founded the University of Naples, the first state university of the Middle Ages.

However, Frederick's policies in Sicily naturally led to the pursuit of his interests in Italy, and this, combined with his continued failure to fulfill his now five-year-old crusade vow, led to strained relations with the papacy. In 1223, he renewed his vow to lead a crusade within two years; in 1225, he appealed for a postponement and promised to go by 1227. Meanwhile in 1225, three years after the death of his wife Constance, Frederick married Isabella, the sister of King Henry III of England. Tensions continued to grow between Frederick and the papacy, especially after Frederick summoned a council to Cremona in Italy, in 1226, to discuss the restoration of his rights there. When Pope Honorius died in 1227, he was succeeded by the much less conciliatory Gregory IX, and the conflict erupted anew.

Pope Excommunicates Frederick

Because of his continual failure to embark upon a crusade, Pope Gregory excommunicated Frederick. Despite this, and much to the exasperation of the papacy, Frederick immediately departed for the Holy Land. From June 1228 to June of 1229, Frederick aroused as many passions in the East as he did back home. His respect for the Muslim princes and their culture led to the successful negotiation of a treaty with El-Kamil, the sultan of Egypt, which saw Jerusalem and much of the Holy Land restored to the Christians. Frederick wrote to Henry III of England that:

> by a miracle, rather than by valour, that undertaking has been achieved which for a long time numerous princes and … rulers of the world … have not been able to accomplish by force.

But this achievement through diplomacy rather than force of arms (and while still an excommunicate) angered the patriarch of Jerusalem and caused more gossip and stories to spread about the emperor: it was even thought that he had a harem of Muslim beauties which accompanied him on his travels.

While Frederick had been away on crusade, the pope had taken advantage of his absence to invade and overrun Sicily. Thus, Frederick's first task upon his return was to reconquer his kingdom, which he achieved with rapidity. He regarded Sicily as the center of his Empire, not Germany. "We are led," he wrote, "by a special affection to think assiduously on how the native population of our Kingdom of Sicily, which demands a more special attention … is the most brilliant of all our possessions." As a result, he was to visit Germany only fleetingly in the remaining 20 years of his reign.

From 1230 to 1250, Frederick was locked almost constantly in conflict with the papacy over the question of Italy and the Empire. After checking a rebellion of German princes in 1231, in the course of which he was forced to offer considerable concessions, Frederick began to move against his Italian enemies, and in 1237 he defeated an Italian army near Cremona. Gregory, increasingly more aware that Frederick was pushing for sovereignty over all of Italy, including Rome, renewed the excommunication decree in 1239. But in 1241, when Frederick's forces virtually advanced to the gates of Rome, the aging Gregory died in the August heat, and Frederick withdrew to Sicily to await events and pressure for the election of a more sympathetic pope. At first Frederick rejoiced at the selection of Innocent IV, but during negotiations to remove the excommunication, the new pope fled to Lyons, and at a council held there in 1245 Frederick was once more excommunicated and declared deposed, while the struggle for Italy continued. In 1248, Frederick suffered a major defeat at Parma, and although his position remained strong and his commanders continued to campaign in Italy, funding for his wars was a major concern. In the aftermath of his defeat, he returned to Sicily, where he remained until his death in 1250.

His Contributions to Learning and Law

Although the conflict with the papacy forms a central and vital strand of Frederick's career (it also led to the belief that he was the Antichrist), he must also be accorded a place in history as a great patron of the arts, and as a poet, philosopher, and scientist. Because of the rich cultural heritage of Sicily, and because of his own character, Frederick went to great efforts to attract learned men from all over Europe, paying little heed to cultural or religious distinctions. This was unusual in a society which tended to be racist and xenophobic, and Frederick was able to attract Christian, Muslim, and Jewish scholars to his court. (Yet it should be noted that, like most people of his time, Frederick harbored the usual medieval suspicion and hatred of heretics.) Although by the 13th century it was not all that unusual for a king to surround himself with poets, Frederick's court was distinguished not only by its multicultural makeup but also because Frederick was a great patron of the sciences (literature and poetry were the more usual interests of medieval princes). He had the works of Aristotle and the Muslim mathematician Averroes translated and eventually sent to the universities of Paris and Bologna. "We believe it to be useful," he wrote in his letter accompanying the books, "and of value to us to provide the opportunity for our subjects to enlighten themselves, because, well-informed, they will more readily do what is right."

Frederick corresponded with Muslim and Jewish scholars on philosophical, mathematical, geometrical, and scientific problems, and he received as a gift from the sultan of Damascus in 1232, "a planetarium ... on which were figures of the sun and moon indicating the hours of the day and night in the course of their determined movements." Much of Frederick's interest in the sciences and particularly astrology must be attributed to Arabic influences in Sicily. However, Frederick also appears as genuinely intellectually curious. He even wrote a treatise called *On the art of hunting with Hawks (De arte venandi cum avibus)*, in which he showed that he was skilled in not only philosophical theory but was also aware of the importance of firsthand observation and investigation. His curiosity is also demonstrated by his interest in the natural and the supernatural, and by his curiosity about animals: he kept a large menagerie which included elephants, camels, leopards, hawks, gyrfalcons, and even giraffes.

In a less savory vein, Frederick is also reported to have conducted somewhat gruesome experiments on humans: for instance, he is reputed to have enclosed a living man in a cask so that he would die there, in order to observe whether the soul departed the body after death. He also conducted linguistic experiments by ordering infants to be raised in complete silence in order to determine which language they would speak. While these stories may or may not be entirely true and are probably exaggerated, Frederick's rather unusual interests and his quest for knowledge did lead to the widespread belief that he was an unbeliever, or, at best, a skeptic. Under Frederick the arts of painting, sculpture, and architecture also flourished, in Germany as well as in Sicily; one of his greatest architectural achievements, which can still be seen today, was the octagonal Castel del Monte in Sicily, built around 1246.

Frederick was also an accomplished administrator and legislator. One of his ambitions was to create a centralized and uniform state in Sicily and, later, Italy, and his legislative achievements are enshrined in the Constitutions of Melfi of 1231, which have been called the most important legal codification of the 13th century. Frederick's conception of law and the state touched on all aspects of public and many aspects of private life: from how to ensure peace to how to legislate and administer courts; from decrees on choosing a bride to regulations governing the running of slaughterhouses outside the cities. He even dealt with the purity of the air. Among these decrees was the first coherent legislation on public health in Europe, as well as a precise definition of the physician's profession.

Salimbene wrote a lively description of the emperor, beginning with the common assertion that:

> Of faith in God he had none; he was crafty, wily, avaricious, lustful, malicious, wrathful; and yet a gallant man at times, when he would show his kindness or courtesy; full of solace, jocund, delightful, fertile in devices.

Salimbene went on to record how Frederick had even written a letter on his behalf once. He described Frederick as "a comely man, and well-formed, but of middle stature," but an Arab observer during Frederick's crusade thought that he was "ruddy and bald; he has weak eyesight." Yet Frederick's cultural interests suitably impressed those Muslims with whom he had dealings. Djemal ad-Din-Ibn Quacel, who had visited Frederick's court in Sicily as an ambassador, said of the emperor that, "He was distinguished among all the kings of the Franks for his talents and for his taste for philosophy, logic, and medicine."

Frederick II died on December 13, 1250, aged only 56, probably of dysentery, in Apulia. He was buried in the cathedral of Palermo, beside his parents, in a red porphyry sarcophagus mounted upon four carved lions. An early inscription on his tomb read: "If probity, reason, abundance of virtue, wealth, Nobility of birth, could forfend death, Frederick, who is here entombed, would not be dead."

Like his contemporaries, the world has not yet reached any agreement on the life and career of Frederick II. Some historians, pointing to his cultural achievements, have regarded him as a man born before his time, while others have stressed that Frederick was very much a product of his medieval environment, pointing to his contempt for heretics and the limited nature of his cultural achievements. But controversial though he may be, his success as a statesman and administrator, as well as a patron of the arts and learning, if not his military ability, must be duly acknowledged. In his time, he was regarded prophetically as a last emperor; by the 16th century, legend had merged him with his grandfather **Frederick Barbarossa,** who was waiting inside the Kyffhauser mountain to return at a crucial moment for the good of the Empire, like a medieval German King Arthur.

SOURCES:

Barraclough, G. *The Origins of Modern Germany.* Norton, 1984.

Leuschner, J. *Germany in the late Middle Ages.* Translated by S. MacCormack. North Holland, 1980.

Tierney, B., ed. *The Middle Ages Volume 1: Sources of Medieval History.* 4th ed. Knopf, 1983.

Van Cleve, T. C. *The Emperor Frederick II of Hohenstaufen.* Clarendon Press, 1972.

FURTHER READING:

Abulafia, D. *Frederick II: A Medieval Emperor.* Penguin, 1988.

Keen, M. *The Pelican History of Medieval Europe.* Harmondsworth, 1968.

Frederick II, the Great

(1712–1786)

King of Prussia, who doubled the size of Brandenburg-Prussia, vastly increased its wealth, made it a great center of learning, and transformed it into one of the most potent military powers in Europe.

"When a man is in a strong position, is he to take advantage of it or not?"

FREDERICK II, THE GREAT

In the 18th century, there were several hundred states in the region of Europe known as "the Germanies," and each state had a separate ruler. Austria, the largest political entity in the Germanies, was ruled by the Habsburg family who retained the medieval title of Holy Roman Emperor while also holding several other titles, including Monarch of Hungary and Monarch of Bohemia (with its capital at Prague, Bohemia is now a part of Czechoslovakia).

One of the weaker German states was ruled by the Hohenzollern family whose lands were scattered throughout the region. The two largest of the Hohenzollern states, separated by several hundred miles, were Brandenburg (located in the northwest of the Germanies with its capital at Berlin) and Prussia (located in the northeast, on the Baltic Sea, with its capital at Konigsberg). The Hohenzollerns held the titles of Elector of Brandenburg and King of Prussia.

On May 31, 1740, Frederick II of the Hohenzollern family succeeded his father as elector of Brandenburg and king of Prussia. By the time of his death, some 40 years later, Frederick would more than double the size of Brandenburg-

Family name: Hohenzollern. Born in Berlin in 1712; died at Potsdam in 1786; son of Frederick William I (1713–40) and Sophia Dorothea (daughter of George I of England); married: Elizabeth Christina of Brunswick-Wolfenbüttel.

Contributed by Joseph Tempesta, Associate Professor of History, Ithaca College, Ithaca, New York

CHRONOLOGY

1712	Born in Berlin
1730	Attempted to flee Prussia; captured and imprisoned by his father
1740	Succeeded his father as king of Prussia and elector of Brandenburg; began First Silesian War
1745	Began Second Silesian War
1756	Prussia and Britain fought the Seven Years' War against Austria, France, Russia, and Sweden
1763	Treaty of Paris concluded the Seven Years' War; Prussia kept Silesia
1772	Participated in the First Partition of Poland and annexed West Prussia
1786	Died at Potsdam

to witness the beheading of a close friend who had been involved in the planned escape.

After 1730, as training for his eventual assumption of duties as ruler of Brandenburg-Prussia, Frederick was exiled to several cities in Brandenburg and given the task of administering them. Three years later, again at his father's insistence, Frederick married the German princess, Elizabeth Christina, though he never loved her. Once he became king in 1740, he had nothing more to do with her. He would later die childless, with a nephew to succeed him.

Throughout both his childhood and adult life, Frederick maintained his closest relationship with his sister Wilhelmina. Corresponding regularly, they discussed literature, philosophy, affairs of state, and anything else of a public or private nature. It was she who provided solace during the darkest days of his relationship with his father.

The Enlightened Despot Rules Prussia

In 1740, when Frederick became king of Prussia and elector of Brandenburg, and was finally empowered to rule as he wished, he won the reputation of being an "Enlightened Despot." In fact, he maintained an active correspondence with many Enlightenment philosophers and literati, including Voltaire. Frederick wrote poetry, composed music (which is still performed on the concert stage), wrote several political studies, and attempted to rule according to Enlightenment principles. He oversaw legal reforms in Hohenzollern lands, abolished torture, and granted religious toleration. He spent lavishly on the royal palace of Sans Souci, at the city of Potsdam near Berlin. To Sans Souci he brought ballet, symphonic, and opera companies from around Europe. Under his rule, Brandenburg-Prussia became one of the great intellectual centers of Europe.

Above all, Frederick sought to make Prussia a great European power. To achieve this, he invested heavily in the army. In his *Competition For Empire*, Walter Dorn observes that while France's army in 1761 amounted to 1.2% of its entire population, Prussia's army amounted to 4.4%. In short, more than any other European state, a larger portion of Prussia's population was under arms.

The *Junkers*, comprised of the impoverished landed nobility, formed the officer corps of the Prussian army. Since service in the army (or government) was their only avenue to wealth and career success, they gave their unswerving allegiance to the state. Knowing this, Frederick

Prussia, vastly increase its wealth, make it a great center of learning, and transform it into one of the most potent military powers in Europe—stronger even than Austria in the Germanies. For his efforts, Frederick would earn the title, "The Great."

Frederick Hohenzollern was born on January 24, 1712, in Berlin. His mother was Sophia Dorothea, the daughter of George I, king of England and elector of Hanover. His father was Frederick William I, who governed the boy's upbringing by appointing tutors and commanding them to teach only the basic skills such as reading, writing, and counting. Believing that these skills would enable Frederick to someday rule efficiently, his father strictly instructed the tutors not to teach music, the arts, literature, or philosophy. Secretly, however, Frederick's mother Sophia and the tutors taught these subjects to the crown prince, who thus became acquainted with Enlightenment literature and philosophy; he even became an accomplished flutist. When Frederick William discovered the transgression, he dismissed the tutors and, beginning about 1728, took personal charge of completing his son's education.

Frederick spent nearly the rest of his young years beside his father. Known to be an extremely irascible man, Frederick William never missed an opportunity to humiliate his son in public. Their relationship became so estranged that in 1730, the young Frederick planned to flee to England, but his father uncovered the plot and imprisoned his son. Several months later, 18-year-old Frederick was released, but not before his father forced him

demanded spartan service from the *Junkers,* punishing failure with severity. As a result, the efficiency of the Prussian military (and governmental bureaucracy) under Frederick was unmatched in Europe.

When Frederick became king in 1740, he annexed Silesia, embarking upon a foreign policy which would occupy him for most of the remainder of his reign. This action resulted in the Two Silesian Wars (1740–45) and proved a major cause of The Seven Years' War (1756–63). Today, Silesia comprises the southwestern part of Poland, but in 1740, with its capital at Breslau, Silesia formed part of the Holy Roman Empire ruled by the Habsburgs. Frederick annexed Silesia for several reasons. First, he detested the lingering medieval notion that the Holy Roman Emperor of Austria had supreme authority over all other German rulers. Considering this anachronistic, Frederick refused to regard the Prussian king as anyone's inferior. Consequently, he intended to diminish Habsburg power in the Germanies. The second reason for the annexation was that Silesia was agriculturally richer and industrially stronger than Brandenburg-Prussia; it was also twice the size, and double the population. Adding Silesia to the Hohenzollern state would make Frederick's kingdom a powerful enough political force to rival Austria in the Germanies.

Finally, Frederick wanted to avenge a humiliation which his father Frederick William I had suffered at the hands of Austria. In 1713, the Holy Roman Emperor **Charles VI** had issued the Pragmatic Sanction which stipulated that if he should die without a male heir, the territories of his Empire were to pass intact to his female heir. In return for Prussian acceptance of the Pragmatic Sanction, Charles promised to support Frederick William's claim to two small German provinces. A few years later, however, Charles reneged on his promise, unaware that Frederick William's son would seek revenge for this slight.

In 1740, when Emperor Charles VI died with no male heir, his daughter **Maria Theresa** became the archduchess of Austria, queen of Hungary, and queen of Bohemia (she did not inherit the title of Holy Roman Empress). As stipulated in the Pragmatic Sanction, she inherited, intact, all of the Habsburg lands. With a woman ruling Austria-Hungary and the emperorship vacant, Frederick II thought the Habsburg position weak and the time right for invasion of Silesia.

Maria Theresa, however, proved to be a formidable foe. The start of the First Silesian War went badly for Frederick; in fact, at Mollwitz in

1741 the Austrians nearly defeated the Prussians. But the Prussians won the day, and as a result the French joined the Prussian attack against the Austrians. For centuries, the Habsburgs had attempted to conquer the French without success; now France saw an opportunity for revenge.

In 1741, France occupied the Habsburg kingdom of Bohemia. Maria Theresa believed that while Frederick wanted only Silesia, France wanted to conquer all of the Holy Roman Empire. Therefore, in order to turn all her forces on France, the more dangerous enemy, Maria Theresa offered to end hostilities with Prussia. Frederick accepted, and in return Austria recognized Prussia's annexation of Silesia. The agreement was cemented by the Treaty of Breslau in 1742, and Frederick pulled out of the war, abandoning France.

With the help of England, France's colonial rival in India and the Americas, Maria Theresa then drove France out of Bohemia. But the Anglo-Austrian force soon occupied the French provinces of Alsace-Lorraine, alarming Frederick. Fearing that a French defeat might lead to an attack upon Prussia by the Anglo-Austrian alliance, he tore up the Treaty of Breslau and again attacked Austria, beginning the Second Silesian War.

In 1745, Frederick took personal command of the Prussian army and executed a series of brilliant maneuvers. Because of his victories on the battlefield, he held on to Silesia, defeated Austria and England, and won the reputation as a military genius. Prussians began referring to him as "The Great." That same year, when England pulled out of the war, Austria was forced to sue for peace. Prussia and Austria signed the Peace of Dresden, in which Austria again recognized Prussia's annexation of Silesia.

These events weakened the European alliances. France was angry with Prussia for pulling out of the First Silesian War; Austria was angry with England for pulling out of the Second Silesian War. In fact, Maria Theresa never accepted the loss of Silesia and wanted to win it back. Her opportunity came in 1756 as a result of a reversal of European alliances known as the Diplomatic Revolution. England is the key to understanding the reversal.

The king of England, **George II,** was also the elector of the German state of Hanover, which was located on Brandenburg's western border. In 1755, King George still considered Prussia his enemy and sought to protect Hanover from attack by concluding a subsidy treaty with Russia. George II agreed to subsidize Russia's maintenance of an army on the eastern border of Prussia, so as to threaten Frederick II and keep him from possibly attacking Hanover.

In 1756, fearing the might of Russia, Frederick negotiated the Treaty of Westminster with England. By this treaty, Prussia agreed to help Hanover should France attack, and England agreed to help Prussia should be it attacked by Russia. Therefore, King George had succeeded in frightening Prussia into an alliance which protected Hanover from French attack in the west, while the subsidy treaty with Russia protected Hanover from Prussian attack in the east.

The Treaty of Westminster proved a blunder for Frederick because for a second time France felt abandoned by him. So when Maria Theresa proposed a Franco-Austrian alliance, France accepted. Thus, in the Treaty of Versailles in 1756, France agreed to help Austria if attacked by Prussia. The Diplomatic Revolution was completed: France and Austria were now allied against England and Prussia.

The Seven Years' War Begins

The same year, Frederick committed a second near-fatal blunder. He surmised that the Treaty of Westminster was offensive to the Russians who might, therefore, join the French and the Austrians against Prussia and England. He invaded Saxony—another possession of Maria Theresa—proposing to return it only if she agreed not to enter an alliance with Russia. Maria Theresa, however, did not succumb to blackmail, and by the terms of the Treaty of Versailles, this attack opened the way for France to declare war on Prussia. The Seven Years' War had begun. In 1757, Russia (and later Sweden) declared war on Prussia as well, and Frederick faced a war on two fronts.

With England concentrating on fighting the war against France in the Americas, Prussia faced the coalition in Europe virtually alone. Though the coalition occupied Berlin, Frederick managed to fight a brilliant defensive war, further enhancing his reputation as a military genius. Then, in 1762, fortune smiled on him when the Russian tsarina Elizabeth died and her successor **Peter III**, an admirer of Frederick, pulled out of the war. The following year, Austria sued for peace. Prussia

returned Saxony, but for a third and final time, Maria Theresa recognized Frederick's annexation of Silesia. Meanwhile, France lost most of her American colonies to England.

Before the end of his life, Frederick took advantage of another opportunity to add to his possessions. Joined by the other Great Powers of Europe in 1772, Frederick participated in the First Partition of Poland, ostensibly because the Roman Catholic majority in Poland refused to protect the religious rights of the Protestant minority. In reality, Frederick used this issue as an excuse to add more territory to the Hohenzollern state. He annexed West Prussia (a strip of land which was later referred to as the Polish Corridor) up to, but not including, the port of Danzig (Gdansk). This annexation joined East Prussia to Brandenburg, and, for the first time, most of the Hohenzollern lands were contiguous.

While Frederick spent the remainder of his life personally governing his lands, he continued to spend lavishly on the arts, and Prussia remained a mecca for the great minds of the Enlightenment. Unfortunately, the rigors of personal rule took their toll. On August 17, 1786, with his body ravaged by disease, Frederick the Great died in the arms of soldiers gathered around him at his beloved Sans Souci. By the time of his death, he had transformed Prussia into one of the Great Powers of Europe. At Frederick's request, he was buried at Sans Souci.

SOURCES:

Dorn, Walter. *Competition For Empire.* Harper, 1965.

Gaxotte, Pierre. *Frederick The Great.* Yale University Press, 1942.

Gooch, G. P. *Frederick The Great.* Knopf, 1947.

Hubatsch, Walther. *Frederick The Great of Prussia.* Thames & Hudson, 1975.

Rosenberg, Hans. *Bureaucracy, Aristocracy, Autocracy.* Beacon Press, 1958.

FURTHER READING:

Horn, D. *Frederick The Great.* English University Press, 1964.

Paret, Peter. *Frederick The Great.* Hill & Wang, 1972.

Redaway, W. *Frederick The Great.* Putnam, 1908.

Weill, H. *Frederick The Great and Samuel Von Cocceji.* Wisconsin State Historical Society, 1961.

Elizabeth Fry

(1780–1845)

British reformer and Quaker lay evangelist, who worked for prison reform, particularly to relieve the physical misery and moral degradation of women prisoners.

"We long to burn her alive. Examples of living virtue disturb our repose and give birth to disturbing comparisons."

REV. SYDNEY SMITH (1821)

An evangelist who relied on prayer and Bible-reading to inculcate virtue, Elizabeth Fry epitomized the reformer inspired by religious motives. She also relied on her access to the politically powerful, an advantage she enjoyed as a member of a well-connected Quaker family and enhanced by the celebrity status that she quickly attained through her prison visits. Her work on behalf of women prisoners caught the popular fancy, and she enjoyed a prestige in her country and in other European countries that few women in a society ruled by men could match. On the other hand, England soon rejected her approach to prison reform.

People worried about the increase in crime that had started with the Industrial Revolution; it had increased even more after the end of the long wars with France brought extensive unemployment. A combination of the 18th-century Enlightenment critique of traditional institutions and a humanitarianism largely rooted in Evangelical (and Quaker) religion encouraged a fresh look at crime and punishment.

Fry inspired confidence as a devout, motherly woman of unquestionable sincerity. Her

Born Elizabeth Gurney in Norwich, England, in 1780; died at Ramsgate, England, in 1845; married: Joseph Fry (tea merchant and banker who became bankrupt in 1828), 1800; children: four sons and seven daughters (one daughter died in childhood).

Contributed by David M. Fahey, Professor of History, Miami University, Oxford, Ohio

CHRONOLOGY

1764	Cesare Bonesana published his *Essay on Crimes and Punishment*
1777	John Howard published *The State of Prisons*
1791	Jeremy Bentham published Panopticon on prison architecture and policy
1798	Fry began the religious conversion that made her a strict Quaker (Society of Friends)
1811	Accepted as full minister in the Society of Friends
1815	Battle of Waterloo ended wars of the French Revolution and Napoleon
1813	Fry visited Newgate Gaol to distribute clothing
1816	Began systematic visits to Newgate
1817	Organized Association for the Improvement of the Female Prisoners in Newgate
1818	Failed to persuade Home Secretary to prevent a condemned woman's execution; Society for the Improvement of Prison Discipline and the Reformation of Juvenile Reformers founded
1821	Fry organized British Ladies' Society for Promoting the Reformation of Female Prisoners
1827	Published *Observations on the Visiting, Superintendence and Government of Female Prisoners*
1835	Passage of Prison Act imposed harsh discipline

Fry was in her teens in 1798 when an American member of the Society of Friends attacked the luxurious "gayness" of the local Quakers and awakened in Fry a sense of God that began her conversion to a strict Quakerism. This was not the common Evangelical conversion experience—a realization of guilt, followed by a sense of God's forgiveness—but instead a mystical communion with God. She never desired religious ceremonies or theology or a highly organized church. Her religion was a very personal one, founded on silent meditation, aided by the reading of the Bible, that sometimes led to informal but eloquent sermons. Virtually alone among religious denominations of the early 19th century, the small Society of Friends allowed women and men an equal right to speak at religious services because of the Quaker principle of direct inspiration.

Fry gradually adopted the strict Quaker policies on dress and Quaker peculiarities of speech (such as saying "thee" and "thou" instead of "you"). She became what contemporaries called a plain Friend. By 1799, she rejected singing as a distraction from true piety. (Her younger brother Joseph John Gurney followed her in reviving many of the old distinctive practices of the Quakers that separated them from other people; although as the leader of the Evangelical Quakers, he encouraged good relations with all Evangelical Protestants.)

After her father's death in 1809, Fry began to speak at Quaker meetings and was recognized officially as a full minister two years later. Her marriage in 1800 to a London Quaker, Joseph Fry, delayed her wider public career; she bore ten children between 1801 and 1816 (and an 11th in 1822).

Prison Ministry Begins

Although at the urging of an American Quaker she had visited Newgate Gaol (jail) in London during 1813, it was at the end of 1816 that Elizabeth Fry began her systematic work as a prison reformer. She visited many prisons in the British Isles during the following years, but she made her special mission the reform of the women imprisoned in Newgate. Approximately 300 women and children were crowded in a women's ward comprising 190 square yards. Hardened criminals guilty of serious crimes were mixed with those jailed for minor offenses. Children lived in the prison with their mothers, in rags, filth, and idleness. As the prison furnished no uniforms, many poverty-stricken women existed half-naked. Prison policy combined occasional brutality with a permissiveness that allowed inmates considerable

prison visits belonged to a tradition of well-off, benevolent women visiting the unfortunate, a kind of unpaid social work. Helping women prisoners appeared to be a respectable philanthropy for pious women with time, energy, and money to spare. Although the Society of Friends had an English membership of less than 20,000 during Fry's lifetime, Quaker women took a disproportionate role in charity and reform.

Elizabeth Fry was born into a happy, prosperous family, the Gurneys, at Norwich in eastern England, blighted only by the early death of her mother. Her father's relaxed Quakerism abandoned many of the restrictions identified with that religion, such as the requirement to wear only simple clothing and to avoid worldly society. She grew up enjoying fashionable parties and dances that earlier Quakers would have avoided. Some of her sisters would eventually withdraw from Quakerism to join the state Anglican Church, and her banker brothers would greatly add to the family riches.

freedom—tolerating drinking and fighting—and made no attempt at rehabilitation, such as training the women for jobs outside prison walls.

In 1817, Fry organized the Association for the Improvement of Female Prisoners in Newgate. Two members visited the prisoners every day to read the Scriptures aloud. When Fry read from the Bible (and preached) at Newgate, so many people wanted to attend that the London magistrates authorized her to issue tickets. Association members adopted a personal approach toward women prisoners and tried to gain their active cooperation through kindness and persuasion. Fry's association put the women prisoners to work, sewing and knitting, under the supervision of prisoner monitors. With a prisoner as the instructor, it also organized a school for the women (and their children) to teach them to read the Bible. One of Fry's rules for the Newgate women declared "that there be no begging, swearing, gaming, card-playing, quarrelling, or immoral conversation."

Fry's work was not confined to Newgate. In 1818, she made a tour of prisons in northern England and Scotland with her brother Joseph John Gurney, described in a book published under his name, *Notes on a Visit Made to Some of the Prisons in Scotland and the North of England in Company with Elizabeth Fry.* Middle-class ladies' committees sprang up to visit prisons all over the country. In 1821, they joined together as the British Ladies' Society for Promoting the Reformation of Female Prisoners.

Fry was an activist, not in most respects an original thinker. Ironically, most of her ideas resembled that of Jeremy Bentham, an earlier prison reformer who often is contrasted with Fry because he despised religion. Like Bentham, Fry favored classifying prisoners (in contrast to the prevalent mixing of all types), providing productive work for them, and establishing healthful living conditions. Her more distinctive opinions favored the employment of matrons to supervise women prisoners, rejected capital punishment (and flogging) in principle, minimized the role of unproductive hard labor such as working the treadmill, and repudiated bread-and-water diets. She tried, with modest success, to mitigate the sufferings of the women sentenced to transportation to Australia, a form of penal exile. Above all, she insisted that women criminals could be redeemed.

Her Influence Wanes

For a few years, Fry had the ear of Cabinet ministers and parliamentary committees, but she soon lost her influence. Overestimating what she could do, she offended those whom she wanted to persuade. This was the case in 1818 when she lobbied the Home Secretary, Lord Sidmouth, to stop the execution of a Newgate prisoner.

By 1827, when she published the short book *Observations on the Visiting, Superintendence and Government of Female Prisoners,* based on her practical experience, her time of importance had already passed. She continued to argue for the importance of local ladies' committees; the influence of public-spirited women was needed to supplement and correct the laws and regulations established by men. For the prisoners themselves, she urged the women visitors to show a spirit of mercy: "Great pity is due from us even to the greatest transgressors among our fellow-creatures."

Fry lost prestige (and money for her prison charities) when her husband's businesses failed in 1828. As a bankrupt, he was excluded from the Society of Friends, and the Fry family became dependent on the financial generosity of the wealthy Gurneys.

By the mid-1820s, other prison reformers increasingly advocated policies contrary to Elizabeth Fry's. Many Quakers (including two of her brothers-in-law) were prominent in the Society for the Improvement of Prison Discipline and the Reformation of Juvenile Reformers (founded in 1818), but after a brief period when it supported her, the Society lobbied for a centralized professional prison administration and detailed bureaucratic rules that left no place for the visits of "meddlesome" ladies' committees. Fry's rivals campaigned for the harsh prison policies pioneered in the United States at Philadelphia, such as solitary confinement and exhausting hard labor. These principles became law when Parliament adopted the Prison Act of 1835.

Although lacking any practical influence, Fry remained a celebrity, particularly on the continent of Europe. Acclaimed in 1838 and 1841 when she visited France and the German states, she was also honored in 1842 by the king of Prussia who visited her Bible-reading at Newgate and lunched at her home.

Two years after Elizabeth Fry died in 1845, two of her daughters published a *Memoir of the Life of Elizabeth Fry with Extracts from her Journal and Letters,* an abridgment in two volumes of her 44 volumes of handwritten journals. The *Memoir* sought to make Fry a saint and left out whatever the daughters regarded as not fitting that image. Until 1980, Fry's biographers failed to read the original journals.

Fry was not the perfect woman that her daughters presented. She embodied many contradictions. She adhered to a strict Quakerism that required plain living and the rejection of worldly vanities; yet, as some fellow Quakers grumbled, her simple clothes were cut from expensive fabrics, and she rejoiced in her opportunities to mingle with politicians, aristocrats, and royalty. Nothing was more important for her than her religion, yet, to her great anguish, she failed to nurture a commitment to Quakerism among her children, nearly all of whom left the Society of Friends when they grew up.

Despite her limitations, Elizabeth Fry deserves to be remembered as a genuinely good woman, as her contemporaries acknowledged, and a much wiser one than the men who belittled her as a naive amateur realized. In the early 19th century, women reformers were loved more often than they were respected. Although far from perfect, Fry's philosophy of prison reform avoided numbing bureaucracy and dehumanizing brutality and encouraged the participation of members of the general public in the conduct of prison life.

SOURCES:

Cooper, Robert Allan. "Jeremy Bentham, Elizabeth Fry, and English Prison Reform," in *Journal of the History of Ideas*. Vol. 42. (1981): 675–90.

Dobash, Russell P., R. Emerson Dobash, and Sue Gutteridge. *The Imprisonment of Women*. Basil Blackwell, 1986.

Kent, John. *Elizabeth Fry*. B.T. Batsford, 1962.

Rose, June. *Elizabeth Fry*. Macmillan, 1980.

FURTHER READING:

Ignatieff, Michael. *A Just Measure of Pain: The Penitentiary in the Industrial Revolution, 1750–1850*. Pantheon, 1978.

Isichei, Elizabeth. *Victorian Quakers*. Oxford University Press, 1970.

McConville, Sean. *A History of English Prison Administration, 1750–1877*. Vol 1. Routledge and Kegan Paul, 1981.

Prochaska, Frank K. *Women and Philanthropy in Nineteenth-Century England*. Clarendon Press, 1980.

Punshon, John. *Portrait in Grey: A Short History of the Quakers*. Quaker Home Services, 1984.

Giuseppe Garibaldi

(1807–1882)

Italian nationalist and guerrilla leader, who was the dominant military figure in the process of Italian unification.

"I offer neither pay nor quarters nor provisions; I offer hunger, thirst, forced marches, battles and death. Let him who loves his country in his heart and not with his lips only follow me."

GIUSEPPE GARIBALDI

Born in Nice on July 4, 1807, Giuseppe Garibaldi was only seven when he saw his city move out from under the control of the Napoleonic Empire and become part of the northern Italian Kingdom of Piedmont-Sardinia. Consequently, it is certainly possible that his later concern over Italian nationalism and frontiers can be traced to his childhood in Nice. Garibaldi's father Domenico, a fisherman who also engaged in coastal trading, introduced his son to the sea. His mother Rosa Raimondi was known to have smothered him with affection, promoting an attachment Garibaldi maintained throughout his life. Both parents were pious and hoped that their son would become a lawyer or priest; instead, the young Garibaldi became deeply anticlerical, harboring an abiding hatred for the Roman Catholic Church. Seized by wanderlust, the 15-year-old headed to sea as a cabin boy.

By 1832, Garibaldi had earned a master's certificate as a trained sea captain. Sailing the eastern Mediterranean, where he survived pirate attacks, he had developed toughness, self-reliance, and a love of adventure. He was also influenced by the revolutionary and nationalist ideas of his day. In

Contributed by Bernard Cook, Professor of History, Loyola University, New Orleans, Louisiana

Pronunciation: English: gar-i-BAWL-de; Italian: gah-ri-BAHL-de. Born in Nice on July 4, 1807; died on his farm on the Island of Caprera, June 2, 1882; married: Anna "Anita" Ribeiro da Silva, 1842 (died during their flight from the Austrians, 1849); married: Giuseppina Raimondi, 1859 (divorced on grounds of nonconsummation, 1879); married: Francesca Armosino (who had already borne him three children), January 26, 1880; children: Menotti, Rosita, Teresa, Ricciotti, Clelia, Rosa, Manlio.

467

1814	Nice became part of the northern Italian Kingdom of Piedmont-Sardinia
1831	Mazzini founded the Young Italy movement
1846	Pius IX elected pope
1848	Piedmont twice defeated by Austria; revolution in Rome
1849	Napoleon III sent a French army to crush the Roman Republic
1852	Camillo di Cavour became prime minister of Piedmont
1858	Aided by France in a war against Austria, Piedmont won Lombardy
1860	Garibaldi led his Thousand Red Shirts against the Kingdom of Two Sicilies
1861	Kingdom of Italy established
1866	Italy joined Prussia against Austria and won Venetia
1870	Franco-Prussian War; Kingdom of Italy occupied papal Rome.

1833, after meeting the apostle of Italian nationalism, **Giuseppe Mazzini,** at Marseilles, Garibaldi joined Mazzini's Young Italy movement dedicated to the liberation and unification of Italy, much of which was controlled by Austria and the papacy.

The following year, Garibaldi, who had been conscripted into the Piedmontese navy, joined in a feeble plot to overthrow the government. When the plan miscarried, he fled across the mountains to France, but the Piedmontese government tried him in absentia and sentenced him to death. Unable to return home, he began a 13-year period of exile and adventure. After a short stint in the service of the bey of Tunis, he shipped out on a French vessel for Brazil, where he tried his hand at coastal trading, only to find himself too trusting to make a wise businessman. Garibaldi's efforts as privateer and soldier, however, proved more successful. In 12 years of fighting, he survived hardship, wounds, shipwreck, capture, and torture.

A Freedom Fighter in South America

Though those years left him with crippling arthritis and rheumatism and a deep distrust for politicians, his heroic idealism was never dampened, and he became an inspiring leader and experienced guerrilla fighter. His exploits became legendary as he fought for freedom in the south of Brazil and Uruguay. Garibaldi's victory at Sant' Antonio over the forces of the Argentine dictator, **Juan Manuel de Rosas,** has been credited with ensuring Uruguayan independence. With a penchant for the dramatic, he adopted the red tunic and gaucho costume which was to become identified with the Italian national cause.

During his exile in South America, Garibaldi never forgot Italy and remained in contact with Mazzini and the Young Italy movement. He too was inspired by the climate of reform and change which had seized Italy following the 1846 election of the seemingly liberal **Pius IX.** Then, on March 23, 1848, Charles Albert, the king of Piedmont-Sardinia, declared war against Austria, which was confronted with a popular rising in Lombardy. The following month, Garibaldi set sail for Nice with 60 members of his Italian Legion and landed in the midst of the patriotic fervor unleashed by the prospect of driving the Austrians from Lombardy and Venetia. Consequently, the old charges against him were ignored. Despite his democratic sentiments, Garibaldi expressed a willingness to fight for the national cause under the leadership of the Piedmontese king. Though his offer was rejected, he went on his own to the city of Milan which was then in rebellion against the Austrians. There, he was welcomed and made a general. A week later, on July 24, 1848, Charles Albert suffered a crushing defeat by the Austrians at Custoza. Defying the king's order to disband and end the fight, Garibaldi, advocating popular insurrection, fought on for 12 futile though inspiring days.

At the end of August, with only 30 men left and wracked with malaria, an exhausted Garibaldi escaped to Switzerland. Deeply disillusioned at the people's failure to join in his struggle, he was, however, convinced that the guerrilla tactics he'd learned in Latin America could be applied in Italy. With the support of the inhabitants, a popular force could prevail through the kind of utter determination that is born of desperation.

Though he had been elected to the Piedmontese parliament, Garibaldi instead chose to lead a small band to fight for Sicilian independence from the Neapolitan king Ferdinand II. En route to Sicily, he was sidetracked by developments in Rome. When the pope's chief minister, Pellegrino Rossi, was assassinated on November 15, 1848, Pius IX fled to Neapolitan territory. Garibaldi was elected to the Roman Assembly where he spearheaded the drive to establish the Roman Republic. Commanding his men against French troops dispatched to assist the pope, he was wounded, but on April 30, 1849, he succeeded in throwing the French back from the walls of Rome in a fierce engagement at the Janiculum Hill. In May, his force repulsed a Neapolitan advance at Palestrina. In pressing the attack against the retreating Neapolitans, he disobeyed General Pietro Roselli, whose appointment as commander in chief Garibaldi resented. When reined in by Mazzini, who had been elected to serve as one of the triumvirs of the Republic, Garibaldi complied. He believed that a dictator was needed to take charge of the increasingly desperate situation faced by Rome as the French tripled the size of their forces, but Garibaldi later complained that Mazzini lacked the ability and will to take charge.

The renewed French attack came on June 3. Garibaldi lost his best men and officers through reckless frontal charges, and his inexperience in the use of artillery was a serious handicap. Nevertheless, his flair and the heroism of his volunteers won many supporters for his view of a united Italy. Finally on June 30, the battle-weary and bedraggled Garibaldi, wearing a sword so bent that it no longer fit into its sheath, told the Roman Assembly that defense was no longer possible. He was cheered for his efforts and given permission to break through the encircling enemy in order to keep the revolution alive. He rejected the offer of an American ship as refuge, and on July 3 led 4,000 legionnaires out of the city. There were expressions of sympathy in the countryside but little support and even resistance against requisitioning; within a week, his force had dwindled to 2,500. On July 31, Garibaldi accepted asylum for his force from the Republic of San Marino. With a remnant of 250, he broke through the pursuing Austrians. Most of his men were eventually captured as they attempted to embark for Venice, but Garibaldi escaped. Sadly, his wife and longtime comrade was less successful. In 1839, Garibaldi had stolen the not-unwilling Anna "Anita" Ribeiro da Silva from her husband, and the two were married in 1842. For years, Anita had sailed and fought with her husband and the nationalists. Although she was five months pregnant, she had accompanied Garibaldi in this desperate retreat from Rome. Pursued by the Austrians, she died in the marshes of Romagna on August 4, 1849. But Garibaldi, with the assistance of sympathizers, finally reached the Tuscan coast and was rescued on September 2, 1849.

Garibaldi's return to Nice was greeted with consternation by the Piedmontese government. Promptly arrested, he was shipped off to a new exile, which took him to New York City and eventually to Peru. As a Peruvian citizen, he captained a ship and sailed to Asia and North America. Then in 1854, he sailed to England. While there, Mazzini attempted to recruit him for a republican insurrection in Sicily, but Garibaldi decided it was unwise to alienate the Piedmontese who alone might drive the Austrians from northern Italy. This decision facilitated his return to Italy, as Count Camillo di Cavour, the prime minister of Piedmont who distrusted Garibaldi's republicanism, reluctantly allowed him to settle in Genoa.

Garibaldi's hope was fulfilled on April 19, 1859, when Piedmont provoked an Austrian attack. Earlier in July 1858, the Plombières agreement between Cavour and **Napoleon III** had committed France to aid Piedmont. As the French and Piedmontese armies advanced into Lombardy, Garibaldi—by then a Piedmontese general—led a band of volunteers, the *Cacciatori delle Alpe* (the Alpine Hunters), who harassed the Austrian flanks. To his dismay, France withdrew from the war in July, and Venetia was left under Austrian control. The national cause, however, spread through central Italy with a wave of popular uprisings. Garibaldi was persuaded by unrest in Sicily to direct his efforts there. Though Cavour distrusted Garibaldi's republicanism and opposed the venture, public opinion would not permit him to prevent the departure. On May 6, 1859, the meager force sailed in two small steamers from Genoa to the slogan of "Victor Emmanuel and Italy."

The Red Shirts Engage the Neapolitans

Garibaldi and his volunteers, dubbed the "Thousand Red Shirts," landed on May 11, 1860, at Marsala on the western end of Sicily. Marching inland, he gained recruits from the downtrodden peasants who believed that he could improve their conditions. On May 15, his poorly armed force engaged the more numerous and well-armed Neapolitans at Calatafimi and carried the day with a spirited bayonet charge. After that engagement and the occupation of Palermo on May 27, the will of the 25,000-man Neapolitan army, weak at best, was largely broken. In order to win the support of the property owners, Garibaldi, whose principal concern was the unification of Italy, repudiated any idea of a social revolution on the island; by July 20, he controlled the whole island with the exception of the fortress at Messina.

On August 18, he crossed to the mainland with the support of the British fleet. After subduing the Neapolitan garrison at Reggio, his march met little resistance. Entering an undefended Naples on September 7, Garibaldi declared himself Dictator of the Two Sicilies. On October 26, he defeated a large Neapolitan force on the Volturno and demonstrated his mastery of conventional mil-

Ricciotti Garibaldi

(1847–1924)

Ricciotti Garibaldi, the second son of Giuseppe and Anita Garibaldi, was born in Montevideo, Uruguay, in 1847. He was sent along with his mother, brother, and sister to Nice before his father's return in April 1848. In 1866, he successfully fought alongside his father, his brother Menotti, and brother-in-law Stefano Canzio against the Austrians. During the Franco-Prussian War, after the collapse of the imperial government, he fought with his father on the side of republican France and scored a resounding success on November 18, 1870, at Culmier-le-sec when his troops

itary techniques. He was confident that papal Rome could also be added to the forming Italy.

But Cavour was anxious to prevent a clash with the French garrison in Rome and distrusted Garibaldi's political intentions, so on September 10, he sent the Piedmontese army south. Seizing a large stretch of the papal territory, the army placed itself between Garibaldi and Rome. Rather than launch a civil struggle in Italy, Garibaldi—though disgusted with Cavour—submitted to the Piedmontese king **Victor Emmanuel II,** handing over his southern conquests. Rejecting financial rewards for his patriotic service, he returned to his home on the barren Island of Caprera. A plebiscite (vote) was conducted in the former Neapolitan territories on October 21, and they joined an expanded Piedmont to form the Kingdom of Italy, which was proclaimed on March 17, 1861.

Garibaldi, however, could not rest while Rome and Venetia remained apart from Italy. To the consternation of the Italian government, which did not want to provoke joint action against Italy by France and Austria, Garibaldi attempted to seize Rome for Italy in 1862. His march on Rome ended when he was wounded at Aspromonte and taken prisoner by Italian troops; popular sympathy for Garibaldi proved so strong that Victor Emmanuel pardoned him. During the Seven Weeks' War which pitted Italy and Prussia against Austria, he successfully led a corps of volunteers against the Austrians near Verona. He was preparing to attack Trentino when he was restrained by his superior, General Alfonso La Marmora. As a result of the defeat of Austria by Italy's ally, Prussia, Italy gained the province of Venetia.

In an 1864 agreement with the Italian government, France agreed to withdraw its garrison from Rome. Three years later, Garibaldi attempted to take advantage of the opportunity provided by the French exit to seize Rome for Italy. Twice captured, he escaped both times; finally, on October 27, 1867, Garibaldi defeated a papal force. French troops had been rushed to Città Vecchia, however, and, on November 3, 1867, Garibaldi was defeated and captured at Mentana, and sent once again to his farm on Caprera.

When war broke out between France and Prussia in July 1870, Napoleon III was compelled to withdraw the French garrison from Rome. Deprived of French protection, the pope was unable to resist the assault of the Italian forces, which occupied Rome on September 20. Thus, the unification of Italy was complete, except for Trieste and the South Tyrol, which would not be gained until after World War I. Garibaldi, the fervent republican, now offered his services to the French Republic, which replaced Napoleon III's imperial government after its defeat at Sedan on September 2, 1870. His troops impeded the movements of the Germans and defeated German units at Châtillon and Dijon. Garibaldi's popularity resulted in his election to the French National Assembly in February 1871. Out of disgust with the conservative majority, he resigned the post to return to Caprera.

In 1874, he was elected to the Italian Parliament as a deputy from Rome, and the Italian state rewarded Garibaldi's service by voting him a substantial gift and an annual pension. After the completion of Italian unification, his radicalism moved further left from republicanism to socialism; he expressed support for the Paris Commune and became a member of Società Operaie and **Karl Marx**'s First International Workingmen's Association. During this period, he continued his fiction writing begun in 1868. Two novels based on the Sicilian expedition, *Cantoni il volontario* (Cantoni, the Volunteer) and *i mille* (The Thousand), joined his earlier anticlerical novel, *Clelia, o il governo del monaco* (Clelia, or the Government of the Clergy). He died at his farm on Caprera on June 2, 1882.

"Garibaldi has rendered to Italy the greatest services that a man could render it," said Cavour in *Lettere edite ed inedite*, "he has given the Italians confidence in themselves, and he has proven to Europe that the Italians know how to fight and to die on the battlefield in order to win back a fatherland."

SOURCES:

Garibaldi, Giuseppe. *Garibaldi: An Autobiography.* Alexandre Dumas, ed. Routledge, Warne, and Routledge, 1860.

surprised a column of 500 Germans. His men captured 170 prisoners and the German standards. At Dijon, on January 20 and 21, 1871, he and his father also prevailed in an engagement against the Prussians.

He later fought in the Greek army against Turkey in 1897, and was elected to the Italian Parliament. In 1914, he formed the Garibaldi Legion to fight in France during the First World War. Following the war, he welcomed Benito Mussolini to his home on Caprera, and favorably compared the Fascist Blackshirts with his father's Red Shirts. He died in 1924. ■

Hearder, Harry. *Italy in the Age of the Risorgimento, 1790–1870.* Longmans, 1983.

Hibbert, Christopher. *Garibaldi and His Enemies: The Clash of Arms and Personalities in the Making of Italy.* Little, Brown, 1966.

Smith, Dennis Mack. *Garibaldi: A Great Life in Brief.* Knopf, 1956.

FURTHER READING:

Parris, John. *The Lion of Caprera.* Arthur Barker, 1962.

de Poinay, Peter. *Garibaldi: The Man and Legend.* Thomas Nelson, 1961.

Ridley, Jasper G. *Garibaldi.* Constable, 1974.

Smith, Dennis Mack. *Cavour and Garibaldi 1860: A Study in Political Conflict.* Cambridge University Press, 1954.

Trevelyan, George Macaulay. *Garibaldi and the Making of Italy.* Longmans, Green, 1911.

———. *Garibaldi and the Thousand.* Longmans, Green, 1909.

———. *Garibaldi's Defense of the Roman Republic.* Longmans, Green, 1907.

Elizabeth Garrett Anderson

(1836–1917)

English physician, who was the first woman to qualify in medicine in Britain and pioneered in the professional education of women.

Name variations: Elizabeth Garrett, Elizabeth Garrett-Anderson. Born in Aldeburgh, Suffolk, England, in 1836; died in 1917; daughter of Newson and Louisa (Dunnell) Garrett; sister of Millicent Garrett Fawcett, president of the National Union of Women's Suffrage; married: James George Skelton Anderson, 1871 (died 1907); children: (two daughters) Margaret and Louisa Garrett Anderson; (one son) Alan.

lizabeth Garrett was the second of ten children (four sons and six daughters) born to Newson Garrett, a prosperous business-man of Aldeburgh, Suffolk, and his wife Louisa Dunnell Garrett. Believing that all his children—girls as well as boys—should receive the best education possible, Garrett's father saw to it that Elizabeth and her sister, Louie, were first taught at home by a governess. In 1849, they were sent to the Academy for the Daughters of Gentlemen, a boarding school in Blackheath run by the Misses Browning, aunts of poet Robert Browning. Garrett would later shudder when she recalled the "stupidity of the teachers," but the rule requiring students to speak French proved to be a great benefit. On her return to Aldeburgh two years later, she continued to study Latin and mathematics with her brothers' tutors. Garrett's friend, educator Emily Davies (1830–1921), encouraged her to reject the traditional and limited life of the well-to-do English lady. Davies believed that women should be given the opportunity to obtain a better education and prepare themselves for the professions, especially medicine. But Davies, who later became the principal of Girton College, Cambridge, did not feel suited to becoming a pioneer in

"Nowhere in Europe was the woman who wished to study medicine so stubbornly opposed as in Britain, yet nowhere was her final victory so complete.... Among the reasons for victory may be found the character of Elizabeth Garrett, the first woman in this country to qualify as physician and surgeon."

JO MANTON

Contributed by Lois Magner, Professor of History, Purdue University, West Lafayette, Indiana

the field of medicine and encouraged Garrett to take on this role.

Visiting her sister in London in 1859, Garrett met **Elizabeth Blackwell,** the first woman in America to graduate from a regular medical school. Blackwell, who was then practicing medicine in England, had succeeded in having her name placed on the British Medical Register and was delivering a series of three lectures on "Medicine as a Profession for Ladies." Contrasting what she considered the useless life of the lady of leisure with the services women doctors could perform, Blackwell stressed the contributions female doctors could make by educating mothers on nutrition and child care, as well as working in hospitals, schools, prisons, and other institutions. Whereas Blackwell saw in Garrett a "bright intelligent young lady whose interest in the study of medicine was then aroused," Garrett had not yet decided on a career in medicine and was in fact somewhat overwhelmed by Blackwell's enthusiasm. "I remember feeling very much confounded," Garrett later explained, "and as if I had been suddenly thrust into work that was too big for me." Indeed, Garrett thought that she "had no particular genius for medicine or anything else." Nevertheless, Blackwell can be credited with having fueled Garrett's interest in becoming a fully accredited physician.

Despite his encouragement for his daughter to find some form of work outside the home, Garrett's father at first found the idea of a woman physician "disgusting." Her mother was too old-fashioned and inflexible to accept the idea that her daughter go to work, and she warned her family that if her daughter left home to earn a living, the disgrace would kill her. Seeking advice, Garrett was accompanied by her father on visits to prominent physicians; they were informed that it was useless for a woman to seek medical education because a woman's name would not be entered on the Medical Register, an official endorsement without which medicine could not be legally practiced in England. To guard against the circumstances that had made it possible for Blackwell to be entered on the register, foreign degrees had been ruled unacceptable. During their visits, one doctor asked Garrett why she was not willing to become a nurse instead of a doctor. "Because," she replied, "I prefer to earn a thousand rather than twenty pounds a year!" Indeed, throughout her life she remained vehemently opposed to the idea that women should be confined to nursing while men monopolized medicine and surgery.

Eventually, a meeting was arranged with Dr. William Hawes, a member of the board of directors of Middlesex Hospital, one of London's major

CHRONOLOGY

1860	Began private medical studies but was refused admission to medical schools
1865	Obtained license of the Society of Apothecaries, London
1866	Established St. Mary's dispensary for poor women, which became the New Hospital for Women
1870	Obtained M.D. degree in France; served on London School Board and developed fitness programs for girls' schools
1873	Daughter born; Garrett "inadvertently" admitted to membership by the Paddington (London) branch of the British Medical Association
1874	Helped establish the London Medical College for Women
1883–1903	Served as dean
1897	Elected president of the East Anglican branch of the British Medical Association
1902	Retired and moved from London to Aldeburgh
1908	Elected mayor of Aldeburgh
1917	Died at Aldeburgh

teaching hospitals. This led to the suggestion that Garrett try a "trial marriage with the hospital" by working as a nurse for six months. Assigned to the surgical ward, she used the opportunity to attend dissections and operations, meet the medical staff of the hospital, and obtain some of the training provided to medical students. During this probationary period, Garrett found that she enjoyed the work immensely, that it was neither shocking nor repugnant to her feminine sensibilities, and that the difficulties against which she had been so seriously warned were quite trivial. "It is not true that there is anything disgusting in the study of the human body," she said. "If it were so, how could we look up to God as its maker and designer?" After a three-month probationary period, she abandoned the pretense of being a nurse and unofficially became a medical student, making rounds in the wards, working in the dispensary, and helping with emergency patients. She offered to pay the fees charged medical students but was told that no London medical school would admit her. The hospital staff accepted her as a guest, allowing her to study and carry out dissections, but would not accept her as a student.

In December of 1860, she took examinations that covered the work of the past five months and the results proved impressive. Then in May of the following year, she was accepted for some special courses of lectures and demonstrations; instead of providing new opportunities, this opening wedge stiffened the opposition and increased antifeminist hostility. When she received a certificate of honor in each of the subjects covered by her lecture courses, the examiner sent her a note: "May I entreat you to use every precaution in keeping this a secret from the students." When she answered a question in class that no other student could answer, the students drew up a petition calling for her exclusion on the grounds that she was interfering with their progress. The Medical Committee of Middlesex Hospital was glad to follow their recommendation and she left the hospital in July.

Despite further rejections from Oxford, Cambridge, and the University of London which, according to its charter provided education for "all classes and denominations without distinction whatsoever," Garrett would not be deterred. In 1862 the senate of the University of London had decided, however, that women were neither a class nor a denomination, which left the University without the power to admit them. Determined to secure a qualifying diploma in order to place her name on the Medical Register, she decided to pursue the degree of Licentiate of the Society of Apothecaries (L.S.A.); though the L.S.A. was not as prestigious as the M.D., its holders were duly accredited physicians. To qualify, an applicant had to serve a five-year apprenticeship under a qualified doctor, take certain prescribed lecture courses from recognized university tutors, and pass the qualifying examination. The Hall of Apothecaries was by no means an advocate of equal opportunity for women, but its charter stated that it would examine "all persons" who had satisfied the regulations, and—according to legal opinions obtained by Garrett's father—"persons" included women. An apothecary and resident medical officer at the Middlesex Hospital, who had been one of her tutors, accepted Garrett as an apprentice.

In October 1862, Garrett went to St. Andrews in Scotland where Dr. Day, the Regius Professor of Medicine, had invited her to attend his lectures. When university officials discovered that she had been permitted to secure a matriculation "ticket," the clerk was instructed to reclaim it. Garrett's refusal to return the ticket nearly sparked a lawsuit. It was finally decided that the university's constitution permitted the admission of women, but that the senatus had the discretionary power to exclude any particular person, male or female. Garrett was thus excluded. She remained in St. Andrews attending courses until December but had

no chance of completing her studies there. Study in America might have been a possibility, but Garrett believed that her main task was to open the medical profession and medical education to women in England—even if the battle consumed much of her life and delayed her own career.

With great difficulty, she was able to piece together the elements of a course of instruction, including a summer spent studying with Sir James Simpson in Edinburgh and a very unhappy six-month period of service as a nurse in the London Hospital. But when Garrett presented her credentials to the Society of Apothecaries in the fall of 1865, the examining body refused to administer the examination. After Garrett's father threatened to sue, the apothecaries again reversed themselves. She passed the qualifying examinations to see her name enrolled in the Medical Register one year later. The Society of Apothecaries immediately revised their charter to require graduation from an accredited medical school—all of which excluded women—as a prerequisite for the L.S.A. degree. Another woman's name would not be added to the Medical Register for the next 12 years.

Garrett Opens Women's Hospital

Garrett's goal was to establish a hospital for women staffed by women. Thus in 1866, she opened the St. Mary's Dispensary for Women in London "to enable women to obtain medical and surgical treatment from qualified medical practitioners of their own sex." For some years, she remained the only visiting physician and dispenser; three times a week, she attended outpatients, while also visiting patients in their own homes. The dispensary filled a great need; within only a few weeks, 60 to 90 women and children were seen each consulting afternoon. Serving an impoverished community as physician, surgeon, pharmacist, nurse, midwife, counselor, and clerk, Garrett's association with poverty-stricken families led to her involvement with the women's rights movement. In 1872, with a ward of ten beds, the dispensary became the New Hospital for Women and Children. Demand rapidly outgrew the original facilities, and three houses were purchased and converted into additional wards.

Like her friend Emily Davies, Garrett maintained a strong interest in the reform of education and the expansion of educational opportunities for women. At the time, free compulsory education was becoming a reality for the children of the working class, and Garrett was asked to run for election to the school board by the working men of the district in which she practiced. She was elected to the London School Board in 1870, the same year she obtained the M.D. degree from the University of Paris. Commuting back and forth from London to Paris, she passed all five parts of the examination and successfully defended a thesis on "Migraine" which showed her to be an excellent clinical observer who had treated a large number of patients suffering from migraine and other kinds of headache.

In 1869, Garrett applied for a staff position at the Shadwell Hospital for Children. James George Skelton Anderson, head of a large shipping firm, was one of the members of the hospital board of directors who interviewed her; he and Garrett began working together on reforms needed to improve the administration of the hospital. Their engagement was announced in December 1870. Many of her friends feared she would relinquish her work if married but, as Louisa Garrett Anderson explained in her biography of her mother, Garrett believed "that the woman question will never be solved in any complete way so long as marriage is thought to be incompatible with freedom and with an independent career." She was beginning to see her own life as a way of disproving this notion. They were married on February 9, 1871.

Garrett continued to practice medicine, contrary to the common expectation for married women. Like Garrett's father, Anderson supported his wife's commitment to combine marriage and family with a medical career. Their daughter wrote: "From 1871 to the close of her working life, some thirty-five years later, she proved that a married woman can succeed in a profession and that a medical woman need not neglect her family." Three children were born during their first seven years of married life, two of whom, Louisa and Alan, went on to distinguished careers of their own. The second daughter Margaret, however, died of tubercular peritonitis when only 15 months old.

The New Hospital for Women provided a demonstration of what trained professional women could accomplish. "No men or no hospital" served as Garrett's primary rule in guiding its development. In 1878, she became the first woman in Europe to successfully perform the operation of ovariotomy. Regarded as serious and dangerous, the first operation could not be performed in the hospital since the death of a patient would obviously injure its reputation. To deal with this problem, Garrett rented part of a private house and had the rooms thoroughly cleaned, painted, and whitewashed before the patient and nurses were brought in. The cost of the rooms and their preparation was contributed by James Anderson, who was proud of

Suffragists Elizabeth Garrett Anderson (left) and Emmeline Pankhurst meet in Westminster.

his wife's success but who noted, "We shall be in the bankruptcy court if Elizabeth's surgical practice increases." The next ovariotomy was performed in the hospital. Despite her successes, Garrett did not enjoy operating and was perfectly willing to turn this part of hospital work over to other skilled women surgeons as they joined her staff. The hospital moved to larger quarters at a new site in 1899, nearly two decades before being renamed the Elizabeth Garrett Anderson Hospital.

Helps Establish Medical College for Women

In 1874, along with Sophia Jex-Blake and others, Garrett helped establish the London Medical College for Women, where she taught for 23 years. As dean of the institution (1883–1903), she opposed the idea that women planning work as missionaries should come to the school and acquire a little medical knowledge. She "distrusted the capacity of most people to be efficient in two professions." Two years after its establishment, the London School of Medicine for Women was placed on the list of recognized medical schools, ensuring its graduates access to a registrable license. In 1877, the school was attached to the Royal Free Hospital and permitted to grant the degrees that were required for enrollment on the British Medical Register. Garrett's son Alan was born just before the Royal Free Hospital opened its wards to women students; 50 years later he would become its chairman. The school became one of the colleges of the newly constituted University of London in 1901, and two years later, at the age of 67, Garrett resigned as dean to be appointed honorary president.

Whereas in controversial matters she took a quiet, professional position, Garrett was a suffragist and a member of the Women's Social and Political Union (founded 1903). Although she disagreed with women who were protesting against the Contagious Diseases Acts, which were instituted as an attempt to control venereal diseases, she was devoted to rebutting the pseudoscientific charge that intellectual activity harmed women's health and fertility; she was, regardless, condemned by some feminists for supporting the Contagious Disease Acts. Garrett's daughter suggests that her mother's training had provided little information about the venereal diseases and that her experience did not incite her to challenge the views of the medical profession in this particular matter. Later, the feminists were vindicated by evidence that the Acts were quite ineffective for their stated goals and offensive to many; they were repealed in 1886.

"Inadvertently" admitted to membership by the Paddington Branch (London) of the British Medical Association in 1873, Garrett was scheduled to read a paper on obstetrical section in 1875 at the annual meeting in Edinburgh when the error became known to Sir Robert Christison, then president of the association. Sir Robert proved unable to annul or expel Garrett, who was able to read her paper, but he and the association took steps to make sure no other women gained membership. A clause excluding females was added to the articles of the association in 1878, a prohibition not repealed until 1892. The only woman member of the association for 19 years, Garrett was elected president of the East Anglian branch of the British Medical Association in 1897.

In 1902 the Andersons retired to the Garrett family home in Aldeburgh, and six years later she became the first woman mayor of Aldeburgh. At the start of World War I, she traveled back to London to see her daughter Dr. Louisa Garrett Anderson and Dr. Flora Murray leave the city in charge of the first unit of medical women for service in France. "My dears," she said, "if you go, and if you succeed, you will put forward the women's cause by thirty years." During the war, Louisa Garrett Anderson was joint organizer of the women's hospital corps and served as chief surgeon of the military hospital at Endell Street from 1915–1918.

Elizabeth Garrett Anderson had lived a life full of firsts. She was England's first woman doctor, the first woman M.D. in France, the first woman member of the British Medical Association, the first woman dean of a medical school, and Britain's first woman mayor. Years after her death at Aldeburgh on December 17, 1917, her daughter wrote this tribute: "In her girlhood, Elizabeth heard the call to live and work, and before the evening star lit her to rest she had helped to tear down one after another the barriers which, since the beginning of history, hindered women from work and progress and light and service."

SOURCES:

Bell, Enid Moberly. *Storming the Citadel: The Rise of the Woman Doctor.* Constable, 1953.

Garrett Anderson, Louisa. *Elizabeth Garrett Anderson, 1836–1917.* Faber & Faber, 1939.

Hume, Ruth Fox. *Great Women of Medicine.* Random House, 1964.

Manton, Jo Grenville. *Elizabeth Garrett Anderson.* Dutton, 1958.

Wilkinson, M. "Elizabeth Garrett Anderson and Migraine" in F. C. Rose and W. F. Bynum, eds. *Historical Aspects of the Neurosciences.* Raven, 1982, pp. 165–169.

FURTHER READING:

Blackwell, Elizabeth. *Pioneer Work in Opening the Medical Profession to Women.* Longmans, Green, 1895, reprinted, Schocken Books, 1977.

Chaff, Sandra L., Ruth Haimbach, Carol Fenichel, and Nina B. Woodside, compilers and eds. *Women in Medicine: A Bibliography of the Literature on Women Physicians.* Scarecrow Press, 1977.

Hurd-Mead, Kate Campbell. *A History of Women in Medicine.* Haddam Press, 1938, reprinted, AMS Press, 1977.

Marks, Geoffrey, and William K. Beatty. *Women in White.* Scribner, 1972.

Robert Gascoyne-Cecil, Third Marquess of Salisbury

(1830–1903)

Conservative Party leader and last British prime minister to sit in the House of Lords, who was a brilliant practitioner of balance-of-power diplomacy and presided over the zenith of the British Empire.

"Political equality is not merely a folly—it is a chimera.... Whatever may be the written text of a Constitution, the multitude always will have leaders among them, and those leaders not selected by themselves.... But the only consequence will be that they will have bad leaders instead of good."

LORD SALISBURY

Robert Arthur Talbot Gascoyne-Cecil, third marquess of Salisbury, sprang from a wealthy aristocratic family of undistinguished accomplishments. Although the founders of the family, the father and son William and Robert Cecil, were sagacious advisors to Queen **Elizabeth I** and King **James I,** the succeeding generations were insignificant. In the words of his biographer, Lady Gwendolen Cecil, "the general mediocrity of intelligence which the family displayed was only varied by instances of quite exceptional stupidity." His grandfather, the seventh earl of Salisbury, married a very intelligent woman, Lady Emily Hill, whose political entertaining was rewarded by her husband's promotion in the peerage from earl to marquess. His father, the second marquess, showed some interest and ability in politics, serving in a minor capacity in the short-lived Conservative ministries of Lord Derby in 1852 and 1858.

Robert Cecil, the third marquess of Salisbury, was born on February 3, 1830, at the family estate of Hatfield (one of the most glorious stately homes in England). After studying at Eton College and at Oxford University, he spent almost two

Born on February 3, 1830, at Hatfield, Hertfordshire; died at Hatfield on August 22, 1903; son of James, 2nd Marquess of Salisbury, and Frances Mary Gascoyne (heiress of a Liverpool merchant and landowner); married: Georgina Caroline Alderson, 1857 (died November 20, 1899); children: five sons and three daughters. Predecessors: William Cecil, Lord Burghley (Elizabeth I's lord treasurer); Robert Cecil, 1st earl of Salisbury (advisor to Elizabeth I and James I). Descendants: James, 4th Marquess, and Robert, 5th Marquess, Conservative Party cabinet ministers; David Cecil, professor of English literature; Hugh Cecil, professor of history.

Contributed by Denis Paz, Professor of History, Clemson University, Clemson, South Carolina

CHRONOLOGY

1830	Born at Hatfield
1853	Elected Conservative member of Parliament for Stamford
1866	Appointed secretary of state for India in Lord Derby's ministry
1867	Resigned over the Reform Act of 1867
1868	Succeeded his father as Marquess of Salisbury; moved to the House of Lords
1874–78	Secretary of state for India in Disraeli's ministry
1876–78	Russo-Turkish War
1878	Treaty of San Stefano ended Russo-Turkish War; Salisbury appointed foreign secretary; represented Britain at the Congress of Berlin
1880	Fall of Disraeli's government
1881	Salisbury became leader of Conservative opposition
1885–86	Became prime minister and foreign secretary in his first ministry
1886	Resigned; succeeded by Gladstone's short-lived Liberal government; returned as prime minister
1887–92	Served as foreign secretary as well as prime minister
1895–1900	Prime minister and foreign secretary in his third ministry
1899–1902	Boer War
1902	Retired from public life
1903	Died on August 22

years in Australia, returning to Britain in 1853. What to do with his life was a big question. He was the second son; but his elder brother, who in the normal course of events would follow a career in politics and succeed to the title, was in poor health and went blind at an early age. So it was Robert who went into politics instead, representing the family borough of Stamford in the House of Commons from 1853 until his father's death in 1868. (His brother's early death in 1865 meant that he would inherit the title and seat in the House of Lords.)

Cecil's early political career, from 1853 to 1866, was marked by a quick demonstration of ability in parliamentary debate. Those years were not good ones in which to be a Conservative politician, because the Liberals, led by **Lord Palmerston,** dominated Parliament and won elections. The Conservative Party, led by Lord Derby, formed governments in 1852 and 1857, but held power for only 24 months. The ambitions of Conservative politicians thus were frustrated. Cecil made his mark as a speaker of more than ordinary ability, as a defender of the privileges of the Church of England, and as an intelligent Conservative politician who appreciated both abstract theoretical principles and the nuts and bolts of practical legislation. This combination of abilities can be explained by Cecil's dire economic need.

Cecil Writes Political Essays

Against his father's wishes, Cecil married Georgina, eldest daughter of the judge Sir Edward Alderson, on July 11, 1857. His father strenuously opposed the match because Georgina was several years older than Cecil, and because the prospective bride was objectionable on religious grounds. (She was a High Church Anglican, which in those days was deemed worse than being a Roman Catholic.) When Cecil persisted in the match, his father refused to give him an income. Needing money, Cecil supported himself by becoming a professional writer. He specialized in political essays for some of the most outstanding and influential Conservative political magazines of the day, the *Quarterly Review,* the *Saturday Review,* and *Bentley's Quarterly Review,* among others. These political essays were noted at the time for their intelligent and sophisticated exposition of conservative political principles, and their clear and vigorous literary style. They owe much to his wife's influence. Georgina was a well read and intelligent woman who treated her husband as her intellectual equal. They shared common religious and ideological beliefs; discussed the great political, economic, and intellectual issues of the day; and together enjoyed reading French literature. Their personalities complemented each other. Cecil's shyness combined with nearsightedness to make him awkward in social situations; he frequently failed to recognize people (even his fellow cabinet ministers) or remember their names. His family liked to rearrange and even replace furniture in a room, and wait to see how long it took him to notice the change. Georgina enjoyed entertainment, was a good conversationalist, and claimed never to have met a boring person. Thus he relied on her to carry the burden of entertaining and socializing so important for a political career. This partnership was very important to Cecil, and his wife's death in 1899 would grieve him deeply.

Concurrently with his writing, Cecil continued an active political life in the House of Commons. Because his family controlled the borough of Stamford, he never once faced opposition and never had to concern himself with winning elections. Instead, he focused his political energies inside the House of Commons. During the 1850s and early 1860s, he spoke frequently and effectively on controversial issues such as the abolition of compulsory church rates (local taxes for the upkeep of Anglican churches), the admission of Jews to Parliament, the conduct of the Crimean War, and welfare for the poor. On all these issues he espoused a conservative line, arguing that the Church of England deserved support as the national church, that the membership of Parliament should reflect Britain's identity as a Christian nation, that the Liberal Party was unfit to prosecute war vigorously, and that the poor were entitled to a basic standard of living. Reward for his political activities finally came in June of 1866, when the Liberal ministry fell and Lord Derby formed his third Conservative government. Cecil was appointed secretary of state for India, charged with responsibility for administering that most important part of the British Empire. During his nine months in office, Cecil demonstrated remarkable administrative abilities and proved himself an effective defender of the Indian budget.

Cecil broke decisively with the leadership of his party, and especially with **Benjamin Disraeli,** the Conservatives' chief spokesman in the House of Commons, over the issue of parliamentary reform. Disraeli had long been interested in finding an issue that might bring his party success at the polls. He concluded that, under the existing requirements for the franchise, the Conservatives had no hope of winning elections. (In fact they had not won an election since 1841.) Therefore, he thought that the party should espouse the cause of extending the vote to working-class males, figuring that the new voters would thank the Tories by returning them to power. When Disraeli convinced the cabinet to introduce what became the Reform Act of 1867, Cecil refused to go along, resigned his office, and attacked the measure in Parliament and in the press. He argued that the expansion of the electorate would create an American-style mass political system in which the natural leaders of the country would be displaced by professional politicians, and in which the independent member of Parliament voting his own conscience would be displaced by party functionaries pandering to a fickle electorate. Furthermore, he charged his party leaders with treachery and dishonesty, maintaining that they had abandoned their principles in an effort to stay in power. Cecil's antipathy to Disraeli would have made it difficult to remain in the House of Commons. With the death of his father in April

1868, however, he transferred to the House of Lords as the third marquess of Salisbury. That was his political stage for the rest of his life.

Salisbury, as he was now called, was in Opposition in the House of Lords during the Liberal prime minister **William Ewart Gladstone**'s government of 1868–74. In the latter year, however, the Conservatives at last won an election, and Benjamin Disraeli became prime minister. Despite their estrangement, Disraeli appointed Salisbury secretary of state for India. His main concern in that office was to protect India from the threat of Russian expansionism. Russia had long been interested in controlling Afghanistan (which bordered India), and unrest among the Afghan tribes led to fears of Russian meddling. The main Russian threat, however, turned out to be in the Balkans, then under Turkish rule. The Bulgarians revolted against Turkish rule in 1876 and appealed to the Russians, fellow Slavs, for help. Russia won the war that followed, and the Treaty of San Stefano (March 1878) seemed to ensure Russian domination of the Balkans, the fatal weakening of Turkey, and the opening of the eastern Mediterranean Sea to the tsar's fleet. At this juncture the foreign secretaryship fell vacant, and Salisbury was appointed to it in April 1878. Salisbury at once demanded that the Treaty of San Stefano be renegotiated at a conference of all the great powers on the grounds that the Turkish concessions to Russia represented a threat to the peace of Europe. The result of Salisbury's demand was the Congress of Berlin, which managed to create a delicate balance of power in the Balkans that lasted for 30 years, although not without periodic conflict.

Salisbury Espouses Balance-of-Power Policy

Salisbury's diplomacy at the Congress of Berlin was based on the traditional idea of the balance of power, and thus rejected the idea of noninterference espoused by Victorian Liberals such as Lord Palmerston, **Richard Cobden,** and **John Bright.** Writing in the *Quarterly Review* in 1860, Salisbury encapsulated the policy that he advanced at the Congress of Berlin, and that he was to follow for the rest of his diplomatic career. "England did not meddle with other nations' doings when they concerned her not. But she recognised the necessity of an equilibrium … among the states of Europe. When a great Power abused its superiority by encroaching on the frontier of its weaker neighbours, she looked on their cause as her cause and on their danger as the forerunner of her own."

The Conservatives were defeated in the election of 1880 and replaced by Gladstone's second

Liberal government of 1880–85. Disraeli's death in 1881 resulted in a divided Opposition, with Salisbury leading the Conservatives in the House of Lords. Because Gladstone's reformist domestic policy was popular with the voters, it was difficult to attack. The Liberals, however, were vulnerable in their foreign and imperial policies to charges of weakness and even of cowardice in the face of events that could be taken as threats to British interests and insults to British honor. This was especially the case in the Sudan. Reluctantly, Gladstone had ordered the occupation of Egypt, which controlled the Sudan, to protect the Suez Canal, but had ordered the popular general **"Chinese" Gordon** to evacuate the Sudan. Instead, Gordon decided on his own to make a stand against the Sudanese at Khartoum. Gladstone's government opposed Gordon's step but failed to do anything about it. When a relief expedition was eventually sent, it arrived at Khartoum two days after the town had been stormed and Gordon killed. Salisbury was able to excoriate the Liberals and Gladstone for betraying Gordon and failing to defend British honor. When Gladstone's government fell in June 1885, Salisbury took office as both prime minister and foreign secretary.

Salisbury's first ministry was short-lived, lasting only until January of 1886. Salisbury had called elections in December, and had campaigned on the platform of British chauvinism. Gladstone had matched that with calls for justice to Ireland. The result was a split Parliament with the Irish Nationalists holding the balance of power. Gladstone appealed to the Irish by announcing his conversion to Home Rule for Ireland, but Salisbury remained staunchly for union between Ireland and Britain. The Irish Nationalists switched their votes to the Liberals in January 1886 and the Conservatives resigned. Gladstone resumed office and introduced the first Home Rule Bill; after its defeat he called for a general election on the question. Aided by defections from the Liberal ranks, Salisbury won the election by appealing to the union and by declaring that what Ireland needed was "government that does not flinch, that does not vary, … that she cannot hope to beat down by agitations."

Salisbury's second ministry lasted from 1886 to 1892. Once again he combined the offices of prime minister and foreign secretary. Africa, and the implications of Africa for the diplomatic relations among Britain, France, and Germany, took up most of his time. Salisbury wanted to promote the balance of power in Europe and to achieve a good understanding with Germany. To those ends, he negotiated an adjustment of competing colonial claims in Africa. Germany abandoned its claims to Uganda and acknowledged the British protectorate over Zanzibar in East Africa in return for Britain's returning the North Sea island of Heligoland to German control. Similarly, Britain accepted the French takeover of Madagascar in return for France's acceptance of the British takeover of Zanzibar. In both cases, the British thought that they had the better end of the deal. Salisbury encouraged British penetration of Africa by semiprivate means, granting royal charters to the British East Africa Company (1888) and the British South Africa Company (1889). The latter company colonized what became Rhodesia and was to get Britain involved in the South African War in Salisbury's last ministry.

In domestic affairs, Salisbury allowed his cabinet ministers, especially George Joachim Goschen, the chancellor of the exchequer; Henry Matthews, the home secretary; and A. J. Balfour, the chief secretary for Ireland, to set their own policies—although of course they had to be policies that he approved. Among the most noted domestic achievements were the County Councils Act, 1888, which established elected bodies to administer local government, and the Free Education Act, 1891, which eliminated school fees. Ireland, however, was the most contentious area of domestic government. The ministry had come to power because of its opposition to Home Rule and its promise of law and order, and it continued that policy throughout its life. The Crimes Act, 1887, which Balfour was responsible for, appealed to English sentiment at the same time that it alienated Irish sentiment. The government was especially concerned to neutralize the charismatic leadership of the Irish leader **Charles Stewart Parnell.** The government had attempted to blacken Parnell's reputation by publicizing several letters apparently written by the Irish leader, which condoned terrorism in the pursuit of Irish self-rule. Parnell denied having written the letters, and an investigative committee eventually discovered that they were forgeries. What saved the ministry was the public scandal that erupted when it was revealed in 1890 that Parnell was living with another man's wife. The ministry limped on for another two years but was defeated in the election of 1892.

He Faces International Crises

Gladstone became prime minister again at the age of 82, and promptly reintroduced the Irish Home Rule Bill. This time it passed the House of Commons, only to be rejected by the House of Lords. Salisbury played a prominent role in the debates on this issue. Unable to convince his colleagues to fight an election on the issue, Gladstone resigned. The Liberals limped on under Lord Rosebery's leadership until 1895. Salisbury formed a coalition with Joseph Chamberlain, a former Liberal who had joined the Conservatives over Home Rule. Salisbury served as foreign secretary as well as prime minister, while Chamberlain took responsibility for colonial affairs. Salisbury almost immediately faced international crises with the United States, France, and Germany. The United States claimed that the boundary dispute between Venezuela and British Guiana violated the Monroe Doctrine, and threatened to enforce its own view of the boundary's location. Salisbury, however, defused American hotheadedness by presenting documentation that proved the British case, by opposing European intervention in the Spanish-American War, and by allowing the Americans to displace British interests in Samoa and Central America. The Anglo-French dispute came over the Fashoda Crisis of 1898, in which a French expedition penetrated the Sudan, thereby threatening British control of the Nile River. Salisbury deftly dislodged the French by combining the threat of force with diplomatic pressure. He sent Sir **Herbert Kitchener** to Fashoda with a superior force of troops, and the French commander was forced to withdraw. The French government protested, but Salisbury stood firm, and eventually the French backed off.

The conflict with Germany was the most serious and had the worst long-term consequences for world diplomatic relations. Colonial Secretary Joseph Chamberlain supported British expansion in southern Africa, and had given **Cecil Rhodes** secret encouragement to take over the Afrikaner republics of the Transvaal and the Orange Free State. Acting on this secret understanding, Rhodes arranged for the Jameson Raid of 1895, in which a guerilla force invaded the Transvaal in order to compel President **Paul Kruger** to give the right to vote to British residents there. The raid was a failure, and Germany, to Salisbury's dismay, supported the Afrikaner republics. Encouraged by this support, Kruger became intransigent. When Chamberlain sent troops to South Africa, Kruger issued an ultimatum demanding that the troops be removed. Britain refused to remove the troops, and Kruger declared war. The South African (Boer) War, fought between 1899 and 1902, was Salisbury's last great diplomatic success. Although the Afrikaners were hardly models of innocent victims, they were so treated by those powers which did not like Britain for other reasons. The United States, for instance, denounced the British for fighting a war of annexation in South Africa at the same time

that it was occupied in fighting a war of annexation in the Philippines. The French, the Russians, and, especially, the Germans also denounced the British. Despite this diplomatic isolation, Salisbury was able to convince the Great Powers to confine their opposition to words. Britain's isolation during the South African War led Salisbury's successors to abandon balance-of-power diplomacy and to seek allies against German hostility. The battle lines for the First World War were being drawn.

Salisbury's health had been failing for some time in the 1890s, and the deaths of his wife in November 1899 and of Queen **Victoria** in January 1901 had saddened him. He regarded it his duty to remain in office, however, until the end of the war. In 1900, he relinquished the Foreign Office. The South African War ended in May 1902, and Salisbury retired from public office in July. He lived quietly at his ancestral estate of Hatfield until his death a year later.

Lord Salisbury's life coincided with the zenith of British economic prosperity and imperial domination. Britain in 1830, the year of his birth, was entering a period of unrivaled economic prosperity, thanks to the Industrial Revolution. During his active political life as Conservative Party leader, Britain expanded her empire in Africa, India, and China. At his death, she stood at the pinnacle of power. Both economic and political decline were to come as the growing economic and political rivals of the United States, Germany, and Japan challenged British dominance. It was in large part due to Salisbury's leadership, however, that Britain's decline was a slow process.

SOURCES:

Cecil, Algernon. "Robert Arthur Talbot Gascoyne-Cecil, third Marquis of Salisbury," in *Dictionary of National Biography, 1901–1911*. Oxford University Press, 1912.

Cecil, Gwendolen. *Life of Robert, Marquis of Salisbury*. 4 vols. Hodder & Stoughton, 1921–32 (reprinted by Kraus, 1971).

Kidd, Charles, and David Williamson, eds. *Debrett's Peerage and Baronetage*. St. Martin's Press, 1990.

Marsh, Peter. *The Discipline of Popular Government: Lord Salisbury's Domestic Statescraft, 1881–1902*. Harvester Press, 1978.

FURTHER READING:

Blake, Lord, and Hugh Cecil, eds. *Salisbury: The Man and His Policies*. St. Martin's Press, 1987.

Pinson, Lillian. *Foreign Affairs Under the Third Marquis of Salisbury*. Athlone Press, 1962.

Taylor, Robert. *Lord Salisbury*. St. Martin's Press, 1975.

Charles de Gaulle

(1890–1970)

Leader of the French Resistance against Nazi Germany during World War II, who came out of retirement in 1958 to end the French Algerian War and create his country's present government.

Born on November 22, 1890, in Lille, France; died in 1970; son of Henri (a teacher) and Jeanne (Maillot-Delannoy) de Gaulle; married: Yvonne Vendroux, 1921; children: (one son) Philippe; (two daughters) Elizabeth and Anne (died 1948). Predecessors: Paul Reynaud, premier, Third Republic (in 1940), Pierre Pflimlin, premier, Fourth Republic (in 1958). Successors: Felix Gouin, premier, Provisional Government (in 1946), Georges Pompidou, president, Fifth Republic (in 1969).

Although General Charles de Gaulle was very controversial during his lifetime, both inside and outside France, virtually everyone now agrees that he was one of the most significant statesmen in 20th-century Europe. A career military man, de Gaulle first attracted attention in 1934 with his support of a mechanized army for France. With the defeat of France by Nazi Germany in 1940, he called upon the French to resist. The honor of France had been tainted, he argued, by a weak republican system dominated by political parties which had failed to prepare France adequately for the threat from Nazi Germany. Throughout the period of the German occupation, 1940–44, General de Gaulle led the Free French in London.

After the liberation of France in 1944, he headed the Provisional Government, but he resigned in 1946 when it became clear to him that the political parties would once again dominate French political life. In 1958, he was called back to power when France teetered on the brink of civil war over the Algerian revolt. He wrote a new constitution, providing for a strong presidency, to which he was named in 1959; he then presided

"There is a pact of twenty centuries between the grandeur of France and the liberty of the world.

CHARLES DE GAULLE, 1941

Contributed by Bertram M. Gordon, Professor of History, Mills College, Oakland, California

over the French withdrawal from Algeria in 1962 and an expanding French economy in the mid-1960s. In May 1968, his government was shaken by a student revolt and workers' strike that paralyzed France for a month. His prestige tarnished by these events, General de Gaulle resigned the presidency after a decentralizing reform bill he supported was defeated in a referendum in April of 1969. He died the following year.

Charles André Marie Joseph de Gaulle was born on November 22, 1890, in the northern city of Lille into a family with roots going back to medieval France. One of his ancestors had fought in the battle of Agincourt against the English in 1415. The early de Gaulles held lesser ranks in the French nobility, but the 19th-century generations turned to the practice of law. His father Henri de Gaulle was educated for a military career but, during the war with Prussia in 1870, was wounded and subsequently took up teaching as a career. In 1886, he married Jeanne Maillot-Delannoy, a second cousin on his mother's side. The marriage produced four boys and a girl. Born in 1890, Charles de Gaulle was the second child. He grew up in a family that was strongly Catholic, conservative and steeped in French history, one which advocated a sense of service and traditional values. From his parents, Charles de Gaulle also learned an appreciation for the elegance of the French language. There was warmth but also seriousness of purpose in the de Gaulle household.

By 1890, the French Third Republic, established after defeat by Prussia in the war of 1870, was firmly entrenched, having survived several major crises and scandals. De Gaulle's early years were spent against a background of the unfolding Dreyfus affair, which began in 1894 when Captain Alfred Dreyfus, the highest-ranking Jewish officer in the French army, was convicted of passing military secrets to the Germans. The "Affair," as it came to be known in France, ultimately ended with the exoneration of Dreyfus, but not before France had been split into two hostile camps. One camp was composed of Republicans, liberals, and Socialists, who supported the secular state and demanded the revision of the guilty verdict. The other camp was a composite of high military officials, Church leaders, Royalists, anti-Semites, and a mixed coalition of those who believed Dreyfus guilty, who argued that a reopening of the case would weaken the French army in the face of a powerful and hostile German neighbor. France came close to civil war. The victory of the Dreyfusards, or pro-Dreyfus camp, led in 1905 to a legal separation of church and state in France. Young de Gaulle, who had been studying at a Jesuit school in Paris, was sent by

CHRONOLOGY

1890	Born in Lille, France
1913	Joined Pétain's 33rd Infantry Regiment
1916	Taken prisoner at the battle of Verdun
1918	Released from prison; WWI ended
1924	Assigned to French occupation army in Germany; published first book
1934	French Republic threatened; hostile demonstrations by fascists and communists
1940	France overrun by Nazi Germany; de Gaulle fled to England; broadcast call for Resistance
1944	Returned to Paris with armies of liberation; became head of Provisional Government
1945	World War II ended
1946	Resigned as head of Provisional Government; French Indochina War began
1947	French Fourth Republic created; de Gaulle organized the *Rassemblement du Peuple Francais* (RPF), a political party
1953	RPF disbanded
1954	French defeated in Indochina War
1958	Uprising in Algeria; de Gaulle named premier
1959	Introduced constitution for the Fifth Republic; named president
1968	Student revolt in Paris
1969	Resigned after defeat in referendum; died the following year

his father to continue his studies at another Jesuit college in Belgium, where, apparently, he decided on a military career.

To all appearances, de Gaulle was a serious young man, especially where the interests of France were concerned. He believed that the parliamentary institutions of the Republic were weak and that he could better serve France in her army. After spending two years at a preparatory school, de Gaulle enlisted in 1909 in the 33rd Infantry Regiment, stationed at Arras, near Lille, and a year later was accepted into the prestigious military academy at Saint-Cyr, the French equivalent of West Point, in the suburbs of Paris. Two of de Gaulle's physical traits would be focal points for cartoonists throughout his public life: his exceptional height (he was six feet five) and his exceptionally large nose, which

earned him the sobriquet "Cyrano." Upon his commission following graduation from Saint-Cyr, de Gaulle asked to be posted with his old regiment, the 33rd Infantry, to which he was assigned in 1912. His commanding officer was Colonel Henri *Philippe Pétain,* a man with whom de Gaulle would forever after be linked.

De Gaulle Wounded, Taken Prisoner

Like the young de Gaulle, Pétain was austere and aloof but knew his men and won their respect. Like de Gaulle, Pétain was an outsider, critical of established military strategies in the French army and, therefore, repeatedly passed over for promotion. Most importantly, while the French general staff promoted a strategy of constant attack, Pétain supported one of defense and economy in the use of both human and material resources. When the German onslaught came at the beginning of World War I, de Gaulle was wounded in both 1914 and 1915 fighting on the western front. During the battle of Verdun, which cost France approximately 600,000 casualties in 1916, de Gaulle was again wounded and this time taken prisoner. Pétain, now a general, had been put in charge of the entire Verdun front. Following Pétain's strategy of relying more on artillery to conserve manpower, the French held out against repeated German offensives, and Pétain became a national hero. Impris-

oned in Germany, de Gaulle made five unsuccessful attempts to escape and ended up a prisoner of war for the duration of hostilities. During this time, he gathered materials for his later books and learned German. In 1917, at the nadir of French military fortunes, Pétain quelled a mutiny, further burnishing his image in France.

With the armistice of November 1918, de Gaulle returned home, only to go to Poland in 1919 when French forces aided the new Polish state in its struggle against the Bolshevik forces of revolutionary Russia. With significant French help, the Poles were able to ward off a Russian attack in 1920, and de Gaulle was given Poland's highest military decoration. Upon his return from Poland in 1920, de Gaulle, now a captain, courted and the following year married Yvonne Vendroux, the daughter of a biscuit maker from Calais. He was appointed a history lecturer at Saint-Cyr, and the two settled down to a quiet domestic life, raising a family in Paris. According to biographer Don Cook, "He was already absorbed with his feelings about France and destiny, and [Madame de Gaulle] was absorbed in him." In 1922, he was accepted as a student in the École Supérieure de Guerre, a military school conducted by generals who had led France during the First World War. De Gaulle saw that the military doctrine of the French General Staff had shifted after the war from its emphasis on attack to exclusive concentration on defensive firepower. Some of the younger officers, however, argued for offensive use of the tank, which had been introduced in the closing stages of the war.

Like Pétain, who was now a marshal of France, de Gaulle rebelled against the military doctrines taught by the General Staff and, like Pétain, who became his patron, de Gaulle saw promotions go to other candidates. In 1924, he published his first book, *La Discorde chez l'ennemi (Discord among the Enemy)*, an analysis of the German defeat of 1918, which attributed Germany's problems to a Nietzschean cult and showed de Gaulle's willingness to present his ideas to an audience wider than the military. At the same time, de Gaulle was sent to join the French occupation forces in western Germany; he was recalled by Pétain in 1925 to work on a history of the French military that Pétain hoped would help rally opinion against projected cuts in the military budget by the Socialist government of Édouard Herriot. With his immense personal prestige as the victor of Verdun, Pétain in the mid-1920s used his influence to help build the Maginot line, a wall of fortresses on the Franco-German border intended to protect France from future attack. Even though Pétain continued to sponsor occasional lectures by de Gaulle, the Maginot line represented the victory of the defensive strategy that de Gaulle opposed. In 1927, de Gaulle, finally promoted to major, was sent back to Germany to command the 19th Battalion of Light Infantry, a unit of the famous Alpine Chasseurs. From 1929 through 1931, he was posted with the army in Beirut, Lebanon, then a French Mandate sanctioned by the League of Nations. Back in France in 1931, de Gaulle continued to write and in 1934, a year after **Adolf Hitler** came to power in Germany, published a book, entitled *Vers l'armée de métier (The Army of the Future)*, which argued that France, rather than rest on her laurels after her victory in World War I, should adopt new forms of mechanized warfare, notably the coordinated use of tanks. His book went largely unheeded until 1940, though in 1937 he was named to command the 507th Tank Regiment at Metz, near the frontier with Germany. The outbreak of World War II in September 1939 found de Gaulle in command of the tanks of the 5th Army, stationed in support of the Maginot line along the Rhine in Alsace in eastern France.

From September 1939 until May 1940, the Franco-German frontier was relatively quiet in what was called the "Phoney War," while German forces cut through Poland, then Denmark and Norway. The German attack in the West on May 10, 1940, led to a rout in which, although de Gaulle's tank forces fought well, the French army was effectively broken within three weeks by the kinds of coordinated tank attacks de Gaulle had favored for France. On June 17th, Marshal Pétain, now 84 years old and a known supporter of a cease-fire, was named premier. De Gaulle, having just been promoted to general, refused to accept the finality of defeat. He and his family left France for London, from which he broadcast back to France on the 18th of June, calling for the French to defend their national honor and resist the German forces then in the process of overrunning their country. Few heard this radio appeal, and most of the French welcomed the armistice that the Pétain government was able to sign with the Germans. The Germans occupied roughly the northern three-fifths of France, including Paris, and allowed the establishment of a French government, headed by Pétain, with its capital in the spa resort of Vichy in the unoccupied zone. Known as the Vichy government, the new regime supported collaboration with Hitler's Germany in the belief that Germany had won the war and that England, the lone country opposing her in the summer of 1940, would soon be defeated. Ironically, de Gaulle's patron Pétain now headed a government that sentenced him to death in absentia as a traitor.

Calls on French to Resist Nazis

To de Gaulle, any collaboration with Germany was a dishonor for France and the values of "liberty, equality, fraternity" for which France had stood since her revolution of 1789. From London, he broadcast radio speeches back to France, calling upon his fellow citizens to resist the Nazis, and he organized "Free France," his Resistance movement, after 1942 called "Fighting France." The willingness of the Pétain government to collaborate with the Nazis, according to de Gaulle, had betrayed France. He believed that France had been defeated in 1940 in part because of a weak parliamentary regime during the Third Republic (1875–1940), and that postwar France would need a strong executive power.

After a long struggle to assert control over the various Resistance forces in France and to win over the wartime allies (British prime minister **Winston Churchill** and American president **Franklin D. Roosevelt**) de Gaulle emerged the undisputed leader of the French Resistance. He was said to be austere and even arrogant in his behavior, but de Gaulle saw himself as the incarnation of French ideals and national honor at a time when no one else would speak up. Because of his refusal to compromise on what he considered essential issues of French honor, he quarreled continually with the other Allied leaders, and President Roosevelt looked, in vain, for other potential French leaders. As head of the Resistance, de Gaulle led the victory parade down the Champs-Élysées in Paris the day after the city was liberated by Allied forces in August 1944. He was named to head a Provisional Government while a constitution was drawn up for a new Fourth Republic. Almost immediately afterward, however, de Gaulle quarreled with the leaders of the prewar political parties which were reconstituted in France after the Liberation. In January 1946, he resigned from the government.

With de Gaulle now out of office in 1946, France became involved in a costly war to retain her colony of Indochina, and in 1947 the Fourth Republic was established, very much a copy of the Third. Against a background of an intensification of the Cold War between Soviet Russia and the West and the deepening Communist insurgency in Indochina in 1947, de Gaulle launched a new political party, the RPF (*Rassemblement du Peuple Français,* or "Rally of the French People"), which emphasized anticommunism and the need for a strong French executive. It failed to bring him back to power, however, and he disbanded it in 1953. The following year, French forces in Indochina suffered a shattering defeat at Dienbienphu and the French withdrew from the country. During the same year, a revolt began among the Muslims of Algeria, which had been a French colony since 1830. By 1954, Algeria had a population of some 1.5 million people of European descent as opposed to about 9 million Muslim Arabs. The war, brutally fought on both sides, led in May 1958 to riots among the Europeans in Algiers and other Algerian cities who felt that France needed a stronger government to prosecute the war. The crisis in Algeria, which threatened to spread to continental France itself, led to an invitation for General de Gaulle to return to power. He accepted with the stipulation that he be allowed to sponsor a constitution for a new republic with a stronger executive.

De Gaulle Elected President of Fifth Republic

Once back in power, de Gaulle was given the authority he had requested to draft a new constitution with a much stronger presidency for what was to become France's Fifth Republic. In a strategy he was to use repeatedly, he put his proposal to a vote of the people and made clear that he would resign if the vote went against him. The vote was favorable; the new constitution, which provided that the president be elected indirectly by a vote of "notables" or representatives from throughout France, went into effect in 1959. To almost no one's surprise, de Gaulle was named president of the new republic. He next determined that the only practical solution to the Algerian war was to grant independence to the Muslim insurgents. As his policy became increasingly evident, many of those who had demonstrated on his behalf in 1958 turned bitterly against him, arguing that he had betrayed the cause of French Algeria. De Gaulle had to withstand two coup attempts in 1960 and 1961, but he remained on course, and in March 1962 Algeria was granted independence. Disgruntled partisans of French Algeria formed the *Organisation Armée Secrète* ("Secret Army Organization"), or OAS, which launched a terror campaign to block the independence of Algeria. Several assassination attempts were made against de Gaulle, perhaps the best known in August 1962, described in Frederick Forsyte's *Day of the Jackal.* To provide greater stability for the Republic and to enhance the prestige of the presidency following the assassination attempts, de Gaulle proposed that the president be elected directly by the people. This constitutional revision was also approved by the electorate in a referendum, and in 1965 de Gaulle became the first popularly elected president of the Fifth Republic.

During the mid-1960s, de Gaulle achieved a reconciliation with West Germany, with which he formed a tight bond that dominated the affairs of the developing Common Market (European Economic Community or EEC, founded 1958). To keep France paramount in the Common Market, he twice vetoed British attempts to join the organization, in 1963 and in 1967. He continued the development of French nuclear weapons started under the Fourth Republic, pulled the French military out of the North Atlantic Treaty Organization (NATO), which he argued was dominated by the United States, and, after the 1967 Arab-Israeli war, shifted France from a pro-Israel to a pro-Arab position. To spread the *"grandeur,"* or greatness, of France in the world, he traveled extensively, devoting special attention to the Third World, and gave France a higher profile in world affairs than was justified by her economic and military power. In support of a greater world role for the French language and Francophone communities, while visiting Montreal in 1967 he called for a "free" Quebec, causing a furor in Canada.

In 1968, General de Gaulle was faced with his most serious crisis since the Algerian war. Coalescing around grievances that included authoritarian university structures and outdated curricula, squalid conditions of the growing numbers of foreigners living and working in France, and the American war in Vietnam, protesting university students managed to take over several of the campuses in and around Paris during the spring of 1968. French workers opposing governmental low wages joined the students, and the country was virtually shut down by a general strike in May 1968. Caught off guard by these events, General de Gaulle struck a deal with his military leaders. He won their support against the strikers in return for granting amnesty to the pro-French Algeria military men charged with plotting against him in the early 1960s. He then called for new parliamentary elections which, with increasing numbers of voters growing weary of the strike, resulted in a sweeping victory for his partisans. Nonetheless, de Gaulle's image as a decisive leader had been tarnished. To recoup his prestige early in 1969, he proposed several reforms to decentralize the French government. The package was put to the French voters in a referendum in April 1969, and again de Gaulle staked his personal prestige on the success of the vote, threatening to resign if it went against him. This time, the vote was negative. De Gaulle promptly resigned, and was ultimately succeeded as president by Georges Pompidou, who had been his prime minister from 1961 through the crisis of 1968. Retiring with Madame de Gaulle to their country estate at Colombey-les-deux-Églises, the General worked on his memoirs until his death on November 9, 1970.

Since his death, General de Gaulle has become a national hero in France. His home has been turned into a museum, and a giant Cross of Lorraine, the symbol of the Free French of 1940, has been erected near the village of Colombey. The city of Paris sponsored the celebration of the centenary of his birth in 1990 with a giant sound-and-light show along the banks of the Seine. At events held throughout the year, many of his former political adversaries paid tribute to his enormous role in 20th-century France and the world.

SOURCES:

Bauer, Jean-Louis. "De Gaulle et la Conception de l'Etat," in Institut Charles-de-Gaulle, ed. *Approches de la Philosophic Politique du Général de Gaulle,* Cujas, 1983.

Cook, Don. *Charles de Gaulle: A Biography.* Putnam, 1983.

De Gaulle, Charles. *Discours et Messages.* 5 vols. Plon, 1970.

Dreyfus, François G. *De Gaulle et le Gaullisme.* Presses Universitaires de France, 1982.

Ledwidge, Bernard. *De Gaulle.* St. Martin's Press, 1982.

Remond, Rene. "Comment Charles devint de Gaulle" in *L'Express,* October 19, 1984.

FURTHER READING:

Crawley, Aidan. *De Gaulle, A Biography.* Bobbs-Merrill, 1969.

De Gaulle, Charles. *Memoirs of Hope, 1958–62.* Simon & Schuster, 1971.

———. *The War Memoirs, 1940–46.* Simon & Schuster, 1964.

Lacouture, Jean. *De Gaulle,* Volume 1: *The Rebel, 1890–1944* and II: *The Ruler, 1944–1970.* Norton, 1990–91.

Schoenbrun, David. *The Three Lives of Charles de Gaulle.* Atheneum, 1968.

Werth, Alexander. *De Gaulle, A Political Biography.* Penguin, 1965.

William Ewart Gladstone

(1809–1898)

British statesman who led the Liberal Party during much of the last four decades of the 19th century, while attempting to promote the peaceful settlement of international disputes and resolve the Irish question.

Born in Liverpool, England, on December 29, 1809; died on Ascension Day in 1898, buried in Westminster Abbey; son of John and Anne (Robertson) Gladstone; married: Catherine Glynn, 1839; children: William Henry, Agnes, Stephen Edward, Catherine Jessy, Mary, Helen, Henry Neville, and Herbert John. Descendants: Herbert John, 1st Viscount (first governor general and high commissioner for South Africa). Predecessor: Disraeli. Successor: Lord Rosebery.

William Ewart was the fifth of six children of John and Anne Gladstone, who were both of Scottish descent. His father, who had moved to Liverpool as a youth, had made his fortune in the field of commerce and had purchased the estate of Fasque in Scotland in 1829.

While matriculating at Eton, William Gladstone acquired an interest in politics through his association with James Milnes Gaskell and—as a member of the Eton Society—became prominent during his last two years as a debater. He also developed the practice of reading widely and recording his reading in his daily journal, a practice he would continue throughout his life. In 1828, he entered Christ Church at Oxford, the college most linked with the world of affairs; there he gained double firsts in classics and mathematics and participated in the university debating society (later the Oxford Union), which provided further training for future debates in the Commons.

Many historians maintain that the choice of a career caused Gladstone considerable struggle of conscience. Was he called to serve his church or could he achieve his goals through politics? Others

"[N]o one was a more accomplished master of Parliamentary tactics and Parliamentary management."

OBITUARY IN *TIMES* (MAY 20, 1898)

Contributed by Albert A. Hayden, Professor of History, Wittenberg University, Springfield, Ohio

stress that Gladstone's education and career plans were formulated by his father, and that when the young Gladstone approached him about entering the church, he knew the response would be negative. Certainly he followed his father's educational program, even to the extent of "eating a few of the dinners required by Lincoln's Inn for joining the bar."

But Gladstone's entry into Parliament in 1832 soon presented a dilemma. Though the United Kingdom had abolished the slave trade in 1807, there was continued agitation for the abolition of slavery itself. John Gladstone had plantations in the West Indies where slaves were used, and his son was faced with the task of defending his father's treatment of slaves even though he himself was opposed to slavery. Gladstone's respect for his father outweighed his own convictions, and his father refused to let him go to the West Indies to investigate conditions on his estates. (Slavery in the colonies was finally abolished in 1834.)

Gladstone's entry into Parliament also coincided with angry debates over a series of parliamentary reform bills. At first, as a Tory (Conservative), he was opposed, but he slowly began to drift toward the Whig (Liberal) Party. This transformation in Gladstone's political affiliation was a result of the repeal of the Corn Laws (which restricted free trade) by Sir **Robert Peel** in 1846. The potato blight in Ireland caused Peel, despite the opposition of his land-owning supporters, to introduce the measure which led to the splitting of his Party and the appearance in Parliament of a group of devoted followers of Sir Robert known as Peelites. Eventually, the Peelites gravitated back into either the Conservative Party or into the Liberal Party; Gladstone was one of the Peelites who stayed with the Liberals.

In the years between the split of the Conservative Party in 1846 and Gladstone's first ministry in 1868, Gladstone was occupied by both personal and political affairs. He had married Catherine Glynn in 1839. The depression of 1847 had been hard on Catherine's brother, Sir Stephen Glynn. Since some of Glynn's obligations were secured by the family estate Hawarden, there was danger of losing it. By mutual agreement, the management of the estate was placed in Gladstone's hands, while Stephen Glynn maintained his residence there. The burden of management continued for many years, with Gladstone saving the estate for the Glynne family and eventually his own.

In politics, Gladstone's appointment as chancellor of the exchequer in 1852 launched his career as a financier. His budget of 1853 was to

CHRONOLOGY

1832	Elected member for Newark
1835	Appointed undersecretary for war and the colonies
1841	Appointed vice-president of the board of trade
1843	Member of Cabinet as president of board of trade
1845	Resigned from Cabinet over Maynooth grant; appointed colonial secretary
1847	Elected member for Oxford University
1852–55	Appointed chancellor of exchequer, again from 1859–66
1864	Elected member for South Lancashire
1868	Elected member for Greenwich
1868–74	Became prime minister for first time
1873–74	Appointed chancellor of exchequer
1875	Publicly retired from leadership of Liberal Party
1880	Elected member for Midlothian
1880–86	Served as prime minister; introduced first Home Rule bill
1892–94	Served as prime minister; introduced second Home Rule bill
1898	Died on Ascension Day; buried in Westminster Abbey

move Britain even further in the direction of free trade, leaving only 48 articles on the tariff, and his budget of 1860 reduced that number still more. But the real mark of Gladstone's budgets was his zeal for reducing rather than increasing taxes. His devotion to retrenchment was real and, at times, it was carried to the point of excess. The best illustration of this came in 1886 when he proposed to reduce the salary of Jesse Collings by £300. Collings was Joseph Chamberlain's parliamentary secretary at the Local Government Board, and the attempted salary reduction did nothing to win Chamberlain's support for Gladstone's first Home Rule bill (which would give the Irish legislature more power).

Gladstone also had a desire to strike a balance between direct and indirect taxes, and his budgets were related to his view of political society. Indirect taxation fell essentially on those who did not have the franchise (right to vote), and direct taxation was paid by those who were enfranchised. In proposing to extend the franchise in 1866, Gladstone sought to draw even closer the relation between taxation and the franchise. As historian

H.C.G. Matthew suggests, Gladstone's reform bill of 1866 was devised so that the working class, which "contributed almost half of national income and, through payment of indirect taxes, a third or rather more of the government's revenue," should have a predominance of voters in a third of the boroughs. As Matthew remarks, "Gladstone's franchise proposals of 1866 were designed to consolidate an existing order; Disraeli's destroyed it."

Gladstone Serves as Prime Minister

That new order produced a Liberal majority in the election of 1868 and brought Gladstone into office as prime minister. He first wanted to pacify Ireland; toward that end, he introduced and passed a measure for disestablishing and disendowing the Irish Church in 1869 and a land act in 1870 which provided compensation for tenants who were evicted without cause. He also introduced an education bill in 1873 which would have made higher education accessible to Catholics, but this measure was defeated in the House of Commons. His ministry enacted a host of measures which, as Gladstone put it, opened the windows of opportunity for Englishmen. These measures included the Education Act of 1870, the opening of all branches of the civil service except the foreign service to competitive examination in 1870, the abolition of purchase of commissions in the army by royal warrant in 1871, the opening of the universities to other than members of the Church of England in 1871, and the secret ballot act of 1872. The same degree of support was not given to all these measures by Gladstone, but that fact simply serves to illustrate his view of the role of prime minister, which was to act as a mediator between factions in the Cabinet, to reconcile differences where possible, and, as he said in October 1883, "the supervision, and often the construction, of weighty legislative measures."

As chancellor of the exchequer, he had already done this with respect to fiscal matters; now he had to do the same for domestic and foreign affairs. This meant that Gladstone would not be the radical that **Lord Palmerston** had feared when he said to **Anthony Ashley-Cooper** (Lord Shaftesbury), "Whenever he gets my place we shall have strange doings." Far more than has been realized, Gladstone was adept at bringing people together, and it was not inappropriate that Lord Rosebery should talk in 1885 about Gladstone being the only person who could bring everyone together under the Liberal umbrella.

Perhaps historian Matthew best summarizes Gladstone as a politician. In a very perceptive passage in his biography of Gladstone, he says:

It is certainly the case that Gladstone saw politics as "at once a game and a high art."… He was as alert to political manoeuvring as the most formidable of his opponents, as flexible and resourceful at defending or exploiting a position, and more than a match in stamina for any of his contemporaries when it came to a pitched battle. On the other hand, he appeared to act within a general context of moral objectives which allowed him to personify the moral imperatives of Victorian Liberal politics.

Gladstone's approach to foreign affairs was also established in his first ministry which came into office shortly after the end of the Civil War in the United States. Among other Englishmen, Gladstone had caused considerable consternation in America by supporting the South in that conflict. The North had objected strenuously when ironclads manufactured in Britain were delivered to the South, and after the war there was the need to reestablish normal relations between the two countries. The Treaty of Washington of 1871 agreed that the claim of the United States for damages should be submitted to arbitration. The general significance of the Treaty of Washington, as Matthew states, was that Gladstone was trying to establish "rules for international law for the future." As Gladstone said in his anonymous article in the *Edinburgh Review* on "Germany, France, and England":

Certain it is that a new law of nations is gradually taking hold of the mind, and coming to sway the practice, of the world; a law which recognises independence, which frowns on aggression, which favours the pacific, not the bloody settlement of disputes, which aims at permanent and not temporary adjustment; above all, which recognizes, as a tribunal of paramount authority, the general judgment of civilised mankind.

When Gladstone was defeated in 1873 on his education bill for Ireland, the ministry resigned, but **Benjamin Disraeli** refused to form a government, and as a result Gladstone returned for a year. In the general election of 1874, the Conservatives won a majority for the first time since 1841, and Disraeli spent six years in office. Gladstone retired privately from the leadership of the Liberal Party in 1874; the following year that retirement was made public. He remained a member of Parliament, however, thus creating difficulties for Granville and Hartington who had succeeded him as leaders of the Party in the Lords and Commons, respectively. That ambiguity became especially important when the Eastern Question became the center of attention in the late 1870s. The mistreatment of its Christian subjects by the Turkish government led to Gladstone's publication of a pamphlet entitled *The Bulgarian Horrors and the Question of the East,* of which 200,000 copies were sold, and to the later Midlothian campaigns of 1879 and 1880 where he attacked the forward policy of Disraeli in the Mediterranean, South Africa, and Afghanistan.

Gladstone's attack was partially responsible for Disraeli's defeat in the general election of 1880, and Gladstone returned to active politics and his second term as prime minister. Despite the criticism of Disraeli's forward policy, Gladstone's second ministry was to be beset with the same difficulties in imperial and foreign affairs. In 1882, the Gladstone government went into Egypt, and despite their avowal to withdraw from the Sudan south of Wady Halfa, and their sending General **Charles Gordon** to implement this intention, they did not withdraw. They were also affected by Russian advances against Afghanistan and by the results of Disraeli's actions in South Africa. These misadventures gave some semblance of truth to the myth Disraeli created that the Liberal Party was opposed to empire and was antipatriotic, a point the Conservatives emphasized in the general election of 1885.

The Irish Question

The Irish question was also an important feature of this ministry, and for the rest of Gladstone's political career. In this second ministry there was the enactment of a second Land Act in 1881, the so-called three Fs measure which provided for a fair rent set by a judicial tribunal, fixity of tenure, and free sale. This, however, was the period when **Charles Stewart Parnell** was fashioning an effective Irish party that got the attention of British politicians by obstructing the passing of any legislation in Parliament other than Irish legislation. It was also a time of agrarian crime. Gladstone first attempted to deal with the situation by passing a new crimes act designed to reestablish law and order in Ireland and the enactment of cloture and the guillotine. Parnell was even placed in Kilmainham jail under the crimes act, but by 1882 Gladstone was disillusioned with coercion and resorted to a more conciliatory policy. Parnell was released from jail and W.E. Forster was replaced as chief secretary by Lord Frederick Cavendish, who was murdered in Phoenix Park shortly after his arrival in Ireland. This resulted in the enactment of a new crimes act, for the previous one was soon to expire.

With Parnell developing a cohesive body of supporters and the loyalty of Irishmen generally,

and with the passage of the Franchise Bill in 1884 which gave the vote to the majority of Irishmen, Gladstone was coming to the conclusion that some concession to Ireland was essential to remove the distrust between the two parts of the United Kingdom. When the Parnellites won 85 of the 103 Irish seats in the general election of 1885, Gladstone considered that Ireland had spoken, and when Gladstone's son Herbert announced to newspaper editors in December 1885 that his father was in favor of Home Rule, Parnell turned from his flirtation with the Conservatives to support of Gladstone, and the Liberals returned to office for Gladstone's third ministry.

In that ministry, Gladstone introduced his first Home Rule bill, which was defeated by 30 votes: 93 Liberals, including Chamberlain and Hartington, voted with the Conservatives. This led to a general election in 1886 and the return of the Conservatives and Liberal Unionists (those Liberals who opposed repeal of the Act of Union) to office under Lord Salisbury. Gladstone continued his support of Home Rule, and when the Liberals returned to office after the election of 1892, Gladstone introduced a second Home Rule bill in 1893. This measure passed the Commons but was defeated in the Lords. The following year, Gladstone finally retired when he could not support the naval estimates of his service chief, marking the end of a political career of 61 years. He died on Ascension Day in 1898 and was buried in Westminster Abbey.

SOURCES:

Foot, M. R. D., and H. C. G. Matthew, eds. *The Gladstone Diaries with Cabinet Minutes and Prime Ministerial Correspondence.* 11 vols. Clarendon Press, 1968–90.

Magnus, Philip. *Gladstone: A Biography.* Dutton, 1954.

Matthew, H. C. G. *Gladstone, 1809–1874.* Clarendon Press, 1986.

Morley, John. *The Life of William Ewart Gladstone.* 3 vols. Macmillan, 1903.

Ramm, Agatha. *William Ewart Gladstone.* University of Wales Press, 1989.

Schreuder, D. M. "The Making of Gladstone's Posthumous Career: The Role of Morley and Knaplund as 'Monumental Masons,' 1903–27," in *The Gladstonian Turn of Mind: Essays Presented to J. B. Conacher.* Edited by Bruce Kinzer. University of Toronto Press, 1985.

Shannon, Richard. *Gladstone, 1809–1865.* Vol. I. University of North Carolina Press, 1984.

Stansky, Peter. *Gladstone: A Progress in Politics.* Norton, 1979.

FURTHER READING:

Butler, Perry. *Gladstone: Church, State, and Tractarianism: A Study of his Religious Ideas and Attitudes, 1809–1859.* Clarendon Press, 1982.

Hamer, D. A. *Liberal Politics in the age of Gladstone and Rosebery: A Study in Leadership and Policy.* Clarendon Press, 1972.

Hanham, H. J. *Elections and Party Management: Politics in the time of Disraeli and Gladstone.* Archon Books, 1978.

Knaplund, Paul. *Gladstone and Britain's Imperial Policy.* Frank Cass, 1927.

———. *Gladstone's Foreign Policy.* Frank Cass, 1935, Archon Books, 1970.

Godfrey of Bouillon

(c. 1060–1100)

Medieval knight and duke of Lower Lorraine, who gained fame through leadership in the First Crusade, culminating in his accession as ruler of Jerusalem.

"As a warrior he was without equal, was brave and undaunted; he excelled as a horseman, was expert in the use of his feared sword."

JOHN C. ANDRESSOHN

Godfrey of Bouillon was born around 1060, the second son of Count Eustace II of Boulogne and his wife Ida, daughter of Godfrey II, the Bearded, duke of Lower Lorraine. Little is known about Godfrey's childhood. Even the exact date and place of his birth, which was either at Boulogne or nearby Baisy in Brabant, is unrecorded. Accounts of the life of his mother stress her piety and care in the upbringing of her three sons, Eustace III, Godfrey, and Baldwin. Godfrey's father was probably away for much of his son's youth. Count Eustace participated at the side of **William the Conqueror** in the Norman Conquest of England; he also held substantial lands on both sides of the channel, in England as well as the county of Boulogne in Belgium and north France.

Godfrey probably received some basic education in letters from his mother and clerics. Because of the location of Boulogne between feudal France and imperial Germany, he was fluent in German and French. He certainly was trained in the military skills of knighthood. His later accomplishments in feudal warfare in the service of the German emperor, in protecting his own territories,

Name variations: Godfrey IV, duke of Lower Lorraine; Godefroi de Bouillon (French). Born c. 1060 at either Boulogne (France) or Baisy (Belgium); died on July 18, 1100, at Jerusalem; son of Count Eustace II of Boulogne and Ida (daughter of Duke Godfrey II of Lower Lorraine); unmarried. Predecessor: Godfrey III, duke of Lower Lorraine. Successor: Henry of Limburg as duke of Lower Lorraine; Baldwin of Boulogne, count of Edessa as king of Jerusalem.

Contributed by Karen Gould, Consultant in Medieval and Renaissance Manuscripts, Austin, Texas

493

1056	Henry IV became German emperor
c. 1160	Godfrey of Bouillon born
1066	William, Duke of Normandy, led Norman conquest of England; Count Eustace II of Boulogne at Battle of Hastings
1069	Godfrey II, the Bearded, died; accession of Godfrey III, the Hunchback
1070	Godfrey III married Matilda of Tuscany
1073–85	Pontificate of Gregory VII began
1075	Investiture Controversy began
1076	Godfrey III died; Godfrey of Bouillon named margrave (marquis) of Antwerp
1087	Godfrey invested as duke of Lower Lorraine
1088–99	Pontificate of Urban II
1096	Godfrey departed on First Crusade
1097–98	Crusaders captured Nicaea and Antioch
1099	Jerusalem fell to crusaders; Godfrey became Defender of the Holy Sepulchre
1100	Died in Jerusalem

and finally as a leader in the First Crusade attest to his abilities as a knight.

Although Godfrey could trace a distinguished ancestry back to the emperor **Charlemagne** on both the paternal and maternal sides of his family, as a second son his prospects for being more than one of many minor knights of the feudal nobility seemed slim. However, two important circumstances placed Godfrey in a position to attain a more noteworthy place in medieval history. First, his childless uncle designated him as his heir. Second, Godfrey of Bouillon became one of the key leaders in the First Crusade to the Holy Land.

In 1076, when Godfrey was about 15 years of age, his mother's brother Godfrey the Hunchback was killed, probably by an assassin, while campaigning with Count William of Holland against Robert of Flanders. Several years earlier, around 1070, the elder Godfrey had married Countess **Matilda of Tuscany,** a marriage that was largely political. After one child died in infancy, the couple separated, with Matilda returning to her homeland in Italy. In his early 30s at the time of his death, Godfrey the Hunchback named his

nephew and namesake, Godfrey of Bouillon, as his heir to the duchy of Lower Lorraine.

This inheritance brought the adolescent Godfrey into the turbulent affairs, both political and religious, of the German Empire. Lorraine (Lotharingia in German) was an important territory for the Germans, primarily because of its strategic location as a buffer between German and French lands. At this period, it was divided into two duchies. Upper Lorraine was to the south adjoining Burgundy, while Lower Lorraine was just to the north located between Flanders and Holland on the west and Saxony on the east.

Because both the German emperors and the powerful ecclesiastical leaders wanted to exert firm control in this key area, the emperor Henry IV did not automatically follow Godfrey the Hunchback's wishes by investing his young, inexperienced nephew with the duchy of Lower Lorraine. Instead, to maintain control of this strategic province, Henry IV named his two-year-old son Conrad to the duchy of Lower Lorraine and conferred upon Godfrey the march (border region) of Antwerp. In addition, Godfrey succeeded to the allodial possessions (those to which he was entitled independently of feudal ties), principally the counties of Bouillon and Verdun as well as a few smaller territories.

The Conflict Between Church and State

For the next decade, as Godfrey matured to manhood, he was occupied with two related endeavors: protecting his territorial possessions and serving the German emperor. Between around 1078 and 1084, Godfrey's attentions were given to interconnected religious and political turmoil that the Investiture Controversy caused in Germany. The primary issue was whether the Church whose leader was the pope, or the state whose leader in this case was the German emperor, had the power to elect and appoint or invest Church officials. Emperor Henry IV and Pope **Gregory VII** were strong, forceful personalities who held diametrically opposite views on this question. When Pope Gregory VII used his spiritual power of excommunication on Henry IV, some of the German nobility saw an opportunity to rise against the German emperor and put forward Rudolf of Swabia as ruler of Germany. Thus Henry IV had to battle both religious opposition from the papacy and insurrection within his own kingdom.

The young Godfrey of Bouillon, who was no doubt anxious to prove his loyalty to Henry IV and his worthiness to be duke of Lower Lorraine, supported the German emperor with military service. Although there is some disagreement about the precise nature of his contribution, it is likely that Godfrey took an active part in Henry IV's campaigns against Rudolf between 1078–80. Godfrey was probably a participant in the climactic battle of the Elster in 1080 when Rudolf was killed and his forces were soundly defeated. However, the claim, by William of Tyre (12th-century historian of the crusades), that Godfrey himself killed Rudolf is probably a later elaboration to bolster the perception of Godfrey as an heroic figure.

After Rudolf's death, Henry IV pursued his chief adversary, Pope Gregory VII, by leading troops into Italy between 1081 and 1084, finally capturing Rome. Again, although historical testimony is somewhat ambiguous, Godfrey probably was part of the imperial forces at the sieges of Rome from 1083 to 1084 when Pope Gregory VII fled from Rome under the protection of the Normans of South Italy, and Henry IV was crowned Holy Roman Emperor by his antipope.

Throughout this period, Godfrey had struggled to maintain his control over Bouillon and Verdun. Soon after his uncle died, several parties had allied to contest his possessions. From Italy, Matilda of Tuscany had claimed these lands as widow of Godfrey the Hunchback. Another contender, Count Albert of Namur, supported by Theodoric, bishop of Verdun, had received the county of Verdun as a fief from Matilda. Albert of Namur had effectively taken control of Verdun, but Godfrey had retained possession of Bouillon with its imposing castle.

In 1086, after the height of the Investiture Controversy had passed, Albert renewed his attempts to capture Bouillon. A fierce battle ensued, and Godfrey received military aid from his brothers Eustace and Baldwin as well as from troops from Antwerp. Although no clear victor emerged, the bishop of Liege negotiated a peace settlement in which Godfrey seems to have regained his hereditary possessions, Verdun and Bouillon.

With Godfrey more secure in his allodial holdings and with his record of loyalty to the emperor, he was finally invested as duke of Lower Lorraine. Historical sources advance several dates for this event; the most plausible places it in May 1087 at Aachen when Henry IV had his 13-year-old son Conrad, the nominal holder of the duchy, crowned as king. By both the hereditary designation of his uncle and his service to Henry IV, Godfrey of Bouillon was the logical candidate to fill the vacancy in the duchy of Lower Lorraine.

While Godfrey's elevation may have enhanced his prestige, it did little to increase his broader political influence. Most of his recorded activities during his tenure show his involvement in disputes among religious leaders in the area who were divided in their allegiance to the imperial position of Emperor Henry IV or the Church's adherence to the principles of Gregorian reform now championed by Pope Urban II. Godfrey wavered between support of Henry IV and protection for local bishops and abbots who represented the growing movement of Church reform in and around the duchy of Lower Lorraine.

The historical event that transformed Godfrey's life was the First Crusade. In November 1095, Pope Urban II preached a call for the First Crusade at an ecclesiastical council in Clermont, France. Urban's action was partially a response to an appeal from Byzantium for aid in fighting the Turks. However, the idea of crusade was much more complex and premeditated. From the Church's standpoint, it merged many ideas—including the liberation of Jerusalem and prospects for reuniting the Roman and Byzantine churches—into the concept of a just and holy war whose knightly participants would be making a sacrificial pilgrimage for which they would receive the promise of remission from sins. The crusade aroused an enthusiastic response from people in all walks of life. It was especially well received among the French and Flemish nobility.

Godfrey Takes Part in the First Crusade

The motives of any individual crusader are difficult to determine. In most cases, they were a mixture of true piety and inspiration for the cause, attraction to the adventure, and the possibility of economic gain. Godfrey's vow to participate in the First Crusade probably arose from a pious belief in the enterprise, desire to atone for his vacillation between supporting the emperor and the reform church movement, and an awareness of his lack of firm leadership in the duchy of Lorraine. For whatever reasons, he sold or mortgaged most of his territorial possessions to the bishops of Liege and Verdun. With the proceeds, he was able to equip one of the largest contingents of knights and supporters to undertake the crusade to the Holy Land.

Godfrey and his followers probably left on crusade around August 1096, a date set by Pope Urban. Their route took them overland from Germany along the Danube River through the Kingdom of Hungary and into the Byzantine Empire in modern Bulgaria. For the most part, Godfrey's troops conducted an orderly march and negotiations with the king of Hungary as well as precautions taken by Alexius Comnenus, the Byzantine emperor, assured that they were supervised and usually able to obtain provisions.

Just before Christmas 1096, Godfrey and his crusading army arrived at Constantinople. For the next few months, while his forces were encamped outside the city and other crusaders converged on the imperial capital, Godfrey and Emperor Alexius negotiated over an oath to the emperor which Godfrey finally took in a modified version. By late April 1097, Godfrey of Bouillon and Bohemund of Taranto led their troops from Constantinople to begin their military mission.

Traveling through Asia Minor and Syria, the crusaders took over two years to reach their goal, Jerusalem. Despite many difficulties, including the dangerous terrain, attacks by the Turks, and dissension and disorganization among the leaders, the crusade was successful. Beginning with the siege of the town of Nicaea which surrendered to Emperor Alexius in June 1097, the crusaders achieved a major victory at Antioch in June 1098, along with a number of other military conquests. In addition, Godfrey's younger brother Baldwin led a separate expedition to Edessa where he became count of the first crusading state in 1098.

Godfrey and his forces from Lorraine played a major role in the various battles that the crusaders fought. Because of the large size of his army and his valor in military encounters, he was one of the prominent leaders in the First Crusade. Medieval historians often placed Godfrey in the vanguard of action in battle.

In June 1099, when the crusaders reached Jerusalem and surrounded the city, they prepared for their attack by building wooden scaling ladders and siege towers. Their assault on the holy city took place July 14–15, 1099. In a heated battle, Godfrey and some of his knights were the first to breach the walls and enter the city. Once the crusaders stormed into Jerusalem, the massacre of its inhabitants was so great that blood reportedly ran through the streets. Finally, three years after their departure from Europe, the crusaders took possession of Jerusalem.

In the aftermath of victory, the real difficulty was to consolidate their hold on Jerusalem and the Holy Land. Godfrey of Bouillon was selected to lead this effort taking the title of Defender of the Holy Sepulchre. He had a hard task. The size of the Western forces diminished as many of the crusaders began to return to their homeland. The competition among the remaining leaders for territory in the Holy Land continued to divide their efforts. Godfrey managed to fend off an attack from Egyptian Muslims and subdue the surrounding countryside. With the help of Pisan and Venetian fleets, he was able to begin rebuilding Jaffa, a crucial port for Jerusalem.

Godfrey's initiatives, however, were just beginning when, in June 1100, he became gravely ill on an expedition to aid the south Italian Norman crusader Tancred at Damascus. Taken to Jerusalem, he died about a month later on July 18, 1100. His brother Baldwin succeeded him as king of Jerusalem. Godfrey's ducal title in Lower Lorraine initially went to Henry of Limburg, although the duchy soon became fragmented into smaller holdings.

After Godfrey's death, his fame grew. In medieval chronicles of the crusades, literary romance epics, and troubadour songs, Godfrey became the epitome of the valiant knight. His tall, fair, athletic appearance, his reputation for valor in battle, and his position as defender of the Holy Sepulchre combined to make him an ideal heroic figure. If, in reality, his deeds were less momentous and noble, his constructive leadership during the First Crusade made a significant contribution to the outcome of this important historical event.

SOURCES:

Andressohn, John C. *The Ancestry and Life of Godfrey of Bouillon.* Indiana University Publications, 1947.

Aube, Pierre. *Godefroy de Bouillon.* Librarie Artheme Fayard, 1985.

FURTHER READING:

Peters, Edward, ed. *The First Crusade. The Chronicle of Fulcher of Chatres and other Source Materials.* University of Pennsylvania Press, 1971.

Riley-Smith, Jonathan. *The First Crusade and the Idea of Crusading.* Athlone Press, 1986.

Runciman, Steven. *A History of the Crusades, Volume I: The First Crusade.* Cambridge University Press, 1951.

William Archbishop of Tyre. *A History of Deeds Done Beyond the Sea.* Vol. 1. Translation by Emily A. Babcock and A.C. Krey. Columbia University Press, 1943.

Boris Godunov

(1552–1605)

Russian tsar who attempted the modernization and expansion of Russia but fell victim to famine and the ghost of a dead child.

"Indeed, for all the brilliance of his career and the sagacity and enlightenment of his rule, [Godunov] appeared to be doomed from the outset, like the hero of a Greek tragedy."

IAN GREY

Wishing to make Russia a "modern" nation, **Ivan IV** (1530–84) conquered the Tatar Khanates of Kazan and Astrakhan (1552–56); supported the invasion and colonization of Siberia; invited Europeans to come to Russia as merchants, teachers, and artisans; and attempted to secure control of Livonia (northern Latvia and Estonia). For his accomplishments, he was awarded the title *Grozni*—"The Awe-Inspiring."

Since the reigns of **Ivan III** (1462–1505) and Basil IV (1505–33), the Grand Princes of Moscow had been engaged in a bloody conflict with the other Russian princes. When Ivan IV's father died, Ivan was three years old and his mother Helena became regent. Attempting to reassert their power, the princes poisoned Helen in 1538, and took her son prisoner. For the next five years Ivan was humiliated, until he issued an order on December 29, 1543, which was obeyed: the leading prince, Andrei Shuiski, was arrested, murdered, and his corpse thrown to the dogs. The other princes bided their time. So did Ivan. He turned the government over to his relatives until January 16, 1547, when he was crowned Tsar,

Contributed by J. Lee Shneidman, Professor of History, Adelphi University, Garden City, New York

Name variations: Godunov, Godunoff, or Godounov. Pronunciation: GU-doo-nôf. Born Boris Fedorovich Godunov of Tatar descent in 1552; died in 1605; raised by his uncle Dmitri Ivanovich Godunov; married: Maria Maliuta (daughter of Grigorii Maliuta-Skuratova, the leader of Ivan IV's terror squad); children: (daughter) Xenia; (son) Fedor Borisovich. Predecessor: Fedor I. Successor: Demetrius the False (the 1st Pretender).

Grand Prince and Autocrat of All the Russias, marking the first time a Russian Grand Prince had ever taken the title Tsar-Emperor. It would remain, however, a hollow title for as long as the princes held their power.

On February 13, 1547, Ivan married Anastasia Romanovna, daughter of a non-titled landowner. Ivan made it clear that he intended to appoint non-princely advisors (*boyars*). Among his early supporters was another non-titled landowner by the name of Dmitri Ivanovich Godunov.

The origins of the Godunov family are shrouded in legend. It is written that around 1330 Chet-Murza, a Tatar emir, came to Russia, converted to Christianity, entered the service of the Prince of Moscow, and was granted lands near the town of Kostroma. Chet-Murza's descendants took many family names, one of which was Godunov. By 1550, the Godunovs were one among thousands of non-titled landowners, a position Dmitri Ivanovich hoped to improve by his support of the Tsar.

Little is known of the early life of Dmitri Ivanovich's nephew Boris Fedorovich Godunov. He was born in 1552, his sister Irina was born five years later and, in 1560 or so, they were orphaned and settled in Kostroma with their uncle.

Ivan IV, meanwhile, continued his struggle with the princes, creating in 1550 the *Streltsy* (Musketeers)—a standing army under his control. This small force of approximately 3,000 was not only to protect Russia from invasion but also to be used against the princes whose military force was cavalry and bow-and-arrow infantry. The Tsar also established a private chancery and invited Dmitri Ivanovich to live behind the stone walls of the Kremlin; thus, Godunov and his sister Irina became playmates to the Tsar's sons: Ivan, born in 1554, and Fedor, born in 1557. Then in 1565, Ivan divided Russia—half to be ruled by the princes, the other half which became known as the *Oprichnina*, ruled by himself.

Dmitri Ivanovich became part of the Tsar's inner circle, and in 1570, his nephew Boris Godunov married Maria Maliuta, daughter of Grigorii Maliuta-Skuratova, the leader of Ivan's terror squad against the princes. On October 28 of the following year, Ivan married his third wife (Anastasia died in 1560, his second wife in 1569). Boris served as best man and was promoted to the position of *Kravchi*—food taster.

When the bride died within three weeks and Ivan quickly remarried, it sparked concern in the Orthodox Church. By Canon Law only three marriages were legal, and any issue from the fourth marriage would be considered a bastard. Meanwhile, a marriage was arranged between the Tsar's heir, Ivan Ivanovich, and Evdokiia Saburova, a relative of the Godunovs, while Boris Godunov was appointed his uncle's assistant in the chancery.

The battle with the princes continued. In October 1575, Ivan abdicated, naming the Christianized ex-Khan of Kasimov, Simeon Bekbulatovich as Tsar, and retired to his *Oprichnina* lands where he instituted a reign of terror against the princes. Slowly, the meaning of *Grozni* changed from "The Awe-Inspiring" to "The Terrible." For a year, Tsar Simeon reigned while Ivan wreaked havoc on the countryside; then suddenly Ivan removed Simeon and resumed his office.

Ivan's fourth wife died, and wives numbers five and six each lasted for a few weeks before being exiled to a convent. In 1581, he took his seventh wife, Maria Nagaia, daughter of a minor landowner. It was a double wedding: Ivan had ordered his second son, Fedor, to marry Godunov's sister, Irina.

A family quarrel changed Boris Godunov's future and that of Russia. In November 1581, Ivan and his heir argued and Godunov tried to intercede. The Tsar was furious. In a rage, he clobbered his son, Ivan Ivanovich, with the scepter. Godunov attempted to stay a second blow, but he too was felled. Sobered, Ivan clutched the bloodied heir while Godunov summoned a physician. Four days later the Tsarevich died, and Fedor became the heir.

Ivan IV understood Fedor's limited ability, and secretly planned a Regency Council which eventually had five members: Prince Ivan Mstislavski, Prince Ivan Shuiski (relative of the unfortunate Prince who had been fed to the dogs), Nikita Romanov (brother of Anastasia), Bogdan Belskii, and Boris Godunov. To make matters worse, on October 19, 1582, Maria Nagaia gave birth to Dmitri, a son who posed a potential threat to Fedor even though he was legally a bastard. About the same time, Godunov's wife gave birth to a daughter, Xenia.

On March 18, 1584, as Ivan sat down to play chess with Bogdan Belskii, the Tsar suddenly keeled over, dead. When word of Ivan's death reached Maria's family, the Nagoi's planned a coup to place Dmitri on the throne. But when the Regency Council learned of the plot, the Nagoi clan were arrested and exiled to Uglich, where they were permitted to have a small court for the Tsarevich under the surveillance of Council appointed administrators. Attempting to usurp the leadership of the Council, Belskii was foiled by Mstislavski and Nikita Romanov before being exiled to Nizhni-Novgorod.

On May 31, 1584, Fedor was crowned. He was flanked by his uncle, Nikita Romanov, and his brother-in-law, Boris Godunov; just behind them stood his cousin, Prince Mstislavski. After the ceremony Godunov was named "Master of the Stable," "Privy Grand Boyar," and Governor of Kazan and Astrakhan, titles accompanied by vast estates giving Godunov an income equal to that of any of the princes.

The English merchant Giles Fletcher described Fedor as "simple and weakminded, hardly capable of formulating policy and extraordinarily superstitious." Likewise, the Lithuanian Ambassador noted that Fedor had "little intelligence." In reality it was the Council that ruled, but the Council was divided. Godunov and Nikita Romanov, considered parvenues by the princes, united against Ivan and Basil Shuiski who wanted to remove Fedor and have either Mstislavski or "Tsar" Simeon, who had married Mstislavski's sister, ascend the throne. But Mstislavski refused to betray Fedor and the Shuiski princes left Moscow in December 1584.

Godunov Directs National Affairs

In August of the following year, Nikita Romanov became ill and slowly withdrew from state affairs. Mstislavski had been deprived of most authority after the Shuiski plot, which left Godunov to direct national affairs. He ordered the building of a string of fortresses along the lower Volga to protect Russia from Tatar, Turkish, or Persian attack. The chief fortress was Tsaritzn (Stalingrad), named in honor of his sister Irina. A truce was arranged with Poland, and taxes were levied on princely and religious estates.

With the death of Nikita Romanov in April 1586, Godunov became sole ruler. But his authority still rested on his being the Tsar's brother-in-law. The Shuiski princes, using Metropolitan Dionisii (Bishop of Moscow) as a cat's-paw, tried to convince Fedor to divorce Irina because she had not provided an heir—there had been three miscarriages and two stillbirths. Fedor refused and, in October 1586, the Metropolitan was deposed and exiled to a monastery. Aware of the precariousness of his power base, Godunov sent letters to Queen **Elizabeth** of England and **Emperor Rudolph II** of Germany seeking medical personnel to aid Irina. The Queen sent a doctor.

By 1587, Godunov ruled while Fedor reigned. Queen Elizabeth addressed Godunov as "most glorious prince and beloved cousin"; the Habsburgs referred to him as "most lofty privy councillor of the whole Russian land." Georgian kings and the Persian Shah sought his favors. When the Polish king died, the Polish nobility suggested that Godunov convince Fedor to accept that position. Fedor refused, and the Poles elected Zygmunt Vasa, son of John III of Sweden, an election that posed a threat to Russia. Godunov countered by seeking alliances with England, Spain, and Austria, while constructing stone walls around Smolensk and Moscow.

In July 1588, Jeremiah, Patriarch of Constantinople, arrived in Moscow complaining of his treatment by the Sultan. "If they wish, I shall remain here as Patriarch," he told one of his entourage. But Godunov did not wish a Greek patriarch in Moscow; he suggested that Jeremiah could reside in the ancient See of Vladimir if he established an independent Moscow Patriarchate. The haggling began. Godunov "was in all things able, intelligent and cunning. He managed everything and everyone obeyed him," reported Greek Metropolitan Herotheus, and it soon became evident that Jeremiah would not be permitted to leave Russia without creating an independent Patriarchate. On January 26, 1589, Moscow's Metropolitan Job was consecrated patriarch and placed after the Patriarchs of Constantinople and Alexandria in the Orthodox hierarchy. Godunov then had the Russian Church reorganized and Moscow declared "The Third Rome," the true center of Christianity.

Godunov became a national hero. He was called *Privatel* (ruler) and addressed as "Your Majesty." As Prince Zvenigorodski informed **Shah Abbas** of Persia, "No one is like unto Boris Fedorovich." After the birth of his son, Fedor Borisovich, in 1589, Godunov began an extensive building program. New towns were established on the eastern and southern periphery: Voronezh, Belgorod, Kursk, Samara, Ufa, Tobolsk; new churches were built, including the Great Belfry, the tallest building in Moscow; and streets were widened and paved with logs.

In the evening of May 17, 1591, word reached Moscow that Tsarevich Dmitri was dead and that a mob had butchered all government agents in Uglich. Troops were dispatched immediately, and a commission chaired by Basil Shuiski was convoked to investigate. The investigators arrived in Uglich on May 19 and began taking testimony.

Dmitri had been an epileptic who suffered frequent seizures. On Saturday, May 15, having recovered from a seizure on Wednesday, he was permitted to play with four friends. The children, with two nurses, went into the castle courtyard to play a game called *tychka* (something like mumblety-peg) in which a small knife is tossed in the air, then flips and sticks in the target. Dmitri took his turn and collapsed, falling onto the knife which lodged in his throat. The nurses tried to help, the children screamed, the castle was aroused. Dmitri's uncle Mikhail arrived, yelling that the boy had been murdered by Godunov's agents. Maria arrived, charging that the nurses were in on the plot. A mob gathered as Mikhail harangued. Government agents were hunted and murdered, and Mikhail replaced the toy knife with a dagger.

When the commission arrived, Grigori Nagoi, another uncle, disputed the murder tale. Shuiski gathered the evidence and presented it on June 2 to Tsar Fedor, who passed it to Metropolitan Job. A Church Council ruled the death "an act of God," but blamed Mikhail for the murder of the officials. Mikhail was exiled and Maria was forced to become a nun, taking the name Martha.

Godunov had little time to dwell on the incident because a Tatar army had invaded. But on July 4, when Tatar khan Kazy Girei saw his opponent's artillery, he withdrew without a battle, and Godunov relaxed. If he heard the rumor that it was not Dmitri who had died, he paid no heed. Even the accession of Zygmunt to the Swedish throne posed no problem because his spies had reported that Lutheran Sweden would never accept a Catholic sovereign. When Irina gave birth to Fedosia in 1592, all seemed tranquil. Unfortunately, Fedosia died before her second birthday.

The line of Muscovite princes that had started in 1325 with Ivan I came to its end when Tsar Fedor died at 1 A.M., January 7, 1598. Job announced later that day that Fedor had "handed the scepter to his lawful wife"; Irina, however, had no desire to reign. Who was to reign? Tsar Simeon had been proclaimed Tsar by Ivan IV; both Mstislavski and Basil Shuiski were descendants of the royal family; Fedor Romanov claimed the throne as the nephew of Ivan IV's wife Anastasia. All observers, however, agreed that Boris Godunov was both the most able and popular, but he refused to accept the throne unless it were granted by a *Zemski Sobor*, a national council.

Godunov Becomes Tsar

While Irina entered a monastery from whence she acted as interim head of state, Metropolitan Job summoned a national council and tried on February 17 to convince the council to elect Godunov. But Shuiski objected and the council was adjourned. Three days later, Job asked Godunov, who also had entered a monastery, to assume the throne. When he refused, Job again summoned the council and threatened to excommunicate all who refused to accept Godunov. Returning to the monastery the next day, Job threatened Godunov with excommunication if he did not accept the throne. Irina supported Job's plea. Four days later Godunov accepted the "offer" and went to the Kremlin, only to return to the monastery the following day, insisting on a formal offer from the *Zemski Sobor*. Finally, the council made the offer and, on April 30, Godunov returned to Moscow.

Meanwhile, word arrived that Tatar Khan Kazy Girei was again on the march. On May 2, Godunov left Moscow with his army and the two forces prepared for battle June 29. As before, the Tatar saw the strength of the imperial force and retreated without battle.

Boris Godunov was crowned on September 1, 1598. For the next two years, there was peace and prosperity. New cities were established, trade increased, and the new Tsar sought suitable mates for his children, who had been educated along West European models. Through English merchants he asked Queen Elizabeth to send "any lord of spirit whom [she] might vouchsafe to call cousin." Christian III of Denmark sent his younger brother, Hans, who unfortunately died shortly thereafter. The only other blot on this flourishing period was a persistent rumor that Dmitri had never really died and was being hidden by the Romanovs.

The rains came in April 1601, and for the next four months the Russians did not see a day of sun. The frost came in late August, ruining the crops. The price of rye increased 600%; the cost of wheat jumped 25-fold. Attempting to control prices, Godunov distributed grain from the royal granary and issued an edict to "have the poor kept warm." But a hard winter was followed by a cold, wet spring, and famine led people to the unspeakable. Wrote one French soldier: "To see a wife kill her husband or a mother her children in order to eat them were ordinary occurrences." Cannibalism was a last resort, noted a Dutch merchant, but all the "cats and dogs" had been eaten. In Moscow, 120,000 died of starvation.

The "Ghost" of Dmitri Appears

Reports of Dmitri's escape increased, as peasants and urbanites fled to the forests or the steppes where they became brigands, and the unburied dead piled up. In early summer of 1603, a servant informed a Polish prince that he was the Tsarevich, and the prince sent the man claiming to be Dmitri to Zygmunt; if this "Dmitri" became a Catholic, the Poles might help. On April 24, 1604, the youth sent Pope Clement VIII a letter stating his "obedience and submission." A compact was made: Polish landowner Jerzy Mnishek would advance 100,000 florins; in return "Dmitri" would marry Mnishek's daughter Marina, grant the Mnishek family the cities of Pskov and Novgorod, and surrender the fortress of Smolensk to Poland.

When Godunov learned of the proceeding, he had Dmitri's mother, Martha, brought to Moscow, where she refused to state whether her son were dead or alive. Declaring that the imposter "Dmitri" was in reality the defrocked monk Grishka Otrepev, the Russian Church excommunicated him. Scholars, however, remain in doubt as to "Dmitri's" actual identity. A few accept that he was the real Dmitri, most accept that he was Grishka, while still others reject both suggestions but have no named candidate of their own.

Regardless of his true identity, the man known as Dmitri invaded Russia in October 1604, and thousands joined his standard. Godunov, increasingly ill, having suffered a stroke in the spring of 1603, dispatched the imperial army. In January of the following year, "Dmitri's" forces were defeated, but to little avail; he regrouped and grew stronger. During February and March the imperial troops continued to defeat groups of insurgents, but their numbers only increased as peasants, landowners, and Cossacks joined their ranks.

At 1 A.M., on April 13, 1605, Godunov suddenly rose from the supper table, blood gushing from his nose, mouth, and ears. Two hours later he was dead. The next day the Muscovites took the oath to Tsar Fedor Borisovich, Godunov's son. On April 17, the army swore allegiance; ten days later Basil Shuiski and Mistislavski swore to defend Tsar Fedor. But it was not to be. On May 17, the imperial generals joined "Dmitri." By June 2, Shuiski announced that the 1591 report was a lie: Dmitri had not died. Arrested on June 10, Tsar Fedor was murdered a week later along with his mother and cousins; his sister was sent to a convent. "Dmitri" entered Moscow, and on July 18, Martha embraced her son.

But the throne was still not secure. Within a year, Shuiski and Martha recanted, claiming that Dmitri had, indeed, been murdered on Godunov's orders. The new Dmitri was then murdered; the body of the real Dmitri was brought to Moscow for canonization, and Basil Shuiski became Tsar Basil V. Other "Dmitris" appeared; the Poles invaded. Shuiski was captured and sent to a Polish prison. The Swedes invaded to fight the Poles. Civil war and guerrilla warfare ensued. The Poles were defeated. The brigands then joined the guerrillas in a war of national liberation sponsored by the Church. Monk Philaret, the former Fedor Romanov, called for national unity.

On February 21, 1613, Fedor's son Michael Romanov was elected Tsar, and on January 24, 1619, he appointed his father Patriarch of Russia. The Romanovs had inherited Godunov's legacy.

SOURCES:

Barbour, Philip. *Dmitry*. Macmillan, 1967.

Fletcher, Giles. *Of the Russe Commonwealthe*. Edited by Richard Pipes, Harvard University Press. 1966.

Graham, Stephen. *Boris Godunof*. Yale University Press, 1933.

Grey, Ian. *Boris Godunov. The Tragic Tsar*. Scribner, 1973.

Margeret, Jacques. *The Russian Empire and Grand Duchy of Muscovy*. Edited and translated by C. S. L. Dunning. University of Pittsburgh Press, 1983.

Massa, Isaac. *A Short History of the Muscovite Wars*. Edited and translated by G. E. Orchard. University of Toronto Press, 1982.

Platonov, S. F. *Boris Godunov*. Translated by L. R. Pyles. Academic International Press, 1973.

Skrynnikov, R. G. *Boris Godunov.* Translated by H. F. Graham. Academic International Press, 1982.

FURTHER READING:

Berry, L. E., and R. O. Crummey, eds. *Rude & Barbarous Kingdom.* University of Wisconsin Press, 1986.

Emerson, Caryl. *Boris Godunov: Transpositions of a Russian Theme.* Indiana University Press, 1986.

Platonov, S. F. *The Time of Troubles.* Translated by J.T. Alexander. University Press of Kansas, 1970.

Pushkin, A. S. *Boris Godunov* (play). Translated by Alfred Hayes. Viking, 1982.

Wladyslaw Gomulka

(1905–1982)

First secretary of the Polish Communist Party, who led a reform movement in 1956 that loosened Soviet control and created a model for other Eastern European satellite states to reshape their relationship with Moscow.

"Was it possible to be a Pole, a communist and a patriot all at the same time? Most Poles thought not. Gomulka thought yes."

NICHOLAS BETHELL

Wladyslaw Gomulka was a significant figure in Eastern European history for three decades. His career as a leader of Polish Communism not only influenced the development of his own country but helped transform several other Soviet satellites. Although he emerged as an important leader during World War II, Gomulka's career was marked by dramatic turnabouts. Identified as a Communist who was not slavishly obedient to Moscow, he was forced from power in 1948 and persecuted for several years thereafter. His reputation for independent thinking, especially his call for "a Polish road to socialism," brought him back to power in 1956 as a wave of change struck Eastern Europe. Gomulka went on to direct Poland's government and Communist Party for 14 years in the era of Soviet leaders **Nikita Khrushchev** and **Leonid Brezhnev,** but his reputation as a reformer and a nationalist faded. His countrymen found that his Communist ideology and respect for the power of the Soviet Union placed sharp limits on his tolerance for change and liberalization. In the key event of his later years, he supported the 1968 Soviet invasion of Czechoslovakia to snuff out any liberal reform movement there.

Contributed by Neil Heyman, Professor of History, San Diego State University, San Diego, California

Born in Krosno, a town in the Polish territories of the Austro-Hungarian Empire, on February 6, 1905; died on September 1, 1982, in Warsaw, Poland; son of Jan and Kunegunda Gomulka; married; children: one son. Predecessor: Edward Ochab, first secretary of the Communist Party, 1956. Successor: Edward Gierek, first secretary of the Communist Party, 1970–1980.

When Wladyslaw Gomulka was born in Krosno, a small town located in the oil fields east of the city of Cracow, Poland did not exist as an independent country. It had been partitioned among Russia, Austria, and Prussia at the close of the 18th century. Krosno was in a region ruled by Austria.

Before Gomulka's birth in 1905, his father and mother had emigrated to the United States and lived in Pennsylvania. But the family had failed to establish itself in America and returned to Poland, although one of Gomulka's older sisters remained in Detroit. The young boy was still in school at the close of World War I when Poland was reborn as an independent state.

Leaving school at the age of 14, Gomulka was apprenticed to a locksmith before joining his father as a worker in the oil fields. He also became a member of the Polish Socialist Party, and in 1926 moved further to the Left to become a Communist. Both as a Socialist and a Communist, Gomulka acquired a reputation as a skilled labor organizer. He was arrested by the Polish police several times. During one such incident in 1932, he was shot in the leg by a policeman.

The young Polish leader then spent several years in the Soviet Union. One historian has noted that his later objections to forcing Polish farmers into collective farms came from "his own experiences as a young trainee in the Ukraine … when he had witnessed the mass murders and mass hunger at first hand." But in a stroke of good luck, Gomulka was arrested in Poland in 1936 and sentenced to a long prison term. Over the following years, most important Polish Communists were called to Moscow by the Soviet dictator **Joseph Stalin.** In the midst of the great wave of internal terror being waged by Stalin, Gomulka's countrymen were purged and executed. Thus, the jail term saved his life.

Gomulka Heads Party

In the opening weeks of World War II, when Poland was occupied by Nazi Germany in 1939 and the prisons were left unguarded, Gomulka escaped and joined a unit of armed workers in defending the Polish capital of Warsaw. The war years brought him to a prominent position of leadership in the Polish Communist Party. Working within his country, then under enemy occupation, he rose to become a member of the three-man committee directing the Party. In 1943, when the leader of the committee Pawel Finder was arrested and murdered by the Germans, Gomulka—who had nearly been captured along with Finder—became head of the Party.

Gomulka was not the kind of individual likely to reach the top post before the war; he was a labor organizer, not a writer and intellectual. But the war made "his natural cunning, genuine socialist idealism, limitless energy … just what was needed." At the close of the war, when Poland was occupied by the Soviet army, non-Communists like the Peasant Party leader Stanislaw Mikolajczyk returned from London to join in a coalition government. By 1947, however, Polish Communists had taken full control, and Gomulka played a key role in these events. As deputy prime minister, he helped crush non-Communist political parties. As minister of the recovered territories, he established Polish control over regions annexed from Germany. This involved deporting large portions of the population: under Gomulka's direction, 5,000 people a day were being sent westward to Germany at the start of 1946.

But Gomulka fell from power suddenly in 1948. During that year, **Joseph Tito** of Yugoslavia broke dramatically with Stalin to set up a fully independent communist system. The Soviet dictator responded by purging Communist parties throughout Eastern Europe of unreliable leaders. In Poland, Gomulka was replaced by Boleslaw

Bierut, a reliable follower of Stalin. Gomulka represented a portion of the Party that stressed the need to build a socialist system while taking Polish conditions into consideration. That made him unacceptable and dangerous to Stalin in the late 1940s. Between 1948 and 1953, Gomulka was stripped of his Party posts and imprisoned. Following Stalin's death in 1953, he was released from jail.

Gomulka returned to power in 1956. The death of Stalin had given the populations of Eastern Europe hope that they would be allowed some freedom from rigid Soviet control. In February 1956, when Nikita Khrushchev condemned Stalin at the 20th Soviet Communist Party Congress, it seemed a clear sign that reforms would be permitted in countries like Poland. The death of Bierut in early 1956 increased pressure for change. Riots by shipyard workers in Poznan in June 1956 convinced Party leaders that it was vital to call back Gomulka, with his reputation as a reformer, to lead the Party.

A Crucial Agreement with Khrushchev

The turning point in Soviet-Polish relations came in October 1956. Nikita Khrushchev and other Soviet leaders flew to Warsaw; army and naval units were put on alert for use against Poland. In a confrontation between Khrushchev and Gomulka, the two came to a crucial agreement. The Polish leader was permitted to pursue a policy based on the idea that there were "many roads to Socialism." This meant that satellite states like Poland did not need to model themselves completely on the Soviet Union in creating a new political, economic, and social order. For Gomulka, as one historian put it, "Poland's specific traditions demanded a specifically national brand of Communism." At the same time, Khrushchev received assurances that the Communist Party would remain in control in Poland, and Poland would remain loyal to the Warsaw Pact, the Eastern Europe alliance system dominated by Moscow.

Gomulka's agreement with Khrushchev appeared particularly significant in comparison with events in Hungary. There the movement for reform had not stopped with establishing a more liberal communist system. The Hungarian government allowed other political parties to compete with the Communists and tried to take a neutral position in international affairs. The Soviets had responded with a bloody invasion in November 1956. Gomulka's success in Poland thus seemed to many Eastern Europeans to be a more promising approach to loosening Soviet controls.

Over the following years, Gomulka built a system of Polish Communism based on several compromises with Poland's traditions. The Catholic Church in Poland was left independent. Most land was left in the hands of independent peasant farmers. In political life, a degree of open debate was allowed both inside the Communist Party and between Communists and non-Communists.

Gomulka may have thought that the power of the Church and the peasants' traditions of independence would fade away as Communism became established over the years. If so, he was disappointed. Instead, Poland remained a firmly non-Communist country under an increasingly unpopular government. Meanwhile, Gomulka lost his reputation as a reformer. Discontent, ironically resembling the discontent that had brought him back to power in 1956, began to grow.

Gomulka clung to the need for the Communist Party to keep full political power even if this meant the use of violence against the population. Although there were periodic crackdowns on students and intellectuals, Gomulka could not sup-

Wladyslaw Gomulka appears at the United Nations General Assembly in September 1960.

press his opponents. In March 1968, for example, large street demonstrations, like those that had helped bring Gomulka to power in 1956, took place. They were inspired by the reforms being carried out by **Alexander Dubcek** in Czechoslovakia. In August, Gomulka joined the Soviet Union in sending troops into Czechoslovakia to end the Dubcek experiment.

Economic reforms also faded away. For example, the Polish government refused to give peasant farmers resources needed to produce food efficiently. The government tried to introduce drastic price increases for food in 1970. To make matters worse, the announcement of the change came at Christmastime. Riots broke out in industrial centers, and Gomulka was forced to resign as head of the Polish Communist Party in December 1970. The former leader became an "unperson." His name was rarely mentioned in the newspapers or in statements by the government or the Communist Party. He died of cancer in Warsaw on September 1, 1982.

Historians have seen Gomulka as a complex mixture of a devoted Communist, a Polish patriot, and a canny and flexible political leader. After winning a substantial degree of freedom for Poland in 1956, he showed "that a communist government can rule a country, even one with a predominantly non-communist population, … without an exten-sive use of police terror." He also showed other countries such as Hungary that it was possible to loosen Soviet controls over internal development.

Nonetheless, Gomulka's initial popularity in Poland faded after 1956. It became evident that he would liberalize the system, but only within limits, and he would never let the Communist Party lose its monopoly of political power. His rejection by most of the Polish population thus indicated that even a liberalized form of Communism, sensitive to national traditions, could not be implanted successfully in Eastern Europe.

SOURCES:

Bethell, Nicholas. *Gomulka: His Poland, His Communism.* Holt, 1969.

Brzezinski, Zbigniew K. *The Soviet Bloc: Unity and Conflict.* Rev. ed. Harvard University Press, 1967.

Davies, Norman. *Heart of Europe: A Short History of Poland.* Clarendon Press, 1984.

FURTHER READING:

Neal Ascherson. *The Polish August: The Self-Limiting Revolution.* Viking Press, 1982.

Dziewanowski, M. K. *Poland in the Twentieth Century.* Columbia University Press, 1977.

Gilbert, Felix. *The End of the European Era: 1890 to the Present.* 4th ed. Norton, 1991.

Lewis, Flora. *The Polish Volcano: A Case History of Hope.* Secker & Warburg, 1959.

HISTORIC WORLD LEADERS

Maud Gonne

(1865/66–1953)

Irish nationalist, who was called the "Irish Joan of Arc" for her activities on behalf of Ireland's independence movement.

"When I was still quite a little girl I used to go riding through the country on a pony beside my father. It was the time of the evictions and I used to see people standing in front of their unroofed cottages from which the police held them back.... I thought to myself, 'When I grow up I'm going to change all that.'"

MAUD GONNE

Born in England to English parents, Maud Gonne was the daughter of Edith Frith Cook and Thomas Gonne. Her mother was a member of the distinguished and wealthy Cook family, who manufactured silk, linen, woolen, and cotton goods and sold them throughout the world. The Cooks were also a military family, with younger sons joining the queen's service and daughters marrying officers. Edith Cook was no exception, for Thomas Gonne was a captain in the 17th Light Dragoons when they were married on December 19, 1865. It has been suggested that Maud was born the following day, or very soon thereafter. No record exists of her birth, and since it was illegal not to record the birth of a child, it is assumed that her parents wanted to hide the date. While Maud was often vague about her birthdate, she was quoted in an unpublished Dublin newspaper article as saying that she was born "near Aldershot Camp in 1865." Aldershot Camp, approximately 40 miles from London, was the military base at which her father was stationed.

In 1868, when Captain Gonne was assigned a post in Ireland, Maud and her younger sister Kathleen lived with their mother in a small fishing

Contributed by Colleen Carpenter Cullinan, Ph.D. candidate, University of Chicago Divinity School, Chicago, Illinois

Name variations: Maud Gonne MacBride. Born late 1865 or early 1866 (date uncertain); died on April 27, 1953; daughter of a wealthy English family; married: John MacBride, 1903 (separated 1905); children: (son) Sean; and two illegitimate daughters fathered by Lucien Millevoye.

village north of Dublin Bay, while their father visited from the nearby army base on weekends. The girls did not attend school; instead, they spent their time climbing rocks on the coast and playing with the poor Irish children who lived a world apart from the wealthy English Gonnes. While the local children went off to school each day, Kathleen and Maud amused themselves under the watchful eye of their nurse.

The family then moved to Donnybrook, a Dublin suburb. In 1871, Edith Gonne became ill with tuberculosis. Since the Irish climate was terrible for someone suffering from this disease of the lungs, Thomas Gonne soon decided to move his wife to Italy. But her illness had progressed too far, and she died during the trip. Gonne would later recall a comment of her father's, at the time of her mother's wake in London, that had a profound effect: "You must never be afraid of anything," he told his six-year-old daughter, "not even of death."

Thomas Gonne left his daughters in the care of their mother's aunt for a short time, but Aunt Augusta was not the person to be raising two small girls. He then received notice of a posting to India and found a home and a nanny for the children in the south of France. The Frenchwoman who cared for them taught the girls French, history, and literature, as well as cooking skills; she also imbued them with an interest in art and radical politics.

But Maud did not become a child of the French countryside. She spent her summers in Switzerland and her winters in Italy. When her father became a military attaché, traveling throughout Europe, Gonne often met him in various cities. She had a truly cosmopolitan upbringing. Her independence and defiance of the norms were probably rooted in her unconventional youth and her exposure to places, people, and ideas that young English ladies rarely experienced.

As Gonne grew into her teens, it also became obvious that she was going to be stunningly beautiful. As an adult, she was six feet tall, and her figure, face, and wavy red hair classed her among the great beauties of the age. An aunt, the comtesse de la Sizeranne, took great pride in showing her off and introducing her to Parisian high society. Gonne received several marriage proposals before she was 18; legend has it that when King Edward VII of England was the Prince of Wales, he saw her at a dance and longed to marry her.

By 1884, when Thomas Gonne was permanently posted to Dublin and his daughters joined him, Maud assumed her absent mother's role as hostess of the household. She held parties and teas to help her father's career, impressing higher-ranking officers and their wives. But this family life was not to last: Thomas Gonne contracted typhoid fever in the winter of 1886 and died within a week. His body was taken back to England for burial next to his wife, and Kathleen and Maud—now orphans—were taken in by relatives.

The next several months were stormy ones. Scheming relatives, aware of the large inheritance the girls were about to receive and wishing to have legal control over it as their guardians, informed the girls that their father had left them nothing, and that they would have to accept being adopted by an aunt. But the girls were determined to earn their own living. Kathleen decided to become a nurse, and Maud trained to be an actress. Neither succeeded in their plans, but their activities kept them busy until their father's will was probated in the spring of 1887 and each became financially independent. With the greedy relatives left behind, Gonne returned to her aunt, the comtesse, in Paris.

Gonne Gets Involved in Irish Politics

It was there that Gonne met and eventually fell in love with Lucien Millevoye, a French political activist. Since Millevoye was already married, their relationship remained secret throughout her life. It was sharing in his political interests, however, that shaped Gonne's life more than their romantic liaison. Millevoye's passion for his homeland corresponded to his equally deep hatred for England, and he urged Gonne to get involved in Ireland's independence movement as a way to strike at the English. She took him up on this and eagerly began spending time in Ireland, traveling through the countryside to see firsthand the oppression that the Irish were suffering under their English landlords. Witnessing the eviction of tenants who were asking for a fair rent and the starvation of those suffering during famines, she quickly began to get involved with famine relief efforts and the Land League, an organization dedicated to reforming tenancy laws. She gave speeches, rallying the Irish and influencing the decisions and lawmaking of their English overlords.

Becoming involved in Irish politics meant meeting quite a circle of revolutionaries and leaders in Dublin. Gonne's most famous and influential acquaintance—though she didn't know it at the time—was William Butler Yeats, whom she met in 1889. Not yet the world-renowned poet but only a nondescript young man who wrote a bit of poetry, "Willie" Yeats failed to impress her. Though they became friends, her heart was in Paris with Millevoye. Yeats, on the other hand, was totally taken with Gonne's beauty, spirit, and passion for Ireland, and his love for her inspired much of his poetry.

In 1889, Gonne had her first daughter by Millevoye. Named Georgette, the child survived only three years. Devastated by her daughter's death, Gonne threw herself with renewed vigor into her work for Ireland. She founded lending libraries in remote rural areas of the country, thus promoting the cultural revival then going on. During most of English rule of Ireland, Gaelic (the native Irish language) had been suppressed: children were taught only English, English literature, and English history in the state-sponsored schools, and often learned nothing of the language, history, or literary heritage of their own land. The cultural revival of the Gaelic language and literature was a key element in Ireland's becoming a free state and a free people.

In 1896, Gonne had another daughter by Millevoye, this one named Iseult. Shortly after, Gonne left Millevoye. Their break became final in 1898, when she discovered that he had fallen in love with someone else. Iseult Gonne was raised by Maud as a niece.

Gonne then traveled to the United States in an effort to raise money for Irish causes and to work for international condemnation of England's continued rule of Ireland. It was during one of these speaking tours that she met John MacBride, a veteran of the Boer War and an Irishman from County Mayo, who was also traveling the U.S. on behalf of the Irish. In 1903, the two married, which was seen by many as a terrible mistake. MacBride's conservative, rural Irish background clashed terribly with Gonne's cosmopolitan ways: a quiet, homebound, obedient wife was something she could never be. By the time their son Sean was born the following year, the couple's problems had already begun. MacBride was a heavy drinker, and it is rumored that he abused his wife when he was drunk. It is also possible that he discovered that Iseult was Gonne's child. In 1905, in a separation agreement drawn up in France, Gonne was awarded Sean, but she had to avoid Ireland almost completely for the next 11 years, fearful that if she brought her son there his father could take him away. She was also afraid to leave him for long in France due to his fragile health. In addition to worries about Sean, there was also the fact that many of the Irish people were appalled that she had left her husband. Ireland was a profoundly conservative Catholic country, and marriage was nothing to be trifled with. Shortly after the separation, when Gonne appeared in Dublin to speak, she was booed by those who had once adored her.

On Easter Monday in 1916, the Irish Republican Brotherhood attempted a revolution to rid the country of the English. The Easter Rising was a failure. When the English executed many of the captured Irish revolutionaries, John MacBride, now a martyr to the cause of Irish freedom, was among them. Since this meant that Gonne was free to stay in Ireland with Sean, she plunged once again into the work and agitation she had enjoyed in the past. In May of 1918, she was arrested, along with many other Irish nationalists, and imprisoned in England without charges being filed. Never extraordinarily healthy, having inherited her mother's tendency toward tuberculosis, Gonne did not take to prison life. By October, she was desperately ill. Rather than have another martyr on their hands, the English authorities released her. Despite the fact that she had been forbidden, Gonne returned to Ireland immediately.

She Works To Improve Prison Conditions

Spending the 1920s in efforts to improve prison conditions for Irish political prisoners, she visited prisons, wrote letters to prisoners and other activists, and continued to speak out as often as possible. By now Gonne was a fixture in Irish politics: she had been an influential voice for over 40 years. In 1932, the country honored her for her years of service to the cause of Irish nationalism. It would seem a fitting end to a career—but Gonne was far from finished.

The year 1919 had seen the founding of an independent Irish parliament, but it wasn't until 1932, when **Eamon de Valera** was elected prime

Sean MacBride

(b. 1904)

Sean MacBride was born in 1904 to Maud Gonne and John MacBride. Within the year, Gonne left MacBride, taking Sean with her to France. Sean never knew his father, for Gonne was afraid he might take Sean away. An Irish child raised in France and throughout Europe, Sean MacBride experienced much that many of his contemporaries would not. For example, in 1911, while in Italy with his mother, he received his First Communion from Pope Pius X.

In 1916, John MacBride participated in the Easter Rising and was captured and executed by the English. Shortly after this, Sean returned to Ireland with his mother and soon discovered that being the son of an Irish patriot and martyr carried with it recognition and responsibilities. Following in his parents' footsteps, he became involved in Irish politics and the Irish Republican Army. As an adult, he became a lawyer and often defended Irish nationalists. In 1947, he formed a new political party, the *Clann na Poblachta* (Republican Family). The Clann became influential enough within a year that Sean was elected to the Irish Parliament and named minister of external affairs.

Sean MacBride left politics in 1957 and devoted himself wholly to one of his mother's favorite causes, that of political prisoners. He became heavily involved in, and eventually the head of, Amnesty International, a worldwide organization that agitates for the release of political prisoners. In 1974, he won the Nobel Peace Prize for his efforts—the first Irishman to receive that distinction. ∎

minister of the Irish Free State, that the most significant ties between Ireland and England were broken. Abolishing the oath of allegiance to the British Crown that all Irish officials were required to take, de Valera continued a unilateral revision of the treaty that established the relationship (and lack of one) between the two countries. Though Maud Gonne had originally supported de Valera's efforts, she eventually decided that they were not radical enough. Despite the fact that her son Sean had worked for de Valera's election and was his secretary, Gonne began speaking against de Valera and his policies. She also continued to work tirelessly with the Women's Prisoners' Defense League and to agitate for free school lunches for children.

In 1949, the long process of wresting freedom from the English—piece by tiny piece—was finally over. On Easter Monday, when the Republic of Ireland was formally begun, Gonne was one of the great nationalists invited to the ceremonies in Dublin; she attended with her son, who was now an active figure in Irish politics himself. One of the last survivors of her generation, Gonne struggled through the next several years; age and illness were taking their toll. She wrote her memoirs and was interviewed several times for reminiscences about the glory days of the struggle for Irish freedom. In April of 1953, at the age of 87, she died quietly at home, with her daughter Iseult, her son Sean, and Sean's wife at her side.

SOURCES:

Levenson, Samuel. *Maud Gonne.* Reader's Digest Press, 1976.

Marecco, Anne. *The Rebel Countess.* Chilton Press, 1967.

FURTHER READING:

Cardozo, Nancy. *Maud Gonne.* New York: 1990.

MacBride, Maud Gonne. A *Servant of the Queen.* Gollancz, 1938, 1974.

Ward, Margaret. *Maud Gonne: Ireland's Joan of Arc.* London: 1990.

Yeats, William Butler. *The Autobiography of William Butler Yeats.* Macmillan, 1916.

Mikhail Gorbachev

(1931–)

Leader of the Soviet Union and dynamic young general secretary of the Communist Party, who abolished his country's 70-year-old dictatorship and ended the Cold War.

"In just over five years, Mikhail Gorbachev transformed the world.... Then he discovered that he had started a revolution he could not control."

ROBERT G. KAISER

etween 1985 and 1991, the youngest individual in decades to become head of the Soviet Communist Party dominated the history of the Soviet Union. Mikhail Gorbachev launched a program of political and economic reform that dramatically affected domestic life and the place of his country in world affai.... The Soviet dictatorship was transformed into a multiparty state in which the Communist Party had to struggle to maintain a role. Meanwhile, the Soviet Union moved toward a free-market economy. With equal drama, the longstanding Cold War with the United States diminished and then turned into a cooperative relationship.

Gorbachev's reforms became more radical as time went on, and the end of political dictatorship released forces he could not control. Various ethnic groups began to assert themselves, sometimes in armed clashes with one another, sometimes in moves to leave the Soviet Union itself. Meanwhile, the economic problems of the country grew increasingly severe. Boris Yeltsin, once Gorbachev's lieutenant, emerged as a sharp critic of the Communist Party leader. When conservatives launched an unsuccessful coup in August 1991, the

*Pronunciation: GOR-bach-yoff.
Born Mikhail Sergeyevich
Gorbachev on March 2, 1931, in
the village of Privolnoe in the
Northern Caucasus region of the
Soviet Union; son of Sergei
Andreyevich Gorbachev and
Maria Panteleyevna
Gorbacheva; married: Raisa
Maksimovna Titorenko;
children: one daughter.
Predecessor: Konstantin
Chernenko, general secretary of
the Soviet Communist Party.
Successor: Boris Yeltsin, president
of the Russian Republic.*

Contributed by Neil Heyman, Professor of History, San Diego State University, San Diego, California

511

CHRONOLOGY

1950	Gorbachev entered Moscow State University
1952	Joined Communist Party
1953	Death of Stalin
1955	Completed law school; returned to Stavropol
1970	Appointed Party chief in Stavropol
1978	Moved to Moscow as secretary of Central Committee of Soviet Communist Party
1982	Death of Brezhnev
1984	Death of Andropov; Chernenko led Party
1985	Death of Chernenko; Gorbachev became Party general secretary
1986	Nuclear accident at Chernobyl; Sakharov released from exile in Gorky
1988	Ethnic violence in Armenia and Azerbaijan; Gorbachev became president of Soviet Union
1989	Destruction of Berlin Wall
1990	Lithuania declared independence
1991	August coup; disintegration of Soviet Union; Gorbachev resigned

Soviet Union collapsed and within six months Gorbachev was forced out of office by Yeltsin.

When Mikhail Gorbachev was born in the village of Privolnoe, near Stavropol, in the Kuban region of the Northern Caucausus on March 2, 1931, his country was in the midst of massive turmoil and change. The Communist dictator **Joseph Stalin** was conducting a program of industrial expansion under a series of five-year plans; he was also collectivizing agriculture. This meant bringing individual peasants into collective farms where they worked under direct government supervision. When peasants and peasant villages resisted collectivization, they were met by force on the part of the Soviet secret police and the Red Army.

Gorbachev's family consisted of peasants affected by collectivization. Some accounts indicate that one of his grandfathers was arrested for resisting the government's policy, while another grandfather was reputedly a Communist Party member. In 1941, the armies of Nazi Germany invaded the Soviet Union and occupied large regions in the West and South. For a time the village in which Gorbachev lived came under German control.

The young man distinguished himself as a farm worker, and, with the help of his family background, gained admission to Moscow State University, the most distinguished institution of higher education in the Soviet Union. His student years were a crucial background for an ambitious young man. Gorbachev, however, took an unusual turn in his education. He studied law. His friends from these years have remarked that he used his student days to obtain a broad education. He also married Raisa Titorenko, a sociology student he met at the university.

In 1955, Gorbachev returned to Stavropol and began to rise in the Communist Party organization. Since Stavropol was a vacation area for the nation's leaders, the young Party secretary in Stavropol made important contacts. It was also the original home of **Yuri Andropov,** head of the KGB (secret police) from 1967 to 1981 and leader of the Soviet Union from 1982 until his death in 1984.

In 1978, perhaps at the initiative of Andropov, Gorbachev received his key promotion: he was brought to Moscow as the Party official in charge of agricultural policy. Although the next several years were harsh ones for the Soviet farm economy, Gorbachev's ties to Andropov kept him from receiving fatal blame. His standing in the Party was unusual because of his age. The average member of the Communist Party hierarchy was in his 70s. Gorbachev had not yet reached the age of 50.

In 1982, when Andropov took over as Party leader following the death of **Leonid Brezhnev,** Gorbachev emerged as his key assistant. Andropov was soon disabled by illness, and some historians believe that Gorbachev largely directed Soviet policy over these years. Nonetheless, following Andropov's death in early 1984, Gorbachev lost out to a member of the Party's older generation, **Konstantin Chernenko.**

Radical Reforms, World Popularity

It was only upon Chernenko's death, in early 1985, that Gorbachev was chosen Communist Party general secretary, making him the effective leader of his country. Over the next few years, he launched a reform program that become increasingly daring and radical. Historians question whether he had always been inclined to reform, even as he was climbing the Party ladder, or whether his reforming instincts developed later.

Gorbachev soon became an immensely popular figure on the world scene. In 1986, his release of the dissident **Andrei Sakharov,** who had been exiled in 1980 to the provincial city of Gorky for

512

criticizing the war in Afghanistan, was a dramatic sign of political liberalization in the Soviet Union. Gorbachev's policy of ending the Afghan war and, in particular, his willingness to negotiate radical reductions in Soviet military strength made it clear that he was a very different Soviet leader from his predecessors.

In 1986, Gorbachev began a series of summit conferences with President Ronald Reagan and visited the United States on several occasions. Two years later, Gorbachev made a particular impression when he went into crowds of spectators in New York City to shake hands as if he were running for U.S. office. The clearest sign of improving Soviet-American relations came in May and June 1988 when President Reagan, who had criticized the Soviet Union in the Andropov years as "an evil empire," visited Moscow.

Within the Soviet Union, Gorbachev promoted spectacular political changes. His most important measure came in 1989 when he set up elections in which members of the Communist Party had to compete against opponents who were not Party members. That same year, he called for an end to the special status of the Communist Party guaranteed by the Soviet Constitution. This was an astonishing change: ever since the Bolshevik Revolution of November 1917, the Communist Party had sought a monopoly of political power. In 1988, Gorbachev took the post of Soviet President, giving himself a base of political power outside the Communist Party.

Two issues, however, caused growing difficulty for Gorbachev. First there was the problem of nationalities. The Soviet Union consisted of nearly 100 different ethnic groups. As the political dictatorship began to disappear, many of these groups—like the Christian Armenians and the Moslem Azberbaijanis—began to engage in open warfare against one another. Such bloodshed came from longstanding local quarrels that had been suppressed under Moscow's earlier control. Even more serious, some ethnic groups like the peoples of the Baltic, for example, the Lithuanians, and the Ukrainians, began to call for outright independence. Second, the country's economy was sinking deeper and deeper into crisis. Both industrial and agricultural production were declining, and the old system installed by Stalin in which the economy ran under the centralized control of the government no longer seemed to work.

Gorbachev turned out to be more willing to make changes in government and international affairs than to shift course in the area of the nationalities and the economy. Perhaps pushed by more conservative rivals, he cracked down on the Lithuanians when they declared their independence in the summer of 1990. He tried to move in a gradual way toward a private system of farming and privately owned industry.

At the same time, a powerful rival emerged in the person of Boris Yeltsin. Once an ally of Gorbachev, Yeltsin became the country's leading advocate of radical economic reform. Although forced from the Politburo, the small group at the top of the Communist Party, in 1987, Yeltsin soon established his own political base. He formally left the Communist Party in 1990—something Gorbachev refused to do—and was elected president of the Russian Republic in June 1991. Gorbachev, on the other hand, had been made president of the Soviet Union without having to win a national election. Thus, Yeltsin could claim a greater degree of popular support.

Captured in a Coup

In August 1991, a group of Communist Party conservatives captured Gorbachev while he was on vacation in the Crimea and moved to seize power. Some of these men, like Prime Minister Valentin Pavlov, were individuals Gorbachev had put in power to balance off conservative and liberal political forces. But Yeltsin, not the kidnapped Gorbachev, led the successful resistance to the coup, which collapsed within a few days. When Gorbachev returned to Moscow, he was overshadowed by his former ally. There were even rumors Gorbachev had been involved in the coup.

By the end of 1991, the Soviet Union had fallen apart. When most of its major components like the Ukraine and the Baltic states declared themselves independent, real power began to rest with the leaders of those components, chief among them Yeltsin, the hero of August 1991 and president of the Russian Republic. Gorbachev formally resigned his remaining political office on Christmas Day, 1991.

As a private citizen, Gorbachev faded from public view, but he continued to write and to travel. On one notable occasion, his travels struck an important symbolic note. On May 6, 1992, he spoke at Westminster College in Fulton, Missouri. There, in 1946, **Winston Churchill** had given his classic speech coining the term, "the Cold War." Gorbachev's appearance was a vivid reminder of the changes he had helped to bring about. The Cold War had ended during his seven years in power. In referring to that long and dangerous conflict, he noted that it had not ended in a victory for the West. Rather the defeat of Communism was "altogether a victory for common sense, reason, democracy and common human values."

Like any individual who contributes to a great historical turning point, Gorbachev will find his role interpreted in varying ways. The debate has already been joined. Was he a bold and imaginative leader who courageously moved his country away from a dangerous and decaying system? Or was he more often a timid, indecisive figure, pushed by events he could not resist until eventually they overcame him?

SOURCES:

Doder, Dusko, and Louise Bransom. *Gorbachev: Heretic in the Kremlin.* Viking, 1990.

Kaiser, Robert. *Why Gorbachev Happened: His Triumphs and His Failure.* Simon & Schuster, 1991.

Medvedev, Zhores A. *Gorbachev.* Norton, 1986.

FURTHER READING:

Doder, Dusko. *Shadows and Whispers: Power Politics Inside the Kremlin from Brezhnev to Gorbachev.* Random House, 1986.

Gorbachev, Mikhail S. *Perestroika: New Thinking for Our Country and the World.* Harper & Row, 1987.

Hosking, Geoffry. *The Awakening of the Soviet Union.* Harvard University Press, 1990.

Lewin, Moshe. *The Gorbachev Phenomenon: A Historical Interpretation.* University of California Press, 1991.

Klement Gottwald

(1896–1953)
and Other Leaders
Involved in the Rise of
Communist Power
in Czechoslovakia

Communist leader and president of Czechoslovakia, who was instrumental in organizing the Communist takeover of his country, imposing a Stalinist-type regime that resulted in economic dislocation, bloody purges, and political and social repression.

K lement Gottwald claims the dubious distinction of having presided over the destruction of what had been until 1948 the most successful democratic system in Central Europe. He died in Prague on March 14, 1953, nine days after the death of his Soviet mentor, **Joseph Stalin,** and only four months after the execution of a group of fellow Communists on trumped-up charges of treason. His biography and the fate of his nation are closely linked to the massive political and social upheavals that convulsed Europe in the first half of the 20th century.

The area that became Czechoslovakia in 1918 had a long and complex history starting in the ninth century, when a Moravian kingdom organized itself in the chaos that followed the collapse of **Charlemagne**'s empire. The city of Prague was one of the great cultural and intellectual centers of the Middle Ages and became famous for its university founded in the year 1348. Czech national consciousness was first created in the Hussite movement [see **Jan Hus**] of the early 15th century, which attempted to create a reformed Christian society free of exploitation by German nobles and a corrupt church. Although these aspi-

Born on November 23, 1896, in the village of Dedidocz, in the Mana region of Moravia; died in Prague on March 14, 1953; son of poor peasants; married: Martha; children: daughter, Martha. Predecessor: Edvard Benes. Successor: Antonin Zapotocky.

Contributed by John Haag, Associate Professor of History, University of Georgia, Athens, Georgia

rations were crushed in the Thirty Years' War (1618–48), the desire for an independent Czech nation was kept alive throughout the 19th century when Bohemia and Moravia became a prosperous and highly industrialized part of Austria, while impoverished Slovakia remained part of Hungary.

The collapse of Austria-Hungary in 1918 made possible the creation of an independent Czechoslovak Republic. This new state was burdened from the start by nationality tensions between its Czech, Slovak, German, and Hungarian ethnic groups, but it could also count on a number of positive factors including a highly literate citizenry and democratically-minded humanist political leaders, particularly **Thomas G. Masaryk** and Edvard Benes. In the first national elections, held in April 1920, the Social Democratic Party called for sweeping social and economic changes and was able to win about 25% of the total vote, but the next year a Communist Party was created from the radical faction of the Party, and as a result working-class unity was greatly weakened.

Despite the upheavals within the Marxist spectrum of Czech political life, the Communists continued to be popular because under their leader Bohumir Smeral (1880–1941) they remained a large and heterogeneous Party of 350,000 members. The Party permitted significant amounts of internal debate and called for the creation of a socialist society that was democratic and uniquely suited to the needs of Czechoslovakia. Even with 36 political parties participating in the November 1925 parliamentary elections, the Communists emerged as the second largest party in the nation, electing 41 deputies out of 300. But by the late 1920s, when Klement Gottwald emerged as the leader of a Stalinized Czechoslovak Communist Party, the organization had been severely demoralized and could no longer claim a mass following.

The political career of Klement Gottwald began during his years as a cabinetmaker's apprentice in Vienna, when he joined the Social Democratic movement. Joining the Communist Party of Czechoslovakia (CPC) at its founding in 1921, within a few years he had proven his reliability as an editor. By 1928, supported by Joseph Stalin, he had entered the bureaucracy of the Communist International (Comintern) in Moscow. Certain of backing from Stalin, and promising absolute loyalty to the Stalinist faction in the U.S.S.R. in return, Gottwald was able to oust the pragmatic leadership of the CPC in 1929. As CPC general secretary, Gottwald was absolutely loyal to the orthodox Stalinist line, but the new "leftist" ideological position of the Communists made them much less popular than they had been under Smeral's leadership. In

the October 1929 parliamentary elections, they suffered significantly at the polls, electing only 30 deputies as opposed to 41 four years earlier; by that year, Party membership reached an all-time low of 20,000—only 5% of the total in 1921.

Slavishly embracing the Stalinist line that the greatest enemy of the working class was not Fascism and Nazism but the moderate Social Democrats, Gottwald echoed this position in no uncertain terms when in 1929 he told the delegates to the Fifth Congress of the CPC that he would ensure that the Party would always "hit social Fascism over the head." "Social Fascism" meant the Social Democrats, and during this leftist phase Gottwald relentlessly attacked all within the Communist Party leadership who advocated a policy of cooperation with Social Democrats and others to effectively combat the growing threat of Fascism. In 1933, Gottwald condemned and expelled Josef Guttmann from the Party leadership for advocating a vigorous anti-Nazi united front.

Under Gottwald's leadership, the CPC remained paralyzed and unable to effectively deal with Nazism, which now threatened Czechoslovak democracy both from abroad (**Hitler**'s Third Reich) and from within (the pro-Nazi Sudeten German Party led by Konrad Henlein). Not surprisingly, in the last free elections in prewar Czechoslovakia, held in May 1935, despite the Nazi threat and widespread suffering brought on by economic depression, the Communists were not able to increase their parliamentary representation, which remained at 30. Only with a radical shift in policy announced by the Comintern in 1935 that halted the struggle against "Social Fascism" and called for a united anti-Nazi front including Communists did the CPC again appeal to a broad spectrum of the nation's people.

Gottwald and his Party reached the height of their prewar popularity in the late summer of 1938, when the Sudeten crisis revealed the tragic error of President Edvard Benes (1884–1948), who held the belief that Czechoslovak independence would be guaranteed by Western allies, France and Great Britain. In 1935, Benes had signed a mutual-assistance treaty with the Soviet Union, hoping that this would ensure the security and territorial integrity of his nation. But due to their fear of a war with Germany and deep-rooted fears of an intrusion of Soviet power into Central Europe in the event of war, the Western Allies abandoned their pledge to defend Czechoslovakia. At the Munich conference of September 1938, the Allies gave in to Hitler's demands for the strategic Sudeten territory (an area along the Czech border occupied by 3 million Germans).

Czechoslovakia Falls to Germany

Since the 1935 shift in Comintern policy, Communist parties had based their anti-Nazi stance on the concept of a broad coalition of forces. It was therefore possible for Gottwald and the CPC to argue passionately for a defense of the Czech nation through policies that did not exclude war with Germany. Gottwald's speeches in September 1938—the most eloquent in his political career—made him a spokesman for an embattled democracy, and gave to him and his fellow Communists immense prestige and political capital that would be of value in later years. Benes, however, having been abandoned by his Western allies and fearing a bloodbath if his nation stood against Hitler alone, resigned as president a few days after the signing of the Munich Pact (in which the Allies pressured Czechoslovakia to give in to Hitler's demands), and the cabinet that succeeded him consisted of weak-willed individuals who hoped that by appeasing the Nazis the life of their mutilated nation might be spared. Accordingly, the Communist Party was banned in December 1938. The work of the CPC continued on an underground basis, and Gottwald returned to his Comintern post in Moscow. Czechoslovakia was taken over by German forces in March of 1939. There was no resistance.

The signing of the Hitler-Stalin non-aggression treaty in late August 1939 sealed the fate of Poland and made World War II inevitable. Although the pact caused consternation among Communist and left-wing circles, bringing about the resignation of many militant Marxists who accused Stalin of treason to the cause of world revolution, loyalists like Gottwald held firm to their belief in the Soviet dictator's course of action, defending it in speeches and articles. Back in Czechoslovakia, the Nazi-German occupiers systematically tightened the screws of their repressive machinery, concentrating on the elimination of the educated elite that clearly constituted a nucleus of active resistance. In the fall of 1939, Prague university students and professors were arrested and imprisoned, and many were executed as a warning not to engage in resistance activities. Since the Communists were under orders from Stalin in 1939–41 not to antagonize the Nazis, their role in the resistance was minimal until June 1941, when Hitler attacked the Soviet Union. At this point, Gottwald and the CPC leadership reemerged from obscurity, calling on the people of Czechoslovakia to overthrow their German Nazi and homegrown Fascist oppressors.

The assassination of Nazi governor **Reinhard Heydrich** in June 1942, by parachutists dropped into Czechoslovakia by President Benes's London exile government, led to severe reprisals by the German occupiers. The villages of Lidice and Lezaky, near Prague, were surrounded, all adult males were shot on the spot, women and children were sent to concentration camps, and infants were given to German families in order to be "Germanized." By 1944 a Czech resistance movement, often led by Communists but including men and women of all political beliefs, was firmly in place. In Slovakia, which since March 1939 had been ruled by a pro-Nazi puppet regime headed by Josef Tiso, a Catholic priest and nationalist politician, a massive uprising against the Germans began on August 29, 1944. The Communists played a major role in the Slovak national uprising, and although it was crushed after two months of bloody fighting, it was obvious by the end of 1944 that the Nazi occupation of Czechoslovakia was on its last legs. Because of the dominant role they had played in the anti-Nazi resistance, the Communists would be fated to be a significant factor in postwar political life.

The exile government of President Edvard Benes, which had been operating in London since 1940, now began to plan for the postwar world. As he envisioned it, a peaceful Europe after the defeat of the Nazis would of necessity allocate an important role to a restored Czechoslovakia as a bridge-building society between East and West, one that was firmly rooted in democratic traditions but that also would be able to coexist on the friendliest possible terms with its Soviet neighbor. More than any of the other exiled political leaders, Benes worked to achieve close cooperation with both Western governments and the Soviet regime in order to assure a stable postwar political climate for his people. Accordingly, he signed a Czechoslovak-Soviet Treaty of Friendship, Mutual Assistance and Post-War Cooperation in Moscow in December 1943, a pact in which the Soviet government expressly committed itself (Article 4) not to interfere in Czechoslovak internal affairs. Above and beyond his idealistic vision of a peaceful post-Nazi world, Benes sought friendly relations with the Soviet Union for at least two practical reasons: first of all, he had never forgotten how his nation had been betrayed at Munich by the Western powers, and he saw in the Soviets a guarantee for national survival in the event of a revival of German power; secondly, Benes was convinced he would need Soviet support for the expulsion of the two national minorities (Germans and Magyars) the majority of Czechs and Slovaks would no longer permit to remain in their nation.

In March 1945, Benes, Gottwald, and other Czechoslovak political leaders met in Moscow to draw up a detailed program for the resurrection of political life in their country, parts of which had already been liberated by the Soviet army. As announced on April 4 in the liberated city of Kosice, the nation was to be governed by a coalition called the National Front, which would exclude those who had collaborated with the Nazi occupying forces (this included the entire Agrarian Party). A strong president would share power with a freely elected parliament. The prime minister, Zdenek Fierlinger, was a left-wing Social Democrat known to be friendly to the Communists; there would be three deputy prime ministers, posts reserved for members of the Communist, Catholic People's, and National Socialist parties respectively. Not surprisingly, Klement Gottwald was chosen by the CPC as their choice for deputy prime minister. Significantly, the Communists were given the crucially important Ministry of the Interior as well as those of Education, Agriculture, and Enlightenment (Propaganda). Equally significant was the fact that the Ministry of War was controlled by General Ludvik Svoboda, who, while not a Communist, was extremely pro-Soviet in his sympathies.

Soviet Army Liberates Prague

The Czech resistance rose against the Nazis in Prague in early May 1945, and while American forces under General **George Patton** were close by, it was the Soviet army that actually liberated the Czech capital on May 9. President Benes returned in triumph on May 16, immediately putting into place the political system outlined in the Kosice Program. Gottwald, his close associate Rudolf Slansky, and other Communists arrived in Prague and immediately began to participate in the government, and also reorganized a Communist movement that had been devastated by the Nazi occupation. The number of CPC members in May 1945 was about 40,000, with about 28,000 in Bohemia-Moravia and the rest in Slovakia (a separate Slovak Communist Party had been authorized by the Comintern in May 1939). The fact that the Communists enjoyed immense prestige in the early post-liberation months (they claimed to have lost 25,000 members who died in the anti-Nazi struggle), as well as the obvious reality that Communism would play a major role in the postwar world, prompted large numbers of Czechs and Slovaks, some of them idealists and others clearly opportunists, to join the CPC.

By early July 1945, the CPCs had registered an astonishing growth in membership to 475,304 men and women, and by the end of the year it reached 826,527. The Czechoslovak Communist Party became the country's largest political party, one with a vision of the future that many Czechs and Slovaks shared. Along with the Social Democrats, many of whom were sympathetic to the Communists, a majority of Czechs in 1945 demanded sweeping social changes and looked forward to friendly relations not only with the Western allies but particularly with the nation that had liberated them, the Soviet Union.

Gottwald Appointed Prime Minister

By the end of 1945, sweeping legislation brought about the first measure of large-scale nationalization in liberated Europe. Presidential decrees in October of that year resulted in the creation of a socialized economic sector containing over three-fifths of the industrial work force. Banks were also nationalized at this time, and it appeared that a national consensus had been created in which a socialist but firmly democratic political system could flourish. This impression was reinforced by the parliamentary elections of May 26, 1946, which resulted in a substantial victory for the Marxist parties. The CPC won 37.9% of the vote, while the Social Democrats were able to win another 12.1%. As a result of the election Gottwald was appointed prime minister on July 3, heading a coalition government whose cabinet of 19 ministers represented eight political parties; the Communists held seven of the 19 ministerial portfolios. Gottwald's governmental agenda included the writing of a new constitution that would guarantee civil liberties, equal rights for women, and socialization of key industries, but also protection for small and middle-sized private enterprises. To many Czechs and Slovaks, as well as to foreign observers in 1946, the fact that Czechoslovakia had a Communist prime minister but had been able to retain its democratic traditions was a positive sign on an otherwise devastated and unstable postwar European political landscape.

Although some journalists described Czechoslovakia as a thriving democracy that was "the Kremlin's showcase in Central Europe," there were signs already in 1946 that Gottwald and the Communists would be willing to go far beyond normal democratic political behavior to enhance their power. In the Sudeten German-Czech border areas where the 3 million ethnic Germans were expelled from 1945 through 1947, the Communists customarily handed over confiscated homes and land to Czechs whose prime qualification for receiving the property was that they were willing to sign up as Communist Party members. Using the pretext of uprooting Nazi collaborators from the political scene, Communist activists branded large numbers of individuals as "enemies of the people" whose only real offense was that they were conservatives and anti-Communists.

Even more ominous was a growing Communist influence within the various branches of the state security apparatus. Control over the Ministry of the Interior in 1945 made it possible for Communist agents to infiltrate the important intelligence and State Security units which were subordinated to "Department Z" of the Interior Ministry. Within the Communist Party itself, a secret "Registry Department" headed by Karel Svab concentrated on compiling compromising facts on political opponents of the Communists, particularly relating to the period of Nazi occupation. Many of these Communist intelligence agents had in fact received their training during the war in the Soviet Union, and by 1947 some of their reports were being read by Stalin and other Soviet leaders in the Kremlin.

By the middle of 1947, Czechoslovak domestic politics were being increasingly affected by the acceleration of East-West tensions. As the United States and the Soviet Union struggled to define their respective spheres of influence in Germany and to control the course of events in the rest of Central Europe, for a brief time it appeared that in at least one nation an exception to these tensions might be possible, guaranteeing a uniquely "Czechoslovak road to Socialism." The American announcement of a generous program of economic recovery assistance, the Marshall Plan, in early June 1947 was initially unanimously accepted by Gottwald and his cabinet. But, when the matter was brought up a few weeks later in Moscow during a previously scheduled Czechoslovak-Soviet conference, Soviet displeasure with the idea was summed up in an ultimatum by Stalin. Either the Czechs dropped their intention to participate in the Marshall Plan, or promised Soviet economic assistance would cease (more serious steps could of course be read between the line). A shaken Gottwald yielded, remarking later that he had "never seen Stalin so angry." Upon returning to Prague, a disillusioned Foreign Minister **Jan Masaryk** could only say to his inner circle, "I went to Moscow a free Minister and I'm coming back a servant of Stalin."

Back in Prague, Gottwald announced that his nation would not participate in the Marshall Plan but that the Soviets would assist with the new Two Year Plan of postwar reconstruction. A further complication was a serious drought in agricultural regions which created a potential food crisis and necessitated an urgent request to the Soviets for aid in the form of grain and fodder. After his display of independence, Gottwald's position in the Communist world during the summer of 1947 was shaky. **Marshal Tito** of Yugoslavia, who would dramatically break with Stalin a year later, openly spoke of Gottwald's "disgrace." Soviet concerns about losing influence in their newly created Central and Eastern European satellite regimes ("People's Democracies") doubtless played a significant role in their creation in September 1947 of the Communist Information Bureau (Cominform), an organization that clearly was designed to act as a "policeman" of Communist parties tempted by nationalistic or other "anti-Soviet" ideals. Significantly, Gottwald was not included in the CPC delegation that attended the Cominform constituent meeting in Poland.

As the nation appeared to be slipping into the Soviet orbit, more and more Czechs and Slovaks reacted negatively. Some of the early enthusiasm for the Communists had now waned, and a secret CPC survey of public opinion indicated that in the next national elections, scheduled for May 1948, the Party would very likely lose at least 10% of its voting strength. In the press and in parliamentary debates, the Communists found themselves increasingly subject to searching criticism. Painfully aware that their prestige was slipping, Communists in Slovakia took the lead in forcing the issue of who would ultimately control the nation. The Communist Gustav Husak used his Interior Ministry's discovery of a "plot" as a pretext for pressuring for the creation of a new, Communist-dominated government. A massive show of support by Communist-dominated labor unions for Husak's plan resulted in a symbolic general strike that served to impress public opinion with the strength and will of the Marxist camp. The Communists went to the streets and psychologically cowed their opponents. Consequently, on November 18, 1947, a new and "purged" Slovak cabinet was formed which was thoroughly dominated by Communists and their allies.

The mood in Czechoslovakia in the first weeks of 1948 was one of growing confidence among both the Communists and non-Communists. The Communists, led by a Klement Gottwald once more in the good graces of the Kremlin, had had their morale boosted the previous November, while the various non-Communist parties were confident that they would win an overwhelming electoral victory in the elections scheduled for May. The crisis that resulted in a Communist seizure of power began with the Communist Interior Minister's transfer of a number of non-Communist police officers from active duty to administrative work. When the non-Communist parties demanded that this action be rescinded, the Interior Minister refused, a cabinet crisis erupted, and several ministers resigned from the government in protest. The non-Communist politicians hoped that President Benes would refuse their resignations, precipitating the fall of the Gottwald government and the holding of early elections they were certain to win.

Gottwald did not appear ready for violence at this juncture, and indeed attempted to persuade President Benes to appoint an entirely new cabinet as a compromise solution. But events now moved quickly. Benes, whose health was poor as the result of two recent strokes, made no moves that might plunge the country into bloodshed. The Communists controlled the Prague police and the city filled up with militant workers' militia members and ex-partisans. Caught by surprise and fearful of violence, the non-Communists did not organize any significant counter-demonstrations. The Communized labor unions, as they had earlier in Slovakia, organized a psychologically effective hour-long general strike in support of Prime Minister Gottwald.

In his Hradschin Palace office, Benes could hear the roar of the Communist-led crowds in the streets of Prague and particularly in Wenceslaus Square. On February 25, Benes accepted the resignations and appointed a new and totally Communist-dominated government approved by Gottwald and the Communists, whose incessant street demonstrations had by now created an atmosphere of general panic. Within hours, the Communists had captured opposition Party headquarters as well as municipal, regional, and national administrative offices; social organizations, and educational institutions had been seized and purged. Czechoslovak democracy had succumbed to a bloodless coup, one that was technically accomplished in a legal and constitutional manner.

The show of constitutional legality was maintained when an intimidated National Assembly approved the new government by a vote of 230 to 70. At first, Gottwald's actions appeared to be those of a leader determined to heal the wounds of a deeply divided nation. In early March he visited the grave of revered Thomas G. Masaryk, Czechoslovakia's George Washington. But the death of Foreign Minister Jan Masaryk on March 10, who either jumped or was pushed from a window, served to heighten tensions. Some Western observers termed Masaryk's death a suicide in response to the Communist coup while others suspected the Communists had murdered him; Gottwald argued that criticism of the new regime

in the West had so unnerved Masaryk that he had taken his own life in despair. The new militancy of the regime was seen in the vigorous steps taken by Alexej Cepicka, Minister of Justice and Gottwald's son-in-law, a hard-liner who announced in mid-March that many politicians of the former government would now be tried on charges of treason. Despite talk of retribution, some were encouraged when the new constitution was announced on May 9, because it revealed many continuities with earlier democratic Czechoslovak traditions, including the principle of the separation of powers and the maintenance of the office of president. Furthermore, unlike the Soviet or other Eastern Bloc constitutions, it mentioned neither the dictatorship of the proletariat nor the Communist Party.

Gottwald Officially Becomes President

From February to the end of August 1948, CPC membership increased from 1,409,666 to 2,674,838—over one-third of the voting population of the country. Rudolf Slansky candidly characterized the goal of the membership drive as "the liquidation of the influence of the other parties." This massive increase in active support of the dominant political party made it easier for the next stage of communization to take place. Gottwald officially became president on June 14, 1948, but a deceptive spirit of calm still dominated certain sectors of public life. Displays of anti-Communist sentiments during the traditional Sokol gymnastic festival in Prague in July 1948 served as a pretext for the now thoroughly pliant National Assembly to pass a series of repressive laws in August. These laws authorized the government to arrest, imprison, and try political opponents, as well as detain them in forced-labor camps. The funeral of President Benes, who died in September 1948, led to further anti-regime demonstrations, resulting in more arrests and repressive measures. In the fall of 1948 a series of show trials handed out long terms of imprisonment to leaders of the old regime as well as to "disloyal" army and police officers.

Gottwald's Czechoslovakia was rapidly being transformed into a Stalinist satellite state. The National Assembly had become a rubber-stamp body, meeting no more than twice a year to dutifully approve laws it had in many cases not even seen. On January 1, 1949, the historical provinces of Czechoslovakia were abolished, replaced by 19 administrative regions. Communist power grew rapidly in the new bureaucratic apparatus as chaos reigned and old loyalties evaporated. Within the Communist Party, a repressive spirit of "democratic centralism" now held sway. In practice, this meant that all major decisions with the Party were made not by its Central Committee or even its full Politburo, but by three individuals: Klement Gottwald, Alexej Cepicka, and Prime Minister Antonin Zapotocky (1884–1957). In virtually all areas of Czechoslovak life, repression was the norm in 1949. Not only had the Security Police come under direct Soviet control, many Soviet "advisers" could be found in key positions in the army as well as in such strategic areas of the economy as the uranium mining industry.

The Five Year Plan that began in 1949 not only nationalized the national economy but also radically restructured it—with disastrous consequences. Stalin's single-minded emphasis on heavy industry was slavishly copied by Gottwald and his economic staff. Czechoslovakia, designated by Moscow to be the heavy industry workshop of the Eastern Bloc, was cut off from its Western markets by the Cold War and now became dependent on the U.S.S.R. for most of its raw materials, with prices dictated by Soviet economists. The original Five Year Plan was drastically revised on direct orders from Stalin. Starting in February 1950, at the height of the Cold War, even greater emphasis was placed on heavy industry, a policy that ignored all other branches of the economy.

By late 1949, with the anti-Communist elements exiled or in prison, Communist functionaries deemed unreliable by their former comrades began to suffer exclusion from power and persecution. By this time the Kremlin's fear of "Titoism" and other forms of independent National Communism had led to show trials, resulting in death sentences against leading Communist Party officials in Bulgaria, Hungary, and Poland. Gottwald's first response to Soviet pressures that he initiate similar trials in Czechoslovakia was to reject the idea that his Party—which had operated legally in the 1920s and 1930s—had ever been infiltrated by such agents. Continued demands by Soviet and Hungarian security officials finally led to Gottwald's "request" for Soviet security advisers in October 1949. Almost immediately after their arrival, a witch-hunt atmosphere began to pervade Czechoslovakia.

Although a few dissident Communists had already suffered expulsion and imprisonment in 1948 and 1949, it was not until the last months of 1949 that serious charges began to be leveled against important officials. The editor of the leading CPC newspaper, Vilem Novy, and the Minister of Foreign Trade, Evzen Loebl, were both arrested and expelled from the Party. In April 1950, the Minister of Foreign Affairs, Vladimir Clementis, was removed from his post on charges of having fostered a spirit of Slovak nationalism. The creation in May 1950 of a Ministry of National Security completely independent of both the Ministry of the Interior and military counter-intelligence was an ominous development. Not surprisingly, the new Ministry staff soon included specialists from the Soviet KGB.

Gottwald, who had misgivings about whether he was still in control of the purge, consulted with Stalin in July 1951, and called a halt to a security check on his close associate CPC Secretary General Rudolf Slansky, whom both Gottwald and Stalin had first considered as a possible scapegoat for the growing economic crisis in the country. But Gottwald's orders were simply ignored, since the internal-security operatives took orders directly from the Soviet Embassy, which had very likely received new instructions from Moscow to create a case against Slansky and other "conspirators." Gottwald's last attempt at a "moderate" purge of his Party was the removal of Slansky in September as secretary general. While he had been demoted to the post of deputy prime minister in charge of economic management, it was clear that Slansky had not been purged. But Gottwald had lost control of the situation. The arrival of a new, hard-line Soviet ambassador in Prague in November 1951 meant that the purge within the CPC had taken on a classic Soviet and Stalinist character. No longer was there talk of individual mistakes and failures, but of deep-rooted plots, conspiracies, and "crimes against the people."

Slansky Arrested, Tried

On November 28, 1951, the arrest of Rudolf Slansky was publicly announced. Almost a year was required to prepare Slansky and 13 other defendants for a show trial obviously modeled after those held in the Soviet Union during the Great Purge of the 1930s. The trial had nothing in common with a normal Western judicial procedure since the sentences were determined from the start, and the defendants' "crimes" were totally fabricated charges of treason, conspiracy, and espionage. Varying amounts of physical and psychological torture were used to break the spirits of the defendants, who were carefully prepared. The show trial began in Prague on November 20, 1952; monotonously, the accused repeated the answers they had memorized while in prison, and none denied their "guilt."

A particularly revolting aspect of the Slansky trial was the appearance of family members and friends who appeared to endorse the verdicts; in one instance, the son of a defendant appeared in the courtroom to request the death penalty for his "treasonous" father. None were surprised when the verdict was announced on November 27. Slansky and ten others were sentenced to death, with the three remaining defendants receiving life sentences. One of the most ominous aspects of the trial was the fact that 11 of the 14 defendants were of Jewish origin. They had been accused not only of the standard "crimes" of bourgeois nationalism, Trotskyism and Titoism, but also of a newly discovered form of treason, namely "Zionism." Government propaganda during the trial was not only anti-Zionist but stridently anti-Semitic in tone. President Gottwald did nothing to intervene in the trial, making no attempt to save the lives of his former colleagues, who were hanged on December 3.

It was obvious in early 1953 in both the Soviet Union and Czechoslovakia that more and bloodier purges were on the agenda of the aged, paranoid Joseph Stalin. But Stalin died in early March (perhaps killed by some of his Politburo associates), and Klement Gottwald dutifully went to Moscow to attend the dead dictator's funeral. In Moscow Gottwald became ill, very likely because his poor health (he was in the advanced stages of alcoholism) could not withstand the rigors of a Russian winter (some have suggested, without proof, that he was poisoned). He died in Prague on March 14, 1953, acclaimed a national hero. Gottwald's embalmed body was placed in a mausoleum in Prague (placing him in the select circle of Lenin and Stalin). As late as 1961, monuments in his memory were still being erected in Czechoslovakia.

Unlike the Soviet Union, which quickly began to experience a "thaw" in 1953, post-Gottwald Czechoslovakia remained a repressive society based on harshly Stalinist principles. Although the raising of living standards was announced as a major government goal in September 1953, the fact remained that Gottwald's "old guard," including his successor Antonin Zapotocky and his son-in-law Alexej Cepicka, retained key positions in the regime. Purge trials continued through 1954, political prisoners were not granted amnesty, and a huge Stalin monument was unveiled in Prague in 1955. Only in 1963 did a cautious CPC leadership begin to criticize Gottwald's "cult of the personality," fearful that their own participation in the events of 1948–54 would thus be open to public scrutiny and debate. The brief "Prague Spring" period of reform under **Alexander Dubcek** in 1968 led to many significant revelations of the full intensity of the terror under the Gottwald regime, but the reimposed orthodoxy of 1969–89 prompted ideological hard-liners to once again praise "the Gottwald legacy" in Czechoslovak (and occasionally, Soviet and East German) ideological journals. In a final irony, when Communism was swept away in the streets of Prague in the last weeks of 1989, the discredited Klement Gottwald's portrait was still to be found on circulating banknotes.

Gottwald's Legacy

Klement Gottwald's legacy to Czechoslovakia was one of severe economic dislocation, massive destruction of the foundations of free intellectual life, and a political system that was based for over 40 years on varying amounts of terror, suffocating bureaucracy and relentless propaganda. Between 1948 and 1952, at least 178 people were executed for alleged political crimes, while over 70,000 individuals were arrested and imprisoned, frequently under extremely harsh conditions, for often ill-defined offenses. Besides the immense human suffering and injustice that permeated the political system, the intellectual life of Czechoslovakia, which had been rich, varied, vibrant, and free from 1945 to 1948, was turned into a mockery. From 1950 to 1954 the Czechoslovak book market was swamped with over 2 million volumes of Gottwald's speeches, while his sycophants outdid themselves praising him as "the best disciple of Stalin" and "the heart and brain of our party." For young people, many leisure activities were only available if one joined the Party-run Gottwald Youth. The remnants of Gottwald's inner circle, led by Antonin Novotny, stubbornly managed to hold onto power until 1968, when an attempt was made to create an open-ended form of Marxism, a "Socialism with a human face." This brave effort was perhaps doomed from the start, but Soviet tanks could not create legitimacy for the regime that followed the destruction of the Prague Spring. Most importantly, the reformers of 1968 were able to plant seeds that burst forth in full bloom in 1989 when Communism was swept out of power in another bloodless Prague people's uprising, the "velvet revolution."

SOURCES:

Cotic, Meir. *The Prague Trial: The First Anti-Zionist Show Trial in the Communist Bloc.* Cornwall Books, 1987.

Ebon, Martin. "Prague's Red Premier," in *Forum.* Vol. 108, no. 1, July 1947: pp. 14–20.

Kaplan, Karel. *The Short March: The Communist Takeover in Czechoslovakia 1945–1948.* St. Martin's Press, 1987.

Luza, Radomir and Victor S. Mamatey, eds. *A History of the Czechoslovak Republic, 1918–1948.* Princeton University Press, 1973.

HISTORIC WORLD LEADERS

Renner, Hans. *A History of Czechoslovakia Since 1945.* Routledge, 1989.

Suda, Zdenek L. *Zealots and Rebels: A History of the Communist Party of Czechoslovakia.* Hoover Institution Press, 1980.

FURTHER READING:

Hruby, Peter. *Fools and Heroes: The Changing Role of Communist Intellectuals in Czechoslovakia.* Pergamon Press, 1980.

Sik, Ota. *Czechoslovakia: The Bureaucratic Economy.* International Arts and Sciences Press, 1972.

Wheeler, George Shaw. *The Human Face of Socialism: The Political Economy of Change in Czechoslovakia,* Lawrence Hill, 1973.

Wolchik, Sharon L. *Czechoslovakia in Transition: Politics, Economics and Society.* Pinter Publishers, 1991.

Marie-Olympe de Gouges

(1748–1793)

French writer and activist, who attacked injustice, especially toward slaves and women; authored a charter of modern feminism; and was guillotined at the height of "The Terror" during the French Revolution.

Name variations: Olympe De Gouges (or de Gouges), Madame De Gouges; though she never used her married name, she was indicted under it in 1793. Pronunciation; Ma-re O-lemp de Gooze. Born Marie Gouze in Montauban in Southwestern France in 1748; guillotined on November 3, 1793, at 4:00 P.M.; legal daughter of Pierre Gouze and Olympe Mouisset; married: Louis-Yves Aubry (a restaurateur and caterer), 1765 (died 1766); children: son Pierre.

According to biographer Benoîte Groult, Olympe De Gouges was "the first modern feminist…. A prime example of Woman—unknown—the great omission in historical works. Throughout history, the woman who was active in political and social life whether saint or queen or courtesan or mother has disappeared from our memoirs, reduced to a line in our dictionaries and our textbooks." Feminists such as Groult assert that her absence from the historical record was caused by a single factor: she was a woman. It appears, however, that in the case of Olympe De Gouges, there were additional reasons. She was legally low-born, denied any formal education, married at 16, a mother and widow at 17, and too proud and too independent to use either her late husband's name or to remarry. Her temperament, politics, and primarily her gender put off possible supporters and employers in the literary world, making it enormously difficult for her to find publishers. The works she did manage to get printed were largely ignored and are only now being collected and published.

Beyond the obstacles associated with meddling in the 18th-century world of male politics

"A woman has the right to mount the scaffold; she must also have the right to mount the rostrum."

MARIE-OLYMPE DE GOUGES

Contributed by Frederic M. Crawford, Professor of History, Middle Tennessee State University, Murfreesboro, Tennessee

and of asserting that woman had rights and responsibilities equal to those of man, De Gouges had three strikes against her. First, like her contemporary **Count Mirabeau,** she supported King **Louis XVI** but, unlike Mirabeau, she lived long enough to meddle in his trial. Second, she supported the losing political party in 1792, the Girondins. Third, in 1793 she attacked the leader of the victorious Jacobin political party, **Maximilien Robespierre.** He targeted her and she—like so many Girondin leaders, like the king and the queen, and like Robespierre himself less than a year later—was guillotined, lost in a crowd. De Gouges's one monument, her *Déclaration of the Rights of Woman and the Female Citizen,* was covered up, neglected until recently. So there are many reasons why Olympe De Gouges is disturbingly unknown.

The only source for De Gouges's early life is her autobiographical novel *Mémoire de Mme Valmont,* and what of the novel is factual remains a question for debate. "My birth," she wrote:

> was so bizare that I tremble to set it in public view. I came from a rich and distinguished family whose fortune had been changed by fate. My mother was a daughter of a lawyer with the Marquis de Flaucourt to whom Heaven had given several children…. The eldest of these, Jean-Jacques, did not view my mother with indifference. Age and cultural interests formed between them a sweet sympathy which pointed toward a *liaison dangereuse.* Perceiving the passion, their parents separated them. My mother was married off and Jean-Jacques was sent to Paris where he began a career in drama…. He returned to his province to find that the one he had loved and was still in love with was married and had several children. How can I say this with modesty and still be believed? I came into this world the same day as his return and the whole town believed that was the result of the love of those two. Jean-Jacques showed tenderness toward me and forbade my being put in a foundling home and publicly recognized me as his daughter. In fact it would have been difficult for him to hide the truth since we looked so much alike. He tried every way to get my mother to let him raise me. Doubtlessly, my education would have been much better, but my mother always refused and this dispute caused them to split up leaving me the victim.

The Jean-Jacques of the novel was Jean-Jacques Le Franc de Pomignan (d. 1784), a magistrate and writer of local fame. His letter answering De Gouges's request for recognition, if not spurious, appears to admit parentage:

CHRONOLOGY

1748	Born in Montauban in Southwestern France
1766	Son Pierre born
1784	Antislavery play accepted by the Comedie Française
1786	"The Loves of Chérubin" performed successfully at the Théâtre Italien
1789	"Slavery of Negroes" performed by the Comédie Française, causing an uproar
1791	Sent *Déclaration des droits de la femme et de la citoyenne* ("Declaration of the Rights of Woman and the Female Citizen") with a cover letter to Marie Antoinette
1792	Received *hommage* from the legislature for "patriotic works"; appeared before the legislature in support of *un pauvre* ("a poor man") who was voted relief
1793	Wrote *The Three Urns,* attacking Robespierre; arrested and accused before the Paris Tribunal for "making a criminal attempt on the sovereignty of the people"; guillotined, according to her obituary, "for sedition and for having forgotten the virtues of her sex"

> Your letter, Madame, has awakened sad and disturbing memories from the past…. I well know, most unhappily for me, that you are not a stranger to me, but you have no right to claim from me the title of paternity. You were born legitimate and under the sanctity of marriage. If it is true, however, that Nature speaks in you and that my imprudent tender affection for you in your infancy and the acknowledgement of your mother assure you that I am your father, imitate me and lament the fate of those who have given life.

Was de Pomignan her biological father, and did De Gouges inherit her intellect and creativity from him? Or did the fiction of a noble birth leaven the rough baker's dough so that it rose beyond itself? De Pompignan was correct about legitimate birth. There are witnesses to a birth certificate showing Marie Gouze born to Pierre Gouze, a butcher at Montauban, and Olympe Mouisset, a trinket seller. De Gouges wrote nothing, however, about these two, and there is no record of any formal education. Of her marriage at 16 to Louis-Yves Aubry, a restauranteur and caterer at Montauban, she wrote little, later calling him an old man she never loved, who was neither rich nor well-born. He died soon after the birth of their son Pierre, leaving a small pension.

In widowhood at Montauban, De Gouges developed a friendship with Jacques Biétrix de

Roziéres, a contractor in military transport, and he took her to Paris. Her biographers believe that she refused to marry de Roziéres because she viewed marriage as "the tomb of faith and love."

De Gouges was known for her beauty, leading Mary Lafon, in her *Ninon* (1789), to describe her "eyes from which spurted out electric sparks of fire of thought and of passion; superb black hair flowing profusely around a face marked by perfect teeth; a greek profile and an admirably designed head." A male colleague at the Comédie Française praised her figure but found her coiffure "flamboyant"—a distraction from her intellect.

She Begins Extensive Writing

In Paris from 1767 or 1768, De Gouges developed the reputation of a "*femme galante*"—an attractive, free-spirited, unattached female with an active social and cultural life replete with many friends, many of them respectable. She may have learned to write during this period, but most of her works seem to have been dictated to secretaries/friends. (In fact, many well-known writers of the day employed assistants.) Even with their assistance, her lack of formal education is reflected in her works. "Si j'ecris mal," she once wrote, "je pense bien." ("I write bad, but I think good.") Her biographer Olivier Blanc has identified 135 writings of De Gouges plus seven articles in six different newspapers—four of which are antislavery pieces. Twenty-nine are novels and short stories, 45 are theater pieces, and 64 are political pamphlets, tracts, brochures, and placards.

De Gouges's first play is considered her best dramatic work. She called it, "the first effort of my feeble talent." "Zamour and Mirza, or the Happy Shipwreck" (happy because two slaves were liberated) was written in 1784 and submitted anonymously to the selection committee of the Comédie Française, which accepted it the following year. Performance of the play was long delayed. Powerful colonial interests feared that sympathetic portrayal of blacks might threaten the profitability of French colonies. De Gouges was threatened with a *lettre de cachet* (arrest order signed by the king) and actors refused to blacken their faces. In 1789, the play was retitled "Slavery of Negroes" and was performed by the Comédie Française. Uproar ensued. The mayor of Paris condemned it as an incendiary piece which would cause revolt in the colonies. One critic reviewed the play in only one sentence: "We can only say that in order to write a good dramatic work, one must have hair on the chin." The production closed after three performances.

During the five years between the writing and the performance of this first play, De Gouges wrote many dramas, of which only a few texts survive. A one-act play "Lucinde and Cardino, or Made Crazy by Love" was considered by the Comédie Française but refused. A full text has not been found. A three-act play "The Loves of Chérubin" was written as a sequel to the popular "Mariage de Figaro" ("Marriage of Figaro") by France's best-known dramatist Pierre-Augustin Le Caron de Beaumarchais (1732–99). Retitled "The Unexpected Marriage of Chérubin," the play was favorably reviewed by La Harpe (Frédéric-César, 1754–1838) in the *Mercure de France* and considered by the Comédie Italien and rejected. De Gouges believed that the refusal was due to a vigorous campaign led by Beaumarchais. A five-act play "The Philosopher Corrected, or The Alleged Cuckhold" was printed and attracted attention in 1787. De Gouges termed it a "blunder" but one pleasing to her. It was not performed, De Gouges believed, due to a cabal incensed by the spectacle of a male portrayed in a less than noble light, especially in his love life.

Early in 1787, Finance Minister Calonne persuaded King Louis XVI to assemble a blue-ribbon panel called the assembly of Notables to consider Calonne's reform package to rescue finances. Calonne hoped that the assembly would endorse his reforms, thus influencing the law courts to enregister them. Enthralled by the constant news reports of the Assembly's proceedings, De Gouges turned her imagination to politics.

In 1788, De Gouges published *Letter to the People, or Project for a Patriotic Bank by a Female Citizen*. She called for a voluntary tax to fund a bank which "would be the envy of all the courts of Europe and shame the law courts" which had refused the king's tax edict. Admitting that some of her sex admired luxury to excess, she called upon women who would ordinarily purchase ten hats to buy only two and bank the difference. "Oh, France, France!" De Gouges wrote. "Raise up your head! Don't let your neighbor pity you! Let the People, the law courts, and the King form one family and let the Nation spread its splendor!" Interestingly, the National Assembly, when later organized, did decree a voluntary tax. It was named *Contribution patriotique* and donors received considerable publicity. Proceeds, however, disappeared into the General Fund. Leaders of the National Assembly and Finance Minister Jacques Necker struggled mightily to establish a national bank. The disastrous consequences of the lack of such a bank (until **Napoleon**) demonstrate that they and the woman De Gouges were correct.

Also in 1788, De Gouges published *Reflections on Blacks*. She used this work to urge performances of her play "Zamour and Myrza" (which would be performed the following year), but also made this argument: everywhere in nature one sees variety—different kinds of trees, different kinds of flowers, different kinds of birds, fish, and so forth. Likewise one sees different kinds of human beings. Every kind of human is as precious as trees and other parts of nature are precious. Soon, the Revolution would abolish slavery. Whether or not her work influenced this progress, she was—as in the case of a national bank—in advance of such change.

In 1790, De Gouges's play "The Convent, or Forced Vows" had 80 performances at the Théâtre Comique et Lyrique à la rue Bondy, but other theaters refused her works; "Rien de la trop arrogante Olympe" ("Nothing by the most arrogant Olympe"), as the Comédiens de l'Illustre Maison put it.

On the second of April 1791, when Mirabeau, president of the National Assembly, died, De Gouges immediately wrote a funeral ode and, within a week, a one-act play "Mirabeau in the Elysian Fields" (in mythology, the home of the blessed after death). This play, performed in Paris on April 14, 1791, by the Comedie Italien, was truly avant-garde. Suffice it to say that among the "blessed" greeting Mirabeau in the Elysian Fields were King Louis XIV, Voltaire, Montesquieu, Rousseau, and Benjamin Franklin.

She Presents Her Declaration of Women's Rights

In the summer of 1791, De Gouges authored her *Déclaration des droits de la femme et de la citoyenne* (Declaration of the Rights of Woman and the Female Citizen) patterned after the *Declaration of the Rights of Man* and *The Citizen* decreed as the first part of the Constitution by the National Assembly in August 1789. De Gouges sent a copy to the National Assembly then ending its term and a copy with a cover letter to Queen **Marie Antoinette.** No one has found evidence that the queen, or the National Assembly, or its successor the Legislative Assembly, ever admitted to having received it. The Legislative Assembly once voted hommage to De Gouges for "patriotic acts" (not mentioning the *Déclaration*) and, in its closing days, even received her. The preamble to the *Déclaration* began with characteristic directness and lack of diplomacy: "Man, are you capable of being just? It is a woman who asks you this question. Who has given you the authority to oppress my sex?" Unspeakably radical then, the *Déclaration* is still

radical today (in it, De Gouges insisted on exact equality, including combat roles in the military).

In 1792, De Gouges wrote a five-act play "France Saved, or The Tyrant Dethroned." Set at the Château des Tuilieres, the play gives lessons in patriotism to valets, lessons in good manners to a princess, and political instruction to Marie Antoinette. That fall, De Gouges enthusiastically endorsed the proclamation of the Republic, but attempted to defend King Louis whom the Jacobins insisted on trying for treason. Having overthrown the constitution, the Jacobins now demanded the king's death for violating that same constitution. De Gouges and the Girondins opposed the death sentence and few still argue that they were wrong to do so. The execution of King Louis XVI on January 21, 1793, Monday morning 8:00 A.M., was followed by the entrance of England into the War of the First Coalition and by a blood bath in France. The Girondin leadership was arrested in the early summer of 1793 and guillotined in the fall.

Increasingly, De Gouges viewed Robespierre as a dictator violating liberty and the Republic. In a public letter, *"Response to the Justification by Maximilien Robespierre, addressed to Jerome Petion, President of the Convention,"* she asked, "Do you know how far you are from Cato?" Then, continuing the comparison of Mirabeau to the virtuous Roman senator who opposed Pompey, Crassus, and Caesar, she added, "As far as Marat from Mirabeau, as far as the mosquito from the eagle, and as far as the eagle from the sun." That did it, of course. It was De Gouges or Robespierre. De Gouges recognized this when she wrote:

> Therefore I propose that you take a bath with me in the Seine River. But in order to wash away the stains which have covered you … we will attach sixteen or twenty-four weight cannonballs to our feet and we will thrust ourselves together into the waves. Your death will calm the public mind and the death of a pure life [De Gouges'] will disarm Heaven.

Such sentiments, directed against someone trying not to appear a dictator, were not actionable even in a Revolutionary Tribunal, but De Gouges's essay *The Three Urns* (assembly ballots were put into vases or urns), calling for free elections, touched every member of the Jacobin ruling party and was actionable. Arrested July 20, 1793, De Gouges was accused before the Paris Tribunal on November 2. The next day she was guillotined. Eight months later, in the Revolutionary month of Thermidor (July), the majority of Robespierre's

Jacobin party surprised and guillotined him. Once again, De Gouges had been ahead of events.

SOURCES:

Blanc, Olivier. *Une femme de libertes: Olympe de Gouges.* Rev. ed. Syros/Alternatives, 1989.

Gouges, Marie-Olympe de. *Politsche Schriften in Auswald (Hamburger Historische Studien).* Hamburg: Helmut Buske Verlag, 1979.

Gouges, Olympe de. *Oeuvres, presente par Benoîte Groult (Collection Mille et une femmes).* Mercure de France, 1986.

FURTHER READING:

Conner, S. "Marie-Olympe De Gouges," in *Historical Dictionary of the French Revolution.* Samuel F. Scott and Barry Rothaus, eds. Greenwood Press, 1995.

Landes, Joan B. *Women and the Public Sphere in the Age of the French Revolution.* Cornell University Press, 1988.

Levy, Darline Gay, Harriet Branson Applewhite, and Mary Durham Johnson. *Women in Revolutionary Paris.* University of Illinois Press, 1979.

Schama, Simon. *Citizens: A Chronicle of the French Revolution.* Knopf, 1989.

Henry Grattan

(1746–1820)

Statesman, skilled orator, and member of Parliament, who championed the causes of Irish legislative independence, freedom of Irish trade, and Catholic emancipation.

"A country enlightened as Ireland, chartered as Ireland, armed as Ireland, and injured as Ireland, will be satisfied with nothing less than liberty."

HENRY GRATTAN

The struggles of the Irish people to secure political and religious liberties, in the late 18th and early 19th centuries, were headed by members of the Protestant minority in Ireland. The influence on, and accomplishments of, Henry Grattan in these matters occurred against a backdrop of Enlightenment thought, imperial wars, and revolutionary changes in European governments.

The Grattans of the 18th century were traditionally Dubliners, and in the early part of the century, the family was in transition from the professional to the landed-gentry ranks of Irish society. Born on July 4, 1746, to a prosperous family, Henry Grattan was the only child of James Grattan, a lawyer and magistrate, and Mary Marlay, daughter of Thomas Marlay, who was later a chief justice. Among the boy's uncles were Colonel Marlay, who had fought with distinction at the Battle of Minden, and Richard, who was later bishop of Waterford.

Henry began school at Mr. Ball's Academy in Great Ship Street, Dublin, where John Fitzgibbon, the future earl of Clare and a Grattan political adversary, was a schoolmate. After receipt of punishment deemed unjust by his father, Henry was

Born on July 4, 1746, in Dublin, Ireland; died in London, England, on June 4, 1820; only child of James Grattan and Mary Marlay; married: Henrietta Fitzgerald, 1782; children: two sons, Henry and James; and two daughters.

Contributed by Donna Beaudin, Ph.D. candidate in History, University of Guelph, Guelph, Ontario, Canada

CHRONOLOGY

1775–83	American Revolutionary War
1775	Grattan entered the Irish House of Commons
1780	Demanded legislative independence for Ireland
1783	Quarreled with Flood on House floor
1784	Pitt's India Act put East India Company under government control
1790	Edmund Burke published *Reflections on the Revolution in France*
1797	Grattan declined to stand for re-election
1798	Irish emigration to British North America began; rebellion in Ireland
1801	Act of Union of Great Britain and Ireland came into force
1805	Grattan entered the English House of Commons as a member for Malton
1820	Died on journey to London
1829	Catholic Emancipation Act permitted Roman Catholics in Great Britain to sit as members in Parliament

moved to a school run by a Mr. Young. Deemed "a forward youth," Grattan enjoyed literature and poetry, rural scenery, and correspondence. As a young man, he began regular correspondences with his uncle, Colonel Marlay, and with a young military man named Broome. The amount of letters exchanged between Grattan and Broome "became voluminous"; Grattan wrote in a manner characterized later by his son as forcible and "even picturesque," borrowing from the mid-1760s style of poet and satirist Alexander Pope.

When Grattan was 15, his father was elected to the Irish House of Commons as a representative, and recorder, for the city of Dublin. The Septennial Act, in effect in England since 1716, did not apply to the Irish legislature where a Parliament lasted as long as the monarch reigned; elections were held only with the accession of a new monarch. Even from his teen years, Grattan disagreed with his father in political matters and philosophies. Biographer Stephen L. Gwynn notes that "the only pleasant thing to remember about the relations between the Recorder and his son is that the father took an interest in the son's education." In 1763, young Grattan entered Trinity College in Dublin as a fellow-commoner where he was encouraged to pursue the passion for the classics that had been developing in the past few years.

Nearly coincident with his graduation from Trinity College was the news of the sudden death of his father. Due to his liberal views, Grattan inherited the Cavan estate but not the house at Belcamp where he had spent most of his youth.

Moving to London, he began legal studies and commenced preparation for admittance to the bar. As a law student, Grattan regularly attended the political debates in Parliament. He particularly enjoyed listening to the elder **William Pitt** speak in the House of Lords. It was during these formative years that Grattan "was determined to learn all the accomplishments of a gentleman." But until he was called to the bar in 1772, Grattan led the high life. There was considerable political excitement in London which fueled his interest. He also enjoyed attending theatrical and operatic performances and, in 1774, acted in the play "The Mask of Comus."

In January 1772, Grattan received his call to the bar and entered legal practice. He soon gave this up, however, as his interest in politics continued to grow, and he returned to Ireland where his income was less than £500 per year. Although he continued to write, mostly poetry, and was a recognized penman by his mid-20s, Grattan gradually settled into a political career. Two periods are readily identifiable in his public life: the first coincides with his involvement in Irish political affairs; the second corresponds roughly with his membership in the Imperial Parliament, following the parliamentary union of Ireland and Great Britain.

Grattan Joins Irish House of Commons

In the late 1760s, statesman and orator Henry Flood asserted, in reference to the Declaratory and Octennial Acts, that Irish patriots could do nothing if they did not have political power. Such leadership spurred Grattan to action in the growing movement advocating autonomy for the Irish legislature. In 1775, Grattan was brought into the Irish House of Commons through the patronage of Lord Charlemont, for the borough of the same name. Charlemont was not a statesman in any sense of the word, but he did provide Grattan with political connections. In the face of the emerging revolution in America, Irish parliamentarians were told by their British counterparts that the Irish case was a dangerous one and that the British Parliament was supreme over the Irish. Following the Irish Parliament's October 1775 condemnation of "the American rebellion," Grattan made his first parliamentary speech in December against a motion that sought to ensure a flat-rate expense payment for absentee vice-treasurers of Ireland. From his first speech until his last, Grattan relied

HISTORIC WORLD LEADERS

heavily on eloquence and the transmission of his political passions to compensate for his lack of impressive physical stature and for his high-pitched voice.

"Grattan meditated on creating the political independence of Ireland," notes Daniel Owen Madden. "He was bent on doing something great and glorious which would transmit his name to remote ages." Later biographers have generally concurred with Madden's assessment. Of Grattan's involvement in the late 1770s with the Irish Volunteers, Stephen Gwynn believes that Grattan wanted "to be the champion of an oppressed nation, rather than of an oppressed class within that nation." By 1779 Grattan had begun to establish his leadership within the Irish House of Commons. High-minded without being arrogant, he fought for the repeal of the 1494 Poyning's Law (which made Irish legislation dependent on English Privy Council approval), though he had opposed the Catholic Relief Bill that was introduced in Parliament the year previous.

In the autumn of 1779, Grattan proposed a motion to lift the parliamentary restrictions that had been imposed upon Irish trade by the British Parliament. It also intended that, in the future, the Irish legislature should alone regulate Irish trade. Early in 1780, freer Irish trade was secured from British Parliament with the help of Prime Minister Lord North, though the Irish were excluded from trading in the area of the East India Company's monopoly. The British mercantile interest considered these results alarming. Grattan, and other patriotic constitutionalists in the Irish Parliament, recognized that freer trade was meaningless without parallel reform that would provide for parliamentary independence for Ireland. On April 19, 1780, Grattan introduced a parliamentary motion to this effect. Fellow Irishman **Edmund Burke**, a member of the British House of Commons, considered Grattan a "madman" on this issue, even though they shared the view that the British constitution was "the very definition of freedom."

As part of the parliamentary motion of April 1780, Grattan delivered a "Declaration of Irish Rights" in which he outlined his objectives:

> I wish for nothing but to breathe … the air of liberty…. I never will be satisfied so long as the meanest cottager in Ireland has a link of the British chain clanking to his rags, he may be naked, he shall not be in irons.

This inflammatory speech caused other Irishmen to regard him as "the prophet of Irish redemption." To this end, Grattan recognized it would be necessary to bring "the people" into politics to fight the corruption. In 1780, he also sponsored a tenantry bill that sought to clarify and protect the legal position of leaseholders in Ireland, and unsuccessfully opposed the enactment of a perpetual mutiny bill. He proposed an amendment to the mutiny bill the following year, which was voted down.

Grattan continued to campaign for legislative independence for Ireland after the fall of the North government in 1782 in Westminster. The pace he set for himself contributed to an illness in April of that year, but he managed to deliver his "Declaration of Irish Independence" which articulated three demands: the repeal of Poyning's Law, the repeal of the 1719 Declaratory Act, and the repeal of the perpetual Mutiny Act. These demands were met. At the age of only 36, Grattan's efforts had effected "the Revolution of 1782," though he had faced and endured the hostility of Henry Flood. Flood advocated independence for the Irish legislature and sweeping reforms while Grattan favored the conciliatory approach. Though the Irish Parliament voted Grattan £50,000 in recognition of his services to Ireland, Flood managed to discredit his opponent and the achievements of 1782.

At this busy time in his political life, Grattan's health deteriorated. In August, he went to Spa (Belgium) to take a rest cure. While there, he was re-elected colonel of the Independent Corps of Dublin Volunteers. A month following his October return, he announced his engagement to Henrietta Fitzgerald, reputedly "a lady of great beauty." Married before the end of the year, the couple eventually had two sons, James and Henry, and two daughters.

Flood and Grattan Quarrel

Feelings of bitter animosity between Flood and Grattan continued for the next two years, erupting into a bitter quarrel on the floor of the House. In November 1783, the two men came close to dueling to resolve their differences. Along with his own position, Flood's efforts managed to effectively destroy "Grattan's Parliament," as it was called. While Grattan eventually regained his leadership, Flood never recovered his earlier stature.

Following the achievement of Irish parliamentary independence, the Volunteers began to press for full political rights for Roman Catholics in Ireland. At their Dublin Convention, they proposed parliamentary reform, but the convention lacked leadership and dissolved, thus ending their "moral power." While the Volunteers espoused strong views, they failed to carry the issue of parliamentary reform into Irish politics. Grattan felt the effects of this. "Harshly censured for his inaction in Volunteer Reform" and criticized for being too much of a neutral in politics, Grattan perceived the Irish aristocracy as more patriotic than they actually were. Following the Volunteers' 1783 breach with Parliament, Grattan's political career was "virtually terminated" though he continued to sit in the Irish House of Commons.

While Grattan's popularity in Ireland fluctuated during the early 1780s, by 1785, he was held in considerable esteem by the general public in both Ireland and England. He sought to establish harmony between the two governments, and his popularity increased, especially in Ireland, by managing to impose the will of Ireland upon the British government. Parliamentary reform, however, continued to elude Ireland.

In 1788, Grattan made a parliamentary motion for an inquiry into the condition and practices of the tithe system in Ireland. As always, he was acting in accordance with his Whiggish principles. Obsessed with constitutionality and steadfastly opposed to corruption, Henry Grattan was at the peak of his oratorical powers in the early 1790s. As a member of the Opposition, he spoke on such issues as pensions, places, the Dublin Police Act, the sale of peerages, abolition of places created by the recent Viceroy of Ireland, raising of taxes on distillers, and limitations on the powers of the Lords Lieutenant of Ireland. Philosophically inclined to reform, by which means "he sought to avoid revolution," he was less consistent in the matter of extending the electoral franchise.

The introduction of Theobald Wolfe Tone into Irish politics in 1791 marked "a new birth" of democracy in England. Though Henry Grattan was Wolfe Tone's senior by only nine years, the two men were of different political generations. In the autumn of 1791, Wolfe Tone organized the first branch of the United Irishmen, an organization that Grattan always distrusted. Grattan advocated "a policy of gradualness" to secure full political right for Irish Catholics as part of a larger objective of Irish unity and, in so doing, Gwynn writes, "dealt too generously with the representatives of England, and left himself without the means to bargain."

By 1794, Grattan believed that Ireland was ready for political and judicial reform, and even asserted that such rational reform as would benefit the country's Catholic population would halt the spread of dangerous Jacobin principles. By the next year, it was clear to Grattan that the real barrier to Catholic Emancipation was the personal feelings of King George III. With his health weakening, Grattan declined to stand for re-election for the city of Dublin in 1797. "Never a robust man," he retired to his home at Tinnehinch in County Wicklow. In retirement, Grattan traveled and was out of the country when the Irish Rebellion began in May 1798. Under United Irishmen leadership, pressure for an independent Irish Republic increased and military aid was sought from France. The rebellion's effects were felt most in Ulster and Wexford Counties. Grattan was denounced by authorities as "an enemy to his county," and troops briefly contemplated blowing up his house in Tinnehinch. A target for attack in contemporary pamphlet literature, his name was struck from the Privy Council, and his portrait at Trinity College was taken down.

When Grattan returned to Ireland in January 1799, his health had completely deteriorated; "a nervous wreck," he was under medical instructions to abstain from reading about or speaking of things political. Upon conclusion of the rebellion, Grattan returned to Parliament, as member for County Wicklow, to fight against British Prime Minister **William Pitt the Younger**'s proposed Act of Union following the Irish Rebellion. Grattan was vehemently opposed to the idea of a legislative union of Ireland and Great Britain and spoke eloquently against it, making his final speech on the topic in May 1800. His efforts were to no avail, and the union was effected in January 1801.

With the union of Ireland and Great Britain, Grattan again retired to private life. At the age of 53, he concluded that his political career was at an end. Again his retirement was short-lived, though he declined an invitation in 1803 to accept a seat in the Parliament of the United Kingdom. Only two years later, Grattan entered the English House of Commons as a member for Malton. In 1806, he was returned as one of the members for the City of Dublin, which he continued to serve until his death. As an MP in the united Parliament, Henry Grattan "never desisted from his endeavor to serve Ireland," though these were years of leisure compared to his Irish parliamentary career. His chief concern while serving in the British Parliament was Catholic Emancipation, for which he fought tirelessly. Grattan, a Protestant, perceived it to be "both the price of the Union and intrinsically just."

Grattan's health continued to decline, and in August 1819 he went to his house in Tinnehinch to rest, with the intention of returning to Parliament. The Catholic cause was too important to be abandoned. George III died in 1820 and elections were held; Grattan was returned, without opposition, as MP for Dublin. His doctors, however, advised a respite from parliamentary activity. By the beginning of May, Grattan was very ill but continued to work, declaring "my last breath belongs to my country." On his return to London, too ill to travel by carriage, the last portion of his journey was accomplished by canal from Liverpool. Though Grattan reached London, he died there on June 4, 1820. Political and literary tributes were paid, and he was buried in Westminster Abbey. His eldest son James served in the 9th Light Dragoons, in Parliament (1821–41) and as a privy councillor. Grattan's younger son, also named Henry, served in Parliament (1826–61), published a collection of his father's speeches in 1820, and a multivolume biography of his father that appeared between 1839–46. Catholic Emancipation, the objective of Henry Grattan's political life, was achieved in 1829.

SOURCES:

Grattan, Henry, Jr. *The Speeches of the Right Hon. Henry Grattan.* 2nd ed. Edited by Daniel Owen Madden. James Duffy, 1874.

Gwynn, Stephen Lucius. *Henry Grattan and His Times.* Harrap, 1939.

O'Connell, Maurice R. *Irish Politics and Social Conflict in the Age of the American Revolution.* University of Pennsylvania Press, 1965.

Powell, John Stocks. "Henry Grattan: Enlightenment in Ireland," in *History Today.* Vol. 27 (1977).

FURTHER READING:

Beckett, J. C. *The Making of Modern Ireland 1603–1923.* Faber & Faber, 1989 (first published 1969).

Koebner, R. "The Early Speeches of Henry Grattan," in *Bulletin of the Institute of Historical Research.* Vol. 30 (1957).

O'Brien, Gerard. *Anglo-Irish Politics in the Age of Grattan and Pitt.* Irish Academic Press, 1987.

———. "The Grattan Mystique," in *Eighteenth-Century Ireland.* Vol. 1 (1986).

Gregory I, the Great

(c. 540–604)

Roman magistrate turned pope, who detached the Catholic Church from reliance on the failing Roman Empire, purified it internally, and adapted it to the political conditions of post-Roman Europe.

Born c. 540; died 604; great grandson of Pope Felix III (483–92) and a relative, possibly nephew, of Pope Agapitus (535–36); son of Gordianus (a wealthy Roman landowner). Predecessor: Pope Gelasius II. Successor: Pope Sabinian (604–06).

Pope Gregory I governed the Catholic Church while the Roman Empire, in which it had grown mighty, decayed around him. The headquarters of the Empire, along with most of its resources and armies, had shifted to Constantinople, leaving the once-proud city of Rome half ruined—prey to successive barbarian invasions, fever, famine, and plague. In his 14-year pontificate (590–604), Gregory managed to set the Church on its feet administratively, come to terms with the barbarian Lombard invaders, establish stricter discipline among lax churchmen, and establish conditions for the Church to survive in a fragmented medieval world. He established a new Christian calendar, a liturgy for Catholics everywhere, and one of the timeless musical forms of Catholic worship, the Gregorian chant. He later achieved sainthood when a cluster of miracles was attributed to his supernatural intervention in the years after his death.

Born in about 540, Gregory came from a rich and powerful Roman family but never enjoyed the palmy days of Roman supremacy. Already in his childhood, Rome had been overrun by the Goths and, as he remarked on assuming the

"Gregory set the papacy and the Church on a path that was to make it the predominant force in shaping a new civilization out of the old—a new political and cultural and social unity called Europe."

Thomas Bokenkotter

Contributed by Patrick Allitt, Assistant Professor of History, Emory University, Atlanta, Georgia

papacy, "I have taken charge of an old and grievously shattered ship." Said one of his biographer's, Jeffrey Richards, Rome "had become a city of ghosts and memories, a crumbling relic of lost imperial splendour." Gregory began life with a classical education, one of the last generations to enjoy the old amenities of civilized Rome, though it was attenuated by his never learning to speak Greek. He appears to have been familiar with Roman law and began a rapid rise as a city administrator, reaching the position of Prefect of Rome by 573. But he was also a devout Christian and was devoting much of his fortune to the Church. Establishing a monastery in Rome and six more on family lands in Sicily, he then decided to give up his worldly life altogether in about 574–75 and become an ordinary monk at the Roman monastery on the Caelian Hill. Following **Jesus'** injunction to the wealthy young man (Matthew 19:21), he sold his remaining possessions, gave the money to the poor, and took the monastic vow of poverty.

Gregory lived as a monk for six years before being called back into the world by Pope Gelasius II, who needed a man gifted in administration and loyal to the Church to act as an emissary *(apocrisiarius)*. Traveling to the imperial court in Constantinople, Gregory pleaded with the emperor Tiberius Constantine for troops and supplies for the defense of Rome, but the expedition sent out by the hard-pressed emperor—who had never been to Rome—was not sufficient to drive back the encroaching Lombard invaders. Ravenna, the imperial stronghold in Italy, was also unwilling to expend forces on behalf of Rome. Gregory, a patriotic Roman, was dismayed by this neglect of the city which, to him, was synonymous with civilization.

Remaining a papal legate back in Rome, Gregory gained wide repute for his administrative integrity and his ascetic life. Like the early Egyptian and Syrian Christian monks, he favored a severe regimen of fasting and self-mortification to drive away the temptations of the flesh and to glorify the spirit. This mortification ruined his physical constitution. When Pope Gelasius II died of the plague in the catastrophic year 590 (also a year of flood and famine in Rome), Gregory—against his will—was acclaimed pope, the first monk ever to hold that position. Already a sick man, he was to remain gravely ill throughout his pontificate.

For reasons of health, as well as from a genuine love of contemplative life, he shied away from this office but decided at last that he was duty-bound to accept it. Like **Augustine of Hippo,** another of the great Church Fathers, Gregory acknowledged that God's purpose requires partici-

CHRONOLOGY

c. 540	Gregory born
573	Appointed Prefect of Rome
574–75	Resigned and formed monastic community on Caelian Hill
579	Appointed papal *apocrisiarius* (legate) to Constantinople
590	Elected Pope Gregory
592	Negotiated Provisional Treaty with the Lombards
596	Sent Augustine on mission to England
598	Negotiated unconditional two-year peace treaty with Lombard Agilulf
604	Gregory died

pation in life on earth as well as in the City of God, and that not all men are called to lives of retreat in monastic seclusion. Groaning with pain (graphically described in dozens of his surviving letters), he took on more tasks from his new throne. On one occasion, when he was already weakened by severe fasting, the monks force-fed him for fear that his death was otherwise certain. It is appropriate that his longest surviving work, the *Moralia*, should be a meditation on the biblical book of Job, the greatest sufferer at God's hands of the Old Testament.

Gregory continued to live an austere life as pope, living collectively with monks, though now in the Lateran Palace; he emphasized that his role was to serve, rather than to command. He was the first to take the papal title—used ever since—"Servant of the Servants of God."

From many figures in that era we have only the most fragmentary remains from which to piece together a life and character, but from Gregory's pen we still possess over 800 letters, along with several of his books on the saints, morality, and the proper conduct of the Church. Acclaimed in his own day as masterpieces of Christian literature, they were copied widely. Catholics through the ages have treated him, along with Saints Augustine, Ambrose, and Jerome, as one of the four Latin Fathers of the Church. His literary remains enable us to gain a sense of how Gregory conducted his papal reign and how he dealt with the burdens of his age.

Gregory is, without question, a puzzle. His administrative letters show him to have been a severe and unbending governor, tough-minded, practical, hard to deceive, and untiring in his work. Yet his contemplative works show a spiritual personality so detached from cares of the world that it is difficult to believe we are in the presence of the same man. Like many Christians in the first centuries after Jesus, he believed that the end of the world was extremely close and that his task was to bring as many people as possible into the Christian faith before the catastrophe struck. Historian Richards writes:

> The psychological effect of the apparently unending onslaught of plague and war was immense. For many religious people, including Gregory himself, they were the scriptural precursors of the Apocalypse. There was a strong stimulus to monasticism, as men and women abandoned the world and took to the cloister in large numbers to prepare their souls for the next life. For many others the constant plagues, and wars provided a powerful stimulus to primitive superstition.

Gregory himself was, by our standards, a thoroughly superstitious man. Every event in the known world seemed to him a portent of motions in the hidden world, evidence of God's pleasure or anger, of devils at work, and of the unraveling of long foretold prophecy. "Natural disasters such as earthquakes, fires, or storms," says historian Carol Straw commenting on Gregory's works, "are expressions of God's wrath, or his trial of man; a nun's indigestion is not caused by the cabbage but by the devil lurking in its leaves." It is tempting to smile dismissively at Gregory's supernatural explanation of events both great and small, but it is important, while doing so, to see him as a powerful intellect nonetheless, and a doughty political opponent of the disorder about him.

Gregory Claims Supremacy of Rome

The supremacy of Rome as the seat of the Church was not yet settled. Rome had risen to preeminence in the first three centuries A.D. because it was the center of the Empire, and, soon after **Constantine**'s conversion in 312, Christianity had become the official religion of the Empire. But now that Rome lay in decay, the patriarch of the new imperial city, Constantinople, appeared to have a better claim to supremacy than his counterpart in Rome. The patriarchs of Alexandria, Jerusalem, and Antioch also laid claims.

Using biblical evidence and the force of tradition to make his case, Gregory worked hard to persuade Emperor Maurice to recognize Rome's continuing supremacy. Remorseless in his complaints against the patriarch of Constantinople, and Maurice himself for slighting the centrality of Rome, Gregory showed an unbecoming glee when the emperor, with whom he had squabbled for years, was murdered by one of his generals in 602. From Gregory's day, nevertheless, we can trace the Roman supremacy of the Catholic Church; indeed, Gregory is the man who in many respects laid the foundations of the papacy as world leader of Catholicism.

Recurrent wars, plundering by the Lombards and imperial soldiers, and the general political instability of central Italy led Gregory to intervene to restore order. Gradually taking upon the Church the old civil duty of distributing free grain in times of famine, he also took over the administration of justice, arbitrating civil cases as well as those concerning the Church. In later centuries, especially at the time of the Reformation, the political interests of the papacy became a scandal, but in Gregory's day they were the only alternative to anarchy.

When necessary, moreover, Gregory could take up the sword. Some letters find him paying soldiers, arranging for monks to help to defend Rome, threatening and cajoling the *exarch* (governor) of Ravenna to send aid, and sending officers to defend threatened imperial positions. This military work seemed to him viable only with a strongly centralized command structure. Historian Straw remarks:

> Increasingly polarized, Gregory's society gradually lost a neutral and civilian middle ground. Too often the Church stood face-to-face with the sword. Only a rigorously hierarchical order could be trusted to contain the violent potential of the secular members of society.

Favoring hierarchy and militarized monarchy as organizational principles blessed by God Himself, Gregory made no objection to slavery; he sometimes gave slaves as gifts to loyal churchmen. But he repeated St. Paul's injunctions to slave owners to act prudently, remembering that they and their slaves alike were brothers in Christ. When warfare broke out, as it did repeatedly in the years of his reign, he would devote Church funds to ransoming prisoners of every social rank, even if it meant selling the gold plate of the Church to raise the money. He also faced a massive logistical problem with refugees from war zones; at one point, he was subsidizing 3,000 displaced nuns in Rome alone and trying to prevent licentiousness and crime among other refugees.

Within the Church, Gregory disciplined bishops who were abusing their powers by buying and selling offices, living adulterously with women rather than obeying the law of celibacy, and deviating from orthodoxy. His earlier life as a civil administrator served him well in organizing and defending a Church which could not depend on civil protection. He was zealously intolerant of paganism and heresy, and he instructed one of his bishops to deal with stubborn "idol-worshippers and soothsayers" in this way:

> If you find them unwilling to change their ways, we desire you to arrest them with a fervent zeal. If they are slaves, chastise them with blows and torments to bring about their correction. But if they are free men, let them be led to penitence by strict confinement, as is suitable, so that they who scorn to listen to words of salvation which reclaim them from the peril of death, may at any rate by bodily torments be brought back to the desired sanity of mind.

Here as always, his iron will was at work.

Gregory's austere, monastic approach aroused the opposition of nonmonastic clerical leaders who in the years after his death struggled to regain control of the Church and relax his severest disciplines. For a man who had sought retreat from the world, Gregory was indeed on a paradoxical course. As Straw puts it:

> Even as the papacy assumed greater responsibilities in the secular realm—maintaining the supplies of food and water, paying soldiers, negotiating treaties, administering estates, and systematizing charitable operations—Gregory still sought to preserve the Church from the pollution of secular values.... He continually preferred clerics over laymen, and monks over clerics.... [O]nly those who despised power could be trusted to exercise it wisely....

His motive was to prepare for the end of the world, but the practical effect was to make the Church much more durable in a world which was not coming to an end.

He Negotiates with the Lombards

Gregory's eagerness to convert as many people as possible to Christianity before the Apocalypse explains in part his conciliation of the Lombards. Many of them were Christians too, though he regarded them as the heretical Arian variety. For Gregory, Catholicism alone was the true faith, all other forms of Christianity being despicable. He hoped that by preserving the Catholic churches in Spoleto, one of the Lombard duchies to the north of Rome, his priests and bishops there could effect conversions. He was delighted by one such priest, Sanctulus, who gained a reputation as a miracle-worker, once for "magically" repairing a wine press and later for "freezing" the hands of an axeman who was about to cut off his head. After these evidences of divine protection, Sanctulus was able to move back and forth between Spoleto and Rome, preaching the orthodox Catholic faith without fear of the Lombards.

Befriending the Lombards' queen Theodolinda, Gregory laid the groundwork for the Lombards' subsequent conversion to Catholicism and was gratified to learn that her son Adaloald, born 603, had been christened according to the Catholic rite. Despite this diplomatic work with the Lombard leaders and his arrangement of several pauses in hostilities, however, Gregory was never politically strong enough to impose a general pacification, and Lombard raids on imperial territory continued sporadically throughout his reign and after his death.

In his efforts to secure peace, Gregory sometimes bribed Lombard leaders; he met the chieftain Agilulf (Theodolinda's husband) on the steps of St. Peter's in 593 and paid him £500 of gold in exchange for Agilulf's retreat out of Rome to Milan. In that volatile political environment, Lombards sometimes changed sides and came over to the imperial cause as mercenaries. Imperial soldiers, on the other hand, were so badly paid that they often preyed on the people they were supposed to be defending.

In a missionary venture outside his immediate areas of concern, Gregory sent Augustine, the abbot of his Roman monastery, along with 40 monks, to attempt the conversion of the Anglo-Saxons in England. An apocryphal story tells that he saw several fair-haired English boys in the Roman slave market, inquired after them, punned that they were more like Angels *(Angeli)* than Britons *(Angli)*, and decided there and then to convert the Britons. Augustine landed on the Isle of Thanet in the Thames estuary, gained permission to preach, and soon converted King Aethelbert of Kent, the dominant figure *(Bretwalda)* among the seven Anglo-Saxon kingdoms of England. Augustine became the first archbishop of Canterbury. The conversion of the Anglo-Saxons to Christianity, as of the other peoples of Europe, was a slow and laborious task. Previously wedded to older religions, they would often simply add Christianity to their rituals rather than give up practices which they believed had served them well in the past. In 597, Gregory wrote to the Frankish queen Brunhild that her ostensibly Christian subjects were still worshipping the heads of animals, which he regarded as tantamount to worshipping demons.

In addition to negotiating treaties with the Lombards and undertaking missionary work at home and abroad, Gregory was also able to come to terms with the Franks and Visigoths in the territories which now constitute France and Spain. Reccared, the Visigothic king of Spain, converted from the Arian heresy to Catholicism in 589, and Gregory, receiving the news as he assumed the papal throne, responded by sending Reccared a cherished holy relic, part of the chains in which **St. Peter** had once been bound.

The Franks and Visigoths paid lip service to the supremacy of Rome, though many decades would pass before Rome could effectively arbitrate Church disputes in their territories except with the monarchs' cooperation. In these contacts, nevertheless, Gregory laid the groundwork for the Church to operate outside politically friendly territory, in this way rivalling **St. Paul** and the early Christian missionaries who had done comparable work in Rome before it accepted Christianity.

During his life and following his death, Gregory's name was associated with many miracles. Historian J.C. Metford has gathered several. Among them, he says, are:

the appearance of Christ as the thirteenth pauper at a supper which Gregory was accustomed to give to twelve poor men; … the deliverance from Purgatory of the soul of Emperor **Trajan** by promising that in compensation he himself would either endure two days there or suffer ill-health for the rest of his life. When Gregory gave the shroud of St. John the Evangelist to the Empress Constantia, she refused it as unauthentic. Gregory cut the cloth with a knife and it dripped with blood as proof that it was genuine.

Whatever we think of such stories, it is historically significant that they were widely believed at the time, and by subsequent generations of Christians who had a different attitude to the supernatural than our own.

At Gregory's death, the fruits of his work were not yet ripe, but in time he could be seen as the originator of both the idea and the realization of "Christendom"; though Europe might be fragmented politically, it would be united in the Catholic faith. Christendom was, says historian Thomas Bokenkotter:

pre-eminently the creation of the Popes but also owed much to the anonymous labors of the peaceful monks and the political prowess of the bellicose Franks. Gregory the Great laid its foundation at the end of the sixth century, but its full realization only occurred when **Charlemagne** accepted a crown from the hands of Pope Leo III on Christmas Day in the year 800.

In retrospect, then, Gregory can be seen as the first decisive figure in the shaping of medieval Christendom, detaching it from a foundering Roman Empire, and setting the standards of discipline and internal conduct which would permit it to flourish through the "Dark Ages" which lay ahead.

SOURCES:

Bokenkotter, Thomas. *A Concise History of the Catholic Church.* Doubleday, 1977.

Metford, J. C. *Dictionary of Christian Lore and Legend.* Thames & Hudson, 1983.

Richards, Jeffrey. *Consul of God: The Life and Times of Gregory the Great.* Routledge & Kegan Paul, 1980.

Straw, Carol. *Gregory the Great.* University of California Press, 1988.

FURTHER READING:

Dudden, F. H. *Gregory the Great: His Place in History and Thought.* 2 vols. London: 1905.

Gregory VII

(c. 1020–1085)

One of the most important popes of medieval Europe, who sought to reform the Church by freeing it from imperial interference and by bringing all ecclesiastical matters under the direct control of the papacy.

"I have loved righteousness and hated iniquity, therefore, I die in exile."

POPE GREGORY VII

Though precise details of his early years are lacking, it appears that Hildebrand, the future pope Gregory VII, was born in the northern Italian village of Rovaca and was brought almost immediately to Rome by his father and mother. On his mother's side he was related by marriage to Benedict the Christian, a converted Jew who was the head of the wealthy banking family later known as the Pierleone. Coming from a family with important connections, Hildebrand would probably have received his early instruction in the monastery of St. Mary on the Aventine whose abbot, Peter, was his maternal uncle. As with other young men destined for careers in government or the Church, it is probable that he continued his education in the Lateran Palace school; there he would have had opportunities to get to know his uncle, John Gratian, the archpriest of the church of St. John at the Latin Gate, which was located next to the school.

During this period, the politics of Rome, as well as the politics of the Christian Church, were controlled by the wealthy and influential noble families of the region, making it not uncommon for certain powerful families to see one of their

Born Hildebrand on July 13, c. 1020; died in Salerno, Italy, on May 25, 1085; son of Bonizo and Bertha. Predecessor: Pope Alexander II (1061–73). Successor: Pope Victor III (1086–87).

Contributed by Peter L. Viscusi, Professor of History, Central Missouri State University, Warrensburg, Missouri

own made pope. Such was the case with Pope Benedict IX—son of the count of Tusculum and nephew of two previous popes—who became pope in 1032. In September 1044, riots broke out against Benedict because of his loose morals and Tusculan connections. After he fled the city, a rival political family in the region established its own bishop in the papacy as Pope Sylvester III (January 20, 1045). But Sylvester reigned for only two months until Benedict rallied his supporters, reasserted his power, and expelled him from the city on March 20.

By May 1, however, Benedict had decided to abandon the papacy which he agreed to sell to his godfather, John Gratian, for a substantial sum. Although Gratian, now known as Pope Gregory VI, said he bought the papacy to keep it safe from "less worthy hands," he was unable to distance himself from the taint of simony ("buying or selling a Church office"). Gregory VI struggled to make his papacy effective but could not break the impasse with Sylvester III as to who was the true pope. This—in addition to the charge that he himself was a simoniac—made it impossible for Gregory to attack one of the two major problems afflicting the Church: simony and clerical marriage. Though he held no formal office, Hildebrand gained his first experience in papal administration under Gregory VI.

In the autumn of 1046, the German king, Henry III, traveled to Italy in an attempt to establish some order out of the chaos of Church affairs. Unable to settle the conflicting claims to the papacy, Henry deposed all three claimants—Gregory VI, Sylvester III, Benedict IX—and appointed Suidgar, bishop of Bamberg, pope with the name Clement II. The next day, Clement II crowned Henry III the Holy Roman Emperor.

Henry then returned to Germany, taking Gregory VI and Hildebrand with him to their exile.

Hildebrand stayed in Hamburg until Gregory VI died late in 1047. While in Germany, Hildebrand devoted himself to the study of the canons ("church laws") and the writings of **Pope Gregory I.** Never claiming to be a canon lawyer, he trained himself to think like one, searching for and applying historical precedents among the canons to support papal positions. It is likely that during this time Hildebrand, now a monk, would have become familiar with the reform movement spreading through Germany (which dealt with the secular clergy rather than the monastic clergy) of Bishop Wazo of Liege.

When Clement II also died in late 1047, Henry III took the initiative and appointed Poppo, bishop of Brixen, as the new pope. Taking the name Damasus II, Poppo was enthroned in Rome on July 17, 1048, but died 23 days later, probably of malaria. In December, Henry nominated his cousin Bruno, bishop of Toul, to be the next pope (Leo IX). Leo chose a number of reform-minded churchmen from Germany and France to accompany him to Rome, and Hildebrand was among this select few.

During Leo's pontificate, Hildebrand studied and gained experience in the papal bureaucracy, eventually becoming a cardinal and traveling to France (1054) as a legate ("personal representative") of the pope. In addition to his responsibilities to the papacy, he was appointed prior of the Abbey of St. Paul in Rome. When Leo died, the most important cardinals, Humbert and Frederick, sent Hildebrand to Germany to request the imperial appointment of a new pope. In the spring of 1055, Henry III, at Hildebrand's urging, selected Gebhard, bishop of Eichstatt, as the new pontiff, and Gebhard took the name Victor II.

Again Hildebrand returned to France as a legate and held local synods to attack simony and clerical marriage. Upon his return to Rome, he served for a time as Victor's chancellor ("head of the papal administration"). But Victor died unexpectedly on July 28, 1057, and the Church reformers in Rome elected as pope Cardinal Frederick, who took the name Stephen IX. The first reforming pope to also be a monk, Stephen unified the Church reform and monastic reform movements.

For the first time during this period, the election of Pope Stephen had been made by the cardinals and clergy of Rome rather than imperial nomination or appointment. Worried about possible negative imperial reactions to this new method for papal elections, the reformers sent Hildebrand to Germany in November 1057, and he notified the empress Agnes (Henry III had died October 5, 1056) of the new pope's election, handled the delicate task of soothing imperial worries about the papacy, and obtained the imperial assent.

When Stephen IX died on March 28, 1058, and local nobles attempted to take control of the papacy, Hildebrand acted quickly to counter their moves. Gathering the Roman clergy in Florence, he arranged for the election of Gerard, bishop of Florence, who took the name Nicholas II. Following the election, the reformers asked for and received the imperial assent. Although the pontificate of Nicholas II was relatively short, the papacy achieved two important goals which were to have long-lasting effects upon the history of the Church: freed of imperial interference, popes would be elected by the College of Cardinals; and, through the diplomatic negotiations of Hildebrand, the Norman king who controlled southern Italy, Richard Guiscard, had recognized Nicholas II as his feudal lord, thereby promising military assistance. In gratitude, Nicholas appointed Hildebrand archdeacon ("administrator of Church finances").

He Leads College of Cardinals

With Cardinal Humbert's death on May 5, 1061, Hildebrand became the leader of the College of Cardinals. When Nicholas died in late July 1061, Hildebrand arranged for the election of Anselm, bishop of Lucca, who became Pope Alexander II. But the first years of the new pontificate were marked by strife because of Empress Agnes's support for the antipope Honorius II (Cadalus of Parma). Using his connections to the family of Benedict the Christian, Hildebrand financed the papacy's armed struggle against Honorius; by the time the fighting stopped, he had successfully centralized the papal administration.

On April 21, 1073, Alexander II died and the next day shouts of "Hildebrand for our Bishop!" were heard in Rome. Hildebrand, described by his contemporaries as short with sparkling eyes and a piercing gaze, was elected pope by acclamation of the people. Because he was one of the original reformers brought to Rome by Leo IX, and because he helped frame the papal election decree of 1059, Hildebrand convened the College of Cardinals for a formal vote. The cardinals ratified the people's choice, and Hildebrand, now twice elected, took the name Gregory VII. Preoccupied with attempting to crush a revolt in Saxony, the German king, Henry IV, offered no opposition. The choice of Gregory "VII" signified

his recognition of Gregory VI as the true pope during the triple papacy of 1046. Though his pontificate began with the usual strong condemnations of simony and clerical marriage similar to the proclamations of the other reforming popes, events soon proved that Gregory's reign was to be extraordinary.

In September, Henry IV sent a conciliatory letter to Gregory in which he, using the royal "we," admitted:

> We have not only trespassed on ecclesiastical affairs, but we have sold the very churches to certain unworthy persons, embittered with the gall of simony.... We shall carefully observe your commands in all things.

The outstanding issue of contention between the king and the pope concerned the appointment of a new archbishop of Milan. The reformers in Milan, known as the Patarines, wanted the appointment of someone free from simony; the Milanese clergy (many of whom were simoniacs) wanted to control the appointment of the archbishop.

At a synod held in Rome (February 24, 1075), Gregory issued a broad ban against lay investiture—the practice whereby laymen gave to a newly chosen bishop the ring and staff which were the symbols of the temporalities ("the property and income of the diocese"). This new regulation ran counter to feudal custom and tradition in general, and to German proprietary law in particular. For Henry, it meant that he could not exercise his traditional authority over churchmen who, in Germany and northern Italy, held territories subject to the crown.

Soon after this synod, Gregory included in his Register (official catalogue of his letters and papers) a document known as the *Dictatus Papae*. The *Dictatus* was a listing of 27 chapter headings that, taken together, were a summary of Gregory's views of the pope's position in the organization of the Church and of the world. Gregory believed that the pope was the spiritual descendant of **St. Peter** and was, therefore, the head of the Church; in addition, he viewed the pope as the overall theocratic ruler on earth under whose lordship the emperors and kings ruled their respective lands. Accordingly, Gregory tried hard, as pope and advisor to popes, to gain recognition for papal supremacy. While he did not specifically list territories he considered to be subject to the papacy, Gregory did stake papal claims when the appropriate opportunity presented itself, and at one time or another he laid temporal claim to Germany, Catalonia, Hungary, Kiev, Denmark, Castile, Corsica, Sardinia, Poland, and Bohemia.

Although Henry IV supported Church reform in Germany, the reform movement was making little progress. In some areas, bishops refused to institute the reform program; in other areas, the clergy refused to obey the newly enforced rules against simony and clerical marriage. Unfortunately for both Gregory and Henry, Church reform became intertwined with the question of centralized royal power versus the local autonomy of the German dukes. Despite the victory of Henry's forces under the leadership of Rudolf, duke of Swabia, against the Saxons in early June 1075, German dukes were reluctant to give Henry further cooperation. Even before this victory, Henry IV had written the pope to warn him that the German dukes wanted their king and their pope to be at odds.

Pope Threatens King with Excommunication

At the end of November, Henry IV appointed Tebald, the subdeacon of the church of Milan, archbishop of Milan—a step viewed by Gregory as a challenge to his authority and to the recently instituted decree banning lay investiture. In late December, Gregory wrote a letter to Henry in which he reminded the king of this decree and threatened him with excommunication if he did not comply. Angered by such an affront to his royal dignity, Henry called the Diet of Worms into session (January 24, 1076). At this meeting, two archbishops, 24 bishops, and some of Henry's lay lords composed a letter of reply to the pope. Their letter, addressed to "Brother Hildebrand," accused Gregory of being illegally elected pope and listed other "unlawful" activities he was accused of practicing. In addition to the letter, Henry IV sent a letter of his own that began: "Henry, not by usurpation, but by God's holy ordinance King, to Hildebrand, not Pope, but false monk." The day after the letters were read aloud at the first meeting of the Lenten Synod of 1076 (February 14), Gregory attacked Henry IV in a prayer to St. Peter: "I prohibit to Henry the King … the rule of the whole kingdom of Germany and of Italy. I absolve all Christians from the fealty they have sworn or shall swear to him, and I forbid anyone to serve him as King." Henry IV, his royal authority suspended, was also excommunicated.

By Easter, a number of important bishops had deserted Henry's cause and joined Rudolf, duke of Swabia, and other nobles in a growing rebellion. In addition, the Saxons were preparing an uprising of their own. On October 16 at the Diet of Tribur, the nobles put Henry on notice: he would have a year and a day from the date of his excommunication to reconcile himself with the pope or lose his throne. In the meantime, they scheduled a meeting in Augsburg, Germany, for February 2, 1077, and invited the Pope to attend.

Once again, Church and state affairs were linked. Henry wrote the Pope, saying that he was willing to come to Italy and submit. Gregory, fearing he would lose his growing political influence in Germany if Henry submitted, accepted the nobles' invitation to meet in Augsburg. The nobles, fearing that they would lose control of the political and military situation in Germany, blocked the mountain passes to make it impossible for Henry to get to Gregory. Henry left Germany before Christmas of 1076 and, with much difficulty, crossed the Alps into France and then into Italy. In the meantime, Gregory had traveled as far north as the castle of the countess **Matilda of Tuscany** at Canossa. Henry arrived outside the castle walls on January 25, dressed as a repentant sinner in woolen shirt and with bare feet. Distrusting the king's sincerity, Gregory kept him waiting outside in the snow for three days before agreeing to forgive him.

Once freed from his excommunication, Henry tried to reassert his royal power in Germany. The nobles, however, had other plans. At the same time that Rudolf wrote Henry on behalf of the dukes, telling him not to return to Germany before he negotiated peace, he also wrote the pope (March 1), telling him that the nobles intended to elect a new king. On March 26 at Forcheim, Rudolf was chosen king and crowned at Mainz, whereupon Henry demanded that Gregory excommunicate Rudolf as a usurper. Gregory, however, insisted that he would have to study the situation. A civil war erupted in Germany.

Gregory ordered both Henry and Rudolf to provide him with an escort so he could come to Germany to decide who was the rightful king. Though neither of the warring factions sent an escort, Gregory began referring to Henry as the "so-called King" while using the title "King" when referring to Rudolf. Despite Gregory's hope that Rudolf would provide a military solution to his problem, the warfare in Germany proved indecisive. When the military situation finally began to favor Henry, Henry demanded that Gregory excommunicate Rudolf and threatened to appoint a new pope if he refused. But Gregory would not be intimidated. At the Lenten Synod of 1080, Gregory reexcommunicated Henry and deposed him as king. Church and state were now at war. Initially, this war was fought by writers who prepared propaganda pamphlets that appealed to canon law or Roman law for precedents.

Henry responded to his deposition by summoning the Council of Brixen on June 25, 1080. With 30 bishops present, Gregory VII was deposed and Guibert, archbishop of Ravenna, was elected Pope Clement III; in addition, the council formally excommunicated Rudolf and his followers. Although the military situation in Germany had changed little, Henry gained a distinct advantage when Rudolf died from wounds received at an indecisive battle fought October 15. With Rudolf dead, all significant resistance to Henry ceased. The king gathered his forces, marched on Rome, and besieged the city several times between 1081 and 1083.

After mounting three attacks on Rome in 1083, Henry captured the part of the city which included St. Peter's and confined Gregory to the Castel Sant' Angelo and the old town. Failing to convince the assembled clergy to renew Henry's excommunication at a synod held November 20, 1083, Gregory's position was further undermined when 13 of his cardinals deserted him for Henry. On March 21, 1084, Henry seized more of the city and held his own synod. Gregory was again deposed and excommunicated. On Palm Sunday (March 24), Guibert was enthroned as Clement III, and on Easter, Clement crowned Henry.

Gregory, now desperate, called upon the Norman king and papal vassal, Robert Guiscard, for military aid. Responding to the pope's plea, Guiscard marched on Rome with 30,000 soldiers and 1,000 horsemen. Henry and his army retreated to northern Italy on May 21, rather than engage the Normans in combat. Despite the German retreat, the Romans refused to open their city gates to Guiscard and his men. Because the Romans forced the Normans to storm the city on May 28 to rescue Gregory, the Normans vented their fury on the city and its population. Looting the city for two days and setting its northern and southeastern suburbs ablaze, the Normans sold hundreds of Romans into slavery and took still others with them back to southern Italy as prizes of war. When riots broke out against Gregory for bringing the Normans to Rome, the pope decided to return with his rescuers to southern Italy.

At Salerno, Gregory's health declined and, after a brief illness, he died May 25, 1085. His final words were: "I have loved righteousness and hated iniquity, therefore, I die in exile." Despite his efforts to oversee the administration of the Church, to exert papal supremacy over emperors and kings, and to defend the rights of the Church and its reform from state interference, Gregory was in his own time defeated. Largely as a result of his actions, however, the Church made significant gains in these areas, with the papacy pursuing the issue of lay investiture. Thirty-seven years after the death of Pope Gregory VII, Pope Calixtus II and Emperor Henry V resolved the problem with the Concordat of Worms.

SOURCES:

The Correspondence of Pope Gregory VII. Translated and edited by Ephraim Emerton. Columbia University Press, 1932.

The 'Epistolae Vagantes' of Pope Gregory VII. Translated and edited by H. E. J. Cowdrey. Clarendon Press, 1972.

Imperial Lives and Letters of the Eleventh Century. Translated by Theodor E. Mommsen and Karl F. Morrison. Edited by Robert L. Benson. Columbia University Press, 1962.

MacDonald, A. J. *Hildebrand: A Life of Gregory VII.* Methuen, 1932.

FURTHER READING:

Blumenthal, Uta-Renate. *The Investiture Controversy: Church and Monarchy from the Ninth to the Twelfth Century.* University of Pennsylvania Press, 1988.

Prinz, Joachim. *Popes from the Ghetto: A View of Medieval Christendom.* Schocken, 1968.

Whitney, J. P. *Hildebrandine Essays.* Cambridge University Press, 1932.

Hugo Grotius

(1583–1645)

Dutch legal scholar and statesman, whose writings laid the basis for modern ideas about international law.

Pronunciation: GROW-tee-us. Born Huig de Groot on April 10, 1583; died at Rostock, on August 28, 1645; son of Jan de Groot (a burgemeister and curator at Delft, Holland) and Alida Borren van Overschie; married: Marie van Reigersberch, July 17, 1609; children: four sons and three daughters, although a son and two daughters died young.

When, at the end of World War II, the United States and its victorious Allies placed a number of Nazi leaders of the defeated German nation on trial as "war criminals" in the famous Nuremberg trials, the German leaders maintained that there was no such crime. They had broken no laws of their own country, they reasoned. The only existing laws were the laws of individual nations. There was no such thing as a law between nations. The Allies did not agree. Finding almost all of the accused guilty of crimes against humanity or the laws of war, they insisted that there are commonly understood standards of decency—in both war and peace.

The idea that there is such a thing as international law—as international standards of decency in diplomacy—is a fairly modern idea, emerging from European experiences in the 17th century. Until the Reformation, standards for the conduct of government leaders in the West were set by the Roman Catholic Church, which in the 10th and 11th centuries declared that warfare might not be conducted on certain days, including Sundays and religious holidays (The Truce of God), and that children, peasants, religious pil-

"Today, by common agreement, the jurist, scholar, statesman, theologian, writer, and world diplomat Hugo Grotius is considered to have been the most renowned man of letters and learning the seventeenth century Netherlands brought forth."

CHRISTIAN GELLINER

Contributed by Niles Holt, Professor of History, Illinois State University, Normal–Bloomington, Illinois

grims, and women were to be protected as non-combatants (The Peace of God).

But the Protestant Reformation split the Church's authority, and, at about the same time, a new development created further problems. The nation-state—a government centered around a single nationality—began emerging in Europe as early as the 16th century. Until that time, Europeans thought of themselves as members of a common religious community—part of "Christendom"—rather than being part of France, or Spain, or Germany.

To a large degree, individual European nations were the creation of new national monarchies, who united their realms through marriage, warfare, and, in some cases, pure deceptions. The monarchs challenged Church authorities by proclaiming that they held the throne by "divine right"; their power derived directly from God. In domestic and international affairs, many of these monarchs proclaimed policies ruled by "*raison d'état*" (reason of state).

The 16th and 17th centuries saw many of these trends come to a head. They were the last centuries in which wars were fought mainly on religious grounds. The Thirty Years' War (1618–48), which was Europe's most destructive war before the 20th century, began as a struggle between Catholic and Protestant nobility in Bohemia. It ended as a dynastic war, in which the Catholic rulers of France attempted to undercut the Catholic ruling family of Austria.

The country of Hugo Grotius was the foremost commercial power in Europe in his time. (A coastal nation about the size of West Virginia, the Netherlands, which literally means "the low lands," occupies the tip of northwestern Europe and is bounded by the North Sea, Belgium, and Germany. It is also called Holland, the name of a region that comprises North and South Holland, and its inhabitants are known as the "Dutch.") The country's prosperous and heavily Calvinist majority sometimes argued among themselves, particularly over religion, but its government, a confederation of individual states or provinces, was the most famous republic in 17th-century Europe. The closest figure to a national executive was the *stadtholder,* the leader of the national army and judiciary. One historian has noted that "the Netherlands were to the seventeenth century what England … was to the eighteenth and early nineteenth centuries, a working model of free institutions, and a central light for the rest of Europe."

The grandfather of international law, Hugo Grotius (the Latinized version of his name) lived

during the height of these trends. He was introduced to politics and religious disagreements very early. His father's family had a tradition of political service in Delft; his mother had converted from her Catholic religion to Calvinism at the urging of her husband.

The Accomplishments of a Child Prodigy

The young Grotius quickly proved himself to be a child prodigy. He composed Latin poetry at age eight, and at age 11 he followed in the footsteps of his father by beginning law studies at the University of Leyden. At age 15, he accompanied a Dutch diplomat on a trip to France. There, he so impressed scholars that he was awarded an honorary doctorate in law by the University of Orleans. The French king **Henry IV** proclaimed that he was the "miracle of Holland."

Upon his return to Holland, Grotius was admitted to the bar at the age of 16 and began practicing law at The Hague, the administrative city of the Netherlands. He gained a reputation as a writer of Greek and Latin poems, and at age 18 became the Latin historiographer of Holland. In 1607, he was appointed fiscal advocate of Holland, Zeeland, and Friesland, and in 1613, he became governor of Rotterdam.

During this period of public service in Holland, Grotius became involved in a dispute between Portugal and the Dutch East India Company, the main trading company of the Netherlands. A Dutch ship had taken possession of a Portuguese ship in the Strait of Singapore. In 1603, Grotius wrote his *Commentary on the Law of Prize and Booty (De jure praedae)* to defend the East India Company. Although the book was not published until the 19th century, it proclaimed that freedom of the seas was an "international law." It also laid down four specific principles that would later haunt the defendants at Nuremberg: (1) no state or individual may attack another state or individual; (2) no state or individual may appropriate what belongs to another state or individual; (3) no state or individual may disregard treaties or contracts; and (4) and no state or individual may commit a crime.

Grotius could not avoid becoming enmeshed in the religious politics of his native country, where a dissident Calvinist group, the Arminians, clashed with more traditional Calvinists. **John Calvin**'s father had sided with the Arminians and had seen to it that his son's teachers included prominent Dutch Arminians. The majority of the Dutch provinces sided with traditional Calvinism; only Utrecht and Grotius's native province of Holland sided with the Arminians. In 1618, the *stadtholder,* Prince Maurits, abolished the armies of the dissident provinces and arrested several men, including Grotius. Grotius was tried and found guilty of an unspecified charge—later announced as treason—and sentenced to life imprisonment at the fortress of Loevestein.

Grotius managed to escape two years later when his wife and her maid hid him a chest of books. He took up residence in France, where he was hailed as a hero. There he composed landmark books on religion and law, as well as plays, dramas, poems, theological commentaries, and histories. Among these was his *Defense of the Lawful Government of Holland* (1622), which pleaded his innocence of the charges against him and accused Prince Maurits of illegal actions. When the government of Holland attempted to seize the book, the French king Louis XIII protected Grotius, declaring that persons "of any quality, nation, or condition are forbidden from molesting or harming" him.

Writes Major Work on War and International Law

While in France, he wrote his major work *De jure belli et pacis (Concerning the Law of War and Peace;* 1621), which argued that even war must be regulated by laws. The book established the important principle that neutral parties or nations should remain unharmed during wars. In war, the lives of innocents (women, children, the aged, and those whose occupations are unrelated to the war, such as priests, scholars, and farmers) should be spared. The book established certain basic principles of international law, such as the idea that a declaration of war is mandatory; that enemies might not be slain in neutral territory; that occupying troops may not rape or otherwise harm civilians (although Grotius argued that destruction of property is permissible); and that defeated peoples should not be made slaves. International law, he insisted, was made necessary by the fact that all of "mankind" is comprised in a "human society."

In 1632, Grotius traveled to Holland, then to Sweden. He was appointed the Swedish ambassador to Paris, with the task of convincing the French government to continue military subsidies to Sweden. The Thirty Years' War was in its second decade, and the French government wished to weaken its European rival, Austria. Leader of the Catholic forces, Austria had almost driven Protestant forces in Germany into the North Sea. The Protestant cause had been saved by the military intervention of the Swedish king **Gustavus Adolphus.** Although he was a cardinal in the Catholic church, **Cardinal Richelieu,** the main minister of the French monarchy, had sent subsidies to Adolphus as a means of weakening Austrian power.

For a time, Grotius was successful in convincing France to continue the subsidy, but when the subsidy was eventually withdrawn, he returned to Sweden in disappointment. The new monarch, Queen **Christina,** accepted his resignation but refused to offer him any other appointment. On his return trip to Holland, Grotius survived a shipwreck in the Baltic Sea but died of exhaustion two days later in Rostock, Germany. He was buried in Delft, the only commoner in a church filled with the graves of nobility or royalty.

Hugo Grotius foresaw that the religious, economic, and diplomatic conflicts of his own time could lead to continual chaos and cruelty. All commerce between nations, he argued, should be regulated by the laws of universal human society. He was the first major writer to insist that international law was an integral part of human society—that, in the words of **Thomas Jefferson,** there were diplomatic laws of "Nature and Nature's God."

SOURCES:

Dumbauld, Edward. *The Life and Legal Writings of Hugo Grotius.* University of Oklahoma Press, 1969.

Gellinek, Christian. *Hugo Grotius.* Twayne, 1983.

Knight, William S. M. *The Life and Words of Hugo Grotius.* London: Sweet and Maxwell, 1925.

FURTHER READING:

Grotius. *The Jurisprudence of Holland.* Edited by R. W. Lee. 2 vols. Oxford University Press, 1926–36.

Kingsbury, Benedict, Adam Roberts, and Hedley Bull. *Hugo Grotius and International Relations.* Clarendon Press, 1990.

Lee, Robert W. *Hugo Grotius.* London: H. Milford, 1931.

van Someren, Liesje. *Umpire to the Nations: Hugo Grotius.* London: D. Dobson, 1965.

Vreeland, Hamilton. *Hugo Grotius: The Father of the Modern Science of International Law.* F. B. Rothman, 1986.

Gustavus I Vasa

(c. 1496–1560)

Rebel leader and king of Sweden, who created a centralized, hereditary monarchy, brutally fought off rivals for 37 years, and plundered the Church to secure his dynasty and make himself rich.

Name variation: Gustav I. Pronunciation: Ge-STAVE-us or GES-tahv-us VAH-sa. Born on May 12, c. 1496, in Uppland; died in 1560; eldest son of Erik Johansson Vasa (lord of Rydboholm, a knight and councillor of state); married: Katarina of Saxe-Lauenburg, 1531 (according to an unconfirmed rumor, he killed her with a hammer); married: Margareta Leijonhufvud, 1536; married: Katarina Stenbock, 1552. Predecessor: Sten Sture the Younger (as regent). Successor: his son, Erik XIV.

Sweden, Denmark, and Norway were politically united by the Union of Kalmar, an agreement of 1397. By this arrangement the Scandinavian aristocracies, which were culturally and linguistically similar, agreed to elect their kings and to fight off the efforts of German princes to gain influence over them. The Union frequently broke down throughout the 15th century but was still recognizably intact at the start of the 16th. Conflict between the Danish king Christian II Oldenburg and the Swedish popular leader Sten Sture in the early 16th century, however, brought the Union to an end, and the Swedish nobility signaled its independence in 1523 by electing one of its own, the young head of the Vasa family, as King Gustavus I. During his reign of 37 years, he consolidated Sweden's independence and laid the foundations for Sweden's coming century of greatness.

Sten Sture, who took the title of regent, had already been in large measure an independent monarch, but nominally ruled on behalf of Christian II of Denmark. Christian, eager like most Renaissance princes to consolidate his power, and willing to act mercilessly in the fashion urged by his

"In the months of crisis that preceded the war Gustav Vasa gave the first large-scale exhibition of that morbid irritability, that intolerable violence of language, that inability to control his terrifying outbursts of rage, which made him so ill a master to serve."

MICHAEL ROBERTS

Contributed by Patrick Allitt, Assistant Professor of History, Emory University, Atlanta, Georgia

contemporary, Machiavelli, isolated Sture diplomatically and then attacked Sweden directly in 1517. His pretext was that he had come to rescue Gustav Trolle, the princely Archbishop of Uppsala (Sweden), who believed Sture was trying to diminish the rights and privileges of the Church. Sture saw Archbishop Trolle as a threat and won the assent of the Swedish Estates, or *Riksdag* (a gathering of the principal nobility) to demolish Trolle's fortress at Almare-Staket. Sture met and defeated Christian II on the battlefield of Brännkyrka in 1518. Among his troops was the 22-year-old Gustavus Vasa, who fought courageously.

In the treaty that followed this conflict, the victorious Sture handed over young Gustavus to the Danish king as a pledge of his good intentions, and Christian II took Gustavus back to a mild form of captivity in Denmark. Gustavus's imprisonment was not onerous but when he heard news of renewed fighting between Denmark and Sweden, he escaped and made his way to the port of Lübeck, a member of the powerful Hanseatic League that dominated Baltic, North German, and Scandinavian trading. In 1520, Christian convinced Pope Leo X to excommunicate Sture and all the Swedish Estates for their insulting behavior toward Archbishop Trolle, and then renewed his attack, this time defeating Sture at the Battle of Lake Asunden. Sture was killed, Christian seized Stockholm, and on November 8, 1520, he presided over the "bloodbath of Stockholm" in which his Danish soldiers chopped off the heads of nearly 100 prominent Swedes who had supported Sture. The massacre continued in the Swedish provinces in the weeks that followed.

Gustavus Vasa Elected King After Bloodbath

The surviving Swedes cast about frantically for a leader and found one in Gustavus Vasa, who, with help from Lübeck, had made his way home. Among the dead in the November 8th massacre were Gustavus's father, his brother-in-law, and two of his uncles, so he had a powerful motive for taking up the fight against the Danes. After a succession of nerve-wracking escapes from capture, he began to gather followers, and won his first victory over Christian at Västerås in the spring of 1521. Advancing on Stockholm, Gustavus met the surviving Swedish aristocrats who appointed him regent. Expecting at first to be able to shape and use him to their advantage, the Swedes gradually recognized his skills as a genuine leader and his determination not to be manipulated. With the backing of Lübeck, which sent him mercenary soldiers and ships to blockade the remaining Danish

CHRONOLOGY

1512–20	Regency of Sten Sture the Younger
1518	Battle of Brännkyrka; Gustavus imprisoned in Denmark
1520	Escaped to Lübeck; Bloodbath of Stockholm
1523	Elected king at Strängnäs
1527	Swedish Reformation inaugurated at Västerås
1533–36	The Count's War
1543–44	Dacke Rebellion
1544	Second Estates of Västerås created standing army and hereditary Vasa monarchy
1554–57	Russian War
1560	Death of Gustavus Vasa; accession of his son Erik XIV

garrisons, Gustavus was able to master the entire country by 1523. As *quid pro quo* for this aid, he had to promise major trading concessions to Lübeck, which thereby had a motive for supporting him in the ensuing years of peril. The aristocracy then elected Gustavus king at Strängnäs.

The most immediate threat to Gustavus's new throne came not from Christian II of Denmark but from the friends of Sten Sture, among them Sture's widow Christina Gyllenstierna and their young son Nils. Planning to make Nils king, and angry that Gustavus had appointed some of Sture's old enemies to major state offices, they rebelled in 1524, posing as true Swedish patriots, and recruited hungry peasants who had admired Sture's patriotism and were now suffering from poor harvests and high taxes. The determined Gustavus attacked their stronghold, the castle of Kalmar, in 1525, and killed all its defenders in the hope that he would silence rebellion with one decisive counterstroke.

For the first years of his reign, Gustavus was beholden to Lübeck, whose changing policies concerning the rest of the Baltic led to complex diplomatic maneuvering. Lübeck managed to dislodge Christian II from the Danish throne and install its own candidate, Frederick I. Ironically, Sweden and Denmark now owed debts to Lübeck and both feared Christian II's vengeance, which might fall at any time, since he was related to the most powerful man in Europe, Holy Roman Emperor **Charles V.** Together Swedes, Danes, and Lübeckers evicted Soren Norby—one of Christian's generals who had taken to plundering—from the strategic island of

Gotland in 1526, and in the years that followed the new kings of Denmark and Sweden found other common points of interest, despite residual tensions from the war that had broken the Union of Kalmar. The unsentimental Gustavus never let gratitude toward Lübeck get the better of him. Wanting to diversify Sweden's trade, rather than see it funnelled into Lübeck on disadvantageous terms, he began negotiations with Holland and signed a trading agreement with Prussia in 1526.

Swedish Reformation Inaugurated

For Gustavus, as for many contemporary rulers seeking to enlarge their power, the Protestant Reformation appeared as an irresistible temptation. Sweden, like every other part of Europe, had long been subject to at least some measure of papal intervention and taxation, and its monarch stood to benefit from gaining control over Church affairs and properties. Gustavus, not a rich man, had pressing debts from the War of Independence, which he could not pay from the small revenues of his estates. The Church, by contrast, gained an income almost five times as much as the king's annual income from tithes alone. It also owned estates, castles, and more liquid forms of wealth in abundance. Determined to lay his hands on this wealth, Gustavus confided his intentions to Bishop Hans Brask of Linköping, who had the temerity to protest: "Necessity overrides the law; and not the law of man only but sometimes also the law of God."

Gustavus's chancellor, Lars Andreae, had converted to Lutheranism under the influence of Olaus Petri, a priest who had been a student in Wittenberg during **Martin Luther**'s confrontation with the Church. Within a year of his accession, Gustavus was defending the small circle of Lutherans in Stockholm and pointedly gave his approval to Petri's marriage. Most Swedes opposed the novelties of the Reformation. Bishop Brask tried to coordinate Church opposition and stamp out Lutheranism, while warning aristocrats that the King would turn on their privileges next if they did not resist his designs on the Church. Brask could not prevail against the King's counteroffer to his nobles that they could share in the booty. At a 1527 meeting of the Swedish Estates in Västerås to decide religious policy, the artful King burst into tears and threatened to abdicate if his plan to strip the churches of their wealth was not endorsed. A new rebellion against the King, led by an imposter pretending to be Sture's son, made the aristocracy afraid of the chaos that might follow. Ignoring Brask's pleas, they agreed to Gustavus's plan in the

"Recess of Västerås." Strictly speaking, the Recess *denied* that Sweden was turning to Lutheranism, but its practical effect was to hasten the dismantling of Swedish Catholicism.

Sweden's Reformation, like England's, left the cathedrals, bishops, and clergy largely intact, while gradually squeezing the monasteries out of existence, but there was surprisingly little doctrinal passion outside a small circle of theologians, especially by comparison with the Reformation in Germany, Switzerland, and England. Instead, as historian Michael Roberts observes:

> No head fell on the block for denying or impugning the king's authority over the church; no heretic went to the stake for adherence to unauthorized doctrines; no attempt was made to invoke the law of treason to enforce ecclesiastical policy; not a single abbot was hanged. The Swedish Reformation—gradual, pragmatic, easygoing—was notably gentle and humane.

The first Lutheran Archbishop of Uppsala, Laurentius Petri, brother of Olaus, was an astute and conciliatory churchman. In 1541, under his guidance, a Swedish language Bible marked the most ambitious publishing venture in Swedish history to that date.

The reform process was anything but painless for the clergy. Even those willing to renounce Catholicism and take up Lutheranism witnessed the King plundering their churches for gold and silver plate, candlesticks, and other wealth convertible into money and seizing, for himself or for his nobles, estates, castles, and lands which had been Church property for centuries. This rapacious policy led to an uprising of Catholic nobles and peasants in the southwestern provinces of Sweden in 1529, but Gustavus soon outwitted the rebels and executed the ringleaders.

A more serious threat appeared when, after eight years of exile in Holland, Christian II finally mounted a campaign to regain what he saw as his rightful inheritance of Sweden and Denmark from the Lübeck-backed usurpers Gustavus and Frederick I. Aided by Emperor Charles V, Christian II landed in Norway and advanced quickly at first, but ran out of energy when he met fierce Swedish resistance. Gustavus, reminding his countrymen of the Stockholm bloodbath which Christian II had caused, urged them to fight back vigorously and they did. Frederick I of Denmark was finally able to capture Christian II in the summer of 1532. Bringing an end to what Frederick and Gustavus had regarded as the most serious threat to their thrones, Christian was imprisoned and confined until his death 26 years later.

The Count's War

But Christian II was more easily disposed of than Lübeck. Gustavus had repeatedly put off repayment of his debts and was eager to abrogate Lübeck's trading monopoly. In 1534, after a period of Byzantine diplomacy, Lübeck declared war on Denmark and Sweden, each of which it regarded, with justice, as having betrayed its promises. All Gustavus's enemies who had been driven into exile during the previous decade—including the Sture faction, disaffected Catholics, and Gustavus's own brother-in-law, John of Hoya—joined forces with Lübeck and against Gustavus in what Swedish historians remember as the "Count's War." Gustavus responded by again allying with Frederick I of Denmark and taking to the battlefield, where he won another victory at the battle of Halsingborg. From the start of his reign he had been collecting ships, hoping to challenge the trading power of the Hanseatic ports, and now his embryonic navy won victories at Bornholm and the Little Belt in 1535, inaugurating the growth of Swedish naval and maritime power. This successful outcome of the "Count's War" showed that from now on Gustavus's Sweden was a more dominant power than the Lübeck to which it owed its birth.

Gustavus was obsessed with gathering financial surpluses to safeguard his kingdom. Fear of usurpers kept him constantly at work concentrating resources, and he would repeatedly warn his subjects that without military and financial preparedness events like the "Bloodbath of Stockholm" could recur. In the late 1530s, Sweden's one silver mine at Sala began to produce. As a royal monopoly it filled Gustavus's coffers and cushioned him against the accelerating inflation of the 16th century. The richest man in the kingdom, the largest farmowner, and ultimately its most enterprising merchant, Gustavus did what he could to stand the Swedish economy on a sounder footing. He imported and financed German iron founders, and created a home industry in this commodity that until then had been exported to German foundries. He also tried to establish direct trade links with Holland and England, once the Count's War had shown his command of the Baltic. These trading ventures yielded no impressive results, however, and the King did not hold his subjects' business acumen in high esteem. "The Swedes are so appallingly stupid that they have no notion of how to deal with other people," he wrote in one frank assessment of his subjects.

In the administration of his kingdom, Gustavus, like most of his European contemporaries, tried to free himself from dependence on the hereditary aristocracy and to build up a practical administrative elite whose advancement depended on his favor rather than on independent estates. But recruiting civil servants in Sweden was no easy matter. The country's one university, at Uppsala, had fallen into disuse in the second decade of the century, and as Gustavus grew rich he showed no disposition to divert any of his wealth into education. Most of the aristocrats were hard-drinking, swaggering illiterates with no administrative skills. Swedes seeking learning had to go abroad, while state servants had to be imported to do the King's business. The most famous pair, whose years in power were remembered as the "Rule of Secretaries," were Germans, Georg Norman and Konrad von Pyhy. They brought problems of a different kind. Not knowing Swedish history and tradition, and winning the furious resentment of the aristocracy, their tactless methods of running the kingdom and raising revenue contributed to the worst domestic upheaval of Gustavus's entire reign.

Dacke Leads Peasant Rebellion

The Secretaries, the Reformation, heavy taxation, and the King's violation of traditional mores, all contributed to the rebellion of Nils Dacke, a prosperous peasant in the Småland district of southern Sweden, which began in 1542. Dacke's peasant volunteers outwitted Gustavus's German mercenaries for over a year; as Roberts says:

> with their cumbrous pikes and stereotyped tactics [the mercenaries] were utterly at a loss in the ambushed wilderness of Småland. Their lack of woodcraft put them at a hopeless disadvantage in the deep forests; their habit of advertising their approach by marching to the tap of a drum exposed them to murderous surprises; their professional contempt for peasant armies led them to neglect elementary precautions. And such military assets as remained to them were further diminished by their refusal, as a matter of professional etiquette, to fight on a Monday.

Despite early setbacks, the resourceful Gustavus was able to isolate the province with a blockade and embargo, and finally, catching Dacke on open ground, defeated him at the battle of Hogsby.

Gustavus now convened the Estates at Västerås in 1544 to ratify his victory and to convert his elective monarchy into an hereditary one claiming, as so often in the past, that without a secure center the nation might again fall victim to a new bloodbath, especially if foreign powers took advantage of internal turmoil, as they had tried to do with Dacke. Gustavus had summoned the Estates frequently in the early years of his reign, as a way of assuring broad support for his actions. Since 1529, however, they had not met, which suggests his growing autonomy and confidence as king. In 1539, without consultation, he had declared that the Church was a department of state—making it completely subordinate to the civil power, as **Henry VIII** had done in England. Now Gustavus wanted the Estates' approval to augment his authority once again. At the same time, he acted in a way Machiavelli had always encouraged, by trying to rid himself of dependence on mercenary soldiers, who were expensive and unreliable, and to create the nucleus of a citizen-army in their place. He succeeded in both objects, establishing a Vasa dynasty and making Sweden the first country in Europe to have a permanent army of its own farmer-soldiers.

From that time until his death in 1560, Gustavus's throne rested secure. He even tried to expand his eastern frontier with Russia in 1554 (Finland was then a Swedish province) and pro-voked an inconclusive three-year war against Tsar **Ivan IV.** The war solved nothing but at least it did not visibly weaken Gustavus, who continued his remorseless mulcting of the Church and his alarms, threats, and cajolery of the cities for ever-larger sums of money. According to his heated rhetoric, Sweden was still hanging on to independence by its fingernails. Gustavus was right to view all his neighbors with suspicion and fear, for all of them would have taken the opportunity to dislodge him if it arose, but his throne was sinking strong roots in the Swedish ground and could no longer be challenged with ease. When Gustavus died in his bed in 1560, a crotchety and vengeful old man, his son (taking the name Erik XIV) was able to carry on the expansion of Swedish power. By the 1620s, Sweden would be a major player in European power politics.

SOURCES:

Andersson, Ingvar. *A History of Sweden.* Macmillan, 1956.

Elton, Geoffrey. *Reformation Europe.* Collins, 1963.

Roberts, Michael. T*he Early Vasas: A History of Sweden, 1523–1611.* Cambridge University Press, 1968.

———. *On Aristocratic Constitutionalism in Swedish History, 1520–1720.* Athlone Press, 1966.

Gustavus Adolphus

(1594–1632)

Soldier king who laid the foundation of the modern Swedish state, carved out an empire in the Baltic, and thwarted a Catholic victory in Germany during the middle phase of the Thirty Years' War.

"He was both heart and head of the kingdom."

ROBERT MONRO

I f asked to offer a word that best sums up Sweden's historical experience, very few would respond with warlike. Sweden, after all, has not been at war since 1814; and, as we all know, the Swedish government disburses Nobel Prizes for accomplishments in literature, the sciences, and most notably, contributions to world peace. This image of peaceful and neutral Sweden has not always been the case. During its "Age of Greatness" (1621–1721), Sweden controlled an Empire that included Finland, much of the south shore of the Baltic Sea, and important possessions in northern Germany. Some empires emerged as products of skillfully engineered royal marriages. Sweden's kings acquired their Empire on the battlefield. In an age of "soldier kings," no European dynasty could match the military accomplishments of Sweden's Vasa kings; and the greatest of them all was Gustavus Adolphus.

The view from Stockholm on December 9, 1594, the day of Gustavus's birth, appeared bleak. In 1587, Sigismund Vasa, heir to the Swedish throne, accepted the invitation of the Polish nobility to be their king. A convert to Roman Catholicism, Sigismund simultaneously held both crowns

Contributed by D. K. R. Crosswell, Lecturer, National University of Singapore, Singapore

Name variations: Gustavus II Adolphus, Gustav Adolf, Gustav II. Pronunciation: Ge-STAVE-us or GES-tahv-us Ah-DOLL-fus. Born in Stockholm on December 9, 1594; died in 1632; son of Karl IX; married: Maria Eleonora (daughter of George William, Elector of Brandenburg), November 25, 1620; children: (daughter) Christina. Descendants: Karl X, Karl XI, Karl XII. Predecessors: Gustavus I Vasa, Erik XIV, Karl IX. Successor: his daughter, Christina.

after 1592. He faced powerful opposition in staunchly Lutheran Sweden. The religious issue developed into a civil war. In 1600, Sigismund's uncle, styled Karl IX, usurped the throne. Four years later, his son, Gustavus, became heir.

Blessed with extraordinary intelligence, Gustavus received a thorough education under the strict supervision of Karl IX. Grounded in the Latin classics—still the language of diplomacy—and able to read ancient Greek, Gustavus spoke fluent German and had varying degrees of facility in eight other modern languages. Additionally, he studied law and avidly read histories, particularly those dealing with Sweden's heroic (and mostly mythic) Gothic past. As future chief of the armed forces, the heir applied himself diligently to his military training. At a theoretical level, he studied mathematics, optics, and mechanics and read histories of the great captains. He also examined contemporary writing, especially those dealing with the new techniques of fortification, siegecraft, and tactics emanating from the Netherlands. At the practical level, he served a brief apprenticeship under Sweden's best general, Jacok de la Gardie.

As he matured, Gustavus began to appear as the living embodiment of those ancient Gothic warrior-kings he read and dreamed of: tall with broad shoulders, his long face crowned with golden hair. He loved music and dancing as well as scholarly pursuits. His one vice, in the opinion of his prudish daughter **Christina,** was his excessive "fondness of the ladies." Little is known of his religious education but as king he demonstrated a remarkable degree of toleration for the period.

In 1611, Gustavus, not yet 17 years old, succeeded to the throne. The Resolution of 1604 provided that power would divert to a council of regents appointed from the high nobility until the King turned 18. However, "seeing that God … ha[d] made up in understanding what [was] lacking in years," the Diet, meeting at Nyköping in December 1611, accepted Gustavus as king. As a condition, he accepted a set of limitations on his royal powers known as the Charter of 1611. The new king promised to give the nobility a monopoly over state offices and to govern with the advice of the council and the constitutional bodies—the Diet and the representative Estates [nobles, burghers, clergy, peasants].

Axel Oxenstierna, a 28-year-old noble, drafted the charter. What might have developed into a disastrous clash between king and Oxenstierna, with serious constitutional ramifications, became the firm foundation for a partnership that lasted the duration of Gustavus's reign. The relationship between Sweden's greatest king and its greatest statesman was one of equals. Each brought different personalities into the equation: the chancellor's self-composed wisdom and attention to detail balanced the King's stormy impetuosity. The high degree of cooperation between Gustavus and Oxenstierna—and the King's popularity and personal prestige—won support for royal policies from the institutions of government.

Sweden Institutes Domestic Reforms

While Gustavus's fame rests primarily on his military reputation, the governmental structure he established laid the basis for Sweden's rise as a major power. The process toward administrative centralization began immediately at the accession with the Charter of 1611. As the King spent half of his time outside Sweden on campaign, a system of delegation of power emerged to enable the exercise of executive authority in Gustavus's extended absences. The administrative reforms that followed formalized procedures and provided offices for the nobility, changing them from hostile faction into loyal servants of the state. Oxenstierna's Chancery, a super-administrative agency, oversaw the other bureaus (colleges): the Treasury, which he reorganized in 1618, collected revenue; the Marshal, in charge of military administration; the Admiralty, for naval programs; and the 23 provincial governors (*landshövding*). The Judicature Ordinances of 1614–1615 created Sweden's first independent supreme court. An advanced system of high schools (*gymnasia*) provided civil servants to staff the new governmental structures. The University of Uppsala profited from direct royal patronage. To train administrators for the Baltic Empire, Gustavus founded a new university at Dorpat in 1632. Gustavus's reign brought higher standards of government (better administration and tax collection), the rule of law, and educational advancement. In 1600, Sweden did not have a central government; by 1626, it boasted the most efficient and well-ordered government in Europe.

Sweden undertook these domestic reforms for reasons of self-preservation. In 1611, the question rotated not around whether Sweden would emerge as the dominant power in northern Europe but rather if it could hold its position, even preserve its independence, in the face of an array of enemies. Oxenstierna summed up the situation when he told the council in 1611:

> First, it is generally known that all our neighbors are our enemies, the Poles, the Russians, and the Danes, so that no place in Sweden, Finland, and Livonia can say that it is safe from the enemy. Second, we have simply no friends who take our difficulties to heart. Third, there are none of our enemies who are not, or do not at least think themselves to be, greater and stronger than we.

The rivalry with Sigismund, with its religious overtones (defense of Protestantism against the Catholic Counter-Reformation), initiated a Swedish-Polish war which lasted, with intermittent truces, for 60 years (1600–60). Both Sweden and Poland tried to further their dynastic and territorial interests at the expense of Russia, then caught in the grips of domestic chaos. Most dangerous of all, the Danish king, **Christian IV,** invaded Sweden, intent upon restoring the Scandinavian Union. War on three fronts and a constitutional crisis at home had greeted the teenage King when he came to power.

Gustavus Accomplishes Foreign Objectives

Gustavus's foreign policy in the period 1612–20 focused on four inherited problems: (1) how to extricate himself from the war with Denmark; (2) how to end Swedish involvement in Russia, while preventing Poland from gaining advantage; (3) how to throw back cousin Sigismund's challenge to his throne; and (4) how to keep Sweden out of the religious war in Germany (Thirty Years' War). Despite long odds, he accomplished all his objectives. The Peace of Knäred (January 21, 1613) ended the War of Kalmar with Denmark on terms generally unfavorable to Sweden. Nonetheless, Denmark failed to restore the union. Sweden profited at the expense of the Russians at the Peace of Stolbova (February 27, 1617), gaining all Russia's territories on the Gulf of Finland. For the next century, Russia remained cut off from the Baltic. Gustavus now concentrated his efforts on Poland, claiming his campaigns against Sigismund lent indirect yet valuable aid to the Protestant cause in Germany. To solidify his position with the Protestant north German states, Gustavus married Maria Eleonora, daughter of George William, Elector of Brandenburg, on November 25, 1620. The marriage failed on all counts: not only did it not bring German support for Gustavus's war in Poland, he and the mentally unbalanced Maria Eleonora never produced a male heir.

From 1620 to 1630, the Baltic remained the sphere of action for Sweden. In October 1620, Poland sustained a ruinous defeat at the hands of the Turks. Gustavus seized the opportunity, cast aside the Truce of Tolberg, in effect since 1618, and invaded Livonia (Latvia). In September 1621, Riga, the richest economic prize in the Baltic, succumbed to a siege.

The whole of Livonia fell under Swedish control after Gustavus's victory at Wallhof (January 1626). Before Wallhof, he would have returned Riga to Poland in exchange for a guaranteed peace. After his military successes, the Swedish monarch decided to retain Livonia as the bulwark of a Baltic Empire. In 1627, he invaded Polish Prussia with the goal of controlling every major river-mouth port in the Baltic and with them the rich trade of northeastern Europe. The Truce of Altmark (September 16, 1629) and the Treaty of Tiegenhoff (February 18, 1630) accomplished the King's strategic objectives—the Baltic Sea was effectively a Swedish lake.

His successes in Poland and Prussia—though significant—did not make Sweden secure. While Sweden carved out its Empire in the Baltic, the forces of Protestantism in Germany suffered a series of setbacks. In contrast to France, England, Spain, and Sweden, Germany was only a loose confederation of separatist states. Although its origins lay in the struggle between Catholic and Protestant

German princes, the Thirty Years' War involved much more than religion. The Habsburg emperor, **Ferdinand II,** wanted to exploit the religious strife to expand his political powers inside the Holy Roman Empire. Whatever their religion, all German princes agreed on one point: the need to protect their independence against the efforts of the Emperor to centralize power. German Catholic states joined the Imperial coalition, not to further the Emperor's ambitions, but to pursue their own interests. Far from united, the Protestant side divided into Lutheran and Calvinist camps. Given this highly confusing and shifting environment, Sweden's attempts at building an alliance among the north German states failed. Gustavus's old rival, Christian IV, made a bid to lead a European-wide Protestant alliance. His efforts ended in disaster at the battle of Lutter (August 24–27, 1626). By the end of 1627, Frederick's Imperialist generals counts Tilly and **von Wallenstein** cleared northern Germany and penetrated mainland Denmark. Christian swallowed his pride and asked Sweden for assistance. Wallenstein, now Duke of Mecklenburg and commissioned "General of the Oceanic and Baltic Seas," clearly threatened Sweden.

To deny Wallenstein the best anchorage in the middle Baltic, Sweden defended and then held the German city of Stralsund in 1628. Gustavus still hoped to avoid a campaign in Germany, but efforts to foster yet another Protestant coalition based on Saxony and Brandenburg failed. Without allies, Gustavus decided to intervene, proclaiming himself champion of the Protestant cause.

Sweden Develops Premier Military Force

By 1630, the Swedish army had evolved into the premier fighting force throughout the world. Having absorbed the most current military techniques from his study of Maurice of Nassau and others, Gustavus applied them in his campaigns in Livonia and Prussia. Rejecting the cumbersome massed squares for linear formations, Swedish military doctrine emphasized rapid tactical movement and the firepower of musketeers over the shock value of pikemen. Light and highly mobile artillery pieces were integrated into the infantry to add weight of fire and psychological effect. The Swedes had learned the value of horses in an assault from Polish adversaries. By 1630, the Swedish cavalry was the equal to any in Europe. Gustavus employed his various arms in complementary offensive roles. The advancing lines of musketeers acted as a "rolling barrage" with the "regimental guns" providing direct artillery support. Next, the pikemen rushed forward to open gaps in the enemy line.

Finally, the impact of cavalry, striking home *á la Polonaise,* completed the combined arms attack. Mobility on the battlefield demanded incessant training and a high order of organization. Modern military organizations—companies, battalions, brigades—and the basic chain of command originated with Gustavus's army.

Nor was the Swedish army just another 17th-century mercenary army. This was the first true professional army. The officers, carefully nurtured by Gustavus, were expected to show initiative. The nucleus of the army—Swedish and Finnish regiments—came from a system of national conscription, unique to Sweden. Since feudalism never existed in Sweden, Swedes fought as free men in a national army. Discipline remained strict based on Gustavus's "Articles of War," which forbade swearing, blasphemy, drunkenness, and fornication. A mixture of Lutheranism and the inspired leadership of Gustavus engendered a crusading zeal among the officers and men. With prayers twice a day and a chaplain in every company, the Swedish army brought a new spirit to the war in Europe. In tactics, organization, and spirit, Gustavus's army ushered in the era of modern warfare.

Without major allies or substantial material resources, Gustavus's position offered few advantages. Not all the news was bad. A few weeks after the Swedish landings at Usedom on July 4, 1630, Ferdinand removed the untrustworthy Wallenstein from command. In January 1631, France joined in alliance with Sweden. Other than a financial subsidy, the French provided only moral support. Relying on revenue from the Baltic ports and French money, Gustavus paused to build up his forces with hired mercenaries before opening his German campaign.

Military operations got off to an unpromising start. Slowly clearing eastern Pomerania and Mecklenburg, the Swedes advanced rapidly up the Oder River to Frankfurt. The Swedish monarch hoped to deflect Tilly from his siege of Magdeburg, Sweden's single stalwart ally. On May 10, 1631, Magdeburg fell with 80% of its population perishing in the violence. The Sacking of Magdeburg dealt a serious blow to Protestant morale and Gustavus's prestige.

The Battle of Breitenfeld

Gustavus now made the fateful decision to cross the Elbe River. Two factors influenced his thinking: (1) the need to revive the Protestant cause; and (2) the desire to support his armies by living off the wealthy bishoprics and Imperial cities of central

Germany. The Swedish King intended to make war pay for itself. Several German princes rallied to Gustavus, including the reluctant Elector of Saxony, John William. On August 25, Tilly crossed into Saxony; on September 7, he was brought to battle at Breitenfeld, five miles north of Leipzig.

Breitenfeld offered the first examples of the superiority of the reformed Swedish army and represented a clear break from existing military practice. The Saxon army disintegrated under Tilly's assault, exposing Gustavus's 26,000 to the full weight of the Imperial army of 36,000. Worse, the Saxon rout left the Swedish flank uncovered. A conventional commander would have ordered a retreat; the Swedes coolly wheeled front to flank and launched a series of coordinated attacks on the tightly massed and disorganized Imperial infantry. The Swedish cavalry easily outperformed that of Count zu Pappenheim, reputed to be the best leader of horse in Europe. By nightfall, the Imperial army melted away, and its commander, Tilly, became a wounded fugitive. Breitenfeld overturned the military balance in the Thirty Years' War. Europe had witnessed the crowning success of a military revolution.

Instead of pursuing and destroying Tilly, logistical considerations once again obliged Gustavus to advance toward the Main and Rhine. Frankfurt-am-Main, Worms, and Mainz all fell under Swedish authority. Gustavus, the savior of Protestantism, celebrated Christmas in the palace of the Catholic Archbishop-Elector of Mainz. In a single campaign, he advanced from the Oder to the Rhine, defeated the invincible Tilly, and controlled the lion's share of Germany. Sweden had arrived as a great power.

The King spent the winter creating an administrative structure to extract "contributions" from the regions under Swedish control. Gustavus expected to raise an army of better than 200,000 men, requiring huge sums of money and an effective organization. Naturally, he brought Oxenstierna from Prussia to Mainz to oversee the administration. The closest thing Germany ever had to a central government took shape during the winter of 1631–32.

Gustavus envisioned a campaign for 1632 of Napoleonic scale. He planned to launch a concentric movement into Bavaria, Bohemia, and Austria with seven distinct armies. The offensive got off to a brilliant beginning when Gustavus staged a surprise crossing of the River Lech on April 5, 1632. The Swedes inflicted a devastating defeat on the Imperial forces. Tilly fell mortally wounded in the engagement. The whole of Bavaria and the road to Vienna now lay open.

Wallenstein, recalled to service by Ferdinand, immediately recognized the weakness of Gustavus's strategic position. The Swede's long and exposed line of communication, centered on the central German city of Erfurt, stretched all the way back to the Baltic. Ignoring the threat to Vienna, Wallenstein shifted his forces toward Nürnberg, threatening Erfurt. Outmaneuvered, Gustavus had to parry the Imperial action. After an exhaustive campaign, the impatient Swedish King received a nasty reversal at Alte Feste when he attacked a strong defensive position. The Imperial forces then moved into Saxony; Gustavus quickly marched to intercept. At Lützen, again near Leipzig, the two celebrated commanders squared off.

Wallenstein had made a careful study of Breitenfeld and decided to fight the battle on the defensive, compelling Gustavus to attack. Fog and wet conditions on this mid-November day delayed the Swedish onslaught and reduced the impact of their artillery. Anxious to carry the Imperialist position before Pappenheim could reinforce Wallenstein, the Swedish King took personal command of a cavalry regiment and prepared for the assault.

Gustavus Dies in Battle of Lützen

Although credited with creating the first modern army, Gustavus cannot be considered a modern commander. Always in the thick of the fighting, like one of his Gothic warrior-king heroes, Gustavus carried a musket ball in his neck as a trophy of but one of his many wounds. During his military career, he had countless brushes with death. Twice horses fell through ice beneath him; another was shot from under him. A legend grew that the Swedish King, as God's instrument, was immortal. At Lützen, his luck ran out. Almost before the attack got under way, Gustavus caught a musket ball. His horse bolted, carrying him into the melee where he died an unheroic death. His body, stripped by looters, lay face down in the mud.

When news of the King's passing spread through the Swedish lines, the psychological damage proved greater than the physical losses sustained in any battle. A regiment wavered until one of its chaplains started to sing a Lutheran hymn. Soon the whole Swedish line solemnly sang along. Inspired by anguish and the thirst for revenge, the Swedes and Finns surged forward. Lützen ended in another Swedish victory but at a terrific cost.

Sweden's military ascendancy, hard won at Breitenfeld and Lützen, ended in September 1634

IRENE HARAND

at the battle of Nördlingen. Sweden's defeat, combined with the Spanish intervention, led to the collapse of Oxenstierna's anti-Imperial alliance, the League of Heilbronn. To preserve the military balance, France directly entered the war in Germany. With the broadening of the war, the bloodletting proceeded for another 14 years. Finally, the exhausted powers signed the Treaties of Westphalia in 1648. One of the few victors, Sweden emerged from the Thirty Years' War as a recognized great power and guarantor of the Westphalian settlement.

Under Gustavus, Sweden consolidated its position in Estonia and isolated Russia. Gustavus's acquisition of Riga and Livonia gave Sweden its Empire. He won an armistice from Poland which temporarily removed the threat to the throne from his Catholic rival. The "Lion of the North" reversed the Swedish-Danish power relationship in Sweden's favor. More spectacular yet, his brilliant intervention into Germany removed the threat of a Catholic-Imperial conquest of the north. While he did not live to see it, his victories recorded a final block to the dangers of Protestantism from the Counter-Reformation. All these deeds were achieved before his death at the age of 38.

While Gustavus left his country with many advantages—an excellent army, social stability, and an efficient government—Sweden did not have the population or economic resources necessary to hold the Empire. Although the Swedish Empire collapsed, Gustavus's accomplishments, which astounded his contemporaries, easily matched those of Peter I and Catherine II of Russia or Frederick II of Prussia—monarchs now called "great." Fittingly, Oxenstierna's report to the council in Stockholm captured most effectively Gustavus Adolphus's place in European and Swedish history:

> In the world is now none that is his equal, nor has there been for centuries such a one; and indeed I doubt whether the future will produce his peer. Yea, truly we may call him King Gustav the wise and great, the father of the fatherland.

SOURCES:

Roberts, Michael. *Gustavus Adolphus and the Rise of Sweden.* English Universities Press, 1973.

Scott, Franklin D. *Sweden: The Nation's History.* University of Minnesota Press, 1977.

FURTHER READING:

Roberts, Michael. *Gustavus Adolphus.* 2 vols. Longmans, 1953, 1959.

———. *The Swedish Imperial Experience, 1560–1718.* Cambridge University Press, 1979.

Hadrian

(A.D. 76–138)

Widely traveled Roman emperor, who ordered the construction of the Pantheon in Rome and a wall across Britain, organized an efficient administration, began the systematizing of Roman law, and turned Rome's military policy from conquest to defense.

Born on January 24, A.D. 76, in Italica, an old Roman military colony in a beautiful region near Hispalis (present-day Seville), Hadrian was a younger cousin of **Trajan,** the first Roman emperor born in Spain. Hadrian's father Publius Aelius Hadrianus Afer, a member of a senatorial family, had held the high office of praetor; his mother was Domitia Paulina, a Roman matron from Gades (Cadiz) on the Atlantic coast 60 miles south of Italica. The couple had one daughter, named after her mother, and one son, destined to become the second emperor of Spanish birth. Only nine years old when his father died, Hadrian became the ward of Trajan, then a military commander often posted in distant places such as the Rhineland. As a result, Hadrian was under the more direct care of the equestrian Acilius Attianus, who took him for five years to Rome where the ruthless **Domitián** was emperor. After that, Hadrian returned for a time to his native Italica.

Earning the nickname *Graeculus* ("The Little Greek"), Hadrian was an intellectual young man who loved Greek literature. Like the former emperor **Nero,** he enjoyed painting, sculpting, singing, and writing poetry, but in other ways he

Name variations: Publius Aelius Hadrianus; his monuments often style him Imperator Caesar Traianus Hadrianus Augustus; his full title as emperor was Imperator Caesar divi Traiani filius divi Nervae nepos Traianus Hadrianus Augustus. Born January 24, A.D. 76 in Italica, a Roman colony near Hispalis (Seville), Hispania Baetica (Spain); died July 10, 138, at Baiae on the Bay of Naples, Italy; son of Publius Aelius Hadrianus Afer and Domitia Paulina of Gades (Cadiz); married: Vibia Sabina (grandniece of the emperor Trajan), 100; children: none. Descendants: although childless, he adopted Titus Aurelius Fulvus Boionus Antoninus, who later became the emperor Antoninus Pius, and ordered him in turn to adopt Marcus Annius Verus, who became Marcus Aurelius, Rome's famed "philosopher-king." Predecessor: Trajan. Successor: Antoninus Pius.

Contributed by J. Donald Hughes, Professor of History, University of Denver, Denver, Colorado

559

did not resemble Nero at all. A lover of the outdoors, he grew tall, handsome, and athletic, and enjoyed hunting above other sports. He had curly hair and would later grow a curly beard to hide a scar received in hunting or military practice, and perhaps to imitate Greek philosophers as well. Hadrian would be the first emperor to grow a beard, initiating a style popular among his successors and Roman men in general.

When Trajan returned to Rome in A.D. 93, he called upon Hadrian to join him there to learn more about Rome's military and political affairs. Not long afterward, at 19, Hadrian was appointed to the first of several military posts as tribune, or company officer, with the Second Roman Legion, *Adiutrix*, at Aquincum (Budapest) on the Danube frontier. He then served in a similar command in Lower Moesia (Bulgaria), and then in Upper Germany, where his hostile brother-in-law, Lucius Julius Ursus Servianus, was governor.

Following Domitián's unlamented death, the emperor had been succeeded by the elderly Nerva who had adopted Trajan as his successor. When Nerva died on January 25, A.D. 98, Hadrian was to take the army's congratulations to Trajan in Colonia Agrippina (Cologne) in Lower Germany and managed to do so despite Servianus's attempt to delay him by sabotaging his carriage. Hadrian traveled the last few miles on foot, pleasing Trajan all the more by his loyalty. The emperor took his young cousin on a tour of the troops along the Danube River, then returned with him to Rome.

Trajan's wife Plotina—a formidable and intellectual woman whose interests included philosophy, literature, mathematics, music, and works of charity—became Hadrian's friend and advocate. It was said that she regarded him as a substitute for the son she never had. Hadrian clearly respected her as well, writing that Plotina's "pity and honored dignity achieve all things." She arranged his marriage to Vibia Sabina, Trajan's grandniece, a union designed purely to benefit Hadrian's political career. Vibia Sabina was only 13 (he was 24). They were never attracted to each other, and the marriage remained childless. Still, in spite of animosity that sometimes emerged openly—with Hadrian calling her "tiresome and irritable" and Vibia Sabina murmuring that he was "inhuman"—she remained faithful to him in spite of his many affairs, and often they were able to fulfill their public duties amicably, cooperating on altruistic projects and traveling together on official tours.

Meanwhile, Trajan was bringing Rome to the height of its military power and the Roman Empire to the peak of its territorial expansion. Hadrian took part in his cousin's efforts, serving him as an officer in both campaigns during which the army crossed the Danube and conquered Dacia (Rumania). When Hadrian, as a member of the imperial secretariat, had to speak to the senate on behalf of the emperor, some of the senators snickered at his Spanish accent, moving him to take lessons to improve his pronunciation and Latin style. He thought Greek was a superior language, however, and spoke it fluently. He became such a master of both languages that Trajan made him his private secretary, entrusting him to write the emperor's speeches.

Hadrian's efforts were rewarded when Trajan made him governor of Lower Pannonia (part of Hungary and Yugoslavia), and then had him elected for the year 108 as one of Rome's two consuls—the highest magistracy in the Roman government and a great honor. The city of Athens complimented Hadrian by choosing him as their *archon* (ruler). The possibility that he was to become Trajan's designated successor had occurred to almost everyone, but for whatever reason, the emperor delayed making the choice.

Trajan Dies; Hadrian Becomes Emperor

In his last campaign, Trajan followed in the footsteps of **Alexander the Great,** attacking the

Parthian Empire that threatened Rome's eastern frontier and conquering Armenia and Mesopotamia (Iraq). In the course of this offensive, he appointed Hadrian governor of Syria, a strategic position on the army's supply lines. But Trajan's attempt to enlarge Rome's dominions met with military failures, and—facing several rebellions at once—he abandoned part of Mesopotamia and started to return to Rome. He had reached Cilicia (southern Turkey) when he suffered a massive stroke. With his death imminent, Trajan adopted Hadrian as son and heir, or perhaps Plotina arranged the adoption in his name. The news reached Hadrian on August 9, 117; two days later, word followed that Trajan had died on the 8th. Hadrian was emperor of Rome.

His first actions as emperor were decisive and intelligent, as were almost all those that followed. He sent generals such as Quintus Marcius Turbo to put down rebellions and deal with barbarian incursions, while using Attianus—then serving as prefect of Rome—to suppress a planned coup, the so-called "Conspiracy of the Four Consulars." The plotters, who were senators, were condemned by the senate and put to death. Secure in his position, Hadrian promoted Attianus out of his job and assured the remaining senators of his good intentions.

Perhaps the most conscientious administrator ever to rule the Roman Empire, Hadrian traveled throughout his dominions, visiting almost every province at least once, examining the defenses and ordering the construction of large public works. Desiring peace and convinced that Trajan had expanded the empire too far, particularly to the east, Hadrian abandoned Mesopotamia and Armenia and altered Rome's military policy from conquest to defense. His first journey as emperor in 120–22 illustrated this change, when he visited Britain and ordered construction of a barrier across the island to keep out the northern tribes and serve as a base for Roman military operations. Later known as Hadrian's Wall, the string of fortifications stretched 80 Roman miles between the North Sea and the Irish Sea a short distance south of the present Scottish border. He also began a customs palisade in Germany between the Rhine and Danube which later became the fortified *limes,* and for a time kept barbarian incursions out of a large and strategically valuable territory.

His former patroness, the widowed empress Plotina, died in 122. Though Hadrian's travels prevented him from holding the funeral in Rome until 124, he dedicated a temple to her in Nemausus (Nimes), her birthplace in Gallia Narbonensis (southern France).

In Athens, a city he visited often and loved even more than Rome, Hadrian extended the walls and added an entire quarter to the city, with an ornate arch, bearing his name, that still stands. He also ordered the construction of an important library and completed the Temple of Olympian Zeus, one of the largest temples in the Greco-Roman world.

In addition to being a prodigious traveler, Hadrian became the most famed mountain climber of Roman times. When in Sicily, reported Aelius Spartianus, he "climbed Mount Etna to see the sunrise, which is many-colored, it is said, like a rainbow." He also ascended Mount Casius in Syria by night, again to see the sunrise. There he made a sacrifice in the summit and, in what appeared to be a spectacular acceptance of the offering by Zeus, "a rainstorm arose … and a thunderbolt descended, blasting the sacrificial victim and the attendant."

Hadrian's most eventful trip to the Eastern Mediterranean occurred in 130. He took with him Sabina, whom he had officially made *Augusta* (empress) two years earlier, and his beloved favorite, the handsome 20-year-old Antinous. While they were in Egypt, Antinous drowned in the Nile River. It was said that he voluntarily committed suicide after soothsayers remarked that such a sacrifice would prolong Hadrian's life. The emperor, who had loved the young man for almost seven years, was consumed with grief. In accordance with the ancient Egyptian belief that anyone who died by drowning in the Nile became a god, Hadrian founded a city near the site of his death, named it Antinoopolis, marked it with a great memorial obelisk, and built a temple where Antinous would be worshipped as Osiris, the god whose body had been recovered from the Nile. Elsewhere in the Empire, countless statues of the young man were made and many of them placed in temples; in Rome, Antinous was identified with Silvanus, god of forests.

During the same journey, Hadrian visited Palestine and ordered the refounding of Jerusalem as Aelia Capitolina, a Roman colony. A temple of Zeus was to be built on the site of Solomon's Temple. Hadrian had observed revolts of the Jews under Trajan, and he knew the history of the Greek ruler Antiochus Epiphanes, who had tried to suppress Judaism and had provoked the Maccabean independence movement, so he should have known that his actions would provoke a reaction. Under the messianic leadership of Simeon Bar-Cochba, the Jews indeed rebelled, fighting an unsuccessful war for liberation between 131 and 135 which was very costly on both sides. After the war, Hadrian completed Aelia Capitolina as a city from which Jews were excluded.

Since the days of **Claudius** (A.D. 41–54), the emperor had appointed a secretariat headed by freemen (ex-slaves) to execute imperial policy. But by Trajan's time, this structure had outlived its usefulness, and Hadrian—devoted to administrative and financial efficiency—replaced it with a proficient civil service employing the equestrian order or "knights," the second rank of Roman citizens under the senatorial class. The most important of these was the prefect of the Praetorian Guard, who performed many of the emperor's duties in his absences from the city. The imperial budget was moved firmly into the black, and tax collection was as regular and honest under Hadrian as it ever became under any emperor. At the same time, he granted exemption from onerous and expensive public duties to philosophers, physicians, and teachers of rhetoric and grammar.

Even more important as a foundation for later developments was his sponsorship of the first major step in the codification of Roman Law under the emperor, which was the promulgation of the Perpetual Edict. In this, he was assisted by the eminent legal scholar, Salvius Julianus, and other brilliant lawyers such as Juventius Celsus and Neratius Priscus. In earlier times, important magistrates called *praetores* issued edicts that had the force of civil law but were valid for only one year, the term of office for praetors. The Perpetual Edict, however, was a standard that was not changed from year to year. When Roman Law was systematized by **Justinian** four centuries later, Hadrian's Perpetual Edict was chosen as the starting point for the jurist's work.

Hadrian Builds in Rome

Most of the last eight years of Hadrian's reign were spent in Rome, where he erected a number of large buildings, many of which showed considerable architectural innovation. The most notable of these is the Pantheon, a temple dedicated to the seven planetary deities (Sol, Luna, Mercury, Venus, Mars, Jupiter, and Saturn), which was a circular drum surmounted by a hemispherical dome whose diameter, 142 feet, was exactly equal to its height above the floor. At the top of the dome was an *oculus*, or open circular skylight, almost 30 feet in diameter, while outside, a more conventional temple facade sheltered the doorway. The Pantheon survives almost undamaged today. Across the Tiber River from the main sector of ancient Rome stands Hadrian's Mausoleum, another circular building which was originally crowned by a conical tumulus of earth planted with trees like a sacred grove and by a statue of Hadrian in a golden chariot pulled by four horses. During the Middle Ages, the mausoleum was turned into a fortress and renamed the *Castel Sant'Angelo.* Hadrian had connected it to the rest of the city by a bridge, the Pons Aelius, later called "The Bridge of the Angels."

Located at Tibur (Tivoli), one of Hadrian's most remarkable constructions was the Villa Tiburtina (Hadrian's Villa), a huge complex of many buildings in different architectural styles reminiscent of Hadrian's journeys through distant parts of the empire. Covering more than a square mile, counting the surrounding gardens and forests, it includes the Canopus, with statuary and a reflecting pool recalling Egypt, the Nile, and Antinous's death; a reproduction of Plato's Academy and Aristotle's Lyceum from Athens; a recreation of the beautiful Vale of Tempe in Greece; and even an underground palace called Hades.

In 135, Hadrian fell ill with a long, wasting disease that finally killed him more than two years later but allowed him ample opportunity to choose his own successors. His closest eligible relative was Cnaeus Pedanius Fuscus Salinator, grandson of his detested brother-in-law Servianus. But Fuscus was a teenager who had not yet demonstrated any talent, and Servianus was near 90, his age a tribute to Hadrian's clemency. Hadrian's mercy, however, was at an end; the two men were put to death to keep them from claiming the throne. Instead, Hadrian adopted Lucius Ceionius Commodus Verus, a pleasure seeking man who, fortunately for Rome, perished of disease before Hadrian did. Making a better choice, Hadrian adopted Titus Aurelius Fulvus Boionus Antoninus, who would later become the emperor Antoninus Pius. Hadrian also took the unusual step of ensuring the succession for another generation by commanding Antoninus to adopt Marcus Annius Verus, who thus became Hadrian's adopted grandson; he would later have a distinguished reign as **Marcus Aurelius,** Rome's "philosopher-king." Marcus's brother Lucius Verus, a much less talented young man, was also adopted, and served for a time as coemperor.

Knowing death was near, Hadrian retired to the pleasant town of Baiae on the Bay of Naples and, in spite of his intense suffering, composed a poem which he repeated as he died. The day was July 10, 138; Hadrian was 62 years old and had been emperor for almost 21 years. His body was placed in his great mausoleum in Rome by Antoninus Pius, who made certain that the senate passed a decree honoring Hadrian as a god and ratifying all his acts as emperor.

SOURCES:

Birley, Anthony, trans. *Lives of the Later Caesars.* Penguin, 1976. (Contains the Life of Hadrian by Aelius Spartianus.)

Henderson, Bernard William. *The Life and Principate of the Emperor Hadrian, A.D. 76-138.* Methuen, 1923.

Perowne, Stewart. *Hadrian.* Norton, 1961.

Smallwood, E. Mary, ed. *Documents Illustrating the Principates of Nerva, Trajan and Hadrian.* Cambridge University Press, 1966.

Breeze, David J., and Brian Dobson. *Hadrian's Wall.* Allen Lane, 1976.

Embleton, Ronald, and Frank Graham. *Hadrian's Wall in the Days of the Romans.* Dorset, 1990.

Lambert, Royston. *Beloved and God: The Story of Hadrian and Antinous.* Viking, 1984.

Yourcenar, Marguerite. *Memoirs of Hadrian* (fiction). Translated from the French by Grace Frick. Farrar, Straus, 1963.

FURTHER READING:

Boatwright, Mary Taliaferro. *Hadrian and the City of Rome.* Princeton University Press, 1987.

Douglas Haig

(1861–1928)

Military leader, who led the British Expeditionary Force through years of horrific trench warfare to victory against Germany in World War I.

Name variations: Sir Douglas Haig; Field Marshal Earl Haig. Born June 19, 1861; died January 29, 1928; son of John (a successful Scottish whiskey distiller) and Rachael Haig; married: Dorothy Vivian, July 11, 1905; children: (two daughters) Alexandra Haig and Victoria Haig; (one son) George Alexander Eugene Douglas Haig.

An ancient Scottish border family, the Haigs could trace their ancestral lineage back to the 12th century. Historically, they had distinguished themselves for fighting on the side of the Scots during the incessant border wars and raids that characterized early English-Scottish relations. By the 19th century, however, members of the Haig clan were successfully engaged in commercial and industrial enterprises as citizens of the United Kingdom. John Haig and his wife Rachael were one such prosperous branch. John directed the distillery bearing the family name, which continues to produce a distinctive and world renowned single malt whiskey.

On June 19, 1861, John Haig's fifth and final son, Douglas, was born in Edinburgh, Scotland. Unlike his ancestors' struggles along the rugged border region, Douglas's childhood was comfortable in this well-to-do and large family (he had four sisters in addition to his four brothers). Though his physical environment might have led young Douglas to a complacent acceptance of his privileged life, as happened with so many other young men of his class in Victorian Britain, his mother Rachael instilled within him a profound faith and sense of duty to the greater good.

"He was, I should say, a man of chivalrous and scrupulous character. He made me feel that the war would last thirty years, and that he would carry it on irreproachably until he was superannuated."

GEORGE BERNARD SHAW

Contributed by Andrew P.N. Erdmann, Ph.D. candidate in American History, Harvard University, Cambridge, Massachusetts

His education was characteristic of his class in the late 19th century. First, he attended a day school near his home in Edinburgh. In his teenage years, he went to Clifton College in preparation for university. Haig's early academic performance gave no harbinger of his later success. As a mediocre student, he distinguished himself more by his dedicated effort than by any innate intellectual ability.

Near the completion of his secondary education his parents died within one year of each other. Thus, when he entered Brasnose College of Oxford University in the fall of 1880, he was an heir, with considerable independent means, in search of a career. While at university, Haig had no ambition to flourish as a scholar; he nevertheless continued with his diligent approach to his studies and heartily accepted the advice offered all entering undergraduates by Brasnose's principal to "ride, sir, ride." While at Oxford, he became a skilled horseman and developed his talents as an accomplished polo player. More than likely, this love of riding, when combined with the mystique that has always surrounded the cavalry, helped convince Haig that he would be happy with a military career.

Accordingly, after completing his Oxford examinations, Haig took advantage of the provision that university graduates gained automatic admission to the Royal Military College, Sandhurst, the British equivalent of West Point. Entrance to Sandhurst by university graduates was uncommon; usually cadets entered directly from secondary school. Therefore, upon his admittance in February 1884, Haig was surrounded by men younger than himself in both age and maturity. Reserved by nature, he was distanced even further from his classmates by this disparity. Following the pattern established earlier in his educational career, Haig rose to the top of his class, not by the power of his intellect or his imagination but by industriously applying himself to his studies. For recreation, and in preparation for a career as a cavalry officer, Haig also honed his considerable skills as a polo player.

On February 7, 1885, Haig was commissioned as a lieutenant in the 7th Hussars, a cavalry regiment. In his early years, his greatest service to his regiment was not as a military leader but as a polo player. Within the British military, rivalries between regiments were endemic. Led by Haig's ability, his regiment won the coveted Inter-Regimental trophy in June 1886. Later that summer, Haig was picked as a member of the English national polo team which easily defeated the United States in competition.

After these athletic successes, Haig's career began in earnest when his regiment was transferred to India. Though his first overseas posting was to a region derisively called the "Sloth Belt" by many officers, the young Scot vigorously resisted any temptation to succumb to this tranquil environment. During this time, Haig impressed his superiors in a series of assignments, alternating between staff posts and cavalry commands, and steadily rose in rank and responsibility. Ever ambitious, Haig recognized that graduation from the prestigious Staff College was a prerequisite for further promotions. Unfortunately, he failed in his first attempt to gain entrance because of his color blindness and his lack of proficiency in mathematics.

This setback proved to be temporary. Haig was soon transferred back to England and assigned to observe French and German army maneuvers. Cultivating important allies in the upper echelons of the military establishment and employing friends' ties to the royal family, Haig's excellent performance did not go unnoticed—nor unrewarded. Though his eyesight never improved, Haig was eventually offered a place at the Staff College.

He Expounds on the Place of Cavalry in War

Before entering, Haig was assigned the duty of completing the new edition of the service's *Cavalry Drill Book*, allowing him an opportunity to expound on his understanding of warfare. The vision

CHRONOLOGY

1880	Entered Brasnose College, Oxford University
1884	Entered Royal Military College, Sandhurst
1885	Commissioned lieutenant in the 7th Hussars
1896	Entered Staff College at Camberley
1898	Battle of Omdurman
1899	Boer War began
1901	Queen Victoria died
1914	First World War began
1915	Appointed commander in chief of British Expeditionary Force
1916	Battle of the Somme began
1917	America declared war on Germany; Lenin led Soviet coup d'état in Russia
1918	Armistice with Germany signed
1928	Died of a heart attack

of war he outlined in 1896 was firmly rooted in his past training, not in an understanding of evolutionary trends: to him, the cavalry charge remained the decisive feature of warfare, even in the face of the increasing firepower of the first generation of machine guns.

During his two years at the college, begun in February 1896, Haig came into his own within the military. Unlike at Sandhurst, his peers were now of comparable age, maturity, ambition, and experience. Though he now saw himself amongst equals, his personality and intellectual approach remained immutable. As one of his classmates, General Barrow, would later describe the reasons for his success:

> It was not his brains that brought him forward.... Neither was it tact, of which he had little; nor imagination of which he had none.... It was his personality and his power of concentration.

The strong impression Haig created at the Staff College was best captured by an instructor's prediction that he would one day be the commander in chief.

Though Haig possessed impeccable credentials within the British military establishment, he needed to prove his mettle in a combat command if he were ever to realize his highest ambitions. Immediately upon graduation from the Staff College, Haig had his chance. He was one of three officers selected from his class for secondment, or loan, to the Egyptian Army. For years Great Britain and her ally Egypt had been trying to suppress a native insurrection in the Sudan, just south of Egypt, and by 1898 the preparations were made for the final offensive against the rebel Dervishes. For ten months, Haig served as an officer in the Egyptian army. He distinguished himself under fire at the Battle of Atbara and then again at the Battle of Omdurman, during which the power of the Dervishes was finally crushed. After Egypt, Haig was back in Britain for only a few months before he was set into combat yet again, this time in southern Africa. His new brigade, the 1st Calvary, was deployed to Great Britain's southern African colonies at the outbreak of hostilities between the forces of the British Empire and the Boers (descendants of Dutch settlers) on October 11, 1899. During the Boer War, Haig again demonstrated his aptitude as both a staff officer and a commander in the field before the conflict finally ended in May 1902.

Haig emerged a colonel from the Boer War and was recognized as one of the leading lights in his generation of officers. As he explained his conception of duty to a nephew following the war, however, he saw himself not simply as an army officer, but as one of the standard bearers of the British Empire:

> Don't let the life of mediocrities about you deflect you from your determination to belong to the few who can command or guide or benefit our Great Empire. Believe me, the reservoir of such men is not boundless. As our great Empire grows, so there is a greater demand for them, and it behoves [sic] everyone to do his little and try and qualify for as high a position as possible. It is not ambition. This is *duty*.

Driven by this sense of duty and repeatedly catching the eye of his superiors, Haig continued his rise through the ranks during the 12 years between the end of the Boer War and the beginning of the First World War. His progress was steady. From the command of the 17th Lancers regiment, he returned again to India in 1903 as the inspector general of cavalry. He was recalled from this post in 1906 to take responsibility for the creation of the Imperial General Staff, a command structure which coordinated the training and organization of all the British Empire's forces. Spending two more years in India as chief of staff to the commander in chief of the Indian Army, Haig returned home in March 1912 as a lieutenant general to be given the Aldershot command. This post carried the responsibility for the First Army Corps, a detachment destined for the European continent in time of war as part of the British Expeditionary Force.

These years of professional advance were filled with personal happiness as well. During his leave from India in June 1905, Haig was invited to spend a week with King **Edward VII** at Windsor Castle. There he met and immediately fell in love with one of Queen Alexandra's maids of honor, Dorothy Vivian. Engaged within two days, they were married within a month on July 11, 1905. When a friend questioned him on the wisdom of such a rapid courtship, Haig responded in true form: "Why not? I have often made up my mind on more important problems than that of my own marriage in much less time." Within three years, this happy marriage bore two daughters, Alexandra and Victoria.

The same self-confidence and decisiveness continued to characterize his understanding of warfare. Haig's faith in the cavalry charge as the decisive element in combat remained unchanged. After the Boer War, he belittled the power of artillery, except against "raw troops." In 1907,

Haig published his only book, *Cavalry Studies, Strategical and Tactical,* in which he outlined the role of the mounted service in future war. Though he correctly predicted that future conflicts would be on a larger scale than the past, he simply could not come to grips with the reality that the increased firepower of modern weapons, most notably the machine gun and modern artillery, had irrevocably changed the nature of warfare. Conceptually trapped within his own past experiences and his detailed historical studies of previous campaigns, Haig concluded that "the role of Cavalry on the battlefield will always go on increasing." Supremely confident in his own abilities and these precepts of war, Haig, now an aide-de-camp general, led his First Corps onto the battlefields of northern France when the First World War began in August 1914.

The first encounters of the war largely fulfilled Haig's expectations. The German army attempted to outflank the main French defenses by driving through Belgium, into northern France, and then southward toward Paris. The war was dominated in its first weeks by the maneuver of large units, thrust and counterthrust. Haig's component of the British Expeditionary Force was deployed in the most crucial sector of the front. His quick thinking, deliberate planning, and tactical skill were then instrumental in thwarting the German advance in the First Battle of Ypres (October 19 to November 22, 1914). Haig now became a national figure in Great Britain.

By the onset of winter in late 1914, however, the war of maneuver had degenerated into ghastly trench warfare. As the war wore on through 1915, the casualties mounted after a series of inconclusive battles changed nothing except the commanders of the British Expeditionary Force. On December 10, 1915, a frustrated Prime Minister Herbert Asquith relieved General John French as commander in chief of the British Expeditionary Force and offered the post to Haig, who unhesitatingly accepted.

Haig Leads British Forces at the Somme

Haig believed that he understood how to crack the seemingly impregnable network of trenches and fortifications that the Germans had constructed: an extended artillery barrage to be followed by an assault by an overwhelmingly superior force. The sight for the assault was to be the Somme. In the spring of 1916, the Germans launched their own offensive against the French at Verdun, to the south of the British sector of the front. Though the timetable for Haig's offensive was accelerated to July 1, 1916, to help relieve the pressure on the deteriorating French army, the plan remained essentially unchanged. British artillery bombarded the German positions for an entire week with over 1,500,000 rounds. On the morning of July 1, the infantry climbed out of their trenches and began to cross the almost lunar-like landscape of No Man's Land toward the German positions. Remarkably, the Germans withstood the bombardment, emerged from their bunkers, and proceeded to mow the advancing British and French infantry down with machine-gun fire. The Allies suffered over 60,000 casualties during the first day alone. When Haig received the first casualty figures on July 2—an estimate of 40,000 total casualties—he recorded in his diary that "this cannot be considered severe in view of the numbers engaged, and the length of the front attacked." Unable to see, or perhaps admit, the disaster as it unfolded, Haig continued the offensive. By the time the operation ended in November 1916, Allied forces had suffered over 600,000 casualties and inflicted a like number on the Germans. For this appalling slaughter, the front hardly shifted and Haig received his promotion to field marshal on January 1, 1917.

Reviewing the carnage of the Somme, Haig's faith in his basic tactics remained unshaken. Rather than revising his belief that the German line could be broken by a concentration of artillery and infantry, Haig shifted the next British offensive northwards to the region where France and Belgium meet the sea. He calculated that the German defenses would be less formidable in this sector. Before the French army's offensive of April 1917, Haig had advised its commander, General Nivelle, that it would become clear after one to two days whether the offensive was decisive; if it was not, then the operation should be suspended. In practice, Haig would ignore this advice. With the extended artillery bombardment and concentration of forces, the Germans were not surprised when the Third Battle of Ypres began on July 31. The British attack literally bogged down within days under early autumn rainfall. After some initial progress, the Germans still commanded what high ground existed. Haig decided that it was better to continue and, as the weather worsened in October, he ordered more attacks in the area near the village of Passchendaele. On October 11, Haig revealed both his unwavering confidence and his remarkable detachment from the realities of the battlefield by telling a group of war correspondents that the mud alone, not the Germans, was slowing the advance and that he was close to the crucial breakthrough. Events proved him wrong. The slaughter continued for insignificant gains measured in yards, not miles. Haig pressed on for another month until the campaign ended on November 10, 1917, at the cost of over 240,000 British casualties.

In the spring of 1918, the German army launched its last major offensive of the war, risking everything on the chance of achieving a decisive victory before the full force of the United States, which entered the war the previous April, could be brought to bear. A few days after the birth of his only son Earl, Haig was greeted by the German offensive. Instead of using mass infantry charges, the Germans successfully exploited new tactics based on small groups of "stormtroopers" operating independently to destabilize the Allied defenses. As the British forces fell into confusion and collapse seemed possible, Haig issued a famous special order to all of his troops on April 11, 1918:

> There is no course open to us but to fight it out. Every position must be held to the last man: there must be no retirement. With our backs to the wall and believing in the justice of our cause each one of us must fight on to the end. The safety of our homes and the Freedom of mankind alike depend upon the conduct of each one of us at this critical moment.

The forces of Great Britain rallied and, along with their French and now American allies, eventually blunted the German offensive.

As he had in 1916 and 1917, Haig thought that an offensive could achieve the decisive breakthrough and conclude the war before the end of the year. This time he was correct. Allied counterattacks along the entire front began to retake the territory recently lost to the Germans. Though the Germans fought tenaciously, the toll of their spring offensive was too much, and by October 1918, Allied forces began to overrun the once mighty and intimidating Hindenburg line. On November 11, 1918, the Armistice was signed.

In the years after the war, Haig supervised the demobilization of British forces until he gave up his command of Home Forces in January 1921. As symbolic appreciation for his services to the realm, Haig was granted a special £100,000 reward by Parliament and created an earl. In his final years, he devoted himself wholeheartedly to the creation of a unified organization, the British Legion, to represent and relieve the distress of veterans of the Great War. He died suddenly of a heart attack on January 29, 1928, and was given the final honor of a full national funeral.

To comprehend the course of Douglas Haig's career, one must return to an understanding of his fundamental nature, as described by his colleague Field Marshal Wavell:

> Haig … had a single-track mind, intensely and narrowly concentrated, like a telescope, on the one object. Except for his profession of soldiering, and later his family, he had no real interests of any kind, and little knowledge; nor had he any desire for knowledge, unless it bore on his own special subject…. Haig, secure in his own self-confidence, seldom listened to the opinion of others.

His vision's restricted focus enabled Haig to motivate himself in peace, as well as in war, to unprecedented efforts. These exertions propelled him to the apex of the British military hierarchy. This same "single-track" outlook, however, also led to Haig's unimaginative and stubborn prosecution of trench warfare. Neglecting surprise, Haig's search for the decisive breakthrough by frontal assault propagated instead a prolonged war of attrition. Though he cannot be faulted for seeking such a breakthrough, he can be faulted for his inability to recognize in a timely fashion when an offensive no longer promised any chance of success. Within his mental constitution, therefore, lay the roots of both the successes and the limitations of Field Marshal Douglas Haig's leadership.

SOURCES:

Blake, Robert, ed. *The Private Papers of Douglas Haig, 1914–1919.* Eyre & Spottiswoode, 1952.

Fussell, Paul. *The Great War and Modern Memory.* Oxford University Press, 1975.

Marshall-Cornwall, James. *Haig as Military Commander.* Batsford, 1973.

Sixsmith, E. K. G. *Douglas Haig.* Weidenfeld & Nicolson, 1976.

FURTHER READING:

Chateris, John. *Field Marshall Earl Haig.* Cassell, 1929.

Cooper, Duff. *Haig.* 2 vols. Faber, 1935.

Davidson, John. *Haig, Master of the Field.* Peter Nevill, 1953.

Keegan, John. *The Face of Battle: A Study of Agincourt, Waterloo and the Somme.* Viking, 1976.

Terraine, John. *Douglas Haig: The Educated Soldier.* Hutchinson, 1963.

Dag Hammarskjöld

(1905–1961)

Swedish statesman and economist, who was posthumously awarded the 1961 Nobel Peace Prize for his work as secretary-general of the United Nations from 1953 to 1961.

"You can only hope to find a lasting solution to a conflict if you have learned to see the other objectively, but, at the same time, to experience his difficulties subjectively."

DAG HAMMARSKJÖLD

When Dag Hammarskjöld became secretary-general of the United Nations in 1953, the world's hopes that the organization would preside over a new era of international cooperation and peace had been dashed.

Eight years earlier, in the spring of 1945, delegates from 50 nations had gathered in San Francisco to write the Charter of the United Nations, committing the world community to use "collective security" to prevent and remove threats to world peace. Aggression would be met by united resistance; international differences would be settled by peaceful means in conformity with principles of justice and international law. Within two years the Cold War intervened, polarizing the world once again. As postwar tensions between the United States and the Soviet Union grew, the working relationship that the two victors had maintained during World War II disintegrated. Eastern Europe became a communist camp under the aegis of the Soviet Union, and Western Europe remained capitalist, taking its direction from the United States. Regional military alliances did and would emerge outside the United Nations framework: NATO in 1949 for Western Europe

Pronunciation: HAM-er-shold. Born Dag Hjalmar Agne Carl Hammarskjöld in Jonkoping, Sweden, on July 29, 1905; killed in a plane crash in September 1961; son of Hjalmar (prime minister of Sweden) and Agnes Hammarskjöld; never married.

Contributed by Kathleen Gefell Centola, Adjunct Assistant Professor, Pace University, New York, New York

and the United States, and the Warsaw Pact in 1955 for Eastern Europe and the Soviet Union.

In the East, Korea and Vietnam were divided into Communist and non-Communist sectors with separate governments. China became the People's Republic of China in 1949 under the Communist leadership of **Mao Zedong. Chiang Kai Shek**'s nationalist government fled to Taiwan, which became the "official" China as far as the West was concerned—the only China with a seat on the United Nation's Security Council.

This contraposition of the new superpowers and their client states created a deadlock in the Security Council where the world's "ruling" powers—the United States, England, France, nationalist China, and the Soviet Union—were permanent members. Without the agreement of all the members, no serious political or military action was possible. Since it was impossible, in most cases, for all to agree on any clear-cut definition of aggression, it had become more and more difficult to translate the U.N. charter's promise into practical action.

The world had grown more dangerous since the formation of the United Nations. The proliferation of nuclear weapons meant that war involving the superpowers would be a global catastrophe unprecedented in human history. At the same time, the end of World War II had stimulated a multitude of independence movements in Asia and Africa, and the colonial empires of the Western imperialist nations unravelled. As the superpowers competed for the allegiance of the emerging nations of the Third World, the possibility of the Cold War becoming "hot" increased.

By 1952, **Trygve Lie,** the first secretary-general, had been forced to resign his post because conflict within the United Nations had rendered him almost totally ineffective. In 1950, Lie supported the Security Council's approval of the U.S. decision to use force to resist North Korea's invasion of South Korea. This decision was made while the Soviet Union was absent from the Security Council, boycotting the refusal to admit Mao's government to China's seat. Lie's support destroyed his relationship with the Soviet Union. Considering him to be biased in favor of the West, the Soviets censured him and refused to communicate with him for two years. Trygve Lie's inability to walk the tightrope between the two hostile superpowers paved the way for Dag Hammarskjöld's tour of duty, which began on April 7, 1953.

Dag Hammarskjöld was born in Jonkoping, Sweden, on July 29, 1905, into an aristocratic Swedish family that for centuries had provided outstanding civil servants and soldiers. Perhaps the most important influence on the boy's later career was his father Hjalmar Hammarskjöld. Autocratic, conservative (though never aligned with any political party), remote, and arrogant, Hjalmar Hammarskjöld nevertheless imparted to his son the importance of self-sacrifice and duty in the service of international justice. The elder Hammarskjöld had a long and distinguished career as a Swedish civil servant. He joined the Swedish cabinet as minister of justice and later served as president of the Gota High Court of Appeals. In 1907, he was appointed governor of the province of Uppsala, where Dag Hammarskjöld grew to manhood in the ancient governor's castle. He was also a member of the International Court of Arbitration and first delegate to the second peace conference at The Hague. From 1914 to 1917, he was Sweden's prime minister. After World War I, he served as chairman of the League of Nations' committee for the codification of international law and as a delegate to the Washington Disarmament Conference in 1921.

From his father's example and personal convictions and because the issues of international law and justice were brought to the dinner table for discussion, Dag realized early the importance of an international order where "society is welded together by that higher 'reason' common to us all, which is the bearer of justice."

From his mother Agnes, a generous, "radically democratic" woman, Dag acquired a love of mankind and a deeply religious sensibility. Agnes Hammarskjöld was an intimate friend of Archbishop Nathan Soderblom, theologian and primate of the Lutheran Church of Sweden, whose children were the constant companions of Dag and his brothers. Soderblom was one of the founders of the 20th-century ecumenical movement for Christian unity. Thus a certain religious internationalism also permeated Dag's early life. Disillusioned over the ineffectiveness of the churches in forestalling World War I, Soderblom dedicated himself to rallying church leaders from all the major affiliations to pressure for "Christian judgments" on the social, political, and international issues of the postwar world. In 1925, he organized and presided over the Universal Christian Conference on Life and Work which in turn resulted in the establishment of the World Council of Churches. This church policy of Soderblom in the 1920s made Uppsala, the episcopal seat, an international center.

As an adult Hammarskjöld seems to have combined the three central themes of his youth—civic duty, Christian self-sacrifice, and internationalism—into a working ethic that determined the direction that his life took and the particular way he was able to find meaning in his life.

From 1922, young Hammarskjöld attended Uppsala University as an undergraduate studying literature, philosophy, and French and specializing in political economy. His quick mind, great energy, and discipline allowed him to complete his B.A. in two years. For his doctorate degree, Hammarskjöld chose law. Though his academic career was outstanding, loneliness consumed him. Shy, reserved, believing his father's conviction about the duty of hard work, Hammarskjöld did not take part in the usual entertainments characteristic of a university town. While others lived in student quarters, he lived with his family in the governor's castle. Though he was quite popular with his fellow students (he was elected First Curator of the Uppsala Nation, a Swedish fraternity), he found real intimacy difficult. In many ways Hammarskjöld's detachment came from habits of mind—his impatience with easy small talk and his tendency to reduce all conversation to "essentials."

His emotional isolation, a lifelong problem that would intensify in later life as he remained unmarried, was recorded in his diary, which was published posthumously in 1964. Without personal intimacy and having rejected the Lutheran Christianity of his parents, Hammarskjöld's inner life was tormented by a sense of meaninglessness. He feared he used work as an anesthetic against loneliness and books as a substitute for people. Yet Hammarskjöld retained tremendous religious sensibilities—if not formal religion—and eventually turned to the writings of the great medieval mystics to work out his inner turmoil that spanned many years.

After receiving his doctorate, Hammarskjöld, like his father, made a career in government service, specializing in economics. He was part of Sweden's "Stockholm School," the group of young economists responsible for advocating and implementing Sweden's planned economy in the 1930s. Between 1932 and 1952, he held a number of positions in government and finance. In 1936, he became permanent undersecretary of state in the Swedish foreign office. He also became associated with the National Bank of Sweden, eventually becoming chairman of the board in 1941. His phenomenal capacity for work, his moral stature, his conscientious sense of responsibility, and his incorruptible sense of justice earned him the respect of his colleagues. Although he became a member of Sweden's Social-Democratic government, Hammarskjöld remained a non-political independent. He held strongly to the belief that the civil servant must serve the community rather than any particular group or private political ends. In 1947, he acquired further diplomatic experience as a delegate to the Organization of European Economic Cooperation and the Council of Europe, which convened after World War II. In 1951, he entered the cabinet as minister of state, and in 1952 he became chairman of Sweden's U.N. delegation. By 1953, he was the secretary-general of the United Nations.

Hammarskjöld came to the U.N. with a distinct vision of international politics and his new role as an international civil servant. From his family background he brought a strong commitment to international diplomacy, and his Swedish heritage disposed him to appreciate the vital importance of international law for the protection and development of the smaller nations of the world. On the other hand, his practical diplomatic experience inclined him to dismiss the excessive hopes and foolish claims which accompanied the founding of the U.N. and which then led to great disillusionment when the realities of power politics became apparent. "The UN," he said, "was not created in order to bring us to Heaven but in order to save us from Hell." In the midst of superpower polarity and deadlock in the Security Council, Hammarskjöld hoped to bring to the office of secretary-general a transcendent integrity that would allow him, in the name of the office, to accomplish what others—representatives of individual governments—could not. As he had in Sweden, he saw his role as a neutral civil servant, a go-between and face-saver and, when things went wrong, a scapegoat. Thus, he relied on a highly personal approach—"quiet diplomacy" he called it—stressing his responsibility as secretary-general and building frequent behind-the-scenes contacts and intimate relationships with key leaders and personalities. While he could not alter the realities of the Cold War, he saw his mission as diffusing those world crises—particularly in the Third World—that could have escalated into superpower confrontations. Receiving the call to be secretary-general also enabled him to solve his inner spiritual crisis. He was finally a happy man, finding at last his life's meaning in this "higher calling." Now he viewed the loneliness of his solitary life as the prerequisite—the sacrifice—for a role that required freedom from the obligations of family life and close emotional ties. He often compared himself to a Catholic priest who renounces marriage in order to give his love in a broader sense to humanity.

Hammarskjöld brought insights from previous diplomatic experience and a unique personal style to the Secretariat. He believed the key to persuading national leaders toward a sensible course often lay in finding a way for them to preserve their prestige. He frequently turned up at trouble spots and gathered impressions long before the Security Council had time to meet. Hammarskjöld's extraordinary sensitivity to the sensibilities of the people with whom he dealt enabled him to suggest new and unexpected options for solutions in situations that appeared hopeless. Gradually the ideas themselves would gain acceptance.

By stressing that the secretary-general transcended the power blocs within the United Nations, he was able in 1955 to gain access to **Chou En-Lai** of the People's Republic of China and persuade him to release 11 U.S. airmen captured during the Korean War. The condemnation of Peking by the General Assembly and the refusal to admit Red China to the Security Council had encouraged Chinese hostility to the U.N. Hammarskjöld's meetings with Chou En-Lai established an extraordinary rapport between them. By establishing the "link of mutual human sympathy"—a fundamental Hammarskjöld method— Chou En-Lai released the airmen as a "birthday gift" to Hammarskjöld, now a friend and representative of the world community.

Although Hammarskjöld made progress in finding peaceful solutions to conflicts in Asia, notably in Laos, and in securing the release of the U.S. airmen, the problems in the Middle East and Africa dominated his tenure of office. The Middle East was a particularly turbulent region in the postwar era. Arab-Israeli feuding over boundaries and rights of passage on the Suez Canal and the East-West competition for client states made the possibility of war a dangerous prospect. It became a reality in 1956 with the "Suez Crisis," a frightening confrontation of world powers, but Hammarskjöld's shining moment as secretary-general.

The Suez Crisis Erupts

On July 26, 1956, Colonel **Gamel Abdel Nasser** nationalized the Suez Canal in retaliation for the United States's withdrawal of an offer to finance Egypt's Aswan Dam Project. England and France, economically dependent on passage through the canal, announced in October that they were going to take control of the canal by force. In preparation, they destroyed Egypt's airforce by aerial bombing and sent an invasion armada to "occupy" the Suez Canal. Israel used the opportunity to invade Egypt's Sinai Peninsula to destroy the bases of the *Fedayeen* (Egyptian guerrillas trained to fight Israel). At the same time the Soviet Union threatened to crush the aggressors and restore peace to the area, a scenario guaranteed to arouse the wrath of the United States. The world was clearly at the brink of major power confrontation.

Hammarskjöld was shaken by England, France, and Israel's total disregard of the U.N. charter, and he feared international anarchy would be the long-term result of this flagrant sidestepping. A fresh approach was needed if the conflict was to be settled, an approach preferably within the framework of the United Nations. Hammarskjöld suggested an international peacekeeping force: temporary, composed of small power nations under his control. It was a novel use of military force—not to wage war, but to keep the peace. England and France agreed, if the force would be sufficient to reopen the canal, if Hammarskjöld could get Israel and Egypt to agree to an unconditional cease-fire and, of course, if Egypt would allow the United Nations Emergency Forces (UNEF) on Egyptian soil.

Hammarskjöld flew to the Middle East for intensive talks with Mahmoud Fawzi, foreign minister of Egypt and **David Ben-Gurion,** prime minister of Israel (he had already established friendships with both men). Hammarskjöld discussed the function of the force, its composition, and its goal, which was to clear the canal of debris from the Anglo-French bombardment and facilitate the withdrawal of Anglo-French-Israeli forces by filling the vacuum with the symbolic presence of the world community's agents.

Hammarskjöld concerned himself with every detail of the UNEF, which consisted of 6,000 men from 16 countries. He supervised every discussion and personally negotiated with Egypt, convincing Nasser that UNEF was not an agency of the West. The crisis abated: English, French, and Israeli troops withdrew and the canal was reopened. Typically emphasizing the importance of international law to all parties as the basis of negotiation and the presence of the U.N. forces, Hammarskjöld tried to establish a common ground of principles— based in law and respect for the charter of the U.N.

He envisioned his role as an umpire—constantly reminding the players of the rules of the game, especially the supreme obligation to settle conflict by peaceful means. Acting as de facto prime minister of a world government in a crisis which required executive action, he introduced a new dimension into the office of the secretary-general. The success of UNEF in settling the Suez Crisis increased the prestige of the U.N. It reaffirmed the organization as the proper sphere for settling international disputes.

The Suez Crisis set the precedent for a U.N. peacekeeping force in trouble spots such as Lebanon in 1958, but this approach to the 1960–61 crisis in the Congo met with mixed results and led to Hammarskjöld's tragic death.

Civil Disorder in the Congo

The Belgian Congo became the Republic of Congo in June of 1960 with **Patrice Lumumba** as premier and Joseph Kasavubu as president. The rich province of Katanga, led by premier **Moise Tschombe,** remained pro-Belgian and favored strong provincial governments and a weak central government, while the Lumumba/Kasavubu government in Leopoldville favored a strong central government. Civil war seemed inevitable. In July, Katanga declared itself an independent state, and Tschombe requested Belgian troops for protection. When civil disorder occurred, Belgian troops took over large sections of the Congo to "maintain order" and protect Belgian nationals. Lumumba then asked for a U.N. peacekeeping force to restore order and pressure Belgian troops to return to the military bases agreed upon at the time of independence.

Tschombe refused to allow U.N. troops into Katanga province, while Lumumba insisted that Hammarskjöld use the troops to quell Tschombe's opposition to the central government. Conflict between Lumumba and Hammarskjöld reached the point where Hammarskjöld threatened to withdraw U.N. forces if Lumumba continued to spread "distrust and hostility" for political ends and misconstrue the purpose of the U.N. forces in the Congo. Kasavubu then ousted Lumumba from the central government, further splintering authority in the Congo. The superpowers soon took sides, with the Soviet Union accusing Hammarskjöld of undermining the Lumumba faction at the behest of the United States. Eventually, in retaliation, the Soviet Union called for a reorganization of the office of the secretary-general as a *Troika*, or three-man collective body, and sought the resignation of Hammarskjöld.

In February 1961, Lumumba was killed, an event that shocked the world and moved the Security Council to authorize Hammarskjöld's peacekeeping detachment to use force to establish a cease-fire. The General Assembly voted an additional $100 million for use by these troops. Finally in March 1961, a Congolese summit was held on the recommendation of the U.N., and a confederation government was established. Katanga did not support the new government. In September, Hammarskjöld attempted to meet with Tschombe to persuade him to reconcile with the new central government. Hoping to find a face-saving device that would allow Tschombe to make this move, the secretary-general flew to Northern Rhodesia for negotiations with the Katanga premier. En route, Hammarskjöld's plane crashed, ending his life.

In many ways the U.N. was on trial in Africa. Could it protect Africa from the Cold War and help the newly emerging nations during their crucial foundling years? Though the situation in the Congo was tense and difficult, civil war was prevented. The African member nations stood firmly behind the U.N. efforts to achieve stability in the Congo and condemned all efforts to weaken the U.N. authority. U.N. agencies, like UNICEF and the World Health Organization, kept the Congo afloat economically and administratively while a working settlement was reached.

Hammarskjöld did his best to keep the promise of the U.N. alive in a world of complex rivalries. He prevented the U.N. from reverting to the ineffectiveness of the League of Nations or from becoming merely a static conference machine. Instead, he pushed it to become a dynamic instrument by which nations could shape an organized world community. This was a mission that finally gave meaning to his life and for which, in the end, he gave his life.

SOURCES:

Jordan, Robert S., ed. *Dag Hammarskjöld Revisited: The UN Secretary-General as a Force in World Politics.* Carolina Academic Press, 1983.

Miller, Richard I. *Dag Hammarskjöld and Crisis Diplomacy.* Oceana Publications, 1961.

Stolpe, Sven. *Dag Hammarskjöld: A Spiritual Portrait.* Scribner, 1966.

FURTHER READING:

Hammarskjöld, Dag. *Markings.* Knopf, 1964.

Lash, Joseph P. *Dag Hammarskjöld: Custodian of the Brushfire Peace.* Doubleday, 1961.

Levering, Ralph B. *The Cold War, 1945–1987.* Harlan Davidson, 1988.

Harald III Hardraade

(1015–1066)

Norwegian king, who bought his throne with mercenary money and died attempting to conquer Anglo-Saxon England.

Name variations: Harold III; Harald Hardrada; Harald Sigurdsson; Harald the Ruthless. Born in 1015; died at Stamford Bridge, England, in 1066; son of Sigurd Syr (king of Ringerike) and Aasta; half-brother of Saint Olaf of Norway; married: Ellisif, 1045; children: (two daughters) Maria and Ingigerd; (two sons) Magnus and Olaf by his concubine, Thora. Predecessor: King Magnus I the Good. Successor: Magnus II Bareleg (1066–69) and Olaf III Kyrri, the Peaceful (1066–93).

Harald III Hardraade of Norway is widely considered to be the last of the Viking kings who exemplified the restless, expansionist energy of Scandinavia's 10th- and 11th-century leaders. His multifaceted career as a mercenary for the Byzantine emperor, as a man who bought his Norwegian throne and then used violence to subdue his subjects, and as a warrior who sought to topple the English king, all contribute to this view. Yet it is not necessarily accurate to call Harald a *Viking* king. The Norway of his time was a country already Christianized by the efforts of **Olaf Tryggvason** and Harald's half-brother King Olaf II, who became the country's patron saint. Harald was certainly not a pagan Viking of the pre-Christian era; further, his expansionist tendencies were shared by many of his day, including **William the Conqueror.**

Most of the sources that shed light on Harald Hardraade's career are Icelandic and English. For instance, 13th-century Icelandic historian Snorri Sturluson wrote an entire saga about Harald as part of his great work *Heimskringla (Saga of the Norse Kings).* The *Anglo-Saxon Chronicle* contains notices of Harald's activities in England. In addi-

"After [Harald] came into his fatherland … he never ceased from warfare; he was the thunderbolt of the north, a pestilence to all."

ADAM OF BREMEN

Contributed by Cathy Jorgensen Itnyre, Instructor, College of the Desert, Joshua Tree, California

tion, German chronicler Adam of Bremen deals with Harald in his *History of the Archbishops of Hamburg-Bremen,* which was the archdiocese under which Norway fell. Adam's view of the Norwegian king was certainly negatively biased, as jurisdiction over the Norwegian church was contested by Anglo-Saxon influence.

Of these accounts, only Snorri provides details of Harald's early life, material contained in two chapters of *Saint Olaf's Saga.* His mother Aasta was previously married to a Westfold king, Harald Graenske, with whom she had a son—a great king and Norway's patron saint, Olaf II Haraldsson. Soon after her husband's death, Aasta married a petty Norwegian king of Ringerike, Sigurd Syr (Sow), with whom she had at least five children. Harald Hardraade was born in 1015.

In *Saint Olaf's Saga,* Snorri relates the following incident of 1018, when Harald was three years old. His half-brother Olaf Haraldsson, by then king of Norway, visited his mother and half-siblings. When he teased his three brothers by pretending to be furious with them, the two older boys, Guttorm and Halfdan, reacted with tears, while Harald simply ignored the feigned anger and pulled the King's beard. Olaf was pleased by Harald's fearlessness. Later, while observing the three brothers playing on the family estate, Olaf inquired about their future occupations. Guttorm declared that he wanted to be a rich farmer, Halfdan coveted a large cattle estate, but Harald announced that he wanted to lead so many warriors "that they would eat all of Halfdan's cattle in one meal." Amused, King Olaf remarked to their mother: "That's a king you're bringing up."

King Harald's Saga begins with Harald at age 15. In 1030, when Olaf was defeated and killed by rebellious Norwegian chieftains at Stiklestad, young Harald was present at the battle. According to *Saint Olaf's Saga,* Olaf had considered his half-brother too young to fight, but Harald insisted:

> Certainly I shall be in the battle, but if I am so weak that I cannot handle the sword, then I know a good plan, namely, of tying the sword-handle to my hand. None is more willing than I am to give the bonders [farmers] a blow."

And so from an early age, Harald showed the martial qualities of courage and strength—attributes that were to characterize his entire career.

Severely wounded in the Battle of Stiklestad, Harald nevertheless escaped and soon after set out for Russia, a land heavily influenced by centuries of

CHRONOLOGY

1015	Harald born
1030	Fought with half-brother King Olaf II at Stiklestad
1030	Fled to Russia
1035–44	Fought for the Byzantine emperor in Constantinople
1046	Became co-king of Norway with his nephew Magnus I, the Good
1047–66	Sole king of Norway
1066	Died at Stamford Bridge, England

Viking incursions; in fact, many areas of Russia had been colonized and politically organized by Vikings. King Yaroslav, Russia's ruler from 1036 until 1054, welcomed Harald and hired him as a mercenary to assist in Russian campaigns against Slavs and Poles. After four or five years, Harald traveled to Constantinople, capital of the Byzantine Empire, to continue his mercenary career as a member of the Varangian Guard; Snorri Sturluson gives a great amount of detail about Harald's time in Constantinople. For many years, Vikings had offered their mercenary services to the emperor of Byzantium, and by 1035, when Harald joined the Varangian Guard, Scandinavians dominated this corps of imperial bodyguards and played a significant role in the overall military operations of the Empire. For example, although Greek Georgios Maniakes was the official commander in chief of the imperial forces, Harald repeatedly challenged his authority, remarking, according to Snorri, that "it was the right of the Varangians here in the Greek realm to be entirely free and independent of all others, and to be owing only to the emperor and empress."

As a member of the Varangian Guard from 1035–1044, Harald participated in numerous campaigns against Bulgarians, the Saracens in Asia Minor, and Sicily. His tactical ability, combined with great personal courage, is attested to in several chapters of his *Saga,* but he did at times rely on other talents, such as trickery. During one attempt to besiege a Sicilian town, he realized that the town's strong fortifications would make a direct assault impossible. He instead ordered his troops to ignore the inhabitants and play athletic games outside the town walls, a move intended to demonstrate the Varangians' contempt for the opposing force. After several uneventful days of games, when the Sicilians became complacent and no longer feared an attack, Harald struck. Having concealed weapons beneath their clothing, his men stormed the unsuspecting town. On another occasion, Harald gained access to an enemy town by circulating the rumor that he had died, then had his grieving men request burial within the city walls. As the funeral procession entered the gates, the mourners suddenly became ferocious warriors, and the Sicilian stronghold fell. Harald's long stay in service to the Byzantine emperor contributed both to his reputation and his personal wealth. According to Snorri he "garnered … an immense hoard of money, gold and treasure of all kinds."

By 1044, after some nine years as a member of the Varangian Guard, Harald returned to Constantinople to hear that his nephew Magnus I, the Good, son of Olaf II, had become king of both Norway and Denmark. As Olaf's half-brother, Harald too had a claim to the throne of Norway. Deciding to return to his native land, Harald encountered an obstacle in the form of the Byzantine empress Zoe who was reluctant to lose such a capable—and handsome—warrior. Snorri suggests that Zoe, with her own designs on the exceptionally tall, golden-haired Harald, was stung by his desire to marry her beautiful niece Maria. Perhaps this jealousy led to her charge that Harald had defrauded the emperor of treasure; regardless of her motivation, Zoe imprisoned Harald to prevent his escape. Secretly set free, Harald abducted Maria, sailed from Constantinople, and perhaps added to his personal fortune by demanding ransom for Maria's safe return to Byzantium.

Returning to Russia the same year, Harald married King Yaroslav's daughter Ellisif. Then in 1045, he began his return voyage to Norway, fortified by the dowry from Yaroslav and the considerable wealth amassed during his Byzantine campaigns. Stopping first in Sweden, he met with the claimant to the Danish throne, Svein Ulfsson, who had been recently defeated by King Magnus I of Norway. The two agreed to collaborate in an invasion of Norway and Denmark, and gained strong Swedish support as well for this plan. Harald, however, engaged in secret diplomacy with his nephew King Magnus, allowing the latter to weaken the pact between the Danish Svein Ulfsson and Harald which resulted in the dissolution of Harald and Svein's friendship.

The Kingdom of Norway Is Divided

In May of 1046, Magnus I and Harald Hardraade arranged a division of the kingdom of Norway between them. In exchange for half of Norway, Harald was to share his personal fortune with his nephew. Yet tension was evident in their arrangement. Snorri relates that the two kings frequently engaged in disputes regarding royal prerogatives. The situation became dangerous when Norwegian earls attempted to foster mutual distrust. Nevertheless, the two kings agreed to invade Denmark to prevent Svein Ulfsson from collecting royal revenues there. They were able to stop Svein, but shortly thereafter Magnus fell ill, declaring on his death bed that Svein should rule Denmark; as for Harald, Norway was enough.

Even though Harald immediately announced his intention to be the Danish king, he was unable to make good his claim. His Norwegian army, which insisted on accompanying Magnus's body back to Norway, compelled Harald to go along. Meanwhile, Svein gathered an army and was accepted by the Danes as their king, setting the stage for constant warfare between Harald and Svein that would end only with the latter's defeat at the battle of the Nissa River in 1062, and the subsequent peace treaty in 1064.

Harald's reign as sole king of Norway was a tumultuous one. Many Norwegians were reluctant to allow him to extract revenues from their districts, and constant friction with powerful men in the Trondelag and Uplands districts fueled his excessively violent reactions. Snorri writes:

> King Harald was a very autocratic ruler, and his imperiousness increased as his position in Norway grew more secure. It came to the point that scarcely anyone dared to argue with him, or to propose anything which was different from what he himself wanted.

His treacherous murder of a prominent Trondelag farmer, Einar Paunch-Shaker, created a climate of extreme resentment towards the King. German chronicler Adam of Bremen, who drew most of his information from Svein Ulfsson, clearly reflects Svein's negative view of Harald. To Adam, Harald was "the thunderbolt of the north," and "a pestilence." Many of the Uplanders and Trondelagers had reason to agree.

Harald's ecclesiastical policy (similar to other European leaders of his day) further angered Adam. Although the archbishops of Hamburg-Bremen were supposed to have jurisdiction over Norway's church, Norwegian bishops were frequently consecrated by Anglo-Saxon clergy. In addition, Harald used church income for his own purposes from time to time, and certainly his personal life did not conform to the ideal standards of his day: despite his marriage to Ellisif, he had a concubine Thora, who bore him two sons, Magnus and Olaf. While Adam is silent regarding the latter issue, he clearly rails against Harald for the injustices committed against the dignity of the archbishopric of Hamburg-Bremen and notes that Pope Alexander II was forced to write a stern letter to King Harald, admonishing him to respect the proper ecclesiastical authority.

Considering himself to be one of the claimants to the throne of Anglo-Saxon England, Harald Hardraade traced this claim to his predecessor King Magnus I Olafsson who had made a treaty with King Edward the Confessor's half-brother Harthacanut. The terms of this treaty stipulated that whichever king (Magnus or Harthacanut) survived the other would inherit all of the deceased's possessions. According to the *Saga of Magnus the Good,* upon Harthacanut's death, Magnus sent a letter to Edward the Confessor, announcing himself as the rightful heir. Naturally, Edward denied the claim, and Magnus, reluctant to press his luck, contented himself with his Norwegian and Danish lands. But in 1066, when Harold Godwineson was elected king of the English, Harald Hardraade asserted his own claim to the throne via the Magnus-Harthacanut agreement. Harald Godwineson's rebellious brother, Tostig, the banished earl of Northumbria, offered to play a vital role in Harald Hardraade's campaign: he promised to enlist local Northumbrian support for a Norwegian-sponsored invasion. The 51-year-old Harald Hardraade determined to attempt the invasion.

Harald's Last Campaign

Gathering a significant naval force of perhaps 300 ships, Harald prepared for what would turn out to be his last campaign. He proclaimed his illegitimate son Magnus as king, and named him regent of Norway. His other son Olaf—by Thora—accompanied Harald, as did Ellisif and their two daughters. En route to England, Harald received reinforcements from Shetland and Orkney, where his wife and daughters were left to await the invasion's outcome. Arriving in Scotland, the Norwegian force received further support, and sailed from there to the vicinity of York. On September 20, 1066, Harald Hardraade encountered the armies of the earls of Mercia and Northumbria, which blocked the way to the important objective of York. In the ensuing fierce battle, the Norwegians prevailed, but their losses were heavy.

The decisive clash between Harald Hardraade and Harold Godwineson occurred at Stamford Bridge in York and, as the *Anglo-Saxon Chronicle* records, "a very stubborn battle was fought by both sides." On September 24, Harald Hardraade, joined by Tostig's supporters, marched into York and found an easy victory; perhaps frightened by Tostig, the inhabitants offered no resistance. The Norwegian army spent the night on board their ships—a fatal mistake. According to *King Harald's Saga,* Harold Godwineson arrived with his army from the south and secretly entered the town that night. When Harald Hardraade approached York the morning of September 25, he found an English army of perhaps 6,000 men.

Before the battle began, an English delegation approached Harald Hardraade's forces and offered Earl Tostig one third of England if he would abandon his alliance with the Norwegians. According to Snorri, Tostig considered the offer, but asked:

> "But if I accept this offer now, what will he offer King Harald Sigurdsson for all his effort?"

> The rider said, "King Harold has already declared how much of England he is prepared to grant him: seven feet of ground, or as much more as he is taller than other men."

Tostig refused, and the battle commenced. Harald Hardraade fought ferociously but was killed by an arrow in his throat. By the time Norwegian reinforcements from the ship arrived, they were exhausted and heat-stricken from their mail coats, which reduced their effectiveness and contributed to the Norwegian defeat.

It is necessary to note, however, that the *Anglo-Saxon Chronicle* places the battle at a different site: instead of Harald Hardraade attempting to enter York the morning of September 25, the English source holds that Harold Godwineson surprised the Norwegians at their camp at Stamford Bridge and overwhelmed them by capturing the wooden bridge. Still, both the Icelandic and English sources agree that both sides suffered extraordinary casualties, among them King Harald Hardraade.

Harald's son Olaf Haraldsson was allowed to leave England and ruled Norway as Olaf III with his brother Magnus II until the latter's death in 1069. Olaf then ruled as sole king until his death in 1093, earning the nickname *Kyrri* (the Peaceful) because he had abandoned his father's policy of constant military activity. Harald Hardraade, then, may be considered the last Viking king of Scandinavia, if perpetual foreign adventures define the term *Viking.* But the threat to foreign lands from the North did not die with Harald Hardraade, for Scandinavians plotted to win England by invasion well into William the Conqueror's reign.

SOURCES:

Adam of Bremen. *History of the Archbishops of Hamburg-Bremen.* Translated by Francis J. Tschan. Columbia University Press, 1959.

Anglo-Saxon Chronicle. Translated by G. N. Garmonsway. Dutton, 1965.

Heimskringla: The Olaf Sagas. Vols. I and II. Translated by Samuel Laing. Dutton, 1964.

King Harald's Saga. Translated by Magnus Magnusson and Hermann Palsson. New York, 1966.

FURTHER READING:

Brondsted, Johannes. *The Vikings.* Baltimore, 1960.

Jones, Gwyn. *A History of the Vikings.* New York, 1973.

Larsen, Karen. *A History of Norway.* Princeton University Press, 1948.

Irene Harand

(1900–1975)

and the Rise and Resistance to Anti-Semitism in Austria

Austrian leader in Vienna who vigorously attacked the evils of Nazism, anti-Semitism and religious intolerance and was honored by Israel for her efforts.

"I fight anti-Semitism because it defames our Christianity."

IRENE HARAND

Only in the mid-1980s did it become apparent that not all of the horrors of Nazism originated in the nation that **Adolf Hitler** and his movement gained control over in 1933. A series of events made it clear that Hitler's Austrian homeland also played a significant role. For many decades Austria had enjoyed a reputation as a land of beautiful Alpine scenery, good food, and glorious musical traditions. Few Austrians and virtually no foreigners seemed interested in the darker sides of their country's recent past. Despite the fact that many Austrians had welcomed the German forces when Hitler annexed his homeland to Germany in March 1938, this was largely forgotten during World War II, when the Allied Powers issued their Moscow Declaration of November 1943, which solemnly proclaimed that Austria had been the "first victim" of Nazi aggression. This policy was as much based on a strong desire on the part of the anti-Nazi coalition to rapidly build up an independent Austrian nation, and thus ensure a permanently weakened Germany after the war, as it was grounded in an accurate understanding of contemporary history. Austrians took advantage of these attitudes after 1945 by creating a stable series of governments that played down internal political

Born Irene Wedl on September 6, 1900, in Vienna; died in New York City on February 3, 1975; married: Frank Harand, 1919; children: none.

Contributed by John Haag, Associate Professor of History, University of Georgia, Athens, Georgia

CHRONOLOGY OF BIGOTRY,
THE RISE OF ANTI-SEMITISM IN VIENNA (996–1932)

996	Jews first mentioned living in Vienna
1420–21	Archduke Albrecht V earned for Vienna the title "City of Blood" when he killed most of city's Jews or baptized orphaned infants
1431	Jews officially banned from Vienna "forever"
1625	"Second Jewish ghetto" officially created
1670	Jews expelled by Emperor Leopold I, whose court preacher Abraham a Sancta Clara blamed them for a recent plague
1693	Small Jewish community again founded in Vienna
1700	Johann Eisenmenger published anti-Semitic book Entdecktes Judentum (Judaism Exposed)
1744	Austrian Empress Maria Theresa expelled Jews from Prague
1764	Austrian law permitted Jews to trade in domestic (but not imported) manufactured goods as well as to continue their activities as money changers, bankers, and jewel traders
1781	Emperor Joseph II freed Jews from obligation to wear yellow Star of David
1782	Patent of Toleration freed Jews from ghetto, required Jewish children to attend German-language schools, and opened the trades and most professions to them
1784	Austrian Jews permitted to practice law
1788	Austrian Jews required to adopt German family names and no longer speak Yiddish or Hebrew in public; all able-bodied Jewish males required to perform military service
1790	Death of Emperor Joseph II led to end of new legislation fostering Jewish emancipation
1795	Jewish rights of toleration limited to three years, not for life
1813–15	35,000 Austrian Jews served in army fighting against Napoleonic France
1846	Jewish population of Vienna was about 4,000
1848	Viennese Jews played a prominent role in revolution against Habsburg regime
1849	Liberal Austrian Constitution declared that civil and political rights were not dependent on a citizen's religion, freeing all Jews of earlier restrictions; they were also permitted to own property, and enter all professions and marry Christians; Jews of Vienna permitted to establish their own religious and charitable organization (Israelitische Kultusgemeinde)

→

differences by ignoring ideology and emphasizing national solidarity. The bloody and deeply divisive Nazi past was simply swept under the rug, to most Austrians' immense relief.

In 1986 four decades of Austrian national amnesia about the Nazi past came to an abrupt end when it was revealed that one of the serious candidates for the office of president that year, former United Nations Secretary-General **Kurt Waldheim**, had not told the truth in his memoirs about his war service in the Nazi-occupied Balkans. The lively debate that grew out of this revelation opened a Pandora's box of details about that nation's recent past, particularly the difficult topic of its historic relationship with its Jewish citizens. This subject was discussed with even more passion starting in March 1988, when the 50th anniversary of the Nazi annexation (*Anschluss*) of Austria was commemorated by both government and private citizens. As a traumatic chapter of Austrian history finally began to be examined, nearly forgotten episodes surfaced from an often painfully repressed national memory.

The history of Christian hostility to Jews is a long and complex story with theological, economic, social, and psychological origins. In short, Europe's Jewish minority even in the Middle Ages was tolerated only when it served a purpose for the Christian majority in each nation. Christian moral teachings forbade the lending of money for interest (usury), but with the rise of a money economy such activity was necessary for any developing society; consequently, the presence of Jewish bankers, money lenders, and merchants became essential for rulers if they wanted to rule strong and powerful states. However, when plagues, famines, or wars destabilized the social fabric it was common to single out the Jews as scapegoats and blame them for the calamities. Bloody persecutions followed. Being at the crossroads of central Europe, Austria had a thriving economic and intellectual life that attracted Jews at various times in its history, but while they enjoyed periods of prosperity and toleration, they also endured episodes of persecution.

Accompanying the religious fanaticism of the Crusades in the 11th and 12th centuries there came specific charges against Europe's Jews—including what was seen to be their collective murder of Jesus and continuing rejection of him as the Messiah. Jews were also accused of economic exploitation because of their involvement with money-lending. But most serious was the charge leveled by some of the clergy that held the Jews responsible for poisoning wells, murdering Christian children, and desecrating the consecrated wafers so as to mock the sacrifice of Jesus. As early as 1420–21, Archduke **Albrecht V** of Austria ordered that Jews be expelled from Vienna, blaming them for supplying arms to the forces of the Bohemian heretic **Jan Hus**. As would be the case in later centuries, these "reasons" were little more than pretexts for attacking the Jews. It was easy to find a scapegoat for one's woes in a group that had stubbornly remained religiously and ethnically distinct within the larger Christian society. Wiping clean the slate of indebtedness to Jewish money lenders was doubtless an attractive idea at a time when the costs of financing a war against Hussite rebels had become onerous. The combination of religious, cultural, and economic motives in Christian persecution of Jews would reappear in later centuries as the two communities continued to interact in an increasingly complex political and economic environment.

Austria's Jews began to emerge from their traditional ghetto world in the mid-18th century when the Empress **Maria Theresa** decreed in 1764 that they could engage in certain types of trade as well as continue their traditional activities as money lenders and changers, bankers, and jewel merchants. The Empress was by no means kindly disposed toward Jews, having once stated that she knew of "no worse plague" afflicting her empire, but she moved in the direction of a limited form of tolerance because her advisers made it clear that her realm stood to benefit economically. Far greater reforms affecting Jews in the Habsburg realm took place in the reign of Maria Theresa's son, Emperor **Joseph II**, which began in 1780. A thoroughgoing reformer, Joseph not only freed the Jews from such traditional burdens as having to wear a Jewish badge—a yellow Star of David—on their clothing but also encouraged their cultural as well as economic integration. The 1782 Patent of Toleration ended the requirement that Jews live in their own ghettos and opened up the trades and most professions to them.

By the mid-19th century, a significant number of Austrian and Hungarian Jews had broken away from traditional Jewish religious and cultural patterns and were now part of the modern economy, actively participating in the cultural and intellectual life of Budapest, Prague, and Vienna. Yet Jews remained second-class citizens, at least in part because the authoritarian nature of the regime denied all its subjects, not only Jews, basic constitutional rights that had been at least partially achieved in Great Britain and the United States. It was therefore not surprising that Jews participated when a massive 1848 uprising took place in Vienna against the reactionary regime of Prince **Klemens von Metternich**, who had headed the Austrian

government for more than a generation. After the revolution was crushed, conservatives often blamed Jews for its excesses, suggesting that Jewish intellectuals were dangerous hotheads who could invariably be found in the vanguard of radical movements.

The Austrian Constitution of December 21, 1867, granted all of Emperor **Francis Joseph II**'s subjects full civil liberties. Vienna's Jews took advantage of their new freedoms by engaging in commercial and financial enterprises as well as by preparing for the medical and legal professions by enrolling in universities. Many fortunes were made in the 1860s and early 1870s by Jewish financiers, and by the end of the 19th century a high percentage of Vienna's physicians and attorneys were of Jewish background; most of the city's newspapers were Jewish-owned. But these successes were threatened by a dark cloud. When the Vienna (as well as the Berlin) stock market experienced a severe crash in 1873, Jewish financiers and speculators involved in the collapse were blamed for the entire scandal despite the presence of non-Jews who were also implicated in the complex web of corruption. The financial catastrophe unleashed a general economic downturn. Workers and small shopkeepers lost their livelihood. While the causes of the depression were multi-factored, and few could prescribe a simple cure, many believed they knew the element responsible—the Jews.

By 1875, when the conservative publicist Baron **Karl von Vogelsang** founded his newspaper *Vaterland*, many Christian Viennese responded to his analysis of the modern causes of poverty and social instability. Vogelsang—whose Catholic conservatism was based on an idealized vision of the social harmony that characterized the Middle Ages—identified Jews with virtually all of the evils of his age, seeing them as the vanguard of such socially disruptive systems as capitalism, economic laissez-faire liberalism, materialism, and atheism. Although Vogelsang was harshly critical of what he defined as a corrosive "Jewish spirit," and advocated the creation of a new and "re-Christianized" social order, he did not attack the Jewish religion. Neither did he consider Jews to be biologically different or inferior to Christians. Rather, he hoped that the situation would be remedied when Jews converted to Roman Catholicism, abandoning their reputed love of secular wealth and power.

Others who criticized Austria's Jewish community looked at the problem from a different perspective. In France and Germany a number of writers claimed to have discovered objective, indeed "scientific," causes of the social ills of the time. First published in the 1850s, the racial theories of French author Count **Arthur Joseph de Gobineau** now appeared to some to hold the key to an understanding of the social chaos confronting the 19th century. Gobineau argued that the only creative element in history was the white race, and that other human races, including the Jews and other Semitic peoples, had acted only as parasites. Gobineau himself was not hostile to Jews, and had hoped to make a strong case for the preservation of the privileges of the French aristocracy, arguing that they were racially the most creative and valuable segment of society. But others adapted Gobineau's pseudoscientific notions to their own ideological agendas, particularly in the troubled decade of the 1870s. In 1879 the German author **Wilhelm Marr** coined the term "anti-Semitic," contrasting the innocent and trusting German "race" to Jews who were forever rootless, cunning, and deceitful, while in the same year the German historian **Heinrich von Treitschke** defined the "Jewish problem" as a question of national survival.

By 1881 German and Austrian anti-Semitism was carried to new extremes when the University of Berlin professor **Eugen Dühring** published a violently anti-Semitic book entitled *The Jewish Question as a Race, Morals and Cultural Question*. Dühring asserted that the Jews were a distinct biological entity, a racial group that could never be assimilated or Christianized. These notions were highly attractive to ambitious politicians who could use them as a means of appealing to social groups in the population that had recently suffered from the ravages of unrestricted laissez-faire capitalism, or who felt themselves threatened by Jewish competitors in the job market. Fear of Jewish job competition was particularly strong at Austrian universities and technical institutes, where the number of Jewish students in many fields—particularly law and medicine—was much higher than that of the Jewish percentage of the overall population. By the late 1870s many student fraternities (*Burschenschaften*) had begun to exclude Jews from membership, arguing they did not possess German moral qualities, could never duel or drink beer as well as pure-blooded "Aryans," and were thus not fitted for membership in such exclusive circles.

Anti-Semitic Political Parties Formed

By the mid-1880s the radicalized racist students of Vienna and Graz had found their champion in an up-and-coming politician named **Georg von Schönerer** (1842–1921). Schönerer's father had been an extremely successful railroad engineer who had at one time worked for the Jewish banking family the **Rothschilds** and who had become wealthy in his own right. Untroubled by money worries, the younger Schönerer entered political life in the 1870s as a left-wing liberal, championing some major social reforms. In June 1882 Schönerer turned decisively from liberalism, which was not a racist ideology, by founding the League of German Nationalists (*Deutschnationaler Verein*). This organization of several hundred journalists, teachers, and businessmen called for an all-out campaign against Jewish influences in the economy and political life, as well as in intellectual life and the arts. Using demagogic arguments, Schönerer and his followers agitated among students, middle-class Viennese shopkeepers, and artisans, trying to persuade them that all of their woes were due not to the economic slump of the period, or the capitalist system itself, but to the nefarious power of Jewish speculators and bankers. Although Schönerer's movement was able to score some successes, by the late 1890s it had been largely outdistanced by a new, much more effective vehicle for anti-Semitic demagoguery, the Christian Social Party.

By the early 1890s anti-Semitic appeals had become commonplace in Austrian public life, and it was scarcely surprising that politicians more pragmatic and adaptive to changing moods should appear on the scene. The most successful of these figures was the Viennese-born popular leader **Karl Lueger** (1844–1910), whose personal charm and political astuteness was combined with a cynical use of anti-Semitic slogans that were immensely appealing to his lower middle-class constituency. In the 1890s, Lueger became undisputed leader of the Roman Catholic political party, the Christian Socials, by creating a mass political movement based largely on the fear artisans and shopkeepers had of "Jewish capitalism." In the closing decades of the 19th century tradesmen and artisans found their livelihoods increasingly threatened by competition from more efficient factories and retail distribution networks. Many of these were Jewish-owned enterprises, and anti-Semitic appeals fell on sympathetic ears—particularly if they were attractively presented in the folksy style perfected by such suave demagogues as Karl Lueger.

Lueger's message was a peculiarly Viennese form of populist anti-capitalism that, while vague in its precise program of how to combat Jewish "threats to the Christian social order," nonetheless proved immensely appealing to the imperial city's populace. Even though Lueger refrained from proposing specific legislation to curb Jewish influences, his Christian Social Party was able to win an absolute majority in the Vienna municipal elections of April 1895. Although Emperor Franz Joseph II refused on four occasions to appoint him to the office of Vienna's lord mayor, Lueger's continuing popularity finally forced the sovereign to relent in April 1897. Thus, Lueger became the first mayor of a major European city to rule on an anti-Semitic platform, and his Christian Social Party was clearly the most successful political movement of the late 19th century to base its appeal on hostility toward the Jews.

In practice, Lueger's bark was much worse than his bite. Indeed, within a few years it became clear to the Jews of Vienna that Christian Social racism was almost entirely rhetorical in nature. No legislation was ever passed against Jews and, while they were greatly underrepresented in the bureaucracy, education and the professions were open to them. Ironically, the years 1897–1914 were a veritable Golden Age in Viennese Jewish history. In a society whose aristocracy continued to look contemptuously on money-making activities, Jews and other newly-arrived immigrants in Vienna found that with hard work they could often succeed in such areas as journalism, medicine, law, and the stock exchange. Although many Christian Austrians retained some anti-Semitic prejudices, in the prosperous years before 1914 even they reluctantly concluded that the many nationalities of the Habsburg empire would have to find ways to tolerate one another for the common good. Among the signs of growing toleration were the decline of Schönerer's influence among the fraternities and the rapid rise of the Social Democratic party, which included many Jewish intellectuals and was based on an ideology of universal social transformation based on working-class fraternity.

This promise was shattered in August 1914 by the coming of World War I. At first, the war acted as a unifying force for the multinational state, and until 1916 there was a remarkable sense of common purpose among the different ethnic groups comprising the Habsburg realm. But by late 1916, war-weariness and extreme privations, particularly food shortages, had sapped the will of most Austrians to continue the war. The death of the aged Emperor Franz Joseph II in November 1916 symbolized the end of an era. By this time, anti-Semitism, particularly among a now impoverished middle class, was rampant. With Vienna overcrowded with tens of thousands of Jewish refugees from war-ravaged Galicia, rumors of black-market profiteering by Jews became a commonplace explanation for the sufferings of average Viennese. Politicians, particularly in the Christian Social Party, seized upon the situation as one

CHRONOLOGY OF BIGOTRY,

THE RISE OF ANTI-SEMITISM IN VIENNA (996–1932)

1910	Jewish population of Vienna was 175,318 (8.63% of total population); death of Karl Lueger
1911	Social Democrats defeated Lueger's Christian Social Party in Viennese municipal elections
1917	Viennese Catholic newspaper Reichspost claimed that all leaders of Bolshevik revolution in Russia were Jewish; food shortages and war-weariness helped feed a new public mood of anti-Semitic hostility, particularly directed against Galician Jewish refugees (Ostjuden)
1918	End of World War I brought on abdication of Habsburg emperor and dissolution of Austria-Hungary; about 35,000 Jews died defending Habsburg monarchy
1919	German translation of "Protocols of the Elders of Zion" published; anti-Semitic rally in Vienna attracted 15,000
1920	Platform of newly founded National Socialist German Workers Party (Nazis) included vehemently anti-Semitic proposals; Jewish students brutally attacked at the University of Vienna; Austrian Nazi leader Walter Riehl demanded at September rally that Vienna's "200,000 Ostjuden" be deported to Poland to make housing space available for the city's 150,000 homeless people
1921–23	Racist students attacked Jews, Socialists and others deemed to be "un-German" in numerous riots (Krawalle), using brass knuckles, knives, and sticks
1924	Vienna Institute of Technology attempted to disenfranchise its Jewish students by placing them into a separate student "nation"
1925	A mob of 10,000 demonstrators screaming "Kill the Jews" marched down the Ringstrasse, Vienna's great thoroughfare, to protest the World Zionist Congress; several hundred demonstrators were arrested, but most of the Viennese press supported the demonstrators and the Catholic Church hierarchy remained silent on the issue
1929	12.3% of the Austrian work force was unemployed
1930	With Moritz Zalman, Irene Harand helped found Österreichische Volkspartei (Austrian People's Party); Academic Senate of University of Vienna passed ordinance for "student nations" which was intended to segregate and discriminate against Jewish-student minority; Nazis won 111,000 votes in parliamentary elections (27,500 in Vienna)
1932	Nazis won 17% of votes in local elections throughout Austria (including over 200,000 votes in Vienna)

The sudden collapse of the Habsburg military in October 1918, and the subsequent abolition of the monarchical regime in November, only accelerated a growing mass psychosis directed against a vaguely-defined "Jewish menace." Pacifist and Marxist Jews were now blamed for spreading defeatist propaganda among the frontline troops, thus hastening the military catastrophe. On the home front, too, Jews were seen as the major culprits of a spiraling inflation and black-market economy that made even the basic essentials of existence unaffordable to the middle class. For a resurgent anti-Semitic movement, Jews threatened the very existence of civilization in Austria, acting as either greedy capitalists or fomenting social unrest leading inevitably to a bloody civil war and Bolshevik dictatorship. At Austrian universities, and particularly at the world-famous University of Vienna, bloody student riots (*Krawalle*) regularly erupted in which Jewish students were beaten up and thrown down flights of stairs. In countless newspapers, magazines, and posters Jews were depicted as inhuman and depraved enemies of civilization whose cunning nature constituted an immediate threat to a supposedly pure Germanic spirit.

The end of inflation and the stabilization of the Austrian economy in the mid-1920s dampened but did not eliminate the deep-seated anti-Semitism. The fact that the leading religious and moral institution of Austria, the Roman Catholic Church, did little to combat such prejudices (and on many occasions actually endorsed and encouraged them), only emphasized the difficulties faced by those Christian groups and individuals who aspired to rid Austria of racial and ethnic hatreds.

The Harand Story Emerges

In the troubled 1930s, before and during World War II, the individual who most effectively challenged Christians in Austria to live up to the teachings of their own religion in regard to the Jewish question was a woman, **Irene Harand**. Later, because the great majority of Austrians felt a need to suppress painful details of their recent history, and because her Nazi enemies almost succeeded in obliterating her memory from the consciousness of her fellow countrymen, the story of Irene Harand has only recently emerged from the shadows.

Irene Wedl was born into a prosperous Viennese family on September 6, 1900. Her father, a manufacturer, was Roman Catholic; her mother was Lutheran. To avoid any religious conflicts in the family, Irene and her three siblings were all raised as Catholics, but one of Irene's

offering immense opportunities for increasing their own popularity at the expense of an increasingly unpopular minority.

aunts was Jewish, making two of her cousins half-Jewish. Such religious and ethnic mixtures were quite common in pre-1914 Vienna, and among the educated elite toleration, rather than disapproval, was the general spirit in which such personal matches were viewed. But anti-Semitism was common among the poorer, less educated groups in society who had been propagandized by the demagogues.

During a summer holiday as a young girl, Irene had a firsthand experience with anti-Semitism when she, an older sister, and her two half-Jewish cousins were surrounded by a group of local peasant children who taunted them with pejorative anti-Semitic slogans. Decades later she recalled running, with her older sister in the lead, to the security of the family cabin. Vividly, she remembered what it had been like to be "on the receiving end" of racist hatred, noting that "one never forgets the first time one feels oneself frightened to death, and sees the world as being full of nothing but enemies."

In 1919 Irene Wedl married Frank Harand, who had served as a captain in the Austrian army during World War I. Like his bride, Frank Harand was a devout Catholic who believed that if the world was to be spared another bloodletting such as the recently ended war, it would have to rebuild its moral values and social institutions on Christian principles of justice, love, and toleration. While both Harands were politically conservative and sympathetic to the principles of monarchism, during the first decade of their marriage they avoided political controversies, concentrating instead on creating a pleasant life for themselves. Although she had not attended a university during the 1920s, Irene Harand read widely and familiarized herself with the major economic and political controversies of the time. During these years she increasingly came to read about, and sometimes discuss with friends, two closely intertwined problems that concerned politically active Austrians: the continuing hostility toward the nation's Jewish minority, and a small but growing ultraradical movement that pledged to solve once and for all Europe's "Jewish problem."

The Austrian Republic that came into existence in November 1918 with the demise of the Habsburg monarchy of Austria-Hungary was given little hope of survival. It was unable to feed itself and was burdened with the metropolis of Vienna that contained more than one-third of the new nation's impoverished population; indeed, most Austrians desired *Anschluss* (union) with the German Republic to the north. Furthermore, Austrian political life was a cauldron of deep-seated hatreds, with the ultraconservative Catholic party, the Christian Socials, facing an often implacably doctrinaire Marxist Social Democratic Workers' Party. With small but militant Pan-German and Nazi parties appealing to returning veterans whose idea of politics was based on physical conflict and annihilation, Austrian political life in the first half-decade of the Republic's existence was often violent and bloody. Ideologically, too, post-1918 Austrian politics exhibited extremely intolerant traits. Except for the Social Democrats, which most Austrian Jews supported, Austrian political parties during these years all campaigned on anti-Semitic platforms.

Although the Catholic Church did not condone the violent anti-Semitism of the Nazis, many Catholic clergymen including the nation's brilliant but often politically uncompromising federal chancellor, **Ignaz Seipel**, regarded the Jews as undesirable agents of social decomposition. The Church saw itself as a "nonpolitical" body that was leading the Austrian "spiritual" struggle against Jewry while the Christian Socials were to be found engaged in the often messy political arena. Yet, in practice, such lines were easily crossed.

Harand Is Drawn into Public Debate

This moral environment deeply distressed Irene and Frank Harand as well as others whose vision of a Christian society was built on justice and compassion, and who were convinced that for society to flourish Christians and Jews must be taught to tolerate and respect one another. But neither of the Harands had a pragmatic plan for infusing Christian ideals into a troubled land's public life. Indeed, Irene Harand would continue to remain aloof from political controversies until a series of events inexorably led her into the arena of public debate. She had become interested in the plight of an aged nobleman whose poverty had recently been compounded by a deep personal disappointment. In the years of inflation, 1920–23, he had seen his fortune evaporate and now, in his extreme old age, he endured the pain of his son's refusal to assist him, though some years earlier he had given the son all of his lands and his castle. Believing she might be able to assist the old man, Irene Harand set out to obtain justice through the law. She consulted a number of lawyers, and even though none accomplished anything of substance, all charged her substantially. After a number of such discouraging encounters, she met with well-known attorney Dr. **Moritz Zalman**.

Zalman differed from the other lawyers in that he showed great enthusiasm for the case, insisting that the old man could—indeed must—obtain justice. When the question of fees came up, Zalman told Harand that if she had managed to volunteer her time, energy, and funds on behalf of the poor nobleman, then he could certainly provide his legal skills gratis. This moment was the start of Irene Harand's political career. Harand realized that even she—who had never knowingly harbored anti-Semitic feelings—had sought out only non-Jewish lawyers prior to consulting with Zalman, who was Jewish. The instant he volunteered assistance, the thought had crossed her mind that by refusing a fee for his work Zalman was not "behaving in a Jewish fashion." At this point, with a probing honesty characteristic of her personality, Harand concluded that she had initially interpreted the situation with an anti-Semitic mindset. Like most Viennese of her day, she had assumed that Zalman by definition would be an avaricious, unscrupulous individual. Immediately realizing that this was not the case, she decided to work closely with Zalman not only to help one old man, but to create the foundations of a movement that would bring new and better ideas into Austrian public life.

Besides being a respected attorney who often volunteered his time to help poor but deserving clients, Zalman had for years been deeply involved in political struggles on behalf of the poor and downtrodden. He was particularly involved in cases where impoverished old-age pensioners were denied their benefits. In one such instance, his efforts had resulted in the passing of a new law that guaranteed pensions to 40,000 men and women who had previously been denied any payments. Both Zalman's tough determination to find practical ways to accomplish a goal and his unquenchable moral concern for justice deeply impressed Harand. Together they created the Austrian People's Party and, in what would turn out to be the last free parliamentary elections in Austria, campaigned in November 1930 on a platform calling for greater support for impoverished pensioners while condemning the increasingly virulent outbreaks of anti-Semitic propaganda and violence.

The election results were a disappointment, indeed a veritable disaster, for the fledgling party. Only 14,980 Austrians cast a ballot for the Austrian People's Party (8,459 of these were in Vienna). As a consequence, no seats were won in the national legislature, and what few contributions had flowed into the party treasury before the election could now, in the middle of a worsening economic depression, no longer be counted on.

At this juncture, many might have withdrawn from political life, but a disturbing incident at the time of the election strengthened Harand's resolve to remain active. While walking on Vienna's busy Wiedner Hauptstrasse, she witnessed a parade of Nazi youths, characterizing them later as "a troop of half-grown youngsters." While marching by, they shouted a standard Nazi slogan: *"Juda verrecke"* (death to the Jews). Pedestrians at the scene seemed indifferent. Deeply shocked by this event, Harand noted that one boy of about 12 seemed transformed before her very eyes "from a human child to a little bloodthirsty beast." Alarmed by what she had seen, Harand decided that Nazism in Austria, while still not a mass movement in 1930, had clearly become a dangerous phenomenon because of its powerful appeals to young people seeking a cause. Nazism, she believed, was "guilty of robbing our children of their childhood, stealing our children from us and making criminals of them."

Soon after the incident, Harand appeared at a Catholic political meeting to warn of the growing menace of Nazism. Instead of a sympathetic reception, the audience dismissed her warnings, mocked her for a lack of political experience or judgment, and booed her off the stage as a "foolish, hysterical woman." But it would take more than public humiliation to discourage Harand, who was determined to awaken the people of her native Vienna to the evils growing in their midst. For over a year, she and Zalman continued to warn about the dangers of Nazism and racial hatred, spreading their message in small groups that met in apartments, cafes, and rented halls. But few seemed interested in their warnings. In both Germany and Austria, the Nazi movement grew alarmingly in size and aggressiveness. Most people were more concerned with the basics of economic survival during the depression and regarded Adolf Hitler as another Karl Lueger, an unscrupulous demagogue whose anti-Semitism would quickly moderate once he was forced to deal with the responsibilities of actually wielding political power.

Resistance Movement Gains Strength

Harand's energies were galvanized when Hitler assumed control over Germany in early 1933. In a small pamphlet entitled *So? oder So?* which included on its cover sketches of a swastika and balanced scales of justice, she communicated with a mass audience on the burning issue of the day—whether Nazism, using anti-Semitism as one of its major arguments, would be able to seize power in Austria. Financed by herself and her husband, *So? oder So?* was printed in an edition of 30,000 copies, and sold for the low price of 20 Groschen. The main thesis of the work was that virtually all of the arguments used by anti-Semites were untruths, or gross distortions, and that Jews as individuals rarely behaved in the ways that racist stereotypes had depicted them. She gave as her motive for writing a basic belief that as an Austrian, a Christian, and an "Aryan" she had a responsibility to speak up for a historically maligned people, pointedly reminding her readers that Jesus Christ had also been a Jew.

Encouraged by a favorable response to her pamphlet, which soon went into a second printing of another 30,000 copies, Harand went about her work with a heightened sense of urgency in the summer of 1933. The Austrian Nazi Party had been declared illegal in June of that year and was now engaged in numerous bomb attacks and other underground activities designed to destabilize and psychologically disarm the Austrian government. Attacks on Jewish shops and homes in Vienna became common, and it was clear that if Nazism triumphed in Austria the fate of its Jewish citizens would be grim at best. Seeking moral and financial support from both Catholics and Jews, Harand was able in early September 1933 to release the first issue of a newspaper dedicated to enlightening the public about the menace of Nazism. Called *Gerechtigkeit* (Justice), it declared as its guiding principles a strong desire to fight against racial hatred and to ameliorate human suffering. In a box featured on the first page of each issue, Harand proclaimed the reason for her defense of the honor of Austria's Jews: "I fight anti-Semitism because it defames our Christianity."

Gerechtigkeit quickly became a popular—and often controversial—publication. Many of Vienna's Jews felt their morale improve when they began reading this clearly written, courageous weekly newspaper. Some Catholics who had never given much thought to their anti-Semitic attitudes began to question some of their own assumptions (and prejudices) when confronted with powerful and passionately argued ideas. Within a short time of its founding, *Gerechtigkeit* reached a circulation of almost 30,000 copies. But Vienna's illegal Nazis regarded the paper as a dangerous weapon in the hands of their enemies and demonstrated their anger by disrupting Harand's rallies and meetings with stink bombs and firecrackers. Threatening letters were often addressed to Harand, warning that her defense of Jews made her a traitor to the "cause of pure Germandom."

Harand was not deterred. Encouraged by the initial successes of her publications, in 1933 she founded a "Movement against Anti-Semitism,

Racial Hatred and Glorification of War." Anyone could join this organization, which was usually simply referred to as the Harand Movement. It appealed to Jews and Christians, young as well as old, and by May 1934 could claim 40,000 members. Although membership dropped slightly in 1936 to 36,000, in that year the Harand Movement could boast of 6,000 non-Austrian members. The religious affiliations of the Movement's Austrian members broke down into 25,000 Roman Catholics, 4,000 Jews, and 1,000 Protestants. Remembering that words alone would not suffice to combat ethnic and religious hatreds, the Harand Movement organized several shelters in Vienna that were able to provide hot drinks, food and warmth for 200 to 300 unemployed and homeless people daily in the city's bitterly cold winter months.

Aware that her message of religious toleration and resistance to Nazi racism could only be effective if disseminated to as many people as possible, Harand showed remarkable creativity in "packaging" the ideas of her movement in many different forms. The successful pamphlet *So? oder So?*, as well as the newspaper *Gerechtigkeit*, served to sound the alarm about Nazism, but other methods of recruitment and persuasion were constantly being tried. To win over alienated youth, an organization called the Austrian Youth League *(Österreichischer Jugendbund; ÖJB)* was created; many of its members came from the Social Democratic youth organizations banned in February 1934. Also popular was a youth chorus that served as an auxiliary of the ÖJB, which gave a number of successful concerts of Austrian folk songs. Another novel idea was the issuance of a phonograph record, one side of which contained a brief statement by Harand, with the other side reserved for a song, *"Gute Menschen"* (Good People), which summed up the humane optimism of the Harand Movement.

A final method of spreading the message was a series of perforated gummed labels which resembled postage stamps but had no postal validity. Printed in several languages, these labels depicted great Jewish thinkers, artists, and scientists and were meant to counter the Nazi slander that Jews had never been cultural benefactors. On at least one occasion, these labels were used in Nazi Germany by underground members of the Harand Movement who were in touch with their Vienna headquarters. In 1937 courageous members of the Movement entered the exhibition hall in Munich housing the Nazi regime's anti-Semitic propaganda exhibition *"Der ewige Jude"* ("The Eternal Jew"). Here they plastered the walls and exhibition frames with many of these labels, which depicted among other individuals the noted Jewish scientists **Paul**

Ehrlich and **Heinrich Hertz** and politicians **Benjamin Disraeli** and **Walter Rathenau**.

Sein Kampf Is Published

In August 1935 Harand published a book that became her most compelling indictment of Nazism and anti-Semitism. Entitled *Sein Kampf,* this work was obviously meant to refute the arguments first raised a decade earlier by Adolf Hitler in *Mein Kampf.* By 1935 some conservative Austrians were clearly thinking of the day when an increasingly powerful Nazi Germany would be able to absorb the weak Alpine republic, and were thus less enthusiastic about supporting an outspoken anti-Nazi like Irene Harand. It was probably for this reason that she was unable to find a publisher among the established publishing houses; undaunted, she had her manuscript privately printed and published. In the first chapter of *Sein Kampf,* she defined as one essential feature of Nazism its reliance on lies, defining a lie as "a filthy weapon... a crime against God, against Nature and against Humanity."

While most of *Sein Kampf* was a vigorous defense of the Jews, Harand's book also analyzed and condemned other destructive forces in the modern world, particularly the long-existing spirit of rabid nationalism that made it possible for Hitler's movement to seduce and control otherwise decent human beings. Arguing that national feelings based on attitudes of superiority toward another people could only act as a poison and lead to war, she made it clear that, while she considered herself to be a good Austrian, such love of country was patriotism—not a narrow-minded and intolerant nationalism. Perhaps realizing that at least in the short run hers was to be a losing battle, Harand wrote in the Preface:

> I hope that [this book] will bring consolation to the victims of National Socialism. It ought to assure them that there are still some people in this world who will not submit to the terror of the Third Reich but who will fight until the danger of Nazi expansion is banished from the earth and the victims of National Socialism are rescued from their torturers.

Sein Kampf ends with both a grim warning and words of shining hope: "National Socialism is the greatest menace of the century. In fighting it, we must use weapons which the Nazis scorn: Idealism and Courage, Common Sense and Love, Truth and Justice!"

The 1935 publication of *Sein Kampf* turned Harand into a declared enemy of the Third Reich. With its provocatively anti-Nazi title it quickly came to the attention of Nazi Germany's supreme censorship board, the *Reichsschrifttumskammer,* which kept tabs on any publication deemed dangerous to the regime. In the board's list of banned books issued in October 1935, *Sein Kampf* was described as being both "dangerous and undesired." With this listing, it became clear that Irene Harand was now regarded as an active and dangerous foe of the Hitler regime. Not only Nazi literary agencies but **Heinrich Himmler**'s feared SS and Gestapo placed her name on lists of those individuals in Austria who would be "dealt with accordingly" at such time that Nazi control extended to her country. Fortunately for Irene and Frank Harand, both were in Great Britain at the time of the *Anschluss* which marked the annexation of Austria to Nazi Germany in March 1938. Had they been in Vienna, there is little doubt that they would have been sent to Dachau concentration camp, where the first anti-Nazis were transported when the Nazi rulers destroyed the vestiges of independent Austria.

After a brief period in Great Britain, the Harands emigrated to the United States, where Irene continued her defense of Jewish honor against Nazi propaganda. By the 1950s, her work was forgotten in both her native Austria and her new homeland America. Only in her final years did her life's work begin to receive the recognition it deserved. In 1969 she was honored by Israel's Yad Vashem Martyrs and Heroes Remembrance Authority as one of the non-Jewish individuals who helped Jews during the Holocaust period and thus deserved recognition as one of the "Righteous among the Nations." One of the members of the commission that recommended her for the award noted the courage necessary in her activities of the 1930s:

> [T]o deliver public speeches at a time when Austria was swept by a wave of political assassinations meant exposing oneself to great risk. This woman waged a desperate and unceasing war which placed her in great peril. She sent her boys to hand out the newspaper at street corners. The children were beaten and she was beaten too. She stood her ground against vilification and threats. If this is not a struggle in which one risks one's life, then I don't know what risk means. She fought to save Austrian Jewry.

After decades of indifference, Irene Harand's Austrian homeland began to take an interest in her achievements in the 1970s. She visited Vienna and was honored there in 1971. It was not, however, until 1990, some ten years after her death, when a public housing project in the heart of Vienna was named after her, that she became known again to the average Viennese. No doubt she would have appreciated the April 20th date chosen for the dedication ceremonies. Every April 20th had been celebrated in the Third Reich with elaborate ceremonies, for it was the birthday of Adolf Hitler. After many decades, at least symbolic justice had triumphed in a small corner of Hitler's homeland.

SOURCES:

Bassett, Richard. *Waldheim and Austria.* Penguin Books, 1990.

"Champion of Justice: Irene Harand," in *Wiener Library Bulletin,* Vol. 9, nos. 3/4, May-August 1955, pg. 24.

Haag, John. "A Woman's Struggle Against Nazism: Irene Harand and Gerechtigkeit," *Wiener Library Bulletin.* Vol. 34, new series 53/54, 1981, pp. 64–72.

Harand, Irene. *His Struggle (An Answer to Hitler).* Artcraft Press, 1937.

Paldiel, Mordecai. "To the Righteous among the Nations Who Risked Their Lives to Rescue Jews," in *Yad Vashem Studies,* Vol. 19, 1988, pp. 403–425.

Pauley, Bruce F. *From Prejudice to Persecution: A History of Austrian Anti-Semitism.* University of North Carolina Press, 1992.

Weinzierl, Erika. "Christliche Solidarität mit Juden am Beispiel Irene Harands (1900–1975)," in Marcel Marcus et al., eds., *Israel und Kirche Heute: Beiträge zum christlich-jüdischen Dialog/Für Ernst Ludwig Ehrlich.* Herder, 1991, pp. 356–367.

FURTHER READING:

Geehr, Richard S. *Karl Lueger: Mayor of Fin Vienna, de Siecle* Wayne State University Press, 1990.

Hallie, Philip. *Lest Innocent Blood be Shed: The Story of the Village of Le Chambon and How Goodness Happened There.* Harper & Row, 1979.

Parkinson, F., ed. *Conquering the Past: Austrian Nazism Yesterday & Today.* Wayne State University Press, 1989.

Pauley, Bruce F. *Hitler and the Forgotten Nazis: A History of Austrian National Socialism,* University of North Carolina Press, 1981.

Whiteside, Andrew G. *The Socialism of Fools: Georg Ritter von Schönerer and Austrian Pan-Germanism.* University of California Press, 1975.

Keir Hardie

(1856–1915)

Coal miner, trade unionist, and Christian socialist, who founded the Scottish Labour Party and Independent Labour Party, and was also instrumental in the creation of the British Labour Party.

Born James Keir Hardie in Legbrannock, Scotland, in 1856; died in Cumnock, Scotland, in 1915; illegitimate child of a farm servant; married: Lillie Wilson, 1879; children: (two sons) James and Duncan; (one daughter) Agnes. Successor: (as leader of the parliamentary Labour movement) James Ramsey MacDonald.

K eir Hardie is the most revered figure in British working-class history; his life story remains one of the sustaining myths of Britain's labor movement. He rose from total obscurity and abject poverty by working tirelessly for the creation of an independent labor party in the United Kingdom. In his later life, he also became an internationally recognized champion of peace, anti-imperialism, racial equality, and women's suffrage.

Keir Hardie grew up in a society transformed by the industrial revolution. By the late 19th century, Britain's rural economy had declined, while its cities were overcrowded, extremely polluted, and totally segregated by class. Landowners and a prosperous business class dominated a political system which still denied poor men and all women the vote. Most people worked long hours for low wages and often suffered from lengthy spells of uncompensated unemployment. Poor nutrition, unsanitary housing, and dangerous working conditions all shortened labor-class lives. Victorian Britain offered workers almost no social mobility, so many of them emigrated to Canada, Australia, New Zealand, and the United States. Others, like

Contributed by Ronald Edsforth, Visiting Assistant Professor of History, Massachusetts Institute of Technology, Cambridge, Massachusetts

Hardie, turned to trade unions and politics to improve the condition of the working class.

James Keir Hardie was born in 1856 in a coal mining village in western Scotland. His mother Mary Keir was a poor farm servant who lived alone in a one-room cottage with a thatched roof and a baked mud floor. James's natural father's identity remains a mystery to this day. In 1859, Mary Keir married David Hardie, a ship's carpenter and sometime miner who moved the family to Glasgow; the couple had five more children, three boys and two girls. Though David Hardie was a hard worker, low wages and uncertain employment made it difficult for him to support his growing family. He sometimes drank heavily, and when he did, he would berate his wife about "the bastard" she had forced upon him. These incidents left young Hardie with a permanent abhorrence of drunkenness.

Keir Hardie did not have a happy childhood. He never attended school and there was little time for play. As the oldest son, he was expected to contribute to the family income at an early age. He began working as a full-time messenger in Glasgow—12 hours per day, six days a week—when he was eight years old. Hardie next worked for a printer but was too poor to be apprenticed.

In 1867, the family left Glasgow and moved back to Lanarkshire where Hardie and his stepfather found work as coal miners. The Hardies eventually settled near Hamilton, in a poverty-stricken, overcrowded neighborhood of company-owned houses known as The Quarter. A pump in the street provided water, and pit toilets in the alley served the sanitary needs of its many residents. Eleven-year-old Hardie worked first as a "trapper," spending 12 hours a day in near total darkness tending the trap that ventilated a mine shaft. His starting wage was one shilling, about 50 cents a day.

For the next 12 years, Keir Hardie worked underground in the mines of Lanarkshire. Coal mining was a physically exhausting, dirty, and dangerous occupation. Mine owners cared little for worker health and safety, and fiercely resisted unions which attempted to improve conditions and raise wages. Black lung disease shortened most miners' lives. Many other miners were killed outright in accidents and explosions. Once, after a tunnel collapsed, Hardie had to spend several frightening hours alone, waiting to be dug out, with the body of a dead mate beside him. In 1877, on another occasion Hardie long remembered, an explosion in a nearby pit killed over 200 miners.

Hardie developed his deep sympathy for the working class and a basic distrust of capitalists

CHRONOLOGY

1867	Began 12 years of work in Scottish coal mines
1880	Led his first miners' strike
1886	Named secretary of new Scottish Miners' Federation
1888	Defeated as independent labor candidate for Parliament; Scottish Labour Party established
1889	Greater London Dock strike; Hardie began publishing *The Labour Leader*
1892	Elected member of Parliament
1894	Independent Labour Party established
1899	British war against South African Boers began
1906	Labour Party won 29 seats in Parliament; Hardie elected chairman of Parliamentary Labour Party
1908	Denounced British rule in India and racial inequality in South Africa
1914	Led movement to avert war in Europe; WWI began

while working as a miner. But his politics were also shaped by other experiences from this period. Somehow finding the time to attend night school, he taught himself history and literature, as well as a little French and Latin. The young man read widely and was particularly fond of Scottish history and the poetry of Robert Burns. He remained a Scottish nationalist to the end of his life.

In 1873, Hardie enrolled in the Good Templars, a temperance organization, which allowed him to develop skills as an organizer and public speaker. By the early 1880s, he was a district official and leading lecturer for the Templars. Although Hardie had joined the temperance crusade for personal reasons, he also believed strong drink degraded the working class; he continued to teach the necessity of abstinence and self-help long after he left the temperance movement.

Although his parents were atheists, Hardie embraced Christianity. For several years he was active in the Evangelical Union, a reform sect which preached that salvation was for all mankind. In 1884, he abandoned organized religion after a favorite minister was dismissed for excessive zeal. Though he never attended church regularly again, Hardie remained a deeply religious man. His later writings reveal his version of socialism to be more influenced by the Christ's Sermon on the Mount than the political-economy of Marx and Engels.

Hardie married Lillie Wilson, an associate from the Good Templars, in 1879. Although she had been a temperance activist, Lillie Hardie never shared in her husband's political crusades. The couple had three children, and for a few years they formed a tight-knit family. However, as Hardie's political career developed, he would travel constantly, while his wife remained home in Cumnock, Scotland. Eventually, with his election to Parliament, Hardie would establish a residence in London where he would live alone for much of the rest of his life.

He Becomes Union Organizer and Journalist

At age 22, Hardie was named local agent of the Lanarkshire Miners' Union. Union organizing in Britain was still risky and difficult. Highly skilled workers had won bargaining rights and some political recognition, but most employers refused to recognize unions, and the courts and police generally supported their intransigence. In 1879, when mining companies reduced wages, Hardie led his Hamilton miners out on strike against the advice of his union's leaders. This strike was broken when the mine owners hired nonunion workers as strikebreakers. In 1880 and 1881, Hardie again led local strikes that were defeated by the importation of "blackleg" (nonunion) workers. Though these walkouts earned Hardie a reputation as a fearless union leader, he was blacklisted by the mine owners and never worked as a miner again.

In 1881, Hardie moved his family permanently from Lanarkshire to Cumnock in Ayrshire. There he found temporary work as a grocery clerk, and then as an insurance agent before finally securing a position as a reporter for the *Cumnock News,* a Liberal Party newspaper. For the rest of his life, Hardie earned a living as a journalist and publisher. Constant writing sharpened his ideas and developed a national audience for his politics.

For five years beginning in 1882, Keir Hardie wrote a regular column on the mining industry for the weekly *Androssan and Saltcoats Herald.* In 1887, he founded *The Miner,* a monthly that vigorously advanced the cause of the newly formed Scottish Miners' Federation. In February 1889, at a time when he was emerging as the undisputed leader of independent labor politics, Hardie started up a monthly magazine in Glasgow. *The Labour Leader* tirelessly promoted his version of socialism and labor independence in politics. He moved the magazine to London in 1894 and published it as a weekly newspaper. Soon functioning as a semiofficial organ of Hardie's own Independent Labour Party, *The Labour Leader* was eventually taken over by the Party in 1904. But in the mid-1890s, when its weekly circulation reached 50,000, Keir Hardie's newspaper played a crucial role disseminating his humane, social democratic critique of British society and politics.

Hardie's transformation from trade union organizer to political agitator paralleled his journalistic endeavors. In August 1886, he was named secretary of the Ayrshire Miners' Union. Shortly thereafter, he drafted a new set of union objectives which declared labor to be the sole creator of wealth and advocated an end to laissez faire in the coal fields. In October 1886, Hardie founded the Scottish Miners' Federation in conjunction with other militant mine union leaders. The new federation called for universal restriction of output through implementation of an eight-hour day and a five-day week. Hardie hoped to be able to negotiate a reduction of the grueling schedule of the miners. But the mine owners refused and then broke the federation's strikes by bringing blackleg labor to the coal fields under police escort.

Despite this total defeat, at age 30 Hardie had begun to develop a reputation outside of Scotland. In 1887, he led a delegation of Scottish miners to London to urge the trade unionists who sat in Parliament as members of the Liberal Party (the so-called "Lib-Labs") to introduce a bill mandating an eight-hour day. The delegation was rebuffed. But later that year, Hardie raised the issue again at a meeting of the Trades Union Congress in Swansea. In a fiery speech, Hardie attacked "Lib-Lab" politicians as too weak to stand up for the majority of the working class. By the end of 1887, Hardie had defined most of the political program he would advocate for the rest of his life. It included the eight-hour day, employers' liability for industrial accidents, national pension and health insurance funds, unemployment compensation, and the nationalization of major industries that refused to improve wages and working conditions. During the 20th century, all these measures would be enacted and become regular features of British life.

In 1888, Hardie decided to run for Parliament in Mid-Lanarkshire when a radical Liberal from that district retired for health reasons. Initially, Hardie hoped for the local Liberal Party's endorsement, but his reputation precluded that possibility. Hardie then put himself forward as an independent labor candidate. This unprecedented action brought socialists and radical unionists from all over Britain into the campaign. The national Liberal Party was so worried that it secretly offered Hardie a safe seat in the next general election if he would withdraw. Hardie refused. In the end,

Hardie suffered an overwhelming defeat at the polls but gained renown for his unwavering independence.

Despite his poor showing in Mid-Lanarkshire, Hardie pressed ahead with plans to create a separate labor party free from all ties to the Liberals and the Tories (also called Conservatives or Unionists). He convened a meeting of trade unionists, middle-class socialists, and Scottish nationalists which proclaimed the establishment of a Scottish Labour Party on May 19, 1888. The group's platform included the main points of Hardie's labor agenda, as well as universal adult suffrage, free public education, a graduated income tax, and home rule for Scotland and Ireland. The new party expressed an ideological compromise between radical liberalism and democratic socialism that nearly matched Hardie's own contemporary views. The Scottish Labour Party never achieved a significant electoral victory. Nonetheless, it developed both labor ideology and future Labour Party politicians. In 1894, the Scottish Labour Party merged with the newly formed national Independent Labour Party, another Hardie-inspired creation.

In these years, Keir Hardie began to demonstrate a concern for international solidarity that would later make him famous around the world. He attended his first International Trades Congress in London in 1888 and gained immediate recognition for a proposal to set up transnational executive committees for each occupation. Hardie held talks with the French miners' union in 1888–89, and played a prominent role in an International Miners' Congress in Belgium in 1890. The positions Hardie took at the meeting which established the Second Socialist International in July 1889 were even more significant. As the representative of both the Ayrshire Miners' Union and the Scottish Labour Party, Hardie urged the international socialist community to reject revolution and accept temporary alliances with middle-class progressives to achieve the passage of specific reform measures. Hardie's pragmatic approach angered some British delegates, as well as a host of continental Marxists. But his moderation and flexibility also won him new respect at home and abroad.

In early 1890, Hardie was unexpectedly proposed as a parliamentary candidate for the West Ham South constituency, a working-class district in London. The district included large populations of gasworkers, dockers, and Irish laborers who had been swept up in the organizing frenzy that surrounded the Greater London Dock Strike of the previous year. Hardie visited West Ham South regularly, making contacts with local labor leaders and giving speeches at prearranged meetings. In early 1892, he resigned his post with the Ayrshire Miners to devote his full energies to the campaign. His hard work paid off in July when the voters in West Ham South gave him an easy victory over a Tory rival.

The Man in the Cloth Cap Enters Parliament

Hardie made a spectacular entrance at the opening of the new Parliament on August 3, 1892. Scorning the traditional formal attire of other MPs (members of Parliament), he appeared in yellow tweed trousers, serge jacket and vest, and a soft tweed cap. The clothes brilliantly announced his Scottish working-class identity, and his intention to remain independent of affiliation with either the Liberal or Tory party. Hardie was of course unable to push through any legislation in this Parliament. But "the man in the cloth cap," as Prime Minister **William Gladstone** referred to him, did gain a national reputation as a spokesman for the needs of the poor and unemployed. Hardie was satisfied to play the roles of agitator and prophet in the Parliament of 1892–94, but away from Westminster he worked doggedly to institutionalize his success. In January 1893, a meeting of labor activists from all over Britain was convened in Bradford. It elected Hardie chairman and proclaimed the formation of the Independent Labour Party (ILP). The new ILP reflected Hardie's dominant influence. At the conference, he argued successfully for decentralization and for flexibility. From the chair, Hardie blocked a proposal to use the word "socialist" in the new party's name and a resolution which would have forced political conformity on ILP members. Keir Hardie was elected chairman of the ILP's new National Administrative Council in 1894, a post he held until 1900.

Within a year, the Independent Labour Party included over 400 local branches with more than 50,000 active members. Over the long run, the Party provided the major vehicle for the growth of independent labor politics in Britain. But in the short run, Hardie experienced great disappointment. In the general election of 1895, all 28 ILP candidates, including Hardie, were defeated at the polls. He suffered yet another election defeat when he stood as the ILP candidate in a parliamentary by-election in East Bradford in the fall of 1896.

An upsurge in industrial conflict at the end of the century set the stage for a dramatic reversal of Hardie's fortunes. When well-organized employers' federations turned to national lockouts to break strikes, and when the courts began to rule decisively against unions, Hardie suddenly found a receptive audience for his political message within the labor movement. In the spring of 1899, the Scottish Trades Union Congress voted to affiliate with the ILP. A few months later, the British TUC voted to convene a special conference of trade unions, socialists, cooperators, and other working-class political clubs to secure better labor representation in Parliament. Hardie's ideas dominated the subsequent meeting in London which established the British Labour Party in February 1900.

The creation of the Labour Party was the crowning achievement of Keir Hardie's career. Although he would not live to see Labour displace the Liberals as Britain's second major party nor have the opportunity to take part in a Labour government, Hardie correctly predicted the rise of Labour in the 20th century. During the last phase of his career, during the years leading up to World War I, Keir Hardie played a crucial role in establishing the Labour Party's voice in Parliament and in setting its long-term domestic and foreign policy agenda.

The Tory government's decision to hold a snap election in 1900 to take advantage of the jingoism aroused by the Boer War caught the newly formed Labour Party off guard. Only ten Labour candidates stood for Parliament, and just two were victorious. Keir Hardie was returned from Merthyr, a mining district in South Wales. Unfortunately, the other Labour member soon made it clear he was content to revert to the old style "Lib-Lab" politics. Thus, until 1906, when the Labour Party elected 29 MPs, Hardie was again a lonely voice in Parliament.

The election of 1906 brought to power a Liberal government that enacted the country's first welfare-state legislation. The Parliamentary Labour Party (PLP) generally supported these Liberal initiatives, but thanks to its first chairman, Keir Hardie, the PLP also staked out independent positions on unemployment compensation, trade union legislation, and women's suffrage. Still, Hardie was not an entirely successful chairman. He seemed temperamentally unsuited for the routine business of leadership and was frequently away from Parliament supporting strikers and attending socialist meetings. In addition, his friendly relations with radical suffragists divided the party.

Speaks Out for Independence, Equal Rights

In 1907, Hardie recognized that his leadership endangered the fledgling Party, so he stepped aside and embarked on a nine-month trip that took him to all parts of the British Empire. This trip, and two others that followed in 1908 and 1912, confirmed Hardie's stature as a remarkably fearless and farseeing political agitator. In Canada, Australia, and New Zealand, he met with labor leaders and spoke at numerous union conferences always urging political independence and democratic socialism. Then Hardie toured the subcontinent with the leaders of the India home-rule movement, speaking out against the harshness of British rule. In South Africa, he advocated both equal political rights and trade unions for the country's black majority. Hardie was reviled in Parliament, scorned in most British newspapers, and even denounced in private by the king for his activity in India and South Africa. But his advocacy of decolonization and racial equality won him millions of admirers around the world. And even more importantly, it established the basis for future Labour government policy toward Asia and Africa.

The last years of Hardie's life were the most tumultuous in modern British history. The Liberal government's plan to grant Home Rule to a united Ireland brought the threat of civil war as Unionist radicals threatened to fight to keep Ulster in the United Kingdom. Militant suffragists repeatedly disrupted Parliament, sabotaged the mails, and fought with police. A series of increasingly violent industrial disputes culminated in a threatened General Strike. And finally, the naval arms race with Germany and rising tensions on the Continent threatened war. Keir Hardie tried to influence the outcome of each of these disputes, but even a man of his seemingly boundless energy could not keep up with events.

Between 1910 and 1914, Hardie seemed to be everywhere, supporting striking workers in Britain and Ireland while protesting the government's tendency to use force to suppress union militants. He also defended the women's rights crusade in Parliament over the protests of some Labour members, and vehemently denounced the forced feeding of jailed suffragists who went on hunger strikes. Within the Labour Party, Keir Hardie was able to block an attempt to establish a permanent electoral alliance with the Liberals. And perhaps most significantly, he organized a peace movement in conjunction with European socialists.

Hardie's antimilitarism had first surfaced during the early days of the Boer War when he denounced the actions of the British government and the jingoism of the Tory Party. In 1909 he had chaired a joint meeting of German, French, and British socialists which called for an end to the

Anglo-German naval arms race. In 1913, he convened a massive peace conference in London's Albert Hall that was attended by delegates from all over the Continent. And in the summer of 1914, when Europe's military machines started to mobilize, Hardie frantically tried to arrange an international general strike to prevent the outbreak of war. His efforts were in vain. World War I was not stopped by international working-class protest. Indeed, most working-class leaders in Europe enthusiastically pledged to support their national governments when the conflict began in August 1914.

Keir Hardie's antiwar efforts showed him once again to be a leader of insight. World War I turned out, as he predicted, to be a futile bloodbath in which the working classes of Europe made the greatest sacrifices. His frantic attempt to rally Europe's socialists against the war left Hardie exhausted, and the war itself seemed to break his spirit. Hardie suffered a stroke in January 1915 but was able to make a few more appearances in Parliament before he completely collapsed. He died in his Scottish home on September 26, 1915. The Labour Party, which he did so much to create, remains a monument to Keir Hardie's memory and his political ideas.

SOURCES:

Hardie, James Keir. *From Serfdom to Socialism.* Fairleigh Dickinson University Press, 1974.

Hughes, Emrys. *Keir Hardie.* George Allen & Unwin, 1956.

Morgan, Kenneth O. *Keir Hardie: Radical and Socialist.* Weidenfeld & Nicolson, 1975.

Reid, Fred. *Keir Hardie: The Making of a Socialist.* Croom Helm, 1978.

FURTHER READING:

Dangerfield, George. *The Strange Death of Liberal England.* Constable, 1935.

Halevy, Elie. *Imperialism and the Rise of Labour, 1895–1905.* Ernest Benn, 1961.

Pelling, Henry. *The Origins of the Labour Party, 1880–1900.* Macmillan, 1953.

Poirer, Philip. *The Advent of the British Labour Party.* George Allen & Unwin, 1958.

Henry II

(1133–1189)

Aggressive and temperamental king of England, who pieced together a large empire which included much of modern France and instigated far-reaching legal and administrative reform.

Name variations: Henry of Anjou; Duke of Normandy. Born in 1133; died in 1189; son of Matilda (daughter of Henry I) and Geoffrey "Plantagenet," Count of Anjou; married: Eleanor, Duchess of Aquitaine; children: Henry, Richard (later Richard I, 1189–99), Geoffrey, John (later King John, 1199–1216). Predecessor: Henry I. Successor, his son, Richard I.

H enry II was born in 1133, the son of Matilda, daughter of Henry I, and Geoffrey, count of Anjou. At Henry's birth, Matilda and Geoffrey were involved in an argument with King Henry I over some castles which Matilda claimed as part of her dowry. By 1135, the quarrel had mushroomed into a small-scale frontier war. In December of that same year, the king died.

The death of the Henry I, while technically at war with his only heir, threw the succession into confusion. Many of the English barons hesitated to put the headstrong and temperamental Matilda on the throne, or even to let her head a regency for her two-year-old son. When a civil war broke out the following year, Stephen of Blois, a nephew of Henry I, seized the throne.

But Geoffrey and Matilda continued to launch invasions against England and Normandy, and Geoffrey finally took control of Normandy in 1148. As king of England, Stephen was weak and indecisive, dominated by his barons, who engaged in frequent skirmishes amongst themselves which, together with Matilda's occasional invasion attempts, brought great unrest and upheaval to the countryside.

"His enemies found [Henry] too brilliant and mercurial, too overwhelming to be forgiven; those close to him feared both his charm and his occasional outbursts of wild anger.... But they all admired him."

CHRISTOPHER BROOKE

Contributed by Kimberly K. Estep, Ph.D. in History, Auburn University, Auburn, Alabama

When Geoffrey died in 1151, his son Henry was almost 18. Now duke of Normandy and count of Anjou in his own right, Henry expanded his domains further by marrying **Eleanor,** heiress to the vast duchy of Aquitaine, in 1152. The following year, Henry launched an invasion of England to claim his birthright and met little resistance. The great barons were more interested in arranging a strategic truce than in engaging in protracted dynastic warfare. The Treaty of Winchester, signed that same year, recognized Henry as Stephen's lawful heir. Nine months later, Stephen graciously died.

Henry II's accession marked the end of the Norman Age and the beginning of the Angevin Age (the Angevin kings are also referred to as the Plantagenet dynasty, after the *plante genet,* or broom flower, which was the family emblem of Geoffrey of Anjou). Reddish-haired with gray eyes, Henry had a large, lionlike head and a powerful build. He was restless and constantly active, with a great love of war and hunting. He was also the first English king to be fully literate. Peter of Blois, a scholar and courtier during Henry's reign, left a famous depiction of life in Henry's court:

> If the king promises to spend the day anywhere … you may be sure that the king will leave the place bright and early, and upset everyone's calculations in his haste…. You may see men rushing about, urging on the pack-horses, fitting the teams to their wagons; everyone in utter confusion—a perfect portrait of hell. But if the prince has announced that he is setting off early to reach a particular place, beyond doubt he will change his mind and sleep until noon. You will see the pack-horses waiting loaded, the wagons silent, the runners asleep, the court merchants in a pother, everyone grumbling…. I believe our plight added to the king's pleasure.

When Henry II took the throne, he set out to end baronial unrest and rebuild the royal prerogative laid down by his grandfather Henry I. To that end, he devised a number of administrative and legal reforms. Most of the prerogatives he exercised had been unofficially implemented during Henry I's rule, but Henry II expanded them, codified them, and made them part of regular royal administration. Under Henry II, a bureaucracy of professional administrators was created to enforce the royal will and safeguard the king's interests.

Institutes Reforms in Taxation, the Military, and the Law

Many of Henry's reforms aimed at modernizing tax collection and military service quotas. The

CHRONOLOGY

1135	Henry I died; nephew Stephen of Blois usurped throne
1153	Henry of Anjou invaded England; Treaty of Winchester recognized Henry as Stephen's legal heir
1154	Henry II crowned king of England
1170	Henry II's eldest son crowned heir; Becket murdered in Canterbury Cathedral
1173–74	Henry's wife and sons involved in an unsuccessful rebellion against him
1183	Young Henry, heir to the throne, died
1186	Geoffrey died
1189	Uprising by remaining sons with the aid of Philip II of France; Henry II died; Richard I succeeded to the English throne

Baronial Charters (1166) required that all tenants-in-chief submit to the king a list of how many knights they had enfoeffed (granted control of a feudal estate) during the reigns of Henry I and Stephen. Henry II used these lists to determine how closely the barons were fulfilling the military obligations imposed by the monarchy. This was the first survey of military service since the reign of **William the Conqueror** (1066–87). The Assize of Arms (1181) attempted to organize the military service based on wealth. Four categories were set up, based on annual income. Those in the top category were required to outfit themselves with a shirt of mail, a helmet, a shield, and a lance. Even the lowest category of knights had to acquire a quilted coat, an iron headpiece, and a lance.

Henry also tried to reorganize England's tax system on more modern lines. Discontinuing the old land tax based on hides, he set up a new tax based on a percentage of annual rents. He also taxed business income and chattels, hoping to tap into the growing wealth of the English cities.

Sometimes referred to as the father of English Common Law, Henry successfully replaced the baronial courts with royal courts to hear criminal cases, questions of royal revenue, and property disputes. His judicial reforms laid the foundation for a new court system, operating under the aegis of the king and dispensing justice based upon a standard common law. He established the Court of King's Bench and the Court of Common Pleas to hear all but the most weighty royal cases. He also sent itinerant justices to the shires to hear cases in the king's name and extended royal jurisdiction to areas previously under the laws of private baronial courts. The Assize of Novel Disseisin, the Writ of Mort d'Ancestor and the Grand Assize were all devised to provide criteria for determining the best title in land disputes; these laws inquired into the status of the land when it passed from the previous owner and legislated heredity based on primogeniture (inheritance by the eldest son).

Before these acts were put into place, property disputes tended to be determined by battle. Under Henry's rule, private warfare and local tradition gave way to a uniform royal law which evolved into English common law. Henry also set the precedent for the use of juries in criminal proceedings, although Angevin juries were used primarily as grand juries—guilt or innocence was still determined by ordeal, relying on divine intervention to render the final verdict.

Perhaps the best-known aspect of Henry II's reign, however, was his protracted quarrel with the Church, personified in the archbishop of Canterbury, **Thomas Becket.** Henry's policies toward the Church stemmed from his ongoing attempts at judicial reform. In the process of expanding the royal courts, he ran afoul of the most powerful institution in 12th-century Europe. During this era, the Catholic Church was at one of the strongest periods of its history. Following a long era of reform, the Church had emerged as a strong advocate of education, and it counted some of the greatest minds of the age among its theologians and leaders.

Henry's problems with the Church began with his attempt to ensure that he had a reliable and cooperative friend at the head of the Church in England. When Theobald, archbishop of Canterbury at Henry's accession, died in 1162, Henry chose Thomas Becket as his replacement. As Henry's longstanding drinking buddy and close friend, as well as a talented Church administrator, Becket seemed to suit Henry's needs perfectly. To Henry's great surprise, however, Becket's appointment to the ancient post of the head of the English Church brought about a genuine conversion. Almost overnight, Becket turned into a fervent and aggressive champion of the rights of the Church.

Differences between Henry and the new archbishop broke out almost immediately, but a real confrontation did not occur until 1164, when Henry extended judicial reform to the English Church in the form of the Constitutions of Clarendon. Henry claimed that these acts, which he required every clergy member to sign, were merely a restatement of the policies implemented by Henry I. While his grandfather on many occasions had exercised his royal pleasure at the Church's expense, he had never dared put these policies in writing, nor did he require the clergy to sanction what they would surely regard as an infringement on their judicial domain.

Henry aimed the Constitutions of Clarendon against what he called "criminous clerics," Church officials who were accused of breaking the criminal laws of England. By tradition, these offenders were turned over to the Church courts for trial. But these courts were notoriously lax—for most offenses, convicted clerics were simply defrocked and sent back out into the streets. The Constitutions of Clarendon demanded further judgment for serious offenses by the royal courts. They also banned appeals to Rome without express royal permission.

Becket Protests Constitutions of Clarendon

When he was informed of the provisions of the Constitutions of Clarendon, Becket immediately cried out against them, insisting that further judgment for convicted Church offenders would submit them to double jeopardy. He also protested against Henry's interference in what he construed to be the internal affairs of the Church. The quarrel which broke out between Henry and Becket has been described as a clash of secular and ecclesiastical governments, representing the global struggle of 12th-century Europe between the universal Church and the rising nation-states. The quarrel was also a personal one, between two former friends who had become bitter enemies. Henry undoubtedly felt that Becket had let him down, and he accused him of breaking his oath of fealty through which he had sworn loyalty to the king when he accepted his office.

Faced with a seemingly insurmountable foe, Becket at first agreed to subscribe to the Constitutions of Clarendon, then in a fit of righteous indignation he backed off and made a formal appeal for support to Pope Alexander III. The pope procrastinated in answering Becket's plea. He was at that time involved in a protracted struggle with Holy Roman Emperor **Frederick Barbarossa** and had little strength to put to Becket's defense. In 1164, therefore, Henry called Becket to stand trial for various offenses against the royal prerogative. Becket refused, claiming clerical immunity from secular courts, and fled the country.

While abroad, Becket actively campaigned for support against Henry's encroachments, while Henry implemented the Constitutions of Clarendon freely in Becket's absence. In the summer of

1170, another direct confrontation arose when Henry determined to have his eldest son crowned as heir. Traditionally, the right to perform royal coronations belonged to the archbishop of Canterbury. Henry, not anxious to call Becket home, simply turned to the archbishop of York, Becket's primary rival, to perform the ceremony.

When Becket received word that the coronation had taken place, he was furious. He angrily threatened to put all of England under interdict, wherein all rites of the Church would be suspended indefinitely, including extreme unction for the dying. Faced with the possibility of eternal damnation for dying unshriven, the English population was certain to force the king to back down. Henry relented, then moved quickly to hammer out a truce whereby Becket could return to England without fear of royal molestation.

The first thing Becket did when he returned to Canterbury was to excommunicate every bishop who had taken part in the coronation ceremony. At news of this, Henry exploded with rage. Turning to his dinner guests, he furiously demanded, "Will no one rid me of the turbulent priest?" Although it is doubtful that Henry would have thought it expedient to have his powerful rival murdered, four knights then in attendance took him at his word. On the night of December 29, 1170, they traveled to Canterbury, surprised Becket in his own cathedral and mercilessly hacked him to pieces before the altar.

All the world was horrified by the brutal murder. Canonized almost immediately, Becket became an instant martyr and his ideas on clerical immunity gained widespread acceptance. Henry was placed in a very difficult position by the incident. When the pope forced him to do penance for the crime, King Henry walked barefoot through the streets of Canterbury while being flogged by the monks of Canterbury cathedral. He was forced to repudiate the Constitutions of Clarendon and to drop his attack on clerical immunity for the time being.

While the Becket incident was a serious embarrassment for Henry, it by no means stripped him of power in matters religious. He carried on his administrative and legal centralization unchecked, and he also continued to exercise a great deal of control over Church affairs. But never again was he able to make his intentions so clear, and for the remainder of his reign he was careful to avoid open conflict with the Church.

In addition to his English concerns, Henry II also had to administer an extensive empire. He was the first English king to hold greater land and wealth outside his kingdom than within it. Henry's possessions were not a unified empire, however. Except for the duchy of Normandy, which had many similar administrative organizations with England, Henry's holdings were a motley assortment of territories, each with its own institutions and governmental systems. There was no central imperial government over the Angevin Empire, and Henry often found many of these areas under the unshakable control of the local lords. Despite these limits, Henry held this massive empire together through sheer force of will.

In spite of the fact that the possessions which Henry had through birth and through marriage were so large they were practically ungovernable, he aspired to increase his holdings still further. He endeavored to make advantageous marriages for his children whenever possible. Through military campaigning, he gained nominal control of most of Ireland, and he made his youngest son **John** (future King John) Lord of Ireland in 1185. Later he had to recall his son after John suffered a series of military disasters. Henry's main focus, however, was the acquisition of more territory in France. Already his French possessions (Normandy, Maine, Anjou, Brittany, Touraine, and Aquitaine) far surpassed those of the king of France, Louis VII. Technically, Henry was Louis's vassal, but historically the Capetian kings had been too weak to exercise any real power beyond the area surrounding Paris known as the Ile-de-France. Henry conducted numerous campaigns in an attempt to gain control of Toulouse, in southern France, but found it to be firmly in the hands of a well-entrenched nobility.

During the reign of Louis VII, Henry's ambitions on the Continent were checked only by the strong local nobles of the provinces. In 1180, however, Louis died and was succeeded by his vigorous young son **Philip II** Augustus. Henry would find Philip the most challenging adversary he was to face outside his own family.

Henry II was "blessed" with a wealthy, landed wife and four strong sons. His wife Eleanor, duchess of Aquitaine (the wealthiest province of France), was well educated and famous in her own right as a patroness of the arts. She was also headstrong and independent. For 15 years, she had been married to Louis VII of France. When her marriage was annulled, the 30-year-old ex-queen of France married the 18-year-old Henry, then count of Anjou. She bore Henry many sons, four of whom grew to adulthood. As Henry's sons became older, however, they exhibited rebellious tendencies that gradually ate away at the strength of Henry's empire during his later years.

As soon as they were old enough, Henry began distributing his various titles among his sons, but he was determined to keep political power firmly in his own hands. His eldest son Henry was named Duke of Normandy and Count of Anjou, and in 1170 was crowned Henry III, king of England. Richard (the future **Richard I, the Lionheart**) received the title Duke of Aquitaine in 1167. Geoffrey became Duke of Brittany in 1181 when he was married to the heiress.

Not content with their lot as Henry II's puppets, his sons, together with their mother, plotted to wrest control from their father by force. In 1173–74, the three eldest fomented a full-scale rebellion, aided by Eleanor and Louis VII. Henry put down the uprising, placed Eleanor in permanent custody in France, and tried giving his sons more control within their provinces. Still he could not satisfy them.

When he ascended to the throne of France in 1180, Philip II proved very adept at exploiting the rebellious tendencies of Henry's sons to his advantage. The young heir Henry died in 1183, followed by Geoffrey in 1186, but the younger two conspired with Philip in another major uprising in 1189. Henry II, ill and near death, was forced to capitulate to the coalition. "Shame, shame on a conquered king," he is reported to have lamented after the successful coup. By this time, though, a changeover of power was imminent, and the rebellion did not change the ultimate outcome of the succession.

Henry II died on July 6, 1189. In spite of the personal humiliation which he suffered, Henry's reign established a firm precedent of royal authority, which enabled his successor, Richard I, to rule England successfully while spending less than six months in actual residence. Henry's legal and administrative reforms outlived him, and today he is regarded as one of England's most effective and powerful rulers.

SOURCES:

Brooke, Christopher. *From Alfred to Henry III, 871–1272.* New York, 1961.
Warren, W. L. *Henry II.* Berkeley, California, 1973.

FURTHER READING:

Jones, Thomas M. *The Becket Controversy.* New York, 1970.
Kelly, Amy. *Eleanor of Aquitaine and the Four Kings.* Cambridge, Massachusetts, 1950.

Henry the Navigator

(1394–1460)

Prince of late medieval Portugal and active crusader, who sponsored the colonization of islands in the African Atlantic and exploratory voyages along the West African coast which initiated the Portuguese colonial empire.

T he voyages of exploration sponsored by Prince Henry of Portugal in the early to mid-15th century were medieval in inspiration yet laid the foundations of a Portuguese empire. Lust for spices, dreams of Christian conversions, and competent navigational technology were significant elements to exploration in an era beset by both political turmoil and economic depression. In this context, Prince Henry's interests and achievements were part of a general European and Christian expansion which dated from the 11th century.

Ferdinand I, the last Burgundian king of Portugal, died in 1383 without male heirs, precipitating a succession crisis and a civil war between Portuguese and Castilian interests. In 1384, recognition by the Portuguese córtes (parliament) of John of Aviz (a bastard of royal blood) as king meant the beginning of the Aviz (Avis) dynasty that would endure for nearly two centuries. Prince Henry, who was called "the Navigator" by English writers, was the third surviving son born to John of Aviz, now John I of Portugal, and Philippa of the English duchy of Lancaster on March 4, 1394, in Lisbon. The marital union of Henry's parents had

Name variations: Prince Henry the Navigator; Don Henrique. Born on March 4, 1394, in Lisbon, Portugal; died at Sagres, Portugal, November 13, 1460; third surviving son of John of Aviz (John I of Portugal) and Philippa of Lancaster; never married; no children.

Contributed by Donna Beaudin, Ph.D. candidate in History, University of Guelph, Guelph, Ontario, Canada

been the physical embodiment of the Anglo-Portuguese alliance of 1386.

Little has been recorded of Prince Henry's childhood. It is known that his mother was a devout Christian with a strong sense of duty, who enforced high moral standards at a court that had previously been perceived as licentious and who raised her sons and daughters in accordance with these personal standards. As a youth, Henry received "bodily training" (which included the development of expertise with arms), as well as clerical education. The character formed by this education was thoughtful, calm, courteous and dignified, qualities that remained evident throughout his life.

Only two contemporary portraits survive, with some dispute as to whether they are actually of Henry. The contemporary chronicler Zurara gives a full description:

> The noble Prince was of a good height and broad frame, big and strong of limb, the hair of his head somewhat erect, his colour naturally fair, but by constant toil and exposure it had become dark. His expression at first sight inspired fear in those who did not know him, and when wroth, though such times were rare, his countenance was harsh.

Zurara went on to praise Henry's courage, intelligence, and ambition, as well as his physical and spiritual purity, and concluded that the prince was "constant in adversity, humble in prosperity."

That Henry had three prominent concerns was clear by the time he reached early adulthood. These objectives were scientific, commercial-political, and religious in scope. It has even been suggested that Prince Henry was sponsoring expeditions as early as the age of 18, when he reputedly sent a ship down the west coast of Africa in 1412.

Given Portuguese proximity to the Muslim world, religious zeal was strong in Henry's family (his father was "an ardent Crusader ... by inclination and profession"). As a governor of the Order of Christ, and by his own disposition, Henry was obliged to wage holy war against the non-Christian infidel. An expedition against Ceuta, a commercial center in Muslim-held North Africa opposite Gibraltar, had been contemplated as early as 1409–10. These plans were put into action in the summer of 1415, despite the death of Queen Philippa due to plague in Lisbon. On her deathbed, this pious woman had given a piece of the true cross to each of her three eldest sons. Prince Henry was deeply affected by his mother's death but kept on with the plans for the campaign against Ceuta. The Portuguese victory in August 1415 marked the beginning of the Christian counterattack against the spread and dominion of Islam. Fighting in such wars, in the service of both one's God and one's king, was how the respectable medieval knight filled his time. The campaign against Ceuta produced rewards for Henry. Not only did he increase his knowledge of the African coast, he received the honors of knighthood when his father named him Duke of Viseu and Lord of Covilham.

Prince Sends Velho to Canary Islands

The year after the Ceuta campaign, Prince Henry sent Gonzalo Velho to the Canary Islands to investigate, in a scientific fashion, the strong current which flowed between the islands. It is from this date that Henry's involvement in commercial and exploratory expeditions can more accurately be reckoned. He also kept vessels at sea to guard the Portuguese coast of North Africa against Moorish pirates. Over the next few years, to about 1420, Henry asserted his independence. Leaving the royal court in Lisbon, he moved to Lagos on the southern coast of Portugal where his father had made him governor. Henry also tried, unsuccessfully, to capture Gibraltar from the Moors.

In preparation for the pursuit of his objectives, Henry studied mathematics, cosmography, medicine, astrology, and nautical astronomy. Edgar Prestage concluded "there can be little doubt [that] in Henry's mind the advance of knowledge was primarily a means to an end" and that these ends were "utilitarian." Thus, Henry's lifelong interest in locating the African country of Guinea included five specific objectives: (1) to obtain scientific knowledge of lands beyond the Canary Islands and Cap Bojador; (2) to determine the extent of Muslim domination in Africa; (3) to trade with any Christian people living beyond Cape Bojador; (4) to enlist the aid of other Christian monarchs in fighting the Muslims; and (5) to spread Christianity. To this list, some have added a sixth, that Henry wished to fulfil the destiny of his natal horoscope. Apparently it foretold that the prince "would be engaged in important and propitious conquests in lands which were hidden from other men."

In a study of *Portugal and the Quest for the Indies,* Christopher Bell writes:

> It is part of the legend of Henry the Navigator that he came to Sagres soon after the fall of Ceuta and spent there most of the rest of his life … that from Sagres he organized the voyages of discovery … and that he founded there a School of Navigation at which he gathered around his cartographers, astronomers, mathematicians, shipwrights and pilots from all over Europe.

While no substantial evidence exists concerning a school in Sagres, Henry did seek the advice of experts: "He possessed the curiosity of a man of science and sought opportunities to satisfy it." Further, he has traditionally been attributed with the establishment of a chair in mathematics at the University of Lisbon. Again, there is little evidence to support this, unlike his subsidy of a university chair in theology.

Henry sponsored an expedition in 1418–20 which effected the discovery of Porto Santo (his first success and Portugal's first "colony") and the rediscovery of the Madeira Islands. Colonization of the latter began in earnest by 1425. Activities such as fishing, dyeing, and sugar-making were particularly encouraged in the new colony. And, from 1418, ships annually left Sagres in search of the Guinea coast. Such endeavors characterized Portugal's "systematic exploration" of the Atlantic islands near the Iberian peninsula and western Africa. With the return of each expedition, Henry had maps brought up to date by incorporating all the new information. Despite great costs, failure, and hostile criticism, Henry persevered: by 1427, the Portuguese had opened trade relations for gold and slaves with Ethiopia. But apart from an attempt to seize Grand Canary Island for the establishment of a military fort, Henry's sailors and navigators made no appreciable progress in finding a navigable sea route to Guinea for nearly 15 years.

In 1434–35, Gil Eanes sailed along the African coast, past Cape Bojador, as far as the mouth of the Rio do Ouro. But the trips by Eanes mark the extent of Henry's sponsorship in navigation during this decade. In the face of criticism from nobles, merchants, and influential men both at court and in the army, his movement was at a nadir and, indeed, in danger of collapsing. Other matters commanded his attention. In September 1433, his father died. Upon accession to the Portuguese throne, his brother Edward I granted to Henry charters for Madeira and Porto Santo, as well as the Grand Mastership of the chivalric Order of Christ. Domestic troubles dominated Edward's brief reign. When Edward died in 1438, Henry's five-year-old nephew became king of Portugal, as Afonso V, and Henry helped to govern the country on his behalf during the early years of the Regency.

Once relieved of the duties of royal government when a Regency Council was established, Henry began to plan (1437) a campaign against Tangier—assisted by his brother Ferdinand who had refused an appointment to the rank of cardinal in the Church of Rome. The expedition was a disaster, the besiegers soon became the besieged, and Ferdinand was imprisoned and died in captivity after five years of suffering. Humiliated by the loss, Henry retired to Sagres in 1443. From there he sent out more expeditions, captains and ships under the Regency's influence to "encourage exploration and legitimate trade."

Still the problem of few real advances in exploration afflicted Henry's efforts, among which commerce was always a secondary concern. Not content with increasing knowledge about the African coast (a further 450 leagues beyond Cape Bojador had been navigated and carefully mapped), Henry also encouraged his seamen to explore the continent through the river systems. To this end, construction of a provisioning base on Arguin Island was undertaken in 1448. His honest and open nature made it easier for a scheming revenue officer to exploit Henry's patronage, and an expedition concerned only with profit was accidentally financed.

Exploration and colonization of the Azores continued apace with "the growing fame of the Prince's explorations." International recognition came, for example, from Edward IV of England, who made Henry a member of the Order of the Garter. This was considered "an unusual honour for the third son of a foreign royal house." But the tenor of Henry's activities gradually changed and trading and commercial interests came to occupy a more central position in expeditions of the late

1440s and the 1450s, predominantly under the captainship of Alvise de Cadamosto. As a struggle for Portuguese retention of the Canary Islands ensued, Henry's personal finances assumed an increasingly desperate nature. Sponsoring exploratory and trading expeditions was costly and the brunt, if not the whole, was borne by the prince.

Pope Recognizes Lands as Portugese Possessions

Now well into his 50s, Henry spent more and more of his time at the royal court. Lands discovered under his sponsorship were granted papal recognition as Portuguese possessions in 1454. From this date, all others would require the permission of the king of Portugal to visit, or make use of, west African lands. Henry always hoped for the conversion of the Africans whom his seamen encountered. Thus, it seemed logical to him to forbid raiding for slaves since this produced limited trade and often failed to produce converts to Christianity.

Under Henry's authority, Cadamosto reported progress in the Madeiras colonization by 1456. Traveling to the Rio Casa Mansa, then on to the Rio Gambia-Cantor, Cadamosto explored the area (including the Rio Senegal and Cape Verde) and returned in 1458 to refit for another voyage. He had gone no further than those who had explored before him, but his contribution was detailed knowledge in anthropology, botany, and mapmaking.

The last significant voyage sponsored by Prince Henry began in 1458, led by Diego Gomez. Although this effort increased Portuguese knowledge of the Cape Verde Islands, the voyages through the 1450s by Cadamosto have been considered as the most notable. The contributions to geography by the Portuguese were an achievement of not only Prince Henry, but also of his successors in exploration.

There has been some discussion of Henry's reclusive behavior during his final years. Sometime between 1454 and his death, he left Sagres to knight his brother Pedro's eldest son as a Constable of the Realm. And Henry's crusading zeal was inflamed by the Turkish capture of Constantinople in 1453. In keeping with his beliefs, Henry's last act of public service was to join his nephew, Afonso V, in campaign against Alcacer (situated between Ceuta and Tangier). Now 64, Prince Henry's involvement and enthusiasm were remarkable, and reminiscent of a much younger man's conduct. Though Henry received the surrender of the opponents' leaders, the conflict was an anticlimax and underscored the decline in European crusading spirit. Following the campaign, Henry returned to Portugal and resumed his sponsorship of exploratory voyages. Little is known of these last expeditions (the Portuguese had always perceived that success was dependent on secrecy).

Retiring to Sagres in 1460, Henry spent a few months putting his personal affairs in order. He granted the islands of Terceira and Graciosa to his nephew and heir-designate Fernando in August, and made his spiritual bequests to the Order of Christ concerning the Madeira Islands. In October, Henry made his will. "In full possession of his faculties almost to the end," he died peacefully in Sagres, Portugal, on November 13, 1460 (leaving a personal debt of 35,000 dobras, or about £130,000), and was buried in the same chapel as his parents. The influence of this "obscure Prince of the fifteenth century" was noted by C. Raymond Beazley in the late 19th century:

> It is not in the actual things done by the Prince's efforts that we can measure his importance in history. It is because his work was infinitely suggestive, because he laid a right foundation for the onward movement of Europe and Christendom, because he was the leader of a true Renaissance and Reformation, that he is so much more than a figure in the story of Portugal.

SOURCES:

Beazley, C. Raymond. *Prince Henry the Navigator: The Hero of Portugal and of Modern Discovery.* Burt Franklin, 1895 (reprinted 1968).

Bell, Christopher. *Portugal and the Quest for the Indies.* Barnes & Noble, 1974.

Prestage, Edgar. *The Portuguese Pioneers.* A & C Black, 1933 (reprinted 1966).

FURTHER READING:

Boorstin, Daniel J. *The Discoverers: A History of Man's Search to Know His World and Himself.* Random House, 1983.

Russell, Peter Edward. *Prince Henry the Navigator: The Rise and Fall of a Cultural Hero.* Clarendon Press, 1984.

Henry IV

(1553–1610)

Calvinist prince and military leader, who became the first Bourbon king of France, ended the devastating Wars of Religion, and promulgated the Edict of Nantes, recognizing freedom of conscience for Huguenots.

"Those who unswervingly follow their conscience are of my religion, as I am of all those who are brave and virtuous."

HENRY IV

The future King Henry IV of France was born on December 13, 1553, at a time of religious upheaval and endemic civil war. In 16th-century France, a relatively powerful minority embraced **John Calvin**'s version of Protestantism. These French Calvinists, or Huguenots, had political and military interests that threatened the crown and the rest of the predominantly Catholic society. Henry was christened a Catholic like his father Antoine of Bourbon, who was a respected soldier and head of the second most powerful noble family in France. Henry's intelligent and capable mother Jeanne d'Albret, who was to exert a tremendous influence on his life, was also of exalted background, being the heiress to the small Kingdom of Navarre which straddled the Pyrenean border with Spain. In 1560, however, she formally adopted Calvinism and made a public profession of her new faith.

Two years later, Antoine banished Jeanne from the French court in Paris, keeping Henry at his side. Up until the death of his father later that year in the first of the French religious wars, the prince received a Catholic education. Then he became the ward of **Catherine de Medici,** the

Name variations: Henri IV; Henri de Bourbon-Navarre, Vert Gallant, Henry the Great, Good King Henry. Born at Pau in Béarn on December 13, 1553; died on May 14, 1610; son of Antoine of Bourbon and Jeanne d'Albret; married: Marguerite of Valois, 1572; married: Marie de Medici, 1600. Descendants: Bourbon kings of France. Predecessor: Henry III of Valois. Successor: Louis XIII of Bourbon.

Contributed by Alan M. James, Ph.D., University of Manchester, Manchester, England

rebellion among the Catholic subjects in her lands, and Henry displayed the personal qualities that would later serve him so well: charm, flattery, clemency, and an ability to inspire personal loyalty. With the outbreak of another civil war in France later that year, Henry and his mother moved to the Huguenot stronghold of La Rochelle, on the western seaboard, where he developed his military skills. The following year, though still a boy, he soon found himself the titular head of the Huguenot forces upon the assassination of his uncle.

In June 1570, Henry commanded his first battle and led a cavalry charge that helped bring about a favorable peace for the Huguenots. As queen regent for the new king Charles IX, Catherine de Medici hoped to improve the volatile relations with the Huguenots by offering her daughter Marguerite of Valois in marriage to Henry; thus, in December 1571, Jeanne left for Paris to negotiate the arrangements. His mother's death the following June, after concluding the marriage treaty, was a blow to Henry, who nevertheless became the Calvinist king Henry of Navarre. After a brief period of mourning, he was married on August 17, 1572, to the royal French Catholic princess in Paris.

Henry Converts, Then Renounces Catholicism

The festivities were marked by a general uneasiness, until an assassination attempt against a Calvinist leader sparked the infamous St. Bartholomew's Day Massacre of the Huguenots in Paris. Amid the slaughter of his fellow Calvinists, Henry of Navarre was compelled to convert to Catholicism for his own safety. Thereafter, he was held at court, masquerading as a loyal Catholic subject of the king, while harboring deep resentment. Early in 1576, on the pretext of a hunting trip, Henry made his escape, which put him in a dangerous political position. Over the last few years, he had disappointed the Huguenots by his actions at court, while his escape threatened to ruin his relations with the Catholic crown. Therefore in June, he renounced the Catholic faith and returned publicly to the profession of Calvinism in order to reclaim his former role as leader of the Huguenots.

From 1576–84, Henry of Navarre was preoccupied with resisting Catherine's attempts to reconcile him with Marguerite and the crown, with consolidating the Huguenot position through recurring civil wars, and with building his own position in the party. He needed strong support, for according to the laws of dynastic inheritance in France, the death of King Henry III's brother, the duke of Anjou, in 1584, left Henry of Navarre the next in line to the French crown. The perceived

queen mother, who for political reasons allowed Henry's return to the Calvinist faith. Thus, almost from the beginning of his life, the prince, who was always conscious of the important political position into which he had been born, was involved as a pawn in the growing religious and civil controversies in France.

Although his childhood stay at the French court was not especially happy, it was an important experience, for he met many of the people who later would shape his political career. These included the future king Henry III, his future adversary Henry Duke of Guise, and his future first wife Marguerite of Valois. In 1566, concerned for her son's education, Jeanne rejoined the court. Shortly thereafter, they escaped to her lands in the south of France. Already at four years of age, Henry had impressed the French king **Henry II** with his active mind and poise; now at 13, he showed great promise, considerable maturity, intelligence, and diplomatic ability. Indeed, the famous soothsayer Nostradamus predicted Henry's accession to the French throne. But such developments were still far off.

Under his mother's tutelage from 1566–72, Henry received a strict Calvinist education and learned much about effective leadership. In 1568, she even entrusted him with the task of subduing a

danger of the Calvinist Henry inheriting the traditionally Catholic French throne sparked one of the greatest political and military crises in French history.

The Wars of Religion resumed the next year with three principal factions in conflict: Henry of Navarre; Henry Duke of Guise, who led the militant Catholic "Holy League" with Spanish backing; and King Henry III, who initially had favored Henry's claim to the throne though insisting on his conversion to Catholicism. Later, Henry III allied himself with Guise as a result of League pressure and Henry of Navarre's refusal to abjure. Appropriately, this conflict is known as the "War of the Three Henrys."

The initial campaigns were inconclusive, but in 1587 at Coutras, just northeast of Bordeaux, Henry of Navarre soundly defeated a royal army in the first major Calvinist victory of the long civil wars. This was offset, however, with an impressive victory by the duke of Guise a month later. Inflated by his triumph, Guise went to Paris against Henry III's expressed command. When it seemed that he would be arrested, the Paris mobs rose in his support and forced the king to flee. After this unfortunate Day of the Barricades (May 12, 1588), the resentful King Henry III was politically isolated and forced grudgingly into a reconciliation. But, in order to reassert his authority late that December, he had Guise assassinated.

The murder only fueled popular resentment of the king (especially in Paris) and, under its new leader the duke of Mayenne, League strength was unaffected. With the aim of winning back Paris, therefore, Henry III joined a successful alliance with Henry of Navarre. But on August 1, 1589, the fanatical monk, Jacques Clément, mortally stabbed the king. Before dying early the next morning, Henry III recognized Henry of Navarre as the legitimate heir to his throne.

Now king of France, though not formally crowned, Henry IV still was faced with opposition from the League based upon his Calvinist religion. He promised to protect the Catholic Church and announced his willingness to receive Catholic instruction by "a good and free council," which many Catholics took as a promise to convert. But as matters of faith were important to him and since he did not wish to appear too opportunistic or insincere to his Calvinist and moderate Catholic supporters, he continually postponed the council. In the meantime, he lifted the siege of Paris and withdrew to Normandy to protect his lines of communication with Protestant England. In September, at Arques outside Dieppe, with inferior forces,

he successfully defeated Mayenne's League army in the first victory of his new reign.

The next year brought mixed results, however. On March 14, 1590, the two sides again met in the open in a major battle at Ivry, 30 miles southeast of Paris. Once more, this victory belonged to the new king. To profit from his triumph, he planned to march against Paris but, for a variety of logistical and tactical reasons, he was unable to begin the siege until two months later. Thus, by the time he arrived on May 12, the capital had had time to prepare, and a long siege ensued. Although the city was on the verge of collapse by August, it was relieved by the timely arrival of Spanish troops which forced Henry to withdraw.

Henry's fortunes did not substantially improve from 1591–93. Although he generally won support in the countryside, it was tactically insignificant. Under increasing pressure from his Catholic supporters, who grew tired of his delays, and by a meeting of the League-dominated Estates-General to discuss the election of a candidate for a new Catholic king of France, Henry made the "perilous leap." On July 25, 1593, his formal conversion to Catholicism was celebrated amid great pomp at St. Denis, near Paris.

Since the sincerity of his conversion was doubted by many, the cynical comment "Paris is well worth a mass" has been attributed to Henry to suggest that his conversion was the height of political opportunism. While this is not entirely true, his conversion did have the effect of removing the last shred of legitimacy his opposition may have had. It did not end the war, however. After formally being crowned king of France on February 27, 1594, at Chartres, Henry IV marched on Paris. Encountering little resistance, he entered the city on March 22 amid supportive cheers.

King Issues Edict of Nantes

Yet the Spanish presence in France continued to support resistance to Henry IV; thus, in January 1595, he declared war on the meddlesome foreign power. After stirring himself from his favorite indulgences: romance, hunting, tennis, and gambling (with a reputation for cheating), Henry displayed great courage and leadership by beating back Spanish forces from Amiens which is dangerously close to Paris. Finally, he led forces into Brittany and easily beat the remaining Spanish-backed resistance. Equally significant, on this trip he also promulgated the famous Edict of Nantes.

For some time, the call from his former coreligionists for protection had been a problem.

Motivated by the desire to come to some sort of domestic religious settlement in order to further reestablish royal authority, the Edict of Nantes granted liberty of conscience and certain civil liberties, but there were also many restrictions. This formal recognition of limited legal status pleased almost nobody. But it came to be accepted generally, and it established a livable modus vivendi for a number of years while denying the Huguenots any pretension to independence from the Crown.

For the remainder of his reign, despite a number of assassination attempts, occasional bouts of illness, and gout, Henry attended to the future of the realm. He had the frontiers fortified and in 1600, took a town in Savoy which he claimed was rightfully French. He also married an Italian princess, Marie de Medici (his marriage to Marguerite having been annulled), in the hopes of begetting an heir so that France would not fall back into civil war. On September 27, 1601, Marie gave birth to a son, the future king Louis XIII. With his young prince, Henry was an attentive (though stern) father. Indeed, sometimes foreign diplomats had to interview him while he carried his son piggyback.

While it is true that Henry could use the powerful symbolism of ostentatious ceremony and pomp to his advantage, he was not fastidious by any means in his daily routine. In fact, he stank personally, and as he loved the food of his native south, his breath reeked of garlic. However, it was undoubtedly Marie's objection to his continued indulgence in mistresses that led to their estrangement, for including his earlier relationship with Gabrielle d'Estrées, for whom he had a genuine fondness, Henry had 54 official mistresses.

With the advice of his competent advisor the duke of Sully, France enjoyed a period of relative stability and commercial growth under Henry IV, including initial efforts to establish colonies in Canada. Also, Henry undertook many great projects such as a network of canals and architectural embellishments to enhance Paris. But the reign was not without its political problems. In 1602, for example, an important military officer, Marshal Biron, was convicted of treason and conspiracy with Spain. Henry had him decapitated at the Bastille, but such affairs revealed lingering concerns: the mistrust of the French nobility and the threat of the House of Habsburg which ruled Spain (and all its possessions) as well as much of Western continental Europe.

Later in his life, with sufficient reserves in the treasury, Henry was able to turn his attention to the Habsburg threat. In Germany, the Protestant princes had united against the Catholic princes and the Habsburg emperor, and in 1609 a dispute over the inheritance of an important duchy threatened the balance of power in Europe generally. Henry began preparations for war against the Habsburgs, among which was the routine plan to meet Sully and inspect the Paris arsenal. But on May 14, when his carriage wound its way through the streets of Paris (ceremoniously prepared for the entry of Marie de Medici, only recently crowned queen consort), it came across congested traffic. As his coachmen dealt with the situation, a lone assassin approached, lunged at the king through a window, and stabbed him three times. With the carriage rushing back to the palace dripping with blood, the end came for Henry IV.

The policy of waging war against the major Catholic powers had not been universally accepted in France. And, several theories immediately arose about great conspiracies and the motives of the killer, François Ravaillac, who suffered a grisly public execution. Though nothing of note came from his military preparations, Henry IV's memory has achieved legendary status, and today he is something of a national hero in France.

He was a successful leader and military strategist. Moreover, he was able to consolidate his position and that of the French monarchy in the face of tremendous opposition. From civil war, he brought peace; from chaos, he restored order. He also granted a measure of tolerance to his Calvinist subjects which lasted until the revocation of the Edict of Nantes in 1685 by his grandson, **Louis XIV.** From his entry into Paris as the king of France, the realm enjoyed relative prosperity and order. Soon France would again suffer from disorder and upheaval, evoking a period of mourning for the days of "Henry the Great."

SOURCES:

Buisseret, David. *Henry IV*. Allen & Unwin, 1984.

Elliot, J. H. *Europe Divided 1559–1598*. Fontana Press, 1968.

Rothrock, George A. *The Huguenots: A Biography of a Minority*. Nelson-Hall, 1979.

FURTHER READING:

Greengrass, Mark. *France in the Age of Henri IV: The Struggle for Stability*. Longmans, 1984.

Love, Ronald S. "Winning the Catholics: Henri IV and the Religious Dilemma in August 1589," in *Canadian Journal of History*. Vol. 24. December 1989, pp. 361–379.

Mahoney, Irene. *Royal Cousin: The Life of Henri IV of France*. Doubleday, 1970.

Henry V

(1387–1422)

King of England, victor of the Battle of Agincourt, who was the most successful English commander of the Hundred Years' War against France.

"The incredible victory of Agincourt, the conquest of Normandy, the diplomatic achievements of the Treaty of Troyes, created a deceptive atmosphere of invincibility around Henry...."

MARGARET WADE LABARGE

In the 14th and 15th centuries, the Hundred Years' War marked the attempt by England's kings to regain control of the French lands their ancestors had held but which King John had lost in the early 13th century. Endless inconclusive campaigning and sieges were punctuated by occasional battlefield victories and treaties. England's greatest victory in the war's early years came at Crecy in 1346, but the most famous took place at Agincourt in 1415, when a badly outnumbered English army under King Henry V routed a far larger body of French knights on St. Crispin's day. Agincourt became a landmark in the development of English patriotism and the scene for one of Shakespeare's great set pieces.

Henry, who at birth seemed remote from the throne, would become king because his father Henry Bolingbroke seized the throne from King Richard II in a coup in 1399. Profligate, neurotic, and suspicious, Richard had resented Bolingbroke's part in the Lords Appellant affair in which Richard's favorites had been removed from court by the senior barons. Claiming that Bolingbroke was guilty of treason, Richard II had him banished in 1397 and then, in his absence, seized all of Bol-

Name variations: (Shakespeare) Prince Hal. Born at Monmouth in 1387; died at Vincennes in 1422; son of Henry Bolingbroke (later King Henry IV) and Mary de Bohun; married: Catherine of Valois (daughter of King Charles VI of France), 1420; children: one son, Henry VI. Predecessor: his father, Henry IV; Successor: his son, Henry VI.

Contributed by Patrick Allitt, Assistant Professor of History, Emory University, Atlanta, Georgia

ingbroke's estates. The young Henry, at the age of 11, accompanied Richard II on campaign to Ireland in 1398 and won a knighthood. Henry was virtually a hostage but appears to have befriended Richard during this campaign.

Bolingbroke meanwhile returned to England with French help while Richard was in Ireland, rapidly gained enough followers to overthrow the unpopular Richard, declared himself King Henry IV by promoting a spurious genealogy, and had the old king murdered in captivity the next year. Young Henry was now Prince of Wales and heir apparent to the throne. Like most medieval princes he was absorbed in hunting and falconry, but unlike most he also read widely and kept up an extensive correspondence throughout his life. His father soon set him to work on the Welsh borderlands and later in Wales itself, combatting the rebellious chieftain Owen Glendower. At first, Prince Henry was supervised by Harry Percy, nicknamed Hotspur, who introduced him to the problems of fighting for and governing a turbulent province. In 1401, the 14-year-old Henry, with the help of Hotspur, besieged Conway Castle to recover it from one of Glendower's adherents, William Tudor, who had seized it while the garrison said its Good Friday prayers. To help his son, the king raided Wales several years in succession with punitive expeditions, but Glendower avoided battles he could not win and never had to wait long before an impecunious Henry IV was forced to withdraw.

One of the men captured by the Welsh was Edmund Mortimer, earl of March, who had been Richard II's heir, and had a stronger claim to the throne than Henry IV himself. Although Mortimer had been captured in the king's service, Henry ordered that he should not be ransomed from the Welsh but left to languish. The decision infuriated the Percy family, Mortimer's cousins. The Percies were also annoyed that they had been denied the chance to get lucrative ransoms from Scottish dukes they had captured in a border incident. These provocations led to an alliance between the Percies, Owen Glendower, and Mortimer, who plotted to overthrow Henry IV and share the kingdom between them.

Appointed Royal Deputy in 1403 to oppose this alliance, Prince Henry pleased his father by showing close attention to detail in his military planning and a dogged adherence to the tasks at hand. The rebellion failed when Henry, supported by his father after a long forced march, won a decisive victory at Shrewsbury. Hotspur was killed in the battle and the other ringleaders were rounded up and executed, averting a severe threat to the Lancastrian regime. Prince Henry completed his military and political training by bombarding and starving Owen Glendower's chief fortress at Aberystwyth into submission. Although Glendower continued to raise raiding forces against England until about 1413, he was no longer a serious threat to the Lancastrians but simply an irritant.

In his early 20s, Prince Henry became a dominant figure on the Royal Council while his father sank into a premature old age, afflicted by horrible boils all over his body and fits of madness. Henry IV died at the age of 46 in 1413, convinced that God was punishing him for executing Archbishop Scrope of York during the Percy rising of 1405. Henry V was crowned during a blizzard on April 9, 1413, but the presence of the earl of March led him, like his father, to feel vulnerable in his claim. Rumors that Richard II was still alive in Scotland fed his insecurity. The chroniclers add that he dismissed all his old friends, forswore amorous adventures, and took on the unbending piety which was to be his hallmark from then on. He put down a rebellion of Lollards, Christian reformers and followers of the Oxford scholar **John Wycliffe** in 1414, led by one of his old Welsh campaigners, Sir John Oldcastle. Henry retaliated by having the heretics roasted alive while hanging in chains over fires.

As king, Henry V believed that the surest way for his dynasty to establish its legitimacy in the English people's eyes was to reclaim the French lands long claimed by the English throne. Accordingly, after acting to secure the internal order of England (which had become chaotic in the last years of his father's reign), he set sail for France with a large army in 1415, scotching another conspiracy against his throne at the moment of embarkation. His army first besieged the port town of Harfleur and took it on September 22 after a shattering artillery barrage. But the besiegers paid a heavy price, nearly a third of them dying or being invalided by dysentery.

Marching to Calais and Battling at Agincourt

Sooner or later dysentery beset every campaigning army in the Middle Ages, but this was one of the worst outbreaks, possibly due to contaminated food supplies. Henry realized he must retreat and cross back to England rather than follow his original plan of pressing on to Paris. But to show the French he was not cowed by rumors of their gathering army, he decided to march to the British outpost at Calais rather than take ship at Harfleur. Ordering his men to take eight days' food supply for the march to Calais, he soon found he had underestimated the difficulties before him. Heavy rains soaked everything and everybody, while swelling rivers became unfordable. The disease-ridden army slogged on, getting steadily hungrier and plundering farms along the way until, to Henry's dismay, he learned that a mighty French army blocked his path at the village of Agincourt. With no choice but to fight, he feared the worst, as did his sick, tired, and hungry men.

As day dawned, the two armies faced one another for several hours before either moved. Then Henry advanced the longbow archers who were to prove his master weapon. The French had few bowmen and so were vulnerable to the English volleys which showered down upon them; every English archer carried a quiver of 50. The muddy ground also favored Henry. The dense pack of French knights was so burdened with armor and equipment that they sank into the quagmire and could hardly move. Those who fell from their horses could not remount, while those who advanced on foot staggered and fell, sometimes piling up on top of one another and dying from suffocation or drowning rather than from English blows.

Soon the English, to their own amazement, found themselves taking droves of prisoners, and anticipated huge ransoms for the 3,000 captives they rounded up. But when the remaining French knights made a final desperate charge, Henry feared that their captive comrades might break free and overwhelm the outnumbered English guard. Accordingly, he ordered death to the prisoners. The English soldiers, dismayed more by the loss of ransoms than by the order's cold-bloodedness,

began to hack away at the helpless captives and killed hundreds of them. When the attack danger passed, Henry told his men to cease the massacre. Over 1,000 valuable hostages remained, to be taken back to England and ransomed later. After giving thanks to God for his victory, Henry's army marched from Agincourt to Calais and then sailed back across the Channel, the king receiving a hero's welcome in England. The ransoming of hostages began, but the price placed on some was so high that they could not be redeemed for years—the duke of Orleans, Henry's own prisoner, did not get back to France until 1440, 25 years after his capture at Agincourt.

Although Henry's victory was popular, the financial cost was high, and England was reluctant to pay for Henry's planned continuation of the war. Nevertheless, he scraped together enough money, men, and equipment to launch a larger campaign in 1417. This time, he planned not merely to cut a swath through northern France but to systematically conquer Normandy and hold it as part of his realm. His navy, consisting of the largest ships ever built until that date in England, swept the Channel clear of French foes; then Henry's invasion fleet, probably more than 1,000 ships strong, sailed to western Normandy. First they attacked the city of Caen. Henry had invested heavily in the most modern siege equipment, including trebuchets (machine for hurling missiles) and cannons which could fire heavy missiles over long distances. The walls of Caen were built to withstand the older cannonballs but not these new weapons, and soon they were breached. The English swarmed in, secured the city, and then marched to the key city of Rouen, on the River Seine.

Henry Starves Rouen into Submission

The French were unable to put an effective army in the field to oppose Henry V, partly because of the decimation they had suffered at Agincourt, partly because there was a civil war raging within the French nobility, and partly because of the threat of invasion further east by the duke of Burgundy. Campaigning armies customarily stopped as the autumn weather cooled into winter, but Henry was determined to press his advantage. Although he found the walls of Rouen thick enough to resist his siege machines, he was able to isolate the city, cut off its water and food supplies, and begin starving it into submission. The garrison and refugees inside the walls waited in vain for relief. The commander sent 12,000 old men and women out, to relieve pressure on supplies, only to find that Henry would not let them pass but herded them into a ditch by the city walls. Several hundred starved to death, but the obdurate Henry insisted that the defenders, who had refused to surrender at his first demand, must bear responsibility. As 1418 began and the plight of Rouen worsened, it finally capitulated. Henry's soldiers ran amok, looting and raping in their habitual lawless way. The king, always ostentatiously pious, went to celebrate mass at the cathedral, while his sense of being God's chosen instrument intensified. He told an itinerant friar who had the nerve to criticize him: "I am the scourge of God, sent to punish the people of God for their sins." He treated the people of Rouen as his own subjects who had been in rebellion against him rather than as foreign nationals, but many of the survivors fled rather than submit to his terrible lordship. In the years that followed, the countryside was full of dispossessed Norman landowners who had turned to lives of banditry.

Henry knew that his conquest could only last if he placed trusted Englishmen in key Norman positions. He did so, rewarding faithful soldiers, often minor gentry, with large French estates and rapid promotion up the social ladder. But these new fiefs were as much burden as benefit to many of the recipients, because they carried the obligation of tax payment and military service on demand. They also faced the hatred of the local population, many of whom followed their former lords' example and fled south or east away from the dreaded English until the whole area became depopulated. Robert Blondel, a French refugee, wrote:

> Before the war we were renowned, rich and powerful. Today, broken and crushed by want, we lead the life of beggars. Many among us who are noblemen are forced to take up the most menial employment; some work at the tailor's trade, others serve in inns, while English cowherds and yokels from the scum strut through our country, grown rich on our inheritances and sporting stolen titles of duke, count, baron, or knight.

After a few years, several of the new English landowners tried to return home from Normandy, but Henry imposed drastic penalties (sometimes death) on those who tried to leave, since without them the entire reconquest scheme would be doomed. Despite his efforts at orderly administration of the conquest, he simply never had the money to pay his troops, and they were all the more ready to live off the countryside and prey on the peasants, intensifying the hatred the English aroused throughout northern France.

In the short term, his victories continued. He captured Pontoise, just 12 miles from Paris, in 1419, and now seemed set to conquer the whole of France. Unable to do so by force of arms alone, he expected that he could negotiate his way into a kingdom, and told French diplomats that he must be granted full sovereignty over Normandy and Aquitaine, along with the hand in marriage of the French king Charles VI's daughter, and the promise of the French crown after Charles's death. His adversaries continued to be divided. At the moment when an alliance between them was essential, the Armagnac faction tricked and murdered Duke John "the Fearless" of Burgundy (he was actually a neurotic coward) and drove the Burgundians into alliance with Henry himself. With Burgundian aid, Henry's conquests advanced all the more quickly. At the Treaty of Troyes, negotiated in 1420 with Charles VI, who was mad except for occasional lucid intervals, Henry got what he was looking for: the succession, Normandy, Aquitaine, and Princess Catherine. After another season of campaigning, marked by his usual ruthlessness, Henry overran the fortress of Melun and at last captured Paris in 1420. It was far larger and richer than any city in England, and completed the loot-bonanza of his loyal soldiers. Henry lived stylishly at the Louvre in an otherwise war-shattered city.

Returning to England in triumph, Henry found his people unwilling to pay for more campaigns; Parliament told him that as heir of France he must raise funds for French wars from his cross-channel subjects. He toured the country frantically trying to raise money, especially when he learned that several of his best generals, including his brother and heir, the duke of Clarence, had died in battle at Bauge. As soon as possible, Henry returned to France and began pursuing the dauphin, later King **Charles VII,** through central France, again refusing to stop for winter and undeterred by heavy casualties, hunger, and epidemics. At the siege of Meaux in early 1422, he followed his usual policy of bombardment day and night with his powerful siege guns and brought the city to surrender after seven months, despite its excellent defenses. While there, he learned that his son and heir Prince Henry had been born, and when the siege was over he hurried to Paris to meet Queen Catherine. But soon after, he fell sick, probably with the dysentery which had afflicted hundreds of his men, and on another expedition against the dauphin he had to be carried on a litter rather than riding.

On August 20, 1422, Henry V died at Vincennes, near Paris, just six weeks before King Charles VI, whom he was to have succeeded, died. Henry's entrails were removed and buried, then his body was dismembered and boiled down in the palace kitchens before being escorted in state back to England in a procession of wagons. His son, not yet a year old, became king Henry VI. Henry's brother, the duke of Bedford, carried on the unending French campaign until his own death in 1435 but had to face a resurgent France under the inspirational leadership of **Joan of Arc.** By 1450, all of Henry V's conquests had been lost, and only the port of Calais would remain an English possession until Queen **Mary I** lost even that a century later.

SOURCES:

Allmand, C. T. *Lancastrian Normandy.* Oxford: Oxford University Press, 1983.

Fowler, K. E., ed. T*he Hundred Years' War.* London: Macmillan, 1971.

Labarge, Margaret Wade. *Henry V: The Cautious Conqueror.* London: Secker and Warburg, 1975.

Seward, Desmond. *Henry V As Warlord.* London: Sidgwick and Jackson, 1987.

Shakespeare, William. *Henry V.*

Henry VII

(1457–1509)

First and most skillful Tudor king of England who, having only a distant claim to the throne, became champion of the Lancastrian cause in the Wars of the Roses, defeated and killed Richard III at the Battle of Bosworth Field, and established a powerful, secure dynasty, defeating all challengers.

Born Henry Tudor in 1457; died in 1509; son of Edmund Tudor, Earl of Richmond (died before Henry's birth) and Margaret Beaufort (a descendant of John of Gaunt); married: Elizabeth of York, 1486; children: (four daughters) Mary, Margaret, Elizabeth and Catherine; (three sons) Arthur, Henry and Edmund. Predecessor: Richard III. Successor: Henry VIII (his second son).

First of the Tudors, last king of England to live and die a Catholic, Henry VII brought to a close the Wars of the Roses which had devastated England through the mid-15th century. His decisive victory at the Battle of Bosworth Field in 1485 killed not only King **Richard III** but also many of Richard's chief supporters, and left Henry free to reward his own followers with the titles, offices, and positions they had held. Shrewd, unsentimental, tight-fisted, and ruthless, Henry VII restored peace and prosperity to England by blending sensible economic and financial policies with intimidation of all rivals. He laid the groundwork of Tudor greatness and ended the chronic domestic warfare which had plagued his weaker predecessors. But the knowledge that his tiny army had won the kingdom left him perpetually aware that another small and dedicated band might oust him in turn, prompting a lifetime of uneasiness.

Henry's claim to the throne was weak. His father's mother was the widow of **Henry V** and his mother (who gave birth to him when she was only 13) was a descendant of **Edward III** and John of Gaunt. Nevertheless, he became the chief hope of the Lancastrians in the Wars of the Roses after the

"The verdict of the God of battles had confirmed such hereditary right as existed.... Thereafter there was nothing to impede Henry from proceeding to coronation."

S. B. CHRIMES

Contributed by Patrick Allitt, Assistant Professor of History, Emory University, Atlanta, Georgia

deaths of Henry VI and his son Prince Edward in 1471. Spending two years as a prisoner of the Yorkists in a Welsh castle, young Henry was rescued by his uncle Jasper Tudor, earl of Pembroke, and raised for the next 14 years in the duchy of Brittany. Richard III, king of England after 1483, was so unpopular that even some Yorkists, the traditional enemies of the Lancastrian cause, offered Henry the throne, and one of them, the duke of Buckingham, raised rebellion in 1483 on Henry's behalf, but was unsuccessful. Henry's own expedition of 1485, supported by the old Lancastrians and other newly discontented Englishmen, began with a landing at Milford Haven in Wales and led to a confrontation with Richard III at Bosworth, in the English midland county of Leicestershire. Although outnumbered, the battle was decided in Henry's favor when the powerful Lord Stanley, whose army stood aloof during the opening rounds of the battle, intervened on Henry's side and assured Richard's destruction.

In an effort to reconcile the warring families of York and Lancaster once and for all, Henry married Elizabeth of York, the daughter of Edward IV, in 1486. The *Holinshed Chronicle* explained his reasons, and their effect:

> [P]eace was thought to descende out of heaven into England, considering that the lynes of Lancaster and Yorke were now brought into one knot, and cornered togither, of whose two bodies, one heire myghte succeede to rule and enjoye the whole monarchie and realme of England.

The marriage enjoyed the support of a papal bull, issued by Pope Innocent VIII who at the same time recognized Henry's place on the English throne and threatened to excommunicate anyone who challenged it. Elizabeth bore seven children, including what to a medieval monarch was all important, three sons. Only one of these sons, Henry, outlived her, however, and she herself died in 1503, aged 41.

Their first child, a son born in September 1486, was the embodiment of the two houses' union, and his birth the occasion of rejoicing. His name, Arthur, reflected Henry's identification with the Arthurian legends of which he had drunk deeply in Wales and Brittany. As Prince of Wales, Arthur was raised largely at Ludlow, on the Welsh border. In line with his father's diplomatic interests, he would be married to a Spanish princess, Catherine of Aragon, when he was 15 and she 16, in 1501. The following year, Arthur would unfortunately die of consumption, leaving his brother Henry (the future **Henry VIII**) as heir both to the

CHRONOLOGY

1457	Henry Tudor born
1485	Battle of Bosworth Field; Richard III died; Henry VII seized the throne
1487	Battle of Stoke; defeated Lambert Simnel
1492	French campaign and Treaty of Etaples
1496	Intercursus magnus: trade agreement with Netherlands
1497	Defeated and captured Perkin Warbeck
1499	Warbeck and the Earl of Warwick executed
1501	Prince Arthur married Catherine of Aragon
1502	Prince Arthur died
1503	Elizabeth of York died; Westminster chapel commissioned
1504	Henry's last Parliament
1509	Henry VII died

throne and to his widow. Henry VII's later dissatisfaction with his son's inability to produce a male heir was to become one of the precipitating causes of the English Reformation.

Henry Defeats Attempts To Overthrow Him

The throne of England had changed hands six times between 1461 and 1485, so Henry VII felt far from secure, despite his marriage, papal endorsement, and male heirs. The early years of his reign were punctuated by Yorkist efforts to regain the throne, most of them egged on by Edward IV's sister Margaret, wife of the duke of Burgundy. Twice he had to face young impersonators posing as claimants to the throne. The first of these, Lambert Simnel, the son of an organmaker from Oxford, was acclaimed King Edward VI in Ireland by a group of Richard III's former supporters and crowned in Dublin Cathedral. Posing as the earl of Warwick, he was coached in his role by an ambitious priest named William Seymour. The Yorkists and Simnel landed in Lancashire in 1487 and marched east to Stoke in Lincolnshire where their army of 8,000 (bigger than Henry's army at Bosworth but comprised largely of German and Irish mercenaries) was defeated by Henry in a bitter fight. Henry recognized that Simnel, aged only ten, was too young to grasp the magnitude of his rebellion or to suffer the full consequences, so he gave Simnel a job as spit-turner in the royal kitchens—a sign surely that Henry had a good sense of humor. From this lowly position, Simnel later rose to be a royal falconer and died an old man in his bed, Tudor loyalist to the end.

Henry spared the coup leaders, preferring to levy huge fines rather than execute them. Indeed, throughout his reign he favored heavy fines to deplete his rivals' resources and enhance his own, rather than the time-honored method of killing them. One of his craftiest maneuvers was to have Parliament declare that his reign had started on the day *before* the Battle of Bosworth Field. In this way, he could claim that anyone who fought on Richard's side had been in rebellion against the king and, as a traitor, must forfeit his estates or pay fines for their recovery.

In 1491, another impersonator, Perkin Warbeck, son of a Dutch boatman on the Scheldt River, posed as the young prince, Richard, duke of York (who had almost certainly died in 1483 at the hands of Richard III). The king of France entertained him as "King of England" and gave him servants with the Yorkist white rose livery. In 1494, Henry, who understood the value of good domestic espionage, uncovered Warbeck's English fellow-conspirators, among them his own Lord Chamberlain Sir William Stanley, the man who had turned the battle at Bosworth in his favor. Dismayed, Henry executed Stanley for treason, but Warbeck persisted in his claims to the throne and launched an expedition which landed in Ireland. There he besieged Waterford but Henry's highly talented regent, Sir Edward Poynings, arrived to rescue the inhabitants and the besiegers decamped. Later, Warbeck gained support from James IV, king of Scotland, who, believing his claim to be the duke of York, arranged for Warbeck's marriage to his cousin Lady Catherine Gordon, and made a large-scale border raid into the north of England to aid his cause.

Henry again took the threat very seriously and retaliated with an expedition large enough to intimidate the Scottish king. His commander, the earl of Surrey, met the Scots at Ayton Castle and made a seven-year nonaggression pact on favorable terms, one of which was that King James should marry Henry VII's daughter Margaret (which he did in 1503), another of which was to repudiate Warbeck. With this treaty, Henry's northern border was secured.

Out of luck in Scotland, Warbeck tried to raise a rebellion in the southwest of England but could not gather sufficient recruits. Finally, unable to escape to the Continent and learning of the Scottish settlement, he threw himself on the king's mercy. Since Warbeck was not English and not technically guilty of treason, Henry treated Warbeck leniently, as he had Simnel, and kept him at court. But Warbeck's repeated efforts to escape and arouse new conspiracies finally led Henry to lose patience and execute him in 1499. At the same time, Henry did away with the feeble-minded earl of Warwick, a Yorkist with a dangerously strong claim to the throne, who had been his prisoner for 14 years, in what most historians regard as little better than a judicial murder. By the turn of the new century, Henry VII's throne appeared secure and was subject to no further rebellions.

The Wars of the Roses had been the result, in part, of the barons' inflated powers. The king often had to compete against the barons rather than act as unquestioned ruler over them all. Occasionally a baron like "Warwick the Kingmaker" had become wealthier and stronger than his ostensible sovereigns. Henry VII was determined to curb the mighty baronies, and to limit the private armies by which many of them assured their independence. In 1487, he summoned Parliament and commissioned them to make private armies wearing their owner's liveries (clothing worn by retainers of a person of rank) illegal. The law was widely flouted: on one occasion, according to Francis Bacon's biography of Henry, the earl of Oxford entertained the king and then drew up his retainers in their livery to bid the king farewell. Henry thanked him for the guard of honor but added that he must fine the earl for violating the livery law. The Parliament of 1504 passed another Act Against Liveries which suggests that they were still commonplace and had once again to be prohibited by name. Moreover, offenders were to be tried in London rather than in their own localities, to prevent lords tyrannizing over, or bribing local jurors in favor of acquittal.

King Raises Money from Rents, Taxes, Trade

Economic historians date the beginnings of capitalism to the early modern period, and Henry VII could certainly stand as an exemplary businessman. He had instantly grasped the relationship between money and power and set about gathering money with an unrivaled single-mindedness, showing none of the profligacy of his European contemporaries or his own successor. After a childhood sharpened by penury, much of the time as a poor guest of the duke of Brittany, Henry appreciated the value of money and the misery and impotence which come from lacking it. He tightened the organization of rents from his own lands (whose yield rose from £4,000 to £30,000 during his reign), and encouraged trade as a way of raising the yield from customs duties. His able archbishop of Winchester, Richard Fox, negotiated the Intercursus Magnus, a trade treaty with the Netherlands in 1496, upon which the prosperity of the British wool trade revived after years of depression. Henry also imposed every possible feudal tax on his subjects, many of which had been in abeyance during the wars.

Eager to live by his own means, he called Parliament only rarely—seven Parliaments met during his reign of 24 years, for a total of only 66 days. Parliament was entitled to raise additional taxes, usually in the event of war, but Henry knew that it should be used infrequently lest repeated exactions provoke further rebellions. When Parliament voted him a large tax grant in 1497 to attack Scotland during the Warbeck affair, it provoked a rebellion in Cornwall (the county farthest from the Scottish border) whose people denied that they should have to contribute to war in such a remote district; 15,000 Cornishmen marched to London, claiming that they were on a mission to rescue the king from his wicked ministers. All the same they were met and defeated by the king's men under Lord Daubeney, at Blackheath in south London. One thousand of them died in the battle, the three ringleaders were put to death, and the rest pardoned on payment of heavy fines. Unlike the Parliaments which would challenge and ultimately overthrow the Crown 150 years later, most of Henry VII's Parliaments meekly did his bidding. The exception was the Parliament of 1504, the first to meet in eight years, which denied Henry's request for £90,000 and offered him only £40,000.

In 1492, like almost every English king since William the Conqueror, Henry attacked France, his new kingdom's venerable enemy, and called on Parliament to finance this campaign. But within three weeks of landing, the French king, Charles VIII, offered him a large sum of money to desist, which he accepted at the Treaty of Étaples. In this way, with minimal casualties, he profited from both ends of the deal, something his spendthrift son Henry VIII was never able to manage. The particularly noteworthy aspect of Henry VII's money-raising methods is that none of them was new. He simply worked systematically at every traditional financial device, kept scrupulous accounts (and paid close attention to them), avoided ruinous extravagances and protracted wars, and in this way died one of the richest men in Europe, certainly the richest in Britain.

Henry VII's archbishop of Canterbury, Cardinal John Morton, who had orchestrated Henry's campaign before Bosworth, was another skilled money raiser who specialized in collecting "benevolent" or "signet" loans from the rich. Morton's "Fork" was an early example of what author Joseph Heller called "Catch 22." According to Francis Bacon, who told the tale with relish, if Morton found an ostentatious man throwing money around on the good life, Morton would say that so wealthy a man surely had plenty to spare as a loan for the king. If he found a miserly man he would declare that much money must have been saved, and could now go as a loan to the king. In either event, the subject had to pay up. Morton, who was nearly 40 years older than Henry, had the absolute trust of the king, and was highly thought of by most contemporaries. He died in 1500, aged 80, still high in the king's favor.

Along with his dogged resistance to rivals and his systematic ways with money, Henry VII was, at least outwardly, a pious man. In these years of the High Renaissance, a succession of scandalous popes disgraced the Throne of Peter, lived riotously, put on their armor to fight for the Papal States, and sold indulgences so shamelessly that they set off **Martin Luther**'s momentous protests and engendered remonstrances from many good Catholics like Erasmus who never joined the Protestant cause. John Colet, dean of St. Paul's in London under Henry VII, reported cases in Britain where, with "abominable impiety" priests "fear not to rush from the bosom of some foul harlot into the temple of Christ." Henry, by contrast, lived a sober and industrious life, went to Mass three times each day, specified in his will an elaborate code of Masses to be said for the welfare of his soul, gave generous aims, and contributed to many Church building projects.

England Becomes Center of Scholarship

His mother, Lady **Margaret Beaufort,** was even more devout, wearing a hairshirt, attending services throughout the day, tending sick paupers, making frequent pilgrimages, and using her time and fortune to aid the Church. Much better educated than many women of her day, she became a patroness of Renaissance scholars and founded King's College, Cambridge, and St. John's College, Oxford. Under the patronage of Margaret and Henry, William Caxton, Britain's first commercial printer, translated and produced books to suit the royal taste, and England became one of the centers of Renaissance scholarship. Erasmus wrote enthusiastically about the thriving intellectual life of Britain when he visited in 1499, comparing it favorably to Italy. This was also the era in which Columbus's voyages to America set off a revolution in Europeans' knowledge of the world. Henry himself patronized John and Sebastian Cabot, Genoese explorers sailing from the English port of Bristol, in search first of the "island of Brasil," later of a northwest passage to China and the wealth of the Orient.

Henry understood that as king he must try to exhibit himself and emphasize the glory of his position and the radiance of his monarchy. He accordingly dressed in expensive clothes and entertained on a large scale, sometimes having 700 dinner guests, but he could not dispel the aura of austerity which surrounded him personally, especially after his wife's death and the failure of various schemes to remarry. "Frugal to excess in his own person," commented one observer "he does not change any of the ancient usages of England at his court, keeping a sumptuous table." The Italian historian Polydore Vergil, who wrote a history of his reign, describes the king, aged about 50 and already beginning to go blind, thus:

> He was gracious and kind and was as attentive to his visitors as he was easy of access.... But all these virtues were obscured latterly by avarice, from which he suffered. This avarice is surely a bad enough vice in a private individual, whom it forever torments; in a monarch indeed it may be considered the worst vice since it is harmful to everyone.

Henry VII died at the age of 52 in 1509, at Richmond Palace, after bringing his son Henry to his bedside and making him promise to marry Catherine of Aragon.

He was buried in the chapel of Westminster Abbey beyond the high altar which he had commissioned in 1503 after his wife's death. Among the relics at his tomb were a piece of the true cross and one of Saint George's legs, both in elaborate display cases. Despite his success in restoring political stability and building up the power and wealth of the monarchy, he had not been widely loved. Lacking a sense of the drama of his position, Henry did not know how to play the public role of national leader. Historian Paul Johnson makes a telling comparison with Henry's son:

> It is significant that Henry VII, a true ... professional, who was far abler and more industrious than his son, was never so secure on the throne, and could not risk putting his authority to the test, because he lacked regal glamour. Henry VIII was idle, irresponsible, ignorant, lacking in judgment and totally oblivious to any sense of duty to the community. But he knew how to beat the big drum of monarchy, and the nation trouped in his wake.

Nevertheless, in his sober, dogged way, Henry VII must rank as one of England's most capable and effective kings.

SOURCES:

Chrimes, S. B. *Henry VII.* University of California Press, 1972.
Elton, Geoffrey. *England Under the Tudors.* London, 1974.
Johnson, Paul. *A History of the English People.* Harper, 1985.
Ross, Charles. *Richard III.* University of California Press, 1981.
Roulstone, Michael. *The Royal House of Tutor.* Balfour, 1974.
Williams, Neville. *Henry VII.* Weidenfeld & Nicolson, 1973.

Henry VIII

(1491–1547)

English king and Renaissance prince, who solidified the Tudor dynasty, broke with the Catholic Church, and oversaw the centralization of government, but who was also plagued by the woes of succession and marital mismanagement.

"Henry's reign in many ways left a deeper mark on the mind, heart and face of England than did any event in English history between the coming of the Normans and the coming of the factory."

J. J. SCARISBRICK

Who does not know at least something about Henry VIII? Here was a king cloaked in as many contradictions and contrasts as he had wives. He was a product of man and a force of nature. He was distinguished as much by what he succeeded in doing as by what he failed to do. He was a reincarnated Prince Hal, characterized by an unparalleled zest for life who metamorphosed into a sour, diseased, and often evil combination of royal Falstaff and grotesque Goliath.

As an infant and child, Henry is little known to us because he was a second son who was inevitably overshadowed by his elder brother Arthur. Ironically, his first public act seems to have come in 1496, at age five, when he witnessed a royal grant by charter to the abbot and convent at legendary Glastonbury; 43 years after this official debut, when he spearheaded the dissolution of the monasteries, King Henry would bring about the ruin of the abbey and have its last abbot hanged for treason.

When Arthur died in 1502, Henry was transported, figuratively speaking, from the back of the palace, where the unneeded but not unim-

Name variations: Henry Tudor. Born June 28, 1491, in the royal palace at Greenwich; died in Whitehall Palace (Westminster), London, on January 28, 1547; third child of Henry VII and Elizabeth of York, the second of their four sons and the only one to grow into adulthood; married—six times: Catherine of Aragon (divorced), Anne Boleyn (beheaded), Jane Seymour (died), Anne of Cleves (divorced), Catherine Howard (beheaded), Catherine Parr (survived); children: (two daughters) Mary and Elizabeth; (one son) Edward. Descendants: Edward VI, Mary I, Elizabeth I, the Stuarts, the Hanoverians/ Windsors. Predecessor: Henry VII. Successor: Edward VI.

Contributed by Robert Blackey, Professor of History, California State University, San Bernardino, California

619

CHRONOLOGY

1509	Succeeded father as king; married Catherine of Aragon
1513	Defeated French and Scots
1516	Princess Mary born; Thomas More wrote *Utopia*
1521	Granted title "Defender of the Faith" by Pope Leo X for written attack against Martin Luther
1527	Sack of Rome by imperial troops of Charles V increased pressure on Pope not to grant Henry divorce from Catherine
1529	Fall of Cardinal Wolsey; Thomas More became Lord Chancellor
1533	Act in Restraint of Appeals to Rome made divorce from Catherine of Aragon possible and national sovereignty a reality; married Anne Boleyn; Princess Elizabeth born
1534	Act of Supremacy confirmed Henry as Head of Church of England
1535	Thomas More executed
1536	Dissolution of monasteries began; Anne Boleyn beheaded
1537	Jane Seymour died giving birth to Prince Edward
1540	Married and divorced Anne of Cleves; married Catherine Howard; Thomas Cromwell executed
1541	Catherine Howard beheaded; married Catherine Parr
1547	Henry died; succeeded by Edward VI

portant second son resided, to the throne room near the king he would soon succeed. But even as heir apparent, Henry seems never to have been given any responsibility for affairs of state nor was he allowed to be independent. (In all fairness, the rigorous supervision under which he lived was at the behest of a father who had lost five of his eight children as well as his wife; young Henry was, indeed, a precious possession.) As such, Henry VIII ascended the throne, in 1509, with little more than a witness' experience in the exacting art of kingship and with his energy to partake in the joys of life finally unharnessed.

Henry's succession—the first peaceful succession since 1422—signaled happy days and deliverance from oppressive sobriety; the new king held out extraordinary promise. "Heaven and earth rejoices," wrote the appropriately named Lord Mountjoy to Erasmus, "everything is full of milk and honey and nectar. Avarice has fled the country. Our king is not after gold, or gems, or precious metals, but virtue, glory, and immortality." Henry

was probably the finest specimen of manhood ever to wear a crown. According to a Venetian visitor, he was:

> the handsomest potentate I ever set eyes on: above the usual height, with an extremely fine calf to his leg; his complexion fair and bright, with auburn hair combed straight and short in the French fashion, and a round face so beautiful it would become a pretty woman.

Henry had charm and intelligence. Fluent in six languages, a gifted musician, a patron of the arts, he had a grasp of theology remarkable for a monarch and was an apt student of mathematics. It was not uncommon for Henry, according to Thomas More's son-in-law and biographer, William Roper, to sit in his private room and confer with the great humanist on "matters of astronomy, geometry, divinity and ... his worldly affairs." Henry was also a superb athlete who could tire out horses in a chase and opponents in tennis; he could shoot an arrow straighter than his archers, and he took the lead in tournaments and jousts. He could also dance women off their feet and drink most men under the table. This truly Renaissance king, at over six feet tall and with a 35-inch waist (based on surviving suits of armor), was in every respects striking.

There was, however, a dark side that would loom larger with the passing years. And in spite of occasional appearances to the contrary, Henry determined to be his own master: "I do not choose anyone to have in his power to command me, nor will I ever suffer it." Early on, **Thomas More** sensed that the man who embraced him with affection would just as easily have his head if it "could win him a castle in France." Henry was high-strung and unstable, and he was capable of gross cruelty. In the first part of his reign, he devoted his energies to the pursuit of pleasure and to war (with some success against France, with more against Scotland, but all at great cost), and he otherwise left the business of government in the capable but greedy hands of **Cardinal Wolsey.** But then, beginning in about 1527 and coinciding with problems of divorce, the beast in Henry began to overwhelm the beauty.

The magnificent young king evolved into a prematurely aged, white-haired, monstrously obese figure. He began to suffer from headaches, and he developed notorious ulcers on his legs which became elephantine and smelled badly; these may have been varicose ulcers which became thrombosed or they may have been a result of osteomyelitis—a chronic septic infection of the thigh bone, in this case caused by a jousting injury and bringing about a discharge of pus. In 1546, his weight was reportedly close to 400 pounds, and his waist had expanded to at least 57 inches. He had to be carried about in a chair and hauled up stairs with ropes and pulleys. As a contemporary wrote, "He had a body and a half, very abdominous and unwieldy with fat."

Some medical historians have suggested that Henry may have been afflicted with syphilis, which could also be responsible for his ulcerated legs and which in turn may have either caused or aggravated his cruelty to friend, foe, and faceless masses. He would become vicious and unbending in pursuit of More, who wished to avoid confrontation, and Thomas Cromwell, who served him loyally and constructively for ten years. He would relentlessly hunt down potential dynastic rivals, including a 68-year-old countess who would be butchered in the Tower of London. He would slaughter religious opponents, Catholics and Protestants alike, and he even oversaw the passage, in 1531, of a new and frightful punishment, "boiling to death." Observing this record from the safety of two generations, Sir **Walter Raleigh** wrote: "If all the patterns and pictures of a merciless Prince were lost in the world, they might all again be painted to life, out of the story of this king." In addition, Henry's problems with fathering children and, therefore, keeping wives might have become more pronounced, or even been caused by syphilis.

Henry Marries Catherine of Aragon

Henry's first marriage, within seven weeks of his accession, was to Catherine of Aragon, his brother's widow and the daughter of **Ferdinand** and **Isabella** of Spain. To overcome the biblical caution (Lev. 20:21) that a man who takes his brother's wife shall be childless, a special dispensation from the pope was received. Henry married Catherine freely and willingly, and although she was five years his senior, she was probably both physically and intellectually appealing; there was also the prospect of a Spanish alliance to support his antagonism toward France plus his hope to rebuild England's continental glory that provided added inducement. The happiness of their early years together was interwoven with disappointments relating to childbirth. Repeated pregnancies produced only one surviving child, Princess **Mary,** born in 1516; by 1525, Catherine was 40 years old and had not been pregnant for five years. Such a natal history, physicians say, is not untypical where one parent is syphilitic. (Mary would later exhibit signs of possible syphilitic congenital infection.)

The extent to which this is true suggests that Henry's difficulties in having a son may have been mostly his own fault.

But having a male heir was of vital importance. As only the second reigning Tudor, Henry was sensitive to the potential insecurity of his family's claim to the throne. (His father's succession came as a result of victory on the field of battle in 1485, but **Henry VII**'s lineage and the fact that he was more Welsh and French than English made him aware of the need to fortify the upstart Tudor dynasty. His own marriage to Elizabeth of York, daughter of Edward IV, and the marriages of his children to the royal houses of Spain and Scotland reflect these concerns. England had no clear-cut laws of succession, and Henry VII's claim was through his mother, an illegitimate Plantagenet whose descendants Parliament had earlier expressly excluded from inheriting the throne.) This claim had to be strengthened, but the succession of Mary as queen in her own right, although not illegal, was without precedent. To a 16th-century mind, this prospect was fraught with danger: disputed succession and civil war at one extreme, domination by a

Henry VIII and his second wife, Anne Boleyn, who was later beheaded after being found guilty of incest and adultery.

foreign power via marriage to a non-English prince at another. So, after rejecting his few alternative courses of action, including the grooming of his illegitimate son, Henry focused attention on divorce and remarriage.

A divorce (an annulment, really) granted by the papacy was not an unreasonable expectation since precedents existed. But there were also complications: Pope Clement VII's hesitation, generated by diplomatic and military pressure from Holy Roman Emperor **Charles V,** who was Catherine of Aragon's nephew, and Henry's growing desire for the new love of his life, Anne Boleyn. For her part, Anne craftily withheld her favors from her anxious suitor because she wished to become his queen, not merely his mistress.

By 1527, another plot line was added to the story of what is known as the King's Great Matter: conscience. Henry became convinced that his marriage to Catherine had been a great sin; the curse of Leviticus was real indeed. Reason might call attention to the existence of Mary to remind Henry he was not childless, and there was also the biblical injunction (Deut. 25:5), which said it was the duty of a man to marry his brother's widow. But to Henry, Catherine's many stillbirths and miscarriages were a more telling reality. When he said his conscience was violently troubled by the sin of his false marriage, he was not being hypocritical. Henry was an egoist and had convinced himself he was right. No doubt it was this conviction that enabled him to survive all the troubles of the divorce and the break with Rome.

Although this was the Age of the Protestant Reformation, and the divorce would pave the way for England's role in it, it should also be remembered that Henry was a Catholic at heart, albeit not one who would be subservient to the papacy, even a papacy that had only recently granted him the title, "Defender of the Faith." In this respect Henry was little different from his fellow European monarchs. Still, there was deprivation and corruption within the Catholic Church, and the general attitude of the English people toward the clergy was unfavorable. Moreover, the rich, corrupt, and uncelibate Cardinal Wolsey, who was also Henry's chief minister, symbolized the worldly aspects of the Church in its worst light. And it was Wolsey who was charged with the responsibility for persuading the pope to grant the divorce. At this task Wolsey failed and, for political reasons, the papacy kept its involvement at a minimum and itself uncommitted. For his failure, Wolsey was forced from his political office in 1529 and surely would have been tried (for exceeding his

authority) and executed had his natural death not beaten the executioner's ax.

Henry then began to pressure Rome and, using the anticlericalism prevalent among members of Parliament, to turn threats into hostile legislation. By 1531, little progress toward divorce had been made. At this point Thomas Cromwell, a former aide to Wolsey and a member of the Privy Council, emerged with a plan that would not only take care of the divorce but also help in creating England as a sovereign national state. Cromwell was the driving force in the decade of the 1530s, and it was he who gave a coherence and purpose to policy that had otherwise been lacking during Henry's reign. In 1532, the English clergy became fully submissive when they accepted the king in the pope's place as their supreme legislator. Also, the machinery for halting the flow of English money to Rome was set in place. By 1533, with the papacy as stubborn as ever, the English Reformation hit full stride.

The crucial Act in Restraint of Appeals became law in March, and henceforth all decisions of the English church court would be final and not subject to appeal to the pope. Two months later, Archbishop Thomas Cranmer opened court; he declared Henry's marriage to Catherine void, and he announced Henry's earlier—and secret—marriage to Anne Boleyn. So ended the King's Great Matter. Catherine was legally and physically cast aside, as was daughter Mary, and the new heir to the throne that Anne had been carrying for several months would be legitimate.

Act Declares England Sovereign State

The Act in Restraint of Appeals, formulated by Cromwell with Henry's support, essentially stated a new doctrine: the king was supreme head and the country was a sovereign state free from all foreign authority. This was a giant step toward total independence and national sovereignty, but among critics of such a posture was the righteous and medieval-thinking Thomas More. An Act of Supremacy in 1534 made Henry the "Supreme Head of the Church of England." It was More's refusal to support this new order which culminated in More's dramatic trial—in Westminster Hall—and beheading in 1535. The man Erasmus had once called "a man for all seasons" died, according to his final words, "the king's good servant, but God's first." While many historians find flaws in the seeming nobility of More's position, none condone Henry's actions. Nevertheless, More's death did not excite much public sympathy, and the English Reformation proceeded, most importantly with the dissolution of the monasteries.

The destruction of the monasteries ("putrified oaks" one contemporary called them) eliminated the last sources of papal support in England, and it provided vast amounts of land (about one-tenth of the country) and income—first from the revenue and then from the sale of more than half of that land—to a financially troubled government. Moreover, the sale of those lands, to the gentry and the nobility, tied these powerful segments of society to the new order.

The last 11 years of Henry's life were filled with much less happiness than the king expected was his due. His doctrinal waverings left the religious position in England unstable. His return to war with France briefly gained the coastal town of Boulogne but cost outrageous sums; this led to other financial ventures, including loans and currency depreciation, which combined to fuel a Europeanwide inflation and to swell the royal debt. And his private life continued to disappoint more than please.

Though Anne Boleyn had been flirtatious with others, her only "crime" was that she had failed to provide the required son; daughter Elizabeth was seen as an unnecessary replication of Mary. Henry's passion for Anne wilted. Evidence against her was gathered, some by the torture of her brother, and so it was no surprise that she was found guilty of incest and adultery. In 1536, shortly after Catherine of Aragon died—an occasion Henry celebrated with a festive ball—Anne's neck rested briefly on the chopping block in the Tower of London before being severed. Wife number three, Jane Seymour, a lady at court, had caught Henry's eye during Anne's waning days, and they married quickly.

Edward Is Born

Jane did not live long enough to be a crowned queen, but her death in childbirth did produce a son, Edward, born at Hampton Court in October 1537. After a year and a half of mourning, a new wife was urged upon Henry by Cromwell. This marriage-by-proxy mismatch was filled with tragicomedic elements (Anne of Cleves, cruelly nicknamed "the Flanders' mare," was somewhere between plain and ugly; upon first seeing her, Henry—no longer the handsome prince himself—kept his distance; they were divorced after six months, although financially she was left secure enough to live as "the King's good sister"); Cromwell was blamed for the fiasco, and he paid for it with his life.

From 1540, no single minister emerged to serve the king as loyally and as effectively as had Cromwell. Government, dominated by religio-political factions, weakened. As the French ambassador noted:

> This King, knowing how many changes he had made, and what tragedies and scandals he has created, would fain keep in favour with everybody, but does not trust a single man, expecting to see them all offended, and he will not cease to dip his hand in blood as long as he doubts his people.

With his fifth wife, Catherine Howard, a vivacious and frivolous 17-year-old, Henry believed the vigor of his youth to be reborn. He called her his "rose without a thorn," and he believed she had married him for love. But his self-delusion barely lasted a year as her infidelities cost her her head in 1542. Henry's last wife, the twice-widowed Catherine Parr, managed to survive the reign by dealing with the increasingly angry and vile temper of an aging and soured egoist, made much more bitter by ill health and by a complex that led him to believe he had had more than his share of tribulations. Henry retained the reins of power until the end, despite his physical decay. Having arranged the hoped-for smooth succession of his son Edward (VI), he died on January 28, 1547, convinced, no doubt, of his own righteousness.

On balance, Henry VIII achieved some critical successes: the position of the Crown was strengthened and monarchy in England was raised to near-idolatry; control of the country was exercised—and not without some justification since there was neither a police force, nor a standing army, nor a modern bureaucracy—through fear and the suppression of dissent; the papacy was excluded and the clergy subdued; the administration was reformed; a navy was created (Henry inherited only five ships from his father, but he left 53 to his son); Wales was incorporated and Welshmen were granted equal rights; and much of the great wealth of the Church came under royal control.

There were, however, notable failures and shortcomings as well: the succession may have been set by law, but the prospects—one sickly son and two princesses—were grim and questions of legitimacy would shadow Henry's children; the religious settlement was so far from being resolved that a dangerous schism resulted; the wealth of the Church may have paid for government policies, but it also strengthened the gentry and nobility and helped to move them to positions whereby they could begin to resist the Crown; cooperation with Parliament to effect the Reformation also provided lessons and precedents with which that body would later be able to challenge the monarchy; the new world and the new trade routes that were being brought to European attention were ignored by the king and, larger navy aside, maritime expansion languished; the wars with France and Scotland cost far more than was ever gained; the debasement of English coins hastened the country into runaway inflation; and the king, who prided himself on being a Renaissance prince and who built more than any other Tudor, was also responsible for the destruction of more beautiful structures and other works of art than the Puritans.

Both for good and for ill, Henry VIII was a man who left his mark on history. Sadly, it seems, he had it in himself to be so much more than he was. Perhaps that is why we can still identify with this larger-than-life man.

SOURCES:

Cannon, John, and Ralph Griffiths. *The Oxford Illustrated History of the British Monarchy.* Oxford University Press, 1988.

Rosebury, Theodor. *Microbes and Morals: The Strange Story of Venereal Disease.* Ballantine, 1973.

Scarisbrick, J. J. *Henry VIII.* University of California Press, 1968.

Starkey, David. "Destruction and Renewal: An Introduction to Henry VIII" in *History Today.* Vol. 41. June 1991.

FURTHER READING:

Dickens, A. G. *The English Reformation.* 2d ed. Batsford, 1989.

Elton, G. R. T*he Tudor Revolution in Government.* Cambridge University Press, 1953.

Pollard, A. F. *Henry VIII.* Longmans, 1966.

Smith, Lacy Baldwin. *Henry VIII: The Mask of Royalty.* Academy Chicago, 1982.

Williams, Neville. *Henry VIII and His Court.* Macmillan, 1971.

Paul von Hindenburg

(1847–1934)

Field marshal and president of the German Republic, who had the dubious honor of sealing the fate of German democracy by appointing Adolf Hitler chancellor on January 30, 1933.

"A man who worships authority does not really need imagination. Hindenburg's gifts are, in fact, not imaginative or intellectual at all. His are talents of character: he has almost a genius for sincerity and loyalty."

HINDENBURG:
THE MAN AND THE LEGEND

It is one of the ironies of history that, at key moments during the drama, the stage is often occupied by well-meaning actors of mediocre talent. Certainly that was the case in Germany during the life of the ill-fated Weimar Republic (1918–33). After 1925, when the Republic struggled for its existence, it was assailed by extremists from both the Right and the Left. Unfortunately, its fate depended upon the aging former field marshal and war hero, Paul von Hindenburg.

As the last president of the Republic, Hindenburg possessed constitutional powers that allowed him to rule by emergency decrees. In the face of parliamentary paralysis, the survival of the Republic depended upon a man whose whole life was devoted to absolute obedience to the old order, that is, to his German Fatherland and his liege lord, the emperor. "His fundamental attitude," wrote one of his early biographers, "is, indeed, essentially a feudal one." The man elected to be president was in his own heart what he always had been, a monarchist.

On his father's side, Paul Ludwig Hans Anton von Beneckendorff und von Hindenburg was descended from a long line of Prussian soldier-

Born Paul Ludwig Hans Anton von Beneckendorff und von Hindenburg (a member of the old Prussian aristocracy, the Junkers) on October 2, 1847, in Posen, Prussia (now Poznan, Poland); died on August 2, 1934, at Neudeck (present-day Podzamek, Poland).

Contributed by Paul R. Waibel, Associate Professor of History, Liberty University, Lynchburg, Virginia

625

1847	Born in Posen, Prussia
1866	Served in the Austro-Prussian War; North German Confederation formed
1871	Prussia defeated France
1888	Accession of Wilhelm II as German emperor
1890	Otto von Bismarck dismissed as chancellor
1911	Hindenburg retired from active duty
1914	WWI began; returned to active duty; together with Erich Ludendorff, defeated the Russians at the Battles of Tannenburg and Masurian Lakes
1918	Germany sued for peace; Wilhelm II abdicated; German Republic proclaimed
1923	French and Belgian forces occupied the Ruhr industrial district of Germany, triggering the Great Inflation
1925	Hindenburg elected president following the death of Friedrich Ebert
1929	Beginning of the Great Depression in United States
1933	Appointed Adolf Hitler chancellor; Reichstag fire; Enabling Act effectively ended democracy in Germany
1934	Died on August 2 at Neudeck; Hitler merged offices of president and chancellor

aristocrats. The Beneckendorffs and Hindenburgs had served the Prussian rulers as soldiers since the high Middle Ages. His mother's family was middle class, but no less devoted to king and Fatherland. As a child, he often heard stories of the liberal revolution that shook Prussia and all of Germany during the year following his birth on October 2, 1847. He was taught to hate those who rebelled against their king and sought to establish a united Germany under a constitutional monarchy. The Black-Red-Gold flag of the Revolution of 1848 remained for him a symbol of disloyalty, if not treason. Ironically, it was the flag under which he later served as president of the Weimar Republic.

As was true of virtually all the elder sons of the Prussian Junker families (aristocracy), Hindenburg's entire education had but one objective—to produce a loyal and efficient Prussian officer. The atmosphere in his childhood home, of which he always spoke with fondness, was harsh by modern standards. When he and his two brothers and sister "were addressed by their elders, they clicked their heels together and stood at attention, holding their hands tightly against their sides." He was taught never to question the authority of his parents, nor later in life the authority of his king-emperor.

Hindenburg's initial education occurred at home: his father taught him geography and history; his mother gave him religious instruction; and a private tutor taught reading, writing, and simple arithmetic. While his father was stationed in Glogau, Hindenburg attended a private preparatory school until he was 11, when he enrolled in the Cadet School at Wahlstatt. He always considered the influence of his parents as a crucial factor in his education, later writing in his autobiography, *Out of My Life* (1920):

> My parents gave me the best thing that parents can give their children, a faith in God the Omnipotent, an unbounded love for the Fatherland, as well as a devotion to the individuals whom they considered the strongest support of the Fatherland: our Prussian Kings.

Before leaving for the Cadet School, the 11-year-old Hindenburg made out a will disposing of most of his earthly possessions (e.g., his toys). For him, when he put on the uniform of his king, a new life began. But the new life at Wahlstatt was brutal. The cadets rose at 5:30 A.M. and retired at 9:00 P.M. The atmosphere was Spartan in the extreme. Discipline was maintained by horsewhips and humiliations.

The educational system at Wahlstatt, as at other Prussian cadet schools, was designed to produce Prussian officers conditioned "to obey and fight whomsoever [they] were told to fight." The emphasis was on physical training, with a minimum of intellectual instruction. Later in life, Hindenburg proudly remarked: "Since my days as a cadet, I have never read a book that did not deal with military affairs." A good Prussian officer was not one who concerned himself with world affairs, or the causes of a war. Rather, he was one trained to obey his lord instinctively.

In 1863, Hindenburg transferred to a cadet school in Berlin. After graduating, he was commissioned a lieutenant in the Third Infantry Guard Regiment, just in time to serve in the Austro-Prussian, or Seven Weeks', War of 1866. Before departing to begin his career as a Prussian officer, Hindenburg took a voluntary oath of lifelong obedience to his sovereign, the king of Prussia. Administered by "priests with a solemn ritual," the oath remained very real to him throughout his life.

The young Hindenburg served with distinction in both the Austro-Prussian War and the

Franco-Prussian War (1870–71) and was decorated for acts of bravery in both. His regiment was stationed in the vicinity of Paris when the Franco-Prussian War ended. Always popular with the officers and men he served with, he was elected to represent them at the proclamation of the German Empire and the crowning of the German emperor **Wilhelm II** on January 18, 1871, in the Hall of Mirrors at the Palace of Versailles.

With the unification of Germany completed in 1871, Europe remained at peace until 1914. From 1871 until his retirement in 1911, Hindenburg's military career consisted of what the Germans liked to call "military peace time work." For 40 years, he conscientiously performed the duties of a peacetime career officer. Slowly, he advanced through the ranks to lieutenant general, each promotion being granted as he reached the appropriate age. When he retired in 1911, at the age of 65, he was commander general of the fort at Magedeburg.

Hindenburg's name would have been forgotten by historians if not for the events of June–August 1914. It was the assassination of the Austro-Hungarian crown prince, Francis Ferdinand, on June 28, and the outbreak of the "Great War" that catapulted Paul von Hindenburg onto the stage of history.

Hindenburg and Ludendorff Become Military Dictators

In accordance with their plans for a general European war, the Germans on August 4, 1914, launched an invasion of France through Belgium. The Schlieffen Plan called for a swift victory over France, while the much slower Russian army was mobilizing. Surprisingly, the Russians were able to invade East Prussia with two armies in mid-August. To meet the Russian threat, the German Emperor recalled Hindenburg to active duty on August 22, 1914. He was given command of the Eighth Army. Together with his brilliant chief of staff, General **Erich Ludendorff,** Hindenburg crushed the Russians at the battles of Tannenburg (August 26–30) and Masurian Lakes (September 10–14). Overnight, Hindenburg became a national hero and a legend. From then until August 1916, he was supreme commander of the eastern front; then, elevated to the rank of field marshal, he became chief of the Greater German General Staff, with Ludendorff as his first quartermaster-general and deputy. Until the end of the war two years later, Hindenburg and Ludendorff were the effective military dictators of Germany. Neither the emperor nor the chancellor and the popularly elected *Reichstag* ("parliament") could effectively check their influence.

As prospects for a German military victory became ever more remote, Hindenburg and Ludendorff forced the removal of chancellors and ministers who suggested that Germany should seek a negotiated peace. While resisting all calls for democratic reforms within Germany, they continued, as late as early 1918, to demand an all-out military victory and a peace of annexations. Something of their objectives can be seen in the harsh Treaty of Brest-Litovsk (March 3, 1918), which they imposed upon the defeated Russians. Russia was forced to surrender to Germany: the Ukraine, Finland, the Baltic Provinces, the Caucasus, White Russia, and Poland.

But neither the tactical genius of Ludendorff nor the living legend, Hindenburg, could stave off the inevitable defeat of Germany on the western front. A final all-out German offensive in mid-July 1918 failed. An Allied counteroffensive, including fresh American troops in mid-September, forced Hindenburg and Ludendorff to acknowledge that the war was lost. Hence, they demanded that the civilian government seek an immediate armistice.

On September 28, 1918, when a new civilian government was formed under the moderate prince Max von Baden, General Ludendorff was dismissed and fled to Sweden in disguise. Hindenburg's heroic image with the German people was enhanced by his faithfully remaining at his post, seeing to it that the German armies returned to Germany in good military order. As revolution broke out in various parts of Germany and chaos threatened, Hindenburg remained as a symbol of order.

On November 11, 1918, the armistice was signed. Two days earlier a Republic had been proclaimed. Although Hindenburg resisted demands for the emperor's abdication, he consented when faced with the fact that Wilhelm II no longer had the support of the army. The fact that he urged the emperor to seek refuge in Holland did not mean that Hindenburg had broken his oath to his lord. For him, as for many Germans, the Republic was a necessary interregnum until the situation permitted the restoration of the monarchy. Even when Hindenburg subsequently served as president of the Republic, he always saw his role as one of a stand-in for the rightful ruler of Germany, the emperor.

During the chaotic days between the armistice of November 11, 1918, and the signing of the Treaty of Versailles on June 29, 1919, Hindenburg kept the officer corps above the political strife and used the army to suppress all left-radical revolutionary stirrings. He then retired once more, cultivating the role of a living symbol of the "good old days" of the old order. Remaining a confirmed monarchist, he closed his memoirs:

> Then from the tempestuous sea of our national life will once more emerge that rock to which the hope of our fathers clung in days of yore—the German Imperial House!

In 1925, following the death of the Republic's first president Friedrich Ebert, Hindenburg was prevailed upon to run for the office as a candidate for the nationalist parties. He was elected due largely to the communists' insistence upon voting for their own candidate rather than the Catholic Center Party's candidate, Wilhelm Marx. Although he continued to hope for a restoration of the monarchy, Hindenburg faithfully honored his oath as president.

The Republic never had the support of the majority of the German people. After the outbreak of the Great Depression, what little support there was rapidly eroded. Political life became increasingly polarized as the extreme Left and Right grew at the expense of the moderate, pro-Republican parties.

Nationalists Support Hitler

In 1932, Hindenburg was re-elected, but not with the support of most conservative nationalists who deserted him for the National Socialist (i.e., Nazi) candidate **Adolf Hitler.** Hindenburg won re-election because Catholics and Social Democrats saw him as the only hope for stemming the rising tide of Nazism. Known to dislike and distrust Hitler, Hindenburg referred to him as "that little Bavarian corporal."

But Hindenburg was 82 years old and showing signs of senility when he began his second term as president. Since July of 1930, Germany had been governed by presidential decree because no government was able to command a parliamentary majority. Under the circumstances, the constitution allowed for the president to declare an emergency and issue decrees in place of parliamentary passed laws. Germany had become a presidential dictatorship.

As the aging President Hindenburg fell more and more under the influence of a right-wing nationalist camarilla ("unofficial and scheming advisors"), a democratic solution to the parliamentary crisis became virtually impossible. Neither Hindenburg nor those close to him were sufficiently committed to saving the Republic. The Nazis, having won 6.5 million votes in the elections of 1930, won 14.5 million votes in the parliamentary elections in 1932, making it the largest party in the German Parliament.

Convinced by his advisors that Hitler could be controlled in a coalition government, Hindenburg reluctantly agreed to appoint him to the office of chancellor on January 30, 1933. Hitler quickly outmaneuvered those who thought they could hold him in check. In failing health, Hindenburg faded into the background, becoming an increasingly remote, but revered, symbol of national unity. On August 2, 1934, when the old soldier died at his estate at Neudeck, the last constitutional check on Adolf Hitler and the Nazi movement was removed.

SOURCES:

Goldsmith, Margaret, and Frederick Voigt. *Hindenburg: The Man and the Legend.* Morrow, 1930.

Ludwig, Emil. *Hindenburg.* John C. Winston, 1935.

Orlow, Dietrich. *A History of Modern Germany: 1871 to Present.* Prentice Hall, 1991.

Pinson, Koppel S. *Modern Germany: Its History and Civilization.* Macmillan, 1966.

Weterstetten, Rudolph, and A. M. K. Watson. *The Biography of President von Hindenburg.* Macmillan, 1930.

Wheller-Bennett, John W. *Wooden Titan: Hindenburg in Twenty Years of German History, 1914–1934.* Archon Books, 1963.

FURTHER READING:

Dorpalen, Andreas. *Hindenburg and the Weimar Republic.* Princeton University Press, 1965.

Hiden, J. W. *The Weimar Republic.* Longmans, 1974.

von Beneckendorff und von Hindenburg, Paul. *Out of My Life.* 2 vols. Harper, 1920.

Nositz, Helene (von Hindenburg). *Hindenburg at Home: An Intimate Biography.* Duffield, 1931.

Rosenburg, Arthur. *The Birth of the German Republic, 1871–1918.* Oxford University Press, 1931.

Ybarra, Thomas Russell. *Hindenburg: The Man With Three Lives.* Duffield, 1932.

Adolf Hitler

(1889–1945)

Austro-German political leader, who rose from total obscurity to lead a powerful mass movement that destroyed democracy in Germany, proclaimed a Third Reich that would "last a thousand years," and started the second World War, which ended with Hitler's suicide and the death of 50 million people globally.

"Germany will either be a world power or there will be no Germany."

ADOLF HITLER
MEIN KAMPF

Despite his attempts in later years to paint a picture of a poverty-stricken childhood, Adolf Hitler grew up in comfortable if not luxurious circumstances. His father, despite his illegitimate birth, was an ambitious, tenacious man who had been able to work his way up the bureaucratic ladder to a responsible position in the Austrian Customs Service, and was thus able to provide his family with social status and economic security. Although intellectually above average, the student Hitler did well only in those school subjects that interested him. As a consequence, he was easily bored by required lessons, and by age 16 had dropped out of school, never taking the *Matura* examination required in Austria for admission to a university. By his mid-teens, Hitler regarded himself as destined for a future as an artist. He was particularly impressed by the music of Richard Wagner, having attended a performance of Wagner's opera "Rienzi" in which the hero liberates his people from national oppression and humiliation.

During these formative years, the young Hitler was surrounded by the increasingly harsh rhetoric of political confrontation that was commonplace in the Austrian Empire of the Habsburg

Contributed by John Haag, Associate Professor of History, University of Georgia, Athens, Georgia

Born April 20, 1889, in the town of Braunau am Inn, Upper Austria; son of Alois Hitler (who changed his name in 1876 from Alois Schicklgruber) and Klara Hitler; had five brothers and sisters but only one other, Paula, survived infancy; married: Eva Braun, April 29, 1945 (both committed suicide the following day in the bunker under the Reich chancellery in Berlin). Predecessor: Chancellor Kurt von Schleicher. Successor: Grand Admiral Karl Dönitz.

the confusion and disorder that seemed to be an inevitable part of democratic government. These prejudices were strengthened by such authority figures as his history teacher in Linz, Dr. Leopold Pötsch, whose anti-Slavic and antisocialist ideology was based on the belief that German culture was superior and had to be defended against "inferior" nations.

After his mother died of cancer in 1907, Hitler moved to Vienna to make his mark on the world. But these were to be years of extreme frustration. He was denied admission to the Academy of Fine Arts, his submitted drawings being judged artistically inadequate, and any hope of starting a career in architecture was made impossible because he failed to complete his secondary education. When a small inheritance ran out, he still refused to take a regular job, subsisting instead on the unpredictable earnings from sales of watercolors he drew of Viennese landmarks. During these early adult years, Hitler read voraciously, but all evidence points to the fact that his mind was already closed to any ideas running counter to his prejudice that history was made by great men, and that German culture could only be saved by taking radical measures against the "subversive" Jewish, socialist, democratic, and liberal forces in society. One of his heroes was the popular mayor of Vienna, Dr. Carl Lueger, whose political career was based on a mass movement combining demagogic anti-Semitism with effective municipal reforms.

Although he regarded war as a noble and necessary part of human society, there is compelling evidence that Hitler hoped that by moving to Munich in May 1913 he would be able to avoid military service in the Austrian army. He was arrested in Munich and, after briefly returning to Austria to take his physical, was declared medically unfit to serve. The start of World War I in August 1914 completely transformed the young drifter's life. Volunteering to serve in the Sixteenth Reserve Infantry Regiment of the Bavarian army, he spent the entire four years of the war at the front. He proved his bravery under fire on numerous occasions, taking great risks as a dispatch runner between trenches, and was twice awarded the coveted Iron Cross. Years later, he would recall that he "passionately loved soldiering," and that the four years of carnage were quite simply "the greatest and most unforgettable time" of his "earthly existence." But despite his courage, Hitler's military superiors did not believe him to be worthy of recommendation for promotion to officer rank, noting that they failed to detect in him the "requisite qualities of leadership" required for an individual to serve successfully as an officer.

dynasty. Because of growing national antagonisms between the different ethnic groups, personal insults and riots (including the throwing of chairs and inkwells) were common occurrences during parliamentary sessions in Vienna. Representative democracy appeared to have failed, and it was this political crisis that provided Hitler with the notion that only strong leadership could save society from

During the war, Hitler had already come to believe that his extraordinary good fortune in surviving the dangers of the front had singled him out for a unique mission. Temporarily blinded in a gas attack in October 1918, he was evacuated to a hospital in Silesia. It was there, a few weeks later, that he received the traumatic news of Germany's defeat. As he was to recount this crucial period years later in *Mein Kampf,* the news of Germany's military humiliation brought tears to his eyes—the first time he had cried since his mother's death 11 years earlier. Convinced that Germany had not been defeated on the battlefield, he believed that the collapse was the result of a conspiracy of "un-German" forces determined to subvert morale on the home front. Regarding the military collapse of November 1918 as "the greatest villainy of the century," Hitler was determined to play a role in restoring Germany to a position of power and respect on the world stage. The hardened war veteran vowed to keep fighting for national glory: "I, for my part, decided to go into politics."

In 1919, Hitler found himself in Munich, still in the army but seeking, like millions of other young demobilized German men, a path into civilian life. Munich had been convulsed by revolutionary upheavals, including two brief failed experiments with communistic "Soviet Republics," and was a city seething with rumors, ideological confusion, and the spirit of political violence. Since the military commanders of Munich feared that some of their troops had become "soft" on radical political ideas, Hitler was chosen to act as a spy and agitator in the affected units; part of his intelligence assignment was to report on the activities of an insignificant right-wing organization called the German Workers' Party. Soon Hitler became an active participant in the meetings of this little sect which hoped to win over the "Marxist-infected" workers of Germany to the cause of extreme nationalism.

Hitler Recruits for German Workers' Party

Adolf Hitler joined the German Workers' Party as its 55th member, and quickly distinguished himself not only by the passionate nature of his debating but also through his organizing skill. Appointed recruiting officer of the group, he showed extraordinary energy and determination by making countless speeches in the streets, in beer halls, or in the meeting rooms of public organizations. Underneath the passionate delivery, Hitler's message was always a simple one: Germany had been "stabbed in the back" rather than militarily defeated, and the traitors were easily identified—

they were Jews, socialists, liberals, pacifists, and all Germans who believed in democracy. Lashing out at the Versailles Treaty, which was universally hated by Germans, Hitler demanded that Germany be given back her honor, her colonies, and her rightful place as a great military and economic power. His solution for these woes was to demand that Germany discard the divisive system of democracy, replacing it with a strong regime, a "national dictatorship" that would remilitarize a demoralized nation and "cleanse" it of subversives.

Although some held Hitler to be little more than an unscrupulous demagogue, he was able to recruit new members for the German Workers' Party and make it well known in Munich and Bavaria. In 1920, the name of the group was changed to the more imposing National Socialist German Workers' Party *(Nationalsozialistische Deutsche Arbeiter-Partei* or NSDAP—usually shortened to Nazi Party), and by July 1921 Hitler had pushed aside his rivals and become the Party's undisputed leader. His word was law, and this fact was soon raised to the *Führerprinzip,* or leadership principle. By 1923, Adolf Hitler had become the focal point of a cult of leadership that defined him to be virtually infallible and above criticism. Long before it seized power in Germany, the Nazi Party functioned as an ironclad dictatorship.

Deeply impressed by the example provided by **Benito Mussolini**—whose Fascist Party of violent Blackshirts had come to power in Italy in October 1922 by intimidating their political opponents with a dramatic "March on Rome"—Hitler was convinced that he too could seize power in Germany. Believing that most conservative politicians, as well as the army high command in Bavaria, were sympathetic to his movement, he attempted to seize power in Munich in November 1923 as a prelude to a successful "March on Berlin." But Hitler had seriously miscalculated the political mood in Germany which—after almost a decade of war, social turmoil, and rampant inflation—desired stability rather than revolution. The revolt against the "November Criminals" (Hitler's description of the German government) failed to receive the support of influential politicians, who turned against the Nazis at the last minute and turned their *putsch* ("attempt to seize power") into a bloody disaster; 16 Nazis and three policemen were killed, while many were seriously injured.

Hitler himself fled unheroically from Munich and was arrested several days later at the lakeside home of a friend. His trial and that of other leaders of the attempted *putsch* in the spring of 1924 provided him with an opportunity to plead his case, arguing that his motives had been pure

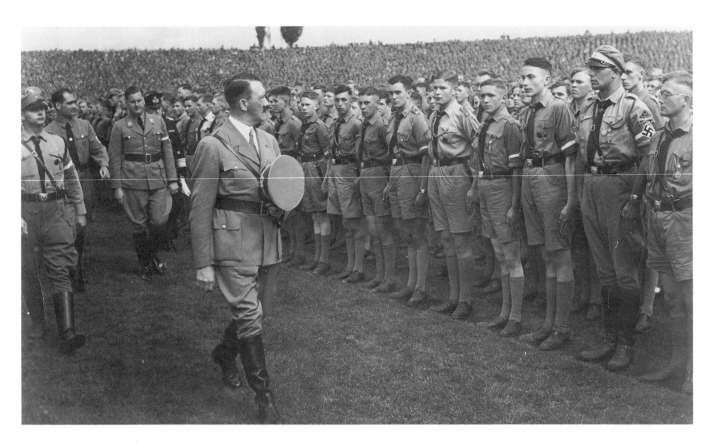

and patriotic in nature. A sympathetic judge sentenced him to a lenient term of five years of comfortable confinement (not hard labor), and chose not to expel him from Germany for his treasonous behavior (Hitler did not become a German citizen until 1932). In the fortress at Landsberg am Lech, Hitler used his enforced leisure to dictate *Mein Kampf (My Struggle)*, a book combining autobiography and an exposition of his world view and ideology *(Weltanschauung)*, the first volume of which was published in the fall of 1925.

Although *Mein Kampf* was long, clumsily written, and poorly organized, it did serve to outline Hitler's fundamental ideas. Defining nature as a relentless struggle between superior and inferior species, and between strong and weak individuals within each species, the Nazi conception of the world saw racial struggle as a "ubiquitous instinct for racial purity." The iron laws of biology that underlay all change in human history, asserted Hitler, had created three types of human races. Repeating racist arguments much in vogue in European thought since the late 19th century, notions that had been used to justify European imperialism on a world scale, Hitler reduced human races to three types: "creators of culture," "bearers of culture," and "destroyers of culture." Not surprisingly, the only culture-creative race was the "Aryans," a vaguely defined group headed by the Germans, while the next group of humanity

was, like the Japanese, culture-bearing but incapable of significant achievements. The lowest category of mankind were the destroyers of culture, and in modern times this negative role was being filled by the Jews, a people Hitler defined as not only incapable of creating culture but indeed as being responsible for virtually all of the political, economic, and moral ills of the modern world.

Released from prison in early 1925, Hitler used his considerable political skills to reconstruct the shattered Nazi movement. He was able to outmaneuver potential rivals for leadership as well as attract new talent to the Party's inner circles, including the cynical but gifted propagandist **Joseph Goebbels.** While membership grew, it did so slowly as long as the German economy was prosperous in the late 1920s; the poor showing of Nazi candidates in the 1928 national elections (they won only 2.6% of the popular vote) makes this clear. But the Nazis thrived on crisis and chaos, and when the world economic situation began to rapidly deteriorate after the 1929 New York stock market crash, they were well prepared to attack what was still a fragile German democracy. With the onset of widespread unemployment, Hitler's demagogic message of a Nazi Third Reich as a foolproof cure for the nation's ills, previously ignored by the great majority of Germans, now began to sound plausible to increasingly desperate people. Nazi anti-Communism and anti-

Semitism, propagated throughout Germany by thousands of trained speakers, now reaped a rich harvest. In September 1930, the Nazis won an astonishing 18.3% of the votes cast for parliamentary delegates, making them—after the Social Democrats—the second most important political party in the country.

Vowing not to repeat the mistake of 1923, Adolf Hitler pledged to respect the laws and democratic constitution of Germany. This was, of course, essentially a deception. While they avoided a *putsch,* the Nazis nevertheless demagogically played on the immense fears of 6 million unemployed Germans and countless others afraid of losing their livelihoods. In their psychological warfare against a weak and faltering democracy, the Nazis could count on Hitler's extraordinary oratorical gifts. As a public speaker, he could bend audiences to his will, fanaticizing them and making them shed their normal intellectual rationality. Much younger than the other politicians (he was only 41 when the Nazis burst on the national scene), Hitler capitalized on his youth and energy, appearing in countless towns and villages to deliver speeches.

Nazis Seize Power

In January 1933, as the result of a behind-the-scenes deal among politicians who naively believed that they could control him once he was entrusted with governmental responsibilities, Hitler was appointed chancellor of Germany by the aged and infirm president **Paul von Hindenburg.** The Nazis now moved quickly and brutally to seize power, using a fire that destroyed the Reichstag building as a pretext to unleash a reign of terror against Communists and other political enemies. Failing to win a clear majority in the March 1933 elections (the Nazis won 43.9% of the vote), the small Nationalist Party helped Hitler to push through constitutional changes that culminated in an Enabling Act in late March that granted the Nazis "legal" dictatorial powers. Within weeks, concentration camps were created throughout Germany to punish political opponents and keep the population terrorized. By the end of 1933, the Nazi Party had been declared the only legal political entity in Germany, and Adolf Hitler, while technically only chancellor, was in fact the unchallenged dictator of a frighteningly efficient totalitarian state.

In June 1934, Hitler purged the Nazi Party of its leadership as well as settling accounts with political enemies; hundreds were shot in a bloody "Night of the Long Knives" that made it clear how brutal the regime was. In a speech to the Reichstag after the purge, Hitler took personal responsibility for the deaths, noting that his word alone was now law in Germany. A few weeks later, when President von Hindenburg died, Hitler seized the opportunity to abolish the presidential office, combining the office of chancellor and führer in his person; the Nazi dictatorship was now solidly established—legally as well as factually. In interviews with the foreign press, Hitler continued to insist that he wanted only peaceful changes in Europe, while at the same time calling for a scrapping of the Versailles Treaty. But all this was a brilliant deception, based on the deep desire for peace by Germany's former foes; secretly, Nazi Germany was rearming as quickly as possible in order to achieve the goals Hitler had outlined a decade earlier in *Mein Kampf.*

By 1935, Hitler restored Germany to great-power status by announcing that the country was scrapping the military restrictions of the Versailles Treaty. The rights of Germany's Jews were also severely abridged through the racist Nuremberg Laws. When, in 1936, German troops occupied the demilitarized zone of the Rhineland, forbidden by the Versailles Treaty, France and Great Britain issued feeble protests even though the action signaled a change in the European balance of power. Jubilant that this great gamble had succeeded, he boasted in a speech, "I go the way that Providence dictates with the assurance of a sleepwalker." In that same year, Adolf Hitler basked in the reflected glory of being host to the Olympic Games. Nazi anti-Semitism was temporarily toned down, and most foreign visitors came away with positive impressions of Hitler's Reich.

But under the surface glitter, Hitler's regime was becoming more repressive. In 1936, the power of the feared SS and Gestapo (secret police) were combined under one man, **Heinrich Himmler.** For enemies of the state, torture and death in numerous concentration camps was almost a certain outcome of deviant behavior. In late 1937, Hitler announced to his inner circle his timetable for war. Believing that he was fated to die young, Hitler was determined to make Germany the greatest power in the world in the immediate future. First he would create a Greater German Reich in the heart of Europe, then seize the rich agricultural lands of Poland and the Soviet Union, enslaving their "inferior" Slavic populations in the process, and then—in alliance with Japan and Italy, and possibly including the British Empire as a junior partner—turn Germany into the paramount power in the world.

Hitler greets troops at the front.

Germany Attacks U.S.S.R.

That Hitler's plans were not fantasies was made chillingly clear in 1938 when Nazi Germany was able to annex Austria and the German-speaking regions of Czechoslovakia without a shot. Led by politicians who believed that Nazism could be appeased, the Western powers did not oppose the conquests. Instead, they hoped to persuade Germany to attack not the Western nations, but the Soviet Union. But Hitler confounded the analysts in August 1939 by signing a nonaggression pact with Stalin which sealed the fate of Poland and made it possible for him to attack and easily conquer France in May 1940 without having to worry about a two-front war. In the summer of 1940 only Great Britain remained to be subdued in the West, but the British under **Winston Churchill** stubbornly refused to capitulate. Frustrated, in June 1941 Hitler attacked the U.S.S.R. in order to fulfill the goals of *Mein Kampf:* conquer *Lebensraum* ("living space") for the Aryan race by destroying the "Jewish-controlled" Soviet state and the source of the "bacillus" of communism. Given the superb weaponry and training of the German military, Hitler (and most observers) expected a quick and easy victory over the Soviets. But the Russian people resisted fiercely when it became clear that Nazi policy was not liberation but genocide. Quickly adapting to the situation, Stalin defined the war not in Marxist but nationalistic terms.

By December 1941, the outcome of the war was in doubt when the German forces were stopped at the gates of Moscow and Leningrad and the United States entered the conflict as a result of the Japanese attack on Pearl Harbor. Hitler responded to these crises with his gambler's instinct of all-or-nothing; he declared war on the United States and pursued the war in the east with increasing recklessness, regarding it as a war of extermination between Aryan supermen and "subhuman" Slavs and their Jewish allies. Dismissing generals he saw as "defeatist," he began to personally direct all phases of military strategy. In January 1942, at the Wannsee Conference, Hitler's lieutenants finalized the precise plans of the "Final Solution of the Jewish Question"—the systematic extermination of Europe's Jews.

The defeat at Stalingrad in January 1943 signaled the beginning of the end for Nazi Germany. After this military disaster, Hitler cut off contact with the German people, refusing to address them publicly or visit their bomb-destroyed cities. His health deteriorated rapidly as a result of stress, lack of exercise and fresh air, and a growing reliance on drugs dispensed by his physician, the quack Dr. Theodor Morell. When it became clear the war was lost, military leaders who had plotted against him as early as 1938 renewed their efforts. But their assassination attempt, on July 20, 1944, failed, and Hitler was only slightly injured. He took vicious revenge, however, placing the conspirators on trial and killing around 5,000 individuals involved in the plot. In his final months, living in his bunker in Berlin, Hitler dictated his last will and testament in which he blamed all but himself (particularly the Jews) for the disasters that had engulfed the world since 1933. A day after marrying his mistress Eva Braun, and with Soviet troops only hours from capturing his bunker, he and his bride both committed suicide. As a legacy to the world, he left at least 50 million dead and many millions more injured, as well as incalculable economic, social, and moral devastation. His "Thousand Year Reich" had lasted 12 years and three months.

SOURCES:

Evans, Richard J. *In Hitler's Shadow: West German Historians and the Attempt to Escape from the Nazi Past.* Pantheon, 1989.

Fest, Joachim C. *Hitler.* Vintage, 1975.

Hitler, Adolf. *Mein Kampf.* Houghton, 1943.

Kershaw, Ian. *The "Hitler Myth": Image and Reality in the Third Reich.* Oxford University Press, 1987.

FURTHER READING:

Allen, William Sheridan. *The Nazi Seizure of Power: The Experience of a Single German Town, 1922–1945.* Franklin Watts, 1984.

Stern, Fritz. *Dreams and Delusions: National Socialism and the Drama of the German Past.* Vintage, 1989.

Zentner, Christian, and Friedemann Bedürftig. eds. *The Encyclopedia of the Third Reich.* 2 vols. Macmillan, 1991.

Hitler's Generals

Karl Dönitz, Adolf Eichmann, Joseph Goebbels, Hermann Göring, Rudolph Hess, Reinhard Heydrich, Heinrich Himmler, Albert Speer

Karl Dönitz

(1891–1980)

Born on September 16, 1891; died on December 24, 1980; son of Emil and Anna Beyer Dönitz; married: Ingeborg Weber (daughter of a German general); children: (two sons) Peter and Klaus (who were killed in the Second World War); (daughter) Ursula. Predecessor: Erich Raeder.

Grand admiral of the navy of the Third Reich, who revolutionized German submarine tactics and succeeded Adolf Hitler as Nazi Germany's last head of state.

K arl Dönitz's childhood was disrupted by the untimely death of his mother when he was a child of four. His father, an optical engineer who deeply mourned the loss of his wife and never remarried, worked for Karl Zeiss of Jena. Raised in a strict Prussian home, Dönitz attended gymnasium (a secondary school based on the study of the classics) in Weimar and earned the coveted *Abitur* diploma in 1908.

In April 1910, Dönitz entered the German imperial navy as a sea cadet, received his commission shortly before the outbreak of the First World War, and served aboard the cruiser *Breslau* which nominally became a part of the Turkish navy during the course of the war. While serving in Turkey in 1916, Dönitz met his future wife Ingeborg Weber, the daughter of a German general serving

Contributed by Bryan Towslee, M.A. candidate, Purdue University, West Lafayette, Indiana

"I ask myself whether I am guilty as an accomplice from the human point of view. But I do not consider myself guilty from the legal point of view. I received orders and I executed orders."

ADOLF EICHMANN

"Whether the other peoples live in comfort or perish of hunger interests me only in so far as we need them as slaves for our culture; apart from that it does not interest me."

HEINRICH HIMMLER

with a military mission to Turkey. Dönitz then returned to Germany to train for his new assignment as an U-boat (submarine) officer. He served aboard several U-boats with distinction and earned the Knight's Cross.

After Germany's defeat in the Great War, Dönitz secured a position in the drastically reduced postwar navy. A leading advocate of U-boat warfare, he developed submarine tactics as he rose through the ranks during the interwar years and served as commander of the U-boat arm on the eve of the Second World War. The initial effectiveness of his submarine strategy in the Battle of the Atlantic earned him a promotion to full admiral in 1941. Dönitz was the epitome of the professional German officer; he demanded the best from his subordinates and was quite severe in dealing with breaches of discipline. An effective leader who took a personal interest in his men, he inspired them to perform fanatical acts of bravery.

In 1943, Dönitz succeeded his chief, Grand Admiral Erich Raeder, and became commander in chief of the German navy. A favorite of Hitler, Dönitz managed to remain in good graces with the Führer until the end of the war. As a result, Hitler designated Dönitz as his successor, a position the admiral assumed on May 1, 1945. The Dönitz government was dissolved by the arrest of its leaders on May 22, 1945.

Tried and convicted on war crimes charges, Dönitz was sentenced by the Nuremberg Tribunal to 10 years in the Berlin fortress prison of Spandau. After his release in 1956, he penned his memoirs, *Ten Years and Twenty Days.* Grand Admiral Karl Dönitz died in his home on Christmas Eve in 1980.

Adolf Eichmann
(1906–1962)

Lieutenant colonel in the SS, who was the organizational mastermind behind the deportation and mass murder of European Jews during the Second World War.

Perhaps the most infamous mass murderer in human history, Adolf Eichmann was the son of a successful businessman who provided him with a comfortable childhood. Little is known about Eichmann's schooling. Preferring horseback riding, he appears to have been a mediocre student who left school at the age of 16 to begin an apprenticeship in his father's electrical construction company. When the family business was crippled by the post-World War I depression, the young Eichmann spent the early 1920s doing odd jobs and drifting about. He was working as a traveling salesman when he first heard Hitler speak; he joined the National Socialist German Workers' Party (NSDAP) in 1931.

After becoming a member of the *Schutzstaffeln* (SS) in 1934, Eichmann—who was good with languages and had acquired some knowledge of Hebrew and Yiddish—established himself as an "expert" on Jews. Three years later, he was sent to Palestine to persuade Arab leaders to take action against Jews in the British mandate. Making a name for himself as director of the "Jewish Emigration Office," an organization that kept track of Jews and forced them out of areas conquered by the Wehrmacht, Eichmann's activities were broadened as a result of the Wannsee Conference (January 20, 1942) where he and other top Nazi officials laid down the organizational details for the "final solution" (the destruction of European Jews).

Working out of the Reich Main Security Office, Eichmann was responsible for the deportation of over 3 million Jews who were ultimately sent to death camps such as Auschwitz. But he managed to keep a low profile and was able to avoid arrest at the end of the Second World War. In 1945, followed by his wife and children, he made his way to Argentina where he worked for German-Argentine Mercedes-Benz in Buenos Aires. After years of rumors and false leads, Israeli agents captured Eichmann in 1960 and took him to Israel where he stood trial for crimes against the Jewish people. Found guilty and sentenced to death, Eichmann was executed by hanging on May 29, 1962.

Joseph Goebbels
(1897–1945)

Reichsminister of propaganda and gauleiter of Berlin, who controlled German cultural life for over a decade.

Raised in the Rhineland town of Rheydt by working-class Catholic parents, Joseph Goebbels was a promising student who was encouraged by his parents to develop his intellect. After earning the Abitur, the young Goebbels enrolled in the University of Bonn and studied German philology.

When the First World War erupted in August 1914, Goebbels rushed to volunteer for the

Adolf Eichmann:
Name variations: lived in Argentina under the alias Ricardo Klement. Born Klaus Adolf Eichmann on March 16, 1906, in Solingen, Germany; executed in Israel on May 29, 1962; married: Veronica Leibl, 1932; children: four.

Joseph Goebbels:
Born Paul Joseph Goebbels on October 29, 1897, in Rheydt, Germany; died on May 1, 1945, in Berlin; married: Johanna Maria Magdalena Quandt, December 1931; children: Hedda, Heide, Helga, Helmut, Hilde, Holde.

front. Much to his disappointment, he was rejected because of his clubfoot (right) and his diminutive size (Goebbels rarely weighed over 100 pounds). Thus, his only taste of military service came in 1917 when he was called up to serve as a "desk" soldier.

Transferring from one university to another in the immediate postwar period, Goebbels completed the requirements for his doctorate in literature in 1922 at the University of Heidelberg. Joining the Nazi party while still a student, he worked his way up through the ranks. In 1926, Dr. Goebbels became the Nazi *gauleiter* ("district leader") of Berlin-Brandenberg. His writing ability and considerable skills as an orator earned him the office of Reichsminister of propaganda after Hitler's ascension to power in 1933.

As such, Goebbels enjoyed enormous powers of censorship that touched nearly every part of life in the Third Reich. He dictated what Germans saw, read, and heard. His propaganda ministry had a particularly heavy hand when it came to the movie industry, for the Reichminister had an extreme fondness for beautiful movie stars. Although he was part of Hitler's inner circle, the sordid details of Goebbels's extramarital affairs sometimes leaked to the public, erupting into scandals that embarrassed both Hitler and the Nazi party.

Nevertheless, Goebbels remained loyal to Hitler and the Nazi cause to the bitter end. He and his family stayed with Hitler in his underground bunker until the Führer took his own life on April 29, 1945. As Russian troops fought toward the Reich Chancellory, Goebbels ordered an SS doctor to poison his six children, then committed suicide with his wife on May 1, 1945.

Hermann Göring
(1893-1946)

Reichsmarshal and commander in chief of the Luftwaffe, who was designated Hitler's successor as Nazi head of state.

Hermann Göring: Born in Bavaria on January 12, 1893; committed suicide on October 15, 1946, after being sentenced to death at the Nuremberg trials; son of Dr. Heinrich (a German colonial official) and Franziska (Tiefenbaumn) Göring; married: Karin von Fock-Kantzow (a Swedish baroness), 1923 (died October 17, 1931); married: Emmy Sonnerman (an actress; 1935); children: (first marriage) Edda Göring.

Hermann Göring was the son of Dr. Heinrich Göring, a German colonial official whose last post was the governorship of German Southwest Africa (present-day Namibia), and Franziska Tiefenbaumn, his father's third wife. Sixty-four at the time of his son's birth, the elder Göring fostered a close relationship between his son and Hermann von Epenstein, an Austrian physician who became Göring's godfather. Von Epenstein owned a castle in Franconia in which the young Göring was raised after his father's retirement from colonial service. Although he spent some of his youth in boarding schools, Göring was largely educated by private tutors. After attending the Karlsruhe Cadet School, he went on to the prestigious Gross Lichterfeld Military Academy, where he passed his officer qualification exams in 1913.

At the beginning of the First World War, Göring served with the 112th Baden Infantry Regiment before transferring to the 25th Field Air Detachment. Distinguishing himself as a pilot, he was awarded Germany's highest honor for an aviator, the *Pour le Mérite* (Blue Max). On July 7, 1918, he was appointed the last commander of the famed Richthofen Squadron (named after the great ace, Manfred von Richthofen).

After the war, Göring flew for the Swedish airline, Svenska Luftrafik, and took up residence in Stockholm. It was during this period that he met and married his first wife, Swedish Baroness Karin von Fock-Kantzow. That same year, 1923, he also joined the Nazi party. Severely wounded by a bullet in the groin during the "Beer Hall Putsch" of November 8–9, he fled to Austria for treatment. His doctor's liberal use of morphine resulted in a lifelong addiction.

Göring rose quickly in the Nazi hierarchy and accumulated an impressive number of titles and positions which included: president of the Reichstag, Reichminister for aviation, Prussian minister of the interior, president of the Prussian State Council, Reich Forrestry commissioner, commander in chief of the Luftwaffe, and commissioner for the Four-Year-Plan. An avid hunter and art collector, he was a charismatic leader who was as popular as Hitler. However, the man designated as Hitler's successor fell into disfavor during the course of the Second World War. Göring was largely responsible for the failure of the Luftwaffe to supply Germany's surrounded 6th army at Stalingrad and for the declining protection afforded by the Luftwaffe during the massive allied bombing campaigns against German cities and industry.

In the last days of the Third Reich, Göring was stripped of his responsibilities due to his premature request to assume leadership of the German government (Hitler was not ready to relinquish control). Captured and tried as a war criminal after the war, Göring cynically attempted to defend his actions before the Nuremberg Tribunal. Nonetheless, the court sentenced him to death by hanging. Cheating the hangman, he swallowed a hidden cyanide vial on October 15, 1946.

Rudolph Hess

(1894–1987)

Hitler's deputy and confidant, who was one of the Führer's most loyal followers.

R udolf Hess was born in Alexandria, Egypt, where his father worked in the export-import business. Although his upbringing was traditionally strict, he looked back on those early childhood years with fondness, having grown up in a villa that overlooked the sea: "Our garden on the edge of the desert was paradise." At the age of 14, he was sent to a boarding school in Germany, followed by a business school in Neuchâtel, Switzerland. When World War I started, Hess immediately volunteered and served with some distinction in the 16th Bavarian Reserve Infantry. He was wounded three times, once seriously, before transferring to the Imperial Air Corps at the end of the war.

After the war, Hess briefly served in a *Freikorps* unit before he gave up soldiering to become a student of political science at the University of Munich. Joining the Nazi party shortly after its establishment in 1920, he was arrested and imprisoned with Hitler in Landesberg prison after the failure of the November 1923 "Beer Hall Putsch." While in prison, Hitler dictated *Mein Kampf* to Hess, who typed and edited the political manifesto.

A true believer in Hitler and the Nazi movement, Hess served as Hitler's personal secretary until 1932. His loyalty was rewarded with a number of positions within the Nazi party; he became Hitler's deputy in 1933, served as chairman of the Central Political Commission, was a member of the Secret Cabinet Counsel, and carried the title of Minister without Portfolio.

His career in the party came to an abrupt end on May 10, 1941, when he took it upon himself to allay British fears about German aggression toward England. Flying a Messerschmitt 110 fighter to Scotland, he bailed out near the home of an English acquaintance, the duke of Hamilton, hoping that the duke would serve as his emissary to the British government. There has been a great deal of historical speculation concerning Hess's bizarre peace mission; the most probable explanation is that Hess thought he was acting in Hitler's best interests, demonstrating the führer's peaceful intentions toward the British. An eccentric, Hess was a hypochondriac and displayed a sense of loyalty that bordered on fanaticism.

After sitting out the war as a British prisoner, he was tried and convicted of crimes against peace by the Nuremberg Tribunal. Sentenced to

Adolf Hitler is flanked by generals Hermann Göring (right) and Heinrich Himmler at a Nuremberg rally.

Rudolph Hess: Born on April 26, 1894, in Alexandria, Egypt; died on August 17, 1987, in Spandau prison, Berlin; eldest son of a businessman; married: Ilse Pröhl, 1927; children: Wolf Rüdiger Hess.

After receiving the Abitur, Heydrich joined the *Kriegsmarine* ("navy") and worked in naval intelligence. His career ended in 1931 as the result of a scandal that involved a shipyard director's daughter. After his discharge, Heydrich joined the NSDAP and the SS. Quickly becoming a favorite of SS Chief **Heinrich Himmler,** Heydrich worked closely with him on the 1934 purge of the Nazi party that came to be known as the "Night of the Long Knives." Heydrich also helped to organize "Kristal Nacht," in which thousands of Jewish businesses were looted and vandalized in 1938.

Rising rapidly through the SS ranks, Heydrich became chief of the Secret Police in 1936, and when several secret police agencies were combined under Heydrich in 1939, he became one of Hitler's most powerful paladins. Requesting permission to fly combat missions as a pilot in 1940, Heydrich distinguished himself by winning the Iron Cross First Class, but an emergency landing behind Russian lines in 1941 put an end to his flying career. Himmler was concerned for his safety.

Heydrich's position as chief of the Secret Police made him an important figure in the implementation of the "Final Solution." It was Heydrich who led the infamous Wannsee Conference (January 20, 1942) which finalized the details of the Holocaust. Heydrich's last position was deputy Reich Protector of Bohemia and Moravia, giving him absolute control over the administration of the annexed Czechoslovakian territories incorporated into the Greater German Reich.

Bold and reckless, Heydrich refused to travel with an escort, a refusal that cost him his life. While en route to Prague on May 27, 1942, his car was machine-gunned and bombed by English-trained Czechs who had parachuted into Czechoslovakia. Heydrich died eight days later, touching off a wave of reprisals that cost a number of innocent Czechs their lives.

life in prison, a sentence he served until his death in 1987, Hess was the sole prisoner in Spandau after the release of **Albert Speer** and Baldur von Schirach in 1966.

Reinhard Heydrich

(1904–1942)

Reinhard Heydrich: Born on March 7, 1904, in Prussian Saxony; died on June 4, 1942, from wounds sustained in an assassination attempt in Czechoslovakia on May 27, 1942; son of a music teacher; married: Lina von Oster, 1931; children: four.

Chief of the Third Reich's secret police, who was the main architect of the "Final Solution" (destruction of European Jews).

An accomplished violinist, horseman, and fencer, Reinhard Heydrich was one of the only leaders of the Third Reich who bore a resemblance to the Nazi racial ideal: tall, blond, athletic, and ruthless. The son of a music teacher, the "Blond Beast" (as he was known in Nazi circles) was a principal character in the formulation of the "Final Solution" which condemned millions of European Jews to deportation and death.

Heinrich Himmler

(1900–1945)

Chief of the *SS (Schutzstaffeln)* and Reichminister of the interior, who was one of the most sinister figures of the Third Reich.

Born in Lüneberg, Bavaria, on October 7, 1900, Heinrich Himmler was the son of a gymnasium instructor whose career was greatly enhanced by his employment as a tutor for Prince Heinrich Arnulf of Wittelsbach of the

Bavarian ruling family. A sickly child who nearly died of a lung infection at the age of four, Himmler grew up in a pious middle-class Catholic family. In 1910, he entered Wilhelms Gymnasium and proved to be a distinguished student, partially attributable to his stern father's insistence on excellence.

The First World War was an event of great excitement for Himmler, who developed an interest in the military that stayed with him into adulthood. Much to his despair, he was rejected for officer training by several regiments. Although he finally became an officer candidate in the 11th Bavarian Infantry Regiment in December 1917, and completed officer training, he was demobilized in 1918 before receiving his commission.

After the war, Himmler experimented with right-wing political groups and served with paramilitary organizations in Munich. After receiving the coveted Abitur in 1919, he decided to train for a career in agriculture, enrolling in the agronomy program at Munich's Technische Hochschule; he continued to play soldier in paramilitary groups during breaks in his studies.

Completing his schooling in 1922, Himmler landed a job with a fertilizer company. But, when his part-time soldiering brought him into contact with Ernst Röhm, Himmler joined the Nazis in 1923, in time to participate in the failed "Beer Hall Putsch" as a member of the *Reichskriegsflagge*. His association with the NSDAP was rekindled when the party was refounded in 1925. Himmler also joined the *Sturmabteilung* (SA) and the *Schutzstaffeln* (SS), becoming a local SS leader in Gau Niederbayern (a district of lower Bavaria). A highly efficient party functionary, Himmler was rewarded with a promotion to *Reichsführer* of the fledgling SS in 1929. Membership then totaled 280. Expanding the elite bodyguard unit into an enormous military and economic empire, Himmler was in charge of 50,000 members by 1933. In the process of establishing the SS, Himmler acquired a number of offices which included: Reichminister of the interior and chief of the Replacement Army.

Himmler's fanatical loyalty and pseudoscientific ideas concerning racial ideology combined to make this otherwise gentle personality into one of the coldest mass murderers in history. His SS empire included the administration of the death camps and concentration camps which consumed the lives of millions of Jews, gypsies, and political dissidents.

During the last days of the Third Reich, Himmler vainly attempted to conclude an armistice with the Western Allies which resulted in Hitler's disfavor and the loss of his rank and offices. On May 21, 1945, while disguised as a sergeant major of the *Geheime Feldpolizei* ("secret military police"), Himmler was stopped at a British checkpoint. Panicking, he committed suicide by ingesting the poisonous contents of a vial hidden in his mouth.

Albert Speer

(1905–1981)

Hitler's architect, Reichminister of armaments, war criminal, and best-selling author, who was the driving force behind Nazi Germany's war economy.

The son of an architect, Albert Speer grew up in extremely comfortable circumstances with the help of maids, a butler, a chauffeur, a cook, and a governess. Educated in private schools until he entered gymnasium from which he received the Abitur in 1923, Speer was an excellent math student. When his father encouraged his son to follow in his footsteps and become an architect, Speer attended the Karlsrühe and Munich institutes of technology before transferring to the Berlin Institute of Technology in 1925. At Berlin, the young Speer studied under Heinrich Tessenow and passed the architect's license examination in 1929. From 1927 to 1932, Speer worked as Tessenow's assistant and established a Berlin residence with his wife, Margarete.

Joining the Nazi party in 1931 after hearing **Adolf Hitler** speak, Speer's membership opened the way for small refurbishing jobs on Nazi buildings. His work for the party attracted the attention of Hitler, who had his own architectural aspirations. Quickly becoming a favorite, Speer was retained as Hitler's personal architect and commissioned to construct a number of buildings, most importantly the Reich Chancellory. In addition, Speer had a flair for organizing spectacular Nazi events and rallies. Few people knew Hitler better than Speer. On intimate terms, the two spent hours poring over plans for the renovation of Berlin and a number of other German and Austrian cities.

But Speer's life changed abruptly with the death of Minister of Armaments and Munitions Fritz Todt in 1942. Charged with the herculean task of administering the production of Germany's weapons, Speer was also led into several other related areas, increasing his enormous responsibilities. A capable technician and bureaucrat, he boosted German production of vital tanks and aircraft to their highest levels, despite the damage done by the Allied air campaign.

Heinrich Himmler:
Born on October 7, 1900, in Bavaria; committed suicide with a poison capsule on May 26, 1945; son of a gymnasium instructor and tutor to the house of Wittelsbach; married: Margarethe Boden (daughter of a large landowner in West Prussia), 1928; children: Gudrun.

Albert Speer:
Born on March 19, 1905, in Mannheim; died in 1981; son of an architect; married: Margarete Weber, 1927; children: five.

As the Third Reich started to collapse in 1945, Speer began to doubt the sensibilities of his Führer and personally intervened to halt much of the destruction of German buildings and communications ordered by Hitler. After Hitler's death, Speer joined the Dönitz government and was arrested on May 22, 1945.

As the only defendant to accept full responsibility for the crimes of the Nazi government, Speer's testimony at the Nuremberg war crime trials caused a sensation. He was found guilty of using forced labor in his armaments factories and sentenced to 20 years in Spandau prison. Released from Spandau in 1966, Speer published his best-selling memoirs *Inside the Third Reich* in 1969, sparking a historical debate that revolved around the extent of his integrity. Some historians were skeptical about the sincerity of Speer's claims to accept total responsibility for the crimes of the Nazi government. Speer went on to publish several more books and became something of a celebrity in West Germany. He died in 1981.

SOURCES:

Clarke, Comer. *Eichmann: The Man and His Crimes.* Ballantine, 1960.

Conot, Robert E. *Justice at Nuremberg.* Harper, 1983.

Douglas-Hamilton, James. *Motive for a Mission: The Story Behind Hess's Flight to Britain.* St. Martin's Press, 1971.

Fest, Joachim C. *The Face of the Third Reich: Portraits of the Nazi Leadership.* Pantheon, 1970.

Heiber, Helmut. *Goebbels.* Hawthorn, 1972.

Irving, David. *Göring: A Biography.* Morrow, 1989.

MacDonald, Callum. *The Killing of SS Obergruppenfuehrer, Reinhard Heydrich.* Free Press, 1989.

Padfield, Peter. *Dönitz, The Last Fuehrer: Portrait of a Nazi War Leader.* Harper, 1984.

Pearlman, Moshe. *The Capture and Trial of Adolf Eichmann.* Simon & Schuster, 1963.

Reif, Adelbert, ed. *Albert Speer: Kontroversen um ein Deutsches Phaenomen.* Bernard & Graefe Verlag, 1978.

Smith, Bradley F. *Heinrich Himmler: A Nazi in the Making, 1900–1926.* Hoover Institution Press, 1971.

Speer, Albert. *Inside the Third Reich.* Macmillan, 1970.

Wistrich, Robert, ed. *Who's Who in Nazi Germany.* Macmillan, 1982.

Zentner, Christian, and Friedemann Bedürftig, eds. *The Encyclopedia of the Third Reich.* Macmillan, 1991.

FURTHER READING:

Arendt, Hannah. *Eichmann in Jerusalem.* Viking, 1963.

Boldt, G. *Hitler's Last Days.* Sphere, 1973.

Deschner, Gunther. *Heydrich: The Pursuit of Total Power.* London, 1981.

Dönitz, Karl. *Memoirs.* Weidenfeld & Nicolson, 1959.

Graber, G. S. *The Life and Times of Reinhard Heydrich.* London, 1980.

Gregory, Frank Huston. *Göring.* London, 1974.

Herzstein, Robert E. *The War That Hitler Won: Goebbels and the Nazi Media Campaign.* New York, 1986.

Hess, Ilse. *Prisoner of Peace.* London, 1954.

Lee, Asher. *Göring: Air Leader.* London, 1972.

Lehmann-Haupt, Hellmut. *Art Under a Dictatorship.* New York, 1954.

Levai, Jeno, ed. *Eichmann in Hungary.* Fertig, 1987.

Manuell, Roger, and Heinrich Fraenkel. *Heinrich Himmler.* London, 1965.

Overy, R. J. *Göring the "Iron Man."* London, 1984.

Raeder, Erich. *Struggle for the Sea.* Kimber, 1959.

Rees, J. R. *The Case of Rudolf Hess.* Surrey, 1947.

Reitlinger, Gerald. *The SS: Alibi of a Nation, 1922–1945.* New York, 1957.

Schmidt, Matthias. *Albert Speer: The End of a Myth.* St. Martin's Press, 1984.

Skipper, G. C. *Göring and the Luftwaffe.* Chicago, 1980.

Speer, Albert. *Infiltration.* Macmillan, 1981.

———. *Spandau: The Secret Diaries.* Macmillan, 1976.

Thompson, H., and H. Stutz. *Dönitz at Nuremberg: A Reappraisal.* Amber, 1976.

Wighton, Charles. *Heydrich: Hitler's Most Evil Henchman.* London, 1962.

Zilbert, Edward E. *Albert Speer and the Nazi Ministry of Arms.* Associated University Presses, 1981.

Jan Hus

(c. 1369/75–1415)

Fifteenth-century religious reformer who, along with John Wycliffe, was one of the most important forerunners of the 16th-century Reformation.

"The Council, which had hoped to eradicate heresy by Hus's condemnation, had only awakened it."

EDWARD M. PETERS

Name variations: John Huss. Pronunciation: Hus, rhymes with bus. Born sometime between 1369 and 1375, in the village of Husinec in southern Bohemia, modern Czech Republic; convicted of heresy and burned at the stake on July 6, 1415; little is known of his family background or youth.

Among the many, no doubt apocryphal, stories of Jan Hus's life is one that relates an incident in his youth, which foreshadowed his fate as a Christian martyr. According to the account, the youthful Hus was sitting beside a fire one winter evening reading about the martyrdom of St. Lawrence. Suddenly, he thrust his hand into the flames. When a fellow pupil pulled him away from the fire and questioned his intentions, Hus replied: "I was only trying to see what part of the tortures of this holy man I might be capable of enduring."

What truth, if any, there is in the story cannot be determined. But what is historical fact is that on July 6, 1415, condemned as an arch-heretic by the Council of Constance and turned over to the state for execution, Jan Hus sang a hymn as the flames engulfed his body in a meadow just outside the city walls of Constance. Hus was charged with propagating the heretical teachings of the late 14th-century English reformer **John Wycliffe,** "the Morning Star of the Reformation," whose bones the Council of Constance ordered disinterred and burned. One hundred years later, **Martin Luther** was charged with heresy by the church

Contributed by Paul R. Waibel, Associate Professor of History, Liberty University, Lynchburg, Virginia

643

CHRONOLOGY

hierarchy for espousing views associated with Hus and condemned as heresy by the Council of Constance. Therein lies the historical significance of Jan Hus. He was a vital link in the chain of reformers who sought to reform the late-medieval church, and whose efforts, often punctuated by martyrdom, culminated in the 16th-century Reformation.

The period of the Renaissance church (roughly the mid-14th through 16th centuries) was, spiritually speaking, the bleakest chapter in Church history. In 1303, Pope Boniface VIII was taken captive by the French king Philip IV, and the papal court moved to Avignon in southern France. An attempt in 1378 to end the "Babylonian Captivity" and return the papal court to Rome led only to the election of two rival popes, one in Avignon and the other in Rome. Both were dominated by men who often made no pretense to spiritual interests. But as destructive as it was, the worldliness of the Renaissance popes did not damage the spiritual authority of the church nearly so much as the Great Schism, the scandal of two popes.

According to the teachings of the medieval church, the pope, or bishop of Rome, was "the vicar of Christ, the successor to St. Peter, the keeper of the keys, the *servus servorum Dei*, the servant of the servants of God." How then could the authority of Christ be divided? Only one of the two popes could

be the true successor of St. Peter according to apostolic succession. The other had to be an antipope. But which was the pope and which was the antipope? And were the sacraments, held to be necessary for the salvation of the individual, valid if performed under the authority of the antipope?

It is within the context of this crisis of faith within the late-medieval church that the life of Jan Hus must be considered. But it also must be viewed against the backdrop of imperial politics within the Holy Roman Empire and the emergence of Bohemian (or Czech) nationalism. The two are so closely intertwined that they cannot be separated. The cause of religious reform in Bohemia at the turn of the 15th century was also the cry of Bohemian nationalism within the Holy Roman Empire.

The exact date of Jan Hus's birth cannot be determined. It has been variously given as the year 1369, 1372, 1373 or 1375. Popular legend placed the exact date as July 6, 1369, but *July 6* is believed to be nothing more than an imaginative analogy with the date of his martyrdom. In any event, he was born in Husinec (meaning "Goosetown") in southern Bohemia on the border of Bavaria.

In his youth, Jan Hus was known simply as "Jan, son of Michael," since it was customary in Bohemia to identify a man by giving his Christian name and the name of his father. In the register of the University of Prague, he is inscribed as "Jan of Husinec," or "Jan from the village of Husinec." Between 1398 and 1400, he signed his name as "Jan Hus," or "Jan Hus of Husinec." After 1400, he always signed his name as simply "Jan Hus." Thus he derived his last name "Hus" from the name of his birthplace, and his actual family name is lost to history.

Of Jan Hus's family even less is known. It is assumed that his parents were humble people of peasant background. Nothing is known of his father, who apparently died when Jan was very young. His mother was a very pious woman. A casual mention in one of his surviving letters leads scholars to assume that Jan Hus had brothers, but nothing is known of them or any possible sisters.

Jan Hus received his "elementary" schooling in the Latin school of the nearby town of Prachatice. When 18 years old, he enrolled at the University of Prague. From then until his death in 1415, his life and fate were shaped by the political and religious struggles that characterized this divided university. In 1393 or 1394, he received his bachelor's degree, and by 1396, his master of arts. That same year, he became a member of the faculty of arts at the university. At first, he lectured on the philosophy of the ancient Greek philosopher Aristotle and the realist philosophy of John Wycliffe. While teaching, Hus also pursued theological studies and in 1404, he earned a bachelor of divinity degree. Three years later, he was in the process of earning his doctorate but never received it. Instead, he earned the martyr's crown.

At what point in his life Jan Hus made the transition to a religious reformer is also unknown. He once commented that the reason he wanted to become a priest was "to secure a good livelihood and dress and be held in esteem by men." During his early years at the university, he lived what he characterized as a lighthearted lifestyle. Hus nowhere records a "conversion" experience as do Martin Luther and other religious reformers. Rather, he simply states that "when the Lord gave me knowledge of the Scriptures, I discarded from my foolish mind that kind of stupid fun making."

Hus Is Appointed a Rector

Following his ordination in 1402, he was appointed rector and preacher of the Bethlehem Chapel in Prague. Founded in 1391, the Bethlehem Chapel was the point at which the Czech national movement coalesced with the cause of religious reform. Under the patronage of Charles IV, king of Bohemia, and his son Wenceslas IV, both of whom were also Holy Roman Emperors, Bethlehem Chapel was a refuge for a group of reform-minded Bohemian clergy, including John Milič of Kroměříž and Matthew of Janov. They preached in the Czech language, rather than Latin, and hence were very popular with the common people.

Jan Hus soon became the leader of the reform party centered in the Bethlehem Chapel and shared their condemnation of the corrupt clergy. Matthew of Janov characterized the priests as:

> worldly, proud, mercenary, pleasure-loving, and hypocritical…. They do not regard their sins as such, do not allow themselves to be reproved, and persecute the saintly preachers. There is no doubt that if Jesus lived among such people, they would be the first to put him to death.

Such outspoken opinions ran the risk of incurring the wrath of the church hierarchy. But so long as Hus and his associates enjoyed the protection of Wenceslas and Zybněk Zajic, the young reform-minded Archbishop of Prague, they were safe.

What drew upon the reformers the charge of heresy was their acceptance of many of the theological teachings of John Wycliffe, a leading exponent of the philosophical position known as "real-ism." Prior to 1401, Hus knew only Wycliffe's philosophical works, but this was enough to incur the enmity of the German-dominated faculty of the university, for they were committed to the opposite philosophical position, "nominalism." The realists believed that universals have objective reality, whereas the nominalists held that universals or abstract concepts are mere names. For Wycliffe and his followers, this meant that in theology they emphasized the priority of faith over reason and the authority of the Scriptures (Bible) over church tradition.

After the marriage of Wenceslas's half-sister Anne of Bohemia to Wycliffe's patron and defender, Richard II of England, a number of Bohemian students went to study under Wycliffe at Oxford University. As these students returned to the University of Prague, they brought with them the theological works of Wycliffe. Many of Wycliffe's views were congenial to the Bohemian reformers of the Bethlehem Chapel and accepted by them. Among them was Wycliffe's doctrine of the true Church. According to Wycliffe's understanding of Scripture, which he held to be authoritative, the true Church consisted of all those—past, present, and future—predestined by God to salvation. Since the Roman Catholic Church included both those predestined to salvation and those "foreknown" to damnation, it was not, as it believed itself to be, the true body of Christ. Hence, Wycliffe rejected the divine origin of the Roman Catholic Church and the alleged authority of the pope.

Wycliffe also advocated "territorial churches, each protected, regulated, and supported by the territorial lords and princes." There was, of course, much more to Wycliffe's theological teaching, but the attraction it held for the Bohemians trying to liberate themselves from German cultural domination should be clear. Likewise, the connection with the 16th-century Reformation is clear. The fundamental doctrines of the Protestant Reformation are present in Wycliffe's teaching, and hence that of Hus, also.

Jan Hus did not accept carte blanche all that Wycliffe taught. He did not, for example, accept Wycliffe's doctrine of remanence with respect to the Eucharist, or Mass. The doctrine of remanence held that in the celebration of the Eucharist, the bread and wine retain their material substance. Thus it denied the alleged miracle of transubstantiation by which, according to the Roman Catholic Church, the bread and wine became the flesh and blood of Christ. Transubstantiation was the key to the whole edifice of medieval theology. Remove it, and one removed the need for the priesthood and the medieval institutional church as it then existed.

Although Hus did not agree with all that Wycliffe taught, and which his associates at Bethlehem Chapel and the university were teaching, he refused to denounce those views which he did not hold. The Bohemian party at the university was locked in a struggle with the German party for control of that institution. The Germans soon realized that their most effective way of countering the Bohemian party was to focus on its Wycliffism. Many of Wycliffe's teachings had been condemned by Pope Gregory XI and the English prelates, although Wycliffe died officially orthodox ("conforming to established doctrine").

A Test of Orthdoxy Threatens Hus

In 1403, Johann Hübner, one of the German masters at the university, drew up a list of 45 articles from Wycliffe's writings. Among them were the doctrine of remanence and the teaching that the Bible is the sole source of Christian doctrine. Hübner was able to have the 45 articles condemned as heresy. As they became a test of orthodoxy at the university, Hus was in danger of being branded a heretic and soon lost the support of both Archbishop Zbyněk and King Wenceslas, although for different reasons. The change of events grew out of efforts to end the Great Schism.

Wenceslas and the king of France (Charles VI) sought to end the Great Schism by convening a church council in Pisa in 1409. The Council deposed both Gregory XII (Rome) and Benedict XIII (Avignon), and elected Alexander VI, who was succeeded in 1410 by **John XXIII**. Since neither of the former two resigned, the number of popes was merely increased by one.

The Council of Pisa and its aftermath sealed Hus's fate. Hus supported Wenceslas and recognized Alexander VI as pope. Zbyněk and the German masters at the University of Prague refused to do so. When many of the German masters chose to leave Prague to found a new university at Leipzig in Germany, Zbyněk began to take a closer look at Hus's teachings.

In 1410, Archbishop Zbyněk confiscated Wycliffe's books and ordered them burned. When Hus defended the books, Zbyněk excommunicated him, and the following year Hus was ordered to appear in Rome. Refusing to go, Hus was excommunicated for disobedience. Having lost the support of his onetime ally, the Archbishop, Hus would next lose the support of his King.

John XXIII proclaimed a crusade against King Ladislas of Naples, a supporter of John XXIII's rival, Gregory XII. The cost of the crusade was to be paid for by the sale of indulgences in, among other areas, Bohemia. Since Wenceslas was to receive a portion of the income from the sale of indulgences, he supported the crusade. Hus, however, openly condemned both and accused John XXIII of "trafficking in sacred things." Such action cost him and his associates the support of Wenceslas. Shortly thereafter, three members of the reform party who spoke out against indulgences were arrested and beheaded.

In September 1412, a papal bull of excommunication of Hus was published in Prague. The city was placed under an interdict, and Bethlehem Chapel closed. An interdict was still a powerful weapon against heretics or other enemies of the church hierarchy. An area under interdict was denied the sacraments: "All masses and sermons, all religious functions, even burial with the Christian rites were prohibited." It was intended to turn the people of an area against the one—in this case Hus—who was defying the church authorities. To spare the city the rigors of being under an interdict, Hus withdrew from Prague and took refuge with various Bohemian nobles.

The final act of Hus's life was played out at the Council of Constance (1414–18), called to bring an end to the Great Schism and to deal with the problem of heresy, especially Hus. **Zygmunt,** the king of Hungary and brother of Wenceslas, was elected Holy Roman Emperor in 1410. To strengthen his position in Germany, he pressured John XXIII to call the Council. Then, in the spring of 1415, offering a guarantee of safe conduct, Zygmunt invited Hus to attend. At first Hus hesitated, but with the urging of Wenceslas, he accepted.

Once in Constance, Hus was lured into the papal residence, then imprisoned in a Dominican dungeon. What followed were months of interrogation and suffering. Zygmunt withdrew his safe conduct in January 1415. It was only due to great pressure exerted by Bohemian noblemen that Hus was given any semblance of a public hearing on June 5, 7 and 8, but he was not allowed to respond to the charges made against him. Presented with a list of 30 articles allegedly drawn from his writings but in fact drawn from the writings of John Wycliffe, Hus was ordered to renounce them upon oath. He refused, unless instructed from Scripture as to where his teachings were in error. The Council rejected his appeal to the Bible as a superior authority.

On July 6, Hus was given a final opportunity to recant. Again he refused, saying that since he did not hold all of the views as stated, to recant would be to commit perjury. He was then declared an arch-heretic and a disciple of Wycliffe. He was ceremoniously degraded from the priesthood, his soul was consigned to the devil, and he was turned over to the secular authorities for execution. That same day, he was led to a meadow outside the city wall and burned alive.

Although the Council had consigned his soul to the devil, Hus—singing loudly as the flames consumed him—consigned his soul to God: "Jesu Christ! The Son of the living God! Have mercy upon me." His ashes were then gathered up and cast into the Rhine River.

SOURCES:

de Bonnechose, Emile. *The Reformers Before the Reformation.* Harper and Brothers, 1844.

Estep, William R. *Renaissance & Reformation.* Eerdmans, 1986.

Foxe, John. *Foxe's Book of Martyrs.* Whitaker House, 1981.

Kaminsky, Howard. "John (Jan) Hus," in *Dictionary of the Middle Ages.* Vol. VI. Scribners, 1985.

Lutzow, Count. *The Life & Times of Master John Hus.* J. M. Dent, 1909.

Palmer, R. R., and Joel Colton. *A History of the Modern World.* 6th ed. Knopf, 1984.

Spinka, Matthew. "Jan Hus," in *The New Encyclopedia Britannica.* Vol. IX. 15th ed. 1973.

FURTHER READING:

Bartok, Josef Paul. *John Hus at Constance.* Cokesbury Press, 1935.

Loserth, Johann. *Wiclif and Hus.* Hodder & Stoughton, 1884.

Previte-Orton, C. W. and Z. N. Brooke, eds. *The Cambridge Medieval History, Vol. VIII: The Close of the Middle Ages.* Cambridge University Press, 1964.

Roubiczek, Paul, and Joseph Kalmer. *Warrior of God.* Nicholson and Watson, 1947.

Schwarze, William Nathaniel. *John Hus: The Martyr of Bohemia.* Revell, 1915.

Spinka, Matthew. *John Hus: A Biography.* 1968.

Innocent III

(1161–1216)

Patron of the Fourth Crusade and arbiter of European power struggles in the high Middle Ages, who was a superbly gifted administrator of the Catholic Church at the height of its influence.

Born Lothario de Segni in Italy, in 1160 or 1161; died in 1216; son of Trasimund, Count of Segni, and Clarissa of Scotti. Predecessors: His immediate predecessor was Pope Celestine III (1191–98), but he inherited and furthered the work of Pope Gregory VII (1073–85). Successor: Honorius III (1216–27).

Once called "the most audacious and relentless of all the medieval popes," Pope Innocent III was one of the most powerful men ever to sit on the papal throne. Building on the work of his recent predecessors, especially **Gregory VII,** he asserted the right of the Catholic Church to intervene in the political affairs of all Christian Europe. He overmastered **King John** of England and the Holy Roman Emperor **Otto,** while forcing nearly all other secular rulers to acknowledge his supremacy. He was also a fierce heresy hunter who, in his campaign for Catholic orthodoxy, built up the Franciscan and Dominican orders of friars and laid the foundations of the Inquisition. As pope for less than 20 years, he invigorated the papacy as one of the central institutions of European politics, a status it claimed but could not retain for at least the next four centuries.

His given name was Lothario de Segni. Like most of the popes, he was an Italian whose early life was blessed with advantage and whose connections ensured rapid promotion through the lower ranks of the Church hierarchy. Born in 1160 or 1161 to the noble family of Trasimund, who claimed descent from the Lombards and regarded

"At Innocent III's death… there was no inhabitant, high or low, in that now far distant Europe who did not recognize that the pope and his church contained the center of gravity for all the political and moral order in their lives. Without a pope, Europe was impossible."

MALACHI MARTIN

Contributed by Patrick Allitt, Assistant Professor of History, Emory University, Atlanta, Georgia

themselves as one of the four oldest noble families in Italy, he was well educated at the two great universities of the day, Paris and Bologna, where he specialized in civil and canon law. During his student days, he visited the new shrine of St. **Thomas Becket** who had been killed in Canterbury Cathedral by knights of England's intemperate king **Henry II** when Lothario was 10.

A deacon by the age of 27, he was a cardinal by 30, and the favorite of Pope Clement III (1187–91). Clement's death temporarily checked Lothario's career, because the family of the new pope, Celestine III, was a traditional feuding rival of his own. Lothario spent seven years marking time, writing treatises, and preserving a reputation for learning, legal skill, and good character, until 1198, when Celestine died in his 90s. The old pope was buried on the very day of his death and a conclave to elect the new pope was held at once—the undignified haste occasioned by popular unrest in Rome. To his surprise, Lothario was elected and chose as his papal name Innocent III. As history would show, few men deserved the name less. Aged only 37, he was not even a priest yet, despite his cardinal's hat, and had to be ordained six weeks later in order to properly fulfill his papal functions.

Innocent III held an exalted view of his office from the beginning, declaring in his consecration sermon that he was "less than God but greater than man." He was a born commander whose unimaginative and less than innovative work was to strengthen, consolidate, and administer the Church. His more than 6,000 surviving letters reveal his formidable efforts, discipline, and shrewdness.

Building on the work of Gregory VII, he insisted that *political* power throughout Christendom was derived from the Church and that he, as "Vicar of Christ" (he was the first pope to use this title), was the dispenser and legitimator of earthly power. His letters are riddled with such claims as: "We hold the place of Christ on earth," and "Seated on the throne of dignity we judge in justice even the kings themselves."

As a warrior prince of Italy, willing to use his family and influential friends to enforce his decree, Innocent presided over a chaotic period in European history. Powerful princes, independent-minded townsmen, and unceasing feuds within the Italian cities meant a condition of permanent unrest, treachery, and bloodshed, in which he was thoroughly implicated and over which he struggled to gain mastery. Even Rome, the center of his empire, was not safe from feuds between powerful rival families, and on several occasions he had to

flee the Holy City to prevent capture or assassination when his family and supporters got the worst of a regional dispute. One of his biographers, L. Elliott-Binns, remarks:

> That the Lord of Christendom, the reprover of great monarchs, should have thus been hunted about by the feeble citizens of a decayed metropolis seems a monstrous anomaly, but it was no uncommon experience for the medieval Popes.

Willing to betray political alliances, he was betrayed by a succession of power-driven emperors and princes both great and small. Of these political conflicts, the most significant were with the Holy Roman Emperors, the rulers of present-day Germany. When Innocent became pope, the imperial throne was disputed. Joining in the decade-long struggle between rival contenders for the Empire, Innocent finally appointed his own ward **Frederick II** Hohenstaufen as emperor and deposed a treacherous rival, Otto, with whom he had had an earlier alliance. Innocent's main concern in his dealings with the emperors was to minimize German influence in Italy and to make certain that his influence took its place.

In his efforts to assert dominance, he used a judicious mixture of political and spiritual weapons. Two of the most potent were the power of excommunication, by which a sinner is expelled from the Church, and the interdict, by which the religious activities of an entire community were frozen. After an argument with King John of England over who should become archbishop of Canterbury (the king claimed the right of appointment, the pope said it was his alone), Innocent placed the whole of England under the interdict in 1208, banning all religious activities, and excommunicated the king the following year. As historian Thomas Bokenkotter describes it:

> The interdict dragged on for nearly six years, while the religious life of England virtually ceased; churches boarded up; bells silent, and priests idle, many of them in exile as John, in retaliation, struck back hard by terrorizing the clergy and confiscating their property.

All God-fearing English people began to worry about the destiny of their immortal souls, and their already unpopular king became more and more disliked. Finally when the pope, in alliance with the French king **Philip Augustus** (1180–1223), threatened to invade England and overthrow John by force, John surrendered himself and his kingdom as vassals to the pope.

In a Machiavellian stroke, Innocent now allied himself with King John against the unruly English barons. When the barons trapped John at Runnymede on the River Thames and extorted concessions from him in the Magna Carta (1215), John persuaded Innocent to annul the charter and to excommunicate the barons. No one then foresaw that the Magna Carta would later be regarded as one of the foundational documents of British and American constitutional government. By John's death the following year, the pope had clearly established himself as a central figure to be reckoned with in English politics, as well as in the politics of the Italians, French, and Germans nearer home. Although much in need of political friendship with France's king Philip Augustus, Innocent was incensed by Philip's efforts to abandon his rightful wife in favor of his mistress. For this sin, Innocent placed the interdict on France, until Philip—like John before him—was forced to submit. Rarely capable of matching these monarchs in troop strength, Innocent exerted authority over them by undermining their popular support.

Pope Fosters Canon Law

One of the ways Innocent tried to assert the supremacy of the Church throughout Europe was by fostering the canon law, which he had mastered at the University of Bologna. He claimed that this body of law, based on papal and episcopal precedents, should govern the conduct of clergy and religious (monks and nuns) everywhere, exempting them from many of the civil laws of their own countries. He also claimed canon-law jurisdiction over all human issues related to religion, such as marriage; his own *Compilatio Tertia* was the earliest authorized collection of papal canon law. Although he was never able to enforce canon law everywhere, its potential political consequences were great; like the interdict, it restricted a king's power within his own domain, giving the pope leverage over many of the most influential, highly educated men of Europe.

Despite his political dexterity, it would be wrong to view Innocent as no more than an Italian prince and power broker; he was a zealously religious man who did everything possible to improve the quality of religious life throughout Christendom. He demanded obedience from the men he appointed, and his letters show a superb range of metaphors through which he amplified his message. To the bishop of Sens, who was slow to do his bidding, Innocent wrote in 1203:

> When we named you archbishop we thought we were doing something useful to the Church of Sens and all France. In placing on the candlestick the light which was under a bushel, we thought we had given the service of God a pastor, not a mercenary. But behold, your lamp is out; it is no more than a smoking wick.

He also wrote repeated letters to other archbishops, urging them to stamp out the widespread practice of simony ("buying and selling church offices"), and to reinvigorate the rules of monastic life which had become lax in many parts of Europe. He prevented men of youth and inexperience from being appointed to bishoprics for political reasons and wanted to be certain that the pope, like his chief lieutenants, remained beyond reproach. "It is proper that the pope should be irreproachable" he wrote in one letter "and that he to whom the care of souls falls should shine like a torch in the eyes of all by reason of his learning in doctrine and his example."

At the Fourth Council of the Lateran, which he summoned to Rome in 1215, more than a thousand senior churchmen debated the state of the Church and tried to regulate higher standards for the priesthood. They decreed, for the first time, that every Catholic should go to confession and communion at least once each year. By the 16th century, many Catholics confessed every week, whereas in the fourth century—St. Augustine's day—confession had been a once-in-a-lifetime affair, undertaken as a permanent cleansing of the soul as one joined the Church. Annual confession seemed, at the start of the 13th century, a judicious way of trying to enforce more uniformity in the sacraments. The Fourth Lateran also defined exactly what the Church meant by "transubstantiation," the miraculous transformation of bread and wine into the body and blood of Christ, which Catholics believe takes place at the Mass. On a more practical note, the Council decided that tithes, the tenth of their income which all Christians were supposed to pay to the Church, should be based on gross incomes rather than on the remains of incomes after other taxes had been exacted. It further decreed that all holy relics, then highly treasured, should go first to the pope for his dispensation to deserving recipients.

Innocent III lived in the age of the crusades, holy wars in which Christians tried to recapture Jerusalem from the Muslims. In a succession of wars—in progress for nearly a century by Innocent's day—Christian soldiers overcame severe hardships to attack the Saracens; they also committed horrific atrocities against their enemies and sometimes against other Christians. While crusading was preached as a sanctified task, the brutal reality was usually otherwise. Venice, from which the Fourth Crusade was launched in Innocent's day, was one of many Mediterranean cities which continued a lucrative trade with the "infidels" even while fighting against them.

A believer in the value of crusades, Innocent hoped to reunite the estranged Christian churches of the East with the Church of Rome. Within nine months of his coronation, he had called for a new Holy War against the infidels, one which he aimed to keep out of the hands of Christian kings and under his own control. He hoped that it would have the effect of reconciling the warring European leaders against a common foe. He was aided by the preaching of a charismatic French priest, Fulk of Neuilly, and by his promise that all who joined the crusade would have their sins forgiven and the interest on their debts suspended. Innocent was not able to keep control over the Fourth Crusade, however. Against his wishes, it first attacked Zara in Hungary, a Christian city which the Venetians coveted, and then moved on to Constantinople, the Eastern inheritor of the Roman Empire. For the first time in its 900-year history, Constantinople fell to an enemy invader. The crusaders rampaged through the city searching for treasure, tore open the tombs of the Eastern emperors, and desecrated churches. Appointing one of their leaders, Baldwin of Flanders, emperor of Constantinople, they claimed that they now had a base from which to attack the Holy Land. In reality, they soon became involved in further distracting wars, so that the long-awaited attack on Jerusalem never materialized.

"The Crusade," as Elliott-Binns aptly notes, "became quite openly an enterprise for private profit, very like the one which William of Normandy had led to the conquest of England." Its diversionary attacks and general lawlessness vividly demonstrate the limits of even Innocent's papal power and the compromised character of this ostensibly Christian age of holy wars. Though unable to use the occupation of Constantinople to reunite the separated Latin and Eastern parts of Christendom, Innocent remained undeterred by the disgraceful failure of the Fourth Crusade, and by the abortive "Children's Crusade" of 1211–12, and asked that the Fourth Lateran Council authorize another attempt on Jerusalem for the year 1217. He would, however, die before it could begin.

In Innocent's day, as in most ages of Christianity, heresy was common. Heresy is the Church's name for religious practices and beliefs whose validity it denies. The prevailing heresy of Innocent's day was that of the Cathars or Albigensians, "an antisocial sect," as one unfriendly commentator describes it, "whose members preached that the material universe was the creation and tool of Satan; hence they condemned the use of all things material, prohibited marriage, encouraged suicide, and in general stood for a morality that strangely combined asceticism and immorality." The Albigensian form of Christianity spread widely in southern France and Italy and was often adopted by the pope's *political* adversaries, just as Protestantism was later adopted by 16th-century princes seeking greater political independence.

Innocent Institutes Inquisition

Hitherto, the Catholic Church had responded to heresies by holding councils and by writing justifications of its own beliefs. But now it took a lamentable turn towards force, a resort which was to become commonplace in the next five centuries. Responding with his usual vigor to the Albigensians, Innocent established an Inquisition, a tribunal designed to investigate allegations of heresy. Under the later pope Gregory IX it took its mature form, setting in motion one of the most odious episodes of Catholic history which reached its apogee in 16th-century Spain. Investigations of heresy had earlier been carried out by local bishops, but Innocent, in his efforts to strengthen Roman control, preferred to send out his own agents. When his early investigation of the Albigensians led to the assassination of Peter of Castelnau, his legate in France, he declared a crusade—a holy war—against them, and two large papal armies overwhelmed the Albigensian strongholds of Beziers and Carcassone, massacring their inhabitants. Previously crusades had been launched (at least officially) only against the Muslims; now the savagery of crusading was turned against other Christians as the general level of political-religious violence in Europe escalated.

In contrast, one of Innocent's less objectionable methods for trying to suppress heresy was to use mendicant ("wandering and begging") friars, whose preaching and moral example, he hoped, would act as living propaganda on behalf of orthodox Catholicism. Arising in this period, the friars favored a monastic life of discipline and austerity but not the withdrawal from the world which usually accompanied it. Two of the best remembered and longest lived groups of friars were established during Innocent's pontificate, the Dominicans and the Franciscans.

Francis of Assisi formed his band of 12 in 1208 and appealed to the pope in 1210 for official approval of his plan to wander the countryside preaching penitence. At first this austere visionary with his plans for a life of absolute poverty dismayed the pope; the two men were temperamentally as different as possible. Eventually, Innocent relented, allegedly because he saw in a dream the great Lateran Basilica, on the verge of collapse, being held up only by this small and despised man. His approval set in motion one of the most successful religious experiments of the Middle Ages. Dominic, a missionary to the Cathars, founded his order at about the same time but emphasized rational argument in converting heretics rather than the selfless love of the Franciscans. The Dominicans too at first lived a life of radical poverty but doubled as theological advisors to the Inquisition.

Innocent died of malaria in May 1216 while traveling through his extensive and troubled domains. His body was lavishly laid out but, without a proper guard, was plundered of its robes and jewels, so that the next day it was found half naked. It was an incongruous end to so powerful a man. As Elliott-Binns concludes:

> So the great Pope passed and with him, in some sense, passed the greatness of the medieval Papacy itself, for none was to arise after Innocent who was to be, as he had been, the arbiter of the destinies of Europe.

Though he was certainly widely feared and respected, Innocent had never been much loved. In the long run, his greatest achievement was to institutionalize the central power of the papacy over the Church. In his own lifetime, he was never able to dominate and quieten the chaos of a perpetually war-torn Europe, but he was able to leave a lasting stamp on its religious life.

SOURCES:

Binns, L. Elliott. *Innocent III*. Methuen, 1968.

Bokenkotter, Thomas. *A Concise History of the Catholic Church.* Doubleday, 1979.

Johnson, Paul. *A History of the English People*. Harper, 1985.

Martin, Malachi. *The Decline and Fall of the Roman Church.* Putnam, 1981.

Powell, James, ed. *Innocent III: Vicar of Christ, or Lord of the World?* D. C. Heath, 1963.

FURTHER READING:

Queller, Donald. *The Fourth Crusade: The Conquest of Constantinople*. University of Pennsylvania Press, 1977.

Smith, Charles Edward. *Innocent III: Church Defender.* Louisiana State University Press, 1951.

Isabella I, Queen of Castile

(1451–1504)

Ferdinand II, of Aragon

(1452–1516)

Spanish rulers, who unified Spain, conquered the Moorish kingdom of Granada, and supported Columbus on his voyage to the New World.

"They were kings of this realm alone, of our speech born and bred among us.... They knew everybody, always gave honours to those who merited them, travelled through their realms, were known by great and small alike, could be reached by all...."

THE ADMIRAL OF CASTILE

Isabella I and Ferdinand II, known as the Catholic Monarchs, are among the most famous and significant rulers of Spain. Under their joint rule, they laid the foundations for the modern nation of Spain as a political and cultural entity, and their support of overseas colonies, especially across the Atlantic Ocean in the new world of the Americas, began the formation of a Spanish Empire.

The accomplishment of bringing a greater sense of unity to Spain becomes significant with an understanding of the political and geographical divisions of the Iberian peninsula during the medieval period. When Isabella and Ferdinand were born in the mid-15th century, Spain was divided into five principal kingdoms. Portugal occupied the west coast. Castile, the largest kingdom, stretched from the north Atlantic coast through much of the central part of Spain. Aragon was in the east. The small Kingdom of Navarre was just north of Castile and Aragon along the French border. Finally, the Moorish kingdom of Granada was in the extreme southern tip of Spain. To further complicate these divisions, several provinces comprised the major kingdoms of

Contributed by Karen Gould, Ph.D., Consultant in Medieval and Renaissance Manuscripts, Austin, Texas

Name variations: Isabella the Catholic, Isabel la Católica (Spanish). Born April 22, 1451, at Madrigal de las Altas Torres, Castile; died on November 26, 1504, at Medina del Campo, Spain; daughter of John II of Castile and Isabella of Portugal, his second wife; married: Ferdinand II of Aragon; children (see Ferdinand, below). Predecessor: Henry IV of Castile. Successor: Joan (Juana) and Philip I of Burgundy and Austria.

Name variations: Ferdinand the Catholic, Fernando el Católico (Spanish), Ferdinand V of Castile, Ferdinand III of Naples, Ferdinand II of Sicily. Born March 10, 1452, at Sos, Aragon; died on January 23, 1516, at Madrigalejo, Spain; son of John II of Aragon and Juana Enríquez of Castile, his second wife; married Isabella I of Castile; married: Germaine de Foix; children—of Ferdinand and Isabella: (one son) John (Juan); (four daughters) Isabella, Joan (Juana), María, Catherine (Catalina). Descendants: Charles V (1519–56) and Philip II (1556–98), the Habsburg emperors of the Holy Roman empire, Spain, and the Netherlands; Mary Tudor (1553–1558), queen of England. Predecessor: John II of Aragon. Successor: Charles V (Charles I of Spain).

1469	Ferdinand and Isabella married
1474	Isabella became queen of Castile
1479	Ferdinand became king of Aragon, Sicily and Sardinia; Treaty of Alcáçovas signed; Portugal renounced claims to Castile
1483	Royal council created to direct Spanish Inquisition
1492	Granada conquered; edict ordering expulsion or conversion of Jews promulgated; Columbus landed in New World
1494	Pope Alexander conferred title Catholic Monarchs on Ferdinand and Isabella; Treaty of Tordesillas between Spain and Portugal established line of demarcation for Spanish and Portuguese claims in Atlantic exploration
1501–02	Edicts ordering expulsion or conversion of Muslims (*Mudéjars*) promulgated
1503–04	Ferdinand conquered Kingdom of Naples; Isabella died; Princess Joan (Juana) inherited Castile with her husband, Philip of Burgundy and Austria
1505	Ferdinand married Germaine de Foix
1506	Philip died
1507	Ferdinand assumed regency of Castile
1512	Annexed Navarre

pursuits including Latin and history, and he developed cultural interests in music and rich adornments. He was also fond of women, fathering an illegitimate child by the time he was 17.

With the death of his elder brother Charles in 1461, Ferdinand became heir to the throne of Aragon. He also had to survive the uncertainties of a decade of civil war and revolt in the province of Catalonia during his minority. In 1468, at age 15, his father proclaimed him king of Sicily, one of Aragon's overseas territories in the Mediterranean. Thus, by the time of his marriage to Isabella in 1469, Ferdinand had gained practical experience in politics and government during this turbulent period.

When Isabella was born in 1451, she also was not expected to rule. She was the daughter of John (Juan) II of Castile and his second wife Isabella of Portugal. Her elder half-brother Henry (Enrique) and younger brother Alfonso ranked above her in the line of succession. Initially, she lived a sheltered life, raised and taught by her mother to prepare for the womanly roles of wife and mother and to lead a virtuous Christian life. Indeed, throughout her life, Isabella had a reputation for her strong Christian faith and purity of moral conduct.

After her father's death in 1454, her half-brother became king of Castile as Henry IV. Because of his weakness as a ruler, factionalism among the strong landholding Castilian nobility grew. Isabella was brought to live at court. By the time she was in her teens, she became a marriage pawn to achieve a favorable situation for the ruling party. Two developments changed Isabella's situation: Henry IV's only child was a daughter Juana whose legitimacy was disputed, and in 1468, when Isabella's younger brother died, Henry IV proclaimed her heir to the throne of Castile.

Isabella and Ferdinand married in October 1469. While a dynastic union between Castile and Aragon seemed logical, its political implications caused opposition in Castile. In fact, Isabella asserted her independence by marrying without Henry IV's consent. The marriage was hastily arranged. Even papal documents of dispensation because of their consanguinity (degree of kinship) had to be forged, and official papal approval did not come until 1471.

The early years of Isabella and Ferdinand's marriage were difficult. In 1470, Henry IV disinherited Isabella and declared that his daughter Juana was legitimate and was the heiress of Castile. The Castilian nobility divided in support of either Isabella or Juana. By early 1474, however, Isabella

Castile and Aragon. In Castile, for example, Galicia and León were to the north with Andalusia, among others, to the south. Aragon had three provinces: Aragon proper, Valencia, and Catalonia, each with distinct institutions of government and language dialects.

The differences that Ferdinand and Isabella experienced in their upbringing were primarily caused by contrasting attitudes to preparing men and women for their respective roles and duties. However, the political turmoil in both Aragon and Castile when Ferdinand and Isabella were young schooled them in important skills of resilience, judgment, and political survival.

As the second son of John (Juan) II of Aragon and his second wife Juana Enríquez of Castile, Ferdinand was not immediately destined to become ruler of Aragon. However, his father's quarrels with his first son Charles (Carlos), and his mother's determined backing, gave Ferdinand a favored position. Although the emphasis in his education was on the martial arts, as a Renaissance prince, he was tutored in humanistic intellectual

and Ferdinand had gained greater support in Castile including control of Segovia whose fortress (*alcázar*) held the royal treasury. When Henry IV died in December 1474, Isabella, who was at Segovia, acted decisively to be proclaimed queen of Castile.

Portugal Surrenders Claims to Castile

Although Isabella and Ferdinand were still in their mid-20s, they had to exert strength and maturity to assert their control over Castile. They used a combination of foreign diplomacy, calculated concessions to the nobility, and armed force to gain the advantage over the disparate factions within Castile. The strongest threat to their rule came when King Afonso of Portugal became engaged to Juana, Henry IV's daughter, who continued to maintain her claim to the Castilian throne. But Ferdinand led forces against the invading Portuguese army, and his victory at the battle of Toro in March 1476 signaled the eventual collapse of the Portuguese cause. By 1479, Portugal capitulated in a series of treaties surrendering all claims to Castile, and Juana, who had never married King Afonso, entered a convent.

That same year marked an important point in Ferdinand and Isabella's reign. With John II of Aragon's death, Ferdinand became ruler of Aragon, Sicily, and Sardinia, and the peace treaty with Portugal brought final recognition of Isabella's rulership in Castile.

Although their dynastic marriage brought together the principal Spanish kingdoms of Castile and Aragon, in governing their lands Isabella and Ferdinand retained much of the separate identity and customs of these territories. They were co-rulers in both Castile and Aragon. However, Isabella had the final powers of decision in Castile while Ferdinand was the primary policy maker in Aragon with Isabella as his consort. This union of Castile and Aragon has been characterized as a loose confederation. Each kingdom maintained its own parliaments (*córtes*), courts, and revenue systems of taxation and coinage. Even customs barriers for trade continued between Castile and Aragon.

The idea of Spanish unity was thus a personal one based on cooperation and understanding between Isabella and Ferdinand as marriage partners. In general, and especially in Castile, Isabella concerned herself more directly with internal working of the government and administration of justice. Ferdinand directed his energies toward foreign affairs and military leadership. However, in both Castile and Aragon, the monarchs acted together on important matters. Their formal concord on signed documents apparently reflected a true ability to work together, to advise and counsel each other, and thus to achieve harmony and accord in their policies and actions.

By 1479, with the consolidation of their positions in Castile and Aragon, Ferdinand and Isabella were able to embark on an ambitious effort to capture the Moorish kingdom of Granada. This campaign was the last stage in the reconquest of the Iberian peninsula from the Muslims. In the eighth century, invading Muslim forces had taken most of Spain except an area in the north. Throughout the Middle Ages, a main theme in Spanish history was the reconquest (*Reconquista*) of these lands from the infidel. By the 15th century, Granada was all that remained of the once extensive Moorish domination of Spain.

From 1478, a series of clashes on the frontier between Castile and Granada broke the truce that had existed between these kingdoms. For over a decade, Spanish forces, directed by Ferdinand, fought for control of Granada. The campaign exploited internal divisions among the ruling family in Granada, as well as armed conflict, particularly sieges of cities, to gain the advantage. Finally in early January 1492, the city of Granada, the last stronghold of the Muslim kingdom, surrendered to Ferdinand and Isabella, adding an important geographical region to the territorial unity of Spain. Completing the *reconquista* also enhanced the prestige of Ferdinand and Isabella in Spain, with the papacy, and throughout Western Europe.

Ferdinand and Isabella also sought to impose their authority over their kingdom through religion. Since the church, including the secular clergy, the monastic orders, and the military orders of Santiago, Calatrava, and Alcántara, controlled sizable amounts of land and exercised significant political power, the two were in part motivated by political and economic considerations. The Catholic Monarchs, however, especially Isabella, also had a genuine concern for religious reform and believed in their responsibility for the spiritual life of their subjects.

Ferdinand and Isabella therefore acted to bring religious uniformity throughout Castile and Aragon. The primary difficulty was that throughout the Middle Ages several religions coexisted in Spain. Besides the Christians, the Islamic faith had been a strong presence, and Jews had enjoyed a greater degree of tolerance than in other parts of Europe. Now Ferdinand and Isabella sought either to expel non-Christians or to convert them.

The Catholic Monarchs adopted two approaches to the problem of religious uniformity. One was conversion to Christianity for Jews and Muslims and a demand for strict adherence to the Christian faith. The principal instrument of this policy was the Spanish Inquisition. Unlike earlier medieval inquisitions against heresy under the aegis of the papacy, Ferdinand and Isabella exercised control of procedures through a royal council known as *la Suprema* and through their appointment of the inquisitor general and other officials. Converted Jews (*conversos*) who might have reverted to Judaism were the primary targets. Under inquisitor generals such as Tomás de Torquemada, the Spanish Inquisition gained a reputation for its harsh methods of trial and punishment, including burning at the stake.

Expulsion was a second way to remove adherents to other religions. After the fall of Granada, Ferdinand and Isabella issued an edict expelling the Jews in March 1492. Then, in 1501, the Muslims or *Mudéjars* were ordered to either convert to Christianity or leave the country. The cumulative outcome of these policies was mixed. Conversion, inquisitions, and expulsion brought religious uniformity, and control over the Spanish church strengthened Ferdinand and Isabella's royal power. On the other hand, the Spanish economy lost many talented merchants, bankers, artisans, and intellectuals. These policies also suppressed the rich cultural diversity (*convivencia*) that had characterized medieval Spain.

Monarchs Back Christopher Columbus

As Ferdinand and Isabella increased their power in Castile and Aragon, they also promoted Spanish interests through their foreign policy. One important area lay across the Atlantic Ocean. Portuguese exploration had opened the possibilities of developing new trade routes to India and the Far East. In 1492, Ferdinand and Isabella backed Christopher Columbus, a Genoese sailor, in his plans to reach the Indies by sailing west across the Atlantic. The result was his famous landing on October 12, 1492, on islands in the Caribbean, which opened the way to Spanish colonization in the New World.

While full development of Spanish colonialism lay in the future, Ferdinand and Isabella concentrated their attention on foreign affairs in Western Europe and the Mediterranean. Ferdinand pursued long-standing interests of the Kingdom of Aragon in south Italy. Aragon already controlled Sicily and Sardinia just off the Italian coast. By 1504, Ferdinand also had secured the Kingdom of Naples.

At this time, alliances among European powers shifted rapidly. Since Ferdinand and Isabella's ambitions usually clashed with those of France, they endeavored to join in alliances that would isolate the French king. Marriage arrangements for their children reflected these diplomatic goals. They created a strong alliance with the Habsburg emperor Maximilian of Austria when their son Prince John married Maximilian's daughter Margaret in 1497 and their daughter Joan married Maximilian's heir Philip in 1496. Another daughter Catherine was betrothed to Prince Arthur, heir of the English king **Henry VII**. Eventually, that same Catherine of Aragon married **Henry VIII** after Arthur's death.

By 1504, Isabella had become seriously ill. At age 54, the strains of monarchy and family had taken their toll on her health. In the early years of her reign, she had to simultaneously secure her rule and bear the burdens of motherhood, giving birth to five children. With no permanent court, she and Ferdinand traveled widely and constantly to impose their power in Castile, Aragon, and later Granada. In a short time, between 1496 and 1500, Isabella suffered several family losses. Her mother died in 1496. Prince John, the heir to Castile and Aragon, died in 1497. In 1498 the death of her eldest daughter Isabella followed by the loss of her grandson Miguel added to her distress. In her already weakened condition, Isabella never recovered from an illness contracted in the summer of 1504; she died on November 26, at Medina del Campo and was buried in Granada.

Isabella's death exposed the fragile personal union of Castile and Aragon. The rule of Castile passed to Isabella's oldest surviving child, Joan, known as "the Mad" (*la loca*) because she suffered from mental illness. Her incapacity to govern allowed the Castilian nobility to assert themselves by dividing their support between Ferdinand or Philip, Joan's husband, as regent. By 1506, Philip had gained the advantage, but he died just after Ferdinand had left Castile for Naples.

When Ferdinand returned to Spain in 1507, he continued to rule Aragon and Castile as he had before Isabella's death. From a second marriage to Germaine de Foix, there had been a possibility of an heir to rule Aragon, but their only son died in infancy. Ferdinand's primary achievement for Spain during his last decade was the annexation of the Kingdom of Navarre in 1512. When he died in 1516, he was buried beside Isabella in Granada.

The Spain that Ferdinand and Isabella had ruled was inherited by their grandson Charles I of Spain (**Charles V**), the Habsburg son of Joan and

Philip. Except for Portugal, the Spanish nation now comprised the entire Iberian peninsula. Although the customs and traditions of the various parts of Spain continued, Ferdinand and Isabella had achieved a more unified state in which Roman Catholic Christianity was a dominant force. Their foreign policy and dynastic marriage had set the stage for Spain to become a world empire in Europe and the Americas. The reign of Ferdinand and Isabella had brought Spain from the end of the Middle Ages to the threshold of the modern era.

SOURCES:

Fernández-Armesto, Felipe. *Ferdinand and Isabella.* Weidenfeld & Nicolson, 1975.

Hillgarth, Jocelyn Nigel. *The Spanish Kingdoms, 1250–1516, Volume II: 1410–1516, Castilian Hegemony.* Oxford University Press, 1978.

Prescott, William H. *History of the Reign of Ferdinand and Isabella.* A. L. Burt, 1838.

FURTHER READING:

Elliott, J. H. *Imperial Spain, 1469–1716.* St. Martin's Press, 1963.

Kamen, Henry. *Spain 1469–1714: A Society in Conflict.* Longman, 1983.

Lynch, John. *Spain Under the Habsburgs, Volume One: Empire and Absolutism, 1516–1598.* Basil Blackwell, 1964.

O'Callaghan, Joseph F. *A History of Medieval Spain.* Cornell University Press, 1975.

Ivan III, the Great

(1440–1505)

Grand Duke of Muscovy and first to call himself tsar, who single-mindedly and methodically mastered all his rivals and laid the foundations for the great Russian Empire.

Born in 1440; died in 1505; son of Basil II, Grand Duke of Muscovy; married: Princess Maria of Tver; married: Sophia (née Zoë Palaeologus; niece of the last Byzantine emperor, Constantine XI); children: two sons, two daughters, including Basil and Elena. Predecessor: his father, Basil II. Successor: his son by Sophia, Basil III.

Under Grand Duke **Basil II** in the mid-15th century, Muscovy was one of several Russian duchies, nominally subservient to the Tatar Khanate of the Golden Horde, and hemmed in by powerful rivals on all sides. The Mongols had invaded in the 13th century, overrunning much of Russia and extorting tribute from the old princes there. Basil managed to shake off the Mongols in all but name by 1452. His son Ivan III completed the recovery of full independence, while his wars on many frontiers paved the way for the expansion of Muscovy and the birth of a united Russia. Ivan III was the first grand duke to make systematic plans for expansion, and he laid the foundations on which Ivan the Terrible and **Peter the Great** could build in the following centuries.

The early years of Ivan's life were precarious for his family. When he was born in 1440, his father was involved in a desperate civil war against a cousin, Dmitri Shemyaka. When Ivan was only five, Grand Duke Basil—his position already weakened by internal conflict—suffered a humiliating defeat at the hands of the Kazan Tatars southeast of Moscow. At the Battle of Suzdal (1445), the Tatars overpowered his army and cap-

"[He was] a statesman of vision and above all of astounding single-mindedness. For Ivan III, more than any of his predecessors or followers on the princely throne of Moscow, knew precisely where he was going."

J. L. I. FENNELL

Contributed by Patrick Allitt, Assistant Professor of History, Emory University, Atlanta, Georgia

tured him. Basil regained his freedom by paying a huge ransom to Khan Ulug-Mahmed, the victor of Suzdal, but no sooner had he returned to Moscow than Dmitri seized and blinded him. Prince Ivan and his younger brother were also seized, and their lives spared only when the primate of the Russian church, Iona of Riazan, interceded for them.

But Dmitri's hold on power proved to be shakier than Basil's; the Duke was set free in 1446 and the two men nominally reconciled. Basil, outwardly conciliatory, plotted revenge. He secured an alliance with Prince Boris of Tver, northwest of Moscow, by betrothing Ivan, then just six years old, to Boris's daughter, Maria. After six years of consolidating his position, in 1452, Basil II was able to defeat Dmitri Shemyaka, who fled for sanctuary to the neighboring duchy of Novgorod. The 1452 campaign was led—in name at least—by the 12-year-old Ivan. Basil was furious with the Duke of Novgorod for sheltering Shemyaka, and arranged to assassinate Shemyaka by poisoning the following year. To complete Basil's revenge, a Moscow army defeated Novgorod in battle and imposed a severe treaty on it. In the same year, Basil for the first time refused payment of tribute to the Golden Horde Khan, his nominal suzerain ("overlord")—a policy which Ivan was to continue.

Little is known of the subsequent years, except that Ivan married Maria of Tver in 1452, sired a son in 1458, and fought a campaign against the Dnieper Tatars in the same year. He succeeded to the Grand Ducal throne in 1462, aged 22, after his father's death from gangrene. Muscovy at that time had not established the principle of primogeniture, by which the oldest son inherited all his father's duchy. Although Ivan received the lion's share, Basil was careful in his will to share almost half of his lands and wealth among his four other sons. Ivan honored the will, but for most of his reign he had to face the anger of his resentful brothers without yielding to them any more than was necessary. More than once they rose in rebellion against him when he refused to share the spoils of victory, so that successes abroad were sometimes vitiated by strife at home.

The scanty records left to us from that era give us only occasional clues to Ivan's personality. One traveler reported:

> He generally drank so excessively at dinner as to fall asleep, and while his guests were all struck with terror and sitting in silence, he would awake, rub his eyes, and then first begin to joke and make merry with them.

CHRONOLOGY

1440	Ivan born
1446	Basil II captured and blinded; Ivan imprisoned
1452	Dmitri Shemyaka defeated and killed
1462	Basil died from gangrene; reign of Ivan began
1467	Wife Maria died
1472	Married Zoë (Sophia) Palaeologus of Byzantium
1471	Ivan's army defeated Novgorod
1478	Final annexation of Novgorod
1480	Golden Horde Khanate defeated and death of Khan-Ahmad
1497	The succession controversy: Sophia and son Basil's plan to poison Dmitri was revealed
1502	Successful intrigues of Sophia and Basil restored Basil (III) to favor and right of succession
1505	Ivan III died

If he was a heavy drinker, he certainly was not reckless politically; each of his advances was preceded by a long period of discussion with his Boyar-Duma ("council") and by careful diplomatic planning.

Much of the first decade of Ivan's reign was dedicated to campaigning on his eastern border, against the Tatars. The Golden Horde no longer enjoyed its former power, and two subsidiary khanates, Kazan and the Crimea, had separated from the older branch. Nevertheless, all three were strong enough to threaten him. Kazan had humiliated his father in 1445, and remained a source of anxiety to Ivan for much of his reign. His large expeditionary force of 1469 was unable to subdue or conquer Kazan once and for all.

Ivan's first wife died in 1467. Although she had been forced on him solely for political reasons, Maria's death caused Ivan genuine regret. He was only 27 at the time, and she had borne him only one son. Like all monarchs of the era, he had to think at once of securing the succession by remarrying, lest he outlive this son and expose the state to a fratricidal succession war. Ivan employed a handful of Italian military and architectural advisors and through one of them he learned that the pope, Paul II, was guardian of a princess who might become his new bride. She was Zoë Palaeologus, a huge woman whose uncle had been the last Byzantine emperor, Constantine XI, when that ancient Empire fell to the Turks in 1452.

The Pope hoped that marrying Zoë to Ivan would create a Moscow-Papal alliance against the Turks, and that he might be able to persuade the Orthodox Russians to convert to Roman Catholicism. Ivan in turn saw the match as a way to enhance his European contacts and enlarge his domestic prestige. His agent, Gian-Battista della Volpe, was in fact a deceitful intriguer who gave the Pope an entirely false picture of Muscovy; it was at that stage far less powerful than Volpe implied, and not in the least tempted by the Roman faith. Nevertheless, the wedding took place in 1472 and Princess Zoë made a stately progress through northern Europe and into Muscovy, where she at once abandoned Catholicism, changed her name to Sophia, and became an observant Orthodox Christian, as she had been in early life.

Ivan was the clear winner of the transaction. "After his remarriage," says historian John Bergamini, "Ivan adopted the Byzantine double eagle for the royal coat of arms, and Byzantine ceremonial was deliberately made the daily routine." But, he adds, "if Byzantine stiffness was to dominate the atmosphere of the court for centuries, its architecture owed less to Constantinople and more to Renaissance Italy." With Ivan's encouragement, the Italian builders who had followed Sophia to Russia turned the Kremlin from a rambling wooden fortress into a magnificent stone palace.

In his dealings with his many neighbors, Ivan was willing to fight when necessary, but like all successful rulers he tried to ensure favorable conditions for war, and never fought if he could get his way through diplomacy. He was also markedly less eager to lead his troops in person than many of his contemporaries. What some chroniclers interpreted as cowardice may have been simple political prudence. In any event, he did not subject himself to unnecessary hazards, and he was able to surround himself with a talented group of commanders. His principal rival in the second decade of his reign was Novgorod, at that time a huge territory to the north and west of Moscow and, having Baltic ports, a gateway to the West.

Ivan's Army Defeats Novgorod

Carrying on where his father had left off in 1456, Ivan claimed Novgorod as a traditional part of his "patrimony," and campaigned against it in 1470–71. Novgorod tried to preserve its independence by allying with its own western neighbor, Lithuania (then of far greater extent than it is today), but unsuccessfully. Lithuanian prince Casimir offered vague gestures of support but never acted on them when the time came. Ivan had ensured that all Novgorod's other potential allies were either neutral, or else allied with him, and after summoning all his soldiers, churchmen, and *boyars* ("noblemen") to a national council of war he set his army in motion. Breaking from custom, which dictated campaigning against Novgorod only in the winter when its marshy lake country would be frozen and permit easy access, this army set out in midsummer. By good fortune 1471 was a drought year, and Ivan's cavalry was able to make easy progress over terrain which would have been impassable in many other years. The army won a decisive victory at the Battle of the Shelon River, overwhelming a larger Novgorod army, many of whose soldiers were reluctant tradesmen pressed into service with no prior military experience.

Following his victory Ivan dictated a treaty whereby Novgorod paid him a large annual tribute and lost all power to make treaties on its own account. An ambiguity in the 1471 treaty led to further friction. Novgorodians agreed that Ivan was their "lord" but denied that he was their "sovereign," and many of the *boyars* argued that he had no legal authority over them except when physically present in Novgorod. To many townspeople, on the other hand, Ivan seemed like a useful counterweight to the imperious lords, and several of them began appealing for his judgments while he was still in Moscow. Faced with rebellious *boyars*, Ivan reinvaded in the autumn and winter of 1478, besieged the city of Novgorod itself, and extorted the recognition of his full sovereignty.

Ivan III responded to scattered rebellions in the following six years by executing or deporting all the principal figures in Novgorodian society to areas around Moscow, and replacing them with his own trusted retainers, who could now enjoy the profits of large estates while keeping their soldiers ready for further wars. Historian George Vernadsky commented on this process: "The historical importance of this mass resettlement for Russian political and social history is tremendous, for in the process of resettlement a new type of conditional landholding was created, the kind of military fief known as pomestie. [The settlers] received land to enable them to perform their duties as army officers, and held it conditional on their service to the state" and not as private property. *Pomestie* permitted Ivan III to maintain effective armies at low cost and to ensure internal political stability by tying land tenure to personal loyalty and service. The annexation of Novgorod was probably the most crucial step in Muscovy's rise since it transformed a hitherto landlocked duchy into a state with ports on the Baltic Sea.

The Tatar khanates to Ivan's south and east remained powerful threats throughout Ivan's reign, particularly the Golden Horde under Khan Ahmad, which was still partially nomadic but centered around the Volga River. Ahmad attacked Russia in 1472, moving northwest in the hope of linking up with his ally Prince Casimir of Lithuania. Casimir was no more help to Ahmad than he had been to Novgorod, however, and the campaign fizzled. Ivan was able to play the rival khanates against one another, and reacted to Ahmad's attack by forming an alliance with the Crimean Khanate, west of the Golden Horde. Although he was a defender of the Orthodox Church in Moscow, which had become independent of the Constantinople Patriarch since the fall of Constantinople, Ivan was always ready to deal with non-Christians in his foreign policy, and to extend religious toleration to all his subjects, a policy which facilitated his diplomacy. He faced a more serious invasion from Ahmed in 1480 but managed to hold off the attack, and was pleased to learn that Tatar rivals had assassinated Ahmad the following year. Although Ivan never paid tribute to the Khans he still had to levy taxes on his own subjects in order to buy lavish gifts for his Tatar allies, and the whole of his southern boundary remained vulnerable. Nevertheless, 1480 is the traditional date given in Russian history for the end of the "Tatar Yoke."

Ivan's next step in the east was his role in a family dispute among the Tatar rulers of Kazan. Taking the side of one claimant, Mohammed-Amin, against Khan Ilgam, he welcomed Mohammed-Amin to his court in 1486 and led an expeditionary force against Ilgam's capital the next year. After a 52-day siege, Kazan fell, Ilgam surrendered his title, and Mohammed-Amin became khan as a vassal of Ivan III. This new security in the east compensated Ivan for the rise of Turkish power in the Crimea to his south. Turkish officials there extorted large duties and bribes from Russian merchants, and prompted Ivan to send an envoy to the Turkish Sultan Bayazit explaining his grievances. The envoy was under strict orders not to abase Ivan before the Sultan, and this successful violation of Ottoman court protocol, at a time when such matters carried immense symbolic significance, was a significant step in demonstrating Ivan's growing power as an independent monarch.

Victories over Novgorod, Kazan, and the Golden Horde enabled Ivan in the later decades of his reign to turn his attention westward, where power was shifting in intricate ways, due primarily to the rise of Turkey. Ivan negotiated with the Holy Roman Emperor, with Hungary, and with Poland in an effort to assure himself of as much diplomatic stability as the volatile area permitted. From Hungary, he also imported mining engineers to begin exploiting Russian mineral assets. The most significant development was a treaty with Lithuania, signed in 1494, which he secured by marrying his daughter Elena to the Lithuanian grand duke Aleksandr. For the first time, Ivan wrote into the treaty that his title was now "Sovereign of All Russia." It was hardly a match made in heaven. Under orders from her father, Elena refused to relinquish her Orthodox faith for that of her Catholic husband. Aleksandr continued to negotiate with Ivan's enemies, including the Teutonic Knights of Livonia, on the eastern Baltic shore, and in 1500, Ivan declared war against his son-in-law. Despite his careful preparations, including an alliance with Denmark, Ivan found himself without help in the war against Lithuania and Livonia. Fighting with the odds against it, Ivan's well-disciplined army won a shattering victory at the Vedrosha River on July 14, 1500, and overran much of eastern Lithuania. In the six-year armistice signed between the two rulers three years later, Ivan kept possession of all the areas currently held by his forces. Once more his boundaries expanded.

Ivan Takes the Name of Tsar

The vast extension of his domains, and his concentration of power at home, obliged Ivan to overhaul his system of government. In 1497, he promulgated a general code of laws, the *Sudebnik,* divided the nobility up into carefully graded ranks, settled government affairs among departments, and elaborated a code of court etiquette to go with his new dignity. He was the first grand duke to take the name of tsar (derived from the Roman and Byzantine term Caesar) and he also claimed that Russia was "the Third Rome," successor to Rome and Byzantium, and destined for immortality.

Despite his successes in war and diplomacy, Ivan faced a severe conflict at home. After giving birth to two daughters Duchess Sophia, his second wife, bore Ivan a son, Basil, in 1479. In 1490, Ivan's son by his first wife died, leaving a wife, Elena, and a boy, Dmitri, then aged six. The rest of Ivan III's reign witnessed an ugly intrigue between Sophia and Elena, each of whom schemed to place her son on the throne; their feud was all the deadlier because no strong principle of succession gave either of them clear precedence. Ivan found it difficult to make up his mind on the question of which boy to favor, son or grandson, but his court and the church polarized into antagonistic factions. Ivan had already imprisoned one of his recalcitrant brothers, Andrei Senior, and left him to die in jail in 1493, which showed that he was willing to act forcefully against his kin. In 1497, he discovered that his wife and son, Sophia and Basil, were involved in a conspiracy to poison Dmitri, their rival. Ivan executed the ringleaders (most of them former friends of Andrei Senior and advocates of Russian federation, rather than the growing autocracy). Basil and Sophia's lives were spared but they lived under close surveillance and in disgrace for the next few years.

Dmitri was installed as co-ruler with his grandfather in 1498, victorious at least for the moment. His triumph did not last. Sophia gradually persuaded Ivan that the ministers who had condemned Basil and herself, led by Prince Ivan Patrikeev, were not really loyal to Ivan and had slandered them for personal gain. Luckily for Sophia, her attempt to recover credit coincided with a squabble over foreign policy between Ivan and Patrikeev, making the Grand Duke more receptive to the idea of betrayal than he would otherwise have been. In 1502, he rehabilitated Sophia and raised his son to a ducal title. After a two-year standoff in which both young men had the title of heir, Basil gained full ascendancy over his father; Dmitri was disgraced, and suffered a prolonged house arrest with his mother Elena.

Among Basil's party in the previous decade had been Russia's conservative churchmen, who resented Ivan's effort to expropriate their estates. Ivan wanted the land to increase his *pomestie* system of offering estates in exchange for military service. This thirst for land had prompted him to take a sympathetic view of some church reformers who inveighed against clerical wealth and denied that the church needed its vast estates. Now that Basil was raised in dignity, the conservative churchmen had a supporter almost equal to Ivan, and one who seemed certain to succeed. Through him they protested more forcefully than ever before and brought Ivan's seizures to a halt. Basil showed his growing influence by approving the conservatives' plan to burn at the stake several of the leading reformers. As Ivan's life drew to a close in 1505, he realized that he had lost control of affairs and that Basil (III) was already the sole effective ruler. Just before Ivan died later that year, he witnessed the marriage of Basil to the daughter of a Moscow *boyar*. This couple would soon produce an heir whom we remember as Ivan the Terrible.

Ivan's death left Russia as a growing power on the borders of Europe and Asia. His reign and his consolidation of the state had coincided with those of other nation-builders: **Ferdinand and Isabella of Spain, Henry VII** of England, and **Louis XI** of France. Despite his negotiations with the German emperor and the kings of Denmark and Turkey, however, Russia was still vastly remote from the theater of European affairs, and not until two more centuries had passed, in the days of Peter the Great, would Russia become a major contender in the contest for European supremacy.

SOURCES:

Bergamini, John D. *The Tragic Dynasty: A History of the Romanovs.* Putnam, 1969.

Dukes, Paul. *A History of Russia.* Macmillan, 1990.

Fennell, J. L. I. *Ivan the Great of Moscow.* London: Macmillan, 1961.

Vernadsky, George. *Russia at the Dawn of the Modern Age.* Yale University Press, 1968.

Ivan IV, the Terrible

(1530–1584)

Tsar and Autocrat of All the Russias, who conquered vast regions, wrote poetry, composed music, designed churches, and murdered thousands in order to create the modern Russian state.

"The tragedies of his reign have their source in his childhood fears and... terrors."

ROBERT PAYNE
AND
NIKITA ROMANOFF

Ivan IV inherited a seemingly peaceful land on the western fringes of Asia; at the time of his death, he bequeathed a nation in turmoil and ruin that was the eastern outpost of Europe.

Ivan's grandfather, **Ivan III, the Great** (1462–1505), had forced the other sovereign princes to recognize his rule, but he had to pay annual tribute to the Tatar Khan of Kazan. Ivan III changed Muscovy's direction when he married Sophia Palaelogus, granddaughter of Byzantine emperor Manuel II. Sophia arrived in Moscow in November 1472, bringing with her artisans skilled in masonry, metal work, and the casting of cannon. During the next 12 years, she bore three daughters and five sons, the eldest being Basil, born in 1479.

Some years later, Tsar Basil III (1505–33), had a childless marriage and divorced his wife against church objections. In January 1526, he married Helena Glinskaia, ward of Mikhail Glinski, a Lithuanian mercenary who had migrated to Moscow after years of service in Germany. On August 25, 1530, Helena gave birth to a son, Ivan, and, a year later, to another son, Yuri; rumors circulated that Helena had a lover. At 54, Vasili was old, his wife young, and their sons infants. In

Name variations: Ivan IV "Grozni," Grand Duke of Muskovy (Ivan is the Russian form of John, the Latin form of Ioannes). Born August 25, 1530; son of Basil III and Helen Glinskaia; married: Anastasia Romanovna; married: Maria (daughter of a Circassian prince); married: third wife, October 28, 1571; married: fourth wife, December 1571; married: seventh wife, Maria Nagaia, 1581; children: (first marriage) Dmitri, Ivan Ivanovich, Fedor (Fyodor); (second marriage) Dmitri (Demetrius). Predecessor: Basil III. Successor: Fedor I.

Contributed by J. Lee Shneidman, Professor of History, Adelphi University, Garden City, New York

1530	Ivan born
1533	Became Grand Prince at age three
1547	Crowned Grand Prince, Tsar and Autocrat of All the Russias; fires set in Moscow; revolt led by the Shuiski faction; Ivan formed council to reorganize Russia
1549	Gathering of the *Zemski Sobor*
1552	Began seige against Kazan; entered Kazan and liberated 100,000 Russian slaves
1558	Invaded Livonia
1562	Alliance formed with Denmark against Poland-Lithuania and Sweden
1563	Russian army seized Lithuanian fortress of Polotsk; Ivan suffered a series of personal losses
1564	Russian force defeated at Ula; Tatars sacked Riazan; Ivan signed a truce with Sweden; abandoned Moscow; divided Russia into two states; returned to Moscow
1566	Aborted coup with mass arrests and executions
1571	Moscow pillaged and burned
1572	Tatars crushed; Ivan hailed as savior; reign of terror
1579	Stephen Batory recaptured Polotsk
1581	Ivan killed the Tsarevich
1582	Truce with Batory
1584	Ivan died

remained helpless. Shortly thereafter, Andrei Shuiski, a leading *boyar,* married a granddaughter of Ivan III and moved into a Kremlin apartment. Since his power extended to the church, Metropolitan Daniel (Bishop of Moscow) fled to Grand Prince Ivan's bedroom for protection, but he was dragged away and replaced by Metropolitan Osip. When Osip objected to Shuiski's practice of throwing his opposers into the dungeon and starving them to death, he too was arrested and replaced by Metropolitan Makari (Macarius). The royal boys were but prisoners behind the stone walls of the gilded Kremlin; Ivan later recalled the period well: "What suffering did I not endure through lack of clothing and through hunger."

Overconfident, the Shuiskis did not suspect an opposition plot developing as the Grand Prince approached puberty. On December 29, 1543, when Shuiski appeared before Ivan without his usual armed retainers, Ivan ordered his arrest. Shuiski was then strangled, and his body was thrown to the hounds. Ivan appointed his grandmother, Anna Glinskaia, and her sons to govern in his name while he and Yuri enjoyed the lives of teenagers. But Ivan did more than ride to the hunt. Under the direction of Metropolitan Makari, who had a massive manuscript collection, Ivan began to read history, literature, and theology. What interested him was the world beyond Muscovy (Moscow), especially the world of his Byzantine grandmother Sophia.

An attractive youth—five-foot-ten, thin, and bright eyed—the time arrived for Ivan to be crowned and wed. He entered Red Square and spoke to the people: "During my dreary childhood I was blind and deaf to the people's suffering. I did not give an ear to the cries of the poor." Then, turning to the *boyars,* "You boyars did as you pleased, you were rebels and unjust judges."

Ivan Crowned, Begins Reorganization

Returning to the Kremlin, Ivan rummaged through the pages of Byzantine history and through the regalia in the treasury until he found what he was seeking. His coronation was to be unlike any previous; it would be Byzantine. On January 16, 1547, the teenager became Grand Prince, Tsar and Autocrat of All the Russias—an open challenge not only to the *boyars,* but also to other European rulers as Ivan claimed to be the equal of Emperor **Charles V** and **Suleiman the Magnificent.** Until he destroyed *boyar* power, and the rulers of Europe recognized his imperial title, the coronation appeared but a magnificent charade. At the time, Russia—as it was slowly coming

October of 1533, he developed a boil that would not heal, and a Regency Council chaired by Mikhail Glinski was formed to prevent Basil's brothers from seizing the throne. When Basil died on December 4, the three-year-old Ivan was proclaimed Grand Prince, and the power struggle began.

"The *boyars* [nobles] are at each other's throats," wrote a Polish spy. Within months Helena and her lover, Prince Ivan Obolenski, seized power. During the next three years, Mikhail and Basil's brothers were arrested, imprisoned, and starved to death. The *boyars* objected, but for little Ivan and his deaf-mute brother this was the happiest period of their lives; Helena, Obolenski, and the boys' nanny, Obolenski's sister Agrafina, doted on them. But the joy ended April 3, 1538, when Helena died of either a heart attack or poison.

Within days Obolenski and his sister were imprisoned while the sobbing Grand Prince

to be called—was larger than any European polity except the Ottoman Empire, but its population of less than ten million was no larger than Spain's, a country only a fraction of its size; technologically, it was behind both the Ottoman Empire and European states.

On February 3, 1547, Ivan married Anastasia Romanovna, daughter of a non-titled landowner, offending the princes who considered her family nothing more than "slaves." Two months later, on April 12, a fire broke out in Moscow but was extinguished quickly. The following week another fire erupted in a different section. It too was extinguished but with more difficulty. Then, on June 21, fires erupted all over the city. Before the disaster ended, Moscow lost 2,000 lives and 25,000 homes, and more than 80,000 people were left homeless. Led by the Shuiski faction, the populace revolted on June 26, blaming the Glinskis for the catastrophe. Left without a choice, Ivan had to exile his grandmother and allow the mob to do as they willed with her sons.

The Shuiskis thought that the removal of the Glinskis would restore power to the Boyar Council (*Duma*) which they dominated. Ivan, however, began seeking allies among the friends of Metropolitan Makari. By November 1547, he had his "Chosen Council," an unofficial group of advisors led by the priest Daniil Silvestr and Alexei Adashev. Ivan and the Council began to reorganize Russia, thus beginning a dozen years of political, economic, and artistic growth.

Russia had to be both opened to the West and restructured internally. The former would be difficult, as Ivan discovered when he learned that German officials had prevented the exit of a group of technicians hired for work in Russia; the latter would be difficult because of *boyar* opposition. To counter the *boyars*, Ivan summoned a national council, or *Zemski Sobor*, which gathered on February 27, 1549. Four days later, he entered Red Square and explained to the populace the need for reforms. Backed by the people, the *Zemski Sobor*: (1) restricted the rights of boyar officials in the provinces; (2) established new state officers; (3) created the *Streltsy* ("imperial troops armed with muskets"); (4) allowed the Tsar to appoint field commanders without regard to noble lineage; and (5) prohibited a father from selling either his children or himself into slavery to pay off a debt. It was also agreed that 1,000 new officials would receive estates around Moscow as payment for their service. The following year, the Tsar summoned a church council which confirmed the *Zemski Sobor*'s laws and also agreed to prohibit land grants to the church without imperial approval.

Having instituted the first stage of reforms, Ivan gathered his army and moved against neighboring Kazan, a Tatar stronghold on the Volga east of Moscow. Brushing aside another Tatar force from the Crimea, Ivan reached Kazan and, by August 13, 1552, began the seige. With the aid of new cannons, the fire power of the *Streltsy,* and Danish engineers who sapped the citadel's walls, Ivan entered Kazan on October 2, liberating 100,000 Russian slaves. By the end of the month, the Tsar was back in Moscow where he was hailed as *Grozni* ("Awe Inspiring") and was able to hold the infant son born while he was at Kazan.

To celebrate the conquest of Kazan, Ivan ordered the building of a new cathedral. Italian and Russian architects listened to the Tsar whose fantasy was to be translated into what eventually became St. Basil's. Other churches were built in bold new styles, and the Kremlin was decorated with new frescoes and icons while the Tsar composed hymns for the church and ordered the building of Russia's first printing press. A new crown was made, a new throne constructed, all to glorify the might of the young Tsar.

Then, on March 1, 1553, Ivan took ill. Hoping that he would die, many *boyars* encouraged his cousin, Vladimir Andreevich, to seize the throne. When the bedridden Tsar demanded that the *boyars* swear to support his infant son, Dmitri, many refused; even the Chosen Council was reluctant to permit Anastasia and her family to be regents. When Ivan did not die, many of Vladimir's supporters fled the country, even though the Chosen Council convinced Ivan to pardon all those who had refused to support Dmitri. In June, when the Tsar took his family on a pilgrimage of thanksgiving, Dmitri fell into a river and drowned. The royal family returned to Moscow in tears; within a year, however, Anastasia had a new heir, Ivan Ivanovich.

During the next half-decade, Ivan continued reforms which made him popular with the lower and middle classes; completed the annexation of the entire Volga region; had a brief war with Sweden (1554–57), which gave Russia a small port near present-day St. Petersburg; organized profitable raids into Crimean territory, enlarged the imperial army, and opened trade negotiation with England via the White Sea.

On January 22, 1558, over the objections of the Chosen Council, Ivan invaded Livonia (Latvia and Estonia), whose German rulers had prevented foreign artisans from reaching Russia. By mid-July imperial forces occupied Narva and Dorpat, sending booty and prisoners back to Moscow. As the

Council had warned, the Tatars saw that the army was occupied elsewhere and attacked in February of 1559. But Ivan, having foreseen such an event, dispatched troops south not only to defeat the intruders but to launch a series of profitable raids deep within Crimean territory. With imperial forces engaged in a two-front war, King **Zygmunt Augustus** of Poland-Lithuania proclaimed himself protector of Livonia and, in September 1559, demanded the evacuation of all Russian forces from Livonia. Deciding to intervene, Sweden and Denmark partitioned Livonia.

When Anastasia died on August 7, 1560, something within Ivan snapped. Wailing, he followed the coffin to the crypt. According to one chronicler, the Tsar began to run "along the broad highway that leads to Hell," convinced that his wife had been murdered in a plot by the *boyars,* who also must have murdered his mother and his uncles and who were now plotting against him and his sons Ivan and Fedor (born 1557). Seized by paranoia, Ivan had members of the Chosen Council tried, convicted, and exiled.

On August 21, 1561, Ivan married Maria, daughter of a Circassian prince, who arrived in Moscow with an entourage of Circassian and Tatar nobles. Representatives of the Patriarch of Constantinople also arrived and announced recognition of Ivan's imperial title.

For the next two years, the Tsar's success continued. Laws were promulgated, limiting princely power on their estates; an alliance was formed with Denmark against Poland-Lithuania and Sweden; and the Russian army, led in part by Circassians and Tatars, seized the Lithuanian fortress of Polotsk. Then came a series of deaths in 1563: on May 4, Maria's two-month-old son died, followed on November 24 by Ivan's beloved brother Yuri, followed on December 31 by Metropolitan Makari. As the Tsar's paranoia returned, charges of treason flew and princes fled the country. In January 1564, a Russian force was defeated at Ula. Ivan ordered arrests, while drowning himself in drink and debauchery. In October, the Tatars sacked Riazan, and Ivan signed a truce with Sweden surrendering territory. More arrests and more debauchery followed.

On December 3, 1564, Ivan and his family abandoned Moscow. One month later, he informed the Muscovites that *boyar* treason had forced him to leave: "My body has grown feeble," he said, "my physical and mental scars multiply. I expected someone to be sorry for me, but no one has been. I have found no one to console me." Though the words were those of a 35-year-old

Tsar, the feelings seemed to be those of a little boy who had long ago been abused by the Shuiskis. Ivan divided Russia into two states: the *Oprichnina* ("the part of the father's estate reserved for the widow") was Ivan's section and would be ruled as he wished; the rest, the *Zemschina* (*Zemshtshina*), would be ruled by the *Boyar Duma.*

On February 2, 1565, Ivan returned to Moscow and 1,000 servitors were settled on lands confiscated from the boyars. A year later, Ivan summoned a *Zemski Sobor* which ratified all his policies. Still wanting his cousin Vladimir as ruler, some princes, encouraged by Zygmunt, plotted a coup. When Ivan's spies reported the treason, mass arrests and executions followed. In terror, Ivan asked **Elizabeth I** of England for asylum; she assured him that he would "be friendly received in our dominions." Fortunately, the Danes prevented the Poles, Lithuanians, and Swedes from taking advantage of the turmoil.

When Maria died on September 1, 1569, paranoia reigned. Vladimir was forced to drink poison, while the cities of Novgorod and Pskov were sacked because the citizens were suspected of being part of a plot. All and everything that had failed to protect Ivan when his mother died was to be destroyed. The population of central Russia was moved to the periphery to make room for the people from the periphery who were moving into the center. Many Russians fled of their own accord. Then, on July 25, 1570, Ivan ordered the people to gather outside Moscow. Dressed in battle armor, he asked their approval for his actions. The people "shouted their approval," and 116 *boyars* were executed.

Moscow Is Pillaged

With the government in disarray, the Tatars struck. On May 24, 1571, Moscow was pillaged and burned, and 100,000 Russians were led away as slaves for the marts in the south. The *Oprichnina* had failed to provide security.

Ivan took wife number three on October 28, 1571; she died 16 days later. Witchcraft and "evil spells," he charged, but he sought no executions. His fourth wife followed in December, though only three marriages were permitted under Canon Law. Ivan had made his point—he could do as he willed. The *Oprichnina* was officially disbanded and incorporated into the *Zemschina,* although Ivan still owned all the *Oprichnina* lands. The Tatars returned to conquer Russia, and for a month the horde devastated southern Russia while the imperial army gathered. On August 21, 1572, the armies clashed at Molodi, about 30 miles from Moscow, and the Tatars were crushed. Ivan was hailed as Russia's savior.

Word arrived that Zygmunt had died and that some Lithuanian nobles wanted Ivan's second son Fedor as their king. "Haunted by the fear of total betrayal," Ivan used the opportunity to provoke a war with Sweden and resume a reign of terror. Wives, mistresses, and even male lovers came and went, but nothing could bring peace to the tormented tormentor. On September 1, 1575, Ivan abdicated, appointing Simeon Bekbulatovich, a descendant of **Genghis Khan,** ruler, while he became "Ivan the Little, Prince of Moscow."

Full-scale terror ran through the heart of Russia, and Ivan "The Awe Inspiring" became Ivan "The Terrible." On his *Oprichnina* lands, all opposition—princes, boyars, relatives, officials, merchants, members of the *Oprichnina*, clerics— was exiled or murdered, as the land became increasingly depopulated. After sending Simeon packing to Tver on September 1, 1576, Ivan resumed the imperial title.

Having established a solid autocratic government on his personal lands, Ivan needed the imperial title to deal with foreign affairs. Military victories and terrifying violence continued throughout 1577, but there was a shadow lurking on the steppe; the Poles had elected Stephen Báthory as king. A vigorous general, Báthory was willing to reach an understanding with the Ottomans in order to crush Russia. By the fall of 1578, he occupied most of Livonia and, in the summer of 1579, recaptured Polotsk and was prepared to march on Moscow.

Ivan Kills His Son

Ivan used the dangers to restructure the tax system and confiscate some church lands. Without success he sought alliances with Pope Gregory XIII, Emperor **Rudolph II,** and Elizabeth I. In 1581, he married wife number seven, Maria Nagaia, though the Church had stopped counting at number three. In September of the same year, Báthory besieged Pskov while the Swedes occupied Narva. Ivan, however, did nothing. Even the conquest of Sibir on October 26 did not seem to interest him. When his son and heir, Ivan Ivanovich, demanded the right to lead imperial troops to relieve Pskov, Ivan clobbered him in fury with the royal scepter. The enormity of the crime struck. Wailing, he tried to stop the blood with his hands. Three days later, on November 19, 1581, the Tsarevich died.

Ivan lamented, tore his hair, wore sackcloth. Frequently breaking down in hysterical tears, he never recovered. Eighty percent of central Russia was depopulated, but he seemed to await nothing but death. Not even the birth of a new son, Dmitri, on October 19, 1582, made any impact. A truce with Báthory had been signed on January 15, 1582, and with Sweden on August 5, 1582. All Russian gains in the West were lost. The Tsar—the century's most accomplished Russian writer—spent his time composing the *Sinodik*, a list of people he had murdered. The lists were sent to monasteries with gifts so that the priests and monks could pray for the victims' souls.

A Council was created for the heir, Fedor. On March 18, 1584, after taking a steam bath and being rubbed with mercury ointment for his sores, the Tsar dressed and summoned his loyal friends. A chess set was brought, and Ivan began to set up the pieces. He fumbled, then fell back dead.

Ivan had changed Russia. Though his attempt to secure a window on the Baltic had failed, he had maintained a port on the White Sea and had begun the conquest of northern Asia. Russia was in economic ruin, but it was no longer possible to challenge the will of the Tsar. Some old titles remained, and even some of the old appanage families appeared as servitors, but a new class had risen to govern Russia, a class completely dependent upon the Tsar's will. As weak as Russia was, she was part of the European political system and not a tributary of an Asian horde. Some historians have viewed Ivan's reign as a failure, but for the little boy subject to the caprice of the Shuiskis, his was a successful reign. Aristocrats called him "The Terrible." But in folk tales, Ivan IV was *Grozni,* "The Awe Inspiring."

SOURCES:

Berry, L. E. and R. O. Crummey, eds. *Rude & Barbarous Kingdom.* University of Wisconsin Press, 1968.

Carr, Francis. *Ivan the Terrible.* Barnes & Noble, 1981.

Eckardt, Hans von. *Ivan the Terrible.* Translated by C. A. Phillips. Knopf, 1949.

Graham, Stephen. *Ivan the Terrible.* Archon, 1968.

The Moscovia of Antonio Possevino, S.J. Translated by H. F. Graham. University of Pittsburgh Press, 1977.

Payne, Robert and Nikita Romanoff. *Ivan the Terrible.* Crowell, 1975.

Platonov, S. F. *Ivan the Terrible.* Edited and translated by J. L. Wieczynski. Academic International Press, 1974.

Skrynnikov, R. G. *Ivan the Terrible.* Edited and translated by H. F. Graham. Academic International Press, 1981.

Staden, Heinrich von. *The Land and Government of Muscovy.* Edited and translated by T. Esper. Stanford University Press, 1967.

Vernadsky, George. *The Tsardom of Moscow, 1547–1682.* Yale University Press, 1969.

FURTHER READINGS:

Keenan, Edward L. *The Kurbsky-Grozni Apocrypha.* Harvard University Press, 1971.

Perrie, Maureen. *The Image of Ivan the Terrible in Russian Folklore.* Cambridge University Press, 1987.

Yanov, Alexander. *The Origins of Autocracy: Ivan the Terrible in Russian History.* Translated by S. Dunn. University of California Press, 1981.

James I

(1566–1625)

King of England (and Scotland), who brought the British Isles peace, provided dynastic security, and brought order to the English church, but whose successes were overshadowed by scandal and constitutional clashes.

"Instead of approaching the reign with the idea that James was a Bad King, it is more fruitful to see him as an exceptional man whose qualities fell sadly short of their highest achievement."

S. J. HOUSTON

Queen Elizabeth, speaking on the subject of marriage, prayed that God would send the royal line an heir "that may be a fit governor, and per adventure more beneficial to the realm than such offspring as may come of me." When her Scottish cousin succeeded in 1603, most Englishmen would have acknowledged that Elizabeth's prayer had been answered. If ever there was a man who should have been prepared to ascend the throne of England, it was James VI, king of Scotland for all but the first of his 37 years.

James was the only child of **Mary, Queen of Scots** and her cousin Henry Stewart, Lord Darnley. Though both were tall and handsome and their veins flowed with Tudor blood, they were not a loving couple. If an unborn child can be said to suffer from psychological trauma, James would have been a candidate; three months before his birth, his mother felt the steel blade of a knife held against her belly as she was forced to watch the barbaric stabbing-murder of her secretary, David Rizzio.

Mary had reason to be afraid. Because her death—and that of her unborn son—would have strengthened her husband's claim to the English

Contributed by Robert Blackey, Professor of History, California State University, San Bernardino, California

Name variations: James VI of Scotland; originally James Stewart (Scottish spelling) or James Stuart (English spelling). Born June 19, 1566, in Edinburgh Castle; died at Theobalds, near Hatfield, on March 27, 1625; only child of Mary, Queen of Scots and Henry Stuart, Lord Darnley; married: Anne of Denmark; children: (three sons) Henry, Charles, and Robert; (four daughters) Elizabeth, Margaret, Mary, and Sophia. Predecessor: Elizabeth I. Successor: Charles I.

a powerful and a divisive force, and although the country was officially Protestant, many Scots were still Catholic.

In spite of having these handicaps as his inheritance, James would do surprisingly well during his more than three decades as king of Scotland—even making the monarchy stronger—but the royal path he would follow was never carpeted in red. The first regent who was to govern until the child-king came of age was assassinated in 1570. The next occupied the position for a year before being mortally wounded during a civil insurrection; little James, stunned, witnessed the actual dying. A third regent died of natural causes the following year, while the fourth, and last, survived for a decade before being executed for his earlier complicity in Darnley's death.

By the start of the final regency, James was almost seven years old. Emotional stability was a stranger to him, and he had no memories of his parents. Those who had cared for him included an alcoholic wet nurse and a harsh senior tutor who nonetheless enlightened the bright young boy in the classics, science, languages, and religious studies.

The young king, on the basis of the good looks of Mary and Darnley, might have been handsome. James, however, had sad, watery, and droopy blue eyes; dark hair; a long fleshy nose; and thin lips that dipped at the corners. Of average height with broad shoulders, he possessed a pear-shaped body that was supported by spindly, bent legs. While he played some golf, the royal game of Scotland, he mostly preferred hunting because the powerful legs of his steed transformed him into a gallant centaur. But on the ground, he eventually had to depend on the physical support of courtiers. (He tried strengthening his legs by bathing them in the bellies of freshly killed stags and bucks, but to no avail.) A hostile contemporary observed that when James ate and drank he made a distasteful, splashing noise, like a Great Dane, dribbling liquids into his beard because his tongue was too big for his mouth.

This undistinguished, sometimes comical-looking man grew up in a loveless environment, and the need to love and be loved was apparently strong in him. When James was 13, an older and elegant French cousin arrived in Scotland, and the adolescent king fell in love; this, perhaps, set a pattern whereby he would link sexual love with men. In other matters, James gained political acumen; he was a quick study and had a retentive memory. But to this portrait must be added another brush stroke. As an adult, and especially in the last decade or so

succession, he was one of the conspirators in this calculated attempt to shock his pregnant wife. The fatal attack on Rizzio intensified Mary's hatred of Darnley. Also linked to this episode were damaging stories that David Rizzio had been the queen's lover and thus James's real father. (James would be haunted by such rumors into adulthood; even his contemporary, **Henri IV** of France, who called James "the wisest fool in Christendom," fueled the rumors by joking about James being the modern-day Solomon he believed himself to be since he also was the son of a David.)

Following Darnley's murder in 1567—in which she was said to have been involved—and her imprudent marriage to the suspected murderer, James Hepburn, earl of Bothwell, Mary, Queen of Scots was forced to abdicate in favor of her 11-month-old son, now James VI. Curiously, Scotland had not had an adult succession since the 14th century. The Stewart dynasty, as the name suggests, had risen from the position of royal stewards via the marriage of the sixth of the Great Stewards to the daughter of **Robert the Bruce**. With many among the Scottish nobility related to the monarchy, the Stewarts (or Stuarts, as the English spelled the name) were seen, at best, as only first among equals. Thus there was nothing sacrosanct about the royal family, especially since the monarchy was short of funds and unable to pay for an army of its own. Moreover, the nobility were both

of his life, James apparently suffered from porphyria, a disease he inherited from his mother and which was eventually passed along to the Hanoverians where it would be responsible for the symptoms identified with the madness of George III. Porphyria means "purple urine" and refers to the most obvious sign of the ailment which results from a pigment discoloration in the blood. The disease weakened and incapacitated James for periods of time, and it made him irritable and melancholy. According to some medical historians, James's need for close friends and favorites on whom he could depend and to whom he could delegate state business may be explained more by his frequent bouts with porphyria than on deficiencies of character. In any case, these diverse ingredients formed his character, and the result was a man who was a curious collage of self-confidence and self-indulgence housed in a less-than-glorious frame.

James Marries Young Anne of Denmark

The late 16th century was a time when Europeans were making increasing contacts with the world around them, but James remained an insular man. He did, however, have one overseas adventure, and a romantic one at that: in 1589, he traveled to Norway to rescue his wife-to-be, the 14-year-old Anne of Denmark, from the frozen grip of ice and snow that had stalled her journey to Scotland. Golden-haired, white-skinned, tall, slender and attractive, she was waiting for her prince to come. Into the Oslo palace lumbered James, "boots and all." Though married a few days later, James's love for Anne quickly faded. Drifting apart, though not before seven children were born, they eventually stopped living together. When Anne died in 1619, James did not even attend her funeral.

Throughout his rule in Scotland James VI had to mediate between and contest with religious groups as well as with noble factions. Ultimately he succeeded in bringing about a new respect for law and order, mostly by securing the cooperation of the nobility. He also had to keep foreign interferences at bay while always retaining Queen **Elizabeth**'s goodwill so as not to jeopardize his succession. And James had to deal with both the real threat of occasional attempts on his life and the perceived threat of spiritual violence from the witches he—and most of society—believed existed. All this fed his paranoia, and James came to see himself as "an experienced king needing no lessons."

He also came to believe that the sovereign had an individual right, derived from God, to his throne. This was a hereditary right, as James wrote in a 1598 treatise, *Trew Law of Free Monarchies,* and even a tyrannical king had inalienable rights over his people because he had been sent by God. In Scotland, this doctrine was pronounced, not practiced, but James would soon bring it with him to England. And once he crossed Hadrian's Wall, the doctrine was regularly paraded before the people's representatives in Parliament and the judges at the bar:

> The state on monarchy is the supremest thing upon earth; for kings are not only God's lieutenants upon earth and sit upon God's throne, but even by God himself they are called gods... [1610].

While the people of two nations waited for an old queen to die, Robert Cecil, Elizabeth's chief minister, secretly corresponded with James for two years and tried to instruct the heir apparent in the art of becoming king of England. (Unfortunately, the smooth succession that followed served only to reinforce James's theories on divine right.) Several days after Elizabeth died, King James VI of Scotland, now England's King James I, began a journey that was, as Dr. Samuel Johnson wrote in the 18th century while reflecting on England's everpresent sense of self-importance, "the noblest prospect which a Scotchman ever sees... the high road that leads him to England."

James I was on that high road for a month before reaching London. The journey itself witnessed other events which seemed to presage future problems. The king, for example, knighted more than 300 men who had come to meet him along the way. (In fact, in his first four months as king, James knighted more men than Elizabeth had during her entire 45-year reign—often for a fee to help bolster perennially weak royal finances.) James also ordered a thief, brought before him in one town, to be hanged at once without a trial; however certain the guilt, such summary justice was not according to English law. And James adopted the title "King of Great Britain" without Parliament's consent; he simply expected that his own perception of himself would be accepted without a challenge. He quickly learned otherwise.

For a people who prized tradition and had been nurtured on Crown worship, the English found James something of an anomaly. Although he clearly espoused the divinity of kingship, he cared little for ceremony or cheering crowds. Used to the glory of Elizabeth, the people were at first puzzled, then put off. Where Elizabeth wore clothes meant to dazzle, James wore extra-thick, quilted jackets (to thwart the daggers of would-be assassins) and pleated, fully-stuffed breeches. "He never [even] washed his hands," wrote a disgruntled contemporary, "only rubbed his finger ends slightly with the wet end of a napkin." James may have come to occupy center stage, but he was a mere crown-wearing Everyman to Elizabeth's Gloriana.

In England, James was confronted with a host of issues and problems that tested both his mettle and his stamina, and central to many of those problems was the state of royal finances. Prices had risen about 50% during Elizabeth's reign, and the queen had left a large debt. Political corruption was growing, and James aggravated the situation by his extravagant and generous nature, a nature that would be exploited by friends and favorites. Every year he incurred a deficit, and within five years the royal debt was six times larger than the one he had inherited.

The King Struggles with Parliament

As a result James was compelled to look to Parliament for assistance. When he met his first Parliament in 1604, the members informed him that they had exercised restraint in their resistance to Elizabeth out of respect for her age, but now they expected more cooperation. James, however, used to a subservient Scottish Parliament, had difficulty in grasping just how sophisticated the English Parliament was becoming and how determined the M.P.'s were to increase their participation in government. An initial clash over a disputed election resulted in the House of Commons drawing up *The Form of Apology and Satisfaction* in which, respectfully and apologetically, they informed the king that their privileges were held by right, not by his good graces. Although this difference in understanding would never be formally resolved during James's reign, the Commons slowly cut away the monarch's control.

Still, James had always recognized that the divine right origin of his power did not mean that those powers were absolute. He readily acknowledged that he could not make laws or collect taxes without the consent of Parliament. Thus the struggle between James and Parliament was over the extent of his lawful powers, that is, his prerogatives, relative to statute law and common law. James, unfortunately, cheapened his prerogative when, for example, he agreed to consider the Great Contract (1610), a proposal to yield some of his prerogatives in exchange for an annual parliamentary grant; nothing came of this except the growth of mutual mistrust. And he weakened the independence of the judicial system by bullying judges. This conflict would continue, with growing intensity, into the next reign as perceived government and royal abuses along with attempts at reform resulted in demands for constitutional change.

James had some success in confronting religious issues and in achieving consensus, perhaps more fully than Queen Elizabeth and certainly more so than his succeeding son, Charles I. A reasonably tolerant man who had no wish to preside over an ideologically polarized country, he told Robert Cecil that he did not wish that "the blood of any man shall be shed for diversity of opinions in religion." This did not, however, prevent James from supporting the official church, and his actions sometimes made life difficult for Puritans and Catholics, whose support he had initially sought in securing his peaceful accession to the English throne.

In response to a Puritan petition to reform the Church of England, presented to him on his journey from Scotland, James, to the dismay of his bishops, sponsored the Hampton Court Conference of 1604. Presiding, Solomon-like, he decided some matters in favor of the bishops, some in favor of the Puritans. But afterwards James lost interest, and he allowed the bishops to dominate the commissions. As a result, measures favoring the established church, such as revisions in the Book of the Common Prayer and authorization for a new translation of the Bible, were passed, while Puritan-inspired proposals failed. Since he allowed the Puritans considerable latitude, however, Puritan religious agitation was never a serious problem in his reign.

Guy Fawkes and the Gunpowder Plot

If James, a product of Scottish Presbyterianism, was a disappointment to the Puritans, this son of the martyred Mary, Queen of Scots proved equally disappointing to English Catholics. Not only did James fail to act on his promise of greater toleration, but the peace concluded between England and Spain in 1604 robbed English Catholics of protection and hope. Frustrated by the events, a small but well-placed band of them plotted to blow up the king and his Parliament on November 5, 1605. The explosion would be a signal for general rebellion, and out of the chaos the Catholics would emerge to restore their faith. But word of the notorious Gunpowder Plot reached the government, and palace guards found Guy Fawkes, a Catholic soldier of fortune, patiently awaiting the appointed hour to ignite the barrels of explosives. Fawkes and his fellow conspirators were tried and executed for treason, but the memory of the attempt is still celebrated annually as anti-Catholic sentiments have been kept alive down to the present time. In fact, the Gunpowder Plot was so outrageous in its conception, and so near to success in its execution, that skeptics believed the government might have been complicitous in order to focus popular rage against Catholics. There is no evidence, however, that James was in any way involved except as a potential victim. His horror upon the discovery of the plot was apparently genuine, and to his credit James did not take revenge on English Catholics in general. Following Queen Elizabeth's example, James was more interested in their temporal loyalty than in their spiritual obedience.

Throughout his reign, James kept male favorites close at hand. After Cecil died, in 1612, these favorites relieved him of many of the administrative burdens of monarchy. Unfortunately, they had little else to recommend them, and their growing influence in the second half of the reign gave James and his court an unsavory reputation. James's most important and long-lasting favorite was George Villiers, later the duke of Buckingham (and the first man outside the royal family to be made a duke since the War of the Roses). James may have referred to this handsome, charming, and even dashing young man as his "sweet child and wife," but Buckingham was no lightweight; he immersed himself in politics and, with his immense energy and his undertaking of tasks the king assigned him, he got things done. The problem was that not all his work was for the good. It was he, for example, who accompanied the son and heir Prince Charles to Spain, in 1623, to push a Spanish marriage. But when this failed, Buckingham turned against Spain and toward a war that, by the next reign, would be disastrous for the English monarchy. An ailing King James, uncommitted to war, lurched into it just the same.

In early March 1625, James fell ill while on a hunting trip. His condition deteriorated quickly and he collapsed as a result of what may have been a stroke. Left speechless and severely weakened by dysentery, robbed of his strength and dignity, James died on March 27. He was buried in Westminster Abbey, in the Chapel of Henry VII; thus have the founders of England's first two dynasties of modern times come to share a common resting place.

This once-successful ruler of Scotland courted failure when he ascended his new throne in 1603. He allowed himself to be flattered by the verbal puffery of obsequious courtiers; he expected too much from others, but never enough from himself. Nevertheless, he sought a middle ground in England and peace abroad—which benefitted English trade and the founding of the colonies in America. If he did not achieve everything he hoped, the structure of government and court he left behind was reasonably sound and stable. To be sure, his fiscal policies aggravated already difficult economic times for the crown, but he defused problems with the church and the state. And although he passed along to his son a throne and a kingdom that had serious problems, these were surely not very much worse than those he had inherited from Elizabeth.

James was a man who is easily criticized. The wise and compassionate observer, however, goes beyond the superficial caricature to see the many dimensions of the whole man who, in 1620, advised his son: "Look not to find the softness of a down pillow in a crown, but remember that it is a thorny piece of stuff and full of continual cares."

SOURCES:

Cannon, John, and Ralph Griffiths. *The Oxford Illustrated History of the British Monarchy.* Oxford University Press, 1988.

Fraser, Antonia. *King James.* Knopf, 1975.

Houston, S. J. *James I.* Longman, 1973.

Tanner, J. R. *Constitutional Documents of the Reign of James I.* Cambridge University Press, 1961.

Willson, David Harris. *King James VI and I.* Oxford University Press, 1967.

FURTHER READING:

Ashton, Robert, ed. *James I By His Contemporaries.* Hutchinson, 1969.

Hirst, Derek. *Authority and Conflict: England, 1603–1658.* Harvard University Press, 1986.

Kenyon, J. P. *Stuart England.* 2d ed. Penguin Books, 1985.

Lee, Maurice, Jr. "James I and the Historians: Not a Bad King After All?" in *Albion,* Vol. 16, Summer 1984.

Mathew, David. *James I.* Eyre & Spottiswoode, 1967.

Smith, Alan G. R., ed. *The Reign of James VI and I.* St. Martin's Press, 1973.

Joan of Arc

(c. 1412–1431)

Teenager, who led Charles VII's armies to dramatic victories in the Anglo-French Hundred Years' War, was tried and executed by her enemies, and later exonerated and proclaimed a saint.

Name variations: Jeanne D'Arc. Born at Domremy c. 1412; burned at the stake in 1431; daughter of Jacques and Ysabeau D'Arc. Predecessors and successors: None, though she stood in a tradition of Christian warriors which included Charlemagne, Roland, and El Cid.

Like all figures in history who claim to have been inspired by divine visions, Joan of Arc was widely disbelieved. French patriots and good Catholics think that she saved France in obedience to the demands of saintly visitors; secular souls, who deny the possibility of miraculous visions, assume she was a schizophrenic, albeit an exceptional one. As fascinating today as she has been throughout the five and a half centuries since her death, the historical Joan is obscured by legend and hagiography. But the events of her life, so far as they can be reconstructed, are extraordinary enough to require no embroidery. She caused such a sensation in her lifetime, moreover, that from letters and chronicles, from the transcript of her trial, and from the papal enquiry into her life which exonerated her 25 years later, we can gain a far more distinct impression of her than of most 15th century figures.

Joan was born about 1412 in the village of Domremy, in the Champagne district of northeastern France. By tradition a shepherd girl but probably from a well-to-do farming family, she began to receive divine visions—from about the age of 13— of St. Michael (captain-general of the armies of

"She is the most notable Warrior Saint in the Christian calendar, and the queerest fish among the eccentric worthies of the Middle Ages."

GEORGE BERNARD SHAW

Contributed by Patrick Allitt, Assistant Professor of History, Emory University, Atlanta, Georgia

Heaven), St. Catherine, and Saint Margaret (both early Christian martyrs) and became convinced that she was destined to save France from its English enemies. Refusing an offer of marriage, she pledged herself to perpetual virginity.

In 1415, when Joan was about three, King **Henry V** of England had won a shattering victory over the French at the battle of Agincourt; in the following years, he consolidated this victory by seizing most of France north of the Loire River, lands which had been in English hands in the 11th and 12th centuries but which King John had lost in the early 13th. John's successors had never surrendered their claims, and Henry V said he was simply resuming his rights as king of England and France. Shakespeare makes it clear in *Henry V* that there was a fair degree of cynicism in the claims by then, and is probably correct in believing that Henry used them largely as a pretext for military swagger and self-aggrandizement. Henry V died in 1422, but the regents for his infant son, Henry VI, maintained the pressure on France throughout the 1420s. The siege of Orleans in 1428 brought matters to a crisis. The English were allied with the duke of Burgundy, and the king of France's armies appeared powerless to save the city in the face of these combined foes.

Joan knew that her father would not let her seek the king with word of her visions; so, in an unusual act of disobedience justified by her "voices," she persuaded her uncle to take her to the local authorities, where she reported her visions to Sir Robert de Baudricourt in the nearby town of Vaucouleurs. Skeptical and amused at first (she was only about 17 years old), he was ultimately impressed by her determination and sent her to the king under escort in early 1429. She proved her miraculous gifts to the uncrowned king, **Charles VII,** supposedly by revealing to him several secrets which he had believed were known only to himself and God. Then she told him:

> I have come to raise the siege of Orleans and to aid you to recover your kingdom. God wills it so. After I have raised the siege I will conduct you to Reims to be consecrated. Do not distress yourself over the English, for I will combat them in any place I find them.

Before accepting her services, however, he subjected her to rigorous tests of faith in his castle at Poitiers, to be certain of her orthodoxy. The priests found her blameless, a point she emphasized often at her trial two years later.

CHRONOLOGY

c. 1412	Joan born at Domremy
1415	English victorious over French at Agincourt
1422	Henry V of England and Charles VI of France died
1428	Joan's first visit to Vaucouleurs; audience with Baudricourt
1429	Met with Charles VII; raised the siege of Orleans; successful campaign to Reims; Charles VII crowned
1430	Joan captured at Compiegne by Burgundians; transferred to English custody
1431	Tried; burned at the stake
1456	Papal investigation overturned verdict and exonerated her
1920	Canonized

Joan, about whom claims of beauty were never made at the time, was strongly built, and soon showed that she could wear armor, ride war horses, and use a jousting lance. "As soon as her armor was made she put it on," wrote one observer, "and went out in to the fields of Poitiers with other armed combatants where she handled her lance as well or better than any man there. She rode spirited chargers, the capricious ones that no one else dared mount without fear." The English Holinshed chronicle took the same view: "Of favor was she counted likesome, of person stronglie made and manlie, of courage great, hardie, and stout withal." She told one of the king's armorers to go to the church of Saint Catherine of Fierbois where he would find a finely wrought sword inscribed with five crosses, buried behind the altar, which was to be her weapon. He did! Joan had never been there, and this legend of the empowering weapon soon became a French counterpart to the English tale of King Arthur's Excalibur. At her trial in 1431, the story of the sword's discovery was to be used by her inquisitors to raise the specter of sorcery.

Joan Rides to Battle Against the English

Armed and determined, Joan now led a column of soldiers to the relief of Orleans. Learning of their approach, the British besiegers withdrew temporarily into fortresses they had prepared nearby and let the French enter the town. As soon as reinforcements arrived, Joan moved onto the offensive and, in her distinctive white armor, led her troops against Saint Loup, the small English fort on the south bank of the river. In a brisk fight, she seized the fort, killing or capturing all the defenders. She moved on to the other forts in the following days and, displaying a calm assurance under attack, was always in the midst of the fight. Although she suffered a foot wound from a spiked caltrop and a crossbow wound above the breast, she stayed in action, forcing the English to retreat. "In this way at last to the deep shame, damage, and embarrassment of the English, the city was delivered from the suffering of the siege," wrote early biographers. The British commander felt certain that only enchantment or sorcery could have led to such a defeat.

With the aid of visions of Saint Catherine, Joan recovered in two weeks from her wounds; she now moved along the Loire River, the fortified frontier of the English possessions in France. Her army, purged of camp-followers and blasphemers and white-hot with religious zeal, seized the forts of Jargeau, Meung-sur-Loire, and Beaugency. It then veered north to defeat an English relief column at the village of Patay on June 18, 1429, prompting dozens more fortified towns, which had earlier made terms with England, to swear loyalty to the French king. "In war," said George Bernard Shaw, "she was as much a realist as Napoleon; she had his eye for artillery and his knowledge of what it could do. She did not expect besieged cities to fall Jerichowise at the sound of her trumpet, but, like Wellington, adapted her methods of attack to the peculiarities of the defence."

Joan's dizzying feats of arms inspired the French court, but the bizarre actions she undertook were already the cause of suspicion in some observers. "They could see she went to confession very often and received the Body of our Saviour each week," wrote her first biographer, but "they were aware that she never did any tasks expected of a woman." She was frequently excluded from the King's Council when it discussed future moves, but her advice, often sought belatedly, proved prophetic. She believed that Charles should next advance on Reims, traditional coronation site of French kings, and embrace his kingship in full, rather than remain an uncrowned dauphin. After a short period of equivocation, he agreed, and the army marched northeast. Following early successes, however, it came to the verge of abandoning the siege of Troyes for lack of food. In the face of this logistical crisis, Joan assured Charles that the city would surrender within two days, and she made speeches to invigorate the hungry soldiers. As she had predicted, Troyes surrendered, and the way was open for Charles to advance to Reims, whose inhabitants, despite an earlier oath to the English, also welcomed him. There, on July 17,

1429, he was crowned, with Joan standing nearby bearing her standard.

The *Chronicle of the Cordeliers* says she cut a great figure at about this time.

> The Maid, arrayed in white armor, rode on horseback before the King, with her standard unfurled. When not in armor, she kept state as a knight and dressed as one. Her shoes were tied with laces to her feet, her hose and her doublet shapely, a hat was on her head. She wore very handsome attire of cloth of gold and silk, noticeably trimmed with fur.

Her relish for weapons and her "cross-dressing" continued to fascinate some of the people she met and horrify others. Citizens in newly liberated towns tried to gather round and touch her manly clothes, though she gave them no encouragement and made no claim to be a healer.

Campaigning against the English and Burgundians continued, with Paris as its next goal (Joan and Charles's journey from Orleans to Reims had made a wide arc skirting Paris to the south and east). For the first time, she now suffered serious reverses, failing to take Paris in September 1429 (and receiving another arrow wound, this time in the leg) and failing again at La Charite Sur Loire that November. She remained dissatisfied by Charles's halfheartedness, and hated court life at the home of his favorite, Georges de La Tremouille, who had disliked her from the start. Leaving court to help the besieged garrison at Compiegne, Joan was captured in battle by John of Luxembourg, a vassal of the duke of Burgundy in May 1430, barely a year after her first appearance in combat. Rumors circulated that she had been betrayed by envious French nobles, who resented her glorious rise from obscurity. Certainly the French made little effort to rescue her. She at once tried to escape from an upstairs window but injured herself in a fall when her makeshift rope broke. Some historians consider the incident a suicide attempt, prompted by her learning that she was to be handed over to the English.

The English commanders, delighted by news of her capture, were indeed determined to get hold of her from their allies. "They were happier to have her than five hundred other combatants, because they had never feared and dreaded any other captain or war commander up to the present time as they had this Maid," said one chronicler, Monstrelet. They had to pay 10,000 crowns to their Burgundian ally for her, and then entrusted her interrogation and trial to Peter Cauchon, the bishop of Beauvais. Assured by the law faculty of the University of Paris that he was acting justly, Cauchon wanted to bring her to trial for sorcery, idolatry, invocation of demons, and heresy. "Through her," said the university in its written opinion, "the honor of God is foully sullied, our Faith grievously wounded, and the Church too much discredited. She has occasioned the diffusion of idolatries, vain beliefs, evil doctrines, and other irreparable disorders and depravities in this kingdom." Cauchon himself, though he held a French bishopric, was an English loyalist and a member of the English king's Great Council.

This English king, Henry VI, himself only eight years old (to Joan's 19), posed through his regent the duke of Bedford as a shocked champion of orthodoxy. "It is notorious," said letters written in the king's name, "that a woman who insisted on being called Joan the Maid, discarding the garb and vesture of the female sex, an act repugnant and forbidden by all law, a deed contrary to Divine Law and abhorrent to God, put on and wore men's garments and likewise armed herself as a man." Cauchon brought her to the English authorities in Rouen, who shackled her in a dungeon and set five loutish soldiers to keep watch over her, though as a prisoner accused of heresy she should have been in an ecclesiastical rather than civil jail maintained by jailers of her own sex. The bishop was determined to convict her; he was, said her biographer, "no less determined on the death of the Maid than Caiphas, Annas, and the scribes and pharisees were for the death of Our Saviour." The English could have raised a staggering fortune by ransoming her but seem never to have considered it.

While most historians assume that Cauchon hated Joan, whose military success the year before had forced him to flee from Beauvais, a few have seen him in a more favorable light, as a judge who scrupulously observed the legal forms and who refused to have Joan tortured, as was often the fate of obdurate prisoners suspected of heresy. Cauchon, said playwright George Bernard Shaw, "was far more self-disciplined and conscientious both as a priest and lawyer than any English judge ever dreams of being in a political case in which his party and class prejudices are involved." On the other hand, few historians have doubted that a verdict of guilty was a foregone conclusion and that the heresy and witchcraft trial was designed more to discredit Joan (and hence her king) than to decide a question of real culpability.

Her Trial for Heresy Begins

After extensive interrogations, Joan went on trial; throughout, she refused to swear an oath on the gospels to tell the whole truth, except on "matters touching the faith." Her interrogators were unable, despite endless questioning, to connect her with the usual practices of witchcraft, and the list of charges was gradually narrowed down to the fact that she would not cooperate with this trial and was, for that reason, disobedient to the Church. She steadfastly insisted that her "voices" came from the saints and that she was rigorously orthodox in her religion. The voices, she added, had told her to wear men's clothes and go into battle, and she had felt obliged to obey them. Cauchon used the issue of dress against her; indeed, it became one of the central issues of the case. Her refusal to replace it with women's dress despite his demands was, he said, evidence that she was disobedient to the Church he represented, and he used it as a pretext to deny her access to Mass and confession.

Joan never admitted to the charges against her, but on May 24, 1431, in a public ceremony at the cemetery of St. Ouen outside Rouen, she did sign a general statement of faults and agreed to put on women's clothes. Sick and exhausted from months of prison and fetters, she appears at that point to have given up hope of being rescued by French forces, as she had earlier expected, and was tormented by the fear that her disobedience toward her inquisitors really was a form of disobedience to God.

With this recantation, she expected to be taken to a Church prison, as Cauchon had promised, but was instead returned yet again to the dungeon and its hateful male guards, and again denied the chance to confess and communicate in Church. She scolded Cauchon for his duplicity:

> I would rather die than be kept in these chains. But if you promise to remove them and allow me to attend Mass and put me in a "gracious" prison and let me have a woman attendant, I will be good and do everything the Church wishes and orders.

Apparently determined that she should die, Cauchon brushed her request aside. Joan responded with the most symbolically powerful statement she could make: she donned once more her male attire.

This act made her, in Catholic eyes, a *relapsed* heretic, an abomination. Accordingly, on May 30, 1431, Joan's sentence was read out in the town square of Rouen; it declared that as an incorrigible relapsed heretic, she was to be handed over for punishment to the civil authorities. Wrote her original biographer:

At once the bailiff of Rouen, an Englishman, who was ready, without further formality, without even pronouncing any sentence of death against her, ordered Joan taken to the space for her burning. Joan, listening to this command, wept and cried out in bewilderment, so that she moved the people and all those present to tears of compassion.

Here was another procedural violation. The Church court had no power to pass a sentence of death; there should have been a civil trial. Nevertheless, the fire was lit "and there she was burned shockingly, martyred indeed, an example of monstrous cruelty." Another chronicle added: "The ashes of her body, gathered in a sack, were tossed into the river Seine. This was done so that no attempt could ever be made, nor even a proposal be suggested, to use them for sorcery or any other mysterious evil."

The shameful story of her death has led everyone involved to try *not* to take the blame. English historian Paul Johnson, for example, is at pains to show why her death should be attributed to French rather than English interests. "Joan of Arc was not a victim of English nationalism: only eight of the 131 judges, assessors, and other clergy connected with her trial were Englishmen. She was, rather, the casualty of a French civil war which had a wide theological dimension." Johnson adds that even her accusers had second thoughts.

We are not surprised to learn that one of the judges who originally condemned her, Jean le Fevre, was also a judge at her rehabilitation; or that Thomas de Courcelles, who advised that she be tortured during her interrogation, was promoted to be Dean of Notre Dame the year she was cleared, and lived to preach the funeral panegyric on her hero-Dauphin Charles VII.

The French king was equally eager to disclaim any culpability and twice tried to have the verdict against her overturned. A mere 25 years after her death, with the Hundred Years' War ended at last, Pope Calixtus III set up a commission (1456) which declared that the verdict against her had been obtained by fraud and deceit. After this reversal, Joan of Arc quickly became a central figure in the folklore of French nationalism, while her *religious* rehabilitation was completed in 1920, the year she was made a saint. George Bernard Shaw's superb play *Saint Joan* was a stage success three years later, in 1923, though it was as much about issues in post–World War I England as about 15th-century France. Joan then had the misfortune of becoming a staple Hollywood figure and was played by several stars, usually very badly.

A controversial figure in every age since her death, Joan of Arc has been reinterpreted as a genuine witch, an heroic early feminist, a premature Protestant, a romantic heroine, and even, in the hands of Mark Twain, as an odd Victorian lady. Whatever the virtues of these diverse claims, she remains the most famous fighting woman in European history.

SOURCES:

Belloc, Hilaire. *Joan of Arc.* Declan McMullan, 1929.

Cambridge Medieval History. Vol. 8. Cambridge University Press, 1959.

Johnson, Paul. *History of Christianity.* Atheneum, 1979.

Rankin, Daniel, and Claire Quintal. *The First Biography of Joan of Arc, with the Chronicle Record of a Contemporary Account.* University of Pittsburgh Press, 1964.

Shaw, George Bernard. *Saint Joan.* Penguin, 1963.

Smith, John Holland. *Joan of Arc.* Sidgwick & Jackson, 1973.

Weintraub, Stanley, ed. *Saint Joan: Fifty Years After.* Louisiana State University Press, 1973.

Joseph Joffre

(1852–1931)

Commander of the French army and coordinator of the Allied armies during the first two years of World War I, whose victory over the Germans at the Battle of the Marne saved the Allied cause from quick defeat.

"We are about to engage in a battle on which the fate of our country depends…. Troops that can advance no farther must at any price hold on to the ground they have conquered and die on the spot rather than give way. Under the circumstances which face us, no act of weakness can be tolerated."

JOFFRE'S ORDER OF THE DAY
AT THE MARNE

Name variations: Papa Joffre. Pronunciation: Jhoff'r. Born in Rivesaltes (Pyrenees-Orientales) on January 12, 1852; died in Paris on January 3, 1931; buried at "La Chataigneraie" in Louveciennes (Seine-et-Marne); third (but eldest survivor) of 11 children of Gilles and Catherine (Plas) Joffre; married: Louise (Pourcheyroux) Lafage (a widow who died young); married: Henriette Penon, 1905; children: none.

The date was September 4, 1914. The decision stood at what was probably the most important turning point in the history of the 20th century; and at this moment the entire weight rested on the massive frame of a white-mustached man garbed in regulation black tunic, red trousers, and boots, seated alone and all but motionless for most of a blazingly hot afternoon under an ash tree in a schoolyard at Bar-sur-Aube, France. His plans for a victorious offensive at the start of the war had been shot to bits by the German defenses in Alsace, Lorraine, and the Ardennes Forest, and now the main German force, having swept through Belgium around the French and British left flank, was driving south past Paris in hot pursuit of what its commanders believed were beaten armies. Once he had recognized the full magnitude of the German move, General Joffre, the man in the schoolyard, had been rushing what troops he could spare since August 25 from his hard-pressed right flank to the vicinity of Paris in hopes of using them against the German right wing when the time should come to make a stand. But had that time come?

Contributed by David S. Newhall, Distinguished Professor of the Humanities, Centre College, Danville, Kentucky

He had intended to continue the retreat as far as the Seine. His staff still argued that this would allow more time to rest tired men, gather reinforcements, and persuade the British to turn about. But General Joseph Galliéni, commander of the Paris garrison, Joffre's former mentor and designated successor should he fail, was urging him to strike now before the Germans fully perceived the danger to their flank. Everybody knew that if the counterattack failed, the war was as good as over. Would weary troops, after weeks of losses and retreats, respond to an order to attack? And would the British commander agree?

True to his fixed method, Joffre had listened impassively to all the arguments, showing no sign of anxiety or haste, an island of almost unnatural calm; now, alone in the schoolyard, he weighed the matter in his mind and at last gave the order: Stop and strike across the Marne, not later across the Seine. The troops responded, the British fell into line after Joffre had personally browbeaten their shaken commander, and following four days (September 6–9) of desperate fighting the Germans withdrew northward, their best chance (as it turned out) to win the war spirited away by "the Miracle of the Marne." Years later, Marshal **Ferdinand Foch,** the Allied commander in chief at

the end of the war, reflected on his former chief's refusal to panic and his willingness to shoulder responsibility in desperate circumstances: "If we had not had him in 1914, I don't know what would have become of us."

Joseph-Jacques-Césaire, born on January 12, 1852, in Rivesaltes, a town at the foot of the Pyrénées near the Mediterranean, was the third (but eldest survivor) of the 11 children of Gilles and Catherine (Plas) Joffre. Gilles worked in the family cooperage his brother had inherited, but in time he devoted himself entirely to some vineyards he owned. The family lived simply but comfortably. The parents paid close attention to their children's education. Joseph attended the local Brothers of the Christian Doctrine school and then the lycée in Perpignan, where he won many prizes, especially in mathematics, and was encouraged to try for the famed École Polytechnique. After a preparatory year in Paris at the Lycée Charlemagne, he became the youngest cadet admitted in 1869, ranking a brilliant 14th of 132 on the examination.

The Franco-Prussian War (1870–71) and the Paris Commune uprising (1871) interrupted most of his second year, during which he found himself made a second lieutenant of artillery after one month's instruction and commanding a battery during the siege of Paris after its captain had gone insane; but he saw little action. From prudence or conviction, he declined an invitation to join the rebels of the Commune and returned to Rivesaltes on leave until the Polytechnique reopened that summer. Late that fall, he graduated 33d of 136: "I asked for the Engineer Corps, I have no idea why. I didn't know anyone in the Army and chance alone dictated my choice."

A strapping man, blue-eyed and blond with a fine bearing, intelligent and full of sense, a tenacious worker, taciturn but friendly and optimistic, Joffre consistently drew high ratings. He learned his trade at the army's school and on the job, mostly building fortifications and barracks, and on November 6, 1876, was named captain. Ironically, the first real boost to his career resulted from a personal tragedy: his wife died suddenly. Despondent and wanting to get away, he volunteered for the Colonial Army in the Far East, where France, while conquering Indochina (Vietnam), was now in an undeclared war with China. He was sent to construct fortifications, barracks, and roads at Keelung, Formosa (Taiwan). His chief, the famous Admiral Courbet, was so impressed by his work under extremely adverse tropical conditions that he secured him the Legion of Honor. Later, while assigned to Hanoi as chief of engineers, he was cited on March 21, 1887, for his conduct at the siege of Ba-Dinh.

He returned to France in July 1888, was promoted to major, and spent two years with a railway regiment. His only relatively unsuccessful tour followed: a year as professor of fortification at the School of Application for Artillery and Engineers; students found the material and the soft-spoken lecturer boring. Again, an assignment overseas provided the second, and most important, shove to his career. He won a posting to build a railway linking the Senegal and Niger rivers in West Africa. Unexpectedly, a year after he arrived he was called to command a column of 16 officers, 380 soldiers, 700 native auxiliaries and porters, and 200 horses and mules to carry supplies in support of a force led by Colonel Eugéne Bonnier; the men were hastening to rescue a detachment engaged in an unauthorized attempt to occupy Timbuctu, the chief town on the upper Niger and long an object of French ambitions but of late controlled by the Tuaregs, fierce Muslim nomads. Bonnier reached Timbuctu but was massacred with 76 of his men while trying to clear Tuaregs from Joffre's route. Joffre, who departed Ségou on December 27, 1893, had to detour into the desert due to flooding; having defeated a large Tuareg force, subdued a rebel town, overcome a succession of obstacles, and collected the bodies of Bonnier's force, he entered Timbuctu on February 12, 1894, ending an epic 505-mile march. While building Fort Bonnier and establishing French authority over the region, he became the army's youngest lieutenant colonel of engineers. Back home, press accounts of "the March to Timbuctu" gave him his first brush with fame.

Returning to France that fall, he filled staff positions in Paris, became a colonel (1897), and fortunately stayed clear of political involvement during the height of the Dreyfus affair (1897–99). Once more, service abroad thrust him ahead. General Galliéni, the brightest star in the Colonial Army, needed someone to build a major naval base at Diego-Suarez. Joffre completed the huge project in three years (1900–03), earning promotion to brigadier general (1901) and Galliéni's warm praise. A series of high staff and line posts followed: director of engineers at the Ministry of War (1904–06), with promotion to *général de division* (major general) on January 24, 1905; commander of the 6th Infantry Division; commander of the II Corps (1908); and member of the Conseil supérieur de la Guerre and director of the Rear Area (1910). It was from this post that, over his objections, he was plucked on July 28, 1911, to be chief of the General Staff and the designated commander in chief in case of war.

Joffre Named Chief of General Staff

Galliéni had declined the appointment and recommended Paul Pau or Joffre. Pau set unacceptable conditions, so Joffre was tapped. The choice surprised many. He was firmly republican in politics and a freethinker in religion, hence politically acceptable to the current government, and was liked and well respected in the army. But he essentially was a "technician" who had never commanded large infantry or artillery units in action, studied strategy and tactics seriously, nor even served on the General Staff.

Joffre's arrival coincided with a grave war scare (the Second Moroccan Crisis, 1911–12), during which he had to advise the government that the army was not yet strong enough to risk war with Germany, a war he was convinced was coming soon. Besides pushing for expanded arms production and (in 1913) passage of a bill extending conscripted service from two to three years in order to increase the number of men available at the moment war should come, he framed a new war plan. Because its failure opened the door to a deep penetration by the Germans in 1914 which needed a "miracle" at the Marne to prevent from becoming a fatal catastrophe, Plan 17 and Joffre have been criticized ever since.

Briefly, it called for an immediate all-out offensive focused on the Ardennes and northern Lorraine (admittedly not easy terrain) even though the Germans were expected to invade neutral Belgium in order to turn the French left wing. The French attack would cancel that danger because it would hit the "hinge" of the sweep through Belgium and thus split the German army or force its hasty retreat. The plan also resulted from the army's need for a doctrine of warfare. Joffre founded his doctrine on the emphasis of the offense which was coming into vogue among the army's thinkers. Only the offense, not the defense, can gain the initiative, break the enemy's will, and finally win. Besides, France and her army needed to discard the defensive and defeatist mentality resulting from the German victory of 1870–71. Throughout the war to come, Joffre remained true to this view. In his memoirs, however, he admitted that some officers were marked by an "unreasoning passion" for the offense and fell into "dangerous exaggerations."

Two other considerations shaped Plan 17. France needed Russia's help to defeat Germany; a quick offensive would help keep them committed to *their* promise of an immediate offensive. As for Belgium, if France violated her neutrality first to beat the Germans to the punch, Britain probably would stay out, and Joffre regarded British aid on his left as critical. Thus, there would be (1) a French offensive at the start, and (2) it would have to be launched across less favorable terrain than the Belgian plain.

The first three weeks of the war climaxed in the bloody repulse of the French offensive—a demonstration of the great advantage the technology of the time gave to the defense, one to be repeated with sickening regularity for the next four years. Plan 17 failed basically because it rested on three false assumptions: (1) the offense would have the advantage over the defense; (2) the German move into Belgium would not extend north of the Sambre-Meuse river line; and most important, (3) if it did the Germans would be stretched too thin (and thus even more vulnerable at the "hinge") because they surely would not use reserve troops in the front lines at the start. By the time the French offensive foundered (August 20–24), the Germans had gone well north of the Meuse in great force (including massive reserves) and were now coming southwest in a huge wheeling movement threatening to circle Paris and drive the Anglo-French into a vise.

Not until his own offensive failed did Joffre and the General Staff fully admit that their assumptions had proved wrong and that they were now in mortal danger. Disaster would surely have descended but for Joffre's ability to face the facts and think clearly when so many had begun to panic or grow discouraged. To a staff colonel who returned full of gloom from a mission to the retreating left wing, Joffre calmly remarked, "What, you no longer believe in France? Go get some sleep. You'll see, all will go well." Another (often overlooked) reason for the recovery was his past experience in railway operations, which helped in the complicated moving of troops from the right flank to Paris. He also showed he could be ruthless. In the first month, he sacked 54 generals—2 of 5 army, 10 of 20 corps, and 42 of 74 division commanders—whom he judged deficient in action, whatever their prior reputations. As he is reputed to have told a fired army commander, "I love you well. But I love France more."

He Rallies Allied Forces To Win at Marne

In the end, Joffre recovered from his own huge mistakes and made his opponent, General **Helmuth von Moltke,** pay dearly for his—among

them, weakening his right wing at a critical time by transferring two corps to the Russian front; deciding to pass east of Paris, thus exposing his flank; and losing control of his commanders so that their armies became disjointed, thus opening a gap into which the British would advance.

When the Germans fell back after September 9, the "Race to the Sea" followed, each side trying to outflank the other. Joffre proved unable to react quickly enough, always "one division and one day too late," to turn his win at the Marne into decisive victory. From mid-November 1914 to the end of 1916, he faced what amounted to a gigantic siege on a front from the English Channel to Switzerland.

The Marne made Joffre world-famous. The army repaid his steady confidence with affection, while the public idolized "Papa" Joffre and found his rotund figure a reassuring presence. He continued to believe in the offense and launched a series of horribly costly attacks in 1915. The Allies must hold the initiative whenever possible; prolonged defense saps soldiers' morale; the invader (as the public insisted) must be expelled and every yielded foot promptly won back; and Italy must be encouraged to join up (which she did) and, especially, the Russians, under intense German pressure that year, must be aided.

He attacked in strategically vital sectors (Artois and Champagne), but gains came to be measured in yards and tens of thousands of lives. For 1916, as general coordinator of all Allied armies, he won agreement for attacks on all fronts by late spring. But a huge German offensive at Verdun (February 21–July 11), whose heroic defense turned it into the costliest battle in history, forced modifications. He drew sharp criticism for having weakened Verdun's forts and ignored signs of an impending attack; his concentration on preparing the Somme offensive was largely responsible, and in the end made that operation (now mainly British) more necessary in order to relieve pressure on Verdun. But the Somme turned into another ghastly battle of attrition, not the hoped-for breakthrough.

Criticism in political and some military circles swelled. For example, Joffre was jealous of his authority, resenting having to let politicians inspect the front or question him in committee. He had sacked (in 1915) a darling of the dominant left-wing politicians, General Sarrail, and failed to support him properly in a subsequent command at Salonika (Greece). He had a huge (but in truth competent) staff with which he lived in a grand château (Chantilly). He followed an unvarying routine, ate three hefty meals a day and slept ten hours a night no matter what. His bare walls and desk testified to a total lack of imagination (which he knew was true and was why he recruited a good staff), and despite his impassive facade in trying times, he had a quick-flaring temper. Most of all, he had won no more victories, while in the wings was a successful general with high political friends, Robert Nivelle, who claimed (wrongly, it turned out) to have the key to the breakout. On December 13, 1916, the government, itself under fire, persuaded Joffre to give up the field command and become the government's chief military advisor. Two weeks later, finding he now was given nothing to do, he quietly resigned. To mollify the public, the government revived a disused rank and promoted him to Marshal of France (December 26).

When the United States entered the war, Joffre was sent with former premier René Viviani on a goodwill mission (1917) and to offer advice. Enormous crowds hailed "Papa" Joffre in Washington, New York, and ten other cities. The enthusiasm may have sped passage of the draft bill. He advised that the United States should send troops as soon as possible (**Woodrow Wilson** promised to dispatch of a division within a month), as many as possible (i.e., no ordinary expeditionary force), and keep them in large units under American commanders. This last point would be much disputed in 1918 by the British and French commanders, who wanted to feed Americans into their depleted divisions; but Joffre had judged that it would be impractical and hurt American morale, which was what General **John Pershing** would successfully argue.

In retirement, Joffre represented France in postwar ceremonies (1920–22) in Spain, Rumania, Portugal, Japan, and China. He regularly attended sessions of the Académie Française (elected February 14, 1918), and with a small staff compiled his memoirs, a detailed account of his service as chief of staff. With his beloved second wife, Henriette Penon, whom he married in 1905, he divided his time between Paris and a villa, "La Châtaigneraie," he built in Louveciennes (Seine-et-Oise). He received Catholic rites, probably to please his wife, and died in Paris on January 3, 1931, from complications of high blood pressure and arterial disease. He was accorded a national funeral and buried at his country home.

He once observed, "A great general doesn't need to be intelligent. He has plenty of intelligent men around him. What he needs are character and good sense." True or not, those two qualities were what France and her allies needed at the most critical single moment of the war, and "Papa" Joffre had them.

Large crowds greeted the popular French Army commander Joseph Joffre (left), shown here with French ambassador Jules Jusserand, during his trip to the United States in 1917.

SOURCES:

Aston, Major-General Sir George. *The Biography of the Late Marshal Foch.* Macmillan, 1929.

Cahisa, Raymond. "Le double roman d'amour de Joffre le Pyrénéen" in *Miroir de l'histoire.* No. 81. 1956: pp. 336–42, passim.

Desmazes, General [René]. *Joffre: La Victoire du Caractère.* Nouvelles Editions Latines, 1955.

Joffre, Joseph. *The Personal Memoirs of Joffre, Field Marshal of the French Army.* Translated by Colonel T. Bentley Mott. 2 vols. Harper, 1932.

Recouly, Raymond. *Joffre.* D. Appleton, 1931.

Revue historique des Armées. No. 1. 1984 (issue devoted to Joffre).

Tuchman, Barbara W. *The Guns of August.* Macmillan, 1962.

Varillon, Pierre. *Joffre.* Librairie Arthème Fayard, 1956.

FURTHER READING:

Beaufré, General André. "Joffre" in Field Marshal Sir Michael Carver, ed., *The War Lords: Military Commanders of the Twentieth Century.* Little, Brown, 1976.

Horne, Alistair. *The Price of Glory: Verdun 1916.* St. Martin's Press, 1963.

King, Jere Clemens. *Generals and Politicians: Conflict Between France's High Command, Parliament and Government, 1914–1918.* University of California Press, 1951.

Krumeich, Gerd. *Armaments and Politics in France on the Eve of the First World War.* Translated by Stephen Conn. Berg Publishers, 1984.

Porch, Douglas. *The March to the Marne: The French Army, 1871–1914.* Cambridge University Press, 1981.

Williamson, Samuel R., Jr. *The Politics of Grand Strategy: Britain and France Prepare for War, 1904–1914.* Harvard University Press, 1969.

John of Austria

(1547–1578)

Illegitimate half-brother of King Philip II of Spain, who distinguished himself as a military commander, notably at the Battle of Lepanto.

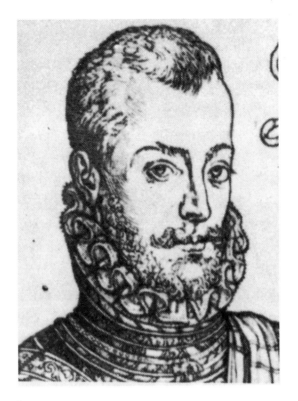

"Don John of Austria has set his people free!"

G. K. CHESTERTON

Name variations: Don John, Don Juan of Austria, Don Juan de Austria. Born on February 24, 1547, in Regensburg, Germany; died on October 1, 1578, near Namur, Belgium; illegitimate son of Emperor Charles V and Barbara Blomberg; never married; children: daughters Doña Juana and Doña Ana de Austria.

The most powerful man in Western Europe in the first half of the 16th century was the Holy Roman Emperor **Charles V** (1519–58), who as King Charles I of Spain (1516–56) inherited from his grandparents **Ferdinand and Isabella** possessions of great wealth and importance in both the Old World and the New. Most of Charles's adult life was spent, however, responding to crises which arose in his German lands as a result of the Protestant Reformation and an accompanying movement for greater local independence from the Empire. Confronted by the challenge of the Schmalkaldic League, a union of princes determined to resist imperial power, Charles traveled in April 1546, to Regensburg, for a meeting of the Diet (imperial parliament) where he hoped to recruit allies for a war against the rebels. While in Regensburg, the ailing, middle-aged widower kept company with an attractive young woman of obscure origin named Barbara Blomberg. Of this brief liaison was born on February 24, 1547, a male child who would later become famous as Don John of Austria.

The emperor at first declined to acknowledge his new offspring, but he did have the infant

Contributed by Stephen Webre, Professor of History, Louisiana Tech University, Ruston, Louisiana

CHRONOLOGY

1559	Royal parentage acknowledged by Philip II
1567	Named general of the sea
1569–70	Put down the Morisco rebellion in the Alpujarras
1571	Commanded Holy League galleys against the Turkish fleet at Lepanto
1573	Captured Tunis
1576	Named governor of the Netherlands to repress the Protestant rebellion

taken from its mother and entrusted to an old friend, Luis Quijada, who arranged for its adoption by Francisco Massi, a musician at the imperial court. In 1550, Massi and his wife Ana retired to Spain and settled at Leganés, near Madrid. There they continued to care for the child, who at that time was known only as Jerónimo. When Jerónimo was eight years old, Massi died and Luis Quijada assumed responsibility for the boy's welfare once again, taking him to live at Villagarcía, his estate near Valladolid. Quijada and his wife Doña Magdalena de Ulloa, who had no children of their own, took great care in the rearing and education of young Jerónimo. Doña Magdalena taught him Latin and read to him from romances of chivalry, while Quijada encouraged his interest in the hunt, horsemanship, and swordplay. Although the emperor seems to have intended his illegitimate son for a career in the Church, it soon became apparent that Jerónimo was better suited to a soldier's life.

In 1556, weary and frustrated, Charles abdicated as both king and emperor and retired to the Hieronymite monastery at Yuste, in western Spain. His imperial crown passed to his brother Ferdinand I (1558–64), while his only legitimate son **Philip II** (1556–98) inherited Spain and its American possessions, as well as Naples, Milan, Franche-Comté, and the Netherlands. Upon his death in 1558, Charles left instructions to Philip to acknowledge Jerónimo as his brother and to provide him with an annual income. The following year, the king brought Jerónimo to court, where he was given the name Juan de Austria, after the house of Austria, or Habsburg, the Spanish royal family.

Secretive and suspicious by nature, King Philip was jealous of this charming, athletic youth of whose existence he had not previously known. Don John's good looks and outgoing personality presented a notable contrast to the king himself

and especially to his son and heir apparent, the morose, psychotic Don Carlos. However, Philip was quick to make use of his newly discovered half-brother, taking advantage of Don John's strengths as well as of his insecurities. The monarch exalted the younger man above the grandees, or upper nobility, whose power and pretense he wished to curb, but at the same time he denied him the rank of *infante* (prince) and with it the right to be addressed as "highness."

Popular at court, Don John became close friends with two nephews of his own age, the heir apparent Don Carlos and **Alessandro Farnese**, the son of Duchess Margaret of Parma, an illegitimate daughter of Charles V by an earlier mistress. In 1561, the three youths were sent to study at the University of Alcalá, but their stay was interrupted when Don Carlos fell and sustained a serious injury to the head. Although he recovered from the accident, the prince's behavior, which was already bizarre, became even stranger. Expressing open hatred for the king, Don Carlos began to intrigue against him. In 1567, the heir apparent attempted to enlist his youthful uncle in a plot to assassinate Philip and seize power, but Don John warned the king. In an action which scandalized the courts of Europe, Philip ordered his son arrested and imprisoned, and the unhappy Don Carlos died in captivity the following year.

Philip Appoints Don John General of the Sea

The loyalty, or at least the prudence, demonstrated by Don John of Austria in his handling of the Don Carlos affair led Philip II to entrust him with a series of significant military commands. In 1567, the king appointed Don John general of the sea, with responsibility for eliminating North African pirates from the approaches to Gibraltar. The ordinarily parsimonious Philip II provided his young general with a squadron of 33 galleys for the purpose, but his confidence in Don John was not absolute. The king may have intended Don John only as a figurehead commander, because he sent along a confidante of his, the experienced officer Luis de Requeséns y Zúñiga, to provide tactical expertise and to report on Don John's competence and loyalty. Apparently, Requeséns's assessment of the young man's performance was favorable, because Philip continued to employ his brother on important assignments.

In 1569, the king sent Don John to the Alpujarras region of southern Spain to suppress a rebellion of Moriscos, former Muslims who had been forced to convert to Christianity in order to avoid expulsion. Once again, Philip provided his brother with a mentor, his onetime foster father Luis Quijada, to whom he was expected to defer in military matters. Don John repeatedly defied the king's wishes, however, exercising command personally and exposing himself to enemy fire. Following Quijada's death in combat, Don John came into his own as a forceful commander, demonstrating both great courage and tactical skill. The emperor's illegitimate son emerged from the Alpujarras campaign a confident soldier, anxious to be employed again against his brother's enemies. "I should be glad to serve His Majesty on some business of importance," Don John wrote to Philip's minister Ruy Gómez da Silva. "I would that he would understand that I am no longer a boy."

Business of considerable importance was even then in the making and it would soon lead to Don John's finest hour. During the 16th century, the southern and eastern frontiers of Christian Europe lived under the constant threat of Islamic aggression in the person of the Ottoman Turks. The Turkish Empire was organized for the acquisition and distribution of plunder and could not, therefore, remain militarily inactive for long. During his long reign, the great sultan **Suleiman** the Magnificent (1520–66) had expanded Turkish dominion into Eastern and Central Europe and along the northern coast of Africa, and was in the process of invading Hungary when death overcame him in September 1566. Suleiman's successor Selim II (1566–74), forced to abandon the Hungarian campaign after some months without significant gain, decided instead to attack the island of Cyprus, an important outpost of the Venetian commercial empire in the eastern Mediterranean.

In spite of the threat posed by Turkish expansionism, there was at no time during the century a unified response on the part of the Christian powers. The division in the Roman Church created by the Protestant Reformation had weakened the West in the face of its adversary, but, even within the remaining Catholic world, jealousy and suspicion undermined attempts to organize a grand alliance. The Valois monarchs of France distrusted the Spanish and Austrian branches of the Habsburg family, and the French king **Francis I** (1515–47) actually signed a formal alliance with Suleiman in 1536. Venice, for its part, was more preoccupied with Spanish intentions in Italy and the Mediterranean than with those of Constantinople. An early attempt by Don John's father Charles V to create a Holy League against the Turk collapsed when the Venetians made a separate peace in 1540.

By 1570, however, conditions were more favorable for an anti-Turkish alliance than before,

in part because of the elevation to the papacy of Pius V (1566–72). A devout ascetic, the new pope called for renewed struggle against both Protestantism in the north and Islam in the east, giving priority to the latter because the threat it posed to Italy was more immediate; there was serious talk of a possible Turkish assault against Rome itself. Efforts to bring the major Catholic powers together benefited also from a change in attitude on the part of the Venetians, who ordinarily preferred to cooperate with Constantinople because of their extensive commercial interests in the East. Selim II's foolhardy decision to attack Cyprus in 1570 drove Venice into the arms of its traditional rivals, Spain and the papacy. More important, the Venetians feared the growth of the Turkish naval base at Lepanto on the Gulf of Patras. With free access to the Adriatic, the sultan's galleys raided at will along the eastern coast of Italy and came within sight even of Venice itself.

By May 1571, Pius had organized a new Holy League composed of Spain, Venice, Tuscany, Savoy, the Knights of Malta, and the papacy itself. Together these powers, large and small, assembled an enormous fleet of war galleys, which the pope proposed to place under the command of young Don John of Austria. Philip II readily agreed to the choice, possibly in order to protect his own investment in the enterprise. Once again, as at Gibraltar and in the Alpujarras, the king revealed his misgivings about his half-brother, stipulating that all orders must be countersigned by Luis de Requeséns. Philip's principal advisors may have shared his skepticism, but the young general's looks, charm, and uncomplicated piety counted for more with the rank and file. As Jack Beeching has observed, "hard-headed men in high places might have private reservations about entrusting the fate of Christendom to a royal bastard aged twenty-four. But to ordinary people... Don John was their man."

Turks Are Defeated at Lepanto

Don John joined the Spanish galleys at Barcelona and proceeded to rendezvous with the other League units off of Messina in August. The following month, with all of his forces gathered, he put to sea and headed east to Corfu, where he learned that the Turkish admiral Ali Pasha had withdrawn his fleet to the safety of the base at Lepanto. There, on October 7, 1571, Don John led the forces of the Holy League against the Turk in the largest naval battle since Octavian had routed Marc Antony at nearby Actium in 31 B.C. Each fleet had more than 200 galleys, but, although it was a relatively even match in terms of numbers, the League had the advantage of superior gunnery. In particular, six immense Venetian galleasses (fast war galleys) served as artillery platforms from which to blast opposing vessels. The traditional techniques of galley warfare, which included ramming, closing, and boarding, had become less significant. By mid-afternoon, the sultan's fleet had been scattered, with a reported loss of 80 galleys sunk and 130 captured. Upon hearing the news, Pius V is reported to have quoted the Gospel, declaring, "There was a man sent from God, whose name was John."

In a few brief, bloody hours at the battle of Lepanto, Don John of Austria's fleet had destroyed the myth of Ottoman naval invincibility in the Mediterranean. There were celebrations throughout Western Europe, even in Protestant England where **Elizabeth I** ordered services of thanksgiving in the churches. At the height of his fame, Don John was the hero of the hour, the dashing young knight who had saved Christendom. Three and a half centuries later in his poem "Lepanto" (1915), the English Catholic writer G.K. Chesterton echoed the spirit of the time:

> Strong gongs groaning as the guns boom far,
> Don John of Austria is going to the war.

In Chesterton's vision, not only was Don John "the last knight of Europe" but also the battle of Lepanto itself was the last chapter in the history of Christian chivalry. Ironically, among the combatants present that day was the Spaniard Miguel de Cervantes (1547–1616), who, although wounded twice, lived to satirize the idea of knight errantry in his great novel *Don Quijote* (1605).

The aura of romance about the memory of Lepanto endures, but the real outcome of the battle was less significant than it appeared at the time. The Holy League failed to follow up on its victory, in part because of Philip II's customary reluctance to put his galleys at greater risk than was absolutely necessary. Meanwhile, Venice once again made a separate peace with Constantinople in 1573. The Turks rapidly rebuilt their fleet and renewed their aggressive operations along the North African coast. Operating from his base at Naples, Don John seized the Turkish position at Tunis in 1573, but Spain was unable to hold it and the sultan took it back the following year.

Some historians believe that Philip II's unwillingness to support aggressive action against the Turk was due to his own jealousy of Don John's new fame. There is evidence that, as the king feared, his half-brother hoped to create somewhere an independent kingdom for himself. As early as 1569, there had been talk of Don John's leading an expedition to rescue Ireland from Protestant rule, and Pius V is believed to have made a proposal regarding a throne for the emperor's son when the two men met at Rome on the eve of Lepanto. By 1574, Don John was at work on a new intrigue, which enjoyed the backing of Pope Gregory XIII (1572–85), to invade England and depose Elizabeth I. The plan called for the rescue of the imprisoned **Mary, Queen of Scots,** who would then be married to Don John and placed on the English throne. Such an ambitious scheme had no hope of success without the support of Philip II, who gave his brother only enough encouragement to keep him cooperative.

Don John's last royal assignment would come in the Netherlands, scene of the greatest challenge facing Spanish power in Europe in the 1570s. Prosperous and independent-minded, the Low Countries had come to Philip II as part of his father's Burgundian inheritance. Resentful of Spanish rule, many Dutch were also attracted to Protestantism. Anabaptism at first, then later Calvinism, made great advances especially in the northern part of the territory (Holland). In 1567, when anti-Spanish disturbances broke out in the Netherlands, Philip sent the duke of Alva with 20,000 troops to suppress them. Alva's harsh measures generated greater resistance, of which **William the Silent** (1533–84), prince of Orange, gradually emerged as the acknowledged leader. Alva stepped down in 1573 and was replaced by Don John's old mentor Luis de Requeséns, who died in 1576, having accomplished little.

To salvage a seemingly hopeless situation, Philip II turned reluctantly to Don John of Austria, whose appointment as governor-general Alva himself had urged as early as 1574. Philip, who hoped to take advantage of his brother's royal connection and fame as the victor of Lepanto to win the Dutch back to their traditional allegiance, was also prepared to be conciliatory, and he empowered Don John to make significant concessions, including the withdrawal of Spanish troops. As usual, Philip considered his brother useful but did not fully trust him; his minister Antonio Pérez planted a spy in Don John's entourage to keep the court informed of his actions.

During a stopover in Paris on his way to his new post, Don John met and became infatuated with the beautiful and uninhibited Marguerite of Valois, sister of King Henry III of France (1574–89), whom she detested, and wife of King

Henry of Navarre (later **Henry IV** of France, 1589–1610), whom she regarded as a mere convenience. Although he never married, the hero of Lepanto was fond of women and had in his time a number of mistresses, by two of whom he had illegitimate daughters. But none of his previous lovers was as powerfully connected or as dangerous as Marguerite. She recognized his usefulness to her own designs, especially in the Low Countries, while, back in Spain, Philip II could not have been pleased to learn of this new affair. According to Jack Beeching, from the time he met the queen of Navarre, "every step Don John took led him downhill."

The new governor arrived in the Netherlands at an unpropitious time. In the so-called "Spanish Fury" on November 3, 1576, the very day on which Don John reached Luxembourg, the king's troops sacked Antwerp in a destructive rage which cost some 8,000 lives and raised anti-Spanish sentiment to new heights. Shortly thereafter, Catholic and Protestant elements joined together to call for the immediate withdrawal of Spanish forces, a demand which Don John had little choice but to grant in February 1577. The agreement called for the evacuation of the troops by land, which meant that Don John must abandon his cherished project of invading England. Without soldiers, he was isolated in the Netherlands, unable to restore Spanish authority or even to keep the peace when Catholics and Protestants fell once again to fighting among themselves.

Deprived of material support from Spain because of demands elsewhere on Philip II's resources, Don John began to take matters into his own hands. In July 1577, without authority from Madrid, he seized the castle of Namur at the strategic confluence of the Sambre and Meuse rivers, a position crucial to military control of the southern, Catholic provinces (Belgium), not to mention a convenient spot to arrange a tryst with Queen Marguerite. Don John also began to reintroduce Spanish troops into the Netherlands, summoning to his side his nephew, friend, and fellow Lepanto veteran Alessandro Farnese, now prince of Parma.

Spanish troops achieved a stunning military victory over the rebels at Gembloux on January 31, 1578, but the triumph resolved nothing. It strengthened the resolve of the Dutch to resist and it failed to regain for Don John the confidence of his royal brother, which apparently he had now lost once and for all. As the situation in the Netherlands deteriorated, so did Don John's health. He suffered several bouts of fever during his time in the Low Countries and visiting dignitaries reported that he had become thin and sallow of complexion. On October 1, 1578, delirious with typhus, the hero of Lepanto died at Bouges, near Namur. On his deathbed, he transferred his command to the prince of Parma and willed his earthly belongings to his brother Philip. It was reported later that among his last words was the declaration that, "During all my life I have not had a foot of land I could call my own." Then he recalled the words of Job, "Naked I came from my mother's womb, and naked shall I return." Don John of Austria's body was smuggled across France and into Spain, where it lies next to that of Charles V in the royal tombs at the Escorial.

SOURCES:

Beeching, Jack. *The Galleys at Lepanto.* Scribner, 1983.

Maxwell-Stirling, Sir William. *Don John of Austria, or Passages from the History of the Sixteenth Century.* 2 vols. Longmans, 1883.

Parker, Geoffrey. *Philip II.* Little, Brown, 1978.

Slocombe, George. *Don John of Austria: The Victor of Lepanto (1547–1578).* Houghton, 1936.

FURTHER READING:

Chuboda, Bohdan. *Spain and the Empire, 1519–1643.* University of Chicago Press, 1952.

Elliott, J. H. *Imperial Spain, 1469–1716.* St. Martin's Press, 1963.

Lynch, John. *Spain Under the Habsburgs.* 2 vols. Oxford University Press, 1964.

Merriman, Roger Bigelow. *The Rise of the Spanish Empire in the Old World and the New.* 4 vols. Macmillan, 1918.

Parker, Geoffrey. *The Dutch Revolt.* Cornell University Press, 1977.

King John of England

(1166–1216)

Third of the Angevin kings, whose indecisiveness led to the loss of England's French territories, whose feud with the pope led to the worst era of Anglo-Vatican relations before the Reformation, and whose taxation and war policies aroused the baronial rebellion which created the Magna Carta.

Name variations: John Lackland. Born in 1166; died in 1216; son of King Henry II of England and Eleanor of Aquitaine; brother of Richard the Lionheart; married: Isabelle of Gloucester; married: Isabelle of Angoulême; children: included Henry, and an illegitimate daughter who married Llewelyn ab Iorwerth (king of North Wales). Successor: Henry III (eldest son).

One of the most villainous kings of England, King John's arbitrary ways led to a baronial uprising that forced him to grant the Magna Carta—the first "Bill of Rights" in the history of the English-speaking peoples. The story of wicked King John can be traced back to the chroniclers Roger of Wendover and Matthew Paris, monks who wrote critically of a king who had come into frequent conflict with their church. Recent historians have found more encouraging things to say about King John as a ruler and lawgiver, especially by comparison with his swaggering, bloodthirsty brother **Richard the Lionheart.** All agree that he was anything but saintly, however, and that his treacherous conduct and almost total lack of religious or moral scruple make him an odious figure for moral contemplation.

John was born in 1166, son of King **Henry II** and eighth child of **Eleanor of Aquitaine.** His belligerent parents were often separated, but John—his father's favorite—grew up in the wandering Angevin court, sometimes in England, sometimes in Henry's extensive French possessions. Violence was a way of life for the Angevins. One chronicler, remarking on their bad tempers,

Contributed by Patrick Allitt, Assistant Professor of History, Emory University, Atlanta, Georgia

recorded that when Henry II heard one of his rivals praised, he "fell screaming out of bed, tore up his coverlet, and thrashed around the floor cramming his mouth with the stuffing of his mattress." John was hardly more temperate; in a bad temper "his whole person became so changed as to be hardly recognizable. Rage contorted his brow, his burning eye glittered, bluish spots discolored the pink of his cheeks." It didn't help that John's ferocious older brothers—Henry, Geoffrey, and Richard—resisting his early efforts to gain estates of his own, gave him the contemptuous nickname "Lackland."

In 1185, when his father made his 19-year-old son overlord of Ireland, John led an expedition of 60 ships there to subdue rebellious chieftains. Wasting his resources on high living, however, John failed to win the allegiance of the Anglo-Norman barons he was supposed to conciliate. The chronicles say that he and his courtiers pulled the Irishmen's long beards and mocked their rustic manners. Defeated by **Donnell O'Brien**, king of Limerick, John's soldiers retreated in disarray. Then, in a family feud of 1189, John joined his brother Richard against their father Henry, and witnessed Henry's final humiliating defeat and death that summer. That same year, he married his cousin Isabelle (or Hadwisa) of Gloucester, to whom he had been betrothed since his tenth year.

When the new king Richard I the Lionheart set off on crusade, he tried to buy his brother John's loyalty by giving him massive gifts of estates throughout England, making him "Lackland" no longer. Far from showing gratitude, John schemed ceaselessly against the new king, anticipating that he in turn would become king at his brother's death. He used Richard's capture on the way home from the Third Crusade as an opportunity to rebel but was humiliated by forces led by his own warrior-mother Eleanor of Aquitaine. After hiding out in Normandy when Richard returned in 1194, John was ultimately forced to throw himself on his brother's mercy. Although John was 27, the king told him, "Think no more of it, John; you are only a child who has had evil counsellors," and with this mortifying act of mercy forgave him.

John Assumes the Throne

During the next five years, John wisely remained loyal to his brother and built up credit among the king's courtiers. Thus, when Richard died at the siege of Chalus in 1199, John was able to assume the throne with Richard's blessing, and despite an immediate conspiracy against him, was able to rebuff his nephew Arthur of Brittany's claim to the

throne. (He later killed this nephew while on a drunken spree in the city of Rouen—allegedly with his bare hands—and threw the body into the River Seine.) Having inherited estates in England and western France which were desperately overburdened with debts incurred during his brother's wars, John lay down his sword and began rebuilding and consolidating his estates. Although his peacemaking efforts drew for him another scornful nickname, "Softsword," most historians agree that he was sensible to come to terms with King **Philip II Augustus** of France. During a royal tour through his southwestern French dominions, however, he decided to marry another Isabelle, the 12-year-old daughter of the turbulent count of Angoulême. For this purpose, he coolly arranged for a papal dissolution of his first marriage on grounds that he and Isabelle of Gloucester were too closely related. Legend has it that lust got the better of his diplomatic instincts when he made this match—it certainly worsened his relations with Philip of France with whom he had been discussing marriage-alliance possibilities.

Having surveyed all his French lands, John next toured his British holdings, visiting more parts of England than any predecessor since the Norman Conquest of 1066. His hard work as an administrator, then and throughout his reign, has impressed historians, especially when they compare his diligence with the absentee Richard I's negligence. His

<table>
<tr><td colspan="2">**CHRONOLOGY**</td></tr>
<tr><td>**1166**</td><td>John born</td></tr>
<tr><td>**1185**</td><td>Failed mission to Ireland</td></tr>
<tr><td>**1189**</td><td>Joined brother Richard in rebellion against father Henry II; Henry died; Richard succeeded</td></tr>
<tr><td>**1192**</td><td>John schemed with Philip Augustus of France, against Richard</td></tr>
<tr><td>**1194**</td><td>Richard returned from crusade and captivity, pardoned John</td></tr>
<tr><td>**1199**</td><td>John succeeded to throne</td></tr>
<tr><td>**1202**</td><td>Victory at Mirabeau</td></tr>
<tr><td>**1204**</td><td>Loss of Normandy</td></tr>
<tr><td>**1208**</td><td>Papal Interdict</td></tr>
<tr><td>**1214**</td><td>Interdict revoked; John defeated at Battle of Bouvines</td></tr>
<tr><td>**1215**</td><td>Magna Carta and baronial rebellion</td></tr>
<tr><td>**1216**</td><td>John died</td></tr>
</table>

purpose was not solely a dedication to good government, of course; he wanted a better grip on his dominions in order to raise more money from them. Having the misfortune to live in an age of inflation, he found that more money was needed to fulfill traditional purposes. His barons resisted his exactions so far as they were able, and the story of their deteriorating relations with John is in large part the story of ever-greater tax burdens laid upon them by the king, coupled with his military failures. Those unable to resist often suffered worst from his demands. On one occasion in 1210, he had all the Jews in England arrested and extorted from them a loan of 66,000 marks.

Like the other Angevin kings, John was constantly on the move, rarely spending more than two or three days in any place, dispensing justice and answering subjects' pleas as he moved. A large household of retainers and servants moved with him, the king's own party often hunting or hawking while the slow baggage train poked along from one site to the next. At times, John showed conspicuous generosity to his retainers and certainly liked to entertain on a grand scale. Historian W.L. Warren lists some of his Christmas bills:

> For 3 blankets, two large knives, twenty four towels, 103 yards of canvas for sacks and cloaks, 1500 cups, 1200 pitchers, 10,000 herrings, 1800 whiting, 4000 dishes, 900 haddocks, 3000 lampreys, and for cartage and work on apartments and tables Thirty Two Pounds, Twelve Shillings and Elevenpence.

No sooner was King John's first tour complete than he learned of renewed conspiracies against him in France. Once his ally, the French king Philip was now trying to break up John's French Empire and seize Normandy, its chief northern province. John began the war for his possessions with a daring march to Mirabeau to rescue his mother Eleanor who was besieged in the castle there. Not only did he rescue her, he also managed to seize nearly all the leaders of the rebellion against him. He imprisoned them in England at Corfe Castle but cruelly and unwisely let them starve to death after an abortive escape attempt.

This loss of hostages and the leverage they would have offered, along with overconfidence in subsequent campaigns, led to disasters. The nobles of Normandy no longer trusted him and resented his practice of replacing them with mercenary captains in positions of responsibility. Several barons went over to Philip's cause. In the long run, the war proved catastrophic, his "impregnable" fortress of Gaillard at Les Andelys (built by his brother Richard) fell by storm after a seven-month siege, and in 1204 John finally had to abandon Normandy completely. Many nobles, who had held estates in England and Normandy since the days of William the Conqueror, were now compelled to choose either to confirm their loyalty to John and hold on to their English lands, or else swear fealty to Philip for their Norman lands and face confiscation in England—an irksome choice to be forced to make.

With a hostile French king on the south shore of the English channel, John had to look to his marine defenses, and became in effect the founder of the Royal Navy. Its principal ships were galleys, but it relied on forcible conscription of supplementary merchant ships in the event of a major conflict (a naval policy continued up to the days of the Spanish Armada nearly 400 years later). From then on for century after century, Britain and France remained enemies on land and at sea, one of the most destructive, long-lasting, and implacable hostilities in the history of Western civilization. Despite this chronic warfare, English admiration for French culture never lapsed, and from King John's time until the years of Napoleon, even to the present, an educated minority of Britons was always eager to travel and study in France. The hatred between the two nations and peoples usually took precedence over this countervailing admiration, however, especially among the lower social classes. Historian Paul Johnson argues that intervals of peace in the long Anglo-French wars were mainly attributable to economic exhaustion:

> [W]henever the English grasped the point that the war was losing money, as from time to time they did, they were abruptly overcome by a rash of pacifism. One might say that much of the history of England has been a conflict between xenophobia and avarice, with the latter usually, in the end, getting the upper hand. The irresistible force of the English desire for war meets the immovable object of the refusal to pay for it.

After the loss of Normandy, John tried every conceivable means of recovering it short of a direct frontal assault, which his vassals were unwilling to finance, believing him too untrustworthy and cowardly to carry it off effectively. His navy won its first notable victory at Zwyn in 1213 against a French invasion fleet. He paid subsidies to all anti-French princes on the eastern borders of France, including the Holy Roman Emperor Otto, and he kept a large force of Flemish knights constantly ready for battle. So long as he was strengthening his fortifications at home and preparing to resist a French invasion, John's English vassals were usually willing to cooperate. They also supported him in successful warring campaigns against Scotland, Ireland, and Wales from 1210 to 1212, whose victories he tried to safeguard by taking hostage the children of Scottish, Irish, and Welsh nobility. Making good on a threat, he hanged 28 of his Welsh hostages in 1212 when the Welsh king Llewelyn ab Iorwerth broke a truce.

Despite John's successes within the British Isles, his barons would not help him retake Normandy directly. Nevertheless, he tried a direct campaign in 1213–14, marching from the southwest after a landing at La Rochelle, and coordinated with an attack by his knights from the northeast. John's army faltered and was defeated at the battle of Roche-au-Moine. Worse, his northern army, replete with Flemish and imperial soldiers, was shattered at the battle of Bouvines, and he was forced to return to England in disgrace once again. After this disaster, his holdings in France shrank irreparably; by the end of his reign, they had been lost with the single exception of Gascony, so that the House of Anjou no longer possessed even Anjou itself.

Baronial Uprising Leads to Magna Carta

No sooner had he landed from his 1214 failure, however, than King John resumed a favored device of charging fines to knights who had refused to accompany him. This provocative act by a man who had just been soundly defeated led to the baronial uprising which culminated in the Magna Carta. Many English barons had been smarting ever since the defeat of their rebellion against John's father Henry II in 1173; Henry had punished the rebels by confiscation of lands and heavy fines, part of the long effort by the Angevin kings to strengthen their financial status vis-a-vis their barons. Already weakened by defeats in Europe, however, John was in a feebler position than his father had been. His situation was particularly precarious because he had only recently emerged from a long controversy with the papacy, which was itself a major player in medieval politics.

Conflict with the papacy was nothing new to the Angevin kings, to be sure; John's father Henry II had scandalized all of Christian Europe by killing Archbishop **Thomas Becket** in Canterbury 35 years earlier. Conflicts between kings, bishops, and Rome were endemic to the age. John's problem stemmed from a disputed appointment. Pope **Innocent III,** one of the most formidable medieval pontiffs, had ordered, in 1205, that the vacant see

of Canterbury should receive as its new archbishop Stephen Langton. The king had appointed a candidate of his own, John de Gray, in accordance with tradition, and refused to accept the pope's nominee. John refused to let Langton enter England at all, and the pope retaliated first by placing an interdict on England (bringing all church business to a halt) and then, in 1209, by excommunicating the temerarious king. John countered by taking all church revenues into his own chronically overstretched treasury, and using it for his Welsh, Irish, and Scottish campaigns. In 1213, Philip of France, seeing an opportunity for exploiting his long-term enemy's embarrassment, raised the odds by declaring that his war against John was no longer simply a secular affair but a crusade, undertaken in God's name. John, afraid of this escalation and of possible desertions from his ranks, then threw himself on the pope's mercy, received his kingdom once more as a fiefdom of the Vatican, and nullified Philip's crusade.

Renewed papal support was not enough to forestall baronial revolt, much of which was strengthened by the discontent of newly impoverished churchmen who had felt the force of the interdict for the last six years. After a succession of negotiations with leading barons under the command of Robert Fitz Walter, John signed the Magna Carta on the island of Runnymede in the Thames Valley, a long document guaranteeing the legal rights of the barons, the king, the administration, and the judiciary.

The charter, which only later took on its name (a function simply of its size) listed many of the grievances the barons felt at John's rule. It specified that his mercenary favorites be relieved of their commands and pension and be banished from the realm. It appealed against arbitrary taxation and tried to establish the principle that barons' consent be gained for all financial exactions. Clause 39, subsequently made famous in British and American constitutional tradition, specified that no freeman could be arrested, imprisoned, outlawed, exiled, "or in any way destroyed" except by lawful judgment of his peers, in accordance with the law of the land. Clause 61 made provision for a baronial council of 25 to ensure that the king was not ruling in an arbitrary way. Few provisions of the Magna Carta took the common people into consideration; it certainly cannot be considered a democratic reform document.

Although it is remembered as the foundation of English liberties and the basis of government by consent, it led rapidly to the outbreak of renewed hostilities when John refused to observe key clauses and when he called on his new ally the pope to excommunicate all rebellious barons. The barons declared that they were now adopting a new king of England—Louis, the son of Philip of France. Civil War broke out in late 1215 and into the next year. John won a succession of victories against his rebellious subjects but could not prevent Prince Louis from landing and advancing to London to receive homage from the rebels.

During this campaign, while crossing the Wash—a shallow estuary in East Anglia—John's army was caught by the inflowing tide and lost its baggage train. Dismayed at the loss of its hugely valuable cargo, which included his collection of jewelry, John retreated to the Cistercian monastery of Swineshead. Here, according to the chroniclers, he overate on a meal of peaches and beer, caught a fever, and died soon thereafter.

The kingdom was left to his infant son, Henry III; Louis of France did not succeed, but the barons were able to reassert the Great Charter as the basis of their liberties. It went on to play a fundamental role in British constitutional tradition despite the deeply compromised character of its origins.

SOURCES:

Crouch, David. *William Marshal: Court, Career and Chivalry in the Angevin Empire, 1147–1219*. Longman, 1990.

Hindley, Geoffrey. *The Book of Magna Carta*. Constable, 1990.

Johnson, Paul. *A History of the English People*. Harper, 1985.

Painter, Sidney. *The Reign of King John*. Johns Hopkins University Press, 1949.

Prestwich, Michael. *English Politics in the Thirteenth Century*. Macmillan, 1990.

Warren, W. L. *King John*. University of California Press, 1978.

John III Sobieski

(1629–1696)

Polish leader, who rejuvenated the faltering Polish state and saved the Habsburg Empire by defeating the Turkish army at the gates of Vienna.

Name variations: Jan Sobieski. Pronunciation: So-BYES-kee. Born on August 17, 1629, in Olesko castle in eastern Poland; died at his Wilanow estate outside of Warsaw, Poland, on June 17, 1696; second son of Jakub Sobieski (a descendant from Polish nobility) and Theophila Danillowiczowna; married: Marie Kazimiere d'Arquien (Marysienka); children: (three sons and one daughter) Jakub, Constantine, Alexander, and Teresa. Predecessor: Michael Wisniowiecki. Successor: Fryderyk August II Mocny (the Strong).

Poland of the 16th and 17th centuries was a place of both continuity and extraordinary contradiction. Sixteenth-century Poland realized her *Zloty Wiek* (Golden Age) under the leadership of her Renaissance kings, Zygmunt I Stary and **Zygmunt II Augustus.** King Zygmunt II, however, died without leaving an heir for the Polish throne, and his death in 1572 brought an abrupt end to Poland's stable and prosperous Jagiellonian dynasty. The continuity and cultural progress of the Jagiellon rulers was soon replaced by a disjointed system of elective monarchy.

During the Jagiellonian period, the Polish nobility greatly increased their political power and finally, with the death of Zygmunt II, they secured the right to elect their future sovereigns. After much debate the nobles of the *Sejm* (Parliament) used their newly gained power to elect a French candidate, Henri of Valois (Henryk III Walezy) to the Polish throne. Henri, however, only remained with his new subjects for a few months before using the cover of night to return to his native France and ascend the French throne. Following Henri of Valois's abdication of the Polish throne, the *Sejm* wasted little time before electing the

Contributed by Christopher Blackburn, Ph.D. candidate in history, Auburn University, Auburn, Alabama

CHRONOLOGY

1648	Peace of Westphalia ended the Thirty Years' War
1655	Beginning of the Swedish-Polish War; Sobieski served in Swedish army of Charles Gustavus
1656	Rejoined the Polish court; given an independent command in the Polish army
1668	Sobieski named Grand Hetman of the Polish army
1674	Elected king of Poland
1677	Purchased his estate at Wilanow
1683	Led a coalition force that lifted the Turkish siege of Vienna
1684	Formation of the Christian League for the expulsion of the Turks from Europe
1686	Formation of the League of Augsburg
1688	Glorious Revolution in England
1696	Sobieski died at his Wilanow estate

Transylvanian Stephen Báthory as the next king of Poland. With the death of Báthory in 1586, the nobility turned to the Swedish Vasa (Waza) family for a king. Friar Tommaso Campanella later wrote of Poland's fascination with electing foreign princes as the kings of Poland:

> For while thou mournest for thy monarch dead
>
> Thou wilt not let his son the sceptre bear
>
> Lest he prove weak perchance to do or dare.
>
> Yet art thou even more by luck misled,
>
> Choosing a prince of fortune, courtly bred,
>
> Uncertain whether he will spend or spare.

The emergence of the Swedes as kings of Poland ultimately led to the Swedish invasion of Poland in the mid-17th century and the chaotic period known as the Polish "Deluge."

John Sobieski was born near the end of the reign of King Zygmunt III Vasa. He was, however, unfortunate enough to spend most of his formative and adult years under the pathetic governments of Ladislas IV and John II Casimir (Jan Kazimierz).

Sobieski was born in 1629 at Olesko castle on the Sobieski family estate in eastern Poland. Although he was a descendant of lesser nobility, his father eventually attained the office of Castellan of Krakow ("warden of the castle"), and his great-grandfather Stanislaw Zolkiewski was a for-

mer *Hetman* ("general") of Poland. Sobieski's patriotic mother educated all her children in their family's history; she never allowed them to forget the brilliant military tradition of their forefathers in protecting Poland's borders against invading Tatars, Cossacks, Turks, and Germans.

Young John and his older brother Marek received much of their education while at the family estate at Zolkiew. Eventually allowed to complete their formal education at the University of Krakow, the brothers then left on a grand tour of Western Europe in 1646. During their two-year trip, they visited and studied military engineering in France, England, Germany, Holland, and Italy. They were, however, forced to end the journey and return to Poland in July 1648, because their father had died suddenly and their mother was trapped by Cossacks in the fortress at Zamosc. Both John and Marek quickly joined the Polish army and financed the formation of two military squadrons. Marek's military career was, however, short-lived. In 1652, he was captured and beheaded by Tatar forces. With the death of his only brother, John Sobieski found himself alone at the head of three reputable and wealthy Polish families: Sobieski, Zolkiewski, and Danillowicz.

Swedes Invade Poland

After an adventurous campaign in 1653 as a young officer fighting and studying Turkish and Tatar forces, Sobieski faced the Swedish invasion of 1654. As the Swedish forces of King Charles X Gustavus swept across Poland, King John Casimir and Queen Louise Marie de Gonzague eluded capture and fled to Silesia. Charles Gustavus soon conquered the halfhearted Polish defenders and proclaimed himself ruler of Poland. The interval from 1648 until 1660 is traditionally known as the "Deluge," one of the darkest periods in Polish history. Faced with internal strife and unrest among the nobility because of the inept rule of John Casimir, Poland was also invaded from without by Swedes, Cossacks, Muscovites, Tatars, Transylvanians, and Germans. In the midst of this turmoil, Sobieski made possibly the worst mistake of his long and illustrious career, he chose to serve the king of Sweden. To his credit, Sobieski abandoned the treacherous Charles Gustavus in 1656, after only eight months of service. With his return to the Polish court of John Casimir, he was made a standard-bearer of Poland and given his first independent command.

In the year 1655, the occupation force of Charles Gustavus committed countless atrocities throughout the Polish countryside and attempted to cart everything of value back to Sweden. This series of endless offenses soon rallied the lethargic and splintered Polish populace to defend their country, and by mid-1656 the Poles were effectively resisting Swedish authority. Jan Pasek, a Polish soldier of the day, vividly described the ruthless nature of the conflict:

> [W]e put to the sword six thousand Swedes who had assembled from various fortresses with much booty acquired in Poland and were trying to cross over to Prussia to join their King. We killed them to the very last man so that as the saying goes [not a single survivor; not even the messenger], not one be left to report to the King the news of the destruction of this army; those who fled from the battlefield to the forest or to the marshes met with an even more cruel death at the hand of the peasants.

Despite their fierce and costly nature, the Polish Wars continued until 1660. By the end of the carnage, Polish forces had regained their country by successfully expelling all occupation troops and repulsing innumerable attacks by Swedes, Cossacks, Tatars, Transylvanians, Muscovites, and Germans.

With the end of the Polish "Time of Troubles," Sobieski turned his attention to politics and Queen Louise Marie's beautiful, and married, lady-in-waiting, Marie Casimere d'Arquien. Marie, commonly known as Marysienka, immediately captivated Sobieski with her independent nature and animated personality. The 1660s proved very successful for Sobieski. His political career, initially launched by his election to the *Sejm*, skyrocketed with his appointment to the post of Grand Marshal and Deputy Hetman of Poland in 1665, and—almost simultaneously—Marysienka's husband conveniently died. Through the promptings of Queen Louise, Sobieski and Marysienka were married later that same year. Sobieski's marriage to the politically aspiring Marysienka clearly marked a new stage of his life, but to say Sobieski was merely the political puppet of his ambitious wife is an obvious overstatement of the facts. As historian L.R. Lewitter illustrates:

> Her beauty and vivacity were to Sobieski and Poland, what Cleopatra's nose had been to Caesar and Rome. Though to explain the whole of Sobieski's conduct from now on in terms of the sublimation of his passion for Marysienka would be a piece of gross over-simplification, it cannot be denied that she was a major and sometimes dominant influence in his life.

In the late 1660s, Sobieski led successful military campaigns against Poland's ancient enemies: the Cossacks, Tatars, and Turks. As reward for his military victories and loyalty during the Lubomirski Rebellion of 1667, Sobieski was named the Grand Hetman of Poland in 1668. That year also witnessed the abdication of King John Casimir and the election of Michael Wisniowiecki as king of Poland. Throughout King Michael's short reign, ending with his abrupt death in November 1673, Sobieski continually proved his military prowess and improved his reputation as a leader. With the death of Michael the nobility once again began the deliberations to determine the next king of Poland. Pasek's memoirs recount the sentiments of the election:

> The election of the new king took place [in May] near Warsaw, but no longer with such a great assemblage as had accompanied that of Michal. Much competition existed also there, but once again God gave us a Piast, [one of our own blood,] the Field Hetman and Commander-in-Chief of the Polish forces, Jan Sobieski.

Sobieski's coronation in 1674 marked the beginning of a period of pro-French policies by Poland. His wife's close ties with France greatly influenced his decision to pursue an amicable relationship with King **Louis XIV** of France, and he ultimately hoped to use French support to establish the Sobieski family as the ruling house of Poland. Also, he imagined a grand military alliance to regain lost Polish territories from the Austrians, Prussians, and Turks. Sobieski soon confirmed his alliance with Louis XIV by signing a secret agreement with the French ambassador at Jaworow. The arrangement called for Poland to drive back the Turks, reclaim East Prussia, and attack Austria when the opportunity presented itself. Although Sobieski waged yet another successful campaign against the Turks, the procrastination of Poland's allies never afforded him the opportunity to begin his campaign against East Prussia.

Turks Are Defeated at Vienna

A noticeable decay of French-Polish relations in 1680, coupled with a Turkish military buildup in the Balkans, brought about a substantial improvement of Habsburg-Polish relations. On April 1, 1683, Sobieski revealed his fear of France's Turkish ally by signing a defensive treaty with the emperor of Germany, Leopold I. In the summer of 1683, Leopold's worst nightmare was realized as he found his Vienna capital surrounded by some 140,000 Turkish troops. Certain of his empire's destruction, the German Emperor was pleasantly surprised, however, as Sobieski and a multinational force of 75,000 men soon appeared near Vienna. As the highest-ranking official of the rescue mission, Sobieski assumed total command of the forces, but it was Sobieski's years of effective campaigning against the Turks that made him the logical choice for the position of commander in chief. The Polish leader conducted the operations brilliantly and on September 12, 1683, at Kahlenberg, inflicted a decisive defeat on the Turkish army. The Duke of Lorrain, who was present that day, later reported:

> All the Cavalry of the Emperor was marching to the Engagement with stedfastness and joy: But the whole action was done by the Polanders alone, who left nothing for the Germans to do.

With the Turkish forces in disarray and heading toward their homeland, Sobieski launched offensives to liberate Hungary from Turkish troops.

Sobieski continued his liberation campaigns until 1691, primarily in an attempt to acquire territory along the Black Sea. Though unsuccessful in his bid for Polish dominance in that area, he was ultimately successful in his struggle to prevent Turkish domination of Eastern and Central Europe. The last years of Sobieski's life dismally concluded an otherwise brilliant career. His final days were filled with sickness and bitter disputes with both family and the Polish nobility. King John III Sobieski died on June 17, 1696, outside of Warsaw, at his rejuvenated Wilanow palace.

SOURCES:

Dalerac, M. *Polish Manuscripts: or the Secret History of the Reign of John Sobieski, The III. of that Name, K. of Poland.* Printed for D. Rhodes, at the Star, near Fleet-Bridge, 1700.

Davies, Norman. *God's Playground: A History of Poland.* Columbia University Press, 1982.

Garlicki, Andrzej, ed. *Poczet krolow i ksiazat polskich.* Czytelnik, 1980.

Lewitter, L. R. "John Sobieski: Savior of Vienna," in *History Today.* March & April 1962.

Milton, John. *A Declaration or Letters Patents of the Election of the present King of Poland, John the Third: Elected on 22d of May last past, Anno Dom. 1674.* Printed for Brabazon Aylmer, at the Three Pigeons in Cornhil, 1674.

Mizwa, Stephen, ed. *Great Men and Women of Poland.* Macmillan, 1941.

Stoye, John. *The Siege of Vienna.* Holt, 1964.

Swiecicka, Maria, trans. *The Memoirs of Jan Chryzostom z Goslawic Pasek.* Kosciuszko Foundation, 1978.

FURTHER READING:

de Battaglia, O. Forest. *Jan Sobieski.* Einsiedeln, 1946.

Laskowski, O. *Sobieski: King of Poland.* Glasgow, 1944.

John XXIII

(1881–1963)

Pope, ruling for less time than any 20th-century predecessor, who set in motion the second Vatican Council which transformed the Catholic Church and its position in the world.

"John XXIII is a man of balance who prefers to pacify rather than affront, to exercise patience rather than cut a knot."

HENRI FESQUET

Pope John XXIII sat on the papal throne for less than five years but set in motion profound changes in Catholic and world history. Soon after his election in 1958, already age 77, he declared his intention to summon a Vatican Council of all the world's bishops and to charge it with the task of *aggiornamento*, opening a window from the Catholic Church out onto the modern world. He hoped the Church could resume its long-lost place at the center of Western civilization. The council met in the fall of 1962 and in the fall of each successive year until 1965. Although Pope John, who died in 1963, saw only the first of these sessions completed, he had lived long enough to put plans into action whose consequences for good and ill are still being felt today. He was the last pope to be almost universally obeyed by his flock, and the first to be widely loved and admired by non-Catholic people throughout the world.

Born Angelo Roncalli in Bergamo, northern Italy, in 1881, he was the son of poor peasant farmers. The Church was then almost the only avenue of advancement for peasant children; when Roncalli proved intelligent and gifted, he was sent

Born Angelo Roncalli in Bergamo, northern Italy, in 1881; died in 1963; son of poor peasant farmers; adopted the papal name John XXIII on his election in 1958. Predecessor: Pius XII (1939–58). Successor: Paul VI (1963–78).

Contributed by Patrick Allitt, Assistant Professor of History, Emory University, Atlanta, Georgia

CHRONOLOGY

1903	Ordained a priest
1921	Promoted to monsignor; made Catholic missions fundraiser
1925	Appointed apostolic visitor to Bulgaria and promoted to archbishop
1934	Moved to Istanbul
1939–45	Second World War (Roncalli still in Istanbul)
1944	Appointed papal nuncio in Paris
1953	Appointed patriarch of Venice
1958	Pius XII died; Roncalli elected pope as John XXIII
1962	Second Vatican Council convened in Rome
1963	John XXIII died; succession of Paul VI

to seminary schools and trained for the priesthood before the age of ten. Ordained a priest in 1903 (soon after a man of even humbler birth had been crowned Pope Pius X), Roncalli showed few remarkable talents at first but gradually developed diplomatic and organizational skills and was repaid with sequential promotions. Much of his early and middle adulthood were, nevertheless, spent in positions of relative obscurity for an ambitious churchman, and the greatest advancements of his life all came when he was beyond the age of 70. Between 1925 and 1934, he was almost an exile in his work as the pope's representative in Bulgaria, where Christianity was a poorly organized minority religion, divided between Roman Catholics and Eastern Orthodox. The Vatican Curia (Vatican civil service), world center of conservative Catholic power, considered him prone to theological literalism and kept him away from centers of influence. The celibate clergy, denied many worldly pleasures, often compensated by pursuing career ambitions and indulging in malicious gossip. Roncalli struggled against both temptations; his letters from these years show him holding himself on a tight rein, trying to silence his discontents, and counseling calm, peace, and resignation.

From Bulgaria, Roncalli was sent by Pope Pius XI to Istanbul, Turkey, where, as archbishop, he faced an even more complicated blend of religions living side by side: Christians were in the minority, Islam dominant, and the regime of Atatürk (**Mustafa Kemal**) militantly secularist. But Archbishop Roncalli was gifted at reconciling antagonists and, unlike many of his Catholic con-

temporaries, kept on good terms not only with the Catholics under his care but with members of all political parties and factions and representatives of all faiths. When the Second World War began, neutral Turkey became a center of international espionage and intrigue, and Istanbul a city through which passed refugees, many of them Jews escaping from Nazism. Roncalli distinguished himself in taking care of the Church's interests and in aiding these refugees, and this work brought him to the attention of Pope Pius XII.

As the Allies swept across Western Europe following D-Day in late 1944, Roncalli was appointed papal nuncio (highest-ranking papal representative) to newly liberated Paris where he undertook the politically sensitive task of reconciling clergy and Catholic citizens who had resisted the Nazis with those who had collaborated, while removing from office the most flagrant collaborationists. He again showed a diplomatic flair and managed to avoid making enemies. Papal delegates in France had traditionally been intrusive in local politics; Roncalli was careful to avoid any heavy-handedness and became correspondingly well liked by Parisian Catholics and politicians. He was, throughout his adult life, bald and fat, and despite a serious interest in history (he wrote books and articles on the Catholic past) was regarded by many contemporaries as dim-witted, even clownish, not an intriguer. This reputation served him well, and he profited from being underestimated; he was never a "holy fool," pious legends to the contrary. His political skill, as well as his orthodox faith and administrative diligence, led to further promotion in 1953 when he was made Patriarch of Venice, now wearing a cardinal's red hat.

The old man who promoted Roncalli, Pius XII (1939–58), was a pope in the old style, monarchical, austerely dignified, a lonely eminence; he expected those to whom he spoke both in person and on the telephone to kneel down. When Pius XII walked in the Vatican gardens, the gardeners were told to hide behind trees so that the pontiff's solitude might be preserved. Former papal nuncio in Berlin, Pius was pro-German and his wartime policy led to much criticism, because of his reluctance to condemn Hitler and his belief that Communist Russia posed a far worse threat than Nazi Germany to the Christian West. Roncalli, untainted by pro-German sympathies, enjoyed advancement partly as a result of Pius's need to recover his and the Church's prestige at the war's end. Venice was a major and much-coveted appointment. As before, Roncalli governed well and, despite a political aversion to the communist and socialist parties then prominent in Italian politics, made sure to be on cordial personal terms with the representatives of each; for reasons of tact and hospitality, he publicly welcomed a socialist convention to Venice in 1956. Pius's death in 1958 led to the final promotion, though Roncalli, who had never worked in the Curia but always away from Rome, was far from assured of election when the conclave opened. But neither was he a shocking choice. As historian Paul Johnson noted:

> His career had brought him into contact with vast numbers of people who needed to be handled with finesse, and a wide range of situations which required tact and intelligence. He had learned to be a diplomat in the best and broadest sense, and this background undoubtedly proved of great value when he assumed the papacy.

As pope, he quickly asserted himself. Taking the name John XXIII was itself a controversial step because the name had previously been taken by one of the Avignon "antipopes" during a Church schism centuries before. Unlike the reclusive Pius XII, he minimized the royal aspects of the papacy and mingled freely with his flock. He visited schools and prisons in Rome and met with representatives of diverse groups, again including non-Catholics. Despite a bulky mythology which has grown up around his memory since the 1960s, he was not really a "liberal" and certainly not a "radical" Catholic. He confirmed Pius XII's ban on the experimental French "worker-priest" movement (in which priests took factory jobs and lived the life of the working men they hoped to bring back to the Church), and he reasserted the tradition of priestly celibacy. He loved Latin, the traditional language of Catholic liturgy, for its precision and its international status among the world's Catholics, and wrote a long justification of Latin, *Veterim Sapientia* in 1962.

But if not radical he was certainly willing to experiment. Catholic representatives appeared at the 1961 meeting of the World Council of Churches in New Delhi whereas earlier popes had spurned the organization. Seeking for some mitigation of the Cold War, John XXIII appealed for peace during the two great power confrontations of his pontificate: the Berlin Wall crisis of 1961 and the Cuban Missile Crisis of 1962. He also received in audience the daughter and son-in-law of Soviet premier **Nikita Khrushchev**. He created more cardinals than tradition dictated, including the first Indian and the first African cardinals, and he set up a secretariat for Promoting Christian Unity under one of his most talented subordinates, Cardinal Augustine Bea. Seeking to bring a close

to a long and shameful tradition of Catholic anti-Semitism, he ordered passages of anti-Jewish language to be omitted from the Good Friday Mass.

Pope Announces Second Vatican Council

By far the most momentous of his decisions was the January 1959 declaration that, at the prompting of the Holy Ghost, he would convene a Second Vatican Council in 1962 to clarify Church teaching and adapt Catholicism to the modern world. His aim was to strengthen and reinvigorate the Church's reputation, which the eccentric recluse Pius XII had let slip. Many Catholics were surprised by this announcement because the First Vatican Council (1869–70) had formally decreed the dogma of papal infallibility on questions of faith and morals, placing the Roman pontiff distinctly above the world's bishops and cardinals in authority. Further Councils seemed, logically, unnecessary, a view which Pius XII had reinforced when in 1950 he declared the dogma of the Assumption of the Blessed Virgin Mary (the belief that upon Mary's death her soul and body were taken into heaven) without the advice of the world's bishops. The First Vatican Council had ended abruptly for external political reasons without ever defining the countervailing powers of the bishops; an issue, said John XXIII, that the second council could now take up.

Distribution of powers was not the only item on the agenda. More generally, how were Catholics and their Church to relate to the modern world from which they had become ever more estranged in the last 100 years, as a blizzard of political, scientific, and technological changes transformed the planet? Catholicism in the 1950s saw itself as actively or latently at war with many aspects of this world. Papal encyclical letters of 1891 (*Rerum Novarum*) and 1931 (*Quadragesimo Anna*) had condemned both capitalism and socialism as political-economic systems based on philosophical materialism rather than divine wisdom; Pius XI and Pius XII had both believed that Catholicism was at war with communism, a tyrannical and atheistical force in world history; in the 1950s, the Vatican supported the Western powers' stern prosecution of the Cold War. Many aspects of intellectual modernism, including the Darwinian and relativity revolutions in science, were prohibited by a restrictive papal "Index" of prohibited books and ideas, in force since 1864. Catholics felt themselves to be on the defensive against the corrosive forces of science and modernity, but they retained the self-assurance to believe that they alone had the solution to the world's woes. Could they step back into the center of the modern world?

John XXIII was eager to modify many characteristic Catholic attitudes and to make Catholicism seem less implacable; his lifelong preparation in diplomacy and interfaith relations made him well-suited to the task. In 1961, a year before the council convened, he issued an encyclical letter, *Mater at Magistra* (Mother and Teacher) which posed many of the great dilemmas of the age in a new and unfamiliar Catholic idiom. It fitted into series with *Rerum Novarum* and *Quadragesimo Anno*, falling on the 70th anniversary of the first and the 30th anniversary of the second. Far from stressing the conflict between the West and communism as a stark polar opposition between good and evil, Pope John criticized the luxury and self-indulgence which he said were often characteristic of the Western nations. He appeared to endorse the notion of economic rights and the welfare state, to encourage trade unionism, and to recognize merit in some practical socialist programs, if not their philosophical underpinnings. The state, he argued, could now be used as an instrument to expand human freedoms rather than limit them. No longer would Italian Catholics voting Socialist automatically be committing a sin. The Italian political right wing was dismayed to see the pontiff, hitherto their anchor, sailing off into these uncharted waters. Some American Catholics also disliked the change of tone, and the conservative journal *National Review* joked that its motto would be: "Mater Si, Magistra No!" (a parody of Fidel Castro's declaration, "Cuba Si, Yanqui No!"). Elsewhere, however, the encyclical was greeted warmly. Protestants and secular people in the West found themselves in the unusual position of warmly endorsing a declaration from a source, the Vatican, which they usually viewed through jaundiced eyes.

Encyclical Urges Peace on Earth

Another encyclical, *Pacem in Terris* (Peace on Earth) 1963, was still more of a surprise in that it was addressed not just to Catholics but to all people of good will throughout the world. Abandoning the Vatican's traditionally militant anticommunist rhetoric, Pope John beseeched the great powers to make peace and to rid the world of the danger of nuclear war. He also abandoned the old double standard whereby Catholics would profit from religious toleration when they were in the minority but would prohibit it when they were in the majority. Encyclical letters are couched in general terms and avoid specifics of policy, but the tone of this letter marked an unmistakable shift in Vatican policy, and led many Catholics to speculate on an *apertura a sinistra* (opening to the left) whereby Catholics and Communists might try to settle their differences and find some philosophical common ground. *Pacem in Terris* coincided with the first European and American mass antinuclear movements and with the Russian-American atmospheric test-ban treaty of 1963. One sign of a possible thaw in the Catholic-Communist confrontation was the release of the Ukrainian cardinal Josef Slipyi after 17 years of Soviet imprisonment. Despite the many auguries of change which Pope John's first years in office had provided, the Vatican Council—when it met in full and mighty pomp at St. Peter's—hardly seemed likely to transform the venerable Catholic branch of Christianity. Documents for discussion had been drawn up beforehand by the Curia under its leaders, Cardinals Tardini and Ottaviani, men who had been, and who remained, potential papal candidates themselves. They asserted, in conformity with John XXIII's will, that all debate was to take place in Latin. There was no opportunity for parliamentary cut and thrust even for those who knew Latin well enough to try it. Cardinal Cushing of Boston, one of the senior American churchmen and a man of pragmatic temperament, offered to pay for the installation of a simultaneous translation system, comparable to that in use at the United Nations and the World Council of Churches, but was frostily turned down. Journalists who clustered thickly about the conference, outnumbering the bishops and cardinals, began to speculate that Curial conservatives had resisted the idea of a council and now wanted to muffle the controversial issues rather than encourage a free and open debate. This may indeed have been the hope of the Curial party, but John XXIII's welcome, and his request for a full airing of all views, encouraged energetic discussion, so that issues not originally planned for debate soon came to the floor and influenced the council's final declarations. In his welcoming address, John XXIII deprecated Catholics who "in the existing state of society, see nothing but ruin and calamity." To the contrary, he said:

> we should recognize that, at the present historical moment, Divine Providence is leading us towards a new order in human relationships, which, through the agency of men... are tending towards the fulfillment of higher and, as yet, mysterious and unforeseen designs. Everything, even those events which seem to conflict with her purposes, is ordered for the greater well-being of the church.

Reform-minded bishops and theologians seized on these words as a mandate for change and were not to be disappointed; from the beginning, they worked to circumvent Curial restrictions. They were the more intellectually powerful group and were better acquainted with the media. Journalists were not allowed to attend the sessions, but the reform party knew how to "leak" information and stories designed to enhance their position in the eyes of the public. Johnson remarks:

> The curialists' vision of a bureaucratic steamroller, advancing remorselessly and crushing opposition according to a prearranged timetable, was replaced by something much closer to an open forum.... [T]he curialists soon discovered that the progressives were far more adept than they at parliamentary business.... In brainpower and in sheer tactical skills, the bureaucrats were heavily outmatched.

Pope John did not attend the daily meetings of the council sessions in St. Peter's, but he followed them closely. A month after the council's opening, on November 21, 1962, he intervened during a dispute over the schema on revelation (an absolutely fundamental document by which the Church defined itself). The Curial schema, drawn up beforehand, was disliked by a plurality of the bishops but not the necessary two-thirds. Rather than force them to accept it, Pope John withdrew the schema and ordered that it be redrafted from the ground up, serving notice thereby that free debate and serious changes were possible and that the council would be more than a rubber stamp on the Curial program. Later he intervened to prevent the expulsion from Rome of two radical theologians, Karl Rahner and Raimondo Spiazzi.

The chief controversies opened to discussion were Catholicism's relations with other branches of Christendom (the "Separated Brethren"), the question of conducting liturgy in vernacular languages rather than Latin, power relations within the Church (John was willing to concede some of the attributes of monarchy in favor of a more harmonious "collegiality"), and the role of the laity in the Church. The documents of Vatican II, promulgated in 1965, shifted the direction of the Church on all these issues. It defined itself henceforth not as a hierarchical organization but as the "People of God" moving through history under God's guidance. The laity were accorded positions of new dignity and importance within the Church, the liturgy was brought into the vernacular, and interfaith relations with other Christians and other world religions strengthened.

Pope John XXIII did not live to see this denouement as he died of gastric cancer in June 1963. The deaths of earlier popes had elicited little or no interest in the rest of the world, but the death of this pontiff occasioned an outpouring of regrets and genuine grief throughout the world. In the four and a half years of his pontificate he had managed to transform the image of the papacy itself, and the image of the Church it headed, diminishing its aloofness; its antagonism to the intellectual, political, and social currents of contemporary life; and its institutional rigidity. His successor Paul VI (Giovanni Montini) inherited the controversial fallout as well as the harmonious benefits of the council, making his own pontificate an era of struggle and dispute. This was particularly true in the case of questions related to sex. John XXIII, like his predecessor Pius XII and his successor Paul VI, opposed the use of contraceptives on the grounds that they impeded the regeneration of life, a gift from God. Paul VI was denounced by many Catholics—theologians as well as laity—in Europe and North America in 1968 when he repeated the traditional prohibition, and this obloquy might well have fallen on John had he lived longer. As it is, however, his brief and incandescent rule has assured him a central position in Catholic history.

SOURCES:

Brown, Robert McAfee. *Observer in Rome.* Doubleday, 1964.
Hebbiethwaite, Peter. *John XXIII.* Doubleday, 1985.
Johnson, Paul. *Pope John XXIII.* Little, Brown, 1974.

FURTHER READING:

Holmes, Derek. *The Papacy in the Modern World.* Crossroads, 1981.
Kaisier, Robert. *Pope, Council and World.* Macmillan, 1963.

Joseph II

(1741–1790)

Habsburg emperor, who attempted to increase the power and efficiency of his state by placing all of his subjects, including the feudal nobility and the Church, under the rule of a benevolent but despotic monarchy.

Name variations: Joseph II, King of Germany, Holy Roman Emperor. Born Joseph Benedict Johann Anton Michael Adam von Habsburg on March 13, 1741, in Vienna, Austria; died in Vienna on February 20, 1790; oldest son of the Empress Maria Theresa von Habsburg and the Holy Roman Emperor Francis I Stephen, former Duke of Lorraine; married: Isabel of Parma, June 1760 (died November 27, 1763); married: Josepha of Bavaria, January 1765 (died 1767); children: (first marriage) Maria Theresa and Christine (who died a few hours after her birth). Predecessor: His mother Maria Teresa. Successor: His brother Leopold II.

As the eldest of the Habsburg empress **Maria Theresa**'s 16 children, Joseph experienced the privileged childhood reserved for an archduke (prince) of one of 18th-century Europe's most important royal families. Rulers of Austria since 1282, the Habsburgs had amassed an empire under the Holy Roman Emperor Charles V (1519–55) that threatened to dominate all of Europe and the New World. Their empire was dynastic, which means that the family created it more through astute marriages than military conquests, a fact that largely explains why its provinces were scattered around Europe. During the reign of Charles V, the territories united under Habsburg family rule included Austria, Bohemia, Hungary, parts of Italy, the Netherlands, Spain and its American colonies, plus the rights of the Holy Roman Emperor in the Germanic states. Hardly anything that happened in Europe escaped the attention of Charles V.

By the time Joseph was born on March 13, 1741, the Habsburg Empire, now largely restricted to Central and Eastern Europe, still retained its place among Europe's Great Powers. In fact, Joseph's great-grandfather Leopold I had enhanced

"Joseph II was the eighteenth century's epitome of political reform. In view of the scope of his operations and the size of the territories under his imperial control, he was perhaps the most significant of the Enlightened Despots of his time."

SAUL K. PADOVER

Contributed by Robert F. Forrest, Assistant Professor of History, McNeese State University, Lake Charles, Louisiana

Habsburg prestige at the turn of the 17th century by defeating his family's two traditional adversaries: the Ottomans and the French. However, Habsburg power stagnated during Maria Theresa's 40-year reign (1740–80), allowing the Prussian king **Frederick the Great** to seize most of Silesia, a mineral-rich province lying just north of Bohemia, and to defeat Habsburg attempts to repossess it in the War of the Austrian Succession (1741–42, 1744–45) and the Seven Years' War (1756–63).

Archduke Joseph grew up constantly surrounded by his family's past glories and uncertain future. When he was eight, his pious and authoritarian mother placed Field Marshall Count Carl Batthyany and Father Franz Joseph Weger in charge of his education. The young archduke liked mathematics and natural science, but his curriculum emphasized subjects more practical for a future emperor. In particular, it stressed history so that he would appreciate his family's greatness and avoid his predecessors' errors. Joseph also studied literature and languages, acquiring an excellent knowledge of French, Italian, and Latin. Maria Theresa intended to instill a deep devotion for the Catholic Church in her son, but his religious training, which included attending Mass daily, had the opposite effect. Instead, Joseph's professor of natural and international law, Anton von Martini, one of the leading adherents of the Enlightenment at the University of Vienna, influenced the archduke to accept the rationalism and anticlericalism of such French philosophes as Voltaire. It seems likely that Joseph also embraced the Enlightenment to rebel against his mother's strictness. In fact, Maria Theresa hoped that Joseph's teachers would be able to eliminate his stubbornness. They failed to achieve the empress's wish, and as Joseph passed through his teenage years, he became progressively more aloof from court life and reserved towards people, especially his brothers and sisters, who competed with him for his mother's affections. Later, as co-regent and emperor, he would ignore all his siblings except Leopold and **Marie Antoinette,** and only correspond with the latter because, as queen of France, she was politically useful.

It was not until Joseph turned 14 that his parents permitted him either to dine or spend much time with them. When he was 18, Maria Theresa finally allowed him to escort a woman to a ball. His sheltered life ended at 19 in June 1760 when his mother had him wed Isabel of Parma, niece of Louis XV of France. The marriage was intended to cement the Franco-Austrian Alliance of 1756, which was directed against Frederick the Great of Prussia. Unlike many political marriages that were thrust upon young aristocrats, Joseph

CHRONOLOGY

1764	Crowned Holy Roman Emperor
1765	Father died; Joseph became joint ruler with Maria Theresa
1767	Wife Josepha died
1770	His only surviving child died
1772	First Partition of Poland
1778	Bavarian War
1780	Maria Theresa died; Joseph ruled alone
1781	Abolished serfdom and most Holy Orders
1786	New penal code introduced
1788	Austria and Russia attacked the Ottoman Empire

and Isabel genuinely liked each other, and Joseph was possibly happy for the first time in his life. His relationship with his mother improved, and she introduced him to governmental affairs by appointing him to the Council of State in 1761.

The joys of 1760 proved fleeting for Joseph. In the first place, his mother refused to grant him any important responsibilities after he shocked her with his plan to increase the monarchy's absolutism by taxing the hitherto exempt nobility. Maria Theresa shared Joseph's desire to make the monarchy more absolute, but she was careful to ensure that any reforms designed to maximize royal power did not in fact weaken her authority. Joseph, on the other hand, believed so strongly in the ability of reason to create an absolutist state that he was prepared to cast caution to the wind to achieve his autocratic goal. Their differing opinions concerning reform led to frequent clashes.

Personal problems also plagued Joseph, compounding his public disagreements with his mother. Despite his constant attention, Isabel became deeply depressed and longed for death. The birth of their daughter Maria Theresa on March 20, 1762, failed to change her mood. When their second daughter Christine died a few hours after birth on November 22, 1763, Isabel succumbed to smallpox a few days later.

Joseph Is Crowned Holy Roman Emperor

Although still grieving over the tragic death of his wife and daughter, Joseph was crowned Holy Roman Emperor at Frankfurt-am-Main in March 1764. On January 23, 1765, he married his second wife Josepha of Bavaria, whom he never liked and who also fell victim to smallpox on May 28, 1767. They had no children. Joseph never remarried, nor did he amuse himself with mistresses. The monarchy and his ambition would fill his remaining days. The death of his surviving daughter on January 20, 1770, seems to have reinforced his decision to renounce a private life.

During the night of August 18, 1765, Joseph's father (Francis I) died suddenly. After some hesitation, the grief-stricken Maria Theresa decided to turn the Empire over to Joseph, confident that her chancellor, Anton von Kaunitz, could control her son's impulsiveness. This proved to be impossible. Joseph's financial retrenchments and other minor reforms so disturbed the privileged courtiers, nobles, and clergy that they coaxed Maria Theresa out of retirement, and on November 17, 1765, Joseph had to accept a co-regency with his mother. The agreement left Joseph once again with only the authority his mother delegated to him. Initially, this meant that he had the largely ceremonial post of Grand Master of all the military orders, plus some minor involvement in foreign affairs and the administration of justice.

Rather than abandon his plans to reform the monarchy, Joseph continued to press his mother for changes. Their renewed conflicts over the proper way to conduct the monarchy's business caused Joseph to seek escape in travel. Between 1765 and 1780, often traveling incognito, he visited most of the Habsburg Empire, along with Marie Antoinette in France, and **Catherine the Great** in Russia. These numerous trips reinforced his conviction that the Empire desperately needed reforming. He also surrounded himself with young men who shared his views on the Enlightenment and reform. By 1771, Maria Theresa's longtime advisors had died, and the empress reluctantly but steadily began to accept some of Joseph's ideas. The result was a series of cautious, mild reforms during their co-regency, which threatened the privileges of neither the nobility nor the clergy.

These reforms embraced a variety of subjects. Heresy ceased to be a crime, and the co-regents banned the practice of torturing defendants to obtain evidence against them. Between 1770 and 1774, they ordered the establishment of secular schools in Austria. Their most important reform was the Urbarial Law of 1774, which Hungary rejected until 1791. This law regulated the amount of robot (forced labor) that serfs owed their lords. While it did not abolish the robot, it reduced its harshness and eliminated some of its worst abuses.

Besides creating an absolute state for the Habsburg monarchy, Joseph had a burning ambition to avenge the loss of Silesia and to regain the Empire's international prestige. During the 1770s, he found several opportunities to achieve these goals. The first in 1771 concerned the desire of Frederick the Great and Catherine the Great to partition the impotent Polish kingdom. Austria could not allow these two neighboring powers to enlarge themselves while the Habsburgs received nothing. Although Joseph urged war at one point, he settled in 1772 for a share of the Polish spoils with Russia and Prussia.

Joseph's second foreign policy adventure occurred in 1777 when he pressed a Habsburg claim for Bavaria following the death of the childless Bavarian elector Maximilian Joseph in 1777. Given the rivalry between Prussia and the Habsburgs for control of Central Europe, Joseph should have known that Frederick the Great would forcefully resist any Austrian attempt to annex territory in Germany. After some diplomatic skirmishing, Frederick prepared for war. Joseph, in spite of his mother's opposition, eagerly mobilized the Austrian army. By defeating his family's bitter enemy, he could prove to everyone that he was the equal of the Prussian king he so admired and feared. Between April and June 1778, as all Europe waited and wondered if the war would begin, the Austrian and Prussian armies faced each other in Bohemia without firing a shot. France supported Frederick. The initially neutral Catherine of Russia broke the deadlock by sending an army to her western border to act as an armed mediator. With all of Europe, his mother, and the court in Vienna against him, Joseph had no choice except to negotiate an end to the crisis he had caused. Austria received a tiny portion of Bavaria in 1779, which cost Joseph dearly in money and prestige. Unable to defeat Frederick the Great, who permanently checked Joseph's ambitions in Central Europe, Joseph turned to Catherine in 1780, hoping to join Russia in partitioning the ailing Ottoman Empire.

On November 29, 1780, Maria Theresa died. Now nothing restrained Joseph II's ambition for personal absolutism and international glory. He began by subjecting every administrative detail to his personal scrutiny. The ever-suspicious emperor established a network of spies whose activities gradually encompassed every aspect of his subjects' public and personal lives. By 1786, Joseph also had centralized the previously provincial police under his personal authority everywhere except in Hungary.

A police state was not Joseph II's conception of the ideal monarchy. As a child of the Enlightenment, he strove to create a paternal despotism devoted to achieving the common good for all his subjects. To determine what constituted the elusive "common good" and to expose corrupt or incompetent bureaucrats, Joseph encouraged his subjects to direct their complaints to him, granting them personal audiences whenever possible. More important, Joseph expanded his sources of public opinion by issuing decrees restricting censorship of the press. The Enlightenment held that men must have the freedom to debate their ideas in public to insure that the state's determination of the "common good" was based on reason. In accordance with this principle, Joseph's censorship decrees granted scholars, scientists, journalists, and writers the freedom to publish their ideas so long as they were not immoral or too mystically religious.

While Joseph believed that public opinion could help him rule reasonably, and thus increase the power of his state, he never allowed it to guide him. He always believed in the supremacy of his own reasonableness over that of his subjects and in his unlimited authority to govern his Empire. Consequently, the reforms necessary to bring the Empire to its full potential of power would emanate from him alone, although all his subjects would benefit equally from the monarchy's increased power and efficiency. What was best for the monarchy was the "common good," which in short is enlightened despotism.

He Introduces Radical Reforms

Since everyone benefited from Joseph II's rule, he believed that everyone should be equally subject to his power, which meant that he had to abolish the privileges of the aristocracy and the Catholic Church. The reforms that he introduced to achieve this were far more radical than the measures his mother had accepted in the 1770s. For example, the new penal code that appeared in 1786 treated all defendants equally regardless of their social class. Convicted criminals were also punished equally, and the code banned the death penalty and brutal punishments for all his subjects. Furthermore, to eliminate all competition with his own judicial system, Joseph abolished all remaining feudal and ecclesiastical judicial rights. In order to bring all the peasants under his authority, Joseph emancipated the serfs in 1781 (1784 for Hungary). Out of respect for property rights, he only regulated rather than abolished the robot and certain fees that the serfs had owed their lords. A later law guaranteed the peasants' right of ownership to the land they occupied but ordered them to pay their lords for it in installments. The last straw for the nobility was the revolutionary tax law of February 10, 1789, which subjected everyone without exception to the land tax and completely abolished the robot. While this law would have greatly alleviated the emperor's financial problems, it would also have destroyed the nobility.

The Catholic clergy's time-honored privileges, which Maria Theresa had protected, blocked his way to personal absolutism as much as they did those of the nobility. To remedy this situation, he issued a series of anticlerical decrees. The first, which appeared on November 29, 1781, abolished most of the monasteries in his eastern lands and confiscated their property. He used some of the money to build a general hospital, a lying-in hospital, a foundling asylum, a medico-surgical academy, and an institution for the deaf and dumb in Vienna, which helped to establish Vienna as a world medical center. Other decrees ended the Church's state-within-a-state status by eliminating the pope's power in the Empire and by placing the clergy completely under Joseph's control. These measures distressed Pope Pius VI so much that he traveled to Vienna in February 1782 where he unsuccessfully pleaded with Joseph to repeal his decrees and restore the Church to its former privileged status.

Joseph was anticlerical, not antireligious. He believed that organized religion could help centralize his authority, but only if he controlled it completely. Since one church could serve his purpose as well as another, he granted religious tolerance to Protestants, Orthodox, and Jews. Although pleased at Joseph's religious tolerance, most people disliked his decree that expanded secular education by ordering parents to send all their children to public secular schools or to pay higher taxes. The major innovation of this educational reform was the special schools created for girls. Every category of school had the same curriculum in order to produce uniformly loyal subjects who shared similar secular ideas.

By 1789, Joseph's radical reforms had brought his Empire to the edge of revolt. Unfortunately, his foreign policy had only intensified the crisis. Between 1783 and 1785, he unsuccessfully tried to open the Scheldt River in Belgium to international shipping. A second attempt to obtain Bavaria by trading it for Belgium also failed. Finally in 1788, he joined Catherine the Great in a war to pillage the Ottoman Empire. Joseph stayed in the field with his troops during 1788 but displayed no talent for military command; he returned to Vienna in December with his health ruined by a fever he caught in the Balkans.

Throughout 1789, the emperor's health continued to deteriorate. The Belgians took advantage of the imperial army's absence in the east and started a revolt in 1788 that left them independent of Joseph II by 1790. The tax reforms of 1789 greatly stimulated discontent among the Hungarian nobles, who resented Joseph's reforms more than any other group. Prussian agents were encouraging them to revolt, and given the level of unrest in Hungary, these plots were dangerous. Joseph also had dissatisfied subjects in Bohemia and Transylvania. Finally, many peasants disliked the fact that the emperor had not given them the land they had worked as serfs. With his dream of enlightened despotism shattered and his health declining more each day, Joseph II became increasingly bitter about the failure of his life's work. On January 30, 1790, with revolution raging in France, he capitulated and signed a decree that formally withdrew his reforms. Hardly anyone lamented his death a few weeks later on February 20, 1791.

SOURCES:

Beales, Derek. *Joseph II, In the Shadow of Maria Theresa.* Vol. 1. Cambridge University Press, 1987.

Padover, Saul K. *The Revolutionary Emperor: Joseph II of Austria.* Archon, 1967.

von Wurzbach, Constant. *Biographisches Lexikon des Kaiserthums Osterreich.* Vol. 6. Austrian State Press, 1860.

FURTHER READING:

Kann, Robert A. *A History of the Habsburg Empire, 1526–1918.* University of California Press, 1974.

Wandruszka, Adam. *The House of Habsburg.* Translated by Cathleen and Hans Epstein. Greenwood Press, 1964.

The Julias of Rome

Julia Domna, Julia Maesa, Julia Soaemias, Julia Mammaea

Empresses of the so-called Severan dynasty, who guided Rome through its last good days before the plague, civil war, barbarian attacks, and famine of the third-century Crisis.

"[Julia Maesa's] brave and venturesome life had brought its disappointments. But at the end she could afford to reflect on the success with which, time and again, she had foreseen danger and had forestalled it. Her courage she shared with the other women of her family."

J. P. V. D. BALSDON

While **Julia Domna** spent much of her husband's reign in political eclipse, her influence was felt again during her son's regime. Her sister **Julia Maesa** revived the Severan dynasty by taking the ruthless actions necessary to place first one grandson and then another on the throne. Her actions staved off the type of civil war that would nearly destroy Rome a generation later, brought Roman jurisprudence to its height, and completed the integration of the eastern and western parts of the Mediterranean world, thereby contributing to the survival of *Romanitas*. Whereas Maesa's daughter **Julia Soaemias** lacked her mother's political acumen, her other daughter **Julia Mammaea** might well have proved a worthy successor as a power behind the throne, had not the army refused her leadership, killing her along with her son and thereby inaugurating the third-century Crisis.

Julia Domna and Julia Maesa were daughters of the high priest of Baal at Emesa. Since Emesa had originally been a kingdom ruled by its high priest, even 200 years after its incorporation into the Roman Empire, the high priest of Baal was wealthy and influential. His children would have

Contributed by Phyllis Culham, Department of History, United States Naval Academy, Annapolis, Maryland

Julia Domna. Name variations: Julia Domna Augusta. Birthdate unknown; died in 217; married: Septimius Severus (later Roman emperor); children: Caracalla and Geta, co-rulers of Rome, both of whom predeceased her.

Julia Maesa. Name variations: Julia Varia, Julia Maesa Augusta. Pronunciation: sound the "æ" dipthong as a long "i." Birthdate unknown; died in c. 224/226; married: Julius Avitus (a Roman senator); children: Julia Soaemias and Julia Mammaea.

Julia Soaemias. Name variations: Julia Soaemias Bassiana, Julia Symiamira, Julia Soaemias Augusta. Birthdate unknown; died in 222; married Sextus Varius Marcellus; children: Elagabalus (Roman emperor, with whom she was assassinated).

Julia Mammaea. (above) Name variations: Julia Avita Mammaea, Julia Mammaea Augusta. Pronunciation: sound the "æ" dipthong as a long "i." Birthdate unknown; died in 235; married: Gessius Marcianus; children: Alexander "Alexianus" Severus (Roman emperor, with whom she was assassinated) and a daughter Theocleia.

Chronology

expected to marry into the richest local families or to contract marriages with other eastern, princely lines. Septimius Severus, an ambitious young senator from Africa, might well have met both daughters at affairs for the local social elite when he commanded a legion in Syria in 179. Julia Domna was about ten at the time, Maesa about 15. Seven years later, when his first wife died, Severus sought Domna's hand. Maesa may have been less attractive to him, she may have already married, or perhaps the following story reported in the ancient sources was indeed true. Supposedly, Domna's horoscope had earlier been cast, predicting she would marry the ruler of the world. Perhaps an astrologer did flatter her with such a reading, and perhaps the superstitious Severus had heard the accompanying local gossip.

Marriage to the 42-year-old Severus meant that the teenage Domna had to leave her family in Emesa and join him on a series of provincial assignments that were necessary for a man hoping to rise in the imperial service. First, she was taken to Lugdunum in Gaul at the other end of the Roman world, where she bore her first son Caracalla. A year later in 189, her second son Geta was born in Sicily. It was probably a relief to the family when the emperor Commodus, who had become suspicious of Severus's ambition, was assassinated in 192. The proclamation of Severus's friend Pertinax as emperor was also surely welcome.

At their new post on the Danube, Domna and Severus received word that the Praetorian Guard back in Rome had killed the disciplinarian Pertinax and auctioned off the empire to the highest bidder—the fabulously wealthy Didius Julianus. Promptly expressing their horror, the Danubian legions declared Severus emperor. As they were not the only legions to so express their esteem for their commander, brutal civil war followed. Predictably, Parthian princelings took advantage of Roman disorder, causing trouble on the borders as well as in areas demanding Severus's attention. Domna accompanied him even into the barren gulleys of Mesopotamia, acquiring the first of many honorific titles: Mother of the Camp. Domna's travels presumably led her to meet many new people with different customs and beliefs, providing experiences that perhaps contributed to her later participation in an intellectual circle.

Unfortunately for the family, Plautianus, Severus's friend from boyhood and his commander of the Praetorian Guard, began undermining Domna's marriage. He may have envied her influence or, as Caracalla insisted, simply aspired to seizing power for himself. In any case, when the civil wars and their travels ended, Domna did not enjoy the fruits of victory in Rome because Plautianus's false accusations of adultery had destroyed Severus's trust in her. She continued to live in the palace with her husband and sons to avoid public scandal, and in 204 was accorded prominence unprecedented for an empress in the Secular Games. This was a rare event, held only once every 110 years. Domna presided as Augusta over a special ceremonial gathering of women—drawn primarily from the most powerful senatorial families—which included her sister Julia Maesa.

Largely excluded from political influence during her time in Rome, Domna encouraged various intellectuals of the day. While some later scholars have questioned the significance of her circle, the first emperor **Augustus** had set the precedent for exercising literary patronage to rally scholars and artists around a new dynasty, and no contemporary would have been surprised by her activities. Philostratus, author of the *Life of Apollonius* which would later prove so influential, was a good friend; Aelian collected stories of exotic (or even fantastic) animals like the manticore and made his contribution to later European folklore; Galen's medical books remained supreme until the later medieval period; even the multitalented Apuleius, best known for the novel *The Golden Ass,* might have been associated with the group. The vitally important historian and senator Dio Cassius was a close associate of the family, and presumably part of the circle—however critical he was of some of its members later, when it was safe.

Though Plautianus's self-serving plots were finally exposed and he was killed, Domna could not have enjoyed the last few years of her husband's reign without wondering what was to come. Her sons had never been friends, and the prospect of having an empire to quarrel over did nothing for their relationship. In an action that offered a solution to the problem of overambitious prefects of the Praetorian Guard while also attributing new importance to legal theory, Severus, for his part, appointed the great legal scholar Papinian—perhaps a member of Domna's circle—to head the guard. The classical Roman law which had such an overwhelming influence on later European, and even Latin American, history is the product of Papinian and Ulpian, about whom more will shortly be said.

Domna Refuses To Divide the Empire

Domna accompanied Severus on what would prove to be his final trip to Britain. When he died there in 211, his final words to their sons were: "Keep peace between yourselves." Their hostility, of course, intensified. According to Herodian, their mother brought them together at one conference with high-ranking senatorial advisors, but no one could see any solution short of cutting the Empire in two. Domna refused to countenance any such measure, responding: "Do you intend to divide your mother's body between you too?" The idea was dropped, rather ironically, considering that later ages would be driven to even finer subdivisions.

Had Domna foreseen the horrible outcome, she might well have agreed to the division. In 212, persuading her that he was ready for a reconciliation with his brother, Caracalla begged that they meet quietly and affectionately in the family chambers without the distractions of attendants. Though ancient sources differ as to whether Caracalla reserved the pleasure of stabbing his brother for himself or had planted assassins to do it, they all agree that Geta died in his mother's lap, drenching her with his blood. Nor was Domna even permitted to outwardly mourn her son's death. Dio, a trustworthy source in this instance, writes: "She was compelled to rejoice and laugh as though at some great fortune, so closely were all her words, gestures, and changes of color observed."

It is true that Domna was raised to even higher horrors during Caracalla's sole reign and that she virtually served as regent in his absence, but that does not mean that she was insensitive or capable of being bribed with grants of power. Turton, who is often more imaginative than scholarly, put it well for once, commenting, "She was a woman of great strength of mind, who refused to let personal feeling impair her political judgment." Having refused to countenance the destruction of the Empire as a unit, she was dedicated to providing it with the best government her power could allow.

But in 217 she lost everything. Caracalla was assassinated, and she was sent back to Emesa to live in seclusion with her sister Julia Maesa. Then only in her mid-40s, she had lost both her children to violent deaths; had seen the destruction, she believed, of everything for which she and Severus had fought; and had only hostility, and perhaps even death, to look forward to at the hands of the new emperor, Macrinus. Some of the ancient sources claim that she missed the exercise of power and influence, and it probably is true that she did not mourn Caracalla as a beloved son. Nonetheless, Domna must have seen in his death the destruction of the hopes of many, including the hope for continued peace and stability. Undoubtedly victim to bitterness and depression described in the sources, she was also afflicted with breast cancer. Refusing food, she starved herself to death.

Her sister **Julia Maesa** was by then a wealthy widow. Her husband's career and fortune had prospered with his brother-in-law's elevation to rule, and her grandson, Bassianus, later called Elagabalus, had inherited his grandfather's position of high priest of Baal. As his grandmother, Maesa could therefore draw on the ages-old treasury of the great temple. Why should a nobody like Macrinus be allowed to usurp the imperial power? She knew that Caracalla had been popular with the troops in the region. Maesa began spreading rumors that her widowed daughter **Julia Soaemias** had had an affair with Caracalla, and that her son Elagabalus was also Caracalla's natural son. Helping the cause of such rumors, Macrinus proceeded to alienate senate, people, and army in a series of errors.

Maesa next enlisted Gannys, Elagabalus's tutor and Soaemias's long-time lover, in her scheme. Maesa, Gannys, Soaemias, Elagabalus, Maesa's other daughter **Julia Mammaea,** and her small son Alexianus all entered a camp of a friendly legion and were effusively welcomed. Though Mammaea's husband was caught on his way and killed by Macrinus's forces, the soldiers proved unwilling to enthusiastically fight other Romans in his name. The young Elagabalus did in fact resemble Caracalla and, having been togged out to strengthen the resemblance, his appearance won over many. In the final confrontation on the battlefield, a determined charge by the Praetorian Guard almost broke the ranks of Maesa's forces, but she and Soaemias jumped down from their chariot in the rear and ran forward to rally the men to stand their ground. When Macrinus's troops discovered that he had fled the scene, they promptly changed sides, and the war was won.

Maesa's Grandson Defies Her

Elagabalus, however, was not mature enough to be emperor, and his first impression on the Romans was disastrous. Maesa could stage rebellions, finance and stage-manage ceremonies to impress and win popular support, but she could not get her rebellious adolescent grandson to wear his toga. Having earlier lived with her sister in Rome, Maesa knew that Elagabalus's heavily made-up face and exotic priestly garb would strike the Romans as combining the worst of effeminacy and eccentricity. But she simply could not convince him that a Roman emperor should look Roman. Thumbing his nose at his grandmother, Elagabalus had a high-camp portrait done and sent it to Rome with instructions that it be hung in the senate. Finally, Gannys was stabbed to death by guards during an argument with Elagabalus. What should have been a triumphant entrance into Rome was significantly tarnished as a result of Elagabalus's outrageous conduct. The sources do not record that Soaemias shared her mother's disquiet nor that she joined Maesa in trying to get Elagabalus to behave with some propriety. Presumably she did not know Rome or Romans as well, or perhaps the ancient sources assessed her correctly as the most flighty member of the family.

Sill, Roman government continued essentially unaffected since it was Maesa who went into the senate, not Elagabalus, who took no interest in anything except Baal and debauchery. Nonetheless, he still threw money around, was generally offensive, and engaged in open corruption with the distribution of horrors and offices. Knowing perfectly well how many emperors had been assassinated in the previous half-century, and what had happened to their families, Maesa must have been quick to see the solution close at hand.

Mammaea's son Alexianus was a precocious little boy who honored his grandmother and mother. Like her aunt Julia Domna, Mammaea was more philosophically inclined and more interested in providing good government than her sister Julia Soaemias. Although some have believed that Maesa hoped Elagabalus could peacefully be persuaded to resign in favor of Alexianus, so that he could devote himself exclusively to his priesthood and sensuality, she almost certainly decided early that Elagabalus would have to be removed. Rumors were spread that Alexianus too was Caracalla's natural son.

Elagabalus, however, was not stupid and knew that once he adopted Alexianus as his grandmother wished, he was expendable. Maesa argued that his almost exclusive homosexuality made it vital for him to adopt an heir to provide for succession, but Elagabalus kept putting it off. Finally, liking and trusting Alexianus as much as everyone else, Elagabalus gave in and adopted him. Then, growing uneasy, he started trying to promote his mother politically, presumably as a counterweight to his grandmother. He sent Alexianus's tutor, the distinguished legal scholar Ulpian, into exile, an action which only cost him more credibility with the senate, as did an abortive assassination plot against Alexianus.

All too late, Soaemias began telling her son to appear for ceremonies appropriately garbed in a toga. She could not, however, make him act with dignity when he got there. The Praetorian Guard became convinced, perhaps correctly, that there was another attempt under way against Alexianus. Modern historians have taken positions ranging from the belief that Elagabalus's ensuing murder at the hands of the Praetorian Guard was a shock to Maesa, who had hoped to prevent it, to the assertion that she had planned all along to eliminate both mother and son. The truth is likely in between. Maesa might well have considered Elagabalus unsalvageable but hoped to get Soaemias out of the predicament. Dio, however, blamed her daughter Mammaea for the final riot in the Praetorian camp in 222, claiming that she had become openly hostile to her sister Soaemias. In any case, Soaemias did not run; on the contrary, she tried shielding her son with her body and died with him. Their corpses were stripped and dragged through the streets.

Mammaea's Son Named Emperor

Mammaea was certainly a different kind of woman than her sister had been. Whereas Soaemias had acquired a shady reputation—although it may well have been exaggerated—Mammaea was known as puritanical. She had always wanted to acquire the best tutors for Alexianus, now Alexander Severus, but after the adoption she had been openly grooming him to be a philosopher king, of the sort Plato wanted to produce. At 13 he had been taught to maintain a dignified public bearing in deliberate contrast with the appearance of his cousin. Though the senate confirmed him, it exacted its price from Maesa and Mammaea. Women could no longer enter the senate. They would have to consult a special advisory group of senators even when a full meeting of the senate was not possible or appropriate. Maesa and Mammaea showed no signs of resenting these measures; they may even have appreciated more genuine involvement in government by the senate. Ulpian was appointed Praetorian Prefect, with lasting consequences for the blossoming of the classical period of Roman law and for the legal traditions of Europe and its colonies.

Unfortunately, Maesa died, probably still in her 50s, just three years later. If she had lived, subsequent tragedies might have been avoided, and the course of European history might have been much different. Though undoubtedly well-meaning (perhaps the most well-meaning of all the women in the family), Mammaea never had the iron will and ruthlessness of her mother and her presence did not evoke the respect that Maesa's had. Ulpian's discipline was uncongenial to the Praetorian Guard, and, in a drunken riot, they pursued him into the royal chambers, where they killed him in the presence of Mammaea and her son Alexander Severus. Even Dio Cassius feared assassination. Mammaea shared Ulpian's devotion to fiscal responsibility, which did nothing for her popularity. Nonetheless, the reign of the popular boy with his comparatively reserved, honest mother seemed later like the last moments of sunshine before the storm.

Had the Romans been left to their own devices, a son of Alexander Severus might have inherited the throne. As it was, Severus's defeat of the Parthians had unleashed a resurgent Persian Empire to overrun the eastern borders. Alexander Severus was only 21 when he and his mother, who was just 40, had to go east to fight a major war. Alexander became sick, and the troops began to think him weak while resenting the suffering they endured in the desert for an expedition aborted through what they believed to be his lack of strength.

The same troops were brought to meet a new threat on the Rhine, the second major wave of Germans who would eventually overwhelm the imperial defenses on the north. A counteroffensive was largely successful but not followed up aggressively as the troops wanted. With his popularity among the troops eroded, and given his reputation for clinging to his mother's skirts, Alexander could not help but appear weak. Malcontents began gathering around a Thracian giant called Maximinus, and one day some of Alexander's troops proclaimed Maximinus emperor. A personal appeal to the assembled troops brought cries that he was a "money-grubbing milktoast." Running to his mother's tent, Alexander found comfort from Mammaea until the assassins came for them both.

In actuality, the Roman Empire had been governed by Syrian princesses of the priestly house of Baal from the time when Caracalla had begun losing interest in civil affairs in about 213 until the death of Alexander Severus in 234. In that way, these two decades were a strange interlude in Roman history; it would be untrue, however, to call it an unhappy one. The dynasty was not responsible for the revival of a brilliantly led Persian Empire, nor for the mass movement of peoples out of central Asia which was just starting to drive the German tribes into the Rhine and Danube frontiers. Subsequent centuries showed that men with military experience were often defeated by these intractable problems. The Julias left Rome's greatest legacy to Europe: classical Roman law of the golden age of Papinian and Ulpian.

SOURCES:

Dio Cassius. *Dio's Roman History.* Vol. IX, Putnam, 1927.

Herodian. Vols. I–II. Harvard University Press, 1969.

The Scriptores Historiae Augustae. Vols. I–II. Harvard University Press, 1959.

FURTHER READING:

Balsdon, J. P. V. D. *Roman Women.* Barnes and Noble, 1962.

Birley, Anthony R. *Septimius Severus: The African Emperor.* Yale University Press, 1972.

Cleve, Robert L. "Some Male Relatives of the Severan Women," in *Historia.* Vol. 37, 1988.

Turton, Godfrey. *The Syrian Princesses.* Cassell, 1974.

János Kádár

(1912–1989)
and the Rise and Fall of Communism in Postwar Hungary

Hungarian Communist leader, who came to power as head of a Soviet-sponsored regime, but who was able to gain control of the domestic political stage and introduce significant economic and political reforms that eliminated Stalinist abuses.

Born János Czermanik (Csermanek) on May 26, 1912, in Fiume, Hungary (today Rijeka, Croatia), for a time used name of Laszlo Gyurko; died in Budapest on July 6, 1989; son of Janos Kressinger and Borbala Czermanik; married: Maria. Predecessor: Imre Nagy. Successors: Karoly Grosz and Miklos Nemeth.

The collapse of Communism in 1989 is an extraordinary story with countless strands of detail, much of it remaining unwritten, but there can be little doubt that when definitive judgments are rendered, Hungary's János Kádár will receive significant credit for making the transition to democracy a peaceful one. Kádár, who dominated his nation's political life for almost a third of a century from 1956 through 1988, underwent a profound transformation in the estimation of his fellow-countrymen, evolving from a man whose power was at first based on a Soviet army that had drowned a national uprising in blood, to a respected leader whose pragmatic, flexible policies brought much-desired stability and prosperity to his people.

Kádár's almost 60 years as a Communist spanned the period from the start of Stalin's dictatorship in the Soviet Union, when the dream of establishing Communist societies in Eastern Europe was held mostly by a handful of underground conspirators, to the last years of the 20th century when discredited Eastern European Communist regimes were swept from power by an angry public because of their inability to create

"All those who are not against us are with us."

JÁNOS KÁDÁR

Contributed by John Haag, Associate Professor of History, University of Georgia, Athens, Georgia

either economic prosperity or a free civil society. Between these two eras were decades of brutal repression, a frustrated uprising in 1956, and a slow but steady economic and political evolution toward a social order free of extreme Stalinist brutality and daily privations. János Kádár was at the center of many of these developments as Hungary found itself transformed, often at high cost, from an impoverished semifeudal agrarian nation to a sophisticated industrial society.

János Kádár was born into grinding poverty in the city of Fiume two years before the start of World War I. His name at birth was János Czermanik but he later changed it to Laszlo Gyurko; finally in the 1940s, as a member of the illegal Communist underground, he adopted the pseudonym János Kádár. His real father, a peasant named János Kressinger, never married his mother, abandoning his family soon after his son's birth. His mother Borbala Czermanik was, according to Kádár's description, a "barely literate… servant girl turned factory hand." After holding a series of odd jobs that helped supplement his family's meager income, he became a journeyman mechanic, but the onset of the world economic depression in 1930 frustrated his plans to become a respected, well-paid skilled worker. With time on his hands, Kádár played either chess (which became his lifelong hobby) or soccer, dreaming of becoming a world-class champion in either field. The almost penniless young worker also enjoyed reading, staying outside during the summer months because his cramped home lacked electricity and his family had little money to pay for kerosene lighting.

Having won the local barbers' union youth chess competition, Kádár's prize was the book *Anti-Dühring* by Friedrich Engels. The book was difficult, but for Kádár its often obscure philosophical vocabulary was profoundly challenging, and its ideas served to introduce the intelligent but spottily educated young man to the complex world of Marxist ideology. Soon convinced that Marxism was the only true path to socialism, Kádár joined the youth section of the Hungarian Communist Party. As a trustworthy and honest comrade, Kádár was chosen by Party leaders to serve as a minor functionary of the illegal Communist movement, which had been banned by Admiral Miklos Horthy, whose semi-Fascist regime governed Hungary in the 1930s. Between 1931 and 1939, Kádár was arrested and imprisoned several times by Horthy's efficient political police.

While the leadership of the Hungarian Communist movement—**Imre Nagy,** Matyas Rakosi, Ernö Gerö, Jozsef Revai, and Zoltan Vas, the so-called "Big Five"—lived comfortably in Moscow during World War II, when Hungary became an ally and then a puppet state of Nazi Germany, János Kádár took great risks as a leader of the underground Peace Party, the name the Communists took from 1939 to 1941.

After the Nazi attack on the Soviet Union, Kádár tirelessly organized a growing anti-Nazi resistance movement, serving as editor of the newspaper *Szabad Nep;* in 1943, he was elected to the ruling Central Committee in recognition of his talent and courage. While trying to establish contact with the Yugoslav partisan movement of Marshal **Josip Broz Tito** in 1944, he was captured by the Gestapo, who tortured him; the resourceful Kádár was able to escape, and in late 1944 he was met by Red Army officers and Hungarian Communists from Moscow, led by Matyas Rakosi who appointed him to the Party Politburo. Kádár's heroic war record made him very useful to the Soviets and the "Muscovite" Hungarian Communists because it gave much-needed prestige to their movement, which the majority of the Hungarian people regarded as being essentially an alien force. Furthermore, Kádár's intimate knowledge of Hungary's indigenous Fascist rulers facilitated his being named deputy chief of police in 1945. Rising rapidly in the regime, in 1949 he succeeded Laszlo Rajk as minister of the interior, becoming at the same time chief of the secret police, the feared AVO.

By 1949, **Joseph Stalin's** paranoia had deeply infected the newly Sovietized satellite states of Eastern Europe. In Hungary, where purges were ordered to crush the specter of "Titoism" or any other variety of independent Communism, Kádár's predecessor Rajk was accused of spying, found "guilty," and executed. According to some accounts, Kádár had conveyed to his old friend Rajk a promise by Party-boss Rakosi that his life would be spared on condition that he confess in court to his Titoist tendencies. Rajk did as instructed but was shot anyway, betrayed not by Kádár but by the brutally cynical Stalinist Matyas Rakosi. Under Rakosi's orders, Kádár was arrested in April 1951 on trumped-up charges of spying, treason, and Titoism. Never placed on trial, he was taken to a concentration camp and suffered intense torture which included the pulling out of his fingernails. Incredible willpower and the desire to destroy the evils of Stalinism enabled Kádár to survive, but upon his release a few months after Stalin's death in November 1953, few would have dared predict that Kádár would be the man who would lead Hungary out of the dark night of Stalinism.

After prison, Kádár worked tirelessly to rebuild his life and political career. He restored his role in the Party by creating a growing network of personal and ideological allies. Even in such minor jobs as membership in the national committee of the ostensibly independent but Communist-dominated Fatherland Front, he was able to impress his fellow members with his honesty and dedication. A master of ward politics, he was able to build a strong political machine in the 13th District of Budapest, a working-class neighborhood that respected uncorrupted and plain-talking politicians. Using this district as his power base, Kádár became a key player in the intrigues that led to the resignation of the hated arch-Stalinist Matyas Rakosi in July 1956. In the same month Kádár was elected to Party Politburo and also became first secretary of the Central Committee, signaling that he had become one of Hungary's principal advocates of Communist-led reform. For a few weeks in the late summer and early autumn of 1956 it appeared that Hungary might be able to undergo a peaceful transition to a reform regime, a process that was taking place at the same time in Poland. In Budapest, a group of passionately reform-minded intellectuals known as the Petöfi Circle discussed the possibility of combining democracy with Socialism or perhaps even breaking free of Soviet domination.

The Hungarian Revolution

By October 1956, Hungary was in the throes of massive discontent. Reformers within the Communist regime, including Kádár, rallied behind Imre Nagy, who had headed a moderate regime from 1953 through 1955. Pressure for peaceful change was dramatically transformed into a national revolution with strong anti-Soviet and anti-Communist overtones on October 23, when a crowd composed mostly of students and intellectuals was fired on by secret police units. Nagy became prime minister, pledging to extend democratic rights, raise living standards, and create a more humane form of socialism. On October 25, Kádár joined the Nagy cabinet as deputy prime minister and also replaced the hated Stalinist Ernö Gerö as first secretary of the Party, promising to democratize the internal life of the organization and begin talks with the Soviet Union "in complete equality" for a prompt withdrawal of Soviet troops from Hungarian soil. Kádár was given his new Party post due to pressure exerted by Soviet Politburo members Anastas Mikoyan and Mikhail Suslov, who had flown from Moscow to Budapest in an attempt to maintain reliable Communist control over a rapidly deteriorating situation. Kádár used his considerable prestige during the next days to argue for a peaceful settlement of the turmoil, urging on October 30 that Communists cooperate with the "Freedom Fighters" who now controlled the streets.

On November 1, 1956, as Soviet troops continued to enter Hungary, Imre Nagy declared his nation neutral in the Cold War and announced its immediate withdrawal from the Warsaw Pact. On the same day, Kádár praised "the people's glorious uprising" and repeated his earlier demand that Soviet forces depart from Hungary. Later that day, however, Kádár and a half-dozen Communists from his inner circle mysteriously vanished from Budapest, being taken by Soviet officers to the Ukrainian city of Uzhgorod. On November 2, Prime Minister Nagy reorganized his cabinet, excluding all Communists other than Kádár and one other anti-Stalinist, but these changes, while doubtless closely reflecting the political mood of the Hungarian people, had become irrelevant. Massive Soviet military force was being readied to crush the brief experiment in nationalist democracy.

A crucial decision was also taken on November 2, but not in Hungary. Meeting with President Josip Broz Tito of Yugoslavia that evening on the Adriatic island of Brioni, **Nikita Khrushchev,** general secretary of the Soviet Communist Party, accompanied by former Soviet Premier **Georgi Malenkov,** discussed the urgent nature of events in Hungary. After being informed of the Soviet decision to militarily intervene in Hungary, Tito recommended that Kádár be appointed head of a new, Soviet-backed government to replace the Nagy regime. While Khrushchev accepted the idea of a Kádár government, he asked of Tito that in return for this favor the Yugoslavs offer political asylum to Nagy and a few of his close associates.

On November 4, Soviet forces attacked Budapest, rapidly crushing the disorganized Hungarian attempts at armed resistance. At the same time, the creation of an exclusively Communist "Hungarian Revolutionary Worker-Peasant Government" was announced, with Kádár as its head. On November 7, a Soviet armored car delivered Kádár and his associates to the Parliament building in Budapest. Within days, Kádár announced a "no revenge" policy to rebels who chose to surrender, abolition of the hated Security Police, as well as the withdrawal of Soviet troops "after the restoration of order." But throughout the last weeks of 1956 the Hungarian population remained sullenly defiant, a general strike was declared, and over 200,000 refugees fled to the West over the Austro-Hungarian border. In January 1957, the United Nations General Assembly voted 59 to 8 to establish a five-nation committee to investigate the situation in Hungary; when its report was issued in June 1957, it was noted that it could find "no evidence of popular support" for the Kádár government.

Reconstruction Begins

Determined to build a new Hungary on the ruins and bitterness of the 1956 uprising, Kádár began the process of reconstruction by taking vigorous steps to rebuild a shattered economy. After the Western powers rejected his request for economic aid, he was able to secure a loan of $250 million from the Soviet Union. A new note of non-ideological realism was struck in December 1956 when a resolution was passed at the first session of the provisional Central Committee of the newly founded Hungarian Socialist Workers Party (HSWP), stipulating that the central principle of economic policy would henceforth be the achievement of rapid and significant increases in the average Hungarian's standard of living.

Rejecting as impractical the traditional Marxist orthodoxy of sacrificing the interests of the generation now alive for the sake of a far-distant and imaginary future, Hungarian Communism under the leadership of János Kádár now looked upon rapid economic improvement as the key determinant in future economic planning. By early 1957, a 20% increase in wages had been decreed, and vigorous measures taken by the authorities made possible a slow but steady increase in the supply of consumer goods available to the average person. The masses, Kádár believed, could be won over to supporting his regime if they could see the tangible results of his policies in their daily lives, particularly in terms of economic improvements.

Despite the fact that the overwhelming majority of Hungarians had opposed his government, it was clear by the fall of 1957 that Kádár's Communist system in Hungary had been able not merely to survive but had the energy and stamina for the long pull, as was demonstrated in the well-attended celebrations for May Day 1957. Consolidation of the Kádár regime now gave it the breathing space necessary to make long-range plans for economic and social reconstruction and build foundations for an eventual national reconciliation. Kádár personally concluded that the previous Soviet-derived system of central planning, obligatory rules, and production quotas would never create a healthy economy and would have to be drastically modified or even scrapped.

In the agricultural sector, rapid collectivization of Hungarian farms took place during the years 1957 to 1960, but unlike the brutal practices associated with the Stalinist period, the authorities showed considerable understanding of peasant psychology. Recognizing and harnessing the skills and energies of the farmers toward the goal of increased agricultural productivity, official policy avoided antagonizing the rural population. Each member of a collective farm was permitted to retain ownership of a household plot of slightly less than three acres, to own several farm animals, and to benefit from a wage system that offered incentives for superior job performance. As a result of these realistic innovations, food production increased significantly. Efficient production methods and wage incentives placed Hungary third in the world in per capita grain and meat production, providing a stark contrast with the chronic food crisis plaguing the Soviet Union. Not surprisingly, Soviet leader Nikita Khrushchev praised the increased productivity resulting from the Hungarian reforms, dubbing the system "goulash Communism."

Encouraged by the impressive performance of Hungarian agriculture in the first half of the 1960s, Kádár and the HSWP Central Committee decided in May 1966 to introduce another set of reforms, the most important of which was a system of pricing which went into effect on January 1, 1968. Using the slogan of "Socialism of the possible," one of Kádár's inner circle of reformers, the economist Rezső Nyers, initiated what was to become a new model for the Communist world, an action which can now be seen as a turning point in the economic development of an Eastern European region that had for two decades uncritically followed the Soviet historical precedent.

Although central planning for the overall economy was retained in what was called the "New Economic Mechanism," Hungarian industrial enterprises were now economically independent in that they were expected to be profitable, fabricating products that were of high enough quality to compete successfully in the domestic and in some cases the world marketplace. Once again, Kádár and his associates were proven correct in their views; agricultural production had long been thriving, and now industrial production also skyrocketed. With bureaucratic brakes removed from the industrial sector of the economy, both enterprises and individuals could (at least in theory) pursue their own interests to a degree never before permitted in a Communist society. As a result, the Hungarian economy enjoyed a "Golden Decade" from the mid-1960s through the mid-1970s.

Intellectually, too, Hungary enjoyed a virtual Renaissance under János Kádár. By the early 1960s, the ideologically stultifying Marxist-Leninist-Stalinist "Socialist Realism" artistic canons of the 1950s had been largely discarded, making possible a great outburst of cultural creativity. Poetry remained popular, producing major voices such as Gyula Illyes, but perhaps even more capable of voicing contemporary concerns in a striking manner was the medium of motion pictures, with the directors Andras Kovacs and Miklos Jancso becoming internationally renowned for their cinematic innovations. While blatantly anti-regime works of art were not permitted, virtually anything short of open defiance was tolerated, echoing Kádár's 1962 slogan of national reconciliation, "All who are not against us are with us." As a result, a great variety of styles of expression in the arts flourished.

The world economic crisis that resulted from the dramatic rise in petroleum prices in 1973 affected Hungary severely. As the price of fuel and raw materials skyrocketed, Hungarian exports also became increasingly difficult to sell in a fiercely competitive world marketplace. The positive balance of trade that had been achieved in the early 1970s became by 1978 a staggering foreign debt burden of eight billion dollars. The resulting economic crisis led to a rapid decline in purchasing power and a marked lowering of the standard of living.

By the early 1980s, Kádár's health was in decline and he began voicing a desire to retire from office and pass the burdens of leadership to a younger generation. Unfortunately, the Kádár government had not seriously responded to the economic crisis until 1979, and even these interventions were a case of too little and too late. It was clear that the limited reforms had failed and that the Hungarian model of reform Communism was not sufficiently innovative and flexible to deal with these new and perplexing conditions.

Kádár's Popularity Plummets

János Kádár's formerly immense popularity plummeted as many Hungarians began to voice the novel idea that in the future meaningful economic changes could not flourish without fundamental political transformations, i.e., the introduction of democracy and the abolition of the Communist monopoly of power. Opposition groups, small in membership but passionately vociferous and comprising some of the greatest talents of the younger generation, now called for radical changes. At a Congress of the HSWP held in April 1985, Kádár lost much of his power; this was, in fact, the beginning of the end of the Kádár era in modern Hungarian history. The Politburo was restructured to give power to a new generation as Karoly Grosz and Imre Pozsgay emerged as the leaders of a post-Kádár Hungary. Sweeping reforms were introduced in the hope that they might be able to stimulate the ailing economy by eliminating subsidies and stripping away layers of bureaucratic fat. By 1987, the crisis continued to deepen, the living standard of the average Hungarian citizen continued to sink, and the government was forced to admit that the inflation rate had reached an excruciatingly painful 17%.

When further austerity measures were announced in July 1987, the smoldering discontent of the Hungarian people burst into a virtual peaceful revolution. While printers and coal miners went on strike, independent trade unions were founded. In late May 1988, the first national conference of the HSWP since 1957 attempted to placate an angry nation by offering them a now unpopular János Kádár as a symbolic sacrifice. Behind his back, many Hungarians had for months been disdainfully referring to Kádár as "Rücksös... the one with warts." His fellow-Communists removed him from his post of Party general secretary as well as evicting him from the Politburo; he was given the powerless and purely honorific position of "Party President." Viewed as cosmetic, these changes did little to halt the collapse of Communist legitimacy throughout the rest of 1988, as many thousands of ordinary Hungarians tore up their membership cards in the HSWP and its subsidiary organizations. In the first months of 1989 some Communist reformers still believed that they could democratize Hungary by making dramatic concessions of power, thus retaining at least some of their previous influence. Accordingly, they authorized a multiparty system, the right to demonstrate in public, and a promise to share power with non-Communist groups.

By spring 1989, the national mood had been dramatically transformed into a "Budapest Spring" in which all ideas and theories could be openly debated. The revolt of November 1956 was now universally held to have been a justifiable national uprising against internal dictatorship and foreign oppression. In June 1989 a massive national funeral honored Imre Nagy and three others who had been executed with him in 1958. Days before this moving event, the aged and ill János Kádár had been removed from his post of Party president and also expelled from the HSWP Central Committee. On the very day that János Kádár died in a Budapest hospital, the Supreme Court of Hungary published its decision to legally rehabilitate Imre Nagy and his colleagues, finally freeing them from charges of treason. With mixed feelings, many Hungarians appeared at Kádár's funeral, perhaps keeping in mind that without him the dramatic events of 1989 might never have taken place.

In the next few months, Hungary officially proclaimed itself to be a democracy, the Communists tried to reconstitute themselves by changing their name to "Socialist Party," and the nation began the long and difficult process of living in a free-market economy. A final assessment of János Kádár's role in modern Hungarian history remains to be written, but few would question the view that the man who began his rule as a hated foreign puppet found ways to evolve to the point where most of his countrymen regarded him as a patriot whose political skill and personal integrity made possible policies that placed Hungary on an evolutionary path that led, in time and without violence, to a new democratic era.

SOURCES:

Hoensch, Jörg K. *A History of Modern Hungary 1867–1986.* Longman, 1988.

Kádár, János. *János Kádár: Selected Speeches and Interviews.* Pergamon Press, 1985.

———. "My First Steps in the Movement," in *New Hungarian Quarterly.* Vol. 28, no. 107. Autumn 1987, pp. 8–14.

Shawcross, William. *Crime and Compromise: Janos Kadar and the Politics of Hungary since Revolution.* Dutton, 1974.

Sugar, Peter F., Peter Hanak, and Tibor Frank, eds. *A History of Hungary,* Indiana University Press, 1990.

FURTHER READING:

Batt, Judy. *Economic Reform and Political Change in Eastern Europe: A Comparison of the Czechoslovak and Hungarian Experiences.* St. Martin's Press, 1988.

———. "Political Reform in Hungary," in *Parliamentary Affairs.* Vol. 43, no. 4. October 1990; pp. 464–481.

Gati, Charles. *Hungary and the Soviet Bloc.* Duke University Press, 1986.

Zinner, Paul E., ed. *National Communism and Popular Revolt in Eastern Europe: A Selection of Documents on Events in Poland and Hungary, February–November, 1956.* Columbia University Press, 1957.

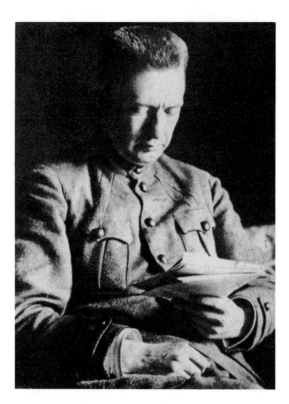

Alexander Kerensky

(1881–1970)

Leading Russian revolutionary, who was swept aside by more skilled and determined rivals in the Bolshevik Revolution of November 1917.

Pronunciation: KER-ensky. Born Alexander Feodorovich Kerensky in Simbirsk, a city in the Russian Empire, May 4, 1881; died in New York City on June 11, 1970; son of Fedor Mikhailovich Kerensky and Nadezhda Alexandrovna Adler Kerenskaya; married: Olga Lvovna Baranovskaya, 1904 (divorced, 1939); married: Lydia Ellen Tritton, 1939; children: (first marriage; two sons) Gleb and Oleg. Predecessor: Tsar Nicholas II. Successor: V. I. Lenin.

Anoted radical leader during World War I, Alexander Kerensky became for a brief time the most powerful figure in Russia during the spring and summer of 1917. In the circumstances of turmoil and revolution, Kerensky seemed to be uniquely able to guide the forces of change. It soon became clear, however, that he was no match for other, more ruthless leaders—like the Bolshevik **V. I. Lenin**—who soon swept him aside.

In 1917, Russia was suffering through the third year of its participation in World War I. A March 8th demonstration by the women of Petrograd—the country's capital, formerly named St. Petersburg—quickly grew into food riots, and over the next few days, the unrest was transformed into full revolt against the monarchy of Tsar **Nicholas II.** The strains of World War I had proven too much for Russia. Based on a fragile society of widespread rural poverty and cities burdened by the pain of the early stages of industrialization, by mid-March the old political system fell apart.

The abdication of Nicholas II on March 15 was followed by the abolition of the monarchy itself. Members of the *Duma*, Russia's recently

"Thanks to his feel for the popular mood, he emerged early as an idol of the Revolution; thanks to his emotionalism, he proved incapable of coping with the responsibilities which he had assumed."

RICHARD PIPES

Contributed by Neil Heyman, Professor of History, San Diego State University, San Diego, California

720

established parliament, set up a Provisional Government, and during the following eight months, the various cabinets and leaders tried to maintain order. Moreover, they attempted to remain in World War I until Russia shared in the Allied victory.

Many historians blame Kerensky for the worst failures and weaknesses of the Provisional Government. Thus, they believe that Kerensky set the stage for the Bolsheviks to seize power. It was Kerensky whom the new leaders, Lenin and **Trotsky,** chased from the Winter Palace and deposed in November 1917. Others, however, focus on his energy and determination in the March Revolution.

Born in Simbirsk, a city on the Volga River, on May 4, 1881, the future revolutionary came from a distinguished family. His father Fedor was an important school administrator whose successes were rewarded in 1889 with the rank of hereditary nobleman; Kerensky's mother was the daughter of a general.

When Kerensky was six years old, the people of Simbirsk were shaken by news that a young man from that city had been arrested and executed in St. Petersburg for attempting to assassinate Tsar Alexander III. The Kerensky family was tied to this shocking event in several ways. The would-be assassin, Alexander Ulyanov, was a graduate of the secondary school where Fedor Kerensky served as director. The elder Kerensky went out of his way to aid the Ulyanov family, helping Alexander Ulyanov's younger brother Vladimir to get admitted to the local university. Young Kerensky did not know Vladimir Ulyanov then. Thirty years later in 1917, however, Vladimir Ulyanov would take the revolutionary name "Lenin," overthrow the Kerensky government, and seize power for his Bolshevik party.

Kerensky spent most of his childhood years in the Central Asian city of Tashkent, where his father was transferred in 1889. There, a guest of the Kerensky family was the young army officer Lavr Kornilov, who was also destined to play a critical role during Kerensky's months as Russia's leader in 1917.

The first years of the 20th century brought a revival of radical politics in Russia, notably among university students. Kerensky was drawn to politics when he left Tashkent in 1899 to attend the University of St. Petersburg. In Russia's capital city, he studied law; met and married Olga Baranovskya, the sister of a classmate; and joined the growing student protests against the monarchy under Nicholas II.

CHRONOLOGY

1904	Outbreak of Russo-Japanese War; Kerensky completed law school
1905	Revolution in Russia
1906	Imprisoned and exiled to Tashkent
1909	Admitted to St. Petersburg bar
1912	Elected to the *Duma*
1914	Russia entered World War I
1917	March Revolution; formation of Provisional Government; July offensive began; Kornilov's march on Petrograd; November Revolution
1918	Kerensky went into exile
1924	Moved from Germany to France
1927	First visit to the United States
1939	Outbreak of World War II
1940	Settled in the U.S.
1965	Publication of *Russia and History's Turning Point*

Kerensky witnessed columns of factory workers marching to petition the Tsar in January 1905. The massacre of many of them in the "Bloody Sunday" incident heightened his opposition to the existing political order and prompted his membership in several organizations tied to the Socialist Revolutionary movement. The Socialist Revolutionaries looked primarily to the peasantry to carry forward the revolution.

In the closing months of 1905, during the last part of the evolution which took place during that year, Kerensky became involved in a group planning to assassinate the Tsar. When the group was betrayed, Kerensky was arrested. Probably due to his distinguished family connections, he got off lightly: his penalty was to spend a few months in Tashkent, where his father still served as director of the school system.

Returning to St. Petersburg in late 1906, Kerensky begin a legal career defending Russian subjects accused of political crimes. The government was cracking down harshly on political dissidents, especially members of non-Russian groups within the Tsar's Empire. Having flirted with a career as an actor while in secondary school, Kerensky quickly obtained a reputation as a dramatic, tireless, and devoted advocate for those facing political accusations. Over the years he defended individuals ranging from Russian peasants to Latvians and Armenians.

In 1912, Kerensky was elected to the Fourth Duma. Although the *Duma* had been established following the 1905 Revolution, conservative election laws had cut down on its independence. As a member of a Socialist Revolutionary faction called the *Trudovik* ("Workers'") Party, Kerensky soon acquired a reputation as the most outspoken critic of the monarchy and its ministers in the entire *Duma*. At this time, during World War I, his involvement with other women also led to problems in his marriage.

Several parts of Kerensky's wartime activities remain controversial. He joined the Freemasons, the Masonic order with origins in Western Europe that called for allegiance to the liberal principles of the French Enlightenment. Because it included numerous *Duma* deputies from several political parties, Kerensky's Masonic connections may have helped him exert influence over political groups in the *Duma* beside his own. Kerensky's biographer, Richard Alexander, has suggested that Kerensky used his prominence in the *Duma* to help promote political strikes during the war. Thus, the young orator not only spent the war years criticizing the government—he actively pushed Russia toward revolution.

Kerensky's Rise and Fall

When the monarchy fell in March 1917, Kerensky immediately took on a leading role in several political bodies. He was a brilliant speaker and a source of apparently limitless energy. In the early confusion of the revolution, he seemed unique in his sense of direction and determination. For example, he took a role at once in the Petrograd Soviet. Soviets, chosen by workers, peasants, and soldiers, sprang up all over Russia as the voice of the country's lower classes. The Petrograd Soviet became the model and center for other Soviets. Eventually, Kerensky became the vice-chairman of this important body.

Kerensky showed his desire to dominate the scene by taking another office. While remaining vice-chairman of the Soviet, he violated its guidelines by taking a cabinet post, minister of justice, in the newly formed Provisional Government. To members of the Soviet, this government was not truly revolutionary but only a middle-class successor to tsarism.

The young Socialist Revolutionary's rise was rapid. He was soon minister of war, and then, in July 1917, prime minister. His dramatic speeches

mesmerized crowds. "I cannot live without the people," he once proclaimed. And he invited his audience to kill him if they ever decided to doubt his democratic ideals. His policies, however, led to increased tension and division. He rejected the idea of pulling Russia out of the war: to Kerensky, if Russia signed a separate peace, it would enable Germany to defeat Britain and France. Then the Germans would turn the full weight of the military power against Russia. Moreover, Kerensky rejected an early program of land reform. It might win the peasants over to the Provisional Government, but it had to wait until the war had been won.

Kerensky sponsored a final offensive for the Russian army in June and July 1917. This "Kerensky Offensive" failed disastrously and provoked the "July Days"—urban unrest in Petrograd in which the Bolsheviks' rank and file pushed their leaders to take power. Although Kerensky imprisoned Bolshevik leaders like Trotsky and forced others like Lenin into exile, he would not allow the Bolshevik chieftains to be executed. Such measures, in his view, smacked of the old tsarist system. Critics have charged that he failed to be ruthless and decisive either in promoting the course of the revolution or in trying to halt it.

Fearing the Left, Kerensky relied increasingly on the army. This led him to appoint a new, hardheaded commander in chief, General Lavr Kornilov. Kerensky's ties to Kornilov remain uncertain, but many historians believe he was hoping to use Kornilov to crush the Bolsheviks and to restore political order. At the same time, however, Kerensky distrusted Kornilov's ambitions to become a military dictator.

In the end Kerensky offended everyone. Kornilov marched on Petrograd in early September, possibly with Kerensky's permission, infuriating the workers and the political Left. Maneuvering frantically, Kerensky released Bolsheviks from prison and called on the workers to help defeat Kornilov. This, in turn, infuriated Kornilov's colleagues among senior military officers.

Kerensky seemed confused and passive, unable to understand the danger in which he found himself. In early November as the Bolsheviks readied their coup, he was making plans for an extended tour of Russia. Instead Kerensky fled Petrograd, rallied a scratch military force, and then failed to retake Russia's capital. After a few months in hiding, he left his country in 1918—never to return.

Alexander Kerensky was a young man of 36 when he went into permanent exile. At first he made his home in Germany. Then, from 1924 to 1940, he lived in France. By this time his marriage to Olga existed in name only, and he had had a series of passionate love affairs. In 1939, he divorced Olga and married Lydia Tritton, the daughter of a wealthy Australian family who had been married to an exiled Russian army officer.

A trip to New York in 1927 showed how isolated he remained even among Russians in exile. On the one hand, he was heckled by Russian monarchists who saw him as a bloody revolutionary. On the other hand, he was heckled by Communists who saw him as a lukewarm socialist and would-be betrayer of the revolution. Kerensky wrote widely, and in books like *The Catastrophe* (1927) and later, *Russia and History's Turning Point* (1965), he tried to defend his actions in 1917.

During the first year of World War II, Kerensky and his new wife made a dramatic escape from France. In June 1940, they were stranded at the Spanish border; only energetic pleas by Kerensky's Australian spouse got them passage to safety on a British naval vessel.

Reaching New York in 1940, Kerensky spent most of the remaining years of his life in the United States. He lived in fear that he would be assassinated by the agents of the Soviet dictator **Joseph Stalin**—something that had befallen Leon Trotsky, one of the makers of the November 1917 Revolution, in Mexico in 1940. Kerensky's second wife died in 1946. In the escalating tensions of the Cold War, he was invited to broadcast to the Russian people over the BBC in 1949.

Establishing a connection with Stanford University in Palo Alto, California, the aging exile—despite his failing eyesight—worked on a massive collection of documents pertaining to the Provisional Government. His feelings about the events of 1917 remained painfully strong, and he clashed with his young American collaborator Robert P. Browder over what documents to include. For example, Kerensky omitted an important statement by General Kornilov and sometimes tried to present the work of the Provisional Government in an overly favorable light.

The Kerensky family showed the effects of exile. His two sons from his first marriage, Gleb and Oleg, settled in England while Kerensky remained in the U.S. After spending almost 63 years in exile following his brief months in power in 1917, Alexander Kerensky died on June 11, 1970, at the age of 89. His place in history rests directly on his conduct during the crucial months between the March and November revolutions of 1917. W. Bruce Lincoln presents a view that many historians share: of all the factors that helped to bring Lenin to power, "perhaps none was more striking than Kerensky's unprecedented paralysis of will."

SOURCES:

Abraham, Richard. *Alexander Kerensky: The First Love of the Revolution.* Columbia University Press, 1987.

Hasegawa, Tsuyoshi. *The February Revolution: Petrograd, 1917.* University of Washington Press, 1981.

Lincoln, W. Bruce. *Passage through Armageddon: The Russians in War and Revolution, 1914–1918.* Simon & Schuster, 1986.

FURTHER READING:

Kerensky, Alexander. *Russia and History's Turning Point.* Duell, Sloan, and Pearce, 1965.

Pipes, Richard. *The Russian Revolution.* Knopf, 1990.

Rabinowitch, Alexander. *The Bolsheviks Come to Power: The Revolution of 1917 in Petrograd.* Norton, 1976.

Nikita Khrushchev

(1894–1971)

Premier of the Soviet Union, who led the first effort to revise the harsh dictatorship of Joseph Stalin, and whose era was distinguished by growing tensions with the U.S. that featured both dangerous confrontation and steps toward detente.

Born Nikita Sergeievich Khrushchev in southern Russia, in the town of Kalinovka, near the Ukraine, on April 17, 1894; died on September 11, 1971; son of Sergei Nicaronovich Khrushchev (a Russian peasant); married: first wife in 1915 (died in the great famine of 1921–22); married: Nina Petrovna, 1924; children: (first marriage) one son and one daughter; (second marriage) one son and two daughters. Predecessor: Joseph Stalin. Successor: Team of party leaders headed by Leonid Brezhnev and Alexis Kosygin.

The death of **Joseph Stalin** on March 6, 1953, opened the Soviet political system for a fierce struggle over his successor. The first question in the spring of that year was how the new leader would be picked. The next was who the new leader would be. The third and most important question was whether or not the individual who followed Stalin at the top of the Soviet system would maintain his harsh and aggressive dictatorship. The new leader turned out to be Nikita Khrushchev, who emerged from a power struggle that lasted more than two years after Stalin's death. In both foreign and domestic affairs Khrushchev led the Soviet Union in sharply new directions.

Nikita Sergeievich Khrushchev was born in southern Russia, in the town of Kalinovka, near the Ukraine, on April 17, 1894. His father was a peasant who worked part of the year in the Ukrainian coal fields, and after a few years of elementary schooling Khrushchev went to work as a coal miner as well. We know little about his place in the two most important events of Russian history during the early part of the 20th century. He apparently did not fight in World War I, perhaps because he was a skilled worker who was needed to

"He moved backward into the future, trying to stand at bay, but always giving ground to the forces he himself, to his greater glory, had unloosed.... [A] peasant, a ward politician, a power-seeker on a grand and ruthless scale... and, towards the end, a statesman."

EDWARD CRANKSHAW

Contributed by Neil Heyman, Professor of History, San Diego State University, San Diego, California

produce coal. More important, he did not take part in the March Revolution of 1917, in which Tsar **Nicholas II** was overthrown, nor did he have a part in the November Revolution, in which **Lenin** and his Bolshevik Party (soon renamed the Communists) took power.

Joining the Communist Party only after the November Revolution, probably in early 1918, Khrushchev fought in the Civil War in which the new government successfully defended itself against a coalition of opposing Russian groups. By 1921, Lenin's new Communist government had taken control of most of the old Russian Empire, defeating the opposing "White" forces. Khrushchev's part in these dramatic events was never described in detail even when he was the Soviet leader, and perhaps he was only a low-ranking officer, *commissar* (political officer), or just a soldier.

As a young man, still without much of a formal education, he received his real schooling in Communist Party institutions during the 1920s. The Party set up schools to give young workers like Khrushchev a basic education and political training. Upon leaving this adult school system, he found a job in the bureaucracy of the Communist Party of the Ukraine, and from 1925 to 1953 Khrushchev's life was tied to the political career of Joseph Stalin, the Soviet dictator, who was building a base of supporters. Lenin had just died, a number of senior Party leaders were competing for the right to succeed him, and Stalin was looking for men who would follow him. Through Stalin's subordinate Lazar Kaganovich, the Party leader in the Ukraine, Khrushchev was brought into Stalin's faction.

Rapid success followed. In 1929, he went to Moscow, the center of national power. His official reason for leaving his Party post in the Ukraine was to continue his education in Moscow; however, Khrushchev spent little time at the Academy of Heavy Industry where he was supposed to be studying. Instead, he moved up the ladder quickly in Moscow's Party organization, and as top man in the Moscow branch of the Communist Party in 1934, the 40-year-old Khrushchev was one of the most powerful people in the country. That same year Stalin appointed him to the Central Committee of the Soviet Communist Party, which consisted of about 100 of the Party's leading figures.

Khrushchev played an important role in strengthening Stalin's fierce dictatorship over Soviet society. From 1934 to 1938, he worked in Moscow, building the city's elaborate subway systems and helping to conduct Stalin's purges. His

CHRONOLOGY

1894	Born in Kalinovka, in Kursk Province of the Russian Empire
1917	Bolshevik Revolution
1918	Joined Red Army as a political commissar
1929	Attended industrial school in Moscow; became an executive in the Moscow Communist Party
1934	Joined Communist Party Central Committee
1938	Made Communist Party chief in the Ukraine
1941	Outbreak of World War II
1949	Brought back to Moscow
1953	Appointed first secretary of Soviet Communist Party
1956	Secret speech criticizing Stalin
1957	Launch of first space satellite (*Sputnik*)
1959	Visit to the United States
1961	Berlin Wall erected
1962	Cuban Missile crisis
1963	Test Ban Treaty signed
1964	Deposed by fellow Party leaders

main success, however, came in surviving the purges himself; most of his colleagues who were in the Central Committee in 1934 were executed.

In 1938, Khrushchev took the top position in the Communist Party of the Ukraine, a crucial position for several reasons. Starting in 1929, farmers both in the Ukraine and elsewhere in the Soviet Union had been forced to give up private land holdings in order to enter collective farms. The Ukraine—the most important agricultural region in the country—had been a center of resistance to Stalin's farm policy, and the loyalty of its people was still uncertain. Moreover, the Ukraine was located along the Soviet Union's border with the countries of Eastern Europe: Poland and Rumania. As Nazi Germany under **Adolf Hitler** expanded eastward, the Ukraine was likely to be hit first by a German military attack. As Stalin's loyal (and brutal) lieutenant in charge of the Ukraine from 1938 to 1941, Khrushchev directed mass arrests and downgraded the Ukrainian language and culture in favor of Russian, a cultural policy used as an important tool by Stalin to bring all regions of the Soviet Union under Moscow's control.

When the Nazi attack came in June 1941, Khrushchev remained in the Ukraine. Although he became a lieutenant general in the Soviet army, he was really a high-level Communist Party official in uniform, making sure that Stalin's wishes were carried out during the war. Khrushchev would later speak of his frustration over the military mistakes made by Stalin. For example, he blamed Stalin for failing to prepare for the German attack even though Hitler's intention to strike the Soviet Union was clear by the spring of 1941. Possibly the first doubts about the man he had so long served began during World War II.

After the war, Khrushchev remained in the Ukraine to supervise reconstruction, a huge task and one which he approached in a novel way. Foreign visitors to the Ukraine came away impressed with Khrushchev; he had developed into a different kind of Communist Party leader, one who circulated among the population and who was interested in the problems of agriculture and the farm population. As the powerful head of an important region, Khrushchev maintained as much of an independent position as anyone could in Stalin's dictatorial system.

In 1949, Khrushchev returned to lead the Communist Party in the Moscow region. Stalin probably had other things in mind for him as the Soviet leader kept his most important and ambitious lieutenants off balance by encouraging rivalries between them. Andrei Zhdanov, a key player in this competition, had just died, and Stalin needed someone to balance off ambitious figures like **Georgi Malenkov.** Thus, the rivalry to succeed Stalin began even before 1953—and it began under Stalin's encouragement.

It took Khrushchev about two years after the death of Stalin to solidify his power and crush his most dangerous rival, Malenkov. Within a few days of the dictator's death, Khrushchev and other Party leaders forced Malenkov to give up the leading position in the Communist Party, the post of first secretary of the Central Committee. Malenkov kept the position of premier, that is, the head of the government. Important changes followed. Without Stalin in charge, the Soviet Union could no longer maintain a brutal dictatorship whose government drained resources from farming and consumer goods in order to feed the military system. Khrushchev became the spokesman for agricultural reform, his special area of interest since his years in the Ukraine, and by the end of 1955, he had enough success to his credit to oust Malenkov and put his own lieutenant, **Nikolai Bulganin,** in charge of the government.

Krushchev Condemns Stalin

The most dramatic moment in Khrushchev's career came in February 1956 at the 20th Communist Party Congress. In a speech on the last night of the Congress, he presented a call for "de-Stalinization." It seemed like a call to reform the Soviet Union. Khrushchev recounted Stalin's crimes against Party members during the purges of the 1930s and condemned Stalin's mistakes during the war. Khrushchev's motives for giving this spectacular speech are still uncertain; perhaps he thought his position as Party leader was endangered by those of Stalin's followers who were still on the scene. Thus, a speech condemning Stalin could serve to heighten his own power.

Regardless of his motives, Khrushchev's move to change the Stalinist system led to a year of calamity. Populations in Eastern Europe, under the control of the Soviet Union since the end of World War II, took this new mood in Moscow as encouragement to make changes in their own countries. With Stalin's system under criticism, the Poles and the Hungarians moved in the fall of 1956 to lessen—or even to end—the power of their ruling Communist governments. While able to reach a settlement with the Poles, Khrushchev crushed the Hungarian rebellion by sending in the Soviet army and killing thousands.

In the spring of 1957, Khrushchev's enemies within the Communist Party like Malenkov came close to removing him from power. Considering him weakened by the uprisings of the previous fall, they confronted him in the Presidium, the small body of individuals that directed Party policy, and demanded his resignation. Khrushchev, refusing to leave, demanded that the larger Central Committee decide the issue, and he won a majority of the members. Following his victory, he attempted to ensure that his Party rivals could not strike again; Malenkov, for example, was exiled to a minor bureaucratic job in a distant province.

Soviets Launch Space Satellite

The 1957 victory over his Party competitors was soon accompanied by a spectacular success in technology and international relations. In early October 1957, the Soviet Union launched *Sputnik,* the first space satellite, leading many foreign observers to speak of the Soviet Union under Khrushchev as the world leader in advanced technology. Still, the success of *Sputnik* gave Khrushchev a new set of difficulties. The United States, possessing far greater wealth, began participating enthusiastically in the space race. This race to be first would prove tremendously expensive for both sides, but the United States would end up winning.

Meanwhile, friction between the Soviet Union and the People's Republic of China grew in the aftermath of *Sputnik.* In the late 1940s, the Chinese had emerged as the second great Communist power in the world while becoming increasingly unwilling to accept the leadership of the Soviet Union in pursuing Communist goals. Restlessness grew when Khrushchev refused to let them have the technology that made *Sputnik* possible, along with help in constructing nuclear weapons, because the Chinese Communists wanted to use missiles and atomic bombs to threaten the Chinese Nationalists on Taiwan. Khrushchev's refusal widened the gap separating China and the Soviet Union.

Thus, faced with growing competition from both Communist and non-Communist countries, his government pushed ahead with "de-Stalinization," freeing many of Stalin's victims from prison and ending the constant threat of police terror that had arisen in the 1930s. He allowed such writers as Alexander Solzhenitsyn to publish books exposing the brutality of life under Stalin. To the Chinese, who now criticized Khrushchev openly, such a policy constituted the betrayal of Communism. They condemned as well his statements that war between the Soviet Union and the United States was not inevitable, statements presenting the view that Communist and non-Communist leaders could "coexist" and compete in non-military areas like economic growth.

The Americans, meanwhile, continued to eye the Soviet Union with suspicion. Khrushchev's efforts at *détente* (the reduction of political and military tensions) were mixed with aggressive moves such as a series of threats to the Western-controlled parts of Berlin in 1958 and again in 1961. Perhaps he made such aggressive moves in order to prevent criticism from the Chinese or from more traditional, Stalinist leaders in the Soviet Communist Party.

To boost his position at home, Khrushchev matched his political reforms with colorful promises of economic abundance. By the early 1960s, he spoke of overtaking and surpassing the standard of living of the United States in the near future. In fact, his farm program—especially the "virgin lands scheme" that opened up large areas of Central Asia for agriculture—did not produce results after an early, promising start.

To Americans, he appeared to be a far different figure from the brutal dictator Stalin during the Cold War years from 1945 to 1953. But Khrushchev had his own record of brutality, especially in Hungary in 1956, and he continued at times to present himself as a bully by threatening Berlin or banging his shoe on a desk at the United Nations to show his displeasure. In the fall of 1959, he made a spectacular tour of the United States, visiting such places as a Hollywood movie set and a Midwestern farm. Two years later, however, in the fall of 1961, a military clash with the United States seemed more likely than it had in years, when Khrushchev, reacting to the growing departure of East Germans to West Berlin, built the wall separating the Communist and non-Communist sectors of the city.

The Cuban Missile Crisis

The following fall brought about the most dangerous confrontation of the Cold War. Placing missiles in Cuba led to an American demand that the Soviet Union back down. After a tense week in which the world stood on the edge of nuclear war, Khrushchev—unable or unwilling to risk a military clash with the United States—agreed to remove the missiles.

The aftermath of the missile crisis of 1962 brought a new wave of Soviet-American cooperation under Khrushchev, along with growing criticism of him by the Chinese. Russia and the U.S. set up an emergency communications system (or "hot line") so that their leaders could speak quickly in times of crisis. The arms race was modified by a ban on nuclear testing in the atmosphere. The Soviet Union began to buy large quantities of food from the United States.

Khrushchev's failures in agriculture and foreign policy reduced him to an even weaker position than the one he had survived in 1957. In October 1964, he traveled to the Crimea in southern Russia on vacation. Hurrying home at the urging of other Party leaders, he discovered they had decided to remove him. This time he went without protest.

Until his death in 1971, he lived in Moscow. He also had a country house, where Western photographers sometimes found him at the polls on voting day or playing with his grandchildren. Unlike political losers under Stalin, Khrushchev was permitted to live out his days in peace.

SOURCES:

Crankshaw, Edward. *Khrushchev: A Career*. Viking, 1966.

Frankland, Mark. *Khrushchev*. Stein and Day, 1966.

Medvedev, Roy A., and Zhores A. Medvedev. *Khrushchev: The Years in Power*. Columbia University Press, 1976.

FURTHER READING:

Hyland, William, and Richard Wallace Shryock. *The Fall of Khrushchev*. Funk & Wagnalls, 1968.

Khrushchev, Nikita. *Khrushchev Remembers*. Little, Brown, 1970.

Linden, Carl. *Khrushchev and the Soviet Leadership, 1957–1964 with an Epilogue on Gorbachev*. Johns Hopkins University Press, 1990.

Pistrak, Lazar. *The Grand Tactician: Khrushchev's Rise to Power*. Praeger, 1961.

John Knox

(c. 1513–1572)

Well-known Scottish Reformer who, through his writings and sermons, was influential in the establishment of Calvinism in Scotland.

"I am a painstaking preacher of the blessed Evangel whose duty is to instruct the ignorant, comfort the sorrowful, confirm the weak and rebuke the proud."

JOHN KNOX

Very little is known about the early life of John Knox; even in his writings, he provided few clues about his childhood years. He was born sometime between 1513 and 1515 in Haddington, during a period when Western Europe was undergoing religious and political upheaval. In 1517, **Martin Luther** posted his 95 Theses in Wittenberg thereby destroying the sacramental system and priestly hierarchy of the medieval church. The reform movement spread rapidly by means of the printing press which published and exported vernacular translations of Luther's works. Politically, the 16th century saw a strengthening of monarchical government through increased centralization and bureaucratization.

These events, however, had little impact upon Knox for the first 30 years of his life. Born into a middle-class family, he was educated at the local grammar school in Haddington until he reached 15 years of age. He left his parents' home to study at St. Salvatore's College at the University of St. Andrews where he studied arts and theology and was awarded a bachelor of divinity. On April 15, 1536, he was ordained as a priest. An avid pupil, historian Jasper Ridley described him as "restless, bursting with energy, and eager to dominate."

Contributed by Margaret H. McIntyre, Ph.D. candidate in History, University of Guelph, Guelph, Ontario, Canada

Born sometime between 1513 and 1515 in Haddington; died in Edinburgh on November 24, 1572; son of a yeoman farmer or merchant; married: Marjory Bowes; married: Margaret Stewart of Ochiltree, 1563; children: (first marriage) Nathaniel, Eleazer; (second marriage) Martha, Margaret, Elizabeth.

CHRONOLOGY

1529	Knox ordained priest
1540	Acted as notary in Haddington
1542	Battle of Solway Moss; James V died; accession of Mary, Queen of Scots
1543	Knox tutored sons of Hugh Douglas
1546	George Wishart burned at stake; Cardinal Beaton assassinated
1548	Treaty of Haddington
1549	Knox set free from galley slavery; appointed preacher at Berwick
1553	Edward VI died; accession of Mary Tudor
1554	Mary of Guise appointed regent; Knox fled to France
1558	Mary Tudor died; accession of Elizabeth I
1559	Treaty of Cateau-Cambrésis; Knox returned to Scotland
1560	Mary of Guise died; Treaty of Edinburgh; Reformation Parliament; Knox appointed first Protestant minister of St. Giles; first meeting of the General Assembly held
1567	Mary, Queen of Scots abdicated; James VI (13 months) crowned king of Scotland
1572	Knox died at age 59; civil war ended the following year

Knox's movements are lost to history for the next four years until 1540 when he found work as a notary in the Haddington area. Performing the same duties as a modern-day lawyer, Knox remained in this position until 1543 when he became tutor to two sons of the Protestant lord, Hugh Douglas of Longniddry. It was during this period that Knox embraced the reformed religion.

Although Scotland was still a Catholic country at this time, Lutheran ideas had been smuggled in through the east coast burghs by students, sailors, and merchants. Attempting to prevent the spread of reformist doctrine, Parliament passed legislation in 1525 which banned the importation of heretical literature. These efforts were largely unsuccessful and a heavier penalty for preaching Lutheran beliefs was meted out to Patrick Hamilton who, in 1528, was the first heretic to be burned. Criticism towards the Church in Scotland was not unfounded. Most of its wealth was concentrated at the top level while parish priests remained poor and uneducated. In order to supplement their meager incomes, many priests held more than one benefice

(office) and were, therefore, often absent from their parishes.

Politically, Scotland was in the midst of yet another royal minority after the death of James V in 1542. The heir to the throne, **Mary, Queen of Scots,** was only seven days old when she succeeded to the crown and, as a result, leadership of the government was given to James Hamilton, earl of Arran. There soon appeared, however, a definitive split among the politically active magnates with one side favoring maintaining the "auld alliance" with France, while the other advocated closer ties with England. In addition, several of the pro-English nobles had converted to Protestantism and sought a rejection of papal authority.

Knox's conversion to Protestantism was an important turning point as it influenced virtually all of his actions and motivations for the rest of his life. During his position as tutor, Knox met George Wishart, a Protestant preacher who had returned to Scotland in 1543 as an envoy sent to negotiate the marriage of the infant queen Mary with **Henry VIII**'s only son and heir, Edward. Wishart was allowed to preach freely throughout southeast Scotland until 1545 when he fell increasingly under the scrutiny of the government. By this time, Henry VIII's belligerent foreign policy had convinced the Scots to reject the marriage alliance with England and actively seek French aid. In December 1545, Knox became a member of a group of Protestant lords which acted as protectors of Wishart. Carrying a two-handed sword, he remained with Wishart for five weeks until January 12, 1546, when it became apparent that Wishart's arrest could no longer be avoided. Twenty-four hours after encouraging Knox to return to his pupils, Wishart was arrested, strangled, and burned at the stake on March 1, 1546.

Knox Preaches to the Rebels

Some Protestant lords focused their revenge on Cardinal Beaton whom they felt had been responsible not only for Wishart's death but for the breakdown of amicable relations with England. On May 29, they took vengeance and stabbed Beaton to death in his castle at St. Andrews. The murderers refused to give up possession of the castle and held Arran's son as hostage. Several lairds (lords) came to join the "Castilians" although they did not receive much support outside of Fife. Nonetheless, the rebels were able to withstand the government's seige with aid from Henry VIII. One year later, in April 1547, Knox made the momentous decision to join the rebels. He brought his two pupils with him and continued to teach them in the castle chapel.

He was soon persuaded by the Castilians, however, to provide them with spiritual support and, from the moment that he preached his first sermon, Knox knew that his calling was affirmed.

Unfortunately, his early career as a preacher was short-lived. By July, 20 French ships had arrived in Scotland and proceeded to bombard the castle. On July 31, the castle fell and Knox was consigned to prison as a French galley slave. Overworked and underfed, Knox's health deteriorated, but he sustained his hopes and his will to live with the belief that God would soon release him from bondage. His prayers were answered 19 months later in March 1549 when he was finally set free.

Fearing persecution in Scotland, Knox went to England where he was appointed preacher at Berwick by the English Privy Council. A permanent residence allowed him to recover his health and, more important, provided him with time to study. His studying was reflected in the sermons he gave to his congregation. Although he could not preach as radically as he had in Scotland, he focused much of his attention on attacking the Mass. These public assaults, however, led him to be summoned before the Council of the North on April 4, 1550, where he was ordered to provide a public defense of his beliefs. The argument he expounded formed the basis of all of his doctrine; namely, that the authority of Scripture was above all, including the pope and the king. Since the Mass was not found in Scripture, Knox concluded, it should not be performed. His reasoning was persuasive, and he was allowed to return home to his congregation.

While he was living in Berwick, Knox met Elizabeth Bowes and became attracted to her daughter Marjory, one of 15 children whose father was captain of Norham Castle. There is very little surviving evidence to provide a clear picture of Marjory Bowe's personality or of their courtship. Historians have tended to focus more on Knox's relationship with her mother due to the existence of letters which Elizabeth Bowes and Knox wrote to one another. Historian W. Stanford Reid concluded that in his letters "we find a warmth, a gentleness, and an understanding that most people do not associate with him." Knox provided moral guidance and spiritual advice to Elizabeth Bowes and, although contemporaries spread rumors that they were lovers, those allegations have no factual basis. Knox was in love with her daughter and, in spite of her father's disapproval, he and Marjory were finally betrothed sometime in 1553.

By 1551, Knox had moved to Newcastle where he preached before John Dudley, duke of Northumberland. Impressed by his obvious abilities, Northumberland invited Knox to accompany him back to London in August 1552. At this time, however, both politics and religion were in a precarious state. Protector Somerset had been executed earlier that year and a radical group of Protestants were challenging the slow-moving Bishop Cranmer to implement sweeping changes to English worship. Knox sided with these reformers who called for a revised and more Protestant *Book of Common Prayer*. A key issue was the presence of kneeling at Communion. In October, Knox preached before the 15-year-old King Edward VI and his council, arguing that kneeling might be considered an act of adoration and thus a continuation of what he considered to be a superstitious and idolatrous practice of Catholicism. His words were strong enough to persuade the council to insert a statement, known as the "Black Rubric," in the second *Book of Common Prayer* which explained that kneeling at the Lord's Supper did not imply adoration of the consecrated elements.

Knox's impression upon the duke of Northumberland was significant. He was offered the bishopric of Rochester but refused the appointment. Prudently, he saw that Edward's reign would not last much longer and would be followed by a resurgence of Catholicism. His prediction was accurate; on July 6, 1553, the young Edward VI died and was succeeded by his Catholic sister, **Mary Tudor.** Fearing for his safety, Knox spent the next five years of his life on the Continent. Here, he wrote several pamphlets and treatises as well as numerous letters to his mother-in-law, Elizabeth Bowes. He also took advantage of his close proximity to the most influential Continental reformers by meeting and speaking with **John Calvin** at Geneva and Heinrich Bullinger at Zurich. To Knox, his responsibilities as a religious exile were clear:

> England and Scotland shall both know that I am ready to suffer more than either poverty or exile, for the profession of that doctrine, and that heavenly religion, whereof it has pleased His merciful providence to make me, amongst others, a simple soldier and witness-bearer unto men.

During his travels abroad, Knox spent some time in Frankfurt where he would have remained as minister had he not quarrelled with moderate English reformers. He finally settled in Geneva which he praised as "the most perfect school of Christ that ever was in the earth since the days of the Apostles." The time that he spent in Geneva had a profound influence upon Knox. Calvin had set up a municipal government which was charged with enforcing strict morality laws. Virtually every aspect of people's lives was under scrutiny and severe punishments were meted out for those who strayed from the Word of God. Thus, not only adultery and fornication were condemned by the authorities as immoral, but also swearing, card-playing, gambling, and wearing ostentatious clothing. Knox was impressed with this moral government and tried, albeit unsuccessfully, to impose it upon Scotland years later.

These formative years in Geneva were interrupted by a trip home to Scotland in September 1555. Although Catholic Mary of Guise had succeeded the Protestant Arran as regent, her rule was characterized by toleration and conciliation towards the reformers. Consequently, Knox was allowed to preach freely in Fife, Angus, the Mearns, Kyle, and Edinburgh. During this period, he finally married Marjory Bowes. Both she and her mother traveled with him when he was asked by his congregation to return to Geneva in September 1556.

Six months later, Knox was again preparing for a return trip to Scotland, this time at the request of a group of Protestant lords. On March 10, 1557, Knox received a letter from some of the leading nobles who supported the Reformation inviting him to return home as their spiritual leader. Knox eventually arrived at Dieppe on October 24 but, to his dismay, found letters from the same lords advising him to go no farther; the time was not yet ripe for a religious revolution. In December, the Scottish nobles signed a bond in which they renounced Catholicism and pledged to work for the recognition of the reformed church. This "First Band" of the Lords of the Congregation, however, failed to attract much support and Knox was forced to wait another two years before his countrymen were able to achieve their religious and political goals.

He Opines on Female Rule

Knox remained in Geneva writing various tracts and pamphlets. Although little is known about his family life, it appears that his wife acted as his secretary, assisting him with his written works and composing some of his correspondence. During this time, Knox wrote what was to become his most famous work. Perhaps out of frustration at having been exiled from England and Scotland, both of which were ruled by female sovereigns, Knox wrote down his thoughts and opinions on the subject of female rule in a pamphlet entitled *The First Blast of the Trumpet Against the Monstrous Regiment of Women.* His views were plain and harsh:

To promote a woman to bear rule, superiority, dominion or empire above any realm, nation or city is repugnant to nature, a disgrace to God, a thing most contrarious to his ruled will and approved ordinance, and finally it is the subversion of good order, of all equity and justice.

Not only did he conclude that Mary Tudor's rule was God's punishment for the sins of the Protestant magnates during Edward VI's reign, but he developed a theory that advocated rebellion against an "ungodly" ruler. In Knox's view, the subjects of a Catholic ruler were legally entitled to overthrow their sovereign by armed rebellion.

His words were prophetic. When he finally returned to Scotland on May 2, 1559, the Protestant Lords of the Congregation were openly rebelling against the regent Mary of Guise. Nine days later, Knox preached a sermon at Perth which stimulated the listeners to loot nearby religious houses. Although Knox attributed these actions to the "rascal multitude," the revolt against Catholicism and French rule in Scotland had begun. By October, the lords had "suspended" Mary of Guise from the regency and were actively seeking aid from **Elizabeth I.** On February 27, 1560, a treaty was signed at Berwick between the rebels and England "for maintenance and defence of the ancient rights and liberties of the country" and an English fleet entered the harbor at Leith which severed the Regent's French support. After the death of Mary of Guise on June 11, another treaty was signed, this time at Edinburgh between France and England in which both English and French troops agreed to withdraw from Scotland. One month later, a parliament was held in Edinburgh which ushered in the Scottish Reformation.

Knox became the first Protestant minister of St. Giles Cathedral in Edinburgh, and he was commissioned, along with five other ministers, to draw up a Confession of Faith, which was passed by Parliament on August 17. Two other acts which abolished the authority of the pope and forbade the celebration of the Mass confirmed the death of Catholicism in Scotland.

Knox was also appointed to an additional committee which was set up to prepare a "book of Reformation." The *Book Of Discipline,* as it came to be known, was essentially a blueprint for the reformers' program and provided for the establishment of ministers throughout the country as well as a national system of education. To Knox, the Reformation in Scotland signaled the triumph of "the saints of God" over those "bloody wolves who claim to themselves the title of clergy." Unfortunately, his "godly council" was soon replaced by an "ungodly" Catholic princess.

When Mary, Queen of Scots returned to Scotland in August 1561, Knox was deeply distrustful. Hoping to set up a system of moral government such as he had witnessed in Geneva, Knox attacked what he believed was sexual immorality at the royal court. In his opinion, Mary's love of dancing was nothing more than lewd and impious behavior. Consequently, he was summoned several times for interviews with Mary where he took the opportunity to criticize the queen for her religion, her marriage plans to Henry Stewart, Lord Darnley, and her deportment. His hostility toward Mary, however, was not shared by all of the reformers, and he was censured in the General Assembly of the Church of Scotland in 1564. In addition, his political views regarding obedience to the sovereign did not win him any favors with the two most important men of Mary's Council, James Stewart, earl of Moray, and William Maitland of Lethington. W. Stanford Reid has concluded that after 1564 "the possibility of his influencing political events on behalf of the reformed religion largely disappeared."

Little is known about Knox's personal activities during this time. His first wife had died in December 1560, and Knox was married again three years later to Margaret Stewart, daughter of Andrew, Lord Ochiltree. The marriage provided ammunition for gossip-mongers as his new bride was 17 years old while he was a man of 50. His physical appearance was daunting. A contemporary described him as:

> rather below the normal height, his cheeks ruddy and somewhat full, the eyes keen and animated, large lips, his thick black beard (flecked with grey) falling down a hand and half long; he bore an air of authority, and in anger his very frown became imperious.

Knox spent much of this time writing his *History of the Reformation in Scotland.* Although he was not heavily involved in political affairs, he made his opinions known to the public through his sermons. He approved of the murder of Mary's Italian secretary, David Riccio, and, though he was absent during the revolution which toppled the queen from her throne in May 1567, upon his return to Scotland in June he demanded that she be executed.

Following Mary's defeat at the battle of Langside in May 1568 and her subsequent flight to England, Scotland became embroiled in a civil war. Knox allied himself with the king's party and he remained in high favor with the various regents who governed the country in the 13-month-old **James VI**'s name. Nonetheless, he became increasingly bitter and frustrated by what he felt was a betrayal by the Protestant lords who joined the queen's party. He continued to criticize Mary and was finally driven from Edinburgh by her adherents. From May 1571 until August 1572, Knox took refuge in St. Andrews. Following a truce between the two opposing sides, he returned to Edinburgh in September 1572. His health, however, rapidly deteriorated and by November 17, he could neither walk nor read. John Knox died, apparently without pain, on November 24 at the age of 59.

SOURCES:

Reid, W. Stanford. *Trumpeter of God: A Biography of John Knox.* Scribner, 1974.

Ridley, Jasper. *John Knox.* Oxford University Press, 1968.

FURTHER READING:

Mackie, J. D. *John Knox.* Historical Association, 1951.

Percy, Eustace. *John Knox.* Hodder & Stoughton, 1937.

Alexandra Kollontai

(1872–1952)

Russian revolutionary, and feminist, whose views were suppressed in Russia because of the growing conservatism and puritanism of the Stalin regime.

Name variations: nickname "Shura." Born Aleksandra Mikhailovna Domontovicha in St. Petersburg on March 19, 1872; died in Moscow on March 9, 1952; daughter of Mikhail Alekseevich Domontovich and Alexandra Alexandrovna Mravinsky (daughter of a Finnish lumber merchant); married: Vladimir Mikhailovich Kollontai (her paternal cousin; divorced), 1893; married: Pavel Dybenko (first Soviet Commissar for Naval Affairs; perished in the Stalin purges in 1937), 1918; children: (first marriage) son Michael (Misha).

Alexandra Kollontai was born to an aristocratic family of Russia, yet early developed a social consciousness. By 1905, she was a published writer and an active feminist. By 1917, she was the only female member of *Lenin*'s revolutionary cabinet. Although she served as Commissar of Social Welfare until 1918, her opposition to Lenin's New Economic Policy (*NEP*) and the increasing dictatorialness of the Communist Party estranged her from Party leadership. Taking refuge in the Soviet diplomatic service, she made a quiet but successful career, ultimately serving as the first female ambassador in modern times. A pacifist and humanitarian, Kollontai represents the best element in the Bolshevik movement and as such was fortunate to have survived the Stalinist terror.

Alexandra Kollontai was born in 1872, the daughter of Mikhail Alekseevich Domontovich and Alexandra Alexandrovna Mravinsky. On her father's side, she was part Ukrainian. Her mother, the daughter of a Finnish lumber merchant in St. Petersburg, was a Russian "new woman" of a type not uncommon in the time of **Alexander II.** She had left her first husband to live with Domontovich, a cavalry officer in the tsar's army and even-

"Kollontai was one of the last of a type, the nineteenth-century radical Russian woman who joined the revolutionary movement from a background of privilege and for motives only peripherally related to main stream Marxism."

BEATRICE FARNSWORTH

Contributed by Robert H. Hewsen, Professor of History, Glassboro State College, Glassboro, New Jersey

734

tually a general, before she secured a divorce; as a result, their daughter was born before her parents were able to marry. As a girl growing up in St. Petersburg, Alexandra enjoyed all the benefits and privileges that her membership in the Russian upper classes entailed, including an English governess, education and training by private tutors in foreign languages, as well as the usual parties, balls, and travel. But the time in which she grew up bred a certain type of rebelliousness and Alexandra had her mother's example before her. In 1893, against her parents' better judgment, Alexandra married her first cousin Vladimir Kollontai, and though she eventually left him, she always spoke well of him and blamed herself for the rupture.

The social and economic ills that beset Russia in the late 19th century were gravely exacerbated by the arrival of the Industrial Revolution. The conscience of the intellectual classes was troubled by the search for social justice and for solutions to deeply rooted problems. Like many of her generation, Alexandra was drawn first to charity work, then to socialism in general, and soon to its Marxist current. Although married with a child, her determination to do something "useful" with her life led her to spend a year (1898–99) in Switzerland studying with prominent Marxists of the day.

Her concern for her child brought Kollontai back to St. Petersburg, but she never resumed living with her husband. Moving with her son into a small apartment, she began to write articles for the leftist press and a book describing the Finnish economy in Marxist terms. In January 1905, overcome by the disastrous defeat of Russia in the Russo-Japanese War and the government's inability to solve the problems at home or to institute reforms needed to bring the country into the 20th century, the Russian people rose in a massive revolt that lasted for the better part of the year. Only the loyalty of the army and the Tsar's "October Manifesto" guaranteeing reforms saved the regime. During that momentous year, Kollontai joined with the St. Petersburg Committee of the Menshevik wing of the Social Democrats who were engaged in fund-raising, communicating with Finnish party members, and inculcating the factory workers of the capital.

It was at this time that Kollontai accepted the notion that feminism was a false means to the solution of the Women's Question because most feminists were middle-class women concerned only with improving their own conditions. In her view, as in that of most Marxists, only the Social Democrats could lead the women of the working class, and the role of women in the movement was

CHRONOLOGY

1872	Born at St. Petersburg
1894	Son Michael born
1898–99	Left husband to study Marxism in Switzerland
1905	Russian Revolution; joined the Menshevik wing of the Social Democratic Workers' Party
1908	Exiled in Western Europe
1915	Joined the Bolshevik Party
1915–16	Five-month propaganda tour of U.S.
1917	Appointed People's Commissar of Social Welfare
1920	Became director of Zhenotdel
1922	Appointed to Soviet trade delegation to Norway
1926–27	Appointed Soviet representative to Mexico
1930–45	Served as Soviet ambassador to Sweden
1952	Died in Moscow

to aid in the bringing about of the great working-class revolution which would result in social justice for all. Nevertheless, Kollontai realized that peasant and working women differed from the men of their respective classes and that a special program was needed to educate them for their role in the revolution and in the post-revolutionary era. Resistance to her views was strong, and her attempts to convince her comrades formed the major thrust of her revolutionary work. As early as 1905, she published her book *The Social Bases of the Woman Question* as well as several pamphlets. One pamphlet, calling for revolution, forced her to flee Russia in 1908.

Alexandra Kollontai spent the next nine years wandering in Western Europe, while developing her thinking on the Women's Question. With the outbreak of the First World War, the Second International of Workers' Parties collapsed as each member party, abandoning its cry for a working-class solidarity against the war, dutifully fell into line, advocating and justifying its own nation's support of the war in progress. Lenin was furious at this betrayal of socialist principles and at the clear defeat of socialism by the forces of nationalism, and Kollontai's identical views on the issue soon brought them together. Impressed by Lenin, she now abandoned her adherence to the Mensheviks and, in 1915, became a member of his Bolshevik Party.

With the fall of the Tsarist government in March 1917, Kollontai immediately left Scandinavia for Russia, arriving even before Lenin. Devoted to the idea that the Revolution would bring a speedy peace, she remained with the Bolsheviks after Lenin's arrival and denunciation of the war. In November of the same year, Lenin's Bolsheviks seized control of Russia in the coup d'état that introduced the Soviet regime. Kollontai, one of the Party's most ardent public speakers, was immediately called upon by Lenin to serve on his cabinet, the Council of Peoples Commissars (SOVNARKOM), as Commissar of Social Welfare—the first female cabinet member in Russia's history.

As Commissar of Social Welfare, Kollontai devoted herself to issues relevant to the effect of the Revolution upon women and the family, including the new marriage law permitting civil marriage and divorce by mutual consent and state support for maternity benefits and child care. She also called for the establishment of an organization devoted to educating women for their roles in the new society. The unpopular Treaty of Brest-Litovsk, which Lenin had **Trotsky** sign in March 1918 to get Russia out of the war at any cost, filled Kollontai with revulsion. Resigning in protest from the SOVNARKOM, she ceased all Party activity for several months.

In the autumn of 1918, Kollontai returned to the fray when, in the company of such other women Party leaders as Inessa Armand and Konkordiya Samoilova, she organized a national Conference of Women Workers held in Moscow in November. As the Civil War (1918–21) deepened, she served as People's Commissar of Enlightenment and Propaganda for the Ukrainian government, and then late in the summer of 1919, as emissary of the Party's Central Committee to its Youth Organization (*Komsomol*). Returning to Moscow, she worked to prepare for the first International Conference of Communist Women to be held in July 1920. There she was cut off from her son in technical school in Petrograd (as St. Petersburg had been renamed) and suffered terrible deprivations but was sustained by the enthusiasm for the long-dreamed-of chance to build a genuine socialist state.

With the support of this conference, Kollontai at last received Party approval for a women's organization to be called the Department for Work among Women Workers and Peasants (*Zhenotdel*), which was placed under the leadership of Inessa Armand. Armand died in 1920, however, and Kollontai inherited her post, the high point of her career. Unfortunately, the *Zhenotdel*'s origins as the pet project of a few dedicated women (Armand, Kollontai, Varvara Moirova, Polina Vonogradskaya, Elena Stasova), rather than as a unique Party initiative, weakened Party support. Yet the *Zhenotdel* did an enormous amount for the Party. Despite their middle-class and upper-class origins, its leaders went out to the factories, bridging the gap between themselves and the women to whom they spoke and gaining their support for the Communist program.

Although devoted to the conviction that the Soviet women's movement must be firmly grounded among the women of the working class, Kollontai did not neglect rural women. Rejecting the categorizing of peasant women in terms of their class, she pointed out that whereas the traditional male peasant might have a stake in the status quo, his downtrodden wife had much to gain by the reforms. Genuinely humane, Kollontai also took an interest in the plight of ruined women from the old privileged classes whose children she felt must not suffer for their mothers' class origins. Although an ardent champion of "free love," she also served on the Interdepartmental Commission for the Struggle Against Prostitution, believing that prostitutes must be reached so that they might be drawn into useful employment. She was adamantly opposed to the punishment of prostitution, believing that since all members of a socialist society must be engaged in useful work, the prostitute should be treated as merely another "deserter." Kollontai was especially radical in regard to the question of the family and, as a Marxist, predicted its extinction. She worked for the establishment of children's homes, daycare centers, and communal dining halls that would make this possible. Here, however, she received little more than the half-hearted support of the Party, which never took the liquidation of the family seriously.

Kollontai's revolutionary views seem to have been tailor-made to fit into the Communist program for the Brave New World Lenin dreamed of creating in the Soviet Union. They foundered, however, upon a basic principle of Marxism that Lenin was unwilling to relinquish: since all problems in society stemmed from the manner in which the means of production and distribution were ordered, the communization of these means would automatically solve all social problems. The duty of women was to support the program of the Party, through which their special concerns would be automatically resolved.

Although there is no question that Alexandra Kollontai took Party discipline most seriously, she did not feel it necessary to remain silent on issues with which she did not agree; on the contrary, she believed that Party discipline required the Party member to speak frankly on such matters. Increasingly, her frankness began to alienate important members of the Party's Central Committee, but what brought about her fall from grace was her role as leader of the so-called Workers' Opposition, which she joined in January 1921.

The end of the Civil War early that year saw Russia a ruined and exhausted country in which the only certainty was the specter of an oncoming famine of staggering proportions. Faced with this menace as well as with serious opposition to his policies in the military and in the countryside, Lenin adopted a New Economic Policy. His purpose was to allow Russia to recover from the disasters of the previous seven years before attempting any further radical reforms. In essence, the *NEP* left the government in control of the "commanding heights" of the economy—heavy industry, transportation, banking, and foreign trade—but allowed the rest of the economy to operate according to a market system. Like many other communists both in Russia and abroad, Kollontai considered the *NEP* to be a capitulation to non-socialist forces and a betrayal of the Revolution.

Kollontai's opposition came to a head at the 10th Congress of the Communist Party in Moscow in March 1921. Here began her conflict with Lenin that was to last until the 11th Congress at which she would meet total defeat. Recognizing herself as the sole opponent who could intellectually match the leadership at the summit of the Party, she emerged as the leader of the Workers' Opposition and her pamphlet by that name, which she distributed at the Congress, particularly enraged Lenin. In Kollontai's view, the collapse of the prewar economy, the pressures of the Civil War, and the difficulties of imposing a working-class revolution upon an essentially peasant society were causing serious problems in Communist Russia that must be solved by a party willing to face the issues squarely rather than silence dissent. Above all, Kollontai feared the increasing bureaucraticization of the Party, the suppression of internal criticism, and the alienation of the Party from the working class. A loyal Party member, she never questioned the Party's domination over the country but only the Party's domination over its members. Shrewdly, in the role of mediator, Lenin skillfully played one faction at the Congress against the other, and Kollontai's attempt to bring about fundamental changes in Party policy failed.

Undeterred, she took her case that summer to what was supposed to be the supreme communist body, the Third or Communist International, founded by Grigori Zinoviev under Lenin's orders in 1919. The *Comintern,* however, was dominated by its Soviet leadership and once again Kollontai failed to have her ideas seriously addressed. In return for her defiance, she was removed from her position with the *Zhenotdel.* Finally, at the 11th Congress of the Party held in 1922, which Lenin was by now too ill to attend, Kollontai and her fellow oppositionists were condemned and barely escaped being ejected from the Party. Thereafter, Alexandra Kollontai was finished as a Communist leader.

In late 1922, Kollontai was sent into genteel exile to Norway as part of a Soviet trade delegation, eventually becoming its head. She was then appointed the Soviet representative to Mexico (1926–27) and finally the Soviet ambassador to Sweden (1930). Although her fall had moved her far from the center of Soviet affairs, Kollontai's talents were never ignored and **Stalin** not only allowed her to live—a most extraordinary concession given his treatment of most of the other "Old Bolsheviks"—but continued to utilize her skills and experience in the diplomatic service. The Soviet government made much of Kollontai in these roles, inaccurately hailing its progressiveness in appointing the first woman ambassador in Russian history (ruler's widowed mothers had served in the past). No one knows how Kollontai survived. Summoned to Moscow in 1937 at the height of the purges, she was allowed to return to her post even though her husband Dybenko, military commander of the Leningrad District, had been executed. She had completely capitulated to the Terror, however, and in her writings participated—at whatever intellectual or personal pain—in the rewriting of Communist history that made possible the Stalin cult. It has been suggested that Stalin needed a few harmless Old Bolsheviks who could be used to bear witness to his supposed closeness to Lenin, and that Kollontai, by accepting this role, perhaps saved her own life.

As ambassador to Sweden, Kollontai worked for a peaceful solution to the Russo-Finnish war (1939–44). Although suspicious at first, the Soviet government accepted her initiatives, and her efforts were appreciated by the diplomats with whom she had to deal. After the war, she was nominated for the Nobel Peace Prize.

Kollontai remained the Soviet ambassador to Sweden until 1945 when, at the end of the Second World War, she retired at the age of 73. Plagued by ill health for much of her life, she had been partially paralyzed by a stroke in 1942 and required constant attention. Unfortunately, she did not live to see the end of the Stalinist dictatorship and, though she lived on a comfortable pension in Moscow and remained unmolested, she was under close surveillance, and her few surviving friends kept their distance. Nevertheless, she drew satisfaction from the existence of the Soviet state which she felt transcended the evils of Stalinism and the destruction of the Communist Party that she had known. He son Mikhail, a non-party engineer, was a source of pride to her, as was her grandson Vladimir who became a professor. Though she continued to write in private, she published nothing. Alexandra Kollontai died on March 9, 1952, just days before her 80th birthday, and was buried in the cemetery at the old Novodevich'e Convent in Moscow.

Alexandra Kollontai was one of the most remarkable women in early 20th-century feminism and certainly the most interesting among the women who participated in the Bolshevik revolution. Gracious, charming, and highly intelligent, she had the respect of Lenin even when he did not agree with her. Her devotion to the cause of women was both sincere and deeply held throughout her life, but, nevertheless, when the Communist Party rejected her views, she submitted to its authority—whatever it may have cost her intellectually—and did so with dignity and grace. In the words of Germaine Greer: "Kollontai herself was eventually persuaded that her ideas had little historical relevance to the state of the Russian nation, and uncomplainingly accepted distinguished obscurity."

SOURCES:

Kollontai, Alexandra. *The Autobiography of a Sexually Emancipated Communist Woman.* Edited by Irving Fetscher. New York, 1971 (repr. 1975 with a foreword by Germaine Greer).

———. *Free Love.* Translated by C. J. Hogarth. London, 1832.

———. *A Great Love.* Translated by Lily Gore. New York, 1929.

———. *Red Love.* New York, 1927.

———. *Selected Writings of Alexandra Kollontai.* Edited by Alix Holt, Westport, Ct., 1977.

———. *The Workers Opposition.* Chicago, 1921.

FURTHER READING:

Clements, Barbara Evans. *Bolshevik Feminist; the Life of Aleksandra Kollontai.* Bloomington, Ind., 1979.

Farnsworth, Beatrice. *Aleksandra Kollontai, Socialism, Feminism and the Bolshevik Revolution.* Stanford University Press, 1980.

Tadeusz Kosciuszko

(1746–1817)

Polish "Hero of Two Worlds," who was both an American Revolutionary War patriot and commander in chief of Polish insurrectionary forces.

"A citizen who wants to take pride on being a good Pole should sacrifice everything for his country and always be humane and just."

TADEUSZ KOSCIUSZKO

Tadeusz Kosciuszko was born a child of the Polish Enlightenment and a subject of the inept Elector of Saxony, King August III. As the youngest son of minor gentry, however, it was many years before he would fully grasp the consequences of being born in such a transformative and volatile era of Polish history.

Kosciuszko grew up in a small wooden country house at Mereczowszczyzna, rather than the unavailable and equally modest family estate at Siechnowicze. Mereczowszczyzna was located in eastern Poland, in Polesie near the head of the Narew River, which is between Brest-Litovsk and Nowogrod. In keeping with the tradition of his social position, young Kosciuszko was kept at home and educated under his mother's direction until the age of nine.

Following his fireside instruction, Kosciuszko began his formal education at the Piarist College in Lubieszow. Established throughout Poland, the Piarist schools were staffed by a Catholic Pietist Order, whose primary goal was the education of the sons of impoverished nobility. Although Kosciuszko showed an average talent for most subjects, in his preferred courses—geometry,

Contributed by Christopher Blackburn, Ph.D. candidate in history, Auburn University, Auburn, Alabama

Name variations: Thaddeus Kosciuszko. Pronunciation: KÄS-ee-ES-koe or Kosh-CHUSH-koe. Born Tadeusz Andrzej Bonawentura Kosciuszko on February 12, 1746, in the small village of Mereczowszczyzna near the city of Brest-Litovsk, in eastern Poland; died in Solothurn, Switzerland, in 1817; youngest of four children of Ludwik and Tekla (Ratomska) Kosciuszko (descended from minor Polish nobility, with a trace of Lithuanian and Byelorussian ancestry); never married; no children.

mie Royale de Peinture et de Sculpture and absorbed the engineering and artillery expertise of private tutors from the renowned École de Genie at Mezieres and École Militaire in Paris.

After Kosciuszko's first year in Paris, the King's monetary subsidies had become erratic and with the first partition of Poland in 1772, had stopped all together. By 1774, Kosciuszko was almost penniless. Compelled to abandon his Parisian studies and return to his homeland, he found no potential position in the diminished ranks of the post-partition army of King Stanislaw. The family estate at Siechnowicze was in disrepair and in dire economic straits. This unexpected and disastrous turn of events led Kosciuszko to support himself by tutoring the children of the affluent General Józef Sosnowski. His lessons with young Ludwika Sosnowski were soon brought to an end, however, when he asked for her hand in marriage. General Sosnowski callously rejected Kosciuszko's request by reportedly saying, "Ring-doves are not meant for sparrows, and the daughters of magnates are not meant for minor gentry." Following this unfortunate incident in 1775, Kosciuszko left Poland in search of a position worthy of his talents. After a brief stay in France, he found himself in Philadelphia offering his services to the Continental Army of General **George Washington.**

Aids Army, Fortifies West Point

In 1776, Kosciuszko's skills as a trained officer and military engineer were a welcome addition to the American army, since the bulk of the colonial troops and officer corps had little or no military education. By October 18, 1776, the Continental Congress granted Kosciuszko the rank of colonel of engineers. He was immediately given the task of designing fortifications for the Delaware River. To prevent the British fleet from sailing up the river and attacking Philadelphia, Kosciuszko designed an intricate system of river-based obstacles, with an overlooking battery of artillery. The fortification of the Delaware occupied most of his time until he was reassigned to General Horatio Gates's Army of the North in April 1777.

Responsible for halting British offensives along the Canadian border, Gates selected the town of Saratoga to challenge the British advance and assigned Kosciuszko the duty of preparing the American position for the upcoming battle. Kosciuszko chose to fortify the high ground of Bemis Heights with some three miles of elaborate earthworks and covering artillery. Intense fighting ensued in August and September 1777, leading ultimately to the surrender of General John Bur-

trigonometry, and drawing—he consistently displayed above average tendencies. Shortly after his father's death, the 14-year-old discontinued his studies in Lubieszow and returned home to help his mother manage the family property at Mereczowszczyzna, along with the newly regained estate at Siechnowicze.

While there, Kosciuszko decided on a career as a professional soldier. In 1765, at the age of 19, he was admitted to the Cadet's Corps of King Stanislaw Poniatowski's newly opened Royal Military Academy in Warsaw. Kosciuszko proved an excellent student of military tactics and was fortunate to have some of the finest instructors Western Europe had to offer. He acquired much of his knowledge of fortifications and training as a military engineer while in Warsaw. After his first year, Kosciuszko was awarded the rank of cadet, later captain, and spent the next two and a half years at the academy as an instructor and as a student in the special engineering course for advanced students.

In 1769, when Kosciuszko's abilities as a military engineer were recognized by the King, he received one of four royal scholarships to study military engineering in France. During his five years in France, he studied drawing at the Acade-

goyne's British forces on October 17. Kosciuszko immediately received the praise of his superiors for his role in the American victory at Saratoga. General Gates said later, "the hills and woods were the greatest strategists which a young Polish engineer knew how to select with skill for my camp."

Kosciuszko's splendid showing at Saratoga also managed to catch the eye of General Washington, who rapidly assigned him the critical task of fortifying the Heights of West Point. West Point's position along the Hudson River was crucial; with that particular area secured, the river systems linking the northern and southern colonies were safe from British attack. Kosciuszko spent nearly three years designing and supervising the construction of the fortifications at West Point. When completed, West Point stood as the crowning achievement of his distinguished career as a military engineer. Historian George Bancroft writes:

> Until 1778, West Point was a solitude, nearly inaccessible; now it was covered by fortresses with numerous redoubts, constructed chiefly under the direction of Kosciuszko as engineer, and so connected to form one system of defense, which was believed to be impregnable

In 1780, Kosciuszko, at the request of his old friend General Gates, was appointed chief engineer of the Army of the South. While in the south, he held many responsibilities, such as: provisioning the army, surveying terrain, engineering river and swamp crossings, commanding troops in battle, and the occasional entrenching of detachments. A year later, in South Carolina, he effectively directed the Battle of Ninety-Six and the protracted blockade of Charleston. With the surrender of General Charles Cornwallis's army at Yorktown, on October 19, 1781, the war and Kosciuszko's American service were nearly over. On October 13, 1783, the American government recognized Kosciuszko's contribution to their victory by granting him both the rank of brigadier general in the American army and U.S. citizenship.

In 1784, Kosciuszko left America for his native Poland. Despite his outstanding military record, he once again found no position in the slimmed-down Polish military and was forced to spend the next five years in near destitution at the Siechnowicze estate. In 1788, the Polish government, in an attempt to strengthen the state, passed several "liberal reforms." A major component of the reform package was a dramatic increase in the size of the Polish army. This rapid military expansion created an opening for Kosciuszko and on October 12, 1789, he was commissioned a major-general.

With the enactment of the Polish Constitution of May 3, 1791, **Catherine the Great** of Russia cooperated with the treasonous Polish Confederates of Targowitz to invade and overturn the Polish reforms. The numerically inferior Polish army was called on to defend its territory from the overwhelming Russian invasion. Kosciuszko, as a divisional commander, was placed in the path of the advancing Russian columns. It was at the Battle of Dubienka on July 18, 1792, that Kosciuszko gained his initial prominence as a Polish commander. His skill on the Dubienka battlefield enabled his 5,000 men to withstand a five-hour assault by some 30,000 Russian troops. This feat prompted King Stanislaw to advance Kosciuszko's rank to lieutenant-general in the Royal Polish Army. Ultimately, however, the Polish king abandoned the reforms of the May 3rd Constitution, and the Polish forces were rapidly overpowered by the numerically superior Russian army. In the wake of the Polish defeat, both Russia and Prussia took advantage of Poland's hapless situation and partitioned her territories for a second time in 1792. Kosciuszko quickly responded to the King's underhanded decision and the second partition by resigning his commission and joining other Polish insurgents and reformers in Saxony.

The Rebellion Against Prussia and Russia

While in exile, Kosciuszko and his associates made plans for a national Polish insurrection against the occupying Prussian and Russian forces. He also traveled to Paris and lobbied for the military support of the French revolutionary government against the partitioning powers. Thus, on March 12, 1794, Kosciuszko's underground militia began resisting the control of the partitioning authorities. Kosciuszko rapidly traveled to Krakow on March 24 and established his control of the insurrectionist government and military organizations. To bolster his small army, Kosciuszko immediately implemented conscription throughout the countryside. The Polish revolutionaries not only faced a shortage of manpower but also a critical shortage of armaments. To overcome the scarcity of firearms, Kosciuszko devised new infantry formations and armed his peasant recruits with pikes and straightened scythes. These scythe-bearing peasants, under the personal command of Kosciuszko, won an unlikely victory over Russian troops at Racławice on April 4.

This success led Kosciuszko to formulate new tactics which used mobile scythe-bearing formations and supporting artillery fire. He sought to increase the size of his army by gaining increased

Tadeusz Kosciuszko is released from prison in 1796 by new Russian tsar Paul I.

support from the peasantry. To do so, he suspended serfdom and reduced required peasant services on May 7, 1794, stating in the "Polaniec Manifesto":

> That every peasant is free and that he is allowed to move freely from place to place, provided he notifies the Orderly Commission of the province whither he goes, and provided he pays all his outstanding debts and national taxes.

The insurgent forces, however, were relentlessly driven back by the better-equipped and numerically superior armies of Prussia and Russia, led by **Alexander Suvorov.** The uprising was eventually brought to an end on the battlefield of Maciejowice. While suffering his greatest military defeat, Kosciuszko was wounded and taken prisoner by the Russian army. Without Kosciuszko's leadership and inspiration, the rebellion soon faltered and dissipated. The uprising was followed by the Third Partition of Poland in 1795. Russia, Prussia, and Austria had now completed the process begun in 1772 of dismembering the Polish state. With this event, Poland disappeared from the European map.

Spending the next two years recovering from his wounds in a prison cell of the Peter-Paul Fortress in St. Petersburg, Kosciuszko was finally released in 1796 by the new tsar of Russia, Paul I. Kosciuszko then made his way to the United

States, where he remained until he returned to France in 1798. He was, however, extremely disillusioned by the French swing from radical republicanism to the authoritarianism of French emperor **Napoleon Bonaparte.**

During the French war with Prussia in 1806, Napoleon tried to add prestige to the Polish uprisings in Prussian Poland by enlisting the support of the Polish "hero of two worlds." On November 3, 1806, Bonaparte wrote to his Minister of Police, Joseph Fouché: "Send for Kosciuszko; tell him to start immediately and join me…. Send me all the Poles you can." Although he had openly opposed Napoleon since 1800, Kosciuszko was considered the chief protector and advocate of the Polish Legions in France. Nevertheless, in 1800, he openly turned against Napoleon, declaring that he never really trusted the French leader's intentions; Kosciuszko said to a friend:

> Do not think that he will restore Poland. He thinks only of himself and not of our great nation, and he will not concern himself with restoring our independence. He is a tyrant, and his only aim is to satisfy his own ambition. He will never create anything durable, of that I am certain.

Furthermore, in 1800, Kosciuszko published an anti-French work entitled *Are Poles Capable of Winning their Fight for Independence?* in which he advanced the idea that Polish troops should not be used within foreign armies to liberate Poland, but rather, that Poles should liberate themselves. This prompted Napoleon to write to Fouché:

> Kosciuszko is a fool, who has not in his own country all the importance that he fancies he has, and whom I shall well do without for reestablishing Poland, if the fortune of arms seconds me.

In spite of his opposition to Napoleon, Kosciuszko remained a resident of France until after the collapse of the French Empire. At the Congress of Vienna in 1815, Tsar **Alexander I** of Russia sought Kosciuszko's support in the creation of a Polish Congress Kingdom. When Kosciuszko demanded too many territorial and political concessions, Alexander disregarded his petition. Retiring to Solothurn, Switzerland, to live out his days, Kosciuszko died on October 15, 1817. In 1819, his remains were transferred for burial among the kings of Poland at Wawel Cathedral in Krakow.

SOURCES:

Budka, Metchie, ed. *Autograph Letters of Thaddeus Kosciuszko in the American Revolution.* Polish Museum of America, 1977.

Chlapowski, General Desire. *Memoires sur les Guerres de Napoleon: 1806–1813.* Plon-Nourrit, 1908.

Halicz, Emanuel. "Tadeusz Kosciuszko and the Napoleonic Wars," in *East Central European War Leaders: Civilian and Military.* Columbia University Press, 1988.

Ier, Napoleon. *Correspondance de Napoleon Ier publiee par ordre de l'Empereur Napoleon III.* Paris, 1858.

Kopczewski, Jan Stanislaw. *Kosciuszko and Pulaski.* Interpress Publishers, 1976.

Mizwa, Stephen, ed. *Great Men and Women of Poland.* Macmillan, 1941.

Nofi, Albert A. "The American Revolution and Kosciuszko," in *East Central European War Leaders: Civilian and Military.* Columbia University Press, 1988.

Poniatowski, Jan. *Wojsko Kosciuszkowskie na plotnie Panoramy Raclawickiej.* Zaklad Narodowy imienia Ossolinskich Wydawnictwo, 1990.

St. Reymont, Wladyslaw. *Rok 1794.* Panstwowy Instytut Wydawniczy, 1988.

FURTHER READING:

Haiman, Miecislaus. *Kosciuszko, Leader and Exile.* New York, 1946.

———. *Kosciuszko in the American Revolution.* Boston, 1972.

Louis Kossuth

(1802–1894)

Hungarian political leader and revolutionary who organized his nation's government and army in 1848–49, declared Hungary free of the Habsburg crown, and spent the rest of his life in exile after the revolt's suppression.

A century after his death Louis Kossuth remains one of the most dramatic revolutionary leaders of 19th-century Europe. His oratorical talents and magnetic personality enabled him to become one of the most charismatic political leaders in an age that produced an extraordinary number of prophetic individuals determined to bring freedom to their peoples.

Kossuth's background was modest in the extreme; his family, which may originally have been Slovak, could trace its noble origins back to the year 1263 and had practiced the Lutheran religion since the 16th century. But, as was quite common among an often impoverished Magyar nobility, Kossuth's father Laszlo earned only a modest living as a lawyer. In view of Kossuth's later stature as a Hungarian nationalist, it is perhaps ironic to note that his mother Karolina Weber was of German ethnic origin. Growing up in an area of mixed nationalities in which the peasants were mostly poor Slovaks and the town burghers were either Magyars (Hungarians) or Germans, young Kossuth accepted as a fact of life the superiority and God-given right to rule of the noble caste into which he was born.

"It is no longer in my power to assist the Hungarian nation by my actions. If my death can benefit it, I will gladly sacrifice my life."

LOUIS KOSSUTH

Contributed by John Haag, Associate Professor of History, University of Georgia, Athens, Georgia

Since the death in 1526 of King Louis II, Hungary had been ruled by the Austrian Habsburg dynasty. A series of bloody rebellions against the Habsburgs ended in 1711 when the Treaty of Szatmar guaranteed Magyar nobles unlimited possession of their estates, full exemption from taxes, and complete mastery over their numerous serfs. Hungary's peasantry now sank into a state of almost total degradation as a feudal regime of powerful landowners, usually aided by a wealthy and morally lax church, tightened its grip on the lives of the poor. By the late 18th century a growing number of liberal-minded nobles, joined by a small contingent of middle-class intellectuals, had decided that Hungarian freedom could only be achieved if the nation accepted a wide-ranging agenda of reforms including the abolition of serfdom. The era of the French revolution and Napoleonic Wars only accelerated these yearnings for national renewal.

Kossuth began his career in the 1820s when the Habsburg Empire was controlled by the ultra-conservative regime headed in Vienna by Prince **Klemens von Metternich.** Metternich despised all manifestations of liberalism, regarding such ideas as inherently wrong and inevitably leading to a disrespect for traditional authority and thus to bloody revolution and anarchy. Before the 1840s, Hungarian opposition to Metternich's absolutist system came almost exclusively from the ranks of the nobility, which desired political independence from Austria and was willing to institute moderate reforms within a constitutional framework, but which by no means believed in democracy or social egalitarianism. Although born a noble, Kossuth went significantly beyond this position, recognizing the need for major reforms that would broaden the base of political life to include the urban middle classes; he did not, however, embrace the increasingly popular ideology of socialism that was evolving in the 1830s and 1840s in France and Germany. As a Magyar nationalist, Kossuth believed that with the achievement of Hungarian national freedom, the minority peoples (Serbs, Croats, Slovaks, and Rumanians) would "naturally" be assimilated and absorbed linguistically and culturally by the dominant Hungarian nationality, despite the fact that taken together these minorities outnumbered the Magyars.

Kossuth delivered his first political speech in 1830, attacking aristocratic privileges. The following year saw a series of speeches opposing extradition of refugee Polish revolutionaries; he also served as local commissioner during a cholera epidemic which claimed 100,000 Hungarian victims. Appointed absentee deputy, representing a local nobleman in 1832, he soon became nationally known for forceful oratory defending liberal ideals including freedom of the press. From 1833 to 1836, he edited a manuscript journal, *Parliamentary Reports,* which provided its 100 subscribers with detailed summaries of parliamentary activities, creating a permanent record of the rise of a liberal opposition in Hungarian politics. After founding the militantly liberal journal *Municipal Reports,* he was arrested on the charge of disloyalty and sedition and sentenced to three years' imprisonment in 1837. Released from prison as result of political amnesty, Kossuth was now viewed by a great majority of Hungarians as a national hero and martyr.

Kossuth's years as a journalist gave him a vast storehouse of information about Hungarian economic and political life, and his years in prison contributed to his maturity as well as providing him with the leisure to learn excellent English by reading Shakespeare and the Bible. Ironically, none other than Prince Metternich provided Kossuth with the presses and financing to launch another publication, the newspaper *Pesti Hirlap* (*Pest Journal*); Metternich apparently hoped that the flamboyant Kossuth would become more moderate in his demands for sweeping reforms once he had been tempered by the responsibilities of managing a journalistic enterprise and responding to fickle public opinion. But Kossuth became even more determined to sweep away the old regime, replacing it with a new society based on national self-assertion, liberal ideals, and constitutionalism. He was elected to the Diet as a representative from Pest.

The Year of Liberal Revolutions

The untested young political novice, who was catapulted into the European spotlight as a result of an electrifying speech (March 3, 1848) to the Hungarian Diet in Pressburg (today Bratislava), used all of his oratorical skills in denouncing the Habsburgs and "the pestilential air blowing from the Vienna charnel house and its deadening effect on all phases of Hungarian life." Only days before, a revolution in Paris had overthrown the unpopular King Louis Philippe, inaugurating 1848 as Europe's year of liberal revolutions. Despite censorship, Kossuth's speech found itself in print as a pamphlet, helping to spread the fever of revolution in Vienna, 20 miles from Pressburg, as well as in Hungary. On March 13, Viennese students and workers, many of whom had read and been inspired by Kossuth's sentiments, toppled the Metternich regime. Popular disturbances spread to Hungary, and seeing the handwriting on the wall, the Habsburg government gave in to the demands of Magyar liberals on March 17 by appointing the opposition leader Count Louis Batthyany prime minister of the first responsible government in Hungarian history. A series of reform laws passed in Pressburg the next three weeks received approval from Vienna in mid-April, transforming Hungary into a virtually independent state.

As the emerging star of his nation's reborn political life, Kossuth had countless admirers, friends, and allies but also potential rivals who hoped to slow his ascent to the top. By nudging him into the post of minister of finance rather than that of interior which he had expressed an interest in, it was hoped that the fiery orator would soon be forgotten. But Kossuth was determined to remain a national leader of the first rank, and he was soon given the opportunity to confront issues of crucial importance for the survival of Hungary's infant revolution. The government of Count Batthyany, believing that an alliance with revolutionary France was unrealistic, accepted the responsibilities of its traditional military alliance with Austria and promised to keep Hungarian troops in Italy, where an anti-Habsburg revolution was now raging. Kossuth consented to this policy unwillingly, realizing that once the Austrian conservative forces had crushed the Italian revolution, they would destroy the radical government in Vienna and then finish their counterrevolutionary agenda by marching on Hungary. The official position of the Hungarian government was a strange and even bizarre one, namely that Hungarian troops would remain stationed in Italy on condition that after the defeat of the Italian revolution Venetia and Lombardy should be granted full autonomy within the Habsburg Empire.

Kossuth's popularity continued to rise in the spring of 1848 as he was elected to a new Diet on the basis of a radically expanded suffrage that included the entire male population. When he called for a military budget that would make possible a national army of 200,000 men, the entire chamber rose to cheer and applaud him, quickly approving his proposal in a unanimous vote of approval. In one of his great moments as an orator, he waited for the thunderous applause to die down, then ended his speech with the stirring phrases: "I bow before the greatness of this nation. If Hungary's energy is equal to her patriotism even the gates of Hell will not prevail against her!" But, as is often true in life, rhetoric and reality did not see eye to eye. The situation in the summer of 1848 was rapidly turning against the Hungarian cause. Officially, the governments of Hungary and Austria enjoyed cordial relations, but power was slipping into the hands of Vienna as the revolutions in Italy and Bohemia suffered major military setbacks. Instead of attempting to win over the Croats and other non-Magyar nationalities, Kossuth and other Hungarian politicians made it clear that in the free Hungary of the future these peoples would be obligated to abandon their languages and cultures in favor of the "superior" Magyar tongue and way of life. Not surprisingly, the response to these ideas of Magyarization was vehemently negative, with such newly emerged leaders as Ban ("Viceroy") Joseph Jellacic, leader of the Croats, organizing a large army to defeat the Hungarians.

In September 1848, a last-ditch attempt at conciliation took place when a Hungarian delegation went to Vienna to discuss the chances for a peaceful resolution of the growing conflict. But, sensing that Jellacic and other enemies of the Hungarian cause were winning on the battlefield, the Habsburg regime essentially ignored the Hungarian negotiating team. Believing that the doors to a peaceful settlement had been irrevocably slammed shut, the Batthyany cabinet resigned in October. With the nation on the brink of anarchy, the Diet created a Committee of National Defense with Kossuth as its president. With superb skill and indefatigable energy, Kossuth quickly organized within weeks a national army (*Honved*) that was able to inflict significant defeats on Croat, Slovak, and Transylvanian rebel forces. For a time it appeared that the Hungarian forces could single-handedly save the revolutionary cause in Central Europe, but these unrealistic hopes were dashed in late October 1848, when *Honved* troops who had hoped to join forces with the besieged Viennese radicals were decisively defeated.

In December 1848, the situation once more changed significantly when the feeble-minded Austrian emperor, **Ferdinand I,** abdicated in favor of his 18-year-old nephew, who would ascend the throne as **Francis Joseph I.** The new Habsburg ruler vigorously backed the aspirations of the non-Magyar nationalities in Hungary, making it clear that he approved of their rebellion against Kossuth's forces. The Hungarian revolutionaries were increasingly divided among moderate and radical factions, with the latter group led by Kossuth, who despite his continuing popularity could not gloss over the fact that many Hungarians were becoming war-weary and disillusioned with political wrangling. Another factor weakening the Hungarian cause was the growing conservatism of the peasants, who had become a satisfied element due to the abolition of feudalism. Despite these problems, Kossuth was able to enlist the skills of a number of gifted military commanders including Arthur Görgey (1818–1916) and the colorful Polish soldier of fortune Josef Bem (1795–1850). It was because of Görgey's tactical genius that *Honved* forces were able to evacuate Budapest in January 1849 essentially intact and able to fight another day.

Kossuth Gambles for Hungarian Freedom

The fateful year 1849 began with Kossuth ordering the evacuation of his government from Budapest (the twin cities of Buda and Pest did not unite to form Budapest until the year 1872) to Debrecen, 100 miles to the east. A string of Hungarian victories in the first months of 1849 made possible the liberation of Budapest, created a mood of often unrealistic optimism, and encouraged Kossuth and his political allies to cross the political Rubicon by declaring full and total Hungarian independence. This took place on April 14, 1849, in Debrecen's Protestant church; Kossuth was proclaimed acting governor of the new state, which was not even defined either as a republic or constitutional monarchy—all that was clear was that Kossuth was now de facto dictator and the Habsburg dynasty had been deposed on Hungarian soil. There was, however, little time to celebrate these events, for in May Russian forces already stationed in the Carpathian mountains now poured into the indefensible Hungarian plains. Despite the bravery of Hungarian troops and the talents of Görgey, Bem and other generals, the 152,000 poorly equipped *Honved* soldiers could not prevail over 200,000 Russian and 170,000 Austrian men enlisted in the coalition of anti-Hungarian forces.

By July 1849, after a series of military catastrophes, it became clear even to Kossuth that his gamble for Hungarian freedom had failed. Since the end of 1848, the keystone of his political and military strategy was the rather unlikely possibility that the revolutionary forces in Germany might yet succeed in setting up a liberal German Republic sympathetic to Hungarian aspirations. Without support from a free Germany, Hungary would be doomed to succumb to the power of a revived Habsburg monarchy. Another negative element of the international balance of power was the fact that an independent Hungary simply could not be tolerated by the reactionary Romanov dynasty ruling Russia. It was more than likely that the impulsive Poles, whose massive revolt of 1830–31 had come close to expelling the Tsar's troops from Polish soil, would seize upon the opportunity to renew their struggle for freedom. Thus it was hardly surprising that Tsar **Nicholas I** would feel a strong obligation to crush the threat of liberalism centered in Hungary, whose armed forces were

attracting growing numbers of Polish revolutionaries including the brilliant Bem.

Kossuth became increasingly unrealistic about the situation in Hungary during the summer of 1849, often disagreeing vehemently with his generals, particularly Görgey, regarding the chances of still achieving a military victory over the combined Austrian and Russian armies. Görgey took the position that with enough military victories Hungary would be able to enter political talks strong enough to achieve significant political autonomy but not the total freedom Kossuth still dreamed of. As late as June, Kossuth reentered Budapest in the regal splendor befitting a national hero, and on July 28 he boasted to the National Assembly, which had fled to the city of Szeged, that "from this city the freedom of Europe will radiate." At this same session a Nationalities Law was passed guaranteeing the national minorities full cultural and local autonomy, legislation which if it had come a year earlier might possibly have saved the revolution. But the war was now lost, with all major Hungarian units defeated (the 20,000 men of Komarom fortress would hold out until October). On August 11, Kossuth transferred his powers to General Görgey who, ever the realist, surrendered to the Russian commander two days later at Vilagos.

A reign of terror now gripped Hungary as the Austrians reestablished their rule. Former Prime Minister Batthyany and 13 generals were executed, as were 40 officers and more than 120 enlisted men. Many revolutionaries received long prison sentences, as General Julius Jacob Haynau fully confirmed the reputation for butchery he had already earned in crushing the Italian insurrection ("the hyena of Brescia"). Kossuth escaped certain death by crossing the Hungarian frontier into the town of Vidin in the Turkish Empire (northwestern Bulgaria). With him were 5,000 or so Hungarian refugees, mostly soldiers, about 3,000 of whom returned to Hungary within weeks as a result of an amnesty offered by the Austrians. The remaining refugees, roughly 800 Poles, 400 Hungarians, and 200 Italians remained with Kossuth but soon their situation became part of world politics as the Austrian and Russian governments applied pressure on the Turks to surrender these "bandits and rebels." Only the backing of France and particularly Great Britain enabled Turkey to grant asylum to Kossuth and his band of defeated revolutionaries. Austrian secret agents were sent to Vidin to kidnap or even murder Kossuth, but these plans were foiled. In early 1850 after the arrival from Hungary of his wife and children, Kossuth and a small group of followers were moved by the Turkish authorities to Anatolia in Asiatic Turkey; here he plotted with revolu-

KOSSUTH'S ENTRANCE INTO THE PARK.

Above we give our readers a third scene from the doings of the grand reception ceremony to Kossuth. It represents the cortege and the noble Hungarian as they entered the Park through the eastern gate under a triumphal arch, amid the shouts of the excited populace, the beating of arms and the firing of cannon. The picture is lifelike, and was sketched by our artist on the spot. Below we give a representation of the Irving House, as it appeared on the evening of Kossuth's arrival there—it being his head quarters as the guest of the "city. The regalia was most excellent and appropriate, and reflects great credit upon the directors of the whole affair. Kossuth was honored by a torchlight procession and serenade, and was compelled many times to appear on the balcony and say a few words to the whole souled multitude, who seemed crazy to have him ever before them. severe exertions through the day and feeble state of health, rendered a long speech on this occasion impossible; but he appeared several times before the multitude, who cheered him to the echo."

TORCHLIGHT PROCESSION AND SERENADE IN FRONT OF THE IRVING HOUSE, NEW YORK.

tionaries still in Hungary, but all of their conspiracies were crushed by the vigilant Austrian police.

From Exile to America

An invitation from the United States government freed Kossuth and his followers from their Turkish exile, and in September 1851 they boarded the U.S. frigate *Mississippi* to begin a triumphant journey that took them to Marseilles, Southampton, and London, where they were welcomed by happy crowds of admirers. In the United States, he was welcomed by dignitaries and a procession up Broadway in which the Hungarian hero stood up in an open carriage to acknowledge the cheers of thousands of New Yorkers. In Washington, he met President Millard Fillmore and was guest of honor at several state dinners, including one hosted by both houses of Congress, an honor previously granted only to Lafayette; Secretary of State **Daniel Webster** angered the Austrian government by asserting that "we shall rejoice to see our American model upon the Lower Danube and on the mountains of Hungary," while in Springfield, Illinois, **Abraham Lincoln** drafted resolutions describing Kossuth as "the most worthy and distinguished representative of the cause of civil and religious liberty on the continent of Europe." Authors such as Ralph Waldo Emerson, Horace Greeley, Harriet Beecher Stowe, and Walt Whitman were inspired by the Hungarian leader's career, while others, including Henry David Thoreau, were annoyed by the nation's "Kossuth fever" noting that the only result of the visit was some Americans now had taken to wearing Kossuth's flamboyant plumed hat.

Despite the immense enthusiasm of his welcome, after a few months many Americans seemed bored by the colorful Hungarian's appeals for money and weapons. Abolitionists were outraged by his refusal to take a stand on the issue of slavery, Southerners suspected that he was hostile to slavery but only kept quiet for purely tactical reasons, and Roman Catholics were angered by his anticlericalism. By the time he departed New York for England in July 1852, traveling with his wife under the name of "Mr. A. Smith and Lady" (he feared an Austrian assassination attempt), Kossuth had become deeply disillusioned with America and Americans, feeling they lacked understanding for Hungary's plight. Americans, on the other hand, now often saw him as a defeated politician who talked too much and was constantly asking for money to finance hopeless revolutionary schemes. Back in England, Kossuth continued to plan for European revolutions with **Giuseppe Mazzini** and other London-based exiles, but in time he was largely rejected by British radical leaders because of his tendency to preach republicanism to the middle classes and democracy to the lower while rejecting out of hand the goals of socialism. **Karl Marx** and Frederick Engels had nothing but contempt for Kossuth, dismissing him as "a swindler who like the apostle Paul is all things to all men," and as "a tightrope walker who does not dance on a rope but on his tongue."

Supremely confident in his own abilities and the justness of his cause, Kossuth ignored these and other criticisms, continuing to organize a dwindling band of followers for the day when he could return to a Hungary completely free of Habsburg rule. The Compromise (Ausgleich) of 1867 that gave Hungary autonomy within the Habsburg state was condemned by the aging Kossuth, who stubbornly refused to return to the land of his birth because it meant acknowledging the sovereign power of the Austrian dynasty (the "Lex Kossuth" law of 1879 resulted in his being stripped of his citizenship in 1890 because he refused to set foot in any Hungarian consulate decorated with the Austrian Emperor's portrait). Thus, Kossuth became a stateless person, who died in exile in Turin, Italy, on March 20, 1894; two weeks later, he was buried in Budapest with a national funeral that attracted thousands.

Louis Kossuth was in many ways the archetypical Romantic hero, courageous to the point of recklessness, and little interested in the new world of science, urban life, and industrialism that was emerging all around him. Intellectually, he was a man of simple concepts derived from the Age of Enlightenment, particularly the idea of the perfectibility of mankind. His legacy to his fellow Hungarians was a mixed one. He kept alive the flame of Hungarian freedom in its darkest hour, so that more moderate and practical politicians could create an essentially free nation in 1867, but his charismatic personality and lack of realism also contributed to an inflated sense of national destiny that led to intolerance of non-Magyar national aspirations and nurtured power illusions that resulted in Hungary allying itself to Germany in this century's two World Wars. In sum, Louis Kossuth was one of the great personalities of the 19th century, a heroic figure who remains in many ways an enigma.

SOURCES:

Deak, Istvan. *The Lawful Revolution: Louis Kossuth and the Hungarians, 1848–1849.* Columbia University Press, 1979.

Hoensch, Jörg K. *A History of Modern Hungary 1867–1986.* Longman, 1988.

Komlos, John H. *Louis Kossuth in America, 1851–1852.* East European Institute, State University College at Buffalo, New York, 1973.

Pachter, Marc, and Frances Wein, eds. *Abroad in America: Visitors to the New Nation 1776–1914.* Addison-Wesley, 1976.

Reynolds, Larry J. *European Revolutions and the American Literary Renaissance.* Yale University Press, 1988.

Sugar, Peter F., Peter Hanak, and Tibor Frank, eds. *A History of Hungary.* Indiana University Press, 1990.

Robertson, Priscilla. *Revolutions of 1848: A Social History.* Harper Torchbooks, 1960.

Taylor, A. J. P. *The Habsburg Monarchy 1809–1918: A History of the Austrian Empire and Austria-Hungary.* Harper Torchbooks, 1965.

Whitridge, Arnold. *Men in Crisis: The Revolutions of 1848.* Scribner, 1949.

FURTHER READING:

May, Arthur James. *The Hapsburg Monarchy, 1867–1914.* Harvard University Press, 1951.

Mikhail Kutuzov

(1745–1813)

Russian general, whose victory over Napoleon was the major factor in the collapse of the Corsican's dream of a European empire.

"As long as there exists an army and it is in a condition to oppose the enemy, so long will I be able to preserve the hope of ultimate victors. But where the army is destroyed, both Moscow and Russia will perish. I order the retreat."

FIELD MARSHAL KUTUZOV,
AS NAPOLEON APPROACHED THE
OUTSKIRTS OF MOSCOW

Unlike his mentor, **Alexander Suvorov,** who was never defeated, Mikhail Kutuzov had a most checkered career and glory came to him late in life. Although he is rarely cited in any biographies of **Catherine the Great,** under whom he served for most of his career, his name is omnipresent in those of **Napoleon** and **Alexander I.** Something less than a military genius but a worthy pupil of Suvorov, he could be weak and indecisive. His greatest achievement was his defeat of Napoleon in 1812, a feat accomplished when he was 67 years old and just a few months before he died. Difficult to deal with, Kutuzov was detested by Tsar Alexander I, who feared and mistrusted him, and he suffered more than one setback before he went on to achieve greatness at an age when many generals would be long retired and musing over past campaigns.

Born in St. Petersburg on September 16, 1745, Mikhail Kutuzov was the son of a lieutenant-general and military engineer who had seen distinguished service under **Peter the Great** (1682–1725) and who served as a Russian senator under the Empress Elizabeth (1740–61), Kutuzov showed early signs of following a military career

Name variations: Golenishchev-Kutuzov; Koutouzoff. Born Mikhail Illarionovich Kutuzov in St. Petersburg, Russia, on September 16, 1745; died on campaign on April 28, 1813; member of a noble Russian family (one ancestor had fought with Alexander Nevsky in the 13th century, while another, Yuri Kutuzov-Shestak, had been Ivan III's ambassador to the Khan of the Crimea in the 15th).

Contributed by Robert H. Hewsen, Professor of History, Glassboro State College, Glassboro, New Jersey

CHRONOLOGY

1745	Born in St. Petersburg
1762	Served as a captain under Suvorov at Astrakhan
1763–68	Served as aide-de-camp to the military governor of Reval (Estonia)
1768–70	Served in Poland; promoted to major
1770–72	Served in the Russo-Turkish War
1773	Lost an eye in the storming of Alushta in the Crimea
1776–86	Served in the Crimea (six years under Suvorov)
1787–91	Served in a second Russo-Turkish War
1792–93	Served in Poland
1793–1801	Served in a variety of capacities including ambassador to Turkey and Prussia
1805	Given a command in the Napoleonic Wars; defeated by Napoleon at Austerlitz
1806	Assigned as military governor of Warsaw
1809	Appointed governor-general of Vilna
1811	Served in third Russo-Turkish War
1812–13	Commander in chief of the Russian army against Napoleon's invasion
1813	Died at Bunslau in Silesia

and at the age of 12 was enrolled in the military-engineering school founded by Tsar Peter. So successful was Kutuzov at his studies that he was a cadet corporal by the age of 14, a quartermaster sergeant and a junior teacher a year later, and a commissioned officer in the army scarcely a year after that. In 1762, while still only 17, he was assigned to the Astrakhan military regiment with the rank of captain, where he served under Suvorov, one of the great military commanders of all time. Although Kutuzov was transferred to Reval to serve as aide-de-camp to the military governor of Estonia less than a year later, this would not be his last service with Suvorov.

Kutuzov saw his first military action on a campaign in Poland in 1764–65 but otherwise remained in Reval until he entered the field a second time to suppress a Polish rebellion (1768–70), during which he was promoted to the rank of major. Discovering that he had a genuine taste for battle, Kutuzov, at the outbreak of the first Russo-Turkish War, requested and received a transfer to

the Southern Army then under the command of Count Nikolai Rumiantsev. The Russian invasion of Wallachia, now a part of Rumania, had already begun, and Rumiantsev had taken Bucharest, but Kutuzov was in time for several other engagements, not the least of which was the great battle to repel the Turkish attempt to recapture the Wallachian capital. Promoted to lieutenant colonel in 1772, Kutuzov's career now suffered a serious blow when he fell out with Rumiantsev, who had him transferred to the Russian Second Army then engaged in battle in the Crimean Peninsula. There, placed in charge of a Cossack attack on Shumla in August 1774, Kutuzov suffered a wound that nearly terminated his career. Shot in the face, he lost an eye, hence his later nickname "the cyclops." Taking a sojourn from military life, Kutuzov traveled to Central and Western Europe where for two years (1774–76) he experienced the glittering world of the Enlightenment, so admired in the Russia of Catherine the Great. Returning to his homeland, Kutuzov resumed his military career in spite of his handicap and was reassigned to the Crimea for the next ten years (1776–86), six of them under the immediate tutelage of Suvorov.

Kutuzov played a prominent role in the new Russo-Turkish War. Although shot again, this time through the cheek and neck, he was promoted to lieutenant-general and went on to distinguish himself under Suvorov at the siege of Odessa in 1790 and at Bender and the Battles of Rymnik, Ismail, and Mashin in 1791. When the fortresses of Ochakov and Ismail were taken, he served with such distinction that he was promoted to the rank of major-general.

Now nearing 50, Kutuzov's military career seemed to be drawing to an honorable close and Empress Catherine found other uses for him in her diplomatic service. He was sent as ambassador to the Ottoman Empire in 1793, and then as ambassador to Prussia. In between these assignments, he served as commander of the Russian army in Finland and as director of the military school for cadets in St. Petersburg. After returning from Berlin, he served as governor-general of Vilna and, after the assassination of Tsar Paul I (1801), as acting governor of St. Petersburg. With the accession of Tsar Alexander I (1801–25), who considered Kutuzov to be wily, immoral, and untrustworthy, the old general's career seemed to have come to its end. Unwilling to displease, Kutuzov retired in 1802 at the age of 57 to live the life of a country gentleman on his estates in the southwestern province of Volhynia.

In 1805, when Russia joined the Third Coalition against Napoleon, Kutuzov was called from retirement to command the Russian First Army Corps, which was to join the Austrian forces invading the southern German states. Before the Russians and the Austrians could come together, however, Napoleon attacked the Austrians at Ulm and administered a crushing defeat. Badly outnumbered, Kutuzov withdrew to Moravia, where he advised the Tsar to allow the army to withdraw further back to Poland where it could rest and reorganize. Rejecting this advice, Alexander, in agreement with his Austrian allies, ordered Kutuzov to advance. At first the combined armies met with great success, defeating Field Marshal Edouard Mortier at Dürrenstein in a brilliant victory (November 17–19, 1805), only to be defeated at the great Battle of Austerlitz where the Russo-Austrian forces were overwhelmed (December 2). Perhaps Napoleon's greatest victory, it is still commemorated in the name of a plaza and railroad station in Paris. In this battle, Kutuzov was badly wounded a third time, while Alexander blamed him for the defeat and removed him from his command. Nevertheless, it was clear that had Kutuzov's advice been followed, the disaster could have been avoided; thus, the defeat actually enhanced the old general's reputation.

Sent away by Alexander to become governor-general of Kiev and then of Vilna, Kutuzov remained in virtual internal exile for five years (1806–11), only to be called back to frontline service by the Tsar in connection with a third Russo-Turkish War (1806–12). Once again, Kutuzov, as commander in chief of the Russian forces, conducted himself brilliantly, encircling and capturing an entire Turkish army at Rushchuk, crossing the Danube, and forcing the Turks to make peace. As a result, the Russians were able to transfer an entire army to join the forces mustered against Napoleon. Kutuzov received from the Tsar the rank of prince and was appointed commander of the St. Petersburg militia.

A complex individual, Kutuzov was at once a rugged soldier and a cultivated gentleman, familiar with European culture, speaking foreign languages, and able to hold his own at the imperial court. Naturally intelligent, he was also a colorful figure. He went on campaign with the finest wines and foods in tow, and in the evenings he and his officers feasted and disported themselves with trollops. Undoubtedly brave, he could be overly cautious, but he would crown his career with one of the great defensive actions in military history.

The Russian Armies Battle Napoleon

After the signing of the Peace of Bucharest concluding the war with Turkey (May 1, 1812), Kutuzov received the command which climaxed his military career: commander in chief of the Russian armies arrayed against the invasion of Napoleon. Making the appointment against his best judgment, Tsar Alexander had acceded to the acclamation of the army, the pleas of the Russian nobility, and especially the recommendation of Rostopchin, governor of Moscow, after it had become clear that the previous commander, Barclay de Tolly, was no match for the French invader; with Suvorov dead, Kutuzov was the only Russian general who had sufficient stature with both the officers and the rank and file to replace de Tolly. The news of Kutuzov's appointment was greeted with the greatest enthusiasm in St. Petersburg, where an enormous crowd swarmed before his home. On the journey to take up his post, he was greeted as a savior by townspeople, peasants, and common soldiers alike.

Napoleon Bonaparte, at the height of his power as emperor of the French and master of almost the whole of continental Europe, crossed the Russian frontier along the Nieman River on the night of June 23–24, 1812, with his Grande Armée, a force of over 450,000 men—the largest army the world had ever seen. It seems unlikely, however, that Napoleon intended to conquer Russia; had that been his plan, he would surely have headed first for St. Petersburg. Rather, many historians believe that he was merely attempting to cow Alexander with a dazzling display of potential force, defeating the Russian armies in combat, while awing his enemies and allies alike in Western Europe. Realizing that the Russian army was unable to meet such a force head on, Kutuzov ordered his men to stage a tactical retreat, adopting what he called a "defense in depth" and drawing the enemy ever further into Russia. Essentially a general of the old school, an 18th-century warrior campaigning in another era, Kutuzov was a less-inspired leader than Suvorov; his great strengths lay in his ability to hearten his weary troops, his concern for their health and morale, and his genius at assessing the military situation in a realistic way.

Although the French bypassed St. Petersburg, their steady advance toward Moscow and Kutuzov's reluctance to engage them in battle distressed a number of people at court who cried out for action. Submitting to this pressure, Kutuzov ordered his troops to turn and engage the enemy at the village of Borodino, some 70 miles west of Moscow (September 7, 1812). As he expected, the Russians were defeated in a bloody battle, and, though they lost only 38,500 men compared to French losses of some 58,000, this was a third of the Russian army. The Russian defeat, however, was not a decisive one and perhaps played a positive role in inducing the invader to push even further into the endless expanses of Russia. In any case, Napoleon was soon faced with the full threat of the Russian winter and everything depended on his vast army reaching and taking Moscow, where it expected to find shelter. To the surprise of Napoleon and to the dismay of the Russians, Kutuzov made no effort to defend the ancient city. But shortly after the French arrived (September 14), the deserted city went up in flames (evidently planned and executed by the Russians), and Napoleon realized that with neither shelter for the winter nor adequate supplies, the Grande Armée had no choice but to withdraw.

Napoleon's immediate plan was to head to the Ukraine, where he might camp during the milder winter of the south. Kutuzov prevented this maneuver, however, by defeating the French at Maloyaroslavets, thereby turning them back upon the road by which they had entered Russia and forcing them into a direct retreat. This withdrawal, begun on October 20, 1812, and accompanied by Kutuzov's merciless harassment of the enemy from the rear, proved to be the most disastrous rout in military history. Though Kutuzov was continually faulted for not pursuing the enemy with greater ferocity, the fact is that he did engage them at Viaz'ma (November 3) and Krasnyi (November 17) and that fewer than 40,000 of Napoleon's troops survived to regain Central Europe. Cautious to a fault, however, Kutuzov generally continued to avoid a direct confrontation with the enemy wherever possible. A last French attempt to engage the Russians took place at Smolensk in November, where Kutuzov bested Napoleon's commanders, Davout and Ney, and the decimated and demoralized Grande Armée. Before the year was out, the enemy had departed Russian soil, Kutuzov had occupied Vilna, and it was clear to all that Napoleon's star had begun to fade. Criticized throughout the campaign for his dilatory tactics, the end result made Kutuzov appear to be a veritable Alexander the Great.

As a result of this rout of Napoleon, Alexander finally relented in his negative view of his commander in chief and nothing was too good for the "Cyclops." Every medal and decoration not previously awarded was bestowed to Kutuzov, and he was promoted to the supreme rank of field marshal and granted the title "Prince of Smolensk." But the Tsar had further tasks for the victor. Early in 1813, Kutuzov was ordered to lead the Russian army into the German states, where, taking command of a joint force of Russians and Prussians, he was instructed to begin to lay plans for nothing less than a final coalition to end the domination of Bonaparte over Europe. But the efforts of the campaigns of the past year proved to have been too taxing for the old warrior. Before he could launch his new campaign, he fell ill at Bunslau in Silesia, where he died March 25, 1813. A statue of Kutuzov was erected in Bunslau and later another in St. Petersburg.

Mikhail Illarionovich Kutuzov stands second only to his great mentor Suvorov as the greatest general in Russian history and was perhaps the first to devise a specific tactic for the defense of so large a territory. Avoiding costly battles wherever possible, he depended upon skillful maneuver in vast spaces and tactical retreat followed by a decisive strike at the critical moment. His strategy of "defense in depth," while lacking brilliance or glamour, allowed the use of the vastness of the Russian land as a major weapon in the defense of the country and was used again most effectively against the German army during Hitler's Russian campaign "Operation Barbarossa" in 1941–42. Kutuzov's name was continually evoked during the Russian defense of the fatherland in the Second World War. Stalin justified the disastrous retreat in the face of the German invasion as being in keeping with the tactics of Kutuzov and, in 1942, the Soviet government announced the creation of an order in his name to be granted for valor on the field of battle. Tsarist and Soviet historians tended to inflate the brilliance of Kutuzov's strategy, however, for in fact he only did what he had to do. In the face of Napoleon's vastly superior forces, he had no other choice. His chief credit is due to his having realized the nature of the situation that faced him and having taken the appropriate action to deal with it.

SOURCES:

Bragin, Mikhail. *Field Marshall Kutuzov.* Moscow, 1944.

Mikhailovsky-Danilievsky, General. *Life of Kutuzov.* French translation by A. Fizelier. Paris, 1850.

FURTHER READING:

Duffy, Christopher. *Austerlitz 1805.* Archon, 1977.

———. *Borodino.* Scribner, 1973.

Holligsworth, B. "The Napoleonic Invasion of Russia and Recent Soi, viet Historical Writing," in *Journal of Modern History.* XXXVIII (1966).

Parkinson, R. *The Fox of the North: Life of Kutuzov.* London, 1976.